Annotations for the History of the Classical Guitar in Argentina 1822-2000 Vol. I

Qué impresión tiene usted de la Argentina?
— preguntan
a Saint-Saëns.

— Es el paraíso terrenal de los músicos...

The composer Saint-Saëns was asked:
"What impression do you have of Argentina?"

He replied:

"It's an earthly paradise of musicians. . ."

This quote is from the weekly magazine "*Caras y caretas*" published in Buenos Aires on December 3, 1932, issue no. 1,783, page 28.

The cover image of Maria Luisa Anido and Miguel Llobet is from *"La Guitarra"* magazine Issue No. 4 of February 1926, drawn by Dr. Samuel Mallo Lopez, his sketches adorn this book.

by Randy Osborne and Héctor García Martínez

Translation and Photo Documentation by Randy Osborne Index by Jan J. de Kloe

Fine Fretted String Instruments
2345 Winchester Blvd. Suite B
Campbell, Ca. USA 95008
First Edition February 2020
www.finefretted.com
M-S 9:00 – 5:30 PM (408) 879-9930

ISBN 978-1-7345294-0-1

This volume represents an enormous compendium of original sources from the 19th and 20th centuries, which up until now has been all but inaccessible to even the most dedicated scholars and researchers. Assembled over many years at great expense and now reproduced here in their original form with translations and notations, this work finally brings the long and rich history of the guitar as it developed in Argentina to the non-Spanish speaker.

Some readers may be familiar with the name Domingo Prat, a Catalan expatriate who in 1934 published his *"Diccionario de Guitarristas y Guitarreros."* This monumental work consisting of well over 2,000 entries of personalities documents the 19th and 20th century personalities of the guitar. Compiled and written in long hand, this labor of love has never been translated into English, and yet it represents but a tantalizing tip of the iceberg in reference to the level of guitar activities present in Argentina during the beginning of the 20th century. With this present volume, many of the prominent teachers, players, dealers, composers, publishers and even luthiers now have not only a face, but in many cases, considerable original source material to considerably augment the abbreviated entries they were given in the Prat Diccionario.

Long before the Guitar Review began its publication in New York City in 1946 there were several Argentinean magazines dedicated to the guitar aficionado including the *Revista Musical Ilustrada "Tárrega", Boletin de la Asociacion Guitarristica Argentina,* and the *Revista de la Guitarra* which documented in precise detail the myriad guitar activities of the times. The Asociacion Guitarristica Argentina had a local membership of over 1400 (Compare with the present day Guitar Foundation of America, which has a worldwide membership of about 2,100! This figure revised in January 2020.).

With a population of active guitarists this large, naturally it follows that luthiers also came to prominence addressing this market, both from Spain and as immigrants, not to mention the large population of native born luthiers already present. This volume documents in detail not only the export activities of makers such as Manuel Ramírez, Santos Hernández, Domingo Esteso, Enrique Garcia, Francisco Simplicio, and even Hermann Hauser of Münich, Germany, whose strings were being sold by the firm Celestino Fernández in the 1930's, but also the Spanish (and other European) makers who immigrated to Argentina to pursue this rich marketplace including Antonio Emilio Pascual Viudes, Francisco Nuñez, and the Galan brothers among others. In many cases, the catalogs of their instruments are presented here for the first time, an extremely valuable research tool for present day dealers and collectors. At the turn of the century, the Antigua Casa Nuñez was producing over 40,000 guitars per year!

Documented here are the activities of Ricardo Muñoz, barely known among non-Spanish speakers. His 1952 publication, *"Tecnologia de la Guitarra Argentina"* is one of the most important and thorough scientific treatises on the instrument to date. Long before guitar collecting became fashionable in North America, Luis Castellano who was the official guitar appraiser for the Municipal Bank of Buenos Aires published his extremely informative and concise *"Prinicipales Caracteristicas de las Guitarras Autores de Renombre Mundial,"* in which he is the first to suggest using a small light to illuminate the interior of the guitar in order to show the bracing structure from the outside, a technique used today by luthiers the world over.

The distinction between amateur and professional levels of involvement with the guitar is addressed in this work, which clearly shows that even at a nonprofessional level, the guitar was taken very seriously in Argentina, and commanded a high level of respect among the general public.

Players, teachers and even luthiers figured prominently in the society pages of the publications of the day. Segovia's crusade to elevate the status of the guitar to that of the violin or piano was achieved in Argentina before Segovia had even arrived on the scene. While in Europe and America the 19th century concept of the artist as a composer/performer was dying, in Argentina this concept continues to be an integral part of the culture of the guitar, and so it is not surprising that many of the finest players and composers for the instrument today hail for this region.

In the rest of the world the involvement of women with the guitar is still rather asymmetrical, but in Argentina women had a significant integration with the instrument and figured prominently as concert artists, and teachers, not to mention amateur involvement. Even today, the integration of women into the inner circles of the art lags behind that of Argentina at the beginning of the 20th century.

The staggering amount of primary source documentation contained in this work is priceless, and of incalculable value to historians, musicologists, luthiers, researchers, and any who have even a modicum of interest in the guitar and its development. No longer is there any excuse to dismiss the activities of these dedicated pioneers of the instrument as being marginal. Clearly, in the beginning of the 20th century, Buenos Aires was the New York, London and Paris of the guitar world. The activities of these pioneers as documented in this work should inspire us all.

Richard Bruné

Evanston, Il 2007, revised in January 2020

Richard E. Bruné

1000 Rand Road, Units 223, 224.

Wauconda Il 60084

847-864-7730

rebruneluthier@yahoo.com

www.rebrune.com

Translator's note

My colleague Dr. Brian Jeffery suggested that this book be written after I had shared with him the depth of knowledge, which Héctor García Martínez has on the tip of his tongue. Brian said when Héctor passes away all that knowledge will be gone as well. I then asked Héctor to go about writing the information, which was only 22 pages of historical text, and later the interviews and I would translate it from Spanish to English. Also, within the scope of this book, I also translated Italian, Portuguese, French and Catalan, and Japanese to English. It was almost impossible to stop writing this book.

In dealing with the guitar in the Rio de la Plata, one telling aspect we need to bear in mind are the population densities of Buenos Aires at different times. In the middle of the 18th century there were about 20,000 inhabitants of the New World port city. When Gaspar Sagreras arrived from Spain in 1869 there were 180,000. Just before the turn of the 20th century, in 1895, there were 670,000. This was the period when Juan Alais, Carlos García Tolsa, Antonio Jiménez Manjón and Julio Sagreras were household names to their concert audiences and students. When the First World War broke out in Europe in 1914 the population was just under 2,000,000. This was when the Academia de Guitarra "Tárrega", directed by Hilarion Leloup, and similar Academias by contemporaries Domingo Prat, Carmelo Rizzuti, Antonio Sinopoli and Pedro A. Iparraguire began. It is also important to remember that this was the era of the advent of radio in Buenos Aires, in the summer of 1920.

In the 1920's Miguel Llobet, Andrés Segovia and Maria Luisa Anido all performed on the radio in Buenos Aires. After the Second World War the population had more than doubled to 4,640,000 in 1947. This was when it was common to hear Ricardo Muñoz give a live guitar lecture that was simultaneously broadcast on radio. Segundo N. Contreras and Carlos Vega were also involved documenting the history of the classical guitar during this period, preserving that which might have been lost. Ricardo Muñoz says in his *"Historia de la Guitarra"*, published in 1930, that there were 5,000 guitarists and aficionados in the port city. To quote my colleague Richard Bruné, Buenos Aires truly was the "World Center of Classical Guitar Activity" in those first few decades of the 20th century. Since Richard Bruné first told me that fact on the phone in the late 1990's, I have now written a book that quotes that fact from the mid 1920's written in Buenos Aires itself. The population of Buenos Aires is presently over 11,000,000. This book contains over 175 biographies of people and businesses, and countless bibliographical references.

Randy Osborne, 12/3/00, revised 9/17/03,8/17/04, 10/15/07,2/15/09 ,7/5 2019, 12-17-19 2/5/20.

This work started as an e-book. It was to be 22 pages of text, written by Héctor García Martínez and a lot of images of the artists and their sheet music covers from over a century ago. I have to thank my colleague, Ronald Louis Fernández , Phd., for convincing me to make it a regular book that sits on a shelf.

Acknowledgements

I would like to thank my co-author Héctor García Martínez for his tireless work in the field of Classical Guitar research. I am deeply indebted to Richard D. "Rico" Stover for his helpful guidance and editing. I have to thank the initial sheet music and record collectors (José Augusto Marcellino, Eduardo Bensadon, Mario Rodríguez Arenas, Ricardo Muñoz, Domingo Prat, Blanca Prat, Consuelo Mallo Lopez and Segundo N. Contreras), whom without their endeavors, this book would be quite a bit smaller and more limited in its scope.

I give the utmost thanks to my parents Stuart Boyce Osborne and Pauline Louise Davey. I want to thank my wonderful son, Byron Stuart Osborne, for his help in so many areas.

I would like to thank my colleagues, Richard Bruné, Dr. Brian Jeffery, Jim Forderer, Matanya Ophee, Lucas Agustín de Antoni of Buenos Aires-for the rare images he was willing to share, José Romanillos, Ronald Louis Fernández , PHD., Jan-Olof Eriksson, Byron Pang-my Classical Guitar maestro 1979-81, Manuel Lopez Ramos, José Rey de la Torre, Josép Maria Mangado i Artigas, Gustavo and Alfredo Breitfield, Ricardo Zavadivker, Jorge Finkielman of the Universidad de Buenos Aires, Dardo Molina Chazarreta, Carlos Guevel, for the rare images he was willing to share, Esmeralda Correale Almiron for her precious photos and history of the Almiron family, Jan J. de Kloe, Ignacio Ramos, Alfredo Escande of Montevideo, Bruno Cespi, Héctor Lorenzo Lucci of Buenos Aires, for his information regarding the Atlanta record company, Federico Sheppard, Vincenzo Pocci, Gregg Miner, Dr. Jack Silver, George Johnson, Omar Facelli of Montevideo, who provided me the purchase of unfound Agustín Barrios records and the Pedro Mascaro y Reissig and Rosendo Barreiro archives, Adrian Ruis Espinos for his information regarding Francisco Tárrega, Professor Julio Gimeno Garcia, for his information about Andrés Segovia's first South American tour departure and the Encyclopedic Discography of Victor Recordings (EDVR) web site: http://victor.library.ucsb.edu. A team of researchers based at the University of California, Santa Barbara Libraries edits the database. I need to thank Santiago Bouzas of the Centro de Investigacion, Documentacion y Difusion de las Artes Escenicas. (CIDDAE) –Teatro Solis, Montevideo, Uruguay.

I want to also thank my friend and colleague, Nobuo Amemiya, for proofreading my Japanese translations of the *"Armonia"* magazines dating from 1954-1957 published in Sendai, Miyagiken, Japan.

In the same field I need to thank Robert Coldwell, for providing images and translations.

Randy Osborne   July 9, 2019

I need to thank the Universidad Catolica Argentina de Buenos Aires for providing me with a copy of the complete issue of the *Revista Musical Ilustrada "Tárrega"* magazine issue No. 26 of September 1926. This has offered the writer the opportunity to make a complete use of all 33 issues of this rare magazine.

I especially need to thank the staff at the Biblioteca Nacional de España in Madrid for the online access to the 2,139 issues of the *"Caras y Caretas"* magazines printed in Buenos Aires from 1898-1939. I viewed all the guitar related pages of every issue between August and November of 2011, although owning 400 issues since 2005. As well I want to thank them for the PDF containing the article on Miguel Borrull and his daughter, Conchita, at the Teatro Eldorado in Barcelona in September 1917. This is from the magazine *"Eco Artistico"* of September 25, 1917 issue No. 281.

I especially need to thank the staff at the Biblioteca Nacional de Uruguay in Montevideo for the access to the *"Montevideo Musical"* magazines from 1885-1952.

I am especially indebted to the late Ronoel Simões and one of his many colleagues, Ivan Paschoito, for the complete series of *"O Violao"* (December 1928 to November-December 1929) and *"A Voz do Violao"* (February to April 1931) magazines, for the images and information they have provided for this book.

Randy Osborne   December 17, 2019

Prologue

When my friend Randy Osborne asked me to write a "History of the Classical Guitar in Argentina", I agreed immediately because the idea appeared very proper. Little or nothing has been written about this subject, though a lot of information has been disseminated. And I understood that it was important to write these annotations in order to document the history of a guitaristic movement originating in this part of South America, the area known as Rio de la Plata, that is one of the most important in the world. But also to do justice to the European maestros who established their presence here, creating outstanding Argentine disciples, all of whom contributed to raise the level of the guitar in concert in these parts, working with courageous spirit and seriousness.

We arrive at the 21st century not understanding why, for example, the name of Domingo Prat is not known to the true dimension of his merits, even in his own land, Spain. The same occurs with Ricardo Muñoz, Hilarion Leloup, Julio S. Sagreras, Carlos García Tolsa and the rest of those who figure in this guitar history.

"The Annotations for the History of the Classical Guitar in Argentina" shows the important musical patrimony that exists of concert artists, authors, composers, luthiers and historical investigators of the instrument who wrote and published important works. Added to this is the sheet music that constitutes a major treasure for collectors and investigators. Since the end of the 19th century until today in Argentina and Uruguay, quite a bit of music has been composed directly for the guitar.

Not in this work, exists any intention whatsoever chauvinist on the part of the author, simply the healthy desire to collaborate a great knowledge of the guitar as an instrument in its diverse aspects, as it has occurred in South America.

And for them, all of our recognition, admiration and affection.

Héctor García Martínez.   September, 2000

Unacknowledgements:

May 4, 2002 On Mel Bay Publications "Guitar Sessions" web page this month is an article I was asked to write. It is a micro-thumbnail sketch of my book that is in progress: "Annotations for the History of the Classical Guitar in Argentina 1822-2000" by Héctor García Martínez and Randy Osborne. The article is entitled: How Buenos Aires Became the World Center of the Classical Guitar. This article is now on my finefretted.org web site.

After giving credit to Victor M. Oxley, for his Barrios related work that I valued to include in this book and give him the credit deserved, I learned he copied and pasted at least 3 paragraphs from the above mentioned article and translated them into Spanish to include in his 2009 publication on page 102 (*Agustín Pío Barrios Mangoré: ritos, culto, sacrilegios y profanaciones*), without giving me credit. Google books gets the credit on this plagiarism discovery, no one will never be able to get away with plagiarism again. My colleague, Rico Stover, said this author is a persona non grata at the U.S. Embassy in Asuncion, Paraguay, and is an armchair historian.

Weeks before César Amaro died in 2012, the book he contributed to: *Recuerdo de un Sueño. Vida y Obra de Agustín Pio Barrios*, published in Paraguay, was released to the public. I bought my copies from the author only to find out that César claimed an Agustín Barrios autographed photo from 1931, included in this book, was "from his archive". This photo was used in Richard Stover's Six Silver Moonbeams 2010 Edition, with my permission and credit for photos used on 8 pages in that book. César never knew how much money was spent to acquire that rare photo.

About Héctor García Martínez

Héctor García Martínez was born in Buenos Aires, Argentina in 1943. He studied guitar in the 1960's with the distinguished guitarist and composer Adolfo V. Luna. Hector has broadcast concerts on LRA Radio Nacional. He also has given concerts in the Centro Cultural General San Martin, Asociacion Estimulo Bellas Artes, Automovil Club Argentino, Fundacion Banco Boston de Buenos Aires, Casa de la Cultura de Victoria, Instituto Magñasco de Gualeguaychu-in Entre Rios and Asociacion Bellas Artes de Pergamino-in Buenos Aires.

Between 1979 and 1986 he gave radio broadcasts and T.V. concerts in the cities of Colonia, Carmelo, Paysandu and Salto (Uruguay). In 1987 Héctor took part when the National Music Direction promoted a series of concerts in the following cities of Argentina: La Rioja, Olta, Chamical, Malanzan, Jachal, San Juan, Huaco, Niquivil, Villa Mercedes and San Isidro. In August of 1987 Héctor gave a concert in the Salon Azul of the National University of the Pampa in Santa Rosa. Since 1988 he has given concerts in the cities of Buenos Aires, Entre Rios and La Pampa.

Lately he has given recitals of a didactic nature, with commentary and reviews on the theme of "The Traditionalism in the Argentine Concert Guitar".

Publications and Historical Investigation:

Héctor is the author of :

"Fasciculo No. 1 Abel Fleury-The Poet of the Guitar", 1st edition 1987, 2nd edition 1988. This is now out of print, and will be made available again soon. Rereleased in 2003 the centenary of Fleury's birth.

"Fasciculo No. 1 Argentino Valle, The Mystery of the Piano", a documental work on the career of the great pianist and composer, who was the first folklore representative in Buenos Aires in 1930.

Acknowledgements and Distinctions :

1989 — The Institute of Folklore Riojano presented Hector with a diploma for his historical investigations.

1992 — Mayor César Uribarri and the City Council of the city of Ranchos awarded Héctor a distinction of "Testimony of Gratitude" for his labor of an extensive biographical work on the career of the great guitarist and composer Justo T. Morales.

Héctor García Martínez contributed to the creation of the Abel Fleury Museum in the city of Dolores, and the Mayor of Dolores especially invites Héctor every year to do a lecture at the Guitar Festival in Memorium of Abel Fleury in Dolores.

Table of Contents

1 Introduction

An important guitaristic movement that originated in this part of South America at the beginning of the 19th century began with the arrival in Buenos Aires, on October 15, 1822, of the Italian musician Esteban Massini, whose activities we will describe more fully, later.

Since then, and with the later arrival of other European maestros, in Argentina as well as Uruguay, there have been notable professors of the guitar, composers, distinguished interpreters and guitar makers, to be added to much later by investigators of the history of the instrument, including some who studied the qualities of the wood to make good guitars.

This group of European musicians left an embedded seed within the South American disciples, that has projected it in the space and time across the generations. Because these maestros transmitted to their students the hereditary schools of Europe, we still have the presence today of Carulli, Sor, Aguado, Tárrega, etc.

Ferdinand Carulli   **and his Rene Lacote guitar**   **Fernando Sor**

Principally they were Spaniards and some Italians, those that came to this zone of the Rio de la Plata (Argentina and Uruguay), and found a favorable environment to develop their professional abilities, which they did not have in their native land.

What was the factor that contributed to the development of such a fruitful guitaristic movement in this part of America?

Argentina at the end of the 19th century and the beginning of the 20th century, was to be found with a flourishing economy and along with that, large social sectors with buying power, belonging to the upper and middle classes, especially owners of cattle ranches, powerful merchants, and groups of professionals with economic solvency, and among them, some government officials, that studied the classical guitar. One proof of this is the great quantity of high-quality guitars that they found, proceeding from Europe, to the Rio de la Plata in this epoch. In respect to this I transcribe a paragraph from the book *"Guitarras y Guitarreros"* (Guitars and Guitarmakers), published in Japan by Tetsukazu Hosokawa that a few years ago was given to me by professor Takeshi Tezuka of Kawasaki, written in bilingual form, Spanish-Japanese.

Dionisio Aguado's autographed *Escuela de la Guitarra* 1825.

This photo is from the archive of Ricardo Muñoz, the rare method itself is from the Mario Rodríguez Arenas archive. This now is in the archive of my colleague, Matanya Ophée.

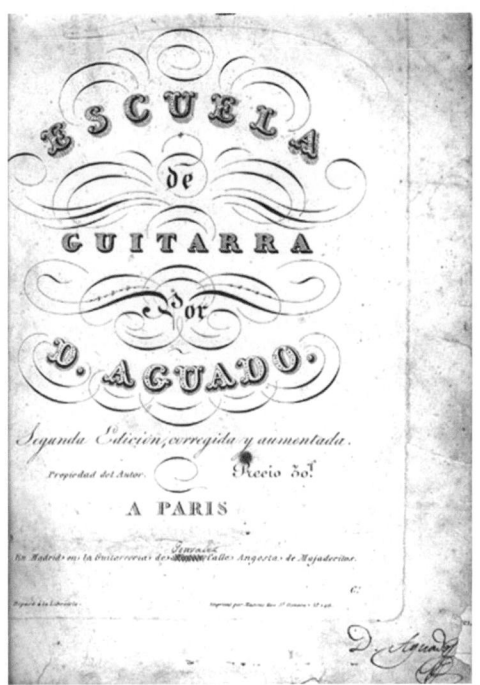

Dionisio Aguado

Autographed *Escuela de la Guitarra* 1825

To be referring to the career of the Spanish luthier Enrique García, we revere a date very interesting: "with a certain confidence in himself, in 1895 he moved to Barcelona to be independent, opening a taller at the address at Aragon 455.

Enrique García Castillo (1868-1922) from a c. 1926 Casa America catalog.

But it was a land strange to him and with few people that knew him, by that, he didn't have orders of expensive guitars. He waited many long and difficult years until in 1912 an exportation contract with an Argentine musical instrument house came. Thanks to that, he would be acquiring great fame in Latin America".

Julio S. Sagreras / Romero, Agromayor and Cia.

Enrique García guitar promotion c. 1918. *Los mejores del mundo* means the best in the world.

The duet of *"Recuerdos de la Alhambra"* was performed at the Salon "La Argentina" by Julio and his student Adela del Valle on September 11, 1917, and this concert is mentioned at the bottom of the first page of the second guitar part.

(Left and Right) The label and headstock of the last
Enrique García guitar made in 1922 (No. 272),
which belonged to Domingo Prat.

"In Argentina at that time Domingo Prat came from Spain,
created his disciple Maria Luisa Anido, Miguel Llobet and Emilio
Pujol transmitted the spirit of the maestro Tárrega to the lands of
Central and South America.

In the Juan Carlos Anido home in 1919, left to right, Miguel Llobet, Emilio Pujol, Juan Carlos Anido,
Maria Luisa Anido and Domingo Prat. Juan Carlos Anido was host to Miguel Llobet for every tour.
Miguel never stayed in a hotel, but in the home of Juan Carlos Anido. Juan Carlos also was Emilio Pujol's
manager and concert organizer. This information is from the *Mundo Musical* issue No. 93 of June 1946-
in an article by Ricardo Muñoz entitled *"Propulsor de la cultura guitarristica del pais"* (Proponent of the
guitaristic culture of the country.)

Miguel Llobet playing for his admirers: Left to Right — Francisco Tárrega Rizo (Jr.),
Leon Farré, Andrés Segovia, Enrique Garcia, Miguel Llobet playing the guitar,
Juan Parras de Moral and Eusebio Gual. Luthier Enrique García had won the
First Prize in the 1893 Exposition of Chicago.

As guitar makers we have Viudes (Antonio Emilio Pascual) and José Ramírez II in Buenos Aires. It was a blossoming epoch of the Spanish guitar in Central America and South America."

(Although this quote is from a published book, my colleague, Richard Bruné, says the stay of José Ramírez II in South America is as a musician and not as a guitarmaker.)

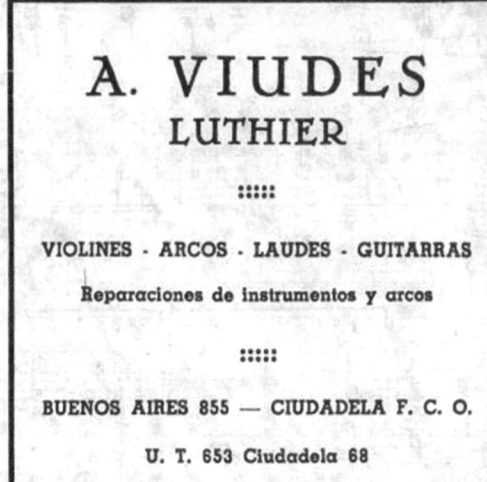

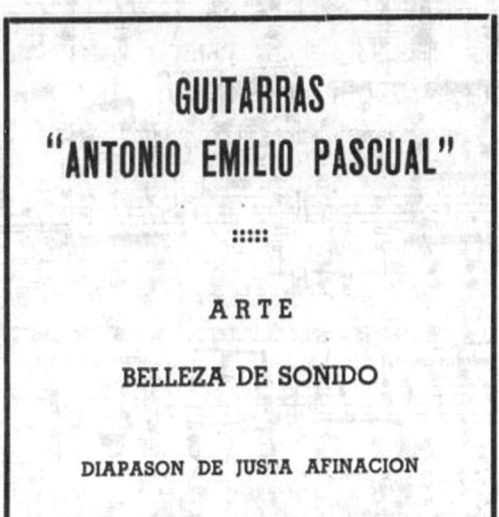

Antonio Emilio Pascual Viudes advertisement from the *Boletin de la Asociacion Guitarristica Argentina*, issue No. 3 June, 1939

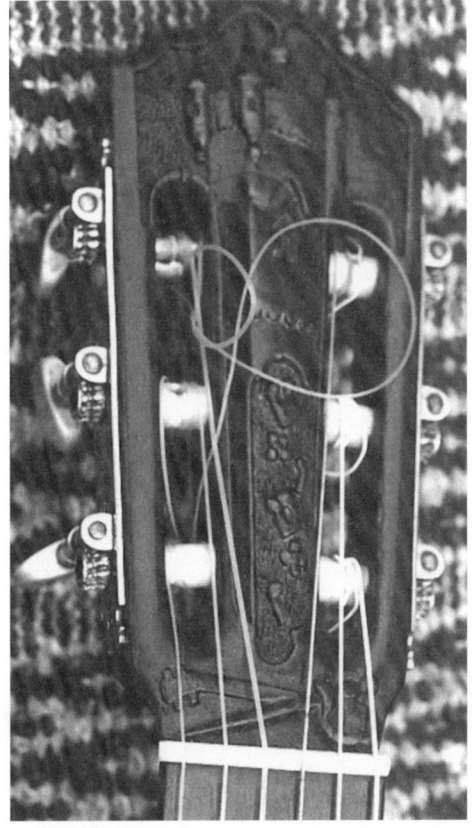

(Left) 1952 Antonio Emilio Pascual Viudes ornately carved headstock.

(Right) Signed label from the same guitar, made very late in his career.

The workshop of Manuel Ramírez in Madrid c. 1911, where the luthiers: Santos Hernández, Domingo Esteso, Modesto Borreguero and Antonio Viudes learned to be masters. (On the far right is the 11 string guitar commissioned by Antonio Jiménez Manjón, which was rejected, and reconfigured to a 6 string instrument and given as a gift to Andrés Segovia in 1912. This information, courtesy of the archive of Richard Bruné.) Later in this work there are excerpts from a c. 1920 Romero & Fernández catalog.

(Left) 1919 Domingo Esteso Flamenco guitar label at the Gravina 7, Madrid address.
(Right) 1920 Santos Hernández Flamenco guitar early label at the Plaza de Nicolas Salmeron 8, Madrid address, this was the home of Santos Hernández. This address is included in the *Dictionnaire Universel des Luthiers* by Rene Vannes from 1931. These are very early examples of the master luthiers going on their own after the death of their maestro Manuel Ramírez in 1916. Modesto Borreguero continued to work for the widow of Manuel Ramírez for many years.

Maria Luisa Anido and Miguel Llobet from "*La Guitarra*" magazine issue No. 3, 1925. In her recorded duets with Miguel Llobet, Maria Luisa Anido used a 1918 Enrique García guitar.

DOMINGO PRAT

Eminente profesor y concertista que en el año 1908 hizo conocer por primera vez en Buenos Aires, la famosa e insuperable guitarra GARCIA.

SIMPLICIO

es el único alumno y sucesor del famoso "luthier" GARCIA y el mejor constructor de guitarras del mundo.

No olvide que Romero y Fernández son los únicos representantes de Simplicio en la República Argentina.

Si desea adquirir una Guitarra Española auténtica visite nuestras casas. Unicas que pueden ofrecerle el más grande surtido en calidad y marcas.

PRECIOS REBAJADOS - VENTA A PLAZOS

Recomendamos las famosas cuerdas
DOBLE DIAPASON

Romero & Fernández

FLORIDA 255 - Bmé. MITRE 947
CANGALLO 1574

Domingo Prat advertisement, for the guitars of Francisco Simplicio, disciple and successor to Enrique García, for the importer, Romero & Fernández , also Prat's publisher. This is from "*Revista Musical Ilustrada "Tárrega"* issue No. 24 of July 1926. My colleague, Richard Bruné, pointed out to me that, the guitar Prat is posing with, is not a Simplicio.

Translation of the previous page:

"Simplicio is the only student and successor of the famous "Luthier" García and the best constructor of guitars in the world.

Don't forget that Romero and Fernández are the only representatives of Simplicio in the Argentine Republic.

If you desire to acquire an authentic Spanish Guitar please visit our music houses. We are the only ones than can offer the largest supply in quality and brands.

REDUCED PRICES — SALES BY INSTALLMENT PLAN

We recommend the famous strings Doble Diapason.

DOMINGO PRAT — Eminent professor and concert guitarist who in the year 1908 made the famous and unsurpassable García guitar known for the first time in Buenos Aires."

This photo is from "*Revista Musical Ilustrada "Tárrega"* magazine, issue No. 22 of May 1926. The translation of the photo caption is: "Standing: Fernando Fausante, Juan Vilatoba, and an unknown gentleman. Seated are: Federico (sic) Francisco Tárrega Rizo Jr., son of the celebrated guitarist, the eminent concert guitarist Emilio Pujol and the constructor of guitars Enrique García."

De pie: Señores Fernando Fausente, Juan Vilatobá y N. N.
Sentados: Señores Federico Tárrega, hijo del célebre guitarrista, el eximio concertista Emilio Pujol y el constructor de guitarras García.

Translation: "Important Notice! Francisco Simplicio is the best constructor of Guitars in the world. The only student and successor of the famous maestro García. The Romero & Fernández house has been distinguished by the celebrated "Luthier" naming us his only representatives in the Argentine Republic. We recommend you visit our music houses before verifying your purchases."

From issue #4 of "*La Guitarra*" magazine in 1926, Enrique Garcia's disciple and successor Francisco Simplicio, one of the most venerated guitarmakers of Barcelona, whose instruments were imported by Romero & Fernández and played by Maria Luisa Anido, Joséfina Robledo, Abel Fleury, Agustín P. Barrios, Martin Borda y Pagola, a friend and patron of Agustín P. Barrios, Celia Salomón de Font, Lalyta Almiron, Domingo Prat and Blanca Prat.

On July 5, 1936 maestro Emilio Pujol gave a discourse at the tomb of Fernando Sor. At this event a plaque was placed that states: "To the brilliant Composer Guitarist Fernando Sor." "Les Amis de la Guitare" (The Friends of the Guitar) July 1936. This is from the *Boletin de la Asociacion Guitarristica Argentina* issue No. 3 of June 1939

The next page is from the *Boletin de la Asociacion Guitarristica Argentina* issue No. 4 of December 1939. This magazine was the sporadic and sometimes monthly digest of the Asociacion Guitarristica Argentina founded in August of 1934.

Translation of the text of the next page:

The Asociacion Guitarristica Argentina in Paris in acts in memory of Fernando Sor on July 2, 1939. (On the hundredth anniversary of his death — July 8, 1939.)

(Upper Left photo) Julien Rousseau reading his discourse.

(Upper Right photo) Attendants in the act of the memento.

(Lower Left photo) The maestro Sarrabio Clavero in his discourse.

(Lower Right photo) The director of "The Friends of the Guitar", Mr. André Verdier.

Part of a postcard printed by the "The Friends of the Guitar" on occasion of the centennial of the death of the renowned musician.

The tomb of Fernando Sor in the Montmartre cemetery in which is seen the wreath that the Asociacion Guitarristica Argentina adhered to this homage.

LA ASOCIACION GUITARRISTICA ARGENTINA EN PARIS
ACTOS EN MEMORIA DE FERNANDO SOR
2 DE JULIO DE 1939

Julien Rousseau
leyendo
su
discurso

Asistentes al acto
recordatorio

El maestro
Sarrablo Clavero
en su
discurso.

El director de "Les
Amis de la Guitare"
Sr. André Verdier

Parte de una tarjeta postal
impresa por "Les Amis de
la Guitarre" en ocasión del
centenario de la muerte del
insigne músico.

CENTENAIRE FERNANDO SOR
(1839-1939)

FERNANDO SOR (1778-1839)

Tumba de Fernando Sor en
el cementerio de Montmartre,
en la que se ve la corona
con que la A. G. A. se adhi-
rió al homenaje.

BREVE RESEÑA DE SU HISTORIA, DE SU RENACIMIENTO Y DE SU FABRICACIÓN

POR JUAN M. MATA

QUE podríamos contaros de la guitarra, que despertara en vosotros, aficionados, sentimientos nuevos? En el lugar más recóndito de España, en casi todas las tierras de Sudamérica, existe un tocador de guitarra. Amparando al instrumento en amoroso abrazo puntea y tensa las cuerdas pacientemente y parece repartir su atención entre el templado y el relato periodístico. Mira acá y allá, y escucha sonriente, arrullado por los balbuceos musicales. Es muy íntimo, muy del corazón, el son de la guitarra española, y el eco de las palabras no suele ser, ante ella, más que una nueva y armónica resonancia de su caja.

TERMINANDO UNA BANDURRIA

La Guitarra Española from the *Blanco y Negro* magazine published in Madrid in 1927.

"A brief review of its history, of its renaissance and of its fabrication. By Juan M. Mata,

Caption "Finishing a Bandurria" 2nd floor of the Ramírez workshop at Calle de Concepción Jerónima, 2, Madrid. (identification: Richard Bruné.)

"What might we be able to say about the guitar, what it awakens in us, aficionados, new feelings? In the most remote place in Spain, in almost all of the lands of South America, exists a guitar player. Protecting the instrument in a loving embrace plucking and holding the strings patiently and appears to distribute his attention between the discipline and the journalistic story. He looks here and there, and listens while smiling, lulled by the musical babble. It is intimate, from the heart, the sound of the Spanish guitar, and the echo of the words are not usually, before it, more than a new and harmonic resonance of its body.

We speak of the guitar, for the reason that, as an instrument it is only as a material creator of the sound. We leave it to stand extended a moment to reach the hands, without daring to try the art of playing it, and we will speak of the other lesser known art, of the modest art of its construction, so interesting and so worthy of the attention of the aficionados.

Spain is the country of the creation of the guitar, the homeland of its best constructors. In Madrid, in Seville, in Granada, in Cadiz were the famous workshops where out came the polished and finely tuned instruments that were the model later for the modern industry, that preserved most carefully the primitive guitars of the 17th century, daughters of the *Vihuela* and granddaughters of the Arabic Lute (*Oud*), that has its ancestors farther away in the instruments of the Orient.

The *Vihuela* of four strings of the 16th century that was skillfully played by Luis de Narvaez, Luis Milan, Miguel Fuenllana and Diego Pisador, was to be converted into the guitar by virtue of the innovation by Vicente Espinel, a musician and poet, who added the fifth string and handed over a new instrument to the Spanish nobility of the Courts of Felipe III and Felipe IV, that spread the unmistakable Spanish art throughout Europe.

The guitar became popular in France and in Italy, but where it found unsuspected roots was in Hispanic America, especially in the lands of the Rio de la Plata that went on to later form the great Republic of Argentina.

In Argentina the guitar has its own and independent history. There it eventually became the national instrument, and today after being hoisted by the public as an emblematic mast, it has passed to the highest social classes, the most aristocratic, they have their most famous makers of the artistic Spanish guitars, and they not only disdain, but they exalt the popular instrument with its grace and with its feminine enchantment.

The great renaissance has been observed in our days, of "the Spanish guitar" as it was called in Europe when it was spreading its art, before its later modification, introduced by the priest Miguel García (Padre Basilio-he is credited with having added the 6th string to the guitar), a popular 18th century player, who utilized the guitar of "seven courses", its previous form didn't prosper, although its use was maintained for a long time and even though it still lingers in Russia, to whose country this instrument of seven strings was exported from Spain.

The guitar that glorified Fernando Sor, the eminent composer and Catalan guitarist; that elevated their contemporaries to sublime conceptions: Dionisio Aguado, Huerta, Ciebra (Ciedra sic), Bosch, Nava (Naya sic), Coste – author of a known study – and in modern times, the great Tárrega, Llobet, Joséfina Robledo, Maria Luisa Anido – Argentine concert guitarist – Sainz de la Maza, Andrés Segovia and others, have a scarce quantity of constructors. It's evident that the guitar can be fabricated in a series, such as an automobile, and that permits the offering of a low price of industrial character, and in such a way, the large workshops of Barcelona and Valencia supply inexpensive guitars to half of the world; but only some small workshops maintain the prestige of the fabrication of a guitar model, of the harmonious instrument, elegant, constructed with refinement and the delicateness of a jewel, that has to be plucked by a well-known artist in front of a select public.

Those workshops aren't abundant. In Madrid maybe they don't exceed more than 2 or 3; in Barcelona another famous one exists, and one very notable one in Paris. They are the owners who inherited the art of Dionisio Guerra, who fabricated magnificent guitars in the 18th century in Cadiz; of Juan Pages,

Hablemos, pues, de la guitarra solamente como instrumento material creador del sonido. La dejaremos reposar extendida un momento al alcance de las manos, sin osar tratar del arte de tañería, y hablaremos de otro arte menos conocido, del arte modesto de su construcción, tan interesante y tan digno de la atención de los aficionados.

España es el país creador de la guitarra, la patria de los mejores constructores. En Madrid, en Sevilla, en Granada, en Cádiz estuvieron los famosos talleres de donde salieron los pulidos y afinadísimos instrumentos que fueron modelo después para los industriales modernos, que conservan cuidadosamente las primitivas guitarras del siglo XVII, hijas de la vihuela y nietas del laúd árabe, que tiene sus ascendientes más lejanos en los instrumentos del Oriente.

La vihuela de cuatro cuerdas del si-

Caption: Drawing placement of the purflings for the guitar

---

another notable Cadiz maker; the maker in Granada Francisco Ortega, of Antonio Torres, of Seville —the Stradivarius of the guitar—; of Llorente, of Carracedo, of Zorzano, the great maker in Logroño, and of Vicente Arias, of Ciudad Real. All of them now passed away. Their names are only memories of other times, who soon will be classics in the art of the guitar, like those of Sor and those of Aguado are today.

GUITARRA POR D. ANTONIO TORRES (EL STRADIVARIUS DE LA GUITARRA), ALMERIA, EN EL AÑO 1886

EL FAMOSO GUITARRISTA Y EMINENTE COMPOSITOR D. FERNANDO SORS. REPRODUCCION DE UN GRABADO DE LA EPOCA PUBLICADO EN LA REVISTA "LA GUITARRA", DE BUENOS AIRES

OTRO MODELO DE GUITARRA CONSTRUIDO POR VICENTE ARIAS, EN CIUDAD REAL, EN EL AÑO 1874

Captions left to right.

Guitar by *Don* Antonio Torres (The Stradivarius of the Guitar.) Almeria, in the year 1886

The famous guitarist and composer, *Don* Fernando Sor, a reproduction of a portrait from that epoch published in the *"La Guitarra"* magazine, in Buenos Aires.

Another model of a guitar constructed by *Don* Vicente Arias, in Ciudad Real, in the year 1874.

───────────────────────

The guitars are constructed with very old woods that are perfectly dried. In a workshop in Madrid where instruments that are beautifully finished come out, they are constructed by the most able hands of the industry, we have contemplated the first grade materials of the guitar, an aspect of the most curious of its fabrication; old chests, the most ancient furniture of strange woods that the guitar makers argue over with antique dealers, paying them a high price. All good guitars have, that as a virtue, a mysterious origin that gives legend a flavor. At times the industry acquires an old key or a manor bed, a raised platform such as a podium, a religious altarpiece, and the first curious impression is deciphering the origin of the wood from which it is formed.

Spain possessed a vast empire when its artists constructed those sofas and objects of many uses and to it arrived from the most remote places from virgin America and of the richest and strangest Oriental deciduous woods, that they employed in the industrial arts. The guitarmaker of today has to sink his hands in those remotest of times to convert the old wood born in ignored forests into harmonic bodies, with the end of which the player brings out the sweet sounds that accompany the laments and the vehemence of the popular songs.

Every guitar is constructed with a different wood. Clearly, it's what we are referring to in the select construction, of expensive models that they usually are to be paid at times up to 1,000 *pesetas* (one year's salary). On some occasions an unknown black wood, that appeared as Ebony, resists being cut by a saw, by the elevated temperature of the untempered steel, that strange piece of furniture had to be abandoned, that one day was the pride of its constructor and he preserved it, through the centuries, a specie of indomitable and aristocratic spirit, when a plebeian leaf wanted to destroy the heart of that

ción de Vicente Espinel, músico y poeta, que la añadió una quinta cuerda y entregó el nuevo instrumento a la nobleza española de las Cortes de Felipe III y Felipe IV, que difundieron el arte españolísimo por Europa entera.

La guitarra se hizo popular en Francia y en Italia, pero donde encontró insospechado arraigo fué en Hispanoamérica, especialmente en las tierras del Plata que habían de formar más tarde la gran República Argentina.

En la Argentina tiene la guitarra una historia propia e independiente. Allí llegó a ser el instrumento nacional, y hoy, después de haber sido izada por el pueblo como un mástil emblemático, ha pasado a las más altas clases sociales. Las muchachas argentinas, las más aristocráticas, tienen sus artísticas guitarras españolas de las marcas más afamadas, y no solamente no desdeñan, sino que enaltecen con su gracia y con su encanto femenino, el instrumento popular.

Se observa en nuestros días un gran renacer de "la guitarra española", como era denominado este instrumento en Europa cuando fué difundido su arte, antes

GUITARRA CLÁSICA, CON ESTA INSCRIPCIÓN: "DIONISIO GUERRA ME HIZO EN CADIZ ESTE AÑO DE 1754"

forma que no prosperó, aunque su uso se mantuvo mucho tiempo y aún perdura en Rusia, a cuyo país se exporta desde España este instrumento de siete cuerdas.

———

La guitarra que glorificó Fernando Sors, el genial compositor y guitarrista catalán; que elevaron a sublimes concepciones sus contemporáneos Dionisio Aguado, Huerta, Ciedra, Bosch, Nava, Coste—autor de un conocido estudio—, y en los modernos tiempos el gran Tárrega, Llovet, Josefina Robledo, María Luisa Anido—concertista argentina—, Sáinz de la Maza, Andrés Segovia y otros, tiene escasos constructores. Es evidente que un instrumento musical puede ser fabricado en serie, como un automóvil, y esto permite ofrecer un bajo precio de carácter industrial, y así, las grandes fábricas valencianas y barcelonesas surten de guitarras baratas a medio mundo; pero sólo algunos pequeños talleres mantienen el prestigio de la fabricación de la guitarra modelo, del instrumento armonioso, elegante, construído con el refinamiento y la delica-

Caption: Classical Guitar, with the inscription: "Made by Dionisio Guerra in Cadiz this year of 1754."

———

great wild tree and formidable for converting it into this so feminine and such subtle thing, that is a guitar.

For constructing the good model guitar they usually employ Cypress, Mahogany, Rosewood, Spruce and Maple. Oak is attractive wood of the expensive sofas, clear and clean, but doesn't serve any use for constructing guitars.

With a thin table it's constructed over a *solera* the harmonic soundboard, is formed egg shaped – according to the professional vocabulary – because it has been observed that the flat ones usually have less life. The placement of the wooden fan braces, glued in different directions, is a delicate work that permits reinforcement of the strength of the body without losing any resonance. The necks are made of Cedar and the fret boards, of Ebony or Rosewood.

The guitar has 19 metal frets, whose separation is studied mathematically. Usually they have templates for their placement, but the distances can be determined by a good fabricator by calculating, a basis of the equality of separation between the nut and the 12th fret and between this and the saddle of the bridge.

The art of the filetry is one of those prodigious remains that stay in Spain of the Arabic labor that enrich our monuments and precious objects of the past. It permits the adornment in mosaic, of the sound hole and, in general, of the whole guitar, and require especially able hands to perform the thorough and patient work.

There consists in the rosette fabrication the usage of small blocks with delicate leaves of pine, colored in several shades, with those which are incrusted in the guitar, the delicate adornment that usually increases the value of the instrument up to the limits that only is fixed by the caprice of the buyer. A delicate cut permits obtaining the pieces of the mosaic that have to form the design, pieces that usually are recorded of 40, 50 or 60 pieces in each one, not being larger than six millimeters or a ¼ of an inch, by three mm or four mm or 1/8 of an inch wide.

REPASANDO FILISTERIA PARA LA CONSTRUCCION DE MOSAICOS

deza de una joya, que ha de ser pulsado por el artista de nombradía ante un público selecto.

Estos talleres no abundan. En Madrid tal vez no excedan de dos o tres; en Barcelona existe otro afamado, y uno muy notable en París. Son sus dueños los herederos del arte de Dionisio Guerra, que fabricó en Cádiz magníficas guitarras en el siglo XVIII; de Juan Pages, otro gadita-no notable; del granadino Francisco Ortega, de Antonio Torres, de Sevilla—el *Stradivarius* de la guitarra—; de Llorente, de Carracedo, de Zorzano, el gran fabricante de Logroño, y de Vicente Arias, de Ciudad Real. Todos han muerto. Sus nombres son sólo recuerdos de otros tiempos, que pronto serán clásicos en el arte de la guitarra, como hoy son los de Sors y los de Aguado.

Se construyen las guitarras con maderas

Caption: Thinning the *filetes* that make up the mosaic of a guitar rosette.

The Spanish guitar, that has its best workshops in Madrid, today exports in very appreciable quantities all over Europe, for all the way from Germany to the Scandinavian countries it advises that there is an increased interest in this genuinely Spanish instrument, that used to be little understood and appreciated in countries of different races and very different temperaments.

viejísimas, perfectamente desecadas. En un taller madrileño de donde salen instrumentos bellísimamente acabados, construídos por las manos más hábiles de la industria, hemos contemplado la materia *prima* de la guitarra, aspecto de los más curiosos de su fabricación: viejos arcones, muebles antiquísimos de extrañas maderas que los guitarreros disputan a los anticuarios, pagándolos a altos precios. Toda buena guitarra tiene, en virtud de esto, un misterioso origen que le presta sabor de leyenda. A veces el industrial adquiere un viejo clave o un lecho señorial, un estrado o un retablo religioso, y la primera curiosa impresión es la de descifrar el origen de la madera de que está formado.

España poseía un vasto Imperio cuando sus artistas construyeron tales muebles y objetos de diversos usos, y a ella llegaron de los lugares más apartados de la virgen América y del caduco Oriente maderas riquísimas y extrañas, que se empleaban en las artes industriales. El guitarrero de hoy tiene que hundir sus manos en estos tiempos remotísimos para convertir la vieja madera nacida en bosques ignorados en cajas armónicas, con el fin de que de ellas saque el tañedor los dulces sonidos con que acompaña los lamentos y las vehemencias de los cantos populares.

Cada guitarra está construída de una madera distinta. Claro está que nos referimos a la construcción selecta, a los modelos caros, que suelen ser pagados a veces hasta a 1.000 pesetas. En cierta ocasión una negra madera desconocida, parecida al ébano, resistió al corte de la sierra, cuyo acero se destempló por la elevada temperatura; hubo que abandonar aquel extraño mueble, que un día fué orgullo de su constructor y que conservó, a través de

REPRODUCCION DE UN RETRATO DEL EMINENTE GUITARRISTA Y COMPOSITOR D. FRANCISCO TARREGA

CONSTRUCCION INTERIOR DE UNA BUENA GUITARRA

los siglos, una especie de espíritu indomable y aristocrático, cuando una hoja plebeya quiso destruir el corazón de aquel gran árbol selvático y formidable para convertirle en eso tan femenino y tan sutil, que es la guitarra.

Para construir los buenos modelos se suele emplear el ciprés, la caoba, el palo santo, el acer y el maple. El roble, esa simpática madera de los ricos muebles, claros y limpios, no sirve para construir guitarras.

Con una delgada tabla se construye sobre las *soleras* la tapa armónica, de forma *ahuevada*—según el vocablo profesional—, porque se ha observado que las que son planas suelen tener menos vida. La colocación de barritas de madera, pegadas en distintas direcciones, es un delicado trabajo que permite reforzar la fortaleza de la caja sin quitarle su resonancia. Los mangos se hacen de cedro, y los diapasones, de ébano o palo santo.

La guitarra tiene 19 trastes metálicos, cuya separación está estudiada matemáticamente. Suele haber plantillas para su colocación, pero las distancias pueden ser determinadas por el buen fabricante por cálculo, a base de la igualdad de separación entre la cejilla y el 12 y entre éste y la cejilla del puente.

El arte de la *filetería* es uno de esos restos prodigiosos que quedan en España de las labores árabes que enriquecieron nuestros monumentos y preciosos objetos del pasado. Permite el adorno, en mosaico, de la boquilla y, en general, de toda la guitarra, y requiere manos especialmente hábiles para ejecutar tan minucioso y paciente trabajo.

Consiste en fabricar pequeños bloques con delgadísimas hojas de pino, coloreadas en diversos tonos, con las que se incrusta en la guitarra. el delica

Captions:

Reproduction of a portrait of the eminent guitarist and composer *Don* Francisco Tárrega. Dedication: "To my beloved friend, the eminent constructor of guitars *Don* Manuel Ramírez, affectionately, Francisco Tárrega." (This photo is in the possession of the José Ramírez family, it was shown in the book "Things about the Guitar.")

Interior construction of a good guitar.

EXAMEN DE UN INSTRUMENTO EN DISPOSICIÓN DE SER BARNIZADO

do adorno que suele avalorar el instrumento hasta límites que sólo fija el capricho del comprador. Un delicado corte permite obtener los trocitos de mosaico que han de formar el dibujo, trocitos que suelen constar de 40, 50 ó 60 piezas cada uno, no siendo más largas de seis milímetros, por tres o cuatro de ancho.

Esta guitarra española, que tiene en Madrid sus mejores talleres, se exporta hoy en cantidad muy apreciable a toda Europa, pues hasta en Alemania y en los pueblos escandinavos se advierte un creciente interés por este instrumento genuinamente español, que solía ser poco comprendido y apreciado en países de distinta raza y de muy diferente temperamento.

La Argentina es nuestro mejor mercado, y en Europa son países importadores Francia, Alemania, Bélgica, Holanda y Rusia. Los Estados Unidos e Inglaterra no acaban de decidirse por la guitarra española.

No obstante, la guitarra tiende a ser señora del mundo. Padecen un error los que la consideran sólo apropiada al acompañamiento o interpretación de nuestros motivos populares. Es un instrumento único, con alma propia, cuyo sonido es muy distinto de todos los restantes. Su conjunto es de los más completos, el armónico es rico en efectos, el arrastre es solo propio de ella. Su son no es intenso, pero es armonioso, muy íntimo, y hoy se interpreta bellísimamente con la guitarra a los grandes clásicos. Falla, Serrano, Turina suelen estudiar y escribir con la guitarra. El triunfo del instrumento español, su consagración mundial, tal vez se logre—y esto es una apreciación personal—cuando alguno de estos grandes músicos que han creado bellísimas obras de concierto sobre aires populares se dejen arrastrar por una original inspiración, fuera de toda corriente mundial, y escriban la gran ópera de música andaluza, o española si queréis, que ha de ser como un gran rayo de sol en este mundo de nuestros días, que va palpando el aire, como un ciego que camina buscando la emoción sin encontrarla.

Juan M. Mata.

(FOTOS LOPEZ BEAUBE)

Caption: Examination of an instrument about to be varnished.

Argentina is our best market and in Europe there are countries importing: France, Germany, Belgium, Holland and Russia. The United States and England haven't ended up deciding for the Spanish guitar yet.

Nonetheless, the guitar tends to be the wife of the world. Those who consider it only for the accompaniment or interpretation of our melodies suffer a mistake. It is a unique instrument, with its own soul, whose sound is very different than all the rest. Its set is the most complete, the harmonics are richly effective, the slide is only its own. Its sound isn't intense, but is harmonious, very intimate, and today it interprets most beautifully with the guitar to the great classics. De Falla, Serrano, Turina usually study and write with the guitar. The triumph of the Spanish instrument, its worldwide consecration, maybe has achieved – and this is a personal appreciation – when some of the great musicians that have created the most beautiful concert works over popular airs they let them drag by an original inspiration, outside of all the world current, and write a grand opera of Andalucian music, or Spanish if you wish, that has to be a great ray of sunlight in this world of our days, that goes breathing the air, like a blind man that walks searching for the emotion without finding it.

Juan M. Mata
(Photos Lopez Beaube)

The photos in this article are of the José Ramírez Guitar Workshop in Madrid. At this time Alfonso Benito, Antonio Gomez and Marcelo Barbero worked for José Ramírez.

Returning to the text of Héctor García Martínez:

About Esteban Massini, we know that he arrived in Argentina in 1822, and that he played guitar, clarinet and flute. When he settled in Buenos Aires, he created the first conservatory of music and music store where imported European instruments and sheet music could be bought.

His commercial advertising announcement read: "Esteban Massini, Italian, has the honor to announce to the public of Buenos Aires, that he has decided to set up permanent residence and offer music lessons for various instruments, such as Flute, French Guitar, Clarinet, etc". (*El Argos* – December 7, 1822)

Throughout commercial announcements, another reads: "Mr. Massini has just received a new collection of superior flutes made by various makers, clarinets, violins, trumpets and octave flutes, French guitars and an excellent collection of military music as well as flute pieces. Everything mentioned is priced very conveniently". (*La Gaceta Mercantil* – March, 1823.)

According to Vicente Jesualdo, in 1829 the debut of Massini's *Gran Rondo* of the guitar with accompaniment of orchestra took place.

During many years Esteban was a flautist in the Orquesta Coliseo, integrating in the orchestra in the greatest seasons 1825-1827, directed by Massini.

Esteban Massini

He had proficient students, belonging to the most select levels of Buenos Aires society, such as Argentine poet Esteban Echeverria, Robles, José Maria Trillo, Santiago Calzadilla (father), Salustiano Zavalia (1810-1873), Nicanor Albarellos (1810-1891), Juan del Campillo (1812-1866) and Dr. Fernando Cruz Cordero (Uruguayan) (who was an official of the government of the controversial Argentine dictator Juan Manuel de Rosas) and who also completed diplomatic functions in later governments in Argentina.

As we've said, Massini performed in a polemic period of Argentina's past, the epoch of Rosas. Precisely in 1835, in Buenos Aires the festivities were held for the inauguration of General Rosas as the Governor and Captain General of the province of Buenos Aires.

The featured work that evening was "*La Italiana*", performed in the Teatro Coliseo, together with the debut of "*Himno de los restauradores*" (Hymn of the Restorers), music by Massini, lyrics by José Ribera Indarte, This work was in homage to General Rosas, the "Restorer of the Laws", for when he assumed power the country was in total anarchy, which he put in order, thus earning him the title of "the Restorer".

About the "*Himno de los restauradores*", Vicente Jesualdo in his "History of Argentine Music", maintains: "This was the song that posed the most predicament in the resistance epoch, and Massini wrote it originally for voice and piano, later transcribing it for various other instruments."

In addition to the above cited works, Massini also composed: "*Duo para guitarra y clarinete*" (1822), "*Duo para guitarra y violin*", "*Contradanza*" (1826), "*Dos canciones historicas*" ("Two Historical Songs") which debuted in Montevideo, Uruguay, "*El Tocado de la Dama*" (1837) and much more.

Esteban Massini died from a heart attack while playing the flute in the Orquesta Coliseo (Coliseo Orchestra) in Buenos Aires in 1838 at 50 of age. Of his disciples we can say that some were public figures.

Salustiano Zavalia: Constitutionist in 1853, he wrote the Constitution of his province, Tucuman. He was an accomplished guitarist, pianist and composer. He composed themes for the guitar, flute, Argentine themes, and danceable pieces.

This biography of Salustiano Zavalia is translated from Ricardo Muñoz's unpublished book "*Historia Universal de la Guitarra*" Volume VII "*La Guitarra en La Argentina*".

"Salustiano Zavalia was born in Tucuman on June 8, 1810, and was a distinguished lawyer who held posts in the Court, Argentine Congress and the Govenorship of his Province. He was a passionate guitarist who studied music in Cordoba with maestro Cambeses and the instrument with *Don* Esteban Massini; who said of him in *La Nacion*: 'Dr. Zavalia in the Lopez family home, playing the guitar and singing aires Tucumanos, with his facility he lost the notion of what hour it was.....'

During his exile of the country, in those fateful days of 1841 and the subsequent ones, playing the guitar and giving lessons living in Lima, Peru for 9 years. His historic guitar is in the possession of his grandson Clemente R. Zavaleta, the ex-Director of the Banco de la Nacion Argentina. Salustiano Zavalia passed away on January 16, 1873, in Tucuman."

This newspaper photo of Salustiano Zavalia and his guitar with case are from the Ricardo Muñoz book.

Esteban Echeverria

Returning to the text of Héctor García Martínez:

Nicanor Albarellos: medical doctor and interpreter of the guitar. He received his medical degree in Paris. He was a friend of poet Esteban Echeverria and Fernando Cruz Cordero with whom he learned the basics, artistically of the guitar of the Rio de la Plata. (Vicente Jesualdo, op. cit.) He is the author of "*Variaciones sobre el Cielito*" (Traditional dance of the Rio de la Plata) (1842) and other works for the guitar.

He was an opponent of General Rosas, and spent many years in exile in Montevideo, where he participated in concerts organized for the benefit of immigrants. After the battle of Caseros, where the regime of General Rosas fell, Nicanor returned to Buenos Aires, to his home, which had been a meeting place for aficionados of music.

Fernando Cruz Cordero: He was born in Montevideo, Uruguay in 1822 and the son of a Sevillian doctor. He was educated in Buenos Aires, where he had lived since a child. He was very young when he began to show an aptitude for music. At the age of 15 he began to study guitar with Massini. Apart from guitar, he began to study law, and passed the bar. He was a functionary in the government of Rosas, as well as in successive governments.

Domingo Prat, in his "*Diccionario de Guitarristas*" says something very important: "It has been said insistently that Esteban Echeverria was the one to introduce in Buenos Aires, the school that cultivated the greatest European guitarists: Sor, Aguado, etc., but the truth is that due to the precise dates we now possess, we can assure that the glory belongs to Fernando Cruz Cordero."

Dr. Fernando Cruz Cordero

Juan Manuel de Rosas

In 1844, Dr. Cordero published a work titled *"Discurso sobre Musica"*, edited in Buenos Aires by Arzac. This cultivator of the guitar was also concerned with didactic study of the instrument, writing a "Method for Guitar". According to dates we possess, this was the first method written in the Rio de la Plata. A copy of this method was part of the music library of the Catalonian maestro Domingo Prat, whose huge sheet music collection was divided (and kept intact) among several of his students, having been dispersed by Carmén Prat after his death. With the passing of time the large collection eventually was purchased by collectors in different parts of the world, and I believe the method by Cruz Cordero ended up in England. About the same subject, Prat said: "to repeat: a polished work of 150 pages and in an order that indicates the didactic personality of Dr. Fernando Cruz Cordero". (Prat op. cit)

In 1852 Cruz Cordero traveled to Europe and performed for Queen Victoria in England at Buckingham Palace. She presented him with gift of a guitar incrusted with mother of pearl. He is the author of *"Six Divertissements pour la Guitare"*, *"Cantos de Marineros"*, *"El Deseo"*, vals (1852), *"Las Olas y el Mar"* (1852). In 1860 he returned to Europe for health reasons and died in Paris the 21st of August 1863. His widow, Petrona Villegas, had his ashes transported to Buenos Aires in a piano case.

After the battle of Caseros in 1852, when the regime of General Rosas fell, the Argentine guitaristic movement had two valuable young proponents: Martin Ruiz Moreno (1833-1919), a student of Bernardo Troncoso, and Juan Alais (1844-1914), a self-taught guitarist. Due to the longevity of both, they would be witnesses to a later movement enriched by the arrival of Spanish maestros and concert artists, who brought the methodologies and music of Sor and Aguado, later followed by the advent of the celebrated Francisco Tárrega.

Carlos Vega, famed Argentine musicologist, speaking of these early guitarists, says this about them: "Contemporaries, disciples and torch bearers of Trinitiario Huerta (1804-1875), Napoleon Coste (1806-1883), Julián Arcas (1832-1882) and Juan Parga (1843-1899)".

Trinitario Huerta   Napoleon Coste   and one of his guitars

(Left) Julián Arcas

(Right) Juan Parga

(Below) Francisco Tárrega playing
for students and friends. left to right:
Tonico Tello, Pascual Roch, José Orellana,
Francisco Corell Pbro, Baldomero Cateura,
Notario Santacruz, Manuel Loscos,
Francisco Tárrega and Vicente Puchol.

Julián Arcas pieces published in two series by: Hijos de Vidal and Roger, Barcelona in 1891, almost a decade after he had passed away.

Juan Parga 1894
Lopez and Griffo, Malaga

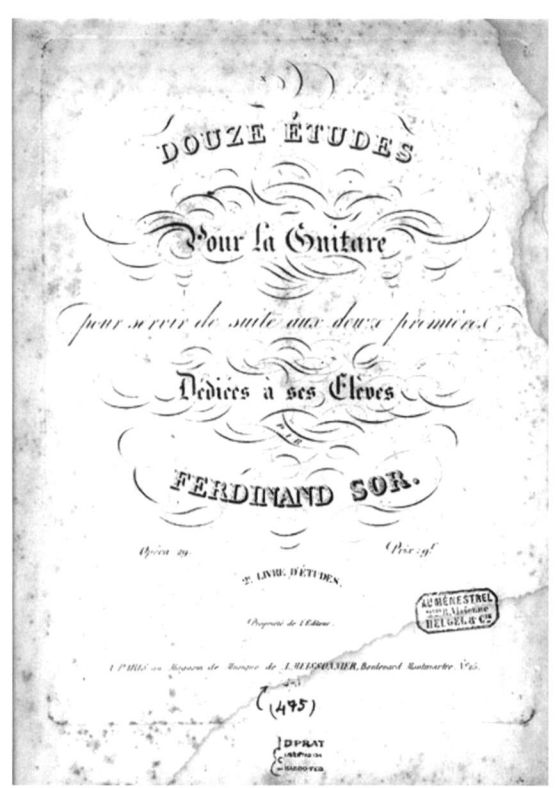

Fernando Sor's Op. 29 published
by A. Meissonnier in Paris, 1825
Archive: Domingo Prat

Juan Carlos Anido and his daughter Maria Luisa in Mar del Plata in 1914. She would study with three Francisco Tárrega students. First with Domingo Prat, who lived in the Anido home, where he had his own servant from 1914-1916, then with Joséfina Robledo, when Prat briefly returned to concertize in Spain, and eventually with Miguel Llobet.

These Spanish maestros that contributed to awaken the fervor for the classical guitar in Argentina in the last decades of the 19th century were the following:

Gaspar Sagreras (1838-1901), who had arrived in 1869, and was father of Julio S. Sagreras,

(Left) Gaspar Sagreras photo from *"Historia de la Guitarra"* by guitar historian Ricardo Muñoz.
(Right) Gaspar Sagreras autograph from *"Giulia"* published by Carlos Schnockel.

It appears that the sequence of publishers for Gaspar Sagreras might be:
Editorial A. Demarchi (1870's)
Ediciones Stefani
Ediciones Carlos Schnockel
E. Oca
Francisco Nuñez y Cia.
Posthumous publishers:
Romero Agromayor y Cia.
Romero y Fernández
Antigua Casa Nuñez, Diego, Gracia y Cia.
Ricordi Americana

Gaspar Sagreras publications by Ediciones Stefani of Buenos Aires, including the flamenco piece *Peteneras*.

"Gaspar Sagreras was born in Palma de Mallorca on October 21, 1838. He became a medical student while simultaneously developing a passion for the guitar. Gaspar proposed to find a maestro to spiritualize on the guitar the hours spent studying a career chose for him by his parents. For these reasons he traveled to Buenos Aires. Soon after his arrival he realized he didn't want to continue in the medical field and devoted himself to the guitar. He renewed his lessons in harmony. He began to perform in public and in private. The members of the bonarense high society frequently solicited him. He was a good friend with his colleagues Juan Alais, Carlos García Tolsa and the cult figure-painter-guitarist Bernardo Troncoso.

In 1887 and 1888 Gaspar, along with Juan Alais and Carlos García Tolsa, offered two concerts playing solos and trios. The concert in 1888 had the greatest success. There is an anecdote to one of those concerts. The trio having stayed until the end of the concert to conclude the last piece in common interest, when all of a sudden Carlos García Tolsa vanished. When the doorman was asked if he had seen Carlos, he replied that he had seen him leave quickly with a friend who had been waiting in the ticket office. With stupefaction Gaspar exclaimed 'Well, we played for the public and the art'. Juan Alais retorted behind his long blond mustache: 'Yes, and...... for García Tolsa' Despite the mischief, that didn't keep them from being friends.

Among the prestigious disciples of Gaspar's were these guitarists: Lorenzo Torres, Mariano Castex Sr., *Doña* Adelina Harilaos de Olmos, and many others who attended the reunions in the home of Gregorio Torres. A frequenter of these get-togethers was Julio A. Roca, twice President of Argentina. His beautiful daughters, who played the guitar, always accompanied him. It was at these reunions that Julio Roca Jr. was presented, a child who played and was highly admired by the high society of Buenos Aires.

Domingo Prat, in his *Diccionario de Guitarristas*, from which this biography is translated, says the composition "*Una Lagrima*" was published and reprinted at least 40 times (sometimes revised, sometimes clandestinely), and that the maestros always included this piece in their repertoire for their students. With his teaching, Gaspar made a name for himself, a modest position and provided an excellent education for his children. Gaspar died on April 14, 1901."

The 1931 Antigua Casa Nuñez catalog lists 47 works by Gaspar Sagreras. The "*Premier Vals Op. 26*" by Godard is not included in that list of 47 works, the publisher is unknown, as well as the lithographer, though in the list of his son, Julio S. Sagreras, No. 130 is the same title.

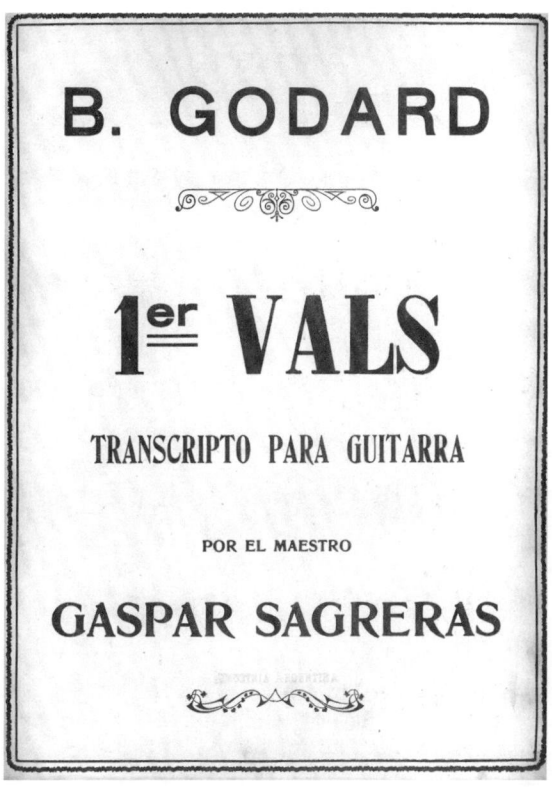

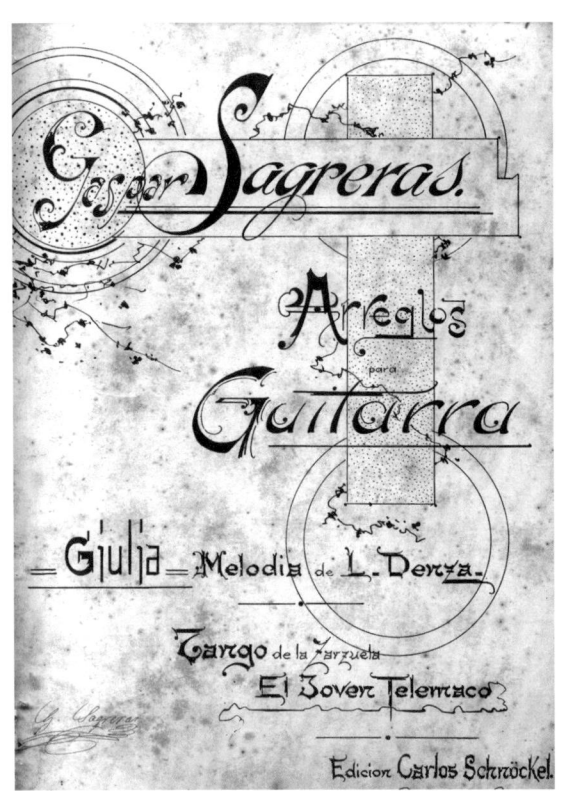

Gaspar Sagreras piece *"Giulia"* published by Carlos Schnockel, *"La Cautiva-Mazurka"*, *"Il Bacio-Vals"* and *"El Carnaval de Venecia"* all published by Francisco Nuñez before the turn of the century. These are numbers 17, 6, 30, 31 respectively in his list of 47 works. The cover for *La Cautiva* is an edition published between 1900-1910, when the name of the street Cuyo was changed to Sarmiento after the centennial of the birth of the nation.

32

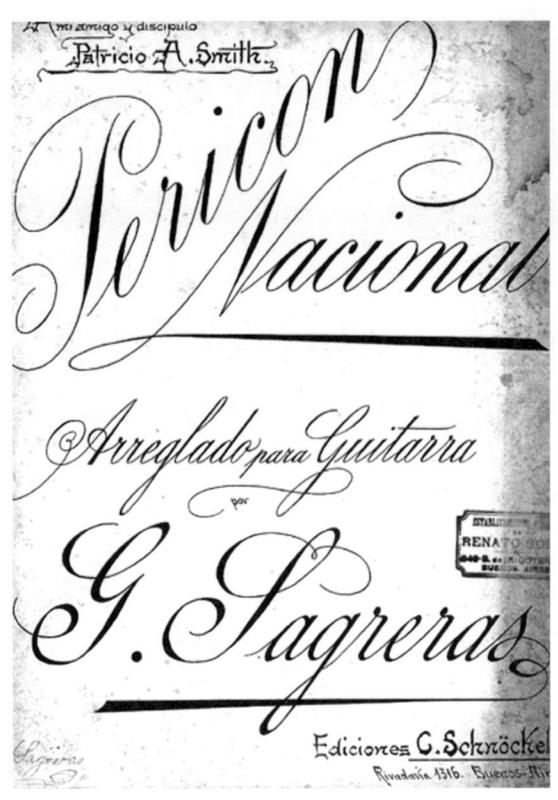

(Above Left) Carlos Schnockel publication of a Gaspar Sagreras transcription and
(Above Right) and another published by E. Oca (Below left) A publication by A. Demarchi and
(Below Right) the 11th edition of the very popular *Una Lagrima* (a tremolo piece) published by Romero
Agromayor y Cia. in 1915. Gaspar Sagreras was dead over a decade and the popularity of many of his
pieces had yet to fade, and they wouldn't for decades.

OBRAS DEL MISMO AUTOR

1	Himno Nacional Argentino	
2	Fantasía sobre motivos de Marta	
3	Una lágrima	fantasía para una guitarra
»	" "	" " " ó dos guitarras
4	Miserere de El Trovador	
5	La Manonga	Mazurca para una ó dos guitarras
6	La Cautiva	"
7	A tu oído	Vals
8	Pericón Nacional	
9	3er Vals Boston	
10	Gorro Frigio	Tango
11	El Brindis	Polka
12	Stephanie	Gavota
13	No me olvides	Habanera
14	El año pasado por agua	Mazurca
15	Spirito Gentil de Favorita	
16	Nanduty	Habanera
17	Giulia romanza de Denza	
18	El Joven Telémaco	Tango
19	La Lira	Vals
20	La Mimosa	Polka
21	Berline Rytmée	Polka militar
22	Tararira	Mazurca
23	La Celestial	"
24	La Cinquantaine	Gavota
25	Colección de estilos criollos	(con canto)
26	Peteneras	para guitarra sola
27	Los Hugonotes	Coro de los bañantes
28	La Traviata	Motivos
29	Ruborosa	Mazurca
30	Il Bacio	Vals
31	El Carnaval de Venecia	Variaciones
32	El Bocaccio	Polka
33	Marcha turca de Mozart	para dos guitarras
34	El Amor es la vida	Habanera para canto y guitarra
35	Lo mejor de una niña	id id id id
36	Oje Carull	canción nap. para mand. id
37	Gita Alpine	Polka
38	Marcha	de la ópera Aida
39	Música prohibita	para canto y guitarra
40	Serenata de Schubert	id id
41	La Voluble	Polka
42	Romanza de la Gitana de El Trovador	
		para canto y guitarra
43	Tango de la zarzuela el Certamen Nacional	
44	La Aurora Vals	Para dos guitarras
45	Trovador	Coro Di Zingari
46	Dolores	Vals
47	Ravvedimento e Perdono	Mazurca

This is a list of the publications of the Gaspar Sagreras originals and transcriptions, it's from the back of the Francisco Nuñez published piece "Vals Boston No. 3" 2nd edition.

Photo of Juan Alais from *"Historia de la Guitarra"* by Ricardo Muñoz. Two weeks after his death, a much smaller photo of Alais was used in the Obituary section of *Caras y Caretas* magazine dated October 31, 1914, issue No. 839 Año XVII.

"Juan Alais Moncada was born in the Federal capital of Buenos Aires on December 7, 1844. His parents were Valentin Alais (English) and Felipa Moncada (Argentine). Juan began to play the guitar when he was 18 years old. By 1870 he had gained a reputation among devotees of music in Buenos Aires. He began to teach the instrument and had acquired the nickname Juan *"El Ingles"*. Domingo Prat, from whose *Diccionario de Guitarristas* this biography is drawn, calls Juan Alais the dean of the instrumentalists of that epoch."

'The distinguished society of Buenos Aires invited Juan to every party to play his vidalitas, chacareras, gatos and estilos. Juan was a self-taught guitarist. Despite not having a maestro to help him advance in an organized manner, Juan's success was such that he played in the orchestra in the old Teatro Colon, under the direction of maestro Bassi. In the political upheaval of the time Juan Alais was at the military campaigns of Cepeda and Pavon. During the war with Paraguay, Juan served as a soldier in the garrison in Buenos Aires. After witnessing battles where men were maimed and killed, young Juan would play his guitar for the enjoyment of his fellow soldiers, who listened with unimaginable enthusiasm'. (Justo Cardenas, from *Caras y Caretas* No. 864. April 24, 1905).

In the year 1882, a group of friends and admirers organized a benefit concert for the great guitarist. It was an important event and was reported in the daily newspapers of Buenos Aires: *"La Nacion"*, Tuesday, November 7, 1882 'Concierto: The commission has resolved the organization of the benefit concert for the Argentine guitarist Mr. Juan Alais, with a part of the proceeds at the same time to be designated to aid the invalids. The music festival will be held on the 18th of the current month in the Florida garden under the direction of maestro Montenegro. There was a reunion in the home of Mr. Saubidet where the initial resolutions regarding the concert were decided, and the following commission was named:

President: Mariano E. Saubidet

Vicepresident: José Villar

Treasurer: Major Sargeant José Poviña,

Secretaries: Pedro Casteroso and José C. Moyano

Subcommission: Torcuato Ocampo, Miguel Lavalle, Rodolfo Araujo Muñoz, José Maria Niño author of "Mitre", Juan A. Argerich, Santiago Duhalde, José S. Alvarez, Belisrio Otamendi, José Mendez, Francisco Delgado, Francisco Mendia, Pedro Barreiro, Alberto J. Kratzenstein and Ignacio R. Mejia.

Mr Alais is considered presently as a complete player of the instrument to which he dedicates himself. "*La Prensa*", "*Las Provincias*", "*La Republica*", "*El Nacional*" and others from the interior of the country such as "*El Eco de Azul*", and the magazine "*El Album del Hogar*", wrote very praiseworthy articles about this concert, to the point that they helped make the event a great success given the congenial popularity enjoyed by the guitarist as well as the legion of friends he could count on. The concert happened in the place mentioned, where they had erected a great triumphal arch to make it the main highlight of the fest, as if the illumination was electric and which gave it a character that "dressed it up". The bands that came were: Army Artillery band, Centro Gallego band, Cuerpo de Bomberos (Firemen), and, to be heard for the first time, the composition entitled "*Fantasia sobre el Himno*", dedicated by the composer Mr. Ratuezno to General Roca. 'To this festival, sponsored by the most distinguished of Buenos Aires, Doctors Albarellos, Mr. Roig and Mr. Moyano contributed as concert artists. The recipient of this benefit, Juan Alais, heard them play on their guitars the symphonies of "*Juana de Arco*" by Verdi and "*La Cenerentola*", accompanied by Dr. Albarellos'. (Justo Cardenas, from *Caras y Caretas* No. 864. April 24, 1905). The festival resulted in reaching the desires of the organizers, producing, according to the above named dailies, the fabulous amount of 33,185 pesos, leaving, after expenses, 17,847 pesos for the benefitee and 5,948 pesos for the disabled. Judging by the funds raised, Juan Alais enjoyed great popularity and sincere affection in his land.

In 1894, His fame extended beyond the limits of the Argentine border, as in 1894 he was named an honorary member of the Central Musical de Chinchu Alta in Peru, sending him the diploma No. 26 signed by the president Romualdo Ibañez. In 1895 Juan took part in a benefit concert in the locality of Almirante Brown which was a great success, principally due to the fact that he was the only one in those times who had the ability to achieve this.

The music of Alais is personal and has the stamp of the author on it: their form is danceable and the works of folkloric character, popular, original works and arrangements. His works conserve some pages of our popular airs, which today are documents for consultation of our folklore, featuring motifs which Alais picked up from the populace to use as the basis for creating a distinct harmonic composition.

Analyzing his compositions, they are of simple harmonization, the originals as well as the arrangements, and they number 87 total. Some of his works are everlasting, such as "*Un Momento*" *(Vals)*, "*La ñatita*", and "*La Perezosa*" (Mazurkas for one or two guitars) and "*Elvira*". The rhythm in the introduction to the waltz "*Un Momento*" is one of the finest examples of his writing. Of course, the value of the works of Alais is great, but always within the genre and ambiance for which he composed, without the pretense of elevated music, technique and spirituality. In his dances, however, the works of Alais do not reach the level of García Tolsa. But they have but an umistakable touch of the popular and the simple, without attempting to give rhythms of high flight that in the end result with little musical merit, such as "*Meditacion*", by García Tolsa, a common melody that is not guitaristic, as well as his sonata "*Al Fin Solos*".

(*"Meditacion"* was concertized by Agustín Barrios (1916-1939), Justo Morales (1917), and recorded on a test pressing by Lalyta Almiron. (1930's) R. O.).

36

To develop his airy melodic themes, Alais utilized the most common positions of the guitar as concerns the left hand. He dedicated his works to friends and many related figures, and the list of dedicatees reveals the depth of appreciation the Argentine aristocracy held for him: Martin Gil, disciple, Dr. Felix Amadeo Benitez, Alberto Luro, Rufino Luro, Horacio Martínez de Hoz, Pastor Luis Obligado (to whom is dedicated the waltz "Caramuru"), Eloisa Lozano (later a disciple of Domingo Prat), Joséfina G. Arana, Susana Maria Luro Cambaceres, Maria Byrne, Esther M. Tobal and Francisco Nuñez. "La Coqueta" was dedicated to Nuñez, his great friend and publisher. Nuñez constructed a splendid guitar for Alais with a good voice, in which the filetes and mosaics in the rosette served not only as adornment but also as reinforcement. The label read "Construida para Juan Alais.- Francisco Nuñez".

This instrument, comparable in its quality of sound to those of Torres, was sold to Guillermo Valdez after a paralysis struck Alais in his 66th year. Valdez bought the guitar for his daughter, a very distinguished player. The author of this Diccionario guards many affectionate memories and a great gratitude for Alais. He never scrimped in his efforts nor did he lack enthusiasm to help his friends and colleagues. Recalling his nobility and kindness with great emotion, I had announced a concert and Alais took to the music store of his great admirer (Casa Nuñez) a respectable quantity of programs without considering the amount of time involved traveling by cablecar with numerous stops, all to help publicize my concert. We could count a succession of works equally eloquent, but that will be known in another opportunity in which we have to record them. In the home of General Leyria in 1908, folks gathered for the typical barbecues, in the company of other guitarists such as E. Gonzalez, with whom there was a friendly guitaristic competition. There were many times that we attended these unforgettable barbecues — which have now passed to a "cuarto menguante" (waning quarter) — at which Alais imposed silence to play for the "catalancito Prat", his personal name for me.

In those reunions distinguished amateurs and friends of the instrument never missed an opportunity to attend, such as police commissioner Pondal, Nuñez and Roberto Lehmann among others. The guitaristic sessions and robust counterpoint that they brought to a head in the grocery store of Raconi, at Peru and Garay streets, and in "La Berbenita", at Belgrano and Saavedra, were faithfully attended by Alais who never missed a gathering, mingling with the payadores (singers) Gabino Ezeiza, Pablo Vazquez and others, and the instrumentalists Caprino, Simeone, Quijano, together with an endless number of artists who so freely gave personality and color to the history of the guitar in those typical corners of Buenos Aires, Republic of Argentina.

In the year 1910 Juan Alais had a partial paralytic attack (stroke), a state that he remained in until his death four years later. The "catalancito Prat" was the only colleague who came to accompany his remains: to say that is painful for those who were his friends; more so for his companion at the time of his death (Domingo Prat), but it is necessary to say that. He died on October 7, 1914. As his nephew, José M. Alais Agrelo stated that Alais will always live in the memory of his fellow citizens, for today many years have passed since his death, and we can only exclaim: "Un Momento!" for Alais." So ends the entry in the Diccionario de Guitarristas by Domingo Prat.

From the "Historia de la Guitarra" by Ricardo Muñoz, published in 1930, we get a slightly different account of various details:

"Juan initially heard the guitar played by his brother Guillermo when Juan was just a child. Guillermo took a long voyage and upon returning, hearing the mastery of Juan, he decided to never play the guitar in front of him again. By the age of 11 years old, Juan had acquired a recognizable expertise, considering he never had a maestro." About the important concert in 1882, Muñoz claims that Juan Alais donated 25% of the receipts, after expenses, to the invalids.

In the 1931 Antigua Casa Nuñez catalog at the beginning of the listing of 87 works by Juan Alias it also mentions for 30 Pesos a bound version of all 87 works was available. The only other artist in the catalogue to have a bound volume offered at that time was Julio S. Sagreras with 110 of the 126 pieces (Nos. 1-126 inclusive.) published by then for *35 Pesos*.

Juan Alais

La tradición de buenos guitarristas siempre la conservaron en nuestro país notables concertistas, pero entre todas el más representativo fué el señor Juan Alais, a quien acabamos de perder hace pocos meses.

Alais nació en esta capital en 1838, y desde su más tierna infancia tomó una decidida afición a la guitarra, resultando un excelente memorista, para quien el instrumento no tenía secretos.

La sociedad distinguida del Buenos Aires que ya pasó, le invitaba preferentemente a toda fiesta para que la concurrencia se extasiase ante aquel prodigio que hacía de la guitarra una caja armónica; y escuchar las vidalitas, chacareras, gatos y estilos ejecutados con una perfección de maestro.

Ya hombre, tomó a lo serio el estudio de la guitarra y se puso a estudiar por su cuenta música, sin maestro que lo guiara, y tan brillantes fueron sus resultados que el maestro Bassi lo incorporó a la orquesta del antiguo teatro Colón.

Hizo las campañas de Cepeda y Pavón y durante la guerra del Paraguay sirvió en la guarnición que quedó en Buenos Aires. Demás está decir que en las horas tristes del campamento el joven Alais recreaba el oído de sus compañeros de armas, haciéndoles oir las piezas de su repertorio, las que eran escuchadas con gran entusiasmo.

La fama del guitarrista criollo fué en aumento, y cuanta pieza componía para guitarra alcanzaba un éxito colosal. Entre sus muchas producciones se hicieron populares la mazurca «La Perezosa» y los valses «Un momento» y «No sé».

La popularidad que gozaba el guitarrista Alais se puso de manifiesto en el concierto que a su beneficio dió en el desaparecido «Jardín Florida», el 18 de noviembre de 1882, cuya entrada alcanzó a la cifra de 33.185 pesos. Dicha fiesta fué patrocina-

Un Momento
Vals

da por lo más distinguido de Buenos Aires; y como concertistas prestaron su concurso el doctor Albarellos, y los señores Roig y Moyano. El beneficiado hizo oir, ejecutadas a la guitarra, las sinfonías de «Juana de Arco», de Verdi, y la de «La Cenerintola», acompañado por el doctor Albarellos.

La simpatía que gozaba Alais, era tal, que fué profesor de lo más distinguido de Buenos Aires.

Los viejos que tuvieron oportunidad de escuchar a Alais en sus buenos tiempos, se deshacen en elogios de la agilidad, destreza y buen gusto del viejo guitarrista criollo, y recuerdan con entusiasmo aquellos aires nacionales que tan brillantemente ejecutaba.

Su gran amigo, el general Leyría, fué uno de los que hasta el último momento se permitió el placer de escuchar los acordes de su guitarra.

JUSTO CÁRDENA.

El célebre guitarrista, en pose de criollo nato.

Portada de «La Perezosa», la composición más popular de Alais.

Alais, en compañía de su amigo íntimo el general Leyría y el guitarrista Emilio González.

This is from a *Caras y Caretas* magazine dated April 24, 1915, issue No. 864 *Año* XVIII.

A little more than six months after Juan Alais passed away, this memorial page was written. Translation of the previous page:

"A *Criollo* Guitarist.

The tradition of good guitarists has always been to preserve the notable guitarists in our land, but among them the most representative was Mr. Juan Alais, who we just lost a few months ago.

Alais was born in this capital in 1838 (sic-1844), and from his most tender infancy he took a decided liking toward the guitar, resulting in an excellent performer, for whom the instrument had no secrets.

The distinguished society of Buenos Aires in which he was involved, invited him preferentially to every party for which the enthusiastic gatherings before that prodigy who toward the guitar's harmonic body; and to hear the *vidalitas, chacareras, gatos* and *estilos* performed with a perfection of mastery.

That man now, undertook seriously the study of the guitar and put by his own music, without a maestro to guide him, and so brilliant were his results that the maestro Bassi, incorporated him into the orchestra of the old Teatro Colon.

He made the campaigns of Cepeda and Pavon and during the war of Paraguay he served in the garrison that stayed in Buenos Aires. The rest is to say that in the sad hours of the encampment the young Alais played to the ears of his companions, having them hear pieces of his repertory, which they listened to with a great enthusiasm.

The fame of the criollo guitarist was augmented, and as for a piece he would compose for the guitar it reached a colossal success. Among his many productions the popular ones became the mazurka *"La Perezosa"* and the waltzes *"Un momento"* and *"No sé"*.

The popularity that the guitarist Alais enjoyed was manifested in the concert, which to his benefit he gave in the now defunct "Jardin Florida", the 18th of November of 1882, whose entrance achieved the amount of 33,185 Pesos. The said party was attended by the most distinguished of Buenos Aires, and as concert artists Doctor Albarellos, and Mrrs. Roig and Moyano lent a hand. The man to receive the benefit was heard, performing on the guitar, the symphonies of *"Juana de Arcos"*, by Verdi, and that of *"La Cenerentola"*, accompanied by Doctor Albarellos.

The kindness that Alais enjoyed, was such, that he was the most distinguished professor of Buenos Aires.

The old folks that had the opportunity to listen to Alais in his good times lavished praise for his agility, dexterity and good taste of the old *criollo* guitarist, and remembered those national airs with enthusiasm that he so brilliantly performed.

His great friend General Leyria, was one of those until the last moment that he permitted the pleasure to hear the chords of his guitar.

Justo Cardenas."

Translations of captions: "The celebrated guitarist, in a pose of being born a *criollo* man.

"The cover of *"La Perezosa"*, the most popular composition by Alais."

"Alais, in the company of his intimate friend General Leyria and the guitarist Emilio Gonzalez."

This photo of Juan Alais is from the
book "*Disertaciones Musicales*" by
Segundo N. Contreras published in 1931.
Of three photos of Juan Alais I am
aware of, Juan appears to be the
youngest in this one. It is probably
taken between 1880-1890. In other
words, Juan was writing and
publishing at the time of this photo,
and not retired or close to retirement
as in the other two photos.

DON JUAN ALAIS

Agustín P. Barrios played this piece
"*La Perezosa*" at the age of 13 in 1898.
This 1st edition of Juan Alais was
published by Francisco Nuñez.

In the *Revista Musical Ilustrada "Tárrega"*, issue No. 8 of February 1925, there appeared an article (with the above photo) written by Mrs. E. Sanchez de Bustamante about Juan Alais:

"It can be said that Juan Alais is the precursor of the guitar in the country. Alais was self-taught, since he never had a professor. He dedicated himself to the guitar as a hobby, and because the instrument was his favorite passion; once he had conquered the difficulties that the guitar offered with its six strings, he lived only for the guitar. The guitar was intimately associated with him and it can be truthfully stated that with it he lived, and with it he died.

Alais has the great merit of having introduced the guitar into the *porteño* halls. He was, in his time, the first to play our music, and as a player he acquired fame promptly.

He was extremely modest in his character and never ostentatious in his art, and without pretensions, willing to be heard in family reunions and concerts, always with amazing success which created a fondness in the public for the guitar. It is due to Alais that we now have a considerable number of enthusiastic followers. Without exaggerating, it can be affirmed that in no part of the world are there so many good guitarists among professors and aficionados as in Buenos Aires. (This statement is the oldest of its kind, in the vein that Ricardo Muñoz said there were 5,000 guitarists and aficionados in Buenos Aires and the English magazine "Guitar News" in 1953 reported: "From the many interesting programs of guitar recitals received from Buenos Aires, it would appear that there is more guitar playing in that City than any other in the world....." R.O.)

But Alais was not of the current era where there are those who attempt to elevate the guitar as an instrument of greatness to the point of performing symphonies of Beethoven, and that is frankly laughable. The music of Alais was less complicated, without a doubt, the most adequate or better said, the most apropos. His most popular pieces were the transcriptions of "*Semiramis*" and "*Juana de Arco*", which he played admirably, together with the fantasies of Julián Arcas and José Viñas, written expressly for the guitar, as well as his own compositions, the criollo airs and regional estilos that he played divinely.

You can't expect the impossible and of the guitar you can't ask more than the six strings can produce, and Alais knew that, and therefore he didn't go beyond it to the classicism of the great musical geniuses.

His characteristics, were a limitless kindness generosity to the point of sacrifice, for his friends and admirers."

Julio Sagreras dedicated "*La Marcial, marcha*" No. 17 to Juan Alais, the homage reading: "To the famous guitarist Juan Alais" (*a afamado guitarrista* Juan Alais), it was published by Francisco Nuñez in 1900.

Carlos Schnockel publication c. 1885

Francisco Nuñez publication

(Lower Left) E. Halitsky publication published at the same address as Carlos Schnockel

Juan Alais was one of the very first Argentine folkloric guitarists, and had established his career by 1875. Julio Martínez Oyanguren recorded *Un Momento* in the 1930's and Abel Carlevaro recorded two *estilos* written by Juan Alais on an LP.

"Carlos García Tolsa was born on November 25, 1858 in Hellin, in the province of Albacete, Spain. He was born to Modesto García and Dolores Tolsa. At the age of 13 he began his guitar studies with an uncle, a distinguished player of the guitar and the bandurria who was blind and who became famous as *"El ciego de Hellin"* ("The blind man from Hellin"). In 1872 he was sent to Madrid to study for his bachelor's degree, alternating his school studies with the practice of his favorite instrument, taking advantage of the visits that were made by the celebrated concert guitarist Julián Arcas, a great friend of his uncle.

In the *Diccionario de Guitarristas,* from which this biography is drawn, it says: "To respect it has been said that Carlos studied for various years with Julián Arcas: following the footsteps of both, and consulting the communications of old, we cannot see how this could have been possible. It is also believed that he was the favorite student of Julián Arcas, to the point that when he was about to die, he said: 'Carlos, I leave the guitar in your hands'. Arcas' death took place in Antequera, Spain on February 16, 1882. During this time García Tolsa had toured with the *"Estudiantina Figaro"* for approximately three years in Europe, and then in parts of America; therefore, when Arcas passed to the "other side", his disciple was already in the New World.

The unyielding temperament to study for a formal career, together with his great facility on the musical instrument, allowed him to deviate, becoming a bohemian in his youth, which is not recommendable. In 1879, Domingo Granados organized the *estudiantina "Figaro"* (Saldoni, Vol. IV, pag. 130), with Carlos García forming part of it. They toured a good part of Spain and the principal capitals of Europe until after a year there was dissention in the group which resulted in Granados leaving the direction and 22-year-old García Tolsa being named in his place from that time forward. That tells us of his intelligence.

Our investigations reveal that the *"Estudiantina Figaro"* was formed without a fixed number of components. The guitarist Joaquín Casanovas tells us that when they played in Barcelona the group was made up of twelve professors, including guitarists, bandurrists, laudists, violinists and a cellist. By another account, the concert guitarist Luis de Soria Irbarne, states that it was composed of nine bandurrias, four guitars, a violin and a cello. Among the players that we know of who of made up the ensemble in distinct periods were Domingo Granados, Victor Mora, Carlos García Tolsa, José Sancho, Manuel Sanchez, José Martínez Toboso, Alfredo de S. Iménez, Joaquín Zamacois, Vicente Zorzano, Gregorio Rodríguez, José Rodríguez (alias *El Colchonero)*; the first three were players, who also acted as directors; the next three, as good guitarists and equally Alfredo de S. Iménez, who joined them in Rio de Janiero; Zamacois and Zorzano, virtuosos on the bandurria and discrete composers; and the two Rodríguez, capable on both instruments. The group was formed with the plan to embark for the island of Cuba. They went to Cadiz where they performed several concerts that were met with great public enthusiasm. The members of this estudiantina were given a banquet in their honor where toasts by the authorities and personalities of the arts and letters were offered. A patriotic and artistic speech was given by the composer of the celebrated pasodoble *"La Giralda"*, Eduardo Juarrauz. (Notes by Luis de Soria Irbarne).

Without a doubt, they left pleasant memories in the distinct parts of America where they performed, only to dissolve their beautiful form of art in Montevideo. The notoriety that Tolsa had achieved in Montevideo and in Buenos Aires supplied him with the motivation to settle in Montevideo. However, with time, due to the demand for his playing in Buenos Aires, he eventually moved there. In the

Uruguayan capital he studied to become a notary public. Upon finishing, he was offered the position of secretary of the Federal Court in the City of La Plata, in which he worked until his last days. In this city he was professor of the Colegio de Escribanos (College of Notaries), and he obtained a prize in the contest about *"Donaciones"* ("Donations"). (Notes facilitated by the guitarist L. Rafael Valdez, residing in La Plata). He was not known to have acted exclusively as a concert guitarist, but he took part in acts and artistic soirées, with a clear, beautiful execution, loaded with color and abundant vibrato, obtaining a pleasant response immediately. We believe that he should not be judged on the level of a serious artist-guitarist-musician, by reasons of culture; the world of art music would never accept a Segovia playing

"*Pienso en Ti*" or of "*Matilde*", the two works in which García Tolsa shone so brightly as author and player. As published 17 original works: four waltzes, four mazurkas, three habaneras, three polkas, a Gavotte, "*Meditacion*", "*Nocturno*" and "*Al Fin Solos*", Sonata. With the exception of the last two, the rest are of a danceable character and they invite the movement of the "tabas mas cansadas" (the most sluggish individual); musically well developed, with fresh inspiration, but with a satiated common melody. "*Meditacion*", a work of the character of the "musica de salon" (salon music), is the most detestable. Where he demonstrates better taste, is in the dedication of "To my friend, the advanced guitarist Martin Gil"; in a "Sonata" of the same class of music as the previous one, but a little better, a very poor "*Al Fin Solos*".

It can be objected to that this composition, like the rest by this author, are a direct result of the musician's ambience and in particular almost a half a century behind as relates to guitar repertoire; this does not improve their value, though it might affirm a good cultural path experimented by that generation. The "*Gran Sonata*" by Sor was written a hundred years ago and was born to be a jewel for all centuries. The Spanish publisher "Ildefonso Alier" published "*Tango*", by Francisco Tárrega, edition no. 5232, that consequently turns out to be the *habanera "Enriqueta"*, by Carlos García Tolsa. For our part we are not inclined to believe whatever of the Valencian guitarist, and it may very well be by Garcia, or then a transcription of some original by Iradier, since this work, from its infancy, was known in our home.

The performance of García Tolsa as a player, aside from his seat in La Plata, developed in salons of very distinguished homes, as a friend or maestro, to stand out in artistic-social reunions: in the home of Dr. Emilio Ocampo of La Plata, in the home of the Governor Julio Costa, being professor to his wife, in the home of the aide-de-camp to the president of the Republic, Teniente Coronel Medardo Latorre; in the sumptuous palace on the calle Callao of Mrs. Castex, music devotee and enthusiast of the guitar; as well, in the home of Adela Castro, Maria Luisa Redounet, Miguez, etc. He was also frequently in the home of my colleague Juan Valler. As we said before, some were disciples and some were friends. In this succession of intimate performances, stimulated by the great affection and admiration that was professed to him, with every attention given and gifts of great value presented to him in the homes of his admirers, where programs were improvised according to the occasion, García being for those people the "*mago de la guitarra*" ("magician of the guitar").

His correct production, inspired and guitaristic, is a model of its class, and at once, without a doubt, the faithful reflection of the author. Carlos García Tolsa died at 47 years of age, in the city Montevideo, leaving a legacy to his wife, the distinguished Uruguayan Elvira Acosta y Lara Medina, a quantity of original works (manuscripts that were purchased from the widow by Eleuterio Tiscornia in 1937 R.O.) that with just interest we would like to know. Carlos died on December 23, 1905." So ends the entry in Domingo Prat's *Diccionario de Guitarristas*.

"Six Silver Moonbeams"/ "*Seis Rayos de Plata*" by Rico Stover provides many dates about the performances by Agustín Barrios playing in concert at least 8 pieces by García Tolsa for several decades. The others being "*Pienso de Ti*",—"*Tanda de Valses*"— "Set of Waltzes" (Stover shows a performance in Bogota in November 1932), "*Meditacion*" (performed in Rio de Janeiro in August, 1916), in Sorocaba, Brazil in May, 1918, in Santos, Brazil in December, 1918, in Montevideo in July, 1920, in Caracas in March, 1930 to a SRO audience, in Bogota in November, 1932, in San Salvador in April and July 1933 and in July and August 1939) , "*Reverie*" (performed in Bogota in December 1932, and in San Fernando, Trinidad in April, 1936), "*La Visita*", "*Mazurka*"— either "*Estela*", "*La Simpatica*" or "*Matilde*", (all *Mazurkas*) and "*Al Fin Solos*" (performed as a duet by Barrios and Escalada in Asuncion, Paraguay in February 1908). Gustavo Sosa Escalada states that he taught Agustín all 17 known pieces by Carlos, as well as all that of Aguado, Sor and Arcas. Abel Carlevaro has recorded an untitled "*Habanera*".

Julio Sagreras dedicated "*Arrullos, vals de salon*" No.22 to Carlos García Tolsa, the homage reading: "To the eminent guitarist *Don* Carlos García Tolsa" (*Al eximio guitarrista Don* Carlos García Tolsa), it was published by Francisco Nuñez c. 1901.

Ricardo Muñoz in his *"Historia de la Guitarra"* paints a somewhat different picture, due to the information he gathered by the individuals he consulted: "Carlos García Tolsa was born in Spain and the great maestro Julián Arcas was lucky to be the selected professor of the one who much later was to be the guitaristic genius of his epoch. Carlos García Tolsa, not only was one of the most celebrated guitarists of his time, also played the bandurria with equal mastery; founded a musical society named *"El Figaro"*, comprised of 25 individuals. In this estudiantina they dressed in the typical garb that University of Salamanca students wore in past epochs: blouse, short pants, long stockings, shoes, cape, a two cornered hat (from the front of which hung a crosswire on which was strung a complete set of tableware — spoon, fork and knife). In a black wardrobe that recalls the historical epochs of troubadours very well, student romances, suits of cast armor and poetry all around, they harmonized everything with the severe tone of black of those galas that have an invisible sweetness.

This estudiantina was formed by great players of the guitar, of the bandurria, a violin and a cello, instruments from which sprang delicate harmonies from the base of the plectrum, but the majority of them, but not all of them, were unknown music. Here the personality of the director stood out, a capable player and very notable musician, who composed or arranged the all the works and, after proofing them with eye and ear, finished with general practice sessions to express the works in public in a brilliant manner never heard before.

So García toured with the estudiantina all over Europe, from Czarist Russia to London, and then on to America, permanently settling there more or less in 1885.

After various concerts that took place in St. Petersburg (Leningrad) and in the great Imperial Palace before the Czar, they went to Vienna, where he played with local musicians one of the most known waltzes by the great musician Strauss, who by coincidence was in one of the box seats of the proscenium of the theater. Upon termination of the piece, the celebrated composer, visibly moved, lifted his legs and climbed over the railing of the box seat to the stage, approached García and gave him a hug in the presence of the numerous public, whose applause served to color an intimate sketch of artistic ties.

The triumphant tour arrived in Montevideo in 1887, where the *estudiantina "El Figaro"* dissolved.

By the year 1890 García had arrived in Buenos Aires, and, like his colleague Antonio Jiménez Manjón, he settled permanently, exercising the profession of notary public/secretary for the Federal Court in the city of La Plata.

A while after his arrival to Argentina, he was invited to play in the presence of the greatest classical guitarist among us, Juan Alais, who listened to him religiously and could appreciate him up close, that small but expressive sound, brilliantly poetic, profoundly romantic, that the new great guitarist Carlos García possessed; endowed of intelligence and of an exquisite artistic spirit, he presented the musical phrases with an elegance never heard before. Unquestionably, he was the most brilliant musician and professional of the guitar that had been in America up to this time.

The following day, our great man of science Martin Gil came to have a guitar lesson with his maestro Juan Alais and found him pondering what he had experienced the previous day ....Alais commented: 'Ah, Martin, my search for a life with the guitar has now been shattered to pieces. We don't know anything; that man is a phenomenon!'

Buenos Aires later verified the reason for Alais' surprise, confirming a new and great artist. He gave many concerts that were valued with just merit that corresponded to his exceptional executions. He earned a lot of money and many bonds from the most select of the porteña society, to whom he dedicated many of his compositions.

Carlos García had few disciples, by reason of not making a profession of his art, maybe because lack of character to that end. A delicate spirit, he was only maestro to a select few friends and families, such as Martin Gil, Ocampo, Latorre, Castex, etc.

García died at 46 years of age, leaving a legacy of 16 works, some of them danceable, but, in their majority, all of concert level, in the classical style and original, that is to say, artistically inspired by his profound creative spirit.

Among those that stand out are two jewels of the most ancient romanticism of the 19th century, the nocturne "Meditacion", dedicated to his friend D. C. Mas de Ayala, and the sonata *"Al Fin Solos"*, that he dedicated to Martin Gil.

The rest are the following: *Estela, Matilde, Simpatica, Una Lagrima, (Mazurkas); Enriqueta, Entre Dos Luces, Maruja, (Habaneras); Irene, Prometida, Travesuras, (Polkas); Lejos di Ti, Pienso en Ti, Visita, (Waltzes); Mercedes (Gavota).* These were dedicated to: Enriqueta Castex, Adela Castro, Maria Felissa Redonnet, M. H. Latorre, A. Mateos, Lieutenant Colonel Medardo Latorre and Dr. Emilio Ocampo.

If we divide the artistic life of García into three periods, one primitive, another of evolution and a third of perfect refinement, we have:

His first epoch, in which he learned the published works known by all and through which we evaluate the degree of guitaristic and musical preparation of this great artist.

His second epoch, when he was only known to his friends and disciples, in which he had yet to publish his studies, romanzas and others; that through them we find beautiful techniques and unimagined music that reveals the artist in the maximum of his fantastic guitaristic powers.

The third epoch was in his last years of his life to which only his disciples and very intimate friends can give testimony of the beauty that this contemporary genius of the guitar expressed, that complicated and difficult music, that modern style of music that we would ultimately hear in the great Segovia, as the last word in musical structure applied to the guitar by the great Spanish musicians. That style, that form, with identical development and musical expression, typical Iberian phrases, of the purest Moorish flavor, García made them hear. His clairvoyance went very far in his epoch, looking far ahead, and his technique, of absolute precision, permitted him to execute admirably those series of rare phrases loaded with exquisitely sublime motifs that today we admire, enchanted by what was the possible repertoire of the future.

The guitaristic genius of García hasn't ever been equaled and he found it easily in the moments when face to face with one or two friends to improvise as they conversed about whatever subject. In between one word and another, accompanied by continuous inhaled puffs of smoke from a cigarette, his fingers would run up and down the fingerboard, halting to play very beautiful chords following the rhythm of an improvisation, a product of the dialogue that internally sustains his thoughts with his soul and the strings of the guitar.

The fingers continued modulating interesting passages hour after hour, exhibiting endlessly all those different aspects of his style: the lovely andante already played, the brilliant allegro or the pleasant moderato, mixed with the magnificent cadence or the romantically enchanting syncopation. Then, when he had amused himself on the guitar, having forgotten the world, concentrating on his spiritual conversation with his instrument, then, and only then, were you able to witness the greatness of this maximum artist.

García wrote down his few works, annoyed by the duress caused by his friends and disciples, who obligated him to do so, achieving their goal only after a thousand discussions. His best work was written in musical shorthand, the only way he could obtain the marvelous fluidity that filled his mind and with naturalness so sublime in the act of playing; therefore, all the best of his beautiful work was lost with him at age of 46.

García married an intelligent and distinguished lady, a capable player of the poetic guitar, Mrs. Acosta y Lara de Garcia; we hope that she will perhaps publish what is supposed to be the sublime art that her genial husband possessed." So ends the account by Ricardo Muñoz.

In the *"Archivo de Guitarra-Catalogo Breve"* (with personal notes by Eleuterio Tiscornia) published by Ricordi in 1948 in Buenos Aires, there is a detailed entry on Carlos García Tolsa and the acquisition of his manuscripts from Elvira Acosta y Lara in 1937.

"García Tolsa, Carlos (1858-1905). Spanish

(Complete Works) 1 Vol.

Although of Spanish origin, García spent all of his life in Argentina. He reunited in one volume his complete works, published in Buenos Aires, which are:

Solos: 2 Fantasies   1 Habenera
    1 Gavotte   Duets. 2 Habaneras
    4 Mazurkas   3 Polkas
    4 Waltzes

The edition of the waltz *Lejos de Ti* published by M. Gray, in San Francisco, California, today is very rare. This, as the remainder of my collection, are the first editions and the majority of them are signed by the author.

In the desire to know what García might have left unpublished for the guitar, I visited Montevideo in 1937 to see *Doña* Elvira Acosta y Lara, widow of the author and distinguished Uruguayan lady, who has now passed away (1940). The wife of Garcia, fine and exquisite in her demeanor, offered to my curious observation three guitars and the collection of published music and manuscripts that she preserved. Of the guitars two were of 6 strings and one of 11 strings. The oldest among them was Spanish, small, of dark wood, almost black, that the Colonel Medardo H. Latorre had given as a gift to her and that she used in duets with her husband. As I had been told that García possessed a guitar by the great Torres, I took advantage of the occasion to reliably verify this: the widow responded that her husband never had such a guitar.

The collection of music was reduced and of little historical value; perhaps it was already diminished, since I didn't find even one old edition of the classics that my eyes searched for avidly. The manuscripts that she preserved there were:

Solos. Gavota for guitar

Sonata No. 14 (Adagio) by Beethoven transcribed for 11 strings by...

Duos. Tuya, Mazurka for two guitars...

Tres hermanas. Mazurka for two guitars...

As for those two mazurkas, only the second guitar parts appeared, I asked the widow for the first parts. She responded: 'Carlos played them with me but never wrote them down'.

In conclusion, as a remembrance of my visit and my interest in the guitar, she gave me those manuscripts of the artist and one of the two examples of the California edition she had of *"Lejos de Ti"*:

Solos. *Lejos de Ti* (Far from thee) Waltz dedicated to Ms. Adela Castro....
Published by M. Gray, San Francisco.

All this is in order and conserved in the volume of my Archive under the identifying label:

C. García Tolsa: Complete Works for guitar."

So ends the entry for Carlos García Tolsa from Eleuteria Tiscornia's *"Archivo de Guitarra-Catalogo Breve"*.

Below is a postcard/promotional card for the *Estudiantina Figaro* from circa 1880. One can see Carlos García Tolsa in the front row on the right. This is courtesy of Roberto Martínez del Rio and Museo Internacional del Estudiante (www.museodelestudiante.com).

This short biography of Tomas Esteban is translated from Ricardo Muñoz's unpublished book *"Historia Universal de la Guitarra"* Volume VI *"America"*.

"Tomas Esteban

He resided in Montevideo, around 1890 he was a famous luthier of the city. The famous *Don* Carlos García Tolsa had his guitar teaching studio in the interior of the workshop. Tomas' son was a first class journeymen guitarmaker for Francisco Nuñez (Antigua Casa Nuñez) in Buenos Aires."

This is translated from the book by Cedar Viglietti "*Origen y Historia de la Guitarra*" published by Editorial Albatros in Buenos Aires in 1973.

Cedar Viglietti says on pages 172-173:

"Muñoz says that in a triumphant tour they (*Estudiantina "El Figaro"*) arrived in Montevideo in 1887, where the association "*El Figaro*" disbanded. However, in the magazine "*Montevideo Musical*" we see already two years before in December to be announced as a professor of guitar on the calle Convencion No. 222. Before, the 1st of November of 1885 we have succeeded to find the possible reason for the end of "*El Figaro*"; in the same magazine it says in this way: 'The *Estudiantina "El Figaro"* has given in San José with very little success its first concert of the second series; that being understood, since now there is nothing new being offered to the public. Its repertoire is very scarce for the many concerts that they have offered in the same city'.

During the year 1888, García offers by way of the press his teaching, now on calle Florida No. 117, and as a pair with another maestro, José M. Parra, on Canelones No. 62. Meanwhile our García continues here in Montevideo as a public notary, until he receives his title. Then he traveled to Buenos Aires and La Plata, that enjoyed his brilliant performances extraordinarily, quickly diffused. Years later he returned to our country and married a Uruguayan lady, Elvira Acosta y Lara Medina, with whom he performed duets of the interpretations of waltzes and mazurkas.

In his manuscripts he had a *Gavota* written for an eleven string, and an *Adagio* of a *Sonata* by Beethoven. It's said he owned a "Torres" guitar, but what is certain is that he had an antique Spanish guitar that he gave to Colonel M. H. Latorre, an aficionado and his admirer. After a long and weighty illness García died in Montevideo at the age of 47."

Cedar Viglietti says on page 246: "Finally we say that there is the custodianship of the eleven string guitar that belonged to García Tolsa, a Nuñez, and his music, a donation by his widow to the Centro Guitarristico Uruguayo "Conrado P. Koch"."

The above statement was certain in the time of Cedar Viglietti, but my colleague, Alfredo Escande, says when he became involved with the Centro Guitarristico Uruguayo "Conrado P. Koch" in 1994, none of that was to be seen, including the photo of Conrado P. Koch, who the society was named for. Those elements have now been dispersed among others involved in the society, as there is no longer a headquarters.

LA LIRA

En la guitarra distinguióse la señorita María Isabel Platero, que ejecutó la mazurka «Estela».

In the November 20, 1900 issue of the magazine "*Montevideo Musical*" Año XVI, No. 156 was the inclusion of the review of the concert involving piano, violin and an *Estudiantina* of six lady players of the "*La Lira*" musical society. Also was the performance by Miss Maria Isabel Platero, on guitar, of the mazurka "Estela", written a decade before by Carlos García Tolsa, published by Carlos Schnockel, c. 1890 in Buenos Aires.

In the December 18, 1888 issue of the magazine "*Montevideo Musical*" Año III, No. 47, the last of Carlos García Tolsa's advertisements in the "*Tarjetas de Visita*" (Calling Cards) section is listed. The 26 illustrious professors include: Gerardo Grasso, maestro of the Flute and Piano, and composer of the "*Pericon Nacional*". At the bottom is the listing of José M. Parra, another maestro of guitar. He is mentioned in Viglietti's book, though nothing is known of his exploits, his ads ran from April 24, 1888 until February 1, 1890, Año V issue No. 5.

Antonia Mollo, profesora de canto, Ituzaingó 203.

Maria Regal, profesora de Arpa, Solfeo y Piano, Zabala 230.

N. Suhr, profesora de piano, Rincon 213.

Leonor Villars, profesora de piano Ciudadela, 46.

Lina L. de Chiesa, profesora de piano Paysandú. 282.

Francisca C. de Castellá, profesora de piano y solfeo, Canelones 152.

Alberta Ader, profesora de piano y canto, Convencion 262.

Albertina Co..tratto. profesora de arpa y piano, Arapey 297.

Catalina Coll, profesora de canto; 25 de Mayo 143.

Alejandro Uguccioni, profesor de violin– José Uguccioni profesor de violin, piano solfeo, Queguay 281.

Gerónimo Piccioli, profesor de canto, Misiones 213.

B. Mazuchi, profesor de violoncello y piano. Colonia 277 a.

Italo Casella, profesor de violin, Arapey 297.

Osea Falléri, profesor de óboe, 25 de Agosto 112.

Gerardo Grasso, profesor de Flauta y piano Maldonado 56.

P. Rossi, profesor de Flauta, Ejido 213.

Amadeo Narbona, profesor de corno, Ciudadela 235.

Carlos Garcia, profesor de guitarra, Florida 117.

nes de idiomas, Ingles, aleman, Sarandi 211.

Juan Galazzo, maestro de composicion, armonia, y contrapunto Venezuela 54.

Santiago Dasso, profesor de violin, Orillas del Plata 131.

Andres de Giovanelli, profesor de idiomas Frances, español, pintura y música Colonia 61 (altos).

E. Faget, afinador y compositor de pianos Convencion 266.

José Coppetti, profesor de piano, Convencion 266.

Alfonso Rodas, profesor de piano, Durazno 159, se ofrece para tocar en bailes.

Nicola Nicastro, profesor de piano; composicion, armonia y contra-punto, Piedad 70.

José M. Parra profesor de guitarra Canelones 162.

Carlos García Tolsa with his Francisco Nuñez 11 string guitar c. 1900.
Courtesy: Gregg Miner. (Archive: FFSI 2012.)

The images on the next few pages are of a guitar that belonged to Carlos García Tolsa (1858-1905). In the photo from the 1930's of the five guitars taken at his home in Montevideo, one can see the 11 string in the center of the top row. This instrument has a Spruce Soundboard and Flamed Maple Back and Sides. The fretboard is Rosewood and is dead straight. The Tuning Pegs are Ebony, the Guitar has its Original Bone Nut and Saddle, as well as Original Frets. The resonance speaks for itself. The height of the 1st String at the 12th Fret is 4/32 and 5/32 on the 8th string.

There are 11 fan braces.

645mm scale, 89mm nut
Body Depth — Lower Bout 96mm, Waist 92mm, Upper Bout 87mm
Body Width — Lower Bout 360mm, Waist 232mm, Upper Bout 262mm
Sound Hole — 80mm
String Spacing — 84mm at the Nut, 111mm at the Bridge
Length of headstock from the Nut to the Top — 200mm

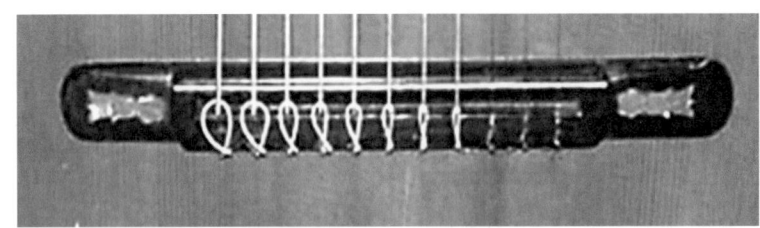

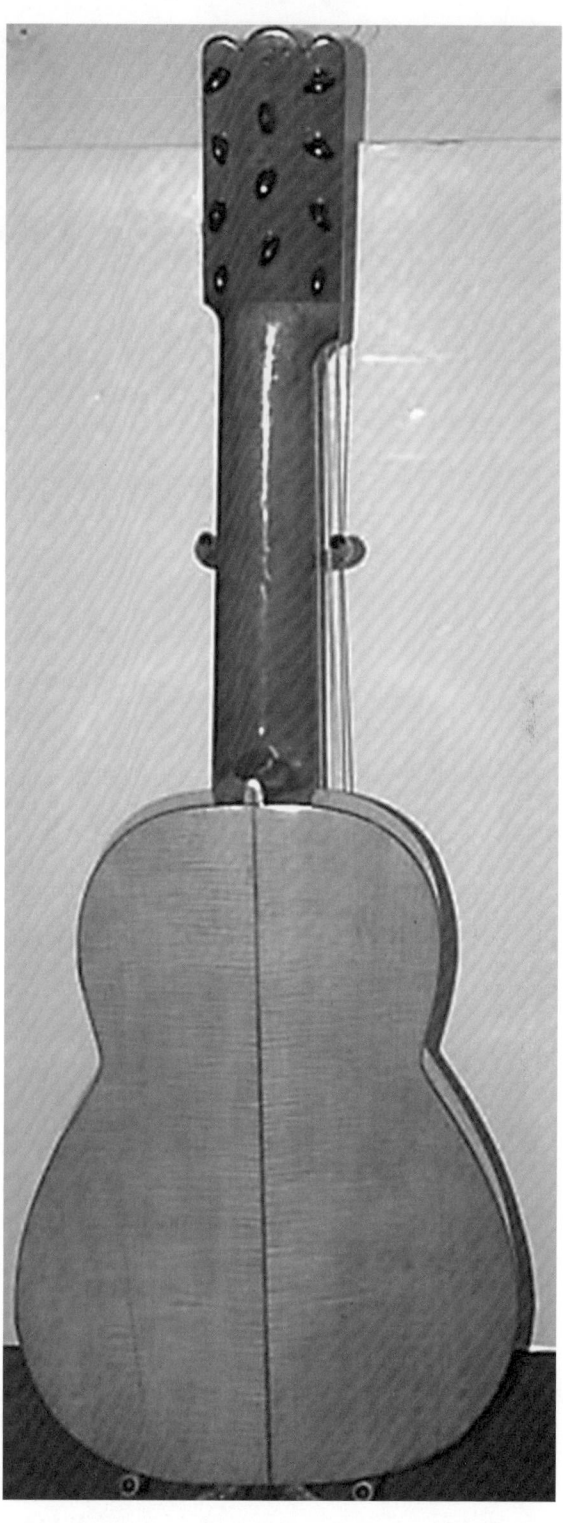

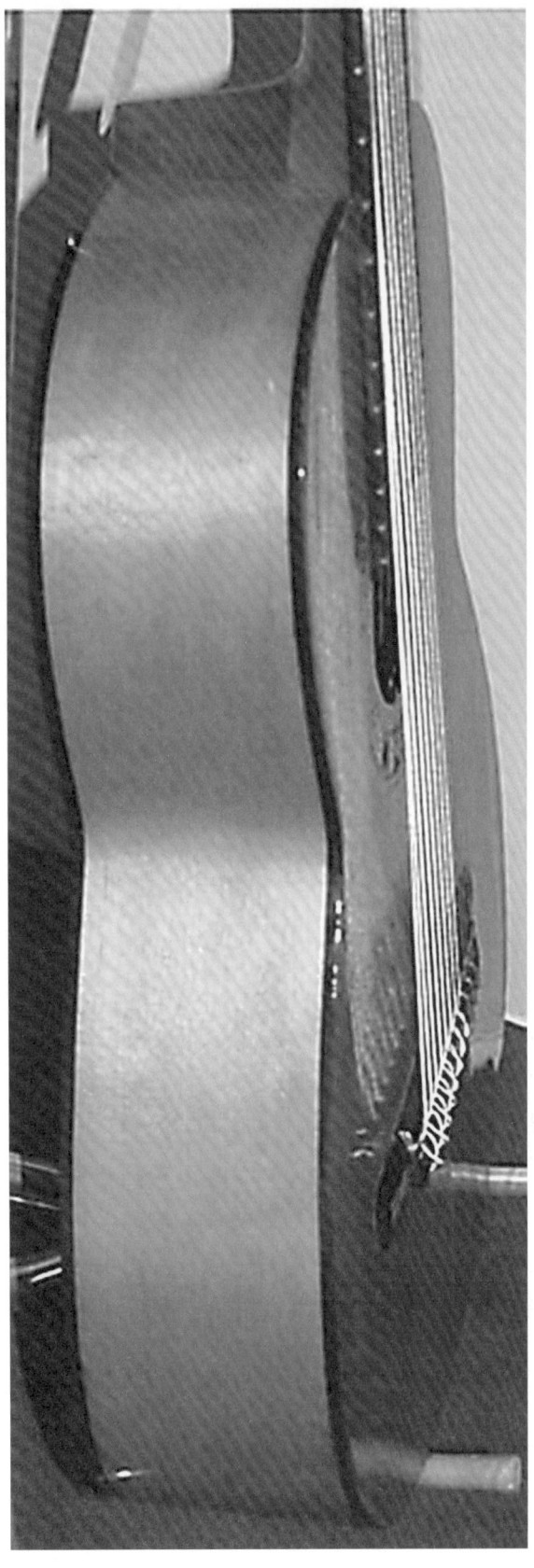

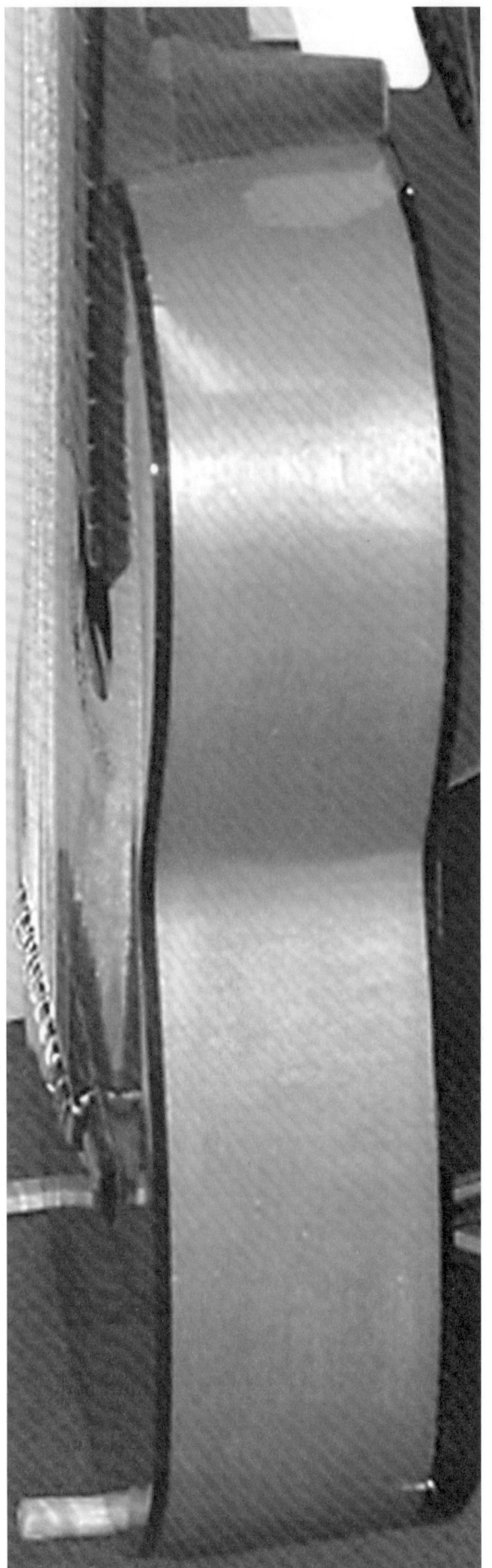

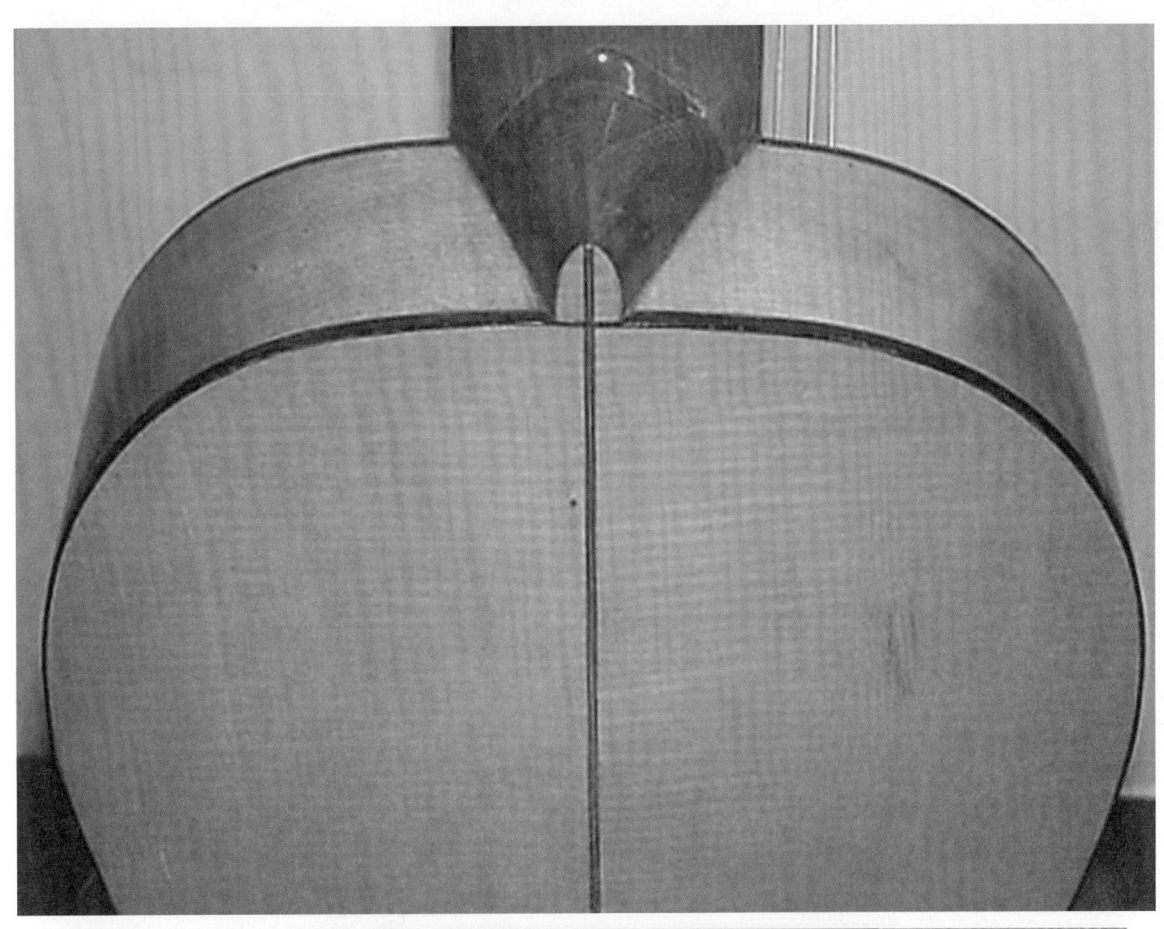

Carlos García Tolsa (1858-1905), who arrived in Montevideo, Uruguay in 1885,

Carlos García Tolsa

(Left) Juan Arcas' favorite student was Carlos García Tolsa. Carlos came to the Rio de la Plata region in 1885 playing bandurria and directing a small orchestra, in which also the guitarists José Martínez Toboso and José Sancho belonged. When the group disbanded then José Martínez Toboso returned to Spain and published his works. José Sancho stayed in Buenos Aires and published several dozen salon pieces, among them *"Melodia Nocturna"*, which has been of some discussion because of Luigi Mozzani publishing the same melody under the title *"Feste Lariane"*.

"Estela" is an early piece published by Carlos Schnockel, c. 1890. This Carlos García Tolsa piece *"Enriqueta"* is for two guitars and is a later piece published by Breyer Hermanos.

(Left) Carlos García Tolsa pieces c. 1887 published by Carlos Schnockel. Carlos García Tolsa was the favorite student of Julián Arcas. The repertoire of Agustín P. Barrios included the tremolo nocturne "*Meditacion*", which was performed for over two decades. Barrios recorded the piece "*Matilde*" for Disco Atlanta in 1913-14. It was his 11th release.

(Left) Francisco Nuñez publication from c. 1890 (Right) Antigua Casa Nuñez publication from c. 1927. Forty plus years after Carlos García Tolsa's arrival and still 20 years after his passing his music was still popular.

Before continuing with the next guitar personality who energized the vitality of the Rio de la Plata region, it's worth a look to see how overwhelmingly influential the *Estudiantina Figaro* was, its legacy lasting right to this very day. It was founded in Madrid in 1878, the first director being Domingo Granados, also being known as Dionisio Granados in some research. According to Ramón Andreu Ricart, in his contribution in 1992 to the *Diccionario Enciclopédico de la Música Española e Hispanoamericana*, they played ten times in the palace before the Czar of Russia, two hundred thirty two concerts in Spain, thirty five concerts in France-where they played at the Paris Exposition in 1878 (source: Scott Hambly), one hundred thirty four concerts in Austria, also concerts in Rumania, Portugal, Italy, Belgium and England. After a year, the director's baton was handed to Carlos García Tolsa in 1879.

According to Scott Hambly, in his article "The Mandolin Comes To America", in the book "Gibson Guitars-100 Years Of An American Icon", "they landed on New Year's Day 1880 in New York City." According to Ramón Andreu Ricart, this concert reviewed by The Times was to be the first of five hundred seventy four concerts that the group would give in the United States and Canada. It was this ensemble that set off the fire for the mandolin in the populace of the New World, not just in the United States, but in other regions we'll examine below. On February 4, 1880 The Times reviewed their concert in Booth's Theatre and noted: "Their darkly picturesque attire, performing melodies in which the true soul of music is perceivable." The Times reviewed their concert on February 16, 1880 saying: "They played an arrangement of the overture to Flotow's "Marta" which was remarkably well done, considering the resources of the mandolin and guitar, quite effective...the unity and finish which these gentlemen show is worthy of praise.... and their proficiency in all they undertake disarms any criticism as to its character." Emulators of the *Estudiantina Figaro* may have begun within a month of their very first New York appearance; an advertisement in The Times on March 4, 1880 for the Booth's Theatre touts the "only and original Spanish Students (as they were billed in the United States), who only appear at this theater." The first documented group imitating the *Estudiantina Figaro* was formed by Carlos Curti with talent readily available in New York: Italian immigrants, many of whom were violinists who took up the bowlback mandolin, being the relative counterpart in their culture.

In the early part of the decade of 1880, the *Estudiantina Figaro* left the United States and began their conquest of the Cuban public. Of the 114 documented concerts on the Carribean island, the daily "*El Almendares*" of Havana offered an account of their performance in the Teatro Tacon: "Caravans of scholars, that in the epoch of vacations, toured around the towns of Spain, with exultation in their countenance, the unpreoccupied mind, the most unfathomable void, in the pockets,"... "with their traditional dress.... transmitting their joy to all parts (of the world). Their joyful manner, their matching resplendent attire and the adventurous spirit that encourages them, roving troubadours that travel around the world, with the guitar in hand and wrapped in the classic dress of the lecture halls of Salamanca, forming an interesting group that brings brotherly affection and love to their divine art."

The *Estudiantina Figaro* performed one hundred thirty-three concerts in Mexico. They also played an unknown amount of stupefying concerts in Guatemala, El Salvador, Costa Rica, Ecuador and Perú. In their tours of Latin America, they were known as: "*Asociación de instrumentistas, Orquesta de guitarras y bandurrias, Compañía de Conciertos, Orquesta Instrumental o Estudiantina Española.*" In October of 1884 they were in Peru in the port just north of the border of Chile. They were to play in Santiago on New Year's Eve, and they arrived by train just moments before the 8:00 PM dinner for 3,600 members of Chilean high society, to celebrate the New Year of 1885. In the local press this announcement later appeared: "We weren't able to get the Teatro Municipal of this city, and in the desire to be judged by a respectable, numerous and intelligent public, we have organized a concert in the Quinta Normal (school), and the proceeds will benefit the Cuerpo de Bomberos (Firemen's Brigade). If our works come to deserve the reception obtained from other publics whom we have had the honor to concertize for, our efforts will have been rewarded and will be a laurel to add to your annals" --*La Estudiantina Española 'Figaro'*."

La Estudiantina Española 'Figaro' at this concert consisted of: Manuel González, José Lombardero, Alejandro Reneses, Valentín Caro, Manuel de Mula, Enrique Olivares, Francisco Cavero, Miguel López, José Sancho, Eugenio Anton, Antonio Gutiez and Juan Ripolli, under the direction of the guitarist Carlos García and his agent, Joaquín Rigalt. The 13 musicians promised a great rich instrumental event with their 7 bandurrias, 4 guitars, violín and cello.

PROGRAM

1ª PART

RUMANIA (March) GRANADOS
A TI (Waltzes) WALDTEUFEL
MARTHA (from the Symphony) FLOTOW

2ª PART

L'INGENUE (Gavotte) ARDITI
GUILLERMO (William) TELL (from the Symphony) ROSSINI
UN BESO (Mazurka)

3ª PART

FANTASIAS DE AIRES ESPAÑOLES, GRANADOS
MISSERERE DEL TROVADOR, VERDI
PUERTO REAL (Pasodoble) JUARRANZ

This program was only a miniscule part of their repertoire of 150 pieces.

La Estudiantina Española 'Figaro' played until 10:15, then offered a *Jota* of Aragon, and a *Zamacueca* of Chile, which just made the crowd roar. The President of Chile, other government officials and the most distinguished members of Santiago society attended this concert. Two days later the Fireman's Brigade, who received 20% of the receipts at the door, held a banquet at the Paseo del cerro Santa Lucía restaurant in honor of the ensemble. On the fifth of January 1885 they left on a train in the direction of San Felipe, enroute to Argentina. They returned in 1886 without their director Carlos García Tolsa. As Ricardo Muñoz says in his *"Historia de la Guitarra"* "The triumphant tour arrived in Montevideo in 1887, where the association *"El Figaro"* dissolved." This statement conflicts with several testimonies. Richard Stover authoritatively shares "In 1894 the Spanish estudiantina group *"Figaro"* arrived to participate in the fourth century anniversary celebrations of the discovery of Puerto Rico. This group was headed by one Pedro Celorio who was a concert player of the guitar and the bandurria." In the P. J. Bone entry of José Sancho in the book "The Guitar and Mandolin", he states that *La Estudiantina Española 'Figaro'* dissolved in 1904, and at that time José Sancho visited Buenos Aires, where he published almost 50 pieces of his guitar compositions with the firm Francisco Nuñez.

La Estudiantina Española 'Figaro' made an enormous impact in the Old and New world. The substantial rise in the quantity of mandolins manufactured in the United States, by Orville Gibson, C. F. Martin and George Washburn, the inspiration in spawning the epoch of mandolin orchestras, making the mandolin as endemic in parts of rural America, where Bluegrass and Country music would sprout generations later, without realizing that the *La Estudiantina Española 'Figaro'* made it all possible. The prevailing institutions of the *estudiantinas* and *tunas* in Chile at the beginning of the 21st century attest to this impact.

Promotion for the *Estudiantina Española Figaro* in New York at Booth's Theatre for the beginning of a performance run on Tuesday February 2, 1880. Twenty musicians are shown.

This reduced image is the outside back cover of "The Musical Record"— A Journal of Music, Art, Literature. Edited by Dexter Smith and published by Oliver Ditson and Co. in Boston in February of 1887. The *Estudiantina Española Figaro* was in Chile and later in Montevideo in the year this was published. The advertisement is for "Winner's Method for the Mandolin, or Mandoline." The impression left by the *Estudiantina Española Figaro* in the United States had not faded at all, to the point it was considered worthwhile of the mention of their ethnicity in the promotion of musical literature.

This account of some of the events of the *Estudiantina Española Figaro* is from the magazine "The Cadenza" Vol. XV No. 12 of June 1909. It is from a lecture, read at the Kotzschmar Club of Portland, Maine by S. A. Thompson, entitled: "The Banjo, Mandolin and Guitar — Their History and Future." The mention of them returning to Spain in 1881 and returning to concertize in Mexico in the 1882 season provides a timeline to believe Carlos García Tolsa was at the death bed of Julián Arcas (February 16, 1882), which was doubted by Domingo Prat in his entry on Carlos García Tolsa. The aspect of Henry Abbey having contracted the *estudiantina* to come to the New World, was very common, as we will see the contracting of Miguel Llobet by Ricardo Diaz Romero to come to Buenos Aires.

> The Spanish Students introduced it in the United States a little more than twenty-five years ago. They used the bandurria instead of the Italian mandolin. The bandurria has 12 strings or 6 double strings, where the mandolin has but four. The original Figaro Spanish Students, twenty-two in number, came to America from Madrid in 1879, under the engagement of Henry Abbey. They returned to Spain in 1881; in 1882 they left Spain again, bound for Mexico. After leaving Mexico they travelled through the States giving concerts. They finally went to South America where they disbanded in 1885.

In continuing on in his lecture, S. A. Thompson, gives just credit to the origin of the mandolin's arrival and addition to the American tradition of Banjo, Guitar and Mandolin.

> So it was through the bandurria that the mandolin came. They were both plectrum instruments, but the Italian mandolin soon crowded out the bandurria. There were no mandolins made in this country at that time, and the only instruments that reached the States were brought by tourists, and Italians coming to this country to live. Soon there was a demand for the Italian product, and as orders began to arrive, the sons of little Italy began to awaken. It is always the unexpected foreign demand that develops the talent at home, for a prophet is without honor in his own country.

Juan Crusans arriving around 1890.

In the short entry in the *Diccionario de Guitarristas* he is described as: "Professor of guitar, Spanish, settling in Argentina around the year 1890; as a player he had performances in the Federal Capital and in the locality of Quilmes, being remembered today by those who could hear him. He is the professor to our colleague Martin F. Alberro (a student of Gaspar Sagreras, then later with maestro Crusans)".

Bernardo Troncoso (1835-1928)

Arriving in 1869, the *Diccionario de Guitarristas* states: "Bernardo Troncoso was born in Seville on March 17, 1835. His artistic temperament led him to study sketching and painting. He shared those disciplines with his study of the guitar under the direction of Manuel Maria de Muro. Meanwhile his fellow students of painting, Villegas and Gimenez Aranda, (afterward great masters) searched for more ample horizons and moved to Rome. Bernardo didn't want to leave the city where he was born, even when flattered by an invitation to visit Madrid, which was not of interest to him. A patriot of the Republic of Spain by his temperament and conviction, he spent most of his youth in his native land devoted to his brushes, the passionate study of his guitar and the dream of his political ideals, until the revolutionary happenings of 1868 that obligated him to search outside the country for the tranquility of his spirit and the future of his family. From Seville he came directly to Buenos Aires in 1869 and, only when he was in his sixties, did he return to Spain to get to know the cities and the things he didn't want to see in his youth. The better part of his life, very long, was spent in the Argentine capital. Due to his artistic knowledge and talent, the generosity of his spirit and the kindness of his character, he found, from the beginning, the support of the government and of society. The pencil and the brush were his combat arms daily. To be a founder of the Escuela Normal de Profesoras, he occupied a position to teach sketching, and shortly afterwards, he entered to dictate the same assignments in the Colegio Nacional de Buenos Aires, under the respective directors Drs. Alcorta and Orma. He maintained his professorship for thirty years, retiring afterwards. During the decades from 1870-1890 Bernardo painted quite a bit, and actively awoke in the youth the pleasure of painting and elevated the level of our national art.

Aside from his principal activity, in the hours of leisure, Troncoso proceeded to cultivate the guitar and gave lessons of technique and interpretation to his passionate students, such as Dr. Wenceslao Escalante, Juan Molina and Dr. Juan Borbon. He played the works of Sor and Arcas to his great friend Dr. Martin Ruiz Moreno, for whom he had acquired a Torres guitar in Spain. More than once Troncoso left the intimate circle of friends and admirers to perform in public concerts organized with social grace and benefit. As a player, the *Sevillano* guitarist approached equally the works of the Spanish classics and Andalucian folklore: interested in the first for the school of technique; delighting in the other for the grace, the taste and the color of the popular. This lyrical vein of the *alegrias* and *tristezas* of the Andalucian soul interested him very much, and to express this interest, he patiently applied the knowledge of composition and harmony that he had acquired studying with Fetis, transcribing for the guitar, with artistic simplicity, the regional airs of his land.

In my private archive I hold, graciously given by Mrs. Sara Escalante de Maura, a practice method of harmony applied to the guitar, unpublished and in original manuscript by the authors: Bernardo Troncoso and the ex-Argentine minister Dr. Wenceslao Escalante. I also have an original manuscript composed by Troncoso entitled *"Danza Rosita"*. It is dated June 3, 1874, Concepcion, Uruguay. The picturesque paintings of Troncoso can be found in the palace of the Legislature and in the Correo (National Post Office building) of the province of Buenos Aires and in the possession of some private parties. At an advanced age Troncoso died in the Federal Capital on December 11, 1928. The daily *"La Nacion"* the following day, in its obituaries, described him as "a painter", adding then: 'Besides bringing his vocation as an artist, he cultivated music, distinguishing himself equally in that art'."

"The impression caused by these lines is, frankly, painful, since the guitar opened the doors for Troncoso in Argentina, allowing him to succeed as never before, gaining the friendship of his disciples, among them the cited minister Escalante, who helped him reach the heights of his talent and knowledge, and who made it possible for him to reside in this country, as witnessed by the children and grandchildren that today distinguish him."

Juan Valler (1835-1926) who arrived in 1878,

Julio Sagreras dedicated two pieces to Juan Valler "*El inspirado, vals*" *No. 16* dated 1900 on the bottom of the cover, and "*Sonatina, estudio No. 5*", No. 45: "To my dear friend and distinguished colleague *Don* Juan Valler " (*A mi estimado amigo y distinguido colega Don* Juan Valler), it was published by Francisco Nuñez c. 1903.

Juan Valler Vilche – Professor, concert guitarist and composer. He was born in the region of Andalucia, in the town of Utrera that belongs to the Province of Seville, on the 11th of April 1835. The venerable figure, pleasant and attractive of the guitarist *Don* Juan Valler has a value that spreads continuously, winning the cordiality of those who know him. We don't say with respect to his arrival in of the guitarist to Buenos Aires, that his suitcase might have been the first guitar that arrived to the country, nor that he was the first virtuoso, no; we know well that this instrument didn't enter into the American terrain before the arrival of Columbus. The first boot that advanced of one of the caravels, with a handful of Andalucians, and in particular Sevillians, they went down and got bogged down in the bow of the fragile ship which the civilizing scalpel, to be nailing for the first time in the virgin body of the Americas, and from the side, they threw the guitar over the soft scrub…; after the first European disembarked and set foot on the American soil. In that moment a fieldfare, from the peg of the guitar, launched its trills in the air as a message of its welcome. That guitar surely came with an Andalucian in 1492. The years passed and on the 15th of April of 1878 the Sevillian whom we are concerned with arrived in Buenos Aires, breathing in his faith in the celebrated virgin of Utrera, and in his beautiful Dulcinea (*Don* Quijote's mistress); a valuable example of a Torres guitar. A little while after his arrival, he performed in public; let's look at the program of the concert in a Buenos Aires Coliseo, now defunct: "Teatro Alegria / Saturday the 24th of August of 1878 / Benefit for the Spanish Concert Guitarist / JUAN VALLER /He will perform "*Fantasia sobre un Tema Aleman*", "*Jota Aragonesa*", "*Tanda de Valses*", and"*Dos Tangos Españoles*". The program finished with a second note that says: "The National Railroad will have coaches going in all directions after the function." His success is to be presumed complete, first, by the Hispanic-Argentine ambiance, and second, by the sensibility that he possessed, augmented by the emotion that it left us with the memory of the most intimate, having left the three mares, the loved wife, and the beloved children. He thought about returning to his homeland; but the pollen of his art had become thickened in the roses in an Argentine gentleman, Dr. Nicanor Albarellos, an aficionado of the guitar, who invited him to his side as a Professor and friend, achieving with it in a short time, to bring his whole family and set up residence in Buenos Aires.

The guitarist Juan Valler had enjoyed, there in Seville, of a just renown; in all of the moment highly considered and distinguished by the society of the capital that presides "*La Giralda*" he knew Huerta, Carnicer, Muro, Antonio Cano, Julián Arcas, who told him: "*Tu chico, vienes conmigo*" (You, come with me.) What could not be achieved, for not liking Valler, found in "*estado humedo*", today is preserved in the archive that belongs to *Don* Juan, a musical autograph that says: "Written by *Don* Julián Arcas in Cadiz for Juan Valler, the year of 1866." Valler with his art was admired by the butler of the palace of *El Alcazar* of Seville, *Don* Ramiro Lapuente, being in a short time presented and appreciated in that royal mansion, bringing in his time, later, the guitarists Arcas, Toboso and Parga. Of the last, the preserved testimonies tell us of the great friendship that they professed: it has to do with a portrait of Parga: "Dedicated to my distinguished friend, *Don* Juan Valler, Seville, the 4th of June, 1877 Juan Parga Bahamonde." Initialed (Foto: Montenegro, Ce. Larga, 15-Jerez). Twenty years later, and with the date the 12th of July of 1897, from Malaga he wrote to Buenos Aires a very extensive letter from which we extract the following: 'My most beloved, excellent and old friend:…the memories jump to my mind….and your daughter? That young beauty of 16 years old that, in her visits to the Alcazar, was so loved by *Doña* Paz. Do you remember Lapuente?…My concerts in the Alcazar?…and those triumphs?…", and a rosary of exaltations is to continue, with a remembrance of daughters.

Don Juan Valler had guitaristic performances in Buenos Aires until the end of the past century. Dr. Nicanor Albarellos who presented him in a hundred and one artistic-family reunions, gave him the opportunity of which, from its beginnings, had had the most distinguished of the porteña society always among his students. We recall the ex-ministers E. Costa, Zavalia, (who trusted his teachings for his sons)

Enrique Berisso, Remigio Gonzalez Moreno, the priest Ogorman, and Dr. Roberto Ezcurra, when he was a child. He was very distinguished by the Argentine President in the Army, Dr. Manuel Quintana, by whom they even have preserved autographed references. Dr. Antonio Bachini, ex-minister of the Republic of Uruguay admired him, working a great friendship. Albarellos gave him in the administration of the ancient Puente Pueyrredon, of Barracas, a position that had been destined for the mentioned doctor, and Harning the engineer for Mr. Rafael Albarellos, whose position he performed until 1884, or maybe until when the State took possession of him, presumably being the good play that would leave such administration. *Don* Juan Valler, in being thankful, gave him as a gift his good guitar made by the eminent Antonio Torres, to his benefactor *"el rengo* Albarellos" (the lame Albarellos), as he was called by his intimate friends for having a defect in his leg.

As a composer, we have consulted in his archive, some *"Preludios" (ensayos*-trials), a *"Plegaria"* (dedicated to the memory of the great guitarist, his friend Juan Parga, another *"Plegaria"* (dedicated to the virtuoso Julián Arcas) and a *"Tema con Variaciones"* (dedicated to his son Antonio), in the year 1918, or when he was 83 years old: all I've mentioned was preserved unpublished and along with a valuable collection of works for the guitar, were in the possession of the distinguished gentleman aficionado *Don* Antonio Valler, his son, thanks to his excessive friendliness and affection we could consult. Juan Valler Vilche passed away at the advanced age of 91 years, in the city of Buenos Aires on September 26, 1926.

So ends the entry in Domingo Prat's *"Diccionario de Guitarristas"*.

Juan Valler was a special person in the Rio de la Plata, in that he saw more than most other guitarists for a period of 48 years. He viewed the emigration from Spain to Argentina of his compatriots, the guitarists who were artists, and became household names through the late 19th century period to that of the advent of radio in 1920. Five of Tárrega's students as well as Andrés Segovia and Regino Sainz de la Maza, were to make their visits and make their impacts on the prosperous society that loved the guitar. Because of that we will continue to read the many accounts of others Juan Valler was involved with that are listed in Domingo Prat's *"Diccionario de Guitarristas"*.

In the entry of Dr. Nicanor Albarellos, "The distinguished professor *Don* Juan Valler, gave the Torres guitar he has brought from Seville as a gift to Albarellos."

In the entry of Julián Gavino de Arcas Lacal: "As a performer, virtuoso and unique concert guitarist, I can say that I have known many persons that I have had the pleasure to hear, almost all of them knowledgeable in the art, such as Juan Valler, Domingo Bonet, José Tey, Severino García Fortea, Juan Moya (from Almeria), the author of my days and many more."

In the entry of Miguel Carnicer y Batlle: "*Don* Miguel Carnicer was named Honorary supporter of the Conservatorio de Madrid the 25th of June of 1832. The distinguished Sevillian Professor Juan Valler who resided in Buenos Aires, where he died, in the year 1926 told me several anecdotes about this Catalan guitarist to which he dealt with quite a bit, and with him he had performed more than once as a duo. Miguel passed away in Seville in 1862.

In the entry of José Maria de Ciebra: "Thanks to Soriano, in his *"Historia de la Musica"*, the grandsons of the "amateur" Argentine guitarist, Dr. Fernando Cruz Cordero, and to the praises that he told us twenty-five years ago, the maestro of the guitar then old, the Andalucian Juan Valler, we have put together some very interesting information for this book. From the first (Volume IV pg. 215) "Well instructed in music and with a surprising performance, he went to Paris and London, where he is presently found (1859), respected by the professors and admired by the intelligent. He performed on the guitar with admirable vigor, with exquisite taste, and with total cleanliness his genre of music that is full and harmonious, he has a particular skill for the imitations; and his compositions are ornamented with harmonics. As an improviser few are equal to him, and in the brilliant hits few imitate him. He plays the six-string guitar with the same ability, as that on the eight-string, and his compositions are extremely difficult." That which Soriano Fuentes tells us, I have corroborated and augmented with the special Andalucian grace, the guitarist and compatriot of Ciebra, Juan Valler, he who, to speak of the Sevillian virtuoso, was enthusiastic, arriving at an exaltation. So great was he, saying, that 'the divine Ciebra' did concerts without a program, nor written music, that is to say: to present to the public, six classes of several airs, and by his choice improvised, with the peculiarity of announcing beforehand their approximate time duration. The possession of this ability to improvise until where he could at will, Soriano Fuertes also tells us".…

In the entry of Carlos García Tolsa: "Also he was very often in the home of his colleague Juan Valler."

In the entry of Medardo Latorre: "Memorable were the reunions that happened there around the year 1890, in the home of Lieutenant Colonel Medardo Latorre, bringing the echoes to us of those who intervened in them many times, Juan Valler and Juan Alais."

In the entry of José Martínez Toboso: "A man of artistic temperament, of a happy and generous character, during many years he was helped by luck and the enthusiastic applause by the public for his performances, remembering the flattering response that he had by the Spanish Royal family, when he was presented in 1875 to them by the guitarist Juan Valler and played in the Alcazar in Seville."

In the entry of Inés Maria Mulcahy de Hammond: "Among other aficionados who achieved a certain notoriety in the guitaristic world, are placed the gentlemen Mrrs. Tomas Vargas, ex disciple of Jiménez Manjón, Ceferino Luque, Santiago Roca, Enrique Peralta Ramos, who is a virtuoso of the instrument, Dr. José M. Armendaris, Guillermo Luzuriaga, dedicated poet of "*El Ritmo del Tiempo*", a disciple of Antonio Sinopoli, Pastor Obligado, ex-disciple of Juan Alais and J. S. Sagreras, Marcos Esnaty, Dr. Roberto Ezcurra, ex-disciple of Juan Valler and Justo T. Morales, Dr. Guillermo Valdes (hijo-Jr.), Aristobulo Durañona, Juan Carlos Anido, who studied with Alais and father of the eminent concert guitarist my disciple Maria Luisa Anido; Eduardo Anido, brother of the former and ex-student of Gaspar Sagreras, who dedicated to him "*No me olvides*", Oreste Negroni, intelligent lover of the music of Coste and Sor, Mariano and Alfredo Villar Saenz, skillful performers especially the last, Ramon Munilla, Ciriaco Gomez, Gregorio and Miguel Centurion, Dr. Enrique Tissoni, who ceded part of his home for the extinguished society "*La Guitarra*", that was directed by Juan Carlos Anido, Dr. Fernando Schweizer, Dr. Nicomedes Antelo, Dr. Servando Gallegos, Dr. Americo H. Albino, the engineer José Escalante Echagüe, Dr. Nicolas Espiro, Dr. Miguel Angel Bermudez, José Kiefl, German, who is owed for some translations in this "*Diccionario*", the military commanders Medardo Hector Latorre, aide-de-camp of General Roca and to whom is owed the publication of the works of Carlos García Tolsa, of who he was a friend and disciple and Leopoldo Funes, who was the captain of the frigate "Rosales"."

In the entry of Manuel Maria de Muro: "From the archive that belonged to the guitarist Juan Valler, who resided afterwards in Buenos Aires, today in our possession, we preserve three works in manuscript, originals of Padre Manuel Maria de Muro one we read says: Tema del Padre Muro, "*Variaciones de Tavira*," the other is titled "*Variaciones en RE*"."

In the entry of Fabian Ortiz de Jea: Domingo Prat describes a method book by Professor Ortiz published in 1890 with a quantity of over 3,100 numbered copies, then states: "That number praises that ambiance of the guitar that I admire so much of Gaspar Sagreras, Juan Alais, Juan Valler, and others of the epoch."

In the entry of Juan Parga Bahamonde: "We count with autographs of Parga, versions of admirers and disciples such as Juan Valler, José Rojo, Eduardo Mistrot, and Eduardo Villar, photographs, printed material and his music.".…

"Various, and perhaps founded, may have been the motives for writing in this certified in the form that it makes, the mother's surname. We minimize ours to a photograph of this guitarist that we have in view and says: 'Dedicated to my distinguished friend *Don* Juan Valler, Seville, the 4th of June, 1877, Juan Parga Bahamonde.

"Already we find in his artistic life at 31 years old in the city of Seville, or in 1876, a date which although he was in the Brigada Topografica of the Spanish army. In this city he contracted a long friendship with the guitarist Juan Valler, with the motive of having been presented to the Royal family in the Alcazar in Seville. . . . In a letter, the date of July 12, 1897 sent from Malaga to Buenos Aires to his colleague Juan Valler he says: 'You already have the knowledge of my first epoch. Apart from that, I completed my artistic education in Madrid, obtaining a seat in the Conservatorio, studying the classics of the piano, and harmony with the late maestro Arrieta. Then it brought the foreign voyages that I got, concertizing in France, Italy, Portugal and all of Spain, until I got tired of the nomadic life as an artist, and I returned to Andalucia with desires to settle in Seville but my destiny was Malaga. . . .'

". . . By the friendship that he had the author of this "*Diccionario*", with Valler, Mistrot and Villar, who to their cultivating the guitar of Parga, we know that he was of a frank and happy temperament; therefore, to coexist in the Andalucian ambiance, he developed his gallant and witty vigor.". . .

In the entry of Mr. Roldan: "In the important collection of works for guitar, that belonged to the Spanish guitarist Juan Valler, is found a precious Minuet by the author of this entry."

In the entry of Antonio Romeo Gulio: "This distinguished maestro was born in Buenos Aires on the 1st of June in 1887, splitting his studies of the guitar with Benito Sarabia and those of the violin with maestro Grassi. Between these two instruments he had more passion for the first, to which he dedicated with earnestness, taking lessons with the great painter as well as a guitarist Bernardo Troncoso, with Carlos García Tolsa and much later with Juan Valler."

In the entry of Oswaldo Soares: "Then the Brazilian professor gives us an "*Estudo em Mi menor*" on page 20 of his method book, as well as by Tárrega: this study belongs to Antonio Rovira (sic-Antonio Rubira), and in the year 1876 was copied by Juan Parga for the daughter of Juan Valler, who was active in Buenos Aires; to be read in respect to the names we're citing."

In the entry of Francisco Nuñez Rodríguez: "To the reunions in the Casa Nuñez, of which we allude to in the continuation of the article we insert, they turn out to be the most celebrated guitarists of the epoch, such as Juan Alais who we lovingly call "*Juan el Ingles*", and for whom Nuñez would construct his best guitar, with an expressive dedication that adorned the rosette of the soundboard, in artistic purflings and mosaics; the old composer, then young, Pedro M. Quijano; the good performer Juan Valler, Julio S. Sagreras, José Vasquez, Romulo Troncoso, and distinguished aficionados, such as General Leyria; Drs. Echayde and Marco; Mrrs. Castells, Quiroga, Villanustre, Diaz, Lopez, Giménez, Méndez, Lafemina, Lara, Centurion: Gregorio and Miguel, Macia, Villagra, Fernández , Avellaneda C., Drs. Servando Gallegos and Guillermo Valdez, and in ending Comandante Funes."

In the entry of Pedro Testuri: "Constructor of guitars. Born the 1st of January of 1863. Resided in the capital of Buenos Aires in the Republic of Argentina around 1870. He did his apprenticeship with Salvador Ramírez. *Don* Antonio Valler possesses two excellent examples by P. Testuri. One was constructed expressly for the Sevillian maestro Juan Valler, father of the above mentioned. This instrument, constructed in 1886, is preserved in a good state, its sounds being of good quality and uncommon sustain."

In the entry of Antonio Torres Jurado: "Owners of "Torres" Guitars: "The concert guitarist and composer Jiménez Manjón possesses two models of eleven-strings, one presently in the possession of his widow, who resides in Toledo, Spain; the other in the hands of the lady Professor Gachitegui in Buenos Aires. José Rojo, a guitarist, presently residing in Neria, Malaga, is the owner of an eleven-string model. The Sevillian guitarist Juan Valler, who has resided in Buenos Aires since 1878, gave a Torres guitar as a gift to the Argentine amateur guitarist Dr. Nicolas Albarellos."

In the entry of Ana Valler: "Distinguished Spanish guitarist. She was born in Utrera, Province of Seville in the year 1859. She did her studies in her home with her father, the notable and cultured Professor *Don* Juan Valler Vilche. By her outstanding merits as an instrumentalist, by her vast and fine culture and by an admirable flower of the Andalucian beauty, she was called for and named professor to the high dames of the court of Queen Isabella II, in the Alcazar of Seville in the year 1875. With her pollen of beauty and youth, she ascended to heaven in the city of Giralda, the 31st of December of 1879."

Antonio Jiménez Manjón (1866-1919), blind Spanish guitarist/composer, played the 11-string guitar, arrived in 1893. (dates of the musicologist Carlos Vega)

This photo of Antonio Jiménez Manjón is from the "*La Escuela de la Guitarra*".

According to the entry in Domingo Prat's *Diccionario de Guitarristas*, "Antonio Giménez Manjón was born in Villacarrillo, Jaen, Spain in 1866, where also were born Juan Parras y Moral and the idolized Andrés Segovia. Antonio studied the guitar with a disciple of Aguado, that resided in the town of his birth, a detail we have heard more than once, but we have been able to affirm that, although a great friend of the school of his maestro, Manjón was a self-taught guitarist. The first years of his career were doubly sad by the lack of support and by the need of the most precious thing in life, sight, which he lost at 13 months in his life.

His interminable Spanish rhapsodies and his dilated operatic potpourris of that epoch were shed mostly in private performances. His colleague David del Castillo stimulated him with sincere and impartial orientations to follow in his artistic career seeing him very soon traveling first to Portugal then on to London and Paris, where he was applauded, recognizing his profound intelligence, insightful musical knowledge and plentiful virtuoso qualities. We have to view a relevant testimony of that epoch, that we are going to copy and comment on, the motive of a concert that took place in the capital of France. {Salle d'Auditions}, 46, Rue Richer. / Saturday, May 11, 1889, 8:30 PM. / Concert / that offers / Mr. G. Manjón / Spanish Guitarist / who will execute on a new guitar of 11 strings.

Program:

Part 1:
1. Second Grand Sonata (Sor)
2. Melodia (Manjón)
3. Fantasia Española (Jota) (Manjón)

Part 2:
1. Andante and Rondo in La menor (Aguado)
2. Adagio de la Sonata 14, Op. 27 (Beethoven)
3. Movimento appassionato (Schumann)
4. Fantasia Española (Fandango) (Manjón)

This program fixed an uncommon personality in the guitaristic world: first as an author, although some find a weakness to execute and promote his own works, a thing, for us, just and humane; second, as an interpreter, now in the program, to Beethoven and Schumann, Manjón, has his own stamp of good taste and vast knowledge; the same in the *Andante-Scherzo, Tema y Variaciones, Minuetto*, of what comprises the first number of the *Sonata* by Sor of the above annotated program, all these pieces oblige the player to perform an exact transcription of the work. In the same year cited of 1889, spoken of in the *"Diario de Avisos"* of Zaragoza, where Manjón offered 4 concerts: "About Manjón, you have to see him, after having heard him play the guitar; you have to hear his full voice, divinely intonated, translating nobility and kindness; you have to admire the admirably correct lines of his visage, and his head, covered with beautiful long hair; and even as the durability of the impression of the music and even the soul holds a cadence of marvelous effects and as the figure disposes itself to abstractions and memories, to the mind come memories of illustrious blind artists and believe one can better imagine Homer reciting verses of his immortal *"Iliad"* to the settings of Chio, and comprehend better of Milton dictating to his wife and his daughters the sublime pages of the work "Paradise Lost". Misfortune robbed Giménez Manjón of sight, and Giménez Manjón fell in love with harmony. When the clarities fell as a cloak of darkness over his insensible pupils, his soul became intoxicated with the ecstasies of the sonorities and cadences. And in the eternal night of those senses, Manjón lives for the music, lives for his love and the love of his guitar. His guitar!, that has 11 strings, and in every string, voices and intonations of a thousand angels; his guitar, that is a temple of his sentiments, of grandiose secrets, that wound and delight and disturb the heart to escape in sighs for those threads that appear as guards of the songs of sirens!..." That is what the writer, Mantestruc said, charmed in reality by that beautiful blindman, scarcely 23 years of age, who possesses adornments of very beautiful wisdom. Mr. Tomas Prat, father of the author of this *Diccionario*, frequently recalled the sublime effect produced by a performance, made by A. Giménez Manjón that took place in the Teatro "El Dorado", in Barcelona, not functioning today. A correspondent for a daily of that locality wrote about the December 18, 1889 performance: "The most inspired works of the classical authors find in Manjón a conscientious interpreter, who plays on the guitar, with admirable properties, his notes, sweet, pathetic, disturbing and his energetic passages, brilliant and dazzling..." Recalling his adolescence, he continues: "At 14 years old Giménez Manjón had forsaken our country, being lead to Paris, alone, without friends, without family, without knowing the French language, and without more than 15 pesetas in his pocket and a heart replete with faith and anxious for glory..." He made a name for himself in Paris and London, says the chronicler nine years after that departure, these beautiful words: "...Manjón possesses a vast and solid education. He knows not only the classics of music, but also those of literature. He knows the sublime concepts of the French, English and Spanish theater, he speaks with exquisite elegance the idioms of Voltaire, Dickens, Camoens, Goethe, and of Dante. He feels a limitless admiration for Shakespeare, Byron, Flamarion, Cervantes, Espronceda and for Zorilla and he is the most fervent apologist for Wagner. When we conversed with him yesterday, he caused us amazement with the respect he felt toward Wagner's compositions and we delighted in the simple story he made clearly of his struggle, of his toils, of his regrets and of his happiness..." He concludes saying: "From that moment his fame was consolidated, and with the growing success he visited Germany, Austria, France, England, and Russia, alternating in the musical sessions with the most eminent artists". That is what they say of the player Manjón. He continued touring on the old continent until 1893, when he departed for America; visiting Buenos Aires, then to Chile and Central America returning to the Argentine capital to be residing in it permanently. Basing himself in a Conservatory, for a certain period of time he was subsidized by the Argentine government, and by him paraded almost an army of disciples, among them the distinguished Margarita Gachiteguy, Romulo Troncoso, Domingo Machado, Luciano Ouviñas and many others that time clouds the memory. In 1912-13 he made a tour of Europe and acted in France, Italy and Spain, where in April of 1913 he gave a concert in the Salon of the Conservatorio in Madrid, with a very guitaristic program leaving perfectly reaffirmed his well-deserved fame.

As a composer he is known to have published 15 works, original, among them some of the popular heritage of Spain and Argentina. These works lay the foundation of his fame. We cite, for example, his "*Célebre Capricho Andaluz*". He has "*3 Estudios Expressivos*" published, and two notebooks of "*La Escuela de la Guitarra*". His list is correct and instrumental, inspired to passages, although they don't review a classical character, decaying many times by the repetition of the phrases. The production of Manjón, doesn't enter into the firmness of the concert literature, neither do they belong to the danceable; is of the genre of the "salon" and the best demonstration is, his *Mazurca Romantica*, known as "*Recuerdos de mi Patria*", published repeatedly many times. That piece is of a melodic line, very pleasant and innocent at once, with good harmony and little enhancement. It has been attempted to compare the labor of Carlos García Tolsa with that of Manjón. That of Tolsa is rhythmically danceable, that of Manjón, although romantic, over that notable blind artist, of having a character, of superior artistic musical culture.

His multiple concerts, given around the cultured world and periodically lasting more than a quarter of a century in Buenos Aires, were continuous demonstrations of art and of great knowledge, that perhaps, we might be able to say weren't appreciated by all those who applauded him. Antonio died in Buenos Aires on January 3, 1919". So ends the entry in the Domingo Prat *Diccionario de Guitarristas*.

The photo is from the *Caras y Caretas* magazine of February 22, 1913 issue No. 751.

The translation is:
"The eminent ones of the guitar: Manjón."

The photo is actually from the "*Caras y Caretas*" magazine of July 5, 1902 issue No. 196.

Las eminencias de la guitarra: Manjon.

EL CONCERTISTA DE GUITARRA MANJON

Ha comenzado á dar conciertos de guitarra, llamando con justicia la atención de los aficionados al armónico instrumento, el artista ciego señor Antonio J. Manjón, que hace diez años visitó por primera vez á Buenos Aires. El señor Manjón agrega á la guitarra vulgar un encordado especial que le permite obtener maravillosos efectos en las piezas de concierto y que solamente él, que es su inventor, puede manejar con tanto resultado y habilidad.

El instrumento que domina el concertista de que nos ocupamos — vulgar y manoseado por todos, desdeñado por muchos á causa de esto, é ingenio de suplicio para las personas que tienen por vecino á alguno de los desaforados guitarreros que abundan por todas partes— es en manos del señor Manjón el mejor intérprete musical del espíritu de los grandes maes-

SEÑOR ANTONIO J. MANJON

tos y sirve para revelarnos la vena lírica y sentimental del que es al propio tiempo autor y ejecutante. Parece que la naturaleza,—así hemos convenido en nombrar lo que antes llamábamos divinidad—hubiese querido conceder á Manjón, en cambio de la vista, un maravilloso instinto de la armonía. Prueba de ello sería el aire vasco de su composición, por no citar otras obras del mismo, que tuvo que repetir en su primera audición, á instancias del público.

El concierto que dió en el antiguo teatro Nacional congregó una numerosa y selecta concurrencia que aplaudió al maestro. Este dará varios otros conciertos auxiliado por su esposa, que es una distinguida pianista, y luego seguirá viaje en jira artística por todas las repúblicas sudamericanas, en donde, de seguro, le esperan nuevos aplausos.

Fot. de Caras y Caretas.

This concert review of Antonio Jiménez Manjón's performance is from the "*Caras y Caretas*" magazine of July 5, 1902 issue No. 196 *Año* V.

The translation is:

"The concert guitarist Manjósn.

He has started to give concerts, calling attention with justice to the aficionados of the harmonic instrument, the blind artist Mr. Antonio J. Manjón, who ten years ago visited Buenos Aires for the first time. Mr. Manjón adds to the common guitar special strings that permit him to obtain marvelous effects in the concert pieces and only he, who is the inventor, can play that it turns out he has such an ability.

The instrument that the concert guitarist that concerns us dominates- common and handled by all, scorned by many because of this, and talent to torment for the person who has by their neighbor some of the earsplitting guitarists that abound in all parts — is in the hands of Mr. Manjón the best musical interpreter of the spirit of the great masters and serves to reveal to us the lyric and sentimental vein of that he in his own time is the author and performer. It appears that nature, in this way we have agreed to name what beforehand we would call divinity — if we had wished to concede to Manjón, instead of vision, a marvelous instinct of harmony. Proof of that will be in his composition "*Aire Vasco*", by not citing other works of the same, that he had to repeat in his first performance, by request of the public.

The concert that he gave in the old Teatro Nacional gathered together a numerous and select audience that applauded the maestro. He will give various other concerts backed by his wife, who is a distinguished pianist, and then he will follow an artistic tour of all the republics of South America, where, you can be sure, they await to applaud him once again."

Photo by "*Caras y Caretas*"— The photo is from the late June 1902 concert, not a "stock" photo.

Suplemento Semanal Ilustrado.

LA NACION

Gratis para los subscriptores y compradores del diario.

Año I. Buenos Aires, 18 de Diciembre de 1902. Nº 16.

LA GUITARRA

Larga es la historia de este instrumento músico. Datan sus primeras páginas de tiempos muy remotos, y está íntimamente ligada á la de otros de cuerda, algunos de los cuales no han alcanzado á entrar en el terreno del verdadero arte.

Aparece, en la antigüedad, á un mismo tiempo en el opulento palacio y en el hogar humilde, obedeciendo sin duda esta generalización á que entonces la música era casi exclusivamente vocal, limitándose el papel de los instrumentos á acompañar los cantos, como así mismo á tocar los aires de danza, y siendo la guitarra (aun con las cuatro cuerdas de que estaba dotada en un principio) capaz, no sólo de emitir los sonidos, diatónica y cromáticamente, sino también de producir los acordes tonales en varias escalas, bastó á satisfacer el sentimiento músico de aquellas épocas.

No es mi propósito hacer la apología del instrumento, refiriéndome á aquellos tiempos en que los soñadores árabes acompañaban con él sus poéticos cantos; ni tampoco á los todavía más lejanos, en que se aunaba á la caprichosa canción egipcia, de extraño ritmo y de tonalidad indeterminada. Voy á ocuparme solamente, y á grandes rasgos, de la guitarra, desde que contribuyó á formar la más moderna de las artes.

Conforme la música fué adelantando, se aumentaba la extensión de los instrumentos y se perfeccionaba el sistema. No fué la guitarra ajena á este movimiento progresista, y en el siglo XVII agregó la quinta cuerda. Más tarde, y cuando el piano alcanzaba ya sus seis octavas y una notable perfección en sus condiciones, los guitarristas añadieron también una cuerda más, llegando á ser el instrumento tal como hoy se usa comunmente. El artista Coste puso la séptima cuerda para engrandecer algunos acordes y facilitar ciertos tonos, y más tarde el constructor Torres inventó la de once cuerdas, que no sólo aumenta la extensión, sino también el sonido; porque las cinco adicionales tendidas sobre el instrumento hacen más intensa la onda sonora. Las seis de la guitarra de Sor (llamémosla así) conservan su primitiva afinación. Por esto es menos explicable que casi no se estudie la nueva guitarra, estando en ella contenida la de seis cuerdas, ni más ni menos que contiene el piano, la extensión del antiguo clavicordio. Pero sea por un extraño fenómeno de rutina, ó porque aun falta un método para la fácil comprensión del nuevo sistema, no se ha generalizado como era de esperar, dada su indiscutible superioridad.

En error craso incurren los que imaginan que con escasa instrucción musical pueda llegarse á dominar este instrumento, que por su naturaleza un tanto complicada necesita de buena preparación.

La guitarra, cual dama recatada, no se manifiesta como es, sino ante aquel que, enamorado de ella, acierta á penetrar en lo íntimo de su carácter.

Su graciosa forma y peculiares efectos la han atraído numerosos apasionados, que la estrechan contra su corazón; pero ¡cosa extraña! casi todos ellos, intentando acariciarla, la maltratan despiadadamente.

¡Pobre caja armónica! Si delicada como una sensitiva, padece hasta con un cambio de temperatura, ¡qué no sufrirá con los rudos golpes que la asestan sus cultivadores no iniciados!

Aparentemente fácil de construir, cualquier carpintero remeda sus contornos; pero escapan á estos profanos constructores las suaves curvas femeninas casi imperceptibles, que son, sin embargo, las que producen los encantadores sonidos que han de animar el esbelto cuerpo.

Si desde la invasión del piano se halla injustamente descuidada, no ha sucedido siempre lo mismo, y era antes adorno de los más encumbrados recintos, y objeto de detenido estudio de los aristocráticos aficionados. Consta que la gran reina Isabel I de Castilla entretenía sus ocios tañendo la guitarra, y posteriormente el rey-sol se complacía en hacer vibrar sus cuerdas. En efecto, quedan aún, y conocemos composiciones sencillas, pero muy apreciables é interesantes desde el punto de vista histórico, de Roberto de Visco, dedicadas á su discípulo Luis XIV, rey de los franceses. Varios artistas antiguos, tales como Ferandière, Arizpacochaga y el padre Basilio, ejecutaban de manera notable, y quedan tradiciones de que producían efectos sorprendentes, que no acertaron á estampar sobre el papel. Sólo por referencia sabemos los que aquellos *virtuosos* realizaban.

Anteriores á Fernando Sor, hay algunas producciones escritas á dos partes, ya de manera precisa, y que despiertan interés. Pero Sor, que puede y debe contarse en el número de los grandes músicos, produjo composiciones de mucho mérito artístico, habiendo algunas entre ellas, que sufren valientemente la comparación con obras notables de célebres autores que han escrito para instrumentos de teclado y de arco. Su estilo es realmente elevado, y admirable la disposición concreta y clara de las voces. En Sor siempre se encuentran melodías de mejor gusto, destacándose de una armonía sabiamente construída. Hay que reconocer que su obra es de difícil mecanismo é interpretación, y tal vez por este motivo no se ha extendido.

13

This is the original publication of Antonio Jiménez Manjón's article "*La Guitarra*" (The Guitar) from the Weekly Illustrated Supplement of "*La Nacion*" published on Thursday December 18, 1902 No. 16 Año I. It is from a hardbound edition that included issues "*Suplemento Semanal Ilustrada*" Nos. 10-35 published from November 6, 1902 to April 30, 1903. The translation is several pages later in the book.

A Sor sigue, no sólo cronológicamente sino en capacidad, Aguado que nos legó á más de su muy conocido y útil método, varias piezas de valor musical incontestable, que he tenido el placer de ver reconocido por los más severos críticos. Su estilo difiere del de Sor principalmente en la tendencia á conceder mayor importancia á una sola voz, que acompaña muy hábilmente, pues sin que su temperamento le permitiera emplear el contrapunto en el alto grado que lo hizo Sor, Aguado era un armonista muy distinguido, y sus producciones son acabadamente estéticas.

En el número de los grandes artistas que han producido para la guitarra, se cuentan: el ya nombrado Coste, Giuliani, que escribió bellísimas obras de una técnica irreprochable, y Regondi, casi desconocido, á pesar de su indiscutible talento.

Desde la desaparición de los autores guitarristas que he nombrado, entró en la era del infortunio, la literatura del instrumento, pues si bien se ha aumentado, ha ido descendiendo en calidad hasta lo inverosímil.

Antonio Cano, hábil ejecutante, compuso muchas piezas, pero carece de ideas importantes, y sus procedimientos son de suma sencillez.

Arcas, notabilísimo *virtuoso*, encantaba con la nitidez y precisión de su mecanismo. Conservo la impresión que cuando niño me produjeron las repetidas audiciones de este artista, que desgraciadamente se limitaba como Cano, á interpretar sus propias composiciones, que son generalmente triviales, acusando una educación musical muy deficiente, con relación á su talento. Algunas de ellas se escuchan, sin embargo, con gusto, porque poseía el singular don de aplicar los efectos de colorido propios de la guitarra.

Genios de la música, universalmente aclamados, han abordado la guitarra, sin haber obtenido en ella resultado feliz. Esto se debe sin duda, á que el mecanismo complicado del instrumento requiere un estudio especial y detenido, que ellos no hicieron.

Conocemos de Weber un *divertimento* para guitarra y piano, de tan escaso valor que denota claramente cuán fuera de camino se encontraba para producir algo digno de su pluma, lo que no logró, pues no supo aprovechar ninguno de los efectos de la guitarra, lo mismo que Ricardo Wagner en las melodías que escribió para canto y guitarra.

No puedo menos de lamentar el errado concepto en que generalmente se la tiene, siendo éste, entre los instrumentos de punteo, el único de solista (incluso el arpa) que puede dar cabida á la música propiamente dicha.

Esa caja, sencilla al parecer, es delicadísima de construir, y sólo muy pocos de lo que á ello se dedican, consiguen llevar á buen término la minuciosa labor que ha menester, si ha de poseer las condiciones requeridas. Los buenos constructores llegan á serlo después de muy larga experiencia, y poseyendo un don de manos y de espíritu tal vez superior al que necesitan los especialistas de instrumentos de arco.

Una buena guitarra bien encordada, y pulsada por un verdadero artista, es susceptible de producir, con sus inimitables sonidos y variados matices, vivas é intensas emociones.

Es de esperar que los músicos esclarecidos, vuelvan á fijar en ella su atención, y estudiándola detenidamente, se compenetren de la infinidad de recursos que encierra. Así podrán coadyuvar al aumento de su repertorio, aportando á los filarmónicos, deleites aun no bien saboreados.

ANTONIO J. MANJON.
Buenos Aires, diciembre de 1902.

This is signed by Antonio Jiménez Manjón in Buenos Aires, December of 1902. His opinions of the 19th century composers and his views of the live performances that he experienced in his youth of Julián Arcas and Antonio Cano are rare accounts indeed.

MONTEVIDEO MUSICAL

ÓRGANO DEFENSOR DE LOS INTERESES ARTÍSTICOS

DIRECCION
Soriano, 93

DIRECTOR:
→ FRANCISCO SAMBUCETTI ←

Este periódico aparece los días
1.º y 15 de cada mes

Año XVIII. † Montevideo, Febrero 15 de 1903 † Número 229.

EL GUITARRISTA MANJON

UNA notabilidad artística de gran valía y ya conocida entre nosotros es el guitarrista Manjon. Su manera delicada de ejecutar le coloca entre los mejores del género; Manjon es el verdadero *virtuoso* de la guitarra y es así que su venida á Montevideo que será en Marzo próximo sea un acontecimiento muy justo para el diletantismo, que va á tener nueva ocasion de admirarla en sus ejecuciones maravillosas.

Mientras tanto damos publicidad al artículo por él escrito y que nos ha sido dado para esta publicación.

LA GUITARRA

Larga es la historia de este instrumento músico. Datan sus primeras páginas de tiempos muy remotos, y está íntimamente ligada á otros de cuerda, algunos de los cuales no han alcanzado á entrar en el terreno del verdadero arte.

Aparece, en la antigüedad, á un mismo tiempo en el opulento palacio y en el hogar humilde, obedeciendo sin duda esta generalización á que entonces la música era casi exclusivamente vocal, limitándose el papel de los intrumentos á acompañar los cantos, como así mismo á tocar los aires de danza, y siendo la guitarra (aún con las cuatro cuerdas de que estaba dotada en un principio) capaz, no sólo de emitir los sonidos, diató-

nica y cromáticamente, sino tambien de producir los acordes tonales en varias escalas, bastó á satisfacer el sentimiento músico de aquellas épocas.

No es mi propósito hacer la apología del instrumento, refiriéndome á aquellos tiempos en que los soñadores árabes acompañaban con él sus poéticos cantos; ni tampoco á los todavía más lejanos, en que se anudaba á la caprichosa canción egipcia, de extraño ritmo y de tonalidad indeterminada. Voy á ocuparme solamente, y á grandes rasgos, de la guitarra, desde que contribuyó á formar la más moderna de las artes.

Conforme la música fué adelantando, se aumentaba la extensión de los instrumentos y se perfeccionaba el sistema. No fué la guitarra ajena á este movimiento progresista, y en el siglo XVII agregó la quinta cuerda. Más tarde, y cuando el piano alcanzaba ya sus seis octavas y una notable perfección en sus condiciones, los guitarristas añadieron tambien una cuerda más, llegando á ser el instrumento tal como hoy se usa comunmente. El artista Coste puso la séptima cuerda para engrandecer algunos acordes y facilitar ciertos tonos, y más tarde el constructor Torres inventó la de once cuerdas, que no sólo aumenta la extensión, sinó tambien el sonido; porque las cinco adicionales tendidas sobre el instrumento hacen más intensa la onda sonora. Las seis de la guitarra de Sor (llamémosla así) conservan su primitiva afinación. Por esta es menos explicable

que casi no se estudie la nueva guitarra, estando en ella contenida la de seis cuerdas, ni más ni menos que contiene el piano, la extensión del antiguo clavicordio. Pero sea por un extraño fenómeno de rutina, ó porque aún falta un método para la fácil comprensión del nuevo sistema, no se ha generalizado como era de esperar, dada su indiscutible superioridad.

En error grande incurren los que imaginan que con escasa instrucción musical pueda llegarse á dominar este instrumento, que por su naturaleza un tanto complicada necesita de buena preparación.

La guitarra, cual dama recatada, no se manifiesta como es, sino ante aquel que, enamorado de ella, acierta á penetrar en lo íntimo de su carácter.

Su graciosa forma y peculiares efectos le han atraído numerosos apasionados, que la estrechan contra su corazón; pero ¡cosa extraña! casi todos ellos, intentando acariciarla, la maltratan despiadadamente.

¡Pobre caja armónica! Si delicada como una sensitiva, padece hasta con un cambio de temperatura, ¡qué no sufrirá con los rudos golpes que la asestan sus cultivadores no iniciados!

Aparentemente fácil de construir, cualquier carpintero remeda sus contornos; pero escapan á estos profanos constructores las suaves curvas femeninas casi imperceptibles, que son, sin embargo, las que producen los

This is the second publication of Antonio Jiménez Manjón's article "*La Guitarra*" (The Guitar) published less than 2 months later in the magazine "*Montevideo Musical*" on February 15, 1903 Año XVIII. Antonio Jiménez Manjón first performed in Montevideo in 1893.

encantadores sonidos que han de animar el esbelto cuerpo.

Si desde la invasión del piano se halla injustamente descuidada, no ha sucedido siempre lo mismo, y era antes adorno de los más encumbrados recintos, y objeto de detenido estudio de los aristócraticos aficionados. Consta que la gran reina Isabel I de Castilla entretenía sus ocios tañendo la guitarra, y posteriormente el rey-sol se complacía en hacer vibrar sus cuerdas. En efecto, quedan aún, y conocemos composiciones sencillas, pero muy apreciables é interesantes desde el punto de vista histórico, de Roberto de Visco, dedicadas á su discípulo Luis XIV, rey de los franceses.

Varios artistas antiguos, tales como Ferandière, Arispacochaga y el padre Basilio, ejecutaban de manera notable, y quedan tradiciones de que producían efectos sorprendentes, que no acertaron á estampar sobre el papel. Sólo por preferencia sabemos los que aquellos *virtuosos* realizaban.

Anteriores á Fernando Sor, hay algunas producciones escritas á dos partes, ya de manera precisa, y que despiertan interés. Pero Sor, que puede y debe contarse en el número de los grandes músicos, produjo composiciones de mucho mérito artístico, habiendo algunas entre ellas, que sufren valientemente la comparación con obras notables de célebres autores que han escrito para instrumentos de teclado y de arco. Su estilo es realmente elevado, y admirable la disposición concreta y clara de las voces. En Sor siempre se encuentran melodías de mejor gusto, destacándose de una armonía sabiamente construida. Hay que reconocer que su obra es de difícil mecanismo é interpretación, y tal vez por este motivo no se ha extendido.

A Sor sigue, no sólo cronológicamente sino en capacidad, Aguado que nos legó á más de su muy conocido y útil método, varias piezas de valor musical incontestable, que he tenido el placer de ver reconocido por los más severos críticos. Su estilo difiere del de Sor principalmente en la tendencia á concader mayor importancia á una sola voz, que acompaña muy hábilmente, pues sin que su temperamento le permitiera emplear el contrapunto en el alto grado que lo hizo Sor, Aguado era un armonista muy distinguido, y sus producciones son acabadamente estéticas.

En el número de los grandes artistas que han producido para la guitarra, se cuentan: el ya nombrado Coste, Giuliani, que escribió bellísimas obras de una técnica irreprochable, y Regondi, casi desconocido, á pesar de su indiscutible talento.

Desde la desaparición de los autores guitarristas que he nombrado, entró en la era del infortunio, la literatura del instrumento, pues si bien se ha aumentado, ha ido descendiendo en calidad hasta lo inverosímil.

Antonio Cano, hábil ejecutante, compuso muchas piezas, pero carece de ideas importantes y sus procedimientos son de suma sencillez.

Arcas, notabilísimo *virtuoso*, encantaba con la nitidez y precisión de su mecanismo. Conservo la impresión que cuando niño me produjeron las repetidas audiciones de este artista, que desgraciadamente se limitaba como Cano, á interpretar sus propias composiciones, que son generalmente triviales, acusando una educación musical muy deficiente, con relacion á su talento. Algunas de ellas se escuchan, sin embargo, con gusto, porque poseía el singular don de aplicar los efectos de colorido propios de la guitarra.

Genios de la música, universalmente aclamados, han abordado la guitarra, sin haber obtenido en ella resultado feliz. Esto se debe sin duda á que el mecanismo complicado del instrumento requiere un estudio especial y detenido, que ellos no hicieron.

Conocemos de Weber un *divertimento* para guitarra y piano, de tan escaso valor que denota claramente cuán fuera de camino se encontraba para producir algo digno de su pluma, lo que logró, pues no supo aprovechar ninguno de los efectos de la guitaara, lo mismo que Ricardo Wagner en las melodías que escribió para canto y guitarra.

No puedo menos de lamentar el errado concepto en que generalmente se la tiene, siendo éste, entre los instrumentos de punteo, el único de solista (incluso el arpa) que puede dar cabida á la música propiamente dicha.

Esa caja, sencilla al parecer, es delicadísima de construir, y sólo muy pocos de lo que á ello se dedican, consiguen llevar á buen término la minuciosa labor que ha menester, si ha de poseer las condiciones requeridas. Los buenos constructores llegan á serlo después de muy larga experiencia, y poseyendo un don de manos y espíritu tal vez superior al que necesitan los especialistas de instrumentos de arco.

Una buena guitarra bien encordada, y pulsada por un verdadero artista es susceptible de producir, con sus inimitables sonidos y variados matices, vivas é intensas emociones.

Es de esperar que los músicos esclarecidos, vuelvan á fijar en ella su atención, y estudiándola detenidamente, se compenetren de la infinidad de recursos que encierra. Así podrán coadyuvar al aumento de su repertorio, aportando á los filarmónicos, deleites aun no bien saboreados.

Antonio J. Manjon.

Los teatros del Plata en 1903

Mucho se habla ya de la próxima estación teatral en ambas capitales del Plata, la cual promete ser de las mejores que hayamos tenido en estos últimos tiempos.

La llegada del célebre director de orquesta Toscanini será el atractivo mayor de la temporada. Los públicos de Buenos Aires y de Montevideo esperan con ansiedad al artista eminente que la vieja Europa aclama como uno de los primeros directores de la época.

Dando una nueva prueba de su *sa-*

I need to thank Cedar Viglietti for finding this in the Biblioteca Nacional de Uruguay and Alfredo Escande for providing this information for the book. The director of the magazine, that lasted from 1885-1952, was Francisco Sambucetti (brother of the musician Luis Sambucetti). Both were founders and managed the Instituto Verdi, where many concerts took place.

This article is from section-Remembering our most distinguished Guitarists and Aficionados of the past —*"Recordando a nuestros mas destacados Guitarristas y Aficionados del pasado."* from the *"Revista de la Guitarra"* magazine issue No. 13 of September 1945 Año VI of the Asociacion Guitarristica Argentina. It reprinted an article titled: *"La Guitarra"* by Antonio Jiménez Manjón from the illustrated weekly supplement of the daily *"La Nacion"* 1902 Año I issue No. 16. (Thursday December 18, 1902-from a bound version FFSI Archives.)

The translation is:

"Although Antonio J. Manjón was Spanish, born in 1866 in Jaen (Spain) he deserves it that we remember him as one of ours, now that a better part of his life passed here in Buenos Aires, where he was a professor of many illustrious Argentine lovers of the guitar; because his best artistic works were conceived and published here, and finally because he wanted to and respected them as their own.

Since we present, to our readers, of this maestro, an article that he would publish in *"El Suplemento Semanal Ilustrado"* of *"La Nacion" Año* I issue No. 16 - 1902, titled:

"The Guitar"

The history of this musical instrument is long. Its first page dates from the most remote times, and this instrument is linked to others of strings, some of which haven't entered into the terrain of the true art.

It appears, in antiquity, to a time of an opulent palace and in the humble home, due to without a doubt the generalization that then the music was almost exclusively vocal, being limited to the paper of the instruments to accompany those songs, as well to play the airs of dance, and the guitar's capacity being (although with four strings as it was given in the beginning), not only to emit the sounds, diatonic and chromatic, but also to produce the tonal chords in various scales, enough to satisfy the musical sentiment of those epochs.

It isn't my purpose to make an apology for the instrument, referring to those times in which the Arab musicians accompanied their poetic songs with it, neither to those still very remote, in which it was the capricious Egyptian song, of a strange rhythm and of an indeterminate tonality. I'm only going to concern myself, and to the great features, of the guitar, since that contributes to form the most modern of the arts.

As for the music, as it was advancing; it augmented the extension of its instruments and was perfecting the system. It wasn't the guitar that was foreign to this progressive movement, and in the 16th century added the fifth string. Later and when the piano reached its sixth octave and a notable perfection in its abilities, as well the guitarists added another string, arriving to be the instrument such as we commonly have today. The artist Coste put the seventh string for enlarging some chords and to facilitate certain tones, and later the constructor Torres invented that of eleven strings, which not only augmented its extension, but also the sound, because its five additional laying over the instrument made the most intense sonorous wave. The six, of the guitar of Sor (we call them in this way) preserve its original tuning. By that it's less explainable that almost no one studies the new guitar, staying with the one that contains six strings, no more no less that the piano contains, the extension of the antique clavichord. But it might be by the strange phenomenon of routine, or because they still lack a method for easy comprehension of the new system, it hasn't been generalized as I would have expected, given its unquestionable superiority.

Those that imagine incur in a gross error that with little musical instruction they can arrive to dominate this instrument, by its nature it's so complicated it needs good preparation.

The guitar, a demure lady which, I don't know to declare as it is, but before that which, in love with her, guesses to penetrate toward the innermost of its character.

Its gracious form and peculiar effects have attracted numerous passionate ones, which have embraced against its heart, but almost all of them a strange case, intending to hug it, have mercilessly treated it bad.

The poor harmonic body! If delicate as a sensitive, victim until with a change of temperature, that doesn't suffer from the rude strikes that its cultivators deal it didn't initiate!

Apparently easy to construct, whatever carpenter mimics its environs; but the almost imperceptible smooth feminine curves escape those profane constructors, which are, however, those that produce the enchanted sounds that have to give life to the slender body.

If since the invasion of the piano it is unjustly and carelessly found, it hasn't always been the same, and before it was adorned of the most distinguished places, and an object of the detailed study of the aristocratic aficionados. There is evidence that the great Queen Isabel I of Castilla was entertained in her leisure playing the guitar, and later the King Sol was pleased to make its strings vibrate. In effect, they still remain, we know simple songs, but very appreciable and interesting from the historic point of view, by Robert de Visée, dedicated to his disciple, Louis XIV, the French King.

Various ancient artists, such as Ferandiere, Arizpacochaca and Padre Basilio, performed in a notable manner and the traditions remain of that to produce surprising effects, which they didn't manage to engrave on the paper. Only by reference do we know that which those Virtuosos made.

Before Fernando Sor, there were some productions in two parts, now of a precise manner, and which have awakened interest. But Sor, who could and must be counted in the number of great musicians, produced compositions of a lot of artistic merit, having some among them, that valiantly suffer the comparison with notable works of celebrated authors who have written for the instruments of the keyboard and of the bow. His style is really elevated, and the specific arrangement and clarity of the voices admirable. In Sor always melodies of the best taste are found distinguished by a knowledgeable constructed harmony. You have to recognize that his work is of a difficult mechanism and interpretation, and perhaps by this motive it isn't widespread.

To Sor follows, not only chronologically but also in capacity, Aguado who left to us, more than his known and utile method, various pieces of undeniable musical worth, which have taken the place to see recognized by the most severe critics. His style differs from that of Sor principally in the tendency to concede major importance to only one voice, that accompanies very ably, since without that its temperament permits it to employ the counterpoint in the high grade that made Sor, Aguado was a very distinguished harmonist, and his productions are aesthetically finished.

In the number of the great artists who have produced for the guitar are found the already mentioned Coste, Giuliani, who wrote the most beautiful works of an irreproachable technique, and Regondi, almost unknown, in spite of his unquestionable talent.

Since the disappearance of the guitarist authors who I have named, they entered an unfortunate era, the literature of the instrument, because although it has been augmented, it has been descending in quality until implausible.

Antonio Cano, an able performer, composed many pieces, but lacks important ideas, and his means are of total simplicity.

Arcas, the most notable Virtuoso, enchanted with his cleanliness and precision of his technique. I preserve the impression that when I was a boy they produced the repeated performances of this artist, who unfortunately limited it as Cano, to interpret his own compositions, which are generally trivial, revealing a very deficient musical education, in relation to his talent. Some of them are heard, however, with taste, because they might contain the outstanding talent to apply the effects of the guitar's own tone colors.

Geniuses of the music, universally acclaimed, have addressed the guitar, without having obtained a happy outcome of it. That must be without a doubt, due to which the complicated mechanism of the instrument that requires a special and detailed study that they haven't done.

We know of a divertimento for guitar and piano by Weber, of such a poor value that clearly indicates how off the path he found to produce something worthy of his pen, with which he didn't succeed, since he didn't know how to take advantage of any of the effects of the guitar, the same as Richard Wagner in the melodies he wrote for voice and guitar.

I can't less than lament the mistaken concept in which generally it has, this being, among the plucked instruments, the only one as a soloist (including the harp) that can make room for its own music.

This box, appears to be simple, is very delicate to construct, and there are only very few of them that dedicate to it, to get carried to a good end in meticulous labor that has to be done, if they possess the required abilities. The good fabricators bring it about after a long experience, possessing a talent of the hands and a spirit perhaps superior to which the specialist of the bowed instruments needs.

A good guitar well strung, and plucked by a true artist, is susceptible to produce, with its inimitable sounds and varied tone colors, live and intense emotions.

It is expected that the illuminated musicians, will return to focus their attention and in a detailed study on it, and they will understand the infinite resources it contains. In this way they might be able to help augment its repertoire, contributing to the philharmonics, delights still not well relished.

Antonio J. Manjón.

This review of Antonio Jiménez Manjón's performance at the homage of Eusebio Blasco is from the "*Caras y Caretas*" magazine of May 23, 1903 issue No. 242 Año VI.

The translation is:

"Teatro Victoria — Homage to Eusebio Blasco

The majority of the resident Spanish families among us gave a meeting Monday evening in the Teatro Victoria, where they owed to celebrate the event organized by the friends of the Spanish writer Eusebio Blasco to benefit the widow and children.

The solidarity that was enjoyed in the life of the notable writer among his companions was shown in relief in the referred to event.

Attractive and well-chosen numbers formed the program of the event.

The part of the concert was the most interesting. The guitarist Mr. Manjón, besides the two pieces of his composition, had performed the melody of Tosti, "*Vorrei morire*", he succeeded to draw abundant applause with it. In their respective parts, Mrs. Montenegro de Gaos and her husband Mr. Andrés Gaos received the ovations of the public. The *Jota Navarra*, by Sarasate, of two violins, that they performed accompanied by the piano by Julián Aguirre, was admirably interpreted.

Mr. *Don* Angel Maria Segovia read a poem of which he is the author and Mrs. Eva Canel and Mr. Alfredo Mendez Caldeira also read various compositions of Blasco with a notable success."

This article is from the "*Caras y Caretas*" magazine of February 21, 1903 issue No. 229.
The translation of the except is:
"*Ladrones Liricos — Robo de una Guitarra y de un Violin valioso.*

Lyrical Thieves — Theft of a guitar and a valuable violin

Mr. Antonio Jiménez Manjón the concert guitarist whose so many and good moments given to our society in the past winter organized musical sessions destined almost absolutely to make known the valuable resources of the favorite instrument suffered a misfortune in the month of November, before that he had to spend many truly bitter hours. A case of being fed up with not having his concert guitar which is worth 2,000 pounds sterling, to be deprived not only of the amount of money that it represents but also of an instrument his hands know to the most minute details and with which he had forgotten of his deficiency of sight. The price perhaps is a little exaggerated, in spite of being a guitar of great richness, but that is very little, if you think that the poor blind man was having complete faith in its conditions and who played it knowing how to find its qualities in another he couldn't succeed to do so, even when he would have the stringing completely for the set of strings which is his exclusive invention. The police follow the path of the pickpocket, but until today their efforts to find the instrument, had been in vain; in the last week, they ended up, they were able to capture it in moments that he was trying to enter the home of the same Mr. Manjón, bringing the stolen guitar, since he, in particular gestures had given with it and promised to rescue it, guarding the reserves of the case. The police and Mr. Manjón have ended up satisfied."

Señorita Maria Eugenia Monty Luro

This article and photo are from the "*Caras y Caretas*" magazine of October 6, 1906 issue No. 417 Año IX.
The translation is:

A concert guitarist

Monday evening an exam of competency as a professor of guitar was offered by, Miss Maria Eugenia Monty Luro, in the Conservatorio de Musica de Manjón. The program was the following:

"Reverie nocturne" Coste
"Rondo en la menor" Aguado
"Adagio de la Sonata, Op. 22" Sor
"Variaciones sobre un aire vasco" Manjón
"Tres estudios" Manjón
Among these studies is one in C minor a specialty in portamentos.

With great security and mastery Miss Monty Luro passed the test of difficulty, and she was outstanding in the "*Aire vasco*" by Manjón, by the sentiment with which she knew how to interpret the most beautiful composition of her maestro.

In the reading, at first look, she demonstrated to possess also an elegant and perfect technique. Miss Monty Luro has, undoubtedly, special abilities to conquer the difficulties of her chosen instrument, and above these endowments, a select spirit impregnated with artistic sentiment.

Maestro Manjón can be proud of her work. Our elegant society, from now on counts on a stimulus that comes to invigorate the tendency of good taste in those who pledge to the lovers of the musical art, opening a path, the costliest at times, amid the plethora of drumming, because if it is, in the immense keyboard of the common. The abundance of musical conservatories, bad in the largest part of them, can bring the disparagement of the rest. It is good, since, to cooperate to the success of those that pledge in the artistic and elevated labor.

Miss Monty Luro (1884-1971) is an artist. Her virtuosity distinguishes, exclusively hers and the high school that she possesses as the favorite student of the inimitable Manjón."

In the "*Montevideo Musical*" magazine on March 8, 1890 No. 10 Año V, on page 2, in the section "*Correo artistico*" (Artistic mail) was the inclusion of a review of a recent performance in Spain by Antonio Jiménez Manjón. This preceded his arrival to play in the Rio de la Plata by 3 plus years. In the case of Miguel Llobet, his international fame was read by the public in Buenos Aires in the "*Caras y Caretas*" magazine, some 6½ years before his arrival in August of 1910.

Correo Artístico

Madrid, Febrero 15 de 1890.

Sr. Director del MONTEVIDEO MUSICAL.

En el Teatro Principal y en el Eldorado ha aparecido el famoso concertista de guitarra, Jimenez Manjon, que sin grande ostentacion, como se presenta siempre el verdadero mérito, ha merecido espontáneos y entusiastas elogios de la escasa pero escogida concurrencia que ha asistido á los conciertos que ha dado.

Interpreta fielmente en la guitarra algunas composiciones clásicas, ejecutadas con pulcritud y delicadeza extremada. Sobresale más, si cabe, en los aires genuinamente populares españoles, pues como verdadero cultivador de este género, no los rebaja para obtener un aplauso no siempre ganado en buena lid.

Jiménez Manjon es otro de los gloriosos pero desdichados ciegos de nacimiento que tantos lauros han conquistado para el arte patrio, y puede figurar en orden de mérito al lado de los más encumbrados artistas privados de la vista.

Translation:

Madrid, February 15, 1890.

Mr. Director of the Montevideo Musical,

In the Teatro Principal and in the Eldorado the famous concert guitarist Jiménez Manjón has appeared, without great ostentation, he is always presented as the true merit, he has deserved thespontaneous and enthusiastic praise by the scarce and chosen gathering that attended the concerts that he has given.

He faithfully interpreted some classical compositions on the guitar, performed with beauty and extreme delicacy. What protrudes more, if possible, is in the popular Spanish airs, since he is a real lover of this genre, he doesn't lower himself to obtain an applause that isn't always won fair and square.

Jiménez Manjón is another one of those glorious but wretched blind from birth players whose many laurels have conquered for the patriotic art, and he can be placed by the order of his merit at the side of the most exalted artists deprived of sight."

This is translated from the book by Cedar Viglietti *"Origen y Historia de la Guitarra"* published by Editorial Albatros in Buenos Aires in 1973.

From pages 177-178:
After citing some information from Domingo Prat's *"Diccionario de Guitarristas"* Cedar Viglietti offers new information about Antonio Jiménez Manjón from other sources.

"At times he used a guitar especially adapted to its eleven strings, eight over the fretboard and three off of it, an innovation that many have adopted after having heard him, only during a certain time, now that this quantity of strings made it difficult to overcome a correct plucking of the right hand. When, years later, he repeated his visit, he now brought one with fewer strings.

We've said, since, that in his first concert, in August of 1893, the journal of yesteryear (*"Montevideo Musical"*) wrote:

'All the judgements that they speak of propagated in respect to the guitarist Manjón have been truly emitted with the most elevated justice, since making him, the said artist, the delicacy of our best society. He is a musician of feeling, most delicate, who makes what, he wants of the instrument, of a marvelous manner.' A little later: 'To the difficulties of this instrument you have to add the complete tuning and the fine performance'.

'He's still a young man of 27 years and of an attractive presence. Blind from birth, it can be said. His wife, who accompanies him on the piano, is a complete professor. (I continue to transcribe faithfully C. V.)

In the program of the piano:

Mendelssohn in a Fantasia

and from Ketterer Vals de las Hadas.

On guitar:

Estudio en Mi, by Cano.

a) Andante. b) Presto, by Sor

Un Recuerdo de mi Patria, by Manjón

Célebre Fandango, Manjón.

Piano:

Melodia e Impromptu, by Rubinstein.

Gran Polonesa en mi bemol, by Chopin.

Guitar and piano:

Suite en Mi menor, by Manjón.

a) Allegro, b) Scherzo a la Sevilliana, c) Romanza, d) Movimiento continuo.

Guitar Solo: Fantasia by Simmer

Peteneras by Manjón.
In another part the writer expressed: 'With reason in his pilgrimage of the entire world he has received many flowers....'"

Full translation from the "*Montevideo Musical*" magazine of August 16, 1893 issue No. 31 Año IX:

"Manjón

"All the judgements that they speak of propagated in respect to the guitarist Manjón have been truly emitted with the most elevated justice, since making him, the said artist, the delicacy of our best society.

In the two concerts Mr. Manjón has given here, with a preference to the latest, he has been favored by an intelligent and relatively numerous audience.

Manjón doesn't search in those countries that make the artistic reputation that he enjoys in Europe another thing known. He is a musician of feeling, most delicate, who makes what, he wants of the instrument, of a marvelous manner. The guitar in the hands of Manjón speaks and sings. Now it is light music, playful, that makes the spirit happy, yet tender, sentimental, that moves the strings most sensatively for whom has the pleasure to hear them. Manjón as a guitarist is a true virtuoso.

To the difficulties of the instrument you have to add the complete tuning and the fine performance all he knows is stamped into what he performs.

With reason, in his artistic pilgrimage, by the entire orbit he has received many flowers, he has gathered the artistic glory to place his name at a great height. He is still young and of an attractive presence.

Blind, at birth (sic), it can be said, God has conceded to him the divine grace of the most intimate artistic sentiment. He deserves all the protection of our public.

His wife who accompanies him on the piano, is a complete professor. For those who haven't heard the artist who we're referring to, it's enough to see the attached program, in which the names of the illustrious composers placed say who Manjón is."

MANJON

Todos los juicios que se habían propagado con respeto al guitarrista Manjón, han sido en verdad emitidos con la justicia mas elevada, pues está haciendo dicho artista las delicias de nuestra mejor sociedad.

En los dos conciertos que aquí ha dado el señor Manjón, con preferencia el último, se ha visto favorecido por un auditorio inteligente y relativamente numeroso.

Manjón no busca en estos países otra cosa que hacer conocer la reputación artística que en Europa gozó. Es músico de sentimiento delicadísimo, que hace lo que quiere del instrumento que maneja, de una manera maravillosa. La guitarra en las manos de Manjón, habla y canta. Ya es música ligera, retozona, que alegra el espíritu, ya tierna, sentimental, que hiere las cuerdas mas sensibles de quien tiene el placer de escucharla. Es Manjón como guitarrista un verdadero virtuoso.

A las dificultades de ese instrumento hay que agregar la afinación completa y la ejecución fina que á todo sabe imprimir en lo que ejecuta.

Con razón, en su peregrinación artística por el orbe entero ha recibido tantas flores, ha conseguido gloria artística para colocar su nombre á gran altura. Es aún joven y de atrayente presencia.

Ciego, de nacimiento, puede decirse, Dios le ha concedido la divina gracia del sentimiento artístico mas íntimo. Merece toda la protección de nuestro público.

Su señora esposa que le acompaña al piano, es toda una profesora.

Para aquellos que no hubiesen oído al artista que nos referimos, basta ver el programa adjunto en que figuran nombres de compositores ilustres que dicen lo que es Manjón.

PRIMERA PARTE

Piano	Fanntasía op. . . .	MENDELSSOHN
	Vals de las Hadas . .	KETTERER
	Estudio en *mi* . . .	CANO
Guitarra . . .	*a* Andante	
	b Presto	SOR
	Un recuerdo á mi pátria,	
	célebre fandango	MANJON

SEGUNDA PARTE

Piano	Melodía	RUBINSTEIN
	Impromptu	
	Gran polonesa en *mi bemol*.	CHOPIN
Guitarra y Piano .	Suite en *mi menor* . . .	
	a Allegro	
	b Scherzo á la sevillana.	MANJON
	c Romanza	
	d Movimiento contínuo .	
Guitarra sola .	Fantasía	SIMMER
	Peteneras . . . , .	MANJON

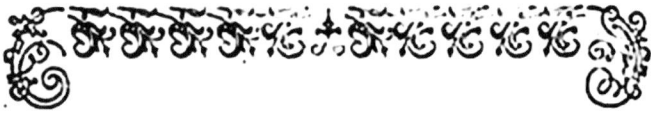

Full translation from the "*Montevideo Musical*" magazine of August 24, 1893 issue No. 32 Año IX:

"Manjón

"Of all the artists who have visited us in the most recent times, he is without a doubt the most notable, the celebrated guitarist Manjón, is an artist of emotion and delicate interpretation on the difficult instrument that he loves.

In the three performances that this artist gave the gathering wasn't so numerous, but in the concert given last Friday there was much more of the public, which demonstrates as proof the great effect that this artist has caused.

What can we say of Manjón that hasn't been said by the European press?

It might take a pen more inspired than ours, to sketch the praise that the king of the guitarists deserves.

As a spectator who was at our side says of the concert on last Friday:

"I believe that the Godmother of Manjón was a fairy who gave him the gift of the enchanted guitar to bewitch the entire world, and and he can scarcely have between his child-like hands in this instrument, the sounds that sprout from the strings that move the listeners.

Some people have assured that Manjón has signed a pact with the devil, who gave him the power of magic, surrendering an enchanted guitar with which he could conquer glory, fortune and love, exchanging his soul and that some years will pass and the demon will appear to reclaim his victim.'

We believe that Manjón is the son of Apollo and Euterpa, who would have him descend from the Olympus, saying to him: "You, go subjugate the universe with your inspiration and propagate the most divine of all the arts in the land."

His performance is marvelous and there isn't a difficulty he can't conquer. The most elegant in thehandling of his instrument, that sings and makes us experience the most varied emotions of an *Andante* that fills our soul with tenderness; an *Allegro*, or those brilliant variations that astonish. Some melodies leave us ecstatic, and when we hear those tangos or caprichos, that appear special to have in front of the eyes a beautiful painting by Goya with its echanting mix of mantillas, and castanets, voluptuously formed black eyes, flowers and sun.

We can't say which of the pieces that he played the best. His classicism and extraordinary ability delighted us to hear him interpret Beethoven, Hummel, Arcas, Aguado and many other illustrious authors.

The concert of last Friday in San Felipe, has been a total triumph for the sublime artist who will always remember it in his career pilgrimage."

MANJÓN

De todos los artistas que nos han visitado durante estos últimos tiempos, es sin duda alguna el mas notable, el célebre guitarrista Manjón, artista de sentimiento y delicada interpretacion en el difícil instrumento que cultiva.

En las tres primeras audiciones que dió este artista la concurrencia no fué tan numerosa pero en el concierto dado el Viernes último hubo mucho mas público, lo que demuestra como prueba el gran efecto que ha causado ese artista.

¿Que podemos deciros de Manjón que no lo haya dicho la culta prensa europea.

¡Se necesitaría una pluma mas inspirada que la nuestra, para trazar los elogios que merece el rey de los guitarristas.

Como decía en el último concierto del Viernes un espectador que teníamos á nuestro lado:

«Se creé que la madrina de Manjón fué una hada que lo regaló una guitarra encantada con que bechizaría el mundo entero, y apenas podía tener el instrumento entre sus manos infantiles, brotaron de sus cuerdas sonidos que conmovían á los oyentes.

Algunas personas aseguran que Manjón ha firmado un pacto con el diablo, el cual le ha dado un poder mágico, entregándole una guitarra encantada con que conquistar gloria, fortuna y amor, en cambió de su alma, y que pasados unos años aparecerá el demonio á reclamar su presa.»

Nosotros creemos que Manjón es hijo de Apolo y Euterpe, que le hicieron descender del Olimpo, diciéndole: «Ve; subyuga el universo con tu inspiracion y propaga en la tierra el mas divino de todas las artes.»

Su ejecución es maravillosa y no hay dificultad que no pueda vencer. Elegantísimo en el manejo de su instrumento, el que canta y hace experimentar las mas variadas emociones: un *andante* llena nuestra alma de ternura; un *allegro*, ó aquellas brillantes variaciones nos asombran. Algunas melodias nos dejan extasiadas, y cuando oímos aquellos tangos ó caprichos, especiales parecénos tener ante los ojos un hermoso cuadro de Goya con su encantadora mezcla de mantillas, y castañuelas, ojos negros formas voluptuosas, flores y sol.

No podríamos deciros cuales son las piezas que toca mejor. Su clasicismo y extraordinaria facilidad nos deleitan al oírlo interpretar á Beethoven, Hummel, Arcas, Aguado y tantos otros autores ilustres.

El concierto del Viernes último en San Felipe, ha sido todo un triunfo para el sublime artista que recordará siempre en su peregrina carrera.

Salon Operai Italiani

CUYO 1374

VIERNES 14 DE SEPTIEMBRE DE 1906

Concierto Manjon

La parte vocal, á cargo de la Sta. Zulema Piñero y uno de los pianos del conjunto, al de la Sta. Irene Lopez, ambas alumnas del Conservatorio de Música que dirige el Sr. Manjon.

Antonio Jiménez Manjón concert held on Friday September 14, 1906 at the Salon Operai Italiani. Some pieces performed were the *2nd Grand Sonata* by Fernando Sor, the *Rondo en Re* by Dionisio Aguado and the *Reverie* by Giulio Regondi. Antonio Jiménez Manjón always had other instruments besides the guitar involved in his concerts. Less than two years later, Francisco Tárrega student, Domingo Prat would perform his first concert at the same theater, in his first visit to Buenos Aires. .

This image and information is from the magazine published in Buenos Aires *Mundo Guitarristico*, September-November 1977 Edition No. 12.

Obras de Antonio J. Manjon

PARA GUITARRA DE SEIS CUERDAS

1	La Mariposa	Mazurka	$	1.00
2	Una flor	,,	,,	1.00
3	Mazurka Lirica		,,	1.00
4	Matilde	Gavotte	,,	1.00
5	Tú y Yó	Duetto	,,	1.00
6	Lola	Habanera	,,	0.80
7	Balada		,,	1.00
8	Vorrei Morir, **(TOSTI)** transcripción.		,,	1.02
9	Adagio de la Sonata XIV **CLARO DE LUNA (BEETHOVEN)** transcripción		,,	1.53
10	Sobre tú corazón Romanza para canto con acompañamiento de			
11	Serenata	para guitarra	,,	2 00
12	La Primavera, **(MENDELSSHON)** Romanza sin palabras, transcripción		,,	1.50
13	Preludio N. 15 **(CHOPIN)** transcripción		,,	1.50
14	Marcha Fúnebre sobre la muerte de un heroe **(BEETHOVEN)** transcripción		,,	1.50
15	Recuerdos de mi Patria		,,	2.00
16	Brisas, Barcarola para violin ó mandolin con guitarra ó piano		,,	1.80
17	Capricho Andaluz		,,	2.20
18	Cuento de Amor		,,	2.00
19	Aire Vasco		,,	

PROXIMAS Á PUBLICARSE PARA LA GUITARRA DE ONCE CUERDAS

Noveletta	Primera sonata
¡Siempre! (Romanza)	Segunda sonata
Leyenda	"Quiero y no quiero"(habanera)
Fantasia Gitana	Danza de Hadas

These are the "Works of Antonio J. Manjón for the six string guitar" published by Francisco Nuñez, this is from the back outside cover of No. 18 *Cuento de amor*. The unnumbered list of eight pieces at the bottom of the page is the "Upcoming pieces for the eleven string guitar to be published". These were a part of a multi-volume hardbound edition made for Mario Rodríguez Arenas by his publisher Francisco Nuñez. Volume 6 contains 86 pieces by a dozen composers. The translation of the text on the cover is: "Album of Music for guitar. A gift that is in Honor of the Argentine Centennial made by Casa Nuñez to the professor and composer Mario Rodríguez Arenas".

Francisco Nuñez
editor
Cuyo 1628 Buenos Aires

Note: The street name Cuyo was changed to Sarmiento after the Centennial in 1910.

This poem *"Oyendo a Manjón"* (Listening to Manjón) by P. Teodoro Palacios is from the *"Caras y Caretas"* magazine of January 3, 1920 issue No. 1110 Año XXIII, and it was published on the 1st anniversary of his death. The translation is:

"His figure was noble, majestic and bizarre;
he appeared like God of the art who was below the ground.
He caresses the pegs of his magical guitar,
and gave to the air those notes that started the instrument.

It was the music of kisses, of tenderness and caresses,
they were fountains of moans, and of tears and regrets,
and they fell over the affectionate and favorable soul,
like rains of prayers, like branches of white lilies.

Sometimes there were yehs and clamors of battle,
other times there were songs of the bravest of patriots,
and mixed with the thunders of the exploding gunpowder,
they were going to be the honey of Vidalitas and the lightning flashes of Jotas.

The retinues of warriors paraded by the strings,
the plains of the pampas with its gauchos and steeds,
the mansisimos herds of cows and calves,
until the sun of Andalucia, made blood of the carnations. . .

And that blindman covered in shades, poured glare
over the enthusiastic public that applauded deliriously,
drunken in the cadences that sprouted like flowers
 of the fingers of that magician, which were fingers of a giant.

And the chords flowed from the box of the artist
like trickles of gold and silver, consolations which dew
and the instrument of the sublime guitarist was trembling
as the wing of an escaped archangel of the heavens. . ."

OYENDO A MANJON
POR P. TEODORO PALACIOS

Manjón, célebre guitarrista.

Era noble su figura, meyestática y bizarra;
parecía el dios del arte que bajó del firmamento.
Abrazóse a las clavijas de su mágica guitarra,
y dió al aire aquellas notas que arrancó del instrumento.

Eran música de besos, de ternuras y caricias,
eran fuentes de gemidos, y de lágrimas y penas,
y caían sobre el alma cariñosas y propicias,
como lluvia de plegarias, como ramos de azucenas.

Unas veces eran ayes y clamores de batalla,
otras veces eran cantos de bravísimos patriotas,
y mezcladas con los truenos de la pólvora que estalla,
iban miel de *vidalitas* y relámpagos de *jotas*.

Desfilaban por sus cuerdas las mesnadas de guerreros,
las llanuras de la pampa con sus gauchos y corceles,
los mansísimos rebaños de las vacas y terneros
y hasta el sol de *Andalucía*, hecho sangre de claveles...

Y aquel ciego envuelto en sombras, derramaba resplandores
sobre el público entusiasta que aplaudía delirante,
embriagado en las cadencias que brotaban como flores
de los dedos de aquel mago, que eran dedos de un gigante.

Y fluían los acordes de la caja del artista
como chorros de oro y plata, cual rocío de consuelos,
y temblaba el instrumento del sublime guitarrista
como el ala de un arcángel escapado de los cielos...

Various Antonio J. Manjón sheet music covers 1900-1910 published by Francisco Nuñez.Antonio J. Manjón arrived in Buenos Aires in 1893, and brought with him the school of the 11-string guitar, his method on the right is written for an 11-string guitar with both treble and bass clefs. This fourth edition was published by Romero & Fernández . He died in Buenos Aires in 1919.

Uncredited published piece Romero, Agromayor and Cia. publication

The "*Estudios Artisticos Op. 25*" was dedicated to Mrs. Maria Eugenia Monty Luro de Crespo who married Eduardo Juan Gil Crespo Pons on May 20, 1916. This edition is not included in the 1931 Antigua Casa Nuñez catalog.

The European maestros formed many Argentine disciples of enormous talent: ladies of high society, aristocratic gentlemen, also a student of humble proportion, who received instruction without tuition, accomplished aficionados, and eminent professionals.

Within this group, of advanced Argentine disciples, we mention: Wenceslao Escalante, lawyer, who was also a professor of philosophy, and in the political arena was a Senator in the Legislature of Buenos Aires. He was director of the National Bank and President of the Hipotecario National Bank, and for a time Minister of Tax Collection. Escalante was a student of Bernardo Troncoso, and later due to his many voyages to Europe on behalf of his political and administrative duties, he received lessons in Paris from Miguel Llobet.

Escalante was born in the province of Santa Fe in 1852 and died in Buenos Aires on March 23, 1912. A monument to his memory was raised on the grounds of the School of Agriculture and Veterinary Medicine of Buenos Aires.

Wenceslao Escalante owned two guitars made by *Don* Antonio de Torres Jurado.

Antonio de Torres Jurado (1817-1892)

Julián Arcas with his Torres guitar

These photos are from "Antonio de Torres" by José Romanillos, published by The Bold Strummer 3rd edition 1997.

ANTONIO TORRES

FROM about 1850 to the time of his death in 1892, a guitar maker named Antonio Torres carried out experiments in the design and construction of the guitar which resulted in improvements, and, to some extent, the stablisation of its design, doing for the guitar, practically what Stradivari had done for the violin.

To demonstrate the importance of the fine-wood sound-board alone, Torres made the rest of a guitar's body of papier-maché—and yet good tone resulted. He established the length of vibrating string at 650 mm. and, among other improvements, used seven bars instead of five as in Panormo's guitars, fanning out from the sound-hole on the under side of the sound-board, in the large bout of the body.

The 650 mm. string measurement naturally affected the size and shape of the guitar, and the increased width of the large bout was a factor which was related to improvements in the technique of playing the guitar.

* * *

This photograph of the great guitar maker was given to the grandfather of Manuel Rodriguez who is now a maker of guitars in Los Angeles, California.

This is from the "Guitar News" magazine issue No. 104 of June-August 1969.

Dr. WENCESLAO ESCALANTE, POR CAO

Do nuestra Agricultura se ha encargado
y aunque es á la guitarra aficionado
ha de ver que no marra
aquel dicho afamado
que afirma que otra cosa es con guitarra.

This is from the *"Caras y Caretas"* magazine of August 3, 1901 issue No. 148.

Actual size view of the rosette of the award winning 1858 Antonio de Torres guitar.
This guitar is known as FE 8 in the maker's biography by José Romanillos.

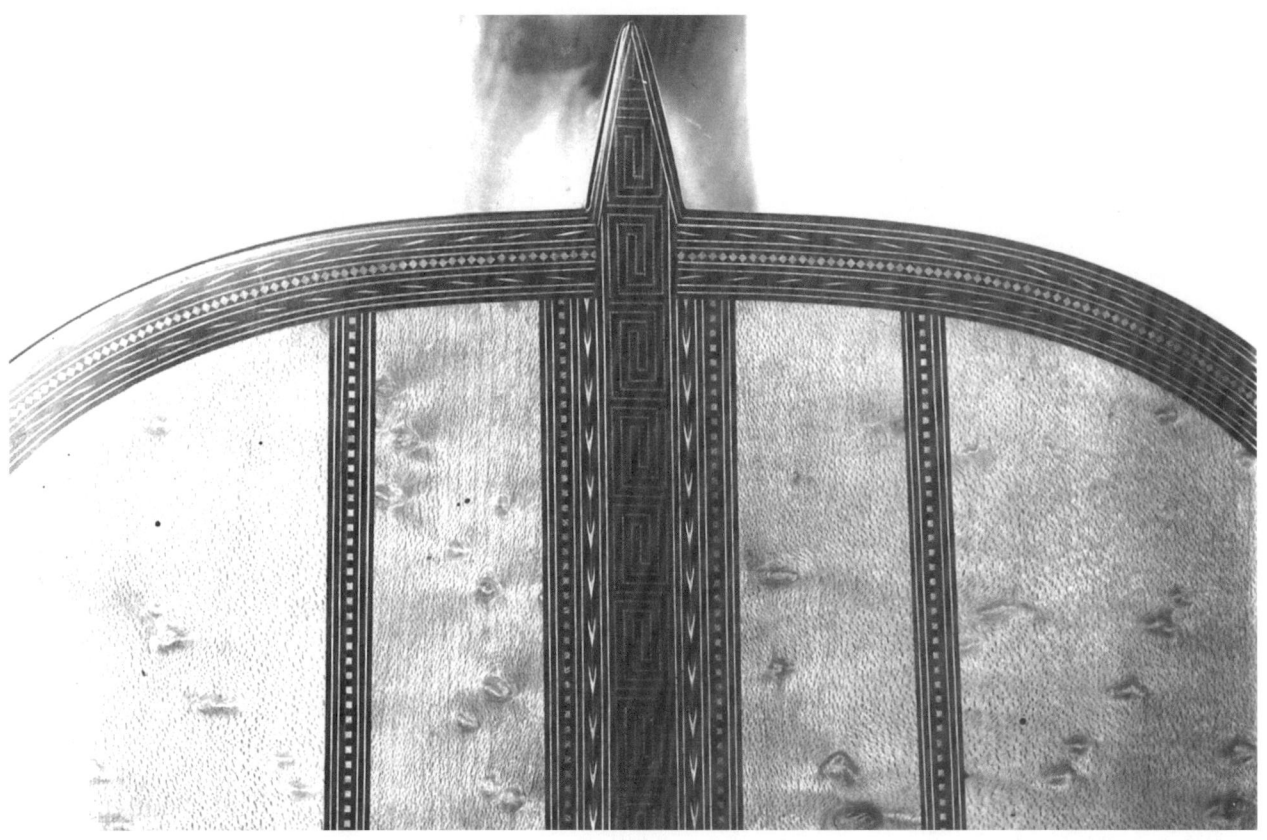

Actual size view of the heel of the 1858 Antonio de Torres guitar.

Actual size view of the end block of the 1858 Antonio de Torres Jurado,
prizewinning guitar at the 1858 Seville exposition.

Archive: All photos from page 82-88 are from Ricardo Muñoz

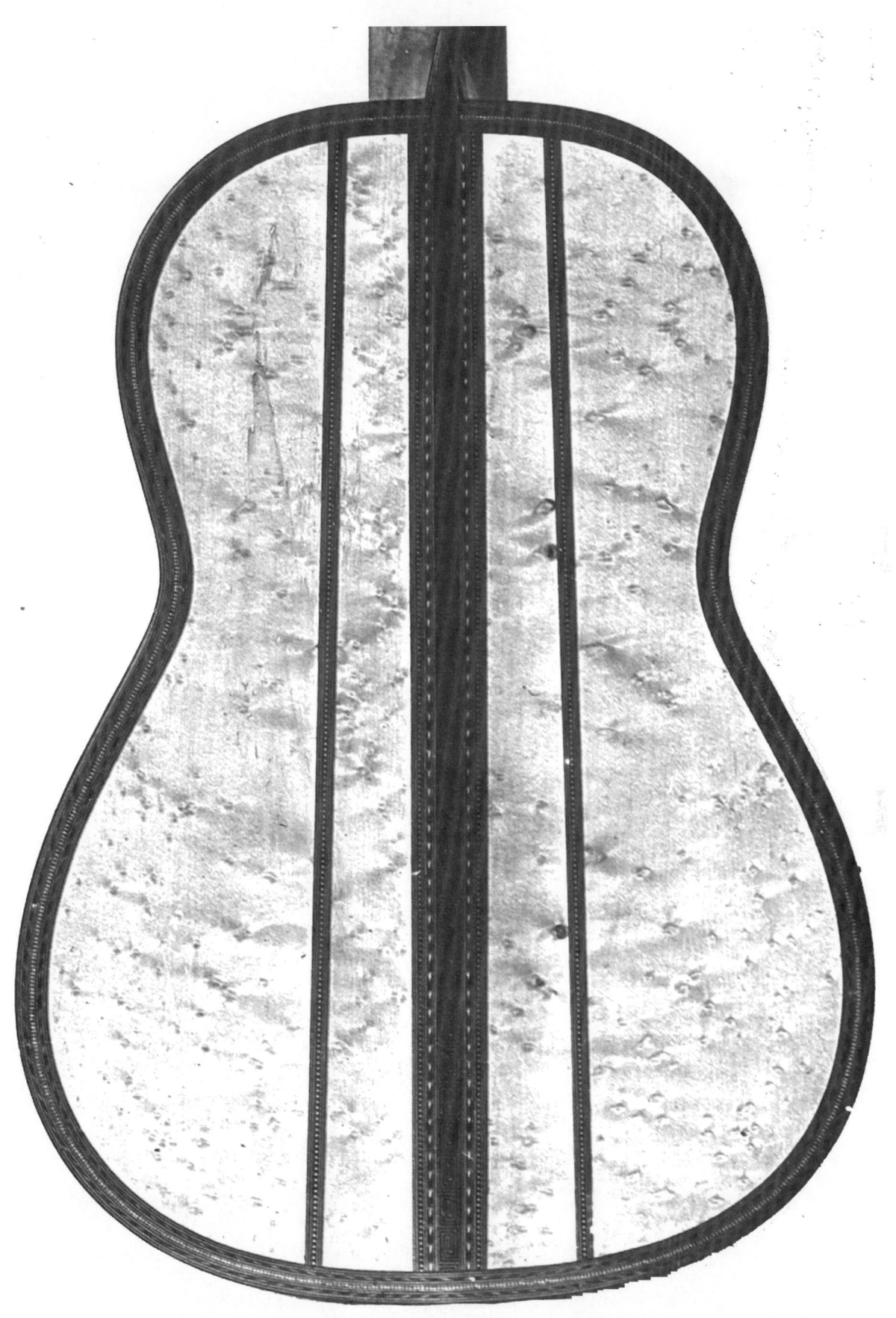

Bird's Eye Maple back of the 1858 Antonio de Torres guitar.

Actual size view of the inlaid maple side of the 1858 Antonio de Torres guitar, showing its extraordinary craftsmanship. This won over all entries at the 1858 Seville exposition.

Actual size headstock of the 1858 Antonio de Torres award winning guitar.

On page 392 of the *Diccionario de Guitarristas* by Domingo Prat is the listing of the *"Poseedores de Guitarras "Torres"*:

"Owners of Torres Guitars

"The concert guitarist and composer Jiménez Manjón owns two models of eleven-strings, one presently in the possession of his widow, who resides in Toledo, Spain; the other in the hands of the lady Professor Gachitegui in Buenos Aires. José Rojo, a guitarist, presently residing in Neria, Malaga, is the owner of an eleven-string model. The Sevillian guitarist Juan Valler, who has resided in Buenos Aires since 1878, gave a Torres guitar as a gift to the Argentine amateur guitarist Dr. Nicolas Albarellos. Another is owned by Dr. Martin Ruiz Moreno, who passed away in 1919, acquired in Seville by the intermediary of the painter and guitarist Bernardo Troncoso, by this same intermediary, the three time Argentine minister Dr. Wenceslao Escalante, who acquired two examples, that are presently in the possession of his daughter Mrs. Sara Escalante de Maura. José Isnardi, distinguished amateur had a Torres, in Buenos Aires, that was stolen from him, from his home in the locality of Florida, in the year 1910. Miss M. Elena Costa Doll, of Buenos Aires, has a beautiful example acquired in Paris in 1909. Mrs. Maria E. Monti Luro de Crespo of Buenos Aires possesses an excellent Torres, without a tornavoz, and constructed in 1884. Federico Cano, has two, one acquired by Emilio Pujol, the other still in the possession of the Cano family. Leon Farré, who passed away in January of 1932, owned two, that have been passed to the possession of Alfredo Opisso; one of them restored and modified in the sides, since these originally were, narrow, that is, to be played in the Flamenco genre, the guitarmaker Enrique Garcia, replaced the sides common for the concert format. Miguel Llobet is the owner of two excellent examples; one of them accompanies him in his artistic life. We make note that these guitars were acquired of a derisory price (ridiculously small). Enrique Crehuet, four examples restored in Barcelona by Simplicio and Fleta. Mario Palmés, in Barcelona owns two examples, and we repeat, without any doubt, he has the *"**guitarra cumbre**"* (ultimate guitar), that previously belonged to the lawyer and amateur guitarist Francisco de Paz. The painter Roberto Ramaugé, Argentine, residing in Paris, possesses two guitars, one of a small format, narrow, a Flamenco type, simple in all senses of the word, acquired in Paris in 1910, gotten away from Spanish guitarist Agustín Andrés; the other is a beautiful work of art by its intrinsic value and its work of mosaics and purflings. Magdalena Cottin, of Paris, sister of the known guitarists Julio and Alfredo, has two Torres guitars of the second epoch. David del Castillo, who passed away, possessed one of the most excellent Torres, for its voices, that previously, was owned by the Spanish General Narciso Ametller. Del Castillo resided for a long time in Paris and his family sold his instrument. In the year 1929, according to the photograph we have in view, the Rowies music house, of Paris, announced it for sale and for the price of 100,000 francs for a Torres. In 1930, Professor José Navas, of Malaga, communicated to the author of this "Diccionario", that a gentleman by the surname of Roldan, in the town of Junquera, of that province, possessed an example of the guitar maker. Dr. Severino García Fortea, an amateur guitarist, who passed away in 1931, had an example. The guitarist, Daniel Fortea, residing in Madrid, offered from that city to Argentina, two guitars for sale. The Spanish guitarist, Roberto Soriano, residing in Buenos Aires, has in his possession an excellent Torres, restored by the guitarmaker Santos Hernández in Madrid. A watch merchant, an amateur of the instrument, established in Antequera, had a beautiful exemplary Torres in 1923, that is to say one of the best, and had belonged to Julián Arcas, who left it in this town when he died. In 1916, in Barcelona a Torres was presented by an Andalucian merchant, of the surname Giménez, who offered it for 25,000 pesetas and it had the peculiarity of being the only one of which the strings came out of the bridge by the six perforations, without being supported by it, the consequence being that the string length began at the exit of every perforation, leaving that in the common guitars it begins from where the strings the rest on the bridge. In Barcelona in 1919, Victoriano Estorch, an owner of a collection of several guitar makers, sold his complete collection to an American multi-millionaire, Mr. Sharpe, who only had interest in acquiring the Torres. Sharpe gave 35,000 pesetas to possess these guitars, this collector died in 1929. Silvio Argerich, residing in Buenos Aires, also is the owner of a "Torres" The author of this "Diccionario" in the year 1917, acquired from Buenos Aires, a Torres guitar constructed in 1864, viewed by some as the best guitar that had belonged to Francisco Tárrega, and as a proof, we attach the following letter of the brother of the artist of Villarreal, directed to my father, a resident of the *"condal"* city:

"Castellon 26th of May of 1917; Mr. *Don* Domingo Prat, Barcelona, Dear Sir and beloved friend: I received your thankful letter of intent of a good desire to acquire the prodigious instrument that belonged in life to my good brother Paco. We would be very pleased to have it go into the hands of your son, this invaluable guitar, worthy to be played so masterfully that you know. We would surrender the guitar to you for the quantity of four thousand pesetas. We await your orders, receive cordial greetings to Maria and strong embraces from your good friend S. S. Vicente Tárrega: S. C. Gonzalez Cherma 105-2o."

This instrument was acquired expressly for ceding it to the brilliant Argentine concert guitarist, my disciple, Maria Luisa Anido, the current owner.

In reference to that guitar, a lecturer said that it was a national shame – for Spain – that it would be acquired in Buenos Aires for the quantity of 4,000 pesetas and is a big shame, that the orator who we are concerned with, may have forgotten that rendering the guitar all the public deserved honors for whom it was the triumphant walk. On the other hand, the professor also omitted that the collection of Victoriano Estorch, which was acquired by an American multi-millionaire, was taken only for the desire of the rich collector.

In ending with the list of owners, the author of this work includes among other things, with an example of a concert instrument and a smaller instrument, that we appreciate their real value. We assure the undeniable authenticity of the guitars, that we don't include by reference, by the fact of having been played as to the others, we attenuate to the veracity of the persons cited.

We won't end without assuring that the Torres guitars have suffered, by the desire of profit that moves many of the unscrupulous, some coarse falsifications, but it's also justice to say, that to others more valuable than many by the great guitarmaker of Almeria."

These paragraphs contain 36 guitars and 33 owners. 11 of the owners lived in the Rio de la Plata. When José Romanillos' biography and catalogue about Antonio de Torres was written there were 5 Torres guitars in the hands of individuals living in Barcelona.

The frontal view of the 1858 Antonio de Torres Jurado, prizewinning guitar at the 1858 Seville exposition.

Francisco Tárrega with his Enrique García guitar. Enrique García closely followed the method of construction by Antonio de Torres. This photo was originally taken in 1906 (The date is courtesy: Rico Stover) and appeared in the magazine "*La Guitarra*" issue No. 1 of July 1923, published by Juan Carlos Anido.

From the column "By the Way" in the B.M.G. magazine published in London from July 1956 Vol. LIII No. 615, the 1859 Torres that actually belonged to Miguel Llobet is mentioned. His daughter ceded it to this museum in 1953.

(Below) This photo of Antonio Jiménez Manjón is from Ricardo Muñoz's unpublished book "*Historia Universal de la Guitarra*" Volume VII "*La Guitarra en La Argentina*". In a much smaller size it appeared in "*Historia de la Guitarra*" published by Ricardo Muñoz in 1930.

A concert by Antonio Jiménez Manjón was listed in the Madrid daily "*El Pais*" on Sunday January 20, 1889. The text translates to:

"The most notable Spanish guitarist *Don* Antonio Jiménez Manjón, who has arrived to his homeland after having acquired in the principal capitals of Europe, overall London, which is where he acquired the merit of the artists, an extraordinary success, presents again in front of his compatriots in a concert, that will take place tomorrow Monday evening at 9PM, in the hall of the Conservatorio. Of course, we predict the "*Sarasate*" of the guitar who the many fans of the beautiful arts penned up in Madrid have flattered, because eminent ones such as Mr. Manjón are the scarcest.

I have here the concert program:

First Part:

1) Segunda gran sonata, en Do – Sor.
2) Recuerdos de mi patria, melodia – Manjón.
3) Jota, fantasia – Manjón.

Second Part:

1) Andante y rondo, en La menor – Aguado.
2) Adagio de la sonata, (op. 28), Beethoven.
3) Canto de amor, estudio, Henselt.
4) Peteneras,

Third Part:

1) Sinfonía de Semiramis, Rossini.
2) Nocturno, Manjón.
3) Fandango, fantasía, Manjón.

The ticket offices are found located in the librería de Fe, Carrera de San Jerónimo; Salon Romero, and portería of the Conservatorio."

Two concerts by Miguel Llobet were reviewed in the Madrid daily "*El Imparcial*" on Sunday, November 17, 1901. The text translates to:

A Notable Guitarist in the "Ateneo" and in "El Evangelio"

A most notable guitarist the night before last presented before the public in Madrid. He isn't an artist whose merit is sanctioned by the applause of the foreign public. Miguel Llobet is a young man of twenty-three years who begins a career of triumphs and of glory. (Same age as Manjón in the above review. R.O.)

The Ateneo applauded him with real enthusiasm. To convert the guitar, the classical instrument, a most delicate box, whose strings respond to a chosen and exquisite art, is only a work that can be gotten by an artist with heart. Miguel Llobet dominates the technique of the instrument, and besides he is a musician. In this way the select public of the Ateneo could appreciate him, who heard the "*Danza*" and the "*Capricho Arabe*" by Tárrega, the "*Minuet*" by Sor-the Beethoven of the guitar; the delicious transcription of the "*Nocturno*" by Chopin, that only the virtuosos of the first rank dare to play, and other compositions transcribed by himself: Catalan folk songs. Miguel Llobet is Catalan.

To the applause of the Ateneo is united with that which Llobet obtained last night in an intimate reunion at the Evangelio. Summoned by the popular newspaper, the editor of the "*El Evangelio*", a great number of journalists, literary writers and musicians turned up last evening. The success of Llobet was real and the ovations that he received by the select gathering must predict sure triumphs.

Besides the works interpreted in the Ateneo, the "*Andante de la sonata décima*" by Beethoven, other classical compositions by Sor and some most delicate "*Seguidillas*" by Mitjana, full of the heat of the Andalucian land, brought enthusiastic applause to the Catalan artist.

It is expected that the numerous public sanctioned the success they obtained in these reunions.

The reunion at the "El Evangelio", finished with the celebrated artists (Miguel) Borrull and (Amalio) Cuenca performing the best of their repertoire.

The two maestros of the Flamenco art also brought a great amount of applause."

Maria Luisa Anido with Tárrega's 1864 Torres, photo taken in November 1922. This is from the magazine "*La Guitarra*" issue No. 1 of July 1923, published by Juan Carlos Anido.

2 | The Modern School — Francisco Tárrega

At the beginning of the 20th century, there was a group of maestros, that assimilated with the arrival of Miguel Llobet, Domingo Prat, Hilarion Leloup, the modern school of guitar that imposed the Spanish rebirth headed by Francisco Tárrega. About this period Carlos Vega maintains: "During the first few years of this century (20th) the transition was prolonged in Buenos Aires, principally fed by the famous guitarist Julio S. Sagreras (1879-1942), by his renowned disciple Antonio Sinopoli (1878-1964), Mario Rodríguez Arenas (1879-1949), Angel del Valle (1874-190?), but these and many more who were of the "2nd row", assimilated what they could of the Tárrega school and the movement it enriched with the generalization of the new technique. To this group is added Hilarion Leloup (1876-1939), who arrived in Argentina in 1912.

Mario Rodríguez Arenas, 1945

Julio S. Sagreras

(Left) Maestro Francisco Tárrega's first publisher, Antich y Tena, in Valencia 1902 and Orfeo Tracio in Madrid 1907 (Right).

(Left) Vidal, Llimona y Boceta in Barcelona 1907 and (Right) Ildefonso Alier located in Madrid, posthumous publications of Francisco Tárrega. When Domingo Prat arrived in 1908, he brought many copies of 12 different published Tárrega pieces. Mario Rodríguez Arenas told Ricardo Muñoz in August of 1945 that when they were available at Casa Nuñez for the very first time, they were sold out in just 8 days.

102

— — — — (front) — — — —

Salones de la Real Academia Filarmonica de Sta. Cecilia
de Cádiz

EL EMINENTE GUITARRISTA
T A R R E G A
CELEBRIDAD EUROPEA

— — — — (back) — — — —

G R A N   C O N C I E R T O
Para el jueves 10 de mayo 1888

Programa

Primera Parte

1. Melodia de las VISPERAS SICILIANAS ......Verdi
2. Fantasia de MARINA ....Arrieta
3. Gran TREMOLO...........................Gottschalk
4. Fantasia Espanola.......................Tárrega
       Descanso de 15 minutos

Segunda Parte

1. Celebre GAVOTA ....Arditi
2. Polonesa de Concierto ....Arcas
3. Carnaval de Venecia ....Tárrega
       Descanso de 15 minutos

Tercera Parte

1. Motivos Heterogeneos ....Tárrega
2. Scherzo y Minuetto ....Prudent
3. Gran Marcha Funebre ....Thalberg
4. Aires Nacionales ....Tárrega
       (A las ocho y media de la noche)

This Thursday May 10, 1888 Francisco Tárrega concert in Cadiz, Spain is from Wilfrid Appleby's "Guitar News" January-March 1970 magazine issue No. 107. The magazine would cease just 12 issues later in 1972, having begun in 1951, and having preserved a lot of priceless data of the Classical and Flamenco guitar world. The classical guitar historian, Thomas F. Heck, found this program, tucked in between the pages of a book, in the archives of Romulo Ferrari in the Liceo Musicale in Modena, Italy. In the next 2 pages of the Guitar News magazine issue Mr. Heck discussed the songs in great detail, but didn't translate the back side of the flyer, which had the Judgements of the Press of Maestro Tárrega. These are some of the earliest impressions by the critics. The translation is on the next page.

There are videos of his works on You Tube.

"The celebrated composers of the classic works never imagined an interpretation so perfect such as that which Tárrega gives on the guitar. To which the most sublime harmonies, the sweetest voices continually occur. . . ." (*El Eco de la Provincia of Alicante*.)

"Last night we heard the famous guitarist Tárrega in the Sala Hass and we have to confess that we never conceived that he could bring out the effects so magical as those the said artist brought forth to his classical instrument. . . ." (*La Renaisement de Barcelona*.)

"Magnificent! Magnificent! Sublime! Never have we heard an artist so polished as Mr. Tárrega."

(*El Litoral de Gandia*.)

"To relate the toughest difficulties mastered by Mr. Tárrega on his humble instrument, it is a superior chore to our efforts. Those which we have heard in the Sonata by Beethoven and in the grand march by Tanhauser, have been convincing that the guitar in the hands of Mr. Tárrega is converted into a large orchestra. . . ." (*La Correspondencia*.)

"The prodigious fingering of Mr. Tárrega, would say that he fabricates real filigrees of the music, if the consideration of the labor with which the eyes can see and with the hands feel is applied what we imagine is immaterial and esthetic. . . ." (*La Publicitat*.)

I need to thank Adrian Ruis Espinos for the identification of the concert location Sala Hass, and for the access to the image to completely translate the judgements of the press.

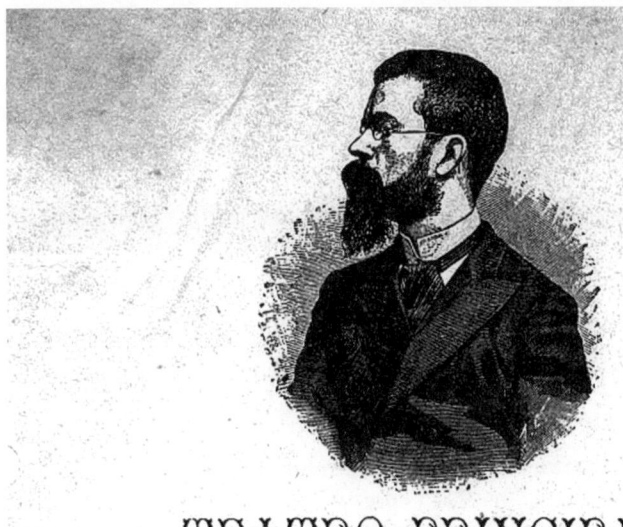

TEATRO PRINCIPAL

GRAN CONCIERTO DE GUITARRA

POR EL CELEBRE ARTISTA

DON FRANCISCO TÁRREGA

PARA EL SABADO 26 DEL CORRIENTE

PROGRAMA

PRIMERA PARTE

1.º	Melodía de las VISPERAS SICILIANAS.	Verdi.
2.º	Fantasía de MARINA	Arrieta.
3.º	Gran TREMOLO	Gottschalk.
4.º	Fantasía Española	Tárrega.

Descanso de 15 minutos.

SEGUNDA PARTE

1.º	Célebre GAVOTA	Arditi.
2.º	Polonesa de Concierto	Arcas.
3.º	Carnaval de Venecia	Tárrega.

Descanso de 15 minutos.

TERCERA PARTE

1.º	Motivos Heterogéneos	Tárrega.
2.º	Scherzo y Minuetto	Prudent.
3.º	Gran Marcha Fúnebre	Thalberg.
4.º	Aires Nacionales	Tárrega.

A las 8 y media de la noche.

PRECIOS DE LAS LOCALIDADES.—Palcos con cuatro entradas, **30** reales.
—Butacas con idem, **5**.—Tablillas bajas, con idem, **4**.—Idem altas con idem,
3.—Entrada general, **2**.—Idem al ultimo piso, **1**¹/₂ reales.

Año 1880

TIPOGRAFÍA DE OLEA.

This Saturday May 26, 1888 Francisco Tárrega Concert program at the Teatro Principal in Valencia, was given as a gift to guitar historian Ricardo Muñoz in 1953, from Francisco Tárrega Rizo (Jr.). In the third part, the first and fourth items suggest Flamenco, which would begin to be recorded by singers and guitarists on wax cylinders, with a usage of 16 plays only beginning in 1881. Julián Arcas had also played and transcribed his own Flamenco pieces. I need to thank Adrian Ruis Espinos for the identification of the concert location. The handwritten date of 1880 is incomplete information by Francisco Tárrega Rizo (Jr.)

—He aquí lo que escribe el *Diario de Avisos* de Zaragoza sobre el concierto dado por el insigne guitarrista Sr. Tárrega en la Escuela de Música de aquella capital:

«El instrumento músico popular en España, la guitarra, con ser tan conocido, con ser del dominio de todos con ser el que encierra nuestros *cantos y ritmos* populares, ofrece en su sencillez un mundo de combinaciones que están completamente vedadas al que no se dedica con afanes de *virtuoso* al estudio de su mecanismo.

La guitarra en mano de Tárrega, es un instrumento distinto á la *guitarra española* (la que solo ejecuta aires nacionales): la guitarra en manos de Tárrega pierde su limitación, es una orquesta, es una caja de música, es un imitador de voces de distinto timbre, de distinto origen, de distinta *tessitura.*

El concertista español D. Francisco Tárrega, ha dedicado sus estudios musicales, que son profundos, al servicio de la guitarra, y tal resultado ha obtenido, ha llegado á tal grado de perfección que ha merecido de críticos notables el sobrenombre de *Sarasate de la guitarra.* Y así es en efecto. Tárrega hacen so en la guitarra de unos sonidos *armónicos,* que sobre aumentar considerablemente la extensión del instrumento, dan á sus voces, mejor al timbre de sus voces, una variedad hermosa: ejecuta con limpieza, corrección y elegancia: conociendo los secretos de la *armonía,* modula con delicadeza y, es claro, contando con todo esto, la guitarra en sus manos es hermoso y completo instrumento que interpreta fielmente los clásicos, y magnífico conjunto de voces distintas que pueden jugar con los temas sosteniendo la atención del que escucha con verdadero interés.

Apoyado á estas excelencias el sonido ya dulce dentro de la percusión de las cuerdas de la guitarra, se comprenderá lo que en manos de Tárrega, puede ser este instrumento.

Ya era conocido este artista en Zaragoza; elementos valiosos le prepararon hace algunos años un concierto en el teatro Lope de Vega y fué aquella fiesta brillante solemnidad musical.

Anoche dió su anunciado concierto en el saloncito de la Escuela de Música y consiguió, como siempre entusiasmar al distinguido público que acudió á la audición.»

This is from the *Montevideo Musical* magazine issue *Año* IX No. 6 February 8, 1894, from the *España Musical* section.

"I have here what the *Diario de Avisos* of Zaragoza wrote about the concert given by the eminent guitarist Mr. Tárrega in the *Escuela de Musica* in that capital:

'The popular music instrument in Spain, the guitar, to be so well known, to dominate all with being that which confines our popular rhythms and songs, offers in its simplicity a world of combinations that are completely forbidden to that which isn't dedicated with slaving away to the study of its mechanism.

The guitar in the hands of Tárrega, is a different instrument than the "*guitarra Española*" (the "Spanish Guitar that is used to play our national airs): the guitar in the hands of Tárrega loses its limitation, it is an orchestra, it is a music box, it is the imitator of voices of a different tones, of a different origin, of a different texture.

The Spanish concert guitarist *Don* Francisco Tárrega, has dedicated his musical studies, that are profound, to the service of the guitar, and such have resulted in obtaining, he has arrived at such a grade of perfection that he has deserved of the notable music critics the nickname: "Sarasate of the guitar." As it's in effect. Tárrega makes use of the harmonics on the guitar, that on it considerably augment the extension of the instrument, give its voices, improve the tone of its voices, a beautiful variety; perform with cleanliness, correction and elegance; knowing the secrets of the harmonics, modulate with delicateness and, it's clear, counting on all that, the guitar in his hands is a beautiful and complete instrument that faithfully interprets the classics, and magnifies the group of different voices that can play with the themes sustaining the attention of those who listen with real interest.

Supporting those excellencies the sound is already sweet within the percussion of the strings of the guitar, what this instrument ultimately can be will be understood in the hands of Tárrega.

This artist is already known in Zaragoza; valuable aspects prepared him some years ago for a concert in the *teatro* Lope de Vega and it was a bright musical solemnity party.

Last night he gave his announced concert in a small hall in the *Escuela de Musica* (School of Music) and received, as always, enthusiasm from the distinguished public that went to the performance."

It appears this column was from the Valencia area, before maestro Tárrega moved to Barcelona.

This is from the *Montevideo Musical* magazine issue *Año* XI No. 2 January 8, 1896, from the *Correo de España* section.

"The notable guitarist *Don* Francisco Tárrega has arrived, who proposes to give some recitals in recreation circles in that capital. Curious Detail: A distinguished English Doctor (Dr. Walter Leckie), of an uncommon education, since he speaks seven languages, of a high social position and passionate lover of our national instrument, is one who follows Mr. Tárrega everywhere."

—Ha llegado el notable guitarrista D. Francisco Tárraga, que se propone dar unos conciertos en los círculos de recreo de aquella capital. Detalle curioso: Un distinguido Dr. inglés, de educación nada común, pues domina siete idiomas, de gran posición social y amante apasionado de nuestro instrumento nacional, que sigue á todos lados al señor Tárraga.

The signature of Francisco Tárrega Rizo (jr.). authorizing a publication of his father. The words below translate to: Note: All copies that don't carry this signature are falsified. (Right) Photo of Francisco Tárrega, from the archive of Maria Luisa Anido, given as a gift to her student, Dr. Edgar Bosco. It is cropped from a Hilarion Leloup photo on page 84.

(Lower Right) Text of the interview by Ricardo Muñoz with Mario Rodriquez Arenas in August of 1945 about how the 12 pieces published by Antich y Tena from 1902-1907 were available for only 8 days before the supply ran out at the Casa Nuñez music store on January 16, 1908. Translation: "But...Who is this Tárrega?...How did you know him?...Impossible! No one knew anything...Everyone, then ran to Casa Nuñez in search of those works by this Tárrega...Do these works exist? In a filing cabinet that says "Tárrega", and that was never opened, they were kept mildewed by the time smelling of humidity, only 12 works, known: *Sueño, Recuerdos de la Alhambra; Marieta, Mazurka en Sol; Adelita, Rosita, Capricho Arabe, Estudio en forma de Minuet; Preludios Nos. 1, 2, 3, 4, 5, 6, 7, 20* and the *Nocturne No. 2* by Chopin.

Eight days later, not a copy existed for sale." *Don* Mario Rodríguez Arenas, was one of the anxious buyers. In these works, he studied and analyzed the how and why of the gyrations....'
From: *"Revista de la Guitarra"* No. 13 Año VI September 1945.

Pero... ¿Quién es ése tal Tárrega?... ¿Cómo saberlo...? ¡imposible...! nadie sabía nada... Todos, entonces, corrieron a la Casa Núñez en busca de aquellas obras musicales de ese Tárrega... ¿existirán esas obras...? En un casillero que decía "Tárrega", y que nunca se abrió, se guardaban enmohecidas por el tiempo oliendo a humedad, sólo 12 obras, a saber: Sueño; R. de la Alhambra; Marieta, Mazurka en Sol; Adelita, Rosita, Capricho Arabe, Estudio en forma de Minuet; Preludios Nos. 1, 2, 3, 4, 5, 6, 7, 20 y el Nocturno Nº 2 de Chopín.

Ocho días después, ni un ejemplar existía ya en venta. Don Mario Rodríguez Arena, fué uno de los ansiosos compradores. En esas obras, estudió y analizó el cómo y porqué de los giros, desarrollos y evolución de ese mecanismo técnico

MÚSICA PARA GUITARRA
Del Mtro. TÁRREGA

1.ª COLECCIÓN

PRECIO FIJO
Pesetas.

Capricho Árabe (Serenata).	2'50
Preludios núms. 1 y 2.	1'50
La Mariposa (Estudio).	1'50
Gran Vals.	2
Adelita, Mazurka.	0'60
Largo de Beethoven, Op. 7.	2
Todas reunidas formando un volumen.	8

2.ª COLECCIÓN

Preludios de Chopín, núms. 6, 7 y 20.	2
Preludios originales, núms. 3, 4 y 5.	2
Rosita (Polka) y Marieta (Mazurka).	1'50
Minuetto de Schubert.	1'50
Minuetto de Beethoven.	1'50
Minuetto de Haydn.	1'50
Todas reunidas formando un volumen.	8

Los pedidos deben hacerse á los Editores Sres. ANTICH Y TENA, San Vicente, 99, VALENCIA, acompañando además de su importe, un sello de veinticinco céntimos para certificar el paquete, sin cuyo requisito no se garantiza la remesa.

The 2 collections of pieces by Francisco Tárrega published by Antich y Tena in Valencia between 1902-1907.

This Francisco Tárrega concert review is from the B. M. G. magazine of January 1966 Vol. LXIII, No. 729.

It took place in the province of Castellon, in the city of Vall de Uxo on Sunday November 13, 1904.

Some of the pieces he performed had been published just 2 years before.

The article was by classical guitarist John D. Roberts.

B.M.G.

THE EXCELLENT COVER PICTURE THIS MONTH IS BY PHOTOGRAPHER TONY B. COES.

Tarrega Concert

By J. D. ROBERTS

FROM the journal *"La Van- guardia"* of Vall de Uxo dated November 19th 1904 we transcribe some interested details about the concert given there by Francisco Tarrega, in the city in which when still a youth he had begun his artistic career.

A MEMORABLE CONCERT: Tarrega, the distinguished artist; the consummate master of the guitar; the superlative concert player admired throughout the world; has been in Vall de Uxo. Last Sunday, Tarrega gave a concert in the Teatro del Centro, the one place in Vall de Uxo where there is intellectual and artistic life. The artist had made the programme up to his own taste and it included his favourite classical works. Together with the Spanish names of Malats, Arrieta, Albeniz appeared the foreign ones of Haydn, Bach, Schumann, Mozart, Gounod and Mendelssohn.

HEAR HIM

To understand what Tarrega does with the guitar, and to feel in tune with his inspiration, it is essential to hear him. We ourselves could not imagine what a guitar was—we had no notion of what the six strings of this instrument could make one feel. There is no one comparable to him. The guitar, when Tarrega plays it, is something more than an instrument; it is a living being which vibrates in accordance with the feelings of the musician.

Tarrega knows the secrets of his instrument in such a manner that not a single chord, harmony, sonority, hidden nuance or unaccustomed sound escapes his marvellous genius. The mastery of inspiration of the player conquers all difficulties of technique, wresting from them with a masterful certainty the true expression and the exact colouring of the musical work. More yet: the execution surpasses the idea which sprang from the mind of the composer. Tarrega feels in such a degree and

executes with such exquisite art the immortal pages of the masters of music that the guitar expresses, with tones that reach to the soul, the feeling and inspiration of its composers. He is not one of those virtuosi who simply demonstrate in concerts the hours they have spent in scales and exercises. He does something more: he imbues himself with the soul of these compositions, with the whole spirituality and essence of the thought, and reflects them with full intensity. When Tarrega, holding his guitar which is a portion of his life, executes the deathless works of the classic composers he becomes transfigured, carried away by a breath of genius. For him the guitar is a necessity of the soul. Without it he would die like a bird without a nest; like a flower torn down by the north wind.

SPECIAL AFFECTION

When he came to play his beautiful "Tremolo" (Recuardos de la Alhambra) he spoke some moving sentences, saying he felt special affection for this town because here he began his artistic career: "Here my concerts began," he said, with a voice clouded with emotion, "and here perhaps they will end, because I am getting old; but even if I live many years yet, my last thoughts will be of Vall de Uxo, which I think of as my second homeland." The audience drowned his last words with great applause and acclamation.

For the finish of such a happy evening, Tarrega and his inseparable disciple Daniel Fortea interpreted some works by Tosti, Bach, Mozart, Haydn, Bizet and Gounod with marvellous precision and agreement, joining the pleasure of listening to Tarrega with that of admiring the fine and finished labour of his pupil Fortea, an honour to his master.

From this night on the name of Tarrega is joined with the lasting memory of a solemn event.

*   *   *

Emilio Pujol, writing in his book "Tarrega", Chapter 5, Section 26, said:

Coming away from this concert, the Master joked with us, his pupils and remarked: "Prepare yourselves! Modern times demand of a guitarist not only that he should play as God commands but that he should likewise speak with the eloquence of Cicero!"

Francisco Tárrega

Don Miguel Llobet wrote an article entitled "Francisco Tárrega" in Paris in January of 1910 in Catalan for the Barcelona musical magazine *"Bulleti"* of the l'Orfeo Catala. Juan Carlos Anido translated it to Spanish to include it on page 14 for issue No. 1 July of 1923 of the *"La Guitarra"* magazine he published in Buenos Aires.

The translation is:

"Completing with a duty of intimate gratitude it appears to me a moral obligation to dedicate a remembrance to the memory of that which was my unforgettable maestro, the prodigious Francisco Tárrega, whose premature end filled my soul with profound mourning.

I don't propose to show biographical dates, because those are, the majority of the times, of little interest to show the personalities in relief and of the power of Tárrega; I will only say two words related pure and exclusively with the artist and his work.

To speak of Tárrega it isn't enough to say: 'He was the first guitarist of such or what epoch,' no! With him the guitar has lost its most eminent figure, the highest of all times of all generations. And it is because Tárrega wasn't only a performer (like another never existed); he was also the creator of a school that could almost be qualified as a New Era for the guitar, opening new horizons and discovering a series of effects and sonorities so unknown, which by this reason, to hear it, the instrument sounded of that manner so unique and sublime at the same time.

It is evident that to bring an end to a work of this artistic importance, it needs, besides, special abilities that Tárrega possessed in a superlative degree, and they were to be a most able musician united to a refined temperament.

If the two most legitimate glories of the past, Sor and Aguado, could come back now, how much they would have been amazed to see the progress and the degree of perfection that was achieved with Tárrega on the instrument that they so much ennobled in their respective epochs!

As a composer, his works constitute the real jewels of the modern literature of the guitar. They all appear to be impregnated with the purist distinction and in particular, the *"Preludios"* can be perfectly placed along side of the most beautiful works which the contemporary music has produced within this genre.

In the genre in which we point out the triumphs achieved, it was in the transcriptions. They can be well qualified as true creations, since it was admirable the mode such as it was appropriated from the idea of the author, to the extreme of which the majority of the compositions of those great maestros produce exactly the effect of having been inspired directly for the guitar. and that was, in part, due to the secret that only he possessed, and which consisted in the most skillful choice of the works. What a shame that their own authors couldn't have tangibly appreciated the relief, the light, the new life that those acquired, overall to be interpreted by that magic exclusive to the great maestro!

He was the ultimate, one of the aspects most characteristic of his marvelous art.

And now, to finish these lines, I must add that Tárrega, as a man, was simply angelical. Since in this way, his memory will remain eternally recorded in the soul of those that, as I, venerate him as an artist and we adore him as a friend."

Miguel Llobet

★ TARREGA CENTENARY NUMBER

GUITAR NEWS

THE OFFICIAL ORGAN OF THE CLASSIC GUITAR ASSOCIATION
(INTERNATIONAL)

No. 9   OCTOBER–NOVEMBER, 1952

FRANCISCO TARREGA was born one hundred years ago on November 21st.

Guitarists in all parts of the world pay homage to this noble artist who devoted his talents to the improvement of a musical instrument of great sensitivity and beauty.

We draw inspiration and encouragement from the example of his life of devotion to his art.

In these pages two of the greatest living guitarists write of Francisco Tarrega. Emilio Pujol, Professor of the Conservatoires of Barcelona and Lisbon, was a friend and disciple of the Maestro. Regino Sainz de la Maza is Professor of Madrid Conservatoire. To their eloquent words of appreciation can be added the feelings of all who have enjoyed Tarrega's music or benefitted by his technical solution of the problems of guitar playing.

From Vadsö in the Arctic Circle came a letter from a student of the guitar who told of the difficulties he experienced, and of his delight in, at last, finding a teacher (Lief Gündhüs) in Norway. To quote from his letter : "The next thing that Gündhüs played for me made me feel like I could cry, and through this little piece (Recuerdos de la Alhambra) I learned to love Tarrega, and since that time he stands for me as the Master of the Guitar."

These words express what thousands of guitarists and audiences feel about **FRANCISCO TARREGA.**

HOMAGE
By Regino Sainz de la Maza

AT this moment when the ancient glories of the guitar are reviving and the instrument is scaling unforeseen heights of artistry, when it is attracting the finest musicians into its rare and beautiful realm, now is the right and opportune moment to remember and to raise up that outstanding artist Francisco Tarrega.

In order better to understand how much the guitar owes to him we have only to consider the decadence into which the instrument had fallen by this time. When he reached the age of twenty-four Sor had been dead for thirty-five years. The guitar, which, thanks to Sor had achieved a peak of unwonted splendour throughout Europe and had come to be regarded as a classical instrument, had fallen into oblivion, just as a century before it had fallen into decay with the arrival in Spain of Domenico Scarlatti, whose harpsichord dethroned the noble guitar.

After the death of Sor neither Aguado nor Coste, the great French guitarist, were able to restore to the guitar its lost prestige. That "style full of invention" of our guitarists of the sixteenth century seemed to be lost beyond redemption until Tarrega appeared. He identified himself with the

Wilfrid Appleby had been a musician since at least the 1920's, and had written about the Classical guitar in his column "The Spanish Guitar" in the B.M.G. magazines since the mid 1940's. The information on the Panormo family and Rene Lacote was initially written by Wilfrid Appleby in the B.M.G. in 1946. Several years later he began his wonderful bi-monthly magazine, "Guitar News" in June-July of 1951, it would last for 119 issues and end in 1972. He would cover the "International News" to a wider range than some contemporary magazines do, having folks translate important texts to be included. It was distributed to at least eight hundred subscribers in 36 countries.

In this issue No. 9, when the Francisco Tárrega centennial was taking place worldwide, the guitarists were remembering he who added so much to their insight of the beloved guitar.

instrument so completely that he learned to discover its finest and inmost shades of expression, finding in it a means of transmitting the formulas and inflexions of a most rich and varied language.

Pedrell spoke of this aspect of his genius. "He gave," he said, "the music for this instrument, so frail of body, but of spirit so sonorous and expressive, wonderful breadth and plenitude of compass." "And," he added, "the art stirred the spirit of the composer, opening up to his inspiration vast horizons. That is why the development of the classic style in modern composition gives to the works qualities which exalt and throw into relief the values of the instrument. Did not Debussy see in the art of Tarrega" he continues, "both orchestral effects and organ sequences"?

Tarrega did for the guitar what Paganini did for the violin. The development and direction of his technique arose—as in the case of Paganini—from a necessity for increase of compass in order to express the spirit of the new romantic music. This meant a complete change of concept, a quite new manner of approach, of penetrating the recesses of the guitar to seize upon the secrets lying therein. His technique was the direct result of this definite aesthetic act. Thanks to his genius, a new revelation was given. At first he turned to transcriptions, and then the work of adapting classical and romantic music to the guitar opened the way to the achievement of higher and more conscious realisation.

The genius which enabled Tarrega to draw from its six strings the whole heart of their music, revealed the possibilities of the instrument and decided its future. He exacted great strength from the fingers, and a greater complexity of execution unknown until his time, which set the art upon secure foundations, provided it with a definite technique, and established its principles, from the manner of placing the hands and producing the sound, to the analysis of all the technical elements. His work was a long process of purification into which he threw the best he had and which he pursued with ardent love.

Tarrega was the St. Francis of Assisi of the guitar. There was something of mystic union in his disinterested undertaking, in his fervent communion with the instrument into which he infused a new and splendid soul.

Tarrega sowed the seed and trained the growth. Thanks to his care and to the fecundity of his art, to his labour bestowed with expansive generosity, we see his work today crowned by this renaissance of the guitar of which he was the inspired founder.

TARREGA AS TEACHER
By Emilio Pujol

IN 1896 the Vicar of Picaña, don Francisco Corell, musician, painter and a fine orator, one of Tarrega's best disciples and friends, invited doña Concha Martinez de Jacobi, her brother and sister Clarita, Ramon Planiol, don Antonio Tello and other friends of the Maestro to a supper at Picaña. After the meal the good priest said grace. Doña Concha could not repress a sob and a few tears. "Why are you crying, Conchita?" asked Tarrega. "Because," she said, "it is many years since I prayed." Tarrega replied : "I am often praying, for he who works, and he who studies, prays."

Tarrega had inherited the capacity for work which is the characteristic of the peasant of Valencia. Some artists have their hours of work ; he worked

Of all of Francisco Tárrega's students, Emilio Pujol, was said to have the interpretation most like his maestro. Here is his reflection of Tárrega as a maestro.

113

all the time. If he enjoyed meeting with difficulties, it was because he wished to prove his strength in overcoming them. He was working when he listened, when he observed, when he meditated . . . Few people came to his door without being met by the sound of his guitar.

His was the exceptional case of a virtuoso of iron will who three times forged a different technique. The first was when, as a boy, he began to play. Then as a man, when, dissatisfied with his technique, in spite of the celebrity he had acquired, he did not quail before privations in order to devise a new method of playing. And then, almost at the end of his life, when his right side was paralysed, he tried daily to force his stricken hand to the agility and touch which had once given it absolute supremacy over the strings.

Although the technique of Sor and Aguado was an advance upon that of their predecessors and contemporaries, the limited scope of the work of each finger prevented any interpretation from having the shading and expression that were required. Tarrega, at the cost sometimes of great sacrifices, worked out the problems of a more expressive and complete musicianship from fundamentals through to the most subtle details. He co-ordinated the elements of instrument, hands and mind, and analysed from their points of view all problems that presented themselves. All combinations of scales, arpeggios, etc., were treated in such a way as to give each finger the greatest independence, strength and sureness possible. No work could present to one thus technically prepared any problem that was not already fundamentally solved.

He taught interpretation by example, teaching his pupil always to listen to what was good and to shut his ears to bad music.

His intense and laborious life was extinguished too soon. He always intended to make a method out of the logical principles of his school, but his intention was cut short by death. A few exercises and studies only were left scattered among friends and disciples like rare pages of a valuable book now forever lost.

Forty three years have passed since the death of the great master. The guitar has reached its zenith after passing through a long and troubled history. And its triumphs are chiefly due to Tarrega.

A TARREGA STORY

By Emilio Pujol

THE eminent poet and artist, Apeles Mestres, who died in Madrid at the age of 82, on July 18th, 1936, the very day of the outbreak of the revolution, had been one of the most intimate friends and admirers of Tarrega.

In the book that he wrote in Catalan, entitled "Volves Musicals" (Musical Fragments), he records, among other things, the following anecdote:

"About the year 1890, Maestro Juan Goula (1843–1917), who had gained world-wide renown as a conductor, was the spoilt darling of the court of St. Petersburg. The Imperial family lavished admiration upon him, and all the members of the Russian aristocracy held it an honour to have his friendship.

He was an ardent friend and admirer of Tarrega, and grieved that his great talent should be left to vegetate here among us, unknown to many even of his fellow-countrymen, instead of bringing him the glory and profit that were due to him. Goula pointed out to him not only the advantages but the obligations that rested upon him to spread his wings and come abroad, where a triumphant career awaited him.

'Leave everything to me' he said, 'all that you will have to do is to pick up your guitar on the date that I give you, get on a train, and allow yourself to be conveyed to the destination I will name.'

And, making use of the authority and prestige that he enjoyed, as I have

These are from the "Guitar News" issue No. 9 of October-November 1952.

said, at court among the aristocracy of St. Petersburg, he began a campaign on behalf of Tarrega, extolling his incomparable art and speaking of him as a star of the first magnitude. He was so successful that he built up an ardent public that longed to hear Tarrega, and began negotiating for halls and impresarios. So Maestro Goula, glowing with the satisfaction of a job well done, wrote to Tarrega: 'Now you can come. Everything is arranged. They await you with open arms.'

Tarrega turned the letter over, pushed it into his pocket, and returned to playing his guitar *for his own pleasure and that of his friends.*

As for Goula, he still awaits his reply in the other world, and St. Petersburg has become Petrograd without having had the happiness of either seeing or hearing Tarrega."

To be a servant of one's art and *To make a servant of one's art* were never one and the same thing for Tarrega.

PROPOSED TARREGA POSTAGE STAMP

IN "Guitar News" (December, 1951) the suggestion was made that it would be appropriate for a postage stamp to be issued by Spain for this centenary.

The "Academia Argentina de la Guitarra" addressed a letter to His Excellency the Ambassador for Spain (in Argentina), don Manuel Aznar, on this matter. We print hereunder a slightly abridged translation of this document:

Your Excellency,

The Twenty-first of November of this year will be the Centenary of the Birth of don Francisco Tárrega Eixea, native of Villareal, Castellon de la Plana, Valencia—a great musician and founder of the modern school of the Classic Guitar. His work raised the instrument to a high concert standard, and it is acclaimed and played by peoples of all five continents and by some of the most accomplished among musicians of all races.

The world has rendered homage to this great master—streets in Villareal, Barcelona and Castellón bear his name, and in the latter place a monument, raised by public subscription, adorns the Paseo Ribalto. Many musical institutions bear his name, not only in Spain but in Tokio (Japan), Buenos Aires, Rosario, Santa Fe, Paraná and several other places.

We can safely generalise and say that all teachers and players of the guitar are influenced by the method of the famous composer of "Capricho Arabe"

Therefore, Your Excellency, the association over which I have the honour to preside, has asked me to request that you should use all the influence of your exalted diplomatic position in begging His Excellency Generalissimo don Francisco Franco, that, as a gift from Spain to the world of guitar-lovers (there are no less than 30,000,000 performers, composers and admirers of the instrument) a postage stamp should be issued in memory of the "IMMORTAL TARREGA" on the anniversary of his birth 21st November 1952.

With the strongest confidence that our request will meet with your most courteous attention, we remain, Your Excellency,

Your Excellency's most humble servants,

(Signed)   Ricardo Muñoz, President.
(Signed)   Leandro A. Castro, General Secretary.

Republic Argentina
Cap Federal, 18th April 1952
"Academia Argentina de la Guitarra"

Professor d. Ricardo Muñoz tells us that this letter was received by the Spanish Ambassador in Buenos Aires with much courtesy and good will.

It is hoped that guitar organisations in other lands will make similar requests.

This article at the bottom is from the "Guitar News" issue No. 8 of August-September 1952.

AROUND THE GUITAR WORLD

ARGENTINA. Senor Don Ricardo Muñoz gave an eloquent address on " Francisco Tarrega " at the centenary commemoration organized by the Asociacion Guitarristica de Rosario—one of the largest guitar societies in the world. After the lecture a young and charming guitarist ,Señorita Fanny Castro, gave a recital which consisted mostly of compositions by Tarrega.

From the many interesting programmes of guitar recitals received from Buenos Aires it would appear that there is more guitar playing in that City than in any other in the world. A very wide range of music is performed by the concert guitarists there--ancient music, Bach and other classics, guitarist composers (Sor, Tarrega, Shand, etc.), modern music (Ponce, Villa-Lobos, Castelnuovo-Tedesco, etc.) and, of course, the characteristic music of Argentina.

AUSTRIA. Karl Scheit, professor of the Academy of Vienna, was recently honoured by being appointed ' State Professor.' He continues to give frequent performances of guitar music as solo recitalist, in duets with Else Gerstl and also in chamber music ensembles with other instruments. Not only is his time occupied in teaching and arranging music for the guitar but he contributed an erudite article on that instrument in " Musikerziehung ". An article about Prof. Scheit (with portrait) also appeared in that publication.

BRAZIL. The enthusiastic society of guitarists in Campinas organized their first GUITAR WEEK during September last. It opened with a broadcast from Radio Educadora de Campinas in which Alberto A. Heinzl gave a talk on The Guitar, followed by Segovia's recording of the Castelnuovo-Tedesco Concerto. On the 22nd two guitarists, G. Santos and J. A. da Silva, gave a recital ; on the 23rd there was a broadcast by Prof. José Ferreira Filho and his pupils ; on the 24th a special Film Show ; on the 25th a recital by Prof. Milton R. Nunes and his pupils ; on the 26th Prof. Nunes broadcast a recital on Radio Brazil—and on the 27th a special meeting, followed by a recital by Prof. Alfredo Scupinari. A full-page report of this Guitar Week appeared in " Messidor."

The São Paulo newspaper " A. Gazeta " of January 7th contained a long and well-written article on the guitar from the pen of Ronoel Simões, whose broadcasts of guitar music have now passed the total of 345 programmes—nearly 1,200 items by 140 guitarists. The Brazilian guitarist Raymundo Lobão gave a recital on December 27th.

These articles are from "Guitar News" magazine issue No. 12 of April-May 1953. Ronoel Simoes, who eventually had the world's largest Classical Guitar record collection, had his name in almost every issue for his radio show playing records of the virtuosos he had begun to collect in 1942.

SPAIN. In Barcelona on January 26th the Society Pena Guitarristica Tarrega held the last of its series of recitals in honour of the Centenary of the Birth of Francisco Tarrega. This was in the hands of Carlos Santias, winner of the ' premio Francisco Tarrega, 1951.' After playing a programme of music by Tarrega, Senor Santias presented two films : " Centenario de Tarrega " and " Huellas de Tarrega ". The former was made during the recent centenary celebrations and the latter is a ' documentary ' on Tarrega's life (Footsteps of Tarrega). Background music was provided for both films by Juan Ruano.

Segovia again visited Barcelona in December for recitals at the Palacio de la Musica.

Radio Malaga broadcast a special programme on November to mark the Centenary of Francisco Tarrega. After an address on Tarrega by Prof. José Navas, compositions by Tarrega were played by Prof. Navas and some of his pupils—Antonio Garcia Azuaga, Evaristo Pujé and Ferdinando Gonzalez Sanchez. The latter also gave a successful broadcast recital on January 12th.

In Valencia a society " Amigos de la Guitarra " has been formed. Manolín Cubedo of Castellon, Valencia, is only fifteen years old but he has already quite a collection of printed programmes of guitar recitals he has given. He is a pupil of Emilio Pujol and plays in the pure Tarrega tradition. Technically speaking the guitar holds no difficulties for him, and his musicianship is good.

During December, at the French Institute in Barcelona, Fernando F. Lavie gave an interesting recital consisting of two groups of songs with guitar—16th and 17th century and folk songs—and a group of guitar solos by de Visée (Suite in D minor), Bach, Sor, Debussy and Albeniz (Rumores de la Caleta).

This is from the "Guitar News" magazine issue No. 12 of April-May 1953.

昭和27年11月16日　第三種郵便物認可

This is from Issue No. 490 weekly publication *Ongakki Shinbun* (Musical Instrument Newspaper) published on November 16, 1952, page 5.

"The Centennial of Tárrega's Birth Approaches" by Shun Ogura

Shun Ogura was a concert guitarist and recording artist since 1931, who had met with Andrés Segovia three times during the maestro's October—November 1929 tour of Japan.

This is item No. 133 from the archive of Ricardo Muñoz in the section about the Centennial of Tárrega's Birth.

The Japanese translation by Randy Osborne is on the next page.

"The Centennial of Tárrega's Birth Approaches"

by Shun Ogura

"Tárrega is the father of modern guitar music.

He was a child born into a humble rural home on November 21, 1852 in Villareal, Valencia, Spain. On December 15,1909 in Barcelona he went to the other world, and the promotion of his guitar music and labor continued. The representatives of the modern guitar music: Segovia, Pujol, the former great Llobet, were all baptized by Tárrega from the beginning.

The guitar was successful in South America's branch family of the Argentine guitar writer Ricardo Muñoz, in the world 3,000,000 guitar lovers, all bathed in Tárrega's grace is the reason for the thank you letters delivered to the representative European angel.

From the homeland of Spain his memorial postage stamp is announced for the contribution by Tárrega to humanity.

Beyond Tárrega's guitar he added a guitar method, instrumental pieces and technique. He wrote singing songs in the manner of the violin on the fretboard.

Therefore, even every string's special note property color naturally has a manner that is dressed.

From that, even Japanese music, which functions becomes a new participation of a thing that came about.

His sheet music, the string's designation, the left and right hand method, the position and other symbols in the eye continues, is the key to the above mentioned technique's materialization.

He wrote about 25 original pieces and innumerable (400 approximately) guitar transcriptions that he left for us. Even when you take one by the master, they show that all of them are good. About, the transparency in his life's charm, it embodied the decree of his have-not ethics.

In one period, he prayed to work and he was expressing his religious view. As for Valencia, Spain's common people, the workers are famous but, he held the same rank's view of life, the thing that the works reflect the problem included in all that our research offers. Our seeing his few photos he appears good. When extracting from the poor man's expression his vocational intention is but deep sculpturing.

When first glimpsing his guitar ascetic to see the peoples depressed force. But our guitar lovers, the guitar fanaticism's most important support of the large base is the thing that will be set in motion. His bulk method book doesn't remain. But, to see his method taught to the disciples has been mentioned when adopting the exceedingly scientific discourse. The identical aim is founded, to use the cello method, in 1914, namely, a period of 5 years after Tárrega's death was written in Paris at the Ecole Normal that was employed by Casals, this method book that is the kind of thing in contrast was a witness to the most important perfection.

Even in Japan the favorable condition of the guitar is progressing. But it is, for an exceedingly difficult instrument, that the growth will have to wait even for a long time to obtain. But, Tárrega is alive in Japan, even Tárrega himself if you think about it. Again, in this break, our thanks to Tárrega is an aspect to be of a special mention."

(Photo caption) Tárrega playing the guitar for his friends.

(The writer is a guitarist.)"

On board the ship "Berenguer el Grande", Domingo Prat signs a copy of a Francisco Tárrega transcription of "*La Paloma*" in D major on Christmas Eve December 24, 1907, a week before he arrived in Buenos Aires.

At the beginning of the 1900's in Buenos Aires, Domingo Prat arrived on January 1, 1908 for the first time to give concerts and is considered to be one of the principal sources, along with Llobet and Leloup, etc. of the modern school.

Mr. J. G. Schroeder of New York sends us the following program of a Guitar Recital given by Senor Arturo Santos of Barcelona, Spain, at Prof. J. G. Withers' studio, Broadway and 65th Street, on May 3, 1908. The endorsement Santos has received from the European press would indicate that he must, indeed, be a great artist on the guitar. We anticipate the pleasure of hearing him in the near future.

PROGRAM

1

a. Eläno pasado por aqua — *Chueca*
b. Minuet (Haydn) — *Santos*
c. Jota aragonesa (Sarassate) — *Tarrega*

2

a. "Inspiration" (Schubert) — *Molats*
b. Moorish Danza — *Tarrega*
c. Fragment from La Boheme — *Puccini*

3

a. Arabian Caprice — *Rossle*
b. "The Little Old Lady" (Spanish Comic Opera) — *Cabalero*
c. Fantasie Hongroise — *J. K. Mertz*

In the June 1908 Cadenza magazine is the listing of this New York recital by Arturo Santos on May 3, 1908. Curriously enough is the Domingo Prat concert just four days later in Buenos Aires, with both concert guitarists playing the *Gran Jota*. Both guitarists had brought the music of Francsco Tárrega to the New World one and half years before the passing of the maestro.

In this debut Buenos Aires concert by Domingo Prat, on Thursday May 7, 1908, at the Salon Operai Italiani (sic) Italia, the *Serenata* by Malats was a Francisco Tárrega transcription. At this time the pieces *Capricho Arabe*, and the immortal piano transcription of Frederic Chopin's *Nocturne* Op. 9 No. 2 had been published.

Archive: Blanca Prat

SALON
OPERAI ITALIA
1374 · Cuyo · 1374

El Juéves 7 de Mayo de 1908
á las 8.45 p. m.
Gran Concierto de Guitarra
POR
DOMINGO PRAT
(Concertista Español)

PRIMERA PARTE

1 - Minuet — *Sor*
2 - Serenata — *Malats*
3) Mazurka (*a*) — { *Chopin*
) Mazurka (*b*) — {
4 - Panaderos — *Arcas*
5 - Sonata 2ª — *Joh. Seb. Bach*
6 - Granada — *Albeniz*
7 - Manchegas — *Chueca*

SEGUNDA PARTE

1 - Andante — *Haydn*
2 - Capricho árabe — *Tárrega*
3 - Romanza — *Mendelshon*
4 - Mazurka — *Chueca*
5 - Nocturno N. 2 — *Chopin*
6 - Gran jota — *Tárrega*

NOTA. - Se ruega al público de no entrar ni salir del Salón durante la ejecución de las piezas.

OTRA - Se dan lecciones á domicilio, razón Casa Núñez y Cia., Cuyo 1628 y D. Prat, Lima 245.

Precios ~ Platea $ 2 ~ Galeria $ 1

But the same Prat, with a flat denial, ignored the existence of the same, letting the doubt exist, being a motive until today of great discussions. He maintains the following: "It's very common to hear "Tárrega School". We deny the existence of such a school by the works of the Valencian guitarist, who left no method or rules for the study of the execution. We don't know of any collections of studies with predetermined exercises: and although a didactic author such as he, that has included in (Prat's) "Scales and Arpeggios" (*Escalas y Arpegios*), three small exercises taken from Tárrega, and other authors that may have done their own, not by that, has been created a school of guitaristic execution: because, with the same right, it can be affirmed that there are as many schools as there are didactic authors".

DOMINGO PRAT MARSAL

Domingo Prat Marsal c. 1910.

"Some nominate that the Tárrega school does support in the pulsation: that is to say, to pluck the string and rest on a lower pitched string, but that is something that is impossible to do, when striking two or more strings together". (D. Prat op. cit-page 317)

With those very clear and precise concepts, remains the doubt of the existence of such a Tárrega school, and if it came to exist it was transmitted by the author empirically to his students, without an integral document remaining in a book. This will be an eternal discussion, as an item to be drawn to the critique of every interpreter or maestro.

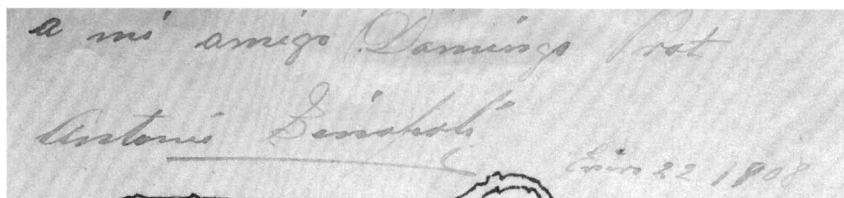

Dedication by Antonio Sinopoli on his 3rd published work "Para todos si no arrebatan" Tango Criollo: "To my friend Domingo Prat, Antonio Sinopoli, January 22, 1908."

This is an important document showing Antonio Sinopoli began publishing in late 1907 and that Domingo Prat had a student three weeks after arriving in the Rio de la Plata.

Antonio Sinopoli's 3rd published work
"Para todos si no arrebatan" Tango Criollo
published by Francisco Nuñez.

Autographed to Domingo Prat.

This is the cover of Domingo Prat's French
dictionary published in 1866 and dated
and autographed December 8, 1910. His
colleague, Miguel Llobet, had invited him
to come to Paris. Miguel had just completed his first tour of the Rio de la Plata, and Domingo Prat
may have left with Miguel from Buenos Aires for Paris after that tour. There is a photo of them from
November of 1910 in Paris in the Index of the *"Diccionario de Guitarristas"*, by Jan J. de Kloe.

Archive: Blanca Prat

In 1910 Romero Agromayor y Cia. began publishing Domingo Prat's works. This image, doubled in size,
is from the back page of *"Seguidillas"* by Mitjana printed in Barcelona by Alessio Boileau y Bernasconi,
though with the logo of Romero Agromayor y Cia. on the front of the sheet music, rather than the Romero
Agromayor y Cia. Buenos Aires version printed by Ortelli Hermanos, often printed in the lower left hand
corner of the the first page. The same case of being printed in Barcelona exists for copies of *"Recuerdos de
Santiago del Estero, triste"* and *"Vidalita (Célebre)"* in my archive, that were once in the hands of José
Augusto Marcellino. In 1913 the name of the Barcelona publisher changed to "Editorial de Musica Boileau".
From the same series is *"Gueya con variaciones"* dated August 15, 1914 and dedicated to Dr. Virgilio
Magnasco and printed by Ortelli Hermanos, at normal size.Boileau y Bernasconi (Taller de Grabada y
Estampacion de Musica A. Boileau y Bernasconi — Provenza 285 — Barcelona)

Taller de Grabado y Estampación de música-A. BOILEAU Y BERNASCONI-Provenza 285-Barcelona

Imprenta Musical-Ortelli Hnos Belgrano 2947-Buenos Aires.

IMPRENTA MUSICAL-ORTELLI Hnos
BELGRANO 2947-BUENOS AIRES

BUENOS AIRES, 15, 8, 1914

The first concerts of Prat in Argentina had great repercussion, what he did was to return on several occasions, his first appearance in the Argentine environment according to our dates was in 1908, and he returned in 1910 and again in 1914, and once more before he permanently settled in Buenos Aires in 1923, arriving married to Carmen Farré, guitarist and teacher. Here, their daughters were born.

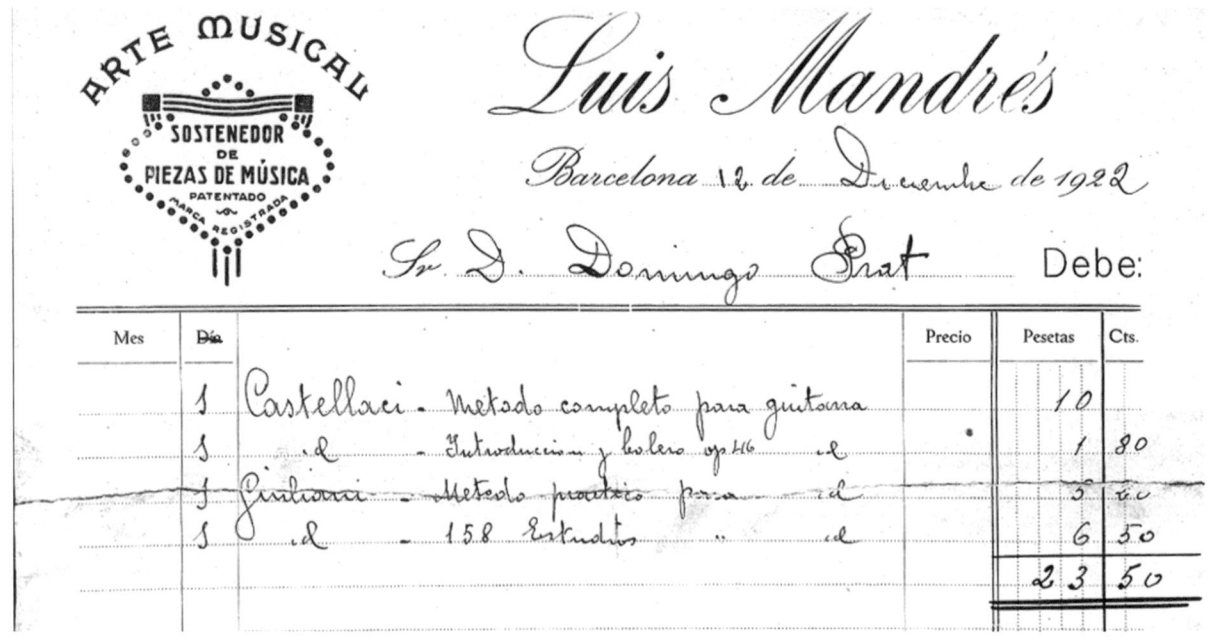

December 12, 1922 receipt for Castellaci and Giuliani methods and pieces, just months before Prat returned to Buenos Aires with his wife, Carmén Farré de Prat.

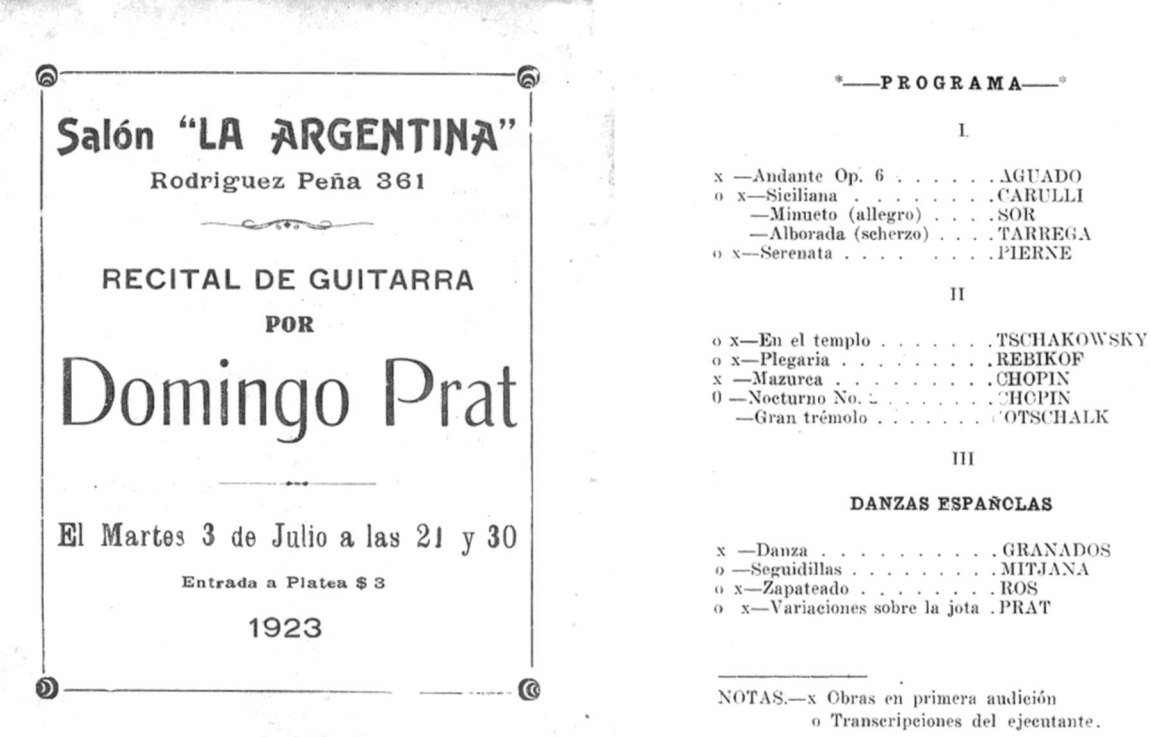

According to "*Historia de la Guitarra*", published in 1930 by Ricardo Muñoz this concert at the Salon "La Argentina" on Tuesday, July 3, 1923 was the first by Domingo Prat after his arrival to stay permanently in Buenos Aires.

PROGRAMA

I

Preludio . . . .
Mazurca . . . .
Pizzicato . . . . } TARREGA
Danza Mora . . . .
Sueño . . . .

II
MINUETOS

En RE mayor . . . .
„ MI menor . . . .
„ FA mayor . . . .
X „ SOL „ . . . . SORS
„ LA „ . . . .
„ SI bemol . . . .
„ DO mayor . . . .

III
CANTOS DE ESPAÑA

Granada . . . .
o x Mallorca . . . . } ALBENIZ
o x Cadiz . . . .
o x Asturias . . . .

NOTAS.—x Obras en primera audición
o Transcripciones del ejecutante.

Domingo Prat concert at the Salon "La Argentina", held just 3 days later on Friday, July 6, 1923. The cover was the same as the previous page.

Domingo Prat and Carmén Farré de Prat in their home at 119 Rodríguez Peña, near the Salon "La Argentina" in 1926.

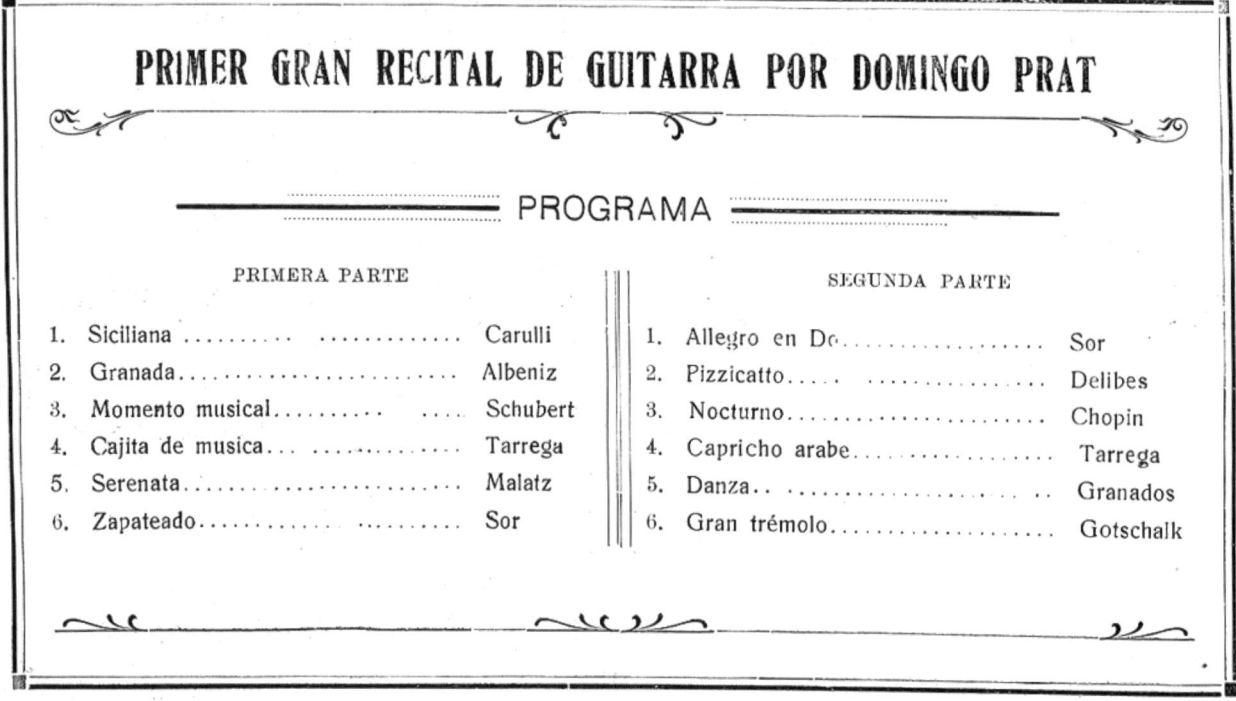

TEATRO IDEAL

Empresa: ANSELMINO

PRIMER GRAN RECITAL DE GUITARRA

— POR —

DOMINGO PRAT

Miercoles 18, a las 21 y 30

The first recital at the Teatro Ideal upon Domingo Prat's return to permanently settle in Buenos Aires, which took place on Wednesday, July 18, 1923.

Archive: Blanca Prat

PRIMER GRAN RECITAL DE GUITARRA POR DOMINGO PRAT

PROGRAMA

PRIMERA PARTE			SEGUNDA PARTE	
1.	Siciliana	Carulli	1. Allegro en Do	Sor
2.	Granada	Albeniz	2. Pizzicatto	Delibes
3.	Momento musical	Schubert	3. Nocturno	Chopin
4.	Cajita de musica	Tarrega	4. Capricho arabe	Tarrega
5.	Serenata	Malatz	5. Danza	Granados
6.	Zapateado	Sor	6. Gran trémolo	Gotschalk

Just a couple of weeks after his most recent debut in the Buenos Aires musical society at the Salon "La Argentina", Domingo Prat offers a program mixed from his previous two concerts. This concert program is not mentioned in *Historia de la Guitarra* by Ricardo Muñoz, such as those of the July 3rd and 6th, 1923 concerts.

Archive: Blanca Prat

Carmén Farré de Prat and her husband Domingo Prat. These photos are from an article in a monthly column entitled "*Cultores de la Guitarra*" (Lovers of the Guitar) in the *Revista Musical Ilustrada "Tárrega"* magazine issue No. 7 of December 1924.

The translation of the article is on the next page.

This is the translation of the article from a monthly column entitled "*Cultores de la Guitarra*" in *Revista Musical Ilustrada "Tárrega"* issue No. 7 of December 1924.

"Lovers of the Guitar

Domingo Prat, Carmén Farré de Prat

Here I have a happy marriage that has arrived at the chasm of the public consecration, after a successful performance in the guitaristic music world.

Mr. Domingo Prat is an old and meritorious professor and a reputable concert guitarist, to the point that his work as an adapter and composer comprises one of the best contributions that has been given among us to the musical art.

Mr. Domingo Prat is a native of Barcelona. At 10 years of age he began his music studies in the municipal school of Barcelona, beginning the following year to study piano. A year later he let go of that instrument to begin the study of the guitar. He studied this instrument with Miguel Llobet.

He was fourteen when he gave his first concert, revealing in his first public appearance his exceptional abilities that he already possessed.

He studied harmony with two maestros; Manuel Burgués and afterward with Joaquín Casado.

He arrived in Buenos Aires at 21 years of age, giving a series of concerts with unusual success, that he decided to reside in our country, dedicating himself to teaching, alternating with public performances. To give an idea of his indefatigable activity, it suffices to record that as a composer, among transcriptions and originals, his works have amounted to more than 200 compositions. Several didactic works among them "*Las escalas y arpegios*", that was published in 1910, and has been reprinted many times. The latest album of "*Danzas y cantos argentinos*", has had a great acceptance that in just a few months his first edition is out of print.

As for Mrs. Carmén Farré de Prat, she studied under the direction of who today is her husband, *Don* Domingo Prat. They made a tour of Spain together, gathering well deserved laurels everywhere.

They returned again to Argentina, that they adore so much, the Prat couple share the labor of the academia that rapidly has come conquering a well built reputation.

The exponent of the work of these distinguished artists, is in the latest student concert, a year after the said academy was founded, about whose brilliant result, our most authorized dailies have spoken in a form quite laudatory."

In 1910 he had published in Buenos Aires his book, "Scales and Arpeggios" (*Escalas y Arpeggios*) by finding a favorable ambiance for the teaching of the guitar, later he published his "The New Technique" (*La Nueva Tecnia*).

(Left) Domingo Prat's "Scales and Arpeggios" first published in 1910 by Francisco Nuñez and Co.
(Right) "The New Technique" (*La Nueva Tecnica*), published in 1929 by Romero & Fernández , that contains arpeggio exercises for using 5 fingers of the right hand.
(Below Left) Domingo Prat transcription of a Robert Schumann piece published by Romero, Agromayor and Cia. c. 1912. (Below right) Anthology of lute music of the 16th-18th centuries.

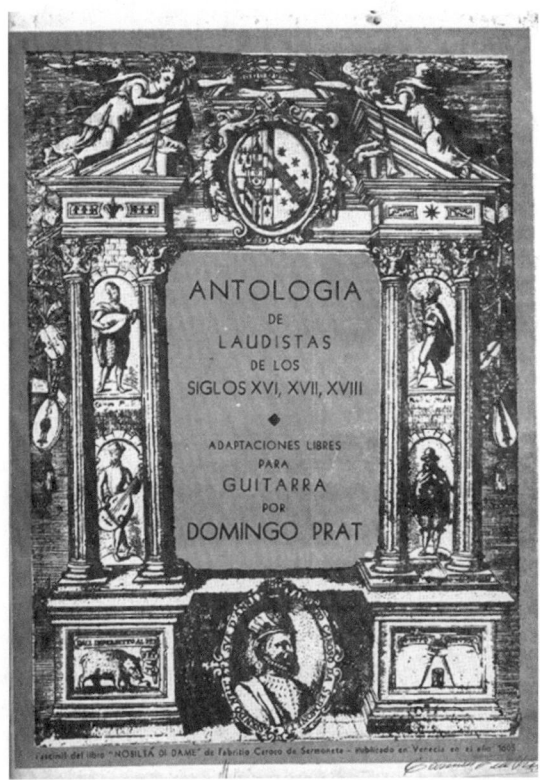

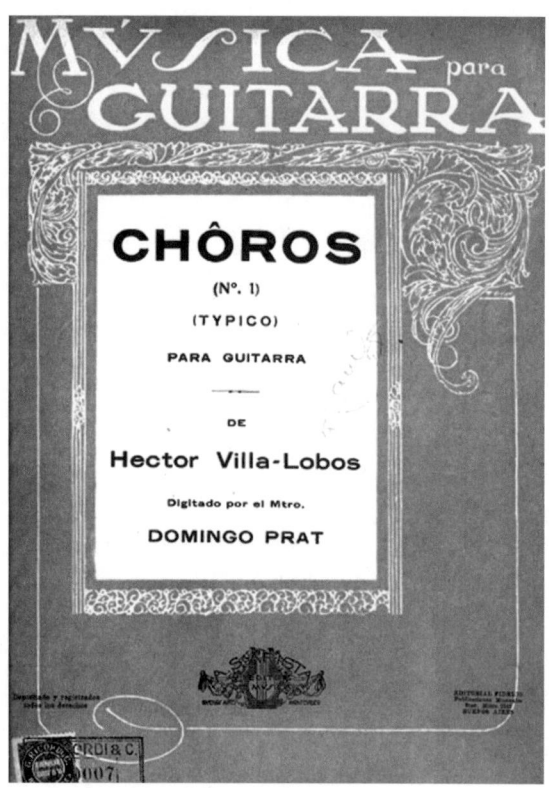

Domingo Prat piece published by:
A. Arista 1925

Romero, Agromayor and Cia. 1912

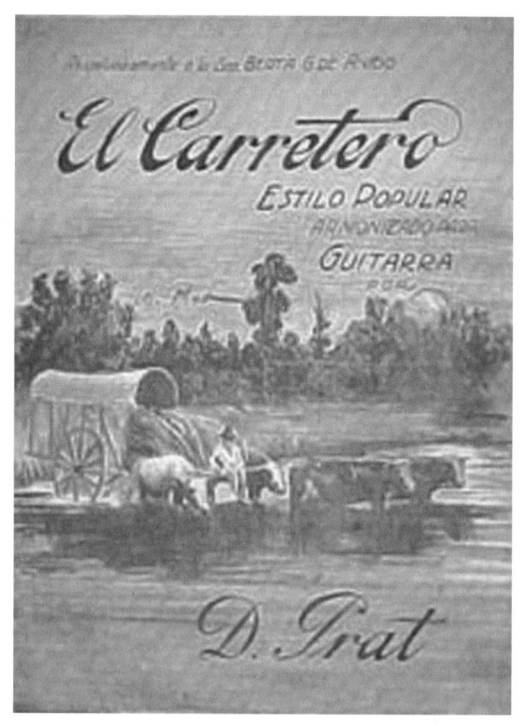

On the lower left is a copy of the "Scales and Arpeggios" published in Barcelona by the "Sociedad Editorial HISPANO-AMERICANA". Archive: Augusto Marcellino. On the lower right a self-published piece, the rarest of all, probably published in a quantity of just a few hundred, compared to an edition of 3,000 such as the "Scales and Arpeggios". It is the 17th piece listed in the 1931 Antigua Casa Nuñez catalog. This is dedicated to the mother of Maria Luisa Anido, *Doña* Berta Gonzalez de Anido.

The song written by Carmén Prat, "Pinina", which is a song for Blanca Prat's sister, Nidya Azucena —"Pinina", was reviewed in Japan by the *"Armonia"* magazine of March 1935 issue No. 49. Chuzaemon Sawaguchi directed and founded this magazine in Sendai Aramachi, Miyayagiken, Japan from 1925 onward.

By the time he was 18 years old Chuzaemon Sawaguchi (1902-1948) had developed the ability to read English, Spanish, Italian and German; therefore it was easy for him to translate information from Guitar and Mandolin magazines to include this information, from sources around the world, in his own *"Armonia"* magazine.

This is from the section:

"Armonia presentations of sheet music, Armonia Library subsection."

Translation by Randy Osborne:

"Pinina (Melody)

Domingo Prat, is a prominent figure of the Argentine guitar world, his wife is known as Carmén Farré de Prat, her tender guitar song is *"Pinina"*. It's a composition of simplicity, as a feminine guitar sentiment, it's intimate, within its brevity its technical skill is simple. This song's title is known by the person's name, Pinina."

(Price 20 sen)

The Japanese translations from 1935 and 1939 used in this book, involved recently studying "pre World War II kanji", where some pictographs are very different or slightly different (some lines going down instead of now going up) than "modern post war kanji", which I studied for over 7 years before doing any translating from the 1954-56 *"Armonia"* magazines.

Archive: Ricardo Muñoz

This is translated from Ricardo Muñoz's unpublished book *"Historia Universal de la Guitarra"* Volume V *"Los Contemporaneos"*.

Ricardo Muñoz says Domingo Prat wrote to him from Barcelona in 1931:

"Very few play the guitar well here, an instrument that can be said has remained relegated to the women, because the men appear to be embarrassed to admit they play the national instrument; such is the present artistic state of the guitar in Spain."

（50）ピニーナ（メロディア）

プラト夫人作曲

アルゼンチンギター界の大立物ドミンゴ・プラトの夫人として知られるカルメン・ファールの優しいギター曲である。單純な構成であるが女性のギターへの感情として、簡單な手法の中に親しさをたべよわせている。ピニーナは人名で此曲が献呈されている。（×頒價二十錢）

Publisher: Diego, Gracia & Co. 1925

Domingo Prat was not only a concert artist, but a composer, transcriber, author and teacher. Along with his wife, Carmén Farré de Prat, the Academia de Guitarra "Prat" taught the most child prodigies who became household names as, concert artists, professors and recording artists in Argentina and beyond. "Pinina" is a song for Blanca Prat's sister, Nidya Azucena — "Pinina".

Hiliarion Leloup, at the age of 13 was in an orchestra that had performed in Spain, and while in France played at the 1889 Universal Exposition of Paris, at the inauguration of the Eiffel Tower.

The Guitar Society of Bilbao, Spain (Seated Left to Right) José Talavera, Hilarion Leloup, Ambrosio Garbisu, Miguel Lamana, (Standing Left to Right)

Board members of the society on both sides of the maestro Francisco Tárrega. This photo is from the biography "Tárrega" by Emilio Pujol published in 1960.

By 1912, four years after the initial arrival of Prat in Buenos Aires, arriving in the same city was the Basque guitarist Hilarion Leloup (Bilbao 1876-Buenos Aires 1939), friend of Francisco Tárrega, from whom he received orientation.

According to Ricardo Muñoz (in his "*Historia de la Guitarra*"), Leloup in 1914, founded a school, that was the first of its type in Buenos Aires, and the first in the Americas. It was called "Academia Tárrega", as a homage to his beloved friend and maestro. From this Academia de Guitarra "Tárrega" graduated notable concert artists as well as professors.

Hilarion Leloup's Academia de Guitarra "Tárrega", with its share of child prodigies, that were to be found everywhere. This photo was dedicated to guitar historian Ricardo Muñoz in June of 1925, and it appeared in the *Revista Musical Ilustrada "Tárrega* magazine in July 1925 issue No. 13.
Archive: Ricardo Muñoz

131

Salón "La Gauloise"

CALLE 4 N° 678   LA PLATA

CONCIERTO DE GUITARRA

El Sábado 10 de Abril de 1920

A LAS 9 P. M.

En honor de mi ex-discípulo profesor Sr. Carlos Novalti

POR EL SEÑOR

HILARIÓN LELOUP

Director de la "Academia Tárrega" de Buenos Aires

PROGRAMA

1ª PARTE

1. Aires Argentinos .... Leloup
2. Cara ingrata (Canción napolitana) .... Cardillo
3. Chacone .... Durand
4. Estudio No. 33 .... Cramer
5. Ave María (Meditación) .... Gounod
6. Aires Vascos .... Leloup

2ª PARTE

1. Chanson Arabe .... Granados-Leloup
2. Granada (Serenata) .... Albéniz-Tárrega
3. Chanson de Solveig .... Grieg-Leloup
4. Mazurca op 33 No 4 .... Chopin-Tárrega
5. Danza Española No. 5 .... Granados-Llobet
6. Variaciones sobre un tema de Mozart .... Sors

---

PRECIOS DE LAS LOCALIDADES

Palco con 4 entradas .... $ 6.—

Platea con entrada .... $ 1.—

Hilarion Leloup concert in the Salon "La Gauloise" on Saturday, April 10, 1920.
Image courtesy of Lucas Agustín De Antoni, Buenos Aires.

"Hilarion Leloup Cabanari was born On October 21, 1876 in Bilbao, Spain. He was the son of Luis Leloup and Carmen Cabanari. Hilarion began to play the guitar when he was five years old but only as a hobby, experimenting with the guitar. When he was seven years of age he began to study under the direction of his father, who was a distinguished professor of guitar.

In 1889 he joined an orchestra organized and directed by his father and toured Spain and France, being very well received in Paris, in the epoch that had celebrated the musical competition of the Universal Exposition.

In the "Sociedad Guitarristica", which was founded in Bilbao, existed a guitar quartet, in which Hilarion distinguished himself with his brilliant playing. At the age of sixteen Hilarion was a concert guitarist and professor; besides having received the professorship of the double bass in the "Sociedad Filarmonica", in the Basque capital, and in a competition he was awarded first chair of the double bass in the "Banda Municipal" and in the "Sociedad de Conciertos". In 1909, along with various other guitarists he performed in the principal cities of Spain, France and England.

In 1912, he moved to Argentina, being fortunately contracted to play in Bahia Blanca, to act as a professor of the double bass in a distinguished musical group. When his committment was up, he was determined to move to Buenos Aires, to act as a bassist and professor of guitar.

In 1915 he became involved in the direction of the "Academia Tárrega" (founded in 1914), sharing the responsibility with Antonio Sinopoli. Later Sinopoli departed and left the "Academia Tárrega" in the hands of Hilarion. In 1916 Hilarion was named artistic director of the "Sociedad la Guitarra", that had been founded by Juan Carlos Anido. Besides having maintained his academia, Hilarion found time to perform in the Argentine capital and in the cities of the interior as well, as he did with Carmelo Rizzuti in 1917.

From 1920 onward he held presentations with his students: Carlos Novatti, Maria Elena McInnes, Adolfo Lopez, Pablo Fleury, Braulio L. Garcia, Amelia Flores Ortega, Francisco S. Aldino, Juan A. Ahumada, Zulema Celia Quiroga, Jacinto Landi, Isidro Figueroa, Armando Sosa Soler, Amelia Amanda Ruggia, Ricardo Morello, Irene Asenjo, Joséfina Romano, Beatriz Romero, Jorge S. Croce, Ana Battiato, Humberto Bianchi, Ofelia Lopez Muñoz, Manuel Sabaté, Julio Alberto Couyet, Margarita Beccaria, Eduardo Correa, Alicia Baez Iriarte, Victor Addesso, Alberto M. Barrenechea, Ricardo Muñoz, Maria Pascual Navas, Ana Maria de Acha Llambias, and others that escape my annotations and many more cited in this book (*Diccionario de Guitarristas* by Domingo Prat) in their respective place.

Academia Tárrega
Director: Hilarion Leloup
B. DE IRIGOYEN 793-U. T. 5763, RIV.
FLORIDA 243 - U. T. 2752, AVENIDA
(Pedir reglamento)

This advertisement for the Academia de Guitarra "Tárrega" is from the *"Musica de America"* magazine, issue No. 11 *Año* II of November 1921. This magazine was founded in December of 1920 and was directed by music critic Gaston O. Talamon. Among its contributors were Joaquín Nin and Felipe Pedrell. The format, font and advertisement "look" of this magazine was the blueprint for Juan Carlos Anido's magazine *"La Guitarra"*, which made its debut in July of 1923.

Archive: J. Augusto Marcellino

As a composer of published original works are known: *"Album de 8 piezas faciles"*, *"Método de solfeo aplicado a la guitarra"*, *"Método Elemental"* and *"Escalas, Acordes y Ejercicios Tecnicos"*, a labor that deserves praising adjectives, done by his intelligence and in part by his orientations which were initiated by Francisco Tárrega in his visit to Bilbao in 1905, which sealed their friendship, as is attested to in the following letter:

"My affectionate and good friend, Mr. Leloup, With great pleasure I was received by your very attentive, thankful affection and attention. And don't think I've forgotten you, very soon I will send you an original for you to study and not to let your enthusiasm be crestfallen, we'll be able to concertize it, to play works of the classics for two guitars, without a doubt, we will make it shine. I've worked a lot, although you are one of the few chosen ones that can reach the heights of the most beautiful guitar..." Said projections that couldn't come to pass, by reasons of illness. Maestro Leloup is, in effect of those that have the real worth by having done it with their own strength.

As a performer and as a teacher he has triumphed there in his land and here, among us, where we believe he has definitely adapted."

So ends the entry in Domingo Prat's *"Diccionario de Guitarristas"*.

Maestro Hilarion Leloup died on February 19, 1939. (Page 2 of the *Boletin de La Asociacion Guitarristica Argentina Año 1 No. 2 of April 1939*.)

Sta. María Elena Mc Innes
Discípula de guitarra del
Profesor Hilarión Leloup
Academia Tárrega

Sta. Rita Flores
De las clases de guitarra del
Profesor Hilarión Leloup
Academia Tárrega

These students of Hilarion Leloup's Academia de Guitarra "Tárrega" appeared in the *"Musica de America"* magazine, issue No. 11 *Año* II of November 1921.They are Miss Maria Elena Mc Innes and Miss Rita Flores.

This advertisement for the Academia de Guitarra "Tárrega" is from the *"Orfeo Revista Musical"* magazine, issue No. 46 *Año* V of June-July 1922.

This photo and that on the following page of the Academia de Guitarra "Tárrega" are from the "*Orfeo Revista Musical*" magazine, issue No. 41 *Año* IV of October 1921. This was the inside front cover and was this month's installment of the "The distinguished players of our Academies" ("*De nuestras Academias — las que se distiguen*").

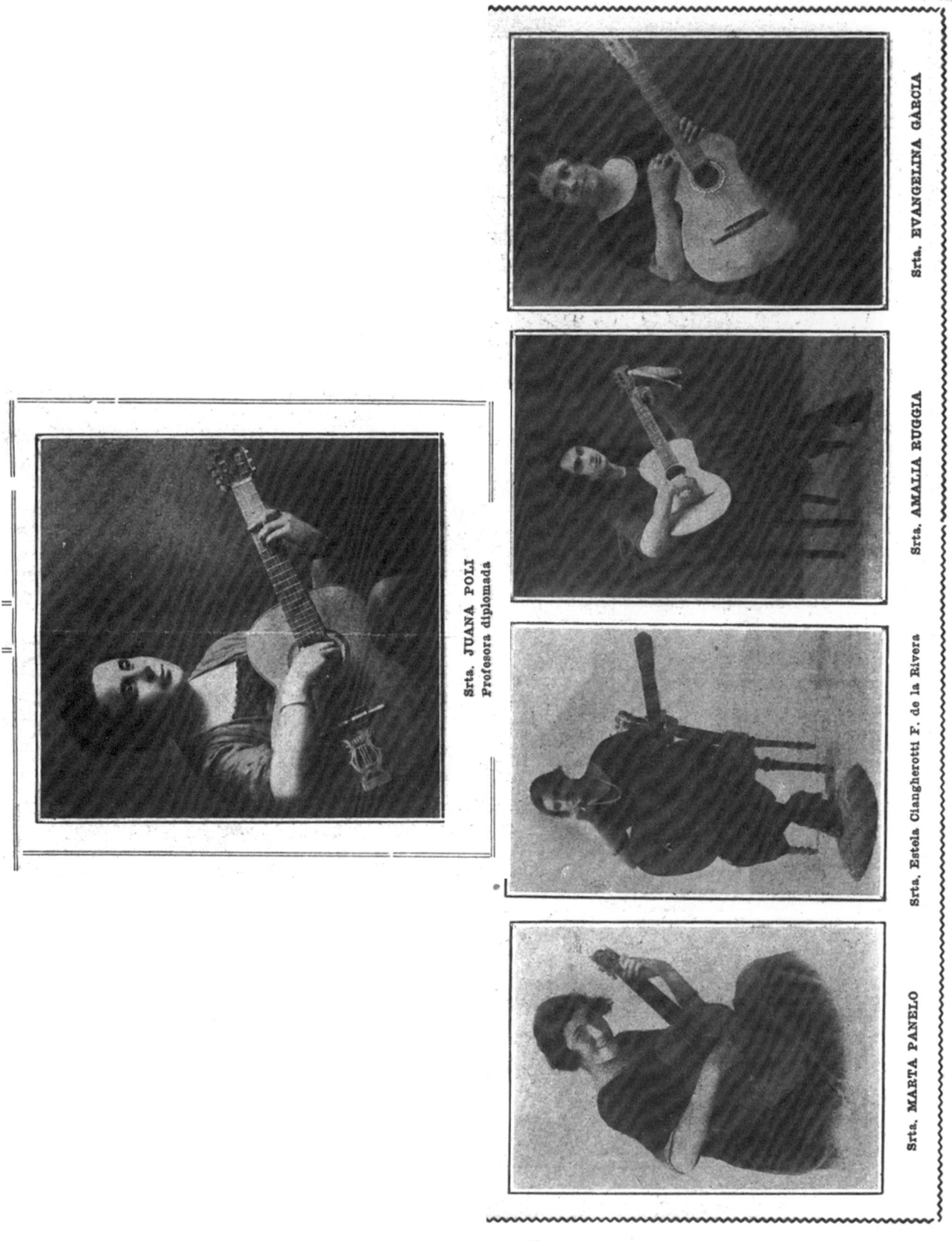

Srta. EVANGELINA GARCIA

Srta. AMALIA RUGGIA

Srta. Estela Ciangherotti F. de la Rivera

Srta. MARTA PANELO

Srta. JUANA POLI
Profesora diplomada

These are the balance of the photos of the Academia de Guitarra "Tárrega" that are from the "*Orfeo Revista Musical*" magazine, issue No. 41 *Año* IV of October 1921.

In 1917, Leloup along with Carmelo Rizzuti, formed a duo of guitars, with which they toured the cities of Argentina's interior. Their duo was to be one of the first of classical guitar in Argentina. With this fact, remains an erroneous opinion that is maintained that the first duo of this type of guitar was that of Miguel Llobet and Maria Luisa Anido, which was a duo that was formed later.

Hilarion Leloup and Carmelo Rizzuti
(Photo courtesy of Lucas Agustín de Antoni, Buenos Aires)

From page 360 of the *Historia de La Guitarra* by Ricardo Muñoz we transcribe the concert of Hilarion Leloup and Carmelo Rizzuti in the Salon "La Argentina" on November 8, 1917.

First part

1. L'Arlessienne – Bizet
2. L'Encouragement (Fantasia) – Sor
Duo Leloup-Rizzuti

3. Recuerdos de Sevilla (Characteristic Fantasy) – Parga
4. Escenas pintorescas – Massenet
5. Gran Tremolo – Gottschalk
6. Tannhauser (March) – Wagner
Hilarion Leloup

Second part

1. Estudio No. 8 – Coste
2. El pescador de perlas – Bizet
3. La Gallegada (pastoral fantasy with variations) – Ferrer
4. Horizontes andaluces (Gran fantasia) – Parga
Carmelo Rizzuti

5. Célebre minuet – Boccherini
6. Aida (Triumphal March)
Duo Leloup-Rizzuti

Antonio Sinopoli and Mario Rodríguez Arenas initially founded the Academia de Guitarra "Tárrega" in 1914 and Hilarion Leloup took over the direction in 1915. Antonio Sinopoli soon had cultivated his Academia "Sinopoli" in San Isidro. Mario Rodríguez Arenas developed a cramp in his right hand in 1917, which curtailed his professional performance, but went on to publish 280 pieces in his lifetime, he was the second most prolific composer and transcriber in Buenos Aires only surpassed by Pedro Antonio Iparraguire who published more than 330 pieces.

The six year study program is also from "*Historia de La Guitarra*". The Academia de la Guitarra

"Tárrega" study program under the direction of Hilarion Leloup was:

"1st year:

Leloup – Método Elemental

2nd year:

Aguado – Exercises for the right hand Nos. 1, 2, 8, 10, 11, 14, 15, 19 and 20.
Leloup – Major and Minor scales, 1st formula.
Aguado – Exercises for the left hand Nos. 18, 20, 22, 26, 27 and 30.
Tárrega – Exercise in Tremolo.
Llobet – three exercises, arpeggio, bar and chromatic scale.
Tárrega —"Prelude No. 1".

3rd year:

Aguado – Studies Nos. 1, 3, 5, 7, 8, 10 and trille study on page 50.
Leloup – Chords in various keys, scales in different positions.
Aguado – Exercises for the left hand Nos. 34, 39, 42, 43, 45, 47, 53 and 55.
Sor – Studies Nos. 1, 5, 11 and 13.
Llobet —Three chromatic technical exercises.
Pujol —"Cancion de Cuna".
Tárrega —"Recuerdos de la Alhambra".

4th year:

Aguado – Studies Nos. 12, 15, 16 and 20.
Tárrega —Three technical exercises.
Aguado – Exercises for the left hand Nos. 58, 60, 68, 69, 73, 74, 87, 88 and examples.
Sor – Studies Nos. 14, 18, 22 and 23.
Leloup – Chromatic and Diatonic scales.
Tárrega —"Minueto" (Pizzicato).
Tárrega —"La Mariposa" (concert study).

5th year:

Coste: Studies (Op.38) Nos. 8, 11, 19, 20 and 22.
Leloup —Two technical studies for the left hand, chords in different positions.
Sor – Study No. 25.
Llobet – Three technical exercises.
Aguado – Study No. 27.
Tárrega – Study in A Major.
Llobet – Spanish Dance No. 5 by Enrique Granados.
Tárrega —"Sueño" (Tremolo Study).

6th year:

Preparation for the concert artist:

1. Special selection of technical studies by Tárrega, Llobet and Leloup.
2. Study of concert works, originals by Leloup and transcriptions."

(Above) Academia de Guitarra "Tárrega" diploma awarded to Ricardo Muñoz in 1923. In his 5th year as a student, Ricardo Muñoz received his "distinguished professor" classification. Juan F. Fontaine, Carlos Novatti and Hilarion Leloup signed it.

Program cover from Hilarion Leloup's Academia de la Guitarra "Tárrega" concert held in the Salon "La Argentina" June 29, 1925.

Eduardo Risler, Berta Singerman and Miguel Llobet at the Academia de Guitarra "Tárrega" concert held in the Salon "La Argentina" on June 29, 1925. The photo is from the *Revista Musical Ilustrada "Tárrega"* No. 13 of July 1925.

(Below) Academia "Tárrega" concert program June 29, 1925, in the Salon "La Argentina".

PROGRAMA

1ª. PARTE

I.—Disertación por el Sr. Adolfo B. Somoza.
Tema: "La guitarra en la Argentina".

II.—Alais — Vidalita.
Por el niño de 7 años Manuel Barrenechea

III.—Tárrega — Preludio.
Por la niña de 9 años Martha Elena Casaravilla Garzón

IV.—Tárrega — Mareta.
Por la niña de 12 años María E. Pascual Navas

V.—Rocca — Leloup; ¡Qué linda es la patria mía....
(Zamba).

Por los niños: María E. Pascual Navas, Martha Elena Casaravilla Garzón, Emilia Casella, Ricardo Morello González, Alfredo Chimondeguy, Eduardo L. Paez de Azevedo, Manuel Barrenechea y Albino Echavarría Coll.

2ª. PARTE

I.—Pujol — Canción de cuna.
Por la niña de 12 años María E. Pascual Navas
II.—Sors — Andante.
Por la Sta. Zulema Celia Quiroga.
III.—Tárrega — Minueto.
Por la Sta. Catalina Reynal
IV.—Llobet — Testamento de Amelia.
Por el Sr. Alfredo Pérez Gauna.
V.—Thomas — Leloup — Mignon (Gavota).
Por las Stas.: Catalina Reynal, Zulema Celia Quiroga, Irene Asenjo, Josefina Aurteneche, Amelia Ruggia, Marta Arraga, María Isabel Gandulfo, María Teresa González Bustamante, Lydia Sabastano, Elida Risso Goñi, y Marta Panelo.

3ª. PARTE

I.—Sors — Minueto en La.
Por el niño de 14 años Ricardo Morello González
II.—Tárrega — Sueño (Trémolo).
Por la Sta. Catalina Reynal
III.—Coste — Estudio N° 20.
Por el Sr. Alfredo Pérez Gauna
IV.—Rosseger — Leloup — Menuet Ancien
Por los Sres. Carlos Novatti, Alfredo Pérez Gauna, Manuel Box, Remigio Comba, Antonio Catuara, Jacinto Landi, Isidro Figueroa, Humberto Agostini, Alfredo Vidal, Juan Lapolla, Armando Sosa y Pablo Gallardo.
V.—Freyre — Leloup — ¡Ay, ay, ay...! Reminiscencias cuyanas.

Conjunto de 46 guitarras por las

Sras.: Luisa M. de Roca y M. Fransen Daalmeyer.

Stas.: Amelia Ruggia, Magdalena Armento, Catalina Reynal, Zulema Celia Quiroga, Irene Asenjo, Josefina Aurteneche, Marta Arraga, María Isabel Gandulfo, Lydia Sabastano, María Teresa González Bustamante, Elida Risso Goñi, Marta Panelo, María Esther Leanes, Julia Hernáez, Felia López Brun, María Esther González Bustamante, Julia Argüello y Elsa Molina.

Sres.: Carlos Novatti, Alfredo Pérez Gauna, Manuel Box, Remigio Comba, Antonio Catuara, Manuel Gallardo, Alfredo Vidal, Jacinto Landi, Humberto Agostini, David Gil Palacios, Juan Lapolla, Isidro Figueroa, Armando Sosa, Juan Reynal, Pablo Gallardo, José Lucas de Lasa, José Bermejo y Aquilino Martín.

Niños: María E. Pascual Navas, Martha Elena Casaravilla Garzón, Emilia Casella, Ricardo Morello González, Alfredo Chimondeguy, Eduardo L. Paez de Azevedo, Manuel Barrenechea y Albino Echavarría Coll.

Esta academia con plan de estudios propios, legalmente autorizada, y su correspondiente reglamento, ha satisfecho mis aspiraciones lo que puede constatarse muy fácilmente; el hecho de saber que en ella han iniciado, robustecido o terminado sus estudios los profesores que a continuación se expresan y que en la actualidad se dedican a la enseñanza:

Sra. Ana S. de Cabrera, (profesora de arte nativo), Stas. Magdalena Armento, Juana Poli y Rita Flores; Sres. Carlos Novatti, Juan F. Fontaine, Ricardo Muñoz (profesores que forman parte de la mesa examinadora de esta academia), Adolfo López, Manuel Lista, Alfredo Pérez Gauna, Remigio Comba, Francisco S. Aldinio, Juan M. Ahumada, Justo T. Morales, Antonio Catuara, Adolfo V. Luna, Luis Verón, Faustino Riglos, Ramón Zeballos, Eduardo Amestoy, Carmelo Rizzuti, Aníbal Ladrú, Benito Fernández y otros.

Este resultado que hago público tiene por único fin, que el lector pueda formar concepto del valer de esta institución artístico-musical.

— Hilarión Leloup.

(Above) The participating students and professors, including Ricardo Muñoz, of the Academia de Guitarra "Tárrega" concert June 29, 1925, in the Salon "La Argentina". An ensemble of 46 guitars performed. Translation of lower right text 4 pages after this page.

The students and professors of the Academia de Guitarra "Tárrega" concert June 29, 1925, in the Salon "La Argentina", from *Revista Columba*.

Archive: Ricardo Muñoz

142

MARIA E. PASCUAL NAVAS

ZULEMA CELIA QUIROGA.

From the *Revista Musical Ilustrada "Tárrega"* issue No. 15 of September 1925. This was the Academia de Guitarra "Tárrega" exam / concert held at the Salon "La Argentina" June 29, 1925. The photos are of those who performed satisfactorily.

MARTHA E. CASARAVILLA GARZON

MANUEL BARRENECHEA

ALBINO ECHAVARRIA COLL

Hilarion Leloup from *Revista Musical Ilustrada "Tárrega"* issue No. 13 of July 1925.

1925 — Leloup presented in the Salon "La Argentina", his first group of guitarists, comprised of 56 students of his Academia. On December 3rd of this year, he offered the same concert, with the same number of interpreters in a radio program, being the first time on Argentine radio that a program of this magnitude, of concert artists had been debuted.

(Below) From the daily newspaper *"La Nacion"* of December 4, 1925, performance by 56 guitarists that was carried on radio L. O. Z.. Ricardo Muñoz says on page 330 in *"Historia de la Guitarra"* that this was the first time this many guitars had performed on radio.

56 GUITARRAS EN UNA AUDICION

La estación L O Z (broadcasting LA NACION) anuncia para mañana por la noche un programa de extraordinario interés para los aficionados a la guitarra; de interés no tan sólo porque la audición la componen 56 guitarras, sino también por la variedad de la música que será ejecutada y los prestigios de muchos de los ejecutantes.

El conjunto de guitarristas pertenece al Conservatorio Tárraga, y ha sido organizado por el director de ese instituto, D. Hilarión Leloup, y por el profesor del mismo, D. Ricardo Muñoz, quienes también lo dirigirán.

El programa preparado es el siguiente:

Primera parte: 1o., María E. Pascual Navas, Marietta de Tárraga; 2o., Irene J. Asenjo, Parrana de Tárraga; 3o., Ricardo Morello González, Minuetto en la de Soro; 4o., profesora Zulema C. Quiroga, Momento musical, de Schubert; 5o., conjunto de seis guitarras: María E. Pascual Navas, Marta E. Casaraviglia Garzón, Ricardo Morello González, Alfredo Chimondegui, Eduardo Paes de Acevedo, Manuel Berrenechea y Albino Chavarría Coll, "Qué linda es la patria mía", zamba de Roca-Leloup.

Segunda parte: 1o., profesor Manuel Boch, Pericón nacional, Grasso Leloup; 2o., Alfredo Pérez Gouna, profesor, Góndola veneciana, de Mendelsshon; 3o., profesor Ricardo Muñoz, Estudio No. 12 de Aguado; 4o., Dúo por María E. Pascual Navas y Ricardo Morello González, "Ay qué linda será", zamba de A. S. Cabrera y Leloup; 5o., conjunto de seis guitarras: Zulema C. Quiroga, Irene Asenjo, Amelia Ruggia, Marta Arraga, María Isabel Gondulfo y Elida Risso Goñi, Mignon Garotta; de Thomas-Leloup.

Tercera parte: 1o., profesor Alfredo Pérez Gauna, Estudio No. 20, de Coste; 2o., profesor Ricardo Muñoz, Gran Tremolo, de Gothchalks; 3o., conjunto de diez guitarras: Carlos Novatti, Alfredo P. Ganda, Manuel Boch, Jacinto Landi, Isidro Figueroa, Humberto Agostini, Alfredo Vidal, Juan Trepolla, Armando Sosa, Pablo Gallardo, Minuetto de Rosseger y Leloup; 4o., conjunto de seis guitarras: Anelia Ruger, Zulema Quiroga, Irene Acenjo, Ricardo Muñoz, Alfredo Pérez Gouna y Manuel Boch, Minuetto, de Mozart; 5o., conjunto de 56 guitarras: todos los anteriormente nombrados, más los siguientes: María E. Leanes, Julia Argüello, Elsa Moliner y Sres. José Bermejo, José L. de Lazo y David Gil Palacios, Reminiscencias cuyanas, Ay, Ay, Ay, de Freire-Leloup.

Translation of "56 guitarras en una audicion":

"56 guitars in a performance"

The station L. O. Z. (La Nacion broadcasting) announces tomorrow night a program of extraordinary interest to aficionados of the guitar; of interest not only because the performance is comprised of 56 guitars, but also for the variety of the music that will be played and the prestige of many of the players.

The ensemble of guitarists belongs to the Conservatorio Tárrega, and it has been organized by the director of this institute, *Don* Hilarion Leloup, and by the professor of the same, *Don* Ricardo Muñoz, who will also direct them.

The prepared program is the following:

First part:

1. Marieta by Tárrega.
   Maria E. Pascual Navas

2. Pavana by Tárrega.
   Irene J. Asenjo

3. Minuetto en La by Sor.
   Ricardo Morello Gonzalez

4. Momento musical by Schubert.
   Professor Zulema Celia Quiroga

5. "Que linda es la patria mia" Zamba by Roca-Leloup.
   Ensemble of six guitars: Maria E. Pascual Navas, Martha Elena Casaravilla Garzon,
   Ricardo Morello Gonzalez, Alfredo Chimondegui, Eduardo Paez de Acevedo, Manuel Barrenechea and
   Albino Chavarria Coll.

Second Part:

1. Pericon Nacional by Grasso-Leloup.
   Professor Manuel Box

2. Gondola veneciana by Mendelssohn.
   Professor Alfredo Pérez Gauna

3. Estudio No. 12 by Aguado.
   Professor Ricardo Muñoz

4. "Ay que linda sera", Zamba by Ana Schneider de Cabrera-Leloup.
   Maria Esperanza Pascual Navas and Ricardo Morello Gonzalez.

5. Mignon Gavotta by Thomas-Leloup.
   Ensemble of six guitars: Zulema Celia Quiroga, Irene Asenjo, Amelia Ruggia, Marta Arraga,
   Maria Isabel Gandulfo and Elida Risso Goñi.

Third part:

1. Estudio 20 by Coste.
   Professor Alfredo Pérez Gauna

2. Gran Tremolo by Gottschalk.
   Professor Ricardo Muñoz

3. Minuetto-Amicu by Rosseger-Leloup.
   Ensemble of ten guitars: Carlos Novatti, Alfredo Pérez Gauna, Manuel Box, Jacinto Landi,
   Isidro Figueroa, Humberto Agostini, Alfredo Vidal, Juan Trepolla, Armando Sosa, Pablo Gallardo.

4. Minuetto by Mozart.
   Ensemble of six guitars: Anelia Ruger (sic), Zulema Celia Quiroga, Irene Asenjo, Ricardo Muñoz,
   Alfredo Pérez Gauna, Manuel Box.

5. Reminiscencias Cuyanas, Ay, Ay, Ay by Freire-Leloup.
   Ensemble of fifty six guitars: with all those previously mentioned and: Maria Esther Leanes,
   Julia Argüello, Elsa Molina, José Bermejo, José Lucas de Lasa and David Gil Palacios."

This photo is of Hilaron Leloup's Academia de Guitarra "Tárrega" performance at the Salon "La Argentina"
on November 1, 1926 and is from the magazine *Revista Musical Ilustrada "Tárrega"* issue No. 28 of
November 1926.

This advertisement for Hilaron Leloup's Academia de Guitarra "Tárrega" is from the magazine
Revista Musical Ilustrada "Tárrega" issue No. 28 of November 1926.

Academia de Guitarra "Tárrega" concert November 1, 1926, in the Salon "La Argentina".

Translation of the text from 6 pages before: "This academy with its own plan of studies, legally authorized, and its corresponding regulation, has satisfied my aspirations to which can be established very easy, the act of learning it that they have initiated, toiled or finished their studies the professors that continue to express it and that in the present dedicate themselves to teaching: Ana S. de Cabrera (professor of native art), Armento, Juana Poli, Rita Flores, Carlos Novatti, Juan Fontaine, Ricardo Muñoz, (professors that form a part of the examining board of this academy), Adolfo Lopez, Manuel Lista, Alfredo Pérez Guana, Remigio Comba, Francisco S. Aldinio, Juan A. Ahumada, Justo T. Morales, Antonio Catuara, Adolfo V. Luna, Luis Veron, Faustino Riglos, Ramon Zeballos, Eduardo Amestoy, Carmelo Rizzuti, Anibal Ladru, Benito Fernández and others.

   This result I make public has by a unique end, that the reader can form a conception of the value of this artistic musical institution." — Hilarion Leloup.

PROGRAMA

PRIMERA PARTE

I. VIÑAS — REVERIE.
Por el niño Manuel Barrenechea.

II. TÁRREGA — COLUMPIO
Por la niña Martha Elena Casaravilla Garzón.

III. BROCÁ — EL ELEGANTE (Vals)
Por el niño Ricardo Morello González.

IV. SORS — MINUETTO EN RE
Por la niña María Esperanza Pascual Navas.

V. ANA S. DE CABRERA — LELOUP — AY QUE LINDO SERÁ... (Zamba)
Por los niños María E. Pascual Navas, Martha Elena Casaravilla Garzón, Ricardo Morello González y Manuel Barrenechea.

SEGUNDA PARTE

I. GRASSO — LELOUP — PERICON NACIONAL
Por el señor Manuel Box.

II. TÁRREGA — PAVANA
Por la señorita Irene Asenjo.

III. PARGA — POLO GITANO
Por la señorita Amelia Ruggia.

IV. LLOBET — DOS MELODÍAS
Por el señor Alfredo Pérez Gauna.

V. MOZART—LLOBET—MINUETTO DE LA SINFONÍA N.° 39
Por las señoritas: Zulema Celia Quiroga, Amelia Ruggia, Irene Asenjo, Lydia Sabastano, Josefina Romano, Julia Hernáez, Elsa Molina y Ofelia López Muñiz.

TERCERA PARTE

I. ROSSEGER — LELOUP — MENUET ANCIEN
Por los señores Manuel Box y Alfredo Pérez Gauna.

II. SCHUBERT — TÁRREGA — MOMENTO MUSICAL
Por la señorita Zulema Celia Quiroga.

III. GOTTSCHALK — TÁRREGA — GRAN TRÉMOLO
Por el señor Ricardo Muñoz.

IV. TÁRREGA — ALBORADA (Cajita de Música)
Por la señorita Josefina Romano.

V. BOCHERINI — LELOUP — CÉLEBRE MINUETTO
Por los señores Carlos Novatti, Ricardo Muñoz, Alfredo Pérez Gauna, Manuel Box, Jacinto Landi, Humberto Agostini, Armando Sosa Soler y José Lucas de Lasa.

VI. PODESTÁ — LELOUP — LA PIEDRA DE ESCÁNDALO (Estilo Criollo)
Conjunto de 50 guitarristas, por la Sra. Elena M. de Rassol, Señoritas Zulema Celia Quiroga, Amelia Ruggia, Irene Asenjo, Lydia Sabastano, Josefina Romano, Julia Hernáez, Elsa Molina, Ofelia López Muñiz, Paula Ricci, Martá Arraga, María Isabel Gandulfo, María Teresa González Bustamante, María Esther González Bustamante, Elida Risso Goñi, María Esther Leanes, María Carmen Leloup, Elsa Gómez Ortega, Elida Olga Fracassi, Angélica Sánchez Bustamante, Carmen García, Francisca Martí, Mercedes Lea Carrere, Angélica María Carrere, Angela Celesia y Margarita Celesia. Señores Carlos Novatti, Ricardo Muñoz, Alfredo Pérez Gauna, Manuel Box, Jacinto Landi, Humberto Agostini, Armando Sosa Soler, José Lucas de Lasa, Alfredo Vidal, José Bermejo, Jorge S. Crooce, Joaquín López Flores, Alejandro Cavenago y Eduardo Correa.
Niños María Esperanza Pascual Navas, Martha Elena Casaravilla Garzón, Margarita Beccaria, María Luisa Niklison, Alicia Báez Iriarte, Ricardo Morello González, Manuel Barrenechea, Eduardo L. Páez de Azevedo, Albino Echavarría Coll y Servando Carlos García.

Academia de Guitarra "Tárrega" song titles November 1, 1926, in the Salon "La Argentina".

148

Leloup is the author of numerous arrangements, besides having written an *"Album de 8 piezes faciles"*, a *"Metodo de solfeggio applicado a la Guitarra"*, *"Escalas, Accordes y Ejercicios Tecnicas"* and *"Metodo Elemental"*.

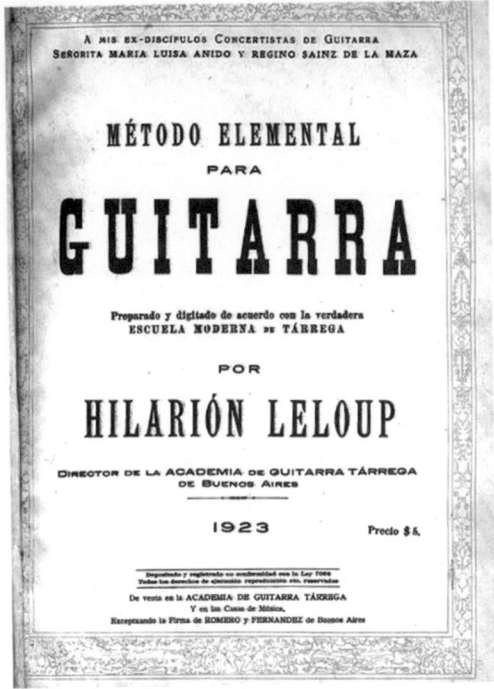 

(Left) 1923 Elementary Method by Hilarion Leloup, endorsed by Miguel Llobet. (Right) Hilarion Leloup's *"Escalas, Accordes y Ejercicios Tecnicas"* published by Romero & Fernández in 1923.

Archive: Mario Rodríguez Arenas

"His labor that deserves well-chosen adjectives, is realized by his intelligence, and in part by those initiated orientations by Francisco Tárrega during his artistic visit to Bilbao in 1905, with whom he began a great friendship, that remains demonstrated in a letter sent by Tárrega from Spain", the text says: "My affectionate and good friend, Mr. Leloup, With great pleasure I was received by your very attentive, thankful affection and attention. And don't think I've forgotten you, very soon I will send you an original for you to study and not to let your enthusiasm be crestfallen, we'll be able to concertize it, to play works of the classics for two guitars, without a doubt, we will make it shine. I've worked a lot, although you are one of the few chosen ones that can reach the heights of the most beautiful guitar". (D. Prat op. cit.). The duo with Tárrega was never realized due to the failing health of the maestro.

Translation of the handwritten endorsement by Miguel Llobet of Hilarion Leloup's method book and dedication to Mario Rodríguez Arenas:

I give below the critique about my method made the best guitarist in the world, Mr. Miguel Llobet.

"Buenos Aires November 30, 1922
Mr. *Don* Hilarion Leloup

My dear friend:

I have reviewed your *Metodo Elemental* for the teaching of the guitar with real pleasure, since the proof of your labor and the fruit of your experience is in it.

Your work is now an appreciable step in the sense to facilitate to the beginner the means to initiate the study of the Guitar.

Given the lack of an easy and progressive method, your work comes to fill the void lending an appreciable service to the beginners and to the Maestros that might guide them, by which it pleases me to congratulate you.

Receive, beloved friend, my cordial wishes, M. Llobet."

"To my friend and colleague Mr. Mario Rodríguez Arenas, affectionately, Hilarion Leloup, Buenos Aires, October 1, 1923.

A CONTINUACIÓN DOY A CONOCER LA CRÍTICA QUE HACE SOBRE MI MÉTODO EL MEJOR GUITARRISTA DEL MUNDO, SEÑOR MIGUEL LLOBET.

Buenos Aires 30 - n.re 1922

Señor D. Hilarión Leloup

Mi muy estimado amigo =
He examinado con verdadero agrado su método elemental para la enseñanza de la guitarra, pues en él se evidencia su labor y el fruto de su experiencia —
Su trabajo es ya un paso apreciable en el sentido de facilitar al principiante los medios de iniciarse en el estudio de la guitarra —
Dada la falta de un método fácil y progresivo, su trabajo viene á llenar un vacío prestando un apreciable servicio á los principiantes y á los maestros que hayan de guiarlos, lo que me complazco en felicitarle —
Reciba, querido amigo, mis cordiales saludos

M. Llobet

HILARIÓN LELOUP

Buenos Aires Enero de 1923

Al amigo y colega
Sr. Mario R. Arenas
Afectuosamente
Hilarión Leloup

ACADEMIA DE GUITARRA
"TÁRREGA"
DIRECTOR
HILARIÓN LELOUP
1688 - SARMIENTO - BUENOS AIRES

Buenos Aires 1 Octubre de 1923

150

(Above Left) Hilarion Leloup c. 1935, possibly published after his passing in 1939.

The 1923 Elementary Method by Hilarion Leloup was given a good review in the "*La Guitarra*" magazine issue No. 2 of December 1923.

(Below Left) publication by Francisco Nuñez of a Bizet transcription by maestro Hilarion Leloup. This song was recorded in Italy by Federico Gallimberti for Odeon Records in 1927.

(Below Right) Transcription of a piece by Edvard Grieg.

This biography of Nedea Ethel Zabala is translated from Ricardo Muñoz's unpublished book *"Historia Universal de la Guitarra"* Volume VIII *"La Escuela Tárrega en La Argentina"*.

"Nedea Ethel Zabala

Her Origin:

She is the daughter of *Don* Antonio and *Doña* Palmira Arriola, born in Pergamino, Buenos Aires the 9th of November of 1923.

Nedea Ethel Zabala, one from the original "La Escuela Tárrega en La Argentina" and the other from the xerox copy-all volumes have copies kept by the author.

Her Education:

She studied theory, solfeggio and harmony in the Conservatorio B. Casi, with professors Delia Carrera and Ercilia de Maria; as to the guitar, at 9 years of age she enrolled in the Academia Tárrega of *Don* Hilarion Leloup, and after his passing on February 19, 1939, she continued her perfection studies with maestro *Don* José Casadey.

Her Virtuosity:

The 19th of July of 1941 she was presented by her maestro Mr. Casadey to the public in the Biblioteca Nacional de Mujeres, interpreting: *"Reverie"* by Schumann; *"Momento Musical"* by Schubert; *"Don Juan"* by Mozart; *"Primer Vals"* by Durand; the 2nd part of the performance was given to the young Juan A. García and the 3rd part both played as a duo, performing: *"Gavota"* from the opera Mignon by Thomas; *"Minuet"* by Mozart; *"Marcha"* from the opera *Aida* by Verdi; *"La Arlessienne"* by Bizet; *"Danza Hungara"* by Brahms. The incessant applause demonstrated the approval of the public who enjoyed the interpretations very much.

The 30th of October of 1943 we see her in the Teatro Salon "Lassalle" performing pages by Correlli, Sagreras, Villa-Lobos, Haydn, Bizet, Mozart, Castelnuovo-Tedesco, Granados, Ross and Tárrega, with skill and excellent musical expression; the following year in the same hall she played works by Centeno, Manjón, Alais, Arcas, Grieg, Schubert, Chopin, Aguado, Schiuma, Espinosa, Albeniz and Tárrega, with public admiration and if anything, more applause. The magazine *"Mundo Musical"* said: '. . . . making a boast of purified technique and great interpretive temperament in the works that comprised the program'.

The 4th of November, after the other performance, she was heard by the musicologist *Don* Oreste Schiuma, who declared; '. . . . she leaves indelible memories. . . .'

The 23rd of June of 1945 she dedicated a concert to her maestro Hilarion Leloup in the "Amigos de la Guitarra", with works transcribed by him; the author of this history on such a occasion published in the program of the performance, the following; 'She possesses very meritorious qualities and a fine musical temperament that makes her a concert guitarist— a pleasure to hear.' — The 28th of the same month she repeated the concert in the Asociacion Tárrega de Rosario, where she received insistent applause. The daily *"La Capital"* then said: '. . . . a purified technique and a musical temperament appreciable enough through her expressive just versions and chords with the spirit of the author, who they valued him with the hottest applause. . . .'

The 21st of September of 1946 she reappeared for the "Amigos de la Guitarra", performing a program dedicated to *Don* Juan Alais, and in which, as a soloist and in duo with the referred to young Garcia, she threshed works of homage and other that *"La Prensa"* the next day praised, declaring: '. . . . Nedea Ethel Zabala due to her endowments as a good instrumentalist and soberly expressive . . . . before the insistent applause she had to add encores.'

The 26th of November of 1949 in the Salon "La Argentina", for the "Amigos de la Guitarra", she gave another concert with the works *"Cancion"* by Schubert-Comba; *"Nocturno"* by García Tolsa; *"Rondo"* by Mozart-Casadey; *"Cajita de Musica"* by Sagreras; *"Chopi"* *(Danza Paraguaya)* by Escobar; *"Nesta Rua"* *(Tema Variado)* by Savio; *"Madrigal"* by Barrios; *"Gran Jota Aragonesa"* by Tárrega and *"Mallorca"* by Albeniz; in the 3rd part, with the string quartet "ESNAOLA" formed by the violins of Alberto Faraday and Felix Marafiott, viola by Francisco Molo and cello by José Bragato, they interpreted the *"Suite Hispana"* by *Don* Manuel del Olmo, in its four parts of *"Musa Andaluza", "Ritmo de Danza", "Nocturno"* and *"Mosaico Flamenco"*; the effort was coronated with the hottest applause by the public filling the hall.

Distinciones:

In 1949 for the outstanding musician-guitaristic performance in the nation, the Asociacion Argentina de Musica de Camara, (Argentine Chamber Music Association) they conceded to her the 1st Prize, of the Concurso, among the instrumentalists of the year."

Saturday June 23, 1945 concert dedicated to Hilarion Leloup.

AMIGOS DE LA GUITARRA

SECRETARÍA: CASTRO 675

4º. CICLO

11º. CONCIERTO

•••

AUSPICIADO POR LA

Asociación Argentina de Música de Cámara

Dedicado a JUAN ALAIS

CONCERTISTA

Nedea Ethel Zabala

con la colaboración de JUAN ANDRES GARCIA

☆ ★ ☆

SABADO 21 de Septiembre a las 18

en el Salón "LA ARGENTINA"

RODRIGUEZ PEÑA 361

ENTRADA GENERAL, $ 1.50.-

Los socios de la As. Argentina de Música de Cámara, tienen derecho a 2 entradas, presentando el carnet social.

Asociaciones Culturales y alumnos $ 1.-

Nedea Ethel Zabala

Nedea Ethel Zabala ,ya bien afianzada en nuestro medio guitarrístico, vuelve a presentarse en nuestro ciclo de conciertos brindando a través de las obras que interpreta su fino temperamento musical.

Esta guitarrista no obstante su juventud, ha alcanzado una madurez que le permite compenetrarse con el espíritu de cada obra que ejecuta. Esta exacta concepción, unida a una depurada técnica, hace que cobre vida en sus manos un todo armonioso que deleita al oyente.

"Amigos de la Guitarra" tiene también el agrado de presentar en esta oportunidad al concertista Juan Andrés García, intérprete brillante, quién se ha presentado en esta capital como solista e integrando con la señorita Zabala, el dúo que vuelve a escucharse dando realce a la parte final.

Esta última parte, compuesta por obras clásicas que hablan por sí solas de su calidad e incuestionable belleza, será ejecutada a dúo por los intérpretes. Dejamos al público la facultad de juzgar la hermosura y justeza de estas ejecuciones.

Saturday September 21, 1946 concert dedicated to Juan Alais.

"Nedea Ethel Zabala, now well established in our guitaristic medium, returns to be presented in our concert cycle offering a fine musical temperament through the works that she interprets.

In spite of this guitarist's youth she has achieved a maturity that permits her to fuse with the spirit of every work she performs. The exact conception, that unites to a purified technique and makes it come alive in her hands and a delight to the listeners.

"Amigos de la Guitarra" also has the pleasure in this opportunity to present the concert guitarist Juan Andrés Garcia, a brilliant interpreter, who has been presented in the capital as a soloist and integrating with Miss Zabala,the duo that returns to be heard embossing in the final part.

This last part, composed of classic works that speak for themselves in their quality and unquestionable beauty, will be performed as a duo by the interpreters. We leave to the public the capacity to judge the loveliness and correctness of these performances."

PROGRAMA

1ª PARTE

E S T I L O	
ZAMACUECA	
G A V O T A	Alais
M A Z U R K A	
V A L S	

2ª PARTE

MEDITACION (Nocturno)	Garcia Tolsa
B O L E R O	Arcas
RONDÓ EL LA	Aguado
GRANADA (Serenata)	Albéniz - Tárrega

3ª PARTE

MINUET ANCIEN	Rossegger - Leloup
V A L S	Viñas - Alais
MARCHA TRIUNFAL	Verdi - Leloup
DANZA PROVENZAL	Bizet - Tárrega
DANZA HUNGARA Nº. 5	Brahms - Casadey

This biography of Juan Andrés García is translated from Ricardo Muñoz's unpublished book *"Historia Universal de la Guitarra"* Volume VIII *"La Escuela Tárrega en La Argentina"*.

"Juan Andrés Garcia

His Origin:

He was born in Chubut, Argentina on the 9th of November of 1922.

His Education:

At the age of 13 years old he began his music studies, he started to play the guitar in 1938 with the brilliant Hilarion Leloup, upon whose death he began to study with maestro José Casadey, receiving his diploma in 1939.

His Virtuosity:

In 1941 he gave a performance in the hall of the Consejo de Mujeres, playing solos and duets with Professor Miss Nedea E. Zabala, both of them obtaining on such an occasion very sincere applause of general approval, sympathy and emulation."

Domingo Prat became permanently settled in Buenos Aires and founded a school with his wife Carmén Farré that carried his name: Academia de Guitarra "Prat".

There he taught numerous students, principally ladies and gentlemen of the high society of Argentina that brought his family a very good salary, that permitted him to totally dedicate himself to teaching, investigation, making transcriptions, writing new methods, forming a voluminous collection of sheet music and writing an important "Diccionario de Guitarristas", for which we need to mention the invaluable collaboration of one of his most notable students, Consuelo Mallo Lopez. The first and only edition of this work has a pencil portrait of the author, drawn by Dr. Samuel Mallo Lopez (who also collaborated, beyond the portrait), brother of Consuelo.

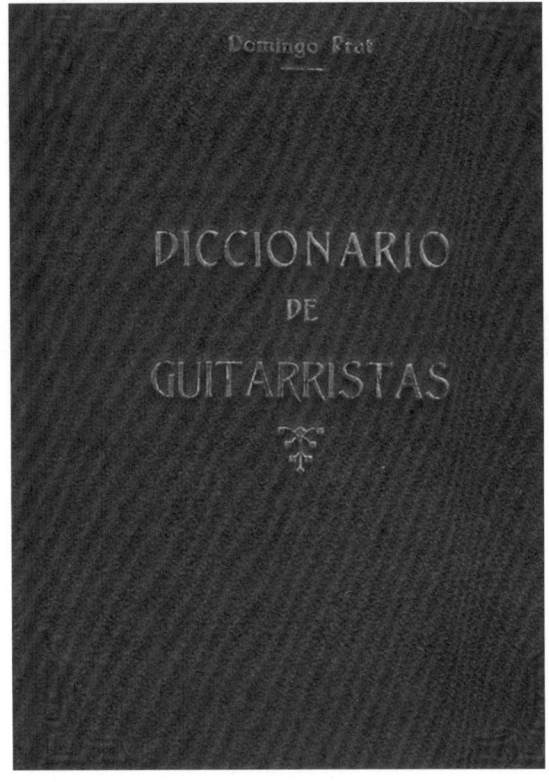

(Left: Outside cover of Domingo Prat's "Diccionario de Guitarristas" published in 1934, autographed and No. 185 of 1605 copies printed.

(Upper Right) Sketch by Dr. Samuel Mallo Lopez drawnin 1933 of Domingo Prat. This is opposite the title page in the "Diccionario de Guitarristas".

This photo with text is from the "Caras y Caretas" magazine of January 11, 1936 issue No. 1945 Año XXXVIII. Translation: "Domingo Prat is the author of a voluminous and interesting "Diccionario de Guitarristas", in which it has history, biography and critique of those dedicated to the guitar and its similar instruments. It is, on the other hand, an outstanding work, and it fills an important void in the musical bibliography of South America and Europe."

Domingo Prat es el autor de un voluminoso e interesante "Diccionario de guitarristas", en el que está la historia, biografía y crítica de cuantos en el mundo se dedicaron a la guitarra y sus similares. Es, por otra parte, obra de singular amenidad, y llenará un importante vacío en la bibliografía musical de América y de Europa.

(In a phone conversation with Héctor in November 1999-he illuminated even further on this subject: Consuelo kept the text in Castellano (Spanish), because Domingo's first language was Catalan. — comment R. O.)

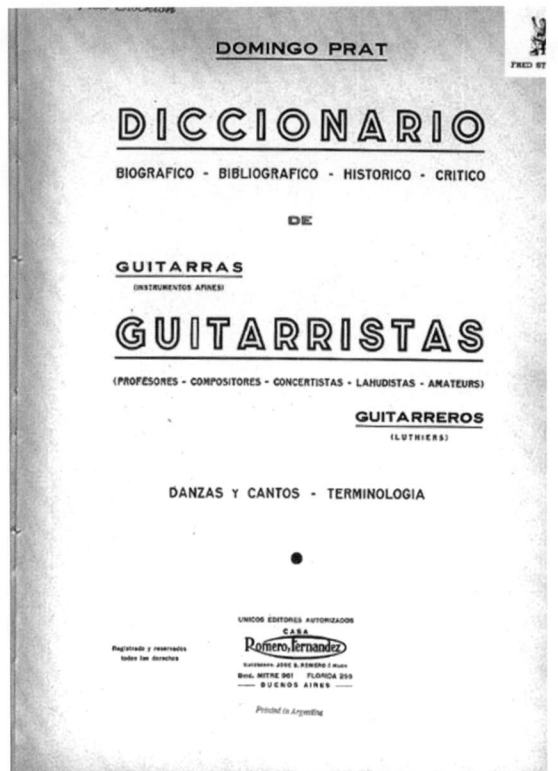

(Left) Inside cover of Domingo Prat's "*Diccionario de Guitarristas*". (Right) Consuelo Mallo Lopez in 1937, she helped Domingo Prat keep the text in Spanish, in his "*Diccionario de Guitarristas*".

(Below Left) Dr. Samuel Mallo Lopez, who did many pencil sketches of artists at gatherings of guitarists, besides the portrait of Domingo Prat. This is from a *Mundo Musical* magazine of the 1940s.

(Below Right) Maria Luisa Anido, who began to study the guitar with Domingo Prat in 1914, when she was 7.

From the Academia Prat, surged virtuoso interpreters, principally women, that distinguished the Academia in their concerts, teaching, and some that drew the admiration of composers who wrote and dedicated pieces to the alumni of Academia Prat, as was in the case of Maria Luisa Anido.

It can be justly affirmed that Prat, along with the maestros previously named: Julio S. Sagreras, Antonio Sinopoli, Mario Rodríguez Arenas and Hilarion Leloup, had consolidated in the Rio de la Plata, the foundation of the systematized guitaristic instruction.

Julio S. Sagreras

Hilarion Leloup from *"Historia de la Guitarra"* by Ricardo Muñoz, 1930.

Antonio Sinopoli

Mario Rodríguez Arenas

"Julio Salvador Sagreras Ramírez was born in Buenos Aires on November 22, 1879. His father was Gaspar Sagreras and his mother Dolores Ramírez. Ricardo Muñoz says in his *"Historia de la Guitarra"* that Julio began his guitar studies with his father Gaspar and Juan Alais. They were the first guitarists that opened the classic period of the instrument in South America. They didn't belong to the school of Tárrega, however, a significant number of disciples received their lessons, whose activity today is embued with genuine enthusiasm and sincere dedication."

Domingo Prat says in his *"Diccionario de Guitarristas"* "Julio began to study at such a young age that by the age of six years old he was the delight of the celebrated reunions in the homes of the porteña high society. By the age of twelve, he was the favorite disciple of Marchal, professor of harmony at the Conservatorio Williams. He passed his exam two years later, becoming a professor of voice and elementary harmony; he continued to take advanced courses until he was seventeen years old. At that time he developed his insight and talent and he began to compose for the theater. He composed three works: *"El cura suplente"*, with lyrics by Lieutenant Spruch, debuted in the old Rivadavia theater, now Liceo, by the actress Lola Membrives; *"La Isla Verde"* and *"Alfilar en bicicleta"* performed in the Teatro "Apolo", on July 4, 1904. He composed 38 pieces for piano, the most notable being: *"Lucila", "Melodia"* and *"Capricho Español"*. This instrument however didn't interrupt anything in his ascension as a guitarist. At the age of twenty he was named professor of guitar in the "Academia de Belles Artes", where he also gave classes in *"Solfeggio"*. In 1905 he founded his "Academia de Guitarra", and in September of the same year he arranged a concert by his students to take place in the Salon "Operai Italiani" (The same theater where Antonio Jiménez Manjón and Domingo Prat gave concerts R.O.). The students that participated were: Inés Maria Mulcahy, Margarita Hau, Leile Brovone, Mercedes Robles, Carlos Pellerano, Antonio Sinopoli, Mario Lamoreaux, Sandalio Salas, Alejandro Méndez and José E. Word. This was an epoch in his life extremely intense, by his untiring activity. His production had reached the respectable number of seventy original pieces for guitar. His friends and admirers were, among others, Enrique H. Chely, Carlos M. Pradére, Francisco Leyria, General of the brigade, Commander Leopoldo Funes, Lieutenant Colonel Romirio T. Valdes, Carlos Avellaneda, Dr. Domingo Machado, Dr. Servando Gallegos, Dr. Martin Ruiz Moreno, Antonio Bachini, Pedro Sicouret, Alfredo Ortiz, Casimiro Causirat, the coleagues Carlos García Tolsa, Juan Valler, Juan Alais, Emilio Bo, Romulo Troncoso, Tancredo Vadell and disciples of that epoch that distinguished themselves: Antonio Sinopoli, Carlos Pellerano, Adela del Valle, Francisca Martin, Victoria Testuri, Amadeo Videla, Martin F. Alberro, etc.

He gave many public performances, as a soloist and in collaboration with his father, Gaspar, with Carlos García Tolsa, Juan Alais, Antonio Jiménez Manjón, Antonio Sinopoli (without a doubt his favorite student), with Domingo Prat in 1909, and much later with Adela del Valle and his daughter Clelia; having performed in the Salon "Nuevo Circulo Napolitano", "Operai Italiani", "La Argentina", "Instituto Verdi", in Montevideo (June 27 and 28, 1902) Salon "Luis MAndrés", in Rosario, Sante Fe province (August 3, 1902), Teatro "Florida", in Santa Rosa (December 7, 1921), Salon "Blanco", of the Club General Pueyrredon, in Mar del Plata (February 21, 1922). Gathering together the reviews of his performances that have taken place, they can form a large book of well-deserved praises; we transcibe the following impression, from the source of one of his performances: '...As surging from infinity, we see being lifted up before us, the excelling figure of the concert guitarist Julio S. Sagreras, in whose hands the guitar vibrates as if over the fingerboard are posed the wings of the immortals of glory. And when we feel that unexplainable something that murmurs to our ears, as a sublime and mysterious symphony, played by invisible beings, the soul sings to the harmonious rhythm of its accents; and over a radiant cascade, nostalgic and wild that flows from the strings, the heart cries, as if over it pass all the yearnings of its intimate singers...'. In similar terms it was expressed in *"El Pais"* (August 19, 1900) by naming Julio's admirers and disciples: Dr. Meyer Pellegrini, Torres Castex, Victorica, Linch, Paz, Costa, Ortega, Rivera, Catelin, Acevedo, Lasalle, Bosch, Monjeaux, Ham and others that formed a legion.

His original production, from 1907 onward, is a bit less prolific, but more original. Mention must be made of his beautiful and inspired very original pages, dignified to study for the history of Argentine folklore, that recall the *"Choros"*, by Villa-lobos, in the Brazilian style. There are the dances (known as *tangos*) *"Muy de la quebrada", "Cancha", "Don Julio", "El Escandaloso", "Cha-Ka-Cha"* and a collection, of simpler construction, published under the pseudonym of S. Resgrasa. As a didactic author he is known for his various volumes of his method, all worthy of praise, in particular his *"Tecnica Superior"*. The intelligence and labor of Julio S. Sagreras have elevated him to an "Ivory Tower" (*"Torre de marfil"*), ornamented with his precious creations; it has had the pleasure to cross the seas and spread around old Europe in a very deserved recognition. Today Sagreras is a beautiful living page in the history of the guitar in Argentina." (Domingo Prat, 1930.)

 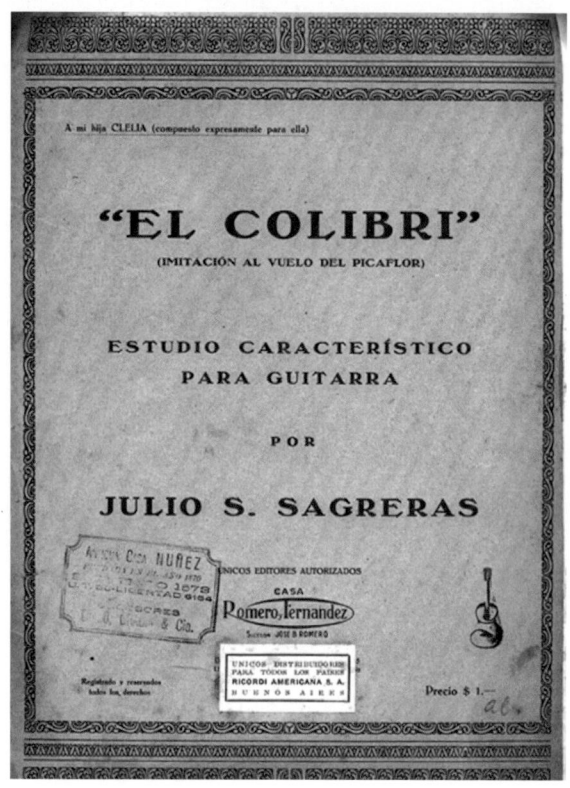

(Left) Volume six in the seven volume series of studies and exercises by Julio S. Sagreras that was published in 1940 by Romero & Fernández .

(Right) *El Colibri"* is the best known of all Julio S. Sagreras' pieces, this edition was published in 1936, though it is the last (146) of Julio's listings in the 1931 Antigua Casa Nuñez catalog.

Julio S. Sagreras was the first president of the Asociacion Guitarristica Argentina, founded on August 26, 1934. He published over 150 works.

Julio S. Sagreras passed away on July 20, 1942. (*Revista de la Guitarra Año IV* issue No. 10 of October 1, 1941 to December 31, 1942.)

In the unnumbered green colored cover *Diccionario de Guitarristas* by Domingo Prat (his own personal copy), in the archives of FFSI, a hand written note states that Julio S. Sagreras passed away on the morning of Monday, July 20, 1942.

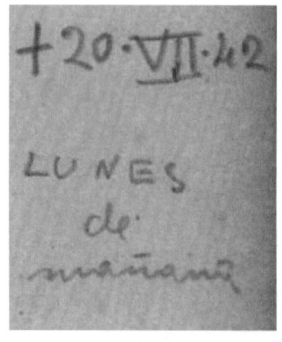

This notice of the initial publishing of his over one hundred pieces of sheet music is from the *"Montevideo Musical"* magazine of November 1, 1900, No. 154 *Año* XVI. This magazine was published by the Instituto Verdi in Montevideo from 1885-1952 and directed by Francisco L. Sambucetti.

Translation:

"Musical News

The guitar Professor Julio S. Sagreras has composed four beautiful musical pieces for this instrument that demonstrate the good artistic taste and the inspiration of the author.

These pieces are: *"Color de Rosa", Vals de salon; "Dulces-Cadenas", Mazurka de salon; "Mis Aspiraciones", Grand concert Fantasy,* and *"Venecia", Barcarola.*

All these are published by the music house Francisco Nuñez y Cia., of Buenos Aires, Cuyo 1628."

These four songs are the listed in the 1931 Antigua Casa Nuñez catalog as numbers: 4, 1, 3 and 7, showing the point when the maestro began to publish his works.

In the July 10, 1902 issue of the *"Montevideo Musical"* magazine No. 215 *Año* XVIII, is the review of the guitar concert at the Instituto Verdi in Montevideo.

Translation:

"The concert guitarist, Mr. Julio Sagreras, whose fame as a performer has such a good name was found to give only one concert here a few days ago in the Sala Verdi, he is now found in Rosario. That artist made known to us that he will return in the following month to Montevideo to give his only solo concert. Many admirers have been known to be conquered by the celebrated artist, who is without a doubt as a guitarist, Mr. Sagreras is of the first rank."

Novedades musicales

El profesor de guitarra Julio S. Sagreras ha compuesto para este instrumento cuatro bonitas piezas musicales que demuestran el buen gusto artístico y la inspiración de su autor.

Estas piezas son: «Color de Rosa,» vals de salón; «Dulces-Cadenas,» mazurka de salón; «Mis Aspiraciones,» gran fantasía de concierto, y «Venecia», barcarola.

Todas han sido editadas por la casa Francisco Núñez y Cia., de Buenos Aires, Cuyo 1628.

El concertista de guitarra señor Julio Sagreras, cuya fama de ejecutante tan buen nombre supo aquí dejar en el solo concierto que dió días pasados en la Sala Verdi, se encuentra ahora en la ciudad del Rosario. Ese artista nos ha hecho saber que el mes entrante volverá á Montevideo para dar un solo único concierto. Muchos admiradores ha sabido conquistarse el celebrado artista, que lo es sin duda el señor Sagreras como guitarrista de primera fuerza.

El señor Julio S. Sagreras.

UN ARTISTA DE LA GUITARRA — JULIO S. SAGRERAS

La tradición entre nuestro pueblo hace que la guitarra sea su instrumento favorito. No hay paisano que no guste de aprender su manejo, y, sea por música o por cifra, ello es que todos saben ejecutar algunas piezas en su querida bordona, como la denomina el paisano.

Aquí siempre hemos tenido buenos guitarristas, pero sin duda, tan artistas como el señor Julio S. Sagreras, puede asegurarse que ha habido pocos; su fama es grande en la ciudad y en la campaña, pues la guitarra en sus manos es un instrumento melodioso, al que sabe arrancarle sus secretos como nadie.

Artista por temperamento e hijo de artistas, inició sus estudios a los seis años, presentándose como concertista a los trece, edad en la que se inició también como compositor. Críticos destacados señalaron en esa época, en el precoz guitarrista, condiciones nada comunes de ejecutante e intérprete. Desde aquellos días ha transcurrido un cuarto de siglo conscientemente, y animado por un grande amor al instrumento y a la disciplina en el estudio, han hecho de él un artista comple-

to, que ha logrado grandes triunfos en cuantos conciertos se ha presentado.

Espíritu exquisito, de una vasta cultura artística, no le son desconocidos ninguno de los grandes músicos clásicos y contemporáneos. Ha estudiado y penetrado las nuevas corrientes renovadoras y, particularmente en la guitarra, adoptado todos los progresos que alcanzara desde Gaspar Sagreras, su padre, pasando por García Tolsa y otros, hasta aquel músico y talentoso artista: Tárrega.

Pero si destaca su personalidad como intérprete, mucho más se hace notar como compositor. Su labor en ese sentido es fecunda y rica. No menos de doscientas obras constituyen su acervo musical.

Ha compuesto numerosas transcripciones de compositores célebres, como: Beethoven, Chopín, Chaminade, Moszkowsky, Godard, Albéniz, etc., adaptadas para guitarra, su música original lo destaca entre todos los compositores nacionales.

El señor Martín Gil, reconocido perito en el arte que nos ocupa, después de reconocer sus méritos y elogiarlo, le ha invitado para una serie de conciertos en Córdoba.

Y para terminar sobre los méritos de Sagreras, lo dijo Llobet: Tienen ustedes, los argentinos, en Sagreras un ejecutante y un ejecutor de gran talento…

El guitarrista Sagreras, con su hijo Romeo.

These photos with the article are from the *"Caras y Caretas"* magazine of January 18, 1919 issue No. 1101 *Año* XXII. The translation is on the next page.

These photos with the article are from the *"Caras y Caretas"* magazine of January 18, 1919 issue No. 1101 *Año* XXII. Translation:

"An Artist of the Guitar — Julio Sagreras

The tradition among our nation makes it that the guitar might be its favorite instrument. There isn't a countryman that doesn't want to learn to play it, and, by music or maybe tablature everyone knows some pieces of its beloved basses, such as is common to the countryman.

We always have good guitarists here, but without a doubt, artists such as Julio Sagreras, we can assure you that there have been few; his fame is great in the city and in the countryside, but the guitar in his hands is a melodious instrument, to which he knows its secrets like no one.

An artist, by temperament and the son of artists, he began his studies at six years of age, being presented as a concert guitarist at thirteen and an age at which he also began to be a composer.

Distinguished critics picked him out as a child prodigy, of uncommon abilities as a player and interpreter. Since those days he is aware that a quarter of a century has passed, and being enthused by his great love for the instrument and the discipline of its study, they have made him a complete artist, who has achieved great triumphs in as many concerts in which he was presented.

An exquisite spirit, of a vast artistic culture, he is not unknown to any of the great classical contemporary musicians. He studied and penetrated the new renovating currents and, particularly the guitar, and adopting all the advances that have been achieved since Gaspar Sagreras, his father, passing by García Tolsa and others, up to that musician and talented artist: Tárrega.

But if he distinguishes his personality as an interpreter, it makes him much more noteworthy as a composer. His labor in this is fertile and rich. No less than two hundred works constitute his musical attainment.

He has made numerous transcriptions of celebrated composers, such as: Beethoven, Chopin, Chaminade, Moszkowski, Godard, Albeniz, etc. adapted to the guitar, his original music distinguishes him among all the national composers.

Mr. Martin Gil, the recognized expert in the art we are concerned with, after recognizing his merits and praising him, he invited him to play a series of concerts in Cordoba.

And to finish about the merits of Sagreras, Llobet said: 'You have, as Argentines, in Sagreras an interpreter and performer of great talent. . .' "

Caption at the bottom: "The guitarist Sagreras, with his son Romulo."

From the book "*Historia de La Guitarra*" by Ricardo Muñoz is the documentation that maestro Julio S. Sagreras and his student Adela del Valle performed 3 concerts of solos and duets in the Salon "La Argentina", the first of those on September 11, 1917.

First Part:

1. Recuerdos de la Alhambra (two guitars) – Tárrega, (This duet was so well received, that this concert date was mentioned at the bottom of page one of the second part of the published duet piece. See page 16 for sheet music cover.)

2. Sonate Pathetique-Allegro (two guitars) – Beethoven

performed by Julio S. Sagreras and his student, Professor Adela del Valle

3. Mercedes, mazurka-romanza – J. S. Sagreras
4. Rondo in A minor – Aguado

performed by Professor Adela del Valle

5. Rapsodia Criolla No. 2 (fantasia sobre la vidalita) – J. S. Sagreras
6. Vals No. 5-Godard – J. S. Sagreras
7. Potpourri sobre motivos españolos – J. S. Sagreras

performed by Julio S. Sagreras

Second Part:

1. Sonate Pathetique-Adagio Cantabile (two guitars) – Beethoven
2. Sonate Pathetique-Rondo (two guitars) – Beethoven

performed by Julio S. Sagreras and his student, Professor Adela del Valle

3. Capricho, tango
4. Vals No. 10-Chopin – J. S. Sagreras
   Crepusculo otoñal (Autumnal)
   Balada – J. S. Sagreras
5. Nocturne No. 2-Chopin – J. S. Sagreras
6. Variations on the Carnival of Venice – J. S. Sagreras

performed by Julio S. Sagreras

The second concert in Salon "La Argentina" was held on October 8, 1918.

First Part:

1. Reverie-Schumann
2. Sonate Pathetique-Allegro – Beethoven

performed by Julio S. Sagreras and his student, Professor Adela del Valle

3. Minuet (from Sonata No. 25) – Sor
   Soñando, capricho – Adela del Valle
4. La Cajita de Musica, Scherzo – J. S. Sagreras

performed by Professor Adela del Valle

5. Andante (from Sonata No. 2) – Mozart
6. Au Matin – Godard
7. Vals Lento Op. 34 No. 2 – Chopin
8. Nocturne Op. 9 No. 2 (transcription by Tárrega) – Chopin
9. Duerme querida! Reverie – J. S. Sagreras

performed by Julio S. Sagreras

Second Part:

1. Sonate Pathetique: a) Adagio, b) Rondo

performed by Julio S. Sagreras and his student, Professor Adela del Valle

2. Mercedes-gavotte – Carlos García Tolsa
3. Gran Jota – Arcas – Tárrega

performed by Professor Adela del Valle

4. Crepusculo otoñal (Autumnal)-Balada – J. S. Sagreras
5. Vals Op. 64, No. 2 – Chopin
6. Le Petit Mourant – Gottschalk
7. Anitra's Dance – Grieg
8. Estudio Melodica Arpegio – J. S. Sagreras
   Estudio caprichoso sobre "La Güeya"– J. S. Sagreras

performed by Julio S. Sagreras

9. Variations on La Vidalita – J. S. Sagreras
performed by Julio S. Sagreras and his student, Professor Adela del Valle

The third concert held in Salon "La Argentina" was held on September 10, 1919.

First Part:

1. Danza Española No. 3 – Moszkowsky
2. Danza Hungara No. 5 – Brahms

performed by Julio S. Sagreras and Professor Adela del Valle

3. Minuet – Mozart
4. Variations on the Carnival of Venice – J. S. Sagreras

performed by Professor Adela del Valle

5. Capricho criollo sobre "El Cielito"– J. S. Sagreras
6. "Pas de Amphores"– air de ballet – Chaminade
7. "Danza de Odaliscas"– (Capricho Oriental) – Sagreras
8. Rumores de la Caleta – (Malagueña) – Albeniz

performed by Julio S. Sagreras

This photo is from Ricardo Muñoz's unpublished book
"Historia Universal de la Guitarra" Volume VII
"La Guitarra en La Argentina".

Second Part:

1. Claro de Luna, Adagio – Beethoven

performed by Julio S. Sagreras and his student, Professor Adela del Valle

2. a) La Cajita de Musica, Scherzo – J. S. Sagreras
   b) Nocturne No. 2 – Chopin

performed by Professor Adela del Valle

3. a) Plegaria, arpeggio study – J. S. Sagreras
   b) Estudio in E Major – J. S. Sagreras
4. Mazurca No. 2 – Godard
5. a) Scherzino, Study in Harmonics in the form of a Gavotte – J. S. Sagreras
   b) Granada-Albeniz

performed by Julio S. Sagreras"

Julio S. Sagreras in the 1930's.

The translation of the handwriting is: "To *Don* Virgilio A. Planas, Julio S. Sagreras, August 20, 1940 Buenos Aires."

This was the photo on the inside cover of volume six in the seven volume series of studies and exercises by Julio S. Sagreras that was published in 1940 by Romero & Fernández .

"Adela Del Valle was born in Buenos Aires in 1897. Her father Angel was born in Asturias, Spain in 1874 and came to Buenos Aires in 1884. Angel was her first teacher whom she studied with until her completion of the elementary level. She pursued her superior studies with Julio S. Sagreras who presented her to the public in 1917, performing solos and duos in several concerts, distinguishing herself most notably, among other works, with the *"Rondo en La"* by Aguado.

As a composer she is known for *"Seis piezas faciles"*, which affirm her belief that the guitar is a marvelous instrument for accompaniment of the voice (like the piano, and, in former times the lute). Professor Del Valle has made a good collection of songs from all regions, some originals and other popular, adapting them to the guitar in a simple manner. That specialty of the art has been practiced in former times and propagated by the great Schubert (1797-1828) with his own material. The quantity of works for this genre published until today by this professor comprises a collection of more than fifty; they fulfill her commitment, and they can serve for consultation in future epochs, as sources for folklore material." So ends the entry in Domingo Prat's *"Diccionario de Guitarristas"*.

There are 58 pieces listed in the 1931 Antigua Casa Nuñez catalog.

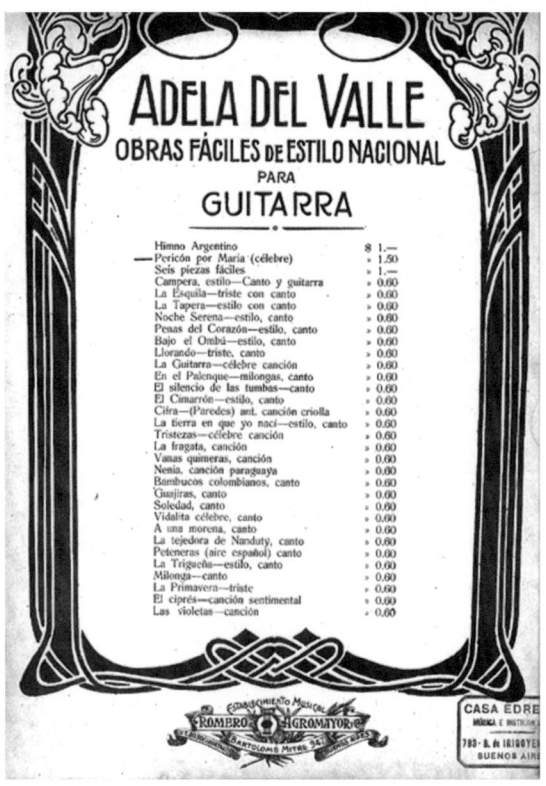

Romero, Agromayor and Cia. c. 1917

Romero, Agromayor and Cia. 1918

Adela Del Valle specialized in easy Argentine folk pieces for voice and guitar to encourage beginning guitarists, though she also had some more intricate solo compositions as well.

Romero & Fernández 1920

Romero & Fernández 1928

"Mario Rodríguez Arenas was born in Buenos Aires on September 30, 1879. He was the son of Manuel Rodríguez and Martina Arenas. He began to study the guitar on June 15, 1903 under the direction of Angel Del Valle. This study lasted for 2 years. At that point Mario began to study harmony with Enrique Morera as well as perfection studies.

In 1907 he began to dedicate himself to teaching. He soon had a distinguished name for himself as well as many wealthy students from the upper classes of the porteño society.

Ricardo Muñoz recounts a story in his biography of Mario Rodríguez Arenas in the magazine "*Revista de la Guitarra*" issue no. 13 of September 1945. Mario told him that in 1908 when Domingo Prat had brought the first editions of Francisco Tárrega to Buenos Aires, the preludes, tremolo pieces, Capricho Arabe, etc. sold out in just 8 days at the Casa Nuñez music store. It was well over a month before the guitar aficionados of Buenos Aires had another opportunity to purchase these works again.

He began publishing works through Francisco Nuñez about 1909. The majority of these pieces were Argentine folk pieces and many of these were so popular that they sold out and had to have subsequent editions reprinted.

According to Ricardo Muñoz in 1913 Mario, along with Antonio Sinopoli founded the Academia de Guitarra "Tárrega". The year after, a student of Francisco Tárrega, Hilarion Leloup, who had arrived in 1912, took over the directorship from Mario and Antonio.

Sometime in 1917 Mario suffered a cramp to his right hand which curtailed his stage performances. His teaching activities kept him busy besides the transcriptions that he produced weekly.

By 1930 Mario Rodríguez Arenas had published over 220 pieces. Besides the Argentine folk pieces there were Chopin, Schumann, Mendelssohn, Grieg and Handel pieces, and method books with the works of Sor, Aguado, Coste, Cano and Tárrega. His seven method books called "*La Escuela de la Guitarra*" were dedicated to his daughter Elba, who became a distinguished guitarist under his direction.

Mario died in 1949."

This biography is drawn three sources: from Ricardo Muñoz's "*Historia de la Guitarra*" published in 1930, Domingo Prat's "*Diccionario de Guitarristas*" published by Romero & Fernández in 1934, in Buenos Aires, and an article in the "*Revista de la Guitarra*" issue No. 13 of September 1945, magazine of the Asociacion Guitarristica Argentina. Different sources provide varied dates for the founding of the Academia de Guitarra "Tárrega", but the date 1914 is used on the concert programs of this academia.

On the right is an image of the *El Diario* daily from Friday May 21, 1909. The translation is: "The known professor of guitar, Mario Rodríguez Arenas has just published a series of national airs that are titled "Rapsodias criollas". The adaptation has been done with exquisite care and with all the art of this professor by the admirers who know him. We especially call your attention to the last edited piece, the arrangements of the traditional *Pericon* and *Vidalita*."

EL DIARIO — Viernes 21 de Mayo de 1909

El conocido profesor de guitarra, Mario Rodriguez Arenas acaba de publicar una serie de aires nacionales que titula "Rapsodias criollas". La adaptacion ha sido hecha con esquisito esmero y con todo el arte que los admiradores de este profesor le conocen. Llama especialmente la atencion en la última pieza editada, el arreglo de los tradicionales pericon y vidalita.

In the 1931 Antigua Casa Nuñez catalog the "*Rapsodias sobre motivos criollas*" is the 16th work.

Archive: Mario Rodríguez Arenas

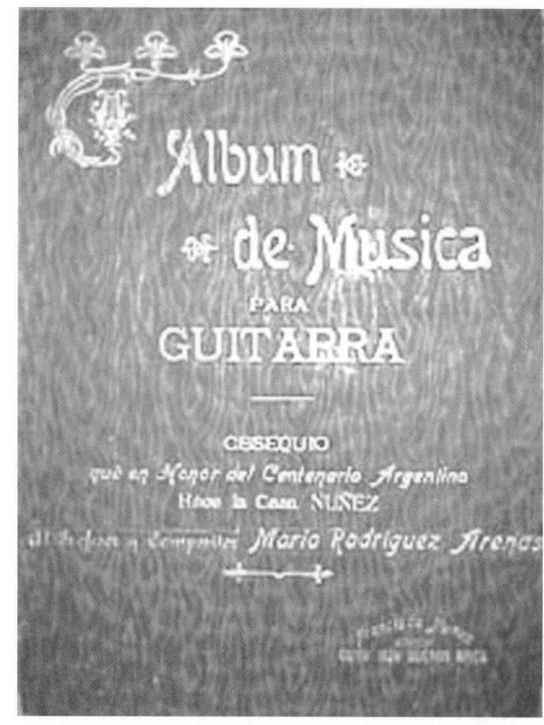

(Left) Mario Rodríguez Arenas c. 1940 (Right) Bound album of sheet music given as a gift from Francisco Nuñez to one of his composers, Mario Rodríguez Arenas in 1910.

(Left) Francisco Nuñez publication of a Mario Rodríguez Arenas transcription of a Roberto Firpo composition at the dawn of aviation. Pianist Roberto Firpo was one of the outstanding composers of the tango. (Right) Julio S. Sagreras transcription of a waltz from Puccini's opera "*La Bohéme*" published by Francisco Nuñez.

Alumnas aventajadas del
profesor de Guitarra M.
Rodríguez Arenas

Srtas. Nelida M. Canepa, Elsa Mohr,
Zulema Ferrezuelo, Maria Teresa Molinari,
Claudia Grillo y Elba Rodríguez Arenas.

The advanced women students of Mario Rodríguez Arenas, including his daughter Elba in the lower left. From *Revista Musical Ilustrada "Tárrega"* issue No. 14 of August 1925.

This biography of Elba Rodríguez Arenas is translated from Ricardo Muñoz's unpublished book *"Historia Universal de la Guitarra"* Volume VIII *"La Escuela Tárrega en La Argentina"*.

"Elba Noemi Rodríguez Arenas

Her Origin:

She is the daughter of the guitarist *Don* Mario Rodríguez Arenas and was born in Buenos Aires on December 28, 1911.

Her Education:

Since she was a youngster she began her study of music and the guitar with her father.

Her Virtuosity:

In a very short time she revealed her exceptional musical-guitaristic abilities, achieving a distinguished artistic hierarchy to perform work of great responsibility, and was heard as such with great applause at the age of 16, on the 24th of July of 1927 in honor of the great Hispanic poet *Don* Francisco Villaespesa, and of the tenor *Don* Miguel Fleta, interpreting *"Preludio"* and *"Recuerdos de la Alhambra"* by Tárrega and *"Testamento de Amelia"* by Llobet. The critics said: "...on the guitar vibrated with all her tears, with all her longings, with all her tenderness. ... Only an artistic temperament as Miss Arenas is capable of interpreting these great difficult works of the great masters so faithfully. " —

Her Compositions:

She has only written 5 original works for the instrument that are native inspired: the *Estilo "Alma Gaucha", "De Tardecita", "A la Luz de la Luna"* and the *Zamacuecas "Ausencia"* and *"Flores del Campo"*, all published by Casa Nuñez.

Her Pedagogy:

She has dedicated herself to teaching, but it was interrupted by the premature and unjust passing at 29 years of age.

Her Passing:

She died in Buenos Aires on January 27, 1941, as a consequence of congested lung failure."

"A remembrance of my daughter Elba for my beloved friend and colleague, Ricardo Muñoz. Mario Rodríguez Arenas February 18, 1941"

Archive: Ricardo Muñoz

172

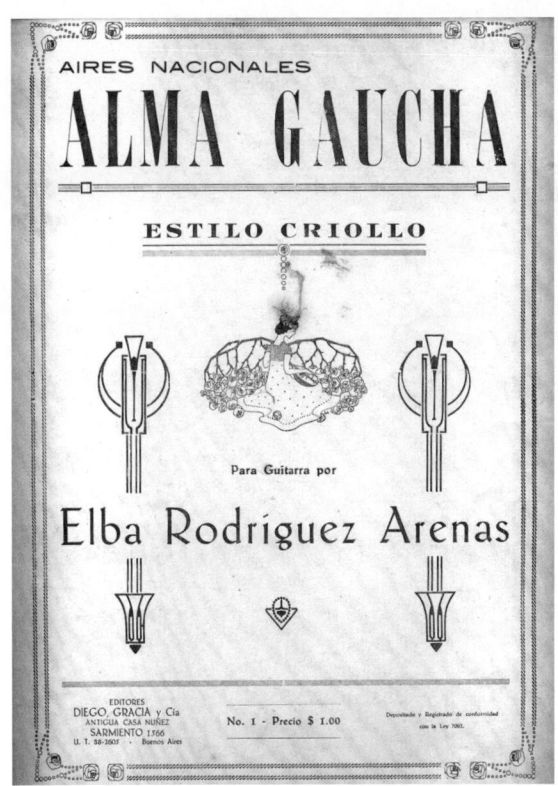

Elba Rodríguez Arenas sheet music pieces, there are five listed in the 1931 Antigua Casa Nuñez catalog. These are all autographed from her father: "A remembrance of my daughter Elba for my beloved friend and colleague, Ricardo Muñoz. Mario Rodríguez Arenas February 18, 1941"— just three weeks after she passed away. The piece on the upper right "*A la Luz de la Luna*" No. 3 was published in March of 1928, when Elba was 16 years old and has the autograph removed. Elba much like Julio S. Sagreras was one of the youngest guitarists to publish pieces of music in the Rio de la Plata. The photo became a postcard and is dedicated on the back:

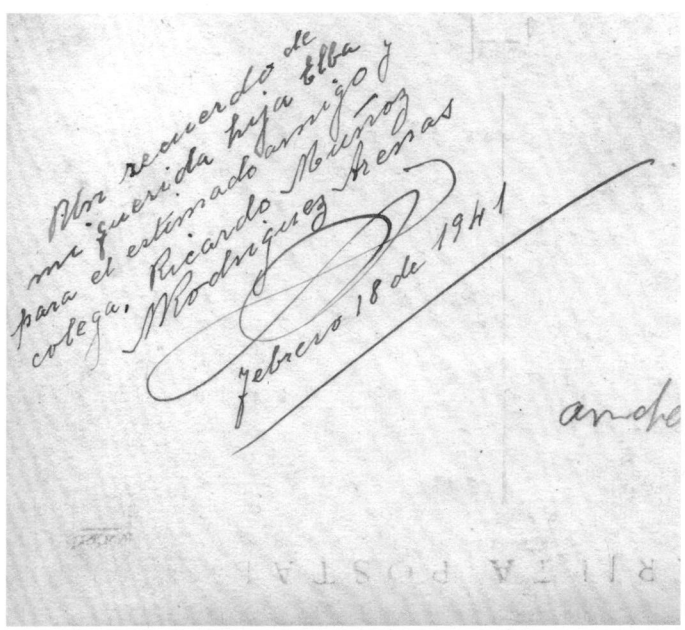

Carlos Molinari   Juan Bosch

Of these Mario Rodríguez Arenas students, the most notable is Geronimo Bianqui Piñero. He was born on September 24, 1905. After beginning the guitar with Mario Rodríguez Arenas, he went on to study with Justo T. Morales. Bianqui became interested in composing and arranging and he published *¡Achalay! (Estilo)* and a Bach transcription of a *Courante* by 1931. In 1943 he published transcriptions of Atahualpa Yupanqui works. Bianqui Piñero was president of the Asociacion Guitarristica Argentina in 1942, 1944 and again in 1947-48.

Photos: *Revista Musical Ilustrada "Tárrega" No. 15* of September 1925

174

As we said before, from the Academia Prat accomplished disciples graduated, especially women. The names at the head of the list of virtuoso concert artists formed by the prestigious Catalan maestro are: Maria Luisa Anido, of international renown, the talented Consuelo Mallo Lopez, who developed an important teaching career, Nellie Ezcaray of Rosario, Santa Fe province, Maria Angélica Funes, Irma Haydée Perazzo, Maria Pascual Navas, Celia Rodríguez Boqué, Adolfina Raitzin, his daughter Blanca Prat, Aurelia Tizon, the last being the first wife of General Juan Domingo Peron, three times President of the Republic of Argentina, equally to General Rosas, a very often debated figure in Argentine politics, Adolfo V. Luna, musicologist Carlos Vega and others.

(Upper Right) Consuelo Mallo Lopez in 1942
This from the magazine *Mundo Musical* issue No. 43 of April 1942.

(Lower Right) Blanca Prat from the magazine *"La Guitarra"* issue No. 1 *Año* I of October 1946, published by the Asociacion Guitarristica Entrerriana in Parana. The photo accompanies an article about a concert Blanca had given at the Biblioteca Popular (library) in Parana on October 20, 1945.

Blanca Prat played:
"Andante Pastoral and Minuetto by Sor.
Tonadilla by Blas Serna
Bolero by Segura
Serenata Andaluza by Zabalza
Hoja de Album, Guitarresca (for left hand alone),
El Triunfo, El Malambo and El Escondido by
her father, Domingo Prat.
Fandanguillo by Moreno-Torroba
Danza No. 5 by Granados
Asturias by Albeniz
Zapateado by Ross."

(Lower Left) Academia de Guitarra "Prat" ad in the issue No. 24 of July 1926 R*evista Musical Ilustrada "Tárrega",* that mentions lessons twice a week.

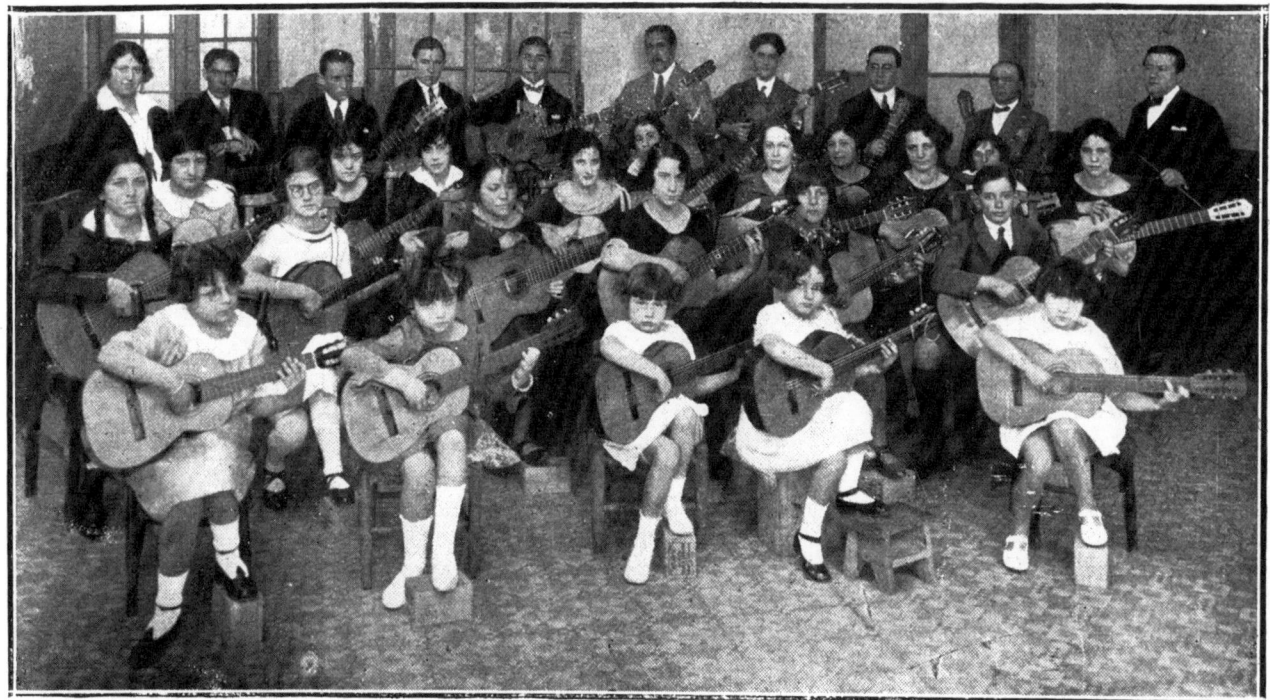

Conjunto de Alumnos del Curso 1924 en el Concierto-Examen realizado el 25 de Noviembre en el Salón "La Argentina".

The photo above is from the *Revista Musical Ilustrada "Tárrega"*, issue No. 7 December 1924. It was also used in the Madrid magazine *"Estampa"* on January 1, 1929, without mentioning who was in the photo, in an interview and article on the luthier Santos Hernández. (Credit to my colleague, Richard Bruné.) The debut of the Academia de Guitarra "Prat" Ensemble of the 1924 Course in the Concert-Exam on November 25, 1924 held in the Salon "La Argentina". The thirty students of the Academia performed this program:

1st part

1) Estudio – Carulli
performed by: Lucia Irene Chapas – 7 years old

2) Vals – Carulli
performed by: Martita Carman – 7 years old

3) Andantino – Carulli
performed by: Ofelia Minardi – 9 years old

4) Estudio – Carulli
5) Gavota – Prat
performed by: Zaira Negroni – 10 years old

6) Recreaciones – Aguado
7) Preludio Lagrima – Tárrega
performed by: Antonia Casas

8) Melodia – Castelli
9) Adelita, mazurka –Tárrega
performed by: Sofia Gasull

10) Romanza – Schumann – Tárrega
11) Sylvia, Pizzicatto – Delibes – Prat
performed by: Haydée Zabalza

12) Estudio No. 7 – Aguado
13) Preludio No. 9 – Tárrega
14) Estudio – Coste
performed by: Celia Rodríguez Boqué – 9 years old

15) Minuetto and Serenata – Mozart – Prat
16) Tarantela – Castina – Prat
performed by: Haydée Fiorini and Haydée Perazzo

17) Sueño-Viñas – Prat
performed by: 10 guitars

Ladies: Maria Amelia Amestoy, Antonia Casas, Sofia Gasull, Laura Molteni, Celia Rodríguez Boqué and Maria Angélica de San Martin

Gentlemen: Leon Carlos, Juan Carlos Artola, Rodolfo A. Luna, Jorge Taullard,

2nd part:

1) Estudio (la gota de agua) – Sor
2) Berceuse – Schumann – Tárrega
performed by: Haydée Fiorini

3) Preludio No. 1 –Tárrega
4) Andante de la Sonata X – Mozart – Prat
5) Capricho Arabe –Tárrega
performed by: Leandro A. Castro

6) Andante largo – Sor
7) Nocturno No. 2 Chopin – Prat
8) Gavota – Tárrega
9) Estudio – Vieuxtemps – Tárrega
10) Asturias – Albeniz – Prat
performed by: Haydée Perazzo

11) Minueto Federal-arranged by Prat
performed by: 30 guitars

Ladies: Maria Amelia Amestoy, Antonia Casas, Martita Carman, Maria Susana Casara, Lucia Irene Chapas, Haydée Fiorini, Alicia Fuentes, Sofia Gasull, Rosa Goyeneche, Sara and Ofelia Lopez Muñiz, Sara Raquel Lanari, Mrs. Angélica de Llera, Laura Molteni, Ofelia Minardi, Ana Mach, Maria Amelia Novion, Zaira Negroni, Ofelia Pérez Cazalla, Irma Haydée Perazzo, Celia Rodríguez Boqué, Maria Angélica de San Martin and Haydée Zabalza.

Gentlemen: Juan Carlos Artola, Ciro E. Arias, Leandro A. Castro, Felipe Gomez, Leon Carlos, Rodolfo A. Luna, Obdulio Lima, Héctor Paillot, Roberto Soriano and Jorge Taullard."

The next page is from the magazine *Revista Musical Ilustrada "Tárrega"* issue No. 11 of May 1925. These are some of the "excellent students" from the Academia de Guitarra "Prat".

Academia de Guitarra Domingo Pratt

ALUMNAS AVENTAJADAS

Niña ZAIRA NEGRONI

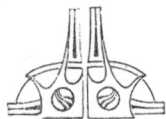

Niña OFELIA A. MINARDI

Niña ANTONIA CASAS

Niña CELIA RODRIGUEZ BOQUE

Niña MARIA HAYDEE ZABALZA

The fifth Academia de Guitarra "Prat" concert on September 15, 1925 at the Salon "La Argentina".
Left to Right are: Amilcar Verdier, Irma Haydée Perazzo, Haydée Fiorini, Celia Rodríguez Boqué, Haydée
Zabalza, Domingo Prat and Leandro Castro. Photo: *Revista Musical Ilustrada "Tárrega"* issue No. 15 of
September 1925.

The audience at the fifth Academia de Guitarra "Prat" concert on September 15, 1925 at the Salon
"La Argentina". Photo: *Revista Musical Ilustrada "Tárrega"* issue No. 15 of September 1925.

The review of the "Academia Prat" student concert from the "*Conciertos*" section of the *Revista Musical Ilustrada "Tárrega"* magazine issue No. 15 of September 1925.

Translation:

"Academia Prat"

"The 15th of last September, in the Salon "La Argentina", the Academia "Prat" offered its 5th concert of students of the academia that is directed by the reputed Spanish maestro Domingo Prat.

The program consisted of two extensive parts that six excellent students of diverse courses carried out.

Miss Haydée Zabalza began the performance with a *"Preludio"* by Tárrega and the popular Catalan song *"El testamento de Amelia"*, harmonized in E minor by maestro Prat. Performed, of course, with knowledge of the fretboard, the new version presents many interesting details.

Mr. Amilcar Verdier played a *"Mazurca"* by Tárrega and a *"Minueto"* by Sor with good taste and then Mr. Leandro A. Castro, an adult student of surplus endowments, offered five pieces. A *"Minuet"* by Sor and a *"Romanza"* by Mendelssohn gave him an opportunity to light up that Castro didn't miss. After with exactness he played an unpublished tremolo piece by Banegas. We must declare that nothing is lost in that it is still unpublished. Castro finished his intervention with *"Granada"* by Albeniz, the deficient version by Tárrega.

Miss Perazzo and Miss Fiorini played a duet of *"Tarentela"* by Castina arranged by Prat. It was a very interesting number by the quality of the performers and the beauty of the guitarization.

In the second part Celia Rodríguez Boque took the initiative. This young girl, of 10 years old, presented in the past year by the Academia, continued her progressive development normally. She played five pieces of considerable difficulty with surprising naturalness. To know the demands that this young girl conquered, which must be known in their serene hidden movement of the *"Preludio No. 4"* by Tárrega. Celia Rodríguez, wisely carried, will yield the best fruits.

Irma Haydée Perazzo is a pleasant reality. She possesses sure technical mediums and a noble temperament. She is very young and has, therefore, a lot of time for proceeding with the cultivation of her spirit in contemplation of the master works of all the arts.

Miss Perazzo offered five works in as many extremely interesting versions. With respect to her presentation in the past year she has shown very serious progress.

The performance ended with a fragment of *"L'Arlesienne"* by Bizet by six guitars. It is the version by Tárrega for two with the parts doubled. It turned out to be a very pleasant number and it was performed under the direction of maestro Prat in a good manner.

The same group afterward offered the *"Minue Federal"* by Prat, corresponding to the insistent applause of the audience."

180

ACADEMIA DE GUITARRA

Director: DOMINGO PRAT
Prof.: CARMEN FARRÉ DE PRAT

119, RODRIGUEZ PEÑA, 119
Unión Telefónica (38), Mayo, 0209

V.º CONCIERTO DE ALUMNOS
: EN EL :
SALÓN "LA ARGENTINA"
RODRIGUEZ PEÑA 361

CURSO DEL AÑO 1925

Martes 15 de Septiembre de 1925
A LAS 21.15 HORAS (9.15 p. m.)

PROGRAMA

PRIMERA PARTE

1 — Preludio N.º 1 . . . . Tárrega
2 — L' testament d' Amelia (en Mi) pop. cat. Prat
        por la Sta. Haydée Zabalza

3 — Mazurka en Sol . . . . Tárrega
4 — Minueto N.º 20 . . . . Sor
        por el Sr. Amilcar Verdier

5 — Minueto No. 19 . . . . Sor
6 — Romanza No. 6 . . . . Mendelshon - Tárrega
7 — Trémolo (inédito) . . . . Banegas
8 — Granada . . . . Albeniz - Tárrega
        por el Señor Leandro A. Castro.

9 —. Tarantela . . . . Castina - Prat
        por las Stas. Irma Haydée Perazzo y Haydée Fiorini

SEGUNDA PARTE

1 — Minueto No. 17 . . . . Sor
2 — Canción de Galicia . . . . Veiga - Prat
3 — Estudio en La . . . . Prat
4 — Preludio No. 4 . . . . Tárrega
5 — Estudio No. 23 . . . . Carcassi
        por la niña de 10 años Celia Rodríguez Bouque

6 — Minueto No. 9 . . . . Sor
7 — Adagio (Sonata 13) . . . . Beethoven - Tárrega
8 — Campanela (estudio) 1a. audición . . . . Prat
9 — Introducción y Variaciones 1a. aud. compl. Sor
10 — Serrana (1a. audición) . . . . Albeniz - Prat
        por la Sta. Irma Haydée Perazzo

11 — L' Arlesienne (Allegro-Adagio-Allegro) . . . . Bizet - Tárrega
        Conjunto por las Stas. Perazzo, Fiorini, R. Bouqué, Zabalza,
                y Sres. Castro y Verdier

Solicitar las entradas por invitación en las Casas de Música
y en la Academia.

The Academia de Guitarra "Prat" produced the largest number of virtuoso child prodigies to become famous. At the time of this Tuesday, September 15, 1925 concert, held at the very prestigious Salon "La Argentina" Celia Rodríguez Boqué was only 10 years old. She would later be the professor of guitar at the Conservatorio Carpi.

Concierto de Guitarra verificado en el Salon "La Argentina" (curso de 1925)
Conjunto de alumnos

The sixth Academia de Guitarra "Prat" concert on November 25, 1925 Salon "La Argentina" concert with 57 students. The works presented were by: Carulli, Regondi, Aguado, Prat, Haydn-Tárrega, Delibes, Chopin-Tárrega, Beethoven, Mendelssohn, Albeniz and Schubert. The entire academia played "Melodia and Minuetto Federal" arranged by Domingo Prat. Academia de Guitarra "Prat", the music school that Domingo and his wife Carmén founded had doubled in size in just one year! It included so many child prodigies, which in most cases performed on Buenos Aires radio when they were 13-18 years old.

The audience at the VI Academia de Guitarra "Prat" concert on November 25, 1925 held in the Salon "La Argentina". Both photos: *Revista Musical Ilustrada "Tárrega"* issue No. 18 of December 1925.

Proemio al Programa

La confección de este "Programa de Estudio" es consecuencia de una larga labor de más de veinte años de enseñanza de la guitarra en esta capital, ella ha producido un número de maestros bien distinguidos que instigado por ellos he determinado la publicación de dicho programa. No creo revelar ningún secreto ni mucho menos ser ello, la piedra filosofal, es nada más que una guía para el maestro y una forma de seguridad para el enseñado. En él hago notar a qué materia pertenece cada cosa anotada, primero para saber donde buscarlo y segundo para insistir en ella si el alumno no lo precisara, es por esto que alguna de ellas y en un mismo año las presento con sobriedad. Quizá en la colocación de algunas cosas no habré estado acertado, pero si quiero creer que su sitio no estará muy distante, formando ellas un correcto trehzado en su totalidad.

Respecto a la egemonía de un METODO COMPLETO de un autor determinado para eliminar a los demás es completamente ilusorio, esto lo dice la práctica, pues opino que de cada uno de ellos se puede tomar, uno, varios o muchos ejemplos, camino seguro para formar un experto idóneo en la materia. El piano, sin duda alguna, es el instrumento más difundido, y para su enseñanza no ha prosperado ningún METODO COMPLETO. Puedo afirmar concretamente que no es posible la formación de un maestro de guitarra a base de un METODO COMPLETO de un autor determinado, en cambio opino que todos o más bien la mayoría de METODOS publicados pueden servir de complemento a la enseñanza completa para hacer un docto en el instrumento, sirviéndose de lo oportuno para los distintos casos que se presentaran.

Hago notar con suma satisfacción que todo lo inscrito en el "Programa de Estudio" es original de guitarra, si en él vemos unas "Variaciones de Arcas sobre un tema de Sor" ello nos dice que tanto lo uno como lo otro su origen ha sido inspirado en y por la guitarra. Otros ejemplos de esta misma índole hay en este programa, así es que repito, todo es original de guitarra.

Debo de hacer presente que por lo dicho en el párrafo anterior, no se cree que no soy partidario de las transcripciones, pues bien sabemos que el gran J. S. Bach, y antes de él, después y hasta nuestros días, grandes músicos han cultivado en más o menos esta rama del arte musical aplicada a distintos instrumentos.

Siendo un profundo admirador del Folk-lore en general y en particular del argentino como lo he demostrado en modestos aportes, no me he descuidado en incluirlos en el "Programa de Estudios" y hago presente sin distinción de autores, que haré efectivas las enseñanzas de hermosas páginas de inconfundible sabor argentino, no habiendo incluido en este programa a la de ningún autor por ser ellas numerosas y por consiguiente merecer un aparte.

Conclusión: Al maestro y al discípulo, para ambos interesados deben de quedar perennes estas simples palabras. Ordenar y observar, es misión del maestro, y atender y estudiar, la del discípulo.

This and the next several pages are of the seven-year program of the Academia de Guitarra "Prat".
The autograph is that of Carmén Farré de Prat.

Translation of the "Proemio al Programa" of the Academia de Guitarra "Prat":

"Preface to the Program"

"The development of this "Study Program" is the consequence of a long labor of more than twenty years of teaching the guitar in this capital which has produced a number of very distinguished maestros who urged me to publish this program. I don't believe it will reveal any hidden secret nor will it be a philosopher's stone — it is nothing more than a guide for the maestro and a form of security for the student. In this method I note which material belongs to which annotation, firstly to know where to locate it, if necessary, and this is particularly important in orienting students who may need it. Perhaps the placement of some items I should not have presumed, but I wish to believe that their placement shall not render them inaccessible, but rather totally strung together as a continuous braid.

In respect to the hegemony of a COMPLETE METHOD of an author determined to eliminate the competition, this is completely illusory in practical experience since every one of these methods can supply a secure path to form a qualified expert in the material. The piano, without any doubt, is the most widely diffused instrument, and for its teaching not any COMPLETE METHOD has prospered. I can concretely affirm that the formation of a maestro isn't possible based on a COMPLETE METHOD of a specific author. Instead, it's my opinion that all, or better said, the majority of METHODS published, can serve to complement a complete instruction for making a thorough study of the guitar to form an expert on the instrument, serving opportunely the distinct kinds of students that may present themselves.

I notate with additional satisfaction that everything in the "Program of Studies" is original and written for the guitar, if in it we look at the "*Variaciones de Arcas sobre un tema de Sor*" included here, it tells us how both musicians have been inspired in and by the guitar. There are other examples in this program of this same disposition, so it is that I repeat all is original for the guitar.

I must point out that what was said in the previous paragraph does not imply that I am opposed to transcription, since we well know that the great J. S. Bach, and those before him, and after until our days, great musicians, who have cultivated more or less this same branch of the musical art and applied it to distinct instruments.

Being a profound admirer of folklore in general and in particular of the Argentine, I have demonstrated in modest contributions, as I haven't neglected including them in the "Program of Studies" which, even though it is without authors, will effectively include beautiful pages of unquestionable Argentine flavor, having avoided including any other author, as they are very numerous and consequently therefore deserve an aside all their own.

Conclusion: To the maestro and to the disciple, for both, these simple words must perennially remain. To order and observe is the mission of the maestro and to pay attention and study is that of the disciple."

184

Año I°

— Considerando el año escolar de nueve meses y descontando de éstos los días feriados y otros que no se pueden asistir involuntariamente a rendir la lección, el profesor tendrá un promedio de ocho meses de enseñanza equivalentes a sesenta y cuatro lecciones, contando éstas dos por semana.

— El desarrollo del programa de cada año el maestro lo realizará según las aptitudes del discípulo.

— Para poder rendir examen el alumno debe tener aprobadas por parte mínima sesenta y cuatro cosas distintas, haciendo presente la variada dificultad que pueden presentar éstas, pues en algunos casos se pueden dar dos y tres cosas por lección, y en otros, un ejercicio o estudio, etc., tendrá que emplear dos o tres lecciones. El total en más, puede determinar en mejorar la nota del examen.

— Para cada año se exponen una cantidad de ejercicios, estudios, etc., muy superiores a lo exigido para el fin de que el maestro tenga un amplio campo de acción en bien de su enseñanza, eligiendo lo oportuno.

— Terminantemente queda bien aclarado que, la colocación de las distintas materias no indica que se deben de realizar en el orden que están expuestas, se empezará por la que se cree más conveniente, y continuando salpicando de una y de otra, volviendo a anteriores o insistiendo en una misma.

ARPEGIOS

PRAT. Ejercicios I° y II° de "La Nueva Técnica". Páginas 4-5. La 1° y 2° Series de dedeos de la 1° fórmula se ordenarán alternando con otras lecciones de distinta materia.

CARULLI. Ejercicios de arpegios varios de las páginas 10-11.

AGUADO. Cuaderno de "50 Lecciones" la 21. Método Lecciones 19-20.

VARIOS

CARULLI. Método 1° parte de N° 1 1al 22 a elección.

AGUADO. Cuaderno de "50 lecciones" Nos. 5, 7, 10, 14, 20, 27, 36, 41, 48.

AGUADO. Método Lecciones Nos. 10, 12, 13, 14, 15.

CANO A. Método Lección N° 13.

CARCASSI. Método 3° parte Nos 1 al 30.

PULGAR

AGUADO. Cuaderno "50 Lecciones" N° 42.

AGUADO. Método Lección 18.

PRAT. Ejercicio I° de "La Nueva Técnica".

FSCALAS

PRAT. Mayores en dos octavas. Cuaderno de "Escalas y Arpegios".

ACORDES

PRAT. Ejercicios I° y II° de "La Nueva Técnica".

AGUADO. Cuaderno "50 Lecciones" Nos. 15, 21, 34.

CEJILLA

PRAT. Ejercicio I. "La Nueva Técnica" realizarlo en cejilla y ascendiéndolo por semitonos como lo indica.

PRAT. Ejercicio Arpegio. Cejilla del Cuaderno de "Escalas y Arpegios".

AGUADO. Cuaderno "50 Lecciones" N° 43.

— Las seis cuerdas hasta el casillero o traste doce de memoria.

Estas se ordenarán en el último cuarto del año y de a una empezando por la prima. Esto no debe ser motivo para que se interrumpe el estudio práctico.

EXPRESION OBRAS

SOR. Minueto N° 1 "Colección de 30 Minuetos revisados por Prat".

VISEO R. Bourré N° 2 del Método de Sor-Coste.

FARRE. Melodía "Billiken" (Vals).

FARRE. Melodía "Tinina"

SAGRERAS J. S. Melodía "Nostalgia" Op. 19. N° 3.

FIN del Año I°

PREPARATORIO

— PRELIMINARES TEORICOS (1).

— Como debe sentarse y el uso del banquito para el pié izquierdo.

— Conocimiento de las distintas partes de que está formada la guitarra para su uso, a saber: Caja, Tapa, Fondo, Boca, Aros, Mango, Diapasón, Pala, Clavijero, Clavijas, Cejillas, Divisiones, Casilleros o Trastes, Puente, Cuerdas.

— Nombre de las cuerdas y su aplicación en las figuras de las correspondientes notas que les pertenece.

— Colocación de la guitarra — Del brazo derecho — Mano derecha — Como se deben pulsar las cuerdas — Del brazo izquierdo — Mano izquierda — Como se deben de pisar las cuerdas.

— Como se debe de Afinar o Templar las cuerdas.

— PRELIMINARES PRACTICOS.

— Ejercicios varios para la mano derecha sola, realizados éstos se procederá a la práctica de ambas manos.

— Mientras duren los ejercicios anteriores, se aprenderán teóricamente y de memoria las notas que hay hasta el cuarto casillero o traste y como están representadas en la música.

— Práctica de la escala cromática por los cuatro primeros casilleros o trastes.

(1)—Se recomendará la lectura de algún texto y para estos casos de iniciación el Método de Aguado, es muy sobrio en detalles, y de éste en donde el discípulo no comprendiese o el maestro disintiera a lo escrito, éste aclarará o explicará al respecto, teniendo presente que en estos casos nada es tan convincente para el iniciado si se le dá una oportuna y correcta explicación verbal.

Academia de Guitarra "Prat", preparatory article and 1st year course.

185

Translation of "Preparatorio"

"Preparatory"

"— Theoretical Preliminaries (1).

— How one must be seated and the use of the footstool for the left foot.

— Knowledge of the distinct parts that form the guitar for your use, to know: Body, Soundboard, Back, Soundhole, Sides, Neck, Fingerboard, Headstock, Gears, Pegs, Barres, Divisions, Frets, Bridge, Strings.

— Name of the strings and application in the figures of the corresponding notes that belong to it.

— Placement of the guitar — Of the right arm — Right hand — How to pluck the strings — Of the left arm — Left hand — How one must press the strings.

— How one must tune the strings.

— Preliminary Practices.

— Various exercises for the right hand alone, having done those one proceeds to practice with both hands.

While the previous exercises last, they will learn theoretically and by memory the notes that there are up to the fourth fret and how they are represented in the music.

— Practice the chromatic scale in the first four frets.

(1) The reading of some text will be recommended and for those cases of initiation the Método de Aguado (Aguado Method) is very sober in details, and of that in where the disciple doesn't understand or the maestro doesn't internalize what I write, this I will make clear or will explain to the respect, of having to point out in those cases nothing is quite convincing for the beginner as being given an opportune and correct verbal explanation."

First Year

"— Considering the school year of nine months and taking for granted those that are holidays and others that aren't their fault that they can't attend to give the lesson, the professor will have an average of eight months of teaching equivalent to seventy-four lessons, counting those twice a week.

— The development of the program of each year the maestro will do it according to the aptitudes of the disciple.

— To be able to give the exam the student must have approved minimally sixty four distinct things, pointing out the varied difficulty that those present, since in some cases they can give two or three things per lesson, and in others, an exercise or study, etc. will have to be employed over two to three lessons. The total en masse, can determine in improving the grade of the exam.

— For every year are exhibited a quantity of exercises, studies, etc., very superior demanding him to by the end that the maestro might have an ample field of action in the good of his student, electing the opportune.

— It remains unequivocally well clarified that, the placement of the distinct materials doesn't indicate that it must be done in the order that they are expressed, it will begin by that which one believes is suitable, and continuing the sprinkling of one or the other returning to previous ones or insisting in the same.

Notes to First Year:

Arpegios (Arpeggios):
Prat: Exercises I and II from Prat's edition: "*La Nueva Tecnica*". Pages 4 and 5 The 1st and 2nd Series of fingerings of the 1st formula to be ordered alternating with other lessons of different material.

Cejilla (Bars):
Prat: Exercise E. from Prat's edition: "*La Nueva Técnica*" to be done with bars ascending by half steps as indicated.

Aguado: — The six strings up to the twelfth fret by memory.
These are to be ordered in the last quarter of the year and by starting on the first fret. This shouldn't be a motive for interrupting the practical study."

— Al empezar el segundo año de estudio el alumno se sabrá de memoria las cuerdas hasta el doce casillero o traste. La prima toda.

— Se pondrá especial atención que dentro de la cantidad mínima de cosas a dar (sesenta y cuatro) se exigirá lo que se cree oportuno de cada materia (arpegios, acordes, ligados, etc.), siendo ésto imprescindible para estar preparado al examen.

— Con respecto a las 3as, 6as, 8as y 10as, que están anotadas, es claro, son a elección insistiendo en realizarlas en su mayoría si así conviniese.

— El párrafo anterior justifica para todos los años, la sobria cantidad de cosas en una materia determinada.

— Recuerdo se tenga presente el último párrafo de esta misma sección que se lee en el AÑO I°.

INTERVALOS

CARULLI — Método: páginas 31 a 33. Ejercicios 3as, 6as, 8as, 10as.

CARCASSI — Método pág. 59, 60. Ejercicios: 3as, 6as, 8as, 10as.

ZURFLU A. — Método: 2° libro (Cahier) pág. 11 a 13. Ejercicios 3as, 6as, 8as, 10as.

PRAT. — Cuaderno "Escalas y Arpegios" pág. 12. Escala cromática de 8as.

AGUADO — Método: pág. de 82 a 85. Ejercicios de 71 a 73 y de 76 al 78.

SOR-COSTE — Método: pág. 26 a 29. Ejercicios 3as, 6as.

SOR-COSTE — Método: Lecciones 6, 9, 13, 10, 27.

TARREGA. — Cuaderno "Escalas y Arpegios" de D. Prat, 3 Ejercicios páginas 14, 15.

CARULLI — Método 2° parte. Nos. 15, 17, 20, 24.

CARCASSI — Op. 60. Estudios 1, 6, 7.

CANO A. — Método Ejercicio N° 2 página 21.

ESCALAS

PRAT. — 1° Escala cromática hasta el doce casillero o traste por las seis cuerdas, página 8.

PRAT.—Mayores, hasta DO sostenido.

" — Cromática en 8as. Cuaderno de "Escalas y Arpegios", pág. 12.

ARPEGIOS

PRAT. — "La Nueva Técnica" Ejercicios III y IV.

PRAT. — C° "Escalas y Arpegios" Ej. y 11 for. pág. 13.

AGUADO — Método Ejercicios Nos. 15, 16, 17, 19.

CARCASSI — Op. 60 Est. 2, 3, 19.

CANO A. — Método Ej. 1 pág. 20.

RITMO

CARULLI — Método 2° parte N° 19.

ACORDES

AGUADO — Método Ej. 12.

PRAT. — "La Nueva Técnica" Ej. III y IV realizarlos en acordes de cuatro y cinco notas respectivamente.

CEJILLA

AGUADO — Método: Ej. 18.

LIGADOS

AGUADO — Método (Sección ligados) Ej. 6, 11, 16, 13. Se realizarán por las seis cuerdas y en los mismos casilleros que den en la prima y con los dedos 1-3 primero, y después 2-4.

VARIOS

AGUADO — Método: Ejercicios del 1 al 5, — 13. Lecciones N° 17. Método.

ARMONICOS NATURALES

AGUADO—Método: Consultar el gráfico y tabla de la página 54 y realizar de memoria el resumen-escala de la página 43 perteneciente al párrafo 184.

AGUADO — (Sección Lecciones) Método Nos. 25 a 36.

GIULIANI — Método 3° parte pág. 31 a 37. Ej. 4 al 10.

CARULLI — Método: Poco Allegretto-Andante. página 25.

CARCASSI — Op. 60 Est. 4-8.

ZURFLUH A. — Método 2° libro (Cahier) Ej. pág. 14.

PORTAMENTO (Arrastre)

Ejercicio preparatorio

Practicar con cada uno de los dedos 1, 2, 3, 4 respectivamente y en una sola cuerda, por ejemplo la cuarta trasladándose en cada uno de ellos del casillero 1° al 13 y continuando ascendiéndolo por semitonos o sea produciendo octavas.

GIULIANI — Método 3° parte. Ej. 11 página 38.

ZURFLU A. — Método 2° libro (Cahier). Ej. página 15.

AGUADO — Método Lección 35-36.

EXPRESION OBRAS

SOR — Minuetos Nos. 2, 3, 4, 11, de la recopilación "Sor 30 Minuetos" revisados por D. PRAT.

VISEO R. — (Método Sor-Coste) Minueto N°. 1.

PRAT. — "Recuerdos de Santiago del Estero" TRISTE.

" Album 3° de "10 PRELUDIOS" el PRELUDIO N° 1.

" Album 2° de "10 COMPOSICIONES" los ESTILOS Nos. 2 y 3.

" "El Carretero" (popular) ESTILO.

VIÑAS-(PRAT) — "Sueño".

TARREGA — "Adelita" Mazurca.

SANCHO — "Melodía Nocturna".

SIRERA J. — "Seguidillas".

PULGAR

AGUADO — Método Ejer. Nos. 6, 7, 8, 11, 20.

SOR-COSTE — Método Est. N° 23 página 11.

FIN del AÑO II°

Academia de Guitarra "Prat", 2nd year course.

Second Year

"—To begin the second year of study the student will know the strings by memory up to the twelfth fret.

— Special attention will have to be put that within the minimum of things to give (sixty-four) it will demand what is believed opportune of every material (arpeggios, chords, slurs, etc.) that being essential for the preparation of the examination.

— With respect to the 3rds, 6ths, octaves, and 10ths, that are annotated, it's clear, they are an elective insisting in doing them in their majority if so agreed.

— The previous paragraph justifies for all the years, the sober quantity of things in a specific material.

— Remember it might have to be pointed out the last paragraph of the same section as that in the First Year.

Notes to Second Year:

Escalas (Scales):
Prat: 1st chromatic scale up to the twelfth fret, on all six strings, page 8.

Acordes (Chords):
Prat: Prat's edition: "*La Nueva Tecnica*" Ex. III and IV to be done in chords of four or five notes respectively.

Ligados (Slurs):
Aguado: *Método* (Slur section) Ex. 6, 11, 16, 13. To be done on all six strings and in the same frets that they give in the first and with fingers 1-3 first and afterwards 2-4.

Portamento (Arrastre-Slide):
Preparatory exercise: To practice with every one of the fingers 1, 2, 3, 4 respectively and on only one string, for example to move the fourth on every one of them from the 1st to 13th fret and continuing ascending by half steps or producing octaves.

*Armonicos Naturales (*Natural Harmonics):
Aguado-*Método*: Consult the graph and table of page 54 and memorize the scale summary of page 43 pertaining to paragraph 184."

— Al empezar el año tercero se ordenará confeccionar la tabla completa de los equisonos, contando la guitarra en 19 casilleros o trastes, o sea veinte notas en cada cuerda. Tómese el modelo de la de Aguado, Lección 16 de su MÉTODO. Se retendrá bien de memoria la posición de los distintos equisonos.

— Téngase presente que en el mínimum de las sesenta y cuatro cosas a realizar intervengan todas las materias.

EJERCICIO COMPLEMENTARIO

CARCASSI — Método. Once ejercicios páginas 51 a 58. Práctica del conocimiento del diapasón en una posición determinada.

CARULLI — Método. Rondó pág. 38.

ZURFLUH A. — Método 2º libro (Cahier) páginas 5 a 10.

MEISSONNIER J. — Método páginas 35 a 58. El estudio final de cada página.

EJ. EXTENSION

AGUADO — Método capítulo 2º Ejer. 87

PRAT. — Cuaderno de "Escalas y Arpegios" pág. 14 el último, pág. 15 el segundo.

PRAT. — Album 1º de "10 Estudios". Scherzo pág. 8.

ESCALAS

PRAT. — Cuaderno de "Escalas y Arpegios". Conclusión de las mayores y todas las MENORES en la 1ª fórmula.

PRAT. — Del mismo Cuaderno: pág. 8, las dos escalas la una MAYOR y la otra MENOR. Estas dos escalas no deben de ordenarse seguidas.

PRAT — Del mismo cuaderno CROMATICAS 2º y 3º.

PORTAMENTO (Arrastre)

ZURFLUH A. — Método 2º libro (Cahier). Andante pág. 15.

PIZZICATO

Practíquese la 1ª Escala cromática por los cuatro primeros casilleros. Ejercicio 1º con el pulgar solo, Ejercicio 2º con los dos dedos i-m.

SOR-COSTE — Método. Estudio 6.

CARCASSI — Op. 60 Estudio 11.

VARIOS

SOR-COSTE — Método. Lecciones 17, 20, 24, 26.

SOR-COSTE — Método. Estudio 16.

CARCASSI — Op. 60. Est. 18, 20, 23.

MOLINO F.
AUBERY du BOULLEY } Recopilación por S. N. Contreras.
MEISSONNIER A.
FERÁNDIERE F.

De este cuaderno algún número a elección.

ARPEGIOS

PRAT. — Cuaderno "La Nueva Técnica" Ejercicio IIº, se procederá a su total desarrollo en sus Fórmulas, Dedeos y Ritmos. Ello se ordenará con cosas de otras materias.

CARCASSI — Op. 60. Est. 13-15.

SOR-COSTE — Método Est. 9-11.

ARMONICOS NATURALES

CARULLI — Método. 2 Ejerc. pág. 34

CASTELLACCI — Método. 5 Lecciones páginas 88-89.

CARCASSI — Método. Ejer. pág. 60.

SOR-COSTE — Método. Ej. 58, 58bis 57, páginas 40 a 42.

ARMONICOS OCTAVADOS SIMPLES

Práctica de la 1ª Cromática por los cuatro primeros casilleros ascendiendo y descendiendo. El dedo i, pisará armónicamente en la octava a realizar y el dedo ch (meñique) pulsará dicha cuerda.

ARMONICOS OCTAVADOS COMPUESTOS

Se pulsarán dos cuerdas simultáneas, una, la aguda, armónicamente y la otra, la grave en sonido natural. Practíquese la escala DO mayor (1ª fórmula) de la siguiente manera, en cada nota armónica que pulsa el dedo ch (meñique), el p. (pulgar) junto con aquel pulsará la VI cuerda al aire.

PULGAR

AGUADO — Método. Estudio 15.

CANO A. — Método. Ejercicio 12 página 15.

VIBRACION

De entre las materias de IIº y IIIº año se elegirá ejercicios oportunos para practicar en un solo dedo, o sea en una cuerda, después en dos, en tres, y cuatro, incluso en posiciones con cejilla.

PRAT. — Ejercicio para la vibración.

LIGADOS

AGUADO — Método. Capítulo IIº mano izquierda. Ejer. 26, 27, 28 (Nº 1) 29 a 31, 74, 79.

CARCASSI. Op. 60. Est. 9,10.

TARREGA — Preludio 9.

TRINO

CARULLI — Método. Capítulo 10. Ejer. página 26.

CASTELLACCI — Método. Ejercicios páginas 61-62.

CARCASSI — Método Ejer. último de la página 49.

AGUADO. — Método. Lección 27, técnicose los párrafos del 146 a 150 página 37. Practíquense los de pág. 50.

OBRAS, EXPRESION

SOR. — Recopilación "30 Minuetos" por D. PRAT, los números 13, 17, 26, 27, 29.

TARREGA — Lágrima — Pavana — Estudio a forma minueto — Preludios Nos. 1, 3, 5.

PRAT. — "Andante" armónicos naturales.

— "L'testament d'Amelia" Canción popular, para la práctica de armónicos naturales.

— "L'noy de la mare" Canción popular, para la práctica de armónicos octavados.

— Preludios Nos. 2, 3, 4, del Album 3º de (10 Preludios).

— Album de "Danzas y Cantos Argentinos" Nos. 1, 3, 5.

PAGANINI. N. — Op. 25 Sonatina.

FIN del AÑO IIIº

Academia de Guitarra "Prat", 3rd year course.

Third Year

"— To start the third year, you will prepare the complete table of the equivalent notes, counting 19 frets on the guitar, or twenty in every string. Take the model of that of Aguado, Lesson 16 in his *Método*. Retain well memorized the position of the distinct equivalents.

— It might have to be brought to attention that in the minimum of sixty-four things to be done all the materials might intervene.

Notes of the third year:
Ejercicio complementario (Complementary exercises):

Carcassi – *Metodo*. Eleven exercises pages 51 to 58. Practice the knowledge of the fingerboard in a specific position.

Pizzicato:

Practice the 1st Chromatic scale in the first four frets. Exercise 1 with the thumb alone, Exercise 2 with the fingers i-m.

Varios (Various):

From this music book select some number referring to the recompilation by Segundo N. Contreras of the works by F. Molino, Aubery de Boulley, A. Meissonnier, F. Ferandiere.

Arpegios (Arpeggios):

Prat: Prat's edition: "*La Nueva Tecnica*" Exercise II, it will proceed to its total development in its Formulas, Fingerings and Rhythms. E: It will be arranged with things from other materials.

Armonicos Octavados Simples (Simple Harmonic Octaves):

Practice the 1st Chromatic scale in the first four frets ascending and descending. The i (index) finger, will land on the harmonic of the octave and the ch (little-pinky finger) will pluck the said string.

Armonicos Octavados Compuestos (Compound Harmonic Octaves):

Two strings will be plucked simultaneously, one, the treble, harmonically and the other, the bass note in its natural sound. The C Major scale (1st formula) is to be practiced of the following manner, in every harmonic note that is plucked by the little finger, the thumb along with it will pluck the open sixth string.

Vibracion (Vibrato):

From among the materials of the 2nd and 3rd year you will select opportune exercises for practicing on one finger, that is to say on one string, after on two, three, and four, including in positions with a barre.

Prat: Exercise for the vibrato.

Obras, Expresion (Works, Expression):

Prat: "*L'testament d'Amelia*" Popular song, for the practice of natural harmonics. "*L'noy de la mare*" Popular song for the practice of harmonic octaves."

Año

— Considerando este año uno de los tramos más difíciles para el estudiante, en este curso se emplearán diez meses de enseñanza efectiva.

VARIOS

LEGNANI L. — Op. 250 "Seis Capriccetti" (a elección).

PRAT. — Cuaderno "La Nueva Técnica" Los Modelos Mayores, Menores y De Séptima.

PRAT — Círculo armónico 1° páginas 17 a 19.

CARCASSI — Op. 60 Est. 25.

SOR — Método. Est. 4.

COSTE N. — Op. 38. Est. 9, 10, 12, 13, 17, 18.

AGUADO — Método. Est. 23.

DAMAS T. — Op. "Amor paterno". Scherzo (Estudio).

CANO A. — Método. Est. 1 a 4-10.

ARPEGIOS

PRAT. — Cuaderno "La Nueva Técnica". Ejercicios III° y IV°, su total desarrollo. Téngase presente que se ordenará alternando con otras materias.

AGUADO — Método. Est. 7 al 10, 12 al 14.

SAGRERAS J. S. — Sonatinas 4-10.

ESCALAS

PRAT. — Cuaderno "Escalas y Arpegios" Cromática 4ª

ARMONICOS OCTAVADOS COMPUESTOS

PRAT. — Cuaderno "La Nueva Técnica" Ejer. II°, en acordes. Se pulsan tres cuerdas simultáneas, una armónicamente (la aguda) y las restantes sonido natural. El dedo i pisará armónicamente y el ch, (meñique) pulsará la cuerda (sonido extremo agudo) y los dedos m, y p, pulsarán las otras dos respectivamente de agudo a grave.

PRAT — C° "La Nueva Técnica" Ejer. III°, se realizará en acordes empleando los dedos p, m, a, ch, de grave a agudo. El i, pisará armónicamente en la misma forma que el ejercicio II°.

LIGADOS

CARCASSI. — Op. 60. Est. 21.

SOR-COSTTE — Método. Est. 18.

AGUADO — Método. Est. 16, 17, 25.

COSTE — Op. 38. Est. 11.

ARCAS-PRAT. — Cuaderno "1° Album de 10 Estudios" el estudio "La Mariposa".

EXPRESION

CARCASSI. — Op. 60 Est. 24.

FAGOT

SOR-PRAT — Op. 29 N° 15. Estudio.

PIZZICATO

SOR-COSTE — Método. Est. 5.

INTERVALOS

SOR-COSTE — Método. Est. 17.

PULGAR

SOR-COSTE — Método. Estudios 12-22

RITMO

SOR-COSTE.—Método. Est. 10, 13, 21.

MANO IZQUIERDA SOLA

PRAT. — Cuaderno "Escalas y Arpegios" 1° Escala cromática. Escalas Mayores y Menores, la 1° fórmula de éstas. Modo de realizarlas. Las notas que se hallen en cuerda libre en la dirección ascendente las realizará cualquier dedo que no tenga que pisar la nota inmediata. En los cambios de posición en dirección ascendente, o sea en la prima, hará la primera nota del cambio, el último dedo que realizó la última nota de la posición que se deja, resultando cuasi siempre que el 4 habrá la nota haciendo oír la que pisa el 1. Al descender resulta menos complicado por simplificarse la acción.

ARMONICOS NATURALES

SOR-PRAT. — Andante obligado de armónicos, (adaptación).

OBRAS

SOR. — De la Recopilación de "30 Minuetos de Sor" revisados por D. PRAT, los Nos. 5 al 10, 14, 19, 24, 25, 30.

PRAT. — Cuaderno "2° Album de 10 Composiciones" YARAVI 1°-2°.
—Album de "Danzas y Cantos Argentinos" Nos. 2, 4, 6.
—Danza Española N° 1.
—Canción popular "L'hereu Riera".

TARREGA. — Preludios 2, 3, 4, 7.
—Pizzicatto (Minueto).
—"Mazurca" (dos) en LA y en SOL.
—"Recuerdos de la Alhambra" (trémolo).
—"Gavota".

PEDRELL C. — "Guitarreo" Op. 121 N° 3 de G. A.

TORROBA F. MORENO — "Preludio" Op. 114 de G. A.

XOUDIS A.—"Barcarola" Op. 100 N° 1

FIN del AÑO IV°

Academia de Guitarra "Prat", 4th year course.

"— Considering this year one of the most difficult spans for the student, in this course ten months of actual teaching will be employed.

Notes of the fourth year:

Arpegios (Arpeggios)"

Prat: Prat's edition: "*La Nueva Tecnica*" Exercise III and IV, its total development. It might be pointed out that it would be arranged with other materials.

Armonicos Octavados Compuestos (Compound Harmonic Octaves):

Prat: Prat's edition: "*La Nueva Tecnica*" Exercise II, in chords. Three strings will be plucked simultaneously, one harmonically (the treble) and the remainder in natural sound. The i (index) finger will produce the note harmonically and the little finger will pluck the string (extreme treble sound) and the m and p fingers pluck the other two respectively the treble and the bass.

Prat: Prat's edition: "*La Nueva Tecnica*" Exercise III, to be done on chords employing the fingers p, m, a, ch, from the bass to the treble. The i finger will land harmonically in the same form as that of the exercise II.

(Note): The "ch" finger is known as the little or pinky finger. The ch stands for *chico* or small finger, it is also known as *menique* or auricular.

Mano izquierda sola (Left hand alone):

Prat: Prat's edition: "*Escalas y Arpegios*" 1st Chromatic scale. Major and minor scales, the 1st formula of them. The mode of doing them. The notes that are found on the open string in the ascending direction do them with whatever finger that you don't need to push the string. In changing the position in the ascending direction, or to say on the first, you will have the first note of the change, the last finger that played the last note of the position that was left, resulting almost always that the 4th will have the note making heard the landing of the 1st. To descend is consequently less complicated by the simplifying the action."

Año V°

— Se proseguirá en este año y hasta al fin de estudio empleando diez meses de lección, no interrumpiendo si así conviniese.

— Considerando este año de un trabajo superior no se medirán con exactitud las (64) sesenta y cuatro cosas anunciadas en años anteriores, pero se exijirá una extricta corrección en la forma.

ESCALAS
PRAT. — Cuaderno "Escalas y Arpegios". Todas las Mayores y Menores en sus fórmulas. En tiempo moderado y en forma de lectura.
" Cromáticas 5° y 6° con sus fórmulas
" Desarrollo de las fórmulas 2°, 3° y 4° de la 4° cromática.

INTERVALOS
SOR-COSTE. — Método. Est. 19. (sextas).

ARPEGIO
SOR-COSTE. — Método. Est. 23.
TARREGA. — Estudio "Sueño" (trémolo).

PULGAR
COSTE. — Op. 38. Est. 22.

LIGADOS
SOR-COSTE. — Método. Est. 20.
COSTE. — Op. 38. Est. 21.

VARIOS
COSTE. — Op. 38 Est. 8, 12, 15, 16, 19, 20, 25.
AGUADO — Método. Est. 26-27.
PRAT. — Cuaderno "1° Album de 10 Estudios" el N° 5 "La Campanella".
" Cuaderno "La Nueva Técnica".
" Continuación de los Círculos armónicos y concluir el Cuaderno.
SOR-COSTE. — Método. Est. 24-25.

ACORDES
SOR-COSTE. — Método. Est. 14.

OBRAS
SOR. — Recopilación de "30 Minuetos revisados por D. PRAT." Nos. 12, 15, 16, 18, 20 al 23, 28.

LABARRE T. — "Sonata" Op. 8 N° 2?
CALL L.-PRAT. — "Sonata".
ARCAS J. — "Polaca fantástica".
PARGA. — Op. 8 N° 1.
TARREGA. — "La Alborada".
" — "Danza Mora".
TORROBA F. MORENO. — "Fandanguillo" Op. 104 N° 1 G. A.
PRAT. — "Gran Jota" Variaciones.
" — "Danza Española N° 3".

BIBLIOGRAFIA (1)
Libros de lectura

Durante el período de estos cinco años el discípulo debe haberse compenetrado bien de los siguientes libros de texto, uno de los complementos básicos de su ilustración, sobre enseñanza: la guitarra y sus cultores.

LAVIGNAC A. "La Educación musical"
CONTRERAS S. N. "La Guitarra".
MUÑOZ R. "Historia de la guitarra".
PRAT D. "Diccionario de Guitarristas, ... (En prensa).

FIN del AÑO V°

Terminación del estudio obteniendo el título de Profesor Elemental.

(1) No se incluyen los siguientes libros "Los maestros de la Guitarra" de F. Buek, y "El Laud y la Guitarra" de Rita Brondi, por presentar el inconveniente de estar publicados en idioma alemán e italiano respectivamente.

Año VI° - VII°

CURSO AL
PROFESORADO SUPERIOR

— Para proseguir los estudios a fin de obtener el título de "Profesor Superior" el director de la enseñanza exijirá una rivalidá de los cinco años anteriores en la forma que él cree oportuna.

— Las obras anotadas en el curso de estos dos años, no se miden por su facilidad o dificultad, ellas se exijirán de memoria y con todos los detalles de expresión que cree deben hacerse según el criterio del que las enseña.

— Hago presente el desequilibrio que pueda existir, respecto a la calidad entre algunas de las obras anotadas, pues son impuestas aquí por el mismo fin que representan, o sea puestas al servicio de un vasto plan de enseñanza.

BACH J. S.
Obras varias. Originales del Laud.

LABARRE T.
"Sonata" Op. 8 N° 11 Moderato — Rondó.

MOLINO F.
"Sonata" Op. 6. N° 1.
Allegro — Andante — Rondó.

SOR.
Op. 3. "Thema y Variaciones".
Op. 5 N° 5 "Andante largo"
Op. 15 N° 2 "Sonata".
Op. 15 N° 4 "Introducción — Thema — Variaciones".
Op. 21 Sexta "Fantasía".
Op. 25 Segunda "Grand Sonata"

DIABELLI A.
"Tres Sonatas" (a elección).

REGONDI J.
Op. 23 "Introducción y Capricho".

CARULLI   (N° 40 G. A.)
"Sonata III°" Largo - - Allegro.

LEGNANI L.
Op. 20 "36 Caprichos" (Estudios).

MERTZ J. K.
Op. 13 N° 6.

AGUADO
Op. 2. "Rondó en LA"
Op. 16 "Fandango Variado".

ARCAS J.
Variaciones sobre un thema de SOR

PARGA.
"Fantasía" Alhambra.

TURINA
"Fandanguillo"

TORROBA F. MORENO.
"Serenata Burlesca".
"Sonatina" Allegretto — Andante — Allegro

CONCLUSION

TESIS — Presentar un trabajo original para la confección de programas de concierto, a base de obras originales y después empleando transcripciones.

Historiar la guitarra. Sus constructores notables, autores de su literatura y cultores que han habido.

TERMINACION AL PROGRAMA

Academia de Guitarra "Prat", 5th, 6th and 7th year courses.

"— It will continue this year and until the end of study employing ten months of lessons, not interrupting if it is to be convincing.

— Considering this year of superior practice they won't measure with exactness the sixty four things announced in the previous years, but a strict correction in the form will be demanded.

Notes for the fifth year

Escalas (Scales)

Prat: Prat's edition: "Scales and Arpeggios" All of the Major and minor scales in their formulas. In moderate tempo and in the form of reading.
Chromatic scales: 5th and 6th formulas
Development of the 2nd, 3rd and 4th formulas and the 4th chromatic scale.

Bibliografia (Bibliography) (1)

Books for reading

During the period of these five years the disciple must have read well the following books of text, one of the basic complements of its illustration, about teaching: the guitar and its proponents.

A. Lavignac "*La Educacion musical*"

Segundo N. Contreras "*La Guitarra*".

Ricardo Muñoz "*Historia de la Guitarra*".

Domingo Prat: "*Diccionario de Guitarristas*" (At the press)

End of Fifth Year

At the termination of the study obtaining the title of Elementary Professor.

(1) This doesn't include the following books "The guitar and its masters" *(Die Guitare und ihre Meister)* by Fritz Buek, and "The Lute and the Guitar" (*il Liuto e La Chitarra),* by Rita Brondi, pointing out the inconvenience of them being published in the idioms German and Italian, respectively."

"— To continue the studies to the end of obtaining the title of "Superior Professor" the director of the teaching will demand a review of the five previous years in the form he believes opportune.

— The annotated works in the course of these two years, aren't measured by the ease or difficulty, they will be demanded of memorization and with all the details of expression that is believed they must be done according to the criteria of what they show.

— I point out the imbalance that can exist, in respect to the equality among some of the works annotated, since they are the duty here by the same end they represent, or to say they are placed to service from a vast plan of teaching.

Conclusion

Thesis — Present an original work for the arrangement of concert programs, a base of original works and afterward employing transcriptions.

— Write the history of the guitar. Its notable constructors, authors of its literature and proponents that they have had."

Reglamento Interno de la Academia

1 — Inscripción abierta permanente.

2 — Hay dos clases de discípulos: "Incriptos al programa" y "Libres". Los primeros son los considerados a seguir la enseñanza bajo el Programa de Estudios, y los segundos como indica su nombre o sea sobre una convención mútua.

3 — El importe de la cuota es 20 $ mensuales, dos lecciones por semana y 15 $ mensuales, una lección por semana.

4 — El importe de la mensualidad es por adelantado debiendo realizarlo del 1 al 5 de cada mes.

5 — Se efectuará examen en cualquier época del año si está preparado el discípulo para ello.

6 — El tiempo a emplear en evacuar la lección lo determina el maestro, no accediendo de treinta minutos. La exijencia de más tiempo será bajo condiciones estipuladas de antemano.

7 — La no asistencia de cuatro lecciones consecutivas sin previo aviso se considera deslindado de la academia.

8 — Se abonarán 20 $ por derecho de examen para cada año que se efectue entregándole al discípulo un "Certificado de estudio" del año correspondiente.

9 — Después de haber rendido el quinto año se entregará el Diploma de "Profesor Elemental" abonando por este derecho 100 $ e ídem para "Profesor Superior". Los discípulos "Inscriptos" en este año no abonarán los derechos de examen.

10 — Los gastos que ocasionen la presentación de uno o más discípulos corren a cargo de los mismos.

11 — Se exxaminarán alumnos externos o sea de otros profesores siempre que puedan responder al mínimum de cosas de distintas materias exijidas en cada año del respectivo "Programa de Estudio". Los derechos de examen son 20 $.

12 — El discípulo "Inscripto", tiene el deber de asistir a las reuniones que se efectuen entre condiscípulos en el local de la Academia.

13 — Serán días feriados todos los que observa y declarase el Consejo Nacional de Educación.

EL DIRECTOR PROFESOR
DOMINGO PRAT

Buenos Aires, Marzo de 1931.

Academia de Guitarra "Prat", with rules of the academy and the graduated students, who now have setup their authentic satellite schools.

"1 — Inscription is open permanently.

2 — There are two classes of disciples: "Enrolled in the program" and "Free". The first are considered to follow the teaching under the Program of Studies, and the second as its name indicates or what might be about a mutual agreement.

3 — The cost is 20 pesos a month, two lessons a week and 15 pesos a month, one lesson a week.

4 — The payment of the month is to be paid in advance between the 1st and 5th of each month.

5 — You will have an examination in whatever epoch of the year and the student will be prepared for it.

6 — The time to employ in leaving the lesson shall be determined by the maestro, not agreeing to be thirty minutes. The demand of more time will be under conditions stipulated beforehand.

7 — The failure to attend four consecutive lessons without prior advisement is considered a drop out of the Academy.

8 — The subscription of 20 pesos for the right to an examination for every year that in effect will give the disciple a "Certificate of study" of the corresponding year.

9 — After having given the fifth year the Diploma of "Elementary Professor" will be awarded of this right by a subscription of 100 pesos and the same for the "Superior Professor". The "Inscripted" disciples in this year don't pay a subscription for the right of an examination.

10 — The expenses that arise for the presentation of one or more disciples will be charged of the same.

11 — They will examine external students or might be by other professors that can respond to the minimum of things of distinct materials demanded in every year of the respective "Program of Study". The rights for the examination are 20 pesos.

12 — The "Inscripted" disciple, has to attend the reunions that are among their fellow students held in the location of the Academy.

13 — There will be holidays that all observe and are declared by the National Council of Education.

The Director Professor Domingo Prat.
Buenos Aires, March of 1931."

This stamp is from the certificate of passing the examination of the Program of Studies (*Programa de Estudios)* of the Academia de Guitarra "Prat" on the following page. Domingo and his family moved to Haedo (Buenos Aires Province) in 1936 and lived at Libertad and Esmeralda.

The translation of the certificate is: "Having overcome the stipulated materials in the "Program of Studies" of the Academia with the previous examination, I certify that the <u>child Edgar A. Bosco</u> has obtained the grade of <u>sufficient</u> in the <u>preparatory</u> year of study. Buenos Aires, March 31, 1944. Signed: Professor Carmén Farré de Prat, Prof. R. Galla, Professor Examiner Francisco J. Delbene and The Director, Professor Domingo Prat."

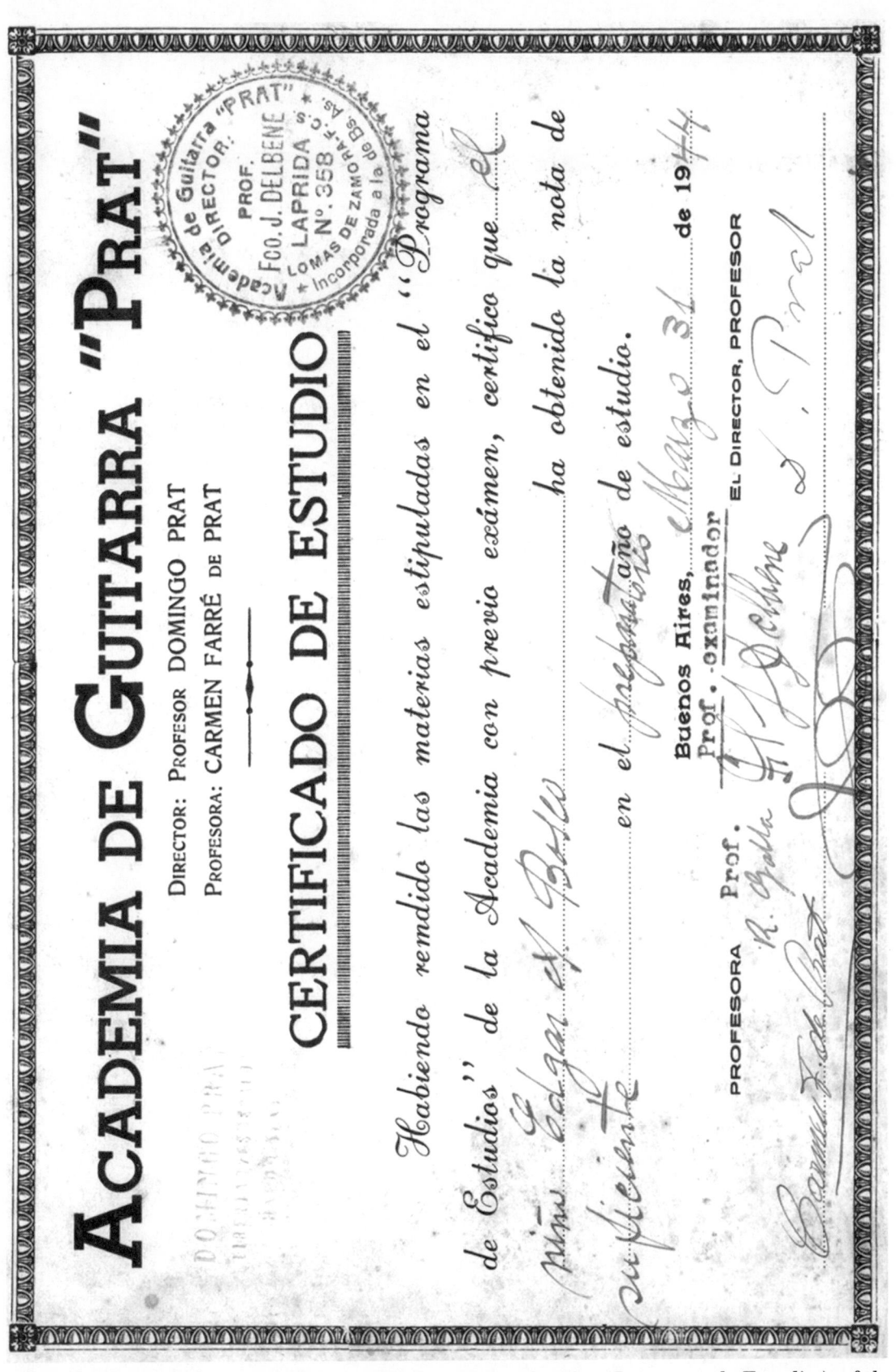

The certificate of passing the examination of the Program of Studies (*Programa de Estudios*) of the Academia de Guitarra "Prat". Edgar A. Bosco was a student of Francisco J. Delbene, a graduate of the Academia, who now had his own annex in Lomas de Zamora. (Buenos Aires Province) Domingo Prat died almost 8 months later on November 22, 1944.

This biography of Amilcar S. Verdier is translated from Ricardo Muñoz's unpublished book *"Historia Universal de la Guitarra"* Volume VII *"La Guitarra en La Argentina"*.

"Amilcar S. Verdier

His Origin:

He was born in Buenos Aires on the 16th of November of 1903.

Amilcar S. Verdier

His Education:

His father, a guitarist, without thinking, possibly, inculcated the passion in his son that he felt for the instrument. Confirming it, he contacted the maestro *Don* Domingo Prat in the year 1923, who gave him his diploma on the 6th of November of 1927.

His Virtuosity:

The quality of the student always distinguished him in his performances of the Academia de Guitarra Prat, affirming the prophecy of his maestro with agility, impeccable technique and noble expression of excellent sounds, which the public always awarded with emotion and congratulations.

In 1929 he offered a concert in the hall of the Damas Catolicas, *"La Prensa"* of the 16th of October delcared: 'His versions are clear and secure, thanks to his clean fingering...there is a musical expression in his performances that is brought to the audience and which constitutes in him the definition of a personality of precise features in his spiritual manifestations and in the form he reveals them.'

The musicologist, Carlos Vega, who attended the concert, said: '...he is an artist. A delicate temperament, a vast musical culture, exquisite taste,...magnificent sound...beauty and cleanliness in his playing and an admirable set of fingering that permits the expression with great richness and a variety of tones.'

He has given many other performances in the Capital and in the Province of Buenos Aires with real success, of the public that follows him, by the critics and knowledgeable.

His Pedagogy:

He is a professor at the Conservatories Williams, Baldasarri, Galvani, Nacional, and the director of his own Academia, incorporated in the center of Buenos Aires, he gives lessons to his students with the best skill and consideration."

Amilcar S. Verdier

Amilcar S. Verdier performed for the Asociacion Guitarristica Argentina as a part of a concert on Sunday June 23, 1940. This is from the *"Revista de la Guitarra"* magazine issue No. 5 *Año* II of May 1940.

IIIª PARTE

Minuetto	Sor
Estudio	Aguado
Mazurka	Wienavski
Romanza	Mendelssohn
Choros	Villalobos
Danza española	Granados

Guitarra: Sr. AMILCAR S. VERDIER.

This is from the *"Revista de la Guitarra"* magazine issue No. 6 *Año* II of June 1940. This performance was broadcast on L. R. 9 Radio Fenix in Buenos Aires on Saturday June 22, 1940 from 9:30 to 10:00PM. It was a part of the second cycle of the weekly radio programs presented in June by the Asociacion Guitarristica Argentina. Translation:

> En el último concierto radial de Junio actuó el concertista señor Amílcar S. Verdier, uno de los valores más sólidos del arte guitarrístico argentino, cerrándose así, con una figura tan ponderable, los programas radiales de Junio que como todos los que proseguirán transmitiéndose en la temporada, encierran loables propósitos culturales y de divulgación del instrumento nacional.

"In the last radio concert of June the concert guitarist Mr. Amilcar S. Verdier performed, he is one of the most solid values of the Argentine guitaristic art, closing in this way, with a figure so considerable, the radio programs of June like those continuing to be transmitted in the season, penned in the praiseworthy cultural purposes and the diffusion of the national instrument."

This biography of Ruth Ada Braceras is translated from Ricardo Muñoz's unpublished book *"Historia Universal de la Guitarra"* Volume VIII *"La Escuela Tárrega en La Argentina"*.

"Ruth Ada Braceras

Her Origin:

She is the daughter of the writer *Don* Guillermo Braceras and the schoolteacher *Doña* Joséfina Vedani, born in Castelar, Buenos Aires, the 22nd of October of 1931.

(Right) Ruth Ada Braceras 1951, one is from the original *"La Escuela Tárrega en La Argentina"* and the other from the xerox copy-all volumes have copies kept by the author.

Her Education:

She began her music studies in the Conservatorio Nacional de Musica y Arte Esencico, undertaking later a superior course with the famous maestros, Ginastera, Palma, Bettucci, Suffern, etc. —

On the guitar she initiated at the age of 7 with *Don* Domingo Prat, studies which she proceeded then to study with his daughter and finally in the Conservatorio Nacional with Maria Luisa Anido.

Her Virtuosity:

In the quality as a soloist she has performed on almost all of the radio stations of Buenos Aires and also in the cultural and social entities with great success.

The 10th of November of 1948 in the Sala de la Sociedad Argentina de Autores y Compositores de Musica she performed works by Bach, Haydn, Sor, San Sebastian, Llobet, Tárrega, Granados, Anido, Aguirre, Prat and Villa-Lobos, with the general approval of the public and knowledgeable ones.

For the Academia Argentina de la Guitarra, in the hall of the Teatro Cervantes, the 25th of June of 1949, in homage to Flag Day, she interpreted Farnaby, Bach, Mozart, Llobet, Granados, Malats, Anido, Prat and Muñoz; *"La Prensa"* reported the following day: '. . . she showed nice endowments as an interpreter and instrumentalist that was to be found in a full evolutionary process.' —

In the same hall on the 30th of August of the same year, in a duo with the guitarist Fanny A. Castro, they performed: *"Allemande"* by Bach-Muñoz; *"Minuetto"* by Beethoven-Muñoz; *"Romanza"* by Mendelssohn; and *"Minuetto"* by Bizet; '. . . with perfect spiritual fusion and correct expressive sonority.'

"La Prensa" August 31, 1949. —

The 12th of October of the same year and in the same hall, for the Academia Argentina de la Guitarra and sponsored by the Comision Nacional de Cultura, she performed solo in the 1st part of the program with works by Morales, Aguirre, Prat, Anido and Cassinelli; the 2nd part in a duo with the guitarist Fanny A. Castro, they interpreted: Torres, Sor, and Granados, being very acclaimed by the specialized public in the musical and guitaristic theme.

The 12th of October of 1949 she reappeared in the Sala Argentina of the Teatro Nacional Cervantes, performing and interesting program for the Academia Argentina de la Guitarra, that the next day "La Prensa" in this way commented: 'This new instrumentalist has evolved. . . . From the technical point of view, her playing is more confident and clearer and her sound has acquired the richest blended tones. As an interpreter her evolution is firmer still. . . . she has achieved interpretations of great flavor.'

Her maestro, Maria Luisa Anido has said: 'I consider Ruth Ada Braceras as one of the most promising figures of our guitaristic environment, by the outstanding abilities of performance beauty, ample and blended sonority and very especially, by her interesting musical personality, intense emotion, of exquisite sensibility, all of it united to extreme youthfulness.' "—

Comisión Nacional de Cultura

❖

Gran concierto en homenaje al

DIA DE LA RAZA

❖

SALA ARGENTINA
Teatro Nacional Cervantes
12 de octubre de 1949, a las 18.30

PROGRAMA

Palabras alusivas al acto por el señor Tesorero, Académico Dr. Don ANTONIO CASACUBERTA, quien en nombre de la Academia hará entrega del 1º y 2º premio, a los señores estudiantes ganadores del Primer Concurso de Guitarra organizado por la entidad.

I PARTE

Vidalita	MORALES
Triste Nº 5	AGUIRRE
Chacarera	PRAT
Canción Nº 4	ANIDO
Gato	Cassinelli

Guitarra sola por la Prof.
RUTH A. BRACERAS

II PARTE

Berceuse	TORRES
Souvenir de Rusia	SOR
Danza Española Nº 11	GRANADOS

Dúo de guitarras por las Profs.
Srtas. RUTH A. BRACERAS y FANNY CASTRO

Comisión Nacional de Cultura

Concierto de Guitarra de
RUTH BRACERAS

24 de junio de 1950
AÑO DEL LIBERTADOR GENERAL SAN MARTIN

SALA ARGENTINA
Teatro Nacional Cervantes
Libertad 815

PROGRAMA

I Parte

Sarabanda	BACH
Andante	HAYDN
Capriccio	ASIOLI DA REGGIO
Pavana	MILAN
Granada	ALBENIZ
Canción Mexicana	PONCE
Polka Paraguaya	ALLENDE
Choros	VILLALOBOS

II Parte

Estilo	PRAT
Triunfo	"
Canción de Cuna	ANIDO
El carretero	MUÑOZ
Milonga del árbol	WILLIAMS
Estío pampeano	FLEURY
Milonga del ayer	"
Pico blanco	"

This Ruth Braceras concert was held on June 24, 1950 at the Sala Argentina of the Teatro Cervantes sponsored by the Comision Nacional de Cultura for the Academia Argentina de la Guitarra. It's interesting to note she played "*Polka Paraguaya*" by Quirino Baez Allende and "*Estilo Pampeano*", "*Milonga del Ayer*" and "*Pico Blanco*" by Abel Fleury.

Archive: Ricardo Muñoz.

This biography of Marta Tejedor is translated from Ricardo Muñoz's unpublished book *"Historia Universal de la Guitarra"* Volume VII *"La Guitarra en La Argentina"*.

"Marta Tejedor

Her Origin:

She was born in Buenos Aires the 19th of November of 1919.

Marta Tejedor

Her Education:

In 1928 she began the guitar with the great Domingo Prat, who presented her in the capacity as a student in distinguished occasions, with a lot of happiness, to play to the public opinion and the journalistic critics judging with praise for her excellent abilities as an instrumentalist, on her interpretation of pages of de Visée, Bach, Sor, Aguado, Paganini, Brunner, Carcassi, Prat, Damas, Alegre, Tárrega, and Sirera.

Her Virtuosity:

After her performance on the 7th of September of 1932 in the Salon "La Argentina", *"La Prensa"* said: '...as to her technique it's secure and brilliant, she approaches all the major difficulties without effort and she conquered them with ease.' She performed with a guitar endowed with an amplifier created by her father, who pursued a better sonority on the instrument with this apparatus.

The 12th of September of 1934 she reappeared in the Salon of the Liga de las Damas Catolicas (Catholic Women's League), interpreting works by Sor, Tárrega, Schumann, Capella, Bickford, Llobet, Oyanguren, André, Suaznabar, Gazcon, and Prat. — Two years later we see her at the Salon "La Argentina" with a select program that was very much applauded and commented on by *"La Prensa"* who said: '...she has undoubtedly made progress; her dominion on the instrument is much better, her sound more ample and more varied, and her musical feeling clarifies her own profile....' "

On the IGRA web site at University of California at Northridge are the massive files of the virtuoso guitarist Vahdah Olcott-Bickford. In the correspondence section are 8 letters written from Marta Tejedor.

Marta Tejedor wrote to Vahdah Olcott-Bickford from 1932 to 1938. She mentions being poor, very poor several times in every other letter. She mentions about playing on 6 different Radio stations in Buenos Aires in 1934 — L.S. 4, L.S. 6, L.R. 9, L.R. 3, L.S. 5 and L.S. 9 in a letter is dated January 7, 1935.

She says her 2nd maestro was Leon Vicente Gascon, and goes on to mention her concerts were reviewed by the newspapers and magazines. She mentions about studying the 5 finger right hand exercises under the direction of Prat. It appears Prat was teaching the 5 finger system before his methodbook was published in 1929.

Marta talks a little about how she is now in the Sociedad de Guitarristas-this would be the Asociacion Guitarristas Argentinas, which was founded on August 26, 1934-just months before she's writing about it.

The most surprising letter is the last one from November 5, 1938, where she mentions having read inthe newspapers about the great alarm of the invasion of Martians in North America-referring to the "The War of the Worlds" Radio Program by H. G. Wells.

This biography of Eduardo Amestoy is translated from Ricardo Muñoz's unpublished book *"Historia Universal de la Guitarra"* Volume VII *"La Guitarra en La Argentina"*.

"Eduardo Amestoy

His Origin:

He was born in Buenos Aires on the 13th of October of 1890.

El profesor E. Amestoy con los alumnos que tomaron parte en el concierto

"The professor Eduardo Amestoy with the students that took part in the concert."

His Education:

In 1903 he began his guitaristic knowledge with the maestro Juan Froie, the following year and for a duration of three years he studied under the celebrated maestro *Don* Julio Sagreras. The military service interrupted his studies, but upon the finish of that engagement he restarted his studies with maestro *Don* Antonio Sinopoli, who by agreement gave him his diploma on the 30th of December of 1916.

His Virtuosity:

He made various performances with a flattering success.

His Pedagogy:

He gave himself completely to the art of teaching, and established his Academia Aguado, for which he published a method: *"Escalas y Arpejios Practicos para la independencia de los dedos"* ("Scales and Arpeggios for independence of the fingers"), which he utilizes for the efficiency of his classes of the distinguished students that attend.

For various consecutive years since 1927, he has presented in public in the Salon "La Argentina" groups of students and as well as soloists that distinguish themselves, such as Maria E. Barrientos, Ida Sitier, Maria J. Scorcelli, Maria E. Rawson, Mercedes Capace and others."

The photo from this biography is from a Buenos Aires daily and was utilized in Ricardo Muñoz's unpublished biography of the artist, a simlar photo of many of the same students was used in Ricardo Muñoz's *"Historia de la Guitarra"*, published in 1930.

Eduardo Amestoy's Method is listed in the 1931 Antigua Casa Nuñez catalog.

≡ Academia de Guitarra "D. AGUADO" ≡

El Director y Alumnos que intervendrán en el concierto que se celebrará el 1.o de Junio.

Esta academia, que dirige el profesor E. Amestoy, celebrará el 1° de junio, un concierto de alumnos, en el salón La Argentina, en el que tomarán parte las señoritas M. Scorcelli, I. Ballesteros, A. Silva, F. Radaelli y E. Resado: y los señores L. Pereyra, M. Chaves, J. Casares, J. Franchini y A. Rolando.

El programa está compuesto por obras de Sor, Cano, Mendelssohn, Carcassi, Tárrega, Haendel, Beethoven, Sirera, Coste, Haydn, Schumann y Aguado.

Creemos que en esta oportunidad el profesor Amestoy, conseguirá obtener un éxito artístico y de público.

• •

This is from the last publication of the *"Revista Musical Ilustrada "Tárrega"* magazine issue No. 33 of May 1927. The above photo was on page 314 in Ricardo Muñoz's book *"Historia de la Guitarra"*.

Translation:

"Academia de Guitarra Dionisio Aguado

Photo caption: The Director and Students who will intervine in the concert that they will celebrate the 1st of June."

This academy, whose director is Professor Eduardo Amestoy, will celebrate a student concert the 1st of June, in the Salon "La Argentina", in it the ladies who will take part: M. Scorcelli, I. Ballesteros, A. Silva, F. Radaelli and E. Resado; and the gentlemen: L. Pereyra, M. Chaves, J. Casares, J. Franchini and A. Rolando.

The program is comprised of works by Sor, Cano, Mendelssohn, Carcassi, Tárrega, Handel, Beethoven, Sirera, Coste, Haydn, Schumann and Aguado.

We believe in this opportunity Professor Amestoy, will obtain an artistic and public success."

Maria Luisa Anido in 1923, from the Hilarion Leloup *"Método Elemental para Guitarra"*. She became professor of guitar at the National Conservatory in Buenos Aires in the fall of 1942. This method was also endorsed by Miguel Llobet, with a copy of his letter, as well as typeset, for ease of reading.

This biography of Maria Esperanza Pascual Navas is translated from Ricardo Muñoz's unpublished book *"Historia Universal de la Guitarra" Volume VIII "La Escuela Tárrega en La Argentina"*.

"Maria Esperanza Pascual Navas

Her Origin:

She is the daughter of Mariano Pascual and *Doña* Anastacia Navas and was born on June 2, 1913 in Buenos Aires.

Maria Esperanza Pascual Navas

"For the guitarist and composer Mr. Ricardo Muñoz and family with admiration and fond affection."

Her Education:

She did her musical studies at the Instituto Musical Fontova and received her title professor of theory and *solfeggio* on December 6, 1925, at 12 years old, awarded with a medallion by the establishment.

In November of 1922 she began to study in Hilarion Leloup's Academia de Guitarra "Tárrega" and received her diploma on December 12, 1925. On November 18, 1926 she began to study in the Academia de Guitarra "Prat".

While still being a student her maestro had her participate in performances by students, that permitted her to begin to know the judgements by the critics then of an artist in formation; "La Opinion" the 19th of June of 1927, said: '... she unites great abilities and reveals as a promise in the sweet and difficult art of the traditional instrument.... the guitar rings tender, smooth, sweet and sad in the hands of the young girl performer ... we would never want — that guitar to stop sounding...'

This and other similar judgements now announced the flattering artistic future that was in store for the young girl, given the correctness of her admirable modern technique and the expression she stamped into the performances; with such a motive she enrolled to complete her musical education in the Conservatorio Nacional de Musica y Declamacion in 1931, and studied higher *solfeggio*, harmony, counterpoint, composition, history of the art and piano, finishing with the classification of outstanding.

Her Virtuosity:

She was presented to the public by maestro Prat the 25th of April of 1929 in the Salon "La Argentina" of Buenos Aires, interpreting works by Sor, Rubinstein, Kuhlau, Prat, Moreno Torroba, Laserna, etc. the critics reported: '. . . she revealed as a complete concert guitarist in the perfect dominion of the faculties of the sentiments and of the technique, indispensable to show that title to know to conserve it . . . It was definite by the praise of the brilliant triumph that conquered the public . . . and she added some numbers at the end of the program that she performed. . . .'

After some other concerts given in the city, she dedicated herself to composition, journalism and in teaching with general satisfaction. —

Her Compositions:

An outstanding musical composer of her instrument and of others, she has written ballets, symphonic poems, chamber music, choral, religious, pianistic, etc. well received by the public and the knowledgeable critics and journalists, works whose quantity will surely be augmented with time given her youth and the anxious inspiration of this author; we recall:

"Danza Incaica"   Unpublished
"Sarabanda"
"Cortejo de Vicuñas"
"El Cholo Pichitonga"
"Danza Orgiastica No. 2"
"Dos cantatas" for choral
"Cancion de Cuna" for three voices, obra (Work) Quicha
"Por un Poquito de Lluvia" for three voices
"Los Ankis Sagrados" (Indigenous work representing making fun of the bad spirits)
"La Piramide de Moche"
"La Rusta Korihuanca" for viola, oboe, female voice, cajons and guitar
"La Chulpa Imperial" dance of the weavers and potters, for piano
"La Vicuña Real"
The great critic *Don* Gaston O. Talamon, said: '. . . exceptional talent to the exclusive service of the Inca music, the mother of the music of our Continent.' —

Her Pedagogy:

In 1930 she took on the classes of the "Club Argentino de Mujeres" (Women's Club), whose students she presented annually; she gave lessons as well in the "Academia de al Asociacion Cultural de Flores", and in her own Academia Prat, incorporated, in which enrolled numerable students of firm technical and musical knowledge, such as the present professors Olga Soria, Marta Bramanti and others already presented in public and praised by the knowledgeable critics and local dailies. —

Her Poetry:

She was dedicated to poetry, with it she also made culture, writing her teachings in the newspapers for children and youth, a source of total energy and of the future, of her works we recall:

"Dientes Perlados" "Pearly Teeth"
—I—   —I—
  "Cuando sonria su boca   When you smile your mouth
de rosa,   that's red,
triunfan tus dientes perlados,   trumps your pearly teeth
nacarados,   pearly,

DIENTES PERLADOS

Cuando sonríe tu boca
de rosa,
triunfan tus dientes perlados,
nacarados,
y se escuchan dulces frases
musicales,
y se aspira el suave aroma
de tu boca.

Son tus frases melodiosas
y armoniosas;
tu sonrisa es de una virgen
soñadora,
y tu cuerpo de gallarda
figura de amor ideal,
como el de Venus de Milo

parece otra vez surgido
de las espumas del mar!

Oh, tus dientes nacarados
y perlados!
Como la nieve de blancos,
como los lirios de Abril.
Oh, la gloria de tus dientes
de marfil!

Eres una mujercita
fascinadora,
la de los dientes perlados
y sonrisa... engañadora.

María E. Pascual Navas.

This poem by Maria Esperanza Pascual Navas is from the *Revista Musical Ilustrada "Tárrega"* magazine issue No. 27 of October 1926. Translation (continuing from the previous page):

y se escuchan dulces frases,
musicales,
y se aspira el suave aroma
de tu boca. —

– II –
Son tus frases melodiosas
y armoniosas;
tu sonrisa es de una virgen
soñadora,
y tu cuerpo de gallarda
figura de amor ideal,
como el de Venus de Milo
parece otra vez surgido
de las espumas del mar!

– III –
Oh, tus dientes nacarados
y perlados!
Como le nieve de blancos,
como los lirios de Abril
Oh, la gloria de tus dientes
de marfil!

– IV– Eres una mujercita
fascinadora,
la de los dientes perlados
y sonrisa........ engañadora. —

and they hear sweet phrases,
that are musical,
and breathes the sweet scent
of your mouth. —

– II –
Your phrases are melodious
and harmonious;
your smile is of a virgin
dreamer,
and your body of a gallant
figure of ideal love
as that of Venus de Milo
it appears again emerged
from the foam of the sea!

– III–
Oh, your pearly teeth
pearled!
Like the white snow
like the Irises of April
Oh, the glory of your teeth
of ivory!

– IV– You are a little woman
fascinating,
and of the pearly teeth
and smile.......... deceiving. —"

Her Lectures:

We know the following given in Buenos Aires:

"Miguel Llobet"; (*Su vida y su obra*-His life and his work), given the 7th of August of 1938 in the Asociacion Guitarristica Argentina, with musical illustrations by the maestros *Don* Remigio Comba, Luis Guido Laurent, José Pla Bort, Roberto Soriano and phonograph recordings.

"Fernando Sor"; (*Su vida y su obra*-His life and his work), in the same institution the 23rd of July of 1939, illustrated on the guitar by Adolfina Raitzin, on the occasion of the Centennial of the death of the great guitarist.

"*Julián Aguirre y otros*"(Julián Aguirre and others); given in the same institution on the 24th of August of 1940 and musically illustrated by the professor Maria Herminia Antola de Gomez Crespo. —

(*La Guitarra y sus Compositoras*" (The Guitar and its Composers), given in the Club Oriental the 22nd of July of 1952, with guitaristic illustrations by her student Marta Bramanti. —

"Enrique Granados"; in the Asociacion Sinfonica Femenina on the 20th of April of 1953, illustrated by Diamela Molina Vedia, singer and accompanied by Adelina Dillet Ferrer and Neti Waiswain.

Her Honors:

She has been cited in the "*Enciclopedia de la Musica*", volume III, page 994, Jackson edition; equally in the book "*Arte y Cultura*" (My colleague, Alfredo Escande, went at my request to the Biblioteca Nacional in Montevideo in search of this book and it couldn't be found, so it's not certain if it exists or if it is a typographical error on the part of the author of this biography, Ricardo Muñoz.) of Montevideo,

Uruguay, on page 313; in the book "*Argentina Musical*"-1943 by O. Schiuma; by the maestro Prat in his "*Diccionario de Guitarristas*" and by Ricardo Muñoz in his "*Historia de la Guitarra*" in 1930, when she was a young girl and had recently begun.

She was the object of a homage by the "Asociacion Renacimiento", that took place on the "*Estacion Radiofonica Cultura*" (The Radio Station of Culture). —

The 25th of July of 1943, the "Asociacion Argentina de Musica de Camara", (Argentine Chamber Music Association) for her musical performances in the country, she was awarded a diploma with a special mention. —

She holds the position of Presidente de la Comision Artistica (President of the Artistic Commission) of the Asociacion Guitarristica Argentina. —"

This photo and article are from the *Revista Musical Ilustrada "Tárrega"* magazine issue No. 25 of August 1926. Translation:

"Maria Esperanza Pascual Navas

Miss Pascual Navas has been incorporated into the increasing numbers of professors of the guitar. She began her guitaristic studies in the Academia "Tárrega", which the Professor Hilarion Leloup directs, the 20th of November of 1922, she was distinguished by her perseverance in the study and by her natural qualities that permitted her to assimilate, the established courses, with total rapidity. The 12th of December of 1925 or to say three years later, she obtained the title of professor, conquering it with the highest classifications. By the indication as a professor and the desire to increase her musical studies she enrolled in the Instituto Fontova, on the 7th of September of 1923, receiving her title as professor of theory and solfeggio, the 9th of December of 1925.

Of a still undesignated date, she will be presented to the public by her Professor Hilarion Leloup, an opportunity that we await to know her artistic merits."

MARIA E. PASCUAL NAVAS

Se ha incorporado al crecido número de profesoras de guitarra, la señorita Pascual Navas. Inició sus estudios guitarrísticos en la Academia "Tárrega", que dirige el profesor Hilarión Leloup, el día 20 de Noviembre de 1922, distinguiéndose por su perseverancia en el estudio y por sus cualidades naturales que le permitieron asimilar con suma rapidez, los cursos reglamentarios. El día 12 de Diciembre de 1925 o sea tres años después, obtuvo el título de profesora, conquistándolo con las más altas clasificaciones. Por indicación de su profesor y a los efectos de robustecer sus estudios musicales, ingresó en el Instituto Musical Fontova, el día 7 de Septiembre de 1923, recibiéndose de profesora de teoría y solfeo, el día 9 de Diciembre de 1925.

En una fecha no designada todavía, será presentada al público por su profesor Hilarión Leloup, oportunidad que esperamos para conocer sus méritos artísticos.

This biography of Olga Soria is translated from Ricardo Muñoz's unpublished book *"Historia Universal de la Guitarra" Volume VIII "La Escuela Tárrega en La Argentina".*

"Olga Soria

Her Education:

She studied music and guitar with Maria E. Pascual Navas and was given a diploma in the year 1947.

Olga Soria

Her Virtuosity:

The 27th of June of 1948 she was presented in the hall of the *Exposicion de Historia y Arte religioso*, in a performance organized by the *"Polifonia"* magazine and in the 2nd part she interpreted an original page by her maestro, titled: *"La ñusta Kori Huanca"*, that the public celebrated insistently given the adequate expression stamped into this beautiful pentatonic page.

The 3rd of November of 1949 we see her in the hall of the Caja Nacional de Ahorro Postal performing works by Carulli, Labarre, Giuliani, Diabelli, Legnani, Coste, Prat, Pedrell, Villa-Lobos, and her maestro Navas.

Five days later she reappeared in the Centro de Musica del Consejo Britanico, performing for the Circulo Feminino Musical, in the first part of the program formed by *"Dos Pastorales, Andantino"* by Carulli; *"Pagina Romantica"* by Pedrell; *"Preludio"* by Villa-Lobos; *"Huaco Funerario y Danza Sagrada"* by Navas. — *"La Prensa"* the following day said: '... a good instrumentalist and praiseworthy interpreter ... she was very much applauded.'

In April of the year 1951 we find her in the Asociacion Guitarristica Entrerriana showing off her artistic and technical endowments, recognized by the gathering which, acclaimed her and obligated her to perform encores.

She gave other performances on the Radio that the elements of the ambiance always awarded her with affection and acceptance."

This biography of Marta Bramanti is translated from Ricardo Muñoz's unpublished book *"Historia Universal de la Guitarra"* Volume VIII *"La Escuela Tárrega en La Argentina"*.

"Marta Bramanti

Her Education:

She began on the guitar, the professor, composer and guitarist Maria E. Pascual Navas, who gave her a diploma in her opportunity when it was deserved, integrally formed her.

Her Virtuosity:

There have been several of her praised presentations on radio broadcasts, of which we recall the 28th of December of 1950 on L. R. 5 Radio Excelsior, in which she interpreted *"Andante"* by Call; *"Rondo"* by Kuffner; *"Romanza"* by Carulli; *"Marcha"* by Sor; *"Preludio"* by Tárrega; *"Triste"* by Prat and *"El Cholo Pichitanga"* by her maestro. — The radio broadcaster made public: 'Marta Bramanti belongs to a group of young players that honors our musical culture.'

The magazine *"Mundo Radial"* declared: '. . . . correct technical and artistic mediums permit her to anticipate a brilliant performance.' —

The 4th of February of 1952 we see her in the Circulo Feminino Musical Santa Cecilia by way of Radio del Estado L. R. A., interpreting works by her maestro; the following year in a duo with the pianist Elena Fischer performing; *"Andante"*, *"Allegro moderato"*, *"Andante con expression"*, *"Rondo"*, *Marcha Funebre"*, *"Allemande"*, *"Adagio"*, *"Marcha"*, *"Minuetto"*, *"Rondo Allegro"* by Diabelli, for the Asociacon Tárrega, with a lot of success and satisfaction.

As well she has performed obtaining a marked triumph for the Centro de Professores Egresados del Conservatorio Nacional de Musica."

From the archive of *Don* Eduardo Bensadon, he wrote down in pen (translated):
"L. R. A. Saturday August 25, 1951 at 1:35PM
The young Argentine concert guitarist: Marta Bramanti

1. Messonier – Siciliana
2. Carulli – Contradanza
3. Tárrega – 2 Preludes
4. Chavarri – Ritmo popular
5. Villa-Lobos – Choros
6. Broqua – Estilo
7. Pascual Navas – Cortejo de Vicuñas"

From the archive of *Don* Eduardo Bensadon, written in pen:
"L. R. A. Saturday August 25, 1951 at 1:35PM
The young Argentine concert guitarist: Marta Bramanti

In the "*L'arte Chitarrística*" magazine Volume 27 of May-June 1951, in the "*Notiziario Internazionale*" section is the listing of a performance on Radio del Estado by the duet of Marta R. Bramanti and Juan Antonio Sivori.

Archive: Ricardo Muñoz

Italian translation by Randy Osborne:

"Marta R. Bramanti and Juan Antonio Sivori are two young Argentine guitarists of Italian ethnicity, who are distinguished by the seriousness of the intentions that motivate them and for the mastering of the instrument. Recently they presented themselves at the microphones of the Radio del Estado for two beautiful broadcasts for which they have been very successful. The pieces for two guitars by De Call, Carulli, Tárrega, Torres, Prat, Luna and Pascual Navas were carried over the waves. Soon Mr. Sivori will make known to Argentine listeners some compositions by our eminent guitarist Maria Rita Brondi, hitherto almost unknown in South America."

— Marta R. Bramanti e Juan Antonio Sivori sono due giovani chitarristi argentini di origine italiana, che si distinguono per la serietà degli intendimenti che li animano e per la padronanza dello strumento. Recentemente essi si sono presentati ai microfoni della Radio del Estado per due belle trasmissioni che hanno avuto molto successo. Furono eseguiti pezzi per due chitarre di De Call, Carulli, Tarrega, Torres, Prat, Luna e Pascual Navas. Presto il Signor Sivori farà conoscere agli ascoltatori argentini alcune composizioni della nostra eminente chitarrista Maria Rita Brondi, finora quasi sconosciuta nel sudamerica.

"Pedro Antonio Iparraguirre — Argentine professor and composer for the guitar. He was born in Barracas al Sud, now Avellaneda, Buenos Aires Province on the 17th of January of the year 1879. Along with the fundamental studies of music he began with the violin, an instrument that later he abandoned to dedicated himself definitely to play the guitar, entrusting his teaching to Professor Luis Taquino, and for harmony and composition with maestro Ciccala. The personality of Iparraguirre is well known in Buenos Aires, where he has resided. We were far from imagining the numerous contribution that this author would give to the guitar, when he published his *Estilo, "El Pampeano" No. 2* of his production, that is dedicated to the *criollo* center "Los Pampeanos", of Avellaneda, today holding the record, according to catalogs of the production for guitar. He has reached the respectable number of 313 works, transcriptions being in its immense majority. Of course this abundant collection, published in less than two decades, hasn't succeeded in such a short time that the guitaristic ambiance can appreciate it in its full worth. Distinguished among them, the Argentine folkloric pieces, mainly some *"Variaciones sobre la Vidalita"*, shows well the eloquence of its originality, in which you can see the composer and the expert of the guitar. As didactic works these are known: "Escalas, arpegios y mecanismo tecnico" and *"10 Estudios diarios de mecanismo"*, well recommended for its end. As a pedagogue, he develops his activity in the Academia "Sors", of which he is the director, periodically making performances of students in his 7th performance on the 30th of July of 1931 in the Salon "Augusteo", where you could appreciate his work, as the teacher. (1931)

So ends the entry written for the *"Diccionario de Guitarristas"* by Domingo Prat.

In the *Revista Musical Ilustrada "Tárrega"* magazine issue No. 29 of December 1926 there was a review of a student concert. Translation:

Academia de Guitarra "Sors"

Monday the 27th of December, it was verified in the Salon "Augusteo", the announced concert by students, of the Academia de Guitarra "Sors" which is directed by Mr. Pedro Antonio Iparraguirre.

The program was in two parts; in the first the works of Sancho, Tárrega, Iparraguirre, Viñas and Sor, originals and transcriptions for this instrument were integrated. Individually the students Elena O. Alegre, Elvira Wilson, Silvano P. Oliva, Maria Angelica Funes, Delfina Rodríguez and Nicanor Iparraguirre intervened. To end the first part with a performance of *"El Pimpollo" Vals* by Iparraguirre, entrusted to a group of guitars. Its audience justifiably applauded this number, for the skillful interpretation.

In the second part the students Juan Falvo, Hilario Rodríguez, Maria Angelica Funes, Nicanor Iparraguirre, Delfina and Hilario Rodríguez and Manuel Rodríguez intervened, who respectively performed the works by Haydn, Tárrega and Iparraguirre.

The end of the program gave a presentation by a group of guitars comprised by the following students:

The Ladies: Delfina Rodríguez, Elvira Wilson, Elena O. Alegre, Maria A. Falco, the young girl Maria Angelica Funes.

The Gentlemen: Juan Cattaneo, Hilario Rodríguez, Juan Falvo, Manuel Rodríguez, Ernesto Wilson, Francisco Gaspar, Camilo Danon, Lorenzo Béttoli, the young boys Silvano P. Oliva and Nicanor Iparraguirre, who gave a pleasant version of the *"Gato Correntino"* by Quijano, gathering applause legitimately received. The director of the academia can feel satisfied, by the performance carried out by his students and by the favorable reception dispensed by the numerous public that attended."

Ricardo Muñoz included details of other compositions and performances not covered by Prat nor the *Revista Musical Ilustrada "Tárrega"* magazine in his biography of Pedro Antonio Iparraguirre.

This information is translated from the biography of Pedro Antonio Iparraguirre in Ricardo Muñoz's unpublished book *"Historia Universal de la Guitarra" Volume VII "La Guitarra en La Argentina"*.

Compositions:

He has written around 400 works for classical guitar, originals and transcriptions, danceable pieces and folkloric, whose details are the following: (with the publishers Ricordi, Nuñez, and his self-published works) they account for approximately 65 works, which can be classified by the following manner: *2 Danzas, 11 Zambas, 3 Chacareras, 3 Cuecas, 5 Tristes, 6 Estilos, 2 Pericons, 2 Gatos, 1 Jota, 2 Milongas, 1 Vidala, 11 Rancheras, 5 Variaciones, 5 Canciones, 1 Cielito, 3 Bailecitos* and *1 Himno.*

He also transcribed music of popular dances of the epoch, so extensive that in the previous case, he proceeded to create an interest in the same: *126 Tangos, 21 Valses, 15 Shimmys, 5 Foxtrots, 5 Paso Dobles, 4 Mazurkas, 3 Polkas, 3 Canciones, 1 Schottisch, 1 Habanera, 1 Estilo* and *1 Milonga.*

His Pedagogy:

He taught numerous students who, he presented annually in public, demonstrating the technical preparation of the same and his pedagogical scope; of those we recall the performance of his Academia de Guitarra "Sors" in homage of the national holiday taking place in the Salon "Augusteo" on the 23rd of May of 1928, in which 20 students took part, among them the present virtuoso Maria Angelica Funes, then a young girl, performing works of the maestro.

The act was repeated in the same hall on the 25th of April of 1930 with the performance of student soloists and in groups, of pages by Carulli, Viñas, Sancho, Coste, Tárrega, Sor, Schumann, of the maestro, etc. with equal success. —

These performances continued repeating including the 13th of July of 1939, on the occasion of the Centennial of the death of Fernando Sor, with the performance of student soloists and ensembles performing works by the maestro, among them Minuet Nos. 1-5-6 and 8, harmonized for two guitars by maestro Iparraguirre; and in this way successively until the voluntary disappearance of the latter.

For the modern technical preparation of his students, besides the methods of Aguado, Sor, Coste, etc. he employed the following:

"Escalas, arpegios y mecanismo tecnico" (Ricordi Edition) and *"10 Estudios diarios de mecanismo"*, by the same publisher; *"Técnica de la Guitarra y Escalas melodicas"* (Nuñez Edition); *"El Principiante, Lecciones Elementales"* by the same publisher; *"Evocacion"* concert study in tremolo" (Nuñez Edition). —

Also the following known methods: *"Método Carulli-Iparraguirre-Corregido, Digitado y Ordenado".* —

"Método Cano-Iparraguirre", Tratado de Armonia, Corregido y Aumentado. —

He was as distinguished as the other Argentine maestros, he published the method of Carrulli, saying he had to correct it, fingering it and put it in order with agreement of the modern school. To think of correcting Carulli, the father of the Italian school of the guitar, forms all audacity, the same as for referring to the treatise of Cano, that didn't need corrections, the technical values of these works, must be attributed to Carulli and likewise to Cano and no way to his pretending to correct them. As much as possible is that Iparraguirre has regularized the said methods adding only the fingering that corresponded in every case, a fundamental recourse of which embraced its origin, which he considers completely important of the works but doesn't qualify as a rectification of the same.

Pedro Antonio Iparraguirre committed suicide in Buenos Aires, on January 14, 1943."

This program of study for the Academia "Sor" is that from guitar historian Ricardo Muñoz's *Historia de la Guitarra*" pages 310-311.

First Year:

Carulli – Part 1.
Cano – First 10 lessons.
Aguado – First 15 lessons.
Iparraguirre – Major scales, 1st pattern.

Second Year:

Aguado – Lessons, Nos. 16-32.
Cano – Lessons, Nos. 11-15.
Cano – Chords in Major Keys.
Cano – Six studies for the right hand.
Iparraguirre – Minor scales, 1st pattern.
Iparraguirre – First chromatic scale, 3rd and 4th patterns.
Iparraguirre – Second chromatic scale.

Third Year:

Aguado – Second section, right hand studies, Nos. 1-10.
Cano – Chords in Minor Keys.
Aguado – Left hand studies, Nos. 1-30.
Cano – Six exercises for the left hand.
Aguado-Second section, Nos. 11-20.
Iparraguirre – Major scales, 2nd pattern.
Sor-Lessons, Nos. 17 and 24, first part.
Iparraguirre – Third chromatic scale, two patterns.
Iparraguirre – Technical exercises, 1st series.
Iparraguirre – Tremolo study.

Fourth Year:

Aguado – Left hand studies, Nos. 31-78.
Cano – Six exercises of medium difficulty (right hand).
Aguado – Wealth of the guitar-including harmonics.
Sor-Studies, Nos. 1, 5, 11, and 13.
Aguado – Third section, Nos. 1-4.
Iparraguirre – Minor scales, 2nd pattern
Iparraguirre – Technical exercises, 2nd series and barred arpeggios.
Iparraguirre – Fourth chromatic scale.

Fifth Year: Elementary professor

Cano – Six exercises of medium difficulty (left hand).
Aguado – Third section, Nos. 5-12.
Sor – Studies, Nos. 14, 18, 21 and 22.
Cano – Studies for both hands, Nos. 1-6.
Coste – Study No. 12.
Damas – Scherzo.
Iparraguirre – Major and minor scales, 3rd pattern.
Iparraguirre – Chromatic scales, diverse patterns.
Iparraguirre – Technical exercises, 3rd series.

Sixth year:

Aguado – Third section, Nos. 13-18.
Coste – Studies, Nos. 5, 6, 19, 20, and 22.
Aguado – Studies 23-27.
Tárrega – Technical exercises.
Iparraguirre – Technical exercises.

Seventh Year:

1) Selection of technical exercises of various authors.
2) Instruction of concert works."

(Left) Pedro A. Iparraguirre from a program of an unknown performance. This was included in the biography by Ricardo Muñoz.

(Upper Right) Pedro A. Iparraguirre from the *"Galeria de Concertistas y Profesionales"* in the 1931 Antigua Casa Nuñez catalog.

(Lower Right) Maria Angelica Funes 1924, at the age when she studied with maestro Pedro Antonio Iparraguirre.

Pedro A. Iparraguirre 1st and 5th pieces published by Francisco Nunez publication c. 1905.

Francisco Nunez publication 1910

Héctor Pirovano publication 1924

Pedro Antonio Iparraguirre was the most prolific composer in Buenos Aires, the Héctor Pirovano piece, *"Triste Entrerriano"*, is his 62nd published work.

This advertisement for Pedro Antonio Iparraguirre by his publisher Héctor Pirovano is from the *Revista Musical Ilustrada "Tárrega"* magazine issue No. 4 of September 1924.

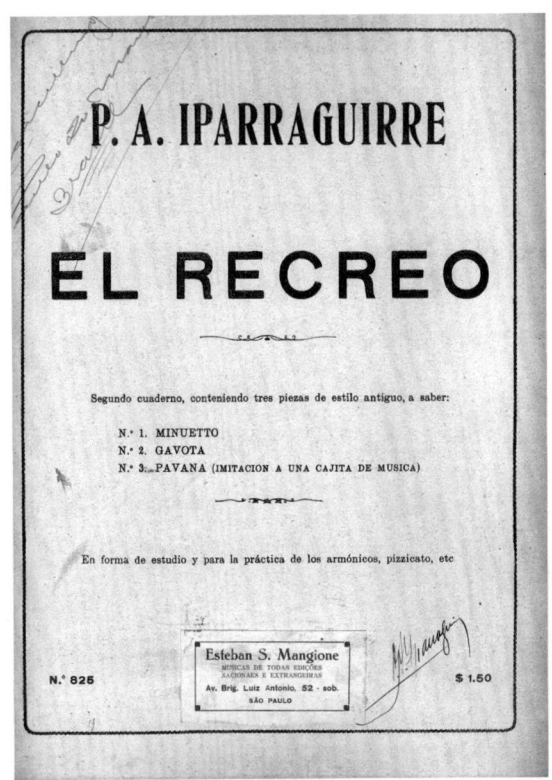

Pedro Antonio Iparraguirre pieces by his publishers Alfredo Perrotti and Hector Pirovano. *"Mate Amargo"* was recorded on Victor by Spina-Baudino.

"Antonio Sinopoli Scalpino was born in San Isidro, Buenos Aires province on October 14, 1878. At the age of twenty three a desire awoke in Antonio to play the guitar, without importance to him as to the sacrifices and without even thinking if the success could be achieved. He studied at the right time with the renowned Julio S. Sagreras in the Academia de Belles Artes, in Buenos Aires, subsidized by the government. As he progressed he eventually distinguished himself in his examination in that Acadamia in December of 1904, where he obtained the honorous qualification of "*Sobresaliente*" in the fourth year, being congratulated by the examiner with a merit for his vast preparation. He began teaching and along with his classmate Carlos Pellerano they opened, in 1907 a modest academia on Bartolomé Mitre and Montevideo streets. When Domingo Prat arrived in Buenos Aires, the professor Sinopoli encountered norms and works to adapt his respectable labor, that being an incentive to augment his love and passion toward the instrument. He performed his first solo concert in 1908 and then with his ex-maestro Julio S. Sagreras and with Domingo Prat repeated instances. He became independent of everything foreign to the ambiance of the guitar, and in 1910 he began to study harmony with the Catalan maestro of counterpoint, Enrique Morera. Antonio began to compose and brought to light some works of value. Sinopoli, by virtue of a sacrifice continued and a sentimental musician awoke within him and arrived in maturity as a concert guitarist, maestro and composer of very appreciated carats. His performance as professor is very distinguished and known; taking into account the very distinguished players that have received his advice, such as Angélica Villanueva Fontana, Petrona Alcira Betnaza, Faustino Riglos and many others that honor him.

His concerts of students that have taken place in the teatros Cervantes and Odeon, of this capital, is evidence of his laudatory labor as a teacher. Above all the one of November 30, 1932 in the Teatro Odeon, given by his consecratory characters for the guitarist Sinopoli and by the number of students that took part, forty-five. Remembering that on November 25, 1925 the Academia "Prat" gave a concert involving fifty-seven students. The presentation on the stage of the Sinopoli concert was filled by a group of harmonious and attention-drawing students, all dressed uniformly with an ambiance that reigned in the theater. As the last number of the concert, a good many of his students played the patriotic and vibrant "*Marcha de San Lorenzo*", which was received with great applause. In general it was a friendly reunion, select by the names of the participants and the audience, that was composed of the illustrious women of the Argentine society. The students that took part were: Elsa Giménez de Becco, Lucila Quesada Urquiza, Silvia and Nélida Perlender, Clelia Piola, Maria Martha de Olivera Saavedra, Elena Delfino, Martha and Anita Nicholson, Catalina Gallo Llorente, Pina Padula, Graciela and Susana Paglietino, Mercedes Bigand, Martha Malbran, Isabel and Clotilde Brea, Delfina Viton, Magdalena Obarrio, Rita Dodero, Julieta and Arminda Vanneli, Lia Marenco, Nelly Piola, Aida and Elsa Bonino, Noemi Rubio, Susana Becco, Maria W. Paris, Maria and Mercedes Marco, Clelia Forte, Beatriz and Perla Arostegui, Maria Angélica and Elena Molinuevo, Elvira Samyn, Julia E. Equia, Maria Arena, Iris Monsa, Alicia Irene Sinopoli, Eleonora and Laura Quesada Urquiza, Maria Esther de la Torre and Nydia L. Samyn.

The magazine "*Caras y Caretas*" No. 1786, that is published in Buenos Aires, concerned its social notes with three pages of photographs with the title "*La mujer argentina, cultora de la guitarra*". ("The Argentine woman, a proponent of the guitar" from December 24, 1932.) See page 153.

This maestro has published originals, some forty works, and the albums "*Ejercicios de escalas*" and "*Ejercicios tecnicos*". Some of his works have reached unique success, to be distinguished among those in the folklore of Argentina. Being as we have seen of a studious temperament and indefatigable, thanks to his experience and knowledge, he invented and patented a "*Modelo de guitarra Sinopoli*" (a mere copy of the double soundhole guitar made by Francisco Simplicio since 1929. The Barcelona guitarmaker and his son made eleven of these. R. O.), about which he tells us that he has 'conquered, in the measure of his efforts, a benefit of unquestionable worth'."

So ends the entry in Domingo Prat's "*Diccionario de Guitarristas*".

Carlos Torretta publication of an
Antonio Sinopoli transcription

Breyer Hermanos publication of
a "*Gato*" folkloric style piece.

Antonio Sinopoli

Romero & Fernández publication of an Antonio
Sinopoli transcription, and cover
of Academia Sinopoli.

The Academia Sinopoli was founded after Antonio Sinopoli renounced his position at the Academia de Guitarra "Tárrega" and was largely comprised of the most select and aristocratic families of Buenos Aires. From Ricardo Muñoz's book *"Historia de la Guitarra"* are transcribed three concerts. The first two have unverifiable locations.

"October 25, 1917

First Part:

1. Estudio Brillante – Alard
Danza Mora-Tárrega

Angélica Villanueva Fontana

2. Serenata – Malats
3. Nocturno No. 2 – Chopin
4. Sonata II, Bourré – J. S. Bach
5. Sevillanas – Albeniz
6. Alhambra – Parga
   a) Introduction and Adios Granada
   b) Aurora
   c) Arabesca
   d) Zambra moruna
   e) Serenata andaluza
   f) Parranda granadina and final

Maestro Antonio Sinopoli

Second part:

1. La colombe – Gounod
2. Andante – Haydn

Mariano Peralta and Ruben Machado

3. L'encouragement – Sor

Maestro Antonio Sinopoli and Mariano Peralta

4. Vidalitas – Sinopoli
5. Serenata Morisca – Chapi
6. Semiramide (fragments of the Symphony) – Rossini

Maestro Antonio Sinopoli, Mariano Peralta and Ruben Machado

Wednesday November 5, 1919

First Part:

1. Minuet in La – Sor
2. Danza Mora – Tárrega

performed by the youngster Arturo Massey

3. Estudio – B. D. de Urquiza
4. Estudio Brillante – Tárrega

5. Canzoneta – Mendelssohn
6. Capricho Arabe – Tárrega
7. Nocturno No. 2 – Chopin

Angélica Villanueva Fontana

8. Minuet – Mozart
9. Tremolo – Gottschalk

Mariano Peralta and Ruben Machado

Second Part:

1. O Matuto – M. Tupinamba
   Cancion Brasileña – A. Sinopoli

   Aires Nacionales

2. a) Milonga No. 2-Sinopoli
   b) La Guardia, zapateado sobre la Huella-Sinopoli
3. Rosa, estudio
4. Spanish Dance No. 5-Granados-Sinopoli
5. Spanish Dance No. 10-Granados-Sinopoli
6. Andante-Haydn (two guitars)
7. Vidalita-Sinopoli (three guitars)
8. Pericon-Sinopoli (three guitars)

Maestro Antonio Sinopoli, Mariano Peralta and Ruben Machado

En el Club Español

Señorita Petrona Alcira Betnaza, que dió un brillante concierto de música española ante una numerosa concurrencia.

Petronila Alcira Betnaza from the *"Caras y Caretas"* magazine of November 4, 1925, issue No. 1415.
Translation:
In the "Miss Petronila Alcira Betnaza, who gave a brilliant concert of Spanish music before a numerous audience."

November 28, 1924 in the Teatro Odeon

First Part:

1. Cancion de los Alpes – Sinopoli

performed by the youngsters Susana Paglietino Eyzoa and Andrés Adolfo Santas

2. Canzoneta – Mendelssohn

performed by the young Zulema Castro Cranwell

3. Danza Mora – Tárrega

performed by the young Edith Escurra

4. Capricho Arabe – Tárrega

Delia Rocha Grondona

5. Minuet – Sor
6. Alhambra – Parga
   a) Introduction and Adios Granada
   b) Aurora
   c) Arabesca
   d) Zambra moruna
   e) Serenata andaluza
   f) Parranda granadina and final
7. Gran Jota – Tárrega

Petronila Alcira Betnaza (right)

Second Part:

1. Cancion Indigena – Sinopoli

Mrs. Haydée Dhers Lecot and Blanquita Dhers,
Maria Christina Fox, Nélida Clara Mosto,
Elena Rosa Olivera, Nélida Ismenia Sinopoli,
and Nydia Dhers Rojas.

2. Gato Santigueño – Sinopoli

**Petronila Alcira Betnaza
(From *Historia de la Guitarra*
by Ricardo Muñoz, 1930.)**

Mrs. Haydée Dhers Lecot, Edith Escurra, Blanquita Dhers, Felicitas Smith Bunge, Nélida Clara Mosto, Elena Rosa Olivera, Susana Benedit.

3. Zamba Cecilia-Sinopoli

Mrs. Haydée Dhers Lecot, Mrs. Arminda de Alvarez Roldan, Blanquita Dhers, Edith Escurra, Nydia Dhers Rojas, Haydée Alberdi, Susana Benedit.

4. Zapateado sobre la Huella – Sinopoli

Laura Alberdi, Edith Escurra, Maria Elena Torres, Maria Esther Alberdi, Elena Rosa Olivera, Haydée Alberdi, Delia Rocha Grondona, Nina Villoldo, Raquel Alberdi.

5. Vidalita – Sinopoli

Laura Alberdi, Nina Villoldo, Raquel Alberdi, Maria Elena Torres, Maria Esther Alberdi, Haydée Alberdi, Delia Rocha Grondona.

6. Pericon por Maria-Antonio Podesta – Sinopoli

Arminda de Alvarez Roldan, Mrs. Haydée Dhers Lecot, Laura Alberdi, Petrona Alcira Betnaza, Maria Elena Torres, Maria Esther Alberdi, Felicitas Smith Bunge, Edith Escurra, Maria Christina Fox, Delia Rocha Grondona, Ana Maria Duhau, Nina Villoldo, Leonor Aphalo, Anita Adano, Blanquita Dhers, Susana Benedit, Nydia and Sarita Dhers Rojas, Carmen Apaolaza, Matilde Kelsey, Elena Rosa Olivera, Raquel Alberdi, Nélida Clara Mosto, Haydée Alberdi, Clarisa Boggio and Nélida Ismenia Sinopoli."

In the February 1929 issue No. 3 of *"O Violao"* magazine published in Sao Paulo, Brazil the guitarist, Oswaldo Soares, writes about a visit by Antonio Sinopoli. Portuguese translation by Randy Osborne

"O Violao" (The Guitar) in Sao Paulo"

"From our beloved representative in Sao Paulo, the competent professor Oswaldo Soares, we have the interesting article that we publish in the lines below.

By that we have an auspicious notice that we find in Sao Paulo, for the holidays, the famous professor and composer Antonio Sinopoli, whom the guitar owes, in a great part, by the great development achieved in Argentina.

Behold the article by Professor Oswaldo Soares:

Professor Antonio Sinopoli

He is in Sao Paulo, for the holidays, the eminent Professor Antonio Sinopoli, composer of distinguishedamong the modern musicians, who enrich the literature of the guitar.

He is residing, during his stay here, in the home of his brother-in-law the kind and amiable gentleman Mr. Angel Carrera.

Sinopoli, was already a friend. By our relationship, it were only of correspondence and data, and when, he launched his Aguado-Sinopoli method with great success, that was unquestionably a service of great utility to the lovers as well for the professors of the guitar. He unites in one volume, that which is necessary of various authors that exists, for the teaching of the guitar, respecting to serve the great work of Dionisio Aguado with admirable artistic sense!

"Maestro Antonio Sinopoli the professor more in evidence in Buenos Aires, by his elevated culture and profound knowledge of the art of teaching. He possesses a large repertoire wherein the most select and most difficult concert works are placed."

Sinopoli, a very cultured and professor of real worthiness, since he knows and rightly so, the guitar and all of its musical and historical literature; and justly by that, and as all the modern guitarists, a great admirer the mourned maestro who advanced our instrument — Tárrega.

In Buenos Aires, he is a professor who has proven by his talent to be a beloved creature.

The Argentine magazines —"*Caras y Caretas*" and "*Plus Ultra*", give us proof of this deserved feature, publishing beautiful photographic pages, of his frequent concerts, in which, a great number of his most advanced disciples take part, and that in the latest of these recitals (December) Mr. Sinopoli, included in the program, a Brazilian song, "*Cabocla Apaixonada*" by Marcello Tupinamba, I had promised him.

These concerts promoted and organized by Mr. Sinopoli, have taken the character of a true consecration to the guitar.

And by this, he counts on in Buenos Aires, with the decided and frank support of the literary, men of letters and journalists, who augment the diffusion and education and give preference to the guitar; therefore Sinopoli is a personality who will mark an epoch in living guitar.

And as naturally, the evolution of the guitar, has been advantageously driven by the surprising results obtained with the modern school of Tárrega, Sinopoli, intelligent as is, have followed that evolution as a modern musician, not only composing pages of like literature to reach everyone, as also smoothing the chore for beginners and students, creating a recreational and interesting mode utile for gymnastic work for the guitar, so much, I take that opportunity for mentioning, his works "*Escalas e Exercicios*" and "*Técnica en todos los tonos*".

The difficult exercises are, however, attenuated, by the rhythmic flavor of the well-chained phrases.

The results of these teachings give us complete and satisfactory demonstrations, by his most gentle and gracious daughter Miss Nelida.

To see and hear the guitar is a satisfaction.

The naturalness, ease and independence with that portal, even on stretches of difficult execution, the predicates that are soon to awaken the attention of those who hear. And I do not know why, the guitar, when played by lily hands, delicate and an agile young woman, and an instrument of incomparable suggestive power; and Nelida, leverages her technique with these gifts of exquisite guitar.

"Miss Nelida Sinopoli, the brilliant Argentine guitarist of exquisite technique and who, in various concerts, has performed with rare brilliance among others the pieces "*Bourée*" by Bach, "*Minueto*" by Schubert, "*Tremolo*" by Gottschalk and "*Sevillanas*" by Albeniz."

And what are these gifts of the guitar? I don't know. The guitar has some inexplicable enchantment. The likes of he who plays. The likes of those who hear. Everyone presents the reason to be of his or her preference. And for one, to its sweet and pleasant voice. For others, the romantic life that it has lived across two centuries, in our regal salons, or in the peasant's hut. For others, is it the companion of a moonlit night in which they sang ballads to someone?

Is it that, the guitar has its strength and its incontestable ascendancy, and especially when its strings are caressed by the most feminine delicacy?

Nights of unequivocal art, are those of a guitaristic reunion, in which our instrument, appears so dignified, in the hands of maestros.

Of his visit to Sao Paulo, I have enjoyed very much. Mr. Sinopoli, combines the qualities of a professor and delicate performer, a very communicative charm. Jovial and modest, his talk is invariably always about a subject that interests us: Music, guitarists and the Guitar.

Sao Paulo, February 3, 1929
Oswaldo Soares."

● Promovió una lucida ceremonia la consagración del enlace de **Alcira Betnaza** con **Enrique J. Daverio**. De izquierda a derecha: S. E. el presidente de la Nación, general **Pedro P. Ramírez**; **María Enriqueta Betnaza, María Inés Lobato Mulle de Ramírez**, esposa del primer magistrado; **María Elena Techera de Arruabarrena, Enrique Betnaza**, los contrayentes, **Celia Daverio de Moscatelli, Agustín Daverio, Ana Betnaza** y **Antonio M. Betnaza**.

This photo, dating from the 1930's, from an unknown daily, possibly "*La Nacion*", of Buenos Aires was found in Domingo Prat's unnumbered *Diccionario de Guitarristas* which had a green cloth cover, unlike all the 1,600 plus editions with the black engraved covers. I acquired this edition from my colleague, Matanya Ophee, who had acquired it from Blanca Prat in the 1990's. It contains Domingo Prat's notes written by hand. This volume was used to create the "Index of the *Diccionario de Guitarristas* by Domingo Prat written by Jan J. de Kloe and published by Editions Orphée.

The translation of the text is:

"They promoted a gracious ceremony for the consecration of the engagement of Alcira Betnaza with Enrique J. Daverio. From Left to Right: S. E. The president of "*La Nacion*", General Pedro P. Ramírez; Maria Enriqueta Betnaza, Maria Inés Lobato, Mulle de Ramírez. Wife of the first magissstrate; Maria Elena Techera de Arruabarrena, Enrique Betnaza, the contracting parties Celia Daverio de Moscatelli, Agustín Daverio, Ana Betnaza and Antonio M. Betnaza.

(Above) Academia Sinopoli that performed in the Teatro Odeon on November 28, 1924, this was the cover photo for the maestro Antonio Sinopoli's publication of "*Las Porteñas*".

(Below) Academia Sinopoli at the National Conservatory later in the 1920's. This photo was on page 313 in Ricardo Muñoz's book "*Historia de la Guitarra*".

Archive: Ricardo Muñoz

Señorita Edith Ezcurra. Señoritas Delia Rocha Grondona y Laura Alberdi. Señorita Alcira P. Betnaza.

Excelentes ejecutantas que tuvieron a su cargo números de música clásica, desempeñándose brillantemente.

En el teatro Odeón, las discípulas del profesor de guitarra, señor A. Sinópoli, dieron un concierto. Una numerosísima concurrencia premió con grandes aplausos la corrección y el arte de las señoritas que tomaron parte. La fotografía muestra el conjunto de guitarras que fué uno de los números más festejados.

FOTOS DE VARGAS.

This photo is from the *Caras y Caretas* magazine of December 6, 1924 issue No. 1366 *Año* XXVII.

"A notable performance of guitar"

Top caption: "The excellent performers who took classical music into their obligation and carried it out brilliantly."

Bottom caption: "In the Teatro Odeon, the disciples of the professor of guitar, Mr. Antonio Sinopoli, gave a concert. The numerous gathering awarded the good manners and the art of the ladies who took part with great applause. The photograph demonstrates the ensemble of guitar in one of their most lively numbers."

In the November 1926 issue No. 28 of the *"Revista Musical Ilustrada "Tárrega"* magazine was a review of a concert by the students of Antonio Sinopoli. Translation:

"Performance by the disciples of Professor Sinopoli

Before an overflowing audience in the Teatro Odeon on Thursday the 25th of November a performance organized by Professor Antonio Sinopoli took place.

The program was in two parts. It began with a *"Zamba"* and *"Gato"* by Sinopoli by the youngsters Delia Gluchlich Pietranera, Sebastian Casares and Ovidio Bolo.

Then Miss Nélida J. Sinopoli demonstrated her excellent abilities in the interpretation of two difficult preludes by Tárrega and the known *"Canzoneta"* by Mendelssohn.

Afterwhich simultaneously, Miss Sinopoli and Miss Angelica Villanueva Fontana, with an astonishing treatment of a tremolo.

The public awarded the performers, who had to play another piece, the difficult *"Estudio"* by Damas, getting, as well here, the sensation of a perfect unity.

The first part concluded with the popular *"Vidalita"* by Sinopoli, entrusted to a group of thirty guitars. The public demanded another work that was *"Chimango"*, by the same maestro.

The second part was entrusted to Petronila Alcira Betnaza. She is, without a doubt, the most advanced disciple of Professor Sinopoli and one of the most distinguished young girl guitarists. She played the *"Minuetto en Mi"* by Sor, *"Asturias"* and *"Danza No. 10"*, both pages translated with a lot of expression, and the *"Gran Jota"* by Tárrega that so many times we have mentioned in this column of reviews.

The performance ended with the *"Pericon Nacional"* correctly performed by a group of students. Again the public demanded works added to the program, and the disciples had to add *"Marcha de Ituzaingo"*.

In the intermission was a raffle among the students that took part and a beautiful concert guitar was donated by Casa Diego Gracia y Cia (Antigua Casa Nuñez). It was won by Miss Lolita Miralles Escudero."

(This review appears to be of the concert presented by *"Caras y Caretas"* magazine 2 months later, Sinopoli's student concerts were an annual event.")

Translation of the text on the next page of the January 1926 concert:

Top caption: "A group of students who took part in the great guitar concert taking place in the Teatro Odeon, being one of the most outstanding spectaculars of the moment."

"A note of bright artistic exponents is what we offer on this page, where as you can see the Argentine woman, renovating a beautiful racial tendency that has come saturating by poetry of time in time of the national legend, it has the fact of a cult of the famous guitar. The vibrant and hot verses sung by almost the majority of our payadors to the classic instrument they incorporate in this way in an eloquent form, and offer us the artistic emotion of performances so interesting as offered in the Odeon by the students of the professor of guitar, Mr. Antonio Sinopoli."

"Miss Petronila Alcira Betnaza, who the principal part of the program was entrusted to and carried it out brilliantly getting abundant applause."

"Misses Angélica Villanueva and Nélida Sinopoli, who performed the *Gran Tremolo* by Gottschalk."

VNA BELLA y NOTABLE

LA GUITARRA TIENE FERVIENTES Y EXIMIAS

Grupo de alumnas que tomaron parte en el gran concierto de guitarras efectuado en el Odeón,
siendo uno de los más salientes espectáculos del momento.

NOTA de claros exponentes artísticos es la que ofrecemos en esta página, donde se ve cómo la mujer argentina, renovando una bella tendencia racial que ha venido saturando de poesía de tiempo en tiempo la leyenda nacional, ha hecho un culto de la famosa guitarra. Las vibrantes y cálidas estrofas cantadas por casi la mayoría de nuestros vates al clásico instrumento se corporizan así en forma elocuente, y nos brindan la emoción artística de ejecuciones tan interesantes como la que ofrecieron en el Odeón las alumnas del profesor Antonio Sinópoli.

Señorita Petronila Alcira Betnaza, que tuvo a su cargo la parte principal del programa, desempeñándose brillantemente y cosechando nutridos aplausos.

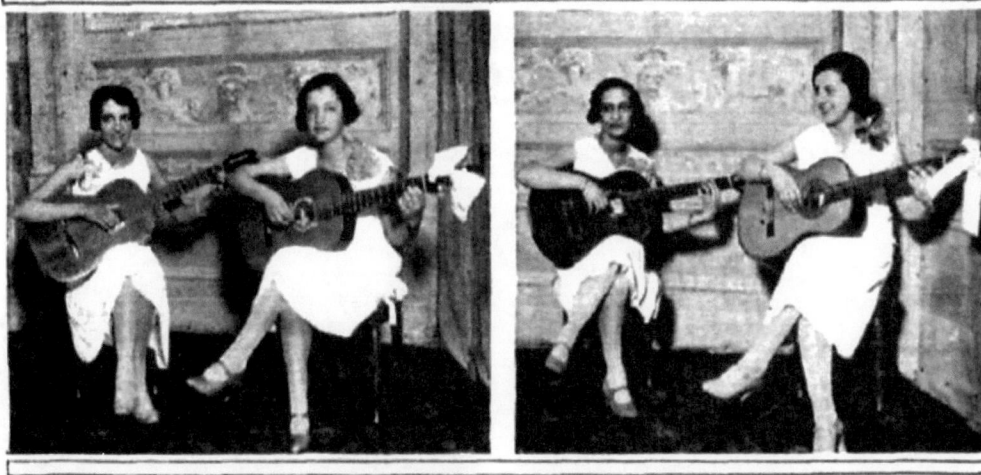

Señoritas Angélica Villanueva y Nélida Sinópoli, que ejecutaron el gran trémolo de Gottschalk.

Señoritas Carmen Josefina Apaolaza y María E. Alchourron.

Fotos de Vargas Machuca.

These photos are from the *Caras y Caretas* magazine of January 24, 1926 issue No. 1470 *Año* XXIX.
"A Beautiful and Notable Fiesta of Art."
"The Guitar has fervent and distinguished players in the girls of our society."

FIESTA DE ARTE

CULTORAS EN LAS NIÑAS DE NUESTRA SOCIEDAD

Señora Haydée Dhers de Lecot y señoritas Nélida C. Mosto, Margarita y

Lolita Miralles Escudero, Sara Mercedes del Castillo y Amanda Rocca.

Señora Arminda B. de Alvarez Roldán, señoritas Ofelia Berrutti y Dora,

Argentina y Ercilia Marta Winterburg.

Señoritas Alchourron, Mosoteguy Paglietino, Apaolaza y Winterburg.

Señoritas Miralles Escudero, de la Serna, Rocca, Sinópoli, Winterburg y Piola.

236

UN
NOTABLE
CONCIERTO
DE
GUITARRA

Señoritas Blanca Medina y Pina Padula, dos de las alumnas del profesor Antonio Sinópoli, que tuvieron destacada actuación en la audición de guitarra dada en el Cervantes.

Señoritas de Pagliostino y de Padula ataviadas con los mantones clásicos, insuperable nota de color.

Señorita Nélida Sinópoli, que interpretó magistralmente obras de Schubert, Bach, Albéniz y Gottschalk.

These photos are from the *Caras y Caretas* magazine of December 22, 1928 issue No. 1577 *Año* XXXI.

Aspecto que ofrecia el escenario del Cervantes con las alumnas del señor Sinópoli, que obtuvieron un rotundo éxito interpretando el pericón nacional.

Niñas de Guerrero Quesada y de Quesada Urquiza Anchorena.

Señoritas Lía, Dalma y María E. Seguí Dávila, que tomaron parte en diversos números del programa.

Interesante grupo de
alumnas que inter-
pretó la "Serenata Mo-
risca", de Chapí, trozo
musical inolvidable que

constituyó uno de los
números de conjunto
que más interesó al
selecto auditorio reu-
-ido en el Cervantes.

Guitarras y mantones, bellos ornamentos para
quienes — los lindos ojos caídos sobre la
caja, —entre rasgueo y rasgueo, dejaron fluir
hondas voces de la raza.

Translation of the photo captions to the 3 previous pages from the *Caras y Caretas* magazine of December 22, 1928 issue No. 1577 *Año* XXXI.

Page One:

"A notable guitar concert"

"Misses Blanca Medina and Pina Padua, two of the students of the Professor Antonio Sinopoli, who had distinguished performances in the guitar concert given in the Teatro Cervantes."

"Misses de Paglietino and de Padula dressed up in classic shawls, unsurpassable in color."

"Nélida Sinopoli, who interpreted masterfully works by Schubert, Bach, Albeniz and Gottschalk."

Page Two:

"A vantage point that was offered on the stage of the Teatro Cervantes with the students of Mr. Sinopoli, who obtained an emphatic success interpreting the *"Pericon Nacional"*."

"The daughters of Guerrero Quesada and de Quesada Urquiza Anchorena."

"Misses Lia, Dalma, and Maria E. Segui Davila, who took part in various numbers of the program."

Page Three:

"An interesting group of students who interpreted the *"Serenata Morisca"* by Chapi, unforgettable musical phrases that constituted one of the numbers of the ensemble which most interested the select audience gathered in the Teatro Cervantes."

"Guitars and shawls, beautiful ornaments for whom — the beautiful fallen eyes over the guitar body — between strum and strum, they let flow the deep voices of the remarkable."

(Right) Enlarged photo from the next concert spread.

Hermoso aspecto que ofrecía el escenario del teatro Odeón,

La mujer argentina,

El profesor Sinópoli con las señoritas María M. de Oliveira Saavedra, Marta Malbrán, Celia E. Forte y Alicia I. Sinópoli.

Señoritas de Rubio, de Piola, de Piola Cotman, de Bonino, de Perfender, de Bigaud, de Nicholson, de Arostegui, de Samyn, de Molinuevo y de Paglietino.

Señorita Nelly Piola Cotman, que interpretó piezas de notables compositores, siendo muy aplaudida.

durante una interesante audición dada recientemente.

cultora de la guitarra

Señoritas Julia Esther Eguia y María Arena, que actuaron interpretando interesantes piezas y arreglos.

Niñas que interpretaron "Serenata morisca", de Chapi - Sinópoli; "La Rinconada", de Sinópoli, y "El delantal de la china", de Pérez Freyre - Sinópoli.

Señorita Susana Becco, que integró varios conjuntos y que, como sus compañeras, actuó con éxito.

This is from *Cara y Caretas* magazine No. 1786 *Año* XXXV of December 24, 1932.

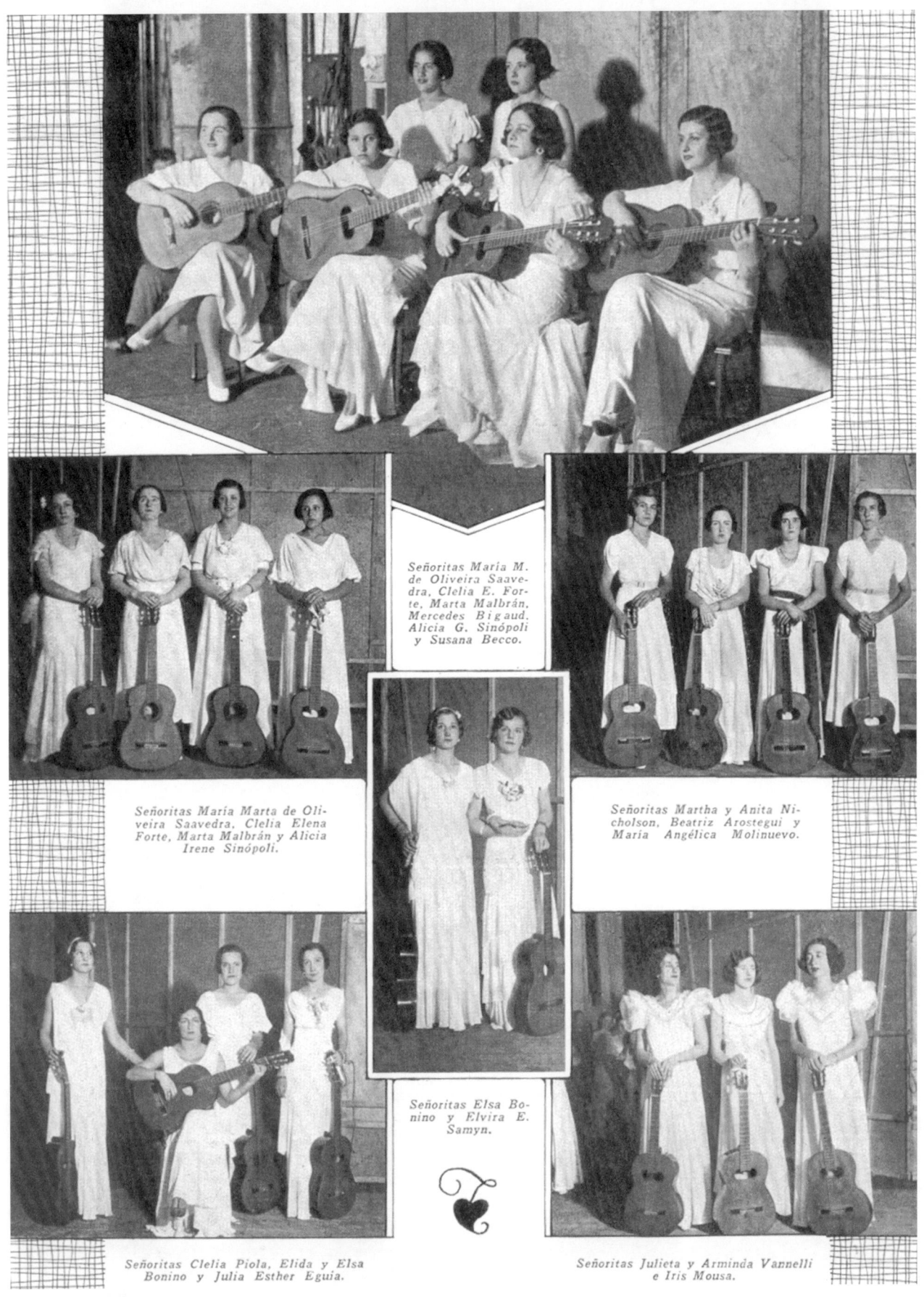

Señoritas María M. de Oliveira Saavedra, Clelia E. Forte, Marta Malbrán, Mercedes Bigaud, Alicia G. Sinópoli y Susana Becco.

Señoritas María Marta de Oliveira Saavedra, Clelia Elena Forte, Marta Malbrán y Alicia Irene Sinópoli.

Señoritas Martha y Anita Nicholson, Beatriz Arostegui y María Angélica Molinuevo.

Señoritas Elsa Bonino y Elvira E. Samyn.

Señoritas Clelia Piola, Elida y Elsa Bonino y Julia Esther Eguía.

Señoritas Julieta y Arminda Vannelli e Iris Mousa.

Of the 23 students, many used the Sinopoli guitar model with the expanded soundhole.

243

This early 1930s Victor recording is of well-known pieces by Antonio Sinopoli. His daughter, Nelida Ismenia, had performed in public with the Academia Sinopoli since the early 1920s.

This listing of *"Vidalita"* is from the *"Catalogo de Discos Victor 1932"* published in Buenos Aires, with a complete list up to January 1, 1932.

Vidalita—Vidalita (Guitarras) Antonio y Nélida Sinópoli| 47589 | 25 | 2.50

Nelida Ismenia Sinopoli — Distinguished Argentine guitarist performer, living in Buenos Aires. She was born in San Isidro in the Capital Federal. She was a student of her father, the notable professor of the same surname, whose solid teachings have made Miss Sinopoli a guitarist of praiseworthy endowments, proving them in the student concerts of her father. She plays pieces by Tárrega, the difficult *"Canzoneta"* by Mendelssohn and the no less difficult "Tremolo" by Gottschalk, being hotly applauded. Also we can appreciate her good qualities in *"Milonga No. 4, "Gato"* and *"Vidalita"* by A. Sinopoli, by the modern media of the recordings of two guitars.

So ends the entry in Domingo Prat's *"Diccionario de Guitarristas"*.

Nelida Ismenia Sinopoli de Lambertini passed away in August of 2010.

Antonio Sinopoli passed away in 1964.

(Right) Antonio Sinopoli at an advanced age.

(Left and Right) Pieces by Antonio Sinopoli that were published by Romero & Fernández and Francisco Nuñez. *"Recuerdos del Rio Lujan"* was the fourth piece Antonio Sinopoli presented to his publisher, Francisco Nuñez, c. 1908.

(Left) Francisco Nuñez publication of an Antonio Sinopoli piece.
(Right) One of the many Antonio Sinopoli pieces published by Breyer Hermanos.

PROGRAMA DE ORDEN PROGRESIVO PARA EL ESTUDIO DE LA GUITARRA

PRIMER AÑO
Primer Término

Método: Página 9-13.		Parte primera: Teórica y Práctica			Leer los capítulos del I al VIII y las lecciones 2ª y 3ª de la página 13.
„	„	14.	Escala Cromática nº 1		Léase la lección nº 4, pág. 15.
„	„	14.	Escala Diatónica nº 2		
„	„	14.	Lección nº 1	Sors —	
„	„	16.	„ „ 5	Aguado —	
„	„	1-2-3	....	„ —	Escalas diatónicas mayores y menores con sostenidos y bemoles. Una octava distribuyendo dos escalas, mayor y menor, por cada lección.
„	„	15.	id.	„ —	Aplíquese el mismo ejemplo para los dedos pulgar e índice que el de la lección 7 de la pág. 17.
„	„	15.	id. „ „	Carulli —	
„	„	15.	id. „ „	Cano —	
„	„	21.	id. „ „	Carulli —	
„	„	26.	id. „ 16	Aguado —	Tabla de los Equisonos.
„	„	16.	id. „ 6	„ —	
„	„	17.	id. „ 7	„ —	Aplíquese el equisono a esta lección.
„	„	17.	id. „ „	Carulli —	
„	„	19.	id. „ „	Cano —	
„	„	14.	id. „ 2	Sors —	
„	„	20.	id. „ „	Aguado —	
„	„	29.	id. „ 19	„ —	

PRIMER AÑO
Segundo Término

Método: Página 1-2-3	....			Escalas diatónicas mayores y menores con sostenidos y bemoles de dos octavas. Deben distribuirse igual que en el término anterior.
„	„	20.	Lección nº 9	Aguado — Trozo A. B. C.

NOTA: Aparte de este programa la Casa Ricordi Americana edita un "Suplemento al Método de guitarra", Aguado, que comprende algunas novedades de ejercicios de escalas y Arpegios con sus cadencias tonales. Además hay cinco ejercicios técnicos y algunas transcripciones de estudios que estimo de gran utilidad digital y musicalmente.

Translation of Antonio Sinopoli's *"Programa de Orden Progresivo para el Estudio de la Guitarra"*.

"Program of the Progressive Order of the Study of the Guitar

First Year
First Term

Method: Pages 9-13. First part: Theory and Practice...Read the chapters from I to VIII and the 2nd and 3rd lessons of page 13.

Page 14. To be read with lesson No. 4, page 15.

Pages 1-2-3. Major and minor diatonic scales with sharps and flats. Distributing two scales of one octave, major and minor, for every lesson.

Page 26. Lesson 16 Aguado — Table of positional note equivalents.

Page 17. The equivalents are to be applied to this lesson.

First Year
Second term

Method: Pages 1-2-3 Major and minor diatonic scales with sharps and flats of two octaves. These must be distributed the same as in the first term.

Page 20. Lesson No. 9 Aguado — Passage A. B. C.

Note: Apart from this program the Casa Ricordi Americana has published a *"Suplemento al Método para Guitarra"* (Supplement to the Method for guitar). Aguado, that included some novelties of exercises of scales and arpeggios with their tonal cadences. Besides there are five technical exercises and some transcriptions of studies that are of great digital and musical regard."

And from the next page (2 of the program):

"Method: Page 19. Lesson No. 9 Sor — The bass notes are to be sustained for their full value.

Final Works of the Term

Supplement: Page 27. Tárrega, Sinopoli

Second Year
First Term

Method: Pages 1-2-3. Major and minor diatonic scales with sharps of three octaves. These must be distributed to those in the previous term.

And from the next page (3 of the program):

Second Year
Second term

Method: Page 3. Major and minor diatonic scales with flats of three octaves. These must be distributed to those in the previous terms

Page 42-43. Lesson No. 41. To study the intervals of the second, minor, major and augmented. The chapter on them is to be read.

Page 52. Lesson No. 41. Practice the same intervals on the fingerboard in No. 1 and 2, letters A. B. C. D. E. F."

Método: Página 19.	Lección nº 9	Sors	— Sosténgase los bajos en todo su valor.
„ „ 22.	id. „ 10	Aguado	—
„ „ 18.	id. „ 1	„	—
„ „ 18.	id. „ 8	„	—
„ „ 23.	id. „ 11	„	—
„ „ 24.	id. „ 14	„	—
„ „ 18.	id. „ 2	„	—
„ „ 21.	id. „ „	Cano	—
„ „ 21.	id. „ „	Aguado	—
„ „ 68-69.	Ejercicio nº 19	„	—
„ „ 24.	Lección	Cano	—
„ „ 30.	id. Nº 20	Aguado	—
„ „ 61.	Ejercicio nº 10	„	—
„ „ 23.	Lección nº 12	„	—
„ „ 24.	id. „ 14	„	—
„ „ 25.	id. „ 15	„	—

OBRAS FINAL DE TERMINO

Suplemento: Página 27 .... **Tárrega** — Lágrima. Preludio.

Sinópoli — Canción de los Alpes.

SEGUNDO AÑO

Primer Término

Método: Página 1-2-3 .... Escalas diatónicas mayores y menores con sostenidos de tres octavas. Deben distribuirse todas éstas igual que en el término anterior.

„ „ 23.	Lección	Aguado	—
„ „ 70.	Ejercicios nº 1 al 5 ..	„	— Capítulo II, ejemplo del 1 al 4.
„ „ 28.	Lección nº 18	„	—
„ „ 25 y 26.	id.	Cano	—
„ „ 58.	Ejercicio nº 6	Aguado	—
„ „ 93.	Preludios nº 1-2-5-6 ..	„	—
„ „ 27.	Lección nº 17	„	—

Suplemento: Página 22. Ejercicio técnico nº 1 Tárrega —

Método: Página 31.	Lección	Sors	—
„ „ 4.	Escala Cromática nº 2	Aguado	—
„ „ 30.	Lección	Sors	—
„ „ 30.	id. nº 21	Aguado	—
„ „ 31.	id. „ 22	„	—
„ „ 29.	id.	Sors	—
„ „ 32.	id. nº 1	„	—

Método: Página 32.	Lección Nº 23	Aguado	—
„ „ 37.	id. „ 30	„	—
„ „ 65-66.	Ejercicio	Cano	—
„ „ 86.	id. nº 70	Aguado	—
„ „ 89-99.	Estudio nº 5	„	—
„ „ 25.	Lección	Sors	—

Suplemento: Página 28 .... **Sinópoli** — Estudio nº 1.

„ „ 30 .... **Sors** — Minuetto de la Sonata, op. 25.

„ „ 32 .... **Tárrega** — Preludio nº 8 y nº 11.

Schumann · Sinópoli — Paisano Alegre.

SEGUNDO AÑO

Segundo Término

Método:	Página 3.	....		Escalas diatónicas mayores y menores con bemoles de tres ostavas. Distribución de todas igual que las anteriores.	
,,	,, 28.	Ejercicio mano izqu. .	Aguado	—	
,,	,, 32.	Lección nº 2	Sors	—	
,,	,, 61.	Ejercicio nº 9	Aguado	—	
,,	,, 73-74.	id. ,, 6 al 12 ..	,,	—	
,,	,, 62.	Estudio	Sors	—	
,, •	,, 58.	Ejercicio nº 38	Aguado	—	
,,	,, 58.	id. ,, 1	,,	—	Sección Segunda — Capítulo I.
,,	,, 101.	Ejercicio, Arpegio y Cejilla			
Suplemento:	Página 22.	Ejercicio técnico nº 2	Tárrega	--	
Método:	Página 42-43.	Lección nº 41	,,	—	Estudiar los intervalos de la segunda, menor, mayor y aumentada. Léase el capítulo de éstas.
,,	,, 52.	id. ,, 41	,,	—	Práctica de los mismos intervalos sobre el diapasón nº 1 y 2, letras A. B. C. D E. F.
,,	,, 52.	id. ,, 21	Aguado	—	
,, •	,, 56.	Ejercicio nº 2	,,	—	
,,	,, 5.	Escala Cromática nº 3	,,	—	
,,	,, 57.	Ejercicio nº 3	,,	—	
,,	,, 81.	id. ,, 48 y 49 ..	,,	—	
,,	,, 39.	Lección nº 34	,,	—	
,,	,, 34.	id. ,, 25	,,	—	
,,	,, 61.	Ejercicio nº 11	,,	—	
,,	,, 81.	id. ,, 50	,,	—	
,,	,, 86-87.	id. ,, 71	,,	—	
Suplemento:	Página 33	....	Sors	—	Minuetto de la sonata op. 22.
,,	,, 36	....	Tárrega	—	Estudio en forma de Minuetto.
,,	,, 38-39	....	,,	—	Preludios nº 9 y 10.
			Schumann · Sinópoli	—	Reverie.

TERCER AÑO

Primer Término

Suplemento:	Página 3	....		Ejercicios de las escalas diatónicas de los tonos Do, Sol, Re y sus relativas menores melódicas, La, Mi, Si.	
,,	,, 15	....		Ejercicios de arpegios — Estudiar los mismos tonos de las escalas. Distribúyanse en este término en la siguiente forma: Una escala; una lección, un arpegio, otra lección.	
Método:	Página 62.	Ejercicio nº 13	Aguado	—	
,,	,, 86-87.	id. ,, 72	,,	—	
,,	,, 68.	id. ,, 18	,,	—	
,,	,, 34-35.	Lección nº 26	,,	—	
,,	,, 40.	id. ,, 35	,,	—	
,,	,, 43.	id. ,, 41	,,	—	Intervalos de 3as. y 4as. Léase el capítulo de éstos.

From the previous page (3 of the program):

Third Year
First Term

"Supplement: Page 3. Exercises of the diatonic scales in the keys of C, G, and D and their relative melodic minors in the keys of A, E and B.
      Page 15. Exercises of arpeggios — To study the same keys as the scales. The following forms are to be distributed in this term: One scale; one lesson, one arpeggio; another lesson.

Method: Page 43. Lesson No. 41. Intervals of 3rds and 4ths. The chapter on those is to be read.

From the next page (4 of the program):

Method: Page 52. Lesson No. 41. Aguado — Practice of the same intervals.
      Page 35. Lesson No. 66. Aguado — Exercise in sixths. Example No. 1 and No. 2.

Third Year
Second term

Supplement: Page 3. Exercise of diatonic scales in the keys of A, E, B, F sharp and their relative melodic minors F sharp, C sharp, G sharp, D sharp.
      Page 15. Exercises of arpeggios. To study those in the same keys as the scales. These are to be distributed among those from the previous term."

From the next page (5 of the program)

Method: Page 43. Lesson No. 41 — Intervals of 5ths and 6ths.
      Page 53. Lesson No. 41 — Practice of the same.

Fourth year
First Term

Supplement: Page 3. Exercises of diatonic scales in the keys of F, Bb, Eb and their relative melodic minors of D, G and C.
      Page 15. Exercises of arpeggios. To study the same keys as the scales. All these are to be distributed in the same manner as in the previous term.

Method: Page 43. Lesson No. 41 Aguado — Intervals of sevenths, octaves and tenths.
      Page 3. Lesson No. 41 Aguado — Practice the same intervals on the fingerboard.
      Page: 88. Exercise No. 75 Exercises in tenths."

From the next page (6 of the program)

Fourth Year
Second Term

"Supplement: Page 3. Exercises of diatonic scales in the keys of Ab, Db and their relative melodic minors of F and Bb.
      Page 15. Exercises of arpeggios. The same keys as the scales and all of them are to be distributed the same as the previous term.

Method: Page 55. Study Aguado — Practice and consequence of the harmonic octaves."

Método: Página 41.	Lección nº 37-38	Aguado	—	
„ „ 52.	id. „ 41	„	—	Práctica de los mismos intervalos.
„ „ 102.	Ejercicio nº 1	Sinópoli	—	
„ „ 36.	Lección nº 28	Aguado	—	
Suplemento: Página 22.	Ejercicio técnico nº 3	Tárrega	—	
Método: Página 93-94.	Preludios 7, 8 y 9 ...	Aguado	—	
„ „ 74-75.	Ejercicios nº 13 al 19 .	„	—	
„ „ 63.	id. „ 15	„	—	
„ „ 67.	id. „ 17	„	—	
„ „ 6.	Escala Cromática nº 4		—	
	Fórmulas 2-3-4		—	
„ „ 33.	Lección	Cano	—	
„ „ 81-82.	Ejercicios nº 51-52-53	Aguado	—	
„ „ 66.	id.	Cano	—	
„ „ 35.	Lección	Sors	—	
„ „ 87.	Ejercicio nº 73	Aguado	—	
Suplemento: Página 11.	Ejercicio sobre la es- cala en Do. 1ª fórmula	Sinópoli	—	
Método: Página 64.	Estudio nº 19	Carcassi	—	
„ „ 42.	Lección nº 39	Aguado	—	
„ „ 42.	id. „ 40-41	„	—	
„ „ 44.	id. „ 42	„	—	
„ „ 85.	Ejercicio nº 66	„	—	Ejercicio en sexta. Ejemplo nº 1 y nº 2.
„ „ 88.	id. „ 76-77 ...	„	—	
Suplemento: Página 39		Heller - Sinópoli	—	Estudio.
„ „ 42		Sors	—	Minuetto nº 4.
„ „ 43		Tárrega	—	Estudio de Campanellas.
„ „ 44		„	—	Preludio nº 6 y nº 12.
„ „ 44		„	—	Trémolo - Recuerdo de la Alhambra.

TERCER AÑO

Segundo Término

Suplemento: Página 3		Ejercicio de escalas diatónicas de los tonos La, Mi. Si, Fa sostenido y sus relativos menores melódicos Fa sostenido, Do sostenido, Sol sostenido, Re sostenido.
„ „ 15		Ejercicios de arpegios. Estudiar estos en los mismos tonos de las escalas. Distribúyanse igual que en el término anterior.

Método: Página 45.	Lección nº 43	Aguado	—
„ „ 46-47.	id. „ 44 y 45 .	„	—
„ „ 69.	Ejercicio nº 20	„	—
„ „ 60.	Lección	Sors	—
„ „ 76-77.	Ejercicio nº 20 al 26.	Aguado	—
„ „ 37.	Lección nº 29	„	—
„ „ 57.	Ejercicio nº 9	Sors	—
„ „ 102.	id. „ 2	Sinópoli	—
„ „ 65.	Estudio nº 3	Carcassi	—
Suplemento: Página 12.	Ejercicio sobre la es- cala de Do. 2ª fórmula	Sinópoli	—
„ „ 23.	Ejercicio técnico nº 4	Tárrega	—
Método: Página 33.	Lección nº 24	Aguado	—
„ „ 67.	Ejercicio nº 16	„	—
„ „ 47-48.	Lección nº 46-47	„	—
„ „ 36.	id. „ 27	„	—

Método: Página 59.   Lección ....   Sors —
  ,,   ,,   7.   Escala Cromática nº 5   Aguado —
  ,,   ,,   62.   Ejercicio nº 12 ......   ,,   —
  ,,   ,,   82.   id.   ,, 54-55 ...   ,,   —
  ,,   ,,   43.   Lección nº 41 ....   ,,   — Intervalos de 5ª y 6ª.
  ,,   ,,   53.   id.   ,, 41 ....   ,,   — Práctica de las mismas.
  ,,   ,, 105.   Estudio nº 9 ....   ,,   —
  ,,   ,,   97.   id.   ,, 2 ....   ,,   —
  ,,   ,,   94.   Preludios nº 10-11-12 .   ,,   —
  ,,   ,,   85.   Ejercicios nº 67-68 ...   ,,   —
  ,,   ,,   97.   Estudio nº 3 ....   ,,   —
  ,,   ,,   91.   Ejercicio nº 88 ......   ,,   —
  ,,   ,, 48-49. Lección nº 48 ....   ,,   —
  ,,   ,,   89.   Ejercicios nº 78-79 ...   ,,   —
  ,,   ,,   38.   Lección nº 32 ....   ,,   —

Suplemento: Página 45 ....   Sinópoli — Estudio nº 2.
  ,,   ,,   47 ....   Sors — Minuetto nº 5.
  ,,   ,, 48-49 ....   Tárrega — Preludio nº 1 y 2.
                                           Granados - Sinópoli — Danza nº 5.

CUARTO AÑO

Primer Término

Suplemento: Página 3 ....   Ejercicios de escalas diatónicas de los tonos de Fa,
                                            Si bemol, Mi bemol y sus relativos me-
                                            nores melódicos de Re, Sol y Do.
  ,,   ,, 15 ....   Ejercicios de Arpegios. Estudiar los mismos tonos de
                                            las escalas. Distribúyanse todas estas
                                            en el mismo modo que en el término
                                            anterior.

Método: Página 39.   Lección nº 33 ....   Aguado —
  ,,   ,, 82-83. Ejercicio nº 60-61-62 ..   ,,   —
  ,,   ,, 100.   Estudio nº 2 ....   Coste —
  ,,   ,, 77-78. Ejercicios nº 27 al 33.   Aguado —
  ,,   ,, 101.   Estudio nº 1 ....   Sors —
  ,,   ,, 43.   Lección nº 41 ....   Aguado — Intervalos de Séptimas, Octavas y Dé-
                                                          cimas.
  ,,   ,, 53.   id.   ,, 41 ......   ,,   — Practicar los mismos intervalos en el
                                                          diapasón.
  ,,   ,, 98.   Estudio nº 4 ....   ,,   —
  ,,   ,, 38.   Lección nº 31 ......   ,,   —
  ,,   ,, 96.   Estudio nº 1 ....   ,,   —
Suplemento: Página 12. Ejercicio sobre la es-
                      cala de Do. 3ª fórmula   Sinópoli —
Método: Página 103.   Estudio nº 7 ....   Aguado —
  ,,   ,,   51.   Lección nº 37. Ej. nº1-2 ,,   —
  ,,   ,,   41.   id.   ,, 36 ....   ,,   —
Suplemento: Página 23. Ejercicio nº 5 ....   Tárrega —
Método: Página 130-31. Estudio nº 26 ....   Aguado —
  ,,   ,,   94.   Preludio nº 13-14-15 ..   ,,   —
  ,,   ,,   63.   Estudio nº 1 ....   Coste —
  ,,   ,, 104.   id.   ,, 8 ....   Aguado —
  ,,   ,, 115.   id.   ,, 4 ....   Sors —
  ,,   ,, 114.   id.   ....   Dumás —
  ,,   ,,   54.   id.   nº 43   Aguado —
  ,,   ,,   88.   Ejercicio nº 75 ......   ,,   — Ejercicios en décimas.

252

Método: Página 49.   Lección nº 49 y 50 ...   Aguado —
  „   „   50.   Capítulo III ....   „   — Imitación Tambora.
  „   „   89-90. Ejercicio nº 80-81-82 .   „   —
Suplemento: Página 50 ....   Sinópoli — Estudio nº 3.
  „   „   52 ....   Sors — Preludio nº 6.
  „   „   53 ....   Tárrega — Preludio nº 5.
                                          „   — Sueño Trémolo.

CUARTO AÑO

Segundo Término

Suplemento: Página 3 ....   Ejercicios de escalas diatónicas de los tonos de La
                                            Bemol ,Re Bemol y sus relativos meno-
                                            res melódicas, Fa y Si bemol.

  „   „   15 ....   Ejercicios de Arpegios. Los mismos tonos de las es-
                                            calas y distribúyanse todos ellos igual
                                            que el término anterior.

Método: Página 106.   Esutdio nº 10 ....   Aguado —
  „   „   113.   id. „ 16 ....   „   —
  „   „   78-79. Ejercicios nº 34 al 39 .   „   —
  „   „   116.   Estudio nº 17 ....   „   —
  „   „   107.   id. „ 11 ....   „   —
  „   „   104-105. id. „ 2 ....   Cano —
  „   „   84.   Ejercicios nº 63-64-65 .   Aguado —
  „   „   55.   Estudio ....   „   Práctica y resultado de los armónicos octa-
                                                       vados.

  „   „   128-130. id.   nº 22 ....   Coste —
  „   „   122.   id. „ 21 ....   Aguado —
  „   „   108-109. id. „ 12 ....   „   —
Suplemento: Página 13. Ejercicio sobre la es-
                cala de Do. 4ª fórmula   Sinópoli —
Método: Página 36.   Ejercicio nº 69 ....   Aguado —
  „   „   51.   Ejemplo nº 13 ....   „   —
  „   „   126.   Estudio nº 24 ....   „   —
  „   „   95.   Preludios nº 16-17-18 .   „   —
  „   „   109.   Estudios nº 13 ......   „   —
  „   „   90.   Ejercicio 83-84-85 ...   „   —
  „   „   124.   Estudio nº 20 ....   Coste —
  „   „   126.   id. „ 23 ....   Aguado —
  „   „   87.   Ejercicio nº 74 ....   „   —
  „   „   120.   Estudio nº 10 ....   Cano —
  „   „   8.   Esc. Cromática Octav.   Aguado —
  „   „   106-107. Estudio nº 12 ....   Coste —
  „   „   92.   Ejercicio nº 90 ......   Aguado —
Suplemento: Página 54 ....   Alard - Tárrega — Estudio nº 2.
  „   „   58 ....   Sors — Minuetto nº 9.
  „   „   59 ....   Tárrega — Preludio nº 3.
                                            Granados - Sinópoli — Danza nº 10.

QUINTO AÑO
Primer Término

Suplemento .... Repaso de todos los ejercicios de las escalas mayores y menores y de los arpegios. Distribúyanse en la forma siguiente. Un día ejercítese las escalas mayores y menores con sostenidos, el otro día todas las mayores y menores con bemoles. Este repaso diario hágase durante el transcurso de este término. Repetir todos los ejercicios de arpegios con la misma distribución para su repaso e igual que el de las escalas.

Método: Página 110-111.	Estudio nº 23	Sors —	
,, ,, 80.	Ejercicios nº 41 al 47.	Aguado —	
,, ,, 112.	Estudio nº 14	,, —	
,, ,, 112-113.	id. ,, 15	,, —	
,, ,, 117.	id. ,, 18	,, —	
,, ,, 127.	id. ,, 25	,, —	
,, ,, 115.	id. ,, 14	Sors —	
,, ,, 121.	id. ,, 20	Aguado —	
,, ,, 95.	Preludio nº 19 y 20 ..	,, —	
,, ,, 50.	Capítulo III	,, —	Imitaciones a Trompeta y Arpa.
,, ,, 118.	Estudio nº 18	Coste —	
Suplemento: Página 14.	Ejercicio sobre la escala de Do. 5ª fórmula	Sinópoli —	
,, ,, 63.	Estudio nº 4	Aguado —	
Método: Página 95.	Preludio nº 21-22	,, —	
,, ,, 90-91.	Ejercicio nº 86-87	,, —	
,, ,, 92.	Ejercicio nº 89	,, —	
,, ,, 123.	Estudio nº 22	,, —	
,, ,, 51.	Ejemplo nº 3	,, —	
,, ,, 132-133.	Estudio nº 27	,, —	
Suplemento: Página 60		Bach - Sinópoli — Courante.	
,, ,, 64		Sors — Minuetto nº 10.	
,, ,, 65		Tárrega — Preludio nº 7.	
		Chopin - Tárrega — Nocturno nº 2.	

QUINTO AÑO
Segundo Término

Suplemento: Página 66	Cramer - Tárrega — Estudio nº 13.
Método: Páginas 134 al 139	Aguado — Rondó en La.
Suplemento: Página 68	Tárrega — Estudio de concierto.
,, ,, 69	Vieuxtemps - Tárrega — Preludio nº 4.
	Bach - Tárrega — Tiempo de Bourré de la Sonata 2ª.
	Parga — Alhambra - Fantasía.

OBRAS DE CONCURSO PARA OBTENER EL PREMIO ESTIMULO
Sors — Gran Sonata op. 25.
Paganini - Tárrega — Variaciones sobre el "Carnaval de Venecia".

Estas dos obras deben aprenderse después de haber terminado el 5º año, 2º término y de haber obtenido el título de profesor. Su estudio detenido comprenderá el plazo de un año y su ejecución se hará cuando el alumno así lo desee, quien debe avisar con tiempo a los fines de fijar la fecha para la reunión del Jurado de la Institución que pertenezca.

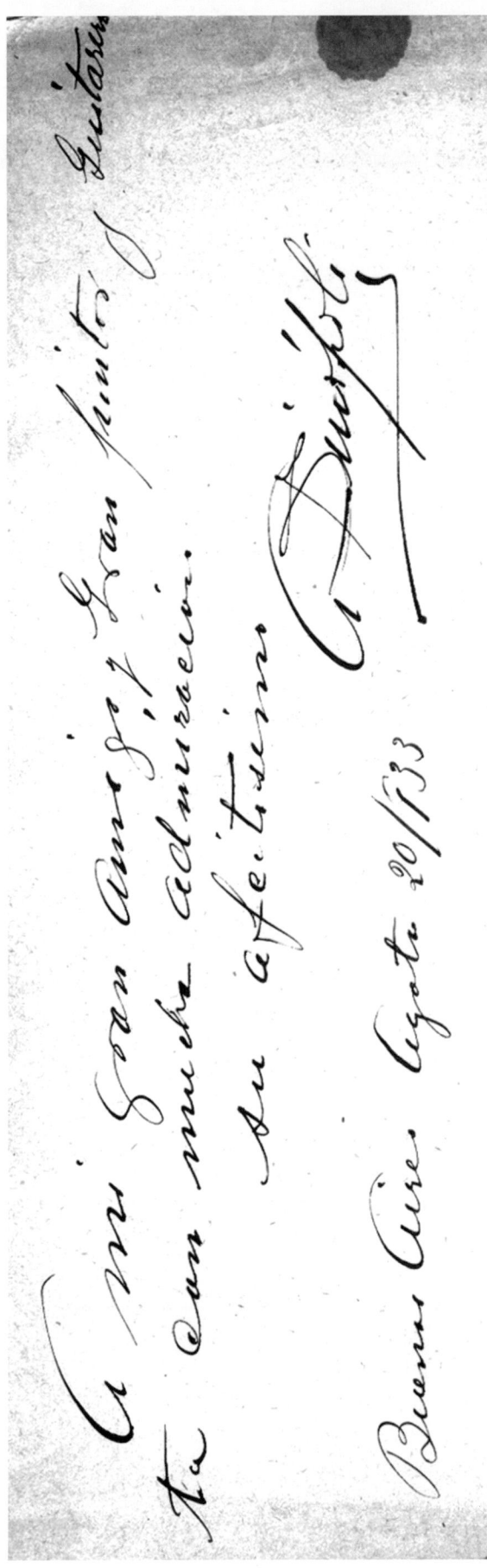

Antonio Sinópoli

SUPLEMENTO
AL
METODO PARA GUITARRA
DE
AGUADO · SINOPOLI

1932
G. RICORDI E C. · EDITORES · IMPRESORES
BUENOS AIRES

B A. 6712 $ 5.—

Antonio Sinopoli's Supplement to his Method.
It was published by Ricordi in 1932. To the left is an
autographed dedication to a great painter in Paris who
is unnamed: "To my great friend and Great painter and
Guitarist with much admiration. Yours affectionately,
Antonio Sinopoli, Buenos Aires. August 20, 1933".

From the previous page (7 of the program):"Fifth
Year First Term Supplement Review all of the exercises
of the major and minor scales and of the arpeggios.
These are to be distributed in the following form. One
day the major and minor scales with the sharps are to
be exercised, and the next day all of the major and
minor scales with flats. This daily review has to be done
during the length of this term. Repeat all the exercises
of arpeggios with the same distribution for their review
and the same as that of the scales.

Concert Works for Obtaining the Award: Sor,
Paganini-Tárrega. These two works must be learned
after having finished the fifth year, second term and to
be done before having obtained the title of professor.
Their thorough study will comprise the period of time of
a year and their performance will be when the student
wants to, whom must advise in time at the end of the
year to set a date of the reunion of the Jury of the
Institution which he might belong."

INDICE

PARTE 1ª: EJERCICIOS

PARTE 2ª: ESTUDIOS, MINUETES Y PRELUDIOS

Above is the index to the *"Suplemento al Metodo para Guitarra"* published by Ricordi in 1932.

This listing is from the *1949 RCA Argentina Catalogo No. 49* as of August 31, 1949.

Many of Domingo Prat's other students would include: Bautista S. Almiron, father of Lalyta Almiron, Severo Rodríguez Falcon, Leon Vicente Gascon, Horacio Maspoli, Carmelo Rizzuti, also receiving their orientations and advice: Justo T. Morales, Abel Fleury and Atahualpa Yupanqui.

BAUTISTA S. ALMIRON

CONCERTISTA DE GUITARRA

Promotional postcard of
Bautista S. Almiron 1913

Photo from cover of self-published pieces

"Bautista Sinobauldo Almiron de Los Santos was born in Buenos Aires on July 29, 1879. When he was very young he began to play the guitar, with a lot of passion and enthusiasm, that not only he dedicated the extra time that his frequent occupations of commerce or national studies needed, but that he sacrificed a lot in those activities in devotion of his vocation, that he felt intensely and intimately.

One of the great worths of Almiron, is in the consideration, of which, in those times, he didn't have a structured program of studies as norms of educative technique that orients the student, imposing him to the rational basis in which rests the domination of the instrument and at once may go forming the musical concept of just what develops in him. The teachers weren't abundant and the maestros with any capacity didn't exist. Almiron de los Santos intuitively drew from his fervent desire, the sufficient will to struggle with the thousand inconveniences that the lack of those pedagogic values represented, without dismay and maintaining his faith unharmed in the triumph and in his future. During the lapse of time between the year 1903 and 1905, in Carmen de Areco, Buenos Aires province, Almiron encountered the Spanish professor Francisco Gonzalez de la Roda, with whom he continued his studies, achieving the domination at his side of the difficult works: Julián Arcas' *"El Delirio"* and Dionisio Aguado's *"Rondo en La"* and others of respectable scope. In the year 1908, in Buenos Aires, Domingo Prat, met Almiron already being a skillful player, manifesting his admiration by having had the opportunity to attend various concerts that Prat had given then; and before his desire to improve, Prat had the great satisfaction of being his friend and maestro.

Almiron being of an artistic temperament and ductile comprehension, under Prat's orientations, very soon eliminated the imperfections of a defective execution, to be saturated in his advice and norms, and to be imposing his new school completely. After some time, Almiron said goodbye to initiate a tour of the interior of the Republic giving concerts, and had succeeded triumph after triumph.

Since then and presently for various years as professor of guitar, he has settled in Rosario, Santa Fe province, and worthy of his capacity, his personality, his enthusiasm, and his passion for the guitar, they have won him the deserved prestige of being the best maestro of that important city.

The value of his teachings have the most praiseworthy testimonies of his numerous disciples, they purify it in the greatest of the pride of a maestro, in the triumphant reality of his daughter Lalyta Almiron, the most notable concert guitarist of the young age of sixteen years of age.

As a composer, Almiron is known for the following works: *Ojos Traicioneros (Vals criollo), La Leyenda (Suite criolla), Lalyta (Vidalita), El huerfano (Andante), Palomitas blancas (Vals lento), Para ella (Romanza), El morrongo (gato criollo), Soñando (Fantasia), Un suspiro (Preludio), Tita (Vidalita), La Oracion (Melodia célebre), Rezos de aldea (Impromtu), Preludio No. 10* and *No. 11*. All of these works, in their distinct genre, are of well considered application to the guitar of its technique and in his emotivity, that make it evident in the impassioned sense, that in the stars of harmony, have molded in them the color of his art and the perfume of his sentiment, as in the flowers of the garden of his dreams.

A little while after finishing these lines, a sad notice arrived that Bautista S. Almiron had died in Rosario, Santa Fe on October 11, 1932. (The year after he accompanied his child prodigy daughter Lalyta Delfina Almiron on a concert tour of Barcelona and Madrid. R.O.)

We believe it opportune to insert the telegram that was published in the daily *"La Prensa"* communicating the said demise: "Rosario, October 11.-This morning in this city the concert guitarist Mr. Bautista S. Almiron died, very well known in artistic circles. The authorities of the cultural institution *"El Circulo"*, sent their note of condolences to the family of the late artist. Other entities of culture did likewise"." Thus ends the entry in Domingo Prat's *"Diccionario de Guitarristas"*.

This photo of Bautista S. Almiron is from the *"Caras y Caretas"* magazine of October 9, 1920 Issue No. 1149. The translation is: "Mr. B. Almiron, professor of guitar, who is giving a series of notable concerts in Rosario."

Señor B. Almirón, profesor
de guitarra que está dan-
do una serie de notables
conciertos en Rosario.

Alais, J. The Washington Post, marcha (Sousa)	$	0.80
— Un momento, valse	»	0.80
— Un recuerdo, valse	»	1.—
— Un suspiro, schottisch, para dos guitarras	»	0.60
— Vita torinesse, polka, para dos guitarras	»	0.80
— Zamacueca y Güeya	»	0.60
Alba, A., Amor naciente, valse	»	0.80
— Andante sentimental	»	0.80
— Brisas porteñas, schottisch	»	0.80
— Caprichosa, polka	»	0.80
— Guagiras célebres	»	0.80
— Marcha española	»	0.60
Alba, A., Mi tesoro, polka	»	0.80
— ¡Penas!, meditación	»	1.—
— Pensando en ti, habanera	»	0.80
— Pitios, mazurka	»	0.80
— Polka militar	»	0.80
— Suspiros del alma, vals	»	1.—
Alba, Luis, T. Preludio (Bach, J. S.)	»	1.20
— Romanza (Mendelssohnn, F.)	»	0.80
Almirón, B. S., Colección de 4 piezas	»	2.—
— Lalita, 2ª. guitarra de la Vidalita María de Alais	»	0.80
— La oración, melodía	»	1.—
Arcas, J., Andante	»	0.80
— Andante y estudio de Prudent	»	0.80
— Ballo in maschera fantasía, (Verdi, G.)	»	1.—
— Barbero de Sevilla, motivos (Rossini, G.)	»	0.70
— Batalla, La, fantasía descriptiva	»	1.20
— Boleras	»	0.70
— Bolero	»	0.70
— Colección de 5 tangos	»	0.80
— Cubana, danza americana	»	0.50
— Delirio, fantasía	»	2.—
— Fantasía sobre motivos heterogéneos	»	1.80
— Fantasía sobre el paño, o sea el punto de la Habana	»	1.20
— Faust, fantasía (Gounod, Ch.)	»	1.60
— Favorita, fantasía (Donizetti, G.)	»	1.20
— Gáetana, mazurka (Ketterer)	»	0.80
— Guayabito, tango	»	0.80
— Guillermo Tell, preludio, y un preludio original (Rossini, G.)	»	0.80
— Il Bacio, valse (Arditi, L.)	»	1.—
— Incógnito, capricho	»	1.50
— Jota aragonesa	»	1.—
— Lucía di Lammermoor, escena y aire final (Donizetti, G.)	»	1.50
— Madrileño, schottisch	»	0.50
— Manuelito, valse	»	0.70
— Marcha fúnebre (Thalberg)	»	1.—
— Marina, tango, y dos estudios	»	0.70

Florida 255. — Cangallo 1574. — B. Mitre 947

Here is a listing of three pieces by Bautista S. Almiron, including the piece "*Lalita*" named for his child prodigy daughter. It is from the c. Fall 1928 "*Romero & Fernández Catalogo No. 5, Métodos y Musica para Guitarra*" catalog of 34 pages. It appears that most of Bautista S. Almiron's pieces were published in the 1920's. See "*Leyenda*" on the next page.

Translation of the photo captions at the top of the next page from a c. 1928 Casa America catalog:

Maria Luisa Anido: "The virtuoso of the guitar, has caused admiration in her concerts by her artistic style."

Irma Haydée Perazzo: "Eminent Argentine concert guitarist, whose artistic temperament has been and is greatly praised."

María Luisa Anido

La virtuosa de la guitarra, ha causado admiración en sus conciertos por su estilo artístico.

Irma Haydée Perazzo

Eximia concertista argentina, cuyo temperamento artístico ha sido y es grandemente elogiado.

PUBLICACIONES MUSICALES

Relacionadas con la técnica de la guitarra

	$ m|n.
Aguado Dionisio..Método completo	5.—
" " " " ed. francesa	6.—
" " "..Cincuenta estudios	2.—
Aguado Sinópoli..Método completo	12.—
Amestoy E. ....Escalas y arpegios	2.—
Cano Antonio ....Método completo, 1ª parte (edición española)	6.—
" " ....Método completo, 1ª parte. (edición argentina)	4.—
" " ....Método completo, 2ª parte. (Tratado de Armonía) ..	4.—
" " ....Veinticinco lecciones fáciles.	3.—
" " ....Dos estudios de concierto ..	2.—
Carcassi Mateo ..Veinticinco estudios melódicos	2.—
Carulli Fernando.Método completo, 1ª parte .	1.20
" " " " 2ª " .	1.40
" " " " 3ª " .	1.50
Coste Napoleón..Veinticinco estudios de salón	4.—
Damas Tomás ...Método completo	7 —
Gascón L. V. ....Estudios elementales y progresivos	3.—
Iparraguirre Pedro.Escalas y arpegios	3.—
" " Escuela del mecanismo	2.—

	$m|n
Leloup Hilarión.. Método elemental	5.—
" " ..Escalas, acordes y ejercicios técnicos	5.—
Ortiz Julián......Teoría de las escalas	2.—
Prat Domingo ..Escalas y arpegios..........	2.—
Rizzuti Carmelo.. Lecciones elementales ...	3.—
R. Arenas M. .... Escalas y estudios de autores varios	5.—
" " "....Escuela de la guitarra, primera parte	4.—
" " "....Escuela de la guitarra, segunda parte	6.—
Roch Pascual.....Gran método I Parte....	7.—
" " ....." " II "	7.—
" " ....." " III "	7.—
Sagreras Julio ....Primeras lecciones	2.50
" " ....Técnica superior	4.—
Segovia Andrés...Escalas diatónicas, primer cuaderno	2.50
Sinópoli Antonio.Ejercicios de escalas	2.50
" " Ejercicios técnicos	2.50
Sors Fernando Gran método completo	5.—
(Coste) ....Edición francesa	8.—

MÚSICA DE SALON

	$m/n.
Alais Juan ......Seis piezas fáciles	1.—
" " ......Plegaria a Moisés, de Rossini	1.—
" " ......Música prohibida, melodía ..	0.60
Alba Luis ......Serenata, de Schubert	0.80
" " ......Romanza, de Mendelsshonn	1.—
Anido M. L. ....Preludio, de Bach	1.20
" " ....Sarabanda, de Bach........	1.50
" " ....Vals, de Grieg........	1.20
" " ....Le petit Berger, de Debussy	1.50
" " ....Rancho abandonado, de Mac Dowell	1.50
Almirón ......Leyenda	1.—
Arcas Julián......El delirio, fantasía	1.30
" " ......El sueño de Rosellén	1.—
" " ......Jota aragonesa	1.—
" " ......Minueto en Sol	1.—
" " " " Mi menor	1.—
" " ......Mi segunda época, fantasía .	1.—
Brocá José......Pensamiento español, fantas.	1.—
" " ......Mi patria, fantasía	1.—
Cano Antonio....La gallegada, fantasía	1.—
" " ....Marcha triunfal	1.—
" " ....Ultimo adiós, romanza ..	0.80
" " ....Andante en Do, Haydn ..	1.—
" " ....Tres valses	1.50
" " ....Tarantella	1.50
" " ....Pomponet, de Durand.....	1.50
Cano Federico ..Catania, siciliana	1.—
" " ....Carmen, romanza..........	1.—
" " ....Bodas de plata, reverie	1.—
" " ....Preludio, estudio	1.—
" " ....Las montañas de la selva, capricho	2.—
" " ....Estudio dedicado a Viñas ..	1.—
" " ....Estudio dedicado a Tárrega .	1.—

	$m/n.
Cimadevilla F. ...Fantasía morisca, serenata .	1.—
" " ...Gran jota aragonesa	1.50
Damas Tomás....Trémolo, nocturno	1.50
Del Valle Adela..Seis piezas fáciles	1.50
Ferrer José......Recuerdos de Montgrí, capricho	2.—
" " ......Los encantos de París	2.—
" " ......Monuet, op. 49	1.—
" " ......Doce minuetos	1.—
" " ......Veladas íntimas	1.—
" " ......El talismán, vals	1.—
Fontaine F. ......En la sierra	1.—
Galluzzo ....Adiós al piano, de Beethoven	0.80
" ....Canción húngara (Alma de Dios)	1.—
García Fortea S.Zambra granadina	2.—
" " Torre bermeja, de Albéniz .	2.—
Gascón L. V. ....Minueto núm. 1	1.—
" " " ....Adiós, Granada (granadinas)	1.50
" " " ....Sonatina en cuatro tiempos	2.—
" " " ...Variaciones sobre una canción	1.—
" " " ...Variaciones de gato a 3 guitarras	2.—
" " " ...Gran jota aragonesa	2.—
Gottschalk J. M.Gran trémolo	1.50
Iparraguirre Pedro El recreo, colección	1.20
" " Sueño de un ángel, de Ludovic	1.—
" " Plegaria de una virgen, de Badarzewska	1.—
" " Serenata, de Toselli	1.—
" " Serenata D'Autrefois, de Silvestri	1.—
" " Berceuse, de Jocelin de Godard	1.—

As a composer Domingo Prat left works of merit that evoked the spirit of Spain and Argentina: *"Danza Española No. 1"*, *"Variations on La Huella"* (huella), *"Bajo el Sauce"* (milonga), are the most well known, also he transcribed for guitar *"Minue Federal"* (from the epoch of Rosas – 1839) and an Album of *"Danzas y cantos Argentinos"* (Songs and Dances of Argentina).

"Danza Española No. 1"

"*Güeya (Huella)* with variations"

"Bajo el sauce"

"Dances and Songs" (Danzas y Cantos)

261

"Abel Fleury Pion was born in Dolores, Buenos Aires province on April 5, 1903. His initial studies of the instrument were very uneven, in spite of having heard good advice, not to be determined by any school nor maestro prefixed that directed his great abilities as an instrumentalist, verified by the author (Domingo Prat) of this *Diccionario* in the year 1928-29, when he was our pupil. As a concert guitarist his activities began in the province of Buenos Aires, in numerous performances where he was well applauded. He played in the Teatro Cervantes of Tandil, on March 24, 1928, in the Circulo de Ahedrez (Chess Club), in Tres Arroyos on June 8, 1928 and in the Teatro Odeon in Mar del Plata in the third occasion of the Fiesta de la Guitarra that was instituted on October 8, 1926, having Fleury responsible for the worldly artistic part and standing out in a distinguished manner. This festival happened on August 17, 1929. His musical culture and present guitaristic orientation are told to us by the works that flow from his performances, where the compositions of Sor, Tárrega, Moreno Torroba, Turina figure and transcriptions of the great musicians: Mozart, Albeniz, Granados, Moszkowsky, Tschaikovsky, etc. However, we will have to make an observation in this particular case, because we believe the order of the pieces isn't good that in the programs by Fleury he has some compositions, which evidently contrast with the quality of the authors that he plays. And this observation we will do in its best form, copying, textually a program where the compositions to play have the right placement due to our criteria:

First Part
1. Gavota: Bach (1685-1750).
2. Sonata: Cimarosa (1741-1801).
3. Allegro from the II Tarantelle: Mertz (1806-1857).
4. Introduccion y Variaciones Op. 9: Sor (Tema Mozart).

Second Part
1. Andante largo: Sor (1778-1839).
2. Romanza Op. 44: Rubinstein (1829-1894).
3. Danza Mora: Tárrega (1852-1909).
4. Kujawiak: Wieniawsky (1835-1880).
5. Tremolo: Gottschalk (1829-1862).

Third Part
1. Campanela (Estudio): Prat (Tema Bach)
2. Sonatina:
a) Allegretto
b) Andante
c) Allegro: Moreno Torroba.
3. Seguidillas: Mitjana (1869-1921).
4. Asturias: Albeniz (1860-1909).

From the audition given by the concert guitarist Consuelo Mallo Lopez in the Sala Wagneriana on May 20, 1932.

Programs ordered as such must serve as a norm to the professors that present theirstudents and to every concert guitarist that considers the same in relation to the guitar, then it won't be of any wonder in them the conviction of which, when they applaud them, he does it as a connoisseur of the public, as a cultured player, and with a program of faultless preparation.

Fleury as a composer has come out with a publication of *"Cuando"*, (Included in the 1931 Antigua Casa Nuñez catalog) Argentine dance, spontaneous page of folklore that indicates the abilities of the author, Abel Fleury." So ends the entry in Domingo Prat's *"Diccionario de Guitarristas"*.

262

This Abel Fleury concert is from the second season of the *Fiesta de la Guitarra*. It took place on Friday September 9, 1927, at the Teatro Colon in Mar del Plata. This concert program originally appeared in "*Abel Fleury-El Poeta de la Guitarra*" written by Héctor García Martínez and published in June 1987.

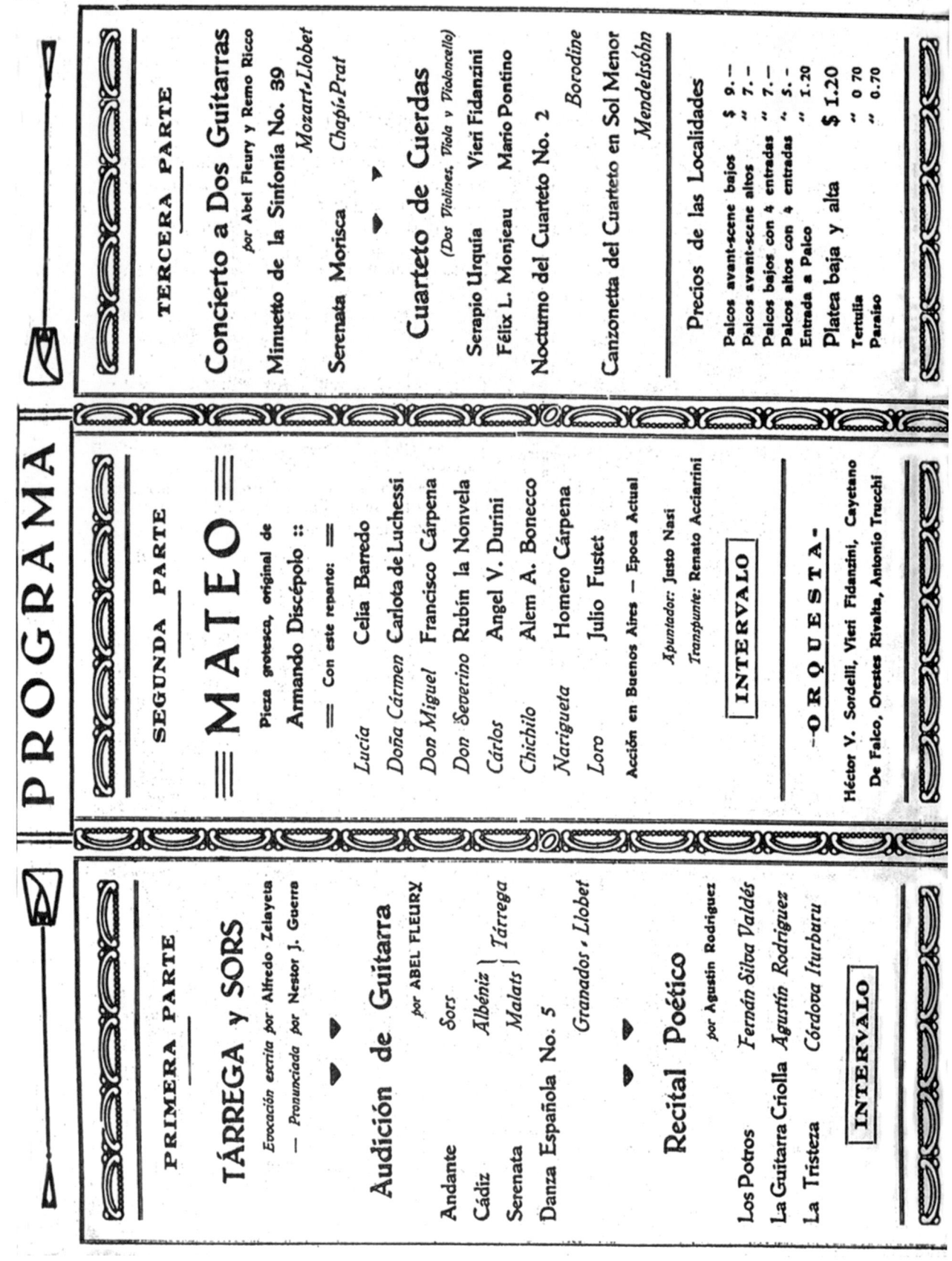

In this Friday September 9, 1927 concert Abel Fleury plays solos of the works of Sor, Albeniz, Mozart, Granados and later duets by Mozart and Chapi with Remo Ricco.

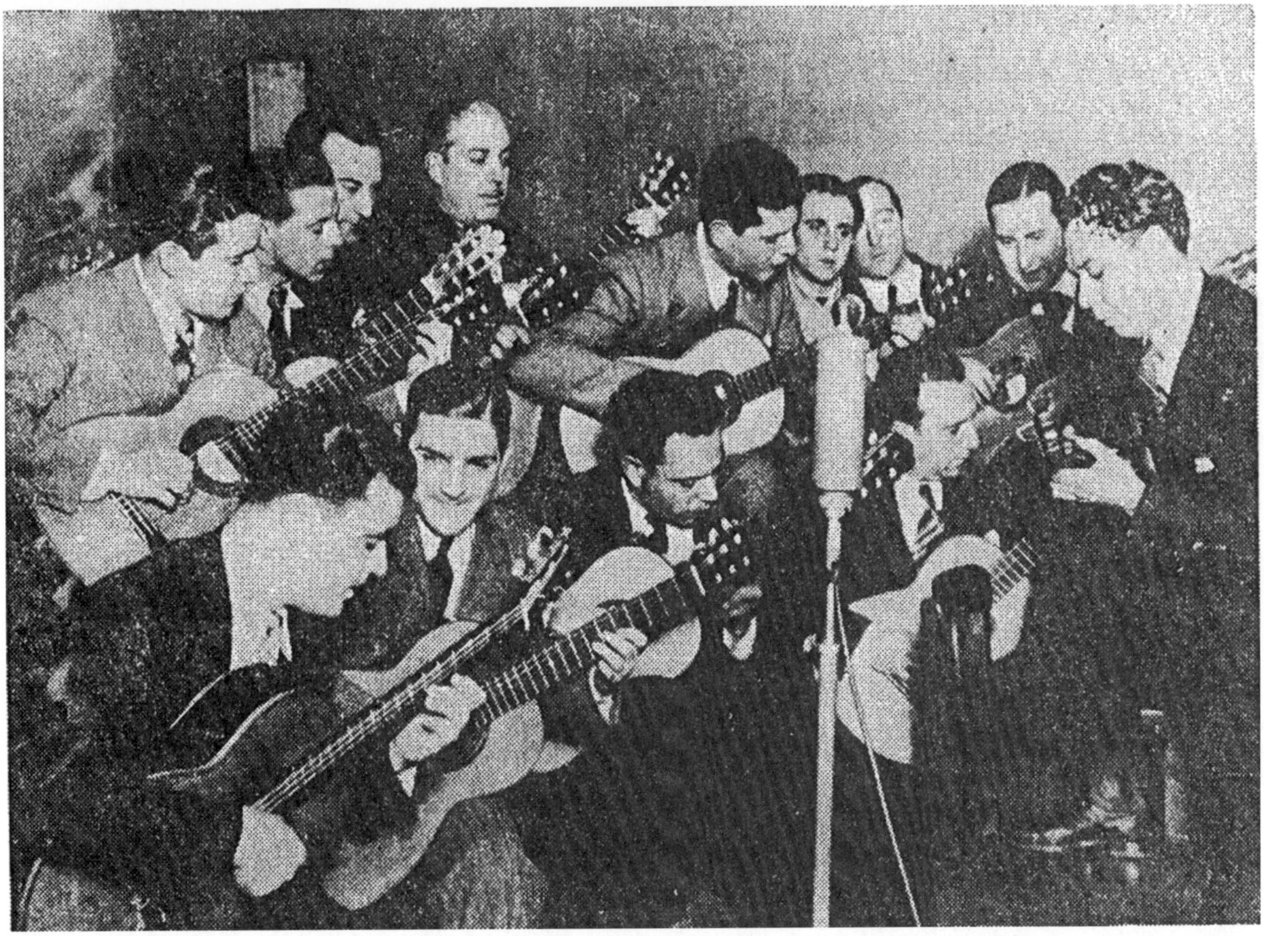

Here is Abel Fleury and his *Escuadrones de Guitarras* (Squadrons of Guitars) performing on radio. There were about a dozen of regular participants, though at times it was augmented to larger occasional outfits, sometimes 40 guitars, and in the Teatro Colon in Buenos Aires with 100 guitars in 1939.

This advertisement appeared the daily *"Nueva Era"* in Tandil in the late 1920's to early 1930's. before Abel went to reside in Buenos Aires in 1933. It originally appeared in *"Abel Fleury — El Poeta de la Guitarra"* written by Héctor García Martínez and published in June 1987.

Here Abel Fleury is with his guitarists of the *Escuadrones de Guitarras* (Squadron of Guitars) in the Teatro Colon in Buenos Aires in an event organized by the Ladies of the Saint Vincent de Paul Society. (Photo courtesy of Horacio Maspoli). This photo originally appeared in *"Abel Fleury-El Poeta de la Guitarra"* written by Héctor García Martínez and published in June 1987.

"Among the principal members of the *Escuadrones de Guitarras* of that epoch were: Luis Guido Laurent, Roberto M. Iglesias (Horacio Maspoli), Enrique Brusso, Exposito, Hector Ayala, Roberto Grela, Ubaldo D'Elio, José Torchia, Humberto Faustino Canataro, Antonio Barraza, Raul Cuello Rodríguez, Guillermo Cesanelli, Santiago Kirchner, Héctor Davis, José Maria Oyhamburu, Raquel Taboada, Horacio Santos, Zulema Fleury, Domingo Laine, the brothers Peralta Toto, and many others."

From pages 33 through 35 of "Abel Fleury" by Gaspar J. Astarita, published in 1995 is a complete list of Abel's solo guitar works: *"Guaymallén, Trinos y Alas, La cimarrona, De clavel en la oreja, Cantar de mi pago, Chamamé, Pegando la Vuelta, Fortin Kakel, Milongueo del ayer, Te vas...milonga, Pico Blanco, Ausencia, A flor de llanto, El desvelao, Estilo pampeano, Pago largo, Sobretarde, Tonada, Vidalita, Cifra, Mudanzas, El tostao, Relato, Pajaros en el monte, Lejania, Real de guitarreros, De sobrepaso, Alma en pena, Cimbronazo, El codiciado, Para Abel Eduardo, La firmeza, El cuando, Genuinia milonga, Venganza gaucha and Maria del Carmen."* The last three solo pieces were not published.

His transcriptions for guitar are: *"Milonga triste, Pena mulata* (Sebastian Piana), *Pajaro Campana (F. Perez Cardozo), Estilo de Los estudios del chiquito (Honorio Sicardi), Preludio No. 21 de clave bien temperado Suite en La (Well Tempered Clavier* by J. S. Bach) *Moto perpetuo-Opus 11 No. 6 (N. Paganini) and Clavel del aire (J. de D. Filiberto)."* This last piece was unpublished but recorded on Victor records.

According to Gaspar J. Astarita: "After Abel's arrival in Buenos Aires, the first radio station he appeared on was Radio Paris. It was Claudio Martínez Paiva that coined the phrase: "*Escuadrones de Guitarras*". With these casts of musicians he performed on different porteña radio stations, but the one he preferred was Radio Belgrano with their special programs and hours that suited him. The "*Escuadrones de Guitarras*" lasted until 1954.

When Abel Fleury arrived in Buenos Aires in 1933, he didn't come empty handed. He had a letter of introduction from the poet, Lauro Viana to the actor Fernando Ochoa. In theaters with Fernando he played background music for criollo poetry readings. In the beginning of Fernando's career, he starred in silent movies and then talkies: *Asi es el tango (1937), Noches de Buenos Aires (1935), Cruza (1942), Joven, viuda y estanciera (1941)* (Abel Fleury with his guitar appeared briefly in the last film.). Abel Fleury provided background music earlier in Santos Vega (1936).

Around 1940 Abel Fleury joined the Cuarteto Argentino de Musica Popular, along side: Pedro Maffia (bandoneon), Sebastian Piana (piano), and Alfredo Corletto (double bass). They performed on Radio Belgrano in many important prime time sessions.

There were four occasions when Abel Fleury went into the recording studio. The initial endeavor was for Odeon on December 4, 1935. he recorded *Estilo pampeana* and the *milonga Ausencia*. Twelve years later, he was given another opportunity to leave, in shellac, his music with the guitar on January 29, 1947. He recorded again for Odeon and the four pieces were: the *malambo Mudanzas, Vidalita*, the pericon *Pajaros en el monte* and the *triste Sobretarde*."

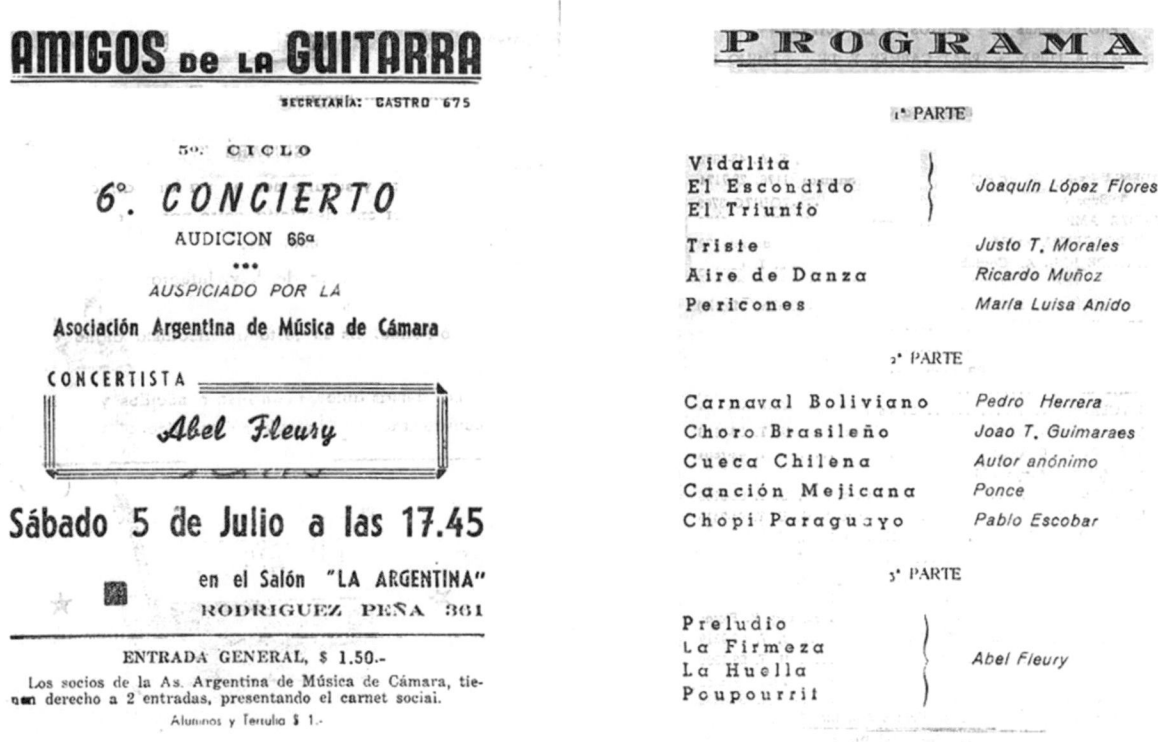

A few months after his second recording session he performed this concert in the Salon "La Argentina" for the Asociacion de Musica de Camara on Saturday July 5, 1947. In 1945 this Chamber Music Association had awarded Abel Fleury with an Honorable Mention for his diffusion of the folksongs of the country, and they reported it to the Direcion de Cultura del Ministerio de Educacion de la Nacion. For thirty years Abel Fleury played in the cities of the interior of Argentina besides Buenos Aires, then he toured to Brazil, Chile and Uruguay.

These photos are from the motion picture *Joven, Viuda y Estanciera (1941)* Abel Fleury, with his guitar appeared briefly in the film, though he provided background music for much it.

El recitador Fernardo Ochoa, intérprete de la poesía gauchesca,
con el guitarrista Abel Fleury. Ambos elementos intervienen en los
"Grandes Espectáculos Radiales"
que viene ofreciendo por su onda
la Radio El Mundo.

This photo of Abel Fleury and Fernando Ochoa is from 1941. The translation is:

"The reciter, Fernando Ochoa, interpreter of Gauchoesque poetry, with the guitarist Abel Fleury. Both elements intervene in the "Great Radio Spectaculars" that comes offered by the waves of Radio El Mundo."

Abel Fleury performed for the Asociacion Guitarristica Argentina on Friday November 29, 1946. This article is from the *"Nuestros Conciertos de la Temporada 1946"* section of the *"Revista de la Guitarra"* magazine issue No. 15 *Año* VIII of July 1947.

Translation:

"Our Concerts of the 1946 Season.

The 29th of November at 6:30PM, entrusted to the Professor Abel Fleury.

The celebrated guitarist was heard playing in the first part the *Sonata* No. Two Op. 25 by Sor, which was comprised of the *Andante Largo, Allegro non troppo, Andantino Grazioso* and *Allegro*. This work presented a series of difficulties that to overcome them a lot of expertise and good technique is necessary. Theabilities Mr. Fleury united, from there his playing was so well proven from all points of view, since it was performed with elegance and good taste. Inthe second part of the program, it's where you could duly appreciate the excellent qualities of the interpreter in our songs that Mr. Fleury embellished. In *"Firmeza", "Pericon", "Vidalita"* etc. as always, he was priceless, deserving the hottest applause by the public. In the third part he returned to the classics, performing a *"Fugue"* by Bach, *"Largo Assai"* by Haydn, and *"Canzonetta"* by Mendelssohn, all with skillful interpretation and sureness. He was applauded a lot by the numerous gathering the filled the location of the Casa del Teatro."

29 de noviembre a las 18.30 horas, a cargo del profesor Abel Fleury.

Este celebrado guitarrista se hizo escuchar en primer término, en Sonata N. II, op. 25 de Sor, que consta de Andante Largo, Alegro non Tropo, Andantino Gracioso y Alegro. Esta obra presenta una serie de dificultades que para salvarlas se necesita mucha pericia y muy buena técnica. Ambas condiciones reúne el señor Fleury, de ahí que su desempeño en tan crítica prueba fué de todo punto de vista encomiable, pues fué dicha con elegancia y buen gusto. En la segunda parte del programa, es donde se pudo apreciar debidamente las excelentes cualidades de intérprete de las cosas nuestras que adornan al señor Fleury. En Firmeza, Pericón, Vidalita, etc., como siempre, estuvo impagable, mereciendo los más cálidos aplausos del público. En la tercera parte volvió al clasicismo, ejecutando una Fuga de Bach, Largo Assai de Haydn y Canzoneta de Mendelshon, todo con acertada interpretación y seguridad. Fué muy aplaudido por la numerosa concurrencia que llenaba el local de la Casa del Teatro.

10

Abel Fleury playing one of two Francisco Simplicio guitars he owned.
Archive: Ricardo Muñoz

RECITAL DE VIOLÃO

— DO —

Consagrado artista

argentino

ABEL FLEURY

Salão Clube Caixeiral

Alegrete, 22 de Agosto de 1948.

(Above) This recital took place at the Salao Clube Caixeiral in Alegrete, Brazil on August 22, 1948.

(Below) Abel Fleury visiting in the home of Isaias Savio in Sao Paulo, Brazil in 1948. Isaias Savio had 38 pieces listed in the 1931 Antigua Casa Nuñez catalog.

I had a conversation with Carlos Barbosa-Lima on April 1, 2007 at San José State University after a Masterclass and he said he saw Abel Fleury in concert and also met him at his teacher's home, that of Isaias Savio. R. O.

NOITE DE ARTE

A ASSOCIAÇÃO ATLETICA BANCO DO BRASIL

tem a grata satisfação de convidar V. S. para o recital de violão que, em sua sede social, ás 21 horas do dia 8 de Outubro próximo, nos proporcionará o grande mestre argentino

ABEL FLEURY

o qual se encontra entre nós em missão cultural e artistica.

RUA 15 DE NOVEMBRO, 228
17.º ANDAR   —   SÃO PAULO

Portuguese translation by Randy Osborne

This concert was held in Sao Paulo.

"Night of Art

The Associacao Atletica Banco do Brasil has the pleasant satisfaction to invite you for a guitar recital that is, in its social headquarters, at 9PM on the 8th of October 1948, we will provide the music of the great Argentine maestro, Abel Fleury who we will find is within our cultural and artistic mission."

The handwritten note about the "*Valsa Scherzo*" by Isais Savio says it is a debut of the piece.

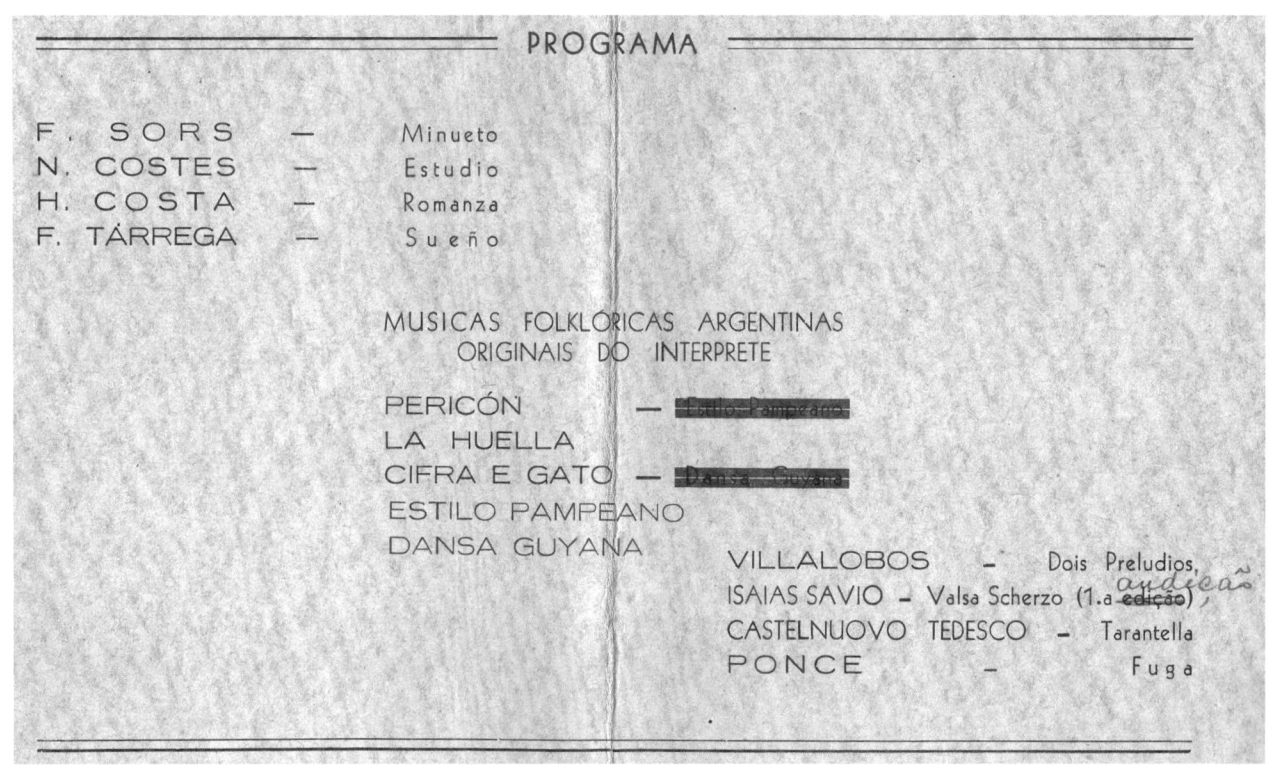

PROGRAMA

F. SORS	—	Minueto
N. COSTES	—	Estudio
H. COSTA	—	Romanza
F. TÁRREGA	—	Sueño

MUSICAS FOLKLORICAS ARGENTINAS
ORIGINAIS DO INTERPRETE

PERICÓN — ~~Estilo Pampeano~~
LA HUELLA
CIFRA E GATO — ~~Danza Guyana~~
ESTILO PAMPEANO
DANSA GUYANA

VILLALOBOS	—	Dois Preludios,
ISAIAS SAVIO	—	Valsa Scherzo (1.a ~~edição~~ audição),
CASTELNUOVO TEDESCO	—	Tarantella
PONCE	—	Fuga

272

This rare photo of Abel Fleury had never been seen by Hector García Martínez in all his decades of research of the artist. The translation is: "To La Casa Galli with all congeniality. Abel Fleury, Mendoza June 22, 1951."

In 1952 he traveled to perform in Spain and France and Belgium. When he performed in Spain he played in Madrid, Granada, Zaragoza, Valencia, Huelva and Barcelona. In this tour he had the opportunity to meet some of the most distinguished students of Francisco Tárrega, Daniel Fortea and Regino Sainz de la Maza.

This photo of Abel Fleury is from a review of a concert in Rosario, Santa Fe province on April 10, 1954, where he played a recital of completely Argentine folk music. It was published in a magazine entitled: *Revista Cultural E Informativa de la Asociacion Guitarristica de Rosario Año III No. 4* of December 1954. This guitar is one of two concert guitars by Francisco Simplicio he owned.

"On the Victor label he recorded on July 28, 1954 a new master of *Estilo pampeana*, and the other side being *Milongueo del Ayer* (78 RPM disc: Victor 681.806). A year later for the same label on July 22, 1955 he recorded the *tango Clavel del aire*, by Juan de Dios Filiberto and his own *Relato* (78 RPM disc: Victor 682.196)." (Gaspar J. Astarita op. cit)

Doctors detected a cancerous tumor in Abel in the early part of 1958. He died at 2:00 pm on August 9, 1958. The poet of the guitar passed away, but was not to be forgotten.

It was the music by Abel Fleury played by Roberto Lara on a Lyrachord LP, that this author, Randy Osborne, purchased in 1976. It sounded like three instruments at once. It was my first experience with guitar music outside the Rock, Blues, Jazz, Country and Western "Americana" that I had played and listened to for twelve years as a guitarist.

On the Victor label he recorded on July 28, 1954 a new master of *Estilo pampeano,* and the other side being *Milongueo del Ayer* (78 RPM disc: Victor 681.806).

(Left) Abel Fleury piece *Estilo Pampeano* in it's 34th edition and dedicated to Fernando Ochoa.
(Right) *Milongueo del ayer* dedicated to Matilde T. Calandra (version for two guitars).

Abel Fleury recorded the *milonga* entitled *Ausencia* and the *Estilo pampeano* for Odeon on December 4, 1935.

He recorded again for Odeon on January 29, 1947. The songs were a pericon entitled *Pajaros en el monte* and the *triste* known as *Sobretarde*.

(Left) Early Abel Fleury piece published by Romero & Fernández . (Right) Early edition of an Abel Fleury piece released by his main publisher Antigua Casa Nuñez.

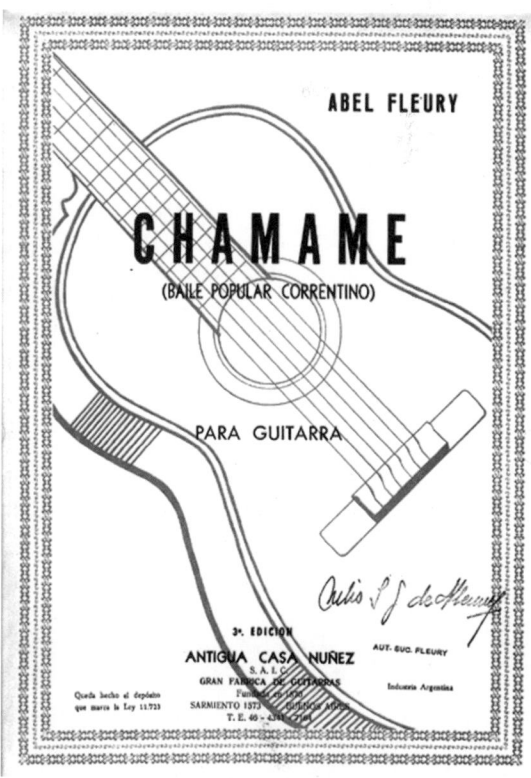

(Left) Abel Fleury pieces published by Antigua Casa Nuñez. Relato was dedicated to Dr. Artemio Moreno and was recorded in Abel's final session. (Right) A piece dedicated to Domingo Prat student, grown up child prodigy Celia Rodríguez Boqué de Beretta.

(Left) Abel Fleury's 34th piece, Fortin Kakel, in it's 1st edition in August 1954 and dedicated to Nellie Ezcaray. (Right) *Ausencia* in it's 9th edition in November 1964, almost 30 years after Abel recorded it in his first session.

El desvelao was dedicated to Maria Luisa Anido and *Real de Guitarreros* to Abel's parents: Eduardo Fleury and Juana Peon de Fleury.

This is the biography of Abel Fleury from Ricardo Muñoz's unpublished book *"Historia Universal de la Guitarra" Volume VIII "La Escuela Tárrega en La Argentina".*

"His Origin

Abel Fleury was born in Dolores, Province of Buenso Aires on April 5, 1903.

His Education

On the guitar he began with his own personal intuition, later with the great maestro Prat he received lessons in 1928 and 1929, meanwhile profound studies of harmony with maestro Sicardi.

His Virtuosity

On March 24, 1928 we see him in the Teatro Cervantes in the city of Tandil, Buenos Aires; on June 8, of the same year in the *Circulo de Ahedrez* in the town of Tres Arroyos, Buenos Aires; on August 17, 1929 in the *Fiesta de la Guitarra* in the coastal city of Mar del Plata, performing works by Sor, Tárrega, Torroba, Turina, Mozart, Albeniz, Granados, Moszkowski, Tschaikowsky and others.

In 1940 and 1941 he appeared in the Salon "La Argentina" playing under the auspices of the "Circulo de la Guitarra" illustrating the lecture by the brilliant professor de Bellas Artes *Don* Fernan Felix de Amador, entitled *"La Guitarra-Instrumento de la Tradicion y la Leyenda"* and *La Guitarra en la Tradicion de la Llanura"*, interpreting pages by Oyanguren, Tárrega, Albeniz, Malats, Granados and his own pieces. *"La Prensa"* said: "He illuminated with perfect dominion of the instrument as it refers to rhythm and intonation, smooth and poetic sound and criollo style, so expressive as accurate..."

In 1944 we see him in the city of Rosario, Santa Fe in the Salon Savoy, sponsored by the "Asociacion Tárrega", playing impeccable versions of his own works of the national folklore; the next year in the Salon "La Argentina" of Buenos Aires, interpreting pages of *criollo* music for the "Amigos de la Guitarra"; and once again for the "Asociacion Tárrega" in Rosario to prolonged applause.

In 1946 he reiterated his eminently criollo music performance for the "Amigos de la Guitarra" and very successfully for the "Asociacion Guitarristica Argentina"; the 6th of June 1947 again for "Amigos de la Guitarra" performing *"Vidalita", "El Escondido" and "Triunfo"* by Lopez; *"Triste"* by Morales; *"Aire de Danza"* which was dedicated by Ricardo Muñoz to the poet of the guitar Abel Fleury; *"Pericones"* by Anido; *"Carnaval Boliviano"* by Herrera; *"Choro Brasileño"* by Guimares; *"Cancion Mexicana"* by Ponce; *"Chopi Paraguayo"* by Escobar and *"Preludio", "La Firmeza", "La Huella"* of his own pen. The next day the 6th of June 1947 *"La Prensa"* wrote: "Fleury is an interpreter of great fidelity and personality, since he knows from the foundation the modalities of our indigenous and criollo folklore and music of the Continent."

On the 29th of November of the same year he interpreted the "2nd *Sonata* Op. 25" by Sor, Bach, Haydn, Beethoven, Mendelssohn, etc. in the Casa del Teatro and so proceeded triumph by triumph without discussion, all over the territory of the country, applauded and paid homage with enthusiasm and affection.

In 1948 he crossed the border and on the 9th of November in Rio de Janeiro he made an appearance at the "Escola Nacional de Musica", interpreting Handel, Haydn, Beethoven, Sor, Ponce, Villa-Lobos, Albeniz, Castelnuovo-Tedesco and his own works. The fact of knowing that this performance produced a ticket to enter of 10,000 cruzeiros, it shows the extent of the admirable artistic success it provoked, then he performed in Sao Paulo and other Brazilian cities to the same public admiration.

In 1950 in Montevideo, Uruguay he performed for the "Centro Guitarristico del Uruguay", the critic of the daily *"La Accion"* said: "He whom has the privilege to hear with new ears the marvelous versions of this guitarist by exception, will enjoy of an indescribable emotion of our sentiments...." In Santiago, Chile the daily *"Zig Zag"* informed us: "He is simple, modest and calm, less with a guitar in his hands. Since he breaks all the lines and he comes back romantic and passionate."

He returned to his homeland, directed 20 guitars for which he personally constructed the music, they applauded him, and called him "The Poet of the Guitar", he continued his tours of art and nationalism by where he set foot and brought his criollo music.

In the year 1952 we see him again in the Brazilian city of Recifes causing a sensational success; the following year he embarked on a tour and visited Valencia, Spain, a city of the guitar and after performing for the public, the daily *"Las Provincias"* on the 19th of February wrote: "His concert was a magnificent lesson of style. Marvelous suggestions were born of his guitar, which in his hands returns to be the mysterious instrument that scarcely we have heard since the great Tárrega. All the spiritual Argentine perfume surged from the mysterious guitar."

From Valencia he went to Madrid and gave three concerts; one in the Instituto de Cultura Medica, another in the Instituto de Cultura Hispanica and the third in the Circulo de Bellas Artes; then he performed in Granada, Zaragoza, and Barcelona, always an artist, applauded, respected and appreciated for his true musical and interpretive values.

His Compositions

Antigua Casa Nuñez publishes these:

"Preludio", relato
"Pajaros en el Monte", pericon
"Estilo Pampeano"
"Milonga del Ayer"
"Mudanzas, malambo", danza
"Pago Largo", huella, danza
"Tonada"
"Cifra y Gato"
"Vidalita"
"Chacarera", danza
"El Cuando", danza
"Guymallén", cueca, danza
"La Firmeza", danza
"Triste"
"Ranchera", danza

Transcriptions of the *"Preludio XXI"* by Bach and the *"Suite en La Mayor"* by Weiss, are published by Ricordi and many others. All of them refer to the flavour and the authentic nostalgia of Argentina. *Don* Carlos Isamitt has said: "The works of Fleury have more unity than those of the Brazilian composer Villa-Lobos."

His Passing

Abel Fleury died in Buenos Aires on August 9, 1958."

INTERNATIONAL NEWS

Argentine. There have been many guitar recitals in Buenos Aires during recent months. Abel Fleury gave a recital of music by Latin-American composers under the auspices of Antigua Casa Nunez.

"ASOCIACION GUITARRIS-AICA ARGENTINA" presented the following guitarists in recitals: Nelly Ezcaray, Enrique Fernandez, Emilio Colombo, Jorge A. Martinez, Oscar A. Devita, Nydia Beatrice Suarez, etc.

"AMIGOS DE LA GUITARRA" presented Nelly Menotti, Osvaldo d'Onofio, Carlos A. Izaguirre Arona, Francisco Orlando La Polla, Manuel Lopez Ramos, Lalyta Almiron, etc. The concert on October 13th was given by the Quintet of Guitars of the Escuela Superior de Musica de la Universidad National del Litoral. Led by Jorge Martinez Zarate the Quintet played music by Byrd, Bach, Mozart, Schubert, Mussorgsky, Stravinsky, Sor and other composers.

Brazil. In Santos and Sao Paulo there is much guitaristic activity. Alfredo Scupinari gave the August recital organised by "ASSOCIA-CAO CULTURAL DO VIOLAO".

A five-column, front-page article on the guitar by Otacilio Colares appeared in the newspaper "Unitario." It was illustrated with a portrait of Tarrega and the headlines—right across the page—were "The Guitar, An Instrument of High and Noble Lineage."

Another newspaper, "A Gazeta" contained an article on "The Repertory of the Guitar" by Ronoel Simoes.

Austria. The Bulletin of the Bund der Gitarristen Osterreichs dated March, 1952, reports many guitar recitals (Luise Walker and others) and concerts in Vienna and other parts of Austria. Maria Luisa Anido gave a recital in the Schubert Saal, Vienna, on April 8th after her visits to London, Paris and Switzerland.

Brazil. Abel Fleury, guitarist and composer, of Argentina, paid a return visit to Sao Paulo, Brazil where he gave a recital of classical and folk lore music on March 1st. He also broadcast some of his own compositions in a programme presented by Ronoel Simoes. On February 9th, Carlos M. Carrion gave a recital which like that of Abel Fleury was organised by Associacao Cultural do Violao. This programme included an original suite in five movements "El Bosque de los Suenos perdidos".

This is from the Guitar News magazine issue No. 7 of June – July 1952.

This is from the Guitar News magazine issue No. 4 of December 1951 – January 1952.

ABEL FLEURY (1903–1958)

WE regret to hear of the death during the autumn of Abel Fleury, one of the greatest of the many famous guitarists of Argentina. He will be known to many of our readers for his musicianly arrangements of Argentine music—on which he was an acknowledged expert. He gave many recitals, his programmes covering a very wide range of music, and did great service to the cause of the guitar.

On November 14th the Asociacion Guitarristica Argentina organised a special recital in Buenos Aires 'en homenaje a Abel Fleury' at which several of his works—Triste, Milonga and Estilo—were included in an interesting programme played by Irma Costanzo.

The following incident will show the esteem in which Abel Fleury was held in South America. Some years ago he visited Brazil on holiday. When the guitarists of São Paulo discovered that he was in their city they pressed him to give a recital. A visitor to Brazil required an official permit for this and he had not applied for one as he was there as a private tourist. However, the guitarists petitioned the authorities to make an exception to the law—with such success that Abel Fleury gave a successful recital and also several radio broadcasts.

This is from the "Guitar News" magazine issue No. 46 of January – February 1959.

"Carmelo Rizzuti was born on July 30, 1889 in Buenos Aires. He had a passion for music and the guitar since he was a child. He began his guitar studies in 1905 with Luis Croce Graciosi, and later with Vicente Caprino, with whom he revealed his good capacity and made great progress in a short time.

Being drafted into the army. interrupted his guitar studies. After his stint in the service he recovered the progress he had achieved. He entered the Academia de Guitarra "Prat" in 1912, and he was a fellow student with the expert guitarists Adolfo Luna, A. Vila, L. Colombié and B. Fernández ; he was presented in concert in the Salon "La Argentina", in whose performance Carmelo Rizzuti achieved an outstanding success.

Not taking a step backward in his studies and always filled with optimism, on Friday March 19, 1915 he gave a Gran Concierto de Guitarra in the Salon-Teatro "Concordia" in honor of Domingo Prat. It was Carmelo's first program with his name on the cover. It was comprised of three parts with works by various authors, which brought applause for the beauty and the difficulty. His success was complete, deserving, besides the cordial congratulations from fellow students and his maestro, but also from the great guitarist: Joséfina Robledo. From that moment onward he was not distracted from the guitar by anything, and in 1916 he dedicated himself to the guitar alone.

He founded his Academia "Superior" de Guitarra "Rizzuti"and became the professor of guitar in the "Conservatorio D'Andrea", presenting a good number of students in his concerts for the institution, Mario and Aquiles de Armas (1923), Graciela Rivas (1925), Delia Solitro (1924); all those maestros, today well known by their performance. Those receiving their diplomas in his academia were: in 1925, Victor Stigliano, Tomas Pomilio; in 1927, Irene Virginia Bordigone, Lolita O. Ala (1st Prize Gold Medal), Lilia A. Cristobal (2nd Prize Silver Medal), Antonio Romero, Severio Cucci, Antonio Giaquinto, Ermano Brandazzi and Isabel Poso; in 1928, Bernabé Alonso (2nd Prize Silver Medal), Aida Lopez Rojas (1st Prize Gold Medal), Noemi C. Toulouse (1st Prize Gold Medal); 1929, Eduardo J. Lagomarsino; in 1930, Etlvina E. Beron, Juanita Arci; 1931, Choly Sanchez, Severo Rodríguez, Olga Abbiate and Rafael Ferraro.

To this respectable quantity of awards given out, he has the great satisfaction and the great honor to have been the only maestro to the notable Argentine concert guitarist Maud Metcalfe. Some of the professors named have become the body of teachers of the academia "Superior", such as: Maud Metcalfe, Delia Solitro, Tomas Pomilio, Alfonso Galluzzo and Victor Stigliano.

In the year 1917 Carmelo formed a duo with Hilarion Leloup, that was being prepared with intelligence in order to undertake a series of concerts in Buenos Aires and a tour of the interior of Argentina, of which a part of their plan took place, though not all because of unforeseen circumstances.

As a composer, he is known for an album "Lecciones elementales". At the end of that album Mr. Santiago A. Marengo (Rizzuti student) dedicates five pages to the history of the guitar (in an outline) and to some artists, it is a work well documented and very appropriate. Besides the cited works, twenty-two of his published works of varied style are known, primarily in the Argentine ambiance: three *Zambas*, three *Tangos, Vidalita, Triste, Gato, Aire Sanjuanino,* etc. This production will undoubtedly be augmented, since he is amply inspired and still young.

Rizzuti has received various musical honors; but we guess that the greatest satisfaction he has obtained, is to have been the maestro to the cited Maud Metcalfe and to be a component of the "Cuarteto Argentino" of guitars." So ends Domingo Prat's entry in his "*Diccionario de Guitarristas*".

This interview with Carmelo Rizzuti is translated from the *"Cultores de la Guitarra"* column in the *Revista Musical Ilustrada "Tárrega"* magazine, issue No. 1, that was published in June of 1924.

"Interview with maestro Carmelo Rizzuti

With the object to put our readers in contact, with one of the most energetic cultivators of the guitar in our country, we have taken the opportunity to celebrate an important interview with the maestro Mr.Carmelo Rizzuti, who has taken the kindness to provide his very valuable time.

We advised him in advance of our visit, and the maestro prepared to respond to our interrogation. We solicit in the first place, a resume of his initiation in the art, and of his fluid and friendly conversation, we can synthesize these declarations.

"Luis Croce, student of Juan Sampoli, a good guitarist," he tells us with certain satisfaction "was who the first time, there in 1904, in a family reunion, revealed to me the harmonius secretos of the guitar."

"A little later, friendly and impartially, I received from the same Croce the first notions of how to pluck the sentimental and popular instrument."

"I made in a relatively short space of time visible progress and later I solicited from the Professor Vicente Caprino his lessons and advice, to the end of perfecting the knowledge adquired."

"During the lapse of two years I received the advantageous teachings of my new maestro, which I had necessity to interrupt, to enter into the army."

The maestro Rizzuti, nostalgic about the life of the conscription, and after he declared to us with an air of triumph.

"Nevertheless, in the hours that were disposed, I dedicated all my desires and enthusiasm in studying in depth the difficulties that characterize many of the works of the great maestros and put in relief the abilities of disposition for the study of an instrument so difficult such as the guitar."

"Coinciding with my completion of my obligations of Argentine citizenship, the arrival to the country of the Spanish maestro Domingo Prat, to whom I was presented by Luis Croce and who I might have received the advantageous teachings and perfection in a new school of the immortal maestro Francisco Tárrega."

And such as who remembers the efforts of a long ascension, he adds:

"I perfected my right-hand technique, I increased the number of works considerably that I performed and in the year 1913 I finished my studies satisfactorily passing the tests."

"In the month of March of 1915, in honor of my unforgettable maestro and friend Domingo Prat, I gave my first concert with flattering success, performing among others the *"Testamento D'Amelia"*, by Llobet;

"Danza Mora", "Sueño" Tremolo-study by Tárrega; *"Minuet en Re"* by Sor; to which I met, with the high honor of the distinguished Spanish guitarist who presently is visiting us, making a artistic tour, Miss Joséfina Robledo."

"A little later I had the honor to hear the applause in the Salon "La Argentina", where I performed on various occasions. In the year 1917, and to the request of Hilarion leloup, I made a artistic tour of the interior, playing concerts in different localities. In this opportunity I was also crowned with the success of our labor. "

"In July of 1922 and in October of the same year, with the competition of my students, I gave, also with success, concerts in the Capital, and in the months of July and December of last year, I presented the most complete group of guitarists that has ever made a presentation in this city."

"My name has been placed with frequency in the programs of acts of concerts of innumerable institutions, such as: Centro Militar de Expedicionarios al Desierto, Cruz Roja Argentina, Asistencia Publica, Asilo Ramon L. Falcon, Ateneo Hispano Americano, etc. etc., and in all those I had the intimate satisfaction to gain spontaneous applause from the attendees."

We recall his work as a professor, and he tells us that, effectively, he has contributed a lot to to the formation and perfection of enthusiastic aficionados.

Some of them have received their respective diplomas which credits them as professors and the rest study insistently and diffuse in our environment the instrument, that our ancestors used, to sing a copla and which has brought from the humble ranch of our Pampas to lord over in the halls for, among one and the other vidalita, to sublimely delight with the transcriptions of the best works of the greatest maestros.

Satisfied in our assignment, we excuse ourselves from the maestro Rizzuti, taking the conviction which the Argentine art has still a lot to expect from the dedication and from the intelligence of this enthusiastic proponent of the guitar.

*

*   *

As a complementary note, we offer to our readers the magnificent program of study to which the students conquered in his accredited Academia de Guitarra.

First Course: Position of the guitar: Rizzuti, Lecciones Elementales; Cano, Method, 8 First lessons; Aguado, Method, 10 First lessons; Prat, Second Form, chromatic scale and major scales of 2 and 3 octaves; Tárrega, Lagrima "Preludio".

Second Course: Prat, Third Form, chromatic scale; Cano, Lessons 9 to 15; Aguado, First section, From 10-20, 26, 28, 30, and 34; Aguado, Second section, First 10 exercises; Prat, minor scales; Tárrega, Estudio en forma de minuetto.

Third Course: Cano, Major tones and their relatives; Prat, Exercises, arpeggio, barres, octave chromatic scale; Cano, Method, continuation; Llobet, Testamento de Amelia; Pujol, Cancion de Cuna.

Fourth Course: Aguado, Second section, exercises 11-21; Tárrega, Exercise (Método Prat, page 15); Aguado, Exercise for the left hand from Nos. 1-30; Llobet, scale (Método Prat, page 14); Prat, arpeggio exercise, 11 forms; Aguado, Third section, studies Nos. 1-8; Tárrega, Preludio No. 5.

Fifth Course: Examination to opt for the Diploma of Elementary Professor; Aguado, Third section, studies Nos. 9-12; Prat, Scales and arpeggios techniques; Sor, Method, studies Nos. 1-5, from the last section; Sainz de la Maza, Preludio.

Sixth Course: Aguado, Exercise for the left hand from Nos. 31-60; Sor, Method, studies Nos. 6-15; Aguado, Third section, studies Nos. 13-18; Sor, Method, studies Nos. 16-26; Tárrega, Recuerdos de la Alhambra.

Seventh Course: Aguado, Exercise for the left hand from Nos. 61-90; Coste, Method, studies Nos. 1-7; Aguado, studies Nos. 19-26; Tárrega, Sonatina.

Eighth Course: Examination to opt for the Diploma of Superior Professor; Aguado, study No. 27; Coste, studies Nos. 8-25; Tárrega, Danza Mora; Aguado, Rondo en la No. 2; Tárrega, Capricho Arabe."

(Left) Carmelo Rizzuti c. 1920, maestro to Maud Metcalfe, who inspired Noemi Toulouse to begin to play the guitar.

(Below) Autograph from a piece of sheet music, which eventually was replaced by an ink stamp.

Carmelo Rizzuti and Rodolfo Alvarez, from the Revista Musical Ilustrada "Tárrega" magazine, issue No. 1, that was published in June 1924.

This program of study for Academia Superior de Guitarra "Rizzuti" is from *"Historia de la Guitarra"* by Ricardo Muñoz, pages 308-309.

"Academia Superior de Guitarra "Rizzuti"-Director: Carmelo Rizzuti

Program study

First course:

Rizzuti – Lecciones Elementales (Elementary Lessons).
Roch – Vol. 1, pages 28-51.
Aguado – Second part, 1st section to lesson 15, Sor-Lessons, Nos. 2, 3, 14, and 19.
Cano – Lessons of Aguado.
Roch – Vol. 1, pages 52-75.

Second course:

Roch – Vol. 1, pages 76-85.
Aguado – Lessons, Nos. 17 and 27.
Aguado-Sor – Lessons, 23, 9, 12, 13, 24.
Cano – Lessons of Aguado.
Roch – Vol. 1, pages 86-89.

Third course:

Roch – Vol. 1, pages 91-108.
Aguado – Lessons 28-36.
Roch – Vol. 1, pages 109-128.
Roch – Vol. 2, pages 3-23.

Fourth course:

Roch – Vol. 2, pages 24-36.
Aguado – Chapter II, lessons 44 to the "Preludes".
Cano-Sor – Lessons 20 and 17.
Roch – Vol. 2, pages 37-69.

Fifth course:

Sor – Studies, Nos. 1-5. (last section)
Roch – Vol. 2, pages 90-98.
Aguado – Third section, Studies Nos. 1-12.
Cano – Study No. 2.
Roch – Vol. 2, pages 99-110.

Sixth course:

Sor – Studies, Nos. 6-15.
Aguado – Studies, Nos. 13-21.
Sor – Studies, Nos. 16-26.
Roch – Vol. 3, pages 3-11.

Academia Superior de Guitarra "Rizzuti"-Director: Carmelo Rizzuti (study program cont.)

Seventh course:

Coste – Studies, Nos. 1-10.
Aguado – Studies Nos. 22-27.
Roch – Vol. 3, pages 12-23.
Coste – Introduction and Allegretto (Sor's method – page 31.)

Eighth course:

Examination for option of professorial diploma.
Coste – Studies, Nos. 11-25.
Coste – "Meditation" (Sor's method, page 65.)
Aguado – Rondo en La, No. 2."

Carmelo Rizzuti solo concert in Salon Augusteo on August 17, 1916, for the "Centro de Cultura Musical de La Guitarra" founded by Juan Carlos Anido. This concert was several weeks before Maria Luisa Anido's public debut in the same location. This is from pages 360-361 of "Historia de la Guitarra" by guitar historian Ricardo Muñoz, published in 1930.

This ink stamp of the Centro de Cultura Musical "La Guitarra" is from the cover of a manuscript of "Serenata Morisca" by Chapi for 2 guitars.

"First part:

1. Marieta – Tárrega.
2. Minuet in Re – Sor.
3. Romanza-Mendelssohn-Tárrega.
4. Meditacion "Nocturno" – Carlos García Tolsa.

Second part:

1. Testament d' Amelia – Llobet.
2. El delirio (trémolo) – Cano.
3. Minuet federal argentino (harmonization) – Prat.
4. La gallegada, (pastoral fantasy with variations) – Ferrer.

Third part:

1. Pavane – Tárrega.
2. Pescadores de las perlas (romanza) – Bizet-Leloup.
3. Minuet – Paderewski-Sinopoli.
4. Danza Mora – Tárrega."

This is the short biography of Mario de Armas from Ricardo Muñoz's unpublished book "Historia Universal de la Guitarra" Volume VIII "La Escuela Tárrega en La Argentina".

He studied guitar with maestro Carmelo Rizzuti, the same as his brother Aquiles de Armas, receiving the title of professional in 1923, giving very admired concerts. In 1933 he committed suicide along with his wife in a hotel in Lomas de Zamora.

Alberto Toulouse

Alfonso Galluzzo
From *Revista Musical Ilustrada "Tárrega"*
Issue No. 1 June 1924, students of the
Academia Rizzuti.

Aquiles de Armas

Mario de Armas

This biography of Alfonso Galluzzo Doldan is translated from the *"Diccionario de Guitarristas"* by Domingo Prat published by Romero & Fernández in 1934.

"Alfonso Galluzzo Doldan — Argentine Guitarist and Composer

He was born in Buenos Aires the 17th of April of 1901. His first maestro of the guitar was Gaspar Cronford Sagreras, continuing his studies until he became a professor under the tutelage of Carmelo Rizzuti, receiving his diploma in December of 1925. He also took musical studies with maestro Luis Hernández Torres. He then used that instruction for forming a part of the teaching faculty of Academia Superior de Guitarra "Rizzuti". Galluzzo Doldan is one of the members of the "Cuarteto Argentino" of guitar, that for the first time was presented in the salon "La Argentina" on October 8, 1929, succeeding as the *"La Nacion"* said on October 9, 1929: 'praiseworthy versions that permitted them proof of a knowledgeable study.' In his capacity as an interpreter he has had an activity that is distinguished, that is reflected by the chronicles of the dailies and magazines in which he was featured. We will extract the following paragraphs: '...the song permitted Galluzo to demonstrate his worth as a performer and as an artist.'

'Once again we could appreciate the unsurpassable technique he possesses and his enviable ability to feel and express the esthetic emotion of the music which he performs.' (*"Diario del Plata"* January 2, 1926).

'Under the modesty of the performer, he hides a soul of an artist, classic, refined, studious. The guitar in the hands of Galluzo unraveled the compositions of the purest maestros, and we felt they were finished with the marvelous expression of the maestro Tárrega, descriptive of the canvas of a painter who exalted the Moorish life.' We are referring to *"Danza Mora"*. (*"Democracia"*, of Rosario de Santa Fe, July 2, 1929). About Galluzzo Doldan the other publications had the same words of praise, such as *"Revista Ferrocarrilera Argentina"* of May 15, 1925, with the character of a report; the magazine "Fantoches" of Rosario, of January of 1925; the *"Revista Nacional"* October 10, 1923, etc. As a composer he has written and published nine works, among them four preludes, that they say are of good orientation, by which they have been captivated. We expect this guitarist now and again will with harmonic surprises undoubtedly enrich the guitar."

The 1931 Antigua Casa Nuñez catalog listed the nine works published until that time. The photo below is from that listing, and was included in Ricardo Muñoz's biography of the artist. The dates are from the *"Boletin Oficial de Registro Nacional de Propiedad Intelectual"* January 11, 1937 published on February 17, 1937, in Buenos Aires.

This list of works by Alfonso Galluzzo Doldan is from Ricardo Muñoz's unpublished book *"Historia Universal de la Guitarra"* Volume VIII *"La Escuela Tárrega en La Argentina"*.

"Preludios" Nos. 1 y 2   Ediciones Antigua Casa Nuñez-Diego, Gracia y Cia.
"Preludio No. 3" June 1931
"Preludio No. 4" October 1931
"Romero", tango July 1930
"Cajita de Musica"
"Adios al Piano" de Beethoven
"Cancion Hungara" de la Zarzuela "Alma de Dios"
"Romanza en RE mayor" April 1931
"Hoja de Album y Romanza No. 2" June 1932
"Tres Romanzas"
"Dos mazurkas"
"Reverie", tremolo
"Plegaria", tremolo
"Ensueño", tremolo
"Trece Preludios mas"
"Diez Caprichos"
"Aire de Pavana"

Alfonso Galluzzo Doldan

"Seis Temas con Variaciones"
"Tres Sonatas de un tiempo"
"Tres Sonatas de 3 tiempos"
"Dos Andantes"
"Andantes"
"Nocturno"
"Dos Romanzas" para 2 guitarras
"Dos Sonatas de 3 tiempos" para 2 guitarras
"Sonata" de 4 tiempos
"4 Tremolos" para 2 guitarras
"Dos Caprichos"
"Preludio" para mano izquierda sola
"Capricho"
"Tres temas con Variaciones" para piano
"Tres Romanzas" para piano
"Dos Sonatas a 3 tiempos" para piano
"Seis Preludios" para piano
"Preludio a 4 manos" para piano
"Bosquejo" a 4 manos para piano
"Allegro y Preludio" para violin y guitarra
"Melodia" sobre la "Gota de Agua" de Sor (3 guitarras)
"Coral" (varias guitarras)
"Tema con Variaciones y Final" para flauta y guitarra
"Andantino" para conjunto
"Pequeño Rondo" para conjunto
"Berceuse" para conjunto
"Coral No. 10"
"9 Romanzas"

Some of the early works by guitarist and composer Alfonso Galluzzo, "*Preludios*" Nos. 1, 2" being the 2nd publication, "*Cancion Hungara*" the 4th work and "*Romanza en RE mayor*" his 6th production, all published by Diego, Gracia y Cia.

290

This biography of Maud Metcalfe is translated from Ricardo Muñoz's unpublished book *"Historia Universal de la Guitarra" Volume VIII "La Escuela Tárrega en La Argentina".*

"Maud Metcalfe

Her Origin:

"Maud Metcalfe was born in Buenos Aires on June 30, 1909.

Her Education:

She studied music and guitar in the Conservatorio "Fanelli" and studied when she was nine years old with Carmelo Rizzuti.

Her Virtuosity:

The 18th of December of 1924 she was presented in public achieving in that and other recitals that she gave the most resonant success by the gathering, knowledgeable listeners critics and journalists, interpreting works by Schumann, García Tolsa, Albeniz, Granados, Tárrega, Chopin, Beethoven, Mozart, Fortea, Sor, Gottschalk and Malats.

The 9th of August of 1925 she gave another concert in the Salon "La Argentina", with works by Granados, Aguirre, Rizzuti, Chopin, Mozart, Tárrega, Massenet, Malats, Beethoven, Mendelssohn and Gottschalk; the critics praised her although they put some objections as to her musical culture.

The 14th of September of 1926 she gave another concert interpreting the classical authors of the piano and guitar. The magazine *Revista Musical Ilustrada "Tárrega"* of October 1926 issue No. 26, said: ". . . she is a guitarist of brilliance and skill. She possesses a delicate sonority, extreme beauty, extraordinary velocity, security and memory. Her potency is uniform . . . and has a great span of tone colors. Her technique is very good, completely outstanding on arpeggios and scales . . . proof of a lot of talent and ability."

The daily *"El Heraldo"* of the 17th of October of 1926, signed by the eminent maestro *Don* Emilio Pelaia, said: "Maud Metcalfe, in her ascending path, won't take much time to be placed on par with the greatest Spanish cultivators of the guitar. Her art is supported by what Ruskin would call *"Grandeza Moral"* (Moral Nobility). above all she possesses a technique that is attained by patience and a lot of work. . . . Without a doubt, already brilliant, she is a real exponent who belongs in the vanguard of the instrumentalists of the guitar in Argentina. Her youth, intelligence, and constancy, can bring her the most complete triumph . . ."

The 18th of July of 1935 she repeated performances in the Sala Lassalle, sponsored by the Asociacion Guitarristica Argentina; *"La Prensa"* of the 20th of the same month reported 'She has made appreciable technical and musical progress . . . she showed great delicacy of sonority, she achieved without force arpeggios of great polish and affirmed a sober and noble expressiveness . . . her very rich tone colors assure the artistically flattering future.'

The following year in the same hall and for the same institution she performed again admirably, her interpretations constituting a noble and legitimate pride for her maestros and the Argentine guitar.

Her Passing:

She died in Buenos Aires on the 3rd of August of 1938, her remains were buried in the British cemetery of this city." So ends Ricardo Muñoz's entry.

This concert review is from the "Conciertos" section of the *Revista Musical Ilustrada "Tárrega"* magazine, issue No. 22, that was published in May 1926.

"Sociedad Argentina de Conciertos

Audicion de Guitarra por la distinguida concertista Argentina Señorita Maud Metcalfe

Argentine Concert Society

Guitar performance by the distinguished concert guitarist Miss Maud Metcalfe

A young concert guitarist, Maud Metcalfe, whose great aptitudes began to be known in Buenos Aires, has given a new and interesting performance in the Salon Augusteo on the 19th of this past May, under the sponsorship of the "Sociedad Argentina de Conciertos".

Maud Metcalfe, of whom we concerned ourselves with great attention in issue 16, to the root of her performance of October, this time, demonstrates a serious progress. A good part of the qualms that we raised in that occasion, don't take place now, but we believe Miss Metcalfe must continue robustly her knowledge, particularly in the sense of her best artistic illustration.

Her technique is by all means satisfactory. while she maintains in medium velocities; but as soon as the rapid passages come, she loses the vigor and dilutes into a misty brushwork, without letting it to be clear and precise.

It is very probable that the lack of vigor might be natural in this young artist and that through no technical procedure achieves to obtain the energy that she lacks naturally by her hands. It's suitable to notice that her mechanism, notwithstanding all, charges a difficult level to overcome. Because the fingering of Miss Metcalfe presents very interesting aspects. Her sound, in the first place, is delicious. When making some phrase sing, simple and heartfelt, she gets to extract notes of purity and truly transparent crystalline, of a quality, which is, itself, expressed emotion.

Maud Metcalfe possesses the arpeggio like few guitarists. She threshes with great clarity even in the best velocities. She has a breath for the difficult and extensive works and, in general a very appreciable agility and tranquility.

It's clear that her technique can improve. There are details of the mechanism that Miss Metcalfe doesn't know, for example, the tendency to utilize a manner to mute the skin of the thumb, characteristic of modern technique. If she would avoid in this way, that, as in some passage of the *"Minuet No. 9"* and of the *"Scherzo"*, to name something specifically, the bass remains ringing when the passage has entered into another chord. Before leaving the point of view of technique, we must remember an important detail. The performance had its maximum balanced expression in the first part; in it, from the point of view, Miss Metcalfe beamed to a great height. But it wasn't the same in the final two parts. She lacked the security and the self-assurance of the first part.

The artists, in general, they say in these circumstances, that they had "a bad night", and they excuse, without anymore, of which is a lack that they can prevent. It is very common that the instrumentalist torments their hands and mind until the last moments before the concert; and it is very common that such conduct produces contrary results. This doesn't mean that the concert guitarist must enter the hall without putting their hands on the instrument, no; that the exercise is always indispensable which isn't to arrive at the muscular and psychic fatigue.

The prudent ones — and these aspects change according to the individuals — it's prudent to rest the eve, trying to worry, and to do in a brief review the day of the performance. Moments before being presented before the public, it is necessary to condition the hands in a series of energetic exercises.

It's evident that who takes ten years of studies, can't augment their technique in fifteen days of desperate exercise and itself, instead, it is clear they can exhaust their energies to the extreme to complete the program of their concert with difficulty.

Let's continue to consider the interpretative labor of Miss Metcalfe. Without a doubt some have at times notable skills, but who can't achieve, with all, to counterbalance the moments in which they run less fortunate.

Miss Metcalfe lacks the complement of a serious artistic preparation, ability to adorn and enrich her smooth and deliciously feminine temperament.

The program begins with *"Minueto No. 8"* (from Domingo Prat's 30 Minuetos) by Fernando Sor. It is a beautiful page, that Miss Metcalfe translates with excellent sound demonstrating her well-awakened sense of blended tones. She continues playing *"Motivo Arabe"*, by Mr. Rizzuti, a page of good effect although it lacks musical interest, that Miss Metcalfe treats with total affection and delicateness.

The third work is *"Recuerdos de la Alhambra"* by Tárrega. There are about the performance of the tremolo on guitar two different criterions, which correspond to contemporary authorities: that of rapid tremolo, who *Don* Miguel Llobet practically supports; and the slow tremolo, who *Don* Domingo Prat covers and upholds. While to carry the opportunity to document our opinion about the particular, we might say now that Miss Metcalfe has decided for the rapid tremolo. But, dispensing with the velocity, it is necessary to be suitable in which, fast or slow, the tremolo first of all must be strong and clear. That which Miss Metcalfe gives is weak and nebulous. In the course of this page the young artist gets some beautiful effects in the sketch that the phrase of her thumb, a finger that she manages with great ease.

She follows with the *"Tema con variaciones"* by Mozart-Sor. The past year we must make, about the interpretation of this page, a declaration somewhat rude. A very different thing it pleases us to say now, but the new version, is totally suitable to us. The *"calderones"* and *"rubatos"* of the past year haven't disappeared, but they are reduced so discreetly, that they can be considered a modality or personal tendency of the young artist.

Miss Metcalfe attacks the theme with a rapidity that isn't suitable to the placidity of the initial phrase. Then it restrains and unfolds the theme attentively hearing the rhythm that dictates the understanding.

The first variation is a real miracle of clarity and exactness. This is the climaxing moment of her concert.

The young concert guitarist with deep sentiment translates the second commentary, a delicious incursion into the minor mode. In the finish of the first part of this variation, something makes us suspect an error in the solfeggio. Here it must be remembered, that the Segovia version presents in the seventh measure a mistake by the typesetter: the two figures below the second beat must be eighth notes instead of quarter notes.

The third variation is excellent by all means, although it returns to be manifested in the preference by the artist for the *"rubatos"*. And more of that in the fourth variation with admirable cleanliness and security. In the fifth the intention is clearly seen to begin with slowness to augment the velocity progressively toward the final part. With a little more discretion, it would appear to us in good taste, in this way as the tempo of the Coda, against the opinion of Llobet, who attributes much more slowness.

Miss Metcalfe was justly applauded. She added the study by Tárrega of the *"Preludio de la Gruta de Fingal"*, excessively rapid and, therefore, it was confused.

The second part begins with the *"Minueto No. 12"* (from Prat's collection) that the concert guitarist performed pleasantly, although with less technical precision. Some phrases can be noted beautifully spoken. Since, in the past year, the *"Triste No. 4"* by Aguirre and as for the *"Scherzo"* by Beethoven, a reserved diagnosis. It seems as a lie that guitarists are so anxious to play at least the *"guitarrizable"* (works playable on the guitar) of all the geniuses.

As an encore, Miss Metcalfe offered the *"Nocturno No. 2"* by Chopin. Mr. Chopin, is another one of the victims of the guitar. It is sensible that artists such as Segovia and Llobet, authorize his performance, including the romantic in their programs, without some persuasion about its guitaribility.

But as this and that refer to Beethoven, they are two orphan affirmations of argument, "Tárrega" promises to the interested readers about this point, to expound later, in separate articles and without referring to any performer, the reasons in which our conviction is founded.

And returning to the *"Nocturno No. 2"*, we believe that Miss Metcalfe wasn't always following the initial rhythm. In this way, for example, in the fifth measure, it appears to us that there isn't a reason to hasten dizzily over a phrase that on the contrary, is asking to be caressed and spoken with smoothness and loving sentiment.

You can plead to the reader that everyone is the owner to sense in his own manner. Very well. To this it can be responded that about the versions of the great musicians exists a tradition slowly forged by the brilliant interpreters of the past and of the present; that all of the personal temperaments find a field exceeded to define their own characteristics through light modifications of detail, but always respecting the general guidelines. And when a new interpreter is fundamentally different from the usual version, it is simply said that he doesn't know how to sing, and it is very easy to prove it.

The music isn't a hieroglyphic that anyone can sense in his own way. The signs of which are served, relatively, complete and the musical ideas are very clearly written for all to know how to read them. As in front of the page of a book, you can vary the intonation, the potency, the velocity, but never the feeling.

Miss Metcalfe played a *"Minueto"* by Beethoven, of which we won't speak, and followed that with one by Sor, the No. 9, that she feels and understands, and in it again lighted up her beautiful sound.

Then she played an *"Andante"* by Mozart, a page of incomparable beauty in whose interpretation Miss Metcalfe didn't achieve being distinguished.

The work began with a portamento. The year before we said: 'The initial little note mustn't sound in the cases in which it is an indirect attack of the original note of the piano.'

The plague of the *portamento* has been introduced by Tárrega; but Tárrega didn't sound like it ever would come to be performed as it's performed now, granting to the adornment, equal or more value than the principal note. Those who listened to Tárrega assured the Valencian maestro just played the initial little note, to slide the portamento swiftly, as a gust.

But it wasn't necessary to have heard Tárrega to perform an adornment. It's enough to read it as it's written. Whatever theory tells us 'that the short appoggiatura is performed rapidly, taking its extremely low value from the following note.'

It will seem somewhat of a bother to the reader our insistence about aspects so elemental of the interpretation, but we beg a little bit of kindness. It is necessary to speak with clarity and to say all, expounding, even though lightly, the grounds of our opinion, because, according as seen, the postulated fundamentals of this tribune of criticism, have its origin for the interested in anything secondary, in anything that the journalist ignores in absolute, in anything less than the truth, less in justice, less in the noble desire and risking to elevate and dignify the dejected prestige of the Argentine guitar.

We're in the *"Andante"* by Mozart. We have seen that Miss Metcalfe begins with an unsuitable portamento. In the course of the first measure the movement remains established with which the artist takes the work; now, by what reason during the five chords of the second measure, this movement hastens breaking the necessary rhythmic and spiritual unity of the work? These alterations of the movement are frequent in the course of this work. There also are errors of reading. In the sixth measure, to mention something specifically, there is a rapid treble passage that connects with the cadence in the seventh measure. Well; the two notes Sol (G) of this passage aren't naturals, because they take the influence of the sharp that alters the Sol (G) of the first chord of the said measure.

The trill, here as in the *"Nocturno No. 2"* by Chopin, mustn't last *"a piacere"* but the time of the note in which it must adorn.

We have come to the same old piece, the indispensable *"Gran Jota"*, whose placement at the end of the programs has remained legalized for the use by who gets with it public and money.

The confection of the program is simply disastrous. Tárrega will return later with all delay about this topic, — in a general thesis, to be limited now in a rapid and clear example:

I.	Minuetto N.o 8	Sors.
	Motivo Arabe	Rizzutti.
	Recuerdo de la Alhambra	Tárrega.
	Tema con variaciones	Mozart-Sors.
II.	Minuetto N.o 12	Sors.
	Triste N.o 4	Aguirre.
	Scherzo de la Sonata op. 2	Beethoven.
III.	Minuetto N.o 9	Sors.
	Minuetto	Beethoven.
	Andante	Mozart.
	Gran Jota Aragonesa	Tárrega.

Supposing that Miss Metcalfe could not offer works of more diverse character, the order of the program should have never been. The logical, series, could have put the works in the following way:

I.	Minueto N.o 8	Sors.
	Minuetto N.o 9	Sors.
	Minueto N.o 12	Sors.
	Variaciones sobre un tema de Mozart.	
II.	Andante	Mozart.
	Minueto	Beethoven.
	Scherzo de la Sonata op. 2	Beethoven.
III.	Nocturno	Chopin.
	Serenata	Malats.
	Recuerdos de la Alhambra.	Tárrega.
	Gran Jota	Tárrega.

Aguirre and Rizutti don't have a logical placement. They could be placed at the beginning of the third set but that would upset the chronology.

In the presented example one can see the first part dedicated to the classics of the guitar. It is clear that the ideal would be an *"Andante"* or *"Andantino"* and an *"Estudio"* instead of the *"Minuetos"* Nos. 9 and 12; but we only put the works performed. The second part continues to be dedicated to the classics. Mozart is the purest figure and representative of that epoch and Beethoven, serially related to Mozart to begin, freely evolves and brilliant to join, in the final stages of his life, with the romanticism. The program remains prepared for the inclusion of the romantics and Chopin — who with Schuman, Schubert and Mendelssohn integrate the prominent group of the epoch — this, well in his place.

Malats and Tárrega are contemporaries. They are well placed at the end of the program although their artistic category might be very inferior to the previous ones. But you already know that being treated to a guitar program there has to be given a preference to the composers of the instrument and it's also known that those don't bear being incomparable to the great masters of the piano or the orchestra.

The essential points of view in the confection of the program are, first the scales of values and second, the chronological order or antiquity.

Besides there is a series of factors such as the grouping by schools and the diffusion of notable contemporary, that can alter in part the essential points of view.

The importance or interest that the performer attributes to a fixed group of new works can be induced to concern with them the central part; and we won't extend ourselves more, but to reproduce those words that with which such good intention and admirable efficacy we insert in our issue number 16 about the same subject: 'It might be vain to intend a mandatory for the confection of the program since that not any formula is absolute. We are no further than the perceptual rigidity. We believe that the order can vary, according to the intention or purpose of the artist, but the permissions always reveal the direction of an illustrated criteria.' "

As you can well imagine the above review filled four pages of the *Revista Musical Ilustrada "Tárrega"* magazine. Maud Melcalfe inspired Noemi Toulouse to play the guitar, and Noemi became Carmelo Rizzuti's favorite student. She received her diploma as a professor in 1924. Below are her photo and repertoire from the Revista Musical Ilustrada "Tárrega" magazine, issue No. 1, that was published in June 1924. This represents quite an ability for a 15 year-old girl, who began to play in 1918, at the age of nine years old. The other previous reviews just filled portions of a page.

Srta. Maud Metcalfe

San Nicolás, Schumann; Nocturno N° 2, Chopín; Sueño trémolo, Tárrega; Cádiz. Albéniz; Danza española N° 5, Granados, M. Llobet; Serenata, Malats; Dos minuetes en "La", Sors; Variaciones de Sors sobre un tema de Mozart; Gran Trémolo, Gottschalk; Granada, Albéniz; Danza Mora Tárrega; Capricho árabe, Tárrega; Recuerdos de Alhambra, Tárrega; Horizontes andaluces, J. Parga; Rapsodia N° 63 de concierto J. Parga; La pavana, Tárrega; Ave María, C. Gounod; Minuet, Paderewski; Preludio español, Albéniz; Canción de cuna, Pujol; Testamento de Amelia, M. Llobet; Chanson árabe, Granados.

Maud Melcalfe

Delia Rodríguez Arias

Maria Teresa Egozcue

Two of Carmelo Rizzuti's students from the *Revista Musical Ilustrada "Tárrega"* magazine, issue No. 1, that was published in June 1924.

Srta. Delia Solitro

Preludios 1, 4, 5, 7 y 8, Tárrega; La Mariposa Estudio, Tárrega; Recuerdos de La Alhambra. Tárrega; Capricho Arabe, Tárrega; Senatina, Estudio, Tárrega; Sueño, Trémolo-Estudio. Tárrega; María, Gavota Tárrega; Góndola Veneciana, Mendelsohn; Granada, Serenata, Albéniz; Andante, Haydn; Gran Trémolo, Gottschalk; Saint Nicolás, Shumann; Fragmento del Septimino, Beethoven; Preludio de la "Gruta del Fineall", Mendelsohn; Preludio Nº 7, Chopín; Pizzicato, Delibes; Reverie, Schumann; Testamento de Amelia Llobet; Variaciones sobre un tema de Mozart, Sors.

Carmelo Rizzuti student, Delia Solitro, with a list of her repertoire from issue No.1 of *Revista Musical Ilustrada "Tárrega"* June 1924 and advertisements from issues Nos. 12 and 15. The ad in No.15 was utilized throughout the remainder of the publication of 33 issues.

Ramon Genen was a Carmelo Rizzuti student who played substantial repertoire. Here is a list of his repertoire from issue #1 of *Revista Musical Ilustrada "Tárrega"* June 1924 and ads from issues Nos. 12 from June 1925 and 15 of September 1925. The ad in #15 was utilized throughout the remainder of the publication of 33 issues. According to Prat's *Diccionario de Guitarristas,* "Ramon was born on July 21, 1900, and he played guitar since his childhood. When he moved from Ojo de Agua to Buenos Aires he entered in the Conservatorio D'Andrea under the direction of Carmelo Rizzuti. In 1924 Ramon received his diploma, and was able to teach at several conservatories, among them, Thibaud-Piazzini. Ramon was also a component in the "Cuarteto Argentino". On November 26, 1930 he presented his students in a concert at the Salon "La Argentina". In the 1931 Antigua Casa Nuñez catalog, six of his compositions are listed.

Sr. Ramón Genen

Lágrima, Preludio, Tárrega; Adelira Mazurka, Tárrega; Pavana, Tárrega; Estudio en Forma de Minueto, Tárega; Preludios 1 y 5, Tárrega; La Alborada, Cajita de Música, Tárrega; Recuerdos de La Alhambra, Tárrega; Capricho Arabe, Serenata, Tárrega; El Testament D'Amelia, Canción Catalana, Llobet; Preludio, Sáinz de la Maza; Canción de Cuna, Pujol; Saint-Nicolás, Schumann; Góndola Veneciana, Mendelsshon; Fragmento en forma de Preludio, Mendelsshon; El Delirio, A. Cano; Allegretto del Cuarteto, Beethoven; El Pescador de Perlas, Romanza, Bizet; Variaciones sobre un tema de Mozart Sors; Rondó en La, Aguado.

This is the back outside cover of the *"Revista Orfeo Musical"* magazine *Año* V No. 43 from February 1922. Carmelo Rizzuti is the Maestro of Guitar at the "Conservatorio D'Andrea".

Archive: Augusto Marcellino.

Palmira Gabba
A Carmelo Rizzuti student at Conservatorio D'Andrea.

Academia Rizzuti students at the Conservatorio D'Andrea on September 27, 1924. Carmelo Rizzuti is standing in the background. From *Revista Musical Ilustrada "Tárrega"* No. 5 October 1924.

Concert at Conservatorio D'Andrea on September 27, 1924

"First part:

1) Zamba-Rizzuti
2) Enriqueta (Habanera)-García Tolsa
performed by: Delia Solitro, Aida Rosa Marchio and Felix Samaniego

3) Pavana-Tárrega
performed by Gaspar Cronford and Rafael Obligado

4) Lagrima-Tárrega
performed by Gaspar Cronford and Alfonso Galluzzo

5) Ensueño Op. 15 No. 7-Schumann
performed by Santiago Marengo and Juan de Dios Peza

6) Minué Federal-harmonization by Domingo Prat
performed by Alfonso Galluzzo

Second part:

1) Los Pescadores de Perlas-Bizet
performed by Alfonso Galluzzo

2) Preludio-Regino Sainz de la Maza
3) Cancion de cuna-Pujol
performed by Ramon Genen and Juan de Dios Peza

4) Variaciones-Mozart (Sor)
performed by Delia Solitro

5) Recuerdos de la Alhambra-Tárrega
performed by Delia Solitro, Santiago Marengo, Alfonso Galluzzo and Ramon Genen"

Santiago A. Marengo
From issue No. 7 of *Revista Musical Ilustrada "Tárrega"* of December 1924.

Academia de Guitarra "Rizzuti" on December 2, 1924 at Prince George's Hall.
From issue No. 7 of *Revista Musical Ilustrada "Tárrega"* of December 1924.

ACADEMIA SUPERIOR DE
GUITARRA "RIZZUTI"

Señor
E. Bensadon y flia

Recuerdo de su 42.º aniversario

Carmelo Rizzuti

30 de Julio
1911 - 1953

Here is a 42nd anniversary card of the Academia Superior de Guitarra "Rizzuti" of July 30, 1953,
dedicated to Eduardo Bensadon and autographed by maestro Carmelo Rizzuti.

CINCUENTENARIO
DE LA
ACADEMIA
RIZZUTI

CINCUENTENARIO DE LA ACADEMIA RIZZUTI
COMISION DE HOMENAJE

Esta comisión tiene el honor de invitar a usted y sus allegados al concierto que se ofrecerá en Homenaje al maestro Carmelo Rizzuti en ocasión de sus bodas de oro con la guitarra.

LEONEL ARCE SCOTT
PRESIDENTE

CARLOS VISCIO
SECRETARIO

JOSE BENEDETTI
TESORERO

NOTA: Con la presentación de ésta invitación en boletería del teatro desde dos días antes del concierto, le serán entregadas sin cargo las localidades numeradas correspondientes.—

Decades later, at the end of his impressionable career, the board of directors of the homage to Carmelo Rizzuti's Academia held a concert in honor of the 50th anniversary of the Academia de Guitarra Rizzuti. It was held at the Teatro Ateneo on July 31, 1961.
Courtesy of Lucas Agustín de Antoni, Buenos Aires.

Translation: "Fiftieth anniversary of the Academia Rizutti. This commission has the honor of inviting you and your close relatives to a concert that is offered as a homage to the maestro Carmelo Rizzuti on the occasion of his golden anniversary with the Guitar. Note: With the presentation of this invitation in the ticket office of the theater from two days before the concert, you will be given the corresponding numbered locations without any charge."

Dicho acto tendrá lugar en el Teatro Ateneo,
Paraguay 918 de esta capital, el 31 del corriente mes
a las 21.30 horas en punto, no se permitirá el
acceso a la sala durante la ejecución de las obras.

Una hora antes de la función estará disponible
en el hall del teatro para ser firmado por los asistentes, el pergamino que le será entregado al
Maestro al finalizar el acto.

Buenos Aires, Julio de 1961.

Back cover of the 50th Anniversary homage to Carmelo Rizzuti. Translation: "The stated act will take place in the Teatro Ateneo, at Paraguay 918 of this capital, the 31st of the current month at 9:30 PM sharp, access to the hall will not be permitted during the performance of the works."

1911 - 30 de Julio - 1962

*La Academia Superior
de Guitarra Rizzuti*

Agradece . . .

Cover of the 51st anniversary homage to the director of the Academia Superior de la Guitarra — Carmelo Rizzuti. This event was held on July 30, 1962.

Invitation courtesy of Lucas Agustín de Antoni, Buenos Aires.

DIRECTOR:

CARMELO RIZZUTI

CUERPO DOCENTE:

HAYDÉE RIZZUTI de CROUZEILLES

ETELVINA BERON

TOMÁS POMILIO

LEONEL ARCE SCOTT

SECRETARIOS:

Dr. JOSÉ C. RIZZUTI

JOSÉ PLA BORT

ADMINISTRADOR:

MARIO B. CROUZEILLES

List of teachers and administration of the Academia Superior de la Guitarra Rizzuti in 1962.

. . . *a sus alumnos, ex alumnos*
y amigos el constante estímulo brindado
a lo largo de 51 años de ininterrumpida
labor en pro de la guitarra.
A todos:

¡Muchas Gracias!

Carmelo Rizzuti
Director

Carmelo Rizzuti thanking his students and ex-students for their support of his 51 year career. Translation: "...to his students, ex-students and friends the constant esteemed salute over the length of 51 years of uninterrupted labor in favor of the guitar. To everyone, Many Thanks." Carmelo Rizzuti, Director.

Courtesy of Lucas Agustín de Antoni, Buenos Aires.

ALUMNOS EGRESADOS

Mariano Peralta - José M. Lasella - Maud Metcalfe - Aquiles de
Armas - Mario de Armas - Lucio A. Avalos - Egidio Smiraglia
Ramón Genen - Delia Solitro - Graciela F. Rivas - Noemí C.
Toulouse - Alfonso Galluzzo - Antonio Romero - Víctor Stigliano
Tomás Pomilio - Lilia A Cristobal - Saverio Cuchi - Eysbel Poso
Antonio Giaquinto - Dolores O. Ala - Irene V. Bordigoni
Ermano Brandazzi - Aída Lopez Rojas - Elisa Orellana de Tapia
Bernabé Alonso Perez - Eduardo Lagomarsino - Etelvina E. Berón
Choly Sanchez - Severo Rodriguez - Olga Abiatte - Rafael
Ferraro - Juan Manuel Barragán Guerra - María Esther Zawels
Lidia Guerrello Oyharzabal - Florencia Padilla - Carlota Bogni
de Nicolussi - Maria E. C. de Thomas - Elsa M. L. Bertoni
José Pla Bort - José M. Molinari - Mary E, Mira López
Dr. Tomás Chamorro - Manuel Martínez - María Inés Rodriguez
Alfredo Latorre - Haydée Elsa Rizzuti - Abel Ortíz Pereyra
Pascual Succi - Dr. Pedro Larrandart - Osvaldo Mele
Humberto Domingo Simuro - Elena Beatríz Pereyra - Ana Otero
María Rosa Lagorio - Carmen Gimenez - Mafalda R. Martínez
Leoni J. Darroux - Aída Eugenia Moyano - Juan Doiglesario
Leonardo M. Denón - Gregorio Fragalá - Aída Nimia Ortíz
Leiva - Salvador V. Lepera - Amaury Mancebo - Santos Duca
María Luisa Natale - Dora E. Contreras - Ricardo Castro
Leopoldo Marquez - Elda Carmen Gazzo - Rosa Alvarez de Simó
Jorge Luis Tosi - María del Rosario Avalos - Juan José De Luca
Manuel Horacio Rodriguez - Leonel Arce Scott - Antonio Berald

Academia Superior de la Guitarra Rizzuti students, which number a total 77.
Courtesy of Lucas Agustín de Antoni, Buenos Aires.

Due to the popularity of the classical guitar there were many maestros and many academias. Another of those maestros was Alejandro Spinardi.

In Domingo Prat's *Diccionario de Guitarristas* it states that: "Alejandro Spinardi was born in Tarnese, Argentina on January 4, 1899. From the time when he was only a youngster he loved reading and music. He was able to acquire a guitar due to the help of his elders. He was self -taught and it took a while for his abilities to unfold into the guitarist he would become. *"El dia que yo me muera"* by Alejandro Spinardi, was published in the *Revista Musical Ilustrada "Tárrega"* issue No. 23 of June, 1926. He established the Academia Argentina de Guitarra." He had composed 15 works for the guitar by the time of Prat's entry and the printing of the 1931 Antigua Casa Nuñez catalog.

Alejandro Spinardi and some students

Srta. ELVIRA WILSON
From *Revista Musical Ilustrada "Tárrega"*
Issue No. 19 from February, 1926

Academia Argentina de GUITARRA

DIRECTOR:

A. SPINARDI

Enseñanza completa y elemental para ambos sexos.

Aires nacionales, tangos, etc.

Cursos rápidos en la Academia y a domicilio.

Calle RIVADAVIA 2542

Dpto. I

U. T. 7879, Mitre   Buenos Aires

Alejandro Spinardi advertisement
From *Revista Musical Ilustrada "Tárrega"*
Issue No. 32 April, 1927

Maria Mila Gramajo Figueroa
From *Revista Musical Ilustrada "Tárrega"*
Issue No. 13 July, 1925

The *Tango, "Dora"* was published in the *Revista Musical Ilustrada "Tárrega"* issue No. 18 of December 1925. The Zamba, *"El dia que yo me muera"* by Alejandro Spinardi, was published in the *Revista Musical Ilustrada "Tárrega"* issue No. 23 of June, 1926.

These two pieces by Alejandro Spinardi were published by Antigua Casa Nuñez in 1936.

According to Domingo Prat's *Diccionario de Guitarristas*: "Faustino Riglos Castillo was born in Buenos Aires on July 29, 1880. Faustino studied with the notable guitarist, Antonio Sinopoli, director of the Academia de Guitarra "Tárrega", and received his diploma in 1913. A little while later Faustino became a part of the body of teachers for the Academia de Guitarra "Tárrega". With his intelligence and vocation as maestro he earned a deserved renown, such that he was named professor of guitar at the Conservatorio "La Nacion". The excessive modesty of Faustino Riglos didn't allow him to be appreciated to his full value, being, however, distinguished among his colleagues."

CONSERVATORIO LA NACION

This photo of Faustino Riglos (the man donning a mustache) with his students of the Conservatorio "La Nacion" was taken on November 7, 1924 at Prince George's Hall and is from the *Revista Musical Ilustrada "Tárrega"* issue No. 6 of November, 1924. This Grand Concert of 120 students involved pianos, the violin family, guitars and vocalists.

The intervention of guitars was:
"I
a) "Marieta"— Francisco Tárrega
Yolanda Echenique

b) "La Natita"— Juan Alais
c) "La Chiquilla"— Jota-Pablo Simeone
Yolanda Echenique, Luisa Frascino, Juana S. Calvo, Edmundo Maggi and José Ruiz Nicueza

II
a) "Vidala con Variaciones"— Antonio Sinopoli
Edmundo Maggi"

This detail about the passing of Faustino Riglos is from Ricardo Muñoz's unpublished book *"Historia Universal de la Guitarra"* Volume VII *"La Guitarra en La Argentina"*.

"Faustino Riglos died in Buenos Aires on the 27th of December of 1952, and was buried in the cemeterio del Oeste, with the attendance of his family, friends and some students."

Edmundo Maggi
From the *Revista Musical Ilustrada "Tárrega"* issue No. 6 of November, 1924.

One of Faustino Riglos' most distinguished students was Edmundo Maggi Zuegers. "Edmundo was born in Buenos Aires on May 10, 1905. At the Conservatorio "La Nacion" he studied with Faustino, and he took his final exam in December of 1925. As a guitarist, he had a beautiful and emotive touch, that made his passages very interesting and he drew frequent applause. Having dedicated himself to the guitar since he was quite young, he has since demonstrated some original pieces of good orientation, those being appreciated and recommended by the populace of the Rio de la Plata. As a composer he is known for his *"Estilo"* and *"Tarantela"*. The *"Estilo facil para Guitarra"* called *"Mi Paisana"* was published in the *Revista Musical Ilustrada "Tárrega"* issue No. 23 of June 1926. Edmundo's *"Tarantela"* was published in the last issue of the *Revista Musical Ilustrada "Tárrega"* issue No. 33 of May 1927. The *"Tarantela"* isn't difficult, but very pleasing in its form of a dance. He is also known for his piece *"Evocacion", Capricho Original,* which reveals the perfection as a composition, and we can expect his worthy contributions to the guitar literature." So ends Domingo Prat's entry, dated 1932, in his *Diccionario de Guitaristas.*

These advertisements are from the *Revista Musical Ilustrada "Tárrega"* issue No. 12 of June, 1925 and issue No. 15 of September 1925, respectively.

Pepito (José) Ruiz Nicueza
This photo is from the *Revista Musical Ilustrada "Tárrega"* issue No. 7 of December 1924.

This photo of Faustino Riglos and his students on November 22 at Prince George's Hall is from the *Revista Musical Ilustrada "Tárrega"* issue No. 28 of November, 1926.

"I

a) Andante-Haydn-Tárrega-Pepito (José) Ruiz Nicueza

II

a) Leyenda — Isaac Albeniz-Edmundo Maggi

b) Vals y Marcha — José Sancho-Angélica M. G. Codino, Delia F. Médici, Mercedes Clucellas, Yolanda Echenique, Rosa D. Demaestri, Edmundo F. Arrigoni, Edmundo Maggi, José Ruiz Nicueza and Antonio Ques Soler"

Leon Vicente Gascon

Another illustrious figure on the scene was Leon Vicente Gascon. In issue No. 6 of *Revista Musical Ilustrada "Tárrega"* of November 1924, there was an article entitled *"Cultores de la Guitarra"*. The following is translated from that article and interview.

"Leon Vicente Gascon was born on July 18, 1896 in Orrios, Teruel province, Spain. He was to arrive in Argentina in 1913.

In the bosom of his home he was to have initiated his apprenticeship that soon, due to the ups and downs of life, he had to abandon it. Leon's father played bandurria and guitar.

"The intrepid struggle, compelling, that sustained me in the first few years of permanent residence in Argentina, smothered to a certain point, momentarily, that strength within that would strive to flourish in my soul, until one night, serene and silently, I heard very remotely the smooth and sweet chords of a guitar, that reached my ears intermittently, brought by the coming and goings of the waves of the air."

"At first I was for a very short time, under the direction of a maestro, Tarantino Nicolau, and later, in 1916, maestro Sinopoli took me on as a student for some four months". For almost a year Leon had to drop the guitar to attend to his obligations.

"I started to study again in 1917 under the direction of Domingo Prat. More than a year had passed since I had to abandon the guitar. Prat returned to Spain and didn't come back until only last year in 1923."

"In 1923 I took some lessons of perfection with the distinguished concert artist Maria Luisa Anido, lessons that undoubtedly, influenced the perfection of my guitar technique."

"Once I had dominated the technique of the instrument and knew all its resources, I dedicated myself to the heavier works, but at the same time more attentively: harmony and composition."

"It was my maestro, in those music studies, an illustrious disciple of Rimsky-Korsakov, the maestro Aboutkoff-professor of Musical History at the Conservatorio Imperial in Russia. The musical science of that man, inexhaustible, translated in great part, to my apprenticeship. About that aspect we must say that the maestro Aboutkoff has departed from Buenos Aires and I had to put myself in the hands of professor Pietro Rubione, another talented artist, who I've gladly entrusted to give the finishing touches to my musical culture."

At the time of this interview Leon Vicente Gascon was the professor of guitar at the Conservatorio Ot. Sevcik. On October 22, 1924 there was a student recital held in the Salon Teatro. The students performed on piano, violin, voice and guitar. The participation of the guitarists was:

Part II

a) Estudio No. 2 — Dionisio Aguado
b) Una Lagrima — Francisco Tárrega

young girl M. E. Ortegui

c) Preludio No. 1 — Francisco Tárrega
d) Cancion Catalana — Miguel Llobet

Laura Dominguez

e) Preludio No. 9 — Francisco Tárrega
f) Fragmento de Septimino — Ludwig van Beethoven

youngster Dante Dominguez

g) Minueto en Re y Andante — Fernando Sor

youngster Pedro Mongelos"

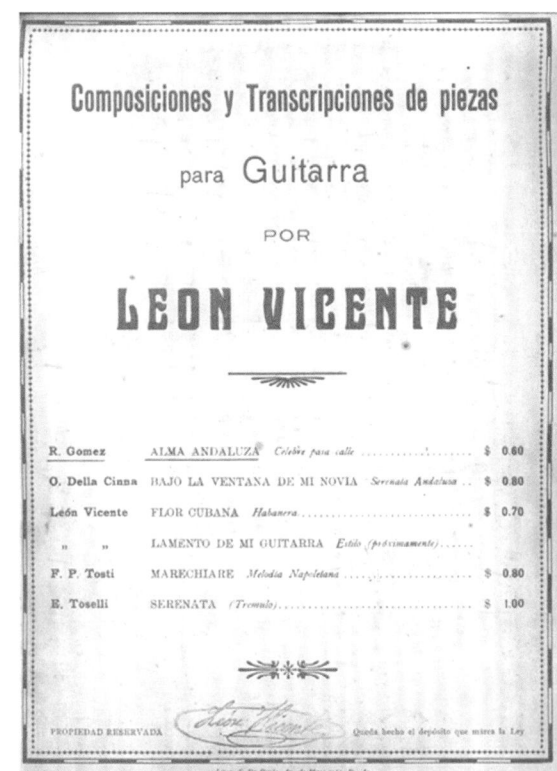

These Leon Vicente pieces are the newest to be listed in the 1931 Antigua Casa Nuñez catalog.

This advertisement is from the *Revista Musical Ilustrada "Tárrega"* issue No. 15 of September, 1925.

314

Leon Vicente Gascon

Cover photo of the *Mundo Musical-Revista Mensual Ilustrada* magazine *Año* XX No. 236 of May 1958. In this issue Nelly Menotti wrote a lengthy homage to Leon (with the help of Inés Neuendorf and Irma Costanzo), that was given at the reunion of the Asociacion Guitarristica Argentina. She quoted Ricardo Muñoz about the gatherings in the Juan Carlos Anido home, in which Leon took part. "In those years the Anido home recalled the memorable reunions that took place in the past century in certain European dinners which were attended by Rossini, Bellini, Liszt, Schubert, Paganini, Sor, etc. At first the home was on calle Cordoba, then on calle Charcas, night after night the candlelit gatherings of friends, poets, writers, musicians, literary critics, Argentine guitarists and bewildered foreigners to hear one ideal solo by Llobet, Pujol, Robledo, Sainz de la Maza, etc.".

Nelly Menotti spoke at great length "about the works of Leon as he had published pieces for over 30 years." (In the 1931 Antigua Casa Nuñez catalog, there were 21 pieces of Leon Vicente Gascon listed.) "They were of Argentine folk dances, Andalucian pieces, Cuban *Habaneras, Minuets,* pieces for 3 guitars and pieces for voice and guitar. As time went on Leon began to number his opuses and wrote a 3-volume method for guitar. Besides this substantial amount of work, he wrote a *Suite La Argentina Op. 10*, containing 5 pieces.

At the conclusion of her musical performance of Leon's Suite Andaluza Op. 13 she says a very eloquent phrase: *"Decir Andalucia es decir guitarra."*—"To say Andalucia is to say guitar"."

Published by Diego, Gracia & Cia.
January 1927

Published by Romero & Fernández
mid 1930's

Published by Alfredo Perrotti
in the 1930's

Vol. 3 of maestro Gascon's Method
published in 1957 by Ricordi

316

Leon Vicente Gascon

レオン・ビセンテ・ガスコンは1896年7月18日スペインのアラゴン州オリオスに生れた。幼少にしてアルゼンチンに移住し、ブエノスアイレスに居住。初め Tarantino について音楽理論とギターを学び、次いで Antonio Sinopoli に師事し1918年には Anido に就いた。現在自らアカデミアを主宰し、後進の指導にあたり、Irma Costanzo, Nelly Menotti などの女流ギタリストを楽界に送つて花々しい活動をしている。

　ガスコンの作曲活動も却々花々しい。最近まで数十曲を手にしているが、教本あり、スペイン風なものあり、アルゼンチン風なものあり、ギター伴奏歌曲あり、二重奏曲あり、独奏曲ありといつた風でまことに多種多彩である。就中次の曲は注目に価する。

　　　Metodo moderno parra Guitarra　（教本）
　　　Album de la Juventudo　（子供のアルバム）
　　　Homenaje a Fernando Sor　（ソルに捧ぐ）
　　　op.　8　　Sonatina　（ソナテイナ）
　　　op.　9　　Suite Espanola　（スペイン組曲）
　　　op. 10　　Suite Argentina　（アルゼンチン組曲）

This is from the Japanese guitar magazine *"Armonia"* from September-October 1956 Vol. III No. 5. The magazine was printed in Sen Dai, Miyagiken, a city heavily damaged by the tsunami after the 8.9 magnitude earthquake on March 11, 2011. Japanese translation by Randy Osborne.

　"Leon Vicente Gascon

　Leon Vicente Gascon was born on July 18, 1896 in Orrios, Aragon Province, Spain. During his childhood he immigrated to Argentina, he resides in Buenos Aires. From his first teacher Tarantino he learned theory and guitar, then he studied under Antonio Sinopoli, in the year 1918 he studied under Anido. Presently he has his own academia that he supervises, a younger generation's leadership by the accomplished women guitarists Irma Costanzo, Nelly Menotti and the like sent from the world of music are doing the magnificent activity.

Gascon's compositional activity is also all the more brilliant. Until recently he has had scores of compositions in his hands, there is a method, Spanish style items, Argentine style things, guitar accompaniment vocal compositions, duet pieces, solo guitar works and truly by means of many kinds of multi-colored pieces. Among other things the following compositions merit your attention.

Método moderno para guitarra (Method)

Album de la Juventud (Album for Adolescents)

Homenaje a Fernando Sor (Homage to Sor)

Op. 8 Sonatina

Op. 9 Suite Española

Op. 10 Suite Argentina"

Leon Vicente Gascon's autograph from the *"Vidalita (Facil)"* published by Diego, Gracia & Cia. in January 1927.

This biography of Leon Vicente Gascon is translated from Ricardo Muñoz's unpublished book *"Historia Universal de la Guitarra"* Volume VIII *"La Escuela Tárrega en La Argentina"*.

"Leon Vicente Gascon

His Origin:

He was born in Orrios, Teruel, Spain, the 18th of July of 1896, settling in Buenos Aires in 1913.

His Education:

In the breast of his family he began to practice the guitar, and once he was in Argentina he began to study with maestro *Don* Tarrantino Nicolau, and in 1916 with *Don* Antonio Sinopoli for only four months, having to stop the guitar to attend to his occupations that didn't bring enough remuneration.

The next year he restarted his guitaristic activities with *Don* Domingo Prat, who, after a little more than a year returned to Spain and Gazcon remained without a maestro; in 1923 the eminent Maria Luisa Anido directed his studies, who made known to him the resources of the instrument and then he dedicated to study higher music, harmony and composition with maestro Aboutoff, who much like Prat, left Buenos Aires and then Leon went to study with maestro *Don* Pietro Rubione, whose talent sculpted his musical personality. —

His Virtuosity:

The 4th of May of 1940 in the Teatro Lassalle he gave a concert with his own works; in the 1st Part a series of compositions from the 1st book of his method: *"El Cucu", "El Eco", "Danzas de los Enanos", "Las Campanas"* and *"Pastor Alegre"*; in the 2nd Part: others from the 2nd book of his method: *"Tamboril", "La Hilandera", "Cabalgata", "Arlequin y Colombina" (Dance), "Campanella"* and "Oracion"; in the 3rd Part: Op. 10 *"Suite Argentina"* and 4th Part: *"Andante"* (Homage to Sor) and Op. 11, *"Suite Noche de Reyes"*, with a great success of approval. —

His Compositions:

His production is constituted by original works of the popular and folkloric genre, some classical and transcriptions, that since then will be augmented with time:

"Desolacion", Tango   Ediciones Nuñez
"Veni pebeta", Tango
"Amor de Gaucho", Zamba
"Sos tan bonita", Zamba
"Vidalita"
"Adios Granada", Cancion
"Minuetto No. 1"
"Asi canta mi guitarra", Estilo

"Album de Juventud"   Ediciones Ricordi Buenos Aires
"La Perchelera", Malagueña
"Suite No. 10 y Op. 11"
"Homenaje a Sor", this is a serious construction of a fine melodic purity, very much in the style of the immaculate personality of the great Sor.
"Acuarela Sevillana", Solea, it transpires his descriptive and impressionistic tendency.

His Pedagogy:

He has taught lessons in the Conservatorio Otto Ševcík and continues imparting them in his private Academia with great success, for whose students he has written a method of modern technical mechanism formed by 2 books that are published by Casa Ricordi and Romero y Fernández , which he uses for his legion of students, many of them now admired virtuosos, such as; Dante Dominguez, Juan Carlos Martínez, Nelly Menotti, Fanny Amanda Castro, etc. —

In several artistic acts he has presented his disciples to the public consideration in order to demonstrate their degree of preparation, of those we recall on the 15th of May of 1930 with his referred to student Dominguez, well applauded; the 5th of December of 1936 he brought 27 disciples to the Teatro Lassalle performing solos, duos, trios and all as a group; on the 15th of June of 1940 he presented the named Martínez with general satisfaction; a new group of 14 guitarists in the same theater; the 25th of October of 1941 he presented to the professional critics his mentioned Nelly Menotti who was highly acclaimed; the 28th of November of 1942 he repeated the success with Fanny Amanda Castro and in this way successively with deserved praise for his continued and constructive work.

Lutherie:

In a union with the maestro of music *Don* Pietro Rubione and the engineer *Don* Hector Ninci, they collaborated in the invention with electric technician Alfredo Caccianini consisting in the application of an electric sound amplifier for our instrument.

The 5th of August of 1931 in the Sala Wagneriana they presented a guitar supplied with the apparatus placed in the interior of the resonant body, over the union of the sides in the endblock, where it came out of the exterior to take current; this was plugged into the common amplifier; Gazcon in his abilities performed some works, as well as strums (Rasqueados), ligados, harmonics, arpeggios and trills with a marked success of admirable proof, since, until the sounds became a harmonic, they were heard for 20 rows, as if the instrument were one meter of distance away, such as the vigor of the soundswithout losing the absolute of its esthetic guitaristic quality, so appreciated and characteristic of the instrument.

The musicologist *Don* Carlos Vega had lectured previously in various passages in the history of the construction, then concerning of the goodness of the invention with praise for the presenters and inventors. However the magnificent result obtained, the negativity of its use is unexplainable, especially in the halls of large dimensions and numerous public."

This adaptation to the guitar by Leon Vicente Gascon is from the *Revista Musical Ilustrada "Tárrega"* magazine issue No. 16 of October 1925.

Now we will look at some of Leon Vicente Gascon's accomplished students:

This biography of Nelly Menotti is translated from Ricardo Muñoz's unpublished book *"Historia Universal de la Guitarra" Volume VIII "La Escuela Tárrega en La Argentina"*.

"Nelly Menotti

Her Education:

In 1936 she began her musical and guitaristic knowledge in the Conservatorio Sgromo with the maestros Elena Fillat and Maria E. Pazos, already a professor in music and guitar, in 1940 she enrolled in the Academia de Guitarra of maestro *Don* Leon Vicente Gascon in 1940, receiving her Diploma in 1941.

Her Virtuosity:

The 25th of October of 1941 her maestro presented her to the public in the Teatro Lassalle, before whom she performed the following program: *"Suite en Re menor"* by de Visée; *"3 Estudios"* by Sor; *"Sonatina" by Paganini; "Vals", "Cancion", "Cifra", "Estilo", "Milonga" and "Zambra"* by her maestro; *"Estilo"* by Pugliese; *"Norteña"* and *"Potpourri"* by Anido; *"Estudio", "Mazurka", "Pavana"* and *"Recuerdos de la Alhambra"* by Tárrega, with great success by the public and art; *"La Prensa"* the next day said: '. . . . she has revealed that she possesses a generous sound and a good dominion of technique.'

Nelly Menotti 1941

The 24th of July of 1943 we see her in the Consejo de Mujeres interpreting Handel, Bach, Beethoven, Gascon, Grieg, Turina, Anido and Albeniz with a lot of success and serenity. The 17th of June of 1946 in the Teatro Lassalle with a very select classical program she obtained insistent applause from the gathering of the public.

For the "Amigos de la Guitarra" she performed in the years 1946-1948 and 1954 with a lot of success, achieving the most emotional congratulations by the public and knowledgeable, whose unending applause obligated her to play encores."

MUNDO MUSICAL

Año XX — N° 237   REVISTA MENSUAL ILUSTRADA   Junio 1958

Nelly Menotti

CONCERTISTA DE GUITARRA

This from the *"Mundo Musical"* magazine of June 1958 issue No. 237 *Año* XX.

This biography of Irma Costanzo is translated from Ricardo Muñoz's unpublished book *"Historia Universal de la Guitarra"* Volume VIII *"La Escuela Tárrega en La Argentina"*.

"Irma Costanzo

Her Education:

She studied guitar with maestro *Don* J. A. Cacciatore, perfecting her skills later with maestro *Don* Leon Vicente Gascon.

Her Virtuosity:

In August of 1954 in the "Asociacion Guitarristica Argentina" she performed a select classical and folkloric program that the public applauded with satisfaction; later she appeared before the "Amigos de la Guitarra" interpreting Sor, Cacciatore, Alard, Moranese, Rubione, Gascon, Tárrega, Albeniz, Falla and Turina demonstrating great temperament, dominion of the instrument, and ample sonority and correct musical expression.

Distinctions:

The composer D. Moranese dedicated to Irma Costanzo his Estilo titled: *"Semblanza Gaucha"* that she performed in various occasions being received with enthusiastic applause."

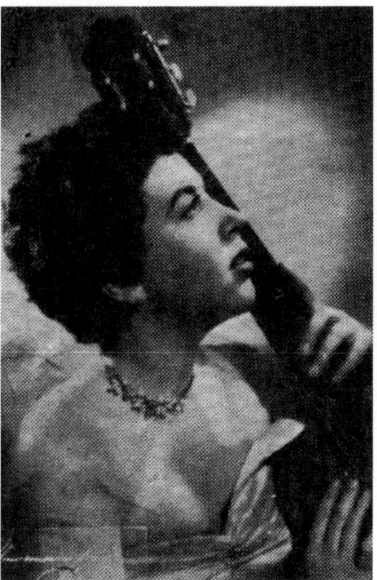

Irma Costanzo in 1958.

There are videos of her on You Tube

Asociación Guitarrística Argentina

CON PERSONERIA JURIDICA

AVENIDA DE MAYO 702
(SUBSUELO)
T. E. 30 - 6371

BUENOS AIRES

QUINTO CONCIERTO

DEL

CICLO 1954

A CARGO DE

IRMA COSTANZO

EL SABADO 28 DE AGOSTO A LAS 18.15 HORAS

EN EL SALON DE ACTOS

MONTEVIDEO 850

Irma Costanzo played for the "Asociacion Guitarristica Argentina"
on Saturday August 28, 1954.

--PROGRAMA--

I PARTE

Viejo Rancho (Estilo)	J. A. CACCIATORE
Bailecito	BIANQUI PIÑERO
(x) Hay! Hay! Hay!	PEREZ FREYRE
Milonga del Arbol	WILLIANS - ANIDO
(x) Bollera (Tonada del Carretero)	RUBBIONE
	DOMENECH

II PARTE

SONATINA Op. 8 en 4 movimientos.

Allegro

Andante

Minueto   L. VICENTE GASCON

Final (a la tarantella)

III PARTE

Marieta (Mazurca)	F. TARREGA
Cajita de Música	
(x) Granada	I. ALBENIZ
(x) Relato del Pescador (del Amor Brujo)	
	M. FALLA
Sevillana	J. TURINA

NOTA: (x) Versión para guitarra del Prof. L. Vicente
      Gascón
      Este programa sirve de invitación
      No se permitira la entrada a la sala durante
      la ejecución

VICENTE CHERUBITO
CONSTRUCTOR DE GUITARRAS
FINAS PARA CONCIERTO

ALBERTI 708

Irma Costanzo's classical and folkloric program with four of the transcriptions
by her maestro Leon Vicente Gascon.

Asociación Guitarrística Argentina

(con Personería Jurídica)

Avda. de Mayo 702

Sub-Suelo Sorocobana

Teléfono 30-6371

BUENOS AIRES

OCTAVO CONCIERTO DEL CICLO 1958

Irma Costanzo

A REALIZARSE

El Viernes 14 de Noviembre

A LAS 21 HORAS

EN HOMENAJE A

Abel Fleury

MONTEVIDEO 850

BUENOS AIRES

ENTRADA LIBRE   PROGRAMA INVITACIÓN

Irma Costanzo's homage to Abel Fleury on Friday November 14, 1958.
"The Poet of the Guitar" had passed away 7 months earlier,
and was dearly missed by his colleagues and his many fans.

Rodolfo Camacho Viera

ORO 2439   Teléfono 71-1516

• • • • • • • • • • • • • • • •

programa

I PARTE

Minuet	Rameau
Gavota	Cacciatore
Andante Largo	Sors
Minueto	Vicente Gascón
Tarantella	Vicente Gascón

II PARTE

Vidala	Almaráz
Polca Paraguaya	García - Ayala
Triste	Abel Fleury
Milonga	Abel Fleury
Estilo	Abel Fleury

III PARTE

Cajita de Música	Tárrega
Preludio	Moreno Torroba
Andante	Moreno Torroba
Garrotín	Turina
Leyenda	Albéniz

Programa dedicado por la intérprete a ABEL FLEURY

Irma Costanzo played a piece by her first maestro *Don* J. A. Cacciatore, Spanish and South American composers and the works *"Triste", "Estilo"* and *"Milonga"* by Abel Fleury.

IRMA COSTANZO IN TOKYO

A BRILLIANT young guitarist, Irma Costanzo of Argentina, achieved resounding success in two concerts at the Tokyo Kudankaikan Hall on October 8th and 12th.

Her first programme opened with Minuet (Rameau), Andante Largo and Minuet (Sor), Alborada and Recuerdos (Tárrega) followed by Boyera (Rubbione), Arco Iris (Ayala) and a South American Suite—Tonada, Vals, Takirari, Gato and Malambo—also by Ayala. Finally, Two Preludes (Villa-Lobos), Danza Espanola No. 5 (Granados), Asturias (Albeniz) and Sevillanas (Turina).

The second programme was entirely different. It included works by Sor, Llobet and Tárrega; Romanza (Barrios), Estilo and Milonga (Fleury), Suite Andaluza (Gascon), Homenaje a Debussy (Falla), Sonatina (Torroba) and Chôro Tipico (Villa-Lobos).

This from the "Guitar News" magazine issue No. 71 of May-June 1963. In her first concert in Tokyo on October 8, 1962 she played the *"Serie Americana"* by Hector Ayala. In the second concert on October 12th, she played *"Romanza"* by Agustín Barrios, *"Estilo* and *Milonga"* by Abel Fleury and *"Suite Andaluza"* by her maestro Leon Vicente Gascon.

Junto a José Jacopi, la concertista Irma Costanzo tañe uno de los instrumentos recién concluidos por el "luthier", que ha construido unas 800 guitarras de concierto

Photo from the article titled *"Lo que deja la polilla"* ("What the moth leaves") from the Buenos Aires daily "La Nacion" of Sunday June 11, 1967. Irma Costanzo visits José Yacopi's workshop. Translation:

"Next to José Yacopi, concert guitarist Irma Costanzo plays one of the instruments recently completed by the "luthier", who has constructed some 800 concert guitars."

IRMA COSTANZO

T HE Argentine guitarist, Irma Costanzo, was presented by the Society of the Classic Guitar, New York, in co-operation with the Consulate General of the Republic of Argentina, in its 116th Concert on November 27th.

Her programme included works by Rameau, Sanz, Sor, Villa-Lobos (5 Preludes and Chôro Tipica), J. Aguirre, H. Ayala, Granados, Falla (Hommage) and Turina.

This November 27, 1967 concert listing is from the "Guitar News" magazine issue No. 98 of March-May 1968.

A decade later the well-known Argentine composer and music critic Pompeyo Camps (1924-1997) wrote a book entitled *"Reportaje a la Guitarra con Irma Costanzo"*, it was published by *Libreria "El Ateneo" Editorial* in May of 1978 with 3,000 copies being printed in Buenos Aires.

> ★ Está la señora María Herminia Antola. Su esposo, ya fallecido, era Jorge Gómez Crespo, un hombre de la élite intelectual y musical de Buenos Aires, que durante muchos años fue titular de la cátedra de guitarra del Conservatorio Municipal. Cuando Segovia llegaba a la Argentina y tenía que recomendar a un profesor, mencionaba a ese matrimonio como los mejores maestros de guitarra del país.
>
> También están Jorge Martínez Zárate y su mujer, Graciela Pomponio, a quienes ya me he referido en alguna de estas conversaciones; Horacio Zeballos, integrante del cuarteto de Martínez Zárate, y la excelente pedagoga Nelly Menotti, quien también estudió con mi maestro, Vicente Gascón, y que es la alumna dilecta de María Luisa Anido.
>
> María Herminia Antola, muy amiga mía me comentó que en una de las últimas veces que vino Llobet a Buenos Aires, anunció: "Ahora vendrá de España un guitarrista, que se llama Andrés Segovia, y veréis que os va a gustar más que yo".

From page 78 is this insight into many personalities included in this book. Translation:

"There is Mrs. Maria Herminia Antola. Her husband, now passed away, was Jorge Gomez Crespo, a man of the intellectual and musical elite of Buenos Aires, who for many years held the professorship of the guitar in the Conservatorio Municipal. When Segovia arrived in Argentina and had to recommend a professor, he mentioned this couple as being the best maestros of the guitar of the nation.

Also there were Jorge Martínez Zarate and his wife, Graciela Pomponio, to whom I have already referred to in some of these conversations; Horacio Zeballos, a member of the Martínez Zarate quartet, and the excellent pedagogue Nelly Menotti, who also studied with my maestro Vicente Gascon, and who is the beloved student of Maria Luisa Anido.

Maria Herminia Antola, my good friend commented on one of the last times Llobet came to Buenos Aires, he announced: 'Now from Spain comes a guitarist, who is called Andrés Segovia, and you shall see that you will like him more than me'."

She says in this book that she paid 5,000 Pesos for her José Yacopi concert guitar, in payments of 1,000 Pesos per installment.

This biography of Fanny Amanda Castro is translated from Ricardo Muñoz's unpublished book "Historia Universal de la Guitarra" Volume VIII "La Escuela Tárrega en La Argentina".

"Fanny Amanda Castro

Her Origin:

She is the daughter of *Don* Armando Castro and *Doña* Isabel Varela. born in Buenos Aires the 2nd of March of 1929.

FANNY AMANDA CASTRO

Her Education:

Maestro *Don* Leon V. Gascon guided her first guitaristic steps since she was 7 years old, and in parallel she studied music with Professor Miss Blanca Diaz. Later she perfected her knowledge with Maria Luisa Anido, privately and in the Conservatorio Nacional de Musica y Arte Esenico, achieving, according to her, to be her favorite student. At the same time and in the referred to establishment she studied theory, solfeggio, harmony, composition, history, psychology and piano, with professors Palma, Quarantino, Bertucci, Suffern, Spena, etc. graduating with the highest grades and congratulations of the jurists, in all of the subjects.

Her Virtuosity:

The 28th of November of 1942 she was presented in public by her maestro Gascon in the Salon Teatro "Lassalle", and she put into evidence her admirable abilities of interpreter and performer in the pages of Haydn, Sor, Prat, Rubione, Boero, Cassinelli, Gazcon, Anido, Sirera, Tárrega, Grieg and Malats, that the public gave her an ovation stimulating the new artist of 13 years of age.

The 27th of November of 1943 she reappeared in the same hall and the public repeated their hottest enthusiastic applause stimulating her notable ascending efforts. two years after, the 12th of October, we see her in the Salon "La Argentina"; '. . . . she is a translator of good musical taste and correct understanding. — These promising endowments make her worth the great applause.'

In 1945 her professor Anido presented her in the Salon "La Argentina" as a child prodigy, performing: *"Preludio y Sarabanda"* by de Visée; *"Sueño y Capricho Arabe"* by Tárrega; *"Danza No. 5"* by Granados; *"Minuetto en Re", "Minuetto en Do", "Estudio No. 12", Andantino y Variaciones"* by Sor; *"Ocaso"* by

Gazcon, *"Cancion"* by Ponce; *"Estilo"* by Fleury and *"Aire Norteño"* by Anido; the author of this history brought to the program some words published: '*Don* Martin Gil, the astronomer and guitarist said some years ago, referring then to the child prodigy Maria Luisa Anido: "In the end, if all follows as I expect, in the harmonic progression, within a few years the name and fame of Maria Luisa Anido will be of world renown. . . ." This was the prophecy that today we admire and is the pride of South America, and hidden again, to be repeated soon in the person of the young girl Fanny Amanda Castro. — History repeats itself! The producer of the spark of its energy in function, is in the great vocation that invades and feeds its soul in formation, in its anxiety to know and understand, always unsatisfied, in its rare modesty, in its personality, in its temperament, fine and extraordinarily poetic and expressive, that which magnifies it decorative robe of its exquisite musical spirit, and its artistic quality of whom in these moments guides and models its guitaristic education, reaffirming its impeccable pedagogic knowledge."

Fanny Amanda Castro, presented to the consideration of the public by her celebrated maestro Maria Luisa Anido, she doesn't have another character that the demonstration by her indicated advanced in the art that we're concerned with; great are the efforts, the intense dedication, both, maestro and student, profoundly love, the music and the guitar, one, exhibiting the secrets that God transmitted from the deepest of his heart, the young girl, evoking in the time of the concert, simple and generously, without pretensions, with the joy and pain of her tender youth. . . . . November of 1945 — (signed) Ricardo Muñoz. —

In 1947 she traveled abroad and visited the city of Montevideo, Uruguay, to be presented on the 25th of October in the Instituto Verdi sponsored by the Centro Guitarristico del Uruguay "Conrado P. Koch", where she threshed out a program of works by Bach, Haydn, Milan, Sor, Mozart, Tárrega, Llobet, San Sebastian, Granados, Malats, Villa-Lobos, Ponce, Muñoz, Fleury and Anido, with great success. —

The 30th of June of 1948 in the Sala de la Sociedad Argentina de Autores y Compositores de Musica, she performed for the Centro de Profesores Egresados del Conservatorio Nacional de Musica. In homage of the *Dia de la Raza;* in the hall of the Club Sirio Libanes, interpreting on the 13th of October of 1948: *"Sarabanda"* by Bach; *"Andante"* by Mozart, *"Tristezas"* by Chopin-Muñoz; *"Andante"* by Floriani-Muñoz; *"El Carretero"* by Muñoz; *"Triste"* by Aguirre-Anido; etc. . . . . Her maestro, Miss Anido wrote: 'Fanny Amanda Castro is, to my judgement, and instrumentalist admirably endowed to contribute with her interesting personality the best exaltation of our guitaristic art, by her fine musical sensibility, as well as by her purified technique notably agile and secure, by clean sonority, that makes Fanny Amanda Castro, an exquisite and extraordinary interpreter in our musical ambiance.'

In the Salon "La Argentina" and sponsored by the Asociacion Argentina de Musica de Camara, the 22nd of March of 1949, dedicated to her maestro Miss Anido, the gathering coronating her effort and action with its sustained ovations.

The 30th of August of the same year, in homage to Santa Rosa the patriarch saint of the guitar, in the Teatro Cervantes and in the 1st part she interpreted works by Floriani-Muñoz, Muñoz, Schiuma, and Anido; in the 2nd part and in a duo with the guitarist Ruth Ada Braceras performed pages by Bach, Beethoven, Mendelssohn and Bizet, and in the 3rd part in a duo with the pianist Miss Marta G. Passalacqua, they interpreted the *"Sonata"* by Call in its tempos of *Adagio, Minuet, Trio, Adagio,* and *Andantino;* the *"Aire de Ballett"* by Carcassi in its tempos of Andante and Allegretto; the *"Nocturno"* by Molino (*Introducion, Romance* and *Rondo*), and *"Evocacion"* by R. Muñoz. — *"La Prensa"* of the following day said: 'With all tact, the interpreters achieved to balance the sonorities and they made considerable expression evident.' This performance was repeated on the 1st of September in the Hemiciclo Musical of the Asociacion Cristiana de Jovenes, with the same considerable artistic triumph.

The 9th of July of 1950, in the town of Salto, Buenos Aires, she musically illustrated a lecture by the author of this history who spoke about: *"La Guitarra en el Espiritu del General San Martin"* (The Guitar in the Spirit of General San Martin); seven days later in the Sala Argentina of the Teatro Cervantes and for the Academia Argentina de la Guitarra, sponsored by the Comision Nacional de Cultura, she performed a program of classic and folkloric works, which *"Mundo Musical"* commented on in this way: 'She proved her dominion and made a boast of musicality. . . . The artist brought forth the hot applause of the audience.' —

The 19th of August in "Homage to General San Martin", sponsored by the Comision Nacional de Cultura, she returned to illustrate the said lecture spoken by the author of this history with the most notable public consideration.

In the hall of the Teatro Cervantes, the 14th of October of 1950, she gave a concert for the Academia Argentina de la Guitarra, she performed in the 1st part works by Morales, Prat, Alcorra and Muñoz; in the 2nd part and with the guitarist Ruth Ada Braceras they performed pages by Bach, Beethoven, Torres, and Sor, and in the 3rd part with the pianist Miss Marta G. Passalacqua, they performed *"Romanza"* by Mendelssohn, *"Ballett"* by Carcassi; *"Chanson paroles"* by Tschaikovsky; *"Evocacion"* and *"Concierto No. 1"* by R. Muñoz. — 'The tact of the pianist deserves to be indicated, which she adjusted to the sound of the piano to that of the guitar.' (*"La Prensa"* of October 15, 1950.)

She then for the Club Boca Juniors and other entities, proceeding in her artistic career progressively, acclaimed by the public who had the fortune to hear her.

The 5th of January of 1956 she got married with the gentleman *Don* Roberto Oscar Cittadini, and nevertheless she continues her life caressing her beloved guitar, without interruption.

Her Compositions:

We know an unpublished work her magnificent *"Romanza"* by Mendelssohn for guitar and piano, and others that are unpublished.

Her Pedagogy:

In March of 1954, the chair of the superior professorship of the Conservatorio Nacional de Musica y Arte Esenico was vacant, to replace the position of Miss Maria Luisa Anido, she was designated to occupy it, due to being the ex-student of the establishment and having gotten the highest grades, that no one had ever achieved before."

This is from the *"Revista de la Guitarra"* magazine issue No. 10 *Año* IV of December 1942. Translation:

"Fanny Amanda Castro. — The 28th of November Professor Leon Vicente Gascon, presented to the consideration of the public the young guitarist Fanny Amanda Castro, who begins her artistic career.

Works of all genres comprised the program that Miss Castro was offering and in every one of the pages, she put into evidence her rare abilities as an interpreter. Among the works offered were several compositions of the maestro Gascon, those were very much applauded."

FANNY AMANDA CASTRO. — El 28 de noviembre, el profesor León Vicente Gascón, presentó a consideración del público a la guitarrista Fanny Amanda Castro, joven que inicia su carrera artística.

Obras de todo género componían el programa que ofrecía la señorita Castro y en cada una de las páginas, puso en evidencia raras condiciones de intérprete. Entre las obras ofrecía varias composiciones del maestro Gascón, las que fueron muy aplaudidas.

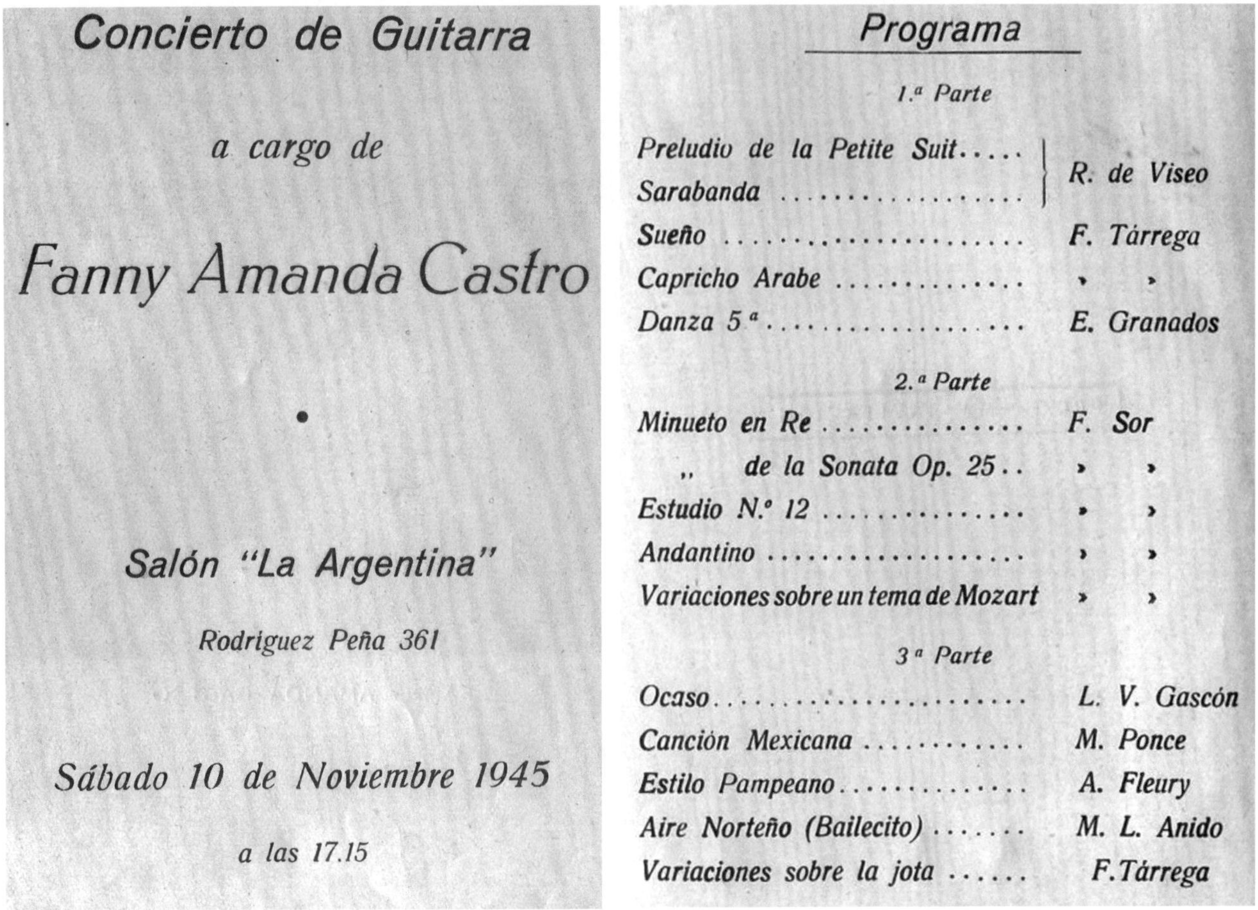

Concierto de Guitarra

a cargo de

Fanny Amanda Castro

•

Salón "La Argentina"

Rodriguez Peña 361

Sábado 10 de Noviembre 1945

a las 17.15

Programa

1.ª Parte

Preludio de la Petite Suit.....	R. de Viseo
Sarabanda	
Sueño	F. Tárrega
Capricho Arabe	" "
Danza 5.ª..................	E. Granados

2.ª Parte

Minueto en Re	F. Sor
„ de la Sonata Op. 25 ..	" "
Estudio N.º 12	" "
Andantino	" "
Variaciones sobre un tema de Mozart	" "

3.ª Parte

Ocaso......................	L. V. Gascón
Canción Mexicana	M. Ponce
Estilo Pampeano.............	A. Fleury
Aire Norteño (Bailecito)	M. L. Anido
Variaciones sobre la jota	F. Tárrega

Fanny Amanda Castro concert on Saturday November 10, 1945 in the Salon "La Argentina"

COMISION DE TEATROS MUNICIPALES

SALA DEL INSTITUTO VERDI

SORIANO 914

SABADO 25 de OCTUBRE DE 1947

A LAS 18 y 45 HORAS

Concierto de Guitarra a cargo de la Sta.

FANNY CASTRO

Organizado por el

"Centro Guitarrístico del Uruguay Conrado P. Koch"

PROGRAMA

I

Sarabanda	Bach
Andante	Haydn
Pavana	Milan
Minueto en Sol	Sor
Tema variado	Mozart-Sor

II

Sueño	Tárrega
Canción del Labrón	Llobet
Dolor	San Sebastián
Danza N.° 5	Granados
Serenata Española	Malate

III

Preludio N.o 3	Villa Lobos
Canción Mejicana	Ponce
El Carretero	Muñoz
Estilo Pampeano	Fleury
Aire Norteño (Bailecito)	M. L. Anido

Este programa sirve de Invitación

NOTA — Por disposición Municipal el público no podrá tener acceso a la sala hasta la terminación de una obra iniciada.

Imp. THEMIS — Colonia 2289

Fanny Amanda Castro concert on Saturday October 25, 1947 in Montevideo, at the Instituto Verdi sponsored by the Centro Guitarristico del Uruguay "Conrado P. Koch".

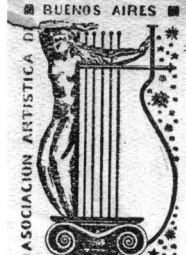

Asociación Artística de Buenos Aires

Secretaría: Muñiz 172 - Capital

ACTO DE HOMENAJE
AL DIA DE LA RAZA

Ofrecido por la institución al Club Sirio Libanés Honor y
Patria a realizarse el día **Miércoles 13 de Octubre de 1948**
a las 18,30 horas en Juncal 857, Capital.

— PROGRAMA —

PRIMERA PARTE

Apertura del acto por el Vicepresidente primero del Club Sirio Libanés
Honor y Patria Don JUAN OBEID.

	1ª.	Sarabanda	J. S. Bach
	2ª.	Andante	W. A. Mozart
(X)	3ª.	Tristezas de Chopin	R. Muñoz
(*)	4ª.	Andante de C. Floriani	R. Muñoz

SEGUNDA PARTE

1ª.	Ño Juan Carlos (Triste)	J. T. Morales
2ª.	El Carretero	R. Muñóz
3ª.	Aire de Danza	R. Muñóz
4ª.	Aire Criollo de Aguirre	M. L. Anido
5ª.	Aire Norteño	M. L. Anido

TERCERA PARTE

1ª.	Canción del Ladrón	M. Llobet
2ª.	Dolor del Pdre. San Sebastián	M. L. Anido
3ª.	Minuetto en Do Mayor	F. Sor
4ª.	Serenata Española	J. Malats
5ª.	Sueño	F. Tárrega

(X) En 1ª. audición dedicada a la ejecutante.

(*) En 1ª. audición.

A cargo de la concertista Srta. FANNY AMANDA CASTRO

PROGRAMA INVITACION

Fanny Amanda Castro concert on Wednesday October 13, 1948 for the Asociacion Artistica de Buenos Aires held in the hall of the Club Sirio Libanes, in homage of the Dia de la Raza. The piece *"Tristezas"* by Chopin-Muñoz was a debut and is dedicated to Miss Castro and the piece *"Andante"* by Floriani-Muñoz also was a debut.

Comisión Nacional de Cultura

❖

GRAN CONCIERTO

Academia Argentina de la Guitarra

❖

SALA ARGENTINA
Teatro Nacional Cervantes
30 de agosto de 1949, a las 18.30

PROGRAMA

Palabras alusivas al acto por la Sra. Pro-Secretaria, Académica
MATILDE TETTAMANTI DE CALANDRA

1ª PARTE

1°—Andante	....	FLORIANI-MUÑOZ
2°—Aire de Danza	....	R. MUÑOZ
3°—Copla	....	A. SCHIUMA
4°—Canción N° 4	....	M. L. ANIDO
5°—Aire Norteño	....	M. L. ANIDO

Guitarra sola por la Prof. Srta. FANNY A. CASTRO

2ª PARTE

1°—Allemande	....	BACH-MUÑOZ
2°—Minuetto	....	BEETHOVEN-MUÑOZ
3°—Romanza	....	MENDELSSOHN-LLOBET
4°—Minuetto (L'Arlessienne)	....	BIZET-TARREGA

Dúo de Guitarras por las Prof. Srtas.
FANNY A. CASTRO y RUTH A. BRACERAS

Fanny Amanda Castro concert with collaboration by Ruth Ada Braceras on Tuesday, August 30, 1949 for the Academia Argentina de la Guitarra in the Sala Argentina.

HEMICICLO MUSICAL
X.° PERIODO

CONFERENCIA Y CONCIERTO

✶

RICARDO MUÑOZ
——
FANNY AMANDA CASTRO
MARTA PASSALACQUA

Jueves 1.° de Setiembre de 1949
21.15 (en punto)

INVITACION ENTRADA

ASOCIACION CRISTIANA DE JOVENES
RECONQUISTA 439 · BUENOS AIRES

Ricardo Muñoz Lecture and Fanny Amanda Castro concert on Thursday September 1, 1949 for the Hemiciclo Musical of the Asociacion Cristiana de Jovenes. Titles are on the next page.

PROGRAMA

"LA GUITARRA CULTA EN LA ARGENTINA DEL SIGLO XIX"

Conferencia por el señor RICARDO MUÑOZ

ilustrada por la concertista FANNY AMANDA CASTRO:

Ocaso (canto indigena)	GAZCON	Estudio	CARULLI
Ño Juan Carlos	MORALES	Minue Federal	PRAT
Minuetto en do mayor	SOR	No me olvides	SAGRERAS
El Triunfo	MUÑOZ	Carlitos	ALAIS

Audición de Guitarra y Piano

Sonata	L. CALL	Nocturno	F. MOLINO
(Adagio, minue, trio, adagio, andantino)		1) Introducción	
Aire de ballet	M. CARCASSI	2) Romance	
a) Andante		3) Rondó	
b) Allegretto		Evocación	R. MUÑOZ

FANNY AMANDA CASTRO, guitarra
MARTA PASSALACQUA, piano

Ricardo Muñoz Lecture and Fanny Amanda Castro concert on Thursday September 1, 1949 for the Hemiciclo Musical of the Asociacion Cristiana de Jovenes.

On Sunday July 9, 1950 Fanny Amanda Castro illustrated Ricardo Muñoz's lecture *"La Guitarra en el Espiritu del General San Martin"*.

CLUB ARTESANO
SALTO (Bs. As.)

Acto Cultural

EN CONMEMORACIÓN DEL

9 de JULIO de 1816

Y DEL

Año Sanmartiniano 1950

A realizarse en su salón de fiestas
el 9 de Julio, a las 18 horas

- PROGRAMA -

Palabras de presentación por el Presidente de la Asociación Prometeo D. **Rodolfo Castagnino.**

LA GUITARRA EN EL ESPIRITU DEL LIBERTADOR, disertación de D. **Ricardo Muñoz,** Presidente de la Academia Argentina de la Guitarra, con ilustraciones en la guitarra por la señorita **Fanny Amanda Castro,** quien interpretará:

TRISTE N.° 5	de Aguirre
DANZA MORA,	de Francisco Tárrega
JOTA ARAGONESA	de Francisco Tárrega
ESTUDIO N.° 11	de Fernando Sor
GRANADA	de Albéniz
GATO	de Cassinelli
EL CARRETERO	de Ricardo Muñoz
MINUETO EN MI MAYOR	de Fernando Sor
VIDALITA	de María Luisa Anido
YARAVÍ	de León Vicente Gazcón

Another influential guitaristic figure was Jesus Gonzalez Yllan. Translating from the *Diccionario de Guitarristas* by Domingo Prat:

"Professor and Spanish concert guitarist. He was born in Villa Otero de Rey, Lugo Province, Spain on September 24, 1893. Being almost a child, when he was 13 years old his family moved to Argentina arriving to these shores in January 1907 and residing in Buenos Aires. After a prudential time to calm the nostalgia of his far away homeland and to give a new direction to follow, he determined to allocate some of his time to rest and some of it to study the guitar, taking as a professor the Spanish guitarist Teodoro Castro known as, *"El niño de Cadiz"*, for a period of almost 3 years, interrupted by his maestro's return to Spain. The confidence, the affection and the hope to a return soon by his maestro, making an involuntary pause in his studies, directing, a little later his steps toward the distinguished professor Hilarion Leloup, with whom his he finished his studies, being awarded a diploma on January 2, 1920. Jesus founded his academia "Escuela Tárrega" on May 25, of the same year. As a performer he played with flattering success. The 24th of October of 1920 along with professor Leloup he played in the Teatro "Menotti Garibaldi" in Olavarria, (Buenos Aires Province), a concert with works of great value, being awarded with hot applause by the audience. Jesus continued to perform concerts in libraries and for societies with increasing renown. With the motive of performing in concert at the Salon de la Federacion de Sociedades Gallegas Agrarias y Culturales, the daily, *"La Oposicion"*, of September 25, 1925 that is published in the capital, spoke in the following manner: "....Professor Gonzalez possesses an ability to make an extensive and delicate program of unquestionable merit, a just technique of the consummate maestro and an emotional sensibility that characterizes him as a true virtuoso, who unites the supreme knowledge of the difficult instrument, making the pieces of sheet music, as known as they are, take a new manner of complete and unique personal character by his rare artistic temperament that distinguishes the incalculable worth of his playing, that, indeed we recommend that the lovers of the guitar go to hear him." These lines and those that we might continue with end up being pale to whatever commentary of praise to which we would add: "...To speak of the Professor Gonzalez in the form which is necessary to let set well the precedent of the colossal effort of his unwavering willpower I need today to salute his emotivity in infinite tenderness to share longings: nostalgia and amalgamated longings with the temperament of the most personal character and to achieve a dominion so absolute to make the listener feel the indomitable energy that vibrates on the strings of his instrument as heartrending shouts of formal protest, it would be necessary to fill a space which we will take advantage of the next opportunity, since who, as our compatriot, to bring today I see the precision to steal the interminable daily rest, to be continued in the future and not too distant glory of Galicia..." (*"Correo de Galicia"*, November 22, 1925). As a professor he has made various concerts with students; we recall one in the Salon "La Argentina" September 26, 1929 and another in the Sala de la Wagneriana on September 25, 1930. Besides in the first hall he presented in public the concert by Maria Rita Flores on December 7, 1924 and Consuelo Mallo Lopez on November 14, 1926. Since the founding of his academy they have received their titles as maestros: Maria Inés Villagra, Rita Zavalla Palmeiro, Maria Zulema Ohteguy, Juana Marcos, Edmundo Arrigone, Alberto Martínez, Raul Palmelo Bruno, Mario Enrique Rablione, Juan Andrés Fernández and Juan Guillermo. The conduct as performer and maestro, which we have pointed out, Jesus Gonzalez gives us a real value in the Buenos Aires guitaristic environment."

The most notable student of Jesus Gonzalez was Consuelo Mallo Lopez. She began with Jesus but later went to study in the Academia de Guitarra "Prat". She had an illustrious teaching, concert, recording, and film career-doing background music with her students.

See page 898 for more on this great professor.

This photo of Jesus Gonzalez is from Ricardo Muñoz's unpublished book *"Historia Universal de la Guitarra"* Volume VIII *"La Escuela Tárrega en La Argentina"*. He is the son of Francisco and *Doña* Dominga Illan. This detail was not found in the Prat biography on the previous page.

Besides his own concerts there were those of his students, such as Maria Rita Flores.

"Maria Rita Flores — Argentine concert guitarist. This instrumentalist was presented for the first time in public in the Salon "La Argentina", the 7th of December of 1924 under the direction of the Professor Jesus Gonzalez; then the 12th of November of 1926 she was heard again in the same hall and in 1927, the 19th of May, then presented under the name Rita Vergara Yanzi. She did that with a program where the authors such as Schumann, Teisseire, Heller, Juan de Dios Filiberto, Tárrega, Pelaia, Albeniz, Vergara Yanzi and Chazarreta were represented."

So ends the entry in the *"Diccionario de Guitarristas"* by Domingo Prat.

(Right) Maria Rita Flores piece published by Ricordi, under the name Rita Vergara Yanzi. It is an Estilo "Dolorido" by Domingo Nocera Netto.

DOMINGO NOCERA NETTO
DOLORIDO
ESTILO

Arreglo para Guitarra por
RITA VERGARA YANZI

BUENOS AIRES
Impreso en los talleres G. RICORDI E. C.

Srta. MARIA RITA FLORES

En pose para "Tárrega", momentos antes de iniciar su recital
de guitarra el 7 de diciembre en el salón "La Argentina"

Maria Rita Flores and maestro Jesus Gonzalez before her concert in the Salon "La Argentina" on December 7, 1924, and the audience that attended the recital.

This is from the *Revista Musical Ilustrada "Tárrega"* magazine issue No. 7 of December 1924.

Sta. MARIA RITA FLORES

Concurrencia que asistió al recital efectuado el 7 de diciembre en el salón "La Argentina"

This is from the *Revista Musical Ilustrada "Tárrega"* magazine issue No. 7 of December 1924.

"Guitar recital

In the Salon "La Argentina" the 7th of December a guitar recital offered by Miss Rita Flores took place.

If we quote what the program says, Miss Flores is a concert guitarist who has studied for only three years, in such a sense the abilities demonstrated by Miss Flores, authorize to expect an interpreter with a great future, if she continues to carry out a tenacious and constant study.

The program performed, is now a palpable demonstration of the aptitudes of Miss Flores, and if we add to it that it was performed with quite a good manner and adjustment, she has shown her merits and plausible labor.

The performance contributed the following program:

I

a) Preludio No. 5 – Francisco Tárrega
b) Romanza – Felix Mendelssohn
c) Capricho arabe – Francisco Tárrega
d) Jota – Julián Arcas

II

a) Pavana – Francisco Tárrega
b) La plegaria – Badarzewska Flores
c) Variaciones sobre "La Flauta Magica" Op. 9 – Amadeus Mozart and Fernando Sor
d) Sueño – Francisco Tárrega

III

a) Granada – Isaac Albeniz
b) Leyenda – Isaac Albeniz
c) El delirio – Antonio Cano and Jesus Gonzalez
c) Gran jota – Francisco Tárrega"

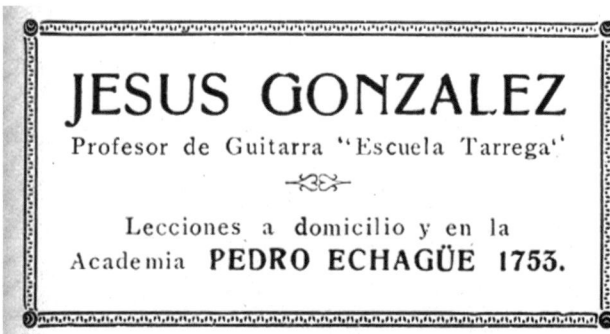

This Jesus Gonzalez advertisement is from the magazine *Revista Musical Ilustrada "Tárrega"* issue No. 19 of February 1926.

This concert review of Maria Rita Flores is from the *Revista Musical Ilustrada "Tárrega"* magazine issue No. 28 of November 1926. Translation:

"Performance by Miss Maria Rita Flores

The 12th of November Miss Maria Rita Flores, now Rita Vergara Janzi (sic- Yanzi), gave a concert again in the Salon "La Argentina".

Miss Vergara isn't very far from offering, from now on, discreet performances, keep in mind that the guitar doesn't show with the procedures of the jazz - band and that, before blows, jumps and bumps of the right hand, it is convenient to caress to polish to refine with sobriety, to ponder the phrase and to say it clearly.

It appears to us here opportune to transcribe the words with which Baillat sketched of the inspired performer.

'He is, who understands the first impression of the different characters of music; he is, who by an instantaneous inspiration, identifies with the genius of the composer, follows him in all of his intentions and discloses as easily as accuracy; he is, who goes to presage the effects to make them brighten with more splendor, he, who knows to join the grace with the sentiment, the simplicity with the gracefulness, the strength with the sweetness and mark all the tones that show the contrasts; he knows to suddenly pass to a different expression, to be accommodating to all the styles, to all the accents; to make the most outstanding passages feel without ostentation and skillfully cast a veil over the most common; to penetrate of the genius of a phrase of music that says nothing to lend charm, create effects that the author abandons many times in the instinct of the artist; to translate all, to encourage all, to transmit to the soul of the listener, that which the soul of the composer felt.'

Miss Vergara is young and has a future. She has to smooth out the playing, not rushing, "ruminating" — is the exact word — the works, not to punish, overall in the harmonic octaves, to be, finally, kinder in technique and diction, and we are sure to hear her in a pleasant concert in the coming year.

This is not to say that Miss Vergara can't be heard today without pleasure; on the contrary. With such a frequency the good taste wanes, that her present performances leave an unpleasant impression."

This concert review of Maria Rita Flores is from the *Revista Musical Ilustrada "Tárrega"* magazine issue No. 33 of May 1927. Translation:

Rita Vergara Yanzi

En el Salón La Argentina, se efectuó la audición de guitarra ofrecida por la señorita Rita Vergara Yanzi.

No conformó la audición ofrecida. La señorita Vergara Yanzi posee conocimientos guitarrísticos que adolecen de evidentes defectos de técnica, que se derivan de un estudio poco sólido y metódico.

Tampoco ha cuidado la selección de las obras inscriptas en su programa.

"Rita Vergara Yanzi

In the Salon "La Argentina", a guitar performance by Rita Vergara Yanzi took place.

The performance offered didn't shape up. Miss Vergara Yanzi possesses guitaristic knowledge that suffers from evident defects of technique, that stem from an insufficient methodical study.

Nor did she take care in the selection of the works written in her program."

342

LUIS ALFFERIN

(Left) A Jesus Gonzalez piece dedicated to and published by José Carratelli.
(Right) This photo of Luis Alfferin, who studied with Jesus Gonzalez, is from the *Revista Musical Ilustrada "Tárrega"* issue No. 19 of February 1926.

Señor Juan Giglio
Prof. J. Gonzalez

Señor Julio Dionisio
Prof. J. Gonzalez

These photos of Jesus Gonzalez's students Juan Giglio and Julio Dionisio are from the *Revista Musical Ilustrada "Tárrega"* issue No. 30 of February 1927.

Julián Ortiz was a guitarist who wrote short articles for the *Revista Musical Ilustrada "Tárrega"* magazine. This March 1925 photo is from issue No. 9 of that magazine. Julián was born on December 21, 1891 in Bilbao, Spain. In Domingo Prat's entry in the *"Diccionario de Guitarristas"*, written in 1930, he states "that at that time, Julián was a teacher and Director of the Colegio Lomas High School in Buenos Aires." He had published 25 pieces and a method to accompany in all keys and positions, by the time of the publishing of the 1931 Antigua Casa Nuñez catalog.

Domingo Prat says: "Julián's most outstanding child prodigy was Maria Angélica Hernández, who at 10 years old and having studied only 1 1/2 years, performed 15 pieces by Sor, Coste, Carulli, Carcassi, Tárrega, Parga, Viñas and Ortiz in the Salon "La Argentina" on August 24, 1928."

These advertisements for Academia de Guitarra "Ortiz" are from the *Revista Musical Ilustrada "Tárrega"* issue No. 12 of June 1925 and issue No. 15 of September, 1925.

This advertisement for Academia de Guitarra "Ortiz" is from the *Revista Musical Ilustrada "Tárrega"* issue No. 29 of December 1926. In this advertisement Julián states that he will teach the student to accompany and play Argentine folk pieces in three months.

(Right) Op. 20 Adios, Muchachos
published by Alfredo Perrotti

Op. 50 Pericon and Gato
published by Antigua Casa Nuñez

Op. 66 Compendio de Escalas y Arpegios
published by Antigua Casa Nuñez
in 1951

In the 1931 Antigua Casa Nuñez catalog Julián Ortiz had 26 works listed.

Of the many figures in Buenos Aires, one came from faraway. "Pablo Escobar Caceres was born in San José de los Arroyos, Paraguay on June 22, 1900. Pablo became fascinated with music and the guitar at a very young age. This inspired him to move to Asuncion, where he entered the "Instituto Paraguayo" to study solfegio and guitar, under the direction of professor Dionisio Basualdo. Soon after, he left the tutelage of his teachers, to be developing on his own in the hard labor of studying the guitar.

He was presented as a soloist in *"La Peregrinacion de Caaupé"*, one of the artistic acts organized by the poet, Martin Barrios, brother of Agustín, in which Pablo received such a flattering reception, wherein he decided to perform a concert in the Salon de la Sociedad Italiana in Asuncion. After that moment, he created programs and left for Brazil, making a debut in San Paulo, giving two concerts in the "Salon del Conservatorio Dramatico y Musical", and a third concert in the "Salon Braz", that was attended by the most select cultured populace. He had the same success in the "Salon Noble Parque" in Santos and in Campinas. A notable aspect of the city of Campinas is that it is where the writer of *"O Guarany"*, A. C. Gomes (1839-1896) was born. Pablo announced one concert, and upon obtaining such success, he had to do two more.

He soon went to Uruguay and on to Montevideo where performed twice in the "Instituto Verdi". His resounding success was to the extent that it prolonged his stay there for 6 months, until he traveled to Buenos Aires. He initiated his concerts with a program sponsored by "Juventud Universitaria Paraguaya" in the Salon "La Argentina" on July 21, 1927, with a return in November to the same hall. He was enthusiastically applauded in "La Peña". He was well paid and received on the radio stations L. O. L. and L. O. Y.. He was named professor of guitar at the "Conservatorio del Plata" and in the "Universidad de Liniers". Pablo, having the desire to improve, studied harmony with composer Alfredo Schiuma." This information is from the *Diccionario de Guitarristas* by Domingo Prat.

He had one transcription of the *Reverie* by Robert Schumann listed in the 1931 Antigua Casa Nuñez catalog. This was the beginning of a long career.

P. Escobar

(Left) This photo of Pablo Escobar is from the *"Galeria de Concertistas y Profesionales"* in the 1931 Antigua Casa Nuñez catalog.

(Right) This photo of Pablo Escobar is from the cover of the *Zamba "Tuya"* shown on the next page.

In 2002 Gilson Uehara Antunes finished a Masters of Musicology thesis in Sao Paolo entitled: *AMÉRICO JACOMINO "CANHOTO" E O DESENVOLVIMENTO DA ARTE SOLÍSTICA DO VIOLÃO EM SÃO PAULO* (Americo Jacomino "Canhoto" and the development of his art of the Solo Guitar in Sao Paolo). He included some of the concerts performed by Pablo Escobar. Portuguese translation by Randy Osborne

"The concert by Pablo Escobar was held in the hall of the Conservatório Dramático e Musical on December 14, 1925, in Sao Paolo, Brazil.

Primeira Parte
— Dr. Pinho: Marcha Paraguaia
— Iparraguirre: El Huerfano
— Escobar: Recuerdos de Zavala
— Barrios: Jha! Che Valle

Segunda Parte
— Barrios: Madrigal
— Garcia: Meditation
— Tárrega: Capricho Árabe
— Barrios: Valsa n.º 4

Terceira Parte
Guitar Duets by Pablo Escobar and Aristodemo Pistoresi.
— Garcia: Mathilde
— Alcântara: Ontem ao Luar
— Sinópoli: Vidalita
— Tárrega: Recuerdos de Alhambra

Aristodemo Pistoresi is the brother of the known industrialist and musical instrument maker of guitars and mandolins, Francisco Pistoresi.

On the 15th of December on the radio station *Sociedade Rádio Educadora Paulista*, Pablo Escobar played some numbers by his contemporary Agustín Barrios, and in a recital the next day in the hall of the Conservatório Dramático e Musical of São Paulo he performed the following pieces:

1. Marcha Paraguaia
2. El Huerfano
3. Recuerdos de Zavala, by Escobar
4. Jha! Che Valle by Barrios
5. Madrigal, by Barrios
6. Meditation, by Garcia
7. Capricho Árabe, by Tárrega
8. Valsa n.º 4, by Barrios

It was the last great guitaristic happening of 1925."

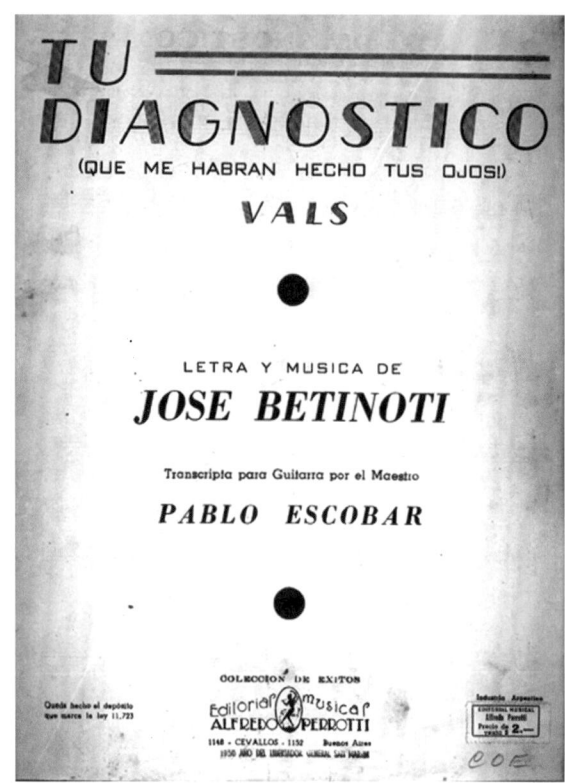

Pablo Escobar published with several different firms. This piece *"Francia"* was written by Carlos Pesce and Octavio Barbero and the transcription published by Alfredo Perrotti in the 1930's. *"Tu Diagnostico"*, also published by Alfredo Perrotti was still available in 1950.

Published by Americo A. Vivona in 1936

Published by Garrot

There are videos of his works on You Tube.

This is the complete photo used in the *La Razon* newspaper piece on Friday, October 22, 1926; a partial view was used in the same newspaper on the 26th, which is seen on the following page. Left to Right are: Uruguayan guitarist Julio Arbelo, Pablo Escobar, Pedro Mascaro y Reissig. The dedication of the photo is from Pablo Escobar to Pedro Mascaro y Reissig. It was written on October 28, 1926.

The translation of the newspaper article text is:

"Pablo Escobar — The Paraguayan Guitarist

The guitarist, with whose name we put above these lines, has just arrived in this capital.

It has to do with a young artist, who thinks of giving some concerts in the principal halls of Montevideo, in which we don't doubt that they will delight the public, since he possesses a correct school and a delicate temperament.

Yesterday during the day, at his invitation, he gave a private performance to the Uruguayan guitarists Pedro Mascaro y Reissig, Guillermo Cocoran, Alberto Segovia and Julio Arbelo, whom have become gratefully impressed by his guitaristic abilities.

Tonight he will give another private performance for maestro Julio Otermin (At that time Julio Otermin had been a recording artist since February 1912 R.O.) and some aficionados of the divine instrument, which takes place in the home of the nationally known guitarist. And Saturday night the young Escobar will give in the Instituto, of the maestro Mascaro y Reissig, another intimate performance for the students of this professor.

In brief we announce the first recitals that the guitarist Escobar will give in this capital, without a doubt he will obtain identical triumphs as those that he just offered in Brazil, in whose principal capitals he has performed in the last several months."

Archive: Pedro Mascaro y Reissig 1917-1938.

El guitarrista paraguayo Pablo Escobar

REPORTAJE AL MAESTRO MASCARO Y REISSIG

Con motivo de la estada en esta capital del concertista señor Escobar, nos entrevistamos con el maestro señor Mascaró y Reissig, a fin de que emitiera su opinión sobre las condiciones guitarrísticas del artista que en estos momentos es nuestro huésped.

Sorprendimos al maestro Mascaró y Reissig en plena labor de enseñanza de su instrumento favorito a uno de sus discípulos.

Enterado de nuestra visita, púsose de inmediato a disposición de nosotros.

—Sabemos que Ud. ha tenido oportunidad de oir intimamente al guitarrista paraguayo Sr. Escobar, respecta a la técnica en la pulsación. No quiero decir con ello que el Sr. Escobar esté equivocado. Este guitarrista utiliza las uñas en su ejecución; también las utilizan Llovet, Segovia y Barrios. Y no diremos, por ello, que estos guitarristas no sean todo lo maravilloso que se pueda pedir. Yo he aceptado, la escuela de Tárrega; y este malogrado guitarrista estableció la supresión de las uñas en la pulsacin; debido a ello es que no estoy de acuerdo con lo que dejo expresado. Pero no por esto voy a negar al joven guitarrista paraguayo sus excelentes condiciones de tal. El señor Escobar tiene mucha semejanza, en su tecnicismo, con su compatriota el concertista Agustín Barrios, con la diferencia única de

El maestro Mascaró y Reissig y el concertista Pablo Escobar

In the *La Razon* newspaper published in Montevideo on Tuesday October 26, 1926, this interview took place with Pedro Mascaro y Reissig about the concert guitarist Pablo Escobar, who was performingin the city at that time. Translation:

"The Paraguayan guitarist Pablo Escobar-News article according to the maestro Mascaro y Reissig.

With the motive of the stay in this capital of the concert guitarist Mr. Escobar, we interview maestro Mr. Mascaro y Reissig, in order for his opinions to be emitted about the guitaristic abilities of the artist that in these moments is our guest.

We surprised the maestro while teaching his favorite instrument to one of his disciples. When he learned of our visit, he immediately put himself at our disposal.

We know that you have had the opportunity to intimately hear the Paraguayan guitarist Mr. Escobar and we expect one use that to declare to us your opinion about the abilities of this artist — they were the words with which we began with the Uruguayan maestro.

In effect — he told us — Mr. Escobar had had the gentility or better said, he had made the honor for me to be, I, the first Uruguayan to have heard his guitaristic manifestations. I have heard many of his delicate musical phrases, where everything is emotional, as are his brilliant performances which has placed the proof of virtuosity within the purest expression. Saturday night he gave a performance to a nucleus of guitarists, having been unanimously considered by all that Mr. Escobar is totally an artist and a notable performer. For my part; this young guitarist deserves my best thoughts, nevertheless, I'm not in agreement with his technique of playing. I don't want to say by that, Mr. Escobar is mistaken. This guitarist uses fingernails in his playing; as well Llobet, Segovia and Barrios use them. And we don't say, by that, which those guitarists are not all the wonders that can be asked for. I have accepted, the school of Tárrega; and that late guitarist established the use of short nails in the plucking; due to that is what I'm not in agreement with, which I let be expressed. But not by that am I going to negate the young Paraguayan guitarist of his excellent abilities as such. Mr. Escobar has a lot of similarity in his technique, with his compatriot the concert guitarist Agustín Barrios, with the only difference is the use of gut strings for the treble register that Barrios utilizes steel. In the performance, to which I referred to beforehand, it left me with various instantances the impression that I had been listening to Barrios, of whom I am a great admirer, since Mr. Escobar let me hear many of the compositions of that concert guitarist, in an admirable interpretation.

In synthesis, I tell them that Mr. Escobar is one of the good guitarists that deserves to let be heard by our public; since he has excellent abilities of performing and an amply acceptable artistic temperament.

With these words, we sufficiently believe we have the impression that the guitarist Escobar has produced in the maestro Mascaro y Reissig, to whom we leave in his reasonable work of going to forming the good guitarists of the future," (end of page-following page to finish article was not in archive).

Archive: Pedro Mascaro y Reissig 1917-1938.

LUNES 17 DE OCTUBRE
a las 18 horas

Audición a cargo del

Profesor Pablo Escobar

PROGRAMA
1ª Parte

1 — Triste, de Pedro Sofía.
2. — Romanza, de Agustín Barrios.
3 — Chopi, (Danza Paraguaya) de Escobar.
    (Por el profesor Pablo Escobar)
4 — Capricho Arabe, de Tárrega. Por la alumna señorita Elena Mario Molle.
5 — Una Lágrima, de Gaspar Sagrera. Por las alumnas señoritas Molle, Roldán, Eggeling y profesor Escobar.
6. — Momento Musical de Schubert, por el conjunto de 10 guitarristas, integrado por los alumnos Srtas. Molle, Roldán, Alvarez, Eggeling. Niños: Barral, Leroi, Villafañe y Sres.: Martínez y Monteagudo y profesor Escobar.

2ª Parte

1 — Vidala de Yupanqui.
2 — Choros de Villa Lobos.
3 — El Abor Brujo de Falla.
    (Por el profesor Pablo Escobar)
4 — Minueto de Beethoven, por las alumnas Srtas. Molle y Eggeling.
5 — Mazurka de Escobar, por el conjunto de once guitarras, integrado por los alumnos: Srtas. Molle, González, Alvarez, Roldán, Eggeling. Niños Barral, Leroi, Villafañe. Sres: Monteagudo, Martínez y Profesor Escobar.

MARTES 18 DE OCTUBRE
a las 18 horas

Audición a cargo del

Profesor Pablo Escobar

PROGRAMA
1ª Parte

1º — Andante, de Escobar.
2º — Asturias, de Albeniz.
3º — Choros, arreglo de Escobar.
    (Por el profesor Pablo Escobar)
4º — Mazurka, de Escobar. Por el alumno Alberto E. Martínez y Prof. Escobar.
5º — La Porteñita, de Simone. Por los alumnos: señoritas Molle, Roldán, Eggeling. Niño Leroi y profesor Escobar.
6º — Pericón, de Podestá. Conjunto de 10 guitarras por los alumnos: Srtas. Roldán, Molle, Alvarez, Eggeling. Niños Barral, Leroi, Villafañe. Sres. Martínez, Monteagudo y Prof. Escobar.

2ª Parte

1º — O'Sole Mío, de Capra.
2º — Cádiz, de Albeniz
3º — Muñeira, de Diana Lavalle.
    (Por el profesor Pablo Escobar)
4º — Desde el Alma, (Vals) de R. Melo. Por el alumno Sr. Manuel Monteagudo.
5º — Enriqueta, (Habanera) de Carlos García. Por las alumnas, señoritas: Molle, Roldán, Eggeling y profesor Escobar.

In October of 1938 Breyer Hermanos held an Exposition of Guitars in the "Salon de Audiciones" (Hall) on their premises of business. There were four concerts weekly for three weeks straight. It's what might be called the first guitar festival of this magnitude. These concerts were also live over the radio on station L. R. 2 Radio Argentina. The radio was in its 18th year in the city of Buenos Aires. Professor Pablo Escobar played in five out of the twelve concerts. We see that 10 or 11 students played pieces in ensemble. In the first concert of Monday October 17 he plays *Romanza* by his compatriot, Agustín Barrios. Besides the performance of Tárrega's *Capricho Arabe,* something very notable is the students playing Gaspar Sagreras' *Una Lagrima.* Gaspar had died in 1901, and almost 40 years later his music was still in favor. Pablo's inclusion of the *Vidala* by Atahualpa Yupanqui is an early footprint of the gigantic influence of that Argentine folk guitarist.

In the 2nd concert held on Tuesday October 18, the performance by the 10 guitar students, of 19th century pieces written by Buenos Aires artists Pablo Simeone, Antonio Podesta and Carlos García Tolsa show what was still in vogue, music written at the time when the population was 20% of what it was at the time this concert took place. At this time also, finding a 1st edition of these works was not easy to accomplish as avid sheet music collector extraordinare Eleuterio Tiscornia would say in his *"Catalogo de su Archivo de Guitarra 1897-1945"*, published by Ricordi Americana in 1948. The piece *Muñeira* is by recording artist Alberto Diana Lavalle, who began playing on radio and making discs in 1930. It is dedicated to Pablo Escobar.

LUNES 24 DE OCTUBRE
a las 18 horas

———

Audición a cargo del
Profesor Pablo Escobar

———

PROGRAMA

1ª Parte

1º — Reverice de Schumann
2º — Nocturno de Chopin.
3º — Aires Sudamericanos, de Barrios.
    (Por el profesor Pablo Escobar)
4º — Romanza, de H. Costa. Alumna Elena M. Molle.
5º — Minueto, de Beethoven. Alumnas Molle y Eggeling.
6º — Vidalita, de Escobar. Conjunto de 8 guitarras, por los alumnos, Srtas.: Alvarez, Molle, Roldán, Eggeling. Niños: Leroi, Barral. Sr. Monteagudo y profesor Escobar.

2ª Parte

1º — "El mistol", (estilo), de Mario Godoy.
2º — Danza indígena, de Escobar.
3º — Marcha militar, (arreglo), Escobar.
    (Por el profesor Pablo Escobar)
4º — Lágrima, de Tárrega. Alumna Sra. Matilde S. Roldán.
5º — Mazurka, de Escobar. Conjunto de 11 guitarras por los alumnos, Srtas: González, Alvarez, Molle, Roldán, Eggeling. Niños: Barral, Leroi, Villafañe. Sres. Monteagudo, Martínez y profesor Escobar.

LUNES 31 DE OCTUBRE
a las 18 horas

———

Audición a cargo del
Profesor Pablo Escobar

———

PROGRAMA

1ª Parte

1º — Sarabanda de Bach.
2º — Primavera, de Escobar
3º — Danza 5ª, de Granados.
    (Por el profesor Pablo Escobar)
4º — Testamento de Amelia de Llobet. Alumna Selma I. Eggeling.
5º — Enriqueta, (habanera), Carlos García. Alumnas: Molle, Roldán, Eggeling y Prof. Escobar.
6º — Pericón Nacional, de Escobar. Conjunto de 6 guitarras por los alumnos Srtas: Molle, Roldán, Eggeling. Niños, Barral, Leroi y profesor Escobar.

2ª Parte

1º — Asturias de Albéniz.
2º — Preludio Nº 2 de Escobar.
3º — Poca ropa, (estilo), Vergara.
    (Por el profesor Pablo Escobar)
4º — Comparsita, de Matos Rodríguez. Niño Enrique A. Barral y profesor Escobar.
5º — Una lágrima, de Gaspar Sagreras. Alumnas Molle, Roldán, Eggeling y Prof. Escobar.

Besides the immortal composers of Europe, in this third concert by Pablo Escobar, he plays *Aires Sudamericanos* by Agustín Barrios, though arranged by Pablo himself. On August 27, 1922 Agustín Barrios had played *Aires Sudamericanos*. at a concert at the Hotel Belvedere in Asuncion, Paraguay. According to Rico Stover it may be *"Aires Criollos"* or *"Armonias de America"*. Pablo's students play in ensemble two of his compositions: a *Vidalita* and a *Mazurka*.

In the fourth concert, Pablo's student Selma Inés Eggeling plays Miguel Llobet's Catalan folksong transcription: *Testamento de Amelia*, available since the 1920's. Miguel had passed away in February of the same year. At this time, pieces such as *Cancion del Lladre*, had yet to be published, and still remained in manuscript by Miguel's hand or that of his student Maria Luisa Anido. In the Ricardo Muñoz archive is a manuscript copy of that song by Maria Luisa Anido. Pablo's students play Carlos García Tolsa's *"Enriqueta"* once again. The *"Pericon Nacional"*, played by his ensemble of 6 guitars, was one of the most popular pieces for many decades ongoing, such that it had arrangements by early composers, such as Gaspar Sagreras and maestros that appeared later such as Antonio Sinopoli.

VIERNES 4 DE NOVIEMBRE
a las 18 horas

———

Audición a cargo del

Profesor Pablo Escobar

———

PROGRAMA

1ª Parte

1º — Tabaré, (yaraví), de Alfredo L. Schiuma.
2º — Cádiz, de Albéniz.
3º — Muneira, de A. Diana Lavalle.
     (Por el profesor Pablo Escobar)
4º — Minueto Op. 25 de Sors. Alumna Salma I. Eggeling.
5º — La Porteñita de Simione. Alumnos, Srtas: Roldán, Mole, Eggeling. Niño Leroi y profesor Escobar.
6º — Mazurka de Escobar. Conjunto de 11 guitarras por los alumnos, Srtas. González, Alvarez, Molle, Roldán, Eggeling. Niños Barral, Leroi, Villafañe. Sres.: Martínez, Monteagudo y profesor Escobar.

2ª Parte

1º — Triste de Pedro Sofía.
2º — Primavera de Escobar.
3º — Marcha militar, arreglo de Escobar.
     (Por el profesor Pablo Escobar)
4º — Loyita, (ranchera), dos guitarras.
5º — Vidalita, de Escobar. Conjunto de 8 guitarras.
6º — Pericón de Podestá. Conjunto de 10 guitarras por los alumnos, Srtas: Roldán, Molle, Alvarez, Eggeling. Niños: Barral, Leroi, Villafañe. Sres. Monteagudo, Martínez y Prof. Escobar.

In the closing concert of the 12 performance, 3-week event: *"Exposicion de Guitarras"* the pianist and composer Alfredo L. Schiuma's piece Tabaré shows the respect of inspirations outside of the "guitar world". The playing of Professor Pablo Escobar's students must have offered a depth of texture to both the audiences in attendance at the Breyer Hermanos premises and to the radio listeners as well.

This photo is from the magazine *"Revista de la Guitarra"* issue No. 6, *Año* II of June 1940. Left to Right are these musicians: Matilde Salomé Roldan, Alfredo Villafañe, Elena Maria Molle, professor Pablo Escobar, Juan Ponce, Selma Inés Eggeling and Alberto Elias Martínez. The accompanying text mentions they have played for the Asociacion Guitarristica Argentina many times and on the 9th of the following month they will play again on *Radio Fenix*, commencing with the *Himno Nacional Argentino* to celebrate the patriotic holiday.

Another maestro was "Miguel Rufino Michelone Teglia. Miguel was born on August 11, 1900 in Buenos Aires. He began his guitar studies with Professor Herminia Baldassari, and then continuing later under the direction of Cayetano Galeano and Antonio Sinopoli. Upon obtaining the mastery of the guitar he was able, according to Domingo Prat's *Diccionario de Guitarristas,* to be appointed professorships at the Conservatorios "Linares", "Valsangiacomo" and "Instituto Musical Diaz Velez" as well as the director of his own "Academia de Guitarra".

In "La Wagneriana" on November 24, 1931 Miguel along with four students perform in a student recital with great success." By the time of the entry in Prat's *Diccionario*, Miguel had published ten pieces, of Argentine folklore styles and easy waltzes for the novice aficionados of the musical landscape of Argentina."

Miguel's most notable student is maestro Manuel Lopez Ramos.

Seven pieces are listed in the 1931 Antigua Casa Nuñez catalog.

Maestro Miguel Michelone from the
"Galeria de Concertistas y Profesionales"
in the 1931 Antigua Casa Nuñez catalog.

Advertisement from 3rd year concert
program of the Asociacion Guitarristica
Argentina for November-December 1937.

This biography of Manuel Lopez Ramos is translated from Ricardo Muñoz's unpublished book "Historia Universal de la Guitarra" Volume VIII "La Escuela Tárrega en La Argentina".

"Manuel Lopez Ramos

His Origin:

He was born in Buenos Aires in the year 1929.

His Education:

At the age of 12 years old he began his music studies of theory, solfeggio, harmony and composition, with maestro *Don* Miguel Michelone, with whom he made his corresponding courses of technical mechanism of the modern school of Tárrega in the culture of the guitar.

His Virtuosity:

The 29th of May of 1948 he performed in the hall of the Damas Catolicas, playing for the Asociacion Guitarristica Argentina: *"Anecdotas"* by Segovia; *"Piezas Caracteristicas"* by Moreno Torroba; *"Preludio, Fuga y Lamento Coya"* by A. Luna; *"Cajita de Musica" y "Movimiento Perpetuo"* by J. S. Sagreras; *"Cancion del Fuego Fatuo"* by de Falla and *"Oriental y Mallorca"* by Albeniz.

The same year, in the Amigos de la Guitarra, he interpreted Moreno Torroba, Turina, Schiuma, Sagreras, Luna, Gomez Crespo, de Falla, Granados and Albeniz, with great success. *"La Prensa"* on the 27th of November said: 'He is an instrumentalist who has absolute dominion over the guitar and who possesses good musical taste and a personality that gives character. . . .'

The 30th of April of 1949 he performed in the Asociacion Tárrega in Rosario, playing an admirable classical program of Spanish and Argentine composers. — The daily *"La Capital"* reported: 'Respectable abilities of the instrumental dominion and expressive virtue were placed into service in a program comprised by works of difficult performance and recognized artistic worth. . . . . .'

The 18th of June he returned to present in the Amigos de la Guitarra a classical program of Hispanic American composers, and the 17th of September he reappeared in the Asociacion Guitarristica Argentina interpreting Rodrigo, Usher, Tansman, Sagreras, Luna, Buchardo, Gomez Crespo, Sainz de la Maza and Albeniz, with great acceptance.

In 1951 we find him in another Amigos de la Guitarra concert; in the Sociedad Argentina de Autores y Compositores de Musica illustrating a lecture by maestro *Don* Francisco Giacobe. — Also performing the *"Concierto de Aranjuez"* by Rodrigo and the *"Sonata Argentina"* by Luna with the orchestra of Bruno Bandini, on the radio station *"Radio del Estado"* (today Radio Nacional) and in the Asociacion Guitarristica de Rosario. He was awarded in all events the warmest applause and congratulations by the knowledgeable and general public.

In 1952 he decided to make a tour of South America and visited Brazil, offering concerts among others in Belo Horizonte, Rio de Janeiro and Sao Paulo, which were very well attended and he was insistently applauded.

Don Arnaldo Marchesotti of the daily *"La Echla de Minas"* in Belo Horizonte wrote: '. . . . he is a great artist, serious and honest, cultured and vibractil, passionate for his smooth instrument whose resources he values and multiplies in his hands. . . . he demonstrates his interpretations a notable maturity, he is, overall, and artist of the sound, and purified and sensible investigator of the surprising blend of tones, that transform through his guitar a harp of ether, clavichord or lute, obtaining contrasts of unforgettable effects. — His agility and bravery are impressive and he knows how to gradually intensify the sound with an admirable intelligence.'

He visited Mexico, the Antilles and in 1952 he stopped in Havana, Cuba, offering performances with works by Rodrigo, Tansman, Gomez Crespo, Sagreras, Ponce, Granados, Turina and Albeniz. — Conchita Gallardo signed in the daily *"El Pais",* the following: '. . . . he dominates the guitar with a magnificent technique and is, besides, a temperamental and dynamic artist.' This collaboration was published after his exciting performance for the Sociedad de Conciertos de Habana.

In 1953 he returned to his homeland and once again made concerts performing for the Asociacion Guitarristica Entrerriana on the 11th of October of 1954. — The next year he visited Brazil again and the 18th of July in the Teatro Cultura Artistica in Sao Paulo, he interpreted works by Scarlatti, Weiss, Castelnuovo-Tedesco, Gomez Crespo, Villa-Lobos, Debussy, Rodrigo and Albeniz, with acclaim of the attending audience.

Later he was presented at competitions in Switzerland and Brussels, in which he interpreted difficult musical pages of the instrument; one of them presided over by Andrés Segovia.

Awards:

In 1948 the Asociacion Argentina de Musica de Camara awarded him the 1st prize, Gold Medal, for his magnificent performances during that year, on the Argentine stages.

The same year, maestro Adolfo V. Luna dedicated his admirable tremolo titled *"Canto Indio"*, that he then played in successive performances.

In 1952 when he visited Mexico, he got to meet the family of the eminent composer *Don* Manuel Ponce, who gave him a gift of the manuscript of *"Concierto del Sur"* for guitar and orchestra, by the great composer, a work that before he left the country he performed at the Bellas Artes under the baton of maestro *Don* Luis Herrera de la Fuente.

His Pedagogy:

He is known for the creation of his new system of plucking by the fingers of the right hand and disposition of the music with which he obtains better facility for the performance, this said, this is very recent and because of that it hasn't been possible to verify if it covers all of the rest of the demands that are required, but remain patient the anxiety praisable of this. . ."

(The Pedagogy section was handwritten and difficult to read the last sentence.)

There are videos of him on You Tube.

Miguel Michelone's notable student, Manuel Lopez Ramos, was born in Buenos Aires on September 4, 1929. In 1940, when Manuel was 11 years old he began his studies with Miguel Michelone. Manuel initiated his career giving concerts in the interior of Argentina and in Buenos Aires in 1948.

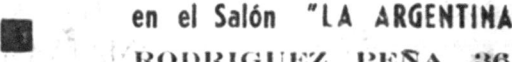

AMIGOS de la GUITARRA

SECRETARÍA: CASTRO 675

6º. CICLO AÑO 1948.

14º. CONCIERTO

(CLAUSURA)

•••

AUSPICIADO POR LA

Asociación Argentina de Música de Cámara

CONCERTISTA

Manuel López Ramos

Viernes 26 de Novbre. a las 21.15

en el Salón "LA ARGENTINA"

RODRIGUEZ PEÑA 361

ENTRADA GENERAL $ 3.—

Los socios de la Asociación Argentina de Música de Cámara, tienen derecho a 2 entradas, presentando el carnet social.

Tendrán rebaja del 50 % los socios de la Asociación Guitarrística Argentina, Círculo de la Guitarra e integrantes del conjunto Cien Guitarras Argentinas.

An early concert program cover in the career of Manuel Lopez Ramos, being for the Amigos de la Guitarra and sponsored by the Asociacion Argentina de Musica de Camara. This concert was held in the Salon "La Argentina" on Friday November 26, 1948. It was the closing concert of the season.

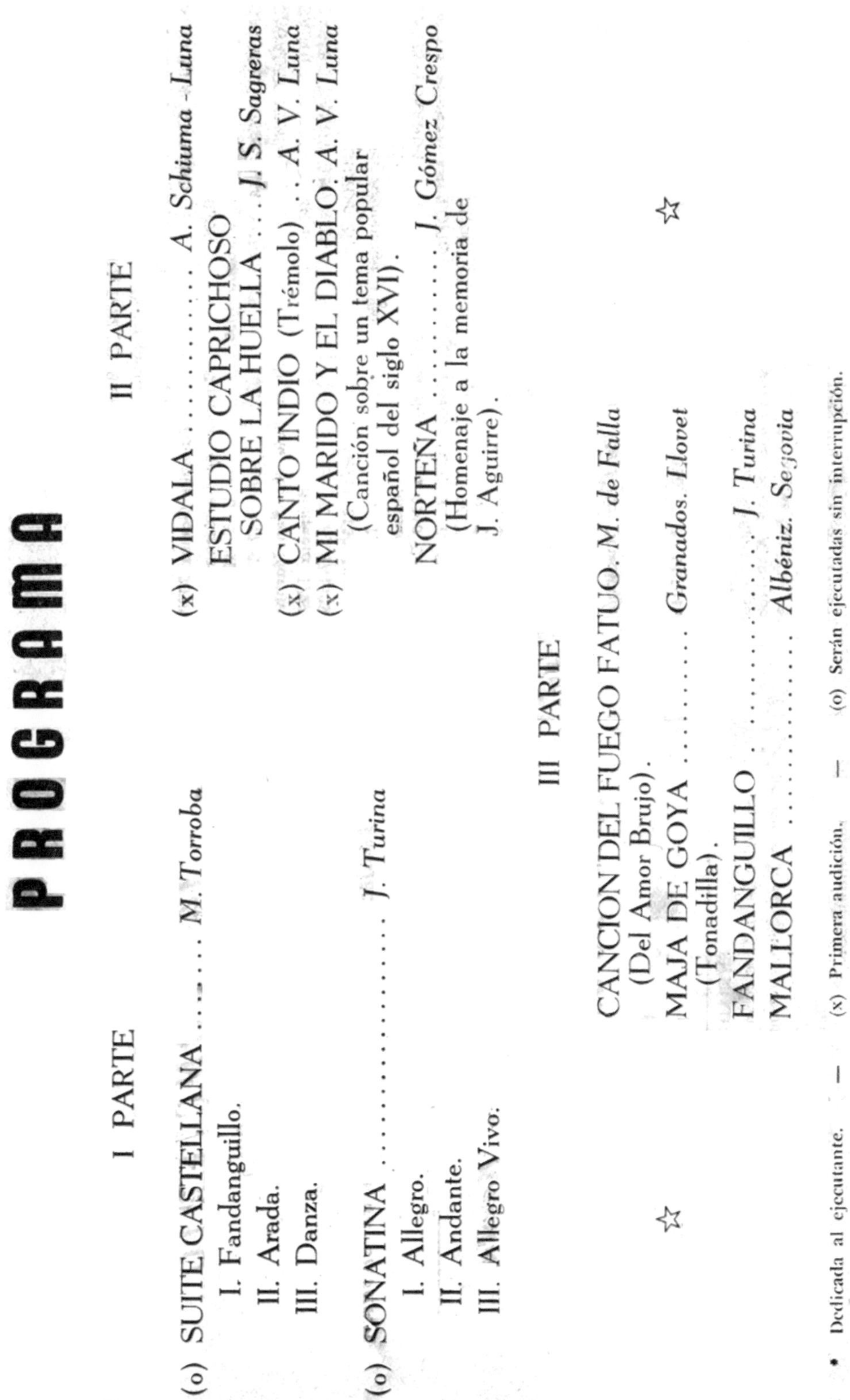

PROGRAMA

I PARTE

(o) SUITE CASTELLANA ...... M. Torroba.
    I. Fandanguillo.
    II. Arada.
    III. Danza.

(o) SONATINA .... J. Turina
    I. Allegro.
    II. Andante.
    III. Allegro Vivo.

☆

II PARTE

(x) VIDALA .... A. Schiuma - Luna

ESTUDIO CAPRICHOSO
    SOBRE LA HUELLA ... J. S. Sagreras

(x) CANTO INDIO (Trémolo) ... A. V. Luna

(x) MI MARIDO Y EL DIABLO. A. V. Luna
    (Canción sobre un tema popular
    español del siglo XVI).

NORTEÑA .... J. Gómez Crespo
    (Homenaje a la memoria de
    J. Aguirre).

☆

III PARTE

CANCION DEL FUEGO FATUO. M. de Falla
    (Del Amor Brujo).

MAJA DE GOYA .... Granados. Llovet
    (Tonadilla).

FANDANGUILLO .... J. Turina

MALLORCA .... Albéniz. Segovia

● Dedicada al ejecutante.   —   (x) Primera audición.   —   (o) Serán ejecutadas sin interrupción.

Manuel's varied repertoire ranges from the Spanish maestros to Argentine folklore pieces. The pieces in part two, *"Vidala", "Mi Marido y El Diablo"* were public debuts, as well as *"Canto Indio"* which was dedicated to Manuel by Adolfo V. Luna.

AMIGOS DE LA GUITARRA

SECRETARÍA: CASTRO 675

7º. CICLO AÑO 1949

2º 1er. **CONCIERTO**

AUDICION Nº. 88

AUSPICIADO POR LA

Asociación Argentina de Música de Cámara

CONCERTIST

Manuel López Ramos

Sábado 18 de Junio a las 18 hs.

en el Salón "LA ARGENTINA"

RODRIGUEZ PEÑA 361

ENTRADA GENERAL $ 3.—

Los Socios de la Asociación Argentina de Música de Cámara, tienen derecho a 2 entradas y los socios de la Peña "El Pial" a 1 entrada, presentando el carnet social.
Socios de la Asoc. Guitarrística Argentina, Círculo de la guitarra y Asociaciones culturales, $ 2.—

This is the first concert of the new season for the Amigos de la Guitarra and sponsored by the Asociacion Argentina de Musica de Camara. It was held in Salon "La Argentina" on Saturday June 18, 1949.

The review of the previous concert on Friday November 26, 1948, from the daily *La Prensa* of Saturday November 27, 1948 in the liner notes. It is as follows: "Amigos de la Guitarra — Last night in the closing concert of the season of this institution in the Salon "La Argentina", Manuel Lopez Ramos showed that as an instrumentalist he has absolute dominion over the secrets of the guitar and that he possesses a good musical taste and personality that is polished".

In these same liner notes it is acknowledged that "Manuel received a 1st Prize, Gold Medal from the Asociacion Argentina de Musica de Camara of Buenos Aires."

PROGRAMA

PRIMERA PARTE

PRELUDIO . . . . *Moreno Torroba*
ZARABANDA LEJANA . . . . *Joaquín Rodrigo*
(Homenaje a la Vihuela de Luis Milán).
SONATA III * . . . . *Manuel Ponce*

    I Allegro Moderato
    II Chanson Adante . . .
    III Allegro non troppo

SEGUNDA PARTE

PRELUDIO Y FUGA
(Tema Criollo).
TRIPTICO **
(Sobre motivos argentinos).

    I Bailecito
    II Pala Pala   *Adolfo V. Luna*
    III Malambo

MI MARIDO Y EL DIABLO
(Canción sobre un tema popular
  español del siglo XVI).

TERCERA PARTE

HOMENAJE A MATEO ALBENIZ *Gustavo Pittaluga*
ALEGRIAS . . . . *Sainz de la Maza*
ORIENTAL . . . . *Albeniz - Segovia*
SEVILLANA . . . . *Joaquín Turina*

* Los tres movimientos serán ejecutados sin interrupción.
** Primera audición.

In this concert Manuel plays pieces by the Spanish maestros Federico Moreno Torroba and Joaquín Rodrigo. He ends the first set with the 3rd Sonata by Mexican composer Manuel Ponce. The second set is completely dedicated to the works of Adolfo V. Luna, including the debut of Adolfo's work *"Triptico"*. Manuel finishes this concert in his third set with more music by the Spanish maestros, which includes the piece from the Flamenco genre *"Alegrias"* by Regino Sainz de la Maza.

"Amigos de la Guitarra"

Secretaría: CASTRO 675

T. E. 46 - 3126

Buenos Aires, Abril de 1951.

El Miércoles 9 de mayo inauguraremos el 9º. Ciclo, teniendo la satisfacción de haber presentado más de 40 guitarristas solistas, Dúos, cuartetos y conjuntos conocidos, en los 109 conciertos organizados.

El concierto inaugural lo tendrá a su cargo MANUEL LOPEZ RAMOS, notable concertista, quién hará escuchar un programa de alta jerarquía musical.

El Miércoles 23 de mayo, actuará, FRANCISCO ORLANDO LA POLLA, destacado guitarrista, con un interesante programa.

Este año iniciaremos una gran conscripción de colaboradores, para contar con recursos permanentes y poder proseguir la obra en favor del bello instrumento: la guitarra.

Invitamos cordialmente a todos los admiradores que deséen escuchar buena guitarra y distintos guitarristas, a suscribir un abono mensual de 4 pesos, o anual de pesos veinte, debiendo organizarse 14 o más conciertos.

Por haberse aumentado la impresión de los programas y el nuevo franqueo que regirá desde el día 16 del corriente, nos vemos obligados a restringir la impresión, enviándose en adelante, unicamente a los abonados e invitados y a quién los solicite.

Saludan a Vd. atentamenete.

Cecilio B. Rodríguez, Manuel López Delgado, Federico de Andreis, Daniel Diego Cruz, Angel Pérez, Miguel A. Ullúa, Ricardo Buccicardi, Andrés Gaviño, Angel Osvaldo D'onofrio.

Nombre y Apellido .... Mensual $ 4.-

Domicilio .... Anual „ 20.-

"We cordially invite all the admirers that desire to listen to good guitar and distinct guitarists, to subscribe by paying 4 pesos per month, or annually twenty, owing to 14 more concerts to be organized.

By having augmented the printing of the programs and the new postage that will begin the 16th of the current month, we see ourselves obligated to restrict the printing, sending in advance, only to the members and invited guests and to those who ask for them.

We greet you attentively. Signed by Cecilio B. Rodríguez and the rest of the board members of the Amigos de la Guitarra April, 1951."

362

Several years later, this was the cover to Manuel Lopez Ramos' Monday April 25, 1955 concert at the Teatro Ateneo. The reviews on the back cover show he had begun his renown internationally in Cuba (April 1952), Mexico (October 1952) and in Sao Paulo, Brazil in 1953.

TEATRO ATENEO
PARAGUAY 918
T. E. 31 - 2888
(CAPACIDAD 737)
(N° 200)

RECITAL DE GUITARRA

MANUEL LOPEZ RAMOS

LUNES 25 DE ABRIL DE 1955 A LAS 22 HORAS

PROGRAMA

I

Sonata .... D. SCARLATTI

Chacona .. .. J. S. BACH

II

Sonata (Homenaje a Boccherini) ..... M. CASTELNUOVO TEDESCO

Allegro con spirito
Andantino, quasi canzone
Tempo di minuetto
Vivo ed energico

Sonatina meridional .... MANUEL M. PONCE

Campo
Copla
Fiesta

III

Tonada .... ADOLFO V. LUNA

Tiento antiguo .... JOAQUIN RODRIGO

En los trigales .... JOAQUIN RODRIGO

La niña de los cabellos de lino .... C. DEBUSSY

Sevillana .... JOAQUIN TURINA

Manuel plays the legendary Bach Chaconne, and pieces by Castelnuovo-Tedesco, Ponce, Luna, Rodrigo, Debussy and Turina.

Manuel Lopez Ramos, Graciela Pomponio, Robert J. Vidal and Jorge Martínez-Zarate at the *1962 Coupe Internationale de la Guitare* held in June 1962 in Paris. This was the cover photo for Wilfrid Appleby's Guitar News issue No. 67 of September-October 1962.

Manuel Lopez Ramos with Graciela Pomponio and Jorge Martínez-Zarate playing submitted compositions that won the competition.

TEATRO ODEON

ESMERALDA 367
TEL. 45-3635

EMPRESA
JOSE PEDRO CARAMBAT

Unico recital del guitarrista

MANUEL LOPEZ RAMOS

JUEVES 24 DE SETIEMBRE A LAS 19 HORAS

Localidades en venta a partir del Sábado 19

Boletería de 10 a 20 horas

This concert at the Teatro Odeon in Buenos Aires took place on Thursday September 24, 1964. The liner notes provide evidence of his past successes. Mentioned are: "Manuel's performances with orchestras of the Radio del Estado and Juvenil under the direction of conductors Bruno Bandini and Luis Gianneo. In 1956 in his first European tour he gave ten concerts in Spain and Italy. Since 1960 he had given concerts in the United States, France, Italy, Switzerland, Holland, Great Britain, Yugoslavia, Belgium and most recently in 1963, Manuel had given fourteen concerts in the USSR, three of the concerts being held in Sala Tschaikovsky in Moscow. Also brought to bear are the radio broadcasts on the B. B.C. in London, the recordings for "Boston Records" and the contract as exclusive recording artist with R. C. A. International." The guitar Manuel Lopez Ramos holds in the photograph on this page was made by Robert Bouchet. As well Manuel currently owns guitars by Hermann Hauser I, Joaquín Garcia, Jeff Elliot.

PROGRAMA

I

Sarabanda y Gavota .... A. SCARLATTI

Sonata .... A. SCARLATTI

Suite III .... J. S. BACH

    Preludio
    Allemanda
    Courante
    Sarabanda
    Bourrée I
    Bourrée II
    Giga

II

Sonata Romántica (Homenaje a Schubert) .... MANUEL PONCE

    Allegro moderato
    Andante espressivo
    Allegretto vivo
    Allegro non troppo e serioso

Berceuse D'Orient .... ALEXANDRE TANSMAN

Danza Pomposa .... ALEXANDRE TANSMAN

Tonada .... ADOLFO LUNA

Serrano (Preludio) .... ANGEL LASALA

Homenaje a Debussy .... MANUEL DE FALLA

Mallorca .... ISAAC ALBENIZ

Danza Nº 11 .... ENRIQUE GRANADOS

In this concert Manuel plays the 3rd Cello Suite by Bach. The John Duarte transcription had been published a short time beforehand. The Mexican composer, Manuel Ponce's Sonata Romantica, that begins the second set, is among the variety of works written by Polish, Argentine and Spanish composers. G. A. Schott had published Alexandre Tansman's *Danza Pomposa*.

MANUEL LOPEZ RAMOS

photo Nisak

This is a promotional postcard by R. C. A. for Manuel Lopez Ramos upon his becoming an exclusive recording artist. Since 1960 Manuel had given masterclasses in the University of Tempe, Arizona, University of Santa Clara, California, Claremont, California Graduate School, San José State College (now University of California at San José), Spring Hill College, Conservatorio Nacional in Guatemala and the Escuela Nacional de Musica of the Universidad Nacional Autonoma de Mexico. In 1965 Manuel founded his Estudio del Arte Guitarristico in Mexico City, which enabled many North American guitarists to attend. In 1969 Manuel received a diploma from the Union Mexicana de Cronistas de Teatro y Musica, given to the most distinguished personalities of the year, for his concerts and pedagogy. As well, in 1971 the Orquesta de Camara of Mexico City gave him a special distinction for his work as a pedagogue and for his diffusion of the art of the guitar in Mexico. The guitar in Manuel's hands is a 1961 Robert Bouchet Spruce and Brazilian concert classical guitar. Robert Bouchet made just over 150 guitars in his different epochs of construction.

As Manuel had begun his career, in 1948, performing concerts in the interior of Argentina, here we find him once again in Rosario, Santa Fe Province on Saturday September 30, 1972, for the Asociacion Guitarristica de Rosario. Manuel's first concert for this institution was on October 31, 1953 in the Salon M. Belgrano. His success was such that he was invited to play in the same location again on June 26, 1954 and a return on June 9, 1956. In this epoch, Abel Fleury and Consuelo Mallo Lopez with her trio were the concert artists playing the back to back performances for the Asociacion Guitarristica de Rosario. Due to his extensive touring outside of Argentina Manuel didn't return to Rosario until October 2, 1964. This September 30, 1972 concert was the first time since 1964, Manuel had paid a visit to the beautiful port city of Rosario.

Photo of Manuel Lopez Ramos from the concert program of September 30, 1972.

The most varied concert by Manuel Lopez Ramos, ranging from ancient music of the Renaissance to Baroque, to Romantic 19th century and living composers of the 20th century. Manuel had played Rodrigo's *Zarabanda Lejana* in concert since 1949. By this time in his career, Manuel had worked with orchestras under the direction of these distinguished maestros: Bandini, Gianneo, Gomez, Lavista, Frausto, Redel, Savin, Ximénez Caballero, Bredo, Lombardi, Goldmann, Ruiz, Vazquez, Spurgeon and Abas.

PROGRAMA

—— I ——

TRES PIEZAS .... **Henry Purcell**
  A New Irish Tune
  Minuet
  Jig
DOS MINUETOS .... **Chr. Fr. Schale**
SUITE III .... **J. S. Bach**
  Prelude
  Allemanda
  Courante
  Sarabanda
  Bourre I
  Bourre II - I
  Giga

—— I I ——

DOS PRELUDIOS y
MINUETO .... **Francisco Tárrega**
PIEZAS
CARACTERISTIQUES ..... **F. Moreno Torroba**
  Los Mayos
  Albada
  Oliveras
  Melodía
SUITE INGLESA .... **John Duarte**
  Prelude
  Folk Song
  Round Dance
SARABANDA LEJANA Y
FANDANGO .... **Joaquín Rodrigo**
GOLONDRINAS .... **M. Castelnuovo Tedesco**
  (de la serie Platero y Yo)
TARANTELLA .... **M. Castelnuovo Tedesco**

LASSALLE

TEATRO COOPERATIVA DE TRABAJO Ltda.

CANGALLO 2263   TEL. 47 - 9388/6280

Unico recital del guitarrista

MANUEL LOPEZ RAMOS

=
=

MIERCOLES 18 DE AGOSTO A LAS 21 HORAS

Localidades en venta a partir del jueves 12 - Boletería de 11 a 23 horas

This Wednesday August 18, 1976 concert at the Lassalle theater was unique one to be performed by Manuel during this particular visit to his homeland. He had been very busy with his international schedule.

MANUEL LOPEZ RAMOS

GUITARRA

PROGRAMA

I

MELODIA .... **EDUARDO GRIEG**

MINUETTO y ALLEGRO .... **FERNANDO SOR**

SUITE 3ª PARA CELLO .... **J. S. BACH**
    (Prelude - Allemande - Courante -
    Sarabande - Bourré I - II - Gigue)

CINCO BAGATELAS .... **WILLIAM WALTON**
    (Allegro - Lento - Alla Cubana
    Andante - Con Slancio)

II

FOLIAS DE ESPAÑA .... **MANUEL PONCE**

FANDANGO .... **JOAQUIN RODRIGO**

SEVILLA .... **ISAAC ALBENIZ**

The liner notes mention that in 1975 Manuel had given fourteen concerts in the Soviet Union and Switzerland. Among the five critiques cited, that of Michael Louvet *"Guia de Conciertos"* in Paris says: "Until this moment, I had never been against neither for the guitar. Thanks to Manuel Lopez Ramos, the instrument has reached me completely. This young musician belongs to the race of the greats. His sound is magnificent, though small, and appeared to me as all that was tenderness and enchantment. With a player of this class, one can easily fall in love with the guitar." Manuel had performed the 3rd Cello Suite by Bach in concert for 20 years.

Manuel Lopez Ramos passed away in Mexico City on June 5, 2006. His widow is the daughter of Miguel Michelone, Manuel's maestro.

"Justo T. Morales Morales was born in Ranchos (today General Paz), Buenos Aires province on March 6, 1877. As a guitarist, he was self-taught, of easy and intelligent assimilation. As a composer he is of a fresh vein and, appears to be, uninterrupted; in distinguishing himself with his original works in the characteristic productions of Argentine folklore. Let's let him speak for himself: "My fondness for the guitar I believe I was born with; since my mother told me that, being very small, of only one or two years old, my best entertainment was to have in my hands a screen that we use for enlivening a fire, according to the story, and making as if I was playing the guitar, passing the hours quite entertained. So that they wouldn't be bothered by my crying, they put the screen in my hands and, an instant remedy, the singer was silenced and replaced by the guitarist." That guitar-screen at nine years old became real: in the home of his grandparents, was hanging and abandoned as unusable, a guitar that caught his eye; it still had three strings in spite of the time; of its being forgotten and their age. With this instrument that he was given as a present, he made his "musical" introduction. His first maestro was Alejandro Cesareo Pérez, a guitarist, pianist and good professor of music. Justo's maestro wanted to initiate his musical education with solfeggio as well, not getting him to do it, but, instead, whatever piece Alejandro played, instantly Justo repeated it, thanks to his formidable perception.

By a method of tablature his maestro taught him pieces of Juan Alais, Gaspar Sagreras, Carlos García Tolsa, and other authors that not even Pérez himself was able to play. The years flew by and the formation of the guitarist had become a reality: influenced without cessation, by the guitar, composition after composition, that didn't come to life from standard notation, but the tablature system his maestro had taught him.

In 1910 the Teatro "Apolo", with sincere approval contracted him. In 1916 his performance was very appreciated in the "La Guitarra" society. (Founded by Juan Carlos Anido). Justo Morales decided to study music, and did so with Professor Eusebio de Miguel, and later with Pietro Rubione. About the guitar: Mario Rodríguez Arenas and Domingo Prat gave him their advice. Dedicated to teaching, today he is one of the most celebrated professors, and Jacinta Arauz, Segundo N. Contreras, Luis F. Benitez, Ricardo Muñoz are among his most distinguished disciples. On October 6, 1920 he presented his twelve-year old student, Maria Esther Benitez Cevallos, in the Salon "La Argentina", playing between them twenty-one works, all well applauded. Among his advanced students we recall Dolores Méndez, Rosita Esmeralda Ginés, Fanny Miro, Sofia Haydée Yungue, and the youngster Jorge C. Sturla. Justo taught many distinguished ladies and gentlemen of the porteña society, among them, to Sara Reybaud, A. de Ezeiza, Maria Angélica A. de Lopez Lecube, Maria Ercilla Yungue de Martínez Toledo, Maria Laura and Susana Alcobendas, Emma M. del Cerro Abella, Rosita del Pilar Gomez, Inés H. Melville, Maria Luisa and Alicia Gonzalez Lagingue, Maria Angélica Llosa, Maria Clara Tormey, Carlota Gallo, daughter of the ex-minister of the Interior Dr. Vicente Gallo, etc. The following aficionados: Dr. Manuel Fernández Cutiellos, President of the Supreme Court of Mercedes and the Doctors Juan Alberto Roth, Alfredo Zakob, Juan Lewis Arauz and Roberto Ezcurra as well had Morales as their maestro. Always working as a teacher, later he took a position in the "El Salvador" college. But where the personality of Morales stands out more so is in his compositions. Undoubtedly his worth is filled with inspiration and whose works are lasting, celebrated in the pages of folklore, to those that know is impressed the unmistakable flavor of Argentina. Justo Morales has had the respectable sum of 34 original works published: *Tristes, Preludios, Rancheras, Milongas, Vidalitas, Zambas, Pericons, Tangos, Gatos* and *Estilos*. All of that pleasant *criolla "mazamorra"* (hodgepodge) is well worth consulting. That old tango, from the war times, *"Diosma"*-not easy, but beautiful — along with his *"Pericon"* and the *"Triste": "ño Juan Carlos"*, form a new Argentine musical trilogy, of popular character. The last work was adapted in the performances by the most excellent guitarist Maria Luisa Anido and by other well thought of players. The *"Triste"* by Morales is different than the *"Triste" No. 4* by Julián Aguirre, it is a true Argentine triste; in the second part it will be as beautiful as you might want, it's well harmonized and to the point it produces sadness in us, but doesn't let it be a song that is a Spanish caprice to us. To Morales, they can't be shirking from those mistakes of the maestros, the ones in European studies; his muse is pure, typical: the smell of ombú and of "patay". Morales believes by spiritual necessity: I have his virtue and success right here. His output is consonant; there aren't any daring ideas that break the melodic line that are characteristic of him. We have lingered with some detail in the personality of Morales, by believing it worthy of study and praise. In him, as in Segovia, his merit is triple fold, by having been his own maestro." So ends the entry by Domingo Prat in his *Diccionario de Guitarristas*.

Justo T. Morales

The above photo is dedicated to Ricardo Muñoz and translates to: "For my student and beloved friend Ricardo Muñoz. Signed Justo T. Morales."

There are 41 pieces by Justo T. Morales listed in 1931 Antigua Casa Nuñez catalog.

From Ricardo Muñoz's *"Historia de la Guitarra"* published in 1930 we glean some other details: "Justo was the son of Vicente Morales and Alejandra Morales. Justo also studied with Hilarion Leloup."

This biography of Justo Tomas Morales is translated from Ricardo Muñoz's unpublished book *"Historia Universal de la Guitarra"* Volume VIII *"La Escuela Tárrega en La Argentina"*.

"Justo Tomas Morales

His Origin:

He was the son of *Don* Justo Vicente and *Doña* Alejandra Morales, born in the town of Ranchos, today General Paz, Buenos Aires Province on the 6th of March of 1877.

His Education:

Since he was a young boy he had a liking for the guitar, which he simulated with a screen that we use for enlivening a fire, which was given to him by his family members when he bothered them by shouting or crying, at 9 years of age, he took hold of an almost broken old guitar in the house, he strung it as he could and in this way he began the first steps in his guitaristic education.

A relative, *Don* Alejandro Cesareo Pérez, a musician, pianist and guitarist initiated him on this instrument performing with a surprising ability when listened to, and nevertheless the gifts, promises and advice that were offered to him, it wasn't possible to get to study music, then maestro Mr. Pérez changed the system and used tablature with great skill, and since in this manner, could convince him to study some pages by Alais, Sagreras, García Tolsa and others, who the youngster assimilated and interpreted magnificently.

In this way he continued during his youth performing important works by memory- works heard by knowledgeable folks that offered to hire him in the Teatro Apolo, where for the first time he received untold applause. In spite of that and as time went on he understood it was impossible to reach his goal by that manner and in 1916, having heard many great maestros and their artistry in the society "Centro de la Guitarra", he decided to study with maestro Eusebio de Miguel and harmony with *Don* Pedro Rubione, while continuing to practice the modern school with maestro Mario Rodríguez Arenas, then later with Hilarion Leloup who gave him his diploma as a professor, proceeding afterward to take his perfection studies with *Don* Domingo Prat.

His Virtuosity:

He made an infinity of good appearances given his particular form of expression, the content of the sheet music that he intelligently adorned with real mastery; these performances consecrated him emphatically before the public, the journalistic critics and the arts in general which, emotional beforehand and so beautiful, couldn't be left in silence; the pencil of the sketch artist D. M. Bonatti did his portrait on the 14th of November of 1951 and the palette and the brush of the notable A. Waingortin put all of the admiration and respectful feeling of the maestro on the marvelous canvas, whose designed portrait and is found in the possession of the Morales family.

The words, in front of the great artist, dedicate to him verses bearing homage of his inspiration and scent; the classic poet *Don* R. Solveyra Casares, Jéronimo Gaid and others, among which is the *"Diptico"* by Eugenio Cardenas, singing in this way:

"To His Hands"
Ah! the blessed prodigious hands
that extract poems on the strings,
to make his notes a language
of virile and harmonious words. —

Saintly Hands. — That at times, quickly
tunes the furies of the swell
and other times calm the landscape. —
Saturated of lilies and of roses.

Knowledgeable hands, that in rhythms and cadences
intoxicate the light to my existence
to make it live full of calm;

I wanted, bearing a homage,
to convert myself, for an instant, into a string
and be able to kiss with all the soul!

To the right is the original from Ricardo Muñoz's unpublished book *"Historia Universal de la Guitarra"* Volume VIII *"La Escuela Tárrega en La Argentina".*

A SUS MANOS

¡ Ah ! benditas las manos prodigiosas
que le arrancan poemas al cordaje,
para hacer de sus notas un lenguaje
de palabras viriles y armoniosas.-

Manos Santas.-Que a veces,presurosas
sintetizan las furias del oleaje
y otras veces la calma del paisaje.-
Saturado de nardos y de rosas.-

Manos sabias,que en ritmos y cadencias
embriagaron la luz a mi existencia
para hacerla vivir llena de calma;

Yo quisiera,rindiendo un homenaje,
convertirme,un instante,en cordaje
¡ y poderlas besar con toda el alma !

376

The 15th day of April of 1921, in a reunion of eminent artists intentionally provoked by the author of this *"Historia"*, in the home of our friend the painter of minatures *Don* M. Martínez Jérez, after the maestro Morales performed, the attendees gave a gift to him a parchment that the brilliant *Don* Luis Macaya, in which the poet Jéronimo Gaid wrote:

The Guitar, which your skillful hand plucks,
makes a miracle with its sounds;
elevates and purifies our senses,
it hurts the most perfect of the human being. —

If the beauty has its mysticism,
A mystic priest of the Beauty,
with anointing performs, as who prays,
and to listen to you pray also I do the same!

For the good that you've done for me, I wish to exalt
the blessed music! The blessed art
that is the most exquisite, being the youngest. —

And, since you love it with such mastery
I proclaim you an apostle of the Harmony,
in the name of Our Mr. Beethoven. —

La Guitarra, que pulsa sabia tu mano,
realiza un milagro con sus sonidos;
eleva y purifica nuestros sentidos,
hiere lo más perfecto del ser humano.-

Si la belleza tiene su misticismo,
místico sacerdote de la Belleza,
con unción ejecutas, como quien reza,
¡ y al escucharte rezo también yo mismo !

Por el bien que me has hecho, quiero ensalzarte,
¡ la música bendigo ! Bendito el arte
que es el más exquisito, siendo el más joven.-

Y, pues tu lo cultivas con tal maestría
Yo te proclamo Apostol de la Armonía,
en el nombre de Nuestro Señor Beethoven.-

Above is the original from Ricardo Muñoz's unpublished book *"Historia Universal de la Guitarra"* Volume VIII *"La Escuela Tárrega en La Argentina"*.

His Compositions:

His musical compositions are divided into originals, classical and folkloric, also the classical, folkloric and dance transcriptions; of the first are the visibly distinguished his most eloquent (su pagina cumbre): *"Alma y Musica",* a fantasy dedicated to his friend and student, the magistrate Dr. Juan A. Roth. — It begins with an introduction of successive chords in an *Andantino* of 3/4 time in G major, continuing the 2nd Part in the same key to the 6/8 rhythm *Andantino,* taking the melody in the form of a tremolo on the 2nd string; the 2nd and 3rd Parts proceed in a (*"Tiempo de Vals"*) waltz tempo, then an *"Allegro"* and it returns to a tremolo for the Lento ending. — It was published by Antigua Casa Nuñez. —

"Cancion de mi Alma", is a spontaneous prelude born in the moments that digress over the fretboard; very sensitive, it was published by the same Casa Nuñez. —

"Baby" (Bailecito de la Muñeca)   Antigua Casa Nuñez
"Preludios Nos. 1, 2, 3 and 4"
"2 Preludios"
"Preludio Melodico"
"Evocacion"
"Filigrana"
"Pavana" (2nd guitar for that of Tárrega)
"Peluquita"
"Preludiando" (Unpublished)

As far as his folkloric compositions, what is written in maestro Domingo Prat's *"Diccionario de Guitarristas"* on page 214 well describes them-see biography by Prat.

"Don Antonio" an original and sensible *Triste,* from a deep inspiration, simple, noble, and emotional, like *"Diosma", "Pericon"* and *"ño Juan Carlos"* for 1, 2 and 3 guitars published 6 times by Antigua Casa Nuñez.

"Santos Vega", is another *Triste* expressing the infinite pain of the *gaucho* singer living in the most indigent misery that the destiny provides; a magnificent original page constructed in just 30 minutes of inspired and fleeting time.

"Fugaz", criollo prelude in E minor, graceful, emotional always developed over a single melody, it ends with legatos of interesting impressions.

"Argentina", Milonga   Antigua Casa Nuñez
"Solo para Ti", Vals
"Aires de mi Patria", Vidalita
"Tambien mi Rancho se Llueve"
"Mimita", Triste
"Cantos de mi Patria": "El Pingo", El Aparo", El Lazo: with 4 lines for singing, written by the poet *Don* R. Solveyra Casares on the 8th of August of 1925; and "El Facon", Estilo.
"Amalia", Zamba
"Lolita" Zamba
"Bajo el Parral", Triste
"Album de 4 piezas y dos Estilos:
    "La Delia", Milonga
    "Mercedes", Mazurka
    "Podhi", Estilo
    "Nenino", Vals
    "La Cuca", Estilo
"El Gaucho Argentino", Estilo
"De mi Epoca", Tango
"Don Cosme", Estilo

378

"9 de octubre", Vals
"Danzas Argentinas", Gato
"De la Rosa"

"La Caprichosa", Tango, by Villoldo   Casa Ricordi
"El Otario", Tango, by G. Metallo
"Flor Porteña", Zamba
"El Riojanito", Gato
"Ojos Negros", Vidalita
"Añorando", Tanda de Valses-a group of waltzes
"Mazurkas No. 1 y 2 —
"La Leyenda", Estilo
"El Chaco", Estilo
"Maria Angelica", Estilo
"Cachito", Vals
"Azul y Blanco", Ranchera
"Cancion Argentina", Vidalita
"Estilo Criollo", —

Of his transcriptions we recall:

"Preludio" by the Padre Manuel Maria de Muro who in 1934 dedicated to his ex-student Ricardo Muñoz, author of this *"Historia Universal de la Guitarra",* and who later returned to dedicate to the distinguished virtuoso Elsa Molina; it was published in the *"Revista de la Guitarra"* issue No. 5 of the Asociacion Guitarristica Argentina in the month of May of 1941. —

It is a solemn religious theme, an Andante, of 18 measures, magnificently adapted to the guitar in the key of D minor.

Besides, transcriptions exist of several waltzes by Chopin, all of them unpublished, whose manuscripts are found in the possession of his family.

His Pedagogy:

Here, paired to his compositions is where begins his great artistic work; chiseled magnificently directed toward concrete forms to the sonorous pages that construct and do interpret by his distinguished students now admired on the stages of the Argentine Guitar, today distinguished professional maestros, men of letters, of the forums, of the finest society, etc. who turn to him in expectation of lessons and advice; of them we recall: the excellent Elsa Molina, Maria Herminia Antola de Gomez Crespo, Elba Rosado de Biancardi, Maria Esther Benitez Cevallos, Sara Reybaud, Maria Angélica A. de Lopez Lecube, Lolita de Menéndez de Barth, Rosita Ques, Maria Haydée Gomez, Lewis Delia Arauz, Dolores and Concepcion Menéndez, Inés H. Melville, the historian and maestro *Don* Segundo N. Contreras, Severo Rodríguez, Vicente M. Vita, Emilio Horroke, Carlota Gallo, daughter of the ex-minister of the Interior Dr. Vicente Gallo, Dr. Manuel Fernández Cutiellos, President of the Supreme Court of Justice in the City of Mercedes, Buenos Aires Province, Doctor *Don* Juan Alberto Roth, Criminal Judge of the City of la Plata, Roberto Ezcurra, Jorge C. Sturla, and the author of this "Historia" and others, who constitute an artistic generation of the Argentine modern guitar.

He was a professor of the Colegio El Salvador, and wrote some pedagogical works of high technique, of which we especially cite:

"Mis Recuerdos"   Antigua Casa Nuñez
"Los Primeros Pasos"
"Dos Estudios faciles"
"Arpejios", estudio en Do mayor   (This and those that follow are unpublished)
"Ejercicio en forma de Preludio"
"Ejercicio" dedicado a Ricardo Muñoz, in 1934

"Divigando", preludio dedicated to R. Muñoz
"Estudio en extension", dedicated to R. Muñoz in 1941
"Principios", 4 Preludes
    1. "Adagio" in chords in E minor
    2. "Melodia", of intense tenderness
    3. and 4. — Ejecuciones continuadas en semicorcheas con cierto colorido de grata satisfaciones. . . . .
    (Continued performance in sixteenth notes with certain colors of pleasant satisfaction....)

"*Método Didactico del Mechanismo Técnico*", Antigua Casa Nuñez; is a complete demonstration of his conscious technical ability and pedagogy on the instrument he practices.

Morales is one of the most lofty figures of the guitar cult of his time, he was a maestro in the most ample acceptation of the word and a virtuoso of outstanding technical and interpretive ability endowed of an ultrasensitive spirit, his name has him united to the other greats in the history of the modern Argentine guitar of the 20th century, surely the posterity will have to appraise a day of artistic importance of such a distinguished maestro. —

Honors:

The 7th of August of 1937, the publisher and guitarmaker Antigua Casa Nuñez, in merit to his quality as an artist and maestro, organized a concert in the Salon Lassalle to the total benefit of Morales, in which took part, the students of the maestro who intervened were: Spinardi, Ladru, Romeo, Casuscelli, Mallo Lopez, Rizzuti, Martin, Amestoy, Benitez, Leloup, Lopez, Gonzalez, Veron, Gascon, Paradella, Michelone, Iparraguire, Soriano, Brugni, and the homaged.

Amigos de la Guitarra sponsored by the Asociacion Argentina de Musica de Camara, the 27th of November of 1947, on the occasion of his goodbye to the Argentine populace that applauded him so much, offered a concert in the Salon "La Argentina", in it which Morales performed in the 1st Part: "*Estudio*" and "*Andantino*" by Sor; "*Cancion*" by Bensadon; "*Preludiando*", "*Melodia*" and "*Bailecito de la Muñeca*" from his own harvest; in the 2nd Part, his student, the Professor Elba Rosado de Biancardi interpreted: "*Allemande*" and "*Preludio*" by Bach; "*Scherzino*" by De Rubertis; "*Choros*" by Villa-Lobos; "*Allegretto*" and "*Allegro*" by Moreno Torroba; and in the 3rd Part: both performed playing "*Milonga*", "*Vidalita*", "*Triste*", "*Gato*" and "*Ranchera*" by the maestro, with a clamorous success. —

The 1st of February of 1949 the "Academia Argentina de la Guitarra" named him a "Miembro Benemérito" (Meritorious Member) of the institution.

The 24th of May of 1952, the "Asociacion Guitarristica Rosario", offered an homage in collaboration with the notable maestro Adolfo V. Luna; the concert guitarist Nelly Ezcaray and the duo Maciel Varela began the act, sponsored by the Sub Comsion de Cultura of the Municipality of Rosario, which took place in the Sala de la Biblioteca Argentina.

Of the friendship Morales always made a following, many times desecrated by the world of the ungrateful, selfish and vain people as he had the soul of a poet, the 3rd of April of 1942, he wrote of his pain to his friend and student *Don* Vicente de Vita, as he unloaded the weight of his grief:

Remember Vita, the Sunday,
that I speaking to you of my life,
I said that the soul wounded
had, There! of suffering?
Good, since, in these lines
he will soon find,
the most eloquent proof
who is to die has to be born. —

The friendship that is for me,
the same life, the heaven!
ungrateful and unconsoled
only is what I was offered. —
My noble aspirations,
that never ever came about
to reality, they were shattered,
always to be at that time.

My ideals already dead,
my life made in suffering,
only a continuous torment,
 the destiny I was offered.
And then as a secret,
I searched in my guitar God!
the inspiration that yearning,
sprouted of the heart.

And I wrote my melodies;
my studies, my Estilos,
 and those were palliatives
for this my great pain.—
Therefore, in my "nights"
in what my spirit is calm
the surrender to my "God" of the soul,
as an offering of love.

And in my eternal solitude
my grief increases!
who will give me the happiness
that doesn't reach to be known
No one now! therefore I say,
except for that I regret
to be born to die
and but, I mustn't be born!

His Passing:

The 1st of November of 1952 Morales visited me at 10:30AM, making it known to me, the only reason he came was to congratulate me on my upcoming birthday on the 4th; we conversed very pleasantly between one and another swallows of appetizers; at 12:30 he left accompanied by his son, Carlos, all the way to Monroe and Andonaegui streets, where he took the cable car No. 35, that conducted him to his home. He arrived at his house, Departmento No. 1 of the calle General Artigas 4533 and had lunch, then took his Santos Hernández guitar and in circumstances that led up to tuning the strings, he fell headlong into a faint where he lost his vision completely, ability to speak and the movement of his right side, the doctor concurred of the diagnosis; brain hemorrhage with total paralysis. — Two hours later, one of his granddaughters communicated to me what had occurred.

The 4th of January of 1953 at 7 o'clock he died; he was buried the following day at 4PM in the Cemeterio del Oeste, with the attendance of representatives of the Asociacion Guitarristica Argentina, Academia Argentina de la Guitarra, Amigos de la Guitarra, his family, a few friends, maestros and students and without one word of goodbye, by not accepting their relatives."

¿ Recuerda Vitta, el Domingo,
que hablándole de mi vida,
le dije que el alma herida
tenía, ¡ hay ! de padecer ?
Bueno, pues, en estas líneas
encontrará prontamente,
la prueba más elocuente
que morir debí al nacer.-

La amistad que es para mí,
la misma vida ¡ el cielo !
ingratitud y desconsuelo
sólo es lo que me ofreció.-
Mis nobles aspiraciones,
que nunca jamás llegaron
a realidad, se troncharon,
siempre al estar en sazón.-

Muertos ya mis ideales,
Mi vida hecha un sufrimiento,
sólo un continuo tormento,
el destino me brindó.-
Y entonces, como un secreto,
busqué en mi guitarra ¡Diosa!
la inspiración que anhelosa,
brotaba del corazón.-

Y escribí mis melodías;
mis estudios, mis estilos,
y ellos fueron paliativos,
para este mi gran dolor.-
Por eso, en mis "noches",
en que mi espíritu está en calma
le entrego a mi "Diosa" el alma,
como una ofrenda de amor.-

¡ Y en mi eterna soledad
acreciento mi amargura !
¡ quien me dará la ventura
que no alcancé a conocer ?
¡Nadie ya ! por eso digo,
sin por ello arrepentirme:
¡ al nacer debí morirme,
y sinó, no debí nacer.!

Above is the original from Ricardo Muñoz's unpublished book "*Historia Universal de la Guitarra*" *Volume VIII "La Escuela Tárrega en La Argentina"*.

SALÓN LA ARGENTINA
RODRIGUEZ PEÑA 361

MIERCOLES 7 DE NOVIEMBRE DE 1917
A LAS 9 p. m.

CONCIERTO DE GUITARRA

DEL

CLUB ATLÉTICO POLICIA DE LA CAPITAL

A BENEFICIO DE SU BIBLIOTECA
Y PANTEON DE ESTA REPARTICION

CON EL CONCURSO DEL

Concertista: JUSTO P. MORALES
Maestro: ENRIQUE SANCHEZ ARANDA
y el Señor R. MUÑOZ

Entrada General . . . . $
Socios (al corriente) del Club . . . . . $

Imp. "Consiglio" Esc. Monteaguão 14

CONCIERTO DE GUITARRA

Verificóse anoche en La Argentina una audición de música de este instrumento á cargo de los señores Justo P. Morales y R. Muñoz, que fué precedida de una conferencia sobre este género musical tan predilecto ahora de nuestro público.

Tanto el conferencista don Enrique Sánchez Aranda, como los ejecutantes fueron muy aplaudidos.

CONFERENCIA

Dió anoche en La Argentina, don Enrique Sánchez Aranda, una conferencia sobre "La guitarra y su música", ilustrada con números que fueron ejecutados en ese instrumento por los concertistas señores Justo P. Morales y R. Muñoz.

Aligerada de todo ese fárrago nomenclatural de fechas y giros técnicos con que se condimentan éstos pesados platos, la conferencia del señor Aranda fué una interesante y amena disertación donde se puso de relieve todas las bellezas y recursos de este instrumento que salido de sus límites populares ya se empieza a considerar por los musicólogos como importante y apto para todo género de armonía.

Al final fué muy aplaudido por la concurrencia como así mismo los que

---

Concert in the Salon "La Argentina" on Wednesday November 7, 1917 headed by maestro Justo T. Morales, Enrique Sanchez Aranda and Ricardo Muñoz. Praises from two unspecified newspapers from November 8, 1917.
Archive: Ricardo Muñoz

Translation of "*Concierto de Guitarra*":

"Last night in "La Argentina" a performance of music took place by this instrument entrusted to Justo Morales and Ricardo Muñoz that was preceded by a lecture about this musical genre our public is so fond of now.

The lecturer, Enrique Sanchez Aranda, as well as the performers were extensively applauded."

Translation of "*Conferencia*" (Lecture)

"Last night in "La Argentina" *Don* Enrique Sanchez Aranda gave a lecture about "The Guitar and its Music", illustrated with numbers that were performed on this instrument by the concert guitarists Justo T. Morales and Ricardo Muñoz.

Without of all the nomenclature medley of dates, technical digressions, with which fill this heavy plate, the lecture of Mr. Enrique Sanchez Aranda was an interesting and pleasing dissertation where all the beauties and recourses of this instrument that has emerged from its popular limits that now have begun to be considered by musicologists as important and capable of all genres of harmony were put in relief.

At the end he was applauded quite a bit by the gathering as so were the concert guitarists."

At the top of the next page is the program of the November 7, 1917 concert.

Justo T. Morales in 1917

Ricardo Muñoz in 1923

PROGRAMA

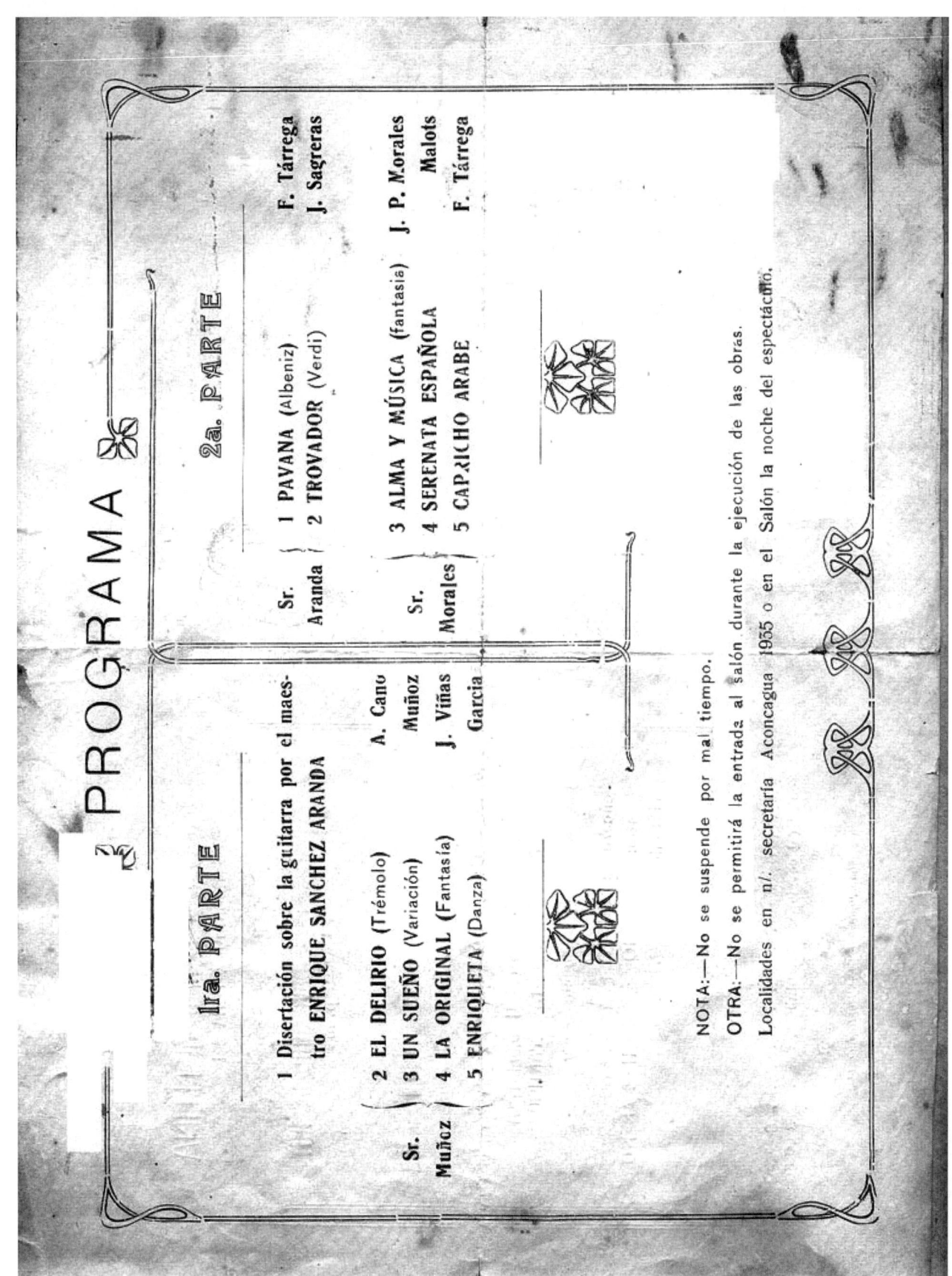

1ra. PARTE

1 Disertación sobre la guitarra por el maestro **ENRIQUE SANCHEZ ARANDA**

Sr. Muñoz {
2 EL DELIRIO (Trémolo)   A. Canu Muñoz
3 UN SUEÑO (Variación)
4 LA ORIGINAL (Fantasía)   J. Viñas García
5 ENRIQUETA (Danza)
}

2a. PARTE

Sr. Aranda {
1 PAVANA (Albeniz)   F. Tárrega
2 TROVADOR (Verdi)   J. Sagreras
}

Sr. Morales {
3 ALMA Y MÚSICA (fantasía)   J. P. Morales
4 SERENATA ESPAÑOLA   Malots
5 CAPRICHO ARABE   F. Tárrega
}

NOTA:—No se suspende por mal tiempo.

OTRA:—No se permitirá la entrada al salón durante la ejecución de las obras.

Localidades en n/. secretaría Aconcagua 1955 o en el Salón la noche del espectáculo.

Concert by maestro Justo T. Morales and students, including Ricardo Muñoz and Anibal Ladru at the Salon Ramon L. Falcon on Saturday August 3, 1918.

(Page 245) 1918 Justo T. Morales concert titles, of particular note is the performance of Carlos García Tolsa's (1858-1905) "Meditacion", which is a tremolo piece. Agustín Pio Barrios in Brazil had also performed it by this time in 1916. "Meditacion" is a piece that Barrios played for over 25 years. Guitar historian, Ricardo Muñoz, also performed in this 1918 Justo T. Morales concert. It is worthy to note the inclusion of Anibal Ladru, who according to Domingo Prat, worked with large guitar ensembles for quite some time.

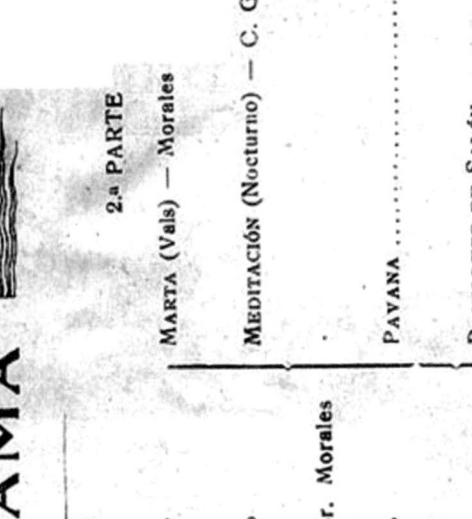

PROGRAMA

1ª. PARTE

1.º—OIMONTE—Ouverture—(Piano—Josefina Padrón)

2.º Sta. Iglesias y { SERENATA— Piano y Violín—VALACCA
niño Iglesias { por G. Bragos.

3.º—Sta. Cabrera (canto) tonadillas.

GUITARRA

4.º Sr. Ladrú y { SERENATA morisca.......... Chapí
Fernández

5.º— id. — ESTUDIO............. Coste

6.º— id. PERICON NACIONAL............... Sinópoli

2.ª PARTE

1.º MARTA (Vals) — Morales

2.º MEDITACIÓN (Nocturno) — C. García

Sr. Morales

5.º PAVANA .... Albeniz

4.º RAMILLETE DE SALÓN .... Pargas

5º. Sr. Morales y Muñoz } PAVANA .... Tárrega

6.º— id. — ENTRE DOS LUCES (Habanera) C. García

7.º— id. — RECUERDOS DE LA ALHAMBRA Tárrega — Sagreras

8.º—Sres. Morales, Muñoz, Ladrú y Fernández } VIDALITAS .... Sinópoli

NOTA—No se suspende por mal tiempo.

OTRA—No se admitirá la entrada al salón durante la ejecución de las obras.

OTRA—La C. D. se reserva el derecho de admisión.

DISTINGUIDAS CULTORAS DE LA GUITARRA

Discípulas del profesor **JUSTO T. MORALES**

Srta. MOÑA MENENDEZ

Srta. LEWIS DELIA ARAUZ · Srtas. DOLORES y CONCEPCION MENENDEZ · Srta. INES H. MELVILLE

The distinguished students of Justo T. Morales: Mona Menéndez, Lewis Delia Arauz, Dolores and Concepcion Menéndez, Ines H. Melville.
From: *Revista Musical Ilustrada "Tárrega"* No. 21 of April 1926

Audición de Guitarra, ofrecida por el conocido profesor señor Justo T. Morales, en casa de sus distinguidas discípulas, las señoritas de Menéndez.

De pié: Señores Teniente Coronel Nicolás Menéndez; Dr. José M. Torres Zárate; señorita Fortunata Echeverría, señora Angélica Menéndez de Cires; Señores Martín Cires Irigoyen; Saul Demetrio Pereyra; Eduardo Talero y Miguel Judez.

Sentados: Señoras Amalia Irigoyen A. de Cires: Concepción Judez de Menéndez: Haydée Amalia Cires de Pereyra; señoritas Concepción Moña y Lolita Menéndez.

(Above) Justo T. Morales performing in the home of Teniente Coronel Nicolas Menendez. From: *Revista Musical Ilustrada "Tárrega"* No. 22 of May 1926.

(Below) Lola and Mona Menendez from *Revista Musical Ilustrada "Tárrega"* No. 23 of June 1926.

Doctor Juan Lewis Arauz
Prof. J. T. Morales

Señor Albino D. Ottonello
Prof. J. T. Morales

Justo Morales' students: Juan Lewis Arauz and Albino Ottonello from the *Revista Musical Ilustrada "Tárrega"* issue No. 30 of February 1927.

In the daily *"El Diario"* of Parana, Entre Rios province of Sunday August 16, 1953, is an article with a photo about Justo T. Morales from a series *"Maestros de la Guitarra"* written by Luis Sadi Grosso. "Justo T. Morales' students are mentioned as: Severo Rodríguez, Bianqui Piñero, Elba Rosado de Biancardi and Maria Angélica Funes. Maria's 78 RPM recording of *"Serenata Burlesca"* by Moreno-Torroba and two Chopin pieces: *"Preludio No. 7"* and *"Mazurka"* are mentioned as being recent. Justo had broken his right arm in April-May of 1948. He passed away on January 4, 1953 at 76 years of age."

Archive: Eduardo Bensadon.

Justo Tomás Morales

Q. E. ✝ P. D.

FALLECIO EL 4 DE ENERO DE 1953

Su esposa e hijos invitan al funeral que por el eterno descanso de su alma se oficiará el 4 de Enero de 1954, en la Iglesia San Juan Bautista María de Vianney, Av. San Martín 4460, a las 10 horas.-

Yo muero, pero mi cariño no muere; os seguiré amando desde el Cielo, como os he amado en la tierra.

San Bernardc

ORACION

La Fe mantiene unidos a los que separa la muerte, Misericordioso Señor dadle el reposo eterno a tu siervo JUSTO TOMAS que redimiste con tu preciosa sangre.

¡Oh Señor, bendigamos tu santa Voluntad.!

Acerca más a ti tu siervo y cuando nuestras almas oprimidas por el dolor, busquen consuelo en el Corazón de tu divino Jesús, ten piedad y misericordia de su alma.

Así sea.

Padre Nuestro, Ave María y Réquiem.

JACULATORIAS

¡Oh Virgen Santísima Auxiliadora rogad por él.!

Sagrado Corazón de Jesús, ten piedad de su alma.

Jesús, José y María.

This is the invitation to the funeral of maestro Justo T. Morales. Archive: Eduardo Bensadon. Translation:

"Justo T. Morales

He died on the 4th January of 1953.

His wife and sons invite you to the funeral that by the eternal rest of his soul will be officiated the 4th of January of 1954 (sic-1953) in the Iglesia San Juan Bautista Maria de Vianney, Av. San Martin 4460, 10AM.—

'I die, but my affection doesn't die, we continue loving from Heaven, as I have loved on the land.'

Saint Bernardine

Oration:

'The Faith keeps united those who are separated by death. Merciful Father give him the eternal repose to your servant Justo Tomas who redeems to you his precious blood.

Oh, Father, please bless us with your saintly will!

Coming closer to you your servant and when our souls oppressed by the pain, search for consolation in the Heart of your divine Jesus, have pity and mercy of your soul.

In this way so be it.

Our Father, Ave Maria and Réquiem'

Aspirations
Oh Most Holy Virgin pray for the helper!
Sacred Heart of Jesus, have pity on his soul.
Jesus, Joséph and Maria."

(Left) Justo T. Morales 3rd publication with Francisco Nuñez c. 1917, dedicated to Julio S. Sagreras.
(Right) Morales piece named for aficionado Juan Carlos Anido, and published by Alfredo Perrotti.

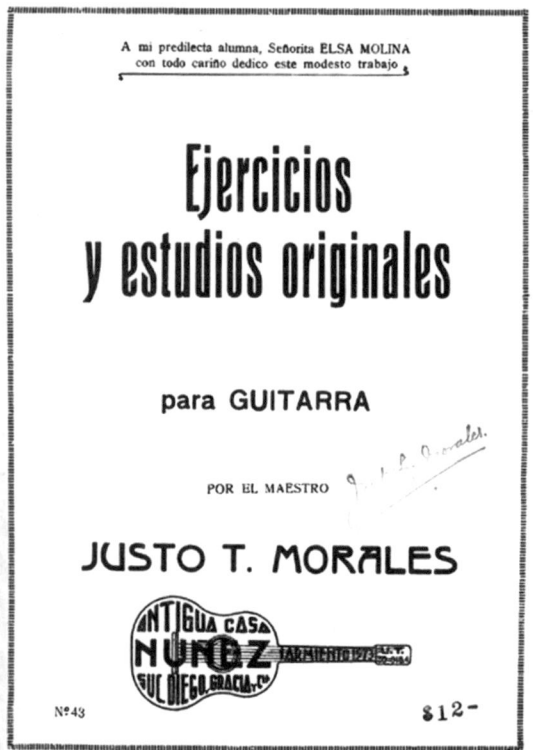

(Left) Morales piece published by Diego, Gracia and Co.
(Right) Justo T. Morales set of exercises and studies published by Antigua Casa Nuñez in the late 1930s.

Anibal Ladru in the home of Juan Carlos Anido c. 1925 (from a larger photo)

"Anibal Ladru was born on January 10, 1882 in Tucuman. By his own inclination he decided to study the guitar, succeeding to be a good self-taught instrumentalist. It was unforeseen circumstances that induced him to become a professor, in a short time by the 1920's it was opening a brilliant path. He was named professor in the "Conservatorio Fracassi", he arranged a program of six *"Cursos"* (courses), and is presented with his title of this institution, with the following words: "Anibal Ladru- He is considered one of the most notable concert guitarists and professor of guitar in the capital. Since he was a youngster he demonstrated his great aptitude for the instrument that Tárrega ennobled, and to whose school he belongs, adopting his methods. The dailies *"La Prensa"* and *"La Nacion"* with the motive of his performances, they filled their pages with complementary articles about his school of guitar, telling of his numerous amounts of distinguished students. As a result of his success as a concert guitarist and teacher, maestro Fracassi named him professor of guitar, not only in the main conservatory but also in their annexes where the number of his students constantly grew, having presented the select and solid ensembles of students in different performances." As a composer his known works are *"Escuela de Mecanismo Tecnico para Guitarra",* that consists of 28 pages of nutritious material for the teacher, as it indicates in its title, being published in 1927. The goodness of this work is praise to the author's guitaristic knowledge. He has also a work of Inca character, entitled *"La Quena, Imitiva"*, quite a successful different composition." *And so ends the entry in the Diccionario de Guitarristas by Domingo Prat.*

In the unnumbered green colored cover *Diccionario de Guitarristas* by Domingo Prat, in the archives of FFSI, a hand-written note states that Anibal Ladru died in Buenos Aires on October 30, 1938. Source: Index of the *Diccionario de Guitarristas* by Domingo Prat by Jan J. de Kloe, Editions Orphée.

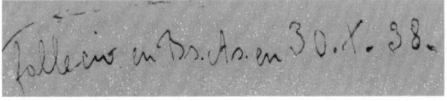

In the *Revista Musical Ilustrada "Tárrega"* issue No. 18 of December 1925 in the Conciertos section there is a concert program from Friday December 18, 1925. The students of Anibal Ladru performed at the hall of the Liga Argentina de Damas Catolicas.

"First part:
Works by Tárrega, Schumann and Llobet-Raul Warschavsky

Minueto de Beethoven- Luisa Virgille and Maria Modesta Diaz Vega

Second part:
pieces by harps, violins and pianos

Third part:
Himno al Sol-Benavente
La Vidala Catamarqueña-Forte
La Flor de Tusca-Luna

Large group of students

La Natita-Alais
Pericon-Sinopoli

Anibal Ladru and students:

Clara Modesta de la Vega
Elsa Arroyo Randle
Maria Modesta Diaz Vega
Luisa Virgille,
Ivonne Lartigue
Elena Lartigue
Blanca Vega
Juanita Flora Ramírez
Angelica Nieves Rodríguez
Margarita Cazenave
Elena Gomez Cornet
Mrs. Laura Ousset de Nardelli
Mr. Raul Warschavsky
Mr. Manuel Levingston.

The applause was such that
unnamed encores were performed."

This photo is from the *Caras y Caretas* magazine of December 27, 1930 issue No. 1682 *Año* "The students of the Professor Anibal Ladru who offered a concert in the Wagneriana."

Recital de guitarra

Los alumnos del profesor Aníbal Ladrú que ofrecieron un concierto en el local de la Wagneriana.

From the October 1958 Ricordi Americana catalog *"Ediciones para Guitarra y otros instrumentos de Rasgueo"*, is the listing of the Ricordi Americana publication of Anibal Ladru's *"Escuela del mecanismo tecnico"*. It was initially published in the 1920's most likely by Romero & Fernández and contains chromatic exercises by Domingo Prat and Miguel Llobet later included in Emilio Pujol's vol. III of his *"Escuela Razonada de la Guitarra"* published in 1953. The *"Escuela del mecanismo tecnico"* is listed in the 1931 Antigua Casa Nuñez catalog.

(Left) *"La Quena"* by Anibal Ladru and published by Romero & Fernández in the late 1920s, the cover of which was drawn by Dr. Samuel Mallo Lopez. This publication was the only piece by Anibal Ladru listed in the 1931 Antigua Casa Nuñez catalog.

(Right) Anibal Ladru transcription of a Paul Lincke piece, published in the 1930s.

(Below) This listing is from the 1949 RCA Argentina Catalogo No. 49 as of August 31, 1949.

CONJUNTO DE VEINTE GUITARRAS (Guitarras)

Pericón Nacional 37539   Rosas Porteñas - Zamba 37539

In 1933 Anibal Ladru, with his ensemble of 20 guitars, made these recordings for Victor in Buenos Aires. *"Pericon Nacional",* from the 19th century, remained a favorite for many generations. Gaspar Sagreras (1838-1901) published *"Pericon Nacional"* as his 8th piece of the 47 he produced. These recordings were listed in The Guitar Review issue No. 1 of October-November 1946. The original label was a "Scroll" Victor label in 1933.

1.º DE JULIO DE 1937   AÑO- 52

Montevideo Musical

ORGANO FUNDADOR DEL "INSTITUTO VERDI"

EL MAESTRO GERARDO GRASSO

"FALLECIO EN ESTA CAPITAL

Después de 2 años de penosa dolencia falleció el 18 del mes pasado el virtuoso y querido Mo. Gerardo Grasso, que fué profesor del Instituto Verdi y examinador de sus clases durante más de 40 años.

Como complemento de éstas líneas publicamos en el presente número el artículo que en "La Mañana" publicó nuestro colaborador **Alexio** y que dice así:

En la tarde de ayer, dejó de existir en nuestra metrópoli, tras las alternativas de una prolongada dolencia, el veterano maestro don Gerardo Grasso, figura destacada de nuestro ambiente musical al que prestara durante 60 años el caudal valioso de sus singulares aptitudes artísticas y de su vivo amor por el sublime arte.

El Mo. D. Gerardo Grasso, a la edad de 23 años, época en que ingresó como profesor de la desaparecida Escuela Nacional de Artes y Oficios.

The composer of the *"Pericon Nacional"*, Gerardo Grasso, from the July 1, 1937 issue *Año* LII of the *"Montevideo Musical"* magazine.

Hijo de Estanislao Grasso, que fué músico experto y director de bandas en pasadas épocas. Gerardo Grasso se incorporó, adolescente, apenas, a la famosa orquesta del teatro Solís, en 1877, destacándose como flautista de grandes condiciones.

Sus progresos hicieron de él un concertista en este instrumento, formando además un buen núcleo de discípulos que son ejecutantes de relieve en nuestro medio.

Si como ejecutante y como maestro, Grasso fué un factor valioso en nuestro desenvolvimiento musical, su labor de compositor no ha sido menos pródiga.

Precisamente, dentro de dos meses se preparaba la conmemoración del cincuentenario del Pericón Nacional, la danza genuinamente criolla que Grasso recogió en la tradición de nuestra vida campera para trasladarla al pentagrama en la época que dirigía la banda de la Escuela de Artes y Oficios.

Suya es también la instrumentación oficial del Himno Nacional, para banda y para orquesta lo mismo que la marcial marcha "Artigas", adoptada por el Ministerio de Defensa Nacional para las bandas del ejército.

Con delicadeza e inspiración suma, Grasso dió igualmente a las masas infantiles que llenan las escuelas primarias bellos cantos, que despiertan en ellas el gusto y la admiración por la más pura y sublime de las artes.

Obra vastísima la suya, apreciada por todos en sus valores positivos, le fué dado al maestro Grasso, en las horas de su ancianidad, recoger el justo reconocimiento a sus singulares méritos de artista y a sus no menores valores de caballero y de hombre virtuoso, siendo objeto repetidamente de homenajes artísticos que halagaron en forma merecida los últimos años de su fecunda existencia.

No sólo los músicos del Uruguay, sino el pueblo todo, tendrá hoy su tributo adolorido y afectivo para la memoria esclarecida del veterano maestro que nos abandona definitivamente."

Translation of the *"Montevideo Musical"* magazine July 1, 1937 issue *Año* LII.

"The Maestro Gerardo Grasso

After two years of a weighty suffering the virtuoso and beloved Maestro Gerardo Grasso passed away on the 18th of the previous month, he was a professor and examiner of his classes at the Instituto Verdi for more than 40 years.

As a complement of these lines we publish in the present issue the article that in the daily *"La Mañana"* our collaborator Alexio who says: 'He passed away in this capital". Yesterday in the afternoon, he ceased to exist in our metropolis, after the alternatives of the prolonged illness, the veteran maestro *Don* Gerardo Grasso, a distinguished figure of our musical ambiance to which he lent his valuable abundance of his outstanding artistic aptitudes and of his living love of the sublime art.

He is the son of Estanislao Grasso, who was a music expert and director of bands in past epochs. Gerardo Grasso joined, scarcely an adolescent, in the famous orchestra of the Teatro Solis, in 1877, to be distinguished as a flutist of great ability.

His progress made him a concert artist of the instrument, besides forming a good nucleus of disciples that are important performers in our environment.

As a performer and as a maestro, Grasso was a valuable factor in our musical development, his labor as a composer hasn't been any less prodigious.

Exactly, within two months of preparing the commemoration of the fiftieth anniversary of the "Pericon Nacional", the genuinely criolla dance that Grasso picked up in the tradition of our rural life for transformation to the sheet music in the epoch in which he directed the band of the Escuela de Artes y Oficios.

Also the instrumentation of the *"Himno Nacional"* was his, for band and the same for the orchestra with the military march *"Artigas"*, adopted by the Ministerio de Defensa Nacional for the Army bands.

With the delicateness and all the inspiration Grasso equally gave beautiful songs to the childhood masses that filled the elementary schools, that awakened in them the fondness and admiration for the purest and most sublime of the arts.

The vastness of his works, was appreciated by everyone for his postive values, and given to him maestro Grasso, in honor of his old age, to pick up the just recognition of his outstanding merits and as an artist and no less as a gentleman and virtuous human being, repeatedly being the object of artistic homages that flattered him in a deserved manner in the last years of his fertile existence.

Not only the musicians of Uruguay, but of the whole populace, will have today his sore and affective tribute for the illuminated memory of the veteran maestro who has left us forever."

Maestro Gerardo Grasso was born in Caposele, Italy in 1860 and came to Uruguay with his parents at a young age.

On the left is a 9th edition cover from the Biblioteca Nacional de Montevideo archives, it was sold in the Julio Mousques music store, on the right is *"el Pericon Nacional"*, by Gerardo Grasso, published by Breyer Hermanos in Buenos Aires c. 1900.

Gerardo Grasso, maestro of the Flute and Piano, is composer of the *"Pericon Nacional"*. In the May 8, 1888 issue No. 18 *Año* III of the *"Montevideo Musical"* it was reported to be selling more and more day by day and was about to have a second edition published due to popular demand. This song is still popular and danced to over a century later. Between 1906 and 1933, there were at least 20 of his compositions recorded, including the *"Pericon Nacional"* by Anibal Ladru and his ensemble of 20 guitars for Victor records.

Severo Rodríguez Falcon concert in Montevideo for the Centro Guitarristico del Uruguay "Conrado P. Koch" Saturday December 23, 1944.

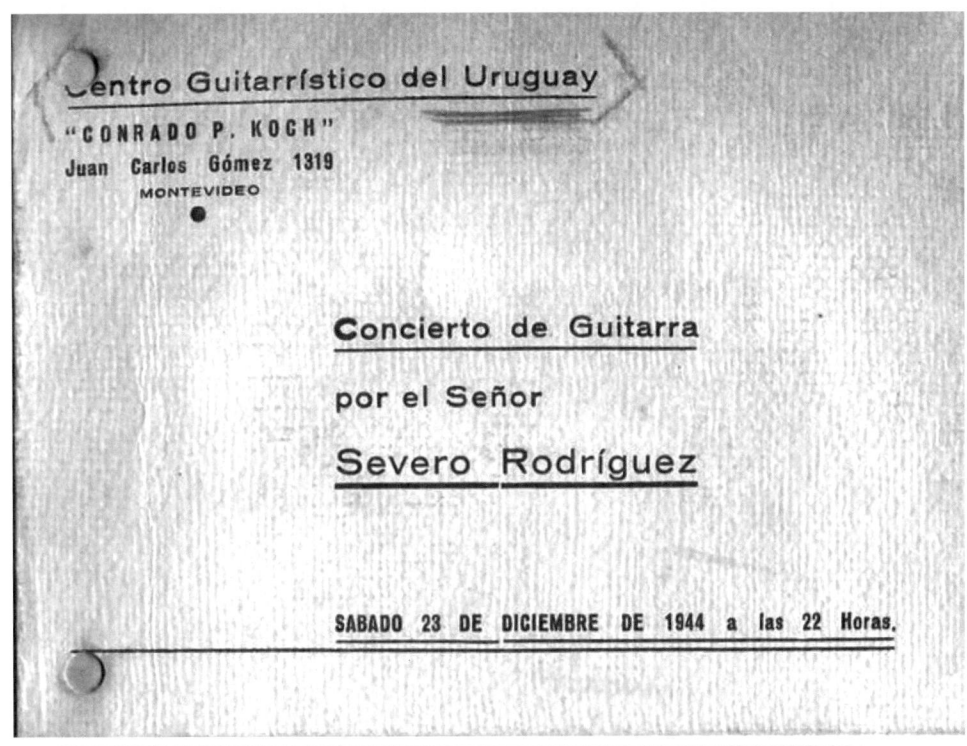

"The Director's Commission of the Centro Guitarristico del Uruguay "Conrado P. Koch" has the pleasure to invite you and your family for the guitar concert that Severo Rodríguez, the distinguished Argentine artist will offer for this Institution on this instrument.

The Centro Guitarristico del Uruguay "Conrado P. Koch" is making an unequaled effort in its fertile life and has assumed the responsibility to toast this performance for the delight of its associates for the best bond and exchange of the guitarists of both sister nations."

Archive: Ricardo Muñoz

```
============ PROGRAMA ============
                    I  Parte

Andantino .................................... SOR
Allegro ...................................... COSTE
Sonatina ..................................... TÁRREGA
Minuet ....................................... MASCARÓ
Tárrega (Impromptu) .......................... R. MUÑOZ

                   II  Parte

Vidalita ..................................... J. T. MORALES
Gato ......................................... A. V. LUNA
Zamba ........................................ ABALOS
Estilo ....................................... M. R. ARENA
Tonada chilena ............................... P. SILVA

                  III  Parte

Minuetto en Si menor ......................... MOZART
Courante ..................................... BACH
Berceuse ..................................... SCHUMANN
Vals Op. 69 N o 2 ............................ CHOPIN
Allegretto ................................... M. TORROBA
```

Severo Rodríguez concert program where he plays music by the European maestros, Uruguayan Classical and Argentine folk music.

On the next page:

A year later in Buenos Aires for the Amigos de la Guitarra, sponsored by the Asociacion Argentina de Musica de Camara, Severo Rodríguez Falcon performs on Thursday July 12, 1945 in the Salon Teatro "Lassalle". Severo Rodríguez performs the music of contemporary Argentine composers in the first set as well as European Baroque and Classical pieces in the second set.

Professor Adolfo E. Paolinelli opens with a lecture on "The Guitar and the Great Maestros of Music".

Archive: Ricardo Muñoz

AMIGOS de la GUITARRA

SECRETARIA: CASTRO 675

...

6º. CONCIERTO
Literario - Musical
3er. CICLO
AUSPICIADO POR LA
Asociación Argentina de Música de Cámara

"LA GUITARRA y
los GRANDES MAESTROS de la MUSICA"
conferencia por el prof. ADOLFO E. PAOLINELLI

CONCERTISTA :
Severo Rodriguez

JUEVES 12 de JULIO a las 21.15 hs.
Salón Teatro "LASSALLE"
CANGALLO 2263

ENTRADA GENERAL $ 1.—

Los socios de la As. Argentina de Música de Cámara, tienen derecho a
2 entradas, presentando el carnet social.

PROGRAMA

Iª PARTE

"LA GUITARRA y los GRANDES MAESTROS de la MUSICA"

conferencia por el prof. Adolfo E. Paolinelli

IIª PARTE

TRISTE	Morales
ZAMBA	Gómez Carrillo
EL SOMBRERITO	A. Schiuma
EL PALITO	Boero
*PAMPA Y ANDES	Luna
EL ESCONDIDO	Prat

IIIª PARTE

COURANTE	Bach
MINUET (del cuarteto en Sol)	Haydn
BERCEUCE	Schuman
ESTUDIO No. 2	Alard-Tárrega
SEVILLA	Albéniz

* Primera audición

"Severo Rodríguez Falcon, was born on September 29, 1918 in the Federal capital of Buenos Aires. He began his guitar studies with Professor Carmelo Rizzuti, receiving his diploma on July 4, 1931. As a player, he has performed in student concerts in the Prince George's Hall and in the Salon "Augusteo", to be heard in cultural acts organized by "Casa del Pueblo". Since 1932 Severo has been in superior classes and perfection studies in the Academia de Guitarra "Prat"."

So ends the short entry from the *Diccionario de Guitarristas* by Domingo Prat.

Severo Rodríguez Falcon

This photo is from a publication of the Asociacion Guitarristica Entrerriana, the magazine *"La Guitarra"* *Año 1, No. 1,* of October 1946, it has listing of a concert program by Severo Rodríguez that took place in the Biblioteca Popular in Parana (Entre Rios Province) on December 18, 1945.

The program he played was:

"Bach – Tárrega: Bourré
Beethoven – Morales: Minuetto
Schumann- – Tárrega: Berceuse
Chopin – Luna: Vals-Op. 69 No. 2
Mendelssohn – Tárrega: Canzonetta
J. T. Morales: a) Vidalita, b) Danza Argentina
Gomez Carrillo: a) Zamba, b) Gato
D. Prat: El escondido
Tárrega: Danza Mora
Alard – Tárrega: Estudio No. 2
Albeniz – Segovia: Leyenda
J. Turina: Fandanguillo

On December 19, 1945 Severo performed on L. T. 14 Radio General Urquiza: Bach: Courante, Haydn: Minuetto, Malats – Tárrega: Serenata Española, Abalos Hnos.: Zamba, J. T. Morales: Vidalita and Ross: Zapateado."

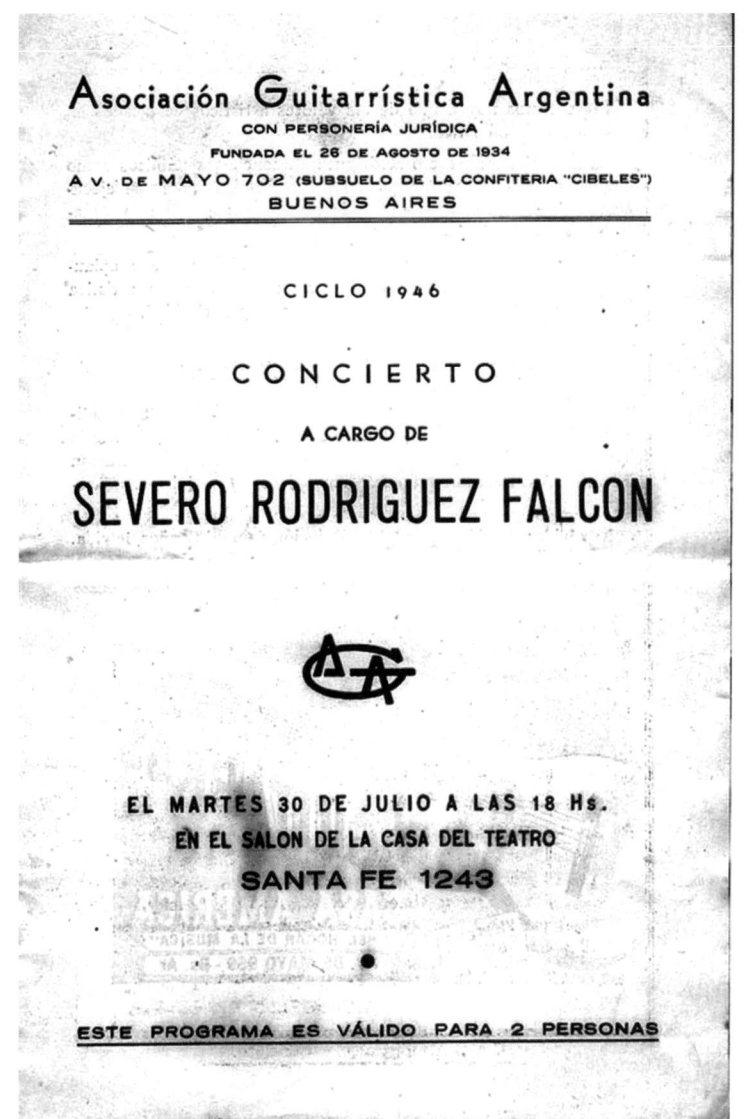

Severo Rodríguez Falcon concert on Tuesday July 30, 1946 at the Salon de la Casa del Teatro, for the Asociacion Guitarristica Argentina.

This biography of Severo Rodríguez Falcon is from Ricardo Muñoz's unpublished book *"Historia Universal de la Guitarra"* Volume VIII *"La Escuela Tárrega en La Argentina"*.

"Severo Rodríguez Falcon

His Origin:

He was born in Buenos Aires the 23rd of December of 1918. (The photo on the previous page was placed in Muñoz"s biography.)

His Education:

He studied music with maestro Luis R. Sanmartino, beginning the guitar with Professor Carmelo Rizzuti, who gave him his diploma on July 4, 1931; later he perfected his knowledge with maestros Justo T. Morales and Adolfo V. Luna.

His Virtuosity:

His first performances began in the capacity as a student in the Principe Jorge and Augusteo halls; to be listened to with interest and goodwill; once he earned his diploma he began his performances in the Asociacion Guitarristica Argentina, the 5th of June of 1938, playing works by Haydn, Bach, Sor, Tárrega and Morales, with positive success.

The 17th of November of the same year, performing with a *"Sinfonia"* guitar from the Antigua Casa Nuñez, in their hall he played works by Morales, to whom he dedicated the program.

The 6th of December of 1939 we find him again in the Salon "La Argentina" interpreting Sor, Coste, Tárrega, Bach, Haydn, Mozart, Beethoven, Schumann, Mendelssohn, Albeniz, Moreno Torroba and Turina, applauded very much by the audience. The following year he appeared for the Asociacion Guitarristica Argentina with the date of the 28th April, playing essentially guitarristic works, which he performed with magnificence, the same in 1941, when he offered again another performance in the Salon "La Argentina".

The 10th of April of 1943 we find him in the Biblioteca Popular of Parana, Entre Rios, sponsored by the Academia Tárrega, interpreting with the maestro Marcelo A. Gonzalez, *"Sonata"* by Scarlatti, *"Minuetto"* by Mozart, *"Serenata"* by Schubert, *"Romanza"* by Mendelssohn, *"Danza Morisca"* by Chapi, *"Vidalita"* by Morales, *"Zamba y gato"* by Luna, *"Murmullos" by Paolinelli;* and *"Recuerdos de la Alhambra"* by Tárrega, both realizing applause and congratulations. The 29th of May and the 24th of June he returned to be presented by the Consejo de Mujeres and in the Salon "La Argentina", respectively, with lots of skill and success.

His concerts proceeded in the *"Agrupacion de Art y Letras"* in the years 1944 and 1945; the 28th of December he again visited the Biblioteca Popular of Parana; the 30th of July of the following year he was presented on the stage of the Asociacion Guitarristica Argentina, performing in the Casa del Teatro to lots of applause; the daily *"La Prensa"* said: "A program of classic, romantic and Argentine and Spanish folkloric works, proving the dominion that he has on the instrument. As an interpreter he always maintains within the limits of good musical taste."

In 1947 we hear him again in the city of Parana, then in Montevideo, and later in the Centro de Arte y Costumbres traditionales "La Brasa" and so he proceeds with his career satisfactorily and with general approval."

404

I PARTE

Bourrée ....⎫
                               ⎬ JUAN SEBASTIAN BACH
Courante ....⎭

Danza (Siglo XVIII .... VIVALDI

Minuet (en sí menor) .... MOZART

Estudio Op. 34 Nº 22 .... COSTE

II PARTE

Vidalita .... JUSTO T. MORALES

Tonada chilena .... P. SILVA

Gato (Danza) .... GOMEZ CARRILLO

Andante (Sonatina indo-criolla)⎫
                               ⎬ A. V. LUNA
Pampa y Andes (Danza) .....⎭

III PARTE

Berceuse .... SCHUMANN

Vals Op. 69 Nº 2 .... CHOPIN

Boceto Andaluz .... SAINZ DE LA MAZA

Allegretto (de sonatina española) MORENO TORROBA

Fandanguillo .... TURINA

Severo Rodríguez Falcon concert titles performed on Tuesday July 30, 1946.

In a publication of the Asociacion Guitarristica Entrerriana, the magazine *"La Guitarra"* issue *Año* 1, No. 2, of April 1947, it has a review of a radio program by Severo Rodríguez that took place on December 16, 1946. Translation:

"Once again, the famed concert guitarist Severo Rodríguez has visited our city, offering two recitals: one on radio, by L. T. 14 Radio General Urquiza, and the other in the performance hall of the Club Progreso, the first with the patronage of the "Asociacion Guitarristica Entrerriana".

The program developed before the microphones of the radio station, and was the following: Beethoven-Morales: *"Minueto"*, Bach-Tárrega: *"Bourré"*, F. Tárrega: *"Tremolo" (Recuerdos de la Alhambra)*, J. T. Morales: *"Vidalita"*, D. Prat: *"Huella"* and J. Ross: *"Zapateado"*.

Severo Rodríguez, one of the top Argentine guitarists, possesses a very careful effective technique that permits him to approach all classes of difficulties with complete success and security. However, his best quality resides in what we call "interpretation". In effect, it is distinguished in our concert guitarist by great rhythmic plasticity, great agility in the forte-piano dynamics-a thing rarely heard in his colleagues; dynamism in the character of the distinct styles and distinct epochs. He is fresh and amiable with his accent of ceremonious antiquity of his interpretation of the *"Bourré"* by Bach. The famous *"Tremolo"* of Tárrega, is always listened to with renewed pleasure, it was played with a purity of uncommon style and with a natural Spanish feel that you can't forget in that composition. The rest of the works verify the qualities that we already know of Severo Rodríguez but, in *"Zapateado"*, by Ross, in the "Rapsodia Andaluza" what rhythmic precision, what colors, what variety of tones, what and how much it is truly typical! *"Zapateado"* by Ross: as a true zapateado is finally heard, as a real Andalucian dance and not as a *"Tarantella"* or as a *"Polonesa"*."

Severo Rodríguez Falcon concert dedicated to his maestro Justo T. Morales held at the Salon "La Argentina" on Saturday April 19, 1947. This concert was sponsored by the "Asociacion Argentina de Musica de Camara" (Argentine Chamber Music Association).

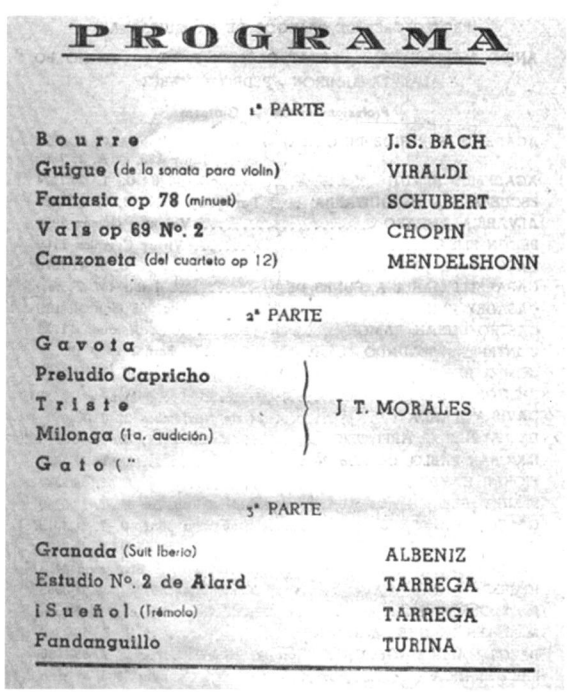

The *"Milonga"* written by Justo T. Morales has its debut in this concert.

Domingo Prat's *"Diccionario de Guitarristas"* (Buenos Aires 1934) in my judgment, in its moment was one of the most important works of the world in its specialty, by the variety of themes it embraces and the form to focus on them.

It contains biographies of guitarists, lutenists, guitar makers of the whole world, a descriptive index of dances, traditional rhythms of Spain and all of the Americas, also it contains a detailing of all the string instruments of the world, or at least almost all that are known. This work is out of print in Argentina, lamentably for many decades, but fortunately reedited in the U.S.A. by Matanya Ophee.

(Left) Contemporary edition of Prat's *Diccionario de Guitarristas* published by Matanya Ophee in 1988.
(Right) Domingo Prat from the cover of the magazine *Mundo Musical* issue No. 76 of January 1945. He had passed away on November 22, 1944.

The valuable and noble work of Prat, it's a shame to say, it isn't known to its true dimension. In spite of today's infinity of students of guitar that revert to their methods when they initiate the study of the instrument. His entrance can be seen today as something overpowered in time. But it is ignored that when he arrived in Argentina at the beginning of the 20th century, that little material existed in the systemized instruction of the guitar.

To finish the sketch of the great Catalan maestro we transcribe a few necessary comments by Carlos Vega, written in the magazine *"Folklore"* of Buenos Aires (1962-63) in what was a series of articles called *"Los Instrumentos Musicales"* (The Musical Instruments). "He was a happy and optimistic man, agreeable and cordial, generous in the extreme, making possible the justice to include the enemies of his own glory. His nerves had become exhausted teaching, studying, and with the medical prescription that confined him to a small house in Haedo. There he was taken by death in 1944".

Referring always to the first few decades of the 20th century, we are going to show other significant works in reference to "the History of the Classical Guitar in Argentina", apart from the arrival of Prat in those epochs, we add the arrival for the first time in Buenos Aires of Miguel Llobet, where he succeeded in one of the most important objectives of his career, as an interpreter outside of Spain. The same Prat makes it known as so: "In 1910 seeing myself in Buenos Aires, with my friend the aficionado Ricardo Diaz Romero trying to encourage him to bring Miguel Llobet, that brought about, his arrival. To answer me, Llobet told me among other things: "Never have I been received, nor believed to experience more happiness than that you have commensurated." Llobet was referring to his arrival in America on the condition where the concert artist would not perform as in Paris, conjointly with other artists, but individually as deemed fit as the artist merits." (D. Prat op. cit) The first performance of Llobet as a soloist, outside of Spain, would be taking place in Argentina, and later in the same manner he would perform in Germany.

(Above) Piece by Ricardo Diaz Romero, who contracted Miguel Llobet to come to Argentina. This piece is dedicated to Miguel Llobet. Translation of the text:

"To my distinguished friend the eminent guitarist Miguel Llobet."

Photo of Miguel Llobet dedicated to Ricardo Muñoz. Miguel and Ricardo were friends from 1918 onward. (This is from the autobiographical material of the Ricardo Muñoz archive.)

408

MIGUEL LLOVET, CÉLEBRE GUITARRISTA

This early photo of Miguel Llobet is from the *Caras y Caretas* magazine published in Buenos Aires on January 9, 1904, issue No. 275, *Año* VII. The translation of the text is:

"A great success has been obtained in the capital of Spain by Miguel Llobet, whose twenty three years of age have succeeded to eclipse the fame of the majority of the concert guitarists, those that are of an abundance in the motherland. Llobet began his studies in the Escuela Municipal de Musica (Municipal School of Music) of Barcelona, and at twelve years old he received lessons from Professor Magin Alegre. He soon began to excel and astonished his audience in Paris, and now in his own Madrid.

In the concerts that he has given in many different theaters in the capital, the public has applauded him with enthusiasm, obligating him to repeat many of the pieces that constitute his extensive repertoire."

This photo and short review are at the beginning of the international fame of Miguel Llobet, who didn't perform in Buenos Aires until six and a half years later in August of 1910.

TEATROS

El célebre concertista de guitarra Miguel Llobet, actualmente en Buenos Aires

La sala de «La Argentina», la noche del segundo concierto de Llobet

The photo of Miguel Llobet playing live in the Salon "La Argentina" and that of his audience are from the magazine *Caras y Caretas* of August 13, 1910, issue No. 619 *Año* 13. This was his second concert of his first tour. This is from page 3, seen by just opening the cover. The translations of the accompanying text and photo captions are on the next page.

Translation of the photo captions on the previous page:

"The celebrated concert guitarist Miguel Llobet, presently in Buenos Aires."
"The salon "La Argentina", the evening of second concert of Llobet."

Translation of the text: "Llobet Concerts".

Conciertos Llobet.—Bien conocido es en el mundo artístico el nombre de Miguel Llobet, considerado actualmente como uno de los más eximios ejecutantes de guitarra, así es que no es de extrañar que sus conciertos en Buenos Aires hayan despertado grandísimo interés. Numeroso público ha asistido en el salón de la sociedad "La Argentina", á los dos conciertos efectuados, manifestándose el fallo del auditório en forma bien entusiasta á favor del artista.

"The name of Miguel Llobet is well known in the artistic world, considered as one of the most excellent guitar players, so it isn't strange that his concerts in Buenos Aires have awakened the greatest interest. A numerous public attended the hall of the society "La Argentina", to the two concerts that have taken place, to be demonstrating in favor of the artist the judgement of the audience in an enthusiastic form."

Two years later enroute to this private recital in Boston, Miguel had written a postcard to Domingo Prat, in Buenos Aires, after his concerts were performed in Chile.

Here is the text in the native tongue followed by a translation.

Santiago 23 de agosto 1912

"Hoy mismo te mandé unos diarios de Valparaiso. Todos los demas diarios en los sitios en donde he tocado, hablan por el exito.
Grandiosos existen en todas partes. Te escribiré detenidamente en el vapor.
Te mando cariñosos recuerdos tu amigo que te quiere."

Miguel Llobet

"En éste teatro di mis dos primeros conciertos.
El 28 presiento que embarco en Valparaíso directamente para los Estados Unidos"

Santiago August 23, 1912

"Today I have sent you some newspapers from Valparaiso. All of the dailies in the sites where I have played, speak of my success.
Everywhere things are great. I'll write you a more detailed account on the ship.
I send you affectionate memories your friend that cares."

Miguel Llobet

"I gave my first two concerts in this theater.
The 28th is when I feel I'll leave on the ship from Valparaiso directly for the United States."

410

This advertisement, of pieces by Francisco Tárrega, is from "The Cadenza" magazine of October 1912 XIX No. 4.

Concert given by Mrs. R. T. Lane and Miss Ethel Lucretia Olcott, assisted by Kruse's Orchestra at Akron, Ohio, May 28, 1913.

1. Overture—The Merry Wives of Windsor ....*Otto Nicolai*
   Kruse's Orchestra.
2. Guitar—
   (a) Caprice, Op. 20, No. 9 ....*Luigi Legnani*
   (b) Capricho Arabe (Serenata)....................*F. Tarrega*
   Miss Olcott.
3. Il bacio (Kiss Waltz)................................*Arditi*
   Mrs. Lane.
4. Kamenoi Ostrow (Cloister Scene), Op. 10, No. 22..*A. Rubenstein*
   Kruse's Orchestra.
5. Concert Waltz, "El Jasmin"....................*Manuel Y. Ferrer*
   Miss Olcott.
6. (a) The Lass With the Delicate Air................*Arne*
   (b) Marchioness, Your Dancing....................*Lemaire*
   Mrs. Lane.
7. Selection from the Opera "Faust"................*Gounod*
   Kruse's Orchestra.

This is from the Crescendo magazine of November 1913, Vol. 6 No. 5, from the "Programs of Concerts and Recitals" page. Miss Ethel Lucretia Olcott later became known as Vahdah Olcott-Bickford. Here we see she performs Tárrega's *"Capricho Arabe"* on May 28, 1913 in Akron, Ohio. It's possible she obtained the sheet music to this piece from the business of J. Rowies in Philadelphia. J. Rowies' main office was located in Paris.

MIGUEL LLOBET

BETWEEN "incident" and "event" there really is a broad differentiation. The first may effectively color the trend of life, thought or action, but the second effectually changes it. To hear a virtuoso exploit an instrument is an intellectual incident, while to listen to a king of virtuosi disclosing the hidden secrets of the same instrument becomes a revealing event, and revelation is the unseen boundary line of intellectuality.

Mr. Paul Eno of Philadelphia was in Boston on Monday, October 7th, and it was through his courtesy that three representatives of THE CADENZA, and several other music-lovers, were treated to a rare exposition of guitar virtuosity. Mr. Eno presented Senor Miguel Llobet, a Spanish guitarist on his way from Chili to France, who graciously played three solos for a small audience of invited guests. To treat of Senor Llobet's performance technically would be criticism trite and effete, though perhaps an easy way out. But to tell of his perfect tonal production, wonderful dynamics, confusing rapidity of execution and strange and bizaare effects would be well nigh impossible. Suffice it to say, that to THE CADENZA it was an event, if not an epoch.

This notice of a private performance by Miguel Llobet on October 1, 1912 in Boston, Massachusetts is from "The Cadenza" magazine issue of November 1912 XIX No. 5. He apparently stunned the listeners.

411

Miguel Llobet

Guitarists and lovers of guitar in Philadelphia enjoyed a rare treat on Tuesday afternoon, Oct.29th, when Mr. Paul Eno presented Miguel Llobet, the famous Spanish guitarist, in recital. 'Tis a pity other cities could not have had the pleasure of hearing this distinguished artist before his return to his home in Paris although the Boston fraternity were fortunate enough to hear him render three or four numbers at an impromptu recital. His program in Philadelphia included "Menuet" (Sor), "Etude de Concert" (Coste), "Nocturne", Opus 9, No. 2 (Chopin), Variations "Sur un theme de Ferdinand Sor" (Llobet), "Bouree" (Bach), "Andante, Sonata X" (Beethoven), "Reve" (Tarrega), "Caprice Arabe" (Tarrega), "Fantaisie Espagnole" (Llobet).

Continued on page 24

Guitarists Round Table
:Contnued from page 21)

The following is a clipping from the Philadelphia "Record".

"A breath of old Castile, as delightful as it was unexpected, floated into Philadelphia yesterday afternoon with the guitar playing of Miguel Llobet. This remarkable young musician, with the face of a Velasquez portrait, had been heralded as a master of that much-neglected instrument—the guitar. We are so accustomed, however, to having musicians labeled extravagantly in advance that the hyperbole no longer is effective. In the case of the young Spaniard the unlooked for happened. A real musician, with the finest and most sensitive appreciation of tonal effects and playing an instrument whose possibilities are rarely exhibited, and which is unique in the concert room, appeared and completely captivated the audience invited to hear him in the Orpheus Club rooms. Llobet's art is gentle—almost tender. It seems the expression of a nature endowed with the rare gift of imparting to his music precisely the degree of suggestion necessary to effective rendition. To hear Bach, Beethoven Chopin and a host of more modern composers exquisitely interpreted by a guitarist, who has at once a thorough appreciation of the best elements in music and a facility of delivery, is a delightful experience. Unfortunately for the musical public, Llobet is returning at once to his home in Paris and will make no public appearances in this country."

The images on this page are from a January 1913 Crescendo magazine, Vol. 5, No. 7. They are from the "Guitarists Round Table" column by Ethel Lucretia Olcott-later known as Vahdah Olcott-Bickford. They document the second recital Miguel Llobet gave in the United States, in Philadelphia on Tuesday October 29, 1912. The review is from the newspaper the Philadelphia "Record".

This is from the *"Revista de la Guitarra"* No. 6
Año II of June 1940.

Translation:

"In Honor of Humberto Allende

In the studios of L. R. 10, Radio Cultura of Buenos Aires, the 14th of the current month a kind homage was paid to the Chilean composer *Don* Humberto Allende, for distinguished performance in South America, thanks to which the nation of Chile could hear in the year 1913 the brilliant guitarist Miguel Llobet, who agreed to the requests that he offered to formulate in the land of O'Higgins a series of concerts, whose memory will last forever."

En Honor de Humberto Allende

En los estudios de L. R. 10, Radio Cultura de Buenos Aires, fué tributado el día 14 del mes en curso un simpático homenaje al compositor chileno don Humberto Allende, de destacada actuación en Sud América, gracias al cual el pueblo de Chile pudo escuchar el año 1913 al genial guitarrista Miguel Llobet, que accediendo a solicitudes que le formulara ofreció en la tierra de O'Higgins una serie de conciertos, cuyo recuerdo perdurará por siempre.

Miguel Llobet's first recording experience, ten years before his initially released recordings for Odeon.

(Trial 1915-12-21-04) December 21, 1915 Manuelito Miguel Llobet Guitar solo

(Trial 1915-12-21-05) December 21, 1915 Sueño Miguel Llobet Guitar solo

This information is from: The Encyclopedic Discography of Victor Recordings (EDVR) web site. A team of researchers based at the University of California, Santa Barbara Libraries edits the database.

It is not known as to what the song *"Manuelito"* is. *"Sueño"* is undoubtedly the Francisco Tárrega composition, published among the first dozen pieces of the maestro's works over a decade before this recording. These were recorded in New York according to web site information-but it's in grey text not black indicating their being unsure about this aspect, the actual location may be Camden, New Jersey.

Miguel Llobet, Spanish Guitarist, Who Will Add Novelty to New York's Concert Season

This photo of Miguel Llobet accompanied the article on the next page from the Musical America magazine of January 15, 1916.

"Master Guitarist" to Play for New York

WE must admit that every master of his art is entitled to a respectful hearing. This does not imply, however, that we need necessarily be interested in the master's particular form of art, or that we are eager to be numbered among those who are called upon to appreciate what he has to offer. For example, you make every effort to attend a Kreisler recital, but might you not have to be persuaded to listen to a Spanish guitarist, even though sensational reports of his playing had preceded him? The answer is obvious, but in the case of Miguel Llobet you might have cause for regret if you did not yield to persuasion.

Señor Llobet, who made the trip to America with Granados, the composer of "Goyescas," the Spanish opera which is to be performed shortly at the Metropolitan, told a MUS'CAL AMERICA interviewer of his early life and of his success with the guitar. He did not find it necessary to apologize for his choice of the guitar as his instrument, for in Spain the guitar is recognized and loved by everyone, especially when it is played as M. Llobet plays it.

Began as a Painter

"I began my work in the art world as a painter," he said. "I had an exhibition of my paintings in Spain, but I was not destined to continue in this field, for my childhood longing to play the guitar was stronger in me. My love for the guitar dates from the time that I received a guitar as a gift when I was very young. At this time I heard Tarrega, who was considered the greatest guitarist in the world, and his playing was a revelation to me. I began to study seriously with Tarrega, and to him I owe whatever success I have attained. I played at the court in Spain, in France and South America and I had planned a tour through Germany when the war broke out and spoiled everything. Fate directed my steps to America, where I hope I shall be as fortunate as in Europe."

A quaint story is told of M. Llobet, who is too modest to repeat it himself. It seems that a poor spinster in Spain, a good soul, but not blessed with a superabundance of beauty, was unfortunate enough to hurt her finger, so that she could not continue teaching the guitar. Mr. Llobet kindly substituted for her and took charge of her pupils for six weeks, turning over the money earned to her. During all that time Mr. Llobet did not play a single note when he was requested to do so by the pupils, for he feared that if they heard him play, the chances of their returning to the spinster would be very slim.

It is interesting to note that Señor Llobet has been most successful with people who hate the guitar as an instrument. They have often come to his concerts with a tolerant attitude, and have left, thrilled and converted. He has won the admiration of such musicians of Debussy, Ravel, Vincent D'Indy, Raoul, Pugno, Dukas and Granados, all of whom are his friends, and all of whom have expressed their desire to write for him. It is almost incredible that hundreds of people were turned away from his concerts in Paris, Munich, and the large cities of South America, and that he could command fabulous prices for his playing. The present writer was interested in reading comments of the leading musical critics in Germany, all of whom are unanimous in according him the position that is given to an artist on the "recognized" instruments.

Classic and Modern Works Given

M. Llobet plays Bach, Chopin, Mendelssohn and almost all of the classical compositions arranged for the guitar by Tarrega, his teacher, and he is also perfectly at home among the moderns, Granados, Albeniz, Debussy and others. He employs none of the tricks frequently associated with guitar playing, and is judged solely upon his merits as a serious musician and artistic interpreter. The question arises: if France, Germany and South America have been educated to guitar recitals, why not progressive America? M. Llobet's first recital in New York will throw more light on the matter.   H. B.

This article is from the Musical America magazine of January 15, 1916. The images on this page have been digitally moved from the oversize original edition.

Miguel Llobet Concert Cover 1918

The Best Guitarist in the World
Miguel Llobet

In his Artistic Season in Argentina

"To my distinguished friend and notable aficionado Rosendo Barreiro with all affinity,
Miguel Llobet
Montevideo October 19, 1918"

Critical judgements by the Principle Dailies of Buenos Aires

La Razon June 1, 1918

Next Tuesday, in the Salon "La Argentina", begins the series of announced concerts by the famous guitarist Miguel Llobet. It isn't necessary to go to his presentation; a few years ago, Llobet affirmed in front of our public his high estimation, not only as an eminent instrumentalist, but as a great artist, that which, without any doubt, he is very significant. Llobet the "virtuoso" in the most noble acception, has never pretended to astonish his audience, and if only to acquire esthetic emotions, at once that how much he gives to his instrument that-as a French writer says-he is believed, by error, otherworldly, only destined to translate an amorous serenata under the starlit sky...

A son of Barcelona, and formed under the direction of the celebrated Tárrega, Llobet began his career as a concert guitarist in Spain. But it was in Paris that he was consecrated, about 15 years ago, as one of the eminent musical interpreters of this epoch-in the same league as Casals, of Thibaud, of Kreisler, of Risler. In the greatest European artistic centers, Llobet has revived his success in Paris, and recently in the United States, he made a successful tour.

The repertoire of Llobet comprises, naturally, the classics of the guitar, but he has added to the works those adaptations of the piano literature, that finally proves that the guitar isn't incompatible with the inspirations of the greatest composers.

La Nacion June 5, 1918

After several years of absence, *Don* Miguel Llobet returns to us more famous and as a musical authority, covered by the renown that has given him applause in front of other audiences; but it is as if he arrived unknown without an announcement, incognito and to the occult, the first *rasgueado* of his guitar he had denounced to the point in front of his audience last night.

He has, in effect, in his hand the admirable delicateness of a wing over the strings of the instrument, and the energetic fortitude of a talon and the sure precision of a governed mechanism by his exquisite and sensible soul of artistic emotion. The guitar becomes a harp or a lute in his arms; it sings a nocturne deeply, a passion burned zealously of the last love, almost like a violin matched with a languid melody, or it vibrates with the trembling sonority and fullness of a chord on the piano. The common guitar of our *gaucho* carried on his shoulder, it is also a psaltery or clavichord. None of them who could have heard him in the Salon "La Argentina" would have been confused. His acquired sound an outright quality, of a voluminous and smooth timbre, without colliding on the strings above the frets of the fingerboard, and that, is the ability of the hands, the finesse of the fingering, perfection of technique, one of good taste, to the purity of style, to the profundity of expression, that communicates to the public the just idea of the composer, without the ridiculous preciousness of the guitar player and with the severe elevation of the interpreter.

The concert artist dignifies the guitar. Still it is her, even in his hands, the personal and intimate instrument by excellence; but to his broad musical field, he makes it by the capacity of a superior musical language, that surprises first, then it enchants.

That could have been noticed last night. The audience that filled the hall where Mr. Llobet gave his first concert, applauded for a longtime for every one of the pieces of the program, and thanked him very lively especially when he played the *Nocturne*, by Chopin, a Spanish dance, by Granados, and the pieces by Albeniz and by Arcas-Llobet, prolonging the ovations unto the end where they obligated him to return to the stage several times.

The concert artist, that has come by measures made by the music center "La Guitarra", by invitation of *Don* Juan C. Anido, will give other concerts on Friday and next Tuesday.

La Prensa June 3, 1918

Last night the great maestro Miguel Llobet gave the announced concert in the Salon "La Argentina". An artist of great merits ….

Missing pages 3-6.

res catalanas armonizadas por el propio Llobet, completaban el programa.

Ya daba la guitarra la impresión de una dulce arpa secundada por un piano agilísimo; ya parecía un conjunto de bandurrias; ya el unísono de una orquesta de cuerdas. No puede darse más energía y más delicadeza a la vez.

La cordial y fervorosa acogida que ha obtenido Llobet, le obligará a aumentar el número de sus conciertos.

❖

«La Nación» *Junio 26 de 1918.*

Anoche tuvo en La Argentina un auditorio tan numeroso como entusiasta el notable guitarrista don Miguel Llobet. Hemos dicho antes de ahora todo el mérito de este artista y cómo ennoblece y eleva el humilde instrumento popular con interpretaciones de impecable estilo y de sorprendente ejecución. Y el concierto de anoche fué nueva demostración de esas admirables cualidades, que el público no puede dejar de reconocer, con largas y frenéticas ovaciones.

Mañana dará el señor Llobet su última audición, y el 7 de julio partirá para Chile, donde dará varios conciertos.

❖

«La Razón» *Junio 26 de 1918.*

Con un auditorio nutrido y atento, dió ayer su penúltima audición de guitarra, en el salón La Argentina, el talentoso concertista don Miguel Llobet. Como en anteriores reuniones, el arte del intérprete llegó en forma amplia y persuasiva a la sensibilidad de sus oyentes. Sonoro, armonioso y elocuente, el instrumento tradujo con precisión y en claro lenguaje, las composiciones del programa. El señor Llobet oyó largos y efusivos aplausos.

Para mañana está anunciado el concierto de despedida.

❖

From page 7.

Catalan popular folk songs harmonized by Llobet himself, completed the program.

He had already given the impression that the guitar was a sweet harp backed up by a most agile piano; it had already appeared like a band of bandurrias; already a unison of an orchestra or strings. He couldn't give a more energetic and more delicate sense at once.

The cordial and fervent reception that Llobet obtained, obligated him to add more concerts to the tour.

La Nacion June 26, 1918

Last night in La Argentina a numerous as well as enthusiastic audience had the notable guitarist Miguel Llobet in concert. We have said before now that all the merits of this artist and as ennobles and elevates this humble popular instrument with interpretations in impeccable style and astonishing performance. The concert last night was a new demonstration of these admirable qualities, that the public can't not recognize, and leave without long and frenetic ovations.

Tomorrow Mr. Llobet will give his last perfomance and the 7th of July he leaves for Chile, where he will give several concerts.

La Razon June 26, 1918

With an abundant and attentive audience, the talented concert artist *Don* Miguel Llobet yesterday gave his next to the last concert in the Salon La Argentina. As in his previous displays, the art of the interpreter came in its ample and persuasive form to the sensibilities of the listeners. Sonorous, harmonious and eloquent, the instrument translated with precision and in clear language, the compositions of the program. Mr. Llobet heard long and effusive applause.

Tomorrow there is the announced farewell concert.

La Epoca Junio 26 de 1918.

En el salón La Argentina tuvo lugar anoche el primero de los dos últimos conciertos anunciados por el que puede llamarse con verdad «el brujo de la guitarra»; el virtuoso y el poeta del humilde instrumento intérprete de las penas y las alegrías de nuestros nativos. Un instrumento de seis cuerdas que se transforma casi milagrosamente en arpa, en piano... en orquesta de dulcísimos sonidos, a la vez robustos y suaves. Miguel Llobet sobrepuja con su interpretación y con su ejecución extraordinaria, cuanto elogio puede tributarse a un artista de «élite»; no diremos, por lo tanto que ha confirmado cuanto afirmara de excepcional en él y a un tiempo nuestra opinión entusiasta de un principio; diremos que ha sido «él», como nunca y que si es posible elevarse sobre la propia perfección, en una ascensión casi milagrosa, él ha realizado anoche esa milagrosa ascensión.

Todo el hermoso programa confeccionado para el concierto de ayer, fué ejecutado con esa indeclinable virtuosidad en él característica; fué delicado y clásico en el «Menuet» de Sor; exactísimo en el «Menuet» de Schubert; profundamente poeta en el «Andante» de Mozart; más que admirable en «Granada» de Albéniz; interpretó con sentida finura el Nocturno N.º 2 de Chopin; estuvo óptimo en las «danzas españolas» de Granados; perfecto en las «melodías populares catalanas» y la «alborada» de Tárrega, y estupendo, realmente estupendo en la «gran jota» de Arcas-Llobet, en la que hizo verdaderos prodigios.

El público congregado en el salón La Argentina (y no tan numeroso como debiera haber sido), le tributó enormes ovaciones a cada final de trozo.

Miguel Llobet dará en el mismo salón, mañana jueves 27, a las nueve de la noche, su «último» concierto; para honra nuestra y satisfacción del gran concertista, esperamos que la sala rebasará de público y que la coronación y consagración de su arte extraordinario serán dignos de él.

La Epoca June 26, 1918.

In the Salon "La Argentina" last night the first of the last two announced concerts took place given by he who can be truly called the wizard of the guitar; the virtuoso and poet of the humble instrument interpreting the sadness and the happiness of our people. An instrument of six strings that transforms miraculously into almost a harp, into a piano... into an orchestra of sweet sounds, at once robust and smooth. Miguel Llobet outbids with his interpretation and with his extraordinary performance, how much praise can be taxed to him "elite"; we don't say, as much that has been confirmed how much can be affirmed of the exceptional in him and, to a time our enthusiastic opinion of a principle; we say that he has been "he" as never and that if it is possible to be elevated over his own perfection, in an ascension almost miraculous, he has made the miraculous ascension last night.

All the beautiful ready-made program for yesterday's concert, was performed with that indeclinable virtuosity in the character; was delicate and classic in the *"Minuet"* by Sor; the very exact thing in the *"Minuet"* by Schubert; profoundly poetic in the *"Andante"* by Mozart; more than admirable in the *"Granada"* by Albeniz; interpreted with such sensual refinement of the *"Nocturne No. 2"* by Chopin; he was in the optimum in the *"Danza Española"* by Granados; perfect in the *"Catalonian Folksongs"* and the *"Alborada"* by Tárrega, stupendous , really stupendous in the *"Gran Jota"* of Arcas-Llobet, in which he was truly prodigious.

The public congregated in the Salon "La Argentina" (It had never been this filled to capacity.) an homage of enormous ovations until the final piece.

Miguel Llobet will give in this same hall, tomorrow Thursday the 27th, at 9 in the evening, his "Ultimate" concert; for honoring our and satisfaction of the great concert artist, we hope that the hall will burst at the seams by the public and that the coronation and consecration of his extraordinary art will be worthy of him.

Photocard featuring Miguel Llobet

Photo featuring Miguel Llobet by Fotografía Joan Vilatobà. © Isabel Vilatoba Estate.

Dedicated and inscribed:

"Para el buen y querido amigo Rosendo Barreiro
como recuerdo de mi segunda tournée por Montevideo. M. Llobet. 27/5/1922".

"For my good and beloved friend Rosendo Barreiro, as a souvenir of my second tour of Montevideo.
M. Llobet. May 27, 1922."

"Miguel Llobet was born on October 18, 1878 in Barcelona, Spain. His entrance into art was to do sketches and paintings, being very young, with the notable maestro Torres Casana. By diverse causes, a consequence of his special manner of being, he abandoned painting, for that which he was splendidly endowed, and he began to study the guitar. He did this with the modest guitarist Magin Alegre, to whom he was presented by "Jaumet de las coplas", a humble singer and player of the instrument. A little while after he began studying with maestro Alegre, his teacher perceived the great abilities in his disciple and he presented Miguel to maestro Tárrega. A short time after Llobet received lessons from the great Valencian guitarist, it being due to he himself, his maestro spoke eloquently of the undoubtable talent of the great concert artist. The aversion that Barcelona felt against the guitar, it was extremely felt in those times: therefore, Llobet already being an instrumentalist and with twenty six years of age, limited his performances to particular societies and to auditions in private, without receiving more than words of thanks. This state of things made him determined to move to Paris in 1904, taking up residence there. But, before making that jump, when the guitarist was twenty, he traveled the limits of his province, getting to know a friend of the guitar a year later, the distinguished Concepcion Jacoby, well to do Valencian lady, admirer and protector until this moment, of he who was the maestro to Llobet, *Don* Francisco Tárrega. *Doña* Concepcion upon hearing the young Catalan marveled at his art, taking him to the warm air of the poetic Malaga, and in 1900 to the Exposition of Paris. Life had become a dream for Llobet, and in the times of his awakening, he gave some performances. In the same Malaga he gave a concert in the "Sociedad Filarmonica", because they had named him an honorary maestro, as they had done previously with Juan Parga; to continue they heard him play in the Sala del Conservatorio de Valencia, and in 1902 in Madrid, where he was applauded twice.

Already in Paris (1904), along with greatly valued musicians, such as Ricardo Viñes, Ribo and others, obtaining resounding triumphs, such as his conquest on January 26, 1905 in the Salon "Washington-Palace", an act in which the great pianist Viñes took part, the violinist M. Chédécal, Llobet and the orchestra of the hall, under the direction of L'Enfant, who opened and closed the session. Together, then, with other artists he acted in "La Trompeta", "Schola Cantorum", etc.; but he never made it in the form as an individual in the city of Paris, impairing his true merits, to not be permanently free of the class of performances that they need the gathering of various artists, such as they put in a contest. Llobet didn't appear to feel his own worth in front of a defined environment, superior to that of Barcelona, and to be finding it better that in this city, it didn't induce any other artistic preoccupation. Concerts such as those, took place often in the Villa Lumiére, being reserved for him the part of honor and assurance of the passing triumph. On the other hand, consequently it was comfortable, by the little amount of preparation it demanded in the renovation of the programs, persisting in this form in his performances for private "soirées", where he was especially sought after. In the French capital he soon enjoyed the renown as a maestro. What a shame that the populace doesn't like our instrument! But the great floating colony and in particular the (south) Americans give the distinctive note of homage to the guitar. Many were from families of those American countries that solicited with interest lessons from Llobet: Mrs. Ortiz Basualdo, Dr. Wenceslao Escalante (Argentines), they weren't only his disciples but also his enthusiastic admirers.

In March of 1910 seeing myself in Buenos Aires, with my friend the aficionado Ricardo Diaz Romero trying to encourage him to bring Miguel Llobet, that brought about, his arrival. To answer me, Llobet among other things told me: "Never have I been received, nor believed to experience more happiness than that you have commensurated." Llobet was referring to his arrival in America on the condition where the concert artist would not perform as in Paris, conjointly with other artists, but individually as deemed fit as the artist merits. With immense success he was crowned in this tour, which he extended in 1913, to Chile. A little later he visited North America in a role of a studious tourist.

And in 1918 he returned to Buenos Aires advantageously contracted by the amateur Juan Carlos Anido; in this tour he culminated the greatest success of his career. He returned to Argentina on repeat occasions contracted by Juan Carlos Anido; but the enthusiasm declined every time: it's that Llobet, now only knew how to demonstrate his great virtuosity, accelerating the vertigo of his playing, weakening the classicism and the expression of the musical phrase. In Europe, since that fateful date, August of 1914, that brought the great conflagration, the artist vegetated until 1919, and, to change the waters to his apparent tranquility, only one country, Germany, rendered, if not money, at least glory, to the concert guitarists, that adventured to play for the German public. In this country Llobet is admired and wanted and he counts on dozens of concerts on every tour made, just as Baldomero Zapater and Francisco Calleja, that are contracted for a long series of performances to make in distinct points.

In Germany, happily, he doesn't have to act as in Paris, where every concert is a musical banquet, formed by intense diverse talent: in the country of Wagner the guitarist is accustomed to act as in Buenos Aires, by way of recitals, as a soloist and in exclusive engagements.

We don't know that Llobet might have played a solo concert by himself, exclusively him, in the capital of France. And if we are mistaken, those won't be unique. You can't deny, however though he might not have triumphed in Paris; but the triumph has been that he succeeded in certain circles. Very few great artists have rarely played the guitar in the same epoch, save the century of gold of our instrument.

Llobet had his great moment and it was a real shame, in the plentifulness of his career, that he didn't dominate the vertigo of his playing that impressed, expressing as it was said earlier, the musical phrase, without stopping the attention in the imaginary phantasm of the public, or, if it does, to dominate it in the sensible part, by the sentiment, that soon let the interest go. Llobet had, however, flourishes of a power and a conducive ability such, that they weren't permitted equality. It was a unfortunate thing for him, that, in his youth, the guitar wasn't a path beaten like that of the piano; he only thought of what the instrument could yield him, this is human; but something much superior, that, without anticipated foresight, he resolved the difficulties, closing in on all the possibilities that mental gymnastics of the calculation in gold paves at times that which breaks into a bad pirouette. His merits as a brilliant guitarist exceeded the expectations of the contractor that brought him to Buenos Aires, without any necessity of accelerating being presented in one year and another. The calculation was unfaithful, by lack of tact and its results gave indifference such that in the Bonaerense public, that shone in "total" absence.

During his stay in the Argentine capital there were a series of concerts for two guitars organized. It hadn't been any bother to originate the failure obtained; on the contrary. The category of both players presumed the success; but the bad, the unforgivable error, was in the works chosen. None of them were originally for the guitar! They only dealt with transcriptions, that never could condition themselves guitaristically to the worth of the *"duos"* of Sor and another guitarist. This lack of judgement, this forgetting of the classical authors of music for the guitar, is simply incredible in the artistic personality of Llobet. The public of Buenos Aires, musically very cultured, understood it so, and lovers of the guitar that are the Argentines, gave the act the only importance that it might have deserved.

As a composer, he is known to have published, as originals, only one work: *"Romanza"*, published by *"Biblioteca Fortea"* (Madrid), of very good musical structure and very guitaristic. As for the publications of arrangements, transcriptions of popular Catalan themes, originals of the populace that he is the only author of, and harmonized for the guitar by Llobet, we won't concern ourselves; because we are only concerned in this Diccionario with the original works, that enrich the pure literature and are exclusively conceived for the guitar." So ends the entry in the *Diccionario de Guitarristas* for Domingo Prat's maestro: Miguel Llobet. Miguel Llobet died of pleurisy in Barcelona on February 22, 1938.

Miguel Llobet and his 1859 Antonio de Torres guitar. This photo is from an article entitled *"Cultores de la Guitarra"* from *Revista Musical Ilustrada "Tárrega"* issue No. 10 of April 1925.

(Left) This review is from an unknown daily of Buenos Aires. "Last concert" in the Salon "La Argentina", of the August 1910 tour that Miguel Llobet made to South America. This was sold out and his reception was to the extent that he drew an encore from the audience at the end of his first set. The encore piece was the Coste etude that was eventually recorded in 1925. The repertoire is quite different than his later tours.

Archive: Mario Rodríguez Arenas

The guitar collection owned by Miguel Llobet was documented by Josép Mangado y Artigas on page 101 of his book *"La guitarra en Cataluña"* (Tecla Editions). This indefatigable author also contributes a lengthy segment on "The Concerts of Lalyta Almiron in Barcelona and Madrid in 1931" at the end of this book.

The guitar collection consisted of: 1) 1783 Joséph Benedid, Cadiz, 2) 1797 Juan Pages, Cadiz, 3) 1824 José Recio, Cadiz, 4) 1841 Francisco Pages, La Habana (Cuba), 5) and 6) Antonio de Torres, Seville 1859 and 1862, 7) 19th century Pedro Pages, Cadiz, 8) 19th century Pablo Hierro, Tortosa (Tarragona), 9) 19th century Altimira, Barcelona, 10) c. 1850 Francisco España, 11) 19th century Pedro Perez, Barcelona, 12) 19th century Ribot y Alcaniz, Barcelona,13) and 14) 1920 J. Ribot and V. Storch Masseguer, Barcelona, 15) unlabeled 19th century French guitar, 16) unlabeled c. 1900 Barcelona guitar, 17) 1921 Alfred Schmid, Munich and 18) c. 1930 American Conservatory, Chicago.

His daughter granted this collection to the Museu de Musica in Barcelona in 1953.

Translation of "Arte y Teatro" (Art and Theater):

"Last Llobet Concert — The most beautiful aspect presented last night in the Salon "La Argentina", completely filled its seats by the most select gathering of aficionados. It is that it had been announced as the last concert of the celebrated guitarist Miguel Llobet, and not to lose the ultimate opportunity to listen to such a brilliant "virtuoso" and an artist of honored style at once. The program on the other hand, was of the most attractive and embraced numbers of very diverse disposition as they were interesting. Sor, the favorite classic composer for the instrument of Mr. Llobet, initiated the evening with a *"Minué"* and two *"Estudios"*. Then a *"Pizzicato"* by Tárrega, the maestro of the concert guitarist, delighting with its delicateness of his playing; Mitjana and Haydn gave a severe note to the first part, that concluded with the most brilliant *"Capricho arabe"* by Tárrega. This captivated, in all truth, the gathering, and a prolonged ovation obligated Mr. Llobet to add *"Estudio",* by Coste, unpublished, in the program.

In the second part Regondi, Chopin, Albeniz and Parga, they prepared, with sentimental and romantic music, to the public, with a "crescendo" of enthusiasm for the *"Scherzo-Gavota", "Estudio"* and *"Un Sueño"* by Tárrega, in them Mr. Llobet made a gala of expression and agility."

Translation of the Romero & Fernández advertisement on the next page from the *Revista Musical Ilustrada "Tárrega"* issue No. 12 of June 1925.

"That the Spanish Guitar is the best in the world, the proof in having been the only ones played by these eminent artists: Sor, Aguado, Arcas, Tárrega, Llobet, Anido, Segovia, Sagreras, Sinopoli and the great maestros.

In spite of the interest that some makers have in wanting to imitate the great constructors of Spanish guitars, it is curious to observe that neither so at least they are able to resemble to those of the less importance, with which is confirmed that a Spanish guitar of little price is equivalent to the one of greater value from any other origin.

We invite you before making your purchase to visit the house of Romero & Fernández .

Time payment sales."

424

Que la ══════
Guitarra Española

es la mejor del mundo, lo prueba el haber sido la única que tocaron los eminentes artistas:

SOR
    AGUADO
        ARCAS
            TARREGA
                LLOBET
                    ANIDO
                        SEGOVIA
                            ROBLEDO
                                SAGRERAS
                                    SINOPOLI

y los más grandes maestros.

A pesar del interés que tienen algunos fabricantos en querer imitar a los grandes constructores de guitarras españolas, es curioso observar que ni tan siquiera consiguen semejarse a los de menos importancia, con lo que se confirma que una guitarra española de poco precio equivale a la de mayor valor de cualquier otra procedencia.

Invitamos a Vd. a que antes de hacer sus compras, visite la casa

ROMERO & FERNANDEZ

FLORIDA 255   **B. MITRE 947**   **CANGALLO 1574**
U. T. 0508 Rivadavia   U. T. 2050 Rivadavia   U. T. 2285 Mayo

VENTAS A PLAZOS

Romero & Fernández advertisement with a photo from the *Revista Musical Ilustrada "Tárrega"* issue No. 12 of June 1925. The photo of Maria Luisa Anido and Miguel Llobet is from their concert at the Salon "La Argentina".

Translation of the *"Cultores de la Guitarra"* Miguel Llobet article from the *Revista Musical Ilustrada "Tárrega"* Vol. 10 April 1925.

"The eminent Spanish guitarist having arrived in our country, we have wanted to dedicate our habitual section to the notable maestro, not only as a deserved homage to his musical genius, but also as a pleasant advance notice of the season which he will soon have to begin among us.

In truth there is nothing in particular we can add which can offer of the best fame to his name, all which once his performance has been brilliantly judged by the most reputable critics and hotly applauded by the public of all the countries.

The *"Courrier Musical"* of Paris says:

You know, in effect, that Spain has been the cradle of the most celebrated guitarists, and is as a competent judge, which the inhabitants of Madrid, Barcelona, Seville, Bilbao, Tolusa, Malaga, San Sebastian, Victoria, etc. acclaim with the most lively enthusiasm to Miguel Llobet in his triumphant concert tours. In Madrid, overall, where he has given a number of recitals, he received an unforgettable reception and the complete royal family managed to congratulate the exceptional virtuoso. The city of Malaga has named him an honorary professor of its Conservatory. Llobet, abandoning a country, which has surrounded him with laurels, wished to conquer Paris. Setting up his residence in the great city where he has dedicated to the professors, since seven years ago. All of the artists, without exception, have demonstrated the sincerest admiration for him. He is the only guitarist that has been invited to play in the most severe and knowledgeable mediums.

Llobet was applauded in the Schola Cantorum in 1905, in the Trompette, and in the "Société Nationale de Musique", in the renowned Matinées Danube (1906) and the Soirées d'Art (1907), etc.

From another source, "Musical America", of New York, says:

We must admit that he is a complete maestro in his art that has a title for respectable fame. That doesn't imply, however, that we pretend to necessarily to be interested in the particular form of the art of the maestro or that we are desire to be among those that are called to appreciate that which he has to offer. For example, you can make all of the efforts to attend a Kreisler recital; but can't be persuaded to listen equally to a Spanish guitarist in spite of the sensational eulogies of which preceded before his performance.

The answer is obvious, but in the case of Miguel Llobet you can have the motive of regret if not having jumped to the persuasion.

Mr. Llobet, who made the trip to America with Granados, the composer of *"Goyecas"*, the Spanish opera which is soon going to be presented in the Metropolitan, has spoken to the reporter of "Musical America" of his early life and of his successes with the guitar. He doesn't find it necessary to praise his selection of the guitar for his instrument because in Spain the guitar is known and loved by all especially when it is played as Mr. Llobet does it.

"La Publicidad" of Barcelona, among other things declares:

A child of this capital, Llobet studied his musical courses here, making the first general education in our Escuela Municipal de Musica. He was a classmate in various classes with Pablo Casals, with which they united some points of beginning, over all in having ennobled the instrument they cultivated expectedly, and he had the "virtue" of being separated from the comfortable path of the "virtuosity". Today, that we see the facility with which it converts into a "virtuoso" all that acquires great notoriety in the dominion of an instrument which, in truth such denomination can't be justified to our great cellist nor our great guitarist. For something commenced to be said among the intelligent ones "Llobet is the Casals of the guitar."

Once he had finished his general studies and defined his inclination towards the guitar, he put himself in the hands of the celebrated Valencian maestro Francisco Tárrega, with whom he verified his complete education of the very difficult instrument. Once he finished studying with his teacher he was opposed to be presented before the public, as is the custom of all the advanced students. Was he very confident in himself? Those of us who know Llobet remember from those old times when we repeatedly told him to make himself known to his compatriots, we know that he took with him to far lands, the desire to what we consider, "a great risk", before a completely unknown audience to avoid being "ridiculed" by his friends.

So Llobet began his first artistic excursion of the Spanish territory in the years 1901-1903, and he commenced to recieve laurels in the principal cities of the Peninsula and especially in Madrid, where he gave a considerable number of performances with the most extraordinary success.

A year later, in 1904 he went for the first time to Paris, and there set up as a center of his artistic excursions to the great European capitals and to Germany and England, where out guitarist is held in the highest of esteem. Rapidly he imposed his art in the principal music centers, such as the "Schola Cantorum", the "Société Nationale de Musique" and other important ones of the French capital. In his own time he was consecrated as a true eminence in his art by the most celebrated masters such as Debussy, Dukas, Fauré, d'Indy, etc.

As a consequence of his success in Paris, they called him to give concerts in other French and Belgian music centers, deserving a special mention is the great triumph in the "Société Royale d'Armonie" of Antwerp.

The great German critic, D. Bauer, expressed that the impression which Llobet's performance produced could be difficult to describe. "It appeared to me that in his time the apparition of Paganini has to have produced a like effect. His technique leaves all that we have known up until now very far behind, a richness of sound in this simple instrument of six strings which no one imagines, and overall an art so musical with which he performs the most diverse pieces, it isn't strange that the public is more and more enthusiastic, in every one of the passages, and which at the end will burst into a true ovation. "Which do you prefer?" The precious *Minuetto* and study by Sor, the study by Coste (masterwork for the right hand), the enchanting and melodius *"Serenata en Sevilla"* by Albeniz-Tárrega and Albeniz-Llobet? The performance of the *Bourée* by Bach was very clear and precise. Therefore we imagine what the old maestro was dreaming. He performed the *Romanza* by Rubinstein with great finesse, which, as the *Bourée,* are transcriptions, very correct by the same maestro, which reveals that he is also a very good harmonist in the transcriptions of the two Catalan airs. And finally the *"Fantasia Española"* by Arcas-Llobet, was really a work of witchcraft, a superior school of the most virtuoso technique, full of the most surprising effects, such as: harmonics, doubly masterfully performed, execution by the left hand alone, (the pizzicato of the left hand on the violin can't compete as for the sound) and like things, those, which you have to see and hear to give account to the same reality. And over all that he possesses the true spirit of art for whose demonstrations are only the most select technical resources. The precious crown of laurels that the Assocation of the Guitar dedicated to the maestro never has been adjudicated to another more deserving and all reconciled in one desire: "Until we see you again". Maybe we will encounter him on another occasion, especially us, the guitarists will submit to a more profound study of the technique of Llobet.

After the concert by Llobet and his two friends, Mr. Nardis and Mr. Souget, they united in a pleasant reunion with our ladies and gentlemen in the cafe Luitpold. Mr. Buek, President of the Assocation of the Guitar, gave in name of all the expressive graciousness to Llobet in chosen words pronounced in the French language, to which Mr. Souget interpreted into German the thanks of the maestro and the pleasure of his stay in Munich. It was a reunion which the Assocation of the Guitar recorded with satisfaction and pride: "It was illuminated by a beautiful star".

In the concert of Llobet, there were expectations that were surpassed by the performer. The pieces that were performed were admirable within the natural limits of the instrument, for example the transcriptions for the guitar by Mozart (Op.9) and the known *Bourée* by Bach, Rubinstein, etc. Others, written for the same cultivators of the instruments, were still the most interesting. The musical historian remembers, to hear the pieces performed, the antique art of the coloratura, it which, by diverse points of view, must have been the most interesting of that which we believe we had heard. — *"Bayrischer Courier"* (German Version)

From "The Globe and Commercial Advertiser", New York:

The culminating point of the concert to be realized on the 17th of April in Bruges, Brussels, a benefit for the Military Hospital No. 28, will be the opportunity of hearing a guitarist of worldly fame. Miguel Llobet is, a native of Barcelona, Spain, and consequently the country where to play the guitar has arrived at its apogee. After attaining fame with the instrument of his country, he traveled all over Europe, awakening the great interest and enthusiasm. The famous classic Vincent d'Indy, declared that his tactical was a revelation and he offered to compose for him. Another admirer that was conquered in France was Debussy. The persons that believe that the guitar isn't an instrument to take into consideration must become aware of the last note by the celebrated musician Richard Epstein, that mentioned, "as the three most celebrated present musicians in the country are Kreisler, Casals and Llobet. — April 5, 1916."

———————

From "The New York Press"

It shouldn't be strange if after hearing the celebrated Spanish guitarist Miguel Llobet which yesterday in the Princess Theater, gave his first concert, the art to play this very difficult instrument in his hands will be taken in more increments.

No one certainly doubts, to finalize his first two pieces; *Minueto* by F. Sor and *Capricho Arabé* by Tárrega, that this admirable artist will win right away the favor of the public. — New York, January 18, 1916. (English Version)"

Translation of *"Conciertos Llobet"* (Llobet Concerts): from *Revista Musical Ilustrada "Tárrega"* magazine issue No. 10 of April 1925.

Various performances of the eminent Spanish guitarist Miguel Llobet are to be announced in the first few days of May. The return of the maestro, originating from Germany, after a tour in which the highest compensation that an artist can aspire for has been received.

The critic says:

"In Vienna, this new visit of Llobet took upon itself the contour of a real happening. The artist had to respond more than twenty times to take the stage to thank the demonstrations of which he was the object, obligating him to exhaust his repertoire in endless encores and, as in 1922, it was necessary to turn off the lights of the theater because the public that filled it didn't show signs of planning to leave.

The illustrious composer Arnold Schonberg, after having heard all of his concerts, solicited a private performance, in which he was enthusiastic of such a manner, that he organized a session in honor of Llobet, having him hear some of his compositions, among them a septet "Serenata", in which the guitar was involved.

CONCIERTOS LLOBET

Anúncianse para los primeros días de Mayo varias audiciones del eminente guitarrista español Miguel Llobet. Torna el maestro, procedente de Alemania, después de una jira en que ha recibido las más altas compensaciones a que pueda aspirar un artista.

Dice un cronista:

"En Viena, esta nueva visita de Llobet asumió los contornos de un verdadero acontecimiento. El artista debió acudir más de veinte veces al escenario para agradecer las demostraciones de que le hacían objeto, obligándole a agotar su repertorio en interminables "bis" y, como en 1922, fué preciso apagar las luces del teatro porque el público que lo llenaba no daba señales de retirarse.

El ilustre compositor Arnold Schönberg, después de haberle oído en todos sus conciertos, le solicitó una audición privada, en la que se entusiasmó de tal modo, que organizó una sesión en honor de Llobet, haciéndole oir algunas de sus composiciones, entre ellas un septeto, "Serenata", en el que entra también la guitarra.

Esta actitud del gran músico austriaco, tan poco pródigo en demostraciones, ha sido muy comentada en los círculos musicales de Viena, donde se la consideró como un hermoso triunfo del eximio guitarrista español".

En la Argentina se le espera con verdadero regocijo y es indudable que no olvida el célebre artista el cariño y devoción con que habitualmente se le recibe, desde que con tan agradable frecuencia nos visita.

This attitude of the great Austrian musician, almost prodigious in his demonstrations, has been quite commented on in the musical circles of Vienna, where it is considered as a beautiful triumph by the most excellent Spanish guitarist.

In Argentina we await him with true joy, and it is indubitable the celebrated artist hasn't forgotten the affection and devotion with which he habitually receives, since that he visits us with such a pleasant frequency."

On the next page is the first concert in Montevideo at the Teatro Solis on May 20, 1922. The text below the list of songs on the program refers to *"Homenaje a Debussy"*, translated it says: "The illustrious maestro Manuel de Falla has reserved the first performance of this work for Miguel Llobet."

This is a special courtesy by the Centro de Investigacion, Documentacion y Difusion de las Artes Escenicas. (CIDDAE)-Teatro Solis.

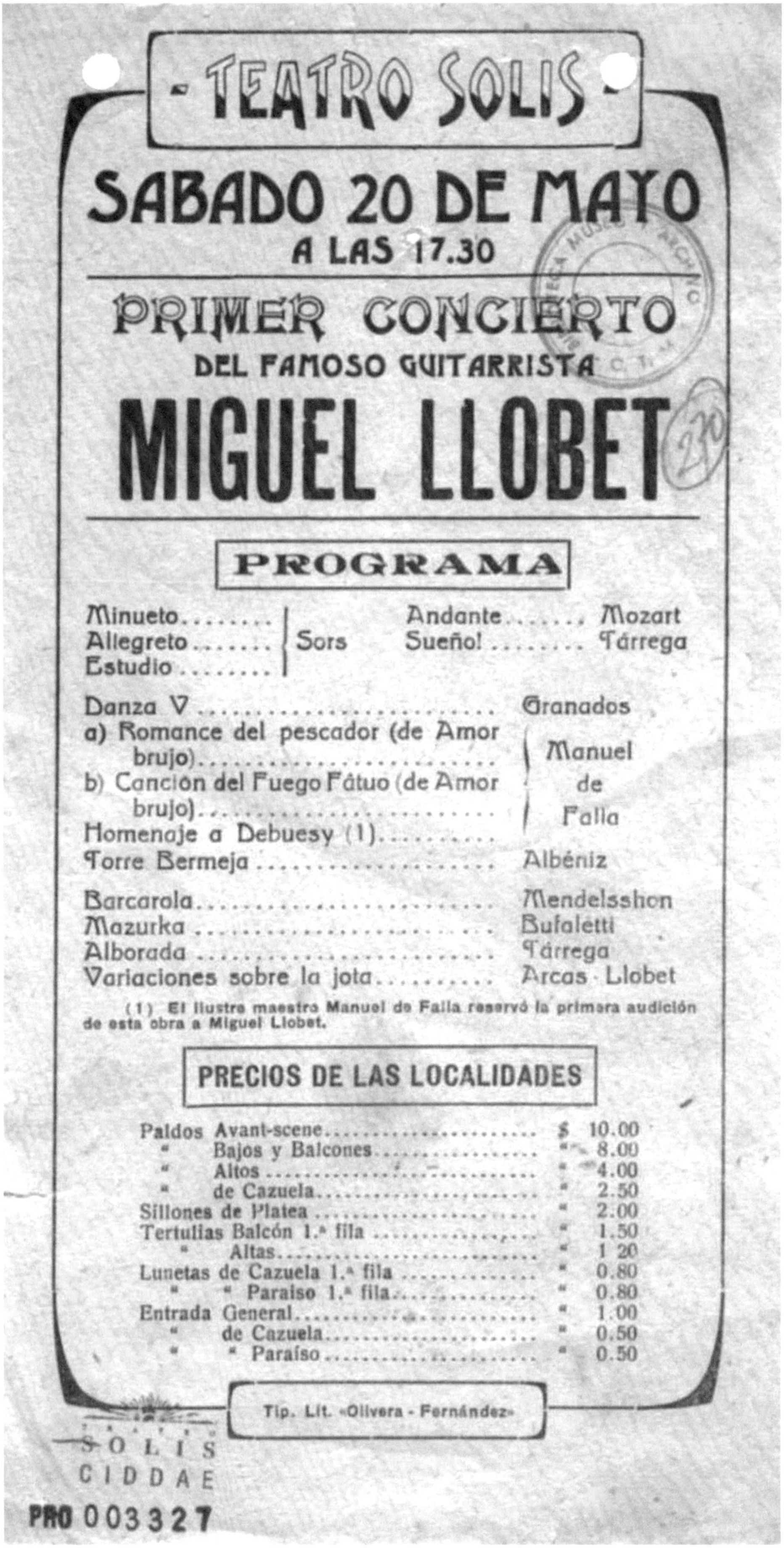

·TEATRO SOLIS·

SABADO 20 DE MAYO
A LAS 17.30

PRIMER CONCIERTO
DEL FAMOSO GUITARRISTA
MIGUEL LLOBET

PROGRAMA

Minueto........		Andante...... Mozart
Allegreto.......	Sors	Sueño! .... Tárrega
Estudio		

Danza V .... Granados
a) Romance del pescador (de Amor brujo)........... Manuel
b) Canción del Fuego Fátuo (de Amor brujo)........ de
Homenaje a Debuesy (1)........... Falla
Torre Bermeja .... Albéniz

Barcarola...................... Mendelsshon
Mazurka .... Bufaletti
Alborada .... Tárrega
Variaciones sobre la jota........... Arcas · Llobet

(1) El ilustre maestro Manuel de Falla reservó la primera audición de esta obra a Miguel Llobet.

PRECIOS DE LAS LOCALIDADES

Paldos Avant-scene.....................	$	10.00
" Bajos y Balcones.................	"	8.00
" Altos	"	4.00
" de Cazuela......................	"	2.50
Sillones de Platea	"	2.00
Tertulias Balcón 1.ª fila	"	1.50
" Altas..........................	"	1 20
Lunetas de Cazuela 1.ª fila............	"	0.80
" Paraiso 1.ª fila...............	"	0.80
Entrada General......................	"	1.00
" de Cazuela....................	"	0.50
" " Paraíso	"	0.50

Tip. Lit. «Olivera - Fernández»

TEATRO
SOLIS
CIDDAE

PRO 003327

430

My colleague, Carlos Salcedo Centurion, went to Rosario, Santa Fe, Argentina in March of 2014, to research the 5-month stay of Agustín Barrios in 1923. He also learned that Miguel Llobet performed at the Biblioteca Argentina on Monday July 3, 1922, Friday July 10, 1925, on Thursday September 3, 1925 with M. L. Anido and again solo on Monday September 2, 1929.

● ●

CONCIERTOS LLOVET

El gran maestro en su segundo concierto realizado en el Salón "La Argentina" acompañado de la señorita Anido y de don Martín Gil.

This photo is from the magazine *Revista Musical Ilustrada "Tárrega"* issue No. 11 of May 1925.

The translation of the caption is:

"Llobet Concerts

The great maestro in his second concert that took place in the Salon "La Argentina" (Friday May 8, 1925), he is accompanied by Miss Anido and *Don* Martin Gil."

On the next page are the concert titles of four performances given on May 6, 8, 12 and 20, 1925.

Miércoles 6 de Mayo

I.—Minuetto, Sors; Allegretto, Sors; Estudio (si menor), Sors; Andante (Don Giovanni), Mozart; Estudio (mi menor), Sors.

II.—Torre Bermeja, Albeniz; Dedicatoria, Granados; Sonatina, a) Allegretto, b) Andante, c) Allegro, Moreno Torroba.

III.—a) Romance del Pescador, b) Canción del Fuego Fátuo (de "Amor Brujo"), M. de Falla; Homenaje a Debussy, M. de Falla; Alborada, Tárrega; Sueño, Tárrega.

Viernes 8 de Mayo

I.—Minuetto, Sors; Estudio, Aguado; Andante, Mozart; Nocturno, Chopin.

II.—Preludio, Sarabanda, Bach; Sonata, a) Allegretto maestoso, Allegro giusto; b) Andante; c) Finale (Allegro), López Chavarri.

III.—Mazurca, Bufaletti; Cinco melodías populares catalanas, armonizadas por Llobet: a) El Testament d'Amelia, b) La Filla del Marxant, c) L'Hereu Riéra, d) El Mestre, e) La Pastoreta. Variaciones sobre la jota, Arcas-Llobet.

Martes 12 de Mayo

I.—Minuetto, Estudio en si bemol, Andante, Sors; Preludio, Bach; Estudio, Coste.

II.—Danza, R. Villar; Córdoba, Albeniz; Danza Nº 7, Danza Nº 5, Granados.

III.—Romanza, Rubinstein; Air de Ballet, Chaminade; Impresión, Mompou; Preludio, Tárrega; Variaciones sobre un tema de Corelli, Sors-Llobet.

Miércoles 20 de Mayo.. 4º. Concierto Extraordinario

I.—Minuetto, Estudio en mi, Sors; Estudio, Aguado; Sarabanda, Preludio, Bach.

II.—Reverie, Schumann; Tonadilla, Granados; Sonata, E. López Chavarri; a) Allegro maestoso. Allegro giusto; b) Andante; c) Finale (Allegro).

III.—Barcarola, Mendelssohn; Dos melodías populares catalanas armonizadas por Llobet: a) L'Hereu Riera, b) La Pastoreta; Sonatina, Moreno Torroba; a) Allegretto, b) Andante, c) Allegro.

These repositioned images are from the magazine *Revista Musical Ilustrada "Tárrega"* issue No. 11 of May 1925. These concerts were held on Wednesday May 6, Friday May 8, Tuesday May 12 and Wednesday May 20, 1925.

Parte de la selecta concurrencia que asistió al segundo concierto efectuado en
el Salón "La Argentina"

This photo is from the magazine Revista Musical Ilustrada "Tárrega" issue No. 11 of May 1925.

The caption translation is:

"Llobet Concerts

This is a part of the select audience that attended the second concert that took place in the Salon "La Argentina" (Friday May 8, 1925)."

On the next page begins a series of Miguel Llobet solo concerts in Montevideo at the Teatro Solis. They are for Friday May 22, Sunday May 24, Thursday May 28 and Saturday May 30, 1925.

The three pages following that series of concerts are two Miguel Llobet-Maria Luisa Anido concerts from Saturday June 27-Maria plays the first two sets as solos then is joined by her Maestro for the last set. On the Sunday June 28, 1925 program of the dozen plus pieces are all performed as duets. The October 3, 1925 is once again Miguel Llobet as solist.

These concert programs are a special courtesy by the Centro de Investigacion, Documentacion y Difusion de las Artes Escenicas. (CIDDAE)-Teatro Solis.

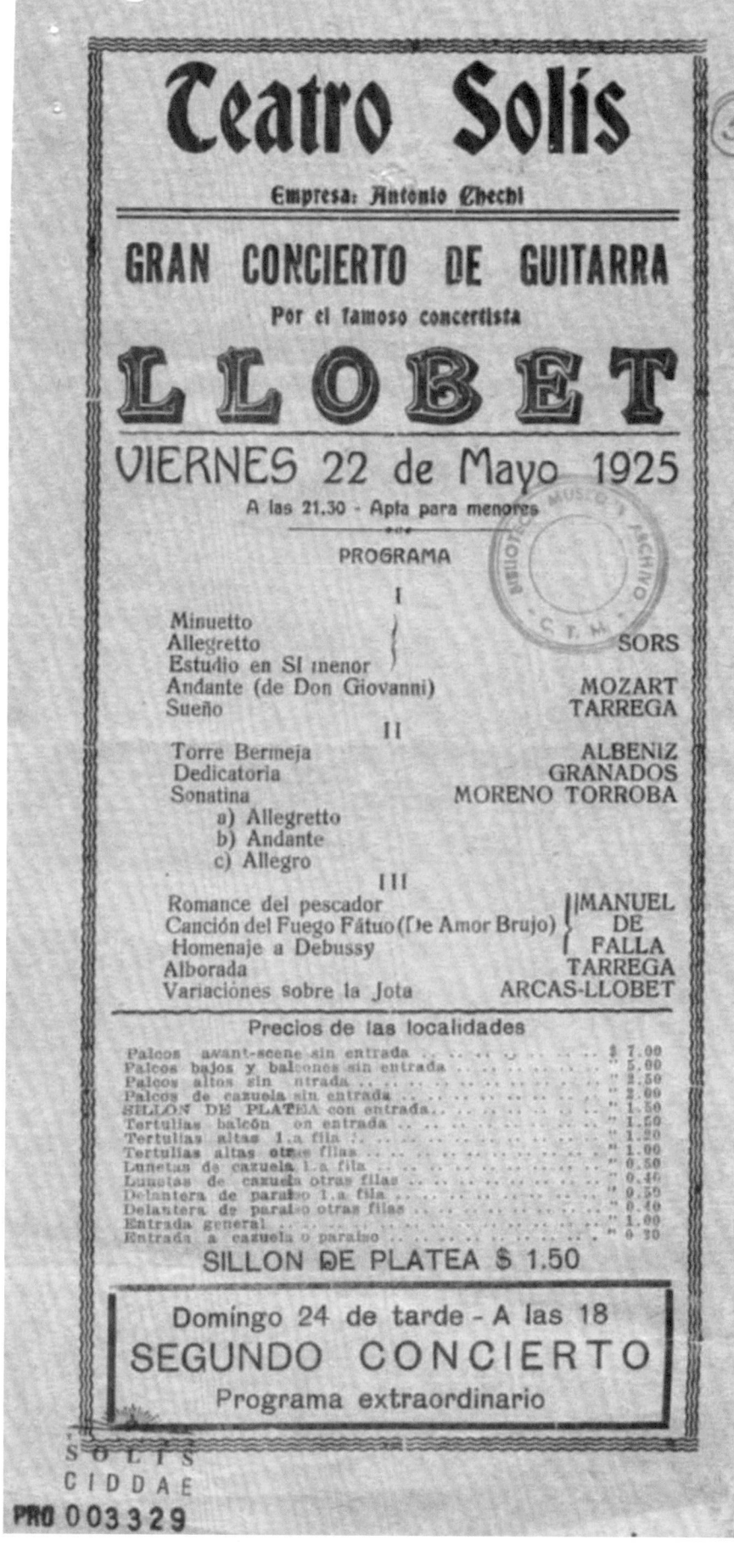

Fernando Sor's *"Estudio en Si menor"* was recorded by Miguel Llobet for Odeon records in Barcelona.

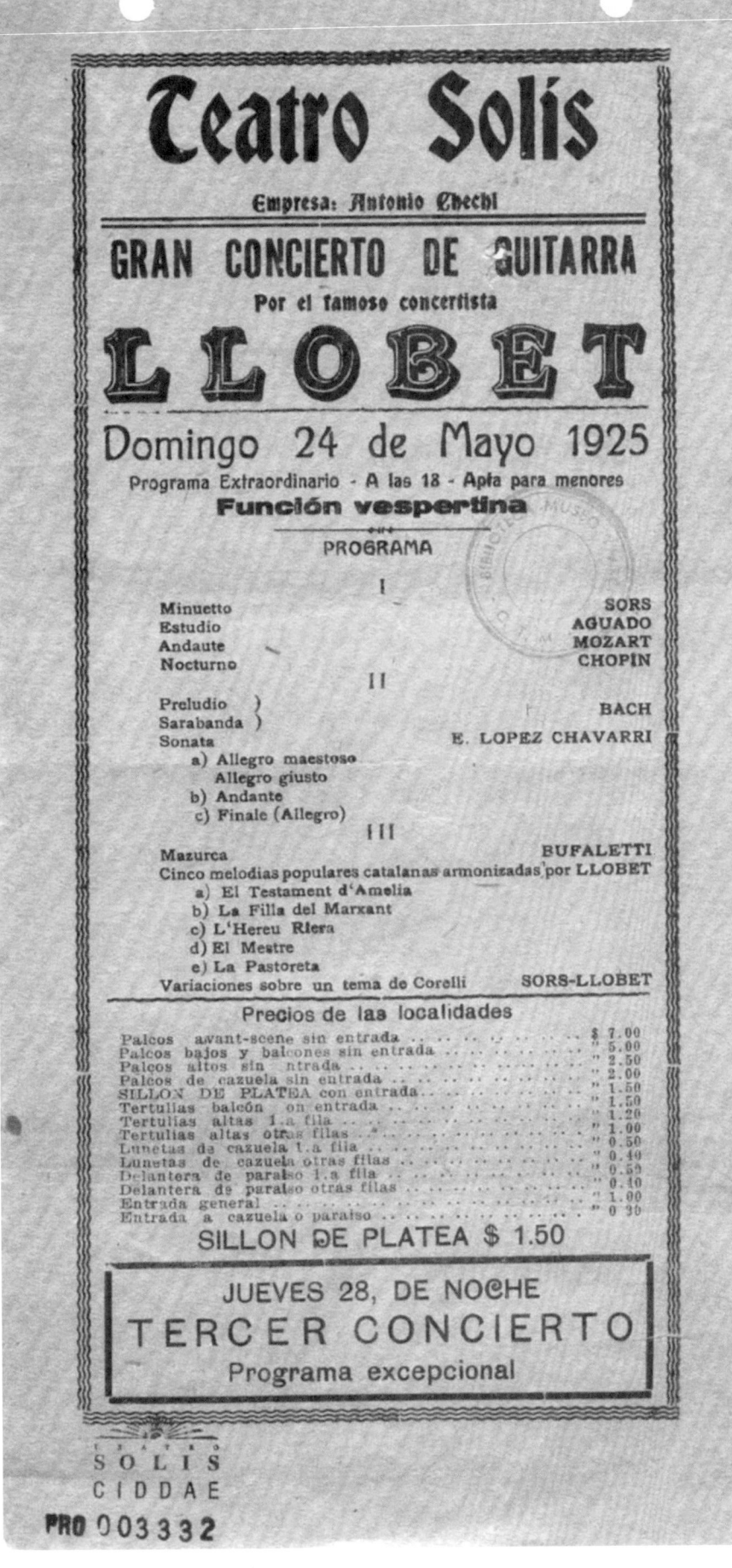

It wasn't until after Miguel llobet had passed away that all of his transcriptions of the Catalan folksongs were published, only three of these were published by 1931. Those being *"El Testament d' Amelia"*, *"L'HereuRiera"* and *"El Mestre"*.

Napoleon Coste's *"Estudio"* was recorded by Miguel Llobet for Odeon records in Barcelona.

436

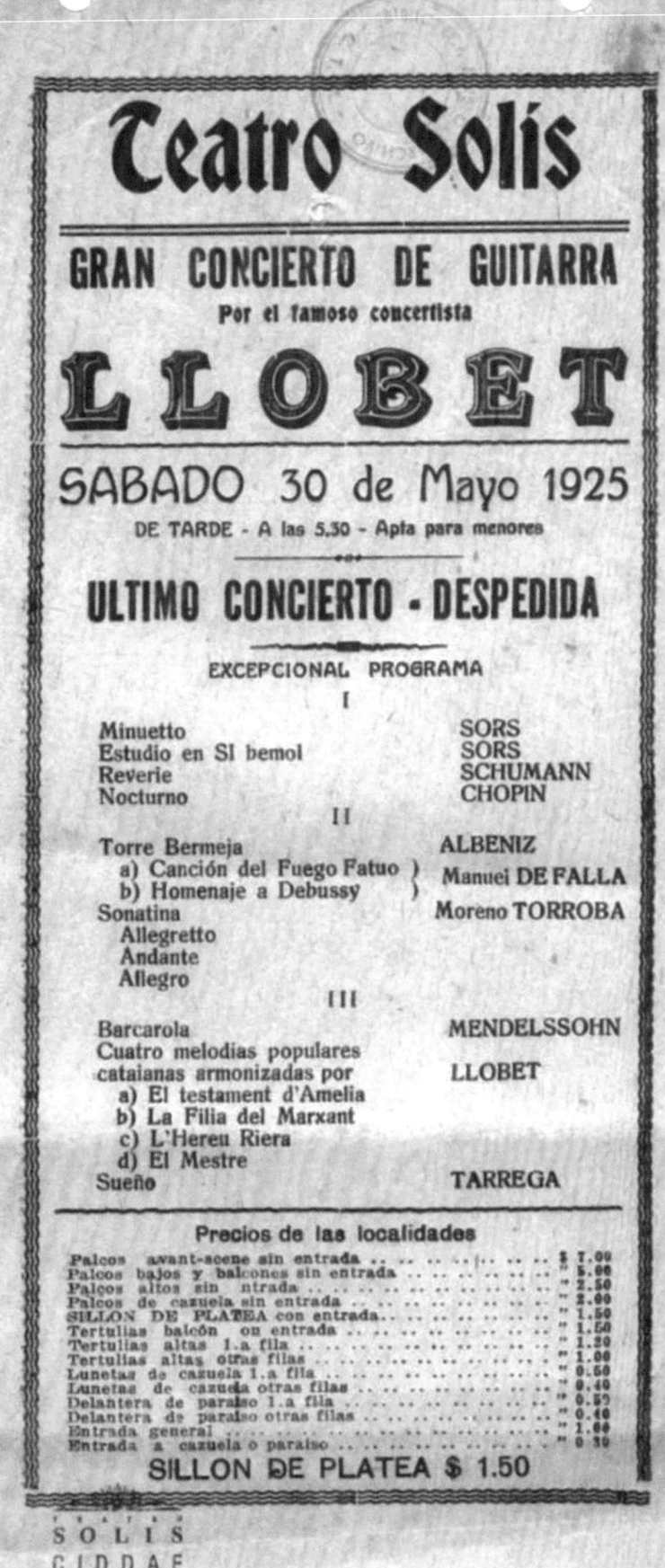

Fredric Chopin's *"Nocturno"* was recorded by Lalyta Almiron for Odeon records in Barcelona in 1931.

Translation of the article by Carlos Vega *"El Mestre" de Miguel Llobet"* from *Revista Musical Ilustrada "Tárrega"* magazine No. 17 of November 1925.

"El Mestre" by Miguel Llobet"

"In the current month in Buenos Aires the impression of *"El Mestre"* has been concluded, the popular Catalan melody harmonized for the guitar by Llobet. By treating it, to us it appears, to be the best work that is in the guitarristic literature, we are going to consider it with great attention.

The guitar, as you know, doesn't climax by the excellence of its original albums. All of its artistic history is to be limited to two names: Sor and Tárrega.

The first, with the *"Andante largo"* and some studies and minuets of great beauty and value, is placed in the first place. Framed in his epoch and considered the deficient knowledge of the instrument at that time, Sor charged a magnitude he couldn't achieve afterward.

Tárrega, celebrated by having proceeded the technical studies of Aguado to endow to the guitar by its present school and having augmented the esthetic possibilities of the instrument with his new concepts, Tárrega, less fortunate as a composer, is placed after Sor varies essentially with some good preludes, neoromantic moments, but without a premonition nor translating impressionism, flowering of the time, nor the previous conquests by the Russians — until where the spirit of these tendencies might have been on the guitar.

After Tárrega the guitar lacks politically active composers. Llobet isn't the same. The most representative of his scarce original production, an *"Impromptu"*, translates an incoherent fragmentary idea, part of which the theme, the development and the cadences don't say anything new. Instead as a conquest of the fretboard it is a marvelous page.

The unquestionable mastery of Llobet, this great experience and rare dominion of the instrument is which, with the delicious popular Catalan melody to his scope; he has brought to make the beautiful page that we comment on. *"El Mestre"*, a song of the people, is an ingenuous and simple melody, astonishing by sobriety and economic with the translation of the noble and deep sentiment. The initial phrase, in a rhythm not very slow rapidly directs to a subdominant for reposing in the dominant.

The repeat concludes initiating a beautiful and original sentence in a modulating cadence that ends with the initial modified phrase in the form of a concluding cadence in the tone of the dominant.

The chorus follows lively and then some independent sentences comment and recalls the initial periods, with those that link later.

The harmonization is masterful. All the timbres, all in color, all the expressive resources of which the guitar is able, have been employed by Llobet in a unique form, very far from his precursor and maestro Tárrega, very far from all which until now he has written and what he is presently writing. *"El Mestre"*, is the work of the guitar that produces the most intense sensation of art.

Because Llobet has put in play springs and unknown concepts by his ancestors; because he has known to take advantage of the technical conquests of the modern music; because he has absorbed the contemporary spirit among the musical aristocracy of the century; because they have subscribed to his extraordinary endowments and his long experience; because he has deeply felt the anonymous song of the birth region; by all that; Llobet surrenders to the guitar a work that ennobles and honors its literature. *"El Mestre"*, comes out of the light of fifteen years of a reserve, under six keys. Because the unique lesson the Llobet didn't learn from the saint and noble Tárrega, was the great lesson of generosity and detachment that the Valencian maestro was giving all his life."

438

Translation of the letter and article by Emilio Pujol *"Los Conciertos Llobet-Anido y "El Mestre"* from the *Revista Musical Ilustrada "Tárrega"* magazine No. 19 of February 1926.

The Llobet-Anido Concerts and *"El Mestre"*

With the motive of the articles published in Tárrega about the performance of the eminent guitarists Miguel Llobet and Maria Luisa Anido and the music of the first, recently published, the eminent Spanish guitarist Emilio Pujol directed a letter to us, whose text we reproduce:

Barcelona January 1926.

Mr. Director of the *Revista Musical Ilustrada "Tárrega"* magazine.

Distinguished gentleman:

I would like to thank you for your exquisite friendliness, the insertion of these lines in the interesting *Revista"Tárrega"* magazine, which I so honorably direct.

As you can see, it isn't more than a simple clarification about erroneous opinions that appeared in the same and in the corresponding issue of the month of last November.

I'm expecting to see myself pleased in the favor that I dare to plead, it pleases me to anticipate to you my profound recognition and most distinguished consideration.

Emilio Pujol

With the greatest pleasure we yield preferential space in another page to the *"Aclaraciones"* (Clarifications) by the illustrious disciple of Tárrega.

The Director.

"Aclaraciones" (Clarifications) by Emilio Pujol

The Christmas holidays contain in their traditional customs a force of irresistible attraction about the home. This spirit that dominates us of an intense manner, this year has given me a happy emotion; that of being able to exchange on our ground, a frank and warm hug with a friend who I love as a brother and admire and respect as a maestro: Miguel Llobet.

The great artist arrived in Barcelona enroute to Buenos Aires, the same day that I came from other lands, to the lap of the family home to saturate myself in a little affection and rest.

In the peace of this circumstantial isolation the maestro had related his triumphs, simply, without pompousness of vanity, with the real emotion that causes the serenity of a complete dignity of an artist, and detailed, with all the necessary meticulousness, reconstructing imaginatively the effects of sonorities obtained with the creation of the repertoire for two guitars, the true conquest for the modern literature of our instrument. Then, he spoke of the progress that the Republic of Argentina has made and does rapidly and intensely in all the Arts; of the profusion of musical works of the best orientation which appear and have appeared in little time, a basis of a future artistic cauldron of priceless national value. And followed in the wake, with that frank spontaneity that goes from the heart to the action, he obliges us to hear two delicious Argentine pages.

They are two *"Estilos"* of the purest character, instrumentalized with an exquisite simplicity; and the felling that gives them life, a sincerity that isn't possible to believe born of a simple intelligent will, but of a profound sentiment of artistic love. After we talked even more: I have learned through him, the intense guitaristic activity that is unfolding and highlighted more every time in all of the Republic of Argentina and meritorious labor of how many champions struggle for the same noble cause of ideals, affirming that if the guitar has so penetrated in the heart of our public it is unique that it can reflect all its soul, the

Argentine "*folklore*", likewise this fused with the guitar because all the indigenous spirituality, has continued the footsteps of its civilization, through the guitar.

In this way my friend the maestro expressed, of this country that he loves as his own and of which he keeps the most pleasant memories as an artist and sensibilities of grateful recognition.

Now as well, some hours after the arrival in my hands an issue of the *Revista"Tárrega"* magazine that corresponds to the month of last November and truly astonishes, I read an article by the editor commenting on the artistic labor of Llobet and Maria Luisa Anido, the Argentine artist prodigy, accusing the great maestro of ingratitude and disdain by the fact of not having placed in his programs any musical production of the country that has managed to lavish so much admiration and affection.

The accusation is unjust. This circumstance doesn't have very far the signification that and excessive patriotic susceptibility has wanted to give him. Llobet is an artist who has among his virtues one that is of a priceless value: sincerity. This makes him avoid the false revealing of his sentiments. And is supported in the confidence of his own sense that can very well have forgotten of officially revealing the admiration and affection that inspires all the display of Argentine art.

I have of that, the most intimate and absolute conviction.

In the same Revista (magazine) we find a commentary by Mr. Carlos Vega that the Catalan melody *"El Mestre"* that was just to be published in Buenos Aires.

After the exposition of various referential considerations to the work of Miguel Llobet, a work nowuniversally consecrated, by the public, critics and musicians of the most elevated artistic category, Mr. Vega ends his commentary attributing to Llobet an unjust sentiment: that of selfishly reserving his productions.

Nothing further from reason that this accusation now which, slighting the material interest that his works may have produced launched time to the edition, hasn't ever haggled the handing over generously to the better part of those who have solicited them. Proof of that, is the fact that the unpublished productions until today by Miguel Llobet come placed in almost all the programs of the present concert guitarists for many years to this part.

We might see well/since Mr. Vega that Miguel Llobet with his generosities and detachment shows having inherited not only the excellencies of the art of Tárrega, but also the virtues that so characterize and ennoble the GREAT MAESTRO."

The Montevideo daily *"El Dia"* on Saturday June 27, 1925 had an announcement of the concert of the distinguished concert guitarists Miguel Llobet-Maria Luisa Anido.

This from the 1917-1938 archive of: Pedro Mascaro y Reissig.

The translation is:

"Disciples of Tárrega

Now that the virtuoso Llobet makes our public vibrate with the magic of his guitar sorcery; now that Maria Luisa Anido moves us more than with youth and her fragile and gracious beauty with the serenity of her art of miracles and dreams, we agree of a great national virtuoso that lives among us his modesty and his art, owner also of a guitar sorcery and that is called Pedro Mascaro y Reissig.

We remember of him, that it isn't being ours that we have to deny his temperament and his technique; we are reminded of him, who admires Llobet and tries to imitate him; we are reminded by him of what is good and simple and humble, such as humble, simple and good were the greats.

Basilio Vizcau."

Here Maria Luisa Anido performs two of Miguel Llobet's most well known Catalan Folksongs.

All of the songs performed at this concert are transcriptions for guitar by Miguel Llobet.

Translation of *"Notas Varias"* from *Revista Musical Ilustrada "Tárrega"* magazine No. 12 of June 1925.

"Various Notes from Montevideo

Our correspondent in that city communicates to us, the success achieved in the three concerts that took place in the Teatro Solis by the notable Miguel Llobet.

The telegram received says in this way: "The concert guitarist Llobet gave three guitar concerts in the Teatro Solis. For some moments it was believed the public wouldn't leave the theater.

The great enthusiasm to hear him again reigned. According to notices he will make a tour again."

NOTAS VARIAS

DE MONTEVIDEO

Nos comunica nuestro corresponsal en esa, el éxito alcanzado en los tres conciertos realizados en el teatro Solís por el notable Miguel Llobet.

El telegrama recibido dice así: "El concertista Llobet realizó tres conciertos de guitarra teatro Solís. Por momenos se creyó público no abandonaría teatro.

Reina gran entusiasmo oírlo nuevamente. Según noticias realizará gira nuevamente."

Translation of "Llobet-Anido" by Carlos J. Vega from *Revista Musical Ilustrada "Tárrega"* magazine No. 12 of June 1925.

"Llobet-Anido

The modern combination of two guitars gives an absolutely new result as an effect and extraordinary as a sensation of art. Such has been able to appreciate in the recitals that, with the collaboration of Miss Anido, *Don* Miguel Llobet, author of the versions has just offered. In the history of the instrument it corresponds, since, the Spanish maestro the most important of all to pass of all the epochs. It hasn't been created, in an absolute sense. In whatever popular reunion that they have sounded and two guitars sang and in the ambiance of the great culture, they have written and transcribed works with the best intention that resulted. Sor himself, left various beautiful pages for two guitars, but the epoch — the 18th century — didn't demand but the fundamental melody of always, faithful escort of sixths and thirds and short horizontal movements, with all which, the instrument of the color by excellence was employed and demanded of mediums, although in the harmonization for two.

Then and afterward, with serious artistic pretension, they have followed trying two guitars without great advantage. The procedure to give to the second guitar already the accompaniment on chords or arpeggios, now one third of the melody with equal bass or of the chord — in the original works; the recourse to transcribe the piano surrendering to each guitar the part reserved to each hand, and other habitual manners, doesn't give the duet the great artistic efficacy.

Tárrega gave the first great step in this sense. The guitars begin to be required and the result is fruitful in beauty and color. *"La Hilandera"* by Mendelssohn, seen and transcribed by Tárrega, it constitutes the most important work of that time, the lively chromatic movement of the left hand achieves on the guitar a beautiful and notable effect.

However, more could be done in every way and has now become.

Miguel Llobet, the great colorist of the popular Catalan melodies, has the responsibility of all the hopes put in his talent and has known imposed, of such an unexpected manner as splendid, endowing to the guitaristic literature of a handful of masterful duos.

Who hasn't attended the recent performances of these works, has a certain right to suppose that two guitars duplicate simply the efficacy of one alone, and that is an error: the twelve strings, treated with the consummate art of Llobet, surpasses all the minor combinations of instruments, achieving, many times, the expressive vigor of the quartet.

The guitars even have over this the advantage of some elements of the orchestra (Percussion, Horns, etc. in a small one) separately of their characteristic timbres, but it isn't necessary to search similarities; now we have said that the modern combination of two guitars gives an absolutely new result.

The principal obstacle for the performance of the duos has to rest on always in the difficulty of uniting two performers of first class, but reckoning maestro Llobet with the collaboration of Maria Luisa Anido, has been finally to offer to the public of Buenos Aires the fruit of a labor that increases considerably its hundred times consecrated artistic personality.

A *Minueto* by Mozart, two pages by Bizet, two *Romanzas* by Mendelssohn and the *Danza Hungara No. 5* by Brahms are all duets of exquisite taste and beautiful realization, which, yet, doesn't offer more news from the historical point of view. But there is more, much more: *"La Hilandera"* by Mendelssohn (Tárrega-Llobet), the *Danza No. 11* by Granados, the *"Evocacion"* by Albeniz, the *"Danza del Molinero"*, *"Cubana"* and the *"Danza Ritual del Fuego"* by De Falla.

As can be said of these marvelous versions is insufficient; the reality is superior to all prejudice, and all opinion. *"La Hilandera", "Evocacion"* and the *"Danza Ritual"* will never find any instrumentation that surpasses the expressive exaltation and the splendid coloring of these two compelling guitars, required to the exhaustion by four masterful hands, the most extraordinary that have ever existed.

Llobet has known to understand and take advantage of the talent and the technique of Maria Luisa Anido, imposing her with decisive authority before the public who acclaim her from several years ago without suspecting — save exceptions — the true magnitude of this figure of privilege."

Translation of "Llobet-Anido" by Carlos J. Vega from *Revista Musical Ilustrada "Tárrega"* magazine No. 13 of July 1925.

"Llobet-Anido

Don Miguel Llobet and his disciple Maria Luisa Anido, the 15th and the 18th gave their latest concerts in the Odeon.

The magazine "Tárrega" has already dealt with some of the extension that such eminent artists deserve, a reason for which only it is possible to add that in both performances they confirm their previous successes, conquering the approval of the public and the dailies' critics.

They finished their commitments in this capital, both guitarists begin a tour of the provinces."

Translation of *"Los Conciertos Llobet-Anido"* from *Revista Musical Ilustrada "Tárrega"* magazine No. 17 of November 1925.

"The Llobet-Anido Concerts

When we pose the bases of action of this magazine, we have — and we continue having — among other fine concerts and of course, those that sustain the norm of artistic nationalism, not precisely as a secondary mobile being cloistered in a closed and sterile localism, but as a breath of necessary renovation in our cultural activities. The musical ambiance, in effect is now found sufficiently prepared for the arrival of our new and effective values, as referred to musical events, from there that we may have seen emerge brilliant figures of composers that have exceeded the horizons of the country with the group so vigorous, serious and systematized, that has imposed to the consideration of the greatest European and South American mentalities.

Buenos Aires, today, constitutes one of the great musical centers, not only by the admirable under-standing of its listeners, but also by the excellence of the national production. To prove this affirmation it suffices to catalog all the series of works of unquestionable merit, that the artistic season of the year in course just left us, many of which have been opportunely marked in the pages of our magazine. On the other hand, they have been the skill to constitute in the authorized interpreters of Argentine works, with a success that brings involved at once the flattering breath for our composers and a plausible act of admiration for the Argentine public.

This necessary antecedent sitting, we are going to refer to the more climactic happening of the year in respect to guitar performances.

With the three latest concerts, two of them celebrated in the Salon "La Argentina", and one in the Asociacion Wagneriana, Mr. Miguel Llobet and Miss Maria Luisa Anido have ended their artistic season.

We have waited for the termination of this cycle of guitaristic performances, for making an analytical study of the corresponding programs to the verified concerts; granted the artistic value of the works, we concern ourselves with the variety and quantity of the works that were utilized for giving such a long series of concerts.

The programs belong to the thirteen latest performances, to the exception of two, are found in our table of work.

We give a summary of the eleven latest concerts, which indicates the times that the same work has been performed:

MENDELSSOHN

Romanza sin palabras	11
La Hilandera	8

GRANADOS

Danza N° 6	8
Danza N° 11	7

FALLA

Danza Ritual del Fuego	7
Danza del Molinero	4
Cubana	4

ALBENIZ

Evocación	6

DAQUIN

Le Coucou	6

BIZET

Minuetto	6
L'Arlesienne	2

MOZART

Minuetto	5

BRAHMS

Danza Húngara	5

TORRES

Berceuse	3

TSCHAIKOWSKY

Humoreske	1

As you can observe, the repertoire is reduced — numerically — for giving the fulfillment of so many concerts, without making abuse of the repetition of some of the works. This circumstance has been by which their latest performances, don't awaken great interest. The fact behaves, from then, a utile lesson for the future.

Mr. Llobet — those are impressions picked up in the guitarristic ambiance — he hasn't felt the desire of flattery to our public; in this way he shows the lamentable error of not having included in his programs works of the national character, which there are and very good, with the addition of that very good could have been replaced, with advantage, to some of those that take place in his repertory. Enough for that, the adaptation of a National Merit to fulfill a legitimate duty of courtesy.

In this opportunity we must remember the pleasant assumed attitude by the concert guitarists; Joséfina Robledo and Andrés Segovia, who transcribed several pages of the late maestro Julián Aguirre, performing some of them, in their performances.

Maestros of world renown, such as: Strauss, Weingartner, Rissler, Ansermet, etc. etc., include in their respective programs music of Argentine composers, which, by their artistic value and by the interpretation that the said maestros knew to give in different opportunities, the critics and the public valued it, with the most ample approval.

This attitude, which honors the maestros mentioned, giving at once a capacity of amplitude, shows that the music, as all the arts, can't have in a field of action closed to the scarce limits of an exclusive trend.

We constitute a populace with incessant impulses of renovation; by the same we must take them into account when the cultural demonstrations are of whatever kind. To not do this in this way, on the part of the maestros that visit us, will only appear as an act of discourtesy, but also an unforgivable oversight, that we mustn't accept by many that might be the merits of the performers that condemn us in a reiterated oversight. We can't therefore pass over in silence the note clearly ungrateful that leaves the maestro Llobet, for whom, given his ample knowledge of our ambiance, in reiterated visits that has made us, can't be unknown now to the enormous cauldron of worthy national compositions transcribed. And our strangeness arises to a point if we consider the compatriot of such ample spirit of understanding such as Miss Anido, has been complicit in this unjustified oversight.

Maestro Llobet also knows that in our capital there is a pleyade of guitar performers, many of those can be submitted to a justified comparison with the greatest world figures of the present. Our musical repertoire is, vast and interesting, able by itself to rejuvenate the somewhat archaic legacy and heavy of many pages of the old time, and consequently, by interest and yet provoking great emotions in its audience. Nothing then justifies that Olympian disdain with which the maestro Llobet has wanted, ignoring local production."

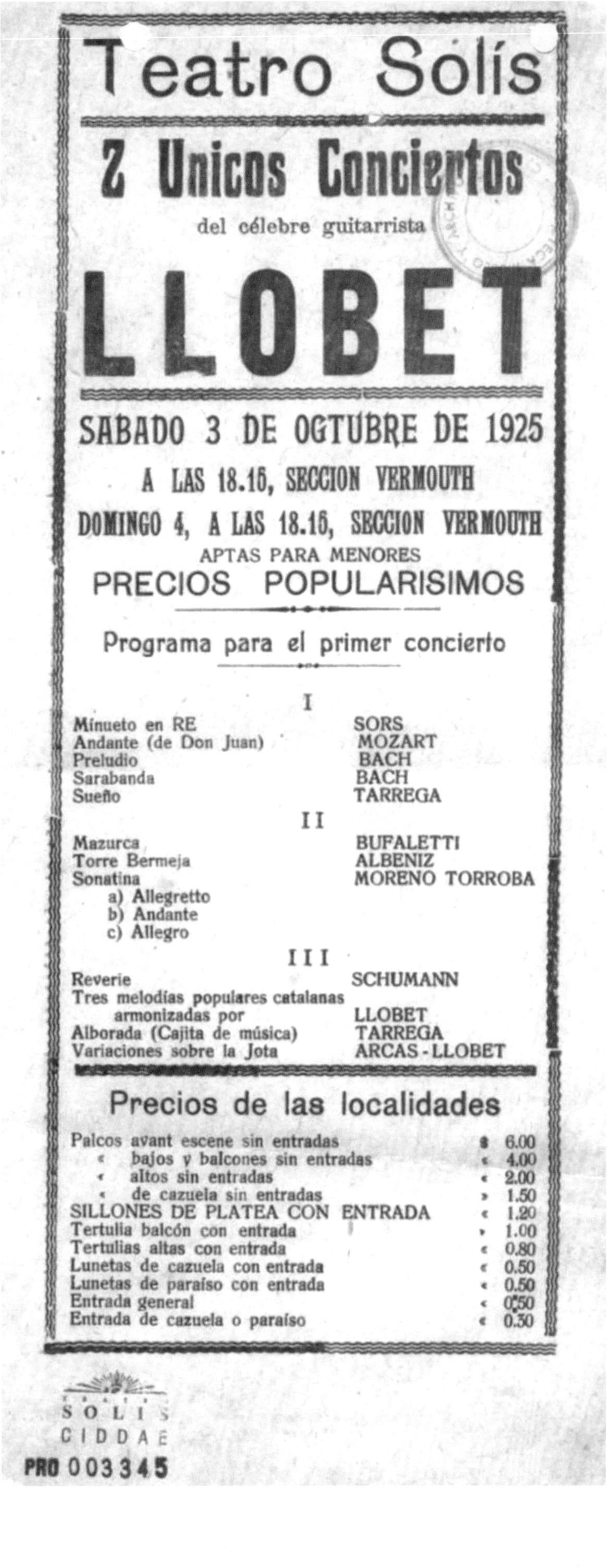

Teatro Solís

Z Unicos Conciertos

del célebre guitarrista

LLOBET

SABADO 3 DE OCTUBRE DE 1925

A LAS 18.15, SECCION VERMOUTH

DOMINGO 4, A LAS 18.15, SECCION VERMOUTH

APTAS PARA MENORES

PRECIOS POPULARISIMOS

Programa para el primer concierto

I

Mínueto en RE	SORS
Andante (de Don Juan)	MOZART
Preludio	BACH
Sarabanda	BACH
Sueño	TARREGA

II

Mazurca	BUFALETTI
Torre Bermeja	ALBENIZ
Sonatina	MORENO TORROBA
a) Allegretto	
b) Andante	
c) Allegro	

III

Reverie	SCHUMANN
Tres melodías populares catalanas armonizadas por	LLOBET
Alborada (Cajita de música)	TARREGA
Variaciones sobre la Jota	ARCAS - LLOBET

Precios de las localidades

Palcos avant escene sin entradas	$	6.00
« bajos y balcones sin entradas	«	4.00
« altos sin entradas	«	2.00
« de cazuela sin entradas	»	1.50
SILLONES DE PLATEA CON ENTRADA	«	1.20
Tertulia balcón con entrada	»	1.00
Tertulias altas con entrada	«	0.80
Lunetas de cazuela con entrada	«	0.50
Lunetas de paraíso con entrada	«	0.50
Entrada general	«	0.50
Entrada de cazuela o paraíso	«	0.30

SOLIS
CIDDAE
PRO 003345

It's is interesting to note that as many times as Miguel llobet performed *"Sueño"* by Francisco Tárrega in Montevideo, he did not play *"Recuerdos de la Alhambra"*.

447

MIGVEL LLOBET

This photo is from the *Caras y Caretas* magazine of September 5, 1925 issue No. 1405 *Año* XXVIII. It was colorized. Translation of the text on the following page.

"Miguel Llobet

In Barcelona, where he was born, he began to play the guitar without a maestro at the age of nine years old. Powerfully attracted by the instrument, he drew the attention of maestro Magin Alegre, who was to be the first to orient him in his artistic steps. Later, as a disciple of Tárrega, he initiated in his school, perfecting his skill rapidly. At the age of sixteen he gave his first concert in public, in the Instituto Musical Rodoreda, in Barcelona, obtaining a marked success. Becoming independent of his family, he began his first true activities as a concert artist in 1900, being presented in the Conservatorio de Valencia in 1901. From there, to Madrid, and afterward, to all the principal cities of Spain. He wanted to be heard by the King of Spain, for whom he played before in the Royal Palace, being lively congratulated. He abandoned Spain to live in Paris, in the year 1904. For ten years he lived in Ville-Lumiére, making short trips outside the country to give concerts. In 1910 he came for the first time to Buenos Aires; he returned in 1918 (sic-1912) and three years ago he distinguished the porteño public as one of its preferred concert guitarists. In this latest performance he initiated the concerts of two guitars with Maria Luisa Anido, obtaining performances of an elevated artistic value. In most of the concerts they gave a guitar almost a century old was used, fabricated by Antonio de Torres, the Stradivarius of the guitar. Sor, the classic, Tárrega, modern, are their preferred authors. Miguel Llobet, the exquisite artist of sensibility and of surprising technique, is the true magician of the guitar, the instrument of the nostalgic nocturnes and the joy of the sun.

In this way he says:

'To the celebrated *Caras y Caretas* magazine,

With all my admiration for the great work of dissemination of all order of ideas that are proposed.

Signed, M. Llobet."

ARTE · NACIONAL

MARIA · LVISA · ANIDO

DISCIPULA PREDILECTA

DE

· LLOBET ·

M

ENUDITA como una musmé, sonriente, me ofrece una mano que al estrecharla parece cartilaginosa.

— CARAS Y CARETAS — le expreso — quiere que usted le diga algo que no sepa el público.

— ¿Algo que no sepa el público? ¿Le diré cómo empecé a estudiar la guitarra?

— Sí, eso interesa.

— Estudiaba yo violín y piano. Según mis maestros, ejecutaba yo con mecanismo sorprendente. Coincidió con un luto de familia mi inclinación por la guitarra: el piano y el violín nos parecían instrumentos que no servían para guardar una buena memoria a los difuntos. Y un día mi padre, gran aficionado a la guitarra, mientras yo estaba enferma con escarlatina, me llevó una a mi cama para que así me distrajera.

This interview is from the *Caras y Caretas* magazine of July 4, 1925 issue No. 1396, *Año* XXVIII.

Fué tal la afición que me despertó, que a los nueve años daba mi primera audición pública, y a los once, mi primer concierto. Lo demás, lo dirá el público. . .

En la sala en que hablamos, una estufa deja pasar una luz roja. María Luisa Anido se frota las manos al resplandor de la llama. Sus ojos vivaces, al evocar el encanto de su precocidad, se hacen más brillantes.

—¿Así es que usted debe su vocación por la guitarra a la escarlatina?

—Ciertamente. Más que todo, a mi padre, un verdadero entusiasta de la música, y mi primer maestro.

—¿Y su emoción artística más intensa, será, sin duda alguna, la primera vez que se presentó en público en su concierto inicial?

—No sabría decirle con toda propiedad. Pero le aseguro que mi mayor emoción la he recibido cuando me he presentado con mi maestro Llobet tocando en dúo. ¡Eso es muy grande para una artista! Llobet es el hombre-cumbre de la guitarra. El ha superado a todos y ha abierto nuevos rumbos a la guitarra... Tárrega, el maestro, fué un creador; Llobet, el artista más completo del mundo, es un renovador. No hay palabra lo suficientemente grande y hermosa para elogiar el arte que sabe encantar el genial artista. ¿Cree, acaso, que no es emoción muy grande el tocar con él, y gran honor para una artista argentina?

—¿Hay ambiente en Buenos Aires para la guitarra?

—Mucho. Y una cosa curiosa: también hay y mucho en Alemania. En la Argentina y este último país hay más entusiasmo que en España misma. Es, a mi manera de ver, el más delicado y expresivo de los instrumentos, ya que cada cuerda es una orquesta. Y éste es el mérito de Llobet: ha sumado todas esas armonías y ha hecho con ellas ese conjunto maravilloso con que llega al público. Es hondo, sincero, sentimental, fuerte, humano. Es todo lo que quiere ser.

—¿Usted ha viajado fuera del país?

—No siendo a Montevideo, no conozco otra ciudad del exterior. Mis deseos serían viajar siempre, y estos deseos se han de cumplir, pues pienso recorrer Europa en unión de mi maestro Llobet. Conozco el interior de mi país y en él he podido apreciar que hay entusiasmo por la guitarra.

—¿Es cierto que la guitarra que usted tiene perteneció a Tárrega?

—Es muy cierto. Fué la predilecta del maestro. Estaba destinada al Museo Histórico de Madrid, y la viuda del maestro prefirió cedérmela a mí. Se trata de un rico instrumento y a quien se tiene por el de mejores voces que existe. Está construído por Antonio de Torres—el Stradivario de la guitarra — en el año 1863. Es decir, que es un poco mayor que yo...

—Sí, unos meses apenas...

—Tengo ahora dieciocho años. María Luisa trae la reliquia.

—Mire—me dice conmovida;—estas manchas son gloriosas: en ellas está el alma maravillosa de Tárrega, el alma que él ponía en sus ejecuciones...

Le pido que toque. Vuelve a llevar sus manos a la estufa. Son sus manos como dos lirios que se acercan a las llamas. Toca «El testament d'Amelia», armonizado por Miguel Llobet. Las cuerdas parecen hablar y expresar el sentimiento de quien las agita. Hay una fina sensibilidad artística en lo que toca. Vibran limpias y parecen traducir el poder de un gran sentimiento.

Luego toca «La Serenata Española», de Albéniz. Y ya esto no es una serenata: un admirable estilo de ejecutante, una sensibilidad maravillosa, una intérprete insuperable, y la serenata es una fantasía que parece surgir de una cosa inmaterial... La frase musical se aclara y se puede leer en la vibración de las cuerdas la emotividad de la eximia artista.

María Luisa Anido, ayer precoz artista—tuvo por maestros a Domingo Prat, a Josefina Robledo y al más grande artista actual de guitarra, Llobet—que a los nueve años ofrece una audición en donde el público de Buenos Aires le tributa una calurosa manifestación de simpatía; que a los once años se presenta en su primer concierto interpretando a Sors, Tárrega, Damas, Llobet, Schumann, Beethoven, Massenet, Chopín, Mendelssohn, y que en la actualidad es una virtuosa que se coloca al lado de Llobet, es una de las primeras figuras femeninas de la guitarra, como lo han testimoniado grandes maestros. Ha hecho transcripciones excelentes.

María Luisa Anido es aún niña y posee un rico temperamento artístico.

—Yo soy haragana—me dice para despedirme.—Yo soy como mi maestro Llobet. ¿Sabe usted lo que hacía Llobet cuando íbamos de viaje? Cuando mediaban unos tres días de un concierto a otro, se cortaba las uñas para así no tener que ensayar... Eso mismo hago yo, aunque no me corte las uñas... Esta es la gran guitarrista argentina que hoy tiene apenas dieciocho años...

A la prestigiosa y popular revista "Caras y Caretas", con todo el afecto de una lectora asidua —

María Luisa Anido

M.   GARCÍA   HERNÁNDEZ

This interview is from the *Caras y Caretas* magazine of July 4, 1925 issue No. 1396, *Año* XXVIII. The translation of this and the previous page begin on the next page.

Translation of the interview of Maria Luisa Anido by M. García Hernández from the *Caras y Caretas* magazine of July 4, 1925 issue No. 1396, *Año* XXVIII:

"Art-National

Maria Luisa Anido-the favorite disciple of Llobet

Petite like a daughter, smiling she offered me her hand which appeared cartilaginous.

M. García Hernández — He expressed — would you like to say something that the public hasn't found out?

Maria Luisa Anido — Something that the public doesn't know? To tell you how I began to study the guitar?

M. García Hernández —Yes, that's interesting.

Maria Luisa Anido — I had studied the violin and the piano. Following my maestros, I performed with surprising mechanism. Coinciding with a mourning of the family was my inclination for the guitar; the piano and the violin appear to us as instruments that don't serve for keeping a good memory of the dead. And one day my father, great aficionado of the guitar, while I was sick with scarlet fever, brought me one to my bed so as to amuse myself. It was such a fondness that awakened in me, that at nine years old I gave my first public performance, and at eleven years of age my first concert. The rest, I will tell the public. . .

M. García Hernández — In the room where we are talking, there is a stove that gives off a red light. Maria Luisa Anido is rubbing her hands to the glow of the flames. Her eyes lively, to evoke the enchantment of her precocity, they make it even brighter.

M. García Hernández — So you would attribute your vocation for the guitar to scarlet fever?

Maria Luisa Anido — Certainly, overall, to my father, a true musical enthusiast, and my first maestro.

M. García Hernández — And your artistic emotion more intense, will be, without a doubt, the first time you performed in public in your initial concert?

Maria Luisa Anido — I wouldn't know how to tell you with all propriety. But I can assure you that my greatest emotion that I have received was when I had been presented with my maestro Llobet playing in a duet. That is very great for an artist! Llobet is the top-man of the guitar. He has surpassed everyone and has opened new directions to the guitar. . . Tárrega, the maestro, was a creator; Llobet, the most complete artist in the world, is a renovator. There isn't a great or beautiful word sufficient to eulogize the art that one knows to enchant the most excellent artist. Do you believe, perhaps, it isn't a very great emotion to play with him, and a great honor as an Argentine artist?

M. García Hernández — Is there an environment in Buenos Aires for the guitar?

Maria Luisa Anido — Very much so. And a very curious thing; as well there is and quite a bit in Germany. In Argentina and in the last country there is more enthusiasm than in Spain itself. It is, in my way of seeing, the most delicate and expressive of the instruments, since every string is an orchestra And that is the merit of Llobet; as he added all these harmonies and has done with them this marvelous grouping brought before the public. He is deep, sincere, sentimental, strong and human. He is everything you want him to be.

M. García Hernández — Have you traveled outside of the country?

452

Maria Luisa Anido — No, being to Montevideo, I don't know another city outside the country. My desires would be to always travel, and those desires will be completed, since I think about touring Europe together with my maestro Llobet. I know the interior of the country and in it I have been able to appreciate the enthusiasm for the guitar.

M. García Hernández — Is it certain that the guitar you have belonged to Tárrega?

Maria Luisa Anido — It is very certain. It was the favorite of the maestro. It was destined to go to the Museo Historico de Madrid, and the widow of the maestro preferred to grant it to me. It has to deal with a rich instrument to which it has the best voices that exist. It's constructed by Antonio de Torres-the Stradivarius of the guitar-in the year 1863 (sic-1864). That is to say, it is a little bit older than I am.

M. García Hernández — Yes, scarcely a few months more. . .

Maria Luisa Anido — I'm eighteen years old now.

M. García Hernández — Maria brings the relic.

Maria Luisa Anido — Look-she tells me disturbingly these marks are glorious: in there is the marvelous soul of Tárrega, the soul that he was putting in his performances. . .

M. García Hernández-I asked her to play. She repeated the warming of her hands over the stove. Her hands are like two lilies that get close to the flames. She plays: *"El testament d'Amelia"* harmonized by Miguel Llobet. The strings appear to speak and express a sentiment of whom is agitating them. There is a fine artistic sensibility in what she plays. They vibrate clearly and appear to translate the power of a great sentiment.

Then she played *"La Serenata Española"* (Cadiz) of Albeniz. And already it isn't a serenata: an admirable style of execution, a marvelous sensibility, an unsurpassable interpreter, and the serenata is a fantasia appears to emerge from an immaterial thing. . . The musical phrase becomes clear and it can be read in the emotivity of the most excellent artist in the vibration of the strings.

Maria Luisa Anido, yesterday the precocious artist, had maestros Domingo Prat, Joséfina Robledo and the greatest artist of the guitar presently, Llobet — that at nine years of age she gave a performance in where the public of Buenos Aires in tribute responded with a very warm manifestation of sympathy; that at eleven years old she presented in her first concert interpreting Sors, Tárrega, Damas, Llobet, Schumann, Beethoven, Massenet, Chopin, Mendelssohn, and that in the present she is a virtuoso placed at the side of Llobet, she is of the first rank feminine figures of the guitar, like the maestros have given testimony to. She has done excellent transcriptions.

Maria Luisa Anido is still a young girl and possesses a rich artistic temperament.

Maria Luisa Anido — I'm lazy—she says to me to say goodbye—I'm like my maestro Llobet. Do you know what Llobet did when we went on a trip? When three days mediated from one concert to the next, he'd cut off his fingernails so he wouldn't have to practice. . . I do the same, although I don't cut my nails. . .

M. García Hernández — That is the great Argentine artist who today is scarcely eighteen years old."

The dedication below the photo on the second page is translated:

"To the prestigious and popular magazine *"Cara y Caretas"* with all the affection from an assiduous reader," (Signed) Maria Luisa Anido.

(Above) Maria Luisa Anido and Miguel Llobet
at the Salon "La Argentina" on June 12, 1925.
From: *Revista Musical Ilustrada "Tárrega"*
issue No. 12 of June 1925.

(Top Right) Newspaper account of an upcoming Miguel Llobet concert on May 3, 1929. He had arrived in Buenos Aires on April 11, 1929, and this was his first concert of his last tour in Argentina. Translation on the next page.
Archive: Eduardo Bensadon

(Bottom Right) From the newspaper *"La Prensa"*, announcement of a concert to be given by Miguel Llobet and Maria Luisa Anido on Wednesday August 21, 1929 at the Teatro Odeon
Translation on 2 pages forth.

Translation of the newspaper account of an upcoming Miguel Llobet concert on May 3, 1929:

"Hoy se presentara en el Cervantes el guitarrista Miguel Llobet."

"Today in the Cervantes theater the guitarist Miguel Llobet will be presented."

"Today, at 5:30 in the Cervantes, the celebrated Miguel Llobet, one of the favorite artists of our public and the most talented initiator of the renaissance of the art of the guitar, will be presented before our public.

The program is the followings:

Minuetto en si bemol, Sor

Andante (*Don* Giovanni), Mozart

Sarabanda en si menor, Bach

Estudio en mi menor, Sor

Estudio en mi mayor, Sor

Serenata, Samazeuilh

Cancion leonesa, R. Villar

Evocaciones criollas, Alfonso Broqua
a) Vidala
b) Ecos del pasaje
c) Ritmos camperos

Romanza, Rubinstein

Betsabé, Carlos Pedrell

Dos melodias catalanas, harmonized by Llobet
a) La filla del marxant
b) El mestre

Danza Española, Granados"

To the right is a photo of Miguel Llobet's study room in the home of Juan Carlos Anido. It is a photo from a Buenos Aires daily and was a part of the archive of Ricardo Muñoz.

Translation of: *"Musica-Maria Luisa Anido y Miguel Llobet iniciaran hoy en el Odeon sus conciertos a dos guitarras."* from the newspaper *"La Prensa"*, of Wednesday August 21, 1929 in Buenos Aires.

"Music-Today Maria Luisa Anido and Miguel Llobet initiate their concerts for two guitars in the Teatro Odeon.

Today at 5:45 in the Odeon the young Argentine concert guitarist Maria Luisa Anido and the celebrated Spanish concert guitarist Miguel Llobet will initiate a cycle of concerts for two guitars, an ensemble of prestigious artists that will play numerous arrangements for two instruments.

The program is the following:

Solo Guitar — Miguel Llobet

Preludio, Sor

Don Juan (Andante), Mozart

Sarabanda, Bach

Ecos del pasaje (from Evocaciones criollas), A. Broqua

Danza Española, Granados

　　Two Guitars — Maria Luisa Anido and Miguel Llobet

Romanza en sol, Mendelssohn

L'Arlesiénne, Bizet

a) Minuetto, Daquin
b) Melodia; Le Coucous, Daquin

Huella, J. Aguirre

　　Two Guitars — Maria Luisa Anido and Miguel Llobet

Leyenda del castillo moro, E. L. Chavarri

Sous le Palmier, Albeniz

Evocacion, Albeniz

El amor brujo, M. de Falla
a) Pantomima
b) Danza ritual del fuego"

From an image 2 pages previously.

456

Program cover of the Miguel Llobet and Maria Luisa Anido concert on Sunday October, 16, 1929 at the Centre Catala (Catalan Center) in Buenos Aires. The program is printed in the Catalan language. Linguists will immediately see the likeness and difference of Catalan and Castellano (Spanish).

MIQUEL LLOBET

En Llobet és l'artista més eximi de la guitarra, avui dia, per la pregonesa, la seriositat i la sobrietat del seu art, d'aquest excels art guitarrístic que, lluny de tota flamenqueria plebea, ha assolit a Catalunya una tradició enlairada, on figuren Sors, el clàssic per excel.lencia, l'anomenat Beethoven de la guitarra, Tárrega, qui, encara que signi fill de Villareal pot dir.se català per la seva llarga actuació a Barcelona i per l'escola magnífica que va deixar-hi, Emili Pujol i Miquel Llobet, ambdós deixebles de Tárrega, etc.

Llobet, que ha visitat l'Argentina, abans d'ara, els anys 1910, 1918, 1922 i 1925, és prou conegut aquí com a tots els paisos amants de la bona música, i encara potser més estimat que en cap altre per les llargues estades que hi ha fet i que l'han permés popularitzar el seu art per totes les comarques de la República, i sobretot per l'eficácia de la seva tasca docent, de la qual n'és una bella prova la seva deixebla predilecta, senyoreta Maria Lluisa Anido.

En invitar, doncs, a Miquel Llobet a donar una audició dedicada als seus conterranis, en el nostre estatge social, el CENTRE CATALÁ está segur d'haver proporcionat als socis una de las més intenses fruicions estétiques. Fem-ne regraciament al genial intérpret.

MARIA LLUISA ANIDO

Els seus mereixements la posen en primer lloc entre les guitarristes de l'Argentina, la seva pátria. Deixebla, des de la seva adolescencia, de Mestre Llobet, ha copsat de tal faisó els seus ensenyaments i la seva musicalitat, que aquell l'ha considerada prou excel.lent per a interpretar junt amb ell les transcripcions a dues guitarres, que són l'obra més remarcable de Llobet com a music i obren un nou horitzó a la literatura guitarrística.

De la maestría d'execució i d'expressió que assoleix el duo de guitarres Llobet-Anido ens n'ofereixen també avui una magnífica mostra, cosa que deven agrair coralment a la gentil concertista argentina.

Translation by Randy Osborne of the Catalan language text of the biographies of Miguel Llobet and Maria Luisa Anido from the concert program for the Centre Catala event held on Sunday October, 16, 1929. In the Catalan language his name is spelled *"Miquel"*.

"Miguel Llobet:

Llobet is the most excellent artist of the guitar, today, by the proclamation, the seriousness and sobriety of his art, that excels the guitaristic art, far away from the flamenco populace, he has succeeded in Cataluña to link a tradition, one figure Sor, the classic by excellence, that was named the Beethoven of the Guitar, Tárrega, whom, that points the sign to the son of Villareal but can be said to be a Catalan because of his long performance in Barcelona and by the magnificent school he left here, Emilio Pujol and Miguel Llobet, both disciples of Tárrega, etc.

Llobet, that has visited Argentina, before now, in the years 1910, 1918, 1922 and 1925, is well known here as by all the local lovers of good music, and points to be perhaps the most esteemed that in another case by his long stays that he has made here and that it has permitted the popularization of his art in all the counties of the Republic, over all by the effectiveness of the knowledgeable teaching, of which there isn't a more beautiful proof than the favorite disciple, Miss Maria Luisa Anido.

One invites, therefore, Miguel Llobet to give a performance dedicated to his compatriots, in our social habitation, the Centre Catala is sure to have proportioned to its society one of the most intense fruitful esthetics. To the endowed interpreter we give our thanks.

Maria Luisa Anido

Her merits have placed her in the first rank among the guitarists of Argentina, her own country. A disciple, since her adolescence, of Miguel Llobet, she has understood such work as his teachings and knowledgeable musicality, that was soon considered excellent by the interpreter together with the transcriptions for two guitars, that are the most remarkable work with music by Llobet, and their work is a new horizon for the guitaristic literature.

Of the mastery to execute and express what the duo of guitars Llobet-Anido succeeds in is that they offer also a magnificent demonstration to us, a thing that they must cordially thank the gracious Argentine concert guitarist."

LI	PARLOPHON
LL	
Llévatelo todo (R. Sciamarella). Tango.	B 25.375
La última copa (J. A. Caruso y F. Canaro). Tango. *Cantor, Juan B. Giliberti y Orquesta Argentina.*	Azul 25 c.
LLOBET, MIGUEL. Guitarrista.	
Andantino (Sor). Estudio (Sor).	B 25.766 Morado 25 c.
El testament d'Amèlia (Llobet). El mestre (Llobet).	B 25.767 Morado 25 c.
Estudio brillante (Coste . Estilo popular criollo.	B 25.768 Morado 25 c.
La filla del marxant (Llobet). Plany (Llobet).	B 25.769 Morado 25 c.
Zarabanda (Bach). Transcripción Llobet. Dos canciones mejicanas (Ponce).	B 25.775 Morado 25 c.
Canción popular leonesa (Villar). Minuetto (Sor).	B 25.778 Morado 25 c.

This is from the *"Catalogo General hasta Agosto 1930 Parlophon El Disco Sonoro"*. This August 1930 catalog lists 12 pieces by Miguel Llobet, showing pieces recorded in 1925 were still in print.

PROGRAMA

I PART

MIQUEL LLOBET

Andantino	*Sors*
Estudi	*Sors*
Andante	*Mozart*
Leonesa	*R. Villar*
Dansa	*Granados*

II PART

MIQUEL LLOBET

Cançó mexicana	*Ponce*
Cançó del foc follet	*M, de Falla*
Tres melodies catalanes armonitza-des per	*M. Llobet*

  a) El mestre.
  b) El testament ð'Amèlia.
  c) La filla ðel marxant.

Variacions sobre la jota .... *M. Llobet*

III PART

MIQUEL LLOBET I MARIA LLUISA ANIDO

Minuet de *L'Arlesienne*	*Bizet*
Huella	*J. Aguirre*
Dansa VI	*Granados*
El cu-cut	*Daquin*
Evocació (de la suite *Iberia*)	*Albéniz*
Dansa ritual del foc (de *El amor brujo*).	*M. de Falla*

NO ES PERMETRÁ L'ENTRADA AL SALÓ DURANT L'EXECUCIÓ DE LES OBRES.

ES PREGA LA PUNTUALITAT

Program titles of the October 16, 1929 Miguel Llobet and Maria Luisa Anido concert. The variety of works stem from European 18th century pieces to modern European and Latin American selections, including pieces especially written for the guitar. (Below the titles in the Catalan language it says: "No one is permitted to enter the hall during the performances of the works. Punctuality is necessary.")

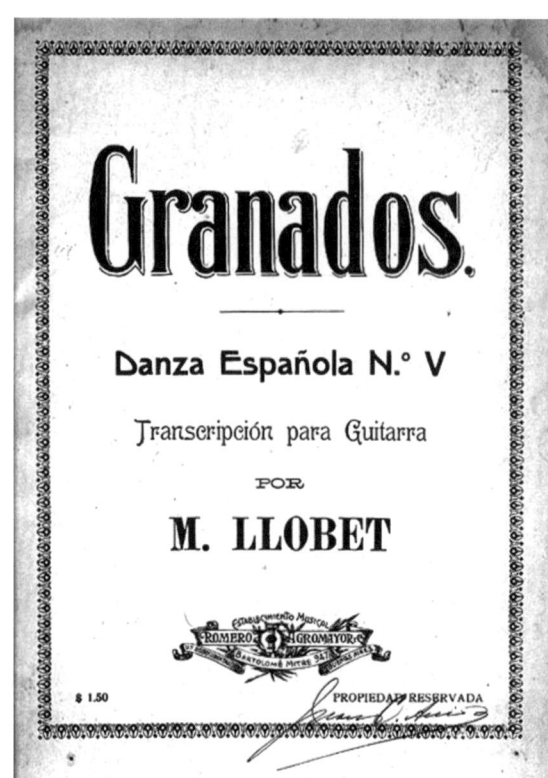

(Left) Daniel Fortea publication of Miguel Llobet in Madrid c. 1915.
(Right) Romero, Agromayor and Cia. publication autographed by Juan Carlos Anido c. 1918.

Miguel Llobet's protege Maria Luisa Anido performed duets with her maestro, and as well, learned to do very fine transcriptions. These pieces published by Romero & Fernández date from c. 1925.

(Left) Romero & Fernández publication.
(Right) Romero & Fernández publication of Tárrega and Llobet.

(Left) *Preludio* from the IV Cello Suite by J. S. Bach a Romero & Fernández publication of Llobet.
(Right) One of Miguel's most well-known transcriptions, a Celestino Fernández publication of Llobet.

Ricardo Muñoz said in his *"Historia de la Guitarra" t*hat Miguel performed on radio, as well as Andrés Segovia and Maria Luisa Anido.Here Miguel Llobet is in the studios of Radio Nacional in 1929. To the right of him is: Juan Carlos Anido.

This postcard was written and sent from Barcelona by Miguel Llobet to Pedro Mascaro y Reissig in Montevideo on August 27, 1930. The translation is on the following page.

From the Pedro Mascaro y Reissig 1917-1939 archive album, translation of the previous page:

"Postcard from Miguel Llobet thanking me for the dedication of my *Minuetto* to him."

Postcard:

"Barcelona, August 27, 1930.

Beloved friend,
A thousand pardons for my delay in writing to you (If you knew the things that I've done!!) but know that in spite of my long silence my affection and consideration for you hasn't lessened in the least. I also received your beautiful *"Minuetto"* (The one that I have already come to like) I thank you for the dedication. The Romero & Fernández music house of Buenos Aires has published my transcriptions of *"Torre Bermeja"* and *"Sevilla"* by Albeniz and *"La Maya de Goya"* by Granados. The last one with a slight error that I'm trying to correct."

Always your affectionate friend,
M. Llobet

On the front of the postcard on the edge:

"Have Pujol and his wife already been giving concerts in South America?"

I want to thank Alfredo Escande for providing the text of the postcard, I couldn't read the first sentence, and my colleague aided me in being able to complete the translation for the sake of the readers.

In the short lived 3 issue magazine *"A Voz do Violao"* (February to April 1931), published in Rio de Janeiro, edited by F. Acquarone, managed by S. Leal, administrated by B. Polazzi, was the issue No. 1 of February 1931, which in its *"Violao no Extrangeiro"* section (The Guitar Abroad), was a report about Miguel Llobet.

Portuguese translation by Randy Osborne:

"Miguel Llobet

The action of this eminent artist, during the past year, was developed in Europe. In London, overall, he conquered receiving hot applause, in recitals that he made in July in that city, by his unequaled technique and impeccable performance.

Playing on British Broadcasting, he had, in his concerts, sharing the radiowaves with the celebrated Spanish singer Carmen Anduvar, who was accompanied on piano by her husband, the brilliant composer Eduardo Chavarri."

This biographical material about Miguel Llobet is translated from Ricardo Muñoz's unpublished book *"Historia Universal de la Guitarra"* Volume IV *"Romanticos y Modernos"*

"His Origin:

He was born in Barcelona the 18th of October of 1878, coming from a family of artists, his father already was a sculptor *Don* Casimiro Llobet, established with a studio in the small square *"Regomir"* on la calle *"Ciutat",* where the slope of the *"Monte Taber"* began toward the ancient port. A brother of Miguel was also skilled in sculpture working along-side his father, living in this narrow apartment with attached romantic furniture and small windows. Later they moved to the wide street Layetana, modern and busy, with his mother *Doña* Joaquína Soler.

His Education:

His artistic culture began in his adolescence, when he studied drawing and painting in the Lonja, with maestro Torres Casana, arts which he profoundly felt making admirable progress; in local expositions various times he won obtaining compensation, these admirable anxieties were evident in his spirit, in the sketch that many years after he made with a pencil, not practicing the drawing, of the portrait of his student Maria Luisa Anido, made in the city of Rosario, in the year of 1922.

MARÍA LUISA ANIDO,
de un dibujo hecho del natural por Miguel Llobet

A sketch of Maria Luisa Anido by her maestro, Miguel Llobet, in Rosario, (Santa Fe Province) June 30, 1922. This appeared in the magazine *"La Guitarra"* issue No. 1 of July 1923. They had made a tour of the interior cities, performing duets to a very pleased audience, this sketch was done at that time. The translation of the caption is: Maria Luisa Anido, of a sketch done from life by Miguel Llobet.

In respect to his musical knowledge he studied the piano and violin. As to the guitar is concerned, the young Llobet had a relative who was the owner of a tavern near the wharf of Barcelona, where one day three Swedish sailors, were drinking abundantly, when it came time to pay the bill their pockets didn't respond to the amount to pay, so they left a guitar as an item to pawn. Those sailors left the Spanish port, perhaps to which they never returned, and it was with this guitar that Miguel Llobet began daily to play it, with true pleasure, until in 1889, when he heard his first serious performance on the instrument, played by maestro Antonio Jiménez Manjón.

It intensely impressed his fine sensibility, without abandoning his pictorial anxieties; he initiated the artistic guitar studies under the direction of maestro Magin Alegre, especially recommended by the common friend the *"Jaumet de las Coplas",* a singer and performer of the instrument.

Months later and being 14 years old, his maestro interpreting the outstanding artistic capacity of his disciple, resolved to speak in this respect with celebrated *Don* Francisco Tárrega, who he knew; he had heard him play in the guitar shop of Ribot y Alcaniz, since then this marvel of youth remained under his direction, by his own solicitation.

Llobet boldly studied, advancing, conquering the difficulties with a surprising nature, he performed in private and was admired. He entered into the "Escuela Municipal de Musica" of Barcelona, where his classmates were Maria Barrientos and Pablo Casals and as Director of the establishment the maestro Rodoreda, who finally arrived in Buenos Aires, where he died being a professor of a private Conservatorio.

Finishing his studies, Llobet traveled around the world working by his conviction and to get our daily bread every day, he wandered all of the continents, taking, as well inspired, fully confident in his future; he excited infinite nostalgias, he emptied out the sublime auditory chore of plucking his six beloved strings, he internalized and interpreted the soul of the populace which visited him breathing life into his spirit, he opened new breaches bursting prodigiously which scored radiant orientations in the emphatic amplitude of a new excellent oratory, whose physiognomy and grandeur, would have to delay, surely, the pen of the historian of the morning.

His thoughts, his ideals, his vision and his hope, constituted the forge in his breast of the determined forms in his intense guitaristic character, personal, dogmatic and perpetual, already by the muse of his melodies, by his romanticism or purified technique, whose line and profile, constitute a creative torrent of perfect modalities.

His Virtuosity:

His first concerts given in Barcelona enthused him acutely, given the triumph he obtained, motivating him to let go of the painting however the laurels he achieved with the same; in 1900 the aristocratic dame *Doña* Mrs. Concepcion Jacoby took the protege to Malaga, where he performed in the "Sociedad Filarmonica", with such success, which promoted him to being named *"Maestro Honorario"* of the same institution; he went to Valencia, and was heard on the hall of the Conservatorio and then went on to Madrid, being fervently applauded; he performed in the Circulo de Bella Artes, in the Ateneo and in the Teatro de la Comedia, where they lacked the seats that the public demanded. Finally, the maestro Tomas Breton, made his presentation in the Palacio Real, performing before the Spanish King and family.

With regard to these performances Rafael Mitjana wrote: "Miguel Llobet is now a true artistic Spanish glory. It is possible that he himself might not have full conscience of his merit, but that isn't important; the intelligent and the real musicians know how to appreciate him in what he is worth.... The Spanish guitar, today rich of six strings in the hands of this artist so skillful as Llobet, he produces marvelous effects. Of sweet and melodious sonority, his timbre highly pleasant, he is quick to express those tones of the sentiments. Laugh and cry, sing and sigh, and over all to howl of an equal manner. It might be said that between his habitual parades a graceful little soul that the plucking of the player awakens, obligating him thanks to the magic to conjure, to tell us mysterious histories and marvelous fantasies, that carry to the auditory another world more noble and elevated, making him forget the trivialities of life. Because the sound of the guitar played is of such a mode, it is highly suggestive and emotional."

"Miguel Llobet is very young, and to dominate such a difficult instrument, unites a solid musical education which permits him to work with knowledge of a cause such as consummate music. He performs compositions of the classic genre with real mastery, of those which constitute the best and most precious richness of such an important branch of the musical literature....."

"As to those who have heard him, they will have to admire his great talent and his exquisite sensibility. And the tell the truth, it causes happiness and satisfaction it is power to applaud without doubts to an artist so notable, who continues making advances in the progressive march of an art genuinely Spanish, makes the laurels of the past come to life again by forgotten misfortunes in the environment of common and crass ignorance in which, by sad fortune, we are submerged."

In 1904 he moved to Paris, and took the Capital of France as the center of his activities and excursions, getting incomparable distinguished ovations and triumphs with his art; he performed in the "Schola Cantorum" in 1905, in the "Societé Nationale de Musique"; in the "Trompete"; in the renowned "Matinés Danube" in 1906, in the "Soirées D'Art" in 1907 and no others less representative.

Composers such as Debussy, D'Indy, Dukas and Faure consecrated him as an eminence in his art given his successes, which were repercussions in all the countries that invited him. He went to Belgium and his recitals in the "Societé Royale D' Armonie" of Antwerp, made the daily *Le Courrier Musical* say the following:

"What Miguel Llobet makes so pleasant to the aficionados and the most intransigent musicians, is the purity of his taste, which he never sacrifices to virtuosity only. To hear him interpret, with noble emotion, with the ideal sound and inaccessible technique, the most beautiful pages of the maestros, we feel spontaneously conquered, subjugated by such art and talent, and added to our praises, the most sincere admiration."

He then went to Argentina and Chile in 1910 and 1912; the events produced among the maestros, students and aficionados was unique in the history of the guitar; from that moment the marked evolution is noted which commenced the development in the soul of the Argentine populace, which saw the guitar as an instrument with character, and a capacity to be placed among the Violin, Cello, Piano, etc. and compete with them, which *Don* Domingo Prat two years before had initiated, the performances on the guitar of works of the times of the romanticism, had been heard but a little among us.

In 1913 he embarked and arrived in Germany; the ovations received in Munich obligated him to return in 1914, Mr. Bauer in the magazine *"Der Gitarrefreund"* saying "The impression, which his performance produces, is difficult to describe. He represents in his time, the apparition of, the same effect Paganini must have produced."

Excellent North American contracts made him to travel to New York twice, the populace and the critics receiving him in an admirable manner; the daily "The New York Globe" said: "The greatest artists of the world on string instruments found here in these moments: Kreisler, Casals and Llobet."

One of the most interesting facts of the artistic life of Llobet took place here in this city, to be the object of intimate sessions in his honor, in the home of the illustrious American pianist *Don* Ernest Schilling, with the public formed by the eminent world class musicians: Paderewski, Kreisler, Godowski, Zimbalist, Sembrich and others, which in those days were found in that great capital; those geniuses, after having heard him, enthusiastically, qualified Llobet as being among the greatest living artists; this is only enough to know the magnitude of this magician of the guitar, glory of the great Spain, glorifying at once his great maestro Tárrega.

So Llobet said: "These concepts satisfy me more than the greatest ovations of an anonymous public composed of thousands of creatures.... but nor in these moments of intense emotion, separate my mind from my daughter, my wife, my father, my brothers all of whom are in Barcelona, it seems to me that my triumphs weren't complete without them;.... I miss being able to communicate with them, who I could share with in the intimacy of the home...." and the great artist, the genius of the guitar of the present century, remains in suspense looking at the vacuum where the images of his loved ones fade away.

In 1918 he visited us again and the critics of the "*La Nacion*" says: "He has, in effect, his hand, the admirable delicacy of a wing over the strings of the instrument and the energetic strength of a talon and the sure exactness of the mechanism, ruled by an exquisite and sensible soul to the artistic emotion. The guitar transforms in between his arms; it is a harp or a lute; it sings deeply in a glowing nocturne by the ardent passion of the last love, almost as a violin intones a listless melody, or vibrates with the trembling sonority and full of a chord on the piano."

The daily "*La Prensa*" said: "He is an artist of great talent, a musician and the most notable interpreter."

The Great War came to an end in 1918, the distinguished artist could renew his travels increasing his triumphs in France, Belgium and England, during the years 1919 and 1920, besides visiting Spain (Barcelona and Madrid); during the months of January, February and March of 1921 he went to Germany and Austria, leaving memories of his visits; of which he had to repeat a few months later in Berlin, Vienna, Munich, Dresden, Leipzig, Weimar, Stuttgart, Frankfurt, Hamburg and many others, where the seats sold out immediately; in Vienna, a city of an elevated musical tradition, the success obligated the lights of the hall to be turned off, since the enthusiastic public didn't think to leave the hall.

The critic expressed it in this way:

In Halle, Germany: "Technically, the artist has caused the most stupendous astonishment. It isn't an exaggeration calling Llobet, the *Sarasate* of the guitar."

"*Leipziger Zeitung*": "Listening to Llobet, the marvelous effects can be appreciated, the mysterious sounds, smooth and harmonic which he has the capacity to produce on the guitar, so unjustly treated until recently."

"*Fränkische Tagespost*": "But even more admirable is such an artist. With that delicacy that he knows how to draw a thousand diverse modalities from the instrument! What magic he knew how to transcribe the "*Andante de la Sonata en Do Mayor*" by Mozart."

Innsbruck: "Llobet is, not only an unsurpassable technician, but a real artist, a musician and unique in his smoothness and beauty of sound without bringing tiresome affects, which leaves very far behind all those you have heard up to now on the guitar."

Without a doubt, the most difficult praises to achieve by a concert guitarist, but also the most valuable, are those which his own and unquestionable merit extracts from the sincerity of a colleague who cultivates the same instrument. The great *Don* Emilio Pujol of proclaimed heredity of Tárrega and the follower of the most pure Spanish guitaristic tradition said:

"Llobet awakened the admiration of the artists such as Kreisler, Paderewski, Severac, Stravinsky some time ago and enjoyed the friendship of Albeniz, Granados, Debussy, Casals and others" In the magazine "*La Guitarra*", he describes the artistic importance of his ex-classmate in the following manner: "Although he is young, he has been the first in revealing the modern orientations of the guitar. Llobet has been in Spain less a student than a disciple of the great Tárrega. Living in Paris since 1904 he bonded with Albeniz, Ravel and Debussy. The frequentation of those innovators and the atmosphere of refined art, in which he lived, had a decisive influence over his spirit. His work and talent as a performer didn't take long to experience his most beneficial influence."

"The musical technique already prodigious in Miguel Llobet was brought to the most conscious accomplishments. He arrived to subordinate all to the music... *Don* Manuel de Fallaattracted by those resources wrote the *"Homenaje a Debussy"* the masterful work of such authority, it is also a homage to the guitar. The productive good seed; a large group of authors wrote since then for the guitar, but it is thanks to Llobet, who motivated and asked all of them that could give."

In 1922 he returned to Argentina; the populace listened to him in delirium and the journalists expressed in this way:

"La Nacion" (May 4, 1922) "It isn't possible to imagine- a equal perfection, a dominion so absolute of the instrument, a similar delicacy in the interpretation, a similar richness of sonority and of timbres. The enormous difficulty of the guitar, with only its six strings, its metal frets that strike snarling the vibrations of those, its little box of resonance, its continuous out of tune notes, it transforms, it magnifies, and it elevates. It has the sweetness of the lute, the smoothness of the harp, the abundance of the piano, it sounds like a violin in the elegance of the portamentos, like a celeste in the full chords, like a clavichord in the pastosity of the ancient counterpoints. This reduced box trembles, howls, sings, cries or it enthuses with the soul so understandable and suggestive, which it might say by used to being superior. And it is in effect, to be superior it possesses and the realm with the marvel of the ability put into service of the talent."

He left South America and embarked for Europe, where he drew new delirious applause and arrived again in Buenos Aires in 1925, prepared to debut works for two guitars, accompanying the already famous Ms. Maria Luisa Anido; transcriptions with all the honors not unworthy for the originals and others already made by himself, including in them works by Argentine authors, to know:

Minuetto by Mozart
Le Cou Cou by Daquin
Romanza sin palabras by Mendelssohn
Danza Hungara by Brahms
Humoreske by Tchaikovsky
Evocacion by Albeniz
2 Danzas by Granados
Cubana by de Falla
Danza del Molinero by de Falla
Berceuse by Torres

For one guitar:

3 Preludios y Sarabanda by Bach
Air de ballet by Chaminade
2 Estudios and 2 Minuettos by Sor
Dedicatoria by Granados
La Pastoreta (Catalan melody) by Llobet
Sonata by Lopez Chavarri
Sonatina by Moreno Torroba
2 Estilos by Quijano

The success of Llobet was emphatic and sensed, possibly better than his previous visits, of which the motive of getting personal satisfaction.

Miguel Llobet was a great musician by instinct and by education; the guitar was the interpretive medium of which it is worth; his extraordinary technique so rich in tones, so clear and transparent, so easily influenced in the expression, in the volume and the dominion of the difficulties which the instrument presents, it is a perfect language with which to reveal the series of states because it pierces his soul, evoked by the works that he interpreted and developed by his own perception, to go deeply into and unravel the thought and someone else's form. The intense musicality of Llobet, is a base about which he lifts the marvels of his sonorous constructions, in those which the spirit of the music and instrumental subtleties, which serve to reveal it, to join and constitute an indivisible unity.

This internal musical life-Alma mater of the true interpretations- they have in Miguel Llobet one of his greatest forms of declaration, "To Make Music", to achieve sonority the best sum of the values and the beauty, to suspend the mind and back away from all relation to the common life, elevating it to a superior region about which the sound reigns with all the power of suggestion; to purify the human nature and reduce it to a state of internal beatitude. It is the mission of the great interpreters, whatever the instrument might be of what it might value, it was the mission which this great artist imposed.

Temperament and culture are the basic principles, which the art of the guitar demands; they are the flowery ornamentation, which emerge and increase in the drum of the essential spirituality of those destined to triumph. Few are artists of the guitar, lamentably, which are found endowed of these magnificent qualities in such a high grade. Miguel Llobet, is, without a doubt one, the most complete figure of all times which the guitar has, and indisputable, the genius guitarist of the present 20th century.

Dario sang as such:

Oh Llobet, lleno de Sol, amor de España	Oh, Llobet, full of Sol, love of Spain!
Artista lleno de purpura y de oros!	An artist full of purple and of gold!
Guitarra que da el clavel, la flor extraña	Guitar that gives the carnation, the strange flower!
Regada por la sangre de los toros!	Sprinkled by the blood of the bulls!
Flor de los gitanos, flor que amor recela!	Gypsy's Flowers, flower that the love distrusts!
Amor de Sangre y luz, pasiones locas!	Love of Blood and light, crazy passions!
Flor que trasciende a clavo y a canela	Flower which smacks of clove and red cinnamon
roja cual las heridas y las bocas!	which offends and the mouths!

The "Asociacion Amigos de España" desiring to perpetuate the memory of one of the greatest interpreters of the homeland entrusted his portrait to the famous painter *Don* José Maria Mezquita, donating it after to the Museo Moderno of Barcelona, where it permanently resides for centuries and centuries. But the emotion he provoked by his admirable performances not only embraced the extensive social and pictorial field, or also of the music in his greatest composers, but which the sculpture, moving equally to equate those which, designed the sketch of his person in the workshop of *Don* José Cardona, whose work is found in the possession of Ms. Maria Luisa Anido.

Sculpture of Miguel Llobet by *Don* José Cardona.

His Compositions:

As a composer Llobet must be studied in the diverse aspects of the originality, of the folklore, the transcriptions and the harmonization of his duets for guitars; in the originals, his production isn't abundant, if the quality well surpasses the imaginable; they register in difficult modulations, faithfully reflecting his musical knowledge, where the expression united with technique, expounds dramatic pictures, sentimental conflicts, landscapes of admirable orgies of auditory colors, he creates scientific formulas in the canvas of the instrumentation and edifies majestic cathedrals which ornament the present literature of the instrument; his works advance until they confuse science with art, because music and poetry are entwined like two angels miraculously united.

He composed the *"Romanza"* in 1896, it is an Andante in 6/8 time in C minor, which changes to C major in the 2nd part; more than a work of inspired melody, it is a sensitive romantic page with simple notes full of intimate emotion; it sends the soul of a man who has lived and profoundly felt fleeting, finding in the music the lenitive of his sadness. His notes arrive to the heart, speak of illusions and they reflect sad waves, whose internal life translate it by the rich and eloquent auditory language.

His *"Preludio",* is an *Allegro ma non troppo,* to the rhythm of 4/4 time in which he distinguishes his pure inspiration in arpeggios and slurs clearly guitaristic; his perfect fingering taken with natural and profound knowledge of the fretboard, conduces, with a simple and admirable melodic line, in his "original" harmonic tours of frequent chromaticism and delicate dissonances, to prove the extraordinary musical talent, an unmistakable stamp of the creative personality of the maestro.

"Impromptu", in 4/4 time, in the Key of E major, is the top work, in which he doesn't know if to admire his modern harmonic factor or his extraordinary mechanism "Absolutely New" on the guitar; this mechanism combines the common arpeggio, with an accented arpeggiated tremolo in a theme of campanellas, resulting in the surprising and delicious effect which surely the ear has experienced at least once; his richness, defies all analysis, his simple and grandiose architecture shuts in a profound impregnated inspiration of the poetic mysticism, in which the unexpected is abundant to the most minimum details; it is a work of mastery which doesn't belong to any art, all the arts are found in it, because it is the sum and synthesis of the art, whose light exceeds classifications and categories.

Meanwhile the bass descends by half steps, the tremolo ascends and ascends in musical whirlwinds which pass to the Key of C Sharp, repeating the theme then in its relative minor, they are melodies which back away and return to return and go and come, it is a song of love, it is a gondola which balances between the risks of a waterfall, of whose amalgam of sounds and colors, symbolically arise and subtle as a little angel hair, the first wave like a song to the humanity.

The melodic line is lively and fragrant rose, it is the nectar of life, which being born between the passions that surround the man, represented by the rumor of the six strings working incessantly, give the majestic impression of turbulences, of gales that approach and go away, while they sing the love that purifies and ennobles..

In the folkloric aspect, it is admirable the manner such as understands the essence of the collective inspiration, since the hearts of the populace in which live, forming the acute coefficient, sentimental of one thousand and one souls that accept and exalt it seeing his instrument converted in the lyrical anonymous poet, coincidental point, mind and soul of the Catalan life, the maestro Llobet, attracted by the mysterious force of the invisible laws, believes, harmonizing new themes for his instrument housed in the collective essence of the multitude, and it says believe, because when the artist constructs a new life, of anonymously born, synthesizing as he feels the popular sensibility, of a fact it consecrates in a flower of the nationality and his race. The history repeats: Liszt, Brahms, Albeniz, Rimski Korsakov and many others, they also studied the popular melodies of their populaces and converted their songs into magnificent descriptive poems which today gloriously impose in the universe, because they are the psychic expression of all a world full of ideas and musical substance.

"Copla", is a variation of a part of the Jota Aragonesa with whose virtuosity he dazzled us with in his last visit; it is a small copla, whose melancholy form is a poetic and sentimental note, among the happy and difficult variations of great technical display; is a enchanting of a Pyrenean *acuarelilla* of smooth tonality, descriptive of the native soil; to be distinguished among strange chords of notable sonority, the devout song full of faith and religion, elevating his prayer to the *"Pilarica"*, spirit and cane of a glorious ground believer, strong and vigorous.

"La Filla del Marxant", is the daughter of the merchant that sings:

Diguen que nes tan bella	They say that she is so pretty
no nes tan bella no	she isn't so pretty
que altres ni an mes que'lla	That others aren't more than her
La virundon	When they see her
ne erau doncella	they aren't there
y ara non sou	and aren't
Cuan ella va sarao	When she goes
sampose boniqueta	
fandilla de orleans	
y devantal de seda	in front of silk

La virundon	When they see her
ne erau doncella	they aren't there
y ara non sou	and are not

It is a simple estilo and fresh pastoral, adapted in the brilliant Key of E Major, the character of the work is very agreeable; it initiates the melody with octave harmonics and the tonic and dominant as a bass pedal to the time of 6/8; then repeats the song on the 4th string, to be distinguished vibrant among the inverted accompaniment, to tour of a delicious effect of campanellas of the 1st and 2nd strings.

"El Mestre"

"El Mestre" or the maestro, is in its genre the top work of the great Llobet; the Catalan critic Joaquín Pena said: "It is a model of its genre, it preserves all the fragrance of the original and of the populace", while the celebrated *Don* Emilio Pujol declared: "It indicates a point of departing toward new orientations, confining the germ of the ulterior polychrome instrumentals."

In effect, it is an Andante of 3/8 time in A major; its profound harmonic development of a modern factor, with strange chords of surprising and fantastic effects, with sonorities full of color and "Absolutely New" on the guitar, it demonstrates, which if to some work by Llobet, it deserves with total justice to be applied to it the words of Berlioz, when he said: "The guitar is an orchestra in miniature."

In the phrase of the latter half of the 7th measure, it begins the form with simple sixths, which then harmonically enlarge to incorporate the 4th string, with a chromaticism that extends to the 6th string; the group is rare, but very beautiful, to be admiring with the nature which resolves those complicated dissonances in the dominant of the key. later on we find chords that put its strange note in a pizzicatto of a curious sonorous effect and in a live contrasts with the trebles, it continues crystalline in the harmonic octaves, with marked popular taste, it repeats the notes and octave below and harmonizes with chords, whose sensation of mystery accentuates the muting of a pizzicato.

So ends the work, after other colored phrases with chords in harmonics and octaves, also in pizzicattos.

As homage to Argentina, Llobet harmonized various national themes, one of them is a *"Triste"*, a lament, a complaint, abandon, amalgam of high emotive value, a Gregorian psalm, imploration, pain which only can translate the music of the native soil of which emerges because if, like a wildflower perfuming the road that might live among the hills, and on the pampas; it is a gaucho song, fertilizing in the Iberian-Argentine cross of all that which he gave to the country, singing its victories, loves and misfortunes, with this box of six strings which from the heaven Columbus *"trujo"* by the mandate of God.

The third aspect of his musicalization is in the transcription, synthetic transplant of the Orchestra, Organ, Piano, Lute, Cello, etc. to the strings of a guitar, what appears at first sight a simple algebraic problem; the problems which the music presents him he solves them in a personal manner, with his own style and is so in this way as the works preserve his fragrance, giving the impression of having been conceived on the guitar.

For example: "Cadiz", is the ardent spirit, tragic and anguished which from the copla jumps to the guitar, raised in the notes of the mystic and emotive saeta; it is a mantilla, combed and adorned, it is a turban, battlements and caliphs, it is the street of the "duels", of the hope and the glory, it is the corduroy of Marsellés, filigree of gold and graceful pony, it is Goyesque acuarela with its classic and embellished pretty girl lost between carnations, lilies and money; all an Andalucian Moorish civilization, living the imaginative caprice of emotions suggested by the word made flesh and the melody of flesh, the hearts rhyming in a world of love and sacrifice.

In Germany and Austria the critics, unanimously, exhausted their repertoire of eulogies to his performances, because his *Andante de la Sonata* en C sharp by Mozart, the *Nocturne No. 2* by Chopin and others, turned out embellished by effects of timbres and vibrations which the piano couldn't obtain.

As to the transcriptions for two guitars by Llobet, they are something completely unpublished; it isn't the sounds that are augmented, nor more liberty conceded to one of the two guitars, because one is entrusted with the accompaniment; it isn't the sum of the sonorous elements, but the product of factors especially musical and personal. There for instance, the *"Romanzas sin Palabras"* (Song without Words) by Mendelssohn, of which, within the frame they were created for, constitutes one of the most complete successes and delicate of the literature of the clavichord, and however, what a torrent of unknown life, vigorous, dynamic, the roughness over the guitaristic harmonies! How pallid and cold to us the whim by where they broke the beautiful pianistic scheme!

The list of his works is the following:

Originals: Copla; Romanza; Scherzo Vals; Impromptu.

Studies: Allegretto; Preludio, Preludio (1916); Escala en MI Mayor para mano izquierda; 3 ejercicios cejilla; 3 ejercicios cromaticos; 3 ejercicios tecnicos en MI mayor; 25 estudios de Carcassi digitados de acuerdo con la escuela Tárrega.

Harmonizations: Testament de Amelia; El Hijo del Rey; El Mestre; La filla del Marxant; L'Hereu Riera; La Pastoreta; Plany; La cancion del Ladron; Triste de Quijano and Estilo de Quijano.

Transcriptions: Sarabanda and 3 Preludios by Bach; Mazurca and Humoresque by Tschaikowsky; La Maja de Goya, Danzas Nos. 5, 6, 7, 11 and Dedicatoria by Granados; Cancion del Fuego Fatuo, Romanza del Pescador de Amor Brujo, Homenaje a Debussy, Sombrero de Tres Picos, Danza del Molinero, Cubana and Amor Brujo by de Falla; Air de Ballet by Chaminade; Impresion by Mompou; Romanza Op. 30 No. 3, Op. 62 No. 25 and Op. 53 No. 20 by Mendelssohn; La Hilandera by Mendelssohn; Hojas de Album and El Mensaje by Schumann; Danza No. 5 by Brahms; Cadiz, Sevilla, Torre Bermeja, Cordoba, Oriental, Evocacion, Sous le Palmier and Rumores de la Caleta by Albeniz; Variaciones by Corelli; Mazurca by Buffaletti; Cancion Leonesa by Rogelio Villar; Ecos del Paisaje by Broqua; Romanza by Rubinstein; Jota by Arcas, Tárrega and Llobet; Melodia Noruega by Grieg; Minuetto and Melodia de L'Arlesienne by Bizet; Minuetto de la Sinfonia No. 39 by Mozart; Le Cou Cou by Daquin; Berceuse by Torres; Leyenda del Castilla Moro by Lopez Chavarri; Huella by Aguirre; Chacarera by Rogatis and Seguidillas by Albeniz.

His Pedagogy:

In his capacity as a maestro, every letter that he wrote and I have read, is a motive to inject optimism; with refinement and good tact he demands that the student inform him of what he does, studies, what he thinks, because he desires to know their aims, their works, ideas and everything, for directing and to be of use with profound affection, because it is his unique satisfaction.

His most known students were *Don* Guido Daunic, a resident of San Francisco, California, *Don* Antonio F. Serra, the celebrated Luise Walker and Maria Luisa Anido, the eminent *Don* Domingo Prat, besides, as I have said, Miguel was an honorary professor of the Conservatorio Provincial de Malaga.

In 1929 he began to write his Method, and I remember in respect that when he embarked from Buenos Aires for Spain on this day he said to me:

"It gives me a lot of work, but it's worth the effort, because it's very necessary, overall, being already antiquated in the present."; this Method never saw the light.

474

His Personality:

In 1910 he arrived in Buenos Aires owner of the prestige that the old Europe had assigned him and, in effect, we can see in the young man an extended face, a Chopinesque type, a curved forehead, tall and wide awake, an indication of a talented creator; clear and big brown eyes, synonymous with sweetness, kindness and extraordinary sensibility; a nose of a long demonstrative line of superior qualities and a mouth whose lower lip outstanding, is the psychological stamp of the good man; all placed on a normal head crowned of abundant brown hair, of regular stature, thin, of fine modes and sad look, as if he were living in an immaterial world. Many, like myself, we try to approach him, and we check that he never lacks in his lips the pleasant smile, the affectionate respect, allowing his intellectual values and the moral quality of his artistic and civic personality to be translucent.

At the end of 1927 he had made up his mind to make a tour of South America, which had to begin in February of 1928, in such circumstances it was known and confirmed by German and Austrian dailies, that *Don* Andrés Segovia would make his own the same year, although some months after, with such a motive in his letter of the 28th of September of 1927, directed to his friend *Don* Juan Carlos Anido, he wrote the following: "If Segovia goes two or three months after my first campaign in Buenos Aires, Montevideo and some important places of the Provinces it is probable that Segovia will encounter the public is already weary...." the letter ended renouncing his project for only this reason. (This was made public in a lecture given in Rosario on April 4, 1943 by Ricardo Muñoz.)

As it can be appreciated, Llobet, keeping profound admiration and respect for the great artist camaraderie, didn't take this tour, in the end to avoid this setback, in spite of being his only medium of life, a fine, delicate and silent generosity, of his soul, whose moral characteristic paints a timbre of nobleness by itself, which possibly the same Segovia ignores.

His life was an uninterrupted ascending line of the sublime spirit, it was one of those chosen with which nature gives us in every century, and which Goethe says: "It was one of those which emerges of the mysterious semi-darkness and armed with magnificent wings that they themselves believe, to strike them powerfully they dominate the reign of the height, from which they emit the shine of their unmistakable light, in paths of progress and civilization."

His work praised with glorification and discussed by others, occupies, in the contemporary music of the guitar, a prominent place; a passionate artist, of noble resources, of evident assimilation, finds the true value of the colors of the musical link, united in the garden of his thought which wanders by the path of the technique and his essence in fantasies combining esthetically, the legends or ingenuous lyricism, tell us the human tradition of all times.

He was a star whose light continues being the leading interpreter of our guitaristic century, because the luminous rays which radiate, continue lighting from North to South and East to West of the planet; his work was a technical and expressive hymn of aristocracy and dignity which is very necessary to discover, already that the personality of a great artist always is instructive and dominant, since it reflects an epoch, to study it, then, is to construct the present and breathe in the future, it is to take possession of an esthetic for then looking further.

His Passing:

To begin the Spanish Civil War of 1937, he commenced to become depressed, to grow weak little by little, while his brothers tore to pieces in the streets and fields; he then died of which is called *"Pasion de Animo"* the 22nd of February of 1938 in his home on the via Layetano 46 of Barcelona; the following Sunday the 23rd he was taken to his last abode in the cemetery of the North, by distinguished musicians of the city and representations of artistic entities, which among them the Orfeo Catala, presided by the maestro *Don* Francisco Pujol, and the Orfeo Gracienc with their director maestro Busells.

Without him we remain very alone, united in our respectful silence; still we vainly hear the noise of the bell of the mourning by the reality; the light has been extinguished and however, it appears that although the masterful strings vibrate to the impulse of his magnificent fingers, with those which he played the cordial phrase, the warm prophecy of his return, the piety, the affection and the pain conceived by the white petal of his beautiful forehead, central constructor and visionary where the eternal shade has perpetuated the clarity of the day.

Llobet has died, nevertheless he lives in the transparent plane of immortality, transfigured in an illuminated star like the anxieties of the human spirit; he lives materialized by the thousand memories that admire his evangelical figure floating in the sacred burial mound of the magnificent symphony of the guitar of all times.

Many remembered his personality, the magazines and newspapers such as *"Il Plettro"* of Milan, Italy, from Havana, North America, and Buenos Aires *"Noticias Graficas"* and *"La Razon"* of the 28th of March, besides *"La Prensa",* in Barcelona *"La Publicitat"* of the 23rd and 24th of February and in *"Dia Grafico"* *Don* Rafael Moragas called him: "Classic?, Romantic?, Very Modern,? Avant-garde?, he is all of those.... in few artists can you find the most intense Internal Heat and the best spiritual effervescence." Others wrote in the magazines *"Catalans", "Radio Barcelona", "Umbral"* and others.

The 18th of October of the same year, in the Hall of the "Pro Arte Musical" of Havana, they paid homage to his memory, the "Sociedad Guitarristica de Cuba" directed by their President Mrs. *Doña* Clara Romero de Nicola, to be developing a concert of selected works, performed by the distinguished guitarists Isaac Nicola, Margot Flores, Maria E. Botet, Rosa de Los Reyes, Aida Plantada, Emilia Lufriu, Debora Cabrera and Mary Leon: this performance and about the homage were covered in the dailies *"Pueblo"* of the 20th of October and *"Noticiero"* of Monday of the same month and the year of 1938.

A special request of the notable artist of the Argentine guitar, the favorite student of the late Llobet, Miss Maria Luisa Anido, I wrote a lecture related with the "Life and Work of Miguel Llobet" with the best care, which I was to give accompanied by illuminated illustrations and the music which the named artist in common agreement would perform, on the 1st anniversary of the death of her maestro.

The "Centre Catala" in whose theater organized the impartial act, with the participation of its chorus, to be taking responsibility of all of the inherent expenditures of the projected homage, all was prepared to such an end, but 48 hours before the fixed date, Miss Anido refused to perform the works which she herself had chosen without an explanation and then she disappeared from the city, motivating her cancellation of the act, which had been solicited and to which she promised to appear.

Nevertheless, the 4th of April, the 29th of May of 1943 and the 30th of September of 1944, I paid homage in the "Biblioteca Argentina" in the city of Rosario, in the *"Circulo de la Prensa"* of that city and in the "Biblioteca Popular" of Parana, accompanied by Professor Mrs. Celia Salomón de Font, who I thanked and dedicated the lecture.

Presently the home of Llobet is a valuable museum entrusted to his only descendant, his daughter Miguelina, whose mother also died in 1948; guitars and more guitars, everyone with its passionate biography, surrounded by magnificent painted pictures selected, with admirable dedications; *Don* Jaime Espinar says: "A harem of guitars; his marvelous harem. And the fairytales of the dream: books of voyages, of esthetics, of poetry, of imagination."

Valuable Gift

To return to Barcelona in 1903, approximately, his patron Mrs. *Doña* Concepcion Martínez de Jacoby, who was the patron beforehand also of the notable *Don* Francisco Tárrega, gave Miguel a magnificent Torres guitar, moreover which this luthier constructed with a body of resonance of paper mache dedicated to the great Tárrega, and which he didn't opportunely return with from the home of the named patron."

This is a photo of Miguel Llobet that was gift from Maria Luisa Anido to Ricardo Muñoz. Copyright Isabel Vilatoba Estate.

From the Ricardo Muñoz archive, in his thick volume titled "Conferencias" (Lectures) is this portrait of Miguel Llobet:

"Vida y Obra de Miguel Llobet- The Life and Work of Miguel Llobet

A lecture first given in the City of Rosario on the 4th of April of 1943 in the hall of the Biblioteca Argentina.—

It was repeated under the sponsorship of the *"Circulo de la Guitarra"* in the hall of the Circulo de la Prensa in Buenos Aires on the 29th of May of 1943.—

It was repeated in the City of Parana on the 30th of September of 1944, in the hall of the Biblioteca Popular, under the sponsorship of the "Academia Tárrega".

Images projected:

1. Head of Maria Luisa Anido (Sketch) by M. Llobet.—

2. Portrait of Miguel Llobet in 1910.—

3. Miguel Llobet (Sketch) by R. Casa.—

4. Portrait of Llobet by L. Mezquita.—

5. Miguel Llobet (Sculpture) by J. Cardona.—

6. Alegoria de la "Cancion Catalana".—

7. Last portrait of Llobet.—

Musical Program all pieces are by M. Llobet

1. Romanza.—

2. Preludio.—

3. La Filla del Marxant.—

4. El Mestre.—

5. Preludio by Bach.—

6. Cadiz by Albeniz.—

7. Triste (Motivo popular argentino)

Vida y Obra de Miguel Llobet-The Life and Work of Miguel Llobet

Mr. President of the "Academia Tárrega"

Ladies:

Gentlemen:

For the first time, in the high platform of artistic culture of the "Academia Tárrega", I have the exceptional honor that for me implies to converse with its very honorable associates and especially those invited to the act, about the eminent personality of the great maestro *Don* Miguel Llobet, whose historical sketch in his most intimate artistic quality, he clearly reveals in his extraordinary works.—

But, within the historical-artistic importance of the act, which I will try not to defraud by the mediums at my reach, it turns out to me highly significant to direct the word, accompanied by the sublime chords of a blessed guitar, plucked by the skillful feminine hands of the artistic director of this Institution, *Doña* Mrs. Celia Salomón de Font, a fine performer, of notable technique and emotional expression, whose place is already a symbol of culture and guitar in this admirable City of Rosario.—

By all that, my most profound recognition of the most charming Board of Directors to the same artist, who with the *Llobetiana* music will bring to our ears, selected passages of the sentimental life of the late great maestro, *Don* Miguel Llobet; the most glorious guitar of our times that has crossed the space of the human life as a fleeting star, leaving on the rock the evergreen of the memory, the monuments of recognition and gratitude that maintain the personality unharmed and latent of a National hero of the Hispanic American art.

Still we vainly hear the noise of the bell clapper in mourning in the reality; the light has been extinguished, and however, still it appears that the vibrations of the strings played by his masterful fingers are heard, in which the friendly phrase is signed, the warm prophecy of his return, the compassion, the affection and the grief conceived by the white petal of his beautiful forehead, center constructor and visionary, where the eternal shadows have perpetuated to the light of day.— He has disappeared, but his soul is here, as much to enter into immortality, which is a negation of his death, since that new life guides the steps of those who proceed in his school, searching in the inexhaustible and marvelous art of his instrument, the perpetual perfection of the sentimental life, whose culture and education, is a fact, that constructs and prepares a man for a better life.—

Llobet hasn't died, he lives in the transparent plane of the immortality, transfigured in an illuminating star for the anxieties of the human spirit; he lives materialized by the thousand infinite evocations that admire his evangelical figure, floating in the sacred mound of the magnificent symphony of the guitar of all times.—

We don't find ourselves in front of another cadaver, no, we are religious spectators devotedly admiring the supreme incarnation of a Holy Saturday, of the ascension of a man, that transposes the threshold of a mansion of the dead to guide a beautiful arc of triumph, by which the creep of the precious life of the father and maestro of an epoch, while neighboring fields harmonize the entrance of a new incorporation to the glory.

His life, was an interrupted ascending line until it reached the highest summit of the sublime human spirit; he was one of those chosen with what nature awards us in every century and as Goethe says: 'He was one of those who emerges in the mysterious semi-darkness and armed with magnificent wings that believe those same, to beat them powerfully to dominate the reign of the height, from which they emit the brilliance of his unmistakable life, in paths of progress and civilization.'

It was an existence constructed above the angular rock of an intimate vocation, a position of declaration from his infancy to his final day of life, ennobled by all the forms and aspects of the beauty, of which he devotedly made a cult, defining the human path run all over the planet, in a group of harmonies and a worthy moral dignified by his gentlemanly irreproachable conduct.

His work, praised with glory and argued by few, holds in the contemporary music of the guitar, a prominent place, a passionate artist, of noble resources, of evident assimilation, found the true value of the colors in the musical trauma, he united them in the garden of his thoughts that wandered by the paths of his technique, and esthetically combined their essence in fantasies, legends or ingenuous lyricism, that told us the human traditions of all times.

Gentlemen of the guitar, Moses, David, Terpander, Timothy, Saint Ambrosio, Saint Remigio, Charlemagne, Milan, Bermudo, Espinel, Corbetta, Sanz, de Visée, Moretti, Legnani and Giuliani; Aguado, Sor, Coste and Tárrega, we stand at the edge of the groove that guards the remains of our longed Messiah, of which was an eternal feast of the grains of our sowing, which was the culmination of our aspirations, in the present epoch, with millions of beings perpetuating a school and a doctrine; his spirit floats incessantly by the lands of the Americas, as the Seville lavender and incense of the temples of Christ.

Llobet was a star, whose light continues being the directing interpreter of our guitaristic century, because the luminous rays that radiate, continue to give light from the North all the way to the South, the Orient and the West of the planet, he was the creator, who as a virtuoso could be forgotten, but who is necessary to discover, his work, is a sonorous technical hymn and expressive of aristocracy and dignity, to study the personality of a great artist, always instructive and subjugating, a position that reflects an epoch, an eternity, to study it, is to construct in the present and to breathe in the future, to take possession of an esthetic, and then look beyond.

In my country he felt the fusion of the spirit and the form between art and nature, between God and man, reaching the miraculous revealed unification to accumulate treasures of live sensations, of reminiscences, of true breathed senses, profoundly merged in the thought and in the soul; there, in his country, he began with sketches and painting in the hands of the maestro Torres Casana, conducing his admirable passion to a distinguished place; his canvases were exhibited in local expositions and rewarded given the quality of the merits of his works.

Not having been able to obtain photographs of his works, it limits me to display the profile of a head done in pencil in the year 1922 in the Argentine City of Rosario, whose model was the eminent guitarist Miss Maria Luisa Anido.

A profile is shown:

Irresistibly attracted by the six strings of the guitar, he enrolled in the Conservatorio Municipal of Barcelona, and began his studies with maestro Magin Alegre, who initiated him in the knowledge of that poor and Cinderella companion of the joy and the tears, consolation of those that circle it, a white dove of those that triumph, a Saintly Spirit of those that sigh, the inspiration in the poet, incarnation of many countries, immortal fulguration of admirable evocations, a model of virtues and ideal guides that in the 15th century, the glorious Hispanic Heraldo brought to the New World sent by the powerful and divine Isabel.

The maestro Alegre tested the special capacity and extraordinary abilities for the instrument of his colossal disciple, then he presented him to the Valencian genius of Villa Real, *Don* Francisco Tárrega, who finding fertile ground in his new student, planted the seeds of his school and gave us one of the most bountiful artistic-musical gardens of the guitar of our century.

Immediately I shall profile his personality and mark paths of a definitive manner in the line of his positive values; I will construct to the virtuoso and to the maestro of the future in an ambiance of respect and devotion, bequeathing to the future precious rocks that proudly show in the present, the most admirable guitaristic musician ornament of the epoch, whose names are: Domingo Prat, Rosita Lloret, Rosita Rodes, Maria Luisa Anido, Luise Walker and others.—

He ran all over the world working by conviction and to get our daily bread; he wandered over all the Continents of the world bringing as all inspired, full confidence in the future, we agitated his infinite nostalgia, he overturned a thousand and one times everything entirely in the sublime auditory chore of his strings, he internalized and took possession of the soul of the nations he visited, he understood them, the following, he interpreted, summed up, harmonized, incarnated, reelected, he elevated and symbolized, and he blew invisibly of his extra creator, he opened new breaches bursting with prodigies that marked radiant orientations, in the rotund amplitude of an excellent new oratory, whose physiognomy and grandeur, will linger over, surely, tomorrow's historian.

480

His thoughts, his works, his ideals, his vision, and his hope constitute the forge in whose breast have wrought intense fixed guitaristic characters, personal, dogmatic and perpetual now by the inspired muse of his melodies, by his romanticism and especially by his purified technique, whose line and profile, constitutes a creator torrent of perfect modalities.

Llobet was always mind and arm, idea and effort, sentiment and expression, thought and action, he was a bridge of mooring and a peg giving the tone, the string that gave the sound and the fretboard that divides it, a left hand performing and a right hand regulating efforts, he was really a sole being conducing the sensible masses toward the most lively brightness of the Sun.

In 1910 he arrived on our shores an owner of the prestige that old Europe had assigned him, in effect, we can contemplate a young long face, a Chopinesque type, of a curved forehead, high and wide-awake, indicator of a profound creative talent; clear large brown eyes, synonymous of the sweetness, kindness and extra sensibility; a nose of a large line, demonstrating superior qualities, and a mouth whose lower lip outstanding, is the psychological stamp of the of the good man; whole, placing a face in a crown of abundant brown hairs; he of a regular stature, thin, of good manners and a sad look, as if he were living in the immaterial world, immersed in an undefined dream.— I present his photograph.—

A photograph of Miguel Llobet is shown:

Many, as I, have tried to get close to him during his artistic South American tours; His lips never fail to show his pleasant smile, the respectful affection, letting be revealed his intellectual values and the moral quality of his artistic and national personality.

Through his private letters that I have seen and have read closely, I have noted the existence of a humble man as a Carthusian; whose outstanding beauty makes him a rare human example.

At the end of 1927 he decided to make an artistic tour of South America, which he would have to initiate in February of the year of 1928; in such circumstances finds and confirms by the German and Austrian dailies, that the celebrated *Don* Andrés Segovia would make his own tour the same year, although a few months later; with such a motive, in his letter dated the 28th of September of 1927 directed to his friend *Don* Juan Carlos Anido, he wrote textually the following: "If Segovia goes two or three months after my campaign beforehand to Buenos Aires, Montevideo and some important places in the Provinces, it is probable that Segovia will find the public fatigued.........etc.etc." and he ended the letter renouncing his own projected tour by this sole reason.

As you can appreciate, Llobet guarding the most profound admiration and respect for the great artist camaraderie, decided to not take his tour, in the end to avoid it by the most minimal inconvenience, nonetheless to be-his only medium of making a living.—This fine, delicate and silent generosity of the soul, this moral characteristic, paints by itself, a ring of nobility that possibly the same Segovia ignored.

In his capacity as a maestro, every letter that he wrote and I have read, is a motive to inject optimism; with delicateness and habitual tact that demands that the student inform him what he does, what he studies, what he thinks, because he wants to know their sights, their works, ideas and everything, to direct and be useful with the most profound affection, because it is his only satisfaction.

His letters also present him as an admirable artistic organizer, in them not only he sends warnings of the fundamental but that embraces the most minimum details with a clear and precise word; the ambient forms, theaters, customs, etc. toward the editing of a simple telegram, it converts him into a perfect mathematician as an actor and spectator.—

Another of those primary aspects of Llobet, is his sensibility, to learn of the passing of his friend *Don* Juan Carlos Anido and of his daughter Bertilda, with the date of the 24th of September of 1933 he wrote to his student Miss Maria Luisa Anido:

"After reading your lines (although disconcerted by the terrible surprise of Bertilda) I relived in a few instants all the performances, almost always at his side, of my South-American campaigns; !!! How much activity, how many memories, how many sets....!!! It has been profoundly emotional............"

Here the writing is completely truncated, the orations interrupted by who knows many things he wanted to say; the pain paralyzed the pen, after, he managed to write only in this way:

However you must, pull yourself together and dedicate all the time that you can to your guitar.— The music, for those that want and feel it, lavishes great consolation.'—

All these private letters contain eloquence, tenderness, finesse, generosity, affection and they inform in his handwriting, anxious hands, hectic, that can only be calmed by the particular freshness that the harmonic body and its fretboard offer.—

His art remained concentrated in his country until 1904, and such admiration awakened, that the Sociedad Filarmonica of the City of Malaga named him *"maestro honorario"* (Honorary maestro), and the notable painter *Don* Ramon Casa, made the sketch that I have the pleasure to present to you.—

The sketch is shown:

To go beyond the border of his country, he played in front of the most demanding public, from the royal courts and princes of the contemporary music, to the possessors of the most mistaken concept by error or ignorance of the guitar; he always amply triumphed provoking the critics most glorious judgements to which, a great artist can aspire, naming him the "Casals of the Guitar", because according to Paderewsky, Schelling, Zimbalist, Sembrich, Godowsky and other emperors of the present music that were his public on a certain day in New York they qualified him among the greatest existing artists; while the daily "The Globe", said: "The greatest artists of the world on string instruments to be found in these moments are: Kreisler, Casals and Llobet".—

His virtuosity awakened the admiration of Stravinsky, Severao, Lopez Chavarri, who wrote and dedicated a magnificent *"Sonata"*; by Manuel de Falla, who composed the *"Homenaje a Debussy"* dedicating it to him; by D'Indy, Dukas, Faure, and cultivated the friendships of Albeniz, Granados, Malats, Villa-Lobos, Ponce, Villar, Pedrell, Mompou, Allende, Broqua, Casals, and many others with whom he conversed in the select artistic dinners of Europe and the Americas.—

The Asociacion "Amigos de España", desiring to perpetuate the memory of one of the greatest interpreters of the country, entrusted the commission of his portrait to the famous Spanish painter *Don* José Maria Mezquita, then, this entity gave it to the Museo de Arte Moderno of Barcelona, where it will remain for centuries and centuries.— I have the pleasure to present a photograph of the said canvas.—

The photo of the canvas by Mezquita is shown:

He was always a romantic guitarist, whose instrument was the sacred soul in the distance; his performances were the virtuoso palette of Goya, whose brush accentuated the maestros strokes of the expression by fingers that unite and separate, what is lengthened and is contracted, what is raised and lowered, what runs, flies and is stopped, before the eyes that are shut and jaws that are widened, while a *"Preludio"* threshes we are speaking of the eternity and always new dreams of the excellent life of all the epochs and all the races; he was a pure musician, without the fatal tendency of being united to the someone else's sensibilities, using intoxicating effects of the public; severe and respectful, he was, as was his artistic interior, as he always was, as was his own personality, he could not be what others would have liked him to be.

His original compositions happened to have difficult modulations, a faithful reflection of his musical knowledge; the expression united to the technique showed dramatic canvases, sentimental conflicts, landscapes of an admirable orgy of auditory colors, he believes scientific formulas in the canvas of the guitaristic instrumentation and edifies the majestic cathedrals that ornament the present literature of the instrument, his works advance until they confuse the science with the art, it is a marvel of vigorous liberty, it is amphora of loyalty, it is severe construction, it is moral of a correct line, it is the summit of the human spirit, it is a sonorous pyramid that elevates the heaven for which God blesses best, it is intelligence interpreting the love in the maximum honesty, clear and pure, exemplary life of all men.

The art was his ideal refuge and while he lived honestly from his guitar, he didn't struggle for unattainable great riches with the art, he coveted gold that at times destroys and degrades, he couldn't corrupt it; and in this way he was this sublime man who disappeared, whose perfumed spirit we experienced within brief moments, when it substitutes my poor word, the music of that man was brought to our ground as a gift of nature.—

We begin the series of his works with *"Romanza"*, which he composed in the year 1896, it is an *"Andante"* in 6/8 time in C minor, which changes to the Major mode in the 2nd part; more than a work of inspired melody and expressive harmonization, it is a romantic page felt, his simple notes full of intimate emotion, sends the fleeting soul of a man that has lived, profoundly felt and has encountered in the music the lenitive of his regrets; his notes arrive at the heart, they speak of illusions and they reflect the sad waves that the sound richly and eloquently translates in his private language.—We listen to this page from his youth:

"Romanza" by Llobet is performed:

Then we will listen to "Preludio", it is an "Allegro non Troppo" in 4/4 time, which highlights its inspiration in arpeggios and legatos clearly guitaristic; its perfect fingering, brought with natural and profound knowledge of the fretboard, conduces with its simplicty and admirable melodic line in his "originals" harmonic tours of frequent chromatics and delicious dissonances, to prove the extraordinary musical talent, unmistakable stamp of the personality of the great creative maestro.

"Preludio" by Llobet is performed:

Another of the admirable aspects of the artistic-musical life of Llobet in the material of his composition, is related with the harmonization of the *"Cancion Catalana"*; to capture the essence of the collective inspiration of the roots of the populace in which he lived, constituting the high-pitched sentimental coefficient of a thousand and one souls that accept and that exalt adapting them to the sonorous range of the instrument, it represents to convert the guitar into the lyrical anonymous poet, coincidental point, the mind and spirit of the Catalan life.

The man of this region, inhabiting mountains and valleys, forests and meadows of gold and emeralds, and its showcased Mediterranean coasts, lives perpetually in contact with nature, without exterior influences a capacity to confuse its personality, and in this way as it has a language that characterizes it, in the way it's the owner of a varied folklore of its own rich themes, whose lyricism, translates the rondallas and songs in smooth nostalgia.

Llobet, a fruit of this Celtibera region, born in Barcelona, ancient City "Julia Augusta" of the Roman Empire, where Ataulfo established his monarchy and Capital of the Visigodos, given its lineage, impossible to remain indifferent to such inspired beauty and beating in the heart of the populace of what emerged; Llobet attracted toward the same by the mysterious force of invisible laws, believes, harmonizing for his instrument new domiciled themes in the collective soul of the multitude, and I say believes, because when the artist constructs a new life of the anonymously born, a capacity to feel as he feels the multiform popular sensibility, of fact he consecrates it in flower and essence of his nationality and of his race.—

He is the son of a populace whose sentiments of beauty have nourished him, the regional model not twisted or deformed, but what gave him the racial substance of his spirit and in this way it speaks to us of the magnificent historical relics, of beggars and feudal, he creates if only immutable artistic rules as a logical consequence of evolution and progress, with Llobet, the history repeats itself, Liszt, Brahms, Albeniz, Rimsky, and many others, as well studied the popular melodies of their nations, converting simple songs into magnificent descriptive poems, that today gloriously impose in the universe, because they are the psychic expression of all a sensible world of ideas and musical substances.— Barcelona, already engraved in a stone monument to its song and erected it in the palace of the Music.— I have the pleasure to show the photograph.—

A photo of the *"Cancion Catalana"* sculpted in Barcelona is shown:

Immediately we will hear the harmonization titled *"La Filla del Marxant"*, or it is *"La Hija del Mercador"*; it is of a simple style and a pastoral painting, adapted in the brilliant key of E major, very adequate for the character of the work; in 6/8 time it begins with octave harmonics the melody and the tonic and dominant as a bass pedal; then it repeats the song on the 4th string, to be distinguished vibrantly between the inverted accompaniment, while the delicious effect passes in campanellas on the 1st and 2nd strings.—

It is as I said, a simple work, but it demonstrates great knowledge of the instrument in its technique, whose admirable fingering permits to faithfully express the content.—We will try to listen to it.—

"La Filla del Marxant" by Llobet, is performed:

To continue we will listen to *"El Mestre"*, or it is *"El Maestro"*; it is one of the top works of the great maestro; the Catalan critic Joaquín Pena, said: "It is a model of its sort, it preserves all of the fragrance of the 'original and of its populace', while the celebrated *Don* Emilio Pujol declared: "It indicates a point of departure toward new orientations, enclosing the germ of ulterior polychrome instrumentals."—

In effect, it is an *"Andante"* of 3/8 time, in the key of A minor; its profound harmonic development of modern manufacture, with strange chords of surprising and fantastic effects, with sonorities full of color and absolutely new in the guitar, they demonstrate, that if some work of Llobet deserves with total justice to have these words of Berlioz applied, when he said: "The Guitar is a Miniature Orchestra.", it really is this work, *"El Mestre"*.

In the phrase of the 7th measure of the 2nd part, it begins the simple form with single sixths, which then is harmonically enlarged to incorporate the 4th string, with a chromaticism that amplifies the 6th string; all this is strange and beautiful, to be admired with the naturalness that resolves to us all the dissonant complications in the dominant of the key; further on we find chords that put a strange note in the pizzicato of a curious sonoral effect, and in a live contrast with the treble, it continues crystalline in harmonic octaves with a marked popular flavor, it repeats the notes an octave lower and harmonizes with chords, whose sensation of mystery accents the damping of the pizzicato.

The work ends in this way, after the other colored phrases with chords in harmonics and octaves as well in pizzicatos.—Let's listen to it.—

"El Mestre" by Llobet is performed:

A third aspect of the musicalizations of Llobetianas, resides in the transcriptions, that is to say, in the synthetic transplanting of the orchestra, of the organ, laud, cello, etc. to the 6 strings of a guitar; it, at first sight and of agreement with the theory, it appears in this way as arithmetical, as the logical result and obligated of an algebraic problem, however, very far from that it is a transcription.

Various factors intervene of a capital manner; the election of the work that is paid to the guitaristic performance and very especially, the election of the key and the strings in the emission of the sonorities now faint or brilliant, of sweet timbres, velvety or tender blends from the violet amethyst to the clear celestial and transparent of a marine water, or a capacity to transmit intense sonorities under the digital force searching the live red of the ruby, the turquoise, the topaz or the brilliance that blinds; here, is where we find Llobet constructing the tracing of the chosen work, resolving the problems that the music presents to him.

Careful of the technique and using the infinite sonoral variety that it offers to the instrument, he resolves the problems in a personal mode, presenting the robust and vigorous physiognomy of his style, embellished by the effects of timbres and vibrations that on other instruments can't be obtained and

484

conserving all the fragrance of the original, as if it was conceived on the guitar, from there, the infinite impression that they produce their performances in the spirit of Albeniz, Granados, de Falla and others, that they say in these transcriptions, can be considered true creations given the excellent and spontaneous manner to make entirely the ideas of the authors his own.

Llobet adapted many works to the glorious guitar, but, in the impossibility to perform them all, we begin with the great Bach, the formidable great classic by excellence, the patriarch of the pure music, the poet who elevated the sonoral beauty to the highest summit with his cantatas and oratorios, by only the inspiration of his extraordinary intellectual faculties.—

We listen to *"Preludio"* of Bach by Llobet:

Lastly we are in front of the great Albeniz, the author of *"Pepita Jiménez"*, to the lyricism that uniting the timbres to the most ardent sentiment of life, it speaks to us of the Alcazares with its marbles, stuccos, and mosaics, of the moldings of jasper and alabaster in the Mezquitas, of the polychrome of Hispalensis tiles and arches of lace sculpted in colonnades, gateways and friezes of the *"Patio de los Leones"*, *"de las Doncellas"*, the *"Generalife"*, where it sends the Christian and Moorish inspirations united in intense artistic displays of the chisel, emerging monumental in the world of joys and flowers under the ardent Sun of the midday.

His serenata "Cadiz", is the ardent spirit, tragic, and anguished from when the copla jumps to the raised guitar in the notes of the mystic and emotional Saeta; it is a mantilla, peineta and caireles, it is a turban, a battlement and califas, it is the street of the Desafios, of the Hope and the Glory, it is the Marsell's of corduroy, the watermark of gold and graceful pony, it is the Goyesca watercolor with its classic gate adorned by the lost girl between carnations, nard and musk; it is all a Moorish-Andaluza civilization living the imaginative capricho of emerged emotions the word made flesh and the flesh a melody rhyming the hearts in the world of love and sacrifices.

The guitar is Spanish, it brings in its body all the Hidalguia of the populace that saw it born, we might see, since, as it feels and as says its own essence.

"Cadiz" of Albeniz by Llobet is performed:

Llobet always said: "Argentina is my second homeland", and dedicated to it many interesting productions; as an homage of his gratitude and his art to the nation, he harmonized various themes with the Argentine flavor, one of those which can be heard as we continue; it is a lament, it is a complaint, it is an abandonment, it is amalgam of a high emotional value, it is a Gregorian Psalm, it is an entreaty, pain that only can translate the music of the terrain, from which arises because if, as the wildflower perfuming the road that lives among the hills or the pampas; it is also consolation after the struggle on the road of life, conquering in the semi-darkness of the night or below the ardent Sun of the day, the relentless elements of nature.

We hear our beloved gaucho, the fertile type in the Ibero-American cross, to which all he gave for the nation shedding his blood and taught to worship to the liberty singing his victories, loves and misadventures, in the chest of six strings that from heaven Columbus *"trujo"* mandated to us by God.— We listen to the Guemes, Lamadrid, Paz and Oribe, to Lavalle, Artigas and the 33 with Lavalleja ahead, a lance in rest and guitar in shoulder strap, seeking death towards the new homelands of Latin America.

Llobet didn't know decadence, he wasn't a painter of gallant scenes nor enchanted by fiction or neurotic, he was simply, the expressive technical follower of his great maestro Francisco Tárrega.

He died on the 22nd of February of 1938 in his native land; the next day, Sunday the 23rd, by the via Laietana he was taken to his last dwelling in the cemeterio del Norte, by the most distinguished musicians of the City and representations of artistic entities, among which included the Orfeo Catala, presided by maestro Francisco Pujol, and the Orfeo Gracienc with its Director maestro Balcells; without him, we remained very alone only united to our respectful silence, his merits and his work, the history with time will accent when it is analyzed in general and in a particular group, without prejudice nor circumstances, and it places him conscientiously in his "epoch".—

The last portrait of Llobet is shown:

Rosario, April 4 of 1943, Ricardo Muñoz"

C X 28 Edison

```
11.    Notic. Edison.
11.15 Orq. Blas.
11.30 Kari Blums.
11.45 L. Lamarque.
12.    Tip. E. Donato.
12.15 Azuc. Maizani.
12.30 Clotilde Denegri.
12.45 Coros Scala.
13.    C. Denegri, Soprano,
         pian. Mastrángelo.
13.15 Coros Hefburg.
13.30 Natv. Shilkret.
13.45 Canc. españolas.
14.    Cámara Mercantil.
14.15 Beethoven Sinfonía
         No 8.
15.    Operetas.
15.30 Mús. de Jazz.
13.45 Bohemios vieneses.
16.    Jerry Wills, Charlas
16.30 Cantores típicas.
17.    Tablada (Inform.)
17.15 Amalia Molina.
17.30 Sindicato Médico.
18.    Preludios
18.15 Miguel Llobet.
18.30 Alicia en el país de
         las maravillas.
19.30 Tierra Adentro. Dir.
         Goyita G. de Fer-
         nández
20.    Radamés Luzzi, ten.
         pian. Mastrángelo.
20.15 R. Mastrángelo (so-
         los de piano).
20.30 Radamés Luzzi (ten.
         pian. Mastrángello
20.45 R. Mastrángello (so-
         los de piano).
21.    Diario sin Tinta.
         Viernes sel. $ 1.50.
22.    Trasm. de Teatro o
         bailables.
```

Miguel Llobet, is listed in this issue of *"Radio Revista — cancionera"* Issue No. 239 *Año* VI Sunday August 23 – Saturday August 29, 1936, published in Montevideo on August 21, 1936. His records were played on Friday August 28 from 6:15PM until 6:30, then followed by a live performance of "Alice in Wonderland" on Radio C X 28 Edison. This play also aired on Mondays and Wednesdays. Miguel Llobet's last tour of the Rio de la Plata area was in 1929 and he was still a very popular virtuoso .The listings in bold text are live performances and the listings in plain text are recordings played for the audience.

On Sunday August 23 there were recordings of *"Solos de Guitarra"* on both Radio C X 26 Uruguay and C X 28 Edison of the 21 radio stations that were operating at the time in Uruguay.

Del diario La Vanguardia de Barcelona Edición del jueves, 24 febrero 1938, página 2.

"ENTIERRO DE MIGUEL LLOBET

Conforme habíamos anticipado, ayer tarda se efectuó el entierro del cadáver de Miguel Llobet.

Las simpatías y admiraciones de que gozaba el que fue guitarrista insigne y valioso defensor del arte hispano en el extranjero, se pusieron de relieve en el fúnebre acto, al que asistieron infinidad de personas, pertenecientes a todos los sectores sociales y principalmente al artístico.

Del «Orfeó Cátala» y del «Orfeó Gracienc» figuraban en la comitiva nutridas representaciones, presididas por los maestros Pujol y Balcells, respectivamente. Reiteramos a la familia' del gran artista legtimo orgullo de Cataluña y de España entera, el testimonio de nuestro pesar."

From the daily: *La Vanguardia* of Barcelona, Thursday edition, February 24, 1938, page 2.

"THE BURIAL OF MIGUEL LLOBET

As we said before, yesterday afternoon the body of MIGUEL LLOBET was buried.

The sympathies and admiration that the notable guitarist and valiant defender of the Spanish art abroad enjoyed, were put into relief in the funeral, to the countless persons attending, who belonged to all the social sectors though mainly to the artistic one.

From the "Orfeó Cátala" and the "Orfeó Gracienc" included in the entourage abundant representation, presided over by maestros Pujol and Balcells respectively. We reiterate, the legitimate pride of Cataluña and Spain, the testimony of our sorrow, to the family of the great artist."

486

Here we see the weekly listings by Max Glucksmann of Miguel Llobet for his Odeon advertisement in the *"Caras y Caretas"* magazine published in Buenos Aires in 1929 and 1930. Miguel Llobet was in the Rio de la Plata area doing concerts and radio programs when the first four of these advertisements were published, though the solos were recorded in Barcelona in 1925.

Miguel Llobet Solo de guitarra

Disco Odeon de 25 cms., $3.50 pesos (10" disc)
196045 August 10, 1929 *"Caras y Caretas"* Issue No. 1610 *Año* XXXII.
Dos canciones mejicanas. Ponce.
Estilo popular criollo. (The composer Pedro Quijano was not mentioned)

196045 August 31, 1929 *"Caras y Caretas"* Issue No. 1613 *Año* XXXII.
Dos canciones mejicanas. Ponce.
Estilo popular criollo. (The composer Pedro Quijano was not mentioned neither on the disc.
   In issue No. 3 (Fall) 1925 of the *"La Guitarra"* magazine published by Juan Carlos Anido, Pedro Quijano is credited as composer, Miguel Llobet as the harmonizer- "written exclusively for *La Guitarra".*)

196046 September 7, 1929 *"Caras y Caretas"* Issue No. 1614 *Año* XXXII.
Andantino. F. Sor
Estudio brillante. Coste.

196046 September 14, 1929 *"Caras y Caretas"* Issue No. 1615 *Año* XXXII.
Andantino. F. Sor
Estudio brillante. Coste.

Miguel Llobet-Maria Luisa Anido Duo de guitarras
Disco Odeon de 25 cms., $3.50 pesos (10" disc)
196067 December 7, 1929 *"Caras y Caretas"* Issue No. 1627 *Año* XXXII.
Huella. Danza argentina. J. Aguirre.
Romanza No. 25. Op. 62. Mendelssohn

Maria Luisa Anido-Miguel Llobet Duo de guitarras
Disco Odeon de 25 cms., $3.75 pesos (10" disc)
196521 January 18, 1930 *"Caras y Caretas"* Issue No. 1633 *Año* XXXIII.
Evocacion. 1ra parte. J. (sic) I. Albeniz
Evocacion. 2nda parte. J. (sic) I. Albeniz

Miguel Llobet Solo de guitarra
Disco Odeon de 25 cms., $3.75 pesos (10" disc)
196523 February 8, 1930 *"Caras y Caretas"* Issue No. 1636 *Año* XXXIII.
Sarabanda. Bach.
Estudio. F. Sors. (Estudio in B minor.)

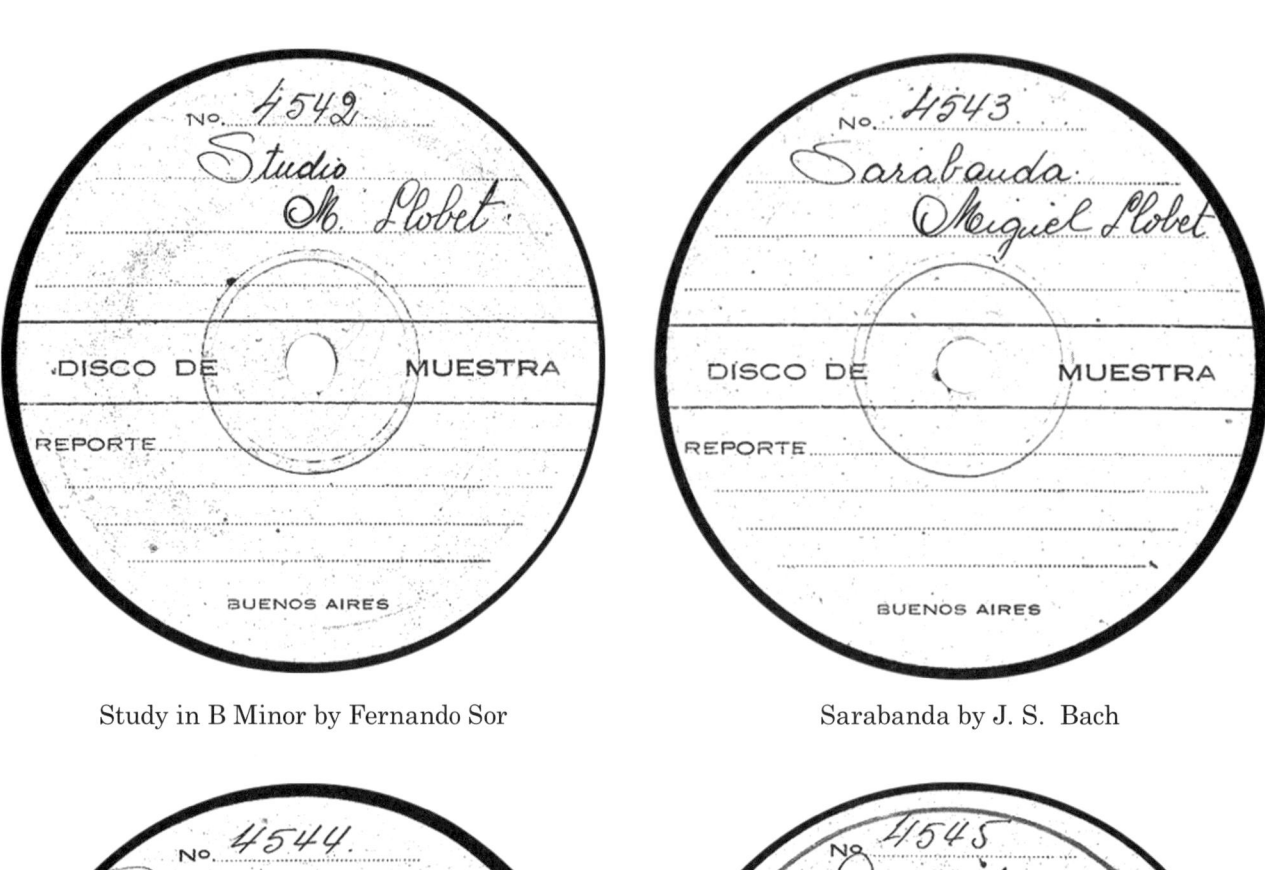

Study in B Minor by Fernando Sor

Sarabanda by J. S. Bach

Estudio Brillante by Napoleon Coste

Andantino by Fernando Sor

Test pressings of Miguel Llobet recordings made in Barcelona in 1925. These are the initial pressings made after the arrival of the master from Europe for manufacture in the Argentine Republic. There is the Study in B Minor by Fernando Sor, the Sarabanda by J. S. Bach, the Estudio Brillante by Napoleon Coste, Op. 38 No. 23 in A Major and the Andantino by Fernando Sor.

Dos Canciones Mejicanas by Manuel Ponce

Estilo Popular Criollo by Pedro M. Quijano

Andantino by Fernando Sor

Estudio Brillante by Napoleon Coste

Odeon Recording Company discs recorded in Barcelona and manufactured in Argentina. In the musical supplement of issue No. 3 of *La Guitarra* magazine published by Juan Carlos Anido in 1925, it states according to the version by Pedro M. Quijano, this piece was harmonized especially for the magazine by Miguel Llobet.

There are videos of his works on You Tube.

These are two of the six songs this duo of Miguel Llobet and Maria Luisa Anido recorded for Odeon in Buenos Aires in 1929. Julián Aguirre wrote the piece *Huella*, and Felix Mendelssohn wrote the *Romanza*. Maria Luisa Anido used her 1918 Enrique García guitar and Miguel Llobet his 1859 Antonio de Torres.

These recordings of Matilde Cuervas and Emilio Pujol performing *"El sombrero de los tres picos"* and *"La vida breve"* are on an Italian pressing of the label *"La voce del padrone"* from 1943 (His Master's Voice).

El Sombrero de tres picos (de Falla) La Voce del Padrone DA 4332 Matrix 110-2349
La Vida Breve (de Falla) La Voce del Padrone DA 4332 Matrix 110-2350

They are both playing guitars made by Antonio de Torres Jurado in his first epoch.

El Testamen de N'Amelia by Miguel Llobet

Andantino by Fernando Sor

Columbia discs made in Kawasaki, Japan by Nipponophone released in Japan in 1939, being the Odeon recordings of the Miguel Llobet made in Barcelona in 1925.

Sarabande in B Minor by J. S. Bach

Dos Canciones Mejicanas by Manuel Ponce

Decca Record Company 78 RPM discs made of the Odeon recordings in the late 1930's in the United States.

LA PUBLICITAT

BARCELONA

Dimecres, 23 de febrer de 1938

MISTER EDEN HA ESTAT APUNYALAT PER L'ESQUE-NA AMB UN PUNYAL ITALIA PELS SEUS MATEIXOS COL·LEGUES.

MIQUEL LLOBET HA MORT

Ahir va morir a Barcelona el que fou famós concertista de guitarra, Miquel Llobet. Ja feia dies que estava malalt. Quan semblava, però, que la malaltia que patia es començava a decantar en un sentit favorable i, per tant, que l'eminent artista es trobaria ben aviat fora de perill, es produïren complicacions que esgotaren la resistència del malalt. I ahir va finir.

Miquel Llobet va començar els seus estudis de guitarra a Barcelona, sota el guiatge del guitarrista Alegre. Després fou deixeble del famós Ramon Tàrrega.

Era molt jove encara que aconseguí remarcar-se com a destacat especialista d'aquest instrument tan delicat de tocar com és la guitarra. I ben aviat i era a París, on va viure durant molts anys.

En el transcurs de la seva vida artística, que fou una cadena d'èxits, efectuà tournés pels principals centres musicals de tot el món. I arreu fou admirat i conceptuat com un dels concertistes més eminents.

Ultra un concertista de primera categoria, Miquel Llobet era un excel·lent músic. Tant és així que deixa escrites moltes composicions inspiradíssimes.

Descansi en pau l'il·lustre artista que tan i tant va enaltir, amb el seu art, el nom de Catalunya, i rebi la seva família el condol sincer de LA PUBLICITAT.

This obituary of Miguel Llobet is from the Catalan language Barcelona newspaper *"La Publicitat"* of Sunday February 23, 1938.

This image of the obituary of Miquel Llobet (Catalan spelling) is from the archive of the concert guitarist José Rey de la Torre and first appeared in the American guitar magazine called "Chelys" Volume 1, No. 5 of November 1976.

The Catalan language translation by Randy Osborne is on the next page.

This obituary of Miquel Llobet (Catalan spelling) is from the archive of José Rey de la Torre and the first paragraph that José translated appeared in the guitar magazine called "Chelys" Volume 1, No. 5 of November 1976. Below is the complete translation.

Translation from the previous page of the Catalan language Barcelona newspaper *"La Publicitat"* of Sunday February 23, 1938:

"Miguel Llobet has died.

Yesterday in Barcelona the famous concert guitarist Miguel Llobet died. He had been in ill health for several days. When it appeared, that the malady, had commenced to go into remission and he was feeling better, so that the eminent artist was out of danger, complications produced set in that weren't resistant to the malady. Yesterday was the end.

Miguel Llobet commenced his guitar music studies in Barcelona under the guidance of maestro Alegre. Later he was the disciple of Francisco Tárrega.

He was very young when he faced the acquisition of remarkable abilities with a distingushed specialist of an instrument with a delicate touch as is the guitar. He went to live in Paris where the duration of his stay was to last for many years.

In the course of his artistic life, that was a chain of successes, he toured the principal musical centers of the whole world. He was regarded to be one of the most eminent concert guitarists.

As well as a concert guitarist of first rank, Miguel Llobet was an excellent musician. He also left many very inspired compositions.

Rest in Peace illustrious artist who not only so ennobled his art, and the name of Catalunya — you leave the family of *LA PUBLICITAT* in sincere sadness."

GUITAR MUSIC

The artistry of Miguel Llobet
(1878–1938)

MIGUEL LLOBET was born in Barcelona and grew up in a family circle where ART, in all its aspects, was accepted as an essential part of life. His father, a sculptor, had his son trained as a painter, but the guitar impelled young Miguel to make music his career, so he studied at Barcelona Conservatory under Tárrega and Casals.

At the age of 23 he won fame as a recitalist in Spain, then went to live in Paris in 1904. Here he associated with the leading contemporary musicians and gave many recitals.

He had a more modern and advanced conception of the guitar than Tárrega and with his keen artistic sensitivity, he made full use of the tonal colours not only of the guitar as a whole, but of *each separate string*.

Thus his arrangements are more artistically satisfying to the discerning ear, though they are more difficult to play.

The ability to make use of subtle variations of tone colour is one of the most important features of the guitar. It gives the discriminating artist a palette of wide range. For this reason Segovia and other artists of the guitar would not use a wire-covered third string, as it robs the guitar of the variation between the covered fourth and the nylon third strings.

Llobet arranged for solo guitar much fine music including Cadiz and Torre Bermeja (Albeniz), La Maja de Goya (Granados), and works by Mozart, Pedrell, Rubinstein, Bufaletti, etc. But perhaps his artistry is best revealed in his enchanting arrangements of simple Catalan melodies such as the well-known 'El Testamen de n'Amelia'.

Ricordi has recently re-published two more of these gems—'El Mestre' and 'La Filla del Marxant'.

Ricordi has also re-issued Llobet's transcription of a Bach Prelude from the 4th Cello Suite and a transcription of Sevilla (Albeniz) by Tárrega and Llobet in collaboration.

Llobet achieved considerable fame in Spain, France, Germany, Austria and most countries of both North and South America. He gave two recitals and a broadcast in London, June 1930.

But it was in Argentina that he achieved his greatest success. In Buenos Aires in 1923 Don Juan Carlos Anido, a man of culture and an aficionado of the guitar, founded a guitar magazine 'La Guitarra'. His daughter, Maria Luisa, then in her early teens, had undoubted talent for the guitar, and had been trained by the best available teachers, including Domingo Prat, compiler of the great *Dictionary of Guitarists*.

On his arrival in Argentina Llobet was engaged to continue the guitaristic training of Maria Luisa. Realising that he had a very talented pupil he set to work to arrange music by Mozart, Mendelssohn, Albeniz, Granados, Falla, etc., for two guitars. The concerts given by Llobet and Maria Luisa Anido in June 1925 were a sensation. Never had such glorious guitar music been heard in the guitar-conscious Argentine capital. The press acclaimed it 'a

new epoch of the guitar; undoubtedly these two artists had demonstrated the truth of Chopin's saying: "There is nothing more beautiful than a good guitar—save perhaps two."

Llobet's arrangements should be studied by all serious guitarists and we hope that more of them, including the duo arrangements, will be made available by publishers.

An interesting account of Llobet's playing is to be found in "Spain of the Spanish" by Mrs. Villiers-Wardell (published 1909):

'Miguel Llobet is a notable guitarist. He was a favourite pupil of Tárrega—the greatest master of the guitar Spain has known during the past fifty years—and, like his illustrious maestro, he is able to make the guitar speak. It was in Paris that I first had the pleasure of making this musician's acquaintance, and I confess to a feeling of intense surprise when I heard him softly playing the opening notes of one of Chopin's most exquisite Nocturnes. I had never thought of associating the guitar with serious music, but in the hands of Miguel Llobet it gave us Bach and Mendelssohn, Chopin and Beethoven. This sounds incredible, but then the guitar is an instrument capable of wonderful things—in thoroughly skilled hands. Towards the end of the evening we pressed the artist to give us something 'really Spanish' and he played—in memorable style—a *jota* composed by Tárrega himself. A glorious piece of music full of brilliant life: music which expressed in delicious sounds what the pictures of Zuloaga express in colour.'

This is from the "Guitar News" magazine issue No. 67 of September-October 1962.

After Llobet, the Spanish concert artist Joséfina Robledo, also a student of Tárrega, presented her program on the Argentine stage. It was in 1914, she arrived forming a part of a Zarzuela company, by advice of her colleagues to become independent, and she commenced to give concerts as a soloist. She returned to Europe and in the next year she was in the Argentine capital again to initiate a series of concerts in the interior cities of the country. After which she toured Uruguay, Paraguay and Brazil. It is in this last South American country, she settled permanently, to dedicate time to teaching, then returned to Buenos Aires where she also had students and offered concerts, until 1924, when she ended up returning to Europe, after spending almost a decade in this part of the Americas.

Joséfina Robledo (1892-1972)

Francisco Tárrega was maestro to both Hilarion Leloup and child prodigy Joséfina Robledo. Leloup began directing the Academia "Tárrega" in 1914 and Joséfina Robledo arrived in the same year and concertized throughout South America. After spending many years in Rio de Janiero, Brazil upon her return to Buenos Aires she was named a professor of guitar in the famed Conservatorio Williams in 1923.

Asistentes al concierto de guitarra dado por la concertista señorita
Joséfina Robledo (×), en los salones del Club Español.

Joséfina Robledo from the *"De Rosario"* page in the *"Caras y Caretas"* magazine of June 6, 1917, issue No. 975. "Attendees at the guitar concert given by the concert guitarist Miss Joséfina Robledo in the hall of the Club Español."

Josefina Robledo

Exim in concertista de guitarra, cuyas recientes audiciones musicales, han puesto una vez más de relieve sus excepcionales dotes de ejecutante. La señorita Robledo une a una impecable técnica un exquisito sentimiento musical.

Joséfina Robledo from the *"Caras y Caretas"* magazine of May 31, 1924, issue No. 1339. "The eminent concert guitarist, whose recent musical performances, have once again put the exceptional endowments of the performer into relief. Miss Robledo unites an impeccable technique with an exquiste musical feeling."

The reason the two photos are so many years apart is: Joséfina Robledo was performing and teaching in Brazil.

Señorita Josefina Robledo, Profesora de Guitarra

Joséfina Robledo from *Revista Musical Ilustrada "Tárrega"* issue No. 3 of August 1924, holding her guitar made by: Enrique García of Barcelona. In *Revista Musical Ilustrada "Tárrega"* issue No. 1 of June 1924 the Joséfina Robledo concerts of May 13 and 16, 1924 were listed:

"May 13, 1924 (possibly in the Salon "La Argentina")

1) Siciliana (1st Sonata for violin solo) Bach — Robledo
2) Scherzo (Sonata Op.2 No.2) Beethoven — Tárrega
3) Vecchio Minueto Op. 18 Sgambati — Robledo
4) Le Cou-Cou (Rondeau) Daquin — Robledo

5) Cancion No. 3 Aguirre — Robledo
6) Aire Criollo Aguirre — Robledo
7) La Mort d'Asis Grieg — Robledo
8) Mazurka Op. 33 No. 4 Chopin — Tárrega
9) Romance Tschaikowsky — Robledo

10) Cordoba Albeniz — Robledo
11) Valencianas Salvador — Robledo
12) Jota Hierro — Robledo

May 16, 1924 (in the Salon "La Argentina")

1) Sarabande (2nd Sonata for violin solo)
Bach — Robledo
2) Largo (Sonata Op. 7 No. 4)
Beethoven — Tárrega
3) Minueto Haendel — Tárrega
4) Romanza No. 43 Mendelssohn — Robledo

5) Cancion No. 4 Aguirre — Robledo
6) Marionettes Españoles César Cui — Robledo
7) Berceuse Ilinsky — Robledo
8) Danza Española No. 7 Granados — Robledo

9) Danza del Molinero
(Sombrero de tres picos) Falla — Robledo
10) Chanson Arabe Granados — Robledo
11) Oriental Albeniz — Robledo
12) Carnival de Venecia Paganini — Tárrega"

Romero & Fernández advertisement of Spanish guitars with a very notable exponent: Joséfina Robledo. There is a prestigous list of guitarists also mentioned. This ad is from: March *1926 Revista Musical Ilustrada "Tárrega"* issue No. 20.

Translation:

"That the Spanish Guitar is the best of the world. The proof of having been the only ones used by the eminent artists: Sor, Aguado, Arcas, Tárrega, Llobet, M. L. Anido, Pujol, Segovia and Robledo.

In spite of the interest that some makers have in wanting to imitate the great constructors of Spanish guitars, it's curious to observe that neither so at least they are able to resemble to those of the less importance, with which is confirmed that a Spanish guitar of little price is equivalent to the one of greater value from any other origin.

We invite you to which, before making your purchases, please visit the house of Romero & Fernández .

In the *Revista Musical Ilustrada "Tárrega"* issue No. 3 from August of 1924, there was an interview with Joséfina Robledo. This biography is from that interview and the biography in Domingo Prat's *"Diccionario de Guitarristas"*. "She was born on May 10, 1897 in the capital of Valencia, Spain. In 1904 she began to study with maestro Francisco Tárrega and did so until his death in 1909. In 1907 she gave her first concert in the Conservatory of Valencia. She studied harmony and music history with maestro Peña Roja. In 1914 she began her artistic tour by traveling to Argentina, where she initiated a series of concerts. In 1915 she began a tour of the interior of the Republic of Argentina, giving concerts in Rosario, Santa Fe, Cordoba, etc. After that successful tour, she traveled to Uruguay, Paraguay and Brazil, where she was celebrated for her divine art of interpretation. She stayed in Sao Paulo for a concert season and then moved to Rio de Janiero where she spent many years teaching until her return to Buenos Aires in 1923. Upon returning to Buenos Aires, she performed concerts in the Wagneriana, Circulo del Rosario and Sociedad Cultural de Bahia Blanca. These three concerts were on September 11, 14 and 20, 1923. In early 1924, she performed in the Salon "La Argentina", Sociedad el Diapason and Sociedad Argentina de Musica de Camara to audiences that were full houses. She was appointed in 1924 as professor of guitar at the Conservatorio Williams, directed by Alberto Williams. Prat says Joséfina had succeeded the most, of those that followed Tárrega and didn't use nails, but mostly flesh, in the plucking of the strings of the instrument. In issue No. 19 of February 1926 of *Revista Musical Ilustrada "Tárrega"*, it mentions in the opening article of the magazine on page 3, that she was triumphant in Europe and had returned to Spain in the middle of 1925. She was receiving rave reviews of a concert she gave in the Teatro Eslava, in the Valencia daily *"Las Provincias"* and by such music critics as: Llopis Piquer, Lopez-Chavari and Manuel Palau. Joséfina Robledo after eleven years duration of being loved for her art in the Rio de la Plata area all the way to Brazil had returned to Europe for the rest of her life." The impact she made on her students would last for decades. She passed away in 1972, and likely born in 1892.

From the *Revista Musical Ilustrada "Tárrega"* issue No. 2 from July of 1924, this advertisement by Romero & Fernández for 13 transcriptions by Joséfina Robledo of Europe's most elite composers.

In 2002 Gilson Uehara Antunes finished a Masters of Musicology thesis in Sao Paolo entitled:
AMÉRICO JACOMINO "CANHOTO" E O DESENVOLVIMENTO DA ARTE SOLÍSTICA DO VIOLÃO EM SÃO PAULO (Americo Jacomino "canhoto" and the development of his art of the Solo Guitar in Sao Paolo). He included some of the concerts performed by Joséfina Robledo. Portuguese translation by Randy Osborne

The official debut of Joséfina Robledo and her husband, cellist, Fernando Molina took place on Sunday July 29, 1917, in the salão do Conservatório Dramático e Musical de São Paulo. The program presented the following pieces:

Primeira Parte
Joséfina Robledo
— Albeniz: Serenata Espanhola
Waltz – Godard
Trêmolo – Gottschalk
Jota Aragoneza – Tárrega

Segunda Parte
Violoncello and guitar – Molina and Robledo
— Squire: Priére
— Pergolese: Nina
— Godard: Sur lê Lac
— Glazounov: Serenata Espanhola

Terceira Parte
Joséfina Robledo
— Albeniz: Granada
— Bach: Bourré
— Chopin: Nocturno op. 9 n.º 2
— Paganini: Carnaval de Veneza

The guitarist appeared again in the capital only in 1923, for the recital at the Conservatório Dramático e Musical.

Primeira Parte
— Tárrega: Capricho Árabe - Serenata
— Mendelssohn: Romanza n.º 6 e 12
— Tárrega: Dois Estudos
— Albeniz: Granada - Serenata
— Pujol: Canção do Berço
— Tárrega: Sueño — Trêmulo

Segunda Parte
— Albeniz: Cadiz
— Beethoven: Minueto del septimino
— Bach: Loure
— Chopin-Robledo: Vals op. 34 n.º 2
— Chopin: Noturno op. 9 n.º 2
— Tárrega: Jota Aragoneza

This advertisement for a guitar model named after Joséfina Robledo is from the *"O Violao"* magazine issue number 1 of December 1928, though Joséfina Robledo had returned to Spain in 1925, her legend remained, she and Agustín Barrios were the first two real virtuosos from outside Brazil to visit various cities and perform musical feats unheard of before their arrival. Portuguese translation by Randy Osborne.

"The Guitar, a Joséphina Robledo model and an instrument by the elite for the elite. Modeled and technically proportioned and of the labor and a type very much for the beautiful sex and satisfaction always for the maestros as well as their students.

Caution!

The Joséphina Robledo model is of our exclusive fabrication and is easy to identify as legitimate it carries inside a label representing the eminent guitarist performing on her instrument.

A Guitarra de Prata-Porfirio Martins and Company Rua da Carioca. 37 — Rio de Janeiro —."

This advertisement for a guitar model named after Joséfina Robledo is from the back cover of a sheet music piece by Alberto Baltar titled: *"Bon Jour, Papa"*. This is a later guitar model maybe from the 1940's. Portuguese translation on the next page by Randy Osborne:

502

"Joséfina Robledo Guitar

A standard of modern guitaristic technique.

The Joséfina Robledo Guitar and a source of harmonic perfection, moderation of workmanship, a style embellished and technical perfection of what is the best that is fabricated until today by the master guitarmakers.

By our exclusive construction, the model that has the name of the notable guitarist and effectively an instrument that unites all of the demanding requirements the end of which is the destiny: sound volume, balance, and overall a timbre that makes it distinguished among its genre. An instrument for concert guitarists, that honors the national industry and a deserved homage a tribute to the favorite disciple of Tárrega, who knew so well that highlight under the sky of Brazil the melody of the instrument of our people.

Constructed of selected Brazilian Rosewood, a rosette finished in Arabic mosaics, Ebony fretboard, ivory purflings, deluxe gears, etc.

<pre>
        Price 400,000
        Case made of cedar, guitar shaped . . . 120,000
</pre>

A Guitarra de Prata — Rua da Carioca. 37 — Rio de Janeiro"

Joséfina Robledo pieces published by Romero & Fernández in 1920.

(Left) Transcription of Beethoven's Moonlight Sonata by Joséfina Robledo for Romero & Fernández.
(Right) Transcription by Francisco Tárrega and revised by Francisco Calleja of the *Serenata* by Malats as performed by Joséfina Robledo.

On the next page is a photo of Joséfina Robledo from the *"A Escola de Tárrega Método completo de Violao"* 2nd edition by Oswaldo Soares, published by Irmaos Vitale. It was not included in the 1st edition. This was a gift to Ricardo Muñoz: "To the eminent Professor and beloved friend Ricardo Muñoz an affectionate embrace from your friend Oswaldo Soares, Rio de Janeiro 1946."

504

Ao meu incomparavel discipulo e brilhante violonista CARLOS COLLET E SILVA com elevadissima admiração, para que o seu nome fique perpetuado neste trabalho, que ofereço aos estudiosos e cultores do violão.

RIO DE JANEIRO, DEZEMBRO DE 1944 — *OSWALDO SOARES*

Josephina Robledo

POSIÇÃO PARA SENHORAS

Text from the previous page. Portuguese translation: "To my incomparable disciple and brilliant guitarist Carlos Collet e Silva with very high admiration, so that his name perpetuated in this work, I offer to students and lovers of the guitar. Rio de Janeiro, December of 1944 — Oswaldo Soares."
Spanish translation: "To my notable disciple Mr. Oswaldo Soares, affectionately Joséfina Robledo, Sao Paulo, February 3, 1923." Portuguese translation: "Position for Women"

This biography of Albor Maruenda is translated from Ricardo Muñoz's unpublished book *"Historia Universal de la Guitarra"* Volume VIII *"La Escuela Tárrega en La Argentina"*.

"Albor Maruenda

Origin:

He is the son of Spanish parents, born in Bahia Blanca, Buenos Aires Province on July 2, 1918.

His Education:

He began the guitar in 1928 with maestro Juan Dozo and later, in the year 1934, he proceeded to study with the celebrated Joséfina Robledo in Valencia, Spain, to whose city he arrived still being very young, studying music afterward with *Don* Eduardo Lopez Chavarri and *Don* Manuel Palau.

His Virtuosity:

He gave some performances in Valencia and other cities of the Province; he returned to Buenos Aires and in 1936 he was presented in the hall of the important music house Casa Breyer, in which he gave a magnificent concert with music of the classics of the guitar and the piano; the 17th of September of the same year we see him in the Sala Lassalle, performing pages by Sor, Haydn, Bach, Moreno Torroba, Padre San Sebastian, Turina, Castelnuovo-Tedesco and de Falla for the Asociacion Guitarristica

Argentina. The daily *"La Prensa"* on the 19th praised him in this way: ". . . besides being an impeccable instrumentalist, in whose technique and richness of sound complement him, he has a temperament tuned by his culture. -- He is very studious and is knowledgeable of his art, his interpretations are always asserted by his musical quality, his sober style and expressivity that is the most effective."

In 1937 he performed in the Biblioteca Bernardino Rivadavia, interpreting Mozart, Tárrega, Bach, Beethoven, Chopin, Moreno Torroba, Malats, Granados and Albeniz, with a real success, reappearing the 17th of June in the same hall, where he reaffirmed his endowed artistic knowledge, and the same some days later in the Salon "La Argentina".

He moved to Santiago, Chile and took the professorship of the guitar of the Conservatorio Nacional de Musica; years later he visited Peru, Central America, Mexico, Venezuela, Bolivia, Brazil, etc.; the great Segovia encountered him in Caracas, and after hearing him said: "He is one of the strongest players of the new generation."

In 1952 we find him offering a concert in the Instituto Pedagogico Nacional de Verones, in the city of Lima where he interpreted Milan, Narvaez, de Visée, Sor and Tárrega.

His Lectures:

He is known to have given lectures in South American Universities, especially about music of the 14th and 16th centuries."

Albor Maruenda has one mention in the *Diccionario de Guitarristas* by Domingo Prat, on page 110 it states: 'He is listed among the most distinguished students of maestro Juan Dozo and that presently he is studying with Joséfina Robledo in Spain.'

Liliana Pérez Corey in the book *"Obras-ineditas para guitarra clasica-de compositores-chilenos"* recalls, having been a student of maestro Albor Maruenda at the Conservatorio Nacional de Musica in Santiago. Later she went to Buenos Aires to study with Consuelo Mallo Lopez until she received her title of Concert Guitarist and Professor. Then she was off to Barcelona to study with the celebrated Emilio Pujol, when she returned to Santiago, she was given the professorship of the guitar at the Conservatorio Nacional de Musica to teach the new generation.

Albor Maruenda

In the *"El Momento Musical -revista mensual ilustrada"* (Illustrated Monthly) magazine published in Buenos Aires in November 1936 Issue No. 2, *Año* 1 in the *"Conciertos"* section is a review of a concert by Albor Maruenda.

'The great virtuoso of the future'-Andrés Segovia has said- 'will be a German or an Austrian, in whose countries they study a lot and very well.' To reveal his opinion the Andalucian artist doesn't ignore how intensely he cultivates this instrument among us, recalling, in effect, the other declaration of his: 'In Buenos Aires they study guitar more than music.' The unquestionable authority who represents the *"Pontifice de la guitarra"* (The Pope of the guitar), we disclaim any commentary. Besides eveything coincides in which the art of Tárrega, in his revelation is the most elevated that comes to us from Spain.

The artist who visits us today is Argentine; he studied with the eminent Joséfina Robledo and his name is Albor Maruenda. He is a young instrumentalist, since he is only 19 years old; but his art is much older. His technique and musicianship is the most interesting. He interprets with absolute sureness, hinting that, if necessary, he would overcome major difficulties easily. His school is classically perfect in which the 'method' has disappeared, he has anulled it to overcome it in a spiritual atmosphere. His hands don't 'listen', instead he directs the strings that vibrate caressed by emotion that flows through his fingers. To the above can be added that the literate culture that Maruenda has isn't limited to the guitaristic field, but also the pianistic, violinistic and symphonic, of whose interpretations he opines with outstanding skill.

After having been presented to the public under the auspicies of the Asociacion Guitarristica Argentina, made in the Salon "La Argentina" reaffirming his exceptional merits. He began his recital with *"Preludio", "Zarabanda", "Menuet"* and *"Gavotta"* by Kuhnau, composer of the 17th and early 18th centuries, to whom the historical critic attributed, without foundation, the first clavichord sonata, forgetting the genius of Pasquini. From those miniatures admirably transcribed in reason of its clavichord origin, it translated the ingenuous purity and the delicate style of a distant epoch. another such happening with the interpretation of a Bach Suite, whose romantic anxiety begins to warn us of the interpreters of the new generation. In the Sonatas of Ponce and Turina, respectively, Albor Maruenda revealed his interpretive qualifications of the modern composers. This artist feels as few do the style of the Spanish music, being, besides, very applauded for his versions of Tárrega, Granados and Albeniz.

Albor Maruenda walks with a firm step towards the few successors of Andrés Segovia. If our prophecy comes to pass the future virtuoso of the guitar will be Argentine."

The photo on the previous page is dated: "Buenos Aires, October 14, 1936."

In the June 23, 1900 issue No. 90 *Año* III of the *"Caras y Caretas"* magazine is the mention on page 7, in an advertisement for the company F. R. Guppy y Cia. located at 368 San Martin, Buenos Aires, of a wax cylinder recording made by Benito Sarabia, who was 26 years old at the time. The translated text reads "New cylinders of all types at reduced prices. The newest. Chosen phrases played on the guitar by Professor Saravia. Chosen phrases played on the mandolin by Professor Palmerino Vitullo. The second general catalog has just been released." These are possibly the first guitar solo and mandolin solos recorded in the Rio de la Plata region.

There was no mention of what label these were produced by, but the finding of a catalog, which they did have, may offer more titles and the name of the producer.

"Benito Sarabia is a Spanish guitarist and composer. He was born in Tudela, in the Province of Navarre on the 21st of May of 1874. From a young age, there in his homeland, he was dedicated to the study of the guitar, to be distinguished on it very soon. After touring several provinces, and having achieved a flattering success, he traveled to Argentina to settle in Buenos Aires. As a performer, he has cultivated his art in a purely personal manner, obtaining a great advantage: his characteristically improvisation on Andalucian (Flamenco) or Argentine airs making this peculiar mode his pleasing clarity of sound. As a composer, a known publication is *"Estilo"* of an Argentine ambiance. he collaborated with the Catalan composer; today the director of the "Conservatorio Fontova", on an Argentine zarzuela titled *"Los visionarios"*. As a maestro within the teaching already mentioned, he has always been very much sought after, a vast illustration adorning his personality which earns him a lot of respect and kindness." So ends the entry in the *"Diccionario de Guitarristas"* by Domingo Prat.

In the 1931 Antigua Casa Nuñez catalog he had one piece listed.

This photo of Benito Sarabia is from a Hermanos Breyer advertisement in a "Caras y Caretas" magazine from July 6, 1918, Issue No. 1031, *Año* XXI.

This concert review of Benito Sarabia is from the *Revista Musical Ilustrada "Tárrega"* magazine issue No. 3 of August 1924.

"Guitar Concert
Guitar performance — The known guitar professor *Don* Benito Sarabia, has given an excellent guitar concert in the Salon "La Argentina", developing the following program with total skill:

"Aires centroamericanos"
"Pequeña rapsodia andaluza"
"Glosa bonaerense"
"Carmen" (arrangement)
"Potpourri de aires nacionales"
"Fantasia militar" (Marcha descriptiva)
"Motivos montañeses"
"San Lorenzo" (Marcha nacional)
"La bruja" (Serenata)
"Canciones peruanas"
"Zamba, triunfo y huella"
"Jota" (Variaciones)"

BENITO SARABIA
Distinguido profesor de guitarra

This photo of Benito Sarabia is from the *Revista Musical Ilustrada "Tárrega"* magazine issue No. 3 of August 1924. "Distinguished Guitar Professor"

This announcement of a Benito Sarabia concert is from the *Revista Musical Ilustrada "Tárrega"* magazine issue No. 26 of September 1926.

"Guitar Performance

Sponsored by the Asociacion Musical de Alumnos del Conservatorio Fontova, a performance with the participation of the guitarist Mr. Benito Sarabia, who completed in his manner the prepared program that took place, on Saturday the 18th of the current month."

Sala de audición de los Discos ‹Rey del Son›, Florida 220

In the July 21, 1900 issue of the *"Caras y Caretas"* magazine No. 94 *Año* III, is this showroom photo for Cassels & Cia., a Buenos Aires record store at the beginning of the 20th century.

This record advertisement for *Criollo* vocals with Guitar, *Zarzuelas*, Police Band, the Teatro Martin Orchestra is from the magazine *"Caras y Caretas"* of August 23, 1902 issue No. 203 *Año* V. As they say at the top of this notice they are "90 days ahead of our competitors, the first to be put on sale in Buenos Aires."

This is from the magazine *"Caras y Caretas"* of September 14, 1901 issue No. 154 *Año* IV. A variety of Flamenco songs with guitar accompaniment available on cylinder recordings. Gaspar Sagreras had published a *Peteneras* piece, he died on April 14, 1901.

In the January 14, 1905 issue of the *"Caras y Caretas"* magazine No. 328 *Año* VII is this ad stating 20,000 discs had just arrived, this shows the demand of the 1,000,000 plus populace.

This Casa Tagini advertisement that states they have just received 25,000 discs and cylinders is from the magazine *"Caras y Caretas"* of March 31, 1906 issue No. 391 *Año* VIII.

This Casa Tagini Criollo vocals with guitar advertisement is from the magazine *"Caras y Caretas"* of January 6, 1906 issue No. 379 *Año* VIII.

514

El Grafófono Columbia
DISCO Y CILINDRO

GRAN PREMIO. PARIS. 1900.

"En el tiempo de mi juventud no habia nada como eso"

GRAN PREMIO. ST. LOUIS. 1904.

Las únicas máquinas parlantes que imprimen y reproducen la voz humana natural, agradable, sin chillidos ni alteración.

Precios al alcance de todos

Pidan CATALOGOS ilustrados gratis á la

Casa Tagini

Perú, 25 al 31.-Av. Mayo 601, 611

Único representante en la República Argentina

Hay constantemente en la casa un surtido de más de **100.000** discos y cilindros artísticos en todos idiomas y de todos los repertorios. **CATALOGOS GRATIS.**

AGENTES: Rosario Santa Fe, A. Ferraris, San Martín, 363; Paraná: Hijos de José Alsina Co.; Córdoba: Angel Sánchez, Constitución, 42; San Juan: A. Zurino G.; Mendoza: A. Zurino G.; Bahía Blanca: Elfersy Co., Chiclana, 202; Río Colorado: Elfersy Co.; Tres Arroyos: Elfersy Co.; La Plata, José Serra, Calle 7 No. 707; Corrientes: Adriano J. Hockner.

This Casa Tagini Columbia records and cylinders advertisement is from the magazine *"Caras y Caretas"* of January 27, 1906 issue No. 382 *Año* VIII. Most notably are the one dozen stores in 12 cities that Casa Tagini is distributing to offering these vocals in all languages and repertoires and the 100,000 units in his own inventory.

In 1909 in the magazine *"Caras y Caretas"* of June 5, 1909 issue No. 557 *Año* XII was this Edison Amberol cylinder advertisement for Flamenco Music. The translation of the text is:

"They have just arrived, the new Flamenco songs. Sung on Amberol cylinders of 4 minutes duration, by the celebrated "Lola la Flamenca" and instrumental pieces performed by the famous flamenco guitarists Amalio Cuenca, Eduardo Salmeron and Miguel Casares, who have received the warm praises and personal congratulations of King Edward of England and of President Diaz of Mexico. These are the first flamenco cylinders of 4 minutes to arrive in the country.

Price 1.70 pesos. You can play them only on the Edison Phonographs, equipped with the apparatus of the Amberol combination.

Of the Edison Regular cylinders, we have 150,000 in existence, of all classes and in all languages. Ask for catalogs."

Previous to this advancement, cylinders were 3 minutes long in duration.

Let's take a look at who these "famous flamenco guitarists" were, after all they were very early recording artists, and their works were available to the listeners of the Rio de la Plata when Domingo Prat was still in his first visit to Buenos Aires.

According to the book "Ethnic Music on Records Volume 4 Spanish, Portuguese, Philippines, Basque: A Discography of Ethnic Recordings Produced in the United States 1893-1942" by Richard K. Spottswood, on page 1810: Amalio Cuenca's Guitar Solo Recordings were:

"Soleares-Aires Flamencos . . . . . . Ed 8010 (4 min) 22342 (4 min)
Potpourri de Tangos Flamencos . . Ed 8011 (4 min) 22343 (4 min)
Guajiras Flamencos . . . . Ed 8012 (4 min) 22344 (4 min)
Granadinas . . . . Ed 8013 (4 min) 22345 (4 min)

These were all recorded in New York on March 3, 1909."

According to the entry in Domingo Prat's *"Diccionario de Guitarristas"*: "Amalio Cuenca is a performing guitarist and professor of the Andalucian genre, "flamenco", a contemporary Spaniard. Since a child he practiced on this instrument, cultivating as a "amateur". His parents influenced him into the profession as a watchmaker and later, when the Basque sport of soccer was in vogue in Europe and Latin America, that is to say, at the end of the 19th century he played as a professional soccer player. That public figure,

Amalio Cuenca

became tired of the Basque "foot-ball" and Amalio Cuenca returned with more passion to practicing the guitar, and in this way in the year 1900 we see him form a part of the body of professors for the now defunct "Sociedad Guitarristica Española", of Madrid, his companions in teaching being the celebrated Rafael Marin, José Rojo, Juan Viñolo, the last two in the class of the *"Guitarra Clasica"*. In the concert that took place by the said entity on May 4, 1900, *"Los tocaores"* (the players) Cuenca and (Rafael Marin) Sanchez were entrusted with one of the numbers of the evening, being awarded with hot applause. Later he moved to Paris where he settled permanently, dedicating himself to teaching and intervening in typical Andalucian artistic acts; in this way we could appreciate him in our visit to the capital of France in 1910, where he presently continues to be surrounded by those who appreciate and admire him. (1930)" So end the entry in Domingo Prat's *"Diccionario de Guitarristas"*

According to the Spanish historian, Mariano Gomez de Caso Estrada (1925-) (Translated by Randy Osborne): "Amalio Cuenca Gonzalez was born on July 10, 1866 in Riaza, Spain to Guillermo and Gregoria, when he was ten they moved to Santa Columba in the Province of Segovia. On April 14, 1898 in the Teatro de la Zarzuela in homage to the Zarzuela singer, Lucrecia Arana, he gave a concert of flamenco airs. In this year he was contracted by diverse impresarios of various spectaculars, being considered a Flamenco maestro.

He formed a duet with Miguel Borrull and they gave many concerts in Madrid. Antonio Chacon contracted Amalio in 1899 as his accompanist. In 1902 he gave more concerts with Miguel Borrull. In 1903 he traveled to Paris, he also gave concerts in Germany and England. Between 1904 and 1906 he accompanied the Flamenco dancers Faico and his wife Lola "La Flamenca" giving concerts in the United States. He returned to Spain, and then was invited by Porfirio Diaz, the President of Mexico to perform in the Presidential Palace. He returned to Spain, and then once again gave concerts with his friend Miguel Borrull. Amalio settled in Paris in 1908 and opened his restaurant in 1912, where the creme de la creme of Flamenco performed their guitars, footwork and great vocals with duende. In May of 1909 he was chosen to record some flamenco pieces for Edison Phonograph, in the United States. This resulted in a great international reputation. In 1910 the Costa Rican Legation opened a new office in Paris, according to the French newspapers Amalio Cuenca was starting a new revolution with his guitar, and he was requested to do a concert, among the attendees was the daughter of Queen Isabel II, *Doña* Eulalia.

The name of Amalio Cuenca was repeated among the cultural mediums and artists in Paris. The commentaries, the concerts and reunions of the powerful classes where he was requested, were saying so much praise that it created a conflict to hear the eminent guitarist of the Segovia Province. In one of these reunions the sculptor, was present. He was motivated to recommend Amalio to his friend, Ignacio Zuloaga, in the summer of 1910.

Rodin, in October, invited the guitarist to give a concert in his studio, for him and a group of friends.

On August 2, 1910, Amalio Cuenca put on a musical extravaganza with four acts and five Flamenco cuadros titled "La femme et la pantin", a work by Pierre Louys, presented in the Théatre Antoine, Regina Badet, Germaine Dermez and Fermin Génier acted.

The French and Spanish newspapers weren't strangers to this representation that they praised.

1912. — Amalio Cuenca had the Grand Opening of his luxurious restaurant, "La Feria", in the most "Chic" area of Paris. He contracted his friend Miguel Borrull and his daughters, celebrated dancers, in this way the best artists of dance and singing of Spain: La Macarrona, Faico, Lola "La Flamenca", La Patita, etc.

Miguel Borrull and his daughter Conchita at the Teatro Eldorado in Barcelona in September 1917. This is from the magazine "Eco Artistico" of September 25, 1917 issue No. 281.

At the inauguration the Ambassador of Spain, the Consul General, Spanish and French nobility, journalists, writers, promoters of ballet, and a good number of artists attended.

In spite of his successes and commitments, he traveled to Spain to contract artists that gave variety to his spectaculars. In September of 1913 he visited the Segovia Province and Riaza, where he gave a concert to family, friends and the distinguished visitors who attended.

1914. — He took on the position of artistic director of the hall of spectaculars "El Kursaal Internacional", in Seville.

He didn't stop doing concerts in Spain and France. For his well-known great merits, in 1922 he was named a member of the jury of the Concurso de Cante Jondo of Granada, organized, among others by Manuel de Falla, and García Lorca. Andrés Segovia, Antonio Ortega Munilla, Antonio Gallego Burín, Gregorio Abril and José López Ruiz joined him on the jury.

Amalio Cuenca had the occasion to perform with his old acquaintances: Ignacio Zuloaga, Ramón Montoya and Antonio Chacón: with the last two he reunited in Seville a few days later.

March 28, 1928. Paris. He had opened an Andalucian tablao. A posh dancer, Teresina Boronat a model of Ignacio Zuloaga and who converted into a Flamenco danced accompanied by Amalio Cuenca. With Manzanilla and other fine wines they toasted the painter and his companion.

He was requested to give two concerts in Spain.

The 26th of May of 1929, in Seville, with his guitar he accompanied the celebrated María Albaicín, who was one of the most distinguished dancers of Spain.

In June of 1930 he was requested by the Ambassador of Spain to give a concert at a banquet for the President of the French Republic, accompanied by the French Ministers of Justice, War, Maritime, Marshal Petain, the Secretary General of Foreign Affairs Philippe Berthelot, and other high officials. The eminent Teresina Boronat danced to the sounds of the guitar of Amalio Cuenca.

The 11th of February of 1931, the Barcelonan residents of Paris opened the new location of *"La Nacion"*. Lolita Benavente presented her *"Danzas Españolas"*, accompanied by Amalio Cuenca.

The 14th of July of this year, as in all, the French commemorated the taking of the Bastille (The 14th of July 1789.). The Spanish artists united for the occasion. Laura Santelmo, the day of 14th presented in the Teatro de la Ópera, Palais Garnier; asked for the guitarist Amalio Cuenca to play as a soloist in her presentation of *"Danzas Españolas"*, to interpret pages of *"Cantos de España"*, by Isaac Albeniz; *"Tango"*, *"Alegria"*, *"La vida breve"* and *"El sombrero de tres picos"*, by Manuel de Falla; and "Escena gitana", by Infante.

Continuing in París, the next year, on April 18, 1932 he celebrated, in the halls of La Sociedad Nueva España, a commemorative fiesta of the proclamation of the Second Republic. La Josélito and Amalio Cuenca performed.

In 1934 Amalio Cuenca was to accompany an exceptional artist, perhaps the best Spanish diva of the ópera of this epoch: Conchita Supervía.

At the beginning of January there were four days of concertos in London, and Amalio Cuenca was brought from Paris.

After being heard in operas by Rossini, alternating with Pergolesi, Respighi, Bizet, the great Spanish contemporaries, on the stage of the "Aeolian Hall" it led to flamenco. He sat next to Amalio Cuenca to sing *"Los siete ritmos más importantes del folklore andaluz y gitano"* (The seven most important rhythms in Andalucian and Gypsy folkmusic.). The *Peteneras, Malagueñas, Fandanguillos, Farrucas, Sevillanas, Garrotins* and *Tangos* emerged. Among the hot applause, emerged the *"Olés"*, and it wasn't from the throats of the Spaniards.

1936. — A performance, in the outstanding hall of concertos Pleyel, of the guitarists Amalio Cuenca, Ramón Montoya and Juan Relámpago who accompanied the dancer La Josélito.

Then came the dark days. The military uprising against the Second Republic brought countless ills. Until those living on foreign soil were affected.

Amalio Cuenca felt the weight of the years and the desires for rest. He wanted to return to Spain. Then he contacted Paco Durrio (François Durrieu); the sculptor he met when he presented a concert supposedly in 1903, as he sought to make his residence permanent, as we have said was in 1908. Durrio wrote to Ignacio Zuloaga, who enjoyed a certain prestige in the French government, that facilitated the crossing of the border and his stay in Spain.

Amalio Cuenca needed diverse documentation. This goes calling for the entry into the offices of the Consulate of Spain in Paris. (Below we see his 1939 passport.)

It is thought that he passed away in the first few years of the 1940's or 1950's in France.

Segovia, December of 2010.
Signed, Mariano Gómez de Caso Estrada."

There are videos of his works on You Tube

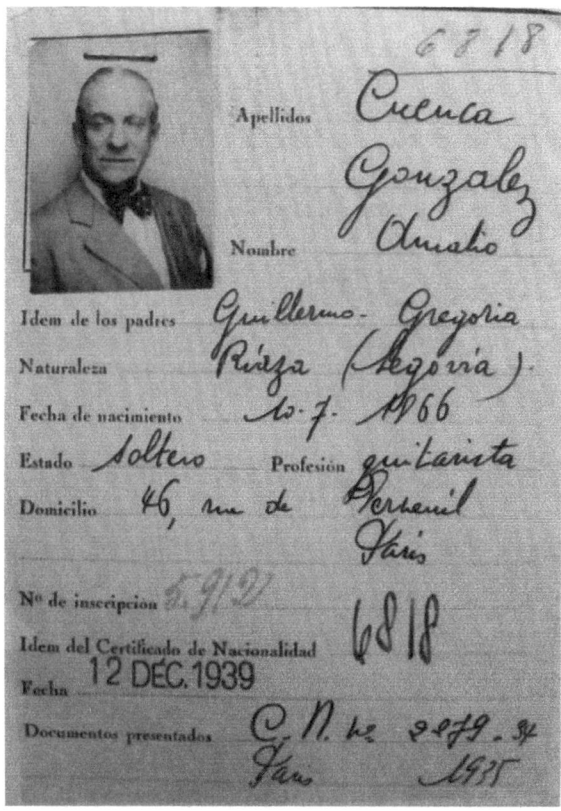

This from the "Guitar News" magazine issue No. 12 of April-May 1953. José Navas, who was the Professor of Guitar at the Conservatorio de Malaga from 1948 until many years later when he retired, shared this comment by maestro Miguel Llobet on the subject of Flamenco Guitar.

Several years ago, the last time the great guitarist Llobet passed through Malaga, I asked him, " What do you make of flamenco, Don Miguel ? ", and he replied : " I cannot explain it, I do not know how it came about." But there are gaps and absurdities. Andalusian music is a popular music and like all popular music it is topical, and the repetition of its topicality opens the door to the ignorant guitarist. The art of flamenco playing is the art of accompanying the singer—and no more. When the flamenco guitarist plays a solo its folk-music charm almost always turns into musical ignorance. He tries to imitate the classic guitarist, but except for rare occasions he cannot avoid cutting a ridiculous figure.

This from the "Guitar News" magazine issue No. 49 of July-August 1959.

Carlos Montoya, flamenco maestro, has given a series of concerts during the Spring of 1959 in Japan. His dancer in the tour of Japan is La Trianita. His program consists of 17 items from a Tarantas — real Cante jondo — to a Jota Aragonesa which is a folk dance rather than flamenco."

Eduardo Salmeron Clemente. "He is one of the most distinguished guitarists from Almeria, Spain, from the last third of the nineteenth century and beginning of the twentieth. He began in the Casino almeriense, by accompanying the Marmolista. He ended his artistic life in the decade of the 1920's, as an official guitarist of the Lion d'Or, alternating with others, with the Niño de Grana, the Niño de Cañete, the Niño de las Moras and Juan Soler (a) el Pescaero. From the beginnings of this twentieth century he made innumerable visits to Europe and America: Paris, Berlin, Bologna, Italy, New York . . ., with recitals in the presence of the Czar of Russia, the Kaiser of Germany and the King of England; he obtained various awards." (Source: Information and photo from the governing body of Almeria, Spain)

Lamentably I could not find any information about Miguel Casares, the third "famous flamenco guitarist" to record for Edison in 1909.

Eduardo Salmerón, guitarrista

In 1910 in Buenos Aires, the guitarist Rodríguez Burgueño recorded guitar solos for both the International Talking Machine Disco Odeon company and Victor Talking Machine Company.

   This information below is from: The Encyclopedic Discography of Victor Recordings (EDVR) web site. A team of researchers based at the University of California, Santa Barbara Libraries edits the database. The information below is from the Victor ledgers, the rare records themselves are not a part of the collection of discs at the University of California, Santa Barbara Libraries.

The six songs were recorded in Buenos Aires.

Matrix No.
R-709   March 27, 1910   Irene (Vals) Victor 62814
Rodríguez Burgueño

Guitar solo
R-710   March 27, 1910   Recuerdos Victor 62815
Rodríguez Burgueño

Guitar solo
R-711   March 27, 1910   Á morón Victor 62815
Rodríguez Burgueño

Guitar solo
R-712   March 27, 1910   Jota aragonesa Victor 62816
Rodríguez Burgueño

Guitar solo
R-713   March 27, 1910   Potpourri de marchas alegres Victor 62816
Rodríguez Burgueño

Guitar solo
R-714   March 27, 1910   Quebracho (Tango) Victor 62814
Rodríguez Burgueño

Número			Tamaño Pulg. c/m

Número			Tamaño Pulg.	c/m
62771	(a) **Entrerriano**—*Tango* (*Trío de Bandurrias y Guitarra*) Estudiantina "Centenario"		10	25
	(b) **Cabañal**—*Polka* (*Trío de Bandurrias y Guitarra*) Estudiantina "Centenario"			
62800	(a) **Pamplona**—*Vals* (*Trío de Bandurrias y Guitarra*) Estudiantina "Centenario"		10	25
	(b) **La Alegría de la Huerta**—*Jota* (**Chueca**) (*Trío de Bandurrias y Guitarra*) Estudiantina "Centenario"			
62801	(a) **Árabe**—*Paso doble torero* (*Trío de Bandurrias y Guitarra*) Estudiantina "Centenario"		10	25
	(b) **Santiago**—*Vals* (*Trío de Bandurrias y Guitarra*) Estudiantina "Centenario"			
62802	(a) **El Esquinazo**—*Tango* (*Trío de Bandurrias y Guitarra*) Estudiantina "Centenario"		10	25
	(b) **La castaña del Gitano**—*Vals* (**García**) (*Trío de Bandurrias y Guitarra*) Estudiantina "Centenario"			
62803	(a) **Retreta Española**—*Marcha* (**Portal**) (*Trío de Bandurrias y Guitarra*) Estudiantina "Centenario"		10	25
	(b) **Triana**—*Paso torero* (*Trío de Bandurrias y Guitarra*) Estudiantina "Centenario"			
62815	(a) **Recuerdos**—*Vals* Solo de Guitarra Burgueño (b) **A Morón**—*Tango* Solo de Guitarra Burgueño		10	25
62816	(a) **Jota Aragonesa**—*Solo de Guitarra* Burgueño (b) **Potpourri de Marchas Alegres**—*Solo de Guitarra* Burgueño		10	25
62841	(a) **San Lorenzo**—*Marcha Militar* (**Silva**) Banda del Pabellón de las Rosas		10	25
	(b) **Viva la Patria**—*Marcha con Canto* (**Mazzocco**) Banda del 6º Regimiento de Infantería			
62855	(a) **Jota Aragonesa**—*Trío de Bandurrias y Guitarra* Estudiantina "Centenario"		10	25
	(b) *En toda la quintana—Canción popular* Meano			
62856	(a) **La faute des roses** (*La culpa la tienen las rosas—Vals* (**Berger**) Banda del Pabellón de las Rosas		10	25
	(b) **La Princesa del Dollar**—*Polka* (**Fall**) Banda del Pabellón de las Rosas			
62868	(a) **El Numantino "Hotel Victoria"**—*Tango* (*Trío de Bandurrias y Guitarra*) Estudiantina "Centenario"		10	25
	(b) **La vuelta al pago**—*Tango* (*Trío de Bandurrias y Guitarra*) Estudiantina "Centenario"			
62878	(a) **Qué cosa bárbara**—*Tango* (**Poggi**) Orquesta de la "Sociedad Orquestral"		10	25
	(b) **Vuelo de Mariposa**—*Vals* (**Sciutti**) Banda del Pabellón de las Rosas			
62925	(a) **Una prueba de Orquesta** (**Sesso**) Banda del Pabellón de las Rosas		10	25
	(b) *En casa del Dentista—Diálogo* Pacheco y López			
62960	(a) *Hijo del Pueblo—Himno Socialista Dúo* (**Caratala**) (Con Orquesta) Quesada-Aldea		10	25
	(b) **El Novillo**—*Vals* (*Trío de Bandurrias y Guitarra*) Estudiantina "Centenario"			

***
***
***

From a 1915 Uruguay Victor Talking Machine Company catalog page 227 are the listings of 4 songs on two discs by Rodríguez Burgueño still available to the public in Argentina and Uruguay. Below is the image from the page 30 (XXX) of the index. It is impossible to not see some the many recordings by the trio *"Estudiantina Centenario"* as well-two bandurrias and one guitar.

On page 37 in the June 1, 1916 issue of the *"Caras y Caretas"* magazine No. 926 *Año* XIX, from an article titled *"Cantores de Contrapunto"* we see the photo of Rodríguez Burgueño (Center-mispelled Brugueño) and Virgilio Magnasco (Right), and Damonte (Left).

Rodrí...ez Brugueño, en medio de los pichones Damonte y **Magnasco**, metiéndole a una clase de punteo, ante pleno auditorio.

Virgilio Magnasco owned a 1916 Enrique García guitar, now in the possession of luthier and historian Richard Bruné.

Virgilio Magnasco-Raffo. He is a notable Argentine aficionado. He was born in Buenos Aires on the 18th of May of 1879. the guitaristic personality of Virgilio Magnasco is well known and admired in the Capital Federal, within the ample environment of culture that the national instrument has achieved. Among our great men, greats where the grandure is seen by the sociological, political, literary, artistic and scientific superiority, has been and continues having excellent guitar culture, who dedicate to it the happiest hours.

Among those of yesterday we mention Juan Bautista Alberdi, Esteban Echeverria, Juan del Campilo, Salustiano Zarabia, etc.; later, in the final stages of the last century, making the list larger the lovers of the instrument are Dr. Nicanor Albarellos, Dr. Wenceslao Escalante; and in our days, the ex-judge of instruction Dr. Servando Gallegos, Martin Gil, Ciriaco Gomez, Dr. Ramon Munilla, Eleuterio Tiscornia, Pastor Obligado, the ex-Vice Presidents of the Republic Elpidio Gonzalez and Enrique Martínez, and to finish Dr. Virgilio Magnasco, of the best Argentine intellectual lineage and brother of the ex-minister of Public Instruction Dr. Oswaldo Magnasco.

The 9th of February of 1899, Virgilio Magnasco entered into the professorship, occupying various categories and positions in the Colegios Nacionales "Domingo F. Sarmiento" and "Nicolas Avellaneda", having achieved in the last, by deserved ascension, the position of Rector, retiring from this position in October of 1928. As a guitarist he cultivates various genres, always with emotion, he possesses a solid technique, based on the school of Aguado, without being subordinated, however, to anyone. He received guitaristically the advice of the Professors Mario Rodríguez Arenas and Antonio Sinopoli, and from the author of the present *Diccionario*. The performer Magnasco, (like the great Segovia), interpreting, certifies that one can play well without a maestro or, a decided school, but with logical norms that mediate all cultivated intelligence.

Virgilio Magnasco is the owner of a guitar that the celebrated luthier Enrique García constructed, a real instrumental jewel, and which he has possessed since 1916. In this guitar he lives and empties his best hours; and of it he brings out the sweetness that it has the capacity of its exquisite sensibility."
So ends the entry in Domingo Prat's *"Diccionario de Guitarristas"*.

This biography of Americo Jacomino is translated from Ricardo Muñoz's unpublished book *"Historia Universal de la Guitarra" Volume VI "America".*

"Americo Jacomino (Canhoto)

His Origin:

He was born in Sao Paulo on February 12, 1887.

His Education:

In 1902 he began his guitar studies intuitively, without a teacher.

His Virtuosity:

In his character as a performer, in the Teatro Lirico of Rio de Janeiro in 1927, he obtained the first prize as a soloist, playing the instrument up-side down, that is to say, with the headstock toward the right and the strings inverted, which obligated him to play the first three strings with the thumb and the bass strings with index, middle and ring fingers.—

They say in spite of this enormous inconvenience, he enraptured the public that listened to him.

His Compositions:

He was a composer inspired by popular music; of his pages we recall the waltz *"Recordacaos de Cotinha", "Belo Horizonte", "Abismo de Rozas", "Luizinha", "Em Pleno Mar", "Rozas Desfolhadas",* etc. the chords *"Beijos e Lagrimas",* the Gavote, *"Alborada de Estrellas",* the Maxixe, *"Invejoso"* and many others.

His Pedagogy:

He was dedicated to the teaching of folklore and gave lessons to Luis Giordano, Rogério Guimarães, Mozart Biscalho and others.

His Passing:

He died in Sao Paulo the 7th of September of 1928."

He began recording in 1913 and all his discs were in the possession of the late classical guitar record collector Ronoel Simoes, making possible the CDs that represent the player. Had he played the guitar in a regular fashion, instead of a manner where professors would not allow a student to attend University classes playing in such an unfortunate position, he could have actually contributed more to history, but alas he was responsible for his own artistic curtailment, and leaves behind a legacy: as one colleague said: "he has more fame than his ability merits".

AMERICO JACOMINO
,, C A N H O T O "

This photo of Americo Jacomino is from a 1920s Odeon catalog of the Casa Edison company in Rio de Janeiro, Brazil, directed by Frederico Figner.

There are videos of his works on You Tube

His ill use of the guitar may set him aside of the importance of early guitar virtuoso recording artists, such as Agustín Barrios-1913, Julio J. Otermin-1912, Rodríguez Burgueño-1910, Mário Pinheiro-1910, Amalio Cuenca, Eduardo Salmeron, Miguel Casares-1909, Octaviano Yañez-1908, etc. He is included here because of when he recorded and the prolific nature of the quantity of 46 songs, not how he hindered his own potential virtuosity.

Sonhando amores,

36280 { Deauville — Polka — Solo Clarinette — com orchestra.
Caprice — Valsa — Solo Clarinette — com orchestra.

ORCHESTRAS

Discos Duplos, Nacionaes, 27 centimetros — 5$000

33346 { Marcha Funebre — Chopin — orchestra.
Os Sinos de Corneville — Banda G. Republicana.

37169 { La Favorita — Coro d'intrudizione atto 1º — com orchestra.
Os Sinos de Corneville — com orchestra.

Serie 120.000

120684 { Voluptuosa — Valsa (A. Camillo)
Sonhando Amôres — Valsa (J. C. Christo)

120685 { Atrevido — Tango (E. Nazareth)
Quem tem amôres não dorme — Valsa (J. G. Christo)

120686 { Deusa — Valsa (C. Pagliacchi)
Lagrimas de Maria — Valsa (O. Carneiro).

Solos de violão pelo festejado artista CANHOTO

120595 { Bello Horizonte — Valsa.
Devaneio — Mazurka.

120596 { Pisando na mola — Polka.
Campos Salles — Dobrado.

— 54 —

This catalog page of Americo Jacomino's first two discs is from 1913 for the Casa Edison company in Rio de Janeiro, Brazil, directed by Frederico Figner.

A Casa Edison *e seu tempo*
FRANCESCHI, Humberto M. A Casa Edison *e seu tempo*. Rio de Janeiro, Sarapuí, 2002, 312 p.

This photo of Americo Jacomino's "Grupo do Canhoto" is from a c. 1914 catalog for the Casa Edison company in Rio de Janeiro, directed by Frederico Figner.

This photo and biographical page of Americo Jacomino is from the magazine *"O Echo-Revista Mensal"* published in Sao Paulo in September of 1916. This is from the Arquivo Publico do Estado de Sao Paulo, online. http://www.arquivoestado.sp.gov.br

Portuguese translation by Randy Osborne

"Concertista de Violao — Concert Guitarist

Americo Jacomino is a guitarist who possesses rare qualities, that one day took another performance in the editor's office of *"Cigarra"* (A very popular magazine), gathering new and deserved praises from the numerous attendees, that accompanied him with interest, with real rapture, to his interpretations, entirely personal, of a series of pieces, some of his own labor, others of celebrated national composers.

On the 6th of the current month, Americo Jacomino gave a concert in the Salão do Conservatório Dramatico e Musical, which was preceded by a lecture by a known man of letters, about — *"O Violao"* (The Guitar)."

In 2002 Gilson Uehara Antunes finished a Masters of Musicology thesis in Sao Paolo entitled: *AMÉRICO JACOMINO "CANHOTO" E O DESENVOLVIMENTO DA ARTE SOLÍSTICA DO VIOLÃO EM SÃO PAULO* (Americo Jacomino "canhoto" and the development of his art of the Solo Guitar in Sao Paolo). I would like to include some of his concerts, as they show usage of Argentine pieces by Gaspar Sagreras. Portuguese translation by Randy Osborne

On the 15th of August of 1923 an event at the Anfiteatro Escola Normal de São Carlos was organized:

Primeira Parte:
— Ouverture by the Orquestrinha da Escola
— Poesias de A. Nobre e Augusto dos Anjos, por Fernando Vargas
— Senhorita Iracema de Arruda Campos – Poesias
— Senhorita Sylvia Toledo – Poesias
— Senhorita Maria Apparecida (sic) M. Vieira – Poesias
— A. Cimino: Guarani, fantasia violin and piano
— S. Cimino: Deuse Negre – Caprice – piano
— Nair G. Veltri: Madrigale – violin solo

Segunda Parte-Here Americo Jacomino accompanies his colleague: Antônio de Barros Leite
— Ouverture pela Orquestrinha da Escola
— Gaspar Sagreras: Uma Lágrima – solo de violão
— Souto: Do Sorriso das Mulheres nascem as flores
— Verdi: Trovador – Miserere – transcrito para violão
— A. Jacomino: Gavota – favorita
— A. Jacomino: Valsa para concerto – Lembrança de um Sonho
— A. Jacomino: Marcha Militar Brasileira
— A. Jacomino: Uma Noite na Roça — cateretê

On the 5th of March 1925 Canhoto gave his first recital on "Sociedade Rádio Educadora Paulista" at 9PM. *"O Estado de São Paulo"* in a program in which the guitarist accompanied the tenor Roque Ricciardi.

The program presented consisted of the following pieces:

— A. Jacomino: Marcha Triunfal Brasileira.
— Frontini: Serenata Árabe
— A. Jacomino: Abismo de Rosas — valsa
— A. Jacomino: Feiticeiro — maxixe de salão

— Sagreras: Uma lágrima — delírio.
— A. Jacomino: Quando os corações se querem
— Calasan: Favorita — gavota
— A. Jacomino: Viola, Minha Viola — samba à moda do Norte.

Radiotelefonia / Sociedade Rádio Educadora Paulista. O Estado de S. Paulo, ano 51, n.° 16813, 6 de março de 1925, p. 06.

And in 1925, on the 23rd de March Jacomino presented in the Salão do Conservatório a recital in homage to Oswaldo Soares and João Avelino de Camargo.

Primeira Parte:
— A. Jacomino: Marcha Triunfal Brasileira (includes "Hino Nacional") —
  Accompanied on guitar by Mr. Carlos R. Souza
— A. Jacomino: Esmeralda – valsa lenta. (ao meu distinto amigo Mr. José Ozório Fonseca),
  Accompanied on guitar by Mr. Carlos R. Souza
— A. Jacomino: Trovador (Miserere) — solo, adapted for guitar
— Sagreras: Uma Lágrima (delírio) — solo
— A pedido: Abismo de Rosas, valsa lenta. Accompanied on guitar by Mr. Carlos R. Souza

Segunda Parte:
— Carlos Gomes: Protofonia do Guarani – Adapted for guitar, por A. Jacomino, Accompanied on guitar by
  Mr. Carlos R. Souza
— A. Jacomino: Feiticeiro – tango de salão – solo
— Calazans: Favorita – gavota – Accompanied on guitar by Mr. Carlos R. Souza
— A. Jacomino: Quando os corações se querem, fox-trot – Accompanied on guitar by Mr. Carlos R. Souza
— Frontini: Serenata Árabe – solo
— A. Jacomino: Viola, Minha Viola — cateretê paulista imitando o grito da
  cabloca. Accompanied on guitar by Mr. Carlos R. Souza

On the 29th of March, presented by Jacomino on rádio the following program:

— S. N. — Padre Nuestro — fox-trot — solo de banjo, with the accompaniment of piano
— A. Jacomino: Sudan — fox-trot — banjo and piano
— A. Jacomino: Tico-tico assanhado — polca característica — cavaquinho with accompaniment of guitar
— G. Verdi: Miserere do Trovador — solo de violão

The accompaniments of guitar and piano were entrusted to Mr. Carlos R. Souza. And it was the first time that Jacomino played presentation on banjo and cavaquinho, a program that included a piece he composed, a maxixe *"A Gente Se Defende"*.

In the same month, on the 30th and on the the 3rd and 5th of May, Canhoto presented in two new recitals presented the following program:

— Silvestre: Serenata d'autre fois.
— A. Jacomino: Sombras do passado — valsa "Boston"
— E. Souto: Do sorriso das mulheres nascem as flores
— A. Jacomino: Por que te vuelves a mi ? — tango Argentino
— Mendelssohn: 3.º Prelúdio
— A. Jacomino: Quando os corações se querem — fox-trot

This text contains excerpts from an article entitled "Gardel and his recording history" by Bruno Cespi and Héctor Lucci and drawn from the Todotango.com web site.

In 1899, imported by the house Enrique Lepage located on Bolívar 375, the first gramophones for 6- and 7-inch diameter flat discs arrived in Buenos Aires. They came from the United States and they showed the mark "Gramophone" registered by their inventor, the German Emile Berliner in 1888.

These talking machines astonished the Buenos Aires population that eagerly wanted to hear them. Because of that they were placed on Calle Florida and on Avenida de Mayo. At these locals audible demonstrations were made for those who paid a fee equivalent to an admission to a popular show. This same experience and modality had already happened in Buenos Aires five years before, in 1893, with the appearance of Edison's phonograph that recorded and played wax cylinders.

In those first years of the 1900s the musical atmosphere of Buenos Aires was largely spread in a domestic way thanks to the gramophone. The local genres included tango, canzonette and arias of Italian operas.

In 1902 the first discs for gramophone were recorded in Buenos Aires. Their diameter was between 165 and 175 mm, and the recordings were carried out by means of a traveling machine sent by the Zonophone Company whose proprietor was a close collaborator to Emilio Berliner in the development of the gramophone.

For those early Zonophone discs recorded their voices and music payadores and singers like Arturo de Nava, Alfredo Munilla, the orchestra of the Teatro San Martín and the Band of the Police of Buenos Aires, conducted by Félix Rizzuti, the father of the pianist José María.

In 1905 the first 10-inch discs (25cm) appeared commercially. They were recorded in Buenos Aires by the same house Zonophone, increasing the number of interpreters: Ángel Villoldo, Andrée Vivianne, Higinio Cazón, Gabino Ezeiza, José Madariaga, the orchestra of the Apolo theater, among others.

Already by this year other companies like Odeon, Victor, Pathé and Columbia also existed and recorded in Buenos Aires with the same traveling system, in which the tango occupied a preferential place.

Then we come to 1910 when the Italian José Tagini, running a bazaar business, sale of discs and phonographic machines, got the license from the Columbia house of North America for recording. He installed at the same place the recording laboratory, on Avenida de Mayo and Perú (Av. de Mayo 601, Perú 25).

Among the first characters that recorded those discs for Columbia Record were Alfredo Gobbi, Ángel Villoldo, Gabino Ezeiza, Eugenio Gerardo López, Arturo Mathon, José Betinotti, Flora Rodríguez de Gobbi, Juan Sarcione and many more.

Appearing as musical groups we have the Municipal Band, Vicente Greco's tango orchestra labeled as "Orquesta Típica Criolla". This name was for the first time printed on a record label. They were followed by groups like those led by Tano Genaro Espósito and Juan Maglio "Pacho" who, with his magnificent quartet, would become the biggest producer of Argentine records in 1912.

The body of participants that occupied the catalog of these Columbia Record discs was very extensive and it is then when José Tagini offered the opportunity to a 21 year-old youth, already called Carlos Gardel, to record seven double discs with a repertoire of his choice.

The announcement advertising the first four discs recorded by Carlos Gardel was published by the Tagini house in the *"Fray Mocho"* magazine on March 28, 1913 and with the following repertoire: T 594: *"La mañanita"*, estilo / *"Me dejaste"*, estilo; T 595 *"Mi madre"*, estilo/ *"Es en vano"*, song; T 637 *"Pobre flor"*, estilo / *"La mariposa"*, estilo; T 638 *"El almohadón"*, waltz / *"Brisas de la tarde"*, song. This announcement said: 'Carlos Gardel, tenor. Artist of the Teatro Nacional. 25 cm Double discs. $2. m/n (national currency)'.

These Columbia Record double discs were cut into matrixes and recorded in North America and they had navy blue labels with golden letters. The three missing discs appeared almost immediately, and they were: T 728 *"Sos mi tirador plateado"*, estilo / *"Yo sé hacer"*, cifra; T 729 *"Mi china cabrera"*, estilo / *"A mi madre"*, estilo; T 730 *"El sueño"*, estilo / *"A Mitre"*, waltz.

Five years passed for Gardel to record again and this time he made it for the Max Glücksmann house in 1917, accompanied by José Razzano. The recordings were carried out in a small room of a vault of Pathé film tapes, of which Max Glücksmann was the agent.

The machine that carried out these acoustic recordings was the same one that Alfredo Améndola brought from Germany for his Atlanta records in 1912 and that, when ceasing his activity in 1915, was acquired in an auction by Max Glücksmann. These early 1917 discs had a purple color label with golden letters and the inscription "Gardel-Razzano".

The first number that the duo chose to commit to record belonged to Ángel Villoldo and was entitled *"Cantar eterno"*, a song released in April of that year, alternating in each double disc the duet with some pieces by Razzano and others by Gardel as soloists.

In this first lot of approximately fifty recordings the interpretation of tango as a song is born in a Gardel's solo: *"Mi noche triste"*, a piece elaborated between Samuel Castriota with his tango *"Lita"* (1915) and Pascual Contursi with his poem *"Mal de ausencia"* (1917).

All these 1917 discs were recorded in wax and they were sent to Brazil for their matrix process and pressing. For that reason, you can read on the labels, in very small fonts and in bas-relief, the legend *"ind. Brasileira"* (made in Brazil).

In 1919 another cycle of recordings began, now in Disco Nacional, entirely manufactured in our country. On the label, also of purple color can be read: "Manufactured exclusively for Max Glücksmann by the First national factory of records in the Argentine Republic".

In Argentina Rosita Quiroga was the first female singer that recorded a disc with microphone (electrical process). It was on March 1, 1926 for the Victor Company with Antonio Polito's and Celedonio Flores's tango *"La musa mistonga"*, disc N° 79.632.

Carlos Gardel recorded his first electric disc in Argentina on November 8, 1926 with Nicolás Verona's and Lito Más's *paso doble*, entitled *"Puñadito de sal"*, N° 1 (matrix). But in fact, his first electric recording was cut in Barcelona on December 26, 1925 with Eduardo Bonessi's and Enrique Dizeo's tango: "Echaste buena".

He continued recording in Buenos Aires until 1927 and in 1928 he recorded in Barcelona again, and in Buenos Aires on June 20 of that same year again.

He returned to Paris and recorded from October 11, 1928 to April 6, 1929; in Buenos Aires between 1919-1930; in Paris in 1931; in Barcelona in 1932; Buenos Aires in 1933 and his last recordings were made in New York, from the 7/27/34 to March 20,1935 with *"Guitarra mía"*, a tune by Gardel and Le Pera."

Atacando los cantares andaluces, con acompañamiento de guitarra y pandereta

Payadores cantando de contrapunto: "La bedera está mojada"...

—Esos dos embudos (también se llaman boc- nas), el de arriba y el de abajo, están en comu- nicación con el aparato registrador, que se encuentra del otro lado de la pared.

—Por eso le decía yo que esto me recordaba á cuando se habla por teléfono. El que canta, es el que habla; el embudo, es el hilo, si usted permite; y el aparato registrador, es el que escucha... ¡Hombre! Y á propósito de aparato registrador, ¿es alguna cosa como el mimeógrafo? Yo he visto una vez un mimeógrafo...

—No, no es como un mimeógrafo, y más se parece á las calesitas que al mimeógrafo. Mientras de aquí se hace ruido, en el aparato registrador hay un disco de metal que efectúa un movimiento de rotación...

—¿De rotación, ó de traslación?

Piano, violín... y tenor. (El violín que se emplea para impresionar, tiene una bocina en lugar de una caja)

—No, de rotación, de rotación.

José Tagini's Columbia Recording Studio in Buenos Aires after 1910. These images are from an undated *"Fray Mocho"* magazine published in Buenos Aires.

These images are from an incomplete article written by Matias Juncal taken from a post 1910 *"Fray Mocho"* magazine. Spanish translation by Randy Osborne.

Photo captions:

Top Left: "The Andalusian singers starting to sing, with accompaniment of guitar and tambourine.
Top Right: "Payadors (Singers) singing in counterpoint: *"La bedera esta mojada"*...
Bottom: "Piano, Violin...and Tenor. (The violin that is employed for impressions has a horn instead of a body.)

"— Those two funnels (also called megaphones), the one above and the one below, are in communication with the recording machine, that is found on the other side of the wall.
    — So I told him that this reminded me of when we talk by phone. He who sings, is he who talks; the megaphone, is the thread, if you will allow me; and the recording machine, is who listens... Man! And by the way the recording machine, is something like the mimeograph?
I have seen a mimeograph once...
    — No, it isn't like a mimeograph, and it appears more like the carousels than the
    mimeograph. Meanwhile here it makes noise, on the recording machine there is a metal disc that performs the rotational movement...
    — Of rotation, or of copying?
    — No, of rotation, of rotation."

Page 2 (Image on the next page.) Photo captions, then text:

Top: "Musicians in front of the megaphone"
Bottom: "The apparatus that presses the sheet of shellac which serves as a matrix."

    — "I told him of copying, because as well there is a movement of copying.
    — But this is of rotation...Well, and to a measure that goes around, it's going to record the sounds on a sheet...
    — Of rubber, of course.
    — No, of shellac, of shellac
    — Of shellac?
    — Yes, sir, of shellac.
    — Look you what is curious! And if it melts?
    — Well you can see for yourself. With everything, it is of shellac.
    — In the end, of shellac or rubber, you say that it records the sounds. And afterward?
    — Later, that sheet, which is the matrix, is sent to the United States, and there they press the discs.
    — That doesn't seem strange, because for those things, there's no place like the United States. The Yankees already have the second-best navy fleet of the world. The first is the English... No, it might be sir, like I say; the first is the English, and the second of them. And why are there two megaphones?

    — The top one is for the voice, and the bottom one for the music. And there's another for the concerts.

Matias Juncal."

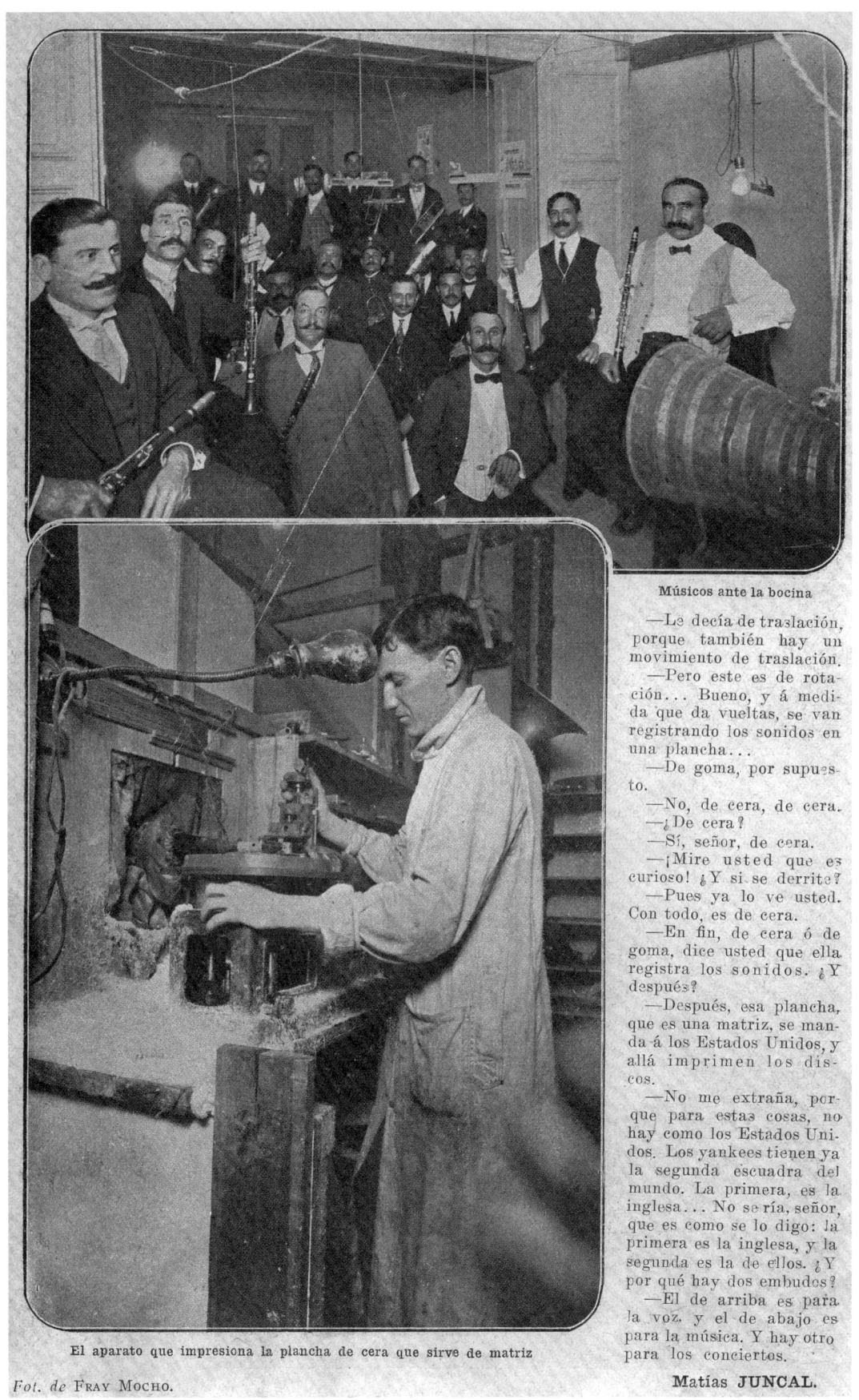

Músicos ante la bocina

—Le decía de traslación, porque también hay un movimiento de traslación.

—Pero este es de rotación... Bueno, y á medida que da vueltas, se van registrando los sonidos en una plancha...

—De goma, por supuesto.

—No, de cera, de cera.

—¿De cera?

—Sí, señor, de cera.

—¡Mire usted que es curioso! ¿Y si se derrite?

—Pues ya lo ve usted. Con todo, es de cera.

—En fin, de cera ó de goma, dice usted que ella registra los sonidos. ¿Y después?

—Después, esa plancha, que es una matriz, se manda á los Estados Unidos, y allá imprimen los discos.

—No me extraña, porque para estas cosas, no hay como los Estados Unidos. Los yankees tienen ya la segunda escuadra del mundo. La primera, es la inglesa... No sería, señor, que es como se lo digo: la primera es la inglesa, y la segunda es la de ellos. ¿Y por qué hay dos embudos?

—El de arriba es para la voz, y el de abajo es para la música. Y hay otro para los conciertos.

El aparato que impresiona la plancha de cera que sirve de matriz

Fot. de FRAY MOCHO.   Matías JUNCAL.

José Tagini's Columbia Recording Studio in Buenos Aires after 1910. These images are from an undated *"Fray Mocho"* magazine published in Buenos Aires.

A TODOS LOS LECTORES

DEL SIMPATICO SEMANARIO

"CARAS y CARETAS"

■

En el nuevo repertorio criollo, los discos marca

"ATLANTA"

no pertenecen a un tipo exclusivamente MERCANTIL, como muchas de las marcas hoy en comercio, con las cuales no se t iene otra mira que la de dar un artículo barato, realizando la mayor ganancia posible y prescindiendo de TODO SENTIDO ARTISTICO. Mientras que manejos parecidos llenan los bolsillos de fabricantes poco escrupulosos, el que PIERDE es el PUBLICO, por cuanto las producciones, que de música tienen SOLO EL NOMBRE, puestas en venta, influyen en el EXTRAVIO del

SENTIDO ARTÍSTICO NACIONAL

menoscabando poco a poco las bellas tradiciones de ARTE PURO que desde tiempos inmemoriales han regido las manifestaciones melódicas de NUESTRO PUEBLO.

Por lo mismo, hablar hoy en día de discos nacionales, es lo mismo que ahuyentar a los compradores de BUEN GUSTO amantes de lucir lo de casa, como buenos PATRIOTAS, pues de todo hay en discos CRIO-LLOS, menos lo que refleje con verdad y pureza la triste y grandiosa ALMA de la PAMPA, cuyos aires parecen emanar de lo infinito, y en los cuales vibra el ESPIRITU que forjó LOS HEROES que nos dieron una PATRIA.

Nosotros, conscientes del respeto que debemos al amor patrio y a las tradiciones nacionales, y con el fin de intimar que LA ARGENTINA no es el mercado de lo MALO y BARATO, como parece haya sido tomado hasta hoy por los importadores de discos, al poner en venta la marca

"ATLANTA"

nos propusimos no ahorrar NINGUN SACRIFICIO, con tal de proporcionar MUSICA CRIOLLA SELEC-CIONADA y AIRES NACIONALES en toda su PUREZA, utilizando para ello ORQUESTAS, BAN-DAS, RONDALLAS, etc., de primer orden, y ARTISTAS de gusto refinado y GARGANTA PRIVI-LEGIADA. De modo que los buenos CRIOLLOS podrán desde hoy en adelante GUSTAR BUENA MU-SICA CRIOLLA y hacerla gustar en los discos:

"ATLANTA"

El respetable PUBLICO se convencerá, y con bien fundado orgullo, que de música tenemos MUCHO Y BUENO, sin necesidad de recurrir al extranjero, y es obra PATRIOTICA popularizarla en debida forma, porque ella concurre a CIMENTAR EL ALMA NACIONAL.

Y del enorme progreso realizado en discos criollos, verdadero paso de GIGANTE que deja lo hecho hasta ahora muy ATRAS, podrá el respetable público darse cuenta parangonándolo con el hermosísimo REPERTORIO EUROPEO, que también pondremos en venta bajo la marca «ATLANTA» y «PANTO-PHONE», en el cual figuran los mejores números tocados y cantados de OPERAS, OPERETAS, ZAR-ZUELAS, DANZAS, BAILABLES, FANTASIAS, etc., primando entre ellos los de los mejores CAN-TANTES ITALIANOS y DE OTROS PAISES, como asimismo los grandes compositores.

PIDAN catálogos a nuestra CASA; son dos para mayor conveniencia de los interesados. En uno van los números criollos, bailables, cantados, españoles, etc. En otro los números Italianos y CLASICOS.

DAMOS DESDE YA LAS GRACIAS a nuestros favorecedores, y su preferencia será INDICE de que estamos en buen camino.

UNICOS CONCESIONARIOS EN LAS REPUBLICAS DEL PLATA:

AMENDOLA & CIA

274, ESMERALDA, 274 - Buenos Aires.— Catálogos Gratis.

Unión Telefónica, 582 (Libertad).　　　　=　　　　Cooperativa Telefónica, 1900 (Central).

This is the first advertisement by Alfredo Amendola's Atlanta record label in the *Caras y Caretas* magazine on April 5, 1913, issue No. 757 *Año* XVI. The translation on next page.

Translation of the previous page:

From the label image:

"Atlanta" Music on both sides for record players of steel needles of all brands.

"To all the readers of the pleasant weekly *"Caras y Caretas"*: In the new criollo repertoire, the "Atlanta" brand records don't belong to a type that's exclusively commercial, as many of the brands in commerce, with which don't have another intent than to offer a cheap article, realizing the best possible profit and dispensing with all artistic sense. So long as the similar operation fills the pockets of unscrupulous makers, it's the public that loses, by how many productions, that of music that only has the name, put on sale, they influence in the going astray of the national artistic sense diminishing little by little the beautiful traditions of pure art that since time immemorial have ruled the melodic demonstrations of our populace.

By the same token, to speak today of national recordings, is the same that frightens away the buyers of good taste of brilliance in the home, as good patriots, since there is everything in criollo recordings, that at least reflect with truth and purity, the sadness and grandiose soul of the Pampa, whose airs appear to emanate the infinity, and in those which vibrate the spirit that forges the heroes that gave us a fatherland.

We, conscious of the respect that we owe to the love of country and to the national traditions and with the end to announce that Argentina isn't the market of the bad and cheap, as appears to have been taking place until today by the importers of records, to put on sale the brand "Atlanta" we propose not to withhold any sacrifice, with such to proportion select *criollo* music and national airs in total purity, utilizing for it orchestras, bands, rondallas, etc., of the first rank, and artists of refined taste and privileged voices. Of the manner that the good criollos can from today henceforth like good criollo music and enjoy it in the records: "Atlanta".

The respectable public will be convinced, and with well founded pride, that of music we have many and good, without necessity of leaving the country, and it is the patriotic work to popularize it in the due form, because it concurs to cement the national soul.

And the enormous progress realized in the *criollo* records, a true giant step that leaves the work until now way behind, the respectable public can take into account comparing it with the most beautiful European repertoire, that we also will put on sale under the brand "Atlanta" and "Pantophone", in which figure the best songs played and sung of operas, operettas, zarzuelas, dances, dance music, fantasies, etc. excelling among them the best Italian singers and of other countries, as well as the great composers.

Ask for catalogs in our store; there are two for the convenience of those that are interested. In one there are numerous criollos, dance music, songs, Spanish, etc. In the other the numerous Italian and Classics.

We give our thanks to those who favor us, and their preference will be an index that we are on a good road.

The only sellers in the republics of the Rio de la Plata area:

Amendola & Co.
274, Esmeralda, 274- Buenos Aires— Free catalogues.
Union Telephone, 582 (Libertad) = Cooperative Telephone, 1900 (Central)."

Algunos de nuestros competidores

al darse cuenta de la superioridad indiscutible de nuestros discos

"ATLANTA"

pretenden contrarrestar el éxito obtenido en pocos días por nuestro disco "ATLANTA", el único con música criolla que circule en EUROPA (lo que demuestra el alto grado artístico conseguido por nosotros y parte de nuestro programa) con difamaciones y mil otros ardides.

TODO EN VANO, pues el respetable público, inteligente en verdadera música criolla, ante tantas difamaciones quiere averiguar la causa de las mismas, y al oir nuestros discos se queda plenamente convencido de sus insuperables cualidades, y de lo infundadas que son las calumnias lanzadas alrededor nuestro. Es decir, que las difamaciones son nuestra mejor réclame, y nuestros competidores reciben la merecida lección.

AUDICIONES GRATUITAS, sin compromiso de comprar.

VENGAN A OIR LOS QUINTETOS **CRIOLLOS** de:

AUGUSTO - CARROTE - FIRPO - BEVILACQUA - TANO GENARO

y **LA RONDALLA** y **BANDA "ATLANTA"**, dirigidas por el festejado autor nacional, maestro **A. DE BASSI.**

LA BANDA MUNICIPAL, dirigida por el genial profesor **ANTONIO MALVAGNI.**

LA FANFARRA DE LA GUARDIA DE SEGURIDAD, dirigida por el maestro **SAMMARTINO,** y finalmente:

LA RONDALLA LAUREADA "VAZQUEZ"

REPERTORIO CRIOLLO, ITALIANO, ESPAÑOL, etc.

CATALOGO GRATIS. Pídanlo á sus únicos importadores:

AMENDOLA & Cía 274, ESMERALDA, 274
BUENOS AIRES

U. T., 582, LIBERTAD. == COOP. TELEF., 1900, CENTRAL.

The second advertisement for Atlanta records from the *Caras y Caretas* magazine of April 12, 1913, issue No. 758 *Año* XVI. The translation is on the next page.

Translation of the previous page:

"Some of our competitors have taken into account the unquestionable superiority of our "Atlanta" records, they pretend to be against the enterprising success obtained in only a few days by our "Atlanta" records, the only with *criollo* music that circulates in Europe (that which demonstrates the high artistic grade achieved by us and the part of our program) with defamanations and a thousand other stratagems.

All in vain, since the respectable public, intelligent in true *criollo* music before so many defamanations want to verify the cause of the same, and to hear our records that stay fully convinced of its unsurpassable qualities, and of the groundless slander that is launched around us. That is to say, that the defaminations are our best reclamation, and our competitors have received the lesson they deserved.

Free listening, without obligation to purchase.

Come and hear the criollo quintets of:
Augusto, Carrote, Firpo, Bevilacqua, Tano Genaro, and the Rondalla and Banda "Atlanta", directed by the nationally celebrated author, maestro A. de Bassi.
La Banda Municipal, (The Municipal Band) directed by the brilliant Professor Antonio Malvagni.
La Fanfarra de la Guardia de Seguridad, (The Fanfare of the Security Guards) directed by the maestro Sammartino, and finally:

La Rondalla Laureada "Vazquez"

Criollo, Italian, Spanish, etc. repertoire.

Free catalog. Ask for it from your only importers:

Amendola & Co. 274, Esmeralda, 274 Buenos Aires
Union Telephone, 582 (Libertad) = Cooperative Telephone, 1900 (Central)."

According to Héctor Lorenzo Lucci of Buenos Aires:, Atlanta records producer Alfredo Amendola opened his doors for business on March 31, 1913. He had traveled to Germany in mid 1912 to purchase a recording machine and obtain the license for the trademark Atlanta. This company lasted until 1917.

The third advertisement for Atlanta records from the *Caras y Caretas* magazine of April 19, 1913, issue No. 759 *Año* XVI. The translation is on the next page.

Translation of the previous page:

"Double sided records "Atlanta" of 25 centimeter diameter, $2.50 national monetary unit each, the best of the world.

The famous laurelled Rondalla "Vazquez", reproduced only and exclusively on the "Atlanta" records.

Ask for the following numbers:

Amendola & Co.
The only sellers in the republics of the Rio de la Plata area.
274, Esmeralda, 274- Buenos Aires
Union Telephone, 582 (Libertad) = Cooperative Telephone, 1900 (Central).
Ask for catalogues. They are free."

Almost 30 years after the *Estudiantina Figaro* arrived in the Rio de la Plata, directed by Carlos García Tolsa, the bandurria was still being constructed, played and even recorded in the Argentine capital. The population of Buenos Aires had tripled in the previous two decades and was now at about two million people. The *Estudiantina Figaro* influenced the culture wherever they went. They started a mandolin and mandolin orchestra boom in the United States cities, small towns and even in the Appalachian mountains, that was of multi ethnic lines.

Of the forty discs listed on the previous page, it should be noted that the catalog numbers are above and below those of the recordings made by Agustín Barrios in early 1913 for Atlanta. Of note also are the compositions by José Sancho, who was an original member of the *Estudiantina Figaro*.

These recordings by the Rondalla (José) Vazquez are listed on the top of the right column of the Disco Atlanta listings on the previous page. The jota entitled *Viva la Rioja* was written by Francisco Calleja's father. Francisco Calleja played a concert with Agustín Barrios and Uruguayan guitarist, Julio J. Otermin in Montevideo in the fall (March, April, May) of 1912. (Six Silver Moonbeams, revised edition pg. 43.)

Bandurria y Guitarra

Discos de 25 c/m., a

62800
- **Pamplona**—*Vals* (*Trío de Bandurrias y Guitarra*)
  Estudiantina Centenario
- **Alegría de la Huerta**—*Jota* (Chueca) (*Trío de Bandurrias y Guitarra*)
  Estudiantina Centenario

62801
- **Árabe**—*Paso Doble torero* (*Trío de Bandurrias y Guitarra*)
  Estudiantina Centenario
- **Santiago**—*Vals* (*Trío de Bandurrias y Guitarra*)
  Estudiantina Centenario

62802
- **El Esquinazo**—*Tango* (*Trío de Bandurrias y Guitarra*)
  Estudiantina Centenario
- **La Castaña del Gitano**—*Vals* (García) (*Trío de Bandurrias y Guitarra*)
  Estudiantina Centenario

62803
- **Retreta Española**—*Marcha* (Portal) (*Trío de Bandurrias y Guitarra*)
  Estudiantina Centenario
- **Triana**—*Paso Doble torero* (*Trío de Bandurrias y Guitarra*)
  Estudiantina Centenario

63694
- **Canción del Vagabundo** (Serrano) (*Dúo de Guitarra y Bandurria*)
  Los Alpinos
- **Genio y Figura**—*Serenata* (*Dúo de Guitarra y Bandurria*) **Los Alpinos**

63695
- **Potpourri de Cantos Flamencos** (*Dúo de Guitarra y Bandurria*)
  Los Alpinos
- **Garrotín**—*Baile Español* (*Dúo de Guitarra y Bandurria*) **Los Alpinos**

63713
- **Fantasía Morisca** (Chapí) (*Dúo de Guitarra y Bandurria*) **Los Alpinos**
- *María Adela*—*Vals* (*Solo de Acordeón*) *Rafael A. Alcorta*

65035
- **De Madrid a París**—*Tercerto de las Cigarreras* (Chueca) (*Dúo de Guitarra y Bandurria*) **Los Alpinos**
- **Machaquito**—*Paso Doble torero* (López) (*Dúo de Guitarra y Bandurria*) **Los Alpinos**

65161
- **Las Bribonas**—*Fantasía* (Calleja) (*Dúo de Guitarra y Bandurria*)
  Los Alpinos
- **Reverte**—*Paso Doble torero* (Arraujo) (*Dúo de Guitarra y Bandurria*)
  Los Alpinos

65392
- **Mazzantini**—*Paso Doble torero* (Martínez) (*Dúo de Guitarra y Bandurria*) **Los Alpinos**
- *De Frente*—*Marcha Militar* (*Solo de Guitarra*) *Julio J. Otermín*

This page from a 1919-20 Discos Victor record catalogue shows the extent of the popularity of the Bandurria besides that of the Guitar. At the bottom of this listing is a guitar solo by Julio J. Otermin (Student of Pedro Maza). He recorded this on February 1, 1912 along with at least 17 other pieces, fourteen months before Agustín Barrios' recorded works by Atlanta/ Artigas were released. He was a prolific recording artist of guitar solos from Uruguay who played in concert on the bill with Agustín Barrios in 1912 in Montevideo along with Francisco Calleja. It was Agustín Barrios' first concert in the Uruguayan capital. The song *Las Bribonas* performed by Los Alpinos was written by Francisco Calleja's father. Some other interesting notes are that the Flamenco pieces *Potpourri de Cantos Flamencos* and *Garrotin* performed in ensemble fashion with a guitar and a bandurria.

The 8 pieces listed here by the *Estudiantina "Centenario"* were recorded on March 5, 1910. That day they recorded a total of 20 songs.

The pieces by Los Alpinos listed here were recorded between January 3rd and 8th of 1912.

This information is from: The Encyclopedic Discography of Victor Recordings (EDVR) web site. A team of researchers based at the University of California, Santa Barbara Libraries edits the database.

These recordings by the *Rondalla Vazquez* numerically are before the Discos Atlanta listings 3 pages previous. This may indicate they are from the earliest (November-December?) 1912 recording sessions in order to offer the public 80 songs on 40 discs by mid-April 1913. They are not listed in the advertisement.

The copyright text on the disc suggests that these were released after the summer of 1910, but in fact they were recorded on March 5, 1910, due to information recently coming to light at the Encyclopedic Discography of Victor Recordings at UCSB therefore predating the release of the *Rondalla Vazquez* discs by more than 2 years. The *Estudiantina "Centenario"* consisted of a trio of two bandurrias and a guitar, the musicians being: Vicente Abad (leader), Fernández, Rodríquez, and Quero. These titles are included in the catalog listing on the previous page. The population of Buenos Aires was about 1.5 million when these were released. These Victor labels are shown at about 90% of original size.

By that time (1910) a young Paraguayan concert artist and composer: Agustín Barrios, of 25 years of age, decided to abandon his country, to be dedicating his time to giving concerts around the world. Initiating his international itinerary in the provinces of northeast Argentina, neighbors of Paraguay. By the end of this year he reached Buenos Aires where he continued concert activities.

Agustín Pio Barrios (1885-1944) from Historia de la Guitarra by Ricardo Muñoz.

From 1913-1929 he recorded his compositions in the Argentine capital for the record company Nacional Odeon, a total of 40 discs of 78 R.P.M. (information we have from the article "Agustín Barrios-Annotations about a Universal Paraguayan", written by Lucio Nuñez in a magazine *"El Encordado" No. 5* – 1993). Soon he traveled to Uruguay and established himself in Montevideo, and what followed was his ascending international career.

The guitaristic ambiance of Buenos Aires wasn't totally favorable to him, due to the fact that he used steel strings, and brought his own South American repertoire, that in this moment, within this medium, where music was predominately influenced by the European repertoire: Sor, Aguado, etc., the public couldn't understand his message. In respect to what Lucio Nuñez says in his article:

"By that epoch of 1920, there was a magazine dedicated to the guitar exclusively, and the critics that made it, they were, out to demolish Barrios. I think because they couldn't comprehend him and didn't understand his Americanistic vocation."

The Argentine guitaristic ambiance in those years was looking mostly at Europe, and the "European Buenos Aires didn't understand his message". In this magazine, among other things, it says that the little success of Barrios, must be due to the porteña public knowing so much, and fully aware of the "Modern" repertoire of the guitar (Sor, Aguado, Albeniz, Tárrega, Granados, etc.).

(Left) pianist and composer Enrique Granados (Right) pianist and composer Isaac Albeniz.

This is an early advertisement for Agustín Barrios' fourth disc *"Ay, Ay, Ay"* released by Atlanta records. This is from the *"Caras y Caretas"* magazine of July 5, 1913, issue No. 770 *Año* XVI. Translation on the next page.

Translation of the previous page:

"Take home the art and the joy!

Ask for a free catalog, of the best records in the world: Atlanta.

No. 304 *"Ay, Ay, Ay,"* a delicate and aristocratic *estilo criollo,* played by the celebrated concert guitarist, Agustín Barrios.

Atlanta records is the only who reproduces the guitar with all of its shades of tones.

Amendola & Co. 274, Esmeralda, 274 Buenos Aires
Union Telephone, 582 (Libertad) = Cooperative Telephone, 1900 (Central).

Only introducers."

In only a few short weeks they had established sales outlets in eight cities, including the capital of Agustín's homeland, Asuncion, Paraguay. *"Ay, Ay, Ay,"* was the most popular of the Agustín Barrios recordings made in the 1913-1914 period, and advertised at least 3 times.

There are videos of his artists' works that he produced for Atlanta records on You Tube

Agustín Barrios' record label of *"Ay, Ay, Ay"* for Atlanta records from the *"Fray Mocho"* magazine of August 1, 1913, *Año II*, No. 66.

This Disco Atlanta advertisement for Ay, Ay, Ay by Agustín Barrios is from January 1914. It is not from a *"Caras y Caretas"* magazine, possibly a *"Fray Mocho"* magazine.

Translation of the previous page:

Atlanta – The best of the world.

(Stamp on the record label) Author's royalties paid.

Ay, Ay, Ay — Estilo (O. Perez Freire)

Celebrated Concert Guitarist

Agustín P. Barrios

No. 65376

Happy New Year.

35 National Monetary Unit. (Peso) (This offer is only good for the next 20 days.) And for this 35 pesos we will send you a beautiful phonograph, being the latest model, 6 double sided 10 inch Atlanta discs, or a total of 12 pieces, to choose in our catalogues, 1 album, 200 fine needles, shipping included all for 35 pesos, its value being 55 pesos.

Hurry and ask for it at:
Amendola and Company — 274 Esmeralda, Buenos Aires.

These are the records still missing, not having surfaced, recorded in Buenos Aires in 1913 and 1914 from the list of 40 discs in "Six Silver Moonbeams-The Life and Times of Agustín Barrios"-revised edition November 1999 by Rico Stover. The *Habanera* and *Romanza* of Disco Nacional 952 recorded in 1924 on this page was acquired in 1999 in time to be included in the revised edition.

Chronological No.	Record No. and Title	Matrix No. of the Atlanta / Artigas record Co.
6)	306 La Morocha Paraguaya (Raccioppi)	Atlanta 65383
	Estilo Regional (Barrios)	Atlanta 65389

Most of these recordings have been found and are included on the 2009 New Edition of Agustín Barrios The Complete Historical Recordings 1913-1942 CD set by Chanterelle, with a total of 68 tracks, adding 9 tracks to the version released in 2005. Rico Stover wrote the liner notes and Randy Osborne was asked to provide some historical information.

One of the rarest later recordings by Agustín Barrios, recorded in 1924 in Buenos Aires. The *Romanza* was recorded again in 1928. Long time Brazilian record collector Ronoel Simões (1919-2010) did not have this among his 8,000 discs, when I acquired it in 1999. The rarity of this disc is due to the producer Max Glucksmann not including it in his full page advertisements in the *"Caras y Caretas"* magazines. It was hidden under a rock.

In May of 2005 two new "unfound" discs were acquired:

2)	302 Ojos Negros (Raccioppi)	Artigas 65368
	Mandolinata Napolitana (Sosa Escalada)	Artigas 65369
15)	Isabel (Barrios)	Artigas 65386
	Oro y Plata (Lehar)	Artigas 65389

The Disco Atlanta Numerical Number of the *Isabel / Oro y Plata* disc is 315.

These appear on the next page.

This is the second disc to be released in 1913 by Disco Atlanta / Artigas of Agustín Barrios' recording debuts. The maestro to Barrios, Gustavo Sosa Escalada, is the composer of *Mandolinata Napolitana*.

Isabel-gavota is a composition by Agustín Barrios. The piece *Oro y Plata*-vals is written by Franz Lehar. The Disco Atlanta Numerical Number of the *Isabel / Oro y Plata* disc is 315. This disc was the 15th release by Discos Atlanta / Artigas. These pieces were recorded in 1914, and only two more discs were released under these labels for the final offerings by Agustín Barrios at this time, until the Odeon recordings were released in 1921.

On the next page is image of a 1913 *Disco "Artigas"* and *"Uruguayo"* 10" disc cover. Juan M. Gonzalez was probably the main distributor of their records in Montevideo. Translation of the text: "Guitar solos performed by the celebrated Paraguayan guitarist Agustín P. Barrios." In 1914 after all the recordings were made another cover stated "Repertorio completo de discos del célebre Guitarrista A. Barrios", which translates to: "The complete repertoire of recordings of the celebrated Guitarist A. Barrios." The size has been reduced.

"ARTIGAS" Y "URUGUAYO"

DISCOS DOBLE FAZ

Sólos de Guitarra
ejecutados por el célebre
Guitarrista Paraguayo
AGUSTIN
P. BARRIOS

SOLICITE
CATÁLOGOS

Cantos Criollos,
Escenas Cómicas,
PIEZAS DE BAILE,
Marchas,
Solos de Acordeón,

Cantos Españoles,
Operas, Operetas.
Canzonetas Napolitanas

EXCLUSIVIDAD:

JUAN M. GONZALEZ

551

This is the first *Disco Atlanta / Artigas* release, the Numerical listing for *Atlanta* was 301. This numbering sequence went up to 317, for a total of 34 songs recorded from late 1912-early 1913 (November-December-January) to 1914.

This Jota is the third release by *Disco Atlanta* of Agustín Barrios, and is an original composition by the maestro.

This fourth disc (304 in Numerical listing) by Agustín Barrios for *Disco Atlanta* is an *Estilo* entitled *Ay, Ay, Ay* composed by Osmán Perez Freire. This *Atlanta* label image and song promotion were in the two advertisements appearing in the *Caras y Caretas* magazine July 5, 1913 and January 7, 1914; and one in *Fray Mocho* magazine on August 1, 1913.

The *Disco Atlanta / Artigas* Numerical Matriz numbering system for Agustín Barrios goes from 65364 to-65397 for a total of 34 guitar solos recorded.

This is the thirteenth release by *Disco Artigas*. These pieces were recorded in late 1913-1914 period, *Divagaciones* is the 21st song of 34 in the matriz numbering system.

This *Disco Atlanta* recording of Carlos García Tolsa's *Matilde* is from the first half dozen pieces Agustín Barrios recorded. Agustín learned all 17 published pieces by Carlos García Tolsa under the direction of his maestro and compatriot Gustavo Sosa Escalada. This piece was not among the known publications studied, nor a song entitled as this was to be found in García Tolsa's widow's archive when it was sold to sheet music collector Eleuterio Tiscornia in the 1930s.

This is from the *"Cronica Musical"* page of the *"Caras y Caretas"* issue of October 22, 1921 issue 1203 *Año* XXIV.

Rico Stover said in a visit on June 7, 2012 that this photo was one he had not previously seen.

"Barrios Concert. —

The Paraguayan guitarist and composer Agustín Barrios with a chosen program did his presentation at the Circulo de la Pensa.

Known by the public of Uruguay, Chile and Brazil, the last country where we were now pleased to hear and applaud him he didn't do that in a year, Mr. Barrios has passed through numerous cities obtaining in all of them a stride and praiseworthy success.

His qualities were proven a few days ago in the concert dedicated to the press and the critics.

He began the performance with a minuet by Beethoven, performed with grace and delicateness. He continued with a nocturne by Chopin, adapted to the guitar. Here Mr. Barrios demonstrated that he possesses such endowments and sufficient resources to really make the instrument sing and obtain some beautiful and perfect slurs.

His excellent interpretation and his correctly measured emotion gave to the composition of the great maestro that special note of sentiment that characterizes it.

Equally well performed were the *"Capricho Arabe"* by Tárrega and the compositions *"Pagina de Album"*, *"Gavota"* and *"Tarantella"* by the same Mr. Barrios, that are pages full of spontaneity.

Mr. Barrios expresses what he feels with great simplicity, without those unpleasant highs and lows such as all of it being fabricated. He possesses a clear technique, perfect, producing the impression of naturalness, which he employs not as an end to dazzle overcoming difficulties, but as a means of which he needs to complete his expression.

His performances review a pleasant character of the pair of modesty and simplicity.

Mr. Barrios has an artistic temperament of great endowment and, in spite of being a thankless and difficult instrument, he gets from it what he wants."

At this time Agustín Barrios was under contract by Max Glucksmann for his record company Disco Nacional Odeon, having recorded *"Pagina de Album"* and *"Tarantella"* on 12" discs, the first title still being unfound.

Though this article was published on October 22, 1921, it doesn't indicate that the concert was recent, such as earlier that month, upon further investigation of the issues of *"Caras y Caretas"*, the issue of September 3, 1921, No. 1,196 it mentions a Barrios photo in issue No. 1,203, in the *"retratos fotograficos"* section. This show that the editors planned some items to be published 8 weeks later after the listing of portrait photos in an index section of a previous issue. None of the other concert reviews in the *"Cronica Musical"* page were dated, so this concert may be from August or even earlier in 1921.

On the subject of Barrios being under contract but not having his recordings advertised by Max Glucksmann in *"Caras y Caretas"* from 1921-1924-not until 1925 were they advertised-the 2nd disc advertised was in June of 1928! In the Six Silver Moonbeams 1999 Edition on page 221-Items 18-26 were not advertised! Nos. 18-23 one sided discs 5 still unfound. Max had advertised Mario Pardo's guitar solos since 1919, having signed the artist in 1918. Mario Pardo's recordings from October 1920-until mid-December 1922 weren't advertised either. Carlos Gardel and José Razzano's discs were advertised at the very top of the page every week until mid 1932 when Max Glucksmann was no longer the distributor for Odeon, his last advertisement was in the *"Caras y Caretas"* magazine on June 25, 1932, issue No. 1,760, page 15. Max Glucksmann's distribution was replaced by THE ARGENTINE TALKING MACHINE WORKS — Fábrica de Discos ODEON located at MONTAÑESES 2150-Buenos Aires, the announcement was in the *"Caras y Caretas"* magazine on April 14, 1934, issue No. 1,854, page 53.

Agustín Barrios Solo de guitarra
Disco Nacional-Odeon de 25 cms., $3. pesos (10″ discs)
954 September 19, 1925 *"Caras y Caretas"* Issue No. 1407 *Año* XXVIII $3. pesos
Capricho arabe. Serenata. Tárrega.
Sarita. Mazurca. A. Barrios.

200 June 16, 1928 *"Caras y Caretas"* Issue No. 1550 *Año* XXXI
Romanza. A. Barrios. Recorded: May 10, 1928
Aire popular paraguaya. A. Barrios. Recorded: May 10, 1928

Agustín Barrios played one concert in Salon "La Argentina" on October 24, 1923 and due to a small audience the November 6 and 8th concerts were cancelled. How many of the ticket buyers at the October 24th concert knew these recordings had been released? Did Juan Carlos Anido, who even went to that concert, know that 6 discs were available? Juan Carlos Anido even went to that concert, apparently, and somehow learned of the November 6 and 8th concerts being cancelled-then he spoke pejoratively about Agustín's performance in issue No. 2 of *"La Guitarra"* magazine, published in December 1923. Maria Luisa Anido in an interview in the mid 1990's said "Agustín sweat profusely"-she probably was speaking of having seen him on October 24, 1923-at what other time in her life would she have seen him? Juan Carlos Anido probably didn't know the records had been released, like every one else at the concert. Juan Carlos also made no mention of the discs in the *"Conciertos"* section page 27 review of the Barrios concert. How could he not be moved by the *"Mazurka Apassionata"*? Or anyone? When we look at the program selected for the 3rd concert it included *"La Catedral"*, which never got to be played for the enjoyment of the audience. Even *"Las Abejas"* didn't move the audience, why? I wonder if Agustín had sequenced the material differently in his first concert, could the 2nd and 3rd concerts have come about?

Here's a reference to the source of Maria Luisa Anido's comments on Barrios:

David Reynolds: On the Cuban School of the Guitar
from: http://columbiaguitarstudio.com/brouwerbarruecoarticles.html

In his 1992 guitarist Aldo Rodríguez published his book "Maria Luisa Anido *Una Vida a Contramano"* (*Editorial Letras Cubanas*) which consists of short conversions between the two guitarists on a variety of subjects relating to the long trajectory of her career.

In Rodríguez's book, the Argentine guitarist relates her encounters with Andrés Segovia (who advised her to disregard her nerves since, "no one can play in front of me"), Miguel Llobet (who "practiced mentally, very seldom physically"), Emilio Pujol ("who practiced eight hours a day and got nervous when he performed"), Alirio Diaz ("a man with integrity"), John Williams ("who always dressed informally"), and Agustín Barrios ("who sweat a lot when he played and got his guitar wet").

According to Rico Stover's investigations, Agustín Barrios was signed by Max Glucksmann in 1921 to produce 5 records a year for his Disco Nacional Odeon record company. Why are the records that were recorded from that time period until those recorded in 1924 so rare and in some cases still unfound? I have found an answer to that question. In 2004 I had purchased at least 400 copies of the *"Caras y Caretas"* magazines dating from 1899-1931. Within those were ads for the *Atlanta / Artigas* 1913-1914 Barrios recordings, and some of the late 1920's *Disco Nacional Odeon* Barrios ads as well. In August of 2011 I became aware that all 2,139 issues of *"Caras y Caretas"* magazines that were published between October 8, 1898 and October 7, 1939 were online as PDFs at the *Biblioteca Nacional de España* in Madrid. I spent several days to download all of them and about 9 weeks to look at all of the issues and print out 4-5" of important pages of information. Spread throughout this book there are listings of various artist's recordings and their release dates via advertising in this weekly magazine. The guitar soloist and vocalist, Mario Pardo, was contracted by Max Glucksmann in 1918 and his discs were made available and advertised beginning in late 1919. The first of Agustín Barrios' recordings that were advertised are listed below beginning in the spring of 1925 — the fall of 1925 in the northern hemisphere, or some 4 years after the beginning of his contract. The 2nd record was not advertised until 1928!

We can see which discs were advertised more than once, and those not advertised.

In Rico Stover's records listings on page 221 of the 1999 revised edition of "Six Silver Moonbeams — The Art and Times of Agustín Barrios Mangoré" we see:

The unadvertised discs:

*means unfound discs
1.-17. These represent Atlanta-Artigas 1913-14 discs. *"Ay, Ay, Ay"*-*"Marcha Paraguaya"* were advertised in the *"Caras y Caretas"* magazine of July 5, 1913, issue No. 770 *Año* XVI, *"Fray Mocho"* magazine of August 1, 1913, *Año* II, No. 66 and in January 1914 possibly in a *"Fray Mocho"* magazine.

18.-23. These are all one sided discs acoustically recorded in 1921.

18. 54231   Madrigal Odeon 609*
19. 54233   El Hijo Prodigo Odeon 610*
20. 54232   Pagina de Album Odeon 611*
21. 54234   Geromita Odeon 612*
22. 54230   Rapsodia Americana Odeon 613*
23. 54235   Tarantela Odeon 614

24.-27. These are all two sided discs acoustically recorded in 1924.

24. 951   Aire de Zamba Odeon 1641
          Minuetto Odeon 1642
25. 952   Habanera Odeon 1643
          Romanza Odeon 1644
26. 953   Minuetto Odeon 1890
          Cordoba Odeon 1891
27. 954   Sarita Odeon 1889
          This disc was advertised on September 19, 1925 *"Caras y Caretas"* Issue No. 1407
          Año XXVIII. Capricho Arabe Odeon 1892
28. 203   Danza Paraguaya Odeon 2474-1 Recorded electrically on April 17, 1928.
          Cueca Odeon 2477-3 Recorded electrically on May 10, 1928.
29. 204   Aconquija Odeon 2692-1 October 20, 1928 *"Caras y Caretas"* Issue No. 1568 *Año* XXXI
          Junto a tu Corazon Odeon 2694-1
30. 205   Oracion Odeon 3881-1 September 20, 1930 *"Caras y Caretas"* Issue No. 1668 *Año* XXXIII
          Vals No. 4 Odeon 3882-2
31. 206   Maxixa Odeon 2681-3 July 5, 1930 *"Caras y Caretas"* Issue No. 1657 *Año* XXXIII
          Mazurka-Sarita Odeon 2682

32. 207   Traumerei Odeon 2800 January 19 and 26, 1929 *"Caras y Caretas"* Issue Nos. 1581 and 1582 *Año* XXXII
        Tarantela Odeon 2801
33. 208   Souvenir d'un Reve Odeon 2951 March 2, 1929 *"Caras y Caretas"* Issue No. 1587 *Año* XXXII
        Souvenir d'un Reve Odeon 2952

We can see which discs were advertised more than once, and those not advertised.

Agustín Barrios Solo de guitarra
Disco Nacional-Odeon de 25 cms., $3. pesos (10" discs)
954 September 19, 1925 *"Caras y Caretas"* Issue No. 1407 *Año* XXVIII $3. pesos
Capricho arabe. Serenata. Tárrega.
Sarita. Mazurca. A. Barrios.
200 June 16, 1928 *"Caras y Caretas"* Issue No. 1550 *Año* XXXI
Romanza. A. Barrios. Recorded: May 10, 1928
Aire popular paraguaya. A. Barrios. Recorded: May 10, 1928
201 July 7, 1928 *"Caras y Caretas"* Issue No. 1553 *Año* XXXI
Loure. Bach. Recorded: April 18, 1928
Luz mala. Estilo. A. Barrios. Recorded: April 18, 1928
202 August 4, 1928 *"Caras y Caretas"* Issue No. 1557 *Año* XXXI
Capricho arabe. Tango. (sic) Tárrega. Recorded: Second take April 17, 1928
Minuet. Beethoven. Recorded: April 17, 1928

   The above recording is of a particular importance, as it was released during the same time as Andrés Segovia's third tour to Buenos Aires, and the first tour in seven years. In fact a review of his first concert performance of July 3, 1928 was also included in this issue. According to Sila Godoy, who related this anecdote to Rico Stover, Andrés Segovia heard this recording of *"Capricho Arabe"* in the home of the guitarist G. Bianqui Piñero during this tour and asked: *"Quien es este?"* ("Who is this?")
203
204 October 20, 1928 *"Caras y Caretas"* Issue No. 1568 *Año* XXXI
Aconquija. (Suite andina). A. Barrios Recorded: May 29, 1928
Junto a tu corazón. Vals. A. Barrios Recorded: May 29, 1928
205
206
207 January 19, 1929 *"Caras y Caretas"* Issue No. 1581 *Año* XXXII
Traumerei. Schumann. Recorded: June 21, 1928
Tarantella. A. Barrios. Recorded: June 21, 1928
207 January 26, 1929 *"Caras y Caretas"* Issue No. 1582 *Año* XXXII
Traumerei. Schumann. Recorded: June 21, 1928
Tarantella. A. Barrios. Recorded: June 21, 1928
208 March 2, 1929 *"Caras y Caretas"* Issue No. 1587 *Año* XXXII
Souvenir D'Un Reve 1ra parte A. Barrios. Recorded: July 28, 1928
Souvenir D'Un Reve 2nda parte A. Barrios. Recorded: July 31, 1928

209 May 25, 1929 *"Caras y Caretas"* Issue No. 1599 *Año* XXXII
Ay, Ay, Ay. (Aire criollo) O. Pérez Freire. Recorded: July 31, 1928
Madrigal. Gavota. A. Barrios. Recorded: May 29, 1928

Disco Nacional-Odeon de 30 cms., $4.50 Pesos (12″ disc)
46071 July 20, 1929 *"Caras y Caretas"* Issue No. 1607 *Año* XXXII
Armonias de America. Potpourri. A. Barrios. Recorded: March 27, 1929
La Catedral. a) Andante religioso. b) Allegro. A. Barrios. Recorded: August 1, 1928

    Why was this gem of a composition, *"La Catedral"*, not released for almost one year after it was recorded, and only heard in concerts by the maestro? There was no 4 minute "B" side to include with it until the recording of *"Armonias de America"* on March 27, 1929.

46071 October 5, 1929 *"Caras y Caretas"* Issue No. 1618 *Año* XXXII
Armonias de America. Potpourri. A. Barrios. Recorded: March 27, 1929
La Catedral. a) Andante religioso. b) Allegro. A. Barrios. Recorded: August 1, 1928

Disco Nacional-Odeon de 25 cms., $3. pesos (10″ discs)
211 December 28, 1929 *"Caras y Caretas"* Issue No. 1630 *Año* XXXII
Confesion. Melodia. A. Barrios.
Aire de Zamba. Zamba. A. Barrios.
210 February 15, 1930 *"Caras y Caretas"* Issue No. 1637 *Año* XXXIII
Minuet. Minuet. F. Sors. Recorded: June 21, 1928
Vals No. 3. Vals. A. Barrios. Recorded: July 31, 1928
206 July 5, 1930 *"Caras y Caretas" Issue No. 1657 Año* XXXIII
Maxixa. Barrios. Recorded: June 20, 1928
Mazurca. Barrios. Recorded: May 23, 1928
205 September 20, 1930 *"Caras y Caretas"* Issue No. 1668 *Año* XXXIII
Oracion. Melodia. A. Barrios. Recorded: March 27, 1929
Vals No. 4. Vals. A. Barrios. Recorded: March 27, 1929

The varied repertoire of Agustín Barrios ranged from the European composers and guitar composers to the South American folk rhythms that he composed in.

These are still acoustic recordings recorded in 1924, as the microphone wouldn't appear in use until 1926.

560

This is a promotional flyer for the Saturday October 17, 1925 concert at the Teatro Solis in Montevideo. This is a special courtesy by the Teatro Solis CIDDAE Centro de Investigacion, Documentacion y Difusion de las Artes Escenicas. The images on pages 353-357 are all due to this courtesy.

TEATRO SOLIS

Sábado 17 y Domingo 18 de Octubre
a las 18 y 30

2 ÚNICOS CONCIERTOS DE GUITARRA 2

Por el genial virtuoso Compositor

BARRIOS

Precios para los 2 Conciertos en conjunto

Plateas y Tertulias Balcón con entrada	$ 2.50
Tertulias Altas " "	" 2.00
Palcos sin "	" 8.00

Imprenta "LA DIADEMA" - Convención. 1241

CIDDAE - Teatro Solis

This is the concert program flyer for Agustín Barrios' two concerts at the Teatro Solis in Montevideo on October 17 and 18, 1925. This lists the price for buying tickets to both concerts.

This is a special courtesy by the Teatro Solis CIDDAE Centro de Investigacion, Documentacion y Difusion de las Artes Escenicas.

PRIMER CONCIERTO

Sábado 17 de Octubre 1925

A las 18 y 15

PROGRAMA

I

Andante ... Mozart
Minuet ... Beethoven
Scherzo ... Coste
LA CATEDRAL
  a) Andante religioso) Barrios
  b) Allegro)

II

Sarabanda)
Preludio) Bach
Romanza ... Mendelssohn
Contemplación)
Capricho Español) Barrios

III

Leyenda ... Albéniz
Réverie ... Schumann-Borda y Pagola
Dos aires típicos andinos armonizados por Barrios
  a) Zamba
  b) Aconquija
Variaciones sobre el Campamento Cerro Leon
canción patriótica tradicional del Paraguay ... Barrios

CIDDAE - Teatro Solis

AGUSTÍN BARRIOS

HACE YA ALGUNOS AÑOS, OYENDO POR PRIMERA VEZ A BA-RRIOS, DIJE QUE ERA UN REVOLUCIONARIO EN SU ARTE, LO QUE NO DEBIERAMOS EXTRAÑAR TRATÁNDOSE DE UN PARAGUAYO. AHORA VUELVO A ESCUCHARLO, Y ME ENCUENTRO CON QUE EL REVOLUCIONARIO HA TRIUNFADO EN TODA LA LINEA, HA-BIÉNDOSE CONVERTIDO EN UN ARTISTA INTERESANTÍSIMO, DE UNA PERSONALIDAD ÚNICA, DENTRO DE UN AMPLIO HORIZONTE QUE LE PERTENECE EXCLUSIVAMENTE PORQUE ÉL MISMO SE LO HA FORMADO, A BASE DE UNA INDEPENDENCIA TEMERARIA Y DE UNA AUDACIA GENIAL.

BARRIOS ES UN INNOVADOR Y UN CREADOR A LA VEZ. CON LA MODIFICACIÓN ¡DE LA CALIDAD DE LAS TRES PRIMERAS CUERDAS CANTANTES Y SU ESPECIAL MANERA DE HERIRLAS, HA LLEGADO A OBTENER SONIDOS DE UN COLORIDO BELLISIMO Y DE UNA SUAVIDAD EMOCIONANTE. SU MANERA DE DECIR Y DE FRASEAR SE PARECE MUCHO A LA FE GARCIA TOLSA, EL ADMIRABLE SENSITIVO DE LA GUITARRA, EL AMIGO Y EL MA-ESTRO PERDIDO.

BARRIOS, AUNQUE CONOCE Y DOMINA LA LITERATURA CLA-SICA DEL INSTRUMENTO, GASTA EN SU ARTE, CAPITAL PROPIO DIRÉ, PUES ES UN CREADOR ORIGINAL Y VIGOROSO.

CUANDO ÉL PUBLIQUE SUS OBRAS SELECCIONADAS, Y ESPE-CIALMENTE SUS ESTUDIOS MELÓDICOS DE ALTA TÉCNICA, CUYA MUESTRA CONOZCO, SE IMPONDRÁ DEFINITIVAMENTE Y PARA SIEMPRE.

POR ÚLTIMO, TRÁTASE DE UN ARTISTA GENUINAMENTE NUES-TRO; DE UN BRILLANTE EXPONENTE SUDAMERICANO, DIGNO DE TODO NUESTRO APOYO Y DE TODA NUESTRA SIMPATÍA.

Martin Gil

****

Precios para los 2 Conciertos en conjunto

Plateas con entrada ... $ 2.50
Tertulias Balcon con entrada ... " 2.50
" Altas " ... " 2.00
Palcos bajos y Balcones sin entrada ... $ 8.00

Imprenta "LA DIADEMA".- Convención, 1241

This concert at the Teatro Solis in Montevideo took place on October 17, 1925. The translation of Martin Gil's article about Agustín Barrios is on the following page.

Agustín Barrios

Already a few years ago, having heard Barrios for the first time, I said he was a revolutionary of his art, which we shouldn't find strange for him being Paraguayan.

Now I return to hearing him once again and I find that with his being revolutionary he has triumphed completely in the line, to being having been converted into the most interesting artist, of a unique personality, within an ample horizon that exclusively belongs to him because he himself has formed it. It is a basis of a rash independence and of an inspired boldness.

Barrios is at the same time an innovator and a creator. With the modification of the quality of the singing first three strings and his special manner of binding them, he has reached obtaining the most beautiful colored sounds and of an emotional smoothness. His manners to say and to phrase appear much like that of Carlos García Tolsa, that admirable and sensitive one of the guitar, my friend and late maestro.

Barrios, although he knows and dominates the classic literature of the instrument, he spends his own capital in his art, since that is to say that he is an original and vigorous creator.

When he published his own selected works and especially his melodic studies of high technique, whose demonstration I know, it would definitely and forever impose.

Lastly, to be treated as an artist genuinely ours: as a brilliant South American exponent, worthy of our support and of all our sympathy.

Martin Gil

564

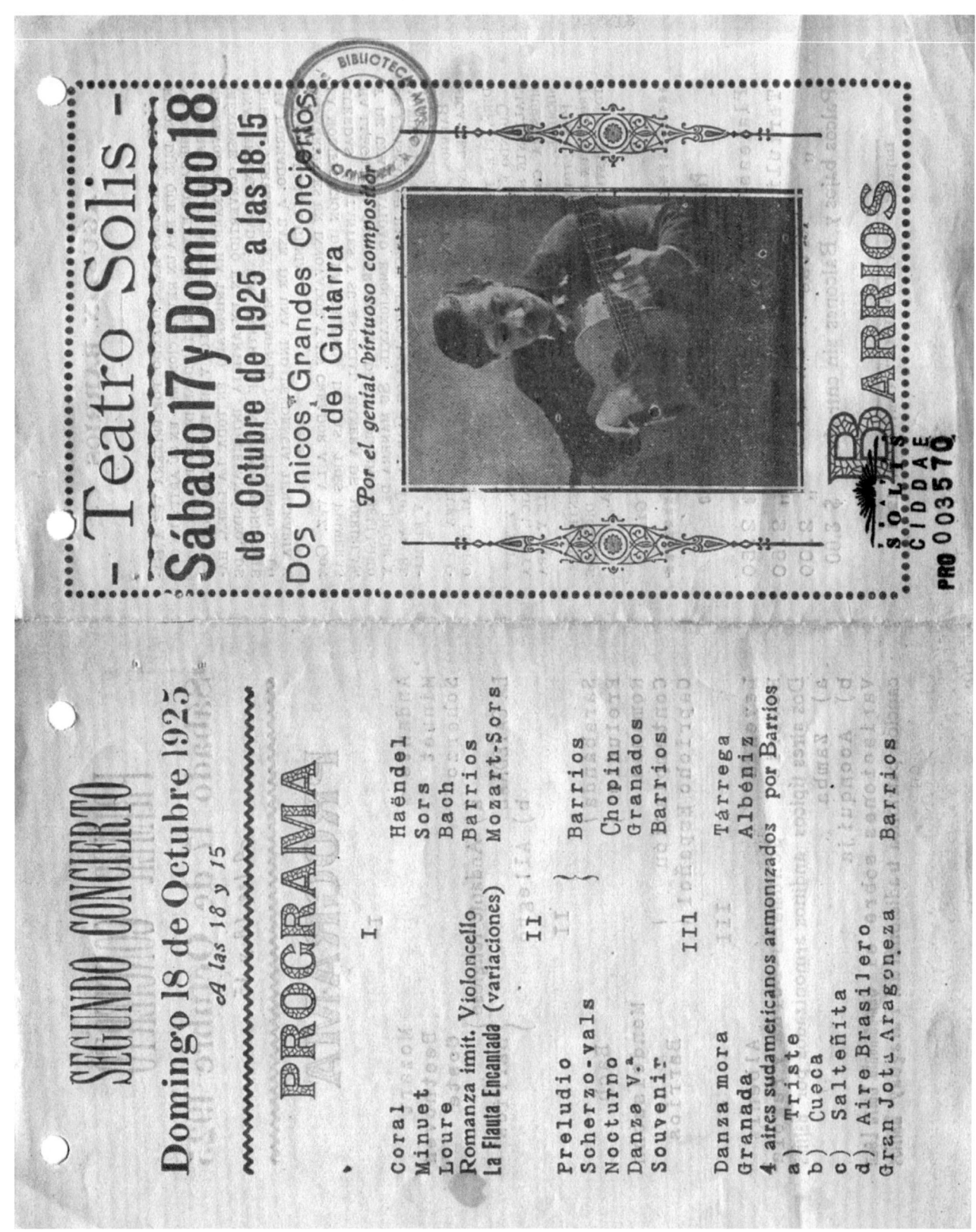

These two concerts held on Saturday October 17 and Sunday October 18, 1925 at the Teatro Solis in Montevideo offered the audience a bouquet of great original and well-known classic works to be heard.

In April of 1928, Agustín Barrios returned before the microphone instead of the megaphone. The disc above was recorded on May 10, 1928.

The *Veroton* logo and words "electric recording" *(grabacion electrica)* indicate the usage of a microphone.

These songs were recorded on April 18, 1928, the 2nd day of the new recording sessions.

The pieces on the next page were recorded for *Disco Nacional Odeon* on April 17, 1928 and May 23, 1928 respectively. The *Mazurca* is "Sarita".

Recordings of Agustín Barrios and enlarged stamps. These are Odeon recordings, and the Columbia disc was produced by Nipponophone in Kawasaki, Japan in 1939. There is an autograph of Agustín Barrios as an ink stamp.

These pieces *Traumerei* and *Tarantella* were recorded on June 21, 1928.

This song commonly known as *Un Sueño en la Floresta* was recorded on two days. Part 1 was recorded on July 28, 1928 and part 2 on July 31, 1928.

This song *"Armonias de America"* was recorded on Wednesday March 27, 1929. The top label was the released 12″ version, being the Odeon 5009 B side to *"La Catedral"*, Odeon 5099 A. This same recorded disc was chosen to replace the worn version from the Ronoel Simões collection on the 2012 edition of "Agustín Barrios The Complete Historical Recordings 1913-1942" CD set.

The bottom label is the unreleased 12″ test pressing version. This rare disc was acquired in November of 2010.

Below is my colleague, Richard "Rico" Stover, holding the disc in a visit to my guitar store on Thursday June 7, 2012.

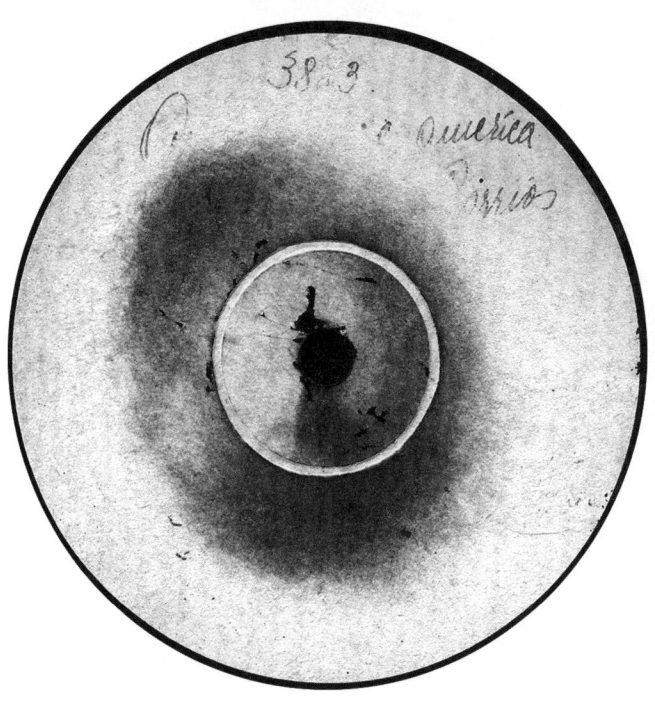

This advertisement for the record company of Agustín Barrios and many other artists is from the magazine *"Caras y Caretas"* issue No. 1550, *Año* XXXI of June 16, 1928.

This is from the July 7, 1928 *"Caras y Caretas"* Issue No. 1553 *Año* XXXI.

This is from the August 4, 1928 *"Caras y Caretas"* Issue No. 1557 *Año* XXXI.

DISCO NACIONAL
La fiel expresión del arte criollo

LAS NOVEDADES DE LA SEMANA Y LOS EXITOS EN BOGA

Impresos por el moderno sistema eléctrico de grabación, son los discos de fabricación argentina más perfectos, por su pureza, volumen sonoro, su fuerza y durabilidad.

MEMBRANA REXOFONICA

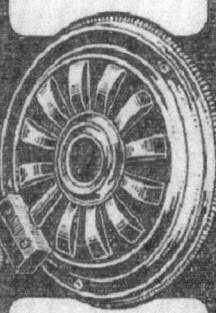

SE HA IMPUESTO POR SU PERFECTA CONSTRUCCION MODERNIZA CUALQUIER MAQUINA PARLANTE.

Dúo Gardel - Razzano
Con acompañamiento de guitarras:
RICARDO - BARBIERI - AGUILAR
Discos Nacional, de 25 ctms.,
a $ 3-25 c/u.
18248 — ¡Che, Bartolo! Tango. (Solo Gardel). R. Sciammarella-E. Cadícamo
Corazoncito. Tango. (Solo Gardel). R. Rossi-J. Rial
18249 — Canción de cuna. Tgo. (Solo Gardel). J. M. Rizzutti-J. A. Díaz-Gómez
Las madreselvas. Zamba. (Solo Gardel). J. Aguilar

Discos Nacional, de 25 ctms.,
a $ 3.— c/u.

ROBERTO FIRPO. Orq. Típica
8790 — Mamarracho. Tango. J. J. Guichandut
Pobre cieguita. Tango. A. Sanders
8792 — Haragán. Tango. E. Delfino
Aquél tapado de armiño. Tango. E. Delfino

F. CANARO. Orquesta Típica
4462 — Otra copa y se acabó. Tango. L. Martini
Marcha atrás. Tango. E. Delfino
4463 — Nelly. Vals. H. Bates
Seguime, si podés. Tango. A. Scarpino-J. Caldarella

O. FRESEDO. Orquesta Típica
5281 — Dandy. Tango. L. Demare
Chorra. Tgo. E. S. Discépolo
5289 — Tus cartas. Tango. A. Bonavena
Obrerita. Tango. A. Russo

J. MAGLIO. Orq. Típica "PACHO"
7588 — Ramona. Vals. M. Wayne
Los distinguidos. Tango. E. Di Cicco

F. LOMUTO. Orquesta Típica
7776 — Cuando mi barrio se duerme. Tango. L. Teisseire
Entre sueños. Tango. A. A. Aieta-J. Polito

ELEUTERIO YRIBARREN
Red Hot Panamerican Jazz
8191 — Final de baile. Pot - pourri. (Canto). 1º parte. S. Ibáñez
Final del baile. Pot - pourri. (Canto). 2º parte. S. Ibáñez

ADOLFO R. AVILES. J. Band
8308 — Noche silenciosa. Vals. J. A. Carluccio
Verbena gitana. Pasodoble. A. F. Frizziani

Discos Nacional, de 25 ctms.,
a $ 3-25 c/u.

IGNACIO CORSINI. Con Acomp. de 3 guitarras: Iriarte-Pesoa-Pagez
18560 — Pillería. Tonada. (Dúo). B. Tagle Lara-C. Flores
La tropilla. Canción. (Dúo). B. Tagle Lara-C. Flores

AZUCENA MAIZANI.
Con Acomp. de piano: E. Delfino y guitarra: M. Parada
11060 — Marcha atrás. Tango. A. R. Bustamante-E. Delfino
Pim, Pam, Pum. Tango. Vacarezza-E. Delfino

GLORIA GUZMAN. Con Acomp. de orquesta: Adolfo R. Avilés
11355 — Pero, hágalo con guantes. Fox Trot. Rastus-Alberti
Guzman and Murray. F. Trot. Alberti. (Arreglo Avilés)

Discos Nacional, de 25 ctms.,
a $ 3.— c/u.

DUO RUIZ-ACUÑA. Con Acomp. de 4 guitarras: GOMEZ-DAVIS
10380 — Vámonos, vida mía. Zamba. Gómez Carrillo
La reina de mis ensueños. (Canción. (Solo Ruiz). Spina-Cárdenas

DELFY. Canto con acompañamiento de piano y guitarra
6537 — Haragán. Tango. E. Delfino-M. Romero
Aquel tapado de armiño. Tgo. E. Delfino-M. Romero

TRIO ODEON.
3 guitarras: Iriarte-Pesoa-Pagez
9614 — En un pueblito de España. Vals. M. Wayne
Mi novia se llama Narda. Fox Trot. A. Pagez

AGUSTIN BARRIOS.
Solo de guitarra
204 — Aconquija. (Suite andina). A. Barrios
Junto a tu corazón. Vals. A. Barrios

Con esta membrana la fonografía llega a su más alto grado de perfeccionamiento. Precio

$ 25.—

PUA CONDOR Son las mejores. En cajitas de 200, $ **1.—**

MAX GLÜCKSMANN
La alegría del hogar moderno

Nuevos Discos

BUENOS AIRES: Florida, 336-44 (edificio propio) — Callao y Mmé. Mitre.
ROSARIO: Córdoba, 1065-69. MONTEVIDEO: 18 de Julio, 966. CORDOBA:
9 de Julio, 76. SANTA FE: Salta, 2661. SANTIAGO DE CHILE: Ahumada. 91.

This is from the October 20, 1928 *"Caras y Caretas"* Issue No. 1568 *Año* XXXI.

Alos advertised in the January 19, 1929 *"Caras y Caretas"* Issue No. 1581 *Año* XXXII.
This is from the January 26, 1929 *"Caras y Caretas"* Issue No. 1582 *Año* XXXII.

This is from the March 2, 1929 *"Caras y Caretas"* Issue No. 1587 *Año* XXXII.

This is from the *"Caras y Caretas"* magazine of May 25, 1929 issue No. 1599 *Año* XXXII.

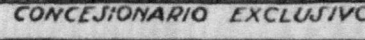

This is from the July 20, 1929 *"Caras y Caretas"* Issue No. 1607 *Año XXXII.*

This is from the October 5, 1929 *"Caras y Caretas"* Issue No. 1618 *Año* XXXII.

DISCO NACIONAL-ODEON

La fiel expresión del arte criollo

GRABADO POR EL MODERNO SISTEMA ELECTRICO VEROTON, ES EL UNICO DISCO DE FABRICACION NACIONAL SIN RUIDO DE PUA DE DURACION ILIMITADA

CARLOS GARDEL. (Del dúo GARDEL-RAZZANO). Con acompañamiento de guitarras: BARBIERI-AGUILAR.

18295 a $ 3.25
De todo te olvidas. Tango. (Primer premio, letra y música, 6º Gran concurso). E. Cadicamo-S. Merico
Bailarín compadrito. Tango. M. Bucino

18296 a $ 3.25
Pensalo bien. Tango. (Segundo premio, letra y música, 6º Gran concurso). A. Calvera-E. López.
¿Por qué soy reo? Tango. Velich-Meaños

ROBERTO FIRPO. Orquesta Típica.

8901 a $ 3.—
Mi secreto. Tango. (Del 6º Gran concurso). G. D. Jeans-G. Cavazza
Un beso. Tango. G. Cavazza

8905 a $ 3.—
Triste memoria. Tango. R. Firpo
Buena pilcha. Tango. (Del 6º Gran concurso). R. Rossi

FRANCISCO CANARO. Orquesta Típica.

4589 a $ 3.—
De todo te olvidas. Tango. (Primer premio, letra y música. 6º Gran concurso). S. Merico
Gallo viejo. Tango. E. Cadicamo

4595 a $ 3.—
Rancho embrujao. Tango. (Primer premio, música. 6º Gran concurso). R. Courau
Canto de amor. Tango. (Del 6º Gran concurso). A. Polito

JUAN MAGLIO. Orquesta Típica "PACHO".

9636 a $ 3.—
Margaritas. Tango. (Premio de Honor 1929. 6º Gran concurso). J. C. Moreno González
Rapaciña. Pasodoble. P. V. Lambertucci

FRANCISCO LOMUTO. Orquesta Típica.

7829 a $ 3.—
Prisionero. Tango. (Seleccionado para el Gran Premio de Honor 1929. 6º Gran concurso). A. A. Aieta
Al caer la tarde. Vals. R. Rossi

ARMANI-COSPITO. Jazz Band.

12003 a $ 3.—
Josefina... por favor. Fox Trot. R. González
Reina mora. Pasodoble. Vázquez Vigo

IGNACIO CORSINI. Con acompañamiento de 3 guitarras: PAGES-PESOA-MACIEL.

18591 a $ 3.25
Amor que muere. Vals. A. Korbeneyer-J. de Dios Filiberto
Saludó y se fué. Tango. A. Supparo-J. Ceglie

DUO RUIZ-ACUÑA. Con acompañamiento de 4 guitarras: GOMEZ-DAVIS.

10417 a $ 3.25
Mi cordobesa. Gato. (Dúo). E. Chavarría.
No quiero que te vayas. Zamba. (Dúo). A. Amaya

CHARLO. Con acompañamiento de 3 guitarras: IGLESIAS-BESADA-ARRIETA.

16237 a $ 3.25
Con tu mirar. Vals. Canosa-Giorno
Anoche la vi. Tango. (Del 6º Gran concurso). Fronti-Díz

PATROCINIA DIAZ. Con acompañamiento de 3 guitarras: FREYRE-DAVILA.

11406 a $ 3.—
Cuando llora la milonga. Tango. Mario Castro-Juan de Dios Filiberto
Barataza. Ranchera. E. Maroni-Juan de Dios Filiberto

RICARDO DOMINGUEZ. Con acompañamiento de rondalla: CAUVILLA PRIM.

16800 a $ 3.25
Axeitam'a polainiña. Canción popular. M. de Adalid
Lonxe d'a terriña. Balada gallega. A. J. Pereira-J. Montes

AGUSTIN BARRIOS. Solo de guitarra.

211 a $ 3.—
Confesión. Melodía. A. Barrios
Aire de zamba. Zamba. A. Barrios

RAFAEL ROSSI. Cuarteto norteño.

9837 a $ 3.—
Adiós Buenos Aires. Tarantela. R. Rossi
A lo lejos. Vals. A. R. Avilés

TRIO GEDEON. Con Acomp. de 3 guitarras.

25603 a $ 3.—
Llevátelo todo. Tango. (Parodia). Trío Gedeón-R. Sciamarella
Ausencia eterna. (A Milonguita). (Parodia). Trío Gedeón-F. N. Bianco

CONCESIONARIO EXCLUSIVO

MAX GLÜCKSMANN

La alegría del hogar moderno

This advertisement, for the record company of Agustín Barrios and many other artists, is from the magazine *"Caras y Caretas"* issue No. 1630, *Año* XXXII of December 28, 1929.

This is from the February 15, 1930 *"Caras y Caretas"* Issue No. 1637 *Año* XXXIII.

This is from the July 5, 1930 *"Caras y Caretas"* Issue No. 1657 *Año* XXXIII.

582

Novedades del Disco

Grabación eléctrica VEROTON — *La fiel expresión*

CARLOS GARDEL. (Del dúo GARDEL-RAZZANO). Con acompañamiento de guitarras: BARBIERI - AGUILAR - RIVEROL.

18823 a $3.25	En la tranquera. (A Mar del Plata yo me quiero ir). Ranchera. P. Laguna-F. Lomuto
	Pordioseros. Tango. G. D. Barbieri
18824 a $3.25	Colorao, colorao. Tango. E. C. Flores-A. H. Acuña
	Aquellas farras. (Argañaraz) Tango. E Cadícamo-R. Firpo

ROBERTO FIRPO. Orq. Típica.

8964 a $3.—	Hula, Fox Trot. A. M. Pioli-A. Taranto
	Triste separación. Vals. P. de Gullo
8965 a $3.—	Luz de esperanza. Vals. L. Castaing. (Con estrib.)
	A mi juego me llamaron. Ranchera. R. Tuegols

FRANCISCO CANARO. Orquesta Típica.

4668 a $3.—	Ya va para un mes. Tango. M. Bucino
	El puehlero. Ranchera. A. A. Aieta. (Con estrib.)
4669 a $3.—	Asuero. Pasodoble. J. Caldarella
	Titiriteros. Tango. S. Mérico. (Con estrib.)
4670 a $3.—	Rosa blanca, Vals. D. Pelle. (Con estrib.)
	Ba'o cuerda. Tango. L. Canaro

JUAN MAGLIO Orquesta Típica "PACHO".

9074 a $3.—	Nostalgia. Vals. A. Sureda. (Con estribi lo).
	El último tango. Tango. V. Salerno
9075 a $3.—	Candombe de barrio. Tango. R. Ventura. (Con Estrib.)
	La forastera. Ranchera. J. Rendón

FRANCISCO LOMUTO. Orquesta Típica.

7855 a $3.—	Pare la marcha. Tango. P. Clausi
	Mi morena. Pasodoble. B. Scaglia. (Con estrib.)

ADOLFO A. LUNA. Solo de guitarra.

1912 a $3.—	Más bien me voy. Zamba. A. V. Luna
	Canto de amor. Estilo. M. Gómez Carrillo - A. V. Luna

IGNACIO CORSINI. Con acompañamiento de 3 guitarras: PAGES-PESOA-MACIEL.

18417 a $3.25	Madre. Tango. Servetto-Pracánico
	Sombras. Tango. Servetto-Pracánico

CHARLO Con Acomp. de orquesta: FRANCISCO CANARO.

16254 a $3.25	Nocturno. Vals. F. García Jiménez-A. Bardi
	El castigo. Tango. (Con acomp. de guitarras). J. Rezzano

Dúo RUIZ - ACUÑA. con Acomp. de 4 guitarras: GOMEZ-DAVIS.

18439 a $3.25	El Triunfo. Triunfo. A. Chazarreta
	Como se guarda un tesoro. Canción. (Solo Ruiz). C. Portela

¡DISCO

Tenor: FERNANDO CINISELLI. Con coro de la Scala y orquesta. Directores: maestros HECTOR PANIZZA y VENEZIANI.

177181 a $5.50	Lohengrin. Signo gentil. Wágner
	Andrea Chenier. Coro di Pastorelle Giordano

Tenor: ROGELIO BALDRICH - CONDESA DE SCLOFANI. Director: maestro ROMERO.

196022 a $3.50	La canción del día. Canción de Amalio. (Por Baldrich). Guerrero-Muñoz Seca-Pérez Fdez.
	La canción del día. Canción de Estrella. (Por la C. de Sclofani). Guerrero-Muñoz Seca-Pérez Fdez.

Tenor: JESUS DE GAVIRIA. Director: maestro CAPDEVILA.

196103 a $3.50	El trust de los tenorios. Jota. Serrano
	La Dolores. El madrigal. Bretón

L'ASSOCIATION ARTISTIQUE DES CONCERTS COLONNE. Director: maestro GABRIEL PIERNE.

177177 a $5.50	Gwendoline. Obertura. 1ª parte. Chabrier
	Gwendoline. Obertura. 2ª parte. Chabrier

DISTRIBUIDOR

MAX GLÜCKMANN

This is from the September 20, 1930 *"Caras y Caretas"* Issue No. 1668 *Año* XXXIII.

NACIONAL - ODEON
del arte criollo — Sin ruido de púa

ADA FALCON. Con Acomp. de orquesta: FRANCISCO CANARO.

11195 a $ 3.25
- Destellos. Tango. J. A. Caruso-F. Canaro
- Cuando llora la milonga. Tango. Luis Mario-J. de Dios Filiberto

PATROCINIA DIAZ. Con Acomp. de guitarras y órgano: FREIRE-DAVILA-FERNANDEZ.

11114 a $ 3.—
- En el baile de Misia Pancha. Ranchera. Falcone-Dima-Ferreyra
- La porteña. Polca. Pesce-Clausi

Dúo ITALO-CASTAÑEDA. Con Acomp. de 3 guitarras: GARRO-PERUSSO.

21007 a $ 3.—
- Mi padecer. Chacarera. C. Perusso
- Noble amigo. Vals. (Solo Castañeda). L. Castañeda

ANA S. DE CABRERA. Canto con Acom. de guitarra.

17014 a $ 3.25
- Me alegra el corazón. Chacarera. A. S. de Cabrera
- Por culpa tuya. Zamba. G. Coria Peñaloza-A. S. de Cabrera

AGUSTIN BARRIOS. Solo de guitarra.

205 a $ 3.—
- Oracion. Melodía. A. Barrios
- Vals Nº 4. Vals. A. Barrios

MARIO A. PARDO. Canto y guitarra.

6606 a $ 3.—
- La guitarrera de San Nicolás. Vals. (Solo de guitarra). E. Maciel
- Velay que soy disgraciao. Zamba. (Canto). Fernández Díaz-Franceschi

MASSOBRIO - CALDARELLA. Acordeón y guitarra.

623 a $ 3.—
- Amor secreto. Vals. Massobrio-Caldarella
- Pastoreando libremente. Ranchera. Massobrio-Caldarella

Trio GEDEON. Con acompañamiento de 3 guitarras.

25014 a $ 3.—
- Con tu mirar. Vals. (Parodia). Trio Gedeón-E. S. Giorno
- Pobre loro. Tango. (Solo Caprara). Montoni-Caprara-Montoni

ODEON

177178 a $ 5.50
- Gwendoline. Obertura 3ª parte. Chabrier
- Ronde villageoise. Chabrier

LEW BRAY. Canto, con acompañamiento de orquesta.

193514 a $ 2.50
- Asomándose a la ventana. (Del film sonoro: Rapsodia del recuerdo). Conrad-Michell-Cottler
- No puedes entender? (William Dutton, con acompañamiento de orquesta). Osterman-Young.

REGINO SAINZ DE LA MAZA. Solo de guitarra.

196100 a $ 3.50
- Mazurka. Tárrega
- El vito. Sainz de la Maza

PAUL MANIA. Solo de órgano.

193503 a $ 2.50
- El molino de la Selva Negra. Pieza característica R. Eilenberg
- Paseo en trineo. Galop. R. Eilenberg

EMILE VACHER. Solo de acordeón con acompañamiento de piano y banjo.

193504 a $ 2.50
- La java des rigoles. E. Vacher
- La más hermosa. Vals. Darlez

DISCO POPULAR "DACAPO"

Discos DACAPO, de 25 centímetros, a $ 2.50 c/u.

FELICIANO BRUNELLI. Solo de acordeón.

D 81905
- Felipe! Tarantela. F. Brunelli
- Polca norteña. Polca. F. Brunelli

ORQUESTA POPULAR "DACAPO".
Dirección: JULIO F. POLLERO.

D 80013
- Copos de espuma. Vals. Bayardo-González
- Prendete fuerte mi china. Ranchera. J. F. Pollero

EXCLUSIVO:

FLORIDA, 336-44

SUCURSALES EN:
ROSARIO: Córdoba, 1065 - 69.
MONTEVIDEO: 18 de Julio, 966.

This is from the September 20, 1930 *"Caras y Caretas"* Issue No. 1668 *Año* XXXIII.

"In my modest opinion Barrios was more modern and he was making his own reality, the American man, and in that, he was ahead of his time. In spite of these adversities, many valued him and he left an inerasable memory." (Lucio Nuñez, ob. cit.) About these last words we refer immediately.

Nuñez is to be referring to: "There was a magazine dedicated to the guitar exclusively", that which had the demolisher's unfavorable concepts to the art of Barrios, he was referring to the magazine *"La Guitarra" No. 2* from December, 1923, created and directed by Juan Carlos Anido, father of the concert artist Maria Luisa Anido. We transcribe the text of the demolishing opinion of the director Mr. Juan Carlos Anido: "Agustín Barrios: Three concerts were announced by Mr. Agustín Barrios, in the Salon Argentina, and of those only one took place." "The distinguished Paraguayan guitarist has had, well, little fortune.and of that, in the greater part can be owed to the modern artistic concept that exists for the guitar in our public." "Mr. Barrios, that has presented himself at once as a performer, composer and folklorist, isn't really, a true exponent of any of these three aludible aspects."

(Left) *"La Guitarra"* magazine, of December 1924 year one, issue two. Published by Juan Carlos Anido.

(Right) An attempt at discrediting Agustín Pio Barrios. The irony is, decades later Juan Carlos's daughter, Maria Luisa Anido, would record and perform in concert, works Information:

Rico Stover

AGUSTIN BARRIOS

Tres conciertos tenía anunciados el señor Agustín Barrios, en el salón «La Argentina», de los cuales sólo realizó uno.

El distinguido guitarrista paraguayo ha tenido, pues, poca fortuna.

Y ello, en gran parte, puede deberse al concepto artístico moderno que en nuestro público existe de la guitarra.

El señor Barrios, que se presenta a la vez como ejecutante, compositor y folklorista, no es, en realidad, un verdadero exponente de ninguno de los tres aspectos aludidos.

Como guitarrista no carece de interés, pues tiene temperamento, pero en ningún caso puede admitirse su figuración entre los concertistas de nota, malgrado una innovación que pretende introducir en el arte guitarrístico.

Esta innovación consiste en substituir las tres cuerdas de registro agudo, (prima, segunda y tercera) que en la guitarra clásica son de tripa, por otras de alambre de acero. Pero el señor Barrios, al incurrir en tan grave falta contra la cultura artística y el buen gusto, no tiene siquiera el mérito de la novedad: la tan desdichada modificación es utilizada por los «tocadores» italianos, y por la mayoría de los «tocadores» de francachelas populares.

Como compositor, tampoco ofrece el señor Barrios características salientes. No puede admitirse, ni remotamente, que sus obras lleguen a formar parte del buen repertorio guitarrístico. Carecen de valor musical y hasta de originalidad. Junto a brevísimos destellos que anuncian ideas de relativo interés, aparecen, apagándolos, períodos vulgarísimos que se prolongan con exceso.

Y como folk-lorista, pensamos que el cancionero ibero-americano espera a otro investigador de mayor enjundia y conocimientos.

Todo lo escrito no pretende, ni mucho menos, indicar la carencia de cualidades innatas en el señor Barrios: quiere significar que éstas de poco sirven si no las sustenta la preparación superior.

"As a guitarist he doesn't draw the interest, while having a temperament, but in no case can it be admitted that he is to be among the concert artists of note, having a disappointing innovation that pretends to introduce the guitaristic art ".

"This innovation consists in substituting the three treble strings (1st, 2nd and 3rd), that on the classical guitar are of gut, with steel strings, but Mr. Barrios, incurs the fault of reprehension of the artistic culture, and in good faith, the novelty is without merit, this extreme modification is utilized by the Italian street players, and for the most part these players perform frankly, popular music".

"As a composer, nor does Mr. Barrios offer any salient characteristics. It can't be admitted, even remotely, that his works come to form a part of the good guitar repertoire. They embrace the musical value of their originality. Along with these little rays of light that announce the idea of relative interest, they appear, shut out, by vulgar periods prolonged to excess".

"And as a folklorist, we think that the Ibero-Americano songwriter waits for another investigator of greater substance and knowledge".

"All I write doesn't pretend, nevertheless, to indicate the lack of innate qualities in Mr. Barrios; but signifies it to be of little value without the sustained superior preparation". The concepts expressed in the magazine by Mr. Anido about the artistic conditions of Agustín Barrios, have been shown over time to be mistaken. Because today Barrios is one of the most extensively referred to guitarists in the guitaristic history of the world. Being the creator of a style with which he gave the universal projection of South American sentiment. Due to these opinions of Mr. Anido, later on, other versions originated and in the Argentine guitar environment at that time they were totally of a negative opinion of Barrios. We reiterate the final concepts of maestro Lucio Nuñez in his article for the magazine *"El Encordado"*: "In spite of these adversities, many valued his work and he left an inerasable memory". A proof of this is, that the guitar personalities then, with more musical and instrumental authority than Mr. Anido, although he was the father of the accomplished concert artist, he was only an aficionado of the guitar, and a great enthusiast of the same, and maestros such as Domingo Prat, Ricardo Muñoz and Martin Gil (astronomer, aficionado of the guitar, writer, newspaper journalist) left documented opinions of favorable remembrances of Barrios.

And it mustn't have been totally adverse for the Paraguayan in the Argentine ambiance of the time, by the quantity of discs he recorded in Buenos Aires from 1913-1928. Being the first recordings of his professional career, when he had only just started, counting in the fact, that he was only a little more than 25 years old.

Photo of Agustín Barrios which was used for the Sao Paulo, Brazil concert program cover at the Municipal Theater on October 13, 1929. At the right of the photo he was described as the "King of the Guitar" (*O Rei do Violao).

According to some judgment, Barrios was the first classical guitarist to record discs in the world. It is certain that they took place in Argentina. And if he wasn't the first guitarist to record, he was one of the firsts to leave interpretations recorded on sound discs. (Julio J. Otermin recorded 18 solos, including three pieces by Fernando Sor in January and February of 1912, fourteen months before Barrios' recordings were available to the public. R.O.)

About the concepts expressed over the art on the part of the personalities mentioned beforehand we commence with Ricardo Muñoz, in his *"Historia de la Guitarra"*, page 361, beginning the biography of this Paraguayan he says: "Barrios, the Paraguayan virtuoso composer, who has succeeded so much in his art, and in what has been given to be said by the South American press, he is one of the most highly accomplished concert artists of the guitar today."

"Endowed with such a rare temperament and an interpretative intuition, his personality is defined with clear and precise lines."

"The artistic figure of Barrios, is the result of successful labor, methodically, intelligently and quite meditated, by a emotional soul and profoundly sentimental." "He is a complete artist, with such moral qualities that ennoble him, that realize the brilliance of his talent, culture, fitting and generous."

Muñoz in this same work includes an opinion by Martin Gil about the *guarany* guitarist (page 368) it says: "Upon his arrival in Buenos Aires in 1928, he was heard privately by our man of the celestial sciences, Martin Gil, and he has made public the following declaration: "At last, after some years I have heard the guitarist Barrios again, revolutionary in his art, that which, is a treatment not to be missed by the Paraguayan".

Teatro Solis in Montevideo, where Agustín Barrios played on October 17 and 18, 1925. Andrés Segovia played there on June 11, 27 and again on July 4, 1920 (Source: Six Silver Moonbeams) Miguel Llobet, Carmen Amaya and Atahualpa Yupanqui also performed there. (Source: *La Historia del Teatro Solis*.) Regino Sainz de la Maza and Julio S. Sagreras also played there as well. The photo is from *Musica y Musicos de Latinoamerica* by Otto Mayer-Serra.

"After hearing him, he found that the revolutionary had triumphed completely, as to having been converted into a very interesting artist, a unique personality, within an ample horizon that belongs to him exclusively, because he himself has formed a base of fearless independence and a gentile audacity. Barrios is an innovator and creator at the same time."

"With the modification of the first three strings, the "singers" of his instrument, and his special manner to strike them, he has shown to obtain sounds of a beautiful color and an emotional smoothness, Barrios although knowledgeable and having dominion over the classical literature of the guitar, all the way to his own art, that is to say, well, he is a vigorous and original creator". "When he published his selected works, and very especially his melodic studies of the technique, whose design I know, it dominated definitively and forever. "Lastly, to be conferred, as an artist genuinely ours, a brilliant South American exponent, worthy of all our support and all of our sympathy".

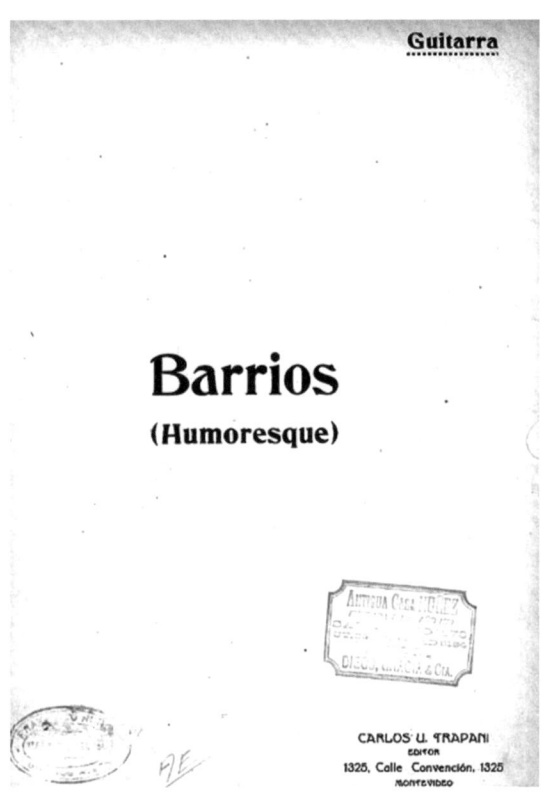

(Left) Piece published by Carlos Trapani in Montevideo, Uruguay, for Agustín P. Barrios in 1921, (Right) 2nd edition of *"Madrigal"* published by Carlos Trapani.

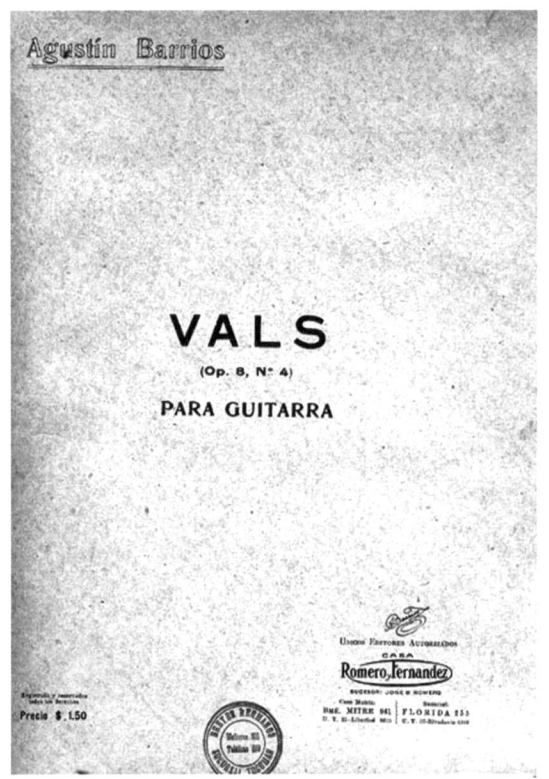

(Left) One of the second series of pieces published by Romero & Fernández , in 1928 for Agustín P. Barrios. (Right) Piece released by Diego, Gracia and Co. in 1928.

Arcas, J., Martha, sinfonía (Flotow)	$ 1.50
— Minueto en Mi menor	» 0.50
— „ en sol	» 0.50
— Mi segunda época, fantasía	» 1.60
— Murcianas	» 1.60
— Norma, sinfonía (Bellini, V.)	» 1.50
— Polaca, fantástica	» 1.50
— Panaderos, Los, bolero	» 1.—
— Polonessa	» 0.50
— Postillón de La Rioja	» 0.70
— Rigoletto, fantasía para dos guitarras (Verdi, G.)	» 1.80
— Rondeña	» 1.80
— Rondó	» 1.50
— Rubia de los lunares, La, habanera	» 0.60
— Saltarina, mazurka	» 0.50
— Soleá	» 1.60
— Sueño (Rosellen)	» 0.80
— Tanda de valses	» 1.20
— Traviata, fantasía (Verdi, G.)	» 1.—
— Trovatore, aria y miserere (Verdi, G.)	» 1.—
— Variaciones sobre un tema de Sors	» 1.20
— Vísperas sicilianas, melodía y bolero (Verdi, G.)	» 1.20
Arias, Célebre Pasodoble español	» 0.70
Ballester, J., Cariñosa, mazurka	» 0.60
— Granadinas	» 0.60
Banegas, A., Milongas clásicas	» 0.60
— Zamba, de la rapsodia de Aires Criollos	» 0.50
Bonet, Guajiras para guitarra y canto	» 0.60
Barrero, V., Himno de Espartero	» 0.50
— Himno de Riego	» 0.50
— La Madrileña, baile español	» 0.50
Barrios, A., Estudio de concierto en La mayor	» 3.—
— Humoresque	» 1.50
— Madrigal, gavota	» 1.50
Bosch, J., Al son de las càmpanas	» 0.80
— Allegro de Sonata	» 1.—
— Amazona	» 0.80
— Balada	» 0.80
— Bolero	» 0.80
— Brimborión, romanza	» 1.—
— Cello	» 0.80
— Coelia, jota-valse	» 0.80
— Colección de 6 piezas fáciles	» 1.60
— Duettina	» 0.80
— Estrellas y flores	» 0.80
— Fantasía dramática	» 1.40
— La Rosa	» 1.40
— Les Echos	» 0.80

ROMERO Y FERNANDEZ

Here is a listing of *"Estudio de concierto en La mayor"* by Agustín Barrios, the first of the series of ten pieces published by Romero & Fernández , in 1928. It is from the c. 1928 *"Romero & Fernández Catalogo No. 5, Métodos y Musica para Guitarra"* catalog of 34 pages.

(Left) The very first anthology of the works of Agustín P. Barrios, published in Brazil by Romeo Di Giorgio c. 1950. Some of the transcriptions are credited to Atilio Bernardini. (This edition was available until c. 1970. Source: Jun Suguwara, store visit on August 11, 2008.)
(Right) Piece transcribed by Atilio Bernardini and published by Del Vecchio in Brazil

(Left) Transcription of *Las Abejas* and published by *Mundo Guarani* c.1955, (Right) Sila Godoy transcription of Barrios' *Danza Paraguaya* c. 1955, he also did a transcription of *La Catedral*.

Agustín Pio Barrios in Asuncion, Paraguay, 1923. Information: Rico Stover

Printed manuscript copy by Hugo Carboni
done in April 1938, of an unpublished Agustín
Barrios piece. This piece that is well-known
today, was a gift to Professor Eduardo Bensadon
from record collector Ronoel Simões of Brazil
in 1946.

Bautista S. Almiron in 1920, says in the
dedication: "To my cherished and distinguished
student A. Rojas Molina." signed B. S. Almiron.

Lalyta Almiron at the
age when she studied
with Agustín Barrios.
Information: Rico Stover

This is from the 1931
Antigua Casa Nuñoz
catalog.

Alfredo Quelu's interview with Agustín Barrios published on June 18, 1928 from the *"La Novela Semanal"* magazine published in Buenos Aires.

The image used to translate is from the book *El Inalcanzable* Agustín Barrios, pages 133 and 134. In this book the source was described as a daily newspaper, though upon close inspection it is a magazine.

"A Magician of the Guitar"

"In the corridor of the hotel. The maid-right out of a French comedy from the end of the 19th century — asks us:

"Quiet..."

Then we crossed on our tiptoes.

"Mr. Barrios is studying" she adds, gathering to his importance the introducer of the importance of the maestro, which is in charge of his tranquility.

Those two important things alarmed us. To bother an artist is to jump into emptiness. One can fall to his feet and sing...

"Come in!"

Hotel room. One hand that tends and a brown face that smiles. In the other hand is a guitar that hangs, as grim, its silence is its frown — because they made it quiet down.

Bohemian atmosphere, but a bohemian place that smells of expensive perfumes, you see a tuxedo and a dinner at top class tables. Bohemian of art.

Here and there suitcases which flirt with the prestige of an innumerable labels of customs houses and hotels of rank....

Portraits... Pieces of music. Concert programs. In the center — in the same center of that sea of graphics — a sculptured profile of a woman, two pieces to stand it up on and a large black frame.

"Good gracious... Does the adventure arise?"

"On the strings of the guitar, that never play in public it is epilogued."

",,,? Its own definition"

Near to the guitar rests a gourd. A fearsome heater-the last word in its genre and, therefore, terror of us those of the familiar brazier — blow and blow with its breath of fire.

"Your beginning...?"

"Giving serenades under the bars of some little brown Paraguayan women. Many times those serenades ended abruptly. You understand...Othello hasn't died... and even a third of his cape the austere commander of Ulloa."

"And the Mejias?"

"To the *guitarrazos* I gave recognition to them many times."

"Greetings, *Don* Juan!"

"I had my Inés, with its mystic anxieties of salvation for my soul and its transport of hallucination.... I was in Asuncion, Paraguay. My father acted as the Argentine Vice Consul; I was a student, but between studying human bones- my father wanted to make me a doctor — and the arpeggios of the guitar, I preferred the latter. There is the greatest enchantment.... Next, which with the first you help your fellow man to die badly, and with the second, instead, to live well."

"Completely. You have been born to be a professor of theology."

"There is something to that, without a doubt. I convince others and easily convinced myself of all, which exalts the love to the guitar. But do you want an instrument more noble?"

"When you play it as you do."

"You might be my substitute for theology, chronicler."

"So much honor!"

"Deserved."

"But, forgive me, we have remained in the serenades and little brown Paraguayan women.... with an Othello...a commander...."

"And the empty pocket...My father died, interrupting my studies and....and the Paraguayan women swim in the bitterness.... They swim, it's indubitable...swim, with what little brown Paraguayan women?"

"I will change the herb...

"But not the theme, didn't you say...?"

"Desiring to get married, I suffered the unspeakable by that empty pocket. Did you know that?"

"We're journalists."

"Then, profoundly knowledgeable. My girlfriend wished in her sighs on her balcony, and me I went to the serenades...One afternoon I told my mother: 'Mother, I'm going to Corrientes... a jump...two days of performances, I'll earn some money, I'll return on Sunday, on Monday I'll vist the Civil Registry, on Tuesday we'll get married'...."

"And on Thursday, get divorced...."

"No, ...The program ended with the marriage, a total week of travels...to form my baker's nest."

"And did you go?"

"Yes, I went. It was a great success, in Corrientes, they contracted me for other cities and so, town by town, my spirit lived the growing emotion of the pilgrimage of art."

"And you returned to Asuncion?"

"Fourteen-years later."

"And then?"

594

"I traveled, studied, I kept traveling and continued studying."

"But, if we're not misinformed, you are in your second reincarnation, right? Because you died, surely one time."

"Man... I'll tell you. Yes, I went to one of my funerals. Do you know what a luxurious thing death is?"

"No, tell me..."

"Of a stupendous theater. You, listen: I was in San Paolo (Brazil). One day, I was walking down the street with my friend, named Camargo, when a so and so came near us, his face showing his circumstances, and he says to my friend: 'Beloved Camargo, I'm sorry, I know you are a great friend of Barrios... The late.....'"

"Atonitos, we kept listening to him: 'Great artist! Quite a man! that Agustín P. Barrios. Quite a man!'"

"But, what are you saying?" Camargo interrupted. "That Barrios was..."

"Dead, beloved, dead, it is lamentable."

"But Barrios is here." shouted Camargo.

"Man... don't digress...has the announcement affected you greatly? Calm down..."

"Enough of your nonsense! Don't you know this man who is accompanying me? Agustín P. Barrios. We're here!"

"Right away I'll clarify everything...In Rio de Janeiro a certain orchestra musician by the surname Barrios has died. As well Agustín. Coincidence? I came to perform there and heard my name and, of course, a sheet music typesetter launched that funeral throng. Some weeks later I read the dailies from Asuncion, the chronicles of my funerals. How many friends I had, and what eulogies!!!"

Admirable. Barrios is one who enjoys the emotion. Friendly or cruel, profound or superficial, all emotion has in its spirit a proportionate receptacle. By that, his works as a composer are, on par that are displays of technique and emotionalized moments, which (missing text) music staff. Such as his *Mazurka appasionada*. Born in (missing text) anguish. In Rio de Janeiro (missing text)

Instinctively they raise, (missing text) to the black frame (missing text) a sculptured profile of a woman.

In the antique rosary, of the waves that pass, Barrios prays thus the fervent prayer of his great emotion.

The life is for the old coffer of harmonies. By his to extract-with the supreme refinement of the centuries, the only note, subtle or profound, of the emotion, whose variations are infinite, such as mankind's thirst for beauty."

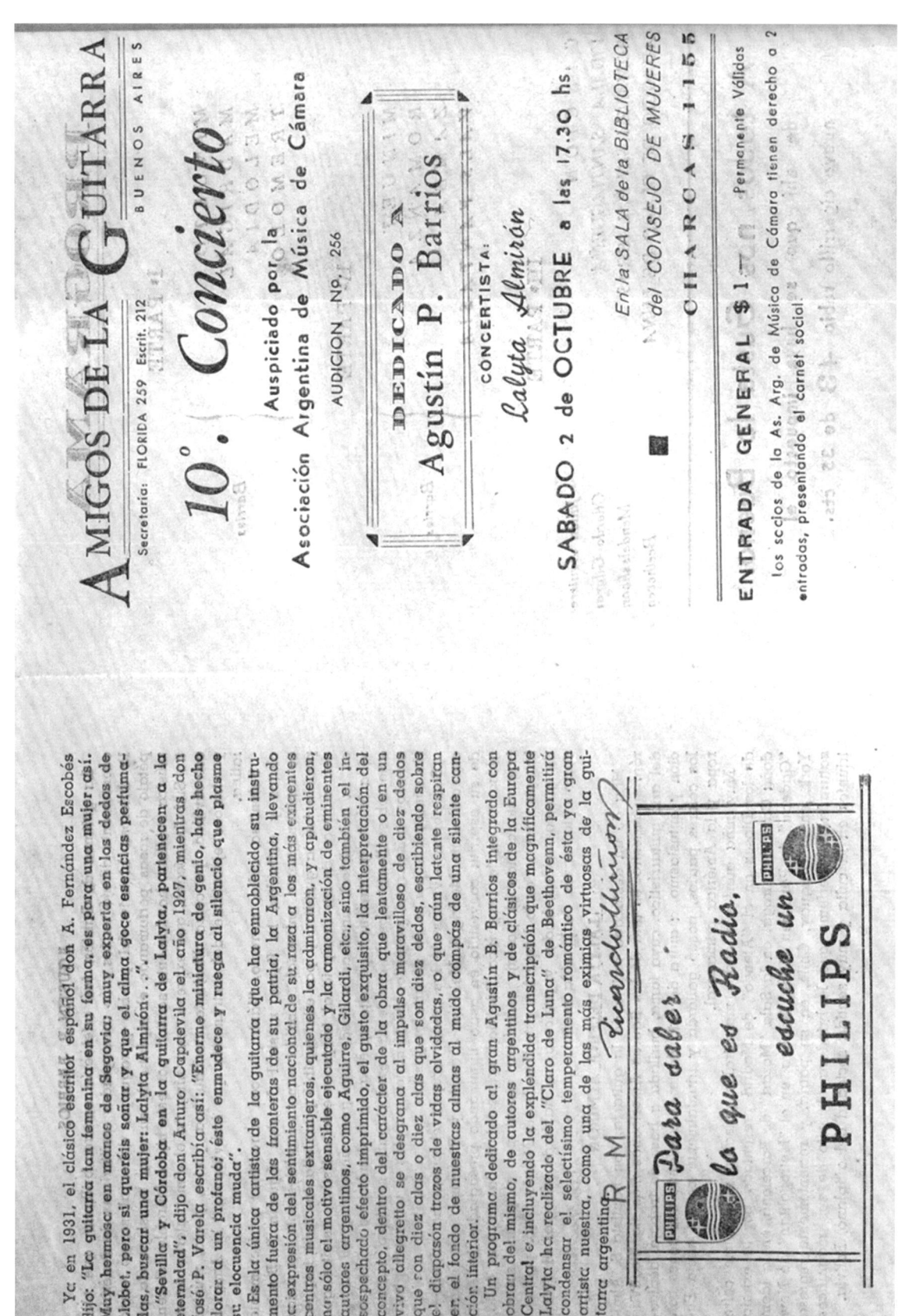

Lalyta Almiron concert dedicated to Agustín Pio Barrios that was held on October 2, 1943, just 10 months before the Paganini of Paraguay died. She certainly was playing pieces that she had learned from Barrios over a five-month period, when she was a child at the age of nine. She had played these pieces for at least 20 years before this concert.

AGUSTIN P. BARRIOS

La guitarra de Barrios, fué orfebrería sonora, brillante, que elocuentemente dibujó en los más consagrados auditoriums de América, la dolorosa historia del pueblo paraguayo, del cual surgió como pétalo de rosas perfumando el espíritu de su raza, transfigurada en música sublime, hondamente sentida por este hijo admirable del centro Sud Americano, que expresó como ninguno el alma interior de su colectividad, ya como dibujante, caricaturista, pintor, poeta, músico y virtuoso ejecutante del instrumento que individualiza la América latina.

Talentoso, culto, correcto, filántropo, con caracteres perfectamente claros y definidos, la figura musical de don Agustín P. Barrios es eminentemente universal; cándido como un adolescente, su única pasión fué la guitarra y por ello escribió para ella los más inspirados motivos de su excepcional temperamento artístico, escritos que en la actualidad, analizados desde cualquier ángulo moral de su vida músico-guitarrística, permite apreciar la deslumbrante calidad de este sobresaliente rapsoda occidental revolucionario, sensitivo, austero, creador, aristócrata, poseedor de fórmulas propias y un extraordinario concepto superior de su arte exquisito.

Sus obras, —varias de las cuales ocupan el programa adjunto—, especialmente Madrigal, Melodía, Trémolo y Romanza, son índices de su espíritu convertido en astro iluminando presagiadas bellezas, glosadas en la magnífica fidelidad orquestal de la guitarra culta, transustanciando el paisaje cromático visual por el poema sonoro imaginativo, volando hacia las estrellas de un Mundo mejor poblado de gnomos, niñas, hadas y princesas, o habitado sólo por el dolor, como única razón de la vida mortal.

Ricardo Muñoz)

¡LALYTA DELFINA ALMIRÓN

Hija de un destacado artista de la guitarra, don Bautista S. Almirón, su maestro, es una de las figuras Americanas más significativas del arte guitarrístico, cuya fama, burilada a base de trabajo, dedicación y entusiasmo, a guisa de estandarte enarbolando sus sones con los colores patrios, paseó gallarda y triunfalmente por la añeja Europa y la América primaveral.

Muy niña aún, sus dedos magistrales pulsaron el sublime cofre de los Dioses en el "Ateneo" de Madrid presentada por la eximia doña Camila Quiroga, en la Sala "Mozart" de Barcelona, en la idem "Gadeau" de París, en Milán, Génova, en el "Metropolitan" de New York, en el Uruguay, Chile, en su patria, y recientemente regresa saturada del perfume que le brindara el éxito de sus magníficos triunfos en la culta y muy sentida sociedad del altiplano, Bolivia.

PROGRAMA

I* PARTE

MINUETO	
MADRIGAL	Barrios
MELODIA	
TREMOLO	

II* PARTE

MINUET	
ROMANZA	Barrios
ZAMBA	
VALS FANTASIA	

III* PARTE

CANCION	Julián Aguirre
VIDALA SANTIAGUEÑA	Gilardo Gilardi
ROMANZA SIN PALABRAS	Mendelsshonn
ADAGGIO DE CLARO DE LUNA	Beethoven

A todos nos Gusta lo Bueno.

de ahí que se haya impuesto el nuevo cigarrillo rubio 43 de 35 cts.

The images on this page and the previous one are from the archive of Ricardo Muñoz.

Translation of the biographies by Ricardo Muñoz of Agustín P. Barrios and Lalyta Delfina Almiron:

Agustín P. Barrios

The guitar of Barrios, was a goldsmith's sound, brilliant, that eloquently sketched in the most consecrated auditoriums of America, the painful history of the Paraguayan populace, from which he surged as a rose petal perfuming the spirit of his race, transfigured in sublime music, deeply felt by this honorable son of the South American center, that expressed as no other the interior soul of his collectivity, since as a sketch artist, caricaturist, painter, poet, musician and virtuoso performer of the instrument that individualizes Latin America.

Talented, cultured, exact, philanthropic, with a perfectly clear and defined character, the musical figure of *Don* Agustín P. Barrios is eminently universal; candid as an adolescent, his unique passion was the guitar and by it he wrote the most inspired motifs of his exceptional artistic temperament for it, written that in the present, analyzed from whatever moral angle of his musician-guitaristic life, permits the appreciation of the dazzling quality of this outstanding occidental revolutionary poetry reciter, sensitive austere, creator, aristocrat, possessor of his own formulas and an extraordinary superior concept of his exquisite art.

His works — various of them fill the attached program — especially *Madrigal, Melodia, Tremolo and Romanza,* are indexes of his converted spirit in a star illuminating foreboded beauties, commenting on the magnificent orchestral fidelity of the worshipped guitar, substantiating the chromatic visual landscape by the sonorous imaginative poem, flying toward the stars of a better World populated by gnomes, little girls, fairies and princesses, or inhabited only by pain, as unique reason of the mortal life.

Lalyta Delfina Almiron

Daughter of a distinguished artist of the guitar, *Don* Bautista S. Almiron, her maestro, she is one of the most significant American figures of the guitaristic art, whose fame, an engraved base of work, dedication and enthusiasm, whose manner of standard raising her sounds with patriotic colors, passing gallantly and triumphantly to the aged Europe and the spring like America.

While still a child, her masterful fingers have played the sublime coffer of the Gods in the *"Ateneo"* of Madrid (1931), presented by Camila Quiroga, in the Sala Mozart in Barcelona, in the *"Gaveau"* of Paris, in Milan, Geneva, in the "Metropolitan" in New York, in Uruguay, Chile, in her own country, and recently returned saturated of the perfume from the toast of the success of her magnificent triumphs in the cultured and sensitive society of the high plains, Bolivia.

Since in 1931, the classical Spanish writer *Don* A. Fernandes Escobés said: "The guitar is very feminine in its form, therefore it is for a woman. Its very beautiful in the hands of Segovia; very expertly in the fingers of Llobet, but if you want to dream and since the soul enjoys perfumed scenes, seek a woman: Lalyta Almiron...."

"Sevilla and Cordoba on the guitar of Lalyta, belong to eternity" Arturo Capdevila said in the year 1927, while *Don* José P. Varela was writing so: "Enormous miniature of genius, you have made cry to a profane one; this one hushes and requests to the silence that shapes its dumb eloquence."

598

She is the unique artist of the guitar that has ennobled her instrument outside the borders of her country, Argentina, taking the expression of the national sentiment of her race to the most demanding foreign musical centers, whom admired and applauded her not only for the sensible motive performed and the harmonization of eminent Argentine authors, such as Aguirre, Gilardi, etc. but also the unsuspected effect impressed, the exquisite taste, the interpretation of the concept, within the character of the work that slowly or in a vivo allegretto is the threshing to the marvelous impulse of ten fingers that with ten wings or ten wings that are ten fingers, writing above the fingerboard passages of forgotten lives, or what still they latently breathe in the bottom of our souls to the mute rhythm of a silent interior song.

A program dedicated to the great Agustín P. Barrios integrated with works by the same, of Argentine authors and of classics of Central Europe and including the splendid transcription that Lalyta has magnificently done of the *"Claro de Luna"* (Moonlight Sonata) by Beethoven, it will permit condensing the most select romantic temperament by our great artist, as one of the most excellent virtuosos of the Argentine guitar."

Ricardo Muñoz

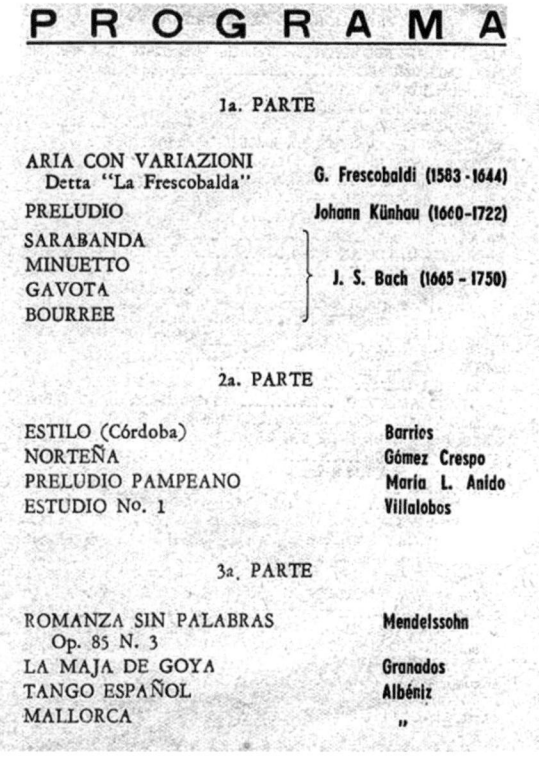

Lalyta on Saturday August 16, 1952 performing an Agustín Barrios composition: *Estilo (Cordoba)*. The images on this page are from the archive of Ricardo Muñoz.

Martin Borda y Pagola, Miguel Llobet, Carlos U. Trapani   Archive: Ricardo Muñoz

Martin Borda y Pagola was a friend of and a financial patron to Agustín Pio Barrios, Agustín left 27 manuscripts written between 1912 and 1921 with him. Carlos U. Trapani was a music storeowner in Montevideo and was Agustín Barrios' first publisher in 1921.

This photo dates from 1922. Source: Rico Stover

1) Allegro Sinfonico
2) La Catedral
3) Las Abejas
4) Danza Paraguaya
5) Fuegos Fatuos
6) Contemplacion
7) Madrigal
8) Estudio en mi menor
9) Vals No. 3
10) Estudio en sol menor
11) Aire de Zamba
12) Minuet
13) Courante
14) Humoresque
15) Capricho Español (Noches de Andalucia)
16) Leyenda de España
17) Serenata Morisca
18) Cordoba
19) Aconquija
20) Vals de Primavera
21) Chinita
22) Luz Mala
23) Minueto
24) Cancion Maternal
25) Sonata (A mi Madre)
26) Plegaria
27) Tango

Manuscript titles: courtesy of Rico Stover

They were written for and dedicated to Martin Borda y Pagola-the Barrios patron. They were in the possession of Martin's daughter, Aida Sosa de Piovano (1915-2002) of Maldonado, Uruguay. In the summer of 2000 I spoke with Aida for 25 minutes in Spanish and she told me about the oldest manuscript that was from 1912. They were living on her grandfather's ranch, which was so big that there was a mountain on it, which inspired the first song. She said Barrios would come and stay for a few days, a week, or a month and then go concertize in another city. Towards the late 1920's they didn't see him so much anymore.

Martin Borda y Pagola is a distinguished amateur Uruguayan guitarist. He learned the guitar with his own enthusiasm in his youth as a son of the Rioplatense lands, so fertile in guitarists of all kinds. Borda y Pagola is the possessor of several instruments of great worth, and by that his home is the center of reunions of good and capable learned guitarists.

So ends the short entry from Domingo Prat's *"Diccionario de Guitarristas"*.

To these favorable opinions and what made his conquests of Argentina, Domingo Prat (European equally as Ricardo Muñoz) sums it up in what he refers to Barrios in his *"Diccionario de Guitarristas"*, saying: "Notable contemporary Paraguayan concert artist and composer. He developed in Asuncion, Paraguay in a musically ambient environment, better said uncertain as to saying a void. Surrendering with fervor to a guitar dreaming of future glory makes his bohemian temperament and instantaneous artistry. As a concert artist we have been able to applaud him many times in his concerts that have taken place in Buenos Aires, always in the Salon "La Argentina".

"Barrios is a capable and intelligent performer, and not of a scarce positive value, there in the Old Continent and in the nations of unquestionable culture, they have dedicated to him laudatory chronicles." Those concepts expressed by authoritative personalities of the epoch, show the falsehood of the of the negative versions originated by the adverse concepts of Mr. Anido, that the whole guitaristic environment ambiance of Argentina was totally adverse to Barrios.

In Richard "Rico" Stover's Six Silver Moonbeams — The Life and Times of Agustín Barrios Mangoré, the revised edition published by GSP, San Francisco, in November of 1999, he says on page 120 that Barrios had played a concert in Manaus and Belem, Brazil in August and September of 1931 as well as one in Cayenne, French Guiana. This photo above is dedicated and autographed by Agustín Barrios on October 22, 1931 in Cayenne. The translation of the dedication is: To my new and very beloved friend Mayor M. B. Blake, (in French) "a good memory". Agustín Barrios, Cayenne, October 22, 1931.

The translation of the text and dedication on the following page is:

THE CELEBRATED GUARANI INDIAN.

To my good friend Mr. Mayor Maurice B. Blake with my best sentiments of sincere congenial affection, October 22, 1931 Agustín Barrios (In this dedication there is no autograph, but rather a large stamp with Barrios' name, similar to the much smaller one used on the postage size stamps on his 78-RPM recordings for Disco Nacional — Odeon.)

BARRIOS the king of the Guitar

The above photo on this page Rico Stover says he had never seen until this one, the one on the following page he says he had seen it before, but not in two color, only black and white. The headband and border are in red, also the full size of the image is 8½" x 11" and had to be reduced for the inclusion. Rico also added that the photos were taken in northern Brazil.

Archive: FFSI

On August 11, 1926 at the Instituto Verdi in Montevideo Guillermo J. Corcoran performed. His maestro was Pedro Mascaro y Reissig. His inclusion of the *Gavota* by Agustín Barrios shows that many guitarists had performed Barrios' works at different periods of the artist's lifetime. A paragraph long biography is also included in the liner notes.

Pedro Mascaro y Reissig archive 1918-1937

Agustín Barrios had also performed at this same Institute on June 19, 1920. Source: (Six Silver Moonbeams page 56. Revised Edition GSP 1999)

Guillermo J. Corcoran — Well deserved thoughts by his maestro Pedro Mascaro y Reissig

Guillermo J. Corcoran has been one of the few, maybe the only one, of my disciples, that, since his first studies, demonstrated an admirable inclination toward the musical works that are the most distinguished by the austerity of the genius, not expressing instead more of a preference for those others whose intensity only suggests a buttress to eclecticism, the child of frivolity.

He has been a jealous student of that which, during a course of studies, deserves, many times, the qualitative of difficulty, and what almost always is the motive of desertion of the infinity of students, that have dedicated to the study of the guitar with only one desire of playing some ballad thing on it, influenced by the very intense ambiance of the GUITARISTS WHO PLAY ONLY BY EAR and of those WHO DON'T READ MUSIC.

Today Corcoran is totally an artist, however he has a certain rebelliousness that only I could assess during my teaching; a rebelliousness always of his temperament, what is exquisite — Corcoran never sacrifices the beauty in altars of established rule. His soul on the strings is all art, all heat, all youth, and all spiritual energy.

And don't believe that this rebelliousness that I mention doesn't deserve my censure, no, on the contrary, this elevates the artist. Albeniz was a rebel in the same sense, according to what Pedrell expresses, and, however, we don't negate that his artistic labor reaches to the limit of the sublime.

After all I have expressed one can believe that my disciple, as happens generally in the very expressive musicians, is weak in that respect to technique, since it might be such a belief, he has studied the mechanism of the guitar so perfectly, that the works of major difficulties, in his hands, are toys. From there we don't wonder why Miguel Llobet, considered the best guitarist of the world, may have qualified him, after hearing him in an intimate performance, as something notable.

As well Agustín Barrios the celebrated Paraguayan guitarist, for whom the exquisite musical diction is the quintessence of the art, awarding him with a hug after hearing him delighting in his original guitaristic phrases of a tremolo.

Precisely in Corcoran the cleanliness with which he performs the tremolos, is meritorious to be admired, that peculiarity of the guitar which, according to Tárrega, is the greatest effect that encloses the richness of the instrument, an effect so careless, lamentably, by some guitarists of this country, that have been heard by the public.

No doubt Corcoran will include that, in the first recitals that he will offer to our public, some work in tremolo, convinced of which in his fingers is a marvel, as neither doubt that he won't omit in programs some production of our colleague Isaias Savio, whose works nevertheless that are unpublished have already had their consecration, my feeling flattered to having been, I, the first that made them heard in public, in my recent artistic tour.

These lines they might be therefore, the expression of the thought that to me Guillermo J. Corcoran deserves as a disciple and artist. P. Mascaro y Reissig Montevideo, May of 1926.

Guillermo Corcoran, with a dedication that translates to: "For my maestro and friend Pedro Mascaro y Reissig, as a memory of my first concert in the Instituto Verdi." Guillermo Corcoran Montevideo August 11, 1926.

Pedro Mascaro y Reissig archive 1917-1939

PROGRAMA

I

Minuet Op. II N.º 5	F. Sors
Estudio	D. Aguado
Andante	Mozart
Allegro	N. Coste

II

3 Preludios	
2 Estudios	
Pequeña Romanza	Isaías Savio
Cajita de Música	
Bourrée	

III

Melodía Catalana	M. Llobet
Barcarola	Mendelsshon
Gavota	A. Barrios
Andante de "Don Giovanni"	Mozart--M. Herrera
Recuerdos de la Alhambra	F. Tárrega

GUITARRA DE CONCIERTO (Modelo propio)
JUAN B. ANFOSSI

The second set pieces written by Isaias Savio were included in the 38 works listed in the 1931 Antigua Casa Nuñez catalog. The *Gavota "Madrigal"* written by Agustín Barrios was possibly in its 2nd edition, published by Carlos Trapani of Montevideo.

Martin Borda y Pagola's daughter, Aida Borda Sosa, performed a concert in Montevideo on Thursday November 22, 1934.

Estudio Auditorio (S. O. D. R. E.) calle Andes

9:45PM

Thursday November 22, 1934

Recital de Guitarra

Program

1st Part:

Sor Andante en La

Aguado Estudio No. 12

Sor Andante en Sol

Barrios Gran Tremolo

2nd Part:

Mendelssohn Barcarola

Bach Courante

Sor Andantino

Tárrega Capricho Arabe

3rd Part:

(Homage to the celebrated Paraguayan composer Agustín P. Barrios)

Barrios "Chinita" Evocacion criolla (dedicated by the author to the performer)

Barrios Vals

Barrios Souvenire d'un Reve

Barrios La Catedral

    (a — Andante religioso

    (b — Allegro solemne

These titles are from Victor M. Oxley's lecture "*La maduracion del genio mangoriano en Uruguay* — 1911-1928" Copyright 2011.

("The maturity of the genius Mangoré in Uruguay — 1911-1928".)

608

C X 28 Edison

11. Notic. Edison.
11.15 Los Matreros.
11.30 R. Rimber.
11.45 Orq. Fresedo.
12. Tip. Paraguaya.
12.15 Orquesta Canaro.
12.30 E. Radamés Luzzi.
12.45 Sopranos.
13. E. Radamús Luzzi.
13.15 Sopranos.
13.30 Barítonos.
13.45 Rondallas.
14. Cámara Mercantil.
14.15 Sinf. de Mozart.
15. Coral Oviedo.
15.15 Aurora Miranda.
15.30 Vals criollos.
15.45 A. Barrios Sol. guit.
16. Jerry Wills.
16.30 Cantores típicos.
17. Tablada semanal.
17.15 Jazz.
17.30 Sindicato Médico.
18. Acto conmemorativo del 4.o aniversario de la Edison Broadcasting con la intervención de los más destacados artistas del ambiente radiotelefónico Montevideano.

Agustín Barrios, is listed in this issue of *"Radio Revista- cancionera"* Issue No. 239 *Año* VI Sunday August 23 – Saturday August 29, 1936, published in Montevideo on August 21, 1936. His records were played on Saturday August 29 from 3:45PM until 4:00 on Radio C X 28 Edison. The listings in bold text are live performances and the listings in plain text are recordings played for the audience.

This same radio station also played records by Miguel Llobet on Friday, August 28, 1936 from 6:15PM until 6:30.

Onda 248   1210 Kilociclos

C X 34 — RADIO URUGUAY

FIGUEIRA, CANEPA Y CIA.

Dirección y Administración: Millán 2370. — Teléf.: Urug. 1500, Aguada

SABADO 3

12. Variedades de la discoteca.
12.30 Fragmentos de las "Campanas de Corneville" y canzonetas napolitanas.
13. Tangos cantados por Tito Schipa y por Gardel.
13.30 Solos de guitarra por Barrios y canciones.
14. Repertorio de bailables.
20. Fox trots americanos (Grabación de Brunswich, exclusiva de Radio Uruguay).
20.30 Conferencia literaria.
21.15 "La otra honra" comedia en tres actos de Jacinto Benavente por el conjunto de comedia española que dirife el señor Luis García Triay.

This comes from the September 27 to October 3, 1931 magazine issue of the *Programa oficial de las estaciones uruguayas de radio* (Official program of the Uruguayan Radio Stations). Recordings of guitar solos by Agustín Barrios and vocal recordings were played on Saturday October 3, 1931 at 1:30 in the afternoon for 30 minutes on radio station CX 34 in Montevideo.

HORA	DOMINGO 10
11.	**Inform. exterior, local e interior.**
11.00	**Servicio propio.**
11.45	Ruddy Vallée.
12.	C. Harmonists.
12.15	Orqs. de salón.
12.30	Pedro Vargas.
13.	**Las campanadas.**
13.15	**La Perchelerita.**
13.30	Canc. españolas.
13.45	Balalaikas.
14.	**"Hora del tango": F. Barthe.**
14.15	
14.30	Orq. Whiteman
14.45	de concierto.
15.	R. Koczalsky.
15.30	**Trasmisión**
16.	
16.15	
16.30	**de bailables**
16.45	
17.	
17.15	**e informaciones**
17.45	
18.	
18.15	**de interés**
18.30	
18.45	**general.**
19.	Selec. de graba-
19.15	ciones selectas.
19.30	Inf. telegráfico
19.45	del interior.
20.	**Las campanadas.**
20.05	del mundo e in-
20.15	form. deport.
20.30	**España Regional**
20.45	por B. Amor.
21.	Inform. mundial
	y local.
21.15	Ag. Barrios.
21.30	Ortiz Tirado.
21.45	Valses vieneses.
22.	Selección de bai-
22.15	lables.
22.30	**Inf. última hora**

Here we see on CX 14 El Espectador radio in Montevideo on Sunday Month? 10, mid to late 1930's Agustín Barrios recordings being played at 9:15-9:30 PM. This is from the magazine entitled: *Programa oficial de las estaciones uruguayas de radio* (Official program of the Uruguayan Radio Stations) The Bold text listings are live events.

Edison Broadcasting
CX 28

Onda 275.2 — Potencia: 3.000 watts — 1090 Kilociclos

EDISON BROADCASTING

MIGUEL BIERE

Administ. y Estudios: Convención 1363
Automático 8-1514. - Estación: Itacumbú 57, Maroñas

DOMINGO 15 DE SETIEMBRE DE 1935
11. **Informativo. 11.20 Síntesis deportiva.**
11.50 Tito Schipa, tenor.
12. **Pascal-Canedo, dúo, y sus guit.**
12.30 **Mariluz, cancion.; piano, S. Oneto.**
13. **Música típica.**
14.30 Alberto Vila, canciones.
15. Mús. de films de dibujos animados.
16.30 Rosita Quiroga, canciones.
17. **Concierto en re, op. 77, de Brahms.**
17.40 Foxtrots; 18. José Moriche, tenor.
18.30 A. Maizani; 19. Ortiz Tirado.
19.30 **Teresa Claramunt, sopr.; piano, señora Costa.**
20. **"El país de los tontos". Frag. zarz.**
20.30 **Roberto Bengoa y sus guitarristas.**
21.30 **Sopranos y tenores.**
22. a 24. **Bailables. Tintorería Biere.**

LUNES 16
11. **Informativo.**
11.20 **Coment. radio-hípicos, por Carrión.**
12. **Polkas paraguayas.**
12.30 **José Marengo y sus guitarristas.**
13. **Canc. españolas; 13.30 E. Barrios.**
14. **"Carmen", de Bizet; óp. completa.**
15.30 Pilar Arcos. 16. Potpourris de óp.
16.30 Mús. típica; 17. Carlos Gardel.
17.30 **Síntesis Deportiva.**
18. Nick Lucas. 18.30 Piano Paderewsky
19. **Comentarios de Cine y Actualidades, por Joan Smiths.**
19.35 R. Luzzi, tenor; piano, Yita Cozzo.
20.15 Lito Bacy y su típ. sinfónica.
21.15 José Mojica. Frag. de films.
21.40 **"Doña Francisquita", frag. zarz.**

MARTES 17
11. **Informativo. 11.20. Maxixas, rumbas.**
12.15 **Raul, chansonnier; piano, S. Oneto.**
12.30 **Radamés Luzzi y Trío Splendid.**
13.30 **Bailables por el Prof. S. Oneto.**
14. **Canciones mejicanas.**
14.30 Gómez-Vila y Gómez.
15. 5ª Sinfonía de Beethoven.
15.40 Rosita Quiroga. 16.30 Canzonetas.
17. **La media hora familiar, con solos de piano, por Chiffon y Lita.**
17.45 **Dr. Cayafa Soca: Comentarios sobre higiene.**
18. Coros rusos; 18.30 M. Chanlee, tenor.
19. Solos de piano, por Godowsky.
19.30 **Teresa Claramunt, soprano; al piano, Sra. Costa.**
20. José Mojica, canciones.
20.30 **Roberto Bengoa y sus guitarristas.**
21.30 **Velada selecta Edison, clás. y liter.**
22.30 **"Los Claveles". zarz. completa.**

MIERCOLES 18
11. **Informativo. 11.20 Polkas paraguay.**
12.15 Carlos Gardel.
12.30 **Trasmisión de la Lotería.**
13. **Azucena Maizani, canciones.**
13.30 Rondalla Uzandizaga.
14. 7ª Sinfonía en La mayor, Beethoven.
14.40 Zarzuelas. 15.30 Magaldi, Mag.-Noda.
16. Mús. típica. 16.30 L. Lamarque.
17. Solos de violín y piano.
17.30 **Bianchi-Zito, dúo de guitarras.**
18. **"Petrouchka", de Strawinsky.**
18.30 **J. Smith: coment. y charlas s. cines.**

19. Rad. Luzzi, ten.; piano, Yita Cozzo.
19.30 Solos de piano, por virtuosos.
19.45 **Diana da Rossa: Media hora selecta.**
20.15 Lito Bacy y su típ. sinfónica.
21.30 **"El barro humano", de Rodríguez Acasuso, por la Cía. Cinema Radio.**

JUEVES 19
11. **Informativo. 11.20 Típica Maffia.**
12. **José Marengo y sus guitarristas.**
12.30 **Radamés Luzzi y Trío Splendid.**
13.30 Ada Falcón. 14. Trío Ciríaco Ortiz.
14.30 **Canc. mejicanas.**
15. **"Del mismo barro", film por Mona Maris y Juan Torena.**
16.30 Pilar Arcos y Joaquín Díaz.
17. Foxtrots y rumbas. Discoteca.
17.45 **Nicader del cartapacio literario.**
18. Al Johnson, canciones.
18.30 **Bianchi-Zito, dúo de guitarras.**
19. Sinfonía Nº 4, óp. 88.
19.30 **Teresa Claramunt, soprano; al piano Srta. Costa.**
20.10 **Roberto Bengoa y sus guitarristas.**
21.10 **"Tosca", de Puccini. Op. completa.**

VIERNES 20
11. **Informativo. 11.20 Mús. típica.**
12.30 **Pascal-Canedo, dúo, y guitarristas.**
13. **Canc. alemanas; 13.30 M. Simone.**
14. **Canciones humorísticas.**
14.30 Andrés Segovia y Agustín Barrios.
14.45 Rondalla "Los Baturros".
15.30 Roberto Díaz y Amalia Molina.
16. Cuarteto en Re menor de Schubert.
16.40 Música española.
17. **La media hora familiar, con solos de piano por Chifon y Lita.**
17.45 **Abuelito Barba blanca. El Rincón de los Niños.**
18. **Dúo de guitarras Bianchi-Zito.**
18.30 Alberto Vila. Dúo Gómez-Vila.
19. **Joan Smith en sus comentarios y charlas sobre cines.**
19.30 **La media hora de Vasa More.**
19.45 Rad. Luzzi, ten.; piano, Yita Cozzo.
20.20 Lito Bacy y su típica sinfónica.
21.20 Lily Pons, B. Gigli, E. Caruso.
22.20 **"El Amor Brujo", de Falla.**

SABADO 21
11. **Informativo.**
11.20 **Síntesis deportiva.**
12. Foxtrots, rumbas, maxixas.
12.30 **Trío Splendid. Dir.: Prof. Vidal.**
13.30 **Agustín Magaldi y Pilar Arcos.**
14. Canzonetas. 14.30 Coros rusos.
15. **"Cuando el amor ríe", por J. Mojica y Mona Maris, film.**
16.30 Canciones chilenas.
17. **Coment. radio-típicos, por Carrión.**
17.40 Alfonso Ortiz Tirado, canciones.
18.30 **La media hora de Vasa More.**
19. **Pascal-Canedo, dúo, y guitarristas.**
19.35 Rad. Luzzi, ten.; piano, Yita Cozzo.
20.10 Solos de piano, por Rubinstein.
20.30 **Diana da Rossa: Media hora selecta.**
20.55 Tito Schipa.
21.15 **"Los cachorros, de Y. Rodríguez, y "La carreta". Cía. Cinema - Radio.**
23 a 1 **Bailables Tintorería Biere.**

Here we see on CX 22 Edison Broadcasting in Montevideo on Friday September 20, 1935 Andrés Segovia and Agustín Barrios recordings played from 2:30-2:45 PM. This is from the magazine entitled: *Programa oficial de las estaciones uruguayas de radio* (Official program of the Uruguayan Radio Stations) The Bold text listings are live events.

C X 26 — RADIO URUGUAY

FIGUEIRA, CANEPA Y CIA. — Millán 2370. — Teléfonos: 2-69-26 y 2-37-16

DOMINGO 12 DE SETIEMBRE DE 1937

- 9. Boezzi: Misa solemne.
- 10. Fantasía de "Boheme", etc.
- 10 30 Carreras por el Dr. Dividendo.
- 11. The Revelers.
- 11 25 Resplandores del Fogón, por el Gaucho Florido, Lucinda e Hilario.
- 12.45 "Guzlares" fragmento y Liberman.
- 13.30 Cortis y octetos.
- 14. Conversaciones evangélicas por el Sr. Hall.
- 14.15 Coros de Ruada.
- 16. Verdi: "Rigoletto" (completa).
- 18. Crawford. 18.30 Bailables.
- 20. Mojica y "La del soto del Parral".
- 20.30 Audición de jazz.
- 20.45 C. Guzman y "Rapsodia azul".
- 21.15 T. Ruffo. 21.30 Chopin: Conc. op. 11.
- 22. Programa español por P. Santaularia y J. de la Cantera.

LUNES 13

- 9. Angelillo y A. Molina.
- 10. C. Miranda. 10.30 Falcón y De Caro.
- 11.15 Carreras por el Dr. Dividendo.
- 11.45 Piano N. Rosa Giffuni.
- 12.30 La Parranda. 13.10 Lucienne Boyer.
- 13.30 Valses. 14. Meller y Chevalier.
- 16. Beethoven: "Septimino".
- 16.30 Schipa y Toti dal Monte.
- 17. Sonata Apassionata, por Bauer.
- 17.30 "Fausto", trío final.
- 18. Frag. de "El Murciélago".
- 18.30 Cía. de zarzuelas Pibernat, con LS2, de Buenos Aires.
- 19.30 Hugo Collerati, piano solo.
- 20. Pilar Arcos.
- 20 30 Il comitato italiano y sus informac.
- 21.15 Casals.
- 21.45 Hora Cultural Alemana.
- 23.45 W. Landowska. "Le cou-cou", etc.

MARTES 14

- 9. Boito: "Mefistófeles", prólogo.
- 9.50 "Norma", obertura.
- 11. Schipa: canzonettas, y E. Morini.
- 11. Maruxa y dúo de Rosa y Pablo.
- 11.30 Cortot y Rethberg.
- 12.15 Audición de armonio: C. Marsiglia.
- 12.30 15 minutos amenos. 12.45 Marsiglia.
- 13. Informativo de Tablada.
- 13.05 Canciones.
- 13.30 Cuarteto Bs. Aires y noved. típicas.
- 16. Brahms: Sonata op. 100.
- 16.40 Chialapin y María Barrientos.
- 17. Massenet: Escenas pintorescas.
- 17.40 O. Tirado. 18.10 Operetas, Strauss.
- 18.45 Carmencita Vargas.
- 19.15 Néstor Rosa Giffuni.
- 19.40 Jazz. 20. Valses de Waldteufel.
- 20. Romito y Anido.
- 20 20 Il comitato italiano y sus informac.
- 21.15 Kreisler. 21.30 Variedades.
- 22. Programa Español, con Pilar Santaularia y Julián de la Cantera.

MIERCOLES 15

- 9. Zarzuelas de Caballero.
- 10. Círculo Mandolinístico.
- 10.30 Sogno de "Manon", y otras romanzas.
- 11. Quiroga y lieders de Schubert.
- 11.45 Pianista Néstor Rosa Giffuni.
- 12.30 Sra. Nilda Müller: lieders y canciones folklóricas internacionales.
- 12.45 P. Goldwin. 13. Inf. de Tablada.
- 13.10 Mojica y balalaikas.
- 13.45 R. Montaner y novedades típicas.
- 16. Saint-Saens: Danza macabra.

JUEVES 16

- 16.30 Falla: 7 canciones.
- 17 "Hollywood Latino": Max Factor.
- 17.15 Dvorak: "El nuevo mundo", sinf.
- 18. M. Berreta.
- 18.30 Compañía de zarzuelas y comedias Pibernat, con LS2 de Bs. Aires.
- 19.30 Canzonettas italianas.
- 20. Ultimas novedades de jazz.
- 20 30 Il comitato italiano y sus informac.
- 21.30 Programa Cultural Alemán.
- 22.30 Rubinstein.

JUEVES 16

- 9. Simone y Lomuto.
- 9.50 Trío Borinquen y E. Pozadas.
- 10.30 Quinteto mejic. 11. Gigli, dúos líricos.
- 12. Piano por Néstor Rosa Giffuni.
- 12.30 Galli Curci y valses.
- 13.05 "Las espigadoras", fragmentos.
- 13.30 "La leyenda del beso" y Mojica.
- 14. Hugo Collerati: piano solo.
- 16. Schubert: Sinfonía Inconclusa.
- 16.30 "Forza del Destino", dúo, y otras.
- 17. Selección Ketelbey.
- 17.40 Caruso. 18. Barrios y Cuevas, guit.
- 18.30 Trov. Romántico y L. Boyer.
- 18.50 Rondalla "Los Baturros".
- 19.15 Resplandores del Fogón: El Gaucho Florido. 20. Melodías de Foster.
- 20 20 Il comitato italiano y sus informac.
- 21.15 Arrau.
- 21.30 "Nelly, te quiero", comedia en 3 actos de Jean Aicard, por la Compañía Santaularia - De la Cantera.

VIERNES 17

- 9. Fregozzi y Jeritza.
- 10. Sinfonía de "Guarany" y otras.
- 10.30 "Bohemios", coros, y Crawford.
- 11.15 Carmencita Vargas.
- 12. N. Rosa Giffuni.
- 12.30 "Scugnizza".
- 13.10 Programa español por Pilar Santaularia y Julián de la Cantera.
- 14. Novedades típicas.
- 16. Berlioz: Sinfonía fantástica.
- 16.30 Ural Cosacos. 17. Debussy: P. suite.
- 17.30 N. Vallin. 18.30 Fabini: "Campo".
- 18.30 Compañía de zarzuelas y comedias, Pibernat, con LS2 de Bs. Aires.
- 19.40 Jazz.
- 20. Gastón Marcel, acompañado al piano por Vernier.
- 20.30 Il Comitato de Italia y sus inf.
- 21.30 Programa Cultural Alemán.
- 22.30 Wanda Landowska.

SABADO 18

- 9. Boero: "El Matrero".
- 9.50 Segovia y Kreisler.
- 10.30 Sofía del Campo y balalaikas.
- 11. Orq. Goldwin y coro de "Nabuco".
- 11.45 Pianista Néstor Rosa Giffuni.
- 12 30 Sra. Nilda Müller, lieders folklóricos.
- 12.45 Art Tatum.
- 13.30 Crawford. 14. Novedades típicas.
- 16. Schubert: Cuarteto en re.
- 16.30 Lily Pons y Martinelli.
- 17. "Hollywood Latino": Max Factor.
- 17.15 "El Escenario del Aire", a cargo de los Hnos. Berreta Galli.
- 18.15 Franck: Quinteto.
- 19. R. Raisa y balalaikas.
- 19.30 "La damita azul". 20. Ortiz Tirado.
- 20.30 Il comitato italiano y sus informac.
- 21.30 "Uruguayita", cancionista.
- 21.50 Hugo Collerati, piano solo.
- 22.30 Debussy: "El mar".

Here we see on CX 26 Radio Uruguay in Montevideo on Thursday September 16, 1937 recorded duets on the Brunswick label, made in 1934 in Cuba by Agustín Barrios and Ezequiel Cuevas (1889-) being played from 6 PM until 6:30 PM. This is from the magazine entitled: *Programa oficial de las estaciones uruguayas de radio* (Official program of the Uruguayan Radio Stations) *Año* VI Setiembre 10 de 1937 No. 320 (September 10th-18th issue.) The Bold text listings are live events. We can also notice Andrés Segovia and Fritz Kreisler recordings being played on Saturday morning September 18 from 9:50-10:30 AM. Ezequiel Cuevas first recorded with Eusebio Delfín for Victor records in 1927. Source: The Encyclopedic Discography of Victor Recordings (EDVR) web site.

According to Rico Stover, Agustín Barrios Mangore had been in Puerto Rico since mid January of 1937, this concert took place on Tuesday March 2, 1937 at 8 PM at the Teatro Ideal in Yauco, Puerto Rico. The theatre had been built the year before. "The eminent Paraguayan guitarist offers his only concert."

Archive: Ramon Vazquez Lamboy

PROGRAMA

I

Giuliani	Fantasía Capricho
Tarrega	Serenata Arabe
Mangoré	La Catedral (a) andante religioso
	(b) allegretto
	Allegro Brillante

II

Beethoven:	Minueto en Sol
Rubinstein:	Melodía en Fa
Sors:	Variaciones sobre un tema de Mozart
Chopín:	Nocturno en mi Bemol

III

Albeniz:	Leyenda
Mangoré:	Invocación a la Luna (rito aborigen)
	Un Sueño en la floresta
	Diana guarani

La sonoridad de la guitarra es infinitamente más blanda y ténue que la del piano; menos penetrante que la del violín; más emotiva y suave que la del arpa.

Para percibir plenamente estas vivas cualidades espirituales del más bello de los instrumentos, se re quiere un absoluto

SILENCIO

En un ambiente quieto y callado, se destaca su delicado sonido, puro y limpio, escuchándose las obras más claramente y el juego de matices en que se revela la calidad del artista no queda obscurecido por los mil ruidos flotantes de un auditorio inatento y distraí do. Se ruega en beneficio de las personas hoy congre gadas, para oír a Mangoré, un riguroso

SILENCIO

En el espacio de obra a obra puede el auditorio descansar de la tensión que la naturaleza de la guita rra le demanda y seguir después el itinerario espiri tual del concierto. Pero mientras toca el Artista el mismo auditorio se percatará de q. cualquier pequeño movimiento interrumpe la coordinación musical de la obra y se anega la sonoridad de la guitarra en una atmósfera falta de transparencia

Por todo lo dicho y deseando dar al concierto ver dadera eficacia emotiva, se ruega y se agradece un perfecto y unánime

SILENCIO

Similar warnings were also a part of Andrés Segovia's programs in Central America. The exact text was used for Andrés Segovia concert in San José, Costa Rica on Friday March 1, 1940 at the Teatro Nacional.

Translation of the previous page.

The sonority of the guitar is infinitely blander and has that of the piano; less penetrating than that of the violin; more emotional and smooth than that of the harp.

To fully perceive these live spiritual qualities of the most beautiful of instruments it requires absolute SILENCE.

In a quiet and hot environment, it distinguishes its delicate sound, pure and clean, the works to be heard are clearer and the range of tones in which the quality of the artist is revealed doesn't remain obscured by the thousand floating noises of an inattentive and distracted listener. It begs the benefit of the persons today gathered to hear Mangore, of a rigorous SILENCE.

In the space of work to work the listener can rest from the tension that the naturaless of the guitar demands and continue after the spiritual itinerary of the concert. But while the Artist plays the same listener will take care whatever small movement interrupts the musical coordination of the work and abnegates the sonority of the guitar in an atmosphere that lacks transparency

By all that is said and desiring to give the concert true emotive efficiency, we beg and thank you for a perfect and unanimous SILENCE.

These recordings of Abel Carlevaro were done in the 1940's, possibly during his 1948 European tour. The manuscript for Las Abejas (Estudio) is from the Martin Borda y Pagola archive. Because of this friendship Abel was one of the first to be able to play these pieces. There are nine pages of information about Agustín Barrios in Abel Carlevaro's "My Guitar My World". This book includes letters from Agustín to Martin. Abel does not talk at all about his recording career. In the Villa-Lobos *Estudio No. 1*, the pianissimo repeats are very well executed, well learned from his maestro Andrés Segovia, to whom the piece was dedicated.

In Alfredo Escande's biography of *"Abel Carlevaro-Un nuevo mundo en la Guitarra"* is this detail.

In London in October of 1949 Abel recorded a 12 inch disc of *"Tarantella"* by Castelnuovo-Tedesco, *"Las Abejas"* by Agustín Barrios and *"Estudio No. 1"* by Villa-Lobos for Parlophone-Odeon records.

Alfredo also mentions in the section when Abel went to Europe that he made a *"corto-metraje"* (short film) for Warner Brothers and performed *"Las Abejas"* by Agustín Barrios.

To the right we see the clipping from page 294 of the January 1, 1944 Odeon-Columbia record catalog. Maria Barrientos had had been an Opera singer in South America since the turn of the century. Agustín Barrios just months before his passing still had 2 discs with 4 songs available for purchase. Evaristo Barrios, a Payador, (Gaucho singer) had been a favorite in the Rio de la Plata for at least 2 decades on radio, records and books, with his comical tales.

BARRIENTOS, MARIA. —
  Soprano
Siete canciones españolas (Falla), El
  paño moruno; Seguidilla murciana;
  Asturiana (Ac. piano M. de Falla) .. C. 264952
BARRIOS AGUSTIN. —
  Solo de guitarra
Capricho Arabe, (Tárrega), Serenata.   O.   202
Minuet, (Beethoven)   O.   202
Oración, Melodía...................   O.   205
Vals Nº 4.........................   O.   205
BARRIOS, EVARISTO. —
  con acompañamiento de guitarras
A contra pelo, Relato Gaucho........ O. 14581
Allá está mi rancho, Tonada.......... O. 14580
¡Ay, si mi flor!, Serrana............ O. 14583
Canción de la siesta, La, Canción
  Campera...................... O. 14581
Canto al hornero, Canción.......... O. 14582
Frente a frente, Relato Gaucho....... O. 14580
—294

Palabras de apertura por el Presidende del Centro, Señor Pedro Mascaró y Reisig.

•

Himno Nacional - *Sres. Américo Castillo y Eugenio Segovia.*

•

1. Parte

Sr. Agustín Carlevaro

    a) Minuet . . . . . Beethoven.
    b) Largo. . . . . . Sor.

•

Sr. Abel Carlevaro

    a) Estudio en si menor   Sor.
    b) Las abejas (estudio)   A Barrios.

Agustín Barrios spent a considerable time in Uruguay, with patrons, musicians and friends. This concert was the inaugural concert of the Centro Guitarristico del Uruguay in Montevideo on Wednesday August 25, 1937. The president of this guitar society was the concert guitarist and professor Pedro Mascaro y Reissig. The version that Abel Carlevaro plays of Agustín Barrios' piece *Las Abejas* was not yet published and is from a manuscript in the Martin Borda y Pagola archive.

PROGRAMA

2ª Parte

Sr. Pedro M. Marin Sánchez

a) Preludio Vasco ... Padre Donostia.
b) Vals Nro. 15 ... Brahms
   (Transcrip. de R. Ayestarán).

Sr. Ramón Ayestaran

a) Rumores de la Caleta ... Albeniz.
b) Danza ... Moreno Tórroba.

3ª Parte

Sra. Olga Pierri y Sr. Atilio Rapat

A) Minuet de la Sinfonia 39 ... Mozart.
b) Berceuce ... Eduardo Torres.
c) Evocación criolla ... J. Ripp.
d) Andante Cantábile ... Sor.

NOTA: Se ruega no entrar a la sala durante la ejecución del programa.

In this concert, besides Agustín and Abel Carlevaro other luminaries such as Ramon Ayestaran, Olga Pierri and Atilio Rapat also performed. Ramon Ayestaran and Olga Pierri would become recording artists in the 1940's-1950's.

The *"Nota"* translated says:
"We beg of you not to enter the hall during the performance of the program."

La Mañana

AÑO XXI—Núm. 157—MONTEVIDE O, VIERNES 27 DE AGOSTO DE 1937

El concierto del Centro guitarrístico "Conrado P. Koch"

Como estaba anunciado, tuvo lugar en el Salon de Actos del Palacio Diaz, el concierto inaugural del Centro Guitarristico del Uruguay "Conrado P. Koch" que resultó un alto exponente de méritos artísticos, no tan solo por la selección de las obras ofrecidas, sino también por la interpretación y técnica que los ejecutantes pusieron de manifiesto.

Con muy sentidas palabras, el Maestro Pedro Mascaró y Reissig, abrió el acto, explicando al selecto auditorio las finalidades del Centro.

Acto seguido los señores Américo Castillo y Alberto R. Segovia ejecutaron el Himno Patrio adhiriéndose de este modo el Centro a la magna fecha que se conmemoraba.

La parte del concierto estuvo a cargo de los señores Agustín y Abel Carlevaro, Pedro Marin Sánchez, Ramón Ayectarán, Atilio Rapal y señorita Olga Pierri, quienes pusieron de manifiesto sus apreciables cualidades de intérpretes.

De notable puede calificarse la actuación que cupo al señor Abel Carlevaro y al dúo formado por la señorita Olga Pierri y Atilio Rapat, quienes dejaron evidenciado en el ánimo de los numerosos oyentes la impresión de hallarse frente a tres intérpretes de relevantes méritos, que hacen presumir la conquista de amplísimos triunfos en un porvenir no muy lejano.

Es de esperar la repetición de estos actos, que tanto bien hacen para el arte y sus numerosos cultores.

On Friday August 27, 1937 the review of the inaugural concert of the Centro Guitarristico del Uruguay appeared in the "*La Mañana*" newspaper. The translation is: The concert of the Centro Guitarristico "Conrado P. Koch".

As it was announced, it took place in the Salon de Actos del Palacio Diaz, the inaugural concert of the Centro Guitarristico del Uruguay "Conrada P. Koch" that resulted in a high exponent of artistic merit, not only by the works offered, but as well by the interpretation and technique that the players put forth.

With very sensitive words Pedro Mascaro y Reissig opened the act, explaining to the select audience the finalities of the Center.

The act followed with Americo Castillo and Alberto R. Segovia playing the *Himno Patrio* to be adding in this way the Center to which the great date that it commemorated.

The concert part was entrusted to Agustín and Abel Carlevaro, Pedro Marin Sanchez, Ramon Ayestaran, Atilio Rapat and Miss Olga Pierri, whom put forth their appreciable qualities of interpretation. Of the notable portion of the program the performance by Mr. Abel Carlevaro and the duo by Miss Olga Pierri and Atilio Rapat, whom had left proof in the liveliness of the numerous listeners, the impression to be found facing the three interpreters of relevant merits that they can impress with the conquest of the amplest triumphs in the not too distant future.

The repetition of these acts is expected, which as well makes art and its numerous followers.

Archive: Pedro Mascaro y Reissig

620

These two concert performances by Remigio Comba were for the Asociacion Guitarristica Argentina, the upper one on Sunday November 14, 1937 held at the Salon Teatro Lassalle, and the lower one on Sunday May 8, 1938 on the premises of the AGA. In the earlier of the two concerts we see he played two pieces by Agustín Barrios, *"Luz Mala"* and *"Vals No. 3"*, and in the later concert *"Romanza"*. At the time of these concerts the composer, Agustín Barrios, had just left Haiti and went to Cuba to stay for a period of six months.

This short biography of Remigio Comba is translated from Ricardo Muñoz's unpublished book *"Historia Universal de la Guitarra"* Volume VIII *"La Escuela Tárrega en La Argentina"*.

"He was born in the city of Parana, Entre Rios on October 1, 1901. He studied music with the Mr. and Mrs. Bargobello-Garcilaza, directors of the Conservatorio Bavio. He studied guitar under the direction of Manuel Montano, later with Eloy Oroño. After coming to Buenos Aires, he entered in the Academia Tárrega with Hilarion Leloup, who awarded him a diploma, and later he studied with Domingo Prat to perfect his knowledge.

He gave his first concert in 1928 in the Teatro 3 de Febrero in Parana, in December of 1929 he played works by Sor, Schubert, Coste, Schumann and Malats. In 1930 he appeared at the Teatro Municipal de Santa Fe and was well applauded. In Buenos Aires he played in 1936 for the Asociacion Guitarristica Argentina, then again in 1937 and 1938. In 1944 and 1947 we find him interpreting Barrios, Schumann, Coste, Chopin, Tárrega, Luna, Allende and his own pieces for the Asociacion Argentina de Musica de Camara; *"La Prensa"* said: 'Comba showed a communicative temperament, that embraced the European and American styles, he has a complete dominion of the sonority and technical resources of the instrument; the public couldn't have been more cordial in its applause.' He's known for: *"Bailecito", "Gato Correntino", "Triste Campero", "Zamba"*, all of them of a rich national flavor."

Remigio Comba

Remigio Comba from the "Galeria de Profesionales" in the 1931 Antigua Casa Nuñez catalog.

Remigio Comba's transcriptions of Schubert published in May of 1948.

"Recordaçao de Agustín Barrios" (Remembrance of Agustín Barrios) was written by Antonio Giacomino in Brazil, it was recorded by the composer for Victor records-disc No. 34076, and it was published by A. Del Vecchio in Sao Paulo c. 1950.

ABEL
CARLEVARO

MARTES, DIA 9 DE NOVIEMBRE DE 1948
A LAS DIEZ Y CUARTO DE LA NOCHE

PALACIO DE LA MUSICA

Abel Carlevaro went on tour to Europe in 1948. This concert program is from the Palacio de la Musica Cataluña in Barcelona. It took place on November 9, 1948. In this concert the artist plays pieces by De Visée, J. S. Bach, Manuel Ponce, Villa-Lobos, Agustín Barrios, Joaquín Turina and Issac Albeniz.

This was one of the first times the music of Barrios' had been performed in Europe since Agustín went there in September 1934.

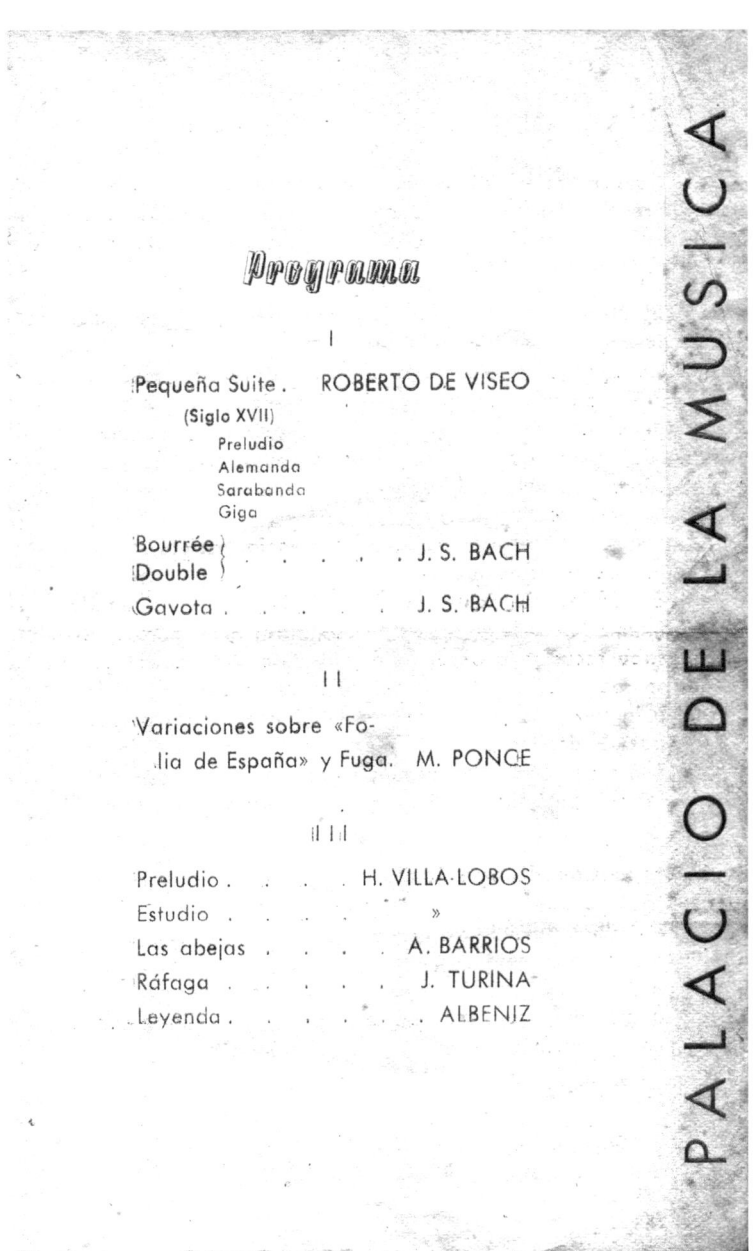

Programa

I

Pequeña Suite .   ROBERTO DE VISEO
(Siglo XVII)
Preludio
Alemanda
Sarabanda
Giga

Bourrée }
Double }   .   .   .   J. S. BACH

Gavota .   .   .   .   J. S. BACH

II

Variaciones sobre «Fo-
lia de España» y Fuga.   M. PONCE

III

Preludio .   .   .   .   H. VILLA-LOBOS
Estudio .   .   .   .   »
Las abejas .   .   .   A. BARRIOS
Ráfaga .   .   .   .   J. TURINA
Leyenda .   .   .   .   ALBENIZ

PALACIO DE LA MUSICA

Abel Carlevaro's tonal development under the direction of his Maestro Andrés Segovia was at a high level at this time. *"Las Abejas"* had been a part of Abel's repertoire since the 1930's.

JUICIOS CRITICOS

Correo de la Mañana. Río de Janeiro, 12 de diciembre de 1943, (Brasil) «...seguro, perfecto, sensible, cualquier género, cualquier repertorio encuentran en él al intérprete magistral.»

El Plata. Montevideo, 17 de diciembre de 1944. «Poseedor del sentido del ritmo, de una lejanía en la cual, las sonoridades, parecen proceder de mucho más allá del espacio físico de la caja de resonancia, y con una perfecta técnica que le permite resolver cómodamente cualquier problema, Abel Carlevaro es, por todos conceptos, un artista de dotes poco comunes. Sus versiones parecen realizadas por la unión de un sentido instrumental, expresado con una conciencia musical de sorprendente capacidad.

En Carlevaro existe, como en muy pocos, el sentido íntimo que el lenguaje de la resonancia tiene para quien sabe escucharlo desde la lejanía. Pero para lograr esto, se requiere, a más, que el alma del mismo artista sea, a la vez, una «caja sonora» infinitamente más perfecta que la del instrumento; y esto es, precisamente, lo que con Abel Carlevaro sucede, y que permite ubicarlo entre los más auténticos realizadores del pensamiento musical»

Roberto Lagarmilla

El Estado de San Pablo. San Pablo, 6 de febrero de 1944 (Brasil). «...su técnica, capaz de vencer las innumerables dificultades del repertorio, está al servicio de su delicada sensibilidad. Con facilidad extrae las resonancias más profundas, da amplitud a la armonía, canta la melodía, y expone con claridad la polifonía; creando una atmósfera de sutil contemplación artística.»

El Debate. Montevideo, 13 de noviembre de 1942. «...estamos en presencia de un artista absoluto: esencia y exterior; espíritu y carne.»

Imp. Riera - Tel. 15575

The translation of the Critic's Judgements is on the following page.

Critic's Judgements

Correio da Manha. Rio de Janiero, December 12, 1943

"Secure, perfect, sensitive, any class, any of his repertoire is found to be interpreted masterfully."

El Plata. Montevideo, December 14, 1944.

"He possesses the sense of rhythm, from a distance of which, the sonorities, appear to proceed from further away than the physical space from the box of resonance, and with a perfect technique which permits him to easily resolve any problem, Abel Carlevaro is, by all concepts, an artist of uncommon ability. His versions appear made by the union of the instrumental sense, expressed with a musical conscience of a surprising capacity.

In Carlevaro exists, as in very few, the intimate sense that the language of the resonance has to be for whomever hears him from the distance. But to succeed at this, it requires, utmostly, that the soul of the same artist might be, at once, a "sonorous box", infinitely more perfect than the instrument; and that is, precisely, to what Abel Carlevaro succeeds at, and what permits his placement among the most authentic makers of the musical thought."

Roberto Lagarmilla

O Estado de S. Paulo. Sao Paulo, Brazil February 5, 1942.

"His technique, a capacity to conquer all innumerable difficulties of the repertoire, is to be of service to his delicate sensibilty. With a facility to extract the most profound resonances, and gives ampleness to the harmony, the singing melody, and exposes with polyphonic clarity; creating an atmosphere of subtle artistic contemplation."

El Debate. Montevideo, November 13, 1942.

"We are in the presence of an absolute artist: essence and composure: spirit and flesh."

The artists of the world performed Agustín Barrios' music at concerts in many countries.

Wilfrid Appleby's "Guitar News" magazine captured these as they were being reported.

This from the "Guitar News" magazine issue No. 3 of October-November 1951.

William Neill of Glasgow, Scotland in the Member's Announcements sought to purchase 78 RPM records by Barrios, Pujol, Presti, Segovia, Arencibia, Lafon, Rodes, Galimberti., etc.

This from the "Guitar News" magazine issue No. 13 of June-July 1953.

At the recent monthly guitar recitals of the Associacao Cultural do Violao, Barrios' *"Vals Op. 8 No. 4"* and *"Tua Imagem"* were performed by Sebastiao Galanti.

This from the "Guitar News" magazine issue No. 15 of October-November 1953.

Oscar Tirao Drago performed Barrios' *"La Catedral"* in his concert program for the first concert of the 1953 season of the Asociacion Guitarristica Argentina. The success of that concert he was invited by the Asociacion Tárrega in Rosario on June 27, 1953. He began performing on Radio Fenix in 1948 at the age of 7 years old. At 8 years old he performed on Radio Provincia de Buenos Aires, and in December 1952, on State Radio. This child prodigy became known as Cacho Tirao.

This from the "Guitar News" magazine issue No. 27 of October-November 1955.

In the "Recitals in Brazil" section it mentions Professor José Alves da Silva performed *"Madrigal"* by Agustín Barrios in his concert program sponsored by the Medical Association for the Associacao Cultural do Violao in Sao Paulo in 1955.

This from the "Guitar News" magazine issue No. 29 of February-March 1956.

At the Peña Guitarristica Tárrega in Barcelona on December 18, 1955 Uruguayan guitarist Oscar Caceres used a guitar made by Santurion to perform Barrios' *"La Catedral"* in his concert program.

Alirio Diaz performed Barrios' *"Medallon Antiguo"* in his short recital on September 23, 1955 on the radio for the Rome National Program.

This from the "Guitar News" magazine issue No. 43 of July-August 1958.

At the Peña Guitarristica Tárrega in Barcelona on April 19, 1958 José Tomas performed Barrios' *Estudio "La Catedral"* in his concert program.

At the Peña Guitarristica Tárrega in Barcelona on April 26, 1958 Manuel Cubedo an unnamed piece by Agustín Barrios in his concert program.

This from the "Guitar News" magazine issue No. 45 of November-December 1958.

For the Associacao Brasileira do Violao in Rio de Janeiro the Uruguayan guitarist, Oscar Caceres, performed Barrios' *"La Catedral"* in his June 26, 1958 concert program.

Nicanor Teixeira, of Rio de Janeiro, gave his first recital in that city on July 13, 1958 performing an unnamed piece by Agustín Barrios.

This from the "Guitar News" magazine issue No. 48 of May-June 1959.

Thirteen year old Antonio Carlos Barbosa-Lima was presented by the Municipal Cultural Comission at a recital in Santos on September 6, 1958 and performed *"As Abelhas"* which is *"Las Abejas"* by Agustín Barrios in his concert.

This from the "Guitar News" magazine issue No. 51 of January-February 1960.

In the "For the Gramophone" section is the listing of fifteen year old Antonio Carlos Barbosa-Lima's 2nd LP (Chantecler CMG-1004). On this recording within the 14 pieces he plays Barrios' *"Choro da Saudade"*.

This from the "Guitar News" magazine issue No. 57 of January-February 1961.

The Society of the Classical Guitar of New York offered its 94th concert presenting Gustavo Lopez and Etta Zaccaria in duet performance at Carnegie Recital Hall on November 4, 1960. Gustavo played solos as well, including *"Danza Paraguaya"* by Agustín Barrios.

This from the "Guitar News" magazine issue No. 69 of January-February 1963.

Peter B. Klausmeyer performed Barrios' *"Preludio en Sol menor, Op. 5 No. 1"* at the Barnes Hall Auditorium at Cornell University on August 6, 1962.

Turibio Santos on August 17, 1962 in Rio de Janeiro performed Barrios' *"La Catedral"* and *"Allegro Sinfonico"* in his concert program.

This from the "Guitar News" magazine issue No. 70 of March-April 1963.

Jodacil Damaceno on June 16, 1962 included Barrios' *"Confession"* in his concert program in Nova Friburgo, Brazil. His concert was repeated for a "Youth" audience the following day.

This from the "Guitar News" magazine issue No. 71 of May-June 1963.

Irma Costanzo performed Barrios' *"Romanza"* in Tokyo at the Tokyo Kudan Kaikan Hall on October 12, 1962.

Alirio Diaz performed Barrios' "Two Paraguayan Dances" at the Great Hall, Cooper Union for the Advancement of Science and Art in New York on February 8, 1963.

In her 2nd tour of Japan in 1963 Maria Lusia Anido performed an unnamed piece by Agustín Barrios in her concert programs. She performed nine concerts, four in Tokyo, the concert program was 24 pages of details on composers from the 13th century to modern composers.

This from the "Guitar News" magazine issue No. 72 of July-August 1963.

Mario Gangi gave a recital at the Teatro del Grande Albergo Quisisana, on the Isle of Capri on April 15, 1963 performing an unnamed piece by Agustín Barrios.

This from the "Guitar News" magazine issue No. 74 of November-December 1963.

At the Peña Guitarristica Tárrega in Barcelona on March 30, 1963 Salvador Alamar Folgado performed an unnamed Barrios' piece in his concert program.

At the Peña Guitarristica Tárrega in Barcelona on April 27, 1963 Jorge Ariza performed Barrios' *"Choro da Saudade"* in his concert program.

This from the "Guitar News" magazine issue No. 75 of January-February 1964.

At the Peña Guitarristica Tárrega in Barcelona on November 27, 1963 Eugenio Gonzalo performed Barrios' *"Danza Paraguaya"* in his concert program.

This from the "Guitar News" magazine issue No. 78 of July-August 1964.

Jodacil Damaceno on April 18, 1964 included Barrios' *"Confesion"* in his concert program in Campos, Brazil.

Seiko Obara, the daughter of Yasumasa Obara, the Secretary General of the Japan Guitar Society performed Barrios' *"Choro da Saudade"* on March 20, 1964 at the Bunka Kaikan in Tokyo.

This from the "Guitar News" magazine issue No. 79 of September-October 1964.

At the Peña Guitarristica Tárrega in Barcelona on May 16, 1964 Jorge Ariza performed Barrios' *"La Catedral"* in his concert program.

The Society of the Classical Guitar, Sydney, Australia presented José Luis Gonzalez in two recitals at Anzac House on June 9 and June 12, 1964 where he performed Barrios' *"Preludio"* and *"Danza Paraguaya"* in his concert programs. The artist continued his tour until the next month. In his 2nd LP the artist also recorded the Barrios songs played in concert (C.B.S. Br. 235066).

This from the "Guitar News" magazine issue No. 87 of July-August 1965.

At the Peña Guitarristica Tárrega in Barcelona on April 4, 1965 Carmen Marina performed Barrios' *"La Catedral"* in her concert program.

This from the "Guitar News" magazine issue No. 90 of September-October 1966.

Sukenori Kyomoto performed Barrios' *"Choro da Saudade"* in a recent concert program in Tokyo.

This from the "Guitar News" magazine issue No. 96 of November-December 1967.

At the Peña Guitarristica Tárrega in Barcelona in June 1967 Eugenio Gonzalo performed Barrios' *"Choro da Saudade"* in his concert program.

This from the "Guitar News" magazine issue No. 98 of March-May 1968.

Leo Affonso Soares an unnamed piece by Agustín P. Barrios in his recent concert program in Brazil.

This from the "Guitar News" magazine issue No. 99 of June-August 1968.

Miguel Rubio, a student of Daniel Fortea, Regino Sainz de la Maza and Andrés Segovia performed Barrios' *"La Catedral"* in his concert program on April 23, 1968 at the Wigmore Hall in London.

This from the "Guitar News" magazine issue No. 108 of April-June 1970.

At the Peña Guitarristica Tárrega in Barcelona on February 1, 1970 Betho Davezac performed Barrios' *"Las Abejas"* in his concert program.

This from the "Guitar News" magazine issue No. 113 of July-September 1971.

Gerard Roussel offers an undated concert review of Turibio Santos in 1971 in Saint-Omer, France at the Theatre Municipal where he performed an unnamed Barrios' piece in his concert program.

This from the "Guitar News" magazine issue No. 115 of January-March 1972.

In his tour beginning June 20, 1971 Betho Davezac performed *"Las Abejas"* by Agustín Barrios in his recitals and radio broadcasts in Tokyo, Nagoya, Osaka, Hiroshima, Kyoto, Dendai and Hamamatsu, Japan.

This from the "Guitar News" magazine issue No. 116 of April-June 1972.

In her 4th tour of Japan in 1971 Maria Lusia Anido performed an unnamed piece by Agustín Barrios in her concerts programs. (Upon looking at the Tuesday November 9, 1971 program we see the *"Danza Paraguaya"* listed, though only stated as *"Danza"*— A. Barrios.)

This from the "Guitar News" magazine issue No. 117 of July-September 1972.

Miguel Rubio, performed Barrios' *"Las Abejas"* in his concert program on March 22, 1972 at the Manchester, Connecticut Community College.

This from the "Guitar News" magazine issue No. 119 of January-March 1973.

Vladimir Mikulka performed Barrios' *"La Catedral"* in his March 15, 1972 concert program at the Prague Conservatory of Music.

These are from the "Guitar News from Overseas" column by Peter Sensier in the "B. M. G." magazine.

This from the "B. M. G." magazine issue of June 1954 issue Vol. LI. No. 590.

At the recital No. 39 of the Associacao Cultural do Violao on February 20, 1954 Sebastiao Galanti performed unnamed piece by Agustín Barrios.

This from the "B. M. G." magazine issue of October 1954 Vol. LI. No. 594.

In Recital No. 41 for the Associacao Cultural do Violao in Sao Paulo, guitarist Orthon Salleiro performed an unnamed piece by Agustín Barrios in his concert program.

This from the "B. M. G." magazine issue of February 1955 Vol. LI. No. 598.

Professor José Alves da Silva performed unnamed piece by Agustín Barrios in his concert program for the Associacao Cultural do Violao in Sao Paulo in 1954.

This from the "B. M. G." magazine issue of August 1955 Vol. LII. No. 605.

Sebastiao Galanti performed *"As Abelhas"* which is *"Las Abejas"* by Agustín Barrios in his concert for the Associacao Cultural do Violao in Sao Paulo in April 1955.

This from the "B. M. G." magazine issue of February 1959 Vol. LVI. No. 646.

Thirteen year old Carlos Barbosa-Lima performed *"As Abelhas" known as "Las Abejas"* by Agustín Barrios in his concert at the Teatro Sao Paulo.

This from the "B. M. G." magazine issue of May 1960 Vol. LVII. No. 661.

Milton Nunes performed unnamed piece by Agustín Barrios in his concert programs around Brazil in 1960.

This from the "B. M. G." magazine issue of September 1960 Vol. LVIII. No. 665.

Ronoel Simões on his radio program played an LP by Geraldo Ribeiro with an unnamed piece by Agustín Barrios.

This from the "B. M. G." magazine issue of April 1962 Vol. LIX. No. 684.

Lauro Blandy performed unnamed piece by Agustín Barrios in his concert program in the Teatro Leopoldo Froes in Sao Paulo on January 22, 1962.

This is from *"L'arte Chitarrista"* magazine Vol. 34-35 of July-October 1952.

Alirio Diaz plays Agustín Barrios' *"Danza Paraguiana" ("Danza Paraguaya")* at an evening concert in the hall of the palazzo Chiablese, during his stay as a student of Andrés Segovia at the Accademia Chigiana in Siena, Italy. Italian Translation: Randy Osborne
Archive: Ricardo Muñoz

MÚSICA PARA VIOLÃO DE

A G U S T I N P. B A R R I O S

The table of contents of the very first anthology of the works of Agustín P. Barrios, published in Brazil by Romeo Di Giorgio c. 1950 titled *Seleçao de Musicas para Violao de Agustín P. Barrios*. Many of the songs performed and listed in the previous pages were from this edition of 23 pieces.

Translation of Portuguese of an article entitled *"O Violao"* (The Guitar) published on April 4, 1953, a column written by Ronoel Simoes, record collector extraordinare.

O violão

Quando Agustin Barrios esteve no Rio de Janeiro, pela primeira vez, onde ofereceu o seu recital de estréia nessa cidade, em 1.o de agosto de 1916, marcou, com este concerto, uma carreira de brilhante sucesso no Brasil. E' interessante frisar que o famoso Barrios, paraguaio, foi um dos violonistas estrangeiros que mais divulgaram o violão em nossa terra. Não existe uma unica cidade, em todos os Estados do Brasil, que Barrios não tenha visitado com o seu nobre instrumento, deixando, até os dias de hoje, profunda admiração naqueles que tiveram a fortuna de ouvi-lo não só como violonista, mas tambem como compositor e poeta. Certa ocasião, quando Barrios esteve em Natal, Rio Grande do Norte, ofereceu naquela cidade um interessante recital de violão em homenagem ao Interventor Federal e esposa, em 28 de março de 1931. Nesse recital, Barrios declamou, dedicada ao violão, a seguinte fantasia de sua lavra: — "Profissão de Fé". Tupã, o Espirito Supremo e protetor da minha raça, encontrou-me um dia em meio de um bosque verdejante, enlevado na contemplação da natureza. E me disse: Toma esta caixa misteriosa e desvenda os seus segredos. E encerrando nela todas as avezinhas cantoras, abandonou-a em minhas mãos. Tomei-a, obedecendo ao mandado de Tupã e, pondo-a bem junto ao meu peito, aconchegado a ela, passei muitas luas à beira duma fonte. E uma noite, Jacy, retratada no liquido cristal, sentindo a tristeza de minha alma india, deu-me seis raios de prata para com eles desvendar os seus segredos. E o milagre se operou: do fundo da caixa misteriosa brotou a sinfonia maravilhosa de todas as vozes virgens da nossa America".

Inumeros escritores famosos dedicaram a Barrios paginas de significativa grandeza, ao lhe ouvirem as interpretações através do seu soberbo violão. Dentre esses, podemos citar os grandes Olavo Bilac e Coelho Neto. São Paulo foi uma das cidades onde Barrios conquistou maior sucesso, tendo aqui efetuado varios concertos e, entre estes, ha alguns que merecem especial atenção, por terem sido realizados no Teatro Municipal, o teatro máximo da Capital paulista. Segundo nos consta, Barrios deixou gravadas, em discos Odeon, cerca de 27 execuções. E' curioso observar que Barrios não tocava com cordas de tripa, porém ele nos explicou a razão desse fato: é que, viajando grande parte de suas excursões pelo interior dos paises percorridos, nem sempre encontrava cordas daquela natureza, que aliás eram de sua preferencia, sendo, portanto, forçado a usar cordas de aço.

When Agustín Barrios was in Rio de Janiero, for the first time, where he was to offer a debut concert in that city on August 1, 1916, setting off, with that concert, a brilliant successful career in Brazil. And interesting to emphasize that the famous Barrios, Paraguayan, was one of the foreign guitarists who diffused the guitar the most in our land. There isn't a city, in any State of Brazil, in which this guitarist hadn't visited with his noble instrument, leaving, until today, a profound admiration for those whom had the fortune to have heard him, not only as guitarist, but as well as a composer and poet. On an occasion in Natal, Rio Grande do Norte (State), he offered an interesting guitar recital in that city in homage to the Interventor Federal and wife on March 28, 1931. In that recital, Barrios declared, the following fantasy of his creation to the guitar:

Profession of Faith:

Tupa, oh Supreme Spirit, and protector of my race, I found myself one day in the green forest, lifted up in the contemplation of nature. And he said to me "Take this mysterious box and unlock its secrets. Locked within are all birdlike singers abandoned in my hands. Taking this mandate of obedience of Tupa and, holding it close to my chest, arriving with it, many moons that passed to the edge of the source. One night, Jacy, portrayed in liquid crystal, feeling the sadness of my Indian soul left me six silver moonbeams with which to unlock its secrets. And the miracle to produce from the depth of the mysterious box a marvelous symphony sprouting of all the virgin voices of our America."

Numerous famous writers have dedicated pages to Barrios of significant greatness, they heard him through the interpretations of his magnificent guitar. Within those we can cite the great Olavo Bilac and Coelho Neto. Sao Paulo was one of the cities where Barrios conquered with great success, having performed various concerts here and, among those there are some that deserve special attention, one having taken place in the Teatro Municipal, or the greatest theater in Sao Paulo. Our second piece of evidence is that, Barrios left recordings, around 27 performed on Odeon records. And it's curious to observe that Barrios didn't play with gut strings, however he explained the reason for this fact: and that, traveling a great part of his excursions through the interior of the countries, he never could find strings of that nature, of high quality that were his preference, being, therefore, he was forced to use steel strings. End of translation.

Archive: Eduardo Bensadon

Though Agustín Barrios was dead for almost a decade, his impact was such that musicians still loved the maestro, and they wrote about the wonderful legend that he had been. R. O.

The photo at the right is Ronoel Simões and is from Ricardo Muñoz's unpublished *"Historia Universal de la Guitarra"* Volume VI *"America"*.

632

This is the translation of the A. B. C. newspaper article *"A 32 años de la muerte del genial Agustín Barrios"* from Asuncion, Paraguay of Sunday September 5, 1976. It is transcribed by Julio Quince and is derived from a conversation with Sila Godoy, a great guitarist and Agustín Barrios investigator for decades. Sila had published transcriptions of Barrios' works in the 1950's. He was also a student of Consuelo Mallo Lopez.

"32 years after the death of the brilliant Agustín Barrios"

The 7th of August completes the thirty-second anniversary of the death of Agustín Barrios (*Nitsuga Mangoré*), the brilliant Paraguayan guitarist whose prestige for the name of Paraguay is in the most quoted artistic centers of the world. In an extensive conversation with Sila Godoy, another guitarist of major prestige of our country that has dedicated years of his life to the recompilation and diffusion of the works of Barrios, he reveals to us details of the last years of the brilliant Mangoré.

"Agustín Barrios — says Sila Godoy — died the 7th of August of 1944 in San Salvador, at the age of 59 years old. He died from a second heart attack; he had an attack in Mexico in 1939. He had passed through Central America and was headed toward the United States to make his first tour of that country, that was to be the culmination of his success, the definite triumph of his career. He was going to enter the United States after his trip to Europe, afterwards having been consecrated in Germany, France, Belgium and Spain. Barrios returned from Europe in the year 1936 to Venezuela, contracted by the Federacion Universitaria of that country. This contract they gave to Barrios took him out of Spain, where the civil war had been taking place. An ambassador, a friend of Barrios, acquired the contract and it opportunely freed him to go to who knows what destiny.

"From Venezuela he went up to Cuba, Costa Rica, Central America and in 1939 he arrived in Mexico, because he carried with him a contract for twenty performances in the United States. He arrived in Mexico with a black Brazilian woman accompanying him, by the name of Gloria. In her epoch she was a ballerina, afterwards she was converted into being the woman who cared for Barrios. She was almost a person of service. Barrios had his world and she was entrusted to take care of him.

"Then Barrios went to the consulate to get his visas. There he had what appeared to be a great displeasure, and when he had left the consulate, he fell down onto the street of a sudden attack. Luckily there was a clinic nearby, they brought him there, and they gave him oxygen and did a special treatment only to discover the great artist that he was.

HE LOST THE CONTRACT

"And when he got his strength back a little bit, more or less in fifteen days, the doctors recommended he leave Mexico. He, with this cardiac arrest lost the contract with the United States and practically remained an invalid. From Mexico he returned to Central America, to be heading towards Costa Rica, where there had been good memories--including having been offered contracts — and he, remembering those offers he headed toward Costa Rica. But in Guatemala, Barrios stayed a few days in a hotel, because he wasn't in the condition to make a continued trip. Because in those days the means of transportation weren't like today, there weren't airplanes and the means were by water or land. The presence of Barrios in Guatemala provoked a reunion of the intellectuals and artists, because only a few days before his attack, Barrios had played his last concert in that country before traveling to Mexico.

"In Guatemala, his admirers and friends went to see him at the hotel where he was a guest. And the journalists made a lot of noise informing about the near-death state that Barrios was in. At that moment President Ubico was governing Guatemala which in those times he had a lot of great political problems. There had been a curfew and there was a prohibition against the assembly of more than two persons. Ubico was one of the greatest strong-arm governors. And the only way to avoid said reunions was to kick Barrios out of Guatemala. And they gave him twenty-four hours to leave the country. It wasn't a measure against Barrios; on the contrary Ubico explained that he had been to the concert of the guitarist and he declared he was an admirer of the same. But he had to cut off the reunion for public well being.

DESTINY: EL SALVADOR

President Martínez of El Salvador took this measure against Barrios as an offense against culture. Martínez was a theosopher, a mystic, as well presided over a strong government, but of a different type than that of Guatemala, of which was its enemy. And when Barrios arrived in El Salvador he felt a little bit freer and stayed a few days in a hotel. The journalists also visited him because thirty days earlier he had given three concerts in San Salvador, one of which was attended by Martínez.

"When Barrios received the visit of the journalists, he told them he was sick, that he couldn't play and that he was heading toward Costa Rica to rest. But the day, which Martínez read that notice in the paper, he made an invitation to Barrios to visit the palace, and he sent a delegate to Barrios' hotel. And when the invitation was announced to Barrios by the person sent by President Martínez, — it shocked him — believing they were going to kick him out once again, he said that he was going to be traveling that very day and couldn't see anyone. But they told him that it had to do with a personal invitation from the President, and he only wanted to speak with him, and if Barrios couldn't come to the palace, the President would come to the hotel.

"They explained to him that everything had been contrary to what he had imagined, that it was to save the prestige of the artist. And then Barrios accepted to go and see President Martínez the following day, to whom he explained the indignation in El Salvador that the expulsion from Guatemala had caused and that the government of El Salvador from that moment on was giving him a lifelong pension, that Barrios could use in whatever part of the world, without being committed to remain in El Salvador neither having to recompense anything to the government. Barrios, affected emotionally, accepted the pension and stayed in El Salvador. With time, his recovery improved and was assisted by the eminent cardiologist who was the personal doctor to President Martínez. And wanting to pay back the medical attention, he offered his services as a professor; he opened up a department of the guitar in the Conservatorio Nacional of San Salvador.

A HUMAN INTRIGUE

"This was the history of the arrival of Barrios to El Salvador. Barrios didn't think of turning around there. On the contrary, with the success that he would've obtained in the United States, he thought about returning to Europe and being converted into a great artist that was the dream of his whole life. He was in the culmination of a career that only Segovia had reached. Because in Europe the dailies of Belgium, after a concert Barrios had given in the Real Conservatorio of Bruxelles, declared that he was very great and equal to Segovia and that included "played music of his own creation".

"Barrios lived for five years in San Salvador under the protection of President Martínez. And there is an anecdote that demonstrates that the affection for Barrios that President Martínez felt was great; because Barrios was an intellectual figure besides being a great guitarist and great composer. He was a man who had perfected his style of life; to the point, to speak with him, visit him, to see him play, to live, was a spectacle in El Salvador that hadn't been known but through the greatest men that had visited the land.

"And the position of Barrios, his personality, his figure, his spirituality, had provoked the jealousy of the director of the Conservatorio de Musica de San Salvador. They made it an intrigue. Then Barrios faithful to his style, explained by reasons of health that he was going to give successive classes in his home. That doesn't explain anything of the jealousy of the director. But at the end of the course, the Minister of Education went to hand out the diplomas in the Conservatorio, and he noted the absence of Barrios, he asked and there begins the intrigue. When Martínez, in his occasion, found out about the sham, he dismissed the director of the Conservatorio, and gave him twenty-four hours to leave the country, and named a new director who was put at the orders of Barrios. That is to say, that Barrios, theoretically was only a professor of guitar, but practically was the super-director. All this world of intrigue, that is human and occurs in whatever part, --the opposition to the men of genius, the gossip, of the weak, as Ortega y Gasset says — Barrios had to take into account.

634

THE END

"And so when President Martínez fell, there was a bloody revolution that began in the months of March-April-May of 1944. Barrios was left without his protector and--he would to have had thought — subject to the will of whatever intrigue. And he prepared to leave El Salvador. He had recuperated once again his great technique and was strong. 59 years is a mature age for a concert artist. An ex-student of Barrios is still alive, Candido Morales, a professor that was a director of a college and a representative in the legislature. Candido Morales accompanied Barrios as a secretary to not have him going out alone. Barrios was going to break up with Gloria in San Salvador, almost as a definite separation, because Gloria had a boarding house where the students of the guitar were guests. Among the boarders there was an Italian Colonel that had stayed in Central America, someone left behind of the intelligence service to Mussolini, that couldn't return to Italy.

"It has to do with a man of money in his country, but in Central America he had stayed isolated, he couldn't return to Italy to recover his fortune. A very intelligent man who admired Barrios very much. When Barrios was preparing to leave the country, it gave him a second heart attack and he died. That was the 7th of August of 1944. His death produced a very great disorientation, because the companion figured only as a wife, they never were married. And Gloria didn't even have documents.

"Fifteen days later Gloria married the Italian Colonel, out of everything, a part they took was the archive of Barrios to Italy. And parts of this archive the Salvadorian government bought. The guitar, the albums, the commemorative medallions, they are to be found in the museum of San Salvador. In reality the Salvadorian government didn't buy those valuable objects, but instead gave an amount of money — it's not known how much — to Gloria. But it must have been considerable, because with this money, Gloria and her husband, the Italian Colonel, they traveled to Italy, leaving a formal brief where the supposed widow of Barrios declared that the extinct wanted all of his things to remain in El Salvador.

PROVINCIAL ROBBERY

"The students, seeing that with the death of Barrios they had definitely lost a great amount, in the evening of the wake they began to empty the home. From a music stand that Barrios had, where he had studied and had his archive of music, what Gloria couldn't put under lock and key, two students that were living in the home of Barrios, entered by a window and they stole an immense quantity of music. It is the only thing that stayed in El Salvador. And this "artistic robbery" (robo artistico) later permitted the recovery of an immense quantity of works. But the other considerable part of the works of Barrios — that is believed to be around three hundred--stayed in a trunk that Gloria took to Italy, with the idea of publishing them.

"Gloria later died in Italy, but before the Italian recovered his fortune — Gloria came to live very well — and then didn't need to make money from the works of Barrios, they remained abandoned. Besides there were no documents and no publisher would risk releasing a work without the legal authorization, of the author's rights and a mountain of other things as well. If it's stumbled upon what with many difficulties it is possible that the trunk may have been thrown away? Because in Italy there exists a custom that one day a year the people throw old trunks, chairs, beds out of windows and other people pick them up or burn them. It doesn't have any certain notice about the trunk. The only thing that can orient the search is that there is a great Italian maestro, who studied with Segovia, which has now announced a publication of an immense amount of unpublished works by Barrios. And possibily investigating a little bit one can come to discover what happened to the works in the old trunk.

"All of this can be investigated. Now, as I have already dedicated more than thirty years of my life to the investigation and recovery of the works of Barrios (When I arrived in Asuncion in 1936, Basualdo had three works of Barrios. Presently we have more than seventy recovered by me, that is supposed to be a third of what Barrios wrote.). I'm no longer in the condition to be able to follow this investigation because the time also comes to me above. Besides the publication of the works of Barrios now in the hands of the Centro de Guitarra Clasica de "Gustavo Sosa Escalada" that is in contact with a grandson of Barrios, that lives in Buenos Aires, son of one of the direct heirs of Barrios — of whose name we have gotten the next testimony — Sadly, this son of Barrios died a year ago, and the Centro de Guitarra Clasica has now a power through the widow of the son of Barrios and with that power and some things that are being legalized, it is opening once again in Buenos Aires for legalizing the rights of the grandson.

"That is to say the situation is very complicated so much that I have come to an agreement with the Centro de Guitarra Clasica for dividing the works of Barrios. I'm going to be in charge of the diffusion of the works of Barrios, as interpreter, to promote them and to have an archive to document the number of recordings that are being made of his music in all parts (of the world). John Williams is recording in London, in Paris they're recording as well. The music of Barrios figures in the conservatory of music in Paris, as a text of teaching and as a high-grade school of technique. As well it's in the conservatory of music in Madrid. All this information, in the part of the diffusion of the works of Barrios, I'm going to follow. But the publication, the contact with the impresarios, including the copies of the works, we would say the technical work, all that the Centro de Guitarra Clasica already has in their possession. And all the rest still to make the revindication definitely for the figure of Barrios needs the support of the Government for its materialization. We must all mobilize to place in the site that corresponds to the Paraguayan that is considered the greatest guitarist of America."

Julio Quince

Translations of photo captions from the
Asuncion, Paraguay A. B. C. daily
September 5, 1976 interview:

"Agustín Barrios dressed for a gala. His
exquisiteness drew the attention in the
places where he went, and it came out in his
concerts, in the manner of his life, in his
conversation."

AGUSTIN Barrios vestido de gala. Su exquisitez llamaba la
atención en los lugares adonde iba, y traslucía en sus conciertos, en su modo de vida, en su conversación.

Translations of photo captions from the
Asuncion, Paraguay A. B. C. daily
September 5, 1976 interview:

"Agustín Barrios, with the portrayal as
Nitsuga Mangoré, and with it he charmed the
most demanding public of Europe and America
for a duration of many years."

On the next four pages are Peter Sensier's October and November 1962 B. M. G. magazine excepts
from Dr. Juan Max Boettner's book *"Musica y Musicos del Paraguay"*. This has to be the earliest massive
English language text written about Agustín Barrios. There are some typos of names.

B.M.G.
Guitar Topics

By Peter Sensier

I THINK it was Gustavo Lopez whom I first heard playing "Danza Paraguaya" in public. Since then many people must have heard it played by Alirio Diaz and John Williams (both of whom play it delightfully) to say nothing of the numerous guitarists who make a bold try at it.

Although it is not too easy and not I believe officially published, it has nevertheless become very popular via MS and photostat copies.

This is understandable because it is both attractive and most guitaristic, although not in my opinion, very Paraguayan. Not for instance as typically Paraguayan as the famous Lauro "Vals" is Venezuelan.

Nevertheless it is well written and I decided recently to dig up what information I could about the composer, Agustin Pio Barrios, and to pass it on to you.

In so doing I discovered quite a lot of interesting information so, before telling you about Barrios, I thought a general outline of the guitar in Paraguay might not come amiss.

POPULAR INSTRUMENT

As in most Latin-American countries the guitar, along with other European instruments, soon made its appearance in the towns and cities established by the Spanish conquerors and by the end of the 18th Century it was the most popular instrument in Paraguay. Today it is still the most widespread.

However in May 1811, Dr. José Gaspar Rodriquez de Francia became the "Supreme Dictator" of Paraguay. He was a stern, severe man who had no love for music or entertainment and in 1816 he sent a group of musicians to prison for playing a serenade in the streets of the capital Asuncion!

The people of Paraguay so feared Dr. Francia that they would only leave their houses if they were obliged of necessity to do so.

Writing of this period Renzgu Longchamp said: "The guitar, inseparable companion of the Paraguayan, was silenced for ever. . . ."

Fortunately this was not entirely true for in the small farms and distant country districts the guitar and the harp were still played, albeit softly, for fear the dreaded El Suprema might hear.

Anyone who knows the Paraguayans would find this hard to believe as music is so much a part of their lives but such was the fear Francia inspired that for some time after he died in 1840 people could not bring themselves to believe they were free of his tyranny.

His successor, Don Carlos Antonio Lopez, although a Dictator, was of happier nature and it is during this era we hear of the first guitarist of note: El Maestro Quintana, guitarist, teacher, clock-maker and mechanic, also credited with writing the first national hymn of Paraguay.

Francesco Solano Lopez succeeded his father Don Carlos in the Dictatorship and both he and his close companion Madame Alicéa Elisa Lynch enjoyed music and entertainment.

Well known among popular musicians of the time were Cangue-Herreros, a self-taught guitarist, singer and poet from Carapegua who taught in a famous regiment during the war of the Triple Alliance (Paraguay versus Argentina, Uruguay and Brazil); Vargas, guitarist and poet; Nicolas Delgardo, guitarist; and Juan Gonzalez, guitarist and watch-maker.

The terrible war of the Triple Alliance that lasted from 1865-1870—and which ended in the heroic death of Francisco Solane and his eldest son at Ceow Caro—left Paraguay in a truly terrible state.

Virtually every able bodied man was killed during the war; the only male survivors being old men and boys.

MUSIC RETURNED

There followed a period of occupation by foreign troops during which time the country came to a standstill but gradually things returned to normal and music once again became a part of everyday life in Paraguay.

The first classical guitarist to appear on the scene was Gustavo Sosa Escalada, from Argentina, around 1890, who later became Professor of Guitar at the Instituto Paraguay.

In 1897 he performed a "Nocturno" by Garcia Tolsa in a concert at the Teatro Nacional and he became the teacher of a whole generation of guitarists, notably Baez Allende, Barrios, Basualdo and Enriqueta Gonzalez.

Chronologically Agustin Barrios fits in here but I am saving him until later.

Quirino Baez Allende (born 3/6/1898) also studied in Buenos Aires under Domingo Prat and gave many concerts in Argentina and Paraguay.

Dionisio R. Basualdo studied later with Barrios and the Spanish guitarist Josefina Robledo in Buenos Aires. He gave concerts in Asuncion and Posadas and is now a Professor of the guitar. Amongst his pupils is Pablo Escoban Cáceies (b. 1900) who has given recitals in Brazil, Uruguay and Argentina.

Then came an interesting personality Carlos Talavera (b. Caazapá, 1900). He was a child prodigy who from his sixth to his fifteenth year played the flute; winning first prize for the best flute player in Paraguay at the age of eight.

At the age of fifteen he turned to the guitar which he taught himself, giving his first concert in Asuncion four years later. Then he toured, giving concerts throughout South America and Spain. In 1931 he went to Central America, returning for concerts in Paraguay in 1932. 1937 saw him back in Spain and he followed this with recitals in Brazil.

He was particularly popular for playing a piece of music called "Güyrá Campana."

Ampelio Villabba, another guitarist from Caazapé, learned this solo—and in his turned passed it on to the famous Paraguayan harp player, Felix Perez Cardozo, who arranged it for harp under the title of "Pájaro Cambana" (The Bell Bird) which, thanks to touring Paraguayan groups, has become known throughout the world.

Other guitarists known to have been active at this time included Candido Fretes, Rudolfo Miranda, Julian Refala and Carlos Abrew Sosa.

BEST KNOWN GUITARIST

Which brings us to Paraguay's best known contemporary classical guitarist, Cayo Sila Godoy. Shortly after his birth at Coronel Oviedo in 1919 his family moved to Villarica, where one of his uncles, Marciano Echauri, gave him his first instruction on the guitar. Later he went to the Ateneo Paraguayo in Asuncion where he studied music under Juan Carlos Moreno. He then received a grant from the Government to study guitar with Consuelo Mallo Lopez in Buenos Aires.

Then followed a busy life giving concerts throughout Latin-America. He is also a composer for the guitar and among his works are "Fiesta Campesina" (based on Paraguayan airs), "Capricho," "Tolderia" (based on Indian themes), a popular series for guitar, Vals, Habanera and Polca and "Fantasia Heroica," dedicated to Cerro Caró, for orchestra.

Cayo Sela Godoy has also spent much time collecting information about Agustin Barrios and it is to him that we owe much of the information available about Paraguay's greatest guitarist.

Of course, an important aspect of the guitar in Paraguay has been its use in popular music of which, with the harp, it has always been an integral part.

Some of the best known contemporary popular guitarists are Samuel Aguayo (singer-guitarist and arranger of a great deal of Folk music), Emigdio Ayala Baez (who has composed many songs, including the beautiful "Me Dicha Lejana"), Dr. Juan Bestard, (medical man and Folk lorist), Mauricio Cardozo Ocampo (guitarist, flautist and composer, with some 200-or-so songs to his credit, including the famous "Galopeia," "Pueblo Ibycui" and "Que linda me Bandria"), Herminio Gurenez (who directed the "Conjunto del Comanchaco" during the Gran Chaco War), Eladio Martinez (guitar and flute, who toured England, France, Spain and Portugal with a Paraguayan company and wrote "Lucento Alba" which David Attenborough used as the signature tune for his B.B.C. T.V. Series "Zoo Quest in Paraguay" and which was played by Martinez' group), Agustin Barboza (Folk singer and guitarist with the original Trio Los Paraguayos, now back in Paraguay where he teaches and has a regular radio programme) and Reinaldo (Ruberto) Medina (composer of a lovely song "Dulce Esperanza" and, until a year or so ago, lead guitarist with Luis Alberto de Parana and his Trio Los Paraguayos).

Naturally in a country where the guitar is so popular one expects to find guitar makers and the most famous was Don Sebastien Chávez who died in 1951 aged 77. He left three sons, all of whom (Prisciliano, Espridéon and Cāsboul) have carried on the tradition of guitar making.

Espefanio Lopez, the best harp maker in Paraguay, also makes good guitars.

And that is a brief outline of the guitar in Paraguay against which, next month, I hope to tell the story of Agustin Pio Barrios.

(To be continued)

Guitar Topics

By PETER SENSIER

(Continued from last month's issue)

AGUSTIN PIO BARRIOS, Paraguay's greatest guitarist, was born in the parish of San Juan Bautista de las Misiones on May 23rd, 1885, to Doreteo Barrios and his wife, Martina Ferreira.

As a small child he showed a great interest in music. While still a boy he was given instruction by the guitarist, Gustavo Sosa Escalada who, realising his great musical potential, advised him to go to the capital, Asunción, where he studied at the Colegio Nacional for a Bachalauriate.

In 1910 he left Paraguay for the first time to give a concert in the Corrientes province of Argentina, which borders on Paraguay.

He had intended staying away for a week only, but it was 14 years before he eventually returned to his native land.

The success he had in Corrientes was such that he felt compelled to seek new horizons, with the result he travelled through Brazil, Uruguay, Argentina and Chile, giving concerts wherever he went.

FIRST HEARD BACH

It was during this time he first heard the music of J. S. Bach and this fired him with a new enthusiasm for composition (which had already interested him as a youth) and he began to compose copiously in three distinct styles: classical, romantic and popular—*i.e.,* folk-based music.

Amongst his compositions of this period are "La Catedral," "Allegro Sinfónico," "Estudios & Preludios," "Lasabeja," "Estudio de Concierto," "Vals Nos. 3 and 4," "Mazurka Appassionata," "Invocación A Mi Madre," "Madrigal," "Contemplación," "Un Sueño en la Floresta," "Confesion," "Oracion," "Danza Paraguay," "Jha Chevalle," etc.

Physically, Barrios was big and muscular, fond of sport and a good athlete. He was not a handsome man, although it is said he became transformed when he played the guitar.

As a person he was friendly and amiable, "delightfully potty but always interesting," according to his pupil, Dionisio Basualdo.

In fact, Barrios was what we would nowadays call "a character." Sometimes he would go for a week without touching the guitar and then would come a period when he would practice for 10 or 12 hours a day without apparently feeling the need for food.

Some days he would be on top of the world, but he would also suffer periods of deep depression and at these times he had the need of good, kind and patient friends to help him regain his morale. Fortunately, although he was "a character" he was a lovable one and he did not lack good companions and kind friends.

Outstanding amongst these was the Paraguayan diplomat, Don Tomás Salomoni and his wife, Doña Luisa Lebrón de Salomoni (a fine classical guitarist) who for two years guided and watched over Barrios and his beautiful Brazilian wife, Gloria.

It was these two kind and generous people who virtually launched Barrios on his highly successful series of concerts in Mexico and immediately afterwards cleared up his debts in Cuba, where he had had an artistic but not economic success.

GUITAR CRACKED

While in Mexico, Barrios' guitar, a beautiful instrument made in Barcelona (in 1920), cracked badly, possibly due to the change of climate (he had recently been in Venezuela). Characteristically, he gave the guitar to Señora Salomoni, who, equally characteristically, bought him a fine Mexican-built guitar in exchange.

Incidentally, Sra. Salomoni later had the guitar repaired and it was as good as new. Barrios' Mexican guitar is now in the Museum of San Salvador.

From Mexico, in 1934, Agustin Barrios and his wife travelled with the Salomonis, by the s.s. Orinoco to Belgium and in Brussels Sr. Salomoni arranged a recital by Barrios before an audience of critics and professors at the Royal Conservatory.

At the end of the first half of the concert, which consisted of the standard "classical" repertoire for the guitar, the critics (whilst admitting his artistry and ability) expressed boredom at the "same old stuff," whereupon Barrios returned to give a second-half made up entirely of his own compositions.

The audience, critics and professors alike, were staggered at his performance and at the end they rose as one man, applauding and shouting "Bravo!"

From Brussels, the four friends went to Belgium for a while and then went to Hamburg, where they finally parted company, Barrios and his wife well provided for.

This was the last they saw of each other.

After a considerable success in Spain, Barrios re-crossed the Atlantic to Venezuela where he gave 20 recitals and enjoyed a greater success than any other guitarist had ever had in that country.

Returning to Mexico for further concerts, he suffered a heart attack and was invited by friends to Costa Rica to recuperate. While there he received an invitation from the President of San Salvador, General Martinez, to visit that country.

Very soon he had gained the love and admiration of the people of San Salvador and before long he was made Professor of Guitar at the National Conservatoire of Music.

There, from 1939-44, he led a peaceful and happy life, surrounded by friends, loved by his pupils and venerated by the people almost as a legend. San Salvador took this elegant Bohemian and extraordinary artistic personality to its heart. As he passed by people would say to each other: "There goes the great Mangore" (Mangore being the name of a Paraguayan Indian chief that Barrios had adopted for his own).

ANOTHER ATTACK

Then one day he suffered another heart attack. He had apparently recovered from it some days later and on August 7th, 1944, while surrounded by his pupils, he asked for a priest to be called for. When the Reverend Father arrived Barrios spoke to him at length, while from another part of the house could be heard the sound of his pupils playing guitars.

By the afternoon he had passed away —surrounded by his pupils, his friends and his wife, Gloria.

His remains lie in the Cementerio de los Illustres, and in the Museum of San Salvador there is a glass case containing his guitar, an album, a gold medal, a diploma and his bust carved in wood.

So loved was Barrios by the people of San Salvador that when his funeral procession passed by the market place of the capital everyone, both merchants and customers alike, left the market to follow him to his last resting place.

As the Paraguayan guitarist, Sila Godoy, says: "The veneration and honour with which his name is held in

San Salvador merits the thanks of all Paraguay."

So ends the story of Agustin Pio Barrios, brilliant guitarist and composer of over 100 works for guitar, who during his life was compared to Paganini for his virtuosity and to Chopin for his instrumental composition and who is still considered by many to be one of the finest musicians of all Latin-America.

NOTE:— Information for this and last month's article was obtained from Dr. Juan Max Boettner's book "Musica y Musieos del Paraguay".

Incorrect spelling of the names of people and places in last month's article were due either to my extremely bad handwriting or a bad attack of "printer's errors".

Agustín Barrios returned to Brazil in 1929 and was covered by the short-lived guitar magazine *"O Violao"*. This photo is from *"O Violao"* Issue No. 9 of October 1929. *"Um astro que reapparece"* (A star reappears)

Portuguese translation by
Randy Osborne:

"A photograph kindly sent to the magazine by our great friend and lover of the guitar in the Estado do Rio Grande do Sul (State of Rio Grande in the South) a doctor in the city of Alegrete, Dr. Miguel Lite de Oliva.

In this we see on the left the great artist Agustín Barrios, who to our readers, they certainly know from the time of his brilliant artistic performances within this city, some years ago. In the center is our mentioned friend, Dr. Oliva and on the right is Mr. Luis Durodoña, the secretary of the maestro."

This photo is from the book *"El Inalcanzable"* published in Asuncion, Paraguay in November 2007. The copies I have of the *"O Violao"* magazine are second generation, and the photos are weak. So, I decided to make use of this very clear photo.

This concert review is from the magazine "*O Violao*" Issue No. 10 of November-December 1929, published in Rio de Janeiro. The director was B. Dantas de Souza Pombo, and he may have been who wrote the concert reviews that follow, there is no signature for them. As Domingo Prat says: B. Dantas de Souza Pombo was a student of, the Argentine guitarist, Juan A. Rodríguez. Portuguese translation by Randy Osborne.

"A Recital by Agustín Barrios

On the 28th of the previous month (November) Agustín Barrios reappeared before our public, in the Theatro Municipal, giving us another recital.

Since 1917, we couldn't hear him, having therefore, an interval of 12 years.

In that space of time, however the Paraguayan artist suffered no modification.

Barrios is unquestionably, the most discussed lover of the guitar in South America, in all of the countries where he has played, since you get various opinions, creating a pleiade of proselytes, that admire him and elevate to the heights, placing him on an elevated pedestal, coming to affirm him to be the best contemporary guitarist.

From there, maybe, the reaction provoked by him, is much bigger than the action. So even, in our groups where the personality of Barrios is discussed, there is no middle ground, or better said, a fair term, not being able to form a sure judgement about his competence, according to the passionate opinions.

From those, however, highlights an evidence: Barrios always gets the majority of the lovers of the guitar excited, perhaps by their rather democratic temperament. Moreover, his repertoire is perfectly accessible to the less cultured spirits. In the case of the pure melodies, not the lacking the sincerity of the more complicated harmonization, to highlight and standout especially because Barrios, appears to us, not to be concerned to please the public en masse as to which he identifies, and which he really pleases.

If it were only art, the Paraguayan artist wouldn't derive restrictions, unfortunately, it isn't only that. Two demands are too severe and from there we see Barrios sustaining the struggle, for many years, it begins by the mode of stringing the guitar. He's the only one to place steel strings on the first three strings of his instrument. Segovia, Robledo, Rodríguez, Llobet, Pujol and Sainz de la Maza, considered the best guitarists of the world, all use gut strings, it doesn't detract from the timbre of the instrument, in reality, a musical heresy. This question and the primary one, when discussing the personality of the Paraguayan artist. He, meanwhile, sustains his point of view, against all of the masters of the instrument and doesn't compromise. To break the shrillness of the steel strings presented us, this time, an innovation of placing rubber dampers over them. However breaking, that shrillness, making his sound pleasing, also diminishing this intensity, making the spectators distances imperceptible, as you could verify in his concert.

Right there, in the Municipal, it hasn't been a long time since, Sainz de la Maza playing on gut strings had twice the sonority obtained by Barrios. Therefore, it seems to us out of doubt that the supporters of steel strings are in error; they judge them as the best sonority.

Really, the less cautious have that impression, when they listen, from up close, to the guitar strung with steel, but putting themselves in the distance, they notice the error. Its use, before that, can only be justified by the greater ease of performance for those not following the classical school, too difficult, but always productive.

It seems to us that the intolerance of Barrios, in this question, about this he has been precisely struggling, studying by himself, without the assistance of some master's experience.

Not having made, naturally, a solid basis, he has to eternally struggle at the difficulties conquered by the masters of the instrument, such as his small sonority and the detraction of the harmonization of the chords by pieces that breathe. Barrios simplifies everything for being able to take the forces of accessible effects.

642

It turns out he presents an imperfect performance and a formidable technique, sometimes even exciting.

Still, the techniques repair what he uses and abuses of effects that outrage the reputed artistic masters, such as, for example the repeated vibrato, prolonged, giving a monotone to the guitar out of character to compare its sorrowful cittern.

Moreover, Barrios still seeks to take effect of antiquated hits such as a bugle and drum, he strikes over the bridge of the instrument of whom the late patriarch of the guitar *"Canhoto"* excited the spectators in the music houses. Tárrega, the immortal innovator of the guitar composing a formidable *"Jota Aragonesa"*, not being able to plagiarize a variation, with such effects, because it is of a musical characteristic that was forced to enrich an elevated harmony and so even, the twenty-six genius variations, those are the most banal.

Today, it would be ridiculous for a Segovia, a Robledo and a Rodríguez to present themselves before a cultured public, playing a march such as the bugle to repeatedly and uninterruptedly having the drums snore annoyingly.

Barrios, however, despises all those objections and prefers to continue his artistic career conceived as such, he is persistent.

We respect his point of view. He, really, has qualities among this that is to be convinced in his artistic process. However it isn't only that which he possesses. Barrios is also sentimental and knows in regard to this communicative soul how to stamp, an essential quality of an artist, that he, is without any favors.

And we can go ahead, Barrios is also a creator. His compositions demonstrate that. Some of them even can be presented as masterpieces of art, as, for example, *"Madrigal"* performed in the first part of his program.

It is a piece of music filled of sentiment, of a rich harmonization, and varying effect. The other compositions of his, not less than eight of them, of the 14 numbers which constitute his program, although pleasant, analyzed in their essence, they leave a lot to desire, by the poor harmonization, by the lack of structure, or by constructing them as imitations of the others. Among these is his "Catedral", together with chords by Bach, melodies of Schubert and common canzonettas.

"Souvenir d'un reve" (Un Sueño en la Floresta), also isn't just a melody modeled but, in the least, it is very similar to *"Meditacao" ("Meditacion")* by Carlos García Tolsa.

In order, as a composer, for Barrios to present to us some qualities, some of the most appreciable, however, it is always resentful for the lack a solid base. The numbers of his compositions were impeccably performed, apart from the restrictions of this assessment. When, however, Barrios performs Bach, Mozart and Chopin, he stumbles too often. In the second part he performed the *"Minueto"* by Beethoven and the *"Preludio"* by Bach, alias, the simplest and shortest by far of the program.

"Sevilla" by Albeniz, was performed in a regular manner.

That is our opinion about the Paraguayan artist.

Although, in his program he announces, "consecrated by the critics as the best contemporary guitarist", we did not judge him as such.

He, in our view, is far from approaching the three great guitarists who have visited us: Robledo, Sainz de la Maza and Rodríguez.

And whosoever shall say to the contrary does so by their own personal sympathy.

This is the program which the Paraguayan concert guitarist Agustín Barrios presented to the public on the evening of Thursday November 28, 1929 in the Theatro Municipal of this capital, Rio de Janeiro.

I
1. Serenata mourisica — Barrios
2. A Catedral — Barrios
   a) Andante religioso
   b) Allegro
3. Madrigal — Barrios
4. Capricho hespanhol — Barrios

II
—
5. Prelude — Bach
6. Loure — Bach
7. Ménueto — Beethoven
8. Tema variado — Mozart-Sor
9. Nocturno — Chopin

III
10. Sevilha — Albeniz
11. Souvenir d'un reve — Barrios
12. Harmonias de America — Barrios
13. Alvorada historica paraguaya — Barrios"

This concert review is from "*O Violao*" Issue No. 10 of November-December 1929.

Translation:

"The 2nd concert of maestro Agustín Barrios

We have already placed in another part of this magazine the impressions of the 1st concert by Barrios. Due to the fact that this issue covers two months, November and December, we went timely to his second concert, still we publish its result.

The artist said how he felt, and it was visible, he was unwell, fearing he couldn't ever successfully complete his program. So even he surprised us. Barrios was brilliant that evening, not only in his performance in which there was nothing left to desire, as well in the repertoire that he chose.

In some pieces, such as "*Leyenda*" by Albeniz and "*Canzonetta*" by Mendelssohn, it was mastery, impeccable. It is a shame that our people are disinterested in some guitar concerts, they kill the stimulus of the artists, who, such as Barrios, Rodríguez, Sainz de la Maza and others that make enormous sacrifices to bring their marvelous art to all corners is well a reward that at least is a relative comfort for one of them.

The program of the second concert of the guitarist Agustín Barrios:

I
Barrios:
1. La Samaritana
2. Menuet em si maior (B Major)
3. Valsa No. 3
4. Allegro brillhante

II

5. Schumann — Traumerei
6. Mendelssohn — Mazurka
7. Mendelssohn — Canzonetta
8. Turina — Fandanguillo
9. Albeniz — Legenda (Asturias-Leyenda)
10. Arcas — Grande fantasia em la (A major)

III

11. Barrios: O choro da saudade
12. Pagina de album
13. Contemplaçao
14. Jota Aragonesa"

From the *"A Voz do Violao"* magazine issue No. 3 of April 1931 is the column *"Os astros Brasileiros do Violao"* (The Brazilian Stars of the Guitar) Portuguese translation by Randy Osborne. In this issue is a biography of José Augusto de Freitas, the most successful of Agustín Barrios' Brazilian students.

Photos of José Augusto de Freitas from *"A Voz do Violao"* and a sheet music piece.

"José Augusto de Freitas is one of the major names in our guitaristic circles. And deservedly so, he has built this renown, deserved for his special taste and an impeccable technique.

He was born on February 20, 1909 in the city of Pomba, Brazil, he came to Rio at the age of only eight years old. Attracted by the guitar of an ascending love, from the first day in which, by the first time, he had the opportunity to hear and sense its marvelous chords, he began his studies alone, learning "by ear", and getting, without the aid of a maestro or method, to make the instrument interpret the sentiments that he thought were in his soul.

After arriving in Rio, however, he had the occasion to receive orientation by a maestro Joaquim dos Santos (Quincas Larangeiras).

They were the most beneficial lessons by the known professor.

José de Freitas, in just a little time, developed with resourcefulness, giving full expansion that he decided by inclining toward the guitar. In a few months as a disciple he satisfied the most difficult demands of his maestro.

José de Freitas then went on to take lessons from Agustín Barrios, the great South American guitarist, then completing his studies perfecting satisfactorily of his performance and of his good taste.

Today, Freitas, is a very distinguished professional, having performed countless times, always achieving the deserved applause of the public that never haggled.

— 'You're marvelous' — they say of him, — 'everyone is impressed, notably of the Rio de Janeiro audiences, with a profound knowledge of the guitar and whose generous applause in my recitals, it has served me to be the stimulus of continuing in the difficult career to which I have dedicated myself. And that generosity has been too much for me, all the times in which I have been presented.'

José de Freitas teaches the guitar. In his course, most frequently, the unquestionable proof of his ability and of his artistic proficiency.

His preferred genre is classical, that he performs with agility and interprets with taste.

Besides his activity as a professor, José de Freitas also has a good discography of repertoire.

And he confesses:

'Even today my discs have reached a very flattering success for me. I attribute that success to the guitar, and because it, — especially for us Brazilians — is the only instrument that can interpret or translate, with faithfulness, our sentiments and our passions.'

He has recorded for Fabrica Odeon (Odeon Rercords): and among those productions, can be cited as the most successful: "*O tempo passa*" (Fox-trot); "*E assim mesmo*" *(Choro)*; "*Lamento d'alma*" *(Choro); and* "*Solucos*" *(Valsa)*.

To one of our questions, about his thoughts in respect to music and the national composers, the known guitarist responded to us:

— "My colleagues are my best brothers; I am proud of all of them, in spite of feeling a great disunity in class . . ."

"A Voz do Violao"

Rico Stover said that he was to have met José de Freitas, but the guitarist died two days before that meeting was to have taken place.

This biography is from the *"Diccionario de Guitarristas"* by Domingo Prat.

José Augusto Freitas — Brazilian concert guitarist and professor of guitar. Born in the city of Pomba, Minas Geraes the 20th of February of 1909. at eight years of age he moved to Rio de Janeiro. By "ear" he learned his first notes; but soon he required a professor, Joaquín dos Santos (Quincas Larangeiras). The progress that Freitas made increased greatly, by which he decided to study with the known Paraguayan guitarist, Agustín Barrios, with whom, he achieved the form to become an able performer. In the Salon Fenix, in Rio de Janeiro, in the middle of the year 1930 he gave a concert that rightly drew the attention of the critics who said praiseworthy attributes. From this concert in Spain, in the magazine "Musica" published in Barcelona in its September issue of 1930, it was said to be one of the most important performances in Brazil. *"A Voz do Violao"* spoke of Freitas in its March (sic-April) issue of 1931, with an interesting article. By that we found out that he had recorded a disc of danceable music as in the same way the preferences that this guitarist has of the original composers of the guitar; those are Carlos García Tolsa, Tárrega, and especially, it says, to Agustín Barrios, the great South American guitarist.

By the preferences of one of the most known Brazilian guitarists it gives us thought with sorrow of which there is even a struggle in Brazil to make known the music of Sor, Carcassi, Coste, Legnani, Regondi and all the great composers of the golden century of the guitar."

On the left are *"Euridice" (Mazurka)* and *"Marlene" (Valsa)* the right is *"Soluços" (Valsa)* by José Augusto de Freitas and all were published by *A Guitarra de Prata* in Rio de Janeiro.
I want to thank my colleague, Ivan Paschoito, for providing the sheet music covers.

Rico Stover told me in 2012 that many years ago he once was set to have the opportunity to interview José Augusto de Freitas, but that the Barrios student died two days before they were to have met.

A contemporary of Agustín Barrios, born just five months later, was Juan Angel Rodríguez Vega. The biography from the *"Diccionario de Guitarristas"* by Domingo Prat follows:

"Juan Angel Rodríguez Vega — Concert Guitarist, Composer and Argentine Professor of Guitar. He was born in Lujan, Buenos Aires Province, the 2nd of October of 1885. He began his studies of music with maestro Carlos Auber, following those up with Juan Gutiérrez, founder of the Conservatorio Nacional; those of harmony, with Ricardo Michalowist. He studied guitar for eight years with Juan Alais. As a concert guitarist, he began his first tour of his country, where he experienced good success: the Centro Guitarristico de Cordoba awarded him with a Gold Medal. In 1927 he decided to perform in Uruguay, under the sponsorship of the President of the Republic, Dr. Juan Campistegui, initiating an artistic tour of the whole nation. In March of 1929 he performed in Brazil, in the cities of Porto Alegre, Santos, Sao Paulo and Rio de Janeiro, with an unquestionable success the greatest he had obtained until that time. The journalistic critics, especially in the guitar magazines: *"O Violao"* and *"A Voz do Violao"*, both of Rio, they consecrated him as the best virtuoso (virtuoso maximo), for his abilities of technique, brilliance, sonority and emotion. The cited magazines published some of hisoriginal compositions and they were received with undeniable value that promoted the personality of the composer. Some are of the classical style, the ultimate folkloric Argentine and Brazilian, the most outstanding are: *"Gota de Agua"* *(Chacarera Jujeña); "Coral del Norte" (Zamba); "Gato Cordobes"; "Herodiades" (Chacarera Jujeña);* etc. published in Buenos Aires. The day before a performance he would announce in Rio de Janeiro, he was surprised by a great ailment in which his left arm was in danger. Luckily, it was answered, and he resided in Bello Horizonte, he was anxious to begin an artistic tour of Europe. In Brazil he conquered an enviable notoriety, shown by the number of students that he counts on having dedicated himself to teaching. Among those we recall the names of: Julieta Mendes, Ophisia Pareto, Carneiro Santiago, Inah de Mello Campos, B. Dantas de Souza Pombo, Juan Pereira Filho (Jr.), Dr. Cristovao Santos, Xavier Bruno, Dr. Armando Werneck, Francisco Guimaraes, José Arry, Lauro Lima and Carlos Sixto."

These details are translated from Ricardo Muñoz's unpublished books *"Historia Universal de la Guitarra"* Volume VI *"America"* and Volume VII *"La Guitarra en La Argentina"*.

"Juan A. Rodríguez is the owner of the beautiful archive of maestro Ricardo Maria Porcel (Born in Mexico City in 1853 — died in Bogota, Colombia in 1899). He published, through Antigua Casa Nuñez, several works of the late maestro: *"Preludio" en re menor, "Crepusculo" vals de salon, "Hilanderas" serenata, aire popular, "Las Violetas" andante, "Bouquet de Salon" mazurka, "Silencio de las Horas" estudio,"Estudio"* by Schumann, *"Polka"*, etc.

Juan Rodríguez, much like Agustín Barrios, went to Brazil and performed his own compositions, and had an enormous success. The magazines published in Sao Paulo: *"O Violao"* and *"A Voz do Violao"* documented his activities to a great degree. The magazines are from the collection of the late Ronoel Simões (1919-2010), and thanks to his colleague, Ivan Paschoito, the information can be included here. Portuguese translation by Randy Osborne.

JUAN RODRIGUEZ

Em outro logar publicamos a musica que o grande concertista portenho nos dedicou.

Por ella se verifica a competencia desse virtuose que, brevemente vem dar uma serie de concertos nesta cidade.

No proximo numero publicaremos tambem um minuetto de sua lavra, que elle gentilmente dedicou á juventude estudiosa do violão no Rio de Janeiro.

This photo from the magazine *"O Violao"* issue No. 5 of April of 1929 translates to:

"In another section we publish the music of this great Rio de la Plata concert guitarist dedicated to us. By that it verifies the competence of this virtuoso who, we will see give a series of concerts in this city shortly. In the next issue we will also publish a minuet of his labor, kindly dedicated to the studious youth of Rio de Janeiro."

Handwritten dedication by the guitarist: "A greeting from an Argentine artist to the precious magazine *"O Violao"*, Sao Paulo, April 8, 1929 Juan A. Rodríguez."

The page before this carried the piece *"Juego de Cuerdas-Estudio Matinal"* by Juan A. Rodríguez.

In the May-June 1929 issue No. 6 of "*O Violao*" was the coverage of a Juan Rodríguez concert.

O professor Juan Rodriguez, na noite de seu concerto no Instituto Nacional de Musica, "posando" especialmente para a revista "O Violão", entre pessoas que o foram cumprimentar. Da direita para a esquerda: Drs. Eustachio Alves, Jayme Tavora, José Vianna, Homero Alvares, Dantas de Souza Pombo e o Sr. Cortez, proprietario da conhecida casa de violões "Cavaquinho de Ouro".

Translation of the text: "The Professor Juan Rodríguez on the night of his concert at the Instituto Nacional de Musica, "posing" especially for the magazine "*O Violao*", among the persons that were present. Right to Left: Drs. Eustachio Alves, Jayme Tavora, José Vianna, Homero Alvarez, B. Dantas de Souza Pombo and Mr. Cortez, owner of the known guitar store "*Cavaquinho de Ouro*".

It should be noted that B. Dantas de Souza Pombo was the director of the magazine "*O Violao*". In Prat's entry in his "*Diccionario*" he is listed as a student of Juan Rodríguez.

In this issue the piece "*Ronda Paulista*" by Juan A. Rodríguez was included.

650

O concerto de violão do grande artista sul-americano Juan A. Rodriguez

Aspecto da assistencia que calorosamente applaudiu o insigne "virtuose", no dia de sua estréa no Instituto Nacional de Musica.

Translation of the text: "The Guitar Concert of the great South-American artist Juan A. Rodríguez."

"Aspect of the attendants warmly applauding the notable "virtuoso", on the day of his debut in the Instituto Nacional de Musica."

Segundo concerto de Juan Rodríguez a realizar-se em 10 de Julho, ás 21 horas, no Instituto de Musica

PROGRAMMA:

PRIMEIRA PARTE

1 — Preludio, op 1 (A), Handel — Porcel;
Preludio, N. 20 (B), Chopin — Tarrega.
2 — Andante, Mozart — Tarrega.
3 — Cantabile, Cetri — Porcel.
4 — Largo, Sors — (1778-1839).
5 — Estudio Brillante, Savio.

SEGUNDA PARTE

(*Dansas Sul Americanas*)
2 — Coral del Norte, (Chilena numero 1 op 29) — Rodriguez.
3 — Minuetto Federal (Época de Rosas 1880) — Rodriguez.

1 — Pericón, (Thema G. Variações op 50) Alais — Rodriguez.
5 — Gran Zapateado, Argentino, — Boliviano op 38) — Rodriguez.
4 — Chôro, op 96, J. dos Santos — Rodriguez.

TERCEIRA PARTE

1 — Allegretto, op 8, Verdier — Porcel.
2 — Divertissement, op 6, Porcel.
3 — Coral, Handel — Tarrega.
4 — Andante Variado, op 63 — Rodriguez.
5 — Flauta — Encantada, (Variações), (A pedido), Mozart — Sors.

Translation of the text: "The Second Concert of Juan Rodríguez to take place on July 10, 1929 at 9PM in the Instituto Nacional de Musica."

Of the pieces that Juan Rodríguez plays here, there are four from the Ricardo Maria Porcel archive, one being a transcription of Handel's *Preludio, op. 1*. There are two Tárrega pieces, one by Isaias Savio, two by Fernando Sor, the closing piece The Magic Flute, and five by the performer.

In the October 1929 issue No. 9 of the magazine "*O Violao*" another concert held in the Theatro Trianon in Sao Paulo on October 15, 1929 by Juan Rodríguez was listed:

First Part:
1-Preludio, op. 1 (A) Handel — Porcel
2-Andante-Haydn — Tárrega
3-Andantino — F. Sor
4-Capricho Arabe (Serenata) Tárrega

Second Part:
Dansas nativas Sul Americanas, harmoisadas por A. Rodríguez
1-Coral del Norte-Chilena N. 3 — Rodríguez
2-Chacarera-Regional argentina — Rodríguez
3-Danza nativa-Uruguay (Estylo) — Rodríguez
4-Tango Brasilero- (O. Dutra) — Rodríguez

Third Part:
1-Grande valsa concerto (Crepusculo) R. M. Porcel
2-Caixinha de musica-Op. 5 — Porcel
3-Baile das Odaliscas (Fragmento arabe) — Porcel
4-Theme e variaçoes-(Mozart) — F. Sor

In the May-June 1929 issue of *"O Violao"* was an article titled: "Juan Rodríguez and Sainz de la Maza — The World's Guitarists-Impressions of who listens and the artistic reality."

The part about Sainz de la Maza will be included in his biographical section-with some very surpising details. Now to our subject at hand translated from Portuguese by Randy Osborne.

"Exactly on the same occasion we were visited by Juan A. Rodríguez who arrived here without any renown, modestly, scarcely with a recommendation of his artistic past, full of eventful journeys, some tragic and others comic.

Without being concerned with another cause than his pure and simple art Rodríguez, the first contact appears by the detached form that two hypotheses forces us to formulate: this man is a great artist or a paltry guitar player.

But conjecture soon disappears, in the first place because he possesses exceptional qualities of an educated man and possesses the secret to become the master of others friendship.

He speaks with such frankness and shows as simple that simplicity attains the root of humility.

Then he tells us how he began his career.

He took a musical course in the Conservatorio Nacional de Buenos Aires and began his first steps with the guitar with the late Juan Alais whose memory he extols and venerates.

He feels the goodness of a man. As for other artists who boast of having had no master, he is not one who was a world celebrity, but had the merit to teach him what he knew.

And continuing Rodríguez tells us what his artistic aim during the years that stroked his dreams to create.

From a certain time to this part, and that, from 1909 until now, the maestros of the guitar kept repeating the same programs of the majority bound by Tárrega.

Studying the fundamental harmony outlined the plan to modify all, firming the purpose of writing in an elevated style of regional Argentine music, making new authors of classical character known.

He spoke about the joy of possessing the music of the Mexican genius — Ricardo Maria Porcel, whose compositions show an uncommon value.

With the old repertoire, more of this author and his competence, instead of playing in the capital of the Rio de la Plata, he went to the interior of the nation, initiating his tour there as a two-fold purpose to display and acquire the themes of compositions that characterize him as a eminent composer.

He was very happy, today he has close to two hundred pages of mastery, in which advocates the development of the technique of the instrument at the same time that it presents the plentitude of its efficiency showing us a new horizon in which it makes one feel inspired.

How many ailments, how many troubles did Rodríguez experience?

A great many, therefore he did not presume the success before it he fondly recalls problems and proceeded on the route drawn beforehand. So, in little time where the field is restricted to performing it became the drive of his spirit.

From there the idea to expand his tour to South America, in the end to collect the regional themes of various lands.

Fleeing the exhibitions without other character without the funds, he went to Uruguay, where he met Savio, one of the new guitarist revelations of the continent.

The author inspired him to produce pages of gold that will immortalize them.

From the Republic Oriental of Uruguay Rodríguez came into our country, entering in the state of Rio Grande do Sul, where he gave several recitals.

From there he moved to Sao Paulo, after his concerts in the Capital and various cities of the interior, then he came to Rio.

Here he had debuted in the Instituto Nacional de Musica with great artistic success.

* * *

Having done his history and description of his personality we now move to analyze the artist.

Juan Rodríguez, is at the same time a performer and composer and under these aspects he can be considered a creative genius.

As a performer he leaves nothing to be desired because he possesses all the great predicates, — distinctness, technique, clarity, sound and color.

Having made a conscious study of the instrument, he dominates it completely, elevating to the highest level of perfection.

From there in a brilliant manner with which he performs the most difficult pieces expressively as they print. His characteristic is to be expressive.

The Guitar in the hands of Rodríguez is divine.

As a composer, he seems to us further, since his works contain what is the most elevated in music.

Conscientious, he doesn't sacrifice to conviction and to the music to obtain an effect.

All that he does is admirable.

Thus, facing him under the two aspects, we are certain that Rodríguez, within a short time, will be recognized as a glory of South America. In fact, he is the guitar to which he owes an effort worthy of men of genius.

Sor marked an epoch; Tárrega another and Rodríguez is the milestone that will pass forever to conquer the Guitar in our days."

In the August - September 1929 issue No. 8 of *"O Violao"* magazine was an article: "Juan A. Rodríguez." Translated from Portuguese:

"Beautiful was a palace of Ipanema that we met the Professor Juan A. Rodríguez in: heavy set, corpulent, with a grin in full face and look lost in the distance; he brought a dark case that he opened carefully, a guitar case.

'The Mr. Rodríguez, the laureled guitarist of the Conservatorio de Buenos Aires, ex-student of Professor Juan Alais.' And a presentation was made.

The man, in diffused light in the room, appeared in the gloom and soon, in which he stood out, his hands were elastic, alive, personalized.

He has the mysterious hands of an artist, a strange vibration and the most intense expression.

The first chords smote the religious silence. . . . and the silence transformed into a harmonious singer!

Rodríguez, he struck the fingers on stretched chords, in masterful polyphony by his performance, he draws scenes, sculptures feelings, now in packed measures, sometimes the guitar cries tears, makes guffaws and groans.

In *"Vagalume"* we see the fireflies enter in the enormous house and, once in a while, in indecision zigzagging flight, making the phosphorescence of their body brilliant, as a point of light damaging the darkness!

Children twirling, happy, wandering, screaming, butterflying, the tense chords vibrate, to play *"O Recreio"*, children in the sunlight, in the grace of innocence, in lightness of childish laughter. . . .

Argentina, Chile, Uruguay, Bolivia live and throb in the compositions of the great performer which, the soul not only the works of others, but also, with the productiveness of admirable inspiration, almost three hundred of his pages, hot and alive already crystalline on the staff. He stylized our popular music, and harmonized this for the guitar, the tangos by Ernesto Nazareth; he will include this music in the programs of his upcoming performances in Europe.

We feel when the hands of the Argentine professor stopped, since the hands of Rodríguez, over the guitar, appear as a magic spider weaving fast, with the thread of inspiration, the plot of the capricious web of harmony, the wide open door of the magnificent temple of the illusion of sound!

Rio — August 1929. Cesar Avila"

O ULTIMO RECITAL DO PROF JUAN RODRIGUEZ NO INSTITUTO NACIONAL DE MUSICA

O Prof. Juan A. Rodriguez na noite do seu 3º e ultimo recital, no Instituto Nacional de Musica entre senhoritas de nossa sociedade que lhe foram levar suas felicitações após á audição.

This photo is from the August - September 1929 issue No. 8 of *"O Violao"* magazine.

Translation of the captions:

"The last recital by Professor Juan A. Rodríguez in the Instituto Nacional de Musica."

"The Professor Juan A. Rodríguez on the night of his 3rd and last recital in the Instituto Nacional de Musica among the ladies of our society that were to congratulate him after the performance."

The *"O Violao"* magazine lasted for 10 issues from December 1928 to November-December 1929.

In the October 1929 issue No. 9 of the magazine *"O Violao"* the piece *"Choro Poesia-Danza nativa-Brazileira- Alcantara-*by Juan A. Rodríguez was included.

The *"A Voz do Violao"* magazine (The Voice of the Guitar) lasted for 3 issues from February 1931 to April 1931. In the issue No. 1 of February 1931 there was an update on the enormous success Juan A. Rodríguez was experiencing. The column was entitled: *"Concertistas extrangeiros"* (Foreign Concert Guitarists) Translation:

"Juan A. Rodríguez

For some years now from Buenos Aires, on tour, Juan A. Rodríguez integrated in such a form into the artistic ambiance of our country, now here until today.

Born in Lujan (Buenos Aires Province), he felt awaken as a child, the attraction to the guitar, having as his first orientator and Argentine maestro, Juan Alais.

Later he completed his studies with Juan Gutiérrez and Ricardo Michalowitz.

A professional of value, a concert guitarist and South American composer, extensive and the number of works (almost four hundred) inspired in all the musical rhythms.

A possessor, besides, of a culture above the common class, he unites with a high spirit, to a journalist that or in an interview, after a special performance to the chroniclers, in Buenos Aires, the impressions that he had of contact with the public.

"The public stage has its secret, that it isn't for everyone. . . ."

The disciples Ophisia Pareto, Joao Pereira Jr., Julieta Mendes, attest to the excellence of his method of teaching.

Juan Rodríguez thus meets his impartial desire of "taking the art to all ambiances of the world!"

When he recorded his pieces on discs for the company Columbia, of Buenos Aires — then in 1927, — he achieved such as the same success an enviable triumph: he received a Gold Medal, in Cordoba and a Diploma of Honor in Uruguay.

Juan Rodríguez affirms that the guitar is a great instrument of the future.

The Brazilian music, which he thinks is the most beautiful, by its varied music themes, enchanting and inspired for typical appreciable compositions, such as *"Choro Villa-Lobos"*, the *"Choros"* by Dutra and Joaquim dos Santos, and *"Canarinho"*.

His preferences that he enjoys are works by Ernesto Nazareth, Octaviano and Heckel Tavares.

For Juan Rodríguez the teaching of the guitar only depends on the subtlety of the spirit of the professor to discover the true mode of sentiment of the disciple, to go down the right track by the true feeling of his artistic temperament. This is the only method or school, that the brilliant Argentine composer recommends to his students: "to put the intelligence into play, covering the useful, and discarding the useless."

Juan Rodríguez, to whom we have the honor to include among our collaborators, assiduous, promised us for our pages of *VOZ DO VIOLAO*, the notes of his best composition."

This article was preceded by *"Rayos de Luar" Estudio Op. 97* by Juan Rodríguez. The photo that accompanied the article was the same as used in the April of 1929 issue No. 5 of *"O Violao"*.

In issue No. 2 of *"A Voz do Violao"* magazine from March 1931 there is the listing of a concert program by Juan A. Rodríguez.

"O proximo concerto de Juan A. Rodríguez (The next concert of Juan A. Rodríguez)

On Friday April 10, the professor and concert guitarist Juan A. Rodríguez will give his last recital in this capital, since that he is going to begin an artistic tour of the States of Brazil, and later, possibly to Europe.

The Professor Rodríguez, to whom the lovers of the guitar owe so much and our illustrious collaborator, of excessive kindness to make his recital under the sponsorship of the *"A VOZ DO VIOLAO"*, to take place in the noble hall of the Instituto Nacional de Musica, on that day at 9PM.

It's enough to name the eminent Argentine concert guitarist, by guarantee of success, still we have the playing by his distinguished student Joao Pereira Jr.

It will be this program, that must be attended by those we dedicate to the guitar, such a variety and carefully chosen:

First Part:

1. Minuet No. 1 — Rodríguez
2. Minuet No. 2 — Rodríguez
3. Andante en Ré menor — Rodríguez
4. El Recreio-Andante gracioso — Rodríguez
5. Sonata No. 2-Adagio presto — Sustenido

Second Part:

1. Preludio sobre las campanelas — Rodríguez
2. Bichito de Luz-Estudio — Rodríguez
3. Estudio de Interpretacion — Rodríguez
4. Romantica-Mazurka — Rodríguez
5. Suite em Mi menor — Rodríguez

Third Part:

1. Lagrima (Tárrega) — Joao Pereira Jr.
2. Estylo popular (Uruguay)-Baco — Rodríguez
3. Evocando-Estudio — Rodríguez
4. Chacarera regional — Rodríguez
5. Chilena No. 5 (Flor de Aroma) — Rodríguez
6. Choro (Dansa typica brasileira) — Rodríguez
7. Gato Regional–G. Carrillo — Rodríguez

The tickets to enter are from now on sale, at the principal houses of music and our editor's office, that attends to your requests, by the telephone number 2-0433."

The three issues of *"A Voz do Violao"* magazine, were produced by F. Acquarone, S. Leal and B. Polazzi with many of their collaborators.

In the 1931 Antigua Casa Nuñez catalog there are 4 pieces by Juan A. Rodríguez.

This Juan A. Rodríguez piece *"Gota de Agua"* is the 1st song of 4 listed in the 1930s Antigua Casa Nuñez catalog, and dates from after 1927, as on the cover it mentions his artistic tours of Argentina and Uruguay.

Archive: José Augusto Marcellino

MUSICAS PARA VIOLÃO

Caminho Solitario - Valsa . . . . 3$000 Prof. José Augusto de Freitas.	**Flor de Aroma** . . . . 3$000 Juan A. Rodrigues
Euridice - Mazurka de Concerto . . . . 3$000 Prof. José Augusto de Freitas.	**Tempo de Gavota** . . . . } 3$000 **Estreia** - Valsa . . . . } A. Lyra
Marlene - Valsa . . . . 3$000 Prof. José Augusto de Freitas.	**Chorinho** . . . . } 3$000 **Sonhando** - Valsa . . . . } A. Lyra
Soluços - Valsa . . . . 3$000 Prof. José Augusto de Freitas.	**Annency** - Valsa . . . . 3$000 Gustavo Ribeiro
Valsa Chopin - Op. 34 n.º 2 . . . . . 3$000 Q. Báez-Alende	**Sonho Gaucho** - Tango . . . . 3$000 Gustavo Ribeiro
Valsa Chopin - Op. 69 n.º 2 . . . . . 3$000 Q. Báez-Alende	**Caixinha de Musica** . . . . } 3$000 **Dansa Infantil** . . . . } Othon Salleiro
Valsa Chopin - Op. 64 n.º 2 . . . . . 3$000 Q. Báez-Alende	**Bon Jour, Papa** . . . . 3$000 A. Baltar
Preludio . . . . 3$000 J. S. Bach e Q. Báez-Alende	**Sons de Carrilhões** - Maxixe - Cho- ro para violão . . . . 3$000 João Teixeira Guimarães (João Pernambuco)
La Despedida (Chilena-Estilisada) . . . 3$000 Juan A. Rodrigues	**Grajahú** - Choro . . . . 3$000 Dilermando Reis
Noites de Insonia (Preludio) . . } **Minueto Antiguo** (Erman Weizel) } 3$000 Juan A. Rodrigues	**Yá** - Valsa . . . . 3$000 Dilermando Reis
Gavota (da 5.a Suite Franceza) . . . . 3$000 Bach e Juan A. Rodrigues	**Leyenda Guarany** . . . . 3$500 Q. Báez-Alende
Ange d'amour - (Berceuse infantil) . . . 3$000 Juan A. Rodrigues	**Clair de Luna** (Adagio da Sonata de Beethoven) . . . . 3$500 Q. Báez-Alende
Pagina de Album . . . . } **Mazurka** (Estudo) . . . . } 3$000 Juan A. Rodrigues	**Album dos principiantes** (4 musicas faceis) . . . . 3$500 Prof. José Augusto de Freitas

EDITORA:

A GUITARRA DE PRATA
Porfirio Martins & Cia.
Rua da Caroca, 37
Tel. 22-5721 — Rio de Janeiro

Juan A. Rodríguez had 8 pieces in 6 publications available in Brazil with the Porfirio Martins and Co. — *A Guitarra de Prata* publishing company in the 1930's. This list is from the back page of *"Confidencia"* — *Serenata* by Professor Antonio Rebello. Of note are the pieces by Quirino Baez-Allende, Joao Pernambuco and José Augusto de Freitas-an Agustín Barrios student.

Archive: José Augusto Marcellino

660

Surely, as maestro Lucio Nuñez had affirmed in his article previously mentioned, the work of Barrios that may have passed inadvertently by certain circles, it must have been in those moments in Buenos Aires, cosmopolitan city, when it was predominated by the European guitar school: Sor, Aguado, Tárrega, Carulli, etc., and he appeared in the Argentine environment with a different style, personal, and with a message even unknown at that time. It can be affirmed that Barrios had to struggle against the obstacles that presented themselves to the precursor in whatever part of the world, who was indeed ahead of his time.

And what he did, with his merits, could not transcend the environment in Europe, understood due to that his international career was conditioned by the two European wars of the 20th century, that they permanently impeded in the nations, the sufficient time to exhibit his ability as an artist and creator. Although, he received favorable critique of prestigious musicians on the European continent, as is in the case of Gino Marinuzzi, the great director of the Palermo Orchestra, in Italy.

We return to the first few decades of the 20th century in Argentina, to view all that occurred within guitaristic matters in this part of South America.

In 1918 another disciple of Francisco Tárrega, Emilio Pujol arrived for the first time in Buenos Aires, invited by amateur guitarist José Maria Escalante, and Emilio returned again in 1930, this time brought by writer Luis Cordero. He performed concerts and in his last visit he gave a lecture on the guitar, as well as solo and duo concerts with his wife, Flamenco guitarist, Matilde Cuervas.

Emilio Pujol and his wife, Matilde Cuervas with their guitars made by Antonio de Torres.

In Buenos Aires, by that time the *"Casa José B. Romero e hijos"* had edited a method by Pujol titled: *"Escuela Razonada de la Guitarra"*. This publishing house also published in 1910 the album *"Escalas y Arpegios"* and in 1929 *"La Nueva Tecnica"*, both works by Domingo Prat, and the *"10 Estudios Varios"* should be added, as well by this Catalan maestro.

With this we see the intense guitar activity that took place in those decades in South America.

GUITARISTS ROUND TABLE

CONDUCTED BY
ETHEL LUCRETIA OLCOTT
Soloist—Teacher—Composer

"The guitar is a miniature orchestra in itself."—Beethoven.

This department is especially for Guitarists but anyone may ask questions pertaining to the guitar or contribute items. Questions or suggestions will receive due consideration. Address "Guitarists Round Table," care of The Crescendo.

London Guitar Recital

On December 14th, 1912, at Bechstein Hall in London, Senor Pujol gave a guitar recital. Senor Pujol is a pupil of the late Francisco Tarrega, and his home is in Barcelona, Spain. His program contained several numbers composed originally for guitar by his teacher, also transcriptions of Bach and Schumann numbers. The following is a comment from The Daily Telegraph.—"The guitar is an instrument one associates principally with serenades and sentiment under southern skies with the moon somewhere about. But that is only because one is ignorant of the possibilities to say nothing of the history of the guitar. For our part, let us frankly confess that until Saturday we did not know it was possible to play a Bach fugue on that instrument. Somebody, an Italian composer, we fancy, once wrote for it a concerto, and Hummel rescued that work for a time from oblivion by rewriting the solo part for the piano. But more often, for obvious reasons, it is the other way about, and in a programme of a guitar recital one naturally expects to find transcriptions. So it was at the recital given on Saturday afternoon, Dec. 14th by Mr. Emilio Pujol. This artist it was—and a most accomplished artist he proved himself—who introduced us to the unsuspected possibilities of the guitar already alluded to, and played on it not only the Bach fugue which has been mentioned, but a Gavotte as well from one of that composer's suites. Schumann's pretty Berceuse with some guitar embroideries and one of the most familiar of Schubert's "Moments Musicals" were also in the scheme, these and the other transcriptions being by Tarrega, who was himself a distinguished guitarist. Mr. Pujol, whose playing of these, as well as of some original compositions from the same pen, showed his possession of a really refined musical temperament, almost made one regret that the great composers failed to discern the possibilities of the guitar in the hands of a skilled and sensitive artist. Incidentally some pianoforte solos were contributed by Count Charles de Souza. But we are bound to confess that we derived far more pleasure from our joyous adventure in the company of Mr. Pujol." Dallas' Musical Monthly says "Senor Pujol is of the opinion that many of the classics are rendered to infinitely greater advantage and with finer musical interpretation on the guitar than on the violin, mentioning in particular the Gavotte and Fugue by Bach which he played at his recital. His opinion is that guitar players are not fed with music of sufficient artistic importance to retain their enthusiasm. His object in coming to England is firstly to endeavor to obtain a greater respect for the guitar from the highest musical authorities here in the same way as it has been accomplished in Spain, viz., that with many of the classics, a more musicianly rendering can be obtained on the guitar than any other instrument. He wants the guitar

to become **necessary** to musicians. When it is considered that a number of the old masters composed the majority of their immortal works on the guitar, possibly from lack of means to purchase the extremely expensive prehistoric forms of pianoforte, it can well be appreciated that the fact of their composition making a most musicianly adaption to the guitar is in no way a phenomena."

Senor Pujol has played before the King of Spain and his aunt, the Infanta Isabella, and was presented with an autograph, on which was inscribed the appreciations of the King who is enthusiastic in upholding the instrument of his people.

D. B.

This Emilio Pujol London recital review is from an April 1913 Crescendo magazine, Vol. V No. 10. He performed for the Spanish royalty at least four years before Andrés Segovia did.

EMILIO PUJOL

A sketch done in 1926 of Emilio Pujol by Samuel Mallo Lopez.

This sketch was published by Juan Carlos Anido in *La Guitarra* magazine issue No. 4 of February 1926.

"Emilio Pujol was born in Granadella, Lerida Province, Spain on April 7, 1886. Since he was a youngster he studied solfeggio and bandurria. With this instrument he formed a part of an *estudiantina*, that went to Paris with the motive of performing in the Exposition of 1900 and distinguishing themselves greatly, as a soloist, he drew the attention of the President of the French Republic, Emilio Loubet, from whom he received effusive congratulations. A few years later Emilio Pujol heard Tárrega privately, and was impressed by the art of the maestro, he abandoned the bandurria to dedicate himself to the guitar under the direction of the Villareal artist. Pujol is an artist of fine sensibility and careful execution, but in his long artistic career, yes, it is certain that he conquered success and deserves the goodwill of the critics, he never gave the sensation to dominate with ease and facility the difficult instrument. He doesn't know in what measure the presence of the public has influenced his execution; but it's evident that this influence is great in whom has the capacity to offer very interesting private auditions. He has been, by this circumstance and in spite of his delicate temperament, a discussed guitarist.

Personally, endowed with congeniality, Emilio Pujol is one learned guitarist. He has written diverse articles and the thesis *"La Guitarra"* in the *"Encyclopédie de la Musique"*, 2nd part pages 1997-2035. Apart from his transcriptions, he is an author of original works. The most spontaneous, correct, delicate and guitaristic of them is his *"Cancion de Cuna"*.

He gave concerts in various cities of Europe. He was invited by the amateurs: the engineer José Maria Escalante Echagüe and the writer Luis Cordero, he came twice to Buenos Aires: in 1918 and in 1930. In this last visit he gave a lecture about the guitar and offered personal performances and with two guitars in collaboration of the guitarist, in the genre *"Flamenco"*, Matilde Cuervas, his wife.

Presently he can be found in the procedure of publishing the work by Emilio Pujol *"Escuela Razonada de la Guitarra"*, that is published by the intervention of the house of José B. Romero e hijos. (and sons), Buenos Aires. This *Escuela Razonada* consists of five parts. Considering its author, we can assure that the work brings a contribution of merit and utility for our instrument. The guitarists will be congratulated, since the piano, instrument well diffused, has an enormous quantity of didactic compositions, something we can't say in respect to the guitar to that which still lacks works of this class. This production, as all those that might appear later with fine didactics, will be very necessary for the guitar; since knowledge is that impossible consequence and besides ineffectual, as we recommend in our program of studies, the teaching and the learning not only of the guitar, but of any other instrument, with a "complete method" only.

We will be the greatest enthusiasts and admirers of this work of Pujol, already that in the year 1910 we lent our contribution for the teaching of the instrument to which we dedicated with the album of *"Escalas y Arpegios"*, and in the year 1929 with *"La Nueva Tecnica"*, with the publisher *José B. Romero e hijos,* Buenos Aires; and with the same house *"10 estudios varios"."* So ends the entry in Domingo Prat's *Diccionario de Guitarristas*.

Emilio Pujol died in Barcelona on November 15, 1980.

(Above) *"La Guitarra y su Historia"*
This lecture given on November 3, 1930, was published in 1934 by Romero & Fernández . Julio J. Otermin and others are mentioned in this work.

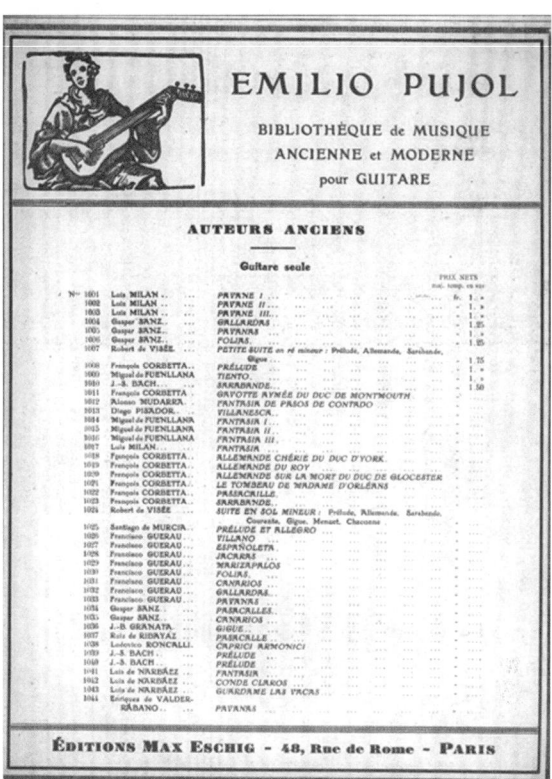

Pieces by Emilio Pujol published by:
Tárrega student, Daniel Fortea in
Madrid in 1915.

Editions Max Eschig in Paris in 1928
44 transcriptions listed

By B. Schott Sohne
in Maine and Leipzig, Germany

Images on this page: Archive: J. Augusto Marcellino

By Romero & Fernández in 1936
in Buenos Aires

" PAVANE."

(Guitar Solo in this issue.)

THE guitar solo " Pavane " is included in our music supplement this month by kind permission of the owners of the copyright, Editions Max Eschig, of 1, Rue de Madrid, Paris, who publish a very excellent catalogue of music.

The following article which describes the solo is by Mr. E. L. Giordan, of Nottingham.—EDITOR.

The guitar solo printed in this issue, with its simple and quaint melody, straightforward style, and well-marked rhythm, seems to belong to the same class of compositions as the old English dances, and ballads, such as some of those embodied in the " Beggar's Opera."

It was taken from a music-book for the " Vihuela," published in 1535 by the famous Spanish vihuellist Luis Milan, and it is the oldest of its kind. The vihuela, a Spanish musical instrument not unlike the guitar, which supplanted it, was at the height of its popularity during the greater part of the 16th century. Its music was written, not in staff notation, but in a peculiar system known as tablature. This system of writing music was also used for the guitar until the 18th century. The modern guitar—as alluded to in " Grove's Dictionary of Music," seems to be particularly well-fitted for transcriptions from the vihuela. It requires, of course, not only a considerable amount of tact and ingenuity, together with exact erudition to interpret and reproduce the meaning of the writers, often imperfectly or very laconically expressed, but also a thorough knowledge of the technique of both instruments.

These qualifications are possessed in a high degree by Senor Emilio Pujol— an accomplished scholar and a great artist—who has undertaken the editorship of a collection of ancient and modern music for the guitar, of which this solo is the first.

The editor could not have chosen a more appropriate number to begin his educational and graded series. In its modern setting and adaptation to the guitar, taking into account the advance made in technique, it remains simple, and yet neither childish nor commonplace ; its style is good all through, and contains nothing that might catch one's fancy at first sight, but soon satiate. Its easy key, chords and few runs are such as can be tackled by a learner of average attainment, and yet appeal to the classical taste of more advanced students. Senor E. Pujol himself does not disdain to play it at his recitals, and with excellent effect, too.

" Pavane " has been carefully marked ; and having no unusual chords or awkward positions, it is unnecessary to give any but general hints.

The Pavan was a slow, stately dance, " a peacock strut," as its name seems to imply ; " the passy-measures pavin " of the *Twelfth Night*—interpreted sometime as " the pacy-measures pavan "—*i.e.,* " the walking-step dance." The present solo played slowly but with plenty of movement, will be a pleasant change from the ordinary music. Need I add that the production of a clear, full, round tone is essential to a true interpretation of its simple beauty ?

This review of a Luis Milan *Pavane* that has been transcribed by Emilio Pujol to guitar notation is from the June 1929 B. M. G. magazine.

(Right) Biography of Francisco Tárrega by Emilio Pujol published in 1960.

EMILIO PUJOL DIO AYER SU PRIMERA AUDICION DE GUITARRA, CON EXITO

Al selecto núcleo de concertistas españoles de guitarra que nos han visitado: Llobet, Segovia y Sáinz de la Maza, debe agregarse hoy uno nuevo: Emilio Pujol, que anoche se presentó, después de más de diez años de ausencia, en la sala de la Wagneriana.

Desde aquella fecha, Pujol ha realizado grandes progresos como artista y como instrumentista: su musicalidad se ha afinado y ha adquirido una personalidad cautivadora; ya es el intérprete consciente que ha sabido compenetrarse de los más ínfimos secretos de las obras, en cuanto a estilo, espíritu de época y expresividad; y el ejecutante que, dominando el instrumento, puede consagrarse de lleno a expresar lo que cada obra le sugiere.

Emilio Pujol es también un erudito musicólogo. La guitarra, desde que ha conquistado en la sala de audición un puesto de primera fila, necesitaba algo más que instrumentistas, lo único que poseyó durante largo lapso, pues cuando un instrumento se incorpora al movimiento artístico, no es posible que quienes lo pulsan no posean una vasta cultura general y conozcan a fondo los recursos y la historia de su medio de expresión.

Este artista español ha consagrado parte de su vida a esos trabajos que vienen a favorecer a todos; ha visitado archivos, estudiado manuscritos y descubierto obras que dormitaban olvidadas en bibliotecas y capillas, lo que le valió que se le pidiera colaborar en una de las obras más completas y más importantes de hoy: "La enciclopedia de la música y Diccionario del conservatorio", fundada por Albert Lavignac, y que actualmente, dirige Lionel de la Laurencie, para la cual Pujol escribió el estudio más serio y concienzudo que exista sobre los orígenes y la literatura de la guitarra.

No es raro, pues, que anoche Emilio Pujol, en obras clásicas, haya logrado interpretaciones tan finamente musicales; dijo con elegancia la "Pavana" del compositor español Luis de Milán, que vivió en el siglo XVI, y la "Gavota favorita del duque de Monmouth", de Corbetta, y con el más puro de los estilos "Alemana y Zarabanda" de R. de Visée, todas ellas trascriptas de la tablatura antigua por el concertista; y en "Minué y Allegro" de Sor y en "Borrega" de Bach, logró también ejecuciones cuidadas y nobles.

De obras españolas modernas, Emilio Pujol dió también versiones muy personales y llenas de vida y de vigor rítmico: así, el "Fandanguillo", de Moreno Torroba, la "Danza española", de Granados y "Serenata española", de Malats, adquirieron todo su castizo españolismo rítmico y expresivo, y el delicado "Dolor", preludio vasco de Fray San Sebastián, conocido aquí en su versión pianística y en la orquestal, encontró en Pujol un intérprete que supo traducir su suave y supraterrenal sentimiento doloroso.

En la tercera parte escuchamos "Vidala", del compositor uruguayo Alfonso Broqua, que, inspirándose en la espiritualidad de la música quichua, ha escrito una página característica y de bello sentimiento; "Chorinho", de Héctor Villa-Lobos, el genial compositor brasileño, obra en la que se afirma una personalidad vigorosa y un americanismo de alto vuelo; "Homenaje a Debussy", de Manuel de Falla, y dos obras de Pujol: "Tonadilla" y "Sevilla", en las que el artista español explaya la exquisita musicalidad arriba elogiada y, un sentido muy nuevo sobre las modalidades del cancionero en el cual se inspira.

El público, muy numeroso, aplaudió con calor a Pujol y le obligó a tocar varias obras fuera de programa.

EMILIO PUJOL

ESCUELA RAZONADA
de la
GUITARRA

Basada en los principios de
la técnica de TARREGA

Libro tercero

RICORDI

(Left) Review of the first 1930 Emilio Pujol concert performed in the Wagneriana theater in Buenos Aires. The translation on the next page.

(Right) Later edition of Emilio Pujol's *"Escuela Razonada de la Guitarra"*, published by Ricordi. The forword of this 4 volume series was written by Manuel de Falla.

From a Buenos Aires daily of 1930, a translation of the previous concert review image:

"Yesterday Emilio Pujol gave his first performance of guitar, with success

To the select nucleus of Spanish concert guitarists that have visited us: Llobet, Segovia and Sainz de la Maza, today a new one must be added. Emilio Pujol, that was presented last night, after more than ten years of absence, in the auditorium of the Wagneriana.

Since that date, Pujol has made great progress as an artist and as an instrumentalist: his musicality has become tuned and he has acquired a captivating personality; he already is a conscientious interpreter that has knowledge to penetrate the most intimate secrets of the works, as for style, spirit of the epoch and expressivity; and the player that, dominates the instrument, can be consecrated from fullness to express what every work would suggest of him.

Emilio Pujol is also an erudite musicologist. The guitar, that ever since has conquered in the concert hall a position of first rank, needed something more than instrumentalists, the only thing it possessed during a long lapse, since when an instrument is incorporated into the artistic movement, it isn't possible that whom plays them doesn't possess a vast general culture and would know from a foundation the resources and the history of the manner of expression.

This Spanish artist has consecrated part of his life to those works that come to favor all; he has visited archives, studied manuscripts and discovered works that had lain dormant and forgotten in libraries and chapels, what was of value that they asked him to collaborate in one of the most complete works and most important of today: *"La Enciclopedia de la musica"* and *"Diccionario del conservatorio"* founded by Albert Lavignac and that presently Lionel de la Laurencie manages, for what they said Pujol wrote the most serious and conscientious study that exists about the origins and the literature of the guitar.

It isn't strange, therefore, that last night Emilio Pujol, in classical works, would have succeeded with interpretations so finely musical; he played with elegance the *"Pavana"* of the Spanish composer Luis de Milan, who lived in the XVI century, and a *"Gavota-*favorite of the Duke of Monmouth", by Corbetta, and with the most pure of styles *"Alemana" and "Zarabanda"* by R. de Visée, all of them transcribed from ancient tablature by the concert guitarist; and in *"Minué" and "Allegro"* by Sor and in *"Bourée"* by Bach, he succeeded as well in careful and notable execution of the pieces.

Of modern Spanish works, Emilio Pujol as well gave very personal versions and full of life and of rhythmic vigor: as in, the *"Fandanguillo"* of Moreno Torroba, the *"Danza Española"* of Granados and *"Serenata Española"* of Malats, they acquired all their noble Spanish rhythm and expression, and the delicate *"Dolor",* a Basque prelude by Fray San Sebastian, known here in its pianistic and orchestral versions encounters in Pujol an interpreter that knew how to translate its soft and nebulous painful sentiment.

In the third part we heard *"Vidala",* of the Uruguayan composer Alfonso Broqua, that, to be inspiring in the spirituality of the *quichua* music, he has written a characteristic page and of beautiful sentiment; *"Chorinho"* of Heitor Villa-Lobos, the genius composer from Brazil, a work that can be affirmed to having a vigorous personality and Americanism in a high flight; *"Homenaje a Debussy",* of Manuel de Falla, and two of Pujol: *"Tonadilla"* and *"Sevilla",* in which the Spanish artist expatiated the exquisite musicality praised above and a very new sense over the modalities of the song book that inspired them.

The public, very numerous, hotly applauded and obliged him to play various works outside of the program (encores)."

668

In the short lived 3 issue magazine *"A Voz do Violao"* (February to April 1931), published in Rio de Janeiro, edited by F. Acquarone, managed by S. Leal, administrated by B. Polazzi, was the issue No. 1 of February 1931, which in its *"Violao no Extrangeiro"* section (The Guitar Abroad), was a report about Emilio Pujol.

Portuguese translation by Randy Osborne:

"Emilio Pujol and his Repertoire of Ancient Music

Emilio Pujol arrived in Buenos Aires in August of the past year, just as Sainz de la Maza was leaving that city.

In his concerts, in the port city, consecrated one more time thanked by the public to prolong his stay there, for many months.

The innumerable applause was well deserved, which Emilio Pujol conquered in good taste by an audience always *"raffine"* (sophisticated, refined).

In all his recitals, the artist was backed by his own wife, *Doña* Matilde Cuervas, a brilliant guitarist.

The programs, varied widely, to include music by F. Corbetta, Roberto de Visée, Luis Milan (1535), Gaspar Sanz (1672), Bach, Sor, Tárrega, Albeniz, Granados, Agustín Grau, Alfonso Broqua (Uruguayan), Manuel de Falla, San Sebastian and our Heitor Villa-Lobos, also his own compositions.

Pujol, with a pure and elegant mechanism, secure and experienced by the most arduous difficult technique, with a profound comprehension of the works and a style so pure, so exact to translate the characteristic modalities of each period of the guitaristic literature, and without patronizing, of the two most noble and representative artists of the present day."

On the next page is the opening page of the B.M.G. magazine published in London in May of 1931. It contains the program by Emilio Pujol and his wife, Matilde Cuervas. The program should be similar to that which was performed in South America, where the performance of Flamenco Guitar Solos by Matilde was not well-received at all in Argentina. There are more details on this facet of that concert tour in the biography of Emilio Pujol by Ricardo Muñoz.

A Monthly Magazine devoted to the Interests of the Banjo, Mandolin, Guitar and Kindred Instruments.

Edited by EMILE GRIMSHAW.

VOL. XXVIII.—No. 313]   MAY, 1931.   [PRICE SIXPENCE.

B.M.G.

Helps, Interests, Enthuses and Entertains all players of the

BANJO, MANDOLIN & GUITAR

and kindred instruments.

Published on the First of each Month

AT

15a, GRAFTON STREET, NEW BOND ST., LONDON, W.1

Telegrams :
"Triomphe, London"   Telephone: GERrard 3418 3419

Annual Subscription, 7/-
American Subscribers, 1 dol. 71c.

The Editor will be pleased to receive from his readers items of general interest (humorous or otherwise) relating to the above instruments, *viz.*, newspaper cuttings, concert notes (with dates), and criticisms, suggestions, queries, correspondence, and articles for consideration, etc

All communications submitted for inclusion in the next issue must arrive at these offices not later than the 20th of each month.

ADVERTISING RATES WILL BE SENT ON APPLICATION.

CONTENTS.

NOTES AND COMMENTS.

BY THE EDITOR.

A FAMOUS GUITARIST.

MR. EMIL PUJOL, the famous Spanish guitarist, and his wife (also a clever exponent of the guitar) who is known professionally as Matilda Cuervas, gave a recital during their recent London visit in the private studio of Mrs. C. Gow, a member of the Philharmonic Society of Guitarists. I give the items that were played because they will probably interest those readers of "*B.M.G.*" who prefer to play the guitar in the classical style.

DUETS by Mr. E. Pujol and
Madam MATILDA CUERVAS.

1. Melodie et Pastoral de l'Arlesienne   -   - *Bizet.*
2. Goyescas   -   -   - *Granadas.*
3. Tango Espagnol   - *Albeniz.*
4. Pantomima de l'Amour Sorcier   -   -   - *M. De Falla.*
5. Danse du Meûnier   - *M. De Falla.*

SOLOS by MATILDA CUERVAS.

6. Granadinas.
7. Soleares.
8. Guajiras.
9. Flaminco.

SOLOS by Mr. E. PUJOL.

10. Pavana   -   -   - *Gaspar Jan.*
11. Menuet   -   -   - *Sor.*
12. Serenade Espagnol   - *Malats.*
13. Caprice Arabe   -   - *Tarrega.*
14. Jota   -   -   - *Tarrega.*
15. Barcarole   -   - *Mendelssohn.*
16. Tonadilla   -   -   - *Pujol.*

DUETS by Mr. E. PUJOL and
Madam MATILDA CUERVAS.

17. Danse de la vie breve *M. De Falla.*
18. Danse du Feu   -   - *M. De Falla.*
19. Le cou-cou   -   -   - *Daquin.*

There was a large and enthusiastic audience present. All the items were well chosen, and the two artistes demonstrated with admirable brilliancy, clarity and expression that the guitar can hold its own with any other musical instrument when properly played.

In honour of Mr. and Mrs. Pujol, the Philharmonic Society of Guitarists gave a dinner at the Spanish Club, Cavendish Square, when the President, Dr. B. A. Perott, proposed a Toast to these great artistes.

*   *   *

MARIO DE PIETRO WRITES.

Many players who attended the Exhibition and Concert at Lysbeth Hall on March 22nd, have written to say how thoroughly they enjoyed the evening and how quickly it seemed to pass.

Mario de Pietro has written :

"I visited the Exhibition of fretted instruments and must say that I was astonished at the high standard of the British goods displayed on the many stands. I sampled one of Clifford Essex' tenor-banjos and was so enchanted with it that I just had to play it for quite a considerable period. I found there the 'Classic' mandolin, which is made by my own factory and is exactly like the one I use myself in all my professional work. I was also greatly pleased with the well-made and beautifully toned guitars exhibited by Messrs. Milners, of Sheffield ; and our old friend Winslow had a fine display of beautifully constructed mandolins. There can be no possible doubt that British-made fretted instruments are honest value and, in regard to tone and fine construction, need fear no foreign competitors."

This Exhibition of fretted instruments was undoubtedly a great success; so much so that arrangements are now being made by the Federation to hold another at the beginning of the next autumn season, the Exhibition will probably be held in a hall twice the size of the Lysbeth Hall, on a Saturday, both afternoon and evening.

*   *   *

This biographical material about Emilio Pujol is from Ricardo Muñoz's unpublished book *"Historia Universal de la Guitarra"* Volume V *"Los Contemporaneos"*.

"His Origin:

Emilio Pujol is the son of Ramon Pujol and Cristina Villarubi, born in Granadella, Lerida, Cataluña, the 7th of April of 1886.

His Education:

Since his childhood he was dedicated to the study of the bandurria, which he arrived to perform in an *estudiantina*, achieving the admiration of who heard him, including the President of the French Republic, *Don* Emilio Loubet, in the Exposition of Paris, who congratulated him.

In the year 1900 he had the opportunity to hear *Don* Francisco Tárrega and remained marveled by the beautiful polyphonics of the poetic instrument and of the extraordinary art of the illustrious maestro, deciding since then to, abandon the bandurria for the guitar, whose studies he made in Villareal under the direction of the artist that he had been so emotionally struck by.

His enthusiasm and determination got him assigned the "favorite student" during the last epoch of the maestro, which thought of him with true paternal affection, corresponded by his disciple with sincere sentiments of profound respect and admiration; by this treatment and teachings Pujol obtained great advantage to be identified with that in such a degree, that his performances, in many cases, appeared to be of his own maestro.

His Virtuosity:

Pujol is without a doubt one of the finest and most delicate artists of the contemporary guitar which, to possess sensibilities so exquisite, he knows how to spill it in abundance with all of the sincerity of his select spirit, admirably perceived by who have had the chance to hear him.

However this dominion demonstrated in various performances, to sense profoundly during the same impresses, of an adverse manner, the presence of the public, he might appear to be bothered like his eminent maestro, a circumstance that doesn't occur when he plays in private and puts free rein to the sublime sentiments contained in his cerebral box.

In 1906 he began with his first concert in Lerida, in 1907 he made his first tour of Spain, with a very flattering success, which influenced in his mind to overcome the borders of his country and move to London; in 1912 he returned to Spain, in 1913 he returned to London where he resided, due to the enthusiastic reception which he made, but he had to give up this purpose and return to Spain because of the break out of the war, in August of 1914.

The judgement about *Don* Emilio Pujol, which the critics produced in the said capital and Valencia, in the years referred to, and which is continued transcribing, offers the exact idea of the artistic worth of this great Catalan musician:

The Morning Post (London December 16, 1912) 'The guitar is little known in this country. As to what you can obtain with it is fully demonstrated by Mr. Emilio Pujol, the Spanish guitarist who made his appearance in London last Saturday at Bechstein Hall. His labor was something superior to the series of arpeggios that are commonly accustomed to expect as the capacity of the guitar. Pujol takes advantage of all the resources of a great technique and right away with a dominion so exceptional of the instrument he arrived to convince us that the guitar deserves to be considered artistically. The transcriptions of classic authors as Bach, Schubert, Schumann and other works by the great guitarist Francisco Tárrega were in the program; of all of them he gave us a pleasant version especially of the *Gavote in Si minor* by Bach, of the delicate sonority and great clarity of performance; he also demonstrated his elevated virtuosity, playing a transcription of the *Fugue en Sol minor* of the first *sonata,* for violin solo, by the same author.'

'But the character of the instrument where the most significant appeared in, was in the group of works especially written for the guitar; that was where he demonstrated qualities that demand paying attention to the capacity of this beautiful instrument.'

Las Provincias (Valencia October 10, 1913) 'Yesterday the announced concert was verified, given by the famous guitarist Pujol in the Conservatorio.'

'The artist (a true and admirable artist), is a disciple of the great Tárrega, and with saying he well deserves the name of the follower of the maestro, this says all. It might be said until a while, which it was impossible that no one could substitute Tárrega, that evocative magician, with the smoothest ideal visions of his guitar. Well, since, Pujol made for us the immense mercy of reviving the prodigious Spanish maestro. That was something mysterious, closing the eyes having heard that immaterialistic sound of the Castellon maestro, that playing, those timbres so his, that interpretation. . . . to be believing that to open the eyes that you're going to see the maestro with his goatee, his eyeglasses, his head of the inclined artist over the famous guitar. . . .; but quickly the new sounds emerge, you don't suspect, purities of sounds heard, energies to us that are unknown. . . and there is the temperament of Pujol, the young interpreter that, guarding jealously, with integrated respect, the tradition of the maestro (it's an admirable case of a purely maintained school!), not allowing by it to let us see, when one wants, the power of the soul of the artist.'

'In a certain work by Bach (the delicious *Loure,* for example), such as those of Mozart or other maestros of that epoch, the transcriptions for the guitar performed by Pujol, don't lose any character, on the contrary, they come close to the grace and inimitable delicateness of the clavichord, more than the modern pianos. As for the admirable *Preludios* of Tárrega, performed by Pujol, they turn out to be unique.'

'Our congratulations to the artist of truth. Signed, E. Lopez Chavarri.'

Such spilled out words by such an authority so eminent as *Don* Eduardo Lopez Chavarri did, surpass as to one can say in a eulogy of the notable guitarist.

672

The Daily Telegraph (London May 25, 1914) 'The guitar so little known as a soloist's instrument in the halls of the concerts of London, and the art of Mr. Pujol, was a revelation for the attendees to the concert given by him in the Steinway hall, that Saturday afternoon.'

'Although the variety of which the instrument offers is quite a lot reduced by the volume which it's permitted, Mr. Pujol demonstrated for us fully that the limits don't exist for the effects of timbre and blend. He produced astonishing sonorities and our admiration was no less recognizing that he worked in a difficult medium.'

'The style of Mr. Pujol is elegant and tidy demonstrating an astonishing ability in reducing the pianissimos until they were almost imperceptible.'

The Standard (London May 25, 1914) 'Considering that the guitar is an instrument limited under the point of view of potency of sonority, the effects of the graduation of blends obtained by Emilio Pujol were truly admirable in the guitar concert he gave, last Saturday in the Steinway Hall.'

'From an element so difficult, it can turn out to be demonstrated how valuable one can obtain an artist so complete as Mr. Pujol. Integrated by diverse Spanish works by Malats, Albeniz, all of which he played was performed with the best delicacy and taste.'

In 1916 Pujol arrived in Barcelona and again in a series of concerts, he returned to demonstrate his marvelous musical technique; J. Balcells, the director of the Orfeo Gracienc, says so in an article of *"La Veu de Cataluña"* on the date of the 15th of November of 1916:

'Under all circumstances, one can qualify the concert dedicated to his associates, given by the eminent guitarist *Don* Emilio Pujol in the performance hall of the Orfeo Gracienc, that of an artistic happening. The select program, was a success of good taste, witnessed by the musical criteria of the marvelous artist of the guitar. Emilio Pujol demonstrated with his interpretations and his excellent diction, he can give a lot to this instrument.'

'.... what impressed the listeners so much, among the distinguished professors and eminent musicians, was in those works adapted to the instrument and which judging by the first impression, could appear as a musical desecration; in this way it occurred with the works of Bach, Mozart, Schumann, Mendelssohn that naturally weren't written for the guitar and by which if it couldn't be affirmed that in their adaptations they were improved, that it could be assured that everything was worthwhile when the performer is the caliber of Pujol and possesses a musical temperament so well balanced....'

'The great maestros have in Pujol and in his guitar, a respectful and fervent interpreter of his conceptions.'

Again, from the month of January of 1917, Pujol made a tour of Spain, leaving in his recitals, in Barcelona, Bilbao and Madrid, indelible fingerprints that were lost behind the time and appear to us that although the timbre is heard of that smooth sound.... all velvet.... which this artist produces...., this Chopin of the guitar his prodigious performances, in this way his compatriots understand and judge by the following manner:

"La Veu de Cataluña" (Barcelona January 13, 1917) 'His name is already known to us, although he is heard but a little here; outside the country he is very well-known, over all in London he habitually resides. He is an artist who has opened a path and he doesn't need our eulogies to have a reputation; one has to speak of him because we can say only the ideas of eulogy after his first recital.'

'One of the best abilities we appreciate in Pujol, is the artistic honor, he avoids prolonged notes and excessive vibrations which sweetening the instrument give it a feminine character. No, Pujol is sincere and says it as the author orders, giving it a clearly masculine character. He has a prodigious mechanism which he employs without abuse, put so only as we have said, to the disposition of the author he interprets; because the artistic power doesn't need to dazzle with acrobatics; the faithful interpretation of the program, is enough.'

'Dominator of the technique of the instrument, *lego* (Tárrega), the notable works such as the *Preludios* which Pujol performed, the *Allegro Brilliante* that he had to repeat; the *Gavota-Scherzo* already known by everyone; the *Alborada* which was played again along with *Recuerdos de la Alhambra, Minuetto* and other *Dos Estudios* admirably conceived for the guitar.'

'The public was numerous and enthusiastic, predicting, and truly was pleasant for us, a resurgence in favor of the instrument, which, in epochs of good taste it had been listened to and moved away from all raucousness.'

"La Vanguardia": (January 18, 1917) 'This time the notable guitarist Emilio Pujol gave us a historic recital, named in this way by understanding from Robert de Visée, vihuelist of the 18th century to the modern maestros of the guitar, Pujol inclusive....'

"Las Noticias" (Barcelona April 3, 1917) 'Emilio Pujol is, perhaps, the direct successor of the great Tárrega; his art is of an admirable beauty, since it has an intimate saying which separates it from those being similar, without letting it be subjected to the indications of the authors. It has its own personality and is played of a smooth percussion, velvety, and the graduations-very clear to obscure are taken with such skill and mastery, which in its intimate saying and playing the guitar, there is such an effect in the harmonic passages, in chords, which appear as continuous sounds; this is an illusion in certain moments. The enthused public, applauds the labor of Pujol, with the warmth of his art that is so exquisite.'

"La Correspondencia de España" (Madrid March 9, 1918) 'The excellent performer, Pujol makes to note by his good taste of diction, which reveals his great artistic temperament. His hands make the strings of the guitar vibrate with such art, which he obtains by this delicious sound.'

In 1919 he visited the Argentine Republic and was duly valued by the intelligent public, and the most select musical circles of the country, leaving in the mind of who had the chance to hear him, the most pleasant memories of his pure, elevated and exquisite sublime art.

In this opportunity the notable musicologist Jeronimo Zanné made a critique of Pujol, reflecting the spiritual image of the distinguished guitarist in the following terms:

'Emilio Pujol is a marvelous guitarist. He possesses a great musicality, admirable technique, exquisite taste, a disciple of Tárrega, he is a perfect classic. He extracts his style of that glorious tradition renovated by Sor, so beautifully developed afterward by Aguado, Tárrega, Llobet and the musician we are concerned with.'

'Pujol is a classic by the purity of his style, by the delicacy of his melodic line, by the perfection of his interpretive art. But classic-we understand well, doesn't mean Cold, rigid, symmetrical; the Classics were Men that felt and expressed with equal intensity that we feel and express today. The scarce critics of those times clearly demonstrated it.'

'The classic Pujol gives the same esthetic value, within the range of interpretations which his temperament admits, to a passage of Sor, the guitaristic composer by excellency, that to a transcription of Bach or of Mozart, or that to a modern composition by Albeniz, Granados or Malats, perhaps more sincere on the guitar than the piano. And the classicism of Pujol extends to all the genres, because it isn't the fruit of a *"parti pris"* (prejudice), but of his temperament.'

'Pujol, whose medium of performance is the pure use of fingertips, suppresses the little stridency which so frequently disfigure the guitaristic interpretations; his diction is clear, warm and expressive, eloquent in his stimulating and moving seriousness in his absence of a *"pose"* and carries out in search of the applause.'

'Hearing him interpret Sor, one appreciates in Pujol the austere, honest and pure guitarist; hearing him interpret Bach or Mozart, Pujol evokes to us the delicate sonorities of the clavichord in the hands of Wanda Landowski; hearing him interpret the modern composers of Andalucian music, Albeniz, Granados, Malats, particularly the *Serenata Española* by the last, which our guitarist played unsurpassable, the passionate artist and the overflowing of enthusiasm is seen in Pujol, always nevertheless, framed in his classicism that come to give the most worth to the harmony and solidity of the little polyphonic group.'

The public of Buenos Aires, which had the opportunity to applaud the eminent guitarist, couldn't be less surprised before the art of Emilio Pujol. the maestro of the intimately human interpretations."

In 1926, solicited by the "Sociedad Cultural Guitarristica" of Madrid, he gave some concerts under their auspices, which were made with great and warm success that is logically explainable, given the exquisite culture of the eminent guitarist.

The 22nd of January of the same year, in the "Sala Parés" of Barcelona, he offered a performance with works by Tárrega, Llobet, Padre San Sebastian, de Falla and two dances of his own, one of them in La and the other in Re, various *Pavanes* and *Folias* by Gaspar Sanz, a *Preludio* and an *Alemana* by Robert de Visée, which provoked the most favorable commentaries of the qualified critics of the moment.

The same year he undertook a tour of Europe, and the dailies of the Continent expressed in this manner:

"Berliner Morgenpost": (Berlin October 21, 1926) 'What Pujol did was something magic. He played with skin of the fingers, obtaining an incredible variety of registrations and an absolute security in all of his technique.'

*"Munichener Post": (*Munich November 3, 1926) 'The Pujol concert has left the happiest memory. Impossible to hear played of a more sonorous manner, more varied nor sweeter.'

"Berlingske Tidende": (Copenhagen November 2, 1928) 'Emilio Pujol is a great artist, not only a virtuoso whose technique includes the absolute dominion of his instrument, but also he is a musician of talent and sensibility which lets him faithfully adapt the diverse music that he interprets.'

"Revue de L'Amerique Latine": (Paris January 1, 1929) 'The transcriptions for two guitars of the works such as *Evocacion* by Albeniz and *Intermezzo* by Granados, have been more than a surprise, a precursor enunciation. Here I have a manner by ultimately serving to the cause of music. (Signed: E. Laroque).'

The 24th of July of 1930 he took the steamship *"Reina Victoria Eugenia"*, proceeding from Paris to Buenos Aires, accompanied by the Andalucian folkloric guitarist *Dona* Matilde Cuervas, with whom he proposed to give performances in duets and lectures on the lines of his important historical investigations about the instrument.

And so it was on the Wednesday 6th of August that he made his first public presentation in the "Sala Wagneriana" at 9:30PM with a program of works by Milan, Corbetta, de Visée, Sor, Bach, Moreno Torroba, Granados, Malats, Fray San Sebastian, Broqua, Villa-Lobos, de Falla and his own; the daily *"La Prensa"* of the following day reported: 'Pujol has made great progress as an artist and as an instrumentalist; his musicality has been tuned and he has acquired a captivating personality; he is already the conscientious interpreter that has known how to penetrate the lowest secrets of the works, as to style, spirit of the epoch and expressiveness; and the performer which, dominating the instrument, can consecrate to the fullest to express what every work suggests.'

'The very numerous gathering applauded with warmth and obliged Pujol to play encores.'

The daily *"La Nacion"* said about the concert: 'We recall that not only a beautiful and elegant mechanism, secure and experienced in the most arduous technical difficulties, but also the profound comprehension of the works and a style so pure in exactly translating the characteristic modalities of each period of the guitaristic literature made by Emilio Pujol, one of the most noble artists and most representative of today.'

The following Saturday the 9th he gave his 2nd performance performing the first two sets with works by Milan, Sanz, Sor, Tárrega, Albeniz, Grau, Broqua and Pujol, as to the 3rd set it was made by performing duets with his companion Matilde Cuervas, playing *"Melodia"* and *"Pastoral"* of *"L'Arlesienne"* by Bizet, *"Intermezzo de Goyesca"* by Granados, *"Cordoba"* by Albeniz, *"Tango"* by Broqua and *"Danza del Molinero"* by de Falla, all those transcriptions by Pujol.

"La Prensa" on the 11th in the eulogy of the labor of the artist, especially of the *"Intermezzo de Goyesca"*, declared: 'Pujol frankly introduces the *rasgueados* (strums) and *golpes* (taps) of the popular guitaristic technique.' These resources are so rich in the power of suggestion for the critic, but not very pleasant for the maestros and aficionados, which suppose, with or without reason, that the artistic technique must be divorced from the popular realm, everyone has to be in its place to which it corresponds, without invading jurisdictions.

These circumstances added, by the performer without fingernails, affected the turnout from his first concert, which hinted that the public really didn't hear the performances more than only filling half the hall.

On the 14th, in the same location Pujol reiterated his presentation, performing solo in the 1st set with works by Sanz, de Visée, Bach, Sor and of the performer; in the 2nd set his companion played flamenco works in the popular style, and in the 3rd set, both played duets, interpreting a *"Minuetto"* by Mozart, *"Tango Español"* and *"El Puerto"* by Albeniz, *"Pantomima" and "Danza"* by de Falla. The turnout wasn't complete.

Immediately both artists traveled to the interior of the country visiting Cordoba, Santa Fe, Santiago del Estero, and Tucuman; the 8th of September in the Wagneriana, organized by the music house Celestino Fernández and Hermanos, he made another concert, in which the 1st set they performed duets, both artists, with works by Mozart, Villa-Lobos, Granados, and de Falla, in the 2nd set Pujol interpreted Sor, Padre San Sebastian, and J. Nin Culmell finishing the performance with popular Andalucian music entrusted to the named Mrs. Cuervas de Pujol. The public following decreased.

In this same way they gave other recitals on the 29th of September in the "Los Amigos del Arte", the 3rd and 13th of October in the Wagneriana, with the same turn of events as in their latest concerts.

As a result of that Pujol complained, as in 1919, he declared his discontent with inadequate expressions which the aficionados picked up on and didn't respond, but it continued that his recitals lacked the turn out and in that aspect, they were a financial disaster.

In 1935 the Comité Honorifique of the "Les Amis de la Guitare" of Paris, named him Président Honorifique of the same entity, and on the 11th of May of 1938 he performed in the Sala Erard, a performance of ancient music accompanied by the singer Conchita Abadia, with works of vihuelists of the 16th century, playing in effect, an authentic vihuela (This was made by Miguel Simplicio in 1935. R.O.), and afterward a very interesting historical lecture about the same subject.

In 1948 he performed duets, with Matilde Cuervas and the collaboration of the singer *Doña* Adelaida Robert, in the Conservatorio Nacional in Lisboa, Portugal, a little later in the Teatro Principal de Castellon, Valencia, giving a concert performing with his companion Cuervas on two guitars. A journalist wrote down his opening words:

'By being the first time that I have the honor to perform in Castellon, cradle and tomb of the greatest guitarist of all times, Francisco Tárrega Eixea, the emotion however reduces my small faculties. The merits of that great artist were many and of such a high lineage, by which the guitarists we have today give us satisfaction, so if we only succeed to evoke the memory of his sublime art from long ago. This performance, serves, well, to sense homage of admiration and affection to which my knowledgeable and beloved maestro, and that he has been, will be an honor of Castellon and the Hispanic art. Glory to Tárrega.'

The first part turned out shining the works of that colossus along with a *Minuetto* by Sor and the known *Serenata* by Malats, a *Vidala* of the Uruguayan composer *Don* Alfonso Broqua. And with his *Guajiras Gitanas*, of a difficult performance, the expressive melody and modern harmonization, Pujol finished this part, being cheered.

Afterward Mrs. Cuervas de Pujol demonstrated her eloquent flamenco art, being applauded and presented by both the Gobernador Civil and the Barrachina orchestra with bouquets of flowers.

The concert finished with duets performing *"L'Arlesienne"* by *Bizet*, *"Goyesca"* and *"Cordoba"* by Granados and Albeniz, *"Danza de la Gitana"* by Halffter and the *"Vida Breve"* with *"El Sombrero de Tres Picos"* by de Falla, transcribed and played in a unique manner by the interpreters.

In 1950 in a central restaurant in Madrid a dinner was celebrated in homage of Pujol, dedicated by a group of enthusiastic friends, with those turning out being Mrs. Cuervas de Pujol, Fernando Rodríguez, Emilita Corral, the favorite student of Pujol, the maestro *Don* Daniel Fortea, Juan Huidobro, Mariano Cubas, Lorenzo del Castillo, Mariano Perea, Emilio Carpio, Rolando Valdés, Miguel Angel Martínez, José Ramírez, Marcelo Barbero, Marcos Herran, Abelardo Corral, Dr. José Perales, Alberto Alvarez, the Professor Samper and others.

This is from the "Guitar News" magazine issue No. 6 of April-May 1952. It mentions the first public performance by Miss Emilita Corral on Friday October 19, 1951.

Ricardo Muñoz said in his unpublished book *"Historia Universal de la Guitarra"* Volume V *"Los Contemporaneos"*: "I expect her to be one of the legitimate promises of the very near future."

APRIL—MAY, 1952   GUITAR NEWS

SPAIN

Lerida. On October 19th, Professor Emilio Pujol presented his youngest pupil, Señorita Emilita Corral, in her first public recital before an audience of distinguished guests at the house of Don Ramon Morell. Introducing the young guitarist Don Emilio Pujol said "The dawn of this young girl's career is a bright one — her technique, her musicianship and good taste show clearly an indisputable master of the guitar." The programme included works by Gaspar Sanz (16th century), Bach and Granados.

Wilfrid Appleby, the editor, of "Guitar News" magazine since 1951, wrote an article titled: "Random Reminiscences" upon the magazine reaching its 100th issue. This is an excerpt:

But in the autumn of 1954 we received a picture so beautiful that we decided to have it printed on the front page of No. 22. The subject of this picture showed a young Spanish lady, as talented as she was charming,

who had studied the guitar under Emilio Pujol. She was Emilia Corral whose performance on Radio Madrid in January 1954 inspired the poet G. Gonzales de Zabala to write this sonnet:

EMILIA CORRAL

Your hands, light butterflies
fluttering over the strings,
change a water-spring of song
into a singing branch of roses.
With the splendour of your gifts
you enrapture the heart,
and scatter your bounty
like a goddess or a fairy.
He trembles who listens in silence.
The obedient guitar is ennobled
in your hands, exquisite and restless,
that weave the intricate music.
Your soul lives in your fingers
and gives life to the notes you interpret.

Here is a hitherto unpublished photograph of Emilia Corral in 1954 (7.) She is now the wife of Andres Segovia, having merged her genius and her love with that of the Grand Maestro of the Guitar.

This is from the "Guitar News" magazine issue No. 100 of September-October 1968.

Everything was simple and without speeches, but to finish the act, Pujol wished to thank the homage and as the emotion which however it didn't permit him to speak, he gave his thanks by a simple and effusive manner.

All those that gathered then went to the home of maestro Fortea where the homage proceeded by Daniel performing first, then Emilita Corral, followed by Perea, del Castillo, etc. Pujol then answered by playing his works *"Salve"* and *"Crepusculo"*, expressed with admirable sweetness, a *"Preludio"* by Tárrega with perfection, then Mrs. Cuervas de Pujol accompanied him on the *"Invencion"* and *"Segunda Fuga"* by Bach, a *"Minuetto"* by Bizet and the *"Intermezzo"* by Granados, elegant, spirited, and saturated of Spanish flavor.

His Compositions:

The musical works composed until this moment are around 100 by this eminent modern artist of the guitar, comprising them are the popular stylized, the classic and the transcriptions of ancient and contemporary pages, by which it makes it necessary to treat them as three distinct aspects.

Whatever might be the line to review all the other works composed by this author, possess the magnificent character of the beauty more carefully and neat difficultly to find errors of the printer, of the music or of whatever other nature in his excellent pages, such is the prolific artistry that he submits to his compositions to be published.

The music publisher Max Eschig of Paris honors him awarding him the direction of his very abundant Archivo Biblioteca de Musique Ancienne et Moderne for the guitar, publishing since then many works of the authors of the 16th and 17th centuries and contemporary, such as Raymond Petit, A. Broqua, A. Grau, Eduardo L. Chavarri, Manuel de Falla, Agustín Salazar, Heitor Villa-Lobos and Pujol himself.

Of his popular and folkloric stylized works we recall his South American themes, *"Chacarera"*, *"Estilo" and "Zamba"* by Broqua; *"Vidala"*, *"Tonadilla" ("Manola del Avapies")* and *"Tiento"* by Fuenllana, etc; which surely will go increasing, to measure what his inspiration and work he permits, for the pride of the aficionados.

As to his labor about classic music, his marvelous *"El Abejorro"*, a modern work of great descriptive effect to imitate, in the 2nd minor, with speedy arpeggios, the flight of this insect; the most important in its performance is in the difficulties that presents the precision, the equality and the exact reproduction of this flight.

Another of the works by Pujol, is his *"Homenaje a Chopin"*, in it he evokes the lyricism of the romantic to whom the homage was written, with fine harmonics and exquisite effects, obtained without neither major complications nor musical displays.

"Villanella" is a lively dance and of stupendous musical effects, full of rhythmic and harmonic varieties, which concede it character to be essentially classic.

Besides, we recall his exceptional *"Cancion de Cuna"*, the most maltreated by the aficionados which, it feels intimately, the desire, and the performance as can be, but it does; in *"Impromptu"*, *"Salve"*, etc.

His transcriptions deserve the qualification of extraordinary, excellent, captivating, by the manner, as treating the voices and the themes, as lifting up the tonalities, the timbres, until arriving to be doubtful the adapted work could be created in another instrument with the comprehension and knowledge finished and perfect of the instrument that performs and its range.

It is also necessary to let constancy, in the actual times which run, of its irreproachable honesty, connected with the respect which it deserves, the works which he transcribes, those which he doesn't disfigure, doesn't chop, or alter their musical sense, add as he likes, as others do, personal passages of the mode, in the epoch, in many distinct occasions to that of the life of the author; this sincere quality makes Pujol, one of the most authentic artists of the guitar of our era, deserving of our profound consideration.

He who has studied and performed his transcriptions, knows well as to our musical literature that this must be an eminent virtuoso, maestro and composer of our instrument; look at the "Sonata" by Scarlatti, for example, whose melodic line is an elegant duet, abundant of precious and sensible jewels of its author, inspiration, freshness, rich effects, admirable harmonic intonation and the marvelous abundance of the succeeded intentions, adapted to perfection. If this doesn't satisfy the rebellious nonconformists who abound, it is possible that it exceeds all classes of demands, his monuments *"Preludios"* or *"Sarabandas"* of the uncontrollable Bach, true organographia written unsurpassable, or *"Cordoba"* by Albeniz and *"Intermezzo" (of Goyecas)* by Granados for two guitars, in which they lift up the Hispanic soul of the midday, with all the strength and warmth of the fire of its existence.

His Pedagogy:

His scattered students by the world diffuse the magnificence of his *Tarregiana* school, the most perfect, unsurpassable, authentic existent, of which Pujol is, the unending fountain, where the guitaristic world attends to stop the thirst of necessary knowledge, which has to take to the selected sure triumph of his artistic musical aspirations.

This maximum knowledge and perfect pedagogy he takes to his method *"Escuela Razonada de la Guitarra"*, divided into five parts, of which the following have been published: the 1st in the month of June of 1934, by Romero y Fernández of Buenos Aires, printed in 104 pages in the musical lithography of Garrot, Tasso and Vita of the said locality; the 2nd by the mentioned publisher and printer the 10th of November of 1935, in 144 pages, both in a format of 34 by 26 centimeters; and the 3rd and last by Ricordi Americana, also of Buenos Aires, the 4th of December of 1954, with 150 pages 31 1/2 by 23 cm; its contents constitute of stock pedagogy carefully, complete and perfect, which in the didactic guitaristic material he has written, across all the times, in French and Spanish; it is top Pujoliana work about the technical mechanism of the instrument, that comprises the least and most complicated details of the movement or general and particular combinations of the fingers of both hands, musically written and as to the great Tárrega believed, without having been surpassed until this date, including, the unequivocal personal suggestions which Pujol, only great maestro of maestros added to the known school.

The discrimination of these marvelous books of the modern epoch of the instrument, is connected in the following Opus II, to describe the techniques and musical writings of the contemporary guitar, but separate of these grandiose disciplines admirably studied, catalogued and progressively expressed and explained, Pujol has written other studies for beginners and players of hierarchy technique, of which these are recommended.

Petite Romance: It is a delicious romantic melody of easy difficulty appropriate for who begin to move the fingers a little bit, getting to taste with the soul the sonorous vibrations of the strings they pluck.

Estudio: Particularly useful for the fingers index, middle and annular of the right hand, to allocate by the harmonic form that is preferred.

Estudio No. 2: Successive scales and chords that initiate in the tone of LA Major, constituting a magnificent support to study the subject, Scale, which, the more they are exercised, the more attention they demand.

680

Ondinas: It deals with a study of agility, with great melodic value for the performance, saving its difficult technical obstacles; it is really a work of mastery, not common in the guitaristic literature, written for virtuosos of a high level, it was dedicated in the year 1921 to Dr. B. Romero Escena, its slurs, generally placed on the last notes of each gruppetto of sixteenth notes to the time *"Vivace"* of 108, its series of difficulties augmented which, once conquered, they permit to assure that one knows how to play a slur in whatever circumstance.

Estudios Superiores: Published by A. Boileau Bernasconi of Barcelona, in the year 1946, in a workbook of VII studies, every one of them is a master of its specialty, scales, arpeggios, chords, etc.

All the careful, plentiful, intelligent, and sensitive labor of the maestro, made to say to his classmate and friend *Don* Daniel Fortea: 'Pujol is a sober judge in this material... he occupies the prominent place in the guitaristic culture in Spain.'; I would have said in the World.

In 1947 he gave his first course of the guitar in the Conservatorio Nacional in Lisbon, Portugal, where he continued teaching as a composer, maestro and musicologist; he was named director of the "Accademia Musicale Chigiana" of Siena, Italy, his student, *Don* Osman del Barco, in his homage founded in Lima, Peru the "Academia Emilio Pujol".

His Investigations:

His invaluable merits brought the public admiration as a logical consequence, whose notoriety influenced in the mind of *Don* Lionel de la Laurencie, Director of the Conservatoire Nationale of Paris, requiring the invaluable collaboration of Pujol, at the end to include in the Encyclopédie de la Musique et Dictionnaire du Conservatoire of the said Conservatoire, a critical study, historical, biographical and didactic about the guitar.

In 1927 his colossal work was added with the title; *"Guitare",* beginning from the pages 1,997 to 2,035; it deals with a historical collaboration deserving of the greatest consideration and respect, however, lamentably various errors which occur on page 2,014 of the IV volume, where it is shown in the following manner:

where Parga is named Pargas;
of Arcas, was born in Malaga in the year 1833 and died the 18th of February of 1884,
his birth took place in Almeria the year 1832 and he died 16th of February of 1882;
of Tárrega, born the 29th of November of 1854, it was the 21st of November 1852.-Etc.etc.

In 1930 he gave a lecture in Buenos Aires, which he then repeated in London, Paris, Barcelona and Montevideo titled: *"La Guitarra y su Historia",* published in 47 pages by Romero & Fernández of Buenos Aires in that date; on page 43 he says: "A page of history must be the faithful reflection of the works and its logical consequences. The exaggerations vagueness, confusion, errors, or omissions are defects which will sooner or later destroy the authority of the text."

However, these knowledgeable appreciations, have almost the same errors included in it as the *Encyclopédie de la Musique et Dictionnaire* du Conservatoire of the Conservatoire Nationale of Paris, with the addition of unjustified declarations not verified about the Argentine guitarists, and other mistakes I will continue to detail:

To *Don* Carlos Amat, the name Carles; to *Don* Roberto de Viseo his name "Visée" by *"suponerlo"* it in French; to the great Tárrega he gives the birth date as born the 29th of November of 1854, instead the 21st of November 1852; on page 31 he says: Joséfina Robledo introduced the technical spirit of the true school of Tárrega in South America in 1914, and then on page 34, he assures that *Don* Domingo Prat in 1908 brought the referred to school to Buenos Aires, on page 37 he says, that *"la plebe"* is the *"LUZ"*.... a thought I can't share.

Those errors indicate, well understood, with the only purpose to authenticate the successes. As to various others not brought into these paragraphs, they can be proven in the lapse of the present *"Historia Universal de la Guitarra"* and as well by the confession which of the same, very honestly Mr. Pujol, gave in the issues Nos. 7 and 8 of *Año* IV of the *"La Chitarra"* magazine, corresponding to July and August of 1937.

In 1934, the same Argentine publisher of Buenos Aires, Romero & Fernández , published in Spanish and English, in 41 pages, of a format of 25 x 17 3/4 cm, his book *"El Dilema del Sonido en la Guitarra";* its content about acoustic (Physical) magnificently assimilated, adapted and explained in the concern to the instrument, treatment of the sound, the timbre in its aspects-historical and physical, the plucking with and without fingernails, the perception- according to the psychic sense, theories and schools of the sound on the guitar, etc.

These themes develop with the profound knowledge which express and desire, naturally, the artists and students of the instrument internalize, that the guitarist already, by reasons of the special culture, not only has to be an able apparatus of plucking strings on its sonorous box. Not one maestro had the technical esthetic vision which, about the subject, the great Pujol studies and presents!

He was appointed to the "Instituto Español de Musicologia" of the "Consejo Superior de Investigaciones Cientificas" of Madrid, in 1945 he reedited: *"Los Seys Libros del Delphin* ...etc.", of the unforgettable Vihuelist *Don* Luis de Narvaez of the year 1538, in a facsimile format, in 1949, in Barcelona, he made his own with the *"Tres Libros de Musica en Cifra"* by *Don* Alonso de Mudarra, pertaining to the year 1546; in 1952 in Zaragoza, he continued with the reproduction of the *"Instruccion de Musica...etc."* by *Don* Gaspar Sanz, 3rd edition of 1674 and the 8th edition of 1697, and even continued working without cessation with the Vihuelists of the 16th and 17th centuries, whose methods can be appreciated in Volume III *"Los Clasicos"* of the present work *"Historia Universal de la Guitarra".* Could it be possible that there is an existence of distracted individuals who are unaware of the reproductions of these treasures of the guitaristic Middle Ages, given by the dedication and tireless work of the great Pujol?

This *"Consejo Superior de Investigaciones Cientificas",* presided by the Ministro de Educacion Nacional, joins in their distinct Institutes the most representative personalities in every specialty and branch of knowledge. For this reason, *Don* Emilio Pujol forms a part of the same, dedicating to the historical and technical investigation of the classic or modern music, organizing a cycle of annual lectures at the institution.

The 16th of June of 1950 Pujol made what corresponded to, dedicating to the eminent guitarist Dr. *Don* Juan Carlos Amat, titling the lecture *"El Tratado de Guitarra Española de Cinco Ordenes de Juan Carlos Amat";* the act he brought to the Salon de la Biblioteca Central de la Diputacion Provincial Catalana, with the warm eulogy for the lecturer; besides, in the Ateneo of Barcelona, he lectured about *"La Guitarra Española en la Musica Portuguesa",* with the unanimous approval of the knowledgeable listeners.

All these investigations, carried out with a lot of dedication and unique love, had their plausible musical results, appeared later, to adapt to the modern music of the guitar, *Seis Pavanas* by Luis de Milan; *Gallardas, Pavanas* and *Folias* by Gaspar Sanz; *Preludio* and *Gavota* by Francisco Corbetta; *Villano,* by Francisco Guerau, etc.; an extraordinary production of the Middle Ages transposed to our epoch, which permits in spite of the true worth of the musicalization and its grandiose authors, almost unknown until today by the aficionados, but, rediscovered by our eminent *Don* Emilio Pujol.

He collaborated as well in newspapers and guitar magazines of diverse countries, in which they feel his artistic knowledge, establishing with his pen, the substantial mastery of the instrument of our days.

Lastly, the esteem which must be includable, to clear up that the errors committed by this great artist, in his writings, which are trivial don't overshadow, the magnitude of his marvelous work in favor of the guitar."

So ends the biography of maestro Emilio Pujol by Ricardo Muñoz.

This interview with Matilde Cuervas by Irene De Falcon is from the daily *"La Voz"* of Madrid published on January 17, 1929.

"Ingleterra — England

Londres y la Guitarra-London and the Guitar

In spite of the constant opposition of the British music critics, the Spanish guitarists have already succeeded in captivating the London public. The guitar has been until now an unknown musical instrument. They have notions that the guitar serves to accompany dancers and singers from Spain; but as a serious musical instrument no one knows it as such. The famous guitarists had come to play classical pieces and the people had ended up being surprised. The critics, in reality, didn't have sufficient knowledge of the guitar to judge the guitarists, and, by frankly not being able to say, it made some critics flatter them very little. What is interesting for the guitarists and us is that every time that those artists risk to arrive in London they succeed to fill the hall. For us that is very important, because the success encourages them to return, and of this mode it is proportionately for us the great pleasure to hear the incomparable music of the guitar, which none of the millions of Englishmen know how to play.

Matilde Cuervas and Emilio Pujol, the famous married couple, gave the latest concert. The English public enjoyed the Flamenco music, because they didn't need a lot of technical knowledge to understand it. Matilde Cuervas has known how to refine, and polish the Flamenco music, getting rid of a little of its savagery. In the Wigmore Hall she appeared solo and later with her husband, playing with an ease and grace that left the English admiring. Her fingers wove the music over the strings like a spider weaves its web. At my side, some English folks, by watching them they had some notions of the guitar music, they observed what turned out to be very gracious and elegant to see the guitar and a woman, an Andalusian woman above all.

Matilde Cuervas honors the Spanish woman with her presence on foreign soil. Besides being an artist she is very cultured, and very dedicated, collaborating with her husband, to adapt ancient music pieces to the guitar composed for string instruments hundreds of years ago.

I. F. 'Were you a guitarist before being married?' I asked Matilde at the exit.

M. C. 'When I was eight years old I gave my first concert'-she answered- 'I'm certain I cried on the stage, out of anger. In my house they had the custom to call me ugly, feucha, as a joke, of course. The day of my first concert I was wearing two stiff braids, and as I was very small that I had to take the guitar by dragging it, the public, seeing me, burst out laughing. I believed they were laughing at me because I was ugly, and crying I left the stage, with the guitar after me. Then they consoled me and I went out again to play; but I looked at the public with rage.'

Matilde continued to tell us as if in the home of her father, where many guitarists frequented, those taught her how to play flamenco. She wrote down the notes, and then played as she read them, leaving the Flamencos marveled. 'But as I was making the notes'-she continued to say- 'I found it the strangest thing that the guitarists never played a piece the same way twice in a row. It always turned out different, without them giving notice to the fact.'

Matilde was purifying the music that she heard, and now has the technique of the Flamenco music.

I. F. 'Where did you meet your husband?'

684

M. C. 'In reality I met him in Spain, at a concert. I was very enthusiastic to hear him, because I had heard a lot about him. But because I was seated in the first row, and he, by his position, he had no choice than to look in my direction, he didn't even see me, and he didn't even take into account of the enthusiasm with which I had listened to him. That bothered me very much, and I took a sure dislike to him. Years later, in Paris although I knew he was there, I didn't have any desire to get to know him. One afternoon, however, I met him in a home of some friends, and …. well, we got married.'

Emilio Pujol listened very proud, full of satisfaction. They are an ideal couple. That I saw, the English public felt his presence and thanked him. They destroyed the legend of which the Spanish woman is, like the women of the Orient, very beautiful, but completely useless. Besides they both play the guitar very well.

Sainz de la Maza, Segovia, the married Pujols, all those guitarists attract us a little when they come to London. I always leave the hall, after hearing one of them, and rub my eyes to see if it's the truth, not to see if it's a lie that I felt under the magic of the guitar.

Irene De Falcon London"

Matilde Cuervas

This photo is from *"La Guitarra"* magazine No. 3 *Año* II published in December of 1941 in Havana, Cuba.

左 **Mathilde Cuervas**　　右 **Prof. Emilio Pujol**

　　　　ドニア・マチルデの想い出

　昔、アルモニアの添附写真にドニア・マチルデの若い美しい姿のものがあった。又、未来
と理想を視つめた射るような眼の壮年のプホール先生の写真も見たことがある。
　マドリードに着いて間もなく、バルセローナに先生御夫妻を訪ねたが、その頃はもう満ち
たりた老夫婦であった。しかし御二人とも壮年の頃の面影を、そのまゝ残していた。
　ドニア・マチルデは私が持参した絹の赤いマフラーを首に巻いて若い娘のように、はしゃ
ぎ、これをリスボンに持って行くのだと喜んでいたのは昨日のことのようである。
　プホール先生のレッスンが終ってから、ドニア・マチルデにフラメンコをきかせてくれと
ねだったことがあったが、不自由な手でマラグーニア風なものをひいた時のプホール先生の
喜びようは一通りではなかった。手足が不自由になってからは、全くギタラから遠ざかって
いたようで、私が我儘を言わなかったら、恐らくギタラを持つことはなかったであろうし、
あの時が最後の演奏だったかも知れない。
　その後、数回マドリードで、又イタリアで先生の御宅を訪ね、勉強させて頂いたが、先生
とドニア・マチルデは、いつも御一緒であった。片ときも離れていることの出来ない若い恋
人のように必ず手をとり合ってバルセローナ、マドリード、リスボン、パリ、イタリアと忙
しい旅行を続けられていたが、先生御夫妻の日常生活を通じて私は偉大な人間愛を教えられ
た。先生はドニア・マチルデなしに一日も居られなかったであろうし、ドニアは『エミーリ
オは完全な人間』だといつも敬愛していた。そして御二人の結びつきが、先生の芸術を推し
進めたのは疑いのないことで、今、独り残された老先生がこれからたった御一人でどのよう
に御暮しになるかと思えば胸をかきむしられるような悲しみを覚える。しかし魂は、たえず
先生と共にあって先生とギタラを愛しつゞけていてくれると信ずるが、先に銘工マルセーロ
を失い、今、母のようなドニア・マチルデの訃を知り、私の心は暗く沈んで浮かない。
　　　　　　　　　　　　　　　　　　　　　　（文及び写真提供・小原安正）

13　　　　　　　　　　　　　　　　　　　　　　　　　　　　　　（ 42 ）

This is from the Japanese guitar magazine *"Armonia"* from March-April 1957 Vol. IV No. 2, and is a remembrance of Matilde Cuervas Rodríguez (1887-1956), written by Yasumasa Obara. The magazine was printed in Sen Dai, Miyagiken, a city heavily damaged by the tsunami after the 8.9 magnitude earthquake March 11, 2011. Japanese translation by Randy Osborne.

"Memories of *Doña* Matilde Cuervas

Doña Matilde Cuervas in a young beautiful form in an old, *"Armonia"* accompanying photo. Furthermore, you can also see the future in the photo and ideally you can see the maestro Emilio Pujol's eyes shine in the prime of life.

686

I arrived in Madrid and before too long, in Barcelona I visited the maestro and his wife, at that time already an old couple. However, with the two, the prime of life's visage of time, remained like that. *Doña* Matilde brought before me a silk red scarf she was wearing rolled up like a young daughter, in Lisbon this she was happy to have from just a few days ago.

Maestro Emilio Pujol was so very glad when *Doña Matilde* played the *Flamenco Malagueña* style, with a little discomforted hand upon my request after the lesson with Professor Emilio Pujol. It seems like she would never touch the guitar again since she got the inconvenience in her hand, so she would not perform on the guitar if I did not state my request, and that might have been her last performance.

After that, a few times in Madrid, and again in Italy I visited the maestro's home, to let myself study but, as for the maestro and *Doña Matilde* they were always together. Even one way like young lovers he couldn't be separating generally hand in hand in Barcelona, Madrid, Lisbon, Paris, Italy busy continuing taking trips but, the maestro's wife's lifestyle, I thought was a great human being's love. As for the maestro even every day *Doña Matilde* couldn't be, as for *Doña Matilde* 'Emilio, the complete human being' always had respect and affection. The couple were united then, but by deduction the maestro's art no doubt moved forward, now, the old maestro left alone from now on is the only one to become spending his time, if you come to think about it, of him leaning against his chest sadly remembering. However as for the soul, constantly the maestro together with the maestro expecting to be with the guitar to continue getting to love it and believing but, before the refined artisan Marcelo (Barbero) died, now, when I read of the mother like *Doña Matilde's* obituary, as for my heart it is dark and depressed it can't be cheerful.

Text and photo offered by Mr. Yasumasa Obara"

Domingo Prat presents this view of the great artist, Andrés Segovia, in his *"Diccionario de Guitarristas"*:

Segovia Torres, Andrés— Concert Guitarist, most excellent in his highest conception and modest composer. He was born in Linares, Spain on March 17, 1893. We will refer to his baptismal certificate, which we copy:

"Don Francisco Morales Aballes, Priest of the San Pedro Parish of this capital-Certify: That the No. 66 folio, in the twenty first book of Baptizims of this Parish Archive appears the following-Entry: In the City of Jaen, the twenty fourth of March of one thousand eight hundred ninety three: I *Don* Juan Garrido y Quesada, Coadjutant Priest of San Pedro, with the license of the Parish of the same, solemnly baptized to a boy, that the according to the declaration given in due form before me and the witnesses that also were in it José Carpio and Miguel Moya, employee of this Church; by that which was said to be and to be named Rosa Torres Cruz, mother of the baptized, was born on the seventh day of the current month at half past six o'clock in the afternoon in the Corredera No. 94 of the City of Linares and residing in it accidentally, son — of Bonifacio Segobia y Montoro and of Rosa Torres Cruz; — Paternal grandparents Andrés and Maria Francisca: natives, the father and paternal grandparents, of this City; the mother and maternal grandmother, of Malaga; the maternal grandfather, of Churriana. The godmother: Teresa Granadino, unmarried, put the name Andrés, I advised her of the spiritual kinship and her obligations. And for what is evident I signed with the Rdo. Parish priest, Juan Garrido, rubricado. Dn. Romero-rubricado. This literal copy of the original that I remitted, Jaén the thirty first of December one thousand nine hundred and thirty. There is a stamp of the Iglesia de San Pedro de Jaén"

It draws the attention that the record his baptizim would belong to the church in Jaén, and not to that of Linares where he was born, presently making that in the transcribed document, the paternal surname that is written with a B, or as Segobia, being known by us and universally as SEGOVIA. A curious detail of biography and perhaps important data for the interested.

We might be able to add little or nothing, if we might attempt it, to the voluminous book of praises of his elevated art. The famous violinist Kreisler, referring to Segovia, declared: "Only two great musicians exist in the world, Casals (cellist) and Segovia".

Without searching in the musical world among its distinct branches and focusing on only sublime instrumentalists, the name of Segovia we can consider placed many steps higher up in the temple of the glory without end, along with others such as Casals, Kreisler, etc.

Through the violoncello and the violin, respectively, the knowledge of the instrumental technique can be a platform where it exactly evaluates the concept which it develops on the guitar. The joining of three or more notes in a single sound (at once, as in a chord) gives beauty, equally to that which the painter obtains by the mixing of two or more colors, and what is usually reserved for the orchestra (joining of violin, violoncello, flute, etc.) or for the piano and for the guitar. The trills of the violin or the slides and vibrations of the violoncello that, to be distinguished, appear by them only as the emotive body in which resides the wealth of sentiments of the sheet music that is heard, and might not give a sensation of beauty so finished and so perfect, if they don't act as over the backdrop that they form of the bass, and the rest of the harmonic part of the orchestra in which they act as primary figures. The rose that, is illuminated by the golden rays of a rising sun, we admire in the foreground of a green luxuriant growth, real in itself all the emotion of the beauty of the frame in which we see it, to the point that, the vision passed, we only remember one thing of it , -the flower-how beautiful! Thus we exclaim, recalling in the sheet music, the cadence of the violin or the vibration of the violoncello; but a rose, violin and violoncello, already out of its favorable frame, are as the sacramental phrase of a Shakespearean drama, which doesn't lose its worth, it has a very distinct appreciation of the emotive sentiment, according to considering it in relation to the ambiance of the drama to which it belongs.

688

To produce or execute, in a sublime degree, atmosphere and phrase is the difference that exists between the guitar and the violin and violoncello, considered as instruments that play solos. The guitar is sufficient in itself on a level of the sum of its refinement, converging in it the tonalities of the harp, chords of the piano, basses of the orchestra, slides of the violin and vibrations of the cello. The other instruments need to be complemented. The violin and the cello represent only the conception of the beauty of a flower, that in our case is the guitar, the rose, of the golden ray of sunlight, and of the green luxuriant growth. Such is the appreciation among the guitar of Segovia, the cello of Casals or the violin of Kreisler. Well understood that I haven't attempted to establish a paragon among personal values, but set a principal, a product of a fair analysis of the instrumental values.

The personality of Segovia presented through the guitar and evaluated by the famous Kreisler doesn't permit the process of the formation, his gestation, his development and his performance up to the pinnacle reached to be highly interesting.

There in Granada, since he was a child, he had played the guitar of *rasgueados* and *falsetas* (techniques of Flamenco guitar). The revelation of the instrumental musician gave to it a friend and disciple of Tárrega, the ventriloquist and Valencian guitarist Paco Sanz, applauded in Buenos Aires in 1912. In one of the continuous tours of of Spain, of this last artist, finding Segovia in Andalucia, he heard some of the repertoire of Tárrega by the modest Sanz (according to data contributed by him): so, he produced the spark. Segovia asked, investigated, analyzed, studied, learned and became independent of the provincial ambiance, to be separating of a regional semiart, and as by the enchantment he began to play in the form that an article of the press tells us that reproduce here: "Segovia, that romantic guitarist that, city by city, town by town, he's going to be carrying light in the magic strings of his guitar pure gusts of wind of art and of poetry that this insensitive public, doesn't appreciate him for what he's worth." (*Boletin* of the *"Biblioteca Fortea"*, January 1914.).

He went to Madrid, then passed on to Valencia, arrived in Barcelona in the year 1915. He was presented. He struggled and triumphed. The guitar on the public concert stage and of payment isn't known there in Barcelona, and it's only in *"capillitas "* of humble aficionados, adorned of bias, admirers of such or whatever maestro. To Segovia from the beginning they admired him, they helped him, and they applauded him, but, although those appreciations they dismissed the rickets in which they lived, they didn't discover or didn't know to see in him the artist that was born for the world. With the guitar he conquered the most representative of the *bellas artes* and of the sciences in the cultured Barcelonan city, where with fear of us making a mistake, we might be able to assure that he won his *"brevet"* to fly in the musical universe. In one of our visits to Barcelona in the year 1916 we met him, we heard and were comrades of Segovia. A group of admirers, among those that had many guitarists, we offered a dinner in "Casa-Juan", a specie of a modest Parisian tavern. Segovia played there. His decision, security, diction, sound and "posse", while he was going to work through his repertoire, well known by us, we affirmed the congratulatory auguries that the father of whom is writing this had made of this portent: "This is the artist that the guitar needs".

He began giving continuous concerts.

The impresarios, shrewd in the matter, see in him a new element for their profits. He goes to Argentina three times (always with a contract), then to New York (the contractors disputed over him), he's applauded in London, Paris, Boston, Mexico, Berlin, Brussels, Saint Petersburg, Stockholm, Budapest, Rome, Vienna and wherever they present him he is the best artist.

Segovia is a psychologist, by excellence, respectful of the public, such is one of the secrets of his triumphs. In his performances he comes on to the stage slowly, gallant, without smiling; but correct. There isn't any stiffness in his movements, neither an affected presentation. Once seated, in front of the audience, with prudent time he calls for silence; when that is absolute, he commences his playing, convinced of which that those present must be quiet to hear, which is to him what they have done. During the performance, he demands religious silence from the devoted, the smallest noise bothers him, and he invites with a smooth gesture that it won't happen again, letting it be understood that whoever makes the noise must leave and let him play whatever passage of the work, if the noise persists in bothering or distracting him. This moral strength and continuous serenity dominates the mass, predisposing it to feel all the beauty of what he plays. He is the genuine actor that, possessed by the same, *"habla"* (speaks) as if in his own home and in his occasion he interrogates the public with a look, that penetrates with happiness or sorrow however, according to the theme that he is playing. The actor with fear of the public can't be abstract and give the complete artistic sensation of what he interprets; so the nervous guitarist never can be presented as a complete artist. Segovia, free of those fears, sure of himself, happy with all his soul the date of the concert has arrived and experiences beforehand the enjoyment of contact with the public, a quality which, separate of all his intrinsic worth, it has reaffirmed him in all his successes. It's perfectly explainable that the nervousness of the guitarist that doesn't possess these abilities would produce in him perturbation of memory and absence of subtle touch, so indispensable for the conquest of the triumph. And if in these abilities he acts to being saved by the effort of his amazed study or playing capacity, it never toasts to the public in full satisfaction of the pleasure of the conquest, obtaining only complacent applause that in the foundation is charity. Segovia never needed gifts; by his own merit he conquered the applause, that almost demanded; because he knew his guitar, his art and his personality had a dominant fascinating worth.

He is therefore, without a school, without maestros, of a very humble cradle and not of a favorable ambiance, but strong and unique, erect with a gesture of a challenge, hurling in the face of failed studies his celebrated phrase: "I feel happy of not having met Tárrega; since of having met him, perhaps I wouldn't be who I am". Just and profound in his independence, it reveals to us not only the concert guitarist, the musician, but also the sharp man and his virile character. His abilities are exceptional that charm and bring to the guitar the knowledge of the music staff; Moreno Torroba, C. Pedrell, Turina, Tansman, Cyril Scott, Samazueilh, Ponce and others that form a legion, obligating them to write beautiful musical pages for the guitar, in whose works shine and honor the composer and player, to be reaffirming with it the beauty of the instrument.

The impressions on discs by Segovia, although having a high value, they suffer from the natural and positive beauty that always escapes the recording. In the sound, as in the color, there are impossible subtlties to confine on a disc as in a photograph; as it is an approximate copy of that, which always establishes a level of approach which enhances the bad and denatures the good. All of the beauty of a beautiful woman is of a totally impossible point to condense in a photograph, as is the subtle art of Segovia that doesn't exist in any of his discs. Grand in all and to be excelling in itself continuously, perhaps he himself, doesn't appreciate all of the worth of the great success achieved in his last visit to Buenos Aires in 1928. He arrived on the 30th of June and gave his first concert four days later; he offered nine concerts, two a week, besides performing in those short intervals in Montevideo and in some province of the public. He embarked to Europe on the 20th of August, forgetting to play an announced concert that on that date was for one of the largest musical associations of the Republic.

The interval of seven years lasted since his second to his latest tour of Argentina. A renovation of almost all of the works of his repertoire was the factor of great importance to awaken the interest that produced the enthusiastic reception that he received; as a beautiful detail and suggestive of his great successes, we recall in his seventh concert, that took place on the 8th of August (in the afternoon, as the rest). At the same hour and the distance of a few meters away, the most excellent pianist Rubinstein gave his 4th concert with a attractive program. In the six previous concerts of Segovia, in spite of their frequency, all of them were an occasion where in the ticket booth of the theater was shown the pleasant little card "Sold Out"; in this 7th concert to which we refer, that coincides the day and hour with that of the Rubinstein, we expected it to be a fortuitous duel that the guitar would remain at a disadvantage. The concert of the pianist took place in the teatro de la Opera, and resulted in being completely full, but the concert of Segovia was a unique public success, an absolute and complete sellout. The cited event, besides of the making by the unique manner of the personality of Segovia, is well implanted the high value of the musical culture of the public of Buenos Aires and the devotees that the guitar has in him; supposing equally a suggestive interrogator, for those that present with the same instrument and don't achieve the success they dream of.

For Segovia, as a composer, we recall the following works: *"Impromptu"*, *"Tres preludios"* and *"Tonadilla" (Biblioteca Fortea)*. The value of these works lies marked with the success that they have reached as the didactic, *"Escalas y Arpegios"*. The personal contribution of fingering in the works that, for him the composers previously mentioned had written, gives opportunity for his originality, to very dignified praises; such as also in the effects of *rasgueado* (Flamenco strum), *tambora* and others, that if they don't improve, the ones already marked that we read in Juan Parga, with it will equip them to a level of worth. We believe of the convenience to annotate, with respect to these works, the many errors and distractions in what Segovia incurs, not only when he fingers the works of other composers, but also in his own transcriptions. We will give various examples of these errors of fingering, from this first ones to the latest editions in the houses "Orfeo Tracio", Madrid; José B. Romero", Buenos Aires; "Sociedad Musical Daniel", Madrid; "Durand", Paris and "Schott", Germany. Those same errors that we will continue to present, they are seen in the original production already cited of this concert guitarist, published before the year 1920, *"Canto del Campesino"*: by Grieg, *Edicion "Orfeo Tracio"*. In the 5th measure, 4th beat, it isn't possible to sharp the quarter note SOL of the chord, if doing a portamento from Mi to Do. The same mistake is repeated in the 10th measure, 2nd beat, which orders a sharped quarter note, while playing two eighth notes. Of the production of transcriptions and fingerings that he left in Buenos Aires, in his second visit, that was published by the house of José B. Romero, in *"Vidalita"* by Aguirre; in the 5th measure, it isn't possible to sharp the LA, for all its value.

"Leyenda" by Albeniz: page 5, 3rd and 4th measures. You can't sustain the time of the DO, as it's indicated.

"Sonatina", by Moreno Torroba, *"Edicion Musical Daniel"*, Madrid, the year 1924. The first initial chord can't be a quarter note.

"Segovia", by Albert Roussel: *Edicion "A. Durand"*, the year 1925. In the 9th measure we don't believe it is necessary to indicate the 3rd beat in two forms, that is to say, with a Bar and without.

"Sérénade", by Gustave Samazeuilh: Editor "A. Durand", the year 1926. In the 9th line, 2nd measure, it isn't possible to sharp the quarter note SOL in the 1st beat, by repeating the same SOL in the 2nd half of the cited time.

The works we will continue to name belong to the house of Schott.

"Nocturno" by Moreno Torroba, the year 1926: In the 5th line, 2nd measure, it isn't possible to sharp the MI. The 3rd measure of the same line is can't be played as written.

"Preludio", by J. S. Bach, the year 1928: 5th measure. In other texts, the FA, the last 16th of the 1st beat, is SOL. The fingering of this measure is barely possible.

"Courante", by J. S. Bach, the year 1928: In the 2nd measure of the 5th line, the fingering of the left hand, could be an error of the printer or of the transcriber.

"Sonata III", by Manuel M. Ponce: In the 3rd page, 6th line, 1st measure, it's impossible to make the 2nd position Bar. We admit that it could be the fault of the printer. But these same errors we find very often in the works fingered by Segovia.

"Preludio", by Moreno Torroba, the year 1928: In the 8th measure it is impossible to play the 16th notes SI and MI, sustaining the SOL sharp of the chord. In the 3rd page, 4th line, 2nd measure, the SI can't be a dotted note, by having to make the FA sharped in the 7th fret of the 2nd string.

"Mazurka", by Alexander Tansman: In the 4th page, last line, 2nd measure. It's impossible to play the initial chord with a 9th position Bar.

"Cuatro piezas breves", by César Franck. In the 6th measure: playing the MI on the 2nd string, as it's indicated, it is impossible to sustain the SI quarter note for a whole beat. In the 9th measure: playing an LA on the 1st string, as indicated, you can't sustain the SI and MI quarter note of the chord.

"Lamento", by Carlos Pedrell: In the 8th measure. You can't sustain the LA , if you have to play an FA on the 6th string. The following measure shows the same error.

"Preludes" VII, by Manuel Ponce, the year 1930: In the 4th line, 4th measure. This measure is really disastrous. It's impossible to analyze.

"Fanstasia / Sonata", by Juan Manen. This work consists of 87 lines. However, in the 1st measure, the 3rd SI can't be sustained, because there has to be a SOL sharp played, 3rd 16th note, with the 1st finger. There is the same defect in the last beat of the same measure. We won't continue the revision of this fantasy by being too extensive...

"Pieces caracteristiques", by Moreno Torroba, the year 1931. Preambulo: the 4th line, 1st measure. It isn't possible to sustain the LA for all of its time, as it's indicated.

"Sonata", by Joaquín Turina, the year 1932: the 4th line, 2nd measure. You might be only able to play this as written, making a 5th position Bar. In the following measure you can't sustain the LA of the chord by having to tie the SI flat.

"Variations sur "Folia de España", by Manuel Ponce. Vaviation I. The faults in the writing are deplorable in the first eight measures. Variation III, in the 4th measure: We believe that in the 2nd beat, the cantabile part, must continue to be written in the same form as in the following two measures, in what I refer to as the notes of the same name are tied.

"Variazioni (attraverso i secoli...) (through the centuries...), by Mario Castelnuovo-Tedesco, the year 1933: 5th line. The first two measures have a fingering that is a little bit capricious. And in the 2nd measure, to be able to play the 2nd LA tied, it is necessary to get rid of the 2nd position Bar.

"The *"Variations sobre un tema"*, by Mozart-Sor, deserve a separate paragraph. We know that Segovia in Buenos Aires published them, in the house of Romero & Fernández in 1921 (?). Many years later, although we don't know why, Schott, in Germany printed them. There are some changes in these two editions; but what's important is that neither of the named publishers that Segovia did contains the Introduction by Fernando Sor. We don't understand why this was done in the house of Schott, when they had published the same work before, with the Introduction, although not revised by Segovia. In our private archive we have the *"Variaciones sobre un tema"*, printed by the editorial Heugel, successor to Meissonnier, with the following cover: *"Variations / Brillantes / sur un Air favori de Mozart/de l'Opera la Flute Enchatée / (O Cara Armonia) / Pour Guitarre Seule / Executées par l'Auteur au Concert donné a l'Ecole Rte. de Musique / et dediées a son Frere / Op. 9".* It is, without any doubt, the most complete of the editions. Another publication in our possession, by the house of N. Simrock, was published in the cities of Bonn and Cologne, with the number 2292 of the editorial. These last three editions named differ in the order of the placement and in the totality of the variations; but, nevertheless, all of them have the Introduction by Sor, that we must respect, since we owe the guitaristic beauty to him.

We also deplore the lack of artistic seriousness by Segovia, not only in what I refer to in the fingering of the works we covered, but as well with respect to his playing on the disc. Besides the lack of the introduction, there are variations that aren't repeated, and that put a large eraser over the halo of Segovia the musician.

We never see in the phonographic impression of a Symphony of Beethoven or a work of Chopin, the lack of repeats in some of its parts, but that they are executed such as they were originally written. We affirm that Beethoven, Chopin and Sor were equally great, and by that, they are dignified of all consideration.

We won't continue an analysis of this work, neither the enunciation of the faults in his works. We have only made note of some errors, taken at random, of one part of the works, transcriptions or fingerings by the great Segovia. We do it with him, by dealing with the top guitarist. We might not do it with a guitaristic mediocrity, because there's no interest in it.

Nevertheless, we let it be constancy of that in the humble original production or transcript by Manjón, the blind guitarist, there aren't any errors of this class; perhaps because his music might have been revised by a competent person. It's our opinion that Segovia must do the same, to not defraud the hopes of the many guitarists that acquire the works they purchase, by one or another cause, his name by the respect it deserves, and for the good of the works of many other great composers, that to him they give, to consider it, with reason, the best player. Of course, if we dedicate ourselves with the pledge to conscientiously revise the works of Manjón and whatever other composer or transcriber, we might encounter the faults of that class; but never with the frequency of those contained in the works where Segovia has put on his personal stamp.

So ends the entry in Domingo Prat's *Diccionario de Guitarristas.*

From page 5 of the daily *"La Correspondencia de España"* Madrid, December 19, 1919:
This translated is: Andrés Segovia to South America. Andrés Segovia, the greatest of all the cultivators of that noble and unjustly denigrated instrument, that is the guitar, who so triumphant for his art as has gallantly struggled, has been contracted by the impresario *Don* Ernesto Quesada for a long tour during the next year to Brazil, Cuba, Peru, Argentina and Uruguay.

Andrés Segovia a Sudamérica

Andrés Segovia, el más grande de los cultivadores de ese noble e injustamente denigrado instrumento, que es la guitarra, por cuyo arte ha luchado tan triunfal como gallardamente, ha sido contratado por el empresario D. Ernesto Quesada para una larga tournée durante el próximo año por Brasil, Chile, Perú, Argentina y Uruguay.

RUBINSTEIN, A SUR AMERICA.—Contratado por el inteligente empresario Sr. Quesada hará este genial artista en el próximo año fuse una campaña por los países suramericanos de cincuenta conciertos, por los que recibirá la suma respetable de 11,000 duros. Esto es un nuevo triunfo de D. Ernesto Quesada, que tiene firmados contratos con el gran pianista Stefaniai e insigne guitarrista Andrés Segovia, también para América. Estos dos artistas darán antes de marchar, y como despedida, otros cuantos conciertos, que se celebrarán en la Comedia el lunes 12 y sábado 17 de enero próximo, respectivamente.

From page 5-6 of the daily *"El Imparcial"* Madrid, December 24, 1919: Rubinstein, to South America-Contracted by the intelligent impresario Mr. Quesada will have this brilliant artist in the next year fuse a campaign of fifty concerts for the South American countries, for those he will receive the respectable sum of 11,000 duros. This is a new triumph for *Don* Ernesto Quesada, who has signed contracts with the great pianist Stefanini and the distinguished guitarist Andrés Segovia, who also will go to the Americas. Those two artists will give before they leave, and as a goodbye, some other concerts, that they will celebrate in the Comedia Monday the 12th and Saturday the 17th of January, respectively.

Source: Professor Julio Gimeno Garcia, Seville

This biographical material about maestro Andrés Segovia is from Ricardo Muñoz's unpublished book *"Historia Universal de la Guitarra"* Volume V *"Los Contemporaneos"*.

Ricardo Muñoz drew from a very large bibliography to write his articles, biographies, etc. I shall leave out the duplication of his usage from Domingo Prat's *Diccionario de Guitarristas*, already included. All other material from the 32 typewritten pages shall be included.

"His Virtuosity

In 1920 Andrés Segovia arrived in Buenos Aires, which hotly applauded him, as few times he had known it to be done, appreciating one of the greatest interpreters of the classics of the epoch in all of his guitaristic musical worth; in regard to that A. Hernández Cata wrote the following: " An now, some words about Segovia. The first, for satisfying the social character of this act and although to risk of being contrary to my Republican heart, it may be said that Segovia has performed twice for the Royalty of Spain. We might say right away that he has played many times more before the distinguished writers and musicians, which are as well the kings of the art. His concerts in Spain and outside of it remove the critic and they kneel around him in admiration. Since Saint Tárrega never has been heard so much musicality, so much tenderness."

"Here I have a guitar, which in case only redeems to all of the guitars of the world that are going to be getting into the mud. The guitar of Segovia makes it a baby girl in his hands or expands it when the hurricane of the passion vibrates on its strings, when he caresses it, it appears a prolongation of his breast. You're going to hear, well, an artist of the glorious lineage of the Casals, of the Kreisler, of the Sauer...."

"To hear the guitar played by my friend Segovia, to convince you, of which not in vain it almost has the form of a heart."

Segovia left Buenos Aires the next year (1921), taking with him two great memories, according to his own expression: "The most emotional of my life, maybe. My first performance in Buenos Aires and my first son (Andrés Jr.) as well being born in this beautiful and charming Argentine land."

Martin Gil the astronomer and select Argentine writer, of the high artistic spirit, made a critical judgement about Segovia saying, writing: "Many times, after having listened to Andrés Segovia, I have attempted to fix my impressions and other times I have failed in my intention, including now. His art is extraordinary, so intense, so subtle, so full of light and at once of tones and the glow of twilight of an acoustic painting illuminated by amazing lights, of truth and of dreams, of reality and of mystery, evoking the pain in a form so noble, so dignified, so serene, that consequently is impossible to materialize them, I'll say, with words on paper. Maybe if it was easier to simply fix such impressions in a diaphanous plaque of the soul, by having to do with an artist that is pure soul."

Segovia continued his recitals in South America, triumph after triumph; in 1923 he returned to Europe visiting Paris in 1924; he arrived in Madrid and performed in January of 1925, in the Teatro Comedia, works by Visée, Giuliani, Sor, Tárrega, Bach, Turina, de Falla, Pedrell and Moreno Torroba; in 1926 we find him in Moscow, proceeding to France, in whose capital he gave two recitals in the first days of February, leaving on the 18th of this month for England, where he stayed until the end of this year. In Paris, heard by the celebrated Stravinsky, admired by his art in the Teatro de la Opera, said: "The guitar does not sound strong, but is heard far." a phrase that has more sense than of which to the first sight seems.

He continues bringing his guitar to Rome, Sweden, Denmark, Belgium, Switzerland, Cuba, Mexico and New York until 1928; the public and the music and newspaper critics consecrated him, unanimously, as the finest guitarist of the world, paying tribute to him with frenetic ovations. The celebrated Max Nordau, profoundly impressed, said: "I'll say and I don't believe it is blasphemy, which renovates to our manner the evangelical miracle of the multiplication of the bread. Because it starts, as he does, of a humble guitar, the sonorities, the brilliances, the movement, the variety, the tone colors, the effects of the sentiments and the force of a complete orchestra, it isn't less prodigal to feed the four loaves of bread to

694

thousands of hungry Galileans. The Middle Ages might have burned us as a wizard to less that venerates as a saint. Less fanatic in our epoch, content with admirers, as he makes us profoundly impressed."

The first tour of Segovia in the United States surpassed the optimum predictions; not only the public deliriously gave him ovations, but a select group of artists among whom we record Mengelberg, Molinari, Koussevitzky, Damarosch, Levinne, Moiseiwitzch, Gabrilowitch, etc. The newspaper fragments, which they transcribe, consigned for the posterity, demonstrate the triumph of the great guitarist.

The day of January 8, 1928, date of his first recital, all the seats of the Town Hall were sold out: "Genius of the Guitar", said Samuel Chotzinof in the World, "This instrument doesn't have any limitation in his hands ."

Olin Downes wrote in the "Times" "... as he is a poet and a maestro, his manner to play is poetic and masterful." Leonard Liebling in the "American" said: "He makes a real miracle completely conquering his audience." In the "Herald Tribune", Lawrence Gilman gave his opinion: "He makes the guitar an instrument that speaks like the cello of Casals or of the violin of Heifetz."

The 30th of June 1928 he arrived at the port of Buenos Aires on board the *"Giulio Césare"* by account of the business Alzati y Cia., and initiated his concerts in the Teatro Odeon on the 3rd of July, performing the *Minuetto* and *Tema Variado* of Sor, *Fandanguillo* by Turina, *Estudio* by Tárrega, *Preludio, Alemana, Fuga, Courante* and *Gavota* by Bach; Minuetto by Haydn, *Sonatina* by Moreno Torroba and *Leyenda* by Albeniz. The obtained result, with an overflowing quantity of the guitaristic public, was clearly reflected the following day, *"La Prensa"* said: "The guitar isn't as, it's been said, the most artistic of the popular instruments, but the only instrument that the populace uses; since; it is the possessor of varied and rich musical resources, of an important literature of its own, cultivated by eminent artists, that can figure on par with the piano, of the violin, or of the violoncello, which this preserve forever to the bagpipes, to the mandolin, the bandurria, the accordion, the quena, or the erque, pleasant, delicate or picturesque in popular songs, but preserve to a musical cult."

"Yesterday Andrés Segovia who after 7 years of absence gave his first concert in the Odeon, is one of the artists which has made the guitar ennobled and dignified the most, who occupies a distinguished seat in the classic art, but has reduced the artistic circles width during more than a century, was overall known as an instrument of the Spanish public and Americans of the Iberian lineage."

"If technically he is a perfect performer, since the point of musical view he has acquired a defined and captivating personality and a style which only is encountered in exceptional artists."

"In the hands of Segovia, the guitar acquires an outstanding artistic signification; if his sonority can't be great volume, due to the nature of the instrument, it achieves the range of sonorities, so varied as tone colors, of a infinite delicacy of a brilliant and incredible vigor...."

"The six pieces of the German composer (Bach), were poured out by Segovia with a purity of style, an elegance and a musicality rarely achieved by known pianists.... (Moreno Torroba, Turina, Albeniz) they had in Segovia an ideal interpreter, that knew to clearly put in with the rhythmic rich supreme art, the popular flavor and so genuine an expression of these pages, which the Spanish soul spoke at length in them".

"In summation, a note of superior art and a new affirmation of which the guitar is an instrument dignified of the appreciation which it dispenses to the rest".

"La Nacion" of the 4th of July of 1928: ".... it appears impossible to achieve a better grade of perfection in a mechanism, which undertakes the most extraordinary difficulties with the most natural simplicity; a better purity and beauty of sonorities, which go from the most delicate and smooth tone colors to the most ample and robust sonority, and maybe which it is the rarest, to be treating of this instrument and of whom cultivate it, a greater musical interest, which demonstrates the nobility, in the sobriety and the respect with which Segovia presents the works that he puts in his program....".

He continued his performances on the dates July 6th, 13th, 17th, 23rd and 27th; August 8th, 12th and 19th, performing the works of Llobet, Tárrega, Sor, Coste, Mozart, Mendelssohn, Grieg, Turina, Moreno Torroba, Albeniz, Giuliani, Pedrell, Milan, Bach, Franck, Ponce, Samazeuilh, Granados, de Visée, Schubert, Scott, Tansman, Roussel, Malats, Chilesotti and Handel; the performances played impeccably by this exemplary virtuoso, the diverse places to reunite all the spiritual classes, from the intuitive cultivators of the popular guitar, to the most prominent figures of out arts and our lyrics.

He finished the last successful concert on August 19th, a select number of artists, writers, aficionados and admirers, offered him a banquet in the Plaza Hotel, surrounding the table were known persons, such as, the Ambassador of Mexico *Don* Alfonso Reyes, the Ambassador Minister of Spain *Don* Francisco Agramonte, *Don* Martin Gil, Artur Rubinstein, Rafael Gonzalez, Dr. Americo Albino, Gaston O. Talamon, Francisco Diego, Enrique Feinman, Carlos Vega, Rodolfo Franco, Jorge Gomez, José Sanchez, Celestino Fernández , Adolfo Luna, V.R. Christensen, Juan Pastor, Dionisio Gracia and many others, including the author of this Volume VII. On the following day *"La Nacion"* quoted the eminent *Don* Martin Gil:

"Before all, I will say with frankness, that I find very little spiritual that to celebrate eating, (one of the most prosaic acts of life) the presence of one of the most spiritual men that I have known and one of the greatest artists which has emerged on the planet. But so an attitude that can be forgiven as if Segovia were a glutton. But it happens all on the contrary. In spite of his aspect of a well fed large child, or of a happy seminary person who has escaped the establishment, or of a pleasant bandit when I see him walk the streets to great strides and in the form to scatter, under the great wings of his grey hat, looking from behind his glasses, whose thick glass magnifies the pupils, which appear as two small spent caramels, however, I say, all those dynamic appearances, Segovia is very sober and more still although it costs to believe him: Segovia is serious and profoundly melancholic. Of a melancholic interior, difficult to describe. Segovia, at first sight, has the simple and sane happiness of the pure and crstalline water which runs without knowing where, in search of its level never found. And poor of the water if you find where it arrives! Like as well: poor of Segovia if he finds his. poor of him and his admirers if they all sometime declare to be satisfied and happy! Because it's understood to be completely happy implies the greatest disgrace. Since from that moment the artist would have to be dead. The same of the water; to find its level in converts into a lagoon.... ! and after that the frogs come!"

"We can say of Segovia what Byron said to Lord Macaulay: That all the fairies gave a meeting around his crib to fulfill with his gifts, except one, which I don't remember which it was."

"Now it can be believed, so, at first sight that the fairy avoids for with Segovia if he had been the dispenser of the physical beauty. However, in this matter, we have to abidecompletely by the verdict of the only competent judge., the beautiful sex and the beautiful sex says, referring to Segovia, that, "the other thing is with the guitar". It is that Segovia has the great talent of the immediate charm; of the warm and suggestive verbal expression. He possesses the smooth surrounding and caressing of the frail confessor intelligent and good:

What an admirable confessor Segovia would have been!"

"What I am seeing with the Franciscan habit, of sandals, tinkling of the medals of the extensive rosary, the walking, silence to the long cold cloisters. It would be common, for me to see, to say that Segovia plays the guitar admirably, because in truth Segovia doesn't play the guitar, Segovia transforms the guitar, the magnificence, the elevated and spiritualized to such a grade, that first to be surprised must be, without a doubt, the guitar itself, to be asked within if she can speak and sing in a form so unknown. Segovia is to be found situated in a plane so distinct to the commonness of the mortals, which in respect to him can't form some comparison. Segovia is only, as was Paganini in his moments. And now, this friendly and great predictor of the beauty of sound and of the expression, after having completed his noble mission among us to spiritualize, proceeds his path around the world, with the naturalness with which the water on the mountain runs, always singing and without knowing why the sadness and mysterious glory of living. Beloved Segovia: please receive these insignificant but affectionate words of mine, in the name of all of those reunited here".

The impressions left by Segovia were fertile in the relation with the variety of an ennoblement of the repertoire, which the great artist deserved considerably enriched by the exhumation of the Spanish, German, French, Italian and English works of antiquity, and those which the modern authors of our epoch are writing.

With Segovia the mediums of expression of the instrument had evolved to the point its richness of tone colors and sonorities give varieties, in the series of pedals that are put in play during the performance, whose musicality and temperament place the artist among the great interpreters of our century, individual endowments that lamentably disappear with him; is one of the most admirable accents which might have unfastened ever of the guitar to be directed to the sensibilities of mankind. Maestro of the same, he possesses in the most intimate accumulated experiences of one hundred generations rich of the aroma that the celebrated *"Triana"* dismisses in the historical *"Zambras"* of the morrish Spain; it pervades his spirit of the little boy the manner of the Andalucian populace dreams on the strings the synthetic pain of the *"Cante Jondo"*, and that hereditary richness and this lesson of the infancy, exalted by a vast culture, they must take him necessarily to say as it says on the guitar.

Don Emilio Pujol in the magazine *"La Guitarra"* expresses about this great artist in the following manner: "Andrés Segovia" is one of the most admired artists in our days. A virtuoso of exquisite gifts, although he's a universal success I've known him since he was very young. His art is expressive and notably sings, of delicate timbres, he possesses a strange power of fascination over the public. The interpretations of this extraordinary virtuoso, carry in themselves the germ of the musical dream. The guitar must be a jealous and tireless propaganda, one of the best reasons of its present prestige. Just like Llobet he possesses a decisive influence over the modern composers, who recently acquired a cause for the guitar. His compatriots, Turina, Chavarri, Moreno Torroba, Salazar, Arregui and the Hispanic Argentine Carlos Pedrell, have dedicated their works to him. To this Hispanic contribution they add happy pieces at times, of music with Spanish character, of the French Roussel, Samazeuilh, Collet, etc. Those that aren't of regional character are Ponce, Migot, Petit, Tansman, and others.

In 1932 we see him in Lausanne, Switzerland and the 13th of April of 1934 in the "Sala Bianco" of the Palazzo Pitti of Florence, Italy, the following day in the "Societa del Quatetto" in Milan, performing works by de Visée, Weiss, Moreno Torroba, Castelnuovo-Tedesco, Granados, Bach, Mozart, Schubert, Ponce and Albeniz. The poets didn't miss it, and sang so:

Al vostro onor d'eccelso chitarrista	To our honor the high guitarist
Bologna applaude dotta ed augurale:	Bologna applauds the scholar and he predicts:
di Voi godra il valor di sommo artista	you will enjoy the value of the great artist
il publico stipato al Comunale.	the audience packed the hall.
Né la perizia sol del chitarrista,	Neither the report of only the guitarist,
esecutor brillante, originale,	the brilliant performer, original,
ammirera, ma il chiaro musicista	you admire, but clearly the musician
di nuovo stile fondator geniale.	brilliant founder of the new style.
Interprete di Bach e dei moderni	He interprets of Bach and the modern
Autori fra i piu celebri e i piu vari	Authors of the most famous and most diverse

suggelli all'opera Vostra offrite eterni.	published works You offer eternal.
I discepoli a Voi devoti e cari *Salutan fra gli accordi e i ritmi alterni* *d'Andrés Segovia el nome senza pari.*	The disciples and devotees dear to you salute between the chords and alternate rhythms the unparalleled name of Andrés Segovia.

In May of the same year he performed in London, in July he made his own in Mexico, of whose capital he left the day of the 14th headed to Panama, he gave three performances in Lima Peru, another three in Santiago, Chile, one in the Province of Mendoza, Argentina, the 18th, 20th and the 24th of August in the Teatro Odeon in Buenos Aires, playing works by Sor, Moreno Torroba, Tárrega, Scarlatti, Bach, Haydn, Ponce, Albeniz, Granados, Weiss, Turina, Castelnuovo-Tedesco, in the debut of his *"Variazioni" (attraverso i secoli)*. The daily *"El Mundo"* on the 21st reported: "His tenderness, regularity and color cause an impression so harmonic and artistic, that it turns out to be impossible to be taken away from the enchantment which awakens.... it is a nobility and a simply admirable quality....the listener lets go of the side of the technical exploits more or less difficult, for concentrating his attention to the spiritual content of the phrases which go to linking with all naturalness, without anything that can resemble affection or ostentatiousness.

Indisputably Segovia is a great psychologist of the public, his brow which tranquilly contemplates and performs, it rests in it, par excellence, one of the most extraordinary factors in his triumph, the serenity in his person, with all the moral strength on his content, silently ordering the human masses which prepare to listen with the maximum attention. It is the absolute security in the true worth of himself; he knows of his eminent artistic gifts of his virtuosity over his instrument, gotten by his own effort, and launches it only to the demanding public critics, disposed to mercilessly criticize of his technical and expressive modes, which then turns out to the most grandiose personal cathedral.

He has given a new direction to the guitaristic performance, a new impulse, with a rich sonority, especially in the color, in the life, strength and warmth of its. musical expressions, without artificially falling in it, banal or juggling, so common in the present hour....

The 20th of January of 1935, the daily *"La Vanguardia"* published by *Don* Eduardo Llosent y Marañon, his verses entitled: *"A la Guitarra de Andrés Segovia"* (To the Guitar of Andrés Segovia) which expressed:

Niña de la voz dolente *y la cintura delgada,* *de cuello negro cisne* *y de aderezo de nacar,* *breve y repartida en curvas,* *mitad mujer, mitad anfora,* *que por parecerte a Venus,* *hasta los brazos de faltan,* *arisca y tierna a la vez,* *a la vez timida y brava,* *y en el amor despiadada.*	Little girl of the sorrowful voice and the thin waist, the neck of a black swan of a dressing of mother of pearl, short and distributed in curves, half woman and half amphora, by that appears to Venus, until the arms lack, and all at once tenderness, at once timid and brave, and in the heartless love.

Niña de seno impuberes	Girl of a prepubescent chest
y caderas de mulata:	and mulatto hips:
en que fuente bautismal	in which baptismal fountain
te dieron nombre las aguas?	they gave you the name the waters?
Se celebro tu bautismo	Your baptism is celebrated
en una blanca alcazaba	in a white fortress
o en algun patio mozarabe	or in some Mozarabe patio
de Sevilla o de Granada?	of Seville or of Granada?
Ay, cuantos nombres te dieron;	There how many names they gave you;
Sistro, Guiterna, Kithara,	Cisterrn, Guitar, Guitar,
Vihuela del romancero,	Vihuela of the romancer,
latina Citara hispanica.	Latin Hispanic Guitar.
He tenido veinte nombres	I have had twenty names
como las mujeres malas,	as the bad women,
y como ellas dando tumbos,	and as them giving falls,
entre aventuras y zambras,	between love affairs and zambras,
quedaste palida y triste	you remained palid and sad
de ver tantas madrugadas.	by seeing many mornings.
Quedo un remedo en sus labios	I remain an imitation in your lips
de tanta amargura y tanta,	of so much grief and so much,
desolacion padecida	endured desolation
por las andaluzas almas;	by the andalucian souls;
angustias de soleares	anguished of being alone
y seguidillas gitanas,	and Gypsy seguidillas,
estertor de malagueña	a death rattle of Malagueña
exclamacion desgarrada	shattered exclamation
del fandanguillo de Huelva,	of the Fandanguillo de Huelva,
de guajira y la caña.	of the Guajira and La Caña.
Te quedo un lubrico sello	You remain a wet stamp
en las ojeras moradas,	in the purple ring under the eye,
de crisparte rasqueando	of strumming
bulerias y tarantas.	Bulerias and Tarantas.
La te la vida andaluza	The Andalucian life
en tu corazon y clamas	in your heart and your cries
por volver a tu bohemia	by returning to your wandering
de perdida y de gitana.	of loss and of gypsy ways.
El puro amor te reclama,	The pure love you reclaim
te retienan sus brazos	you retain in your arms
y te acarician sus palmas,	and you caress in your hands,
y a la propia Andalucia	and to your own Andalucia
nos la entregas transformada,	you surrender to us transformed,
porque Segovia te ha dado	because Segovia has given you
voz andaluza de Albeniz,	Andalucian voice of Albeniz,
voz andaluza de Falla,	Andalucian voice of de Falla,
y voces universales	and universal voices
que embellecen tus palabras.	that embellish your words.
Niña de la voz dolente	Young girl of the sorrowful voice
y la cintura delgada	and the thin waist
por Segovia te conviertes	by Segovia you convert
de perdida, en alta dama.	of loss, into a high dame.

In June of the same year he occupied his accustomed place in the "Salle Gaveau" of Paris; after, Candide published: "There is in art, as in it of the pianist Gieseking, something of sorcery: a windy spell. In the two cases the string loses its materiality: Segovia and Gieseking make it vibrate without which, it appears, to have been played. They serve it as a coherent of waves. Some day science will explain this to us. For the moment we can only premonition it. But it is well evident that certain virtuosos, certain directors of orchestras and some orators, possess a potent abnormal fluidity which lets them conquer the inertia of the material. The study of the *radioestesia* (dowsing) through his guitar, so as the modern magicians utilize their instruments to penetrate to the source of the secrets of emotion buried in our subconscience.... interrogate his strings with a species of modesty and with a light caress lets them ring without awakening them. After that he delivers his practices of enchantment for putting us in direct contact with Bach, Handel, Moreno Torroba, Albeniz or Turina. When we hear the *"Chaconne"* of Bach, we notice that he discovers its true harmonic equilibrium. Segovia has discovered the superior Climate of the guitar constantly maintaining it in a zone of timbres of a perfect distinction. His basses are profound and elastic, his trebles smoother than the distant sound of a vibraphone. All of it is nobility, grandeur, aristocracy, sensibility and musicality.... (Signed: Emile Vuillermoz).

In January of 1936 he reappears in the Town Hall of New York performing *"Variaciones"* by Sor; *"Sonata Meridional", "Tropico"* and *"Rumba"* by Ponce; *"Fuga"* and *"Sarabanda"* by Bach; two *"Minuettos"* by Haydn; *"Hommage a Paganini"* by Castelnuovo-Tedesco and other works by Albeniz and Turina. Olin Downs said: "There is almost an instantaneous transposition of values, a New World of beauties and poetic expression, on an instrument, which has been so slandered, misunderstood and underestimated. Segovia employs the Glissando very rarely and with the same discretion and an infallible good use of as well of Vibrato."

In April we find him in the theater of the Pergola in Florence, then in Monte Carlo, in Nice and in October in London; he visits the United States, Brazil, Uruguay and arrives in Buenos Aires the 6th of May of 1937, performing the next day, 12th and the 19th in the Teatro Odeon, works by Chilessotti, Weiss, Bach, Castelnuovo-Tedesco, Turina, Granados, Albeniz, Scarlatti and Sor, with the tremendous success he always gives, reaffirming once more the Hispanic guitaristic vitality, of which he is a genuine and excellent interpreter.

The 7th of September in the S. O. D. R. E. Hall in Montevideo, he gave a very applauded concert, and after a rest of 4 months he returned to performing in England, Italy, Germany, Hungary, France, North America, Rio de Janeiro, where he visited the great *Don* Heitor Villa-Lobos, who presented him with twelve beautiful preludes for guitar. The Dr. Karl Laux wrote in the *"Dresdner Neueste Nachrichten"* of the city of Dresden, the 10th of November: "He is a phenomenon which has no equal. He is called the Magician of the Guitar. And not only is he the most distinguished guitarist, but as well one of the greatest virtuosos of all time. He can very well have his name cited at the side of Paganini and Liszt. The fact that he doesn't play the piano or the violin, but the guitar, can be a simple design of fate, since if he had chosen another instrument, he would be equally the great artist that he is presently.... the guitar transforms in his hands, to be converted in an instrument of limited power of expression. Segovia has awakened the old and classic literature of the lute to a new life (in particular the original works of J.S. Bach) revealing new aspects of the 18th century".

The Spanish revolution was in full climax in 1937, it produced a mournful note in the spirit of Segovia; the entitled assaulted his home in Barcelona and destroyed part of his valuable materials and those of his soul as well, music and instruments, he was able to save his beloved Ramírez guitar. The Valencian luthier Tatay, residing in New York, immediately presented him with one of his instruments and an important music house in the city of Montevideo gave him another guitar constructed in Paris the 8th of April of 1840 by the celebrated luthier Guillame.

700

In 1938 he finished his new contracts in North America and the 3rd of April he boarded the Western Prince, he embarked for South America, returning to the intelligent and cultured Central Europe; playing in Germany, Czechoslovakia, Switzerland, Scandinavia and in Hungary, with the old success as always. The daily *"Ujság"* of the 24th of November, in Budapest, with the signature P.J. reported: "Listening to Segovia we feel uniquely that a divine music surrounds us and I don't know what occurs for us to think which is the instrument, which serves the artist for our soul to become intoxicated. The instrument of which it is worth to believe in his hands of such a mode, the same emotion which would produce a complete orchestra to us, since, this, won't be able to express more beauties which the guitar of Segovia, so intimate, so delicate. When the Spanish artist rubs the strings, that of tone colors, that of subtleties, and at the same time, what a richness of coloring and vigor of expression there is. The transcendent virtuosity of Segovia might pass to be artificial if the noble and fine art of the great virtuoso didn't rule it. The Wednesday night concert in the great hall of the Academy, filled to the top with the most cultured public of Budapest, he interpreted Sor, Bach, Haydn, Moreno Torroba, Granados, etc., leaving profound emotion in all and every one of the listeners."

The 5th of May of 1939 he returned to Buenos Aires and in the Teatro Politeama he made, using a Hauser guitar, his first concert with works by Moreno Torroba, Castelnuovo-Tedesco, Frescobaldi, Rameau, of Scarlatti-his unpublished *"Sarabanda"* and *Gavota"* whose manuscripts were found in the Conservatory of Naples, works by de Falla, Turina, Pedrell, Albeniz and Villa-Lobos, of this one, a vigorous *"Choros"* which the author dedicated to him and was played for the first time. *"La Prensa"* the following day said: "He constitutes a relevant and noble art..." The second performance took place on the 15th of May in the same hall and others until the 30th of the same month, which was the last, triumphing like no one had triumphed until this moment in this populous city.

In such an opportunity, the celebrated painter *Don* Ramon de Subirate, sketched a portrait of him in pencil.

The 28th of October he reappeared in the S.O.D.R.E. in Montevideo, performing in the 2nd part, of the debut of the *"Concierto para Guitarra y Orquesta"*, which Castelnuovo-Tedesco dedicated and wrote on purpose for the great Segovia the soloist of the instrument; the maestro *Don* Lamberto Baldi directed the orchestra. The local daily newspaper, *"El Pueblo"* reported: "In admirable filling with the orchestra translated his three parts: *"Allegretto"* just and a little pompous, *"Andantino"* to the romance and *"Ritmico"* gentlemanly, in a simply masterful form. He conquered the admiration and enthusiasm of the public, to the orchestra of the miraculous power of seduction of which he is gifted, ennobling, thanks to the surprising musicality of his art-although more if it fits, these noble pages flowed out which gave him a new opportunity of illuminating his technique, his intelligence and sensibility, renowned by a really magical sound, which is the demonstration of an unknown radioactivity and perhaps only science can explain someday." "Segovia, as an artist, is outside of the orbit of all critics... without a doubt!"

The program announcing the performance with its corresponding relations, refers to a brief commentary about Castelnuovo-Tedesco, some other authors and instrumentalists; to express about Segovia, its anonymous writer notes, the very important observations which are reproduced, given its very interesting fundamentals, bases of the artistic aspiration of Segovia toward his never well loved guitar, say as so: "Thanks to this work Segovia made one of his dearest illusions; the restitution of the guitar to superior zones of the musical art. A long time asleep in the arms of the populace, the forgotten musicians of his annexed lineage, that is to say, of the polyphonic flowering it had, under the name of the vihuela in the 16th and 17th centuries, and of its powerful influence in the historical development of the music. The firm will with which Segovia has struggled to elevate the esthetic hierarchy of his loved instrument has been crowned by the best success which he could fancy; The Production of This Beautiful Work! It Won't Be the Last ...."

After performing with the habitual success in Peru, and Chile, again in Buenos Aires the 13th of May of 1940 and the day of the 24th he made his first concert with works by Frescobaldi, Rameau, Sor, Weiss, Bach, Castelnuovo-Tedesco, Villa-Lobos, Turina, Moreno Torroba and Albeniz, and the day of the 27th, for the "Organizacion de Conciertos Iriberri", in the hall of the Teatro Nacional de Comedias, in the capacity as soloist he repeated the *"Concierto para Guitarra y Orquesta"*, already alluded to Castelnuovo-Tedesco, under the baton of the distinguished Conductor *Don* Juan José Castro. *"La Prensa"* the next day, said: "...the work possesses great musical values; constructed with certain refined and subtle science, put to the service of fluid and rhythmic ideas of the slight Hispanic flavor, particularly the final movement, instrumented with personality and sobriety which couldn't escape with the color.... imposed by its beauty across an unsurpassable interpretation by Segovia and the care of Juan José Castro, which achieved the equilibrium of the sonorities of the orchestra, by luck which the guitar is distinguished as is the desire of the composer."

In August, concerts in the Teatro Odeon once again, in one of them which, took place on the 15th, he was presented in the company of his wife, the eminent pianist Mrs. Paquita Madriguera de Segovia, performing the *"Concierto en Re"* written by Castelnuovo-Tedesco for guitar and orchestra, that was reduced for the guitar and piano; both instruments had the occasion to amply illuminate, to make, with extreme correctness, such a noble artistic version of the admirable mentioned reduced work.

The 20th of October of 1941 Segovia gave another magnificent surprise; sponsored by the "Associacion Wagneriana" performing the *"Concierto del Sur"* written for guitar and small orchestra, by the celebrated *Don* Manuel Ponce, conducted by its composer, which dedicated it to him. The daily *"El Mundo"* of the day of the 22nd reported: "Andrés Segovia unsurpassablely interpreted his part as soloist and the orchestra conducted with extreme care by the composer, maintaining the equilibrium of the ingenious instrumental dialogues, without hesitation to the listeners."

The beginning of 1942 he appeared in Viña del Mar; the 18th of March in the Teatro Municipal of Sao Paulo, in April in the Teatro Colon of Buenos Aires, performing the 2nd part of a orchestral concert, conducted by Juan José Castro, *"Concierto para Guitarra y pequeña Orquesta"* by Castelnuovo-Tedesco; both artists deservedly to their works, harvested abundant applause, obligating Segovia to add various interpretations; in this opportunity the Argentine sketch artist, Corace, published an original and well-done caricature.

He did various radio performances and visited Havana in 1943, making his first performance on the 21st of October in the Teatro "Auditorium", in such an opportunity the "Sociedad Guitarristica de Cuba", offered him diverse treats, making his stay in the country more pleasant, the name "Miembro del Comité de Honor" (Member of the Committee of Honor) of the same institution. He continued his tour in diverse North and South American capitals and returned to Buenos Aires, to whose public he was presented on the 26th of June of 1944, in the Teatro Odeon. The daily *"El Mundo"*, among other things said: "It isn't necessary to say Segovia, in full maturity, is the fifth essence of the perfect musicalinterpretation."

He repeated his performances the 3rd and 10th of July, with success, the 24th of the same month he played only in the first part, his wife played on her admirable piano pieces by Beethoven, Albeniz and Castelnuovo-Tedesco in the debut of his poetic *"Nocturno en Hollywood"*; in the third part he ended the performance with the *"Concierto en Re"* written by Castelnuovo-Tedesco, and the *"Concierto del Sur"* by Ponce, their sheet music reduced for guitar and piano. Both versions were the most perfect spiritual unity, of style and flavor, as so said *"La Prensa"* the following day. In October he gave unsurpassable and successful radio performances.

Then he went to Europe and North America, where he arrived in 1947, visiting Los Angeles, Philadelphia, New York, etc. Isabel M. Jones said: *"Segovia and Casals were never unworthy of the highest values and the tradition of the classical Spanish music...."*

Samuel Singer in Philadelphia wrote: "Segovia made his audience frequently forget that it was the old and honorable guitar which they were listening to..... it sounded like the most perfect guitar, or others as the harp or harpsichord, violoncello or violin, and in some opportunities it gave the impression that it was more than one instrument...." Noel Straus said: "Andrés Segovia made it possible to listen to the *"Chaconne"* by Bach of a category of difficulty surpassed in expression, tonal and artistic variety, by none of the greatest violinists of whatever epoch."

In August he returned to Buenos Aires and gave a concert in the Teatro Colon, on the 25th, and gave another in the city of Resistencia, and after visited Holland and made performances in November on the 9th and 10th, and on the 28th he appeared in London; he continued his tour and arrived in Edinburgh, where he played on the 7th of September, 8th and 10th of October of 1948; then he arrived in Italy and, the 5th of December, by acclamation, he is named Honorary President of the "Unione Chitarristica Internazionale" with its headquarters in Modena; he returned to London and performed in Wigmore Hall the 2nd and 7th of November of 1949; in Sao Paulo, Brazil in August of 1950; performing in the Instituto de Educacion Cayetano de Campos, etc. he arrived in Buenos Aires in June 1952 and played his guitar, on Radio Belgrano and in the Teatro Broadway, performing three new works by Paganini, Tansman and Castelnuovo-Tedesco, and then embarked for his homeland after 16 years of absence, arriving in Madrid the 22nd of June, where he immediately headed for Granada.

He participated in the Festival Internacional de Musica y Danzas, distinguishing him with the designation of *"Hijo Muy Ilustre"* of the city of Jaen, which assigned one of the streets with the name of the eminent guitarist. Then he immediately traveled to Stockholm, then to France and Belgium, played in Lausanne, Switzerland the 22nd of October, gave concerts in London and returned to Spain giving performances in November and December of the same year, the most exceeding success that is possible to imagine.

He finished his tour of Europe; in the "Academia de Bellas Artes de San Fernando" in Madrid, for the merit of his international prestige he was named a "Miembro" (Member) of the same institution. In April of 1953 he embarked for the United States, passed to Ecuador giving concerts in the Teatro Colon of Santiago de Los Caballeros, and in the "Sociedad Filarmonica" of Quito, the 22nd of the same month he performed in the Teatro Municipal of Lima, Peru and arrived again in Buenos Aires performing in the "Asociacion Patriotica Española", with the sponsorship of the Spanish Embassy, the 27th of May of 1953, because he was to be the object of homage, conceded by the Government of his country. He received the Gran Cruz de la Orden de Alfonso el Sabio (Order of the Great Cross of Alfonso the Knowledgeable One). The act was initiated with an address by the Vice-President of the entity, Mr. Antonio Cebollero, the distinguished Argentine musicologist *Don* Carlos Vega, emphasized the personality of the homage.

At the beginning of July of the same year, Segovia was admitted to a Madrid hospital for an attack of glaucoma aguda, with a sense of urgency; he yielded to receive a series of surgeries, after some days, of hopeful anguish, the bandages were removed, recovering his normal vision.

Conclusions.

To Segovia are attributed, certain temperamental rarities and of education, conceivable, uniquely, by who doesn't flatter in his pretensions, by concepts or sincere opinions, concrete and real, in many other caustic cases, in pseudo-guitaristic environments, they convert into adversaries, and not into loyal consulted friends. The eternal incomprehension.

Segovia is a man not of tall stature, well-built, of a head with lion-like hair, that was denounced a half a century ago, he uses glasses, obscure eyes, thick lips, is shaved, is simple, pleasant, cultured, patient, graceful and friendly in his treatment of who wants to see him, friends, journalists, musicians, instrumentalists, especially guitaristic aficionados, precocious, consummate, etc.

However, it is sure that, in general, who but do not know the great virtuoso, are those that have covered the marvelous brilliance of the instrument in mud, to who, until the inclusion of a work by Bach in his unequal concert programs, they turn out to be an inconceivable audacity; always, sick and egotistical sentiments.....

This "Great Man of the Guitar", as we have seen, has sacrificed his life for tireless permanent voyages, has walked with his beloved guitar triumphantly and gloriously to the corners of the five continents, exhibiting and demonstrating in 20 years of apostolic life, what everyone since the creation of the Spanish guitar in the 16th century, have propagated limitedly, in all of Europe.

Besides this formidable propaganda, diffuser of his legendary instrument, he has hired it elevating its prestige to the highest artistic dignity, by consequently promoting, it turned out of his greatest aspirations: The Enrichment Of The Literature Of The Guitar And Its Intervention In The Orchestra, Of Equal To Equal, to acquire the intellectual and artistic temple which it deserves, in respect with the rest of the known musical instruments.

He has raised by the magnificence of its majestic sovereignty, a renovated interest toward the guitar, preoccupying to the most eminent contemporary musicians, such as the Hispanics de Falla, Turina, Moreno Torroba, and Salazar, the French Roussel, Samazeuilh, Laparra, Collet, Ferraud and Ibert, the English Cyril Scott, the Mexican *Don* Manuel M. Ponce, the Italian Castelnuovo-Tedesco, the Brazilian Heitor Villa-Lobos and many others, who, not only write beautiful pages for the guitar soloists now, but for small and large orchestras, which, dedicated to the eminent Saint of the Guitar, he performs them with passion in all the cities of the land.

In him, which is connected with the sound, we call, Segoviana, it deals with a much discussed topic among the public, musicians, critics and guitarists; it is indisputable that the gut string produces velvety sounds, and if it is plucked without the fingernail, it converts into marvelous wings that are born and fade away, in a same sonorous current. The nylon string produces the most brilliant crystalline, clean, strong and weak, not smooth and always with a certain metallic tone.

In the past epochs the gut string, in smaller concert halls, fulfilled their mission with the maximum aspiration, the same which today turns out opaque in the immense modern halls and theaters with the capacity of thousands of spectators, whose 50% don't hear it, instead the nylon, without the sublime mellowness of the gut string, have replaced in the best auditory conditions and applaud the emotion heard. The divided guitarists in both tendencies, in agreement or not, as well they are emotional when hearing Segovia, and finally applaud rabidly.

The musician, before the talent of the great virtuoso, not only applaud, but are advised by him write, that, then perform his pages with these prodigious changes of tones which masterfully color the sonorous canvas of the musical landscape; because he is the first and most talented impressionist of the guitar.

As to the critics, we have already seen and read their passionate newspaper writings, to which the very interesting comparative appreciation gathered is noted: "Segovia makes of the guitar what the violoncello is in the hands of Casals, or the violin of Kreisler"; another says: "Clavichordists such as Frescobaldi, Scarlatti and Rameau never had a more extraordinary interpreter", *"La Prensa"* of Buenos Aires of the 20th of May of 1937, to speak about the interpretations of the works of Scarlatti says: "The style and the spirit of the epoch emerges in all its purity, felt by a modern artist which, such as Wanda Landowska on the keys, gives this antique music new life, whose humanity moves us with interpretations of the same category."

In *"El Hogar"* of the day of the 14th of July of 1944, *Don* E. Larroque writes: " I have here the delicate metallic plucks obtained with the fingernail, something similar to those produced by the keys of another magican who is called Wanda Landowska....."; another indicates: "I never listen to Segovia without which certain Attacks of the string with the fingernail remind me of the enchanting keys of Wanda Landowska."; in one more it reads: "The range and color of the instrument in the hands of Segovia at times surpasses that of the clavichord....." It is indisputable which, this admirable reflection of the thousand colors of the sonorous rainbow, which he obtains in the performances of All the works that he interprets, he gets them by plucking with the fingernail, many times near the bridge where the strings are tied and with nylon strings.... and, precisely, to interpret thusly to all the authors, it is what appears very pleasant in our epoch, existing for whom also believes: "it is a dehumanization for the sake of a perfection, which touches the extraterrestrial limits." *Don* Pedro Leloup states: "It leaves an artificial impression."

Of all the manners and whatever might be which the general appreciation every one of the listeners, from the diverse apexes where they are situated, Segovia is the most eminent virtuoso impressionist of the modern guitar accepted and acclaimed by all the public of the universe.

His Compositions:

On many occasions the great Segovia referred to it: "I am not a music composer", however that very noble and sincere declaration, the public opinion of sympathizers, aficionados, guitarists, critics and professionals, are compelled to assure on the contrary, indicating however the musical pages which he has written, are emotional conceptions of the genius composer.

Those reasons obligate it to be spread out so much, by the same in themselves and by the artistic hierarchy of the great instrumentalist, turning out a brief analysis of some of his many works, at the end to clarify affirmations, in benefit of the guitaristic culture. Up until now few have dared to apply the scalpel, whether the outcome coincides or not, they are always angry and don't lack apprehensions that utilize some specifics with caring intentions of the purity and comprehension which the historical correctness demands.

We abstain from all discourtesy, we will say that some musical pages of the Saint of the Guitar yield to a brief exam, only it is necessary for assuring those own manifestations of the author or his infinite modesty, to divide them in three distinct genres, the originals, the popular and his transcriptions.

His first original works were: *"Tres Preludios"* and *"Tonadilla";* published by the *Editorial de Musica Española* in Madrid, by the *Biblioteca Fortea* with the No. 10.445 and as well by Haslinger Tobias of Vienna, under the No. 654 b. It is a modest *Moderato in Mi Major* to the 2/4 time, to equal that of the previous, it lacks technical and harmonic complications, having as a base, successive scales, very appropriate for exercising with them.

In 1945 he published *"Preludio in Chords" a Molto moderato expressivo in Do Major,* released by Celesta Publishing Co. of New York.

Later "The Guitar Review" of New York, published with the title of *5 "Anecdotas",* 1st an *Allegretto,* 2nd an *Allegro,* 3rd a *Lento malinconico,* 4th a *Molto tranquilo* and 5th an *Allegretto Vivo;* also he published a "Preludio" dedicated to Mr. Bobri, Director of the mentioned magazine.

Finally we know of which is written *"Sin Luz",* a work which, the reasons that inspired it are known, in very painful moments for the author and the numerous and interminable guitaristic brotherhood of the world, before all that, we discover it with the profoundest respect and consideration.

All those works don't reach an artistic musical stature, in accordance with the eminent virtuosity of the author.

In connection with his harmonizations of popular airs, original or transcriptions, there are convincing words in the poetry of his *"Cancion Irlandesa"* of the 16th century; in the joy of the *"Canto Finlandes"*; in his very spicy *"Cancion Catalana"*; in the admirable *"Aire Andaluz"*, performed by the maestro *Don* Juan Parras, in the Exposicion de Bellas Artes of Barcelona in the year 1916; in his *"Triste No. 4"* by Julián Aguirre, in which it accumulates all the *gaucho* sadness; with Purcell it pours out his deep poetic English; with Scarlatti the rejoicing and luminosity of his beloved Naples; in *"Sarabanda"* by Handel, it displays all the chivalrous charm of his lineage. Besides it speaks very well of the moving Monteverdean inflections of the *"Canzone e Salterello"* by Chilesotti, so expressive in its rhythm, so expressive in its melodies with the *"Suite"* by Weiss, it approaches the proximity of the great Bach, etc.

However, of all these marvelous things, it isn't the same in the *"Canto del Campesino"* by Grieg, O. Tracio edition, in its 5th measure, on the 4th beat, we find a Sol quarter note of the chord, that can't be held, which also happens in the 10th measure, in the 2nd beat. Something like that happens in the *"Vidalita"* by Aguirre, whose La half note, can't be held for its total value. These mistakes, it's possible that they might have their origin at the printer, by lack of time due to the vigilance and control. As to his music for the popular songs with accompaniment of the guitar, we must affectionately accept, those very respectable lapses or likes of the author.

In respect to his numerable classical transcriptions, published by diverse houses: *"Orfeo Tracio S.A."* of Geneva and Madrid; "Romero y Fernández" of Buenos Aires; "Schott's Sohne" of Mainz-Leipzig, etc. this great instrumentalist didn't want to be content with the guitaristic literature of the first epoch, left in the brilliant century by Carulli, Carcassi, Giuliani, Sor, Coste, Tárrega, etc. he searched as he could and saved the many forgotten jewels dormant in archives and libraries, and transcribed also some others by eminent pianists, clavichordists, lutenists, including by Bach, fervent admirer of the lute, of whose music Segovia contributed valuable arrangements to the guitar, of which we mention some of them:

Preludio: This is magnificently transposed from LA minor on the Lute to RE on the guitar. It isn't a transcription.

Allemande: (from the first Lute Suite) Also transposed from MI minor on the Lute to LA.

Minuetto I and II: (Fourth Lute Suite) Written in the same key of MI Major, only "it's a copy", adapting its fingering to the guitar.

Gavota en Rondo: (Fourth Lute Suite) Written in the same key of MI Major, only "it's a copy", with the deletion of some chords and its fingering adapted.

Chaconne: The transcription is so admirably made, that we reproduce some of the paragraphs of the thoughts of the Secretary of the "Societé de Musicologie Francaise", *Don* Marc Pincherle

"Profoundly admiring the *"Chaconne"*, rarely have I heard it with a certain uneasiness..."

"Nothing is opposed to the idea of which the Iberian origin of the *"Chaconne"* might have inspired for Bach the intention to destine it to the Spanish instrument whose existence, because of the universal curiosity, surely not unknown, and which besides the maestros: de Visée and Corbetta, were having put in the mode of all Europe. It isn't, "will it be necessary to add it?", a risky hypothesis which advises to express this conviction. An argument counts and has weight: conceived or not for the guitar, the *"Chaconne"* is written as if its author might not have thought about another instrument more than this one. There doesn't have to be a change not only in none of the disposition, but that all Comes with entire spontaneity. The chords, which the violin produces with the Arpeggios or Outburst are presented here in only one line. The imitations preserve independence of class and color, the arpeggios give us a harmonic plot equal over that which the melodic movements sketch with full relief. The violin maintains its superiority in certain slurred variations, in whose treble passages turn out livelier and Mordent. More almost all the remaining is more appropriate for the guitar which, outside of the other advantages, makes the bass octave sound of the written note, producing the basses so profound capable to sustain the majestic structure."

"Perhaps it might be a crime against humanity, the *"Chaconne"* to present it as a eager or longing work, wheezing, bristly of difficulties; to make it harmonious, ample, balanced, to give us in the end the equivalent of the most perfect intelligible performance, it can't be rewarded to you more than with great gratitude of all those which listen."

This work as performed for the first time in Buenos Aires, the 7th of May of 1937, the next day the critic Gaston O. Talamon of the daily *"La Prensa"* said: "No matter how little that the transcriptions might be recommendable, you have to recognize that Segovia has succeeded, as it turns out a majority of the moments, better on the guitar than the violin. In this it must have turned out influenced by diverse causes: the Hispanic origin, worth saying, Vihuelistic or Lutenistic of the *"Chaconne"*, and the fact of which the instrumental music of the 17th century, is found developing under the sign of the plucked string instruments, such as the lute and the clavichord, of luck which, as happens for example, with *"Iberia"* by Albeniz, to pass on to the guitar it returns to its instrument of origin. If we add to these reasons varied and refined effects of color and timbre which Segovia gets on the guitar, we will have to indicate the causes which make of the transcription a work essentially guitaristic...."

His Pedagogy:

As to his methods of teaching, it is well known that he imparts lessons in the "Accademia Musicale Chigiana" of Siena-Milan, Italy, where he has students already advanced, besides, they know the distinguished performance of his distinguished disciples, notable artists of the guitar, such as Jesus Silva, Miguel Angel, Abel Carlevaro and others.

In respect to his pedagogic works, it is said that he collects his own progressive studies, which we know opportunely, in whose volumes will include, surely, his *"Estudio Sin Luz"*, a page that due to the solicitation of the Dr. Rubio, the medical surgeon who operated on him, wrote to recuperate his vision, declaring again: "I am not a composer, but the Dr. Rubio compelled me to write it. Still the joy to contemplate the marvelous sets of light and color of the nature and of the life haven't been taken away."

As well "Leccion 12" is known, *Allegretto Moderato e Grazioso, in LA minor* to the time of 3/4, magnificent for insuring the performance of chords.

It has been referred that many authors seduced by the interpretive genius of Segovia and by the sum of resources offered by the instrument, have launched to compose numerous works of refined writing and high artistic significance, which they dedicate to the inspirer, Segovia, which at the same time work by *"cicerone"*(guide) (as he himself says and writes in his collaboration *"La Guitarra y Yo"*, in "The Guitar Review" No. 10), "In the complicated laberinth of the technique of the guitar, how much you can make efforts, for which the musical ideas take in the instrument delicate and suggestive embodiment, to the aim of which the composer remains surprised and delighted by such a rich variety of timbres and subject to the enchantment of the guitar." Without some discussion Segovia amply gets his grandiose intent, fantastically enriching the literature of our instrument.

These circumstances offer him the most important opportunity to practice, leaving unequivocal constancy in these selected pages, of his technical didactic gifts to indicate the pertinent finger of both hands, his respective positions and the chosen string to employ, the success of the sought-after aim and feeling.

All this hasn't developed, lamentably, with the desired felicity, to judge by discipline or too much confidence in the impressions of the works, they contain errors, you have to think as such, already which surrenders, originals in his country, for his edition, and of an immediate part and another for completing his contracts, but, without having controlled, of course, the exactitude of the said impressions."

So ends the biography of maestro Andrés Segovia from Ricardo Muñoz's unpublished book *"Historia Universal de la Guitarra"* Volume V *"Los Contemporaneos"*. The photo is from the same biography.

From the Madrid published magazine *"Hispano-Americana"* of March 31, 1917, two interesting articles stem from the section: *"Otros Conciertos"* both of the nature of the folkmusic of Bandurrias and Guitars of Spain:
Translation of the text:

"Orchestra of Bandurrias and Guitars.

In the Teatro Español, one of these days, an original orchestra of Spanish instruments, has been presented, directed by the young and studious maestro German Lago, with the support and the protection of the Centro de Hijos de Madrid.

It doesn't concern a rondalla, but a real orchestra, comprised of the diverse families of the Laudes and Bandurrias, producing a very artistic group, particularly in some works by Barbieri, Breton, Chapi, Caballero and Chueca.

Also placed in its programs are works by Schubert, Bizet, Grieg, Albeniz, Villar, Giner, Tárrega and others."

Orquesta de bandurrias y guitarras.

. En el teatro Español se ha presentado, uno de estos días, una original orquesta de instrumentos españoles, dirigida por el joven y estudioso maestro Germán Lago, con el apoyo y protección del Centro de Hijos de Madrid.

No se trata de una rondalla, sino de una verdadera orquesta, compuesta con las diversas familias de los laudes y bandurrias, produciendo un conjunto muy artístico, particularmente en algunas obras de Barbieri, Bretón, Chapí, Caballero y Chueca.

También figuran en sus programas obras de Schubert, Bizet, Grieg, Albéniz, Villar, Giner, Tárrega y otros.

Los artistas del Real, y patrocinado por el Comité Hispano-italiano, dieron, el 21 de corriente un concierto vocal en el Palace Hotel a beneficio de la Asociación de Escritores y Artistas Españoles para contribuir a la fundación del Instituto Cervantes.

Acompañados por los maestros Serafín, Saco del Valle, Terragnolo, Anglada y l'eidró, cantaron canciones y fragmentos de óperas las señoritas Lahowska, Bonaplata, Rakowska, Anitúa, Delva, Massip y los señores Massini Pieralli, Crabbé, Pertile, Gigli, Calleja, De Giovani, y Segura Tallien.

La Argentinita y el notable guitarrista señor Segovia tomaron también parte en esta sesión musical que resultó muy lucida.

"The artists of the Real, and sponsored by the Comité Hispano-Italiano, gave a vocal concert the 21st of the current month in the Palace Hotel to benefit the Asociacion de Escritores y Artistas Españoles (Association of Spanish Writers and Artists) to contribute to the foundation of the Instituto Cervantes.

Accompanied by the maestros Serafin, Saco del Valle, Terranolo, Anglada and L'eidro, the ladies Lahowska, Bonaplata, Rakowska, Anitua, Delva, Massip and the gentlemen Massini Pieralli, Crabbé, Pertile, Gigli, Calleja, De Giovani, and Segura Tallien sang songs and fragments of the operas.

La Argentinita and the notable guitarist Mr. Andrés Segovia took part in this musical session that turned out very brilliant."

From the *"Voluntad"* magazine February 1, 1920 *Año* II Num. VI   Madrid

Musical Chronicle by Rogelio Villar-translation by Randy Osborne

Lithograph by Helmut Ruhemann

Andrés Segovia, who is acquiring notoriety and fame worthy of his talent, has fulfilled the miracle, thanks to his persevering efforts and his exquisite art, by taking seriously our national instrument cultivated by such eminent artists as Tárrega and Llobet.

This lithograph by Helmut Ruhermann was done in 1919, as Andrés Segovia says in his autobiography. Upon computer magnification, it appears that the date could have been written over with the year of the magazine publication. This lithograph was utilized for the cover of the August 6, 1920 Cine "Sociedad Española" concert in Buenos Aires.

The sensibility of the guitarist from Granada, purified by a solid cultural esthetic, not only musical but literary and philosophical, is the best guarantee of the seriousness of his art, that he exercises as an apostolate and with the highest fervor of elevating the art of playing the guitar to an artistic level of that which must not descend.

For Segovia technical difficulties don't exist in the guitar; of an instrument, to appear of scarce artistic resources, he brings out a large share, ennobling it with his temperament; well besides the effects of virtuosity, as one who knows the secrets of expression and the art of arousal, in the passages of agility, trills, arpeggios, scales, harmonics, graduations of tone, from the fortissimo to the most dissipated sonorities and fantastic, in a gamut of varied tones, that says exquisitely, he knows how to make the guitar sing, and has an admirable sense of tone; his phrasing is elegant, without mannerisms neither striking in bad taste (to what so many lend the deplorable transcriptions of some works of the piano that are adapted to the guitar) due to all the tenderness of his sentiment, to the clarity and purity of his technique and to the prudence of his artistic faculties well he is one of the few truly intelligent Spanish musicians that I know.

Segovia identifies with the guitar in such a way that, putting his soul in communication with his fingers, the guitar sighs, cries, is happy, having accents of passion at times, other times, languishing trances, and always ineffably carrying dreams and poetry, produced by the medium of the portamento, powerful medium of expression for string instruments when its employed with discretion and in good taste, and what in the guitar produces limitless and beautiful expressive effects when it is an artist such as Segovia that is plucking the guitar.

With a very good sense, the repertoire that Segovia interprets, in general, is comprised of works of the Spanish classical guitarists, with a preference of the composers Sors and Aguado, edited in Paris and London, and those of the contemporaries Tárrega and Llobet. Segovia includes as well in his select programs, works of a national character by Albeniz and Granados, and transcriptions of classical composers by Tárrega and Llobet.

The best eulogy we can make of Segovia, is to say that his concerts are extremely well attended by the public (a thing that isn't attained except by artists of a certain rank), that he is well applauded with great enthusiasm, as just happened to occur in his latest concert that he gave at the Comedia theater.

Rogelio Villar

In Spain, Andrés Segovia's career was moving ahead. He was playing prestigious theaters more month by month, and receiving rave reviews and mounting press reports. Here is an early interview, almost a soliloquy, recorded by R. Villar-translation by Randy Osborne.

From *"La Esfera"* magazine February 14, 1920 *Año* VII Num. 319, published in Madrid.

Artistas Españoles

Andrés Segovia

Andrés Segovia is being in the exuberant Madrid musical life, so full in the reality of Spanish art, an interesting figure at the present.

His concerts in the Comedia (theater) have revealed to the grand public the artistic personality of the eminent guitarist, so learned and so artistic.

To few discreet indications that we have of him for knowing his thoughts about some questions relating to his artistic life and to his passion through the guitar, whose prestige has known to elevate with his talent and his exquisite art, answers us in that which qualifies as the same as intimacies.

Photo by Gonzalez Ragel of Andrés Segovia from *"La Esfera"* February 14, 1920

"I know" — says Segovia — "the ritual questions that the perfect reporter must ask to all men to whom wants to present to the public, and how I have the conviction of what is only the work of the artist-when the name of the artist isn't usurped-it must interest, I will respond with out the necessity of interrogating me. In that way, we will all win: the readers, sincerely; you won't have to ask in vain, and I, won't say only what I want."

"My life? My artistic history? My primary orientation toward the path that today appears to be seen as very slow and deferred but is already straight? Well a life of a man, whose yearning, almost naturally of truth and beauty, had been to replace the lack of stimulation and of cares: one of those aspirations of art and of those acute sensibilities what, isn't so fixed in the laws of inheritance, appearing as prodigious mysteries, and an early instinct for not confusing the magnolias with other flowers, neither the rhetoric-rhetoric of the word and of the spirit-with the true eloquence."

"In the essence of all my memories is the guitar. I began to play it when I was a child, only, and only as well, without trying another instrument over the course of time, I was forming my way, my technique. The love for the guitar has been strengthened while I went and extended my musical studies and my concept of the music. I believe that no other instrument, not even the violoncello, possesses such a richness of timbres, at times truly orchestral, such intimacy and such contagious emotion. The extension of what it needs augments your expressive power; it isn't vast, it's profound, and its popular heritage that makes it apt for expressing that *"aliento de la tierra"* (breath of the land), the source of inspiration of the poets, and the most illustrious musicians. The technicians, a specie of naked trees in which the birds never nest, affirm that, except for the works of the vihuelists, nothing must be played on the guitar.... Bah! I don't pay much attention to them. The music isn't a problem of calculation, but that the calculation is subjected in the guitar to the sentiment, the core of all art. Pages of Bach, of Haendal, of Mozart, of Chopin, by citing only various gain in the guitar such emotive virtue, that is well worth the toil to lose. The musician before the instrumentalist, prefers the orchestra to all else; but after that, the guitar, my guitar, capricious to me is the box of resonance where the echoes of the orchestra, and the passions that can be perfectly evoked."

"Of my successes, I dedicate them to the guitar, for so long it's been debased in ignorant hands without the least instinct, for the most part. Every triumph appears to me as a repair of that, I wouldn't change my performance by that of some concert artist ..... despite they're yearning to conduct orchestras... It would be insincere if I told you I study a lot; that the mechanism, so complex, dissociated in the guitar, demands of me too much effort. No, I play easily, and I'm only preoccupied with the work in itself, and not in its strict relation with the difficulties. And I like the guitar very much, that at times I feel I can't draw away from it, to listen to it myself."

"It has been necessary for many days, many years, through infinite troubles, for acquiring what the public and the critics have come to, with respect to the guitar, to the situation that they are in today. The first concert at the "Teatro de la Comedia" has produced one of the most pure satisfactions of my life, and to those who would have wanted to congregate there self-sacrificing, as much they did by the guitar; Tárrega, almost more of a saint than a musician, in the first place."

"I don't want to elude the inevitable question, because I can respond to it in conscience; of the present guitarists, only two appear to me that join musical ability, artistic temperament, and sufficient technique: Llobet quite in first place, Regino Sainz de la Maza as hope. Of course this appreciation doesn't attempt to be irrevocable, neither to diminish the recognized merits of others. I limit myself to say my truth, which perhaps might not be the truth. The Spanish musicians are interested in the guitar; I have works promised by Espla, Falla, Turina and Villar. When those promises are completed, it will give me the pleasure to organize a Spanish concert, in it that Sors, Albeniz and Granados represented it yesterday. Of course, it will be necessary to study other tunings of the guitar in order to include them in the present modalities. The tuning in effect, is modeled in the canon of the consonance, it has to be expanded for the expressive dissonance in what is so abundant in the latest music, so they might be possible to play. It's the work of tenacity, of study and of time. If I don't lack that, of the other elements I'm sure my temperament is romantic, yes; I am an "expresivista" (expressionist). I don't learn things once to play like that forever, but that I discover them every time. Without that renovated emotion, the art would be just a trade. Besides, rendering of that injustice of nature, that gives and denies talents, I believe that the true art is isn't compatible with ignorance. Those that play and paint "muy bien" (very well) and then don't have common sense neither interests by any of the spectacles of life, neither curiosity by exploring new spiritual horizons are repugnant to me. To know is to live even more, to be more of a man. For me, there isn't a more powerful attraction than a book."

"I'm leaving now for America. My impresario assures me that I will have great success there; I hope he isn't mistaken. I will play as I always play, forsaking myself to that emotion that makes us happy when going before our public. I'm going content, happy, and as a romantic, I figure the guitar, is so many times compared with a woman, it is, in effect; that in those times in what the heroic sense was just dishonored by the Great War (World War I), to include me, humble artist and with pride at the same time, the fortune of the power to go to struggle, according to the supreme formula, by my woman and by my faith."

So expresses the incomparable interpreter of Sors and Tárrega himself, among the classic Spanish composers of the guitar; of Albeniz and Granados, in whose adaptations the great musician-poet of the national instrument puts all of his soul, that just was acclaimed in the "Teatro de la Comedia" with a fervor and an enthusiasm reserved only for the soloists that have the rare talent of knowing how to transmit the emotions of art that produce their exceptional temperament; in the case of Segovia so fine and chosen, of many varied tones, as those that are obtained by plucking the guitar, that in his hands is poetry, ideal and dreamlike.

Rogelio Villar

On May 14, 1920 Andrés Segovia left the port of Cadiz on board the steamer *"Reina Victoria Eugenia"*. The 17-day voyage terminated in Montevideo, where the maestro gave a short performance at a benefit party for widows and orphans of sailors by request of the ship's Captain Martínez. In Buenos Aires the daily *La Nacion* announced the arrival of the ship in its May 30, 1920 edition.

Source: *Andrés Segovia Vida y Obra* by Alberto Lopez Poveda published by the Universidad de Jaen / Ayuntamiento de Linares 2010.

1920 — Maestro Andrés Segovia arrived for the first time in Buenos Aires, the first city outside Europe that he visited where he performed as a concert artist, some time after, here in this metropolis, his first son would be born.

LA RAZON — SABADO 5 DE JUNIO DE 1920

(Top) From *"La Razon"*, at "La Argentina" on Friday June 4, 1920 in Buenos Aires, an announcement of the Tuesday June 8, 1920, concert program works, Tárrega, Granados, Bach, Albeniz and Mozart.

LA RAZON — MIERCOLES 9 DE JUNIO DE 1920

(Middle) Review of the Tuesday June 8, 1920 concert and mention of the concert held in Montevideo, Uruguay on Friday June 11, 1920, as well as on Wednesday June 16, 1920 held in the Salon "La Argentina" and in the Teatro Odeon on Saturday June 19, 1920 for an "extraordinary matinee".

(Bottom) Announcement of two concerts by Andrés Segovia in *"La Nacion"* one on Wednesday June 16, 1920 at the salon "La Argentina", and another in the Teatro Odeon on Saturday afternoon June 19, 1920.

LA NACION — Domingo 13 de junio de 1920

From *"La Razon"*, Saturday June 5, 1920

"For his part the guitarist Andrés Segovia, of great prestige in his land, obtained, in the Salon "La Argentina", a complete clamorous success.

The instrument didn't keep any secret from the concert guitarist, whom doesn't worry about any difficulties of major compromise. But, the most interesting is that, in Segovia, the most excellent instrumentalist, the music of beautiful temperament coincides with the solid culture.

So it explains the intelligent selection, between the best of the literature of the guitar, and a series of adaptations, — we'll indicate, among others, that of the *"Canzoneta"* of the Quartet, in E flat, by Mendelssohn, — the majority of them happy pieces; all of them pages, played in a high artistic style, and in it Segovia displays at once shades of tone that are difficult to obtain, so much as what with the small sonority of the guitar.

At the insistence of the audience, Segovia had to add some encore numbers to the program."

From *"La Razon"*, Wednesday June 9, 1920

"Andrés Segovia, the notable guitarist, last night, in the salon "La Argentina", gave his second concert with a success no less warm than what he will achieve on the night of his presentation. The numerous public attended, demanding that the concert guitarist add a few diverse pieces to his program.

Segovia, whom will perform the day after tomorrow in Montevideo, will reappear in the salon "La Argentina" the 16th, and for the 19th an extraordinary matinee in the Odeon."

From the information above it appears that Andrés Segovia's first appearance in Montevideo was on Friday June 11, 1920. On the following page is the second concert, which took place on Sunday June 27, 1920. This is a special courtesy of the Teatro Solis CIDDAE Centro de Investigacion, Documentacion y Difusion de las Artes Escenicas. A notable inclusion is that of Carlos U. Trapani, who was a music store owner and Agustín Barrios' first publisher.

From page 719: Translation of the review in *"La Razon"* of June 17, 1920: "Andrés Segovia, the most excellent guitarist, returned last night to be very celebrated in a concert given in the salon "La Argentina". Before the reiterated request of a nucleus of admirers, Segovia will give a unique concert, in the Odeon, the day after tomorrow. The program will be comprised of the following:

Estudio — Sor
Tema con variaciones — Sor
Estudio — Tárrega
Serenata — Malats
Fuga de la y Sonata (para violin) — Bach
Minueto — Mozart
Mazurca — Chopin
Momento Musical — Schubert
Canzonetta — Mendelssohn
Danza — Granados
Granada — Albeniz
Preludio Españo — Albeniz
Sevilla — Albeniz"

Andrés Segovia was in Rosario, Santa Fe for a concert on June 25, 1920 and signed an autograph and did a musical sketch to a fan there. I have this image in my archive.

My colleague, Carlos Salcedo Centurion, went to Rosario, Santa Fe, Argentina in March of 2014, to research the 5 month stay of Agustín Barrios in 1923. He also learned that Andrés Segovia performed at the Biblioteca Argentina on Wednesday June 23, 1920, Sunday August 7, 1927 and Tuesday July 7, 1942 .

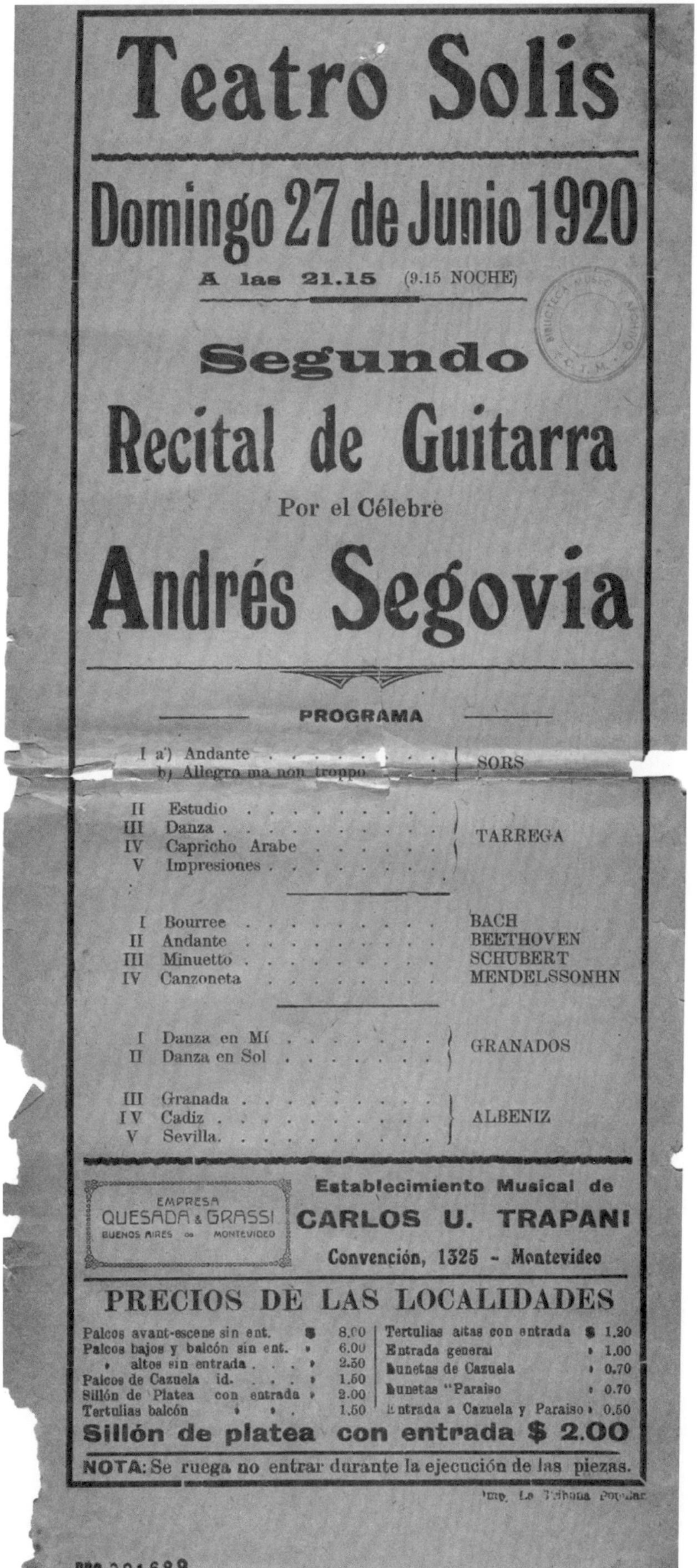

Teatro Solis

Domingo 27 de Junio 1920

A las 21.15 (9.15 NOCHE)

Segundo

Recital de Guitarra

Por el Célebre

Andrés Segovia

PROGRAMA

I a')	Andante	SORS
b)	Allegro ma non troppo	

II	Estudio	
III	Danza	
IV	Capricho Arabe	TARREGA
V	Impresiones	

I	Bourree	BACH
II	Andante	BEETHOVEN
III	Minuetto	SCHUBERT
IV	Canzoneta	MENDELSSOHN

I	Danza en Mí	GRANADOS
II	Danza en Sol	

III	Granada	
IV	Cadiz	ALBENIZ
V	Sevilla	

EMPRESA
QUESADA & GRASSI
BUENOS AIRES — MONTEVIDEO

Establecimiento Musical de
CARLOS U. TRAPANI
Convención, 1325 - Montevideo

PRECIOS DE LAS LOCALIDADES

Palcos avant-escene sin ent.	$ 8.00	Tertulias altas con entrada	$ 1.20
Palcos bajos y balcón sin ent.	6.00	Entrada general	1.00
» altos sin entrada	2.50	Lunetas de Cazuela	0.70
Palcos de Cazuela id.	1.50	Lunetas "Paraiso	0.70
Sillón de Platea con entrada	2.00	Entrada a Cazuela y Paraiso	0.50
Tertulias balcón » »	1.50		

Sillón de platea con entrada $ 2.00

NOTA: Se ruega no entrar durante la ejecución de las piezas.

Imp. La Tribuna Popular

From *"El Hogar"* magazine Buenos Aires June 25, 1920

From *"La Semana Musical"* by Julián Aguirre-translation by Randy Osborne
From "The Week in Music" by Julián Aguirre.

Andrés Segovia. — Among the artists that have visited us presently deserving special attention is the Spanish guitarist whose name begins these lines.

The guitar, that in the hands of the populace is an accompaniment instrument and of scarce resources has, played by this extraordinary artist, sonorities of piano, of violin to the extent of a string quartet in the reductions of Schubert, Mozart and Mendelssohn. They appear in his programs all the way from the specialists such as Sor, Tárrega and Coste to Johann Sebastian Bach, of whom you can't forget were written for the lute, a specie of the guitar with metallic strings, many of the celebrated preludes of the "Well Tempered Clavier".

With all the authors he observes a great beauty in the expression in all the works a grand nobility of sound and an exquisite musicality. It is very profound and subtle in that Segovia makes one forget the perfect virtuosity of his mechanism. The public that has heard him in the "Argentina" and most recently in the "Odeon", in that smaller hall, has made him the object of very enthusiastic demonstrations.

Unknown lithograph of Andrés Segovia from the Julián Aguirre article.

Buenos Aires, Jueves 17 de Junio de 1920.

Andrés Segovia, guitarrista eximio, volvió anoche a ser muy celebrado en el concierto realizado en el salón La Argentina. Ante la petición reiterada de un núcleo de admiradores, Segovia dará un único concierto, en el Odeón, pasado mañana por la tarde. El programa comprende las obras siguientes:

Estudio. Tema con variaciones, de Sor; Estudio, de Tórrega; Serenata, de Malats; Allegro, de Coste; Fuga de la y Sonata (para violín), de Bach; Minueto, de Mozart; Mazurca, de Chopin; Momento Musical, de Schubert; Canzonetta, de Mendelssohn; Danza, de Granados; Granada, Preludio Español, Sevilla, de Albéniz.

(Left) Review in *"La Razon"* of the Andrés Segovia concert in the Salon "La Argentina" on June 16, 1920, and mention of the matinee to be performed on June 19, 1920 at the Teatro Odeon. The translation is on page 716.

Andrés Segovia, célebre guitarrista español, cuyo concierto del teatro Odeón causó admiración extraordinaria.

(Right) From the magazine *"El Hogar"* of July 2, 1920 as he appeared at the Teatro Odeon on June 19. Translation: Andrés Segovia, celebrated Spanish guitarist, whose concert of the teatro Odeon caused extraordinary admiration.

This photo is from the *Plus Ultra* magazine published in Buenos Aires in August 1920. The photo (both by Baldisserotto) on 3 pages ahead, as well, comes from the same magazine.

On the following page is the program of the last concert of this three concert series at the Teatro Solis in Montevideo of the first tour of Andrés Segovia to the Rio de la Plata. It took place on Sunday July 4, 1920. This is a special courtesy by Centro de Investigacion, Documentacion y Difusion de las Artes Escenicas. (CIDDAE) — Teatro Solis

On page 58 of his Six Silver Moonbeams Revised 1999 edition Rico Stover says actually the last concert at the Teatro Solis was on July 25, 1920. It must be an added event to the series.

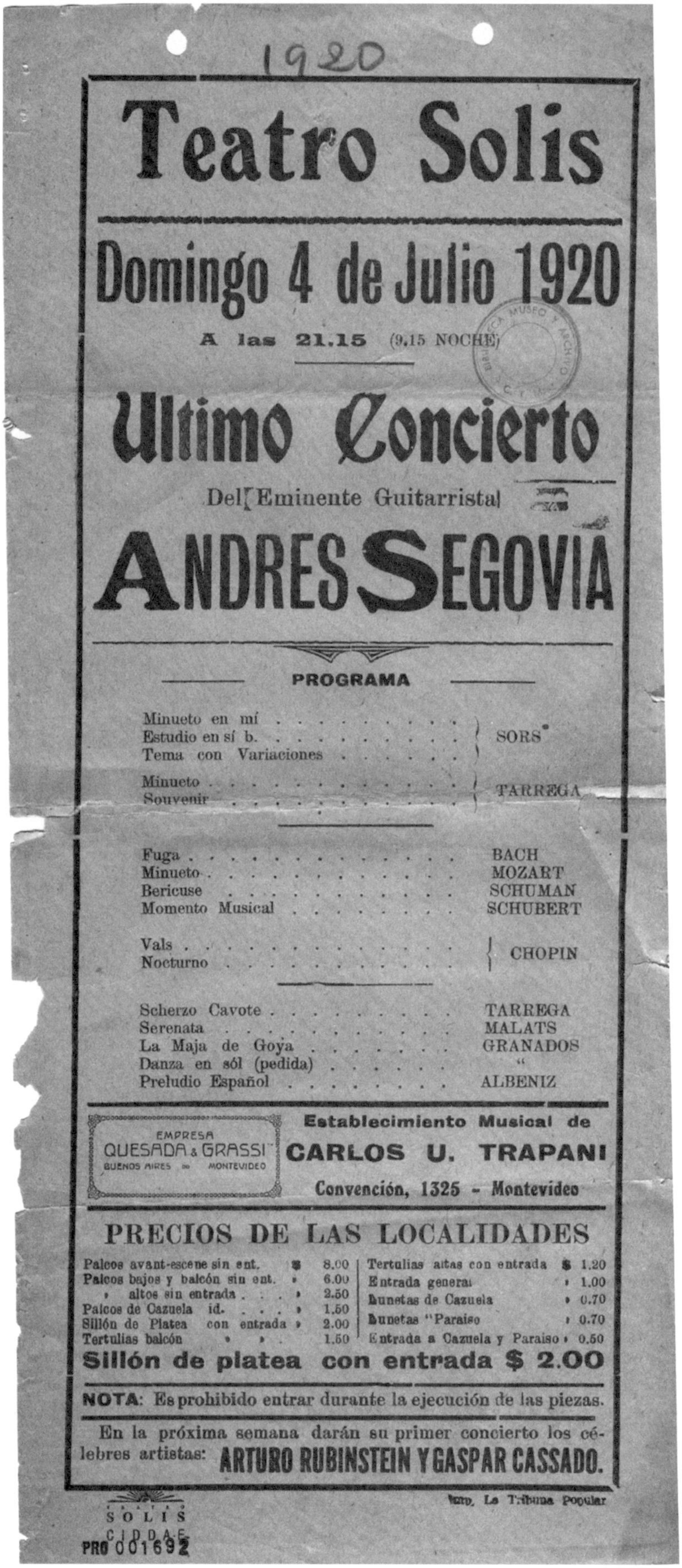

1920

Teatro Solis

Domingo 4 de Julio 1920

A las 21.15 (9.15 NOCHE)

Ultimo Concierto

Del Eminente Guitarrista

ANDRES SEGOVIA

PROGRAMA

Minueto en mí	
Estudio en sí b.	SORS
Tema con Variaciones	
Minueto	
Souvenir	TARREGA

Fuga	BACH
Minueto	MOZART
Bericuse	SCHUMAN
Momento Musical	SCHUBERT
Vals	
Nocturno	CHOPIN

Scherzo Cavote	TARREGA
Serenata	MALATS
La Maja de Goya	GRANADOS
Danza en sól (pedida)	"
Preludio Español	ALBENIZ

EMPRESA
QUESADA & GRASSI
BUENOS AIRES de MONTEVIDEO

Establecimiento Musical de
CARLOS U. TRAPANI
Convención, 1325 - Montevideo

PRECIOS DE LAS LOCALIDADES

Palcos avant-escene sin ent.	$ 8.00	Tertulias altas con entrada $ 1.20
Palcos bajos y balcón sin ent.	6.00	Entrada general	» 1.00
» altos sin entrada	2.50	Lunetas de Cazuela	» 0.70
Palcos de Cazuela id.	1.50	Lunetas "Paraiso	» 0.70
Sillón de Platea con entrada	2.00	Entrada a Cazuela y Paraiso » 0.50
Tertulias balcón » »	1.50	

Sillón de platea con entrada $ 2.00

NOTA: Es prohibido entrar durante la ejecución de las piezas.

En la próxima semana darán su primer concierto los célebres artistas: **ARTURO RUBINSTEIN Y GASPAR CASSADO.**

Imp. La Tribuna Popular

SOLIS
CIDDAE
PRO 001692

720

1920

Teatro Solís

Jueves 22 de Julio

A LAS 21.15 (9.15 NOCHE)

PRESENTACION

del genial violoncellista

Gaspar Cassadó

PIANO: JOSE MARIA FRANCO

— PROGRAMA —

Sonata en lá	L. Boccherini
Adagio	
Allegro	
Siete variaciones sobre un tema de Mozart)	Beethoven

Nocturno	G. Faure
Guitarra	Moszkowsky
Canzonetta	A. Di Ambrosio]
Fileuse	E. Dunkler

Kol Nidrei	M. Bruch
Apassionata	Ch. M. ¡Widor
Humoreska	A. Dvorack
Fantasia Española	J. Cassadó

EMPRESA
QUESADA & GRASSI
BUENOS AIRES – MONTEVIDEO

GRAN PIANO
Steinway & Sons.

DE LA CASA
Julio Mousqués

Precios de las localidades

Palco avant' scene sin ent.	$ 15.00	Tertulias altas	lps. 1.50
" bajos y balcón id. id.	12.00	Delantera cazuela 1.a y 2.a fila	1.20
" altos id. id.	5.00	" " otra fila	1.00
" cazuela id. id.	2.50	Delantera de paraiso 1.a y 2.a fila	1.00
Sillones de platea con ent.	3.00	Entrada a palco	1.00
Tertulia balcón id. id.	2.00	" a cazuela y paraiso	0.70

Sillón de Platea con entrada $ 3.00

NOTA. Es prohibido entrar durante la ejecución de las piezas

Domingo 25 a las 21.15 - Gran Concierto
de Despedida del eximio guitarrista:

ANDRES SEGOVIA

Imp. «La Tribuna Popular»

SOLIS
CIDDAE
PHO 001712

721

The photo of Andrés Segovia playing in the studio of the celebrated painter Emilio Centurion, is by the photographer Baldisserotto. It is from an article entitled *"El Guitarrista Andrés Segovia en Concierto Intimo"* and is from the *Plus Ultra* magazine published in Buenos Aires in August 1920.

722

This translation of the text from an article entitled *"El Guitarrista Andrés Segovia en Concierto Intimo"* is from the *Plus Ultra* magazine published in Buenos Aires in August 1920.

The translation reads:

"With his fingers transformed into nerves, Segovia models the sound. The thumb of the right hand caresses the bass string as a thumb of a sculptor, in as much his companions tickle the sensible string. The left hand, smooth and energeticly crosses the neck to give the clean just tones. And the six nervous strings caressed by the nervous fingers, give melody and harmony. The song, his accompaniment and the rhythm that surge in a miraculous unexplainable evocation.

The nerves hear the music of the guitar and it feels with the nerves, and produces in the soul a sweet anguish. There, in the intimacy of the artistic studio, the guitar of Segovia remains dreaming, as a murmuring supernatural, aided by the silence and the semi-darkness. It isn't a guitar of the large halls, filled with the public, where the performer needs to force the hand a little.

Not even a note of the gift that the guitarist toasts to us is lost. There he models his immaterial sculpture, his small winged figures which the melody dyes of invisible colors. Along and in the deep recess of the spine the shiver of the enthusiasm runs; the nerves are irritated, and the eyes are touched.

The guitar is an inspired flirt. Its accents caress, its laughs are musical, its melodic mime artists are going to direct all, and every one believe to be unique, the exclusive one, the beloved. Segovia--forgive me, maestro-- makes the profession of a trafficker of slaves that ask and light the enchantments of a captive princess, of captive Aspasia. And she, with the essence of a voice of all Them, cries, and laughs, and magically sighs. Segovia appears like Coppelius de Hoffmann, to the knowledge that fabricated that automaton doll, loved by the student until the madness. Segovia knows the secrets of the musical alchemy, and transforms into gold the blinding rays of the melody. Domesticated to a wizard that tames the beats.

Suddenly, the guitar has become muted and the enchantment is broken. It lies down without a soul; abandoned by its owner, Someone comes near and injures one of the strings that launches a whining note, unpleasantly. In as much the trafficker doesn't caress, the Copelius, the alchemist, it will be so, as dead; although the known caress a worthy companion of the music it won't give the sounds with the same style. An hour of ours to live, a chosen hour, brief and grand it embellishes our memory.

Segovia is a great man of the flirtatious guitar.

The text of the previous page from the same article translates to: "Listening to the maestro in the studio of the painter Centurion. Mssrs: Eduardo Alvarez, Emilio Centurion, Jorge Soto Acebal, José M. Franco, Alberto Gelly Cantilo, Maximo Portela, Juan Alonso, Gaspar Cassado, Horacio Quiroga, Arturo S. Mom, Mario Zavattaro, Alejandro Moy and Miguel Petrone."

Of this list of persons in the audience of the maestro, the most notable are the virtuoso cellist Gaspar Cassado and his accompanist on piano José Maria Franco, who began their concert series at the Teatro Solis in mid July 1920.

I need to thank my colleague, Alfredo Escande, for bringing to my attention that Horacio Quiroga, was a Uruguayan writer.

The program of an early concert by Andrés Segovia in Buenos Aires on Friday August 6, 1920 at the Cine "Sociedad Española". The lithograph of Andrés Segovia was done in 1919 in Madrid by Helmut Ruhermann and appears on page 180 in Segovia's autobiography, where he states the year as 1919. The lithograph appeared in a February 1920 "*Voluntad*" magazine, published in Madrid, in which the date is possibly overwritten 1920.

Images on this and the next 3 pages courtesy of Lucas Agustín de Antoni, Buenos Aires.

Viernes 6 de Agosto 1920

—————— :: á las 21 en punto :: ——————

PROGRAMA

I PARTE

Minueto	SORS
Tema con variaciones	›
Danza	TARREGA
Capricho árabe	›

II PARTE

Bourrée	BACH
Andante cantabi.	SORS
Minueto	MOZART
Momento musical	SCHUBERT
Canzonetta	MENDELSOHNN

III PARTE

Danza	GRANADOS
Granada	ALBENIZ
Leyenda	›
Sevilla	›

— PRECIO DE LAS LOCALIDADES —

Platea 2.00 — Palcos 10.00 — Paraíso 1.20

NOTA — Durante la ejecución de las piezas no se permitirá la entrada al Salón.

The program of Sor, Tárrega, Bach, Mozart, Schubert, Mendelssohn, Granados and Albeniz presented by maestro Andrés Segovia on August 6, 1920.

The words of astronomer, scientist, guitarist and friend of Andrés Segovia and Agustín Pio Barrios. In the 1890's Martin Gil first studied with Juan Alais and later on with Carlos García Tolsa.

Andrés Segovia
by Martin Gil

Many times , after having listened to Andrés Segovia, I have attempted to fix my impressions and other times I have failed in my intention, including now. His art is extraordinary, so intense, so subtle, so full of light and at once of tones and the glow of twilght of an acoustic painting illuminated by amazing lights, of truth and of dreams, of reality and of mystery, evocating the pain in a form so noble, so dignified, so serene, that consequently is impossible to materialize them, I'll say, with words on paper. Maybe if it was easier to simply fix such impressions in a diaphanous plaque of the soul, by having to do with an artist that is pure soul!

When they dominate the heights, the horizon is over those whom reach them. Therefore it's that we don't need to speak here of Llobet, neither of Pujol, the rigid and impeccable artist and the friendly and tender poet, neither of the late genius García Tolsa.

Segovia is a prince of the art that deserves the most beautiful carnations of his land and the most beautiful roses of ours.

Martin Gil, Buenos Aires June 19, 1920.

ANDRES SEGOVIA

Por MARTIN GIL

Repetidas veces, después de escuchar a Andrés Segovia, he pretendido fijar mis impresiones y otras tantas he fracasado en mi intento, inclusive ahora.— Es tan extraordinario su arte, tan intenso, tan sutil, tan pleno de luz y a la vez de matices y resplandor de crepúsculos de cuadros acústicos iluminados por luces extrañas; de verdad y de ensueño; de realidad y de misterio, evocando el dolor en forma tan noble, tan digna, tan serena, que resulta posible materializarlas, diré, con palabras sobre papel. Quizá fuese más facil fijar simplemente tales impresiones en la placa diáfana del alma, por tratarse de un artista que es pura alma!

.   .   .   .

Cuando se dominan las alturas, el horizonte sobra para quienes las alcanzan. Por eso es que no debemos hablar aquí de Llobet ni de Pujol, el artista rígido e impecable y el poeta amable y tierno, ni del genio malogrado de García Tolsa.

Segovia es un príncipe del arte que merece los más lindos claveles de su tierra y las rosas más hermosas de la nuestra.

Martín Gil.

Buenos Aires, 19 de Junio de 1920.

726

The words of Max Nordau, describing the stupefying conquest of Andrés Segovia at the Ateneo theatre in Madrid. Segovia had performed for the Queen of Spain long before his arrival in Buenos Aires.

De MAX NORDAU

Segovia en el Ateneo de Madrid

Andrés Segovia apareció anté el público.

Yo experimenté una fuerte sorpresa. Tenía frente a mi un jóven alto, elegante, flexible de abundantes y negros cabellos que dejaban libre la frente grande y luminosa. Una cara llena, fresca, con tez de mujer, radiante de inteligencia, sonriente.

Más, mi sorpresa se cambió en estupefacción, cuando el artista sentado tras de la mesa de la entrada y habiendo empuñado el instrumento que apretaba amorosamente a su corazón, arrancó de él los primeros sones

Un milagro se realizaba delante de mí. Esta guitarra que yo n[illegible]abia tomado jamás a lo serio, se transformaba [illegible]viamente, al primer contacto de la mano de Segovia, en una magnífica orquesta, en una orquesta completa, rica, sonora, variada, produciendo todos los matices y todos los efectos del conjunto de instrumentos que dirige la batuta de un maestro excepcional.

Una vez más me era revelado el hecho de que la materia no es nada, que el espiritu es todo.

El arte de Segovia no se aprende ni se enseña. Es el don, el caudal acordado por la naturaleza a sus favoritos, el «quid divinum.» El lo tiene. Que haga de ello generosamente aprovechar a quienes profesan la religión de lo bello. Que se prodigue. Que permita a los auditorios lo más numerosos posible, admirarle, y su renombre — no tenga la menor duda — llenará bien pronto los dos mundos.

En cuanto a mí, sus conciertos han constituido una de mis mas fuertes impresiones de España.

Andrés Segovia permanecerá para mi como un recuerdo que no evocaré jamás sin una profunda emoción estética.

Andrés Segovia appeared before the public.

I experienced an intense surprise. There was in front of me a tall young man, elegant, with abundant flexible black hair that was let free around the large and luminous face. A full face, fresh, with the complexion of a woman's, radiant of intelligence, smiling.

More so, my surprise changed to stupefaction, when the artist seated behind the table of the entrance and having grasped the instrument that he held lovingly to his heart, he began to make the first sounds.

A miracle happened in front of me. This guitar that I had never taken seriously, was transformed obviously, to the first contact of the hand of Segovia, into a magnificent orchestra a complete orchestra, rich, sonorous, varied, producing all the tones and all the effects of the group of instruments that directed the baton of an exceptional maestro.

Once again it was revealed to me the work that the material isn't anything, that the spirit is everything.

The art of Segovia isn't learned neither is it taught. He is talented, the deemed wealth by the nature of his favorites, the "quid divinum". He has it. What he might make of it generously takes advantage of those whom profess a religion of the beautiful. What a marvel. That permits the listeners the most numerous possible, admire him, and his renown — might not have the least doubt — it will soon fill the two worlds.

As for me, his concerts have constituted one of my strongest impressions of Spain.

Andrés Segovia will remain for me as a memory that I will never evoke without a profound esthetical emotion.

From the *"Caras y Caretas"* magazine of June 11, 1921 issue No. 1184 *Año* XXIV.

"Andrés Segovia

This year you will have the opportunity again to hear our cultivators of the good music, the magnificent performances of this celebrated Spanish guitarist, so favorably judged in his previous tour. Of the extraordinary art of Segovia there is little that can be added to his praise, now that his fame is admirably consolidated."

From the *"Caras y Caretas"* magazine of September 24, 1921 issue No. 1199 *Año* XXIV.

"Asociacion Wagneriana

This important association, that displays so much activity to the end of diffusing the taste of the musical art in our environment, doesn't miss the opportunity to present to our public the quantity of renowned artists that visit us. In this way recently the Asociacion Wagneriana offered us a performance of guitar of the known concert guitarist, Mr. Andrés Segovia.

This guitarist has already conquered among us a well-deserved fame, and his endowments as a good interpreter and artistic spirit have proven once again in the select program with what he delighted us with in this opportunity. It constituted of various numbers of different schools and epochs, all performed with equal mastery and good interpretation; but the compositions that most pleased our public in general were a *"Vidalita"* and a *"Triste"* of the maestro Julián Aguirre."

According to *"Andrés Segovia Vida and Obra"* by Alberto Lopez Poveda, the maestro left Spain on February 10, 1923 on board the ship *Satrustegui* enroute to Cuba. In Havana he offered two concerts in the Teatro Nacional on March 11th and 21st. While in Havana, in a recording studio, using his Manuel Ramírez guitar made by the workshop foreman, Santos Hernández, the maestro recorded Fandanguillo by Joaquín Turina and Recuerdos de la Alhambra by Francisco Tárrega, being the first time he heard his own interpretations, but these recordings were not released commercially.

EMPRESA

QUESADA Y GRASSI

Temporada Oficial de Conciertos

1921

GUILLERMO BACKHAUS	Pianista
PAQUITA MADRIGUERA	Pianista
IGNAZ FRIEDMAN	Pianista
TINA LERNER	Pianista
ANDRES SEGOVIA	Guitarrista
SAINZ DE LA MAZA	Guitarrista
CUARTETO WENDLING DE STUTTGART	Conjunto

This image is from the magazine *Musica de Amercia* issue No. 7 *Año* II of July 1921. It shows the concert artists presented by Quesada and Grassi for the 1921 season. Ernesto Quesada had been Andrés Segovia's manager since the Ateneo concert in Madrid.

Archive: J. Augusto Marcellino
Source: Segovia autobiography 1976.

Among the pianists is: Paquita Madriguera, who was a protegée of Enrique Granados. She became Andrés Segovia's second wife in 1938.

To the right is an autograph from Andrés Segovia to Pedro Mascaro y Reissig. It says: For the notable Professor Mr. Pedro Mascaro y Reissig. A. Segovia.

Montevideo.

Pedro Mascaro y Reissig was a guitarist who had 3 pieces listed in the 1931 Antigua Casa Nuñez catalog.

Archive: Pedro Mascaro y Reissig 1917-1938

ANDRÉS SEGOVIA

THE GUITAR.

The guitar has been very ably demonstrated in London during the past month. First we have had the American artiste, Mr. Nick Lucas, playing solos and accompanying his own songs at the Café de Paris, the Kit-Cat Club, and the Coliseum, in the popular style; and Senor Andrès Segovia demonstrating the instrument in classical selections.

This is what the London *Evening News* says about the great Spanish guitarist :—

"A success—perhaps *the* success of the concert season—has been scored by the guitar.

"A Spanish player, Mr. Andrès Segovia, now in London, has revealed it as deserving a place in the aristocracy of musical instruments.

"After his recital the other afternoon, enthusiasts were saying that they preferred the guitar to violin or piano, as being just as beautiful, more intimate, and less vehement.

"Those who imagined the guitar to be of much the same nature as the vulgar banjo were astounded to hear Mr. Segovia play Bach on it with unsurpassable effect.

"Bach happened to write a few pieces for the lute (which was going out of use even in his day), and all lute music is perfectly suited to the guitar.

"Of course, Mr. Segovia is a most exceptional virtuoso. To reach his degree of mastery one would need to work at the instrument for as long as the violin."

With the exception of just one thing, this is a splendid report; it is just what we require to help the guitar forward to the popularity the instrument really deserves. The exception is the phrase "vulgar banjo," which is infinitely worse than the expressions "ordinary banjo" or "G banjo."

A CLEVER GUITARIST.

ANDRÈS SEGOVIA, the exceptionally clever Spanish guitarist, gave his second London recital at the Wigmore Hall, on January 29th, before a large and fashionable audience. Splendid accounts have appeared in the press about the genius of this wonderful player, and the exquisite tone he produces from his instrument. One paper went so far as to state that the guitar is the most fashionable instrument of to-day, and that there is a big demand for the services of guitar teachers in consequence.

The guitar, strung in the proper way with gut and wire-covered silk strings, and played as it was intended to be played, is unequalled by any other instrument for beauty and quality of tone. It is an instrument for the lover or real music, and as there are excellent books of instruction, and hundreds of charming solos available, I think that many banjo teachers who hitherto have given little thought to the guitar, might with advantage to themselves now give the instrument some of the attention it so thoroughly deserves.

Every teacher who has interested himself in the ukulele or banjuke should certainly play the guitar, for it provides the finest of all accompaniments to these smaller instruments.

A portrait of Señor Andrès de Segovia is reproduced elsewhere in this issue of "B.M.G."

(Left) In this January 1927 B. M. G. magazine issue the reviewer for the London "Evening News" sees Andrés Segovia virtuosity first hand. The Bach Lute pieces must have been very impressionable for the concert going public.

(Right) In this March 1927 issue of the B. M. G. magazine the reviewer is aware of the genius of Andrés Segovia's artistic ability. The mention of tone is something that set him apart from all others. The portrait referred to at the bottom of the article appears on the following page.

GUITAR RECITAL AT THE WIGMORE HALL.

By A. F. Cramer.

THE Second Guitar Recital, given by Señor Andrès Segovia, brought a large and distinguished audience to the Wigmore Hall on Saturday afternoon, the 29th January, and no wonder he was welcomed by such an enthusiastic gathering, for it is seldom the public have the privilege and pleasure of hearing such a wonderful performance on the guitar as that given by Señor Segovia. It must have been a revelation to most of those present, as I think few people ever realized the possibilities and capabilities of this instrument. His playing was delicately superb and his tone-colour delightful. I was much impressed by the performance of the Handel, Bach, and Mendelssohn arrangements, they were prodigiously difficult for the guitar and played exquisitely; the two works by Albeniz were also very beautiful.

It is a great pity we do not hear more of the great guitar players, for I feel sure it would tend to revive the interest in this lovely and romantic old instrument, now almost forgotten.

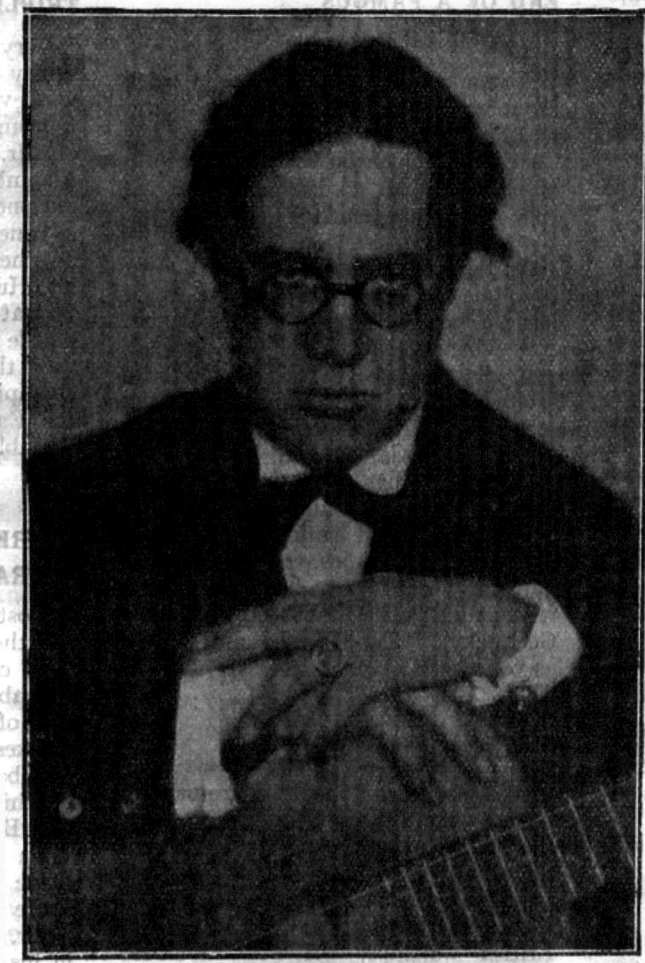

SEÑOR ANDRÈS SEGOVIA.
The Eminent Guitarist.

This second Wigmore Hall concert review, written by A. F. Cramer, is from the March 1927 issue of the B. M. G. magazine.

MID JULY 1927

ANDRES SEGOVIA,
THE WORLD'S GREATEST GUITAR PLAYER.
See page 7.

"His Master's Voice"
New Records
Electrical SILENT SURFACE *Recording*

"His Master's Voice"

In London, just after his Wigmore hall concert, on February 2, 1927 Andrés Segovia began his recording career with the *Gavotte en rondeau* by Bach in the Small Queen's Hall, Studio C recording studios of The Gramophone Co., Ltd., though the majority of his first recordings were done on May 2nd and 20th of 1927. This H. M. V. catalog cover was released about 9 weeks after those recordings were made. The portrait of the maestro was done in 1919 by Helmut Ruhermann. In the lapse of time between 1923 and 1927 the recording industry had adapted to the use of the electric microphone in 1926. The pieces recorded on May 2, 1927 were: *Gavotte* by Bach, *Tema variado* by Mozart-Sor and *Courante* by Bach. Almost 3 weeks later the pieces recorded on May 20, 1927 were: *Allegretto* from the *Sonatina* by Moreno Torroba, *Fandanguillo* by Joaquín Turina and *Recuerdos de la Alhambra* by Francisco Tárrega.

ANOTHER SEGOVIA RECITAL.

I hear that Señor Segovia, the world-famous guitarist, will give another recital at the Wigmore Hall on Saturday, October 29th.

Readers of "B.M.G.," especially those who reside in or near London, should make an effort to hear this celebrated artiste, but it will be necessary to obtain tickets beforehand, otherwise there will be but little hope of gaining admission, owing to the immense attraction of the Segovia recitals to real music lovers.

* *

Finally, there has lately appeared in England a great master of the guitar in the person of Andrés Segovia, a thirty - three years' old Spaniard who, in his own sphere, is of the same calibre as Kreisler and Paderewski in theirs. In London and elsewhere his playing has evoked tremendous enthusiasm, and deservedly so, for it would be difficult to imagine anything more exquisite than the sounds which he draws from the strings. Segovia's popularity has been still further extended by means of the gramophone. The recordings of his playing recently issued are among the finest productions of the Gramophone Company. Many people will desire to emulate Segovia on the guitar, and teachers of the instrument are receiving many enquiries from prospective players.

(Left) This announcement of an upcoming Andrés Segovia recital is from the B. M. G. magazine issue of October 1927.

(Right) The November 1927 issue of the B. M. G. magazine states what a great time was had by all at the recent London concert. The relating his greatness to other well known performers of other instruments had been going on, and would continue as such in many reviews and advertisements.

[December, 1927

THE SEGOVIA RECITAL, OCT. 29th.

W. S. M., writing in the November issue of the *Musical News*, says :—

"Most people associate the guitar with the twanging banjo. They would have had a rude but pleasant disillusionment had they been present at the Wigmore Hall on the occasion of a guitar recital by Andres Segovia. His is an art comparatively new to English audiences, but an ancient one in his native Spain. You cannot get much of a fortissimo on a guitar, in fact the general tone is inclined to be very much on the subdued side and one would anticipate a certain amount of monotony in a long recital. Yet Segovia held his large audience spellbound throughout the afternoon, and even then they demanded encores—as I did also. The range of colour he commands is amazing, ranging from the thin staccato note of the clavichord to the richer notes of the harp. Some Bach pieces sounded as if they were being played on the lute, for which instrument they were probably written. A second group comprised some Cimarosa, Haydn, Mendelssohn (the Canzonetta from the string quartet) and Schubert's sugar plum 'Moment Musical,' which I liked so well that I should like to hear that it has been recorded. Finally, we had some modern Spanish music. They say that there are even better guitarists in Spain than Segovia. I cannot credit it. Segovia does what he wills with his instrument, seemingly produces any effect he requires, bewilders us with his technique, and fascinates us with his wizardry. Above all, he reminds us that the guitar in his hands is an instrument of infinite possibilities."

This October 29, 1927 Andrés Segovia recital review is from the B. M. G. magazine issue of December 1927.

This autographed flyer is from the Saturday November 19, 1927 Andrés Segovia recital that was held in Budapest, it also mentions a Tuesday November 22, 1927 concert coming up in the following week.

735

Hungarian translation by Zsuzsa Racz.

On November 19, 1927, Saturday at 8:30 in the evening
in the great hall of the College of Music
ANDRÉS SEGOVIA's
GUITAR CONCERT will be held

THE PROGRAM:

1. SOR: (1778-1839) Etude
Theme Varié

TORROBA: Sonatina (dedicated to Andrés Segovia)
Allegretto – Andante – Allegro

2. BACH J. S.: Prelude
Allemande
Fuga
Courante
Sarabande
Gavotte

INTERMISSION

1. TURINA: Fandanguillo (dedicated to Andrés Segovia)

GRANADOS: Danza

ALBENIZ: Torre Bermeja
Legenda

   There are a huge number of Bach works in the hands of the public, which are known in violin and
harpsichord, furthermore in guitar transcriptions. Many were of the opinion that the originals were the
violin and harpsichord works, which later got transcribed to guitar. Today this obscure question – thanks
to the researches of Tappert M. M., Bruger H. D. and Bacha E. – has been satisfactorily answered. It is
possible to prove completely from J. S. Bach's original manuscripts that the guitar (lute) transcriptions
were the master's original works. For example, the III. and IV. Suites but also the III. Partita (on solo
violin) exist in transcription form in Bach's own handwriting. The only question remaining is what came
first, the guitar concept or perhaps the other instrumental transcriptions? As this is not a question
of paramount importance, we can relax and let it rest. The main thing is that these works are Bach's
original guitar compositions.

On November 22, 1927, Tuesday at 5:30 in the evening
in the great hall of the College of Music
Andrés Segovia's 2nd. guitar concert will be held

PROGRAM: Bach, Mendelsson, Schubert, M. Ponce, Albeniz etc.

Hungarian translation by Zsuzsa Racz.

GUITAR and LUTE
PRIVATE LESSONS

Solo guitar play. Song accompaniment. Chamber music.
JÁNOS BABRIK A. Jr. classical guitarist
Budapest, VI. Bajza-u. 46, I. 17.
Östereichische Gitarre-Zeitschrift
(Austrian quarterly guitar magazine)
With sheet music of "*Das Lied*" as extra

Printed quarterly (on the 1 st of August, November, February and May) with plenty of extra guitar or sing sheet music included. Our permanent columns are: Guitar News, Concert News,

Literary News, News, Pictures, art and music extras

Issued by J. ORTNER, professor of the Viennese State Music and Applied Arts Academy,formerly guitarist of the court opera
Chief editor: G. MOISSL, Vienna, III., Klimschgasse 16/a.
Subscription for a year is 6 Schilling

Order here: Vienna, II., No. 6., or at Rózsavölgyi and Partner Book and Music Shop

RÓZSAVÖLGYI and PARTNER
Budapest, IV., Szervita-tér 5 and Andrássy-út 45.

THE ONLY GRAMOPHONE AND GRAMOPHONE DISC SHOP IN HUNGARY

Nov. 22 5:30 PM Andrés Segovia's 2nd guitar concert Academy of Music

Nov. 24 7:30 PM Misha Lewitzky (piano subscription second performance) Vigadó

Nov. 25 8:30PM Eve Clare piano recital Academy of Music

Nov. 26 7:30 PM Emil Telemányi's Bach-Mozart program Vigadó

Nov. 27 5:30 PM The second "*nóta*" (popular folksy song) recital of Jóska Nádor Academy of Music

Nov. 28 7:30 PM Verdi program of the Budapest Song and Music Assembly Academy of Music

Nov. 28 8:00 PM Concert of the National Hungarian Singers' Guild Vigadó

Nov. 30 7:30 PM Violin Concert of Fritz Kreisler Vigadó

Dec. 1 8:45 PM Rossini: Missa solemnis – first time in Budapest Academy of Music

Dec. 2 7:30 PM Erno Dohnányi's piano concert Vigadó

Dec. 5 5:30 PM "Vajda János" by author Jeno Köveskuthy Academy of Music Chamber Room

Dec. 5 7:30 PM Chamber Music performance I. with appearances from concert singer Rózsi Fuchs-Fayer and violinist Ibolyka Singer Academy of Music.

America to Hear Segovia, of Spain, Virtuoso Who Plays Bach on Guitar

Andres Segovia, Spanish Guitarist, from a Painting by Miguel del Pino

THE guitar has found a new artistic status in the modern musical world. It has been discovered that its voice rivals that of the harpsichord. Too long regarded as a purely elementary instrument to accompany serenades and the like, it has now asserted its fine and delicate tone as worthy to carry complicated measures of Bach, which were originally written for the lute.

This development of a once despised music-maker has come about largely through the fine demonstrations of the guitar's possibilities which have been made in the last few years on European concert tours by Andres Segovia, a Spanish virtuoso. He is announced to make his first appearances in the United States during the coming winter.

Born in Seville, Spain, Mr. Segovia has for the past fifteen years been appearing as a solo guitarist. Since the war, he has made tours in various European countries, being one of the few foreign artists to make a successful tour of Russia. His recitals have lately become popular in Paris. His London début was made last winter.

Programs of Old and New

Mr. Segovia's programs include the Bach Suite for the lute and classic sonatas. He also presents examples of modern Spanish music by Granados, Albeniz and others, reproducing their fascinating rhythms with authentic racial knowledge of the medium.

The variety of tone-colors and contrapuntal effects which he is able to produce on the guitar were especially remarked by audiences in his Paris and London appearances last year. In particular, he has developed some unusual effects, such as the glissando, which are said to enrich the tonal impressions of his playing.

Mr. Segovia will make his American début at Town Hall, New York, in early January. His tour will be under the management of F. C. Coppicus of the Metropolitan Musical Bureau.

This is from a November or December 1927 Musical America magazine.

This January 14, 1928 Musical America magazinereview by Irving Weil pertains to the United States January 8, 1928 debut of the maestro.

THE DEBUG OF SEGOVIA IN AMERICA
A Guitar, if Kindly Treated, Will Make Fine Music

Those of us who believed that a guitar was merely one of those nuisances that accompanied college glee clubs in "The Spanish Cavalier" era, had one of the shocks of our lives at the Town Hall last Sunday. It was an absorbingly pleasant shock and Andres Segovia, a Spanish guitarist—possibly *the* Spanish guitarist—was responsible for it. This was his first appearance in America and a houseful of people was captivated by the man's unerring skill and resource. He convinced one forthwith that a guitar was unmistakably a musical instrument.

Probably half the audience that packed the hall was made up of our Spanish citizenry who may have known all about Mr. Segovia and what might be done with a guitar even if a few ignoramuses like ourselves didn't. We had, to be sure, heard authentic Hawaiians do strange and fascinating things with authentic ukeleles, but this was of course quite different and even more fascinating.

The guitar, in Mr. Segovia's hands, became something capable of providing an upper-voiced melody supported by varied and ambitious harmony, or an intricate counterpoint sometimes extending to more than two parts. Even a not particularly simple Bach fugue met with no casualties. But the possibilities of the instrument also invaded numerous varieties in tone quality. This gamut of color had to do largely with different ways of plucking the strings, as well as at different places on soundboard or fingerboard. What a violinist would call a left-hand pizzicato, for instance, produced a minuet but beautiful bell timbre and a ponticello effect touched the macabre. An almost vocal portamento and an occasional deft use of vibrato also added their bit of variety.

With all these things at his command and, besides, a sensitiveness and agility of plucking fingers quite amazing in their virtuosity, Mr. Segovia tackled not only Spanish music —some of it actually written for the guitar —but Bach and Haydn and other matters that were not; certainly not primarily, in any case.

He put together a Bach suite from pieces known now as parts of the solo violin suites and sonatas, explaining that Bach may have written them for the lute. The way he played them, however, was sufficient apology, if any were needed, for doing them on a guitar. His instrument indubitably brought out their formal structure less laboriously than the violin does, although we believe we shouldn't care so very much, perhaps, for the D Minor chaconne, in instance, as something for merely tinkling tone. However, he didn't play that.

But what sounded far better than Bach

Andres Segovia, an Extraordinary Artist

and Haydn which, after all were something in the nature of a stunt, was Mr. Segovia's Spanish music. A good deal of this as we have said, was written for the guitar, for of course he is not the only great guitarist Spain has had. There were, indeed, dozens of them and their method has been handed down from generation to generation, together with what they have written for the instrument.

One of the greatest of all of them, according to plenteous contemporary testimony, was Fernando Sor, who toured the Continent and made the instrument fashionable at the beginning of the nineteenth century. Another, of a later generation, was Francisco Tarrega and both these were well represented on Mr. Segovia's programme. But even their pieces were not as interesting as a wholly captivating serenade by Joaquin Malats which, since he was a pianist, was very possibly a piano piece originally.

Nevertheless, after about an hour of the guitar, and in spite of Mr. Segovia's brilliant virtuosity, the inherent poverty of the instrument began to make itself felt. Monotony inevitably crept into the performance. For the guitar, like its remote relatives in the plucked-string family, the lute and the harpsichord, lost their hold on people because something better took their place—the violin and the piano.

From painting by Miguel del Pino

"LOOKS LIKE FRANZ SCHUBERT, PLAYS LIKE CASALS, HEIFETZ"

—*Gilman, N. Y. Herald Tribune*

ANDRES SEGOVIA

The Great Spanish Guitarist

A NEW MUSICAL STAR IN THE FIRMAMENT

By F. C. COPPICUS

F. C. COPPICUS

THE reputation of The Metropolitan Musical Bureau for presenting instrumentalists of the first rank is based on artists of the calibre of Harold Bauer, Ossip Gabrilowitsch, Pablo Casals, Mischa Elman and many others. Therefore, when I sponsored in New York the celebrated Spanish guitarist, Andres Segovia, it was expected that this artist would have a musical success similar to my other instrumentalists.

Not only is a guitar recital a novelty for this country, but I have for a long while felt that the guitar was an instrument of noble lineage and had too long been neglected in our concert halls. When I heard Mr. Segovia in Europe this summer, I realized at once that here was an artist who must have success in America, and whose art was in every way commensurate with the greatest living virtuosi. I felt that Mr. Segovia was such an artist as my clients in this country would expect me to present.

It was gratifying to me to have this opinion supported by the able critics of the New York press, and I was happy that Mr. Segovia's debut recital sold out, with hundreds turned away, which I consider extraordinary.

MADE MUSICAL HISTORY

LAWRENCE GILMAN, *Herald Tribune.*

HE gave one of the most extraordinary and engrossing recitals of music that has ever taken place in a New York concert hall. We think it very likely that this was the first guitar recital ever given in New York, so the player WAS MAKING HISTORY AS WELL AS MUSIC.

We make no bones about saying that Mr. Segovia is one of the most consummate masters of any instrument now before the public. He has made the guitar a thing to be spoken of in the same breath with the harpsichord of Landowska, the 'cello of Casals, the violin of Heifetz. Hearing Mr. Segovia play, one could not but remember, and paraphrase, what Coleridge wrote of a certain singer: "You might have fancied that the voice had a separate being of its own, that it was a living something, the mode of existence of which was for the ear only . . . so perfectly was the utterance without effort, and without the appearance of effort." That effortlessness, that acquired, deceptive spontaneity, is surely the stamp of the supreme technician, the rare and consummate artist.

A POET AND MASTER

OLIN DOWNES, *New York Times.*

THE appearance of Mr. Segovia is not that of the trumpeted virtuoso. He is rather the dreamer or scholar in bearing, long hair, eyeglasses, a black frock coat and neckwear of an earlier generation. He seats himself thoughtfully, strikes a soft chord, then bends over his guitar and proceeds to play like the poet and master he is of that instrument.

He belongs to the very small group of musicians who by transcendent power of execution, by imagination and intuition create an art of their own that sometimes seems to transform the very nature of their medium. Segovia could be if he chose the trick player of this generation. HE DRAWS THE TONE COLORS OF HALF A DOZEN INSTRUMENTS from the one that he plays. He has an extraordinary command of nuances, he seems to discover whole planes of sonority.

This was an unusually significant appearance, and the first of concerts that Mr. Segovia will give here. He is a wholly exceptional artist, a man of mark among the musicians of the day.

This January 21, 1928 Musical America magazine promotion and set of reviews pertains to the United States January 8, 1928 debut of the maestro.

A GENIUS ON THE GUITAR

SAMUEL CHOTZINOFF, *The World.*

THE GUITAR IN THE HANDS OF MR. SEGOVIA SEEMS TO HAVE NO LIMITATIONS WHATSOEVER. It is not given us to know, just how the anatomy of this guitarist's hands differs from ours, nor how he has acquired a mastery of his instrument so perfect that the most intricate polyphony seems as natural to the guitar as to the piano. The fact remains that Mr. Segovia's performance yesterday was aesthetically and emotionally satisfying to the highest degree. If comparisons are at all permissible, I should compare Mr. Segovia to Pablo Casals. I can think of no other artist who possesses the guitarist's delicate musical perceptions, his refinement, his aristocratic reserve and his sense of rhythm. MR. SEGOVIA MUST BE HEARD TO BE BELIEVED.

—⁂—

BOSTON ALSO SUCCUMBS

Marvel at Virtuoso Guitarist
Segovia Amazes Big Audience by Magic of His Art.
—Boston Post, Jan. 16, 1928.

Segovia Shows Wonderful Mastery
His Performance Stirs Enthusiasm.
—Boston Herald, Jan. 16, 1928.

Famous Guitarist Heard in Recital
Segovia Charms and Astonishes.
—Boston Globe, Jan. 16, 1928.

First and Second New York Recitals Sold Out!

Third New York Recital, Gallo Theatre, January 29, at 3 P. M.

Fourth New York Recital, Town Hall, February 4, at 3 P. M.

Everywhere the maestro Andrés Segovia went he astonished his audiences. America in the midst of the Dixieland Jazz era was not used to a guitarist drawing the tones of several instruments as a tone palette. The February 4, 1928 recital was his farewell concert until the next season, which began on December 29, 1928 with his return to perform in the Town Hall.

The following week the Musical America magazine of February 4, 1928 had an article which included comments from the maestro. The article entitled "Granada sends a genius" was written by Hollister Noble. The images on this and the next page are repositioned.

ANDRES SEGOVIA, the young Spanish guitarist who created a generously dimensioned sensation at his first New York recital some days ago, is a remarkable product of his country. It is a pity his present visit will not take him to the West. He is not only a fine distinctive artist of genuine genius, he is a charming, urbane cosmopolitan gentleman with a personality that sparkles.

Among the army of celebrities who have stormed our shores this winter, Segovia, Maurice Ravel, the French composer, and Sir Thomas Beecham, the English conductor, form a triumvirate distinguished for their broad and civilized approach to music.

Mr. Segovia's art has been capably discussed in other columns of this journal. His adventures as he approached his first American tour have been intriguing. Born in Granada not so many years ago, he took to the guitar when about fourteen years of age, and he has made it his permanent interest in life. He is entirely self taught. Although he studied harmony and composition in various schools, he never had a lesson on the guitar. His deep passion for this instrument has nothing of pretence in it.

This interest in his instrument was commented on by Samuel Chotzinoff in a recent discussion of Mr. Segovia in the New York *World* as follows:

"In Munich the more fastidious amateurs are even trying to revive the ancient lute, which to Segovia is a labor that can bear no fruit, for the lute is as extinct as the virginal and it is well for dead things to remain dead. Perhaps the guitar will also vanish presently, but there is much life in it yet, and it has a respectable literature which dates from the dawn of music down to the present day. Boccherini wrote five quintets for strings and guitar; Schubert one. Paganini, who was a great master of the guitar, having devoted three solid years to its practice, composed no less than 104 pieces for it, besides four guitar quintets. Then there is Ferdinand Sor, whose music Segovia disclosed to us for the first time. Sor was a Catalonian who played the guitar with great success all over Europe at the beginning of the nineteenth century. A friend of Spontini, Sor composed a good deal of chamber music and pieces for the guitar, but most of these were destroyed during a fire at his publishers. At Petrograd, Segovia himself discovered a manuscript sonata for guitar by Sor which he expects to knock into shape for one of his New York concerts. "The process of knocking music into shape consumes most of Segovia's spare time, for he explained the old composers could hardly guess the capabilities of the instrument in the hands of the modern artist. * * * * * Segovia's extraordinary artistry touched a responsive chord among modern composers. The piquancy, charm and delicacy of his guitar offered new stimuli for the jaded creative faculties, and Mr. Segovia became the recipient of manuscripts from Roussel, de Breville, Laparra, Samazeuil and Ferroud among Frenchmen; Manen, Ponce, Turina, Espla, Torroba, among his own countrymen; Cyril Scott and Arthur Bliss and others. All these have but an imperfect knowledge of the technique of the guitar, and the manuscripts they sent were musical indications rather than finished products. On the score of a sonata submitted by Cyril Scott the composer had written, "Machen Sie Besser," a legend which is no challenge, but a plea. "I had disturbed the guitarist in the act of complying with this very demand, and Mr. Scott's score was undergoing numerous erasures and additions. The routine question, "What do you think of modern music?" seemed sensible when put to an artist who sincerely cherishes the old music while he encourages the new, and Mr. Segovia's ready answer proved that he had pondered this question at leisure and had arrived at a fairly just settlement.

"'If modern music,' he said earnestly, 'is the natural development o f what has gone before, fine!' Then he added smilingly: 'But so much of modern music glosses over, by startling harmonies and freakish forms, poverty of ideas and emotions. The difficulty that confronts a modern composer is to find originality in orderly advance. You cannot be a hermit in art, you cannot start out in this late day as nude, artistically speaking, as Adam or Eve. Music, like language, is not the creation of an individual. Tradition is but the accumulation of knowledge. The modernist proclaims himself a Robinson Crusoe and sets about making music as if no music had ever been made before him, which is as ridiculous as if a man living in New York today would go about feeding and clothing himself in the manner Crusoe was forced to adopt on his uninhabited island'."

"The guitar for me," Segovia remarked the other day to MUSICAL AMERICA' "is a universal instrument. Contrary to accepted belief, I prefer playing Bach to my native music. This instrument is beautifully designed to bring out the most delicate patterns of polyphonic writing. I play Bach on all my public programs. His music I prefer to play above that of all others."

Mr. Segovia has, of course, played all over Europe countless times. He has toured extensively in Cuba, Mexico and South America. On his tours he notes as an important observation that the appreciation of his music in Germany and Austria seems to be cerebral, objective and more or less intellectualized. In Russia and Spain he finds a sensitive fervor and subjective appreciation quite different.

When final arrangements for his European tour had been made, Mr. Segovia received a cable from his manager that his first American recital would be given in Proctor, Vt. There was consternation in Mr. Segovia's camp. Where was Proctor? Maps and atlases were ransacked. No mention of Proctor. Some American tourists were consulted. They had never heard of the place.

Then came the explanation. Mr. Segovia's formal début would be made in New York, of course. But a very young lady, Miss Proctor, of Proctor, Vt., when asked what she wanted for her birthday, requested a concert (by a guitar player) and Mr. Segovia was finally chosen. With the genial Freddy Schang of the Metropolitan Musical Bureau, Segovia journeyed to Proctor and played for about twenty-five people.

"One of the happiest concerts of my career" was his verdict.

Proctor is in the midst of the Vermont marble quarries and Mr. Segovia has not yet cleared up the discrepancies in his mind caused by marble walks, bridge and masonry of fine marble contrasted with frame houses and wooden barns.

New York Adventures

His New York adventures have been exciting. Nine public and private recitals in his first week here. He often sends someone around to private houses to find out what kind of a chair he will have to use. Fritz Kreisler was the first man to tell him he looked like Franz Schubert (Schubert ought to feel decidedly complimented.)

Mr. Segovia gave his first concert at the age of seventeen in Granada and recently met a Spanish professor of philosophy at Columbia University who was present at his first concert. He plays the piano and composes a good deal for the guitar.

"I am self taught entirely. And I may add that I have not always been very happy with myself either as a professor or as a pupil."

Alexander Tansman has written a work for him which he will play next year. His table the other day was covered with manuscript scores sent him by composers of the modern school all over Europe.

Mr. Segovia is married and has two children. He explained their names very carefully.

"The first I named Andres because neither my wife nor I had the imagination to name him anything else. He developed a great taste for drawing and painting, and when our second boy came along, we called him Leonardo. We had great hopes, but, alas, I fear our youngest boy is going to be a musician."

———

The balance of the article contains some of the maestro's humor.

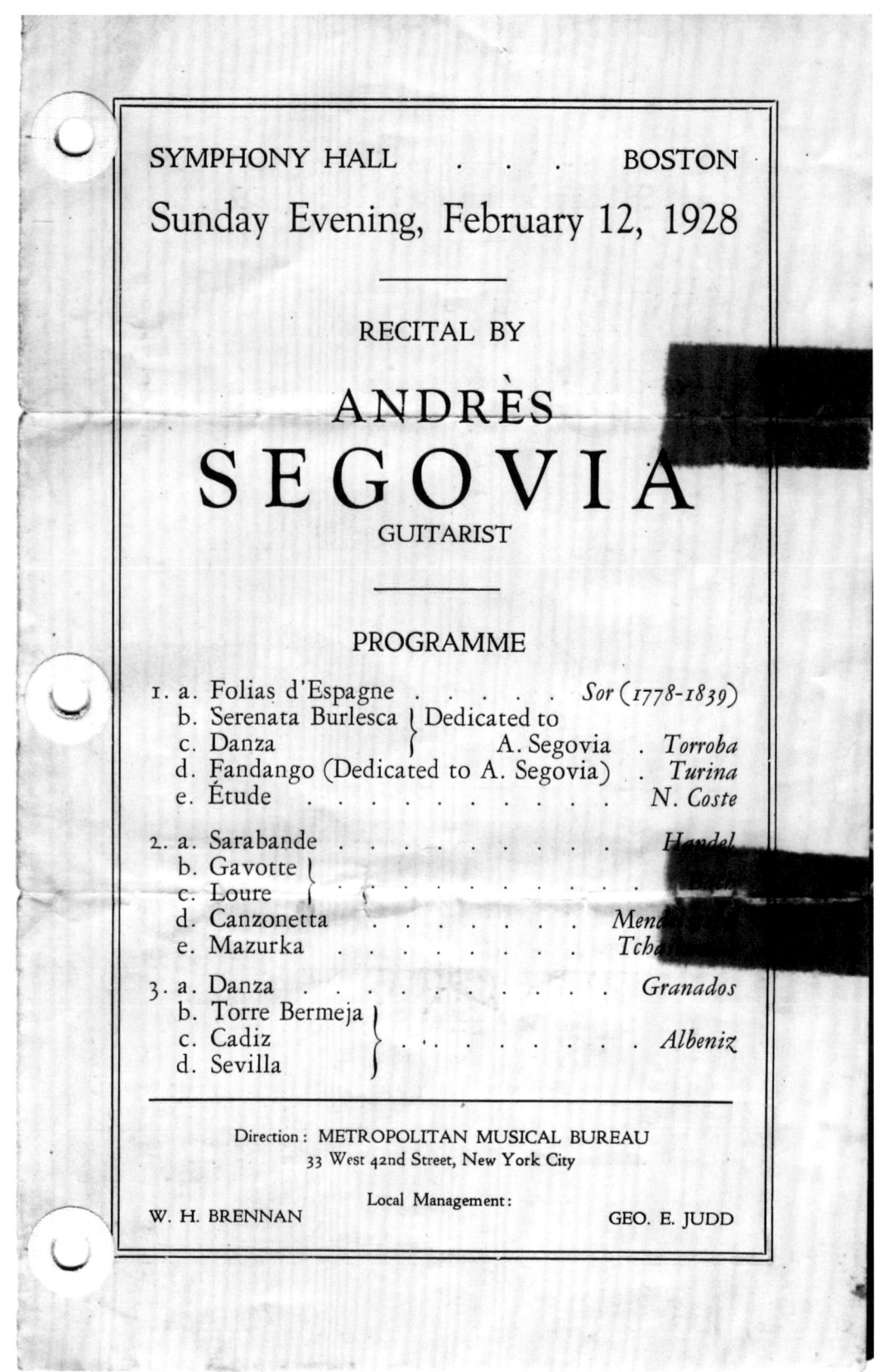

This Sunday February 12, 1928 Concert was held at the Symphony Hall in Boston. These theatre programs belonged to Anna Palmer Coit North (1908-2014), who was the very first female feature writer for Time magazine. I encourage you to watch her You Tube interview made when she was 103 years of age.

Andres Segovia Bids America Farewell

To Return in December for Three Months' Tour Extending to Pacific Coast

Andres Segovia, Spanish guitarist, who met with such sensational success in his American debut, sailed for Europe on February 16 after giving his fifth and last New York recital at Town Hall the day before.

This artist made his American debut on January 8, and in the period of six weeks appeared fifteen times in New

MASTER PIANIST PAYS TRIBUTE TO GREAT GUITARIST

Arthur Shattuck, well-known American pianist, made the above sketch of Andres Segovia, Spanish guitarist, in Paris last summer.

York City, four of which were recitals at the Town Hall and one at the Gallo Theater. He also had four performances in Boston and one each in Baltimore, Washington, Norfolk, East Orange, N. J., and Proctor, Vt. In all, Mr. Segovia played twenty-six concerts in this short period, which is believed to be a record for a new artist visiting America for the first time.

Through his manager, F. C. Coppicus, Mr. Segovia desires to express his personal thanks to the American public for its cordial and enthusiastic reception of his art, which has deeply affected him, particularly in view of the fact that the guitar is a new instrument for the concert hall in New York and its repertory largely unknown to the concert-going public.

Mr. Segovia will return to America next December for a three months' tour, which will take him to the Pacific Coast, from which point he will depart for his first tour of the Orient, including Japan, China, Philippine Islands, Straits Settlements and India.

This review is from the Musical America magazine of February 23, 1928. It mentions that Andrés Segovia performed 26 concerts in his first American tour.

From the Victor records advertisement in the *"Caras y Caretas"* magazine of April 7, 1928 issue No. 1540 *Año* XXXI.

"Op. 9 The Magic Flute" by Sor-Mozart and a *"Gavotte"* by J. S. Bach on a 12" disc, and the *"Sonatina"* by Moreno-Torroba and *"Courante"* by J. S. Bach on a 10" disc.

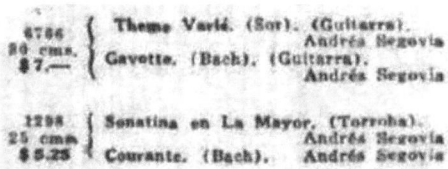

From the Victor records advertisement in the "Caras y Caretas" magazine of May 5, 1928 issue No. 1544 *Año* XXXI.

"Recuerdos de la Alhambra" by Tárrega and "Fandanguillo" by Turina on a 12" disc.

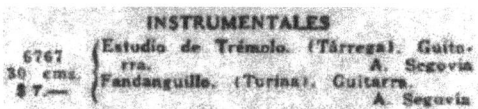

This notice below is from the magazine *"La Revista de Musica"* of July 15, 1928. It translates to:

"As well having reappeared before our public, after having conquered world wide celebrity status, the poet of the guitar, Andrés Segovia. In effect, Segovia isn't only an eminent guitarist, who obtains the intimacy and unexpected sounds and effects of the delicate instrument. Besides the technical aspect, so notable and interesting, to be found in the artist is that characteristic temperament of his musical personality so attractive and congenial. Andrés Segovia is a musician of exquisite sensibility that infuses his art with great poetry of the guitar.

Signed: Ernesto de La Guardia."

44 **LA REVISTA DE MUSICA**

También ha reaparecido ante nuestro público, después de haber conquistado celebridad mundial, el poeta de la guitarra, Andrés Segovia. En efecto, Segovia no es solamente un guitarrista eminente, que obtiene del íntimo y delicado instrumento sonidos y efectos insospechados. Además de este aspecto técnico, tan notable e interesante, se encuentra en el artista ese temperamento característico de su personalidad musical tan atrayente y simpática. Andrés Segovia es un músico de exquisita sensibilidad que infunde con su arte gran poesía a la guitarra.

Ernesto de LA GUARDIA

In Richard "Rico" Stover's revised edition of "Six Silver Moonbeams, The Life and Times of Agustín Barrios Mangoré" on page 103, he includes the program of the first of nine Andrés Segovia concerts to be given in the next month and a half to capacity audiences. This was the premier concert since Andrés' stay in Buenos Aires in 1921. This took place on July 3, 1928 in the Teatro Odeon.

"First Part:

1) Minueto (Sor)
2) Mozart Variations (Sor)
3) Fandanguillo (Turina)
4) Estudio (Tárrega)

Second Part:

1) Prelude, Allemande, Fugue, Courante, and Gavotte (Bach)
2) Minuet Haydn
3) Sonatina (Torroba)
4) Leyenda (Albeniz)"

Andrés' next performance was three days later on July 6, 1928. Before that took place, Carlos Vega, musicologist of the first rank, chronicled his visit to Segovia's hotel room on the evening of July 3, 1928. This was published just one month to the day later, after several other concerts had taken place.

Andrés Segovia by Carlos Vega — translation by Randy Osborne

From: "El Hogar" August 3, 1928 Buenos Aires *Año* XXIV Num. 981

"Segovia is one of the most beautiful accents to ever come from the guitar to go to the sensitivity of mankind. Maestro of the same, the grand temperament free and agile over the obedient technique, to raise it in an individual effort without precedent and showing the art of the epoch magnifying the instrument.

It has to deal with the intimate accumulated experiences by one hundred rich generations of the aroma that the celebrated *Triana* bids farewell in the historic *Zambras* of its Moorish Spain; having impregnated its childlike spirit in the manner with which the Andalusian synthetic pain of the *"cante jondo"* rings on the strings; that rich heritage and that lesson of infancy, exalted by a vast culture, that must take him necessarily to say as it's said, in the guitar the sentiment of all the epochs arrives in the sonority.

There is in the modern guitar something boyish that shows through the first look over the wall into the neighboring garden. And around in amazement in front of the eyes what appears new reflecting the unknown history of the popular "Cinderella", in a struggle for many centuries by reaching the highest artistic destinies.

The guitar "has wings wider than the nest". And in the beginning of the present century the able men arrived to take flight.

Describing a trajectory that can only be explained by those who know the energy of its pulse and spirit, Andrés Segovia appears unexpectedly in the first row. The collaboration of his talent is consequently decisive for the culmination and future of the small *"exacordio"*.

The measurement in what the guitar adjusts to the natural diapason of the spirit has forever generated in its cultivator's devotion and gratitude many times that of the sacrifice.

Andrés Segovia

Por CARLOS VEGA

Photo from *"El Hogar"* (The Home) of August 3, 1928. The caption says it was one of the most recent photos of the great interpreter of the guitar. "Foto Muray". The origin of the sketch is unknown. Photo by Nickolas Muray, © Nickolas Muray Photo Archives

"Since the middle of the 16th century, in what Vicente Espinel added to the instrument -the fifth string with what was to displace the vihuela, until what Francisco Tárrega inaugurated- the modern renaissance; as many as ignored efforts, as much as the secret struggle by reaching what humanity prefers, how impressionable the spectacle of so much fervor and impartial position in the prosperity of the instrument!

Perhaps the guitar realizes in the world of the sensation the ideal sound to what the human soul aspires to; maybe the secular cult of the instrument has identified the aspiration of the spirit with the reality of its sound. It is certain that the soul feels projected outside of itself in the song of the guitar. This is an act without equal in the music; the music is an act without equal in humanity. By that Segovia has succeeded, in comparison with every guitarist, in the human hierarchy.

To hear him as such, having taken possession of the guitar, as far as the miracle is to hear the purest voice of mankind.

Tárrega bequeathed to the 20th century the guitar apt for the most elevation in the sensation of art. With Andrés Segovia arrives one of the best capacities for speaking of a new language. But, what does it say in the guitar? With what music to be presented to the general alternative? How to satisfy the demand of the great European musical centers?

Here begins the labor of Segovia. It was necessary to endow to the guitar of a repertoire able to reach and shake the contemporary sensibility; and it was necessary to renovate the work of the classics that, in the lute and other antique instruments, or lose it by the lack of interpreters. And Segovia, in many years of tenacious labor, has acquired it. That is his first title and this merit that the history of the guitar must recognize.

"The original literature for the guitar"-explains Segovia- "although endowed with many beautiful pages, can't justify the permanent activity of the guitarist in the European centers. The guitar, well, was extinguished in a vicious circle: there weren't concert artists because composers didn't exist, and there weren't composers because guitarists didn't exist. It was necessary to break that. Consequently, I offered to the greatest musicians in Europe the opportunity to compose. I would try it out. I gave them many brief indications as to how they should be adjusted by the creator, and the results weren't long in coming."

Effectively. The mediation of Segovia has generated the greatest and most valuable contribution that the guitar has received of the composers. In all parts of Europe they work for the instrument. In Spain there is a pleyade formally submitted to the work. To the exception of Manuel de Falla, that subsequently to his "Homenaje a Debussy" he hasn't returned to write for the guitar, numerous musicians continue fulfilling interesting works.

"The Andalusian concert artist, that presently has names and titles, enumerated with the certainty of whoever reads". — Moreno Torroba says — "He is the first of the modern guitarists to bring about compositions written directly for the guitar; later, many: Joaquín Turina, with his delicious "Fandanguillo", Lopez Chavarri, Vicente Arregui, Oscar Sola, Adolfo Salazar, Ernesto Halffter, Juan Manén"... Andrés Segovia adds: "In France I have been the object of friendly distinction: Albert Roussel, prominent contemporary figure, has written a worthy page of his name for the guitar. The title "Segovia", and he dedicated it to me"... "As well, they have dedicated works of great interest Gustave Samazeuilh, Jacques Ibert, P. O. Ferroud, Raoul Laparra, Raymond Petit, Pierre de Breville, and Georges Migot"... "But it doesn't have to do with promises. They are works in my possession, and I will play the better part of them in Buenos Aires...You see?-he said to me in his apartment in his hotel-Here they are — And he showed me a pile of manuscripts. Would you like to hear some things?"...

I hesitated for an instant. The maestro just gave his first concert in the Odeon, we dined and, now, when his beautiful triumph of the afternoon would suggest a time for relaxation, consequently he offered me an audition of works that he would have to read from the manuscripts.

But I know Segovia. For the guitar, for the art, The celebrated Andalusian is always fresh. Intellectual and physically, he is strong and resolute. In normal circumstances, he amazes his eloquence of "causer avec guitare" (and without it); in moments of compulsion, that the chronicler recalls, his vigor causes marvels.

I find it convincing that it truly represents an effort for Segovia, not to play the guitar. Meanwhile, the concert artist reads the "Sonata" by Manén. A solemn introduction, slow, very noble; then an "allegretto", in that the popular Spanish song shows refinement, shaped by the culture.

"Three notable Swiss musicians have written for me." -he then tells me- "They are: Aloys Fornerod, William Bastard and Volkmar Andreae".-And he put new manuscripts in front of my eyes. — "Here you have a page by the German composer Hindemith; here one by the Polish composer Alexander Tansman; this other one, of the Portuguese Francisco de Lacerda. In England my instrument inspires a lot of congeniality: Cyril Scott and Arthur Bliss as well have dedicated their works to me, and likewise the Scandinavian composer Hugo Alfvén and the Belgian Raymond Moulaert have done so. Do you know the interesting Mexican musician Manuel Ponce? Well, I owe him for a precious collection of works. Have you already heard them?"

Well then I have verified that in most of the countries of Europe they have collaborated in the work to enrich the guitar forever. We knew here that a lot of music was being written for it; we know a few of the names cited and their works; we can recall, besides, Lopez Chavarri has written as well for Llobet, the Uruguayan Alfonso Broqua for Maria Luisa Anido and for Emilio Pujol, and Eduardo Torres, maestro of the chapel of the cathedral in Seville, has composed some pages for two guitars, but the magnitude of the movement is, for me, a revelation of Segovia.

I think that in Argentina, the country of the world that yields most fervently the cult of the guitar, is one of the few nations whose musicians remain belonging to this well orientated general movement. It appears impossible that no Argentine composer.....

"Yes, yes!"....Segovia interrupted me.- "One of our compatriots, taught very well in Paris, has written for me many and very beautiful pages: he is Carlos Pedrell."

I have a great sensation of relief, which is equal to confessing my belief in that the artists that surge from the populace are votes in favor of its culture. In what measurement lends the coloration of the ambiance in proportion to the artists?...expatriates? "It's best that he stays put". In the uncertainty, I have given up without any more than the satisfaction to corroborate that Argentina is well represented in a tendency that assumes good proportions.

"Here you have the works of Pedrell" — added the artist, handing me various manuscripts.

With total complacency I read the titles and turned pages. There is a "Suite" that consists of four movements: Lamento, Pagina Romantica, Improvisacion and Guitarreo. A "Weberiana", a "Serenata" and, finally, three numbers reunited under the title of "Danzas de las tres princesas cautivos".

"All of them are interesting, particularly the "Weberiana" -says Segovia- "and I'll play them in Buenos Aires."...

It comprises, in the end, which the guitar just acquired a modern repertoire varied and beautiful; and as such the conquest must be almost totally to the determination of Segovia. You already know it isn't enough with asking and to obtain. About the page of the composer it's necessary although to do the difficult chore of the adaptation. In this point the guitar presents more obstacles than any other instrument, and this work, beautifully done by the Spanish concert artist, represents the most noble and important aspect of his efforts.

Segovia talked to me later about the Mexican composer Manuel Ponce with admiration and congeniality. Andrés affirmed that his present compositions for orchestra, trio, piano, and voices, are very superior to his *"folkloric"* pieces written beforehand, they are awakening the attention of the best musicians of Paris. Ponce besides, has penetrated so admirably the nature of the guitar, that hardly is necessary, at times, to modify some chord. His labor up to this date comprises six sonatas, a concerto for guitar and small orchestra, various pages of lesser duration and a collection of studies over formulas that Segovia has given him.

Consequently it's impossible to synthesize the wealth of accounts, about his intervention in favor of a modern repertoire, that the Andalusian guitarist provides us. But it's sufficiently annotated for what the good friends of the instrument comprehend what the guitaristic literature must be to the present epoch.

Now it would be interesting to declare if we are in the presence of the initial impulse or of the favorable moment of the historic process. Boccherini, Kall, Kreutzer, Weber, Schubert, Paganini and other great musicians, haven't they written numerous works for the guitar in past epochs? Yes. But it's fitting to recall that the instrument didn't have then the artistic hierarchy to that which has been elevated by the endowment of technical resources of the later date. An insufficient study of its possibilities hasn't permitted until now the effective exploitation of its attractions, however the noble inspiration with what was in vogue.

The photo below of Andrés Segovia from the Carlos Vega interview for *El Hogar*.

The greatest European critics of the present agree in that the guitar takes its place among the foremost concert instruments. With certainty, well, the affirmation is given today that, in what has passed of the present century, its voice has definitely incorporated to the universal concord of the art.

The instruments give a particular character to the music that is conceived for each one of them. Therefore the popular Spanish music-that is more Moorish than the guitar-has in the instrument of Segovia returns a lot to its primitive confines. And that salutes the presence of Bach in the programs of the guitar by the best musicologists as a just restitution to the ordinary conception of the genre of the plucked string.

But Bach, whose human greatness lives permanently in the present, isn't accessible for the interpreters in his exact manner whether in a great capacity, nourished in a profound culture, hasn't vanished throughout the centuries for returning to the superficiality of the time with the giant German in his pristine fragrance.

The version of Bach on strings and exact interpretation, are conquests that Segovia has succeeded with admirable art. An extensive critical literature has elevated the fulfillment of the eminent Andalusian concert artist to a category of example.

The guitar, in the end, is consecrated as an instrument of art, when happening through Segovia it acquires the majority of the pages with that, it will be able to continue singing in the pure language of the classics and in the complexity of the contemporaries in the future. And meanwhile the name of the Spanish concert artist has prolonged it in a strong relationship with the date most fortunate for the guitar, the remembrance of its happening will subsist as an aroma of the enchantment in the memory of the world.

Signed: Carlos Vega"

TEATRO ODEON

BUENOS AIRES
Empresa ALZATI & Co.

Viernes 6 de Julio 1928, a las 17.30

SEGUNDO CONCIERTO

ANDRES SEGOVIA
GUITARRISTA

(Fotografía del Cuadro al oleo de Miguel del Pino)

Empresa Artística: Sociedad Musical DANIEL

Of this series of concerts, this is the second. For the first time, Andrés Segovia, now the recording artist, has returned to perform for the Buenos Aires public. Many ticket buyers were certainly waiting to hear pieces, that they had only heard on 78 RPM discs since his last concert tour. Andrés Segovia began his recording career on February 2, 1927 in London. A month after this second concert on July 6, 1928, Andrés Segovia performed for "El Circulo" in Rosario, Santa Fe on August 7, 1928.

Tras siete años de ausencia vuelve ANDRES SEGOVIA
después de haber cosechado aplausos fervorosos
en Paris, Londres, Berlin, Viena, Roma,
Budapest, Estocolmo, Petersburgo,
Bruselas, New York, Boston
etc. etc.

El afecto con que se le aguarda en Buenos Aires co-
rresponde perfectamente al que el siente
por el pueblo argentino.

This inside cover page mentions that Andrés Segovia has returned for the first time in seven years, having played and received fervent applause in an array of European and North American cities since his departure. The second paragraph says: "The affection that is kept in Buenos Aires for him perfectly corresponds to what he feels for the Argentine populace."

Breyer Hermanos, guitar maker, publisher and music store concern offers the first series of Victor recordings by the maestro. By this time Miguel Llobet and Regino Sainz de la Maza had already made endorsements for the top of the line luthier models constructed in the Breyer Hermanos (Breyer Brothers) workshop.

PROGRAMA

1. PARTE

ESTUDIO. . . . . *Sor (1778-1839)*

FOLIAS DE ESPAÑA. . . . . „

SUITE (dedicada a Andrés Segovia). . . , . . *Torroba*
    Preludio
    Burgalesa
    Danza

2. PARTE

SARABANDA
BOURÉE   obras escritas
MINUETTO   primitivamente   *J. S. Bach*
GAVOTA   para Laute,

PEQUEÑO VALS . . . . *Grieg*

3. PARTE

SEGOVIA (dedicada al artista) . . . . . . *Albert Roussel*

SEVILLANA (dedicada a Andrés Segovia) . *Turina*

ZAMBRA . . . . *Albeniz*

TORRE BERMEJA . . . . *Albeniz*

Durante la ejecución, no se permite la entrada a la sala.

TERCER CONCIERTO EL MARTES 10 DE JULIO a las 17.45 horas.

Andrés Segovia plays works by Fernando Sor, J. S. Bach, Grieg and Albeniz. Though the most interesting aspect is that of the composers: Moreno-Torroba, Roussel and Turina who have dedicated works to Andrés, which he played on this evening. At the bottom of the page is the announcement of a third concert on Tuesday July 10, 1928.

Guitarras Breyer

FLORIDA 414
BUENOS AIRES

SE HAN CONSAGRADO INSUPERABLES!..

INVITAMOS A LOS ENTENDIDOS
A PROBAR NUESTRAS GUITARRAS
Mod. **"SUPERBA"**

Las más perfectas que se conocen.

Cuerdas para Guitarra

LOS MÁS GRANDES ARTISTAS, SOLO USAN
LA MARCA **"PIRASTRO"**
SIEMPRE FRESCAS Y AL PRECIO MAS REDUCIDO.

BREYER HNOS.

ADQUIERA DISCOS "VICTOR"
de ANDRES SEGOVIA

EN VENTA:
BREYER Hnos. - Dto. GRAMOFONOS
FLORIDA 414

Breyer Hermanos (Breyer Brothers) was in business since the late 19th century, having been founded in 1882 by Adolfo Breyer. By this time in 1928, they had grown to having 8 annexes, serving the public throughout Buenos Aires. Pirastro Strings was also having Andrés Segovia endorse their strings, and they were making promotional postcards with a photograph of the maestro on it.

This transcription of *Leyenda* by Isaac Albeniz by Andrés Segovia was published by Romero & Fernández . By the time of the publication of the 1932 Antigua Casa Nuñez catalog Andrés Segovia had released fifty-four works.

1st edition of Andrés Segovia's "Diatonic Major and Minor scales", published by Romero & Fernández c. 1928-29, after his arrival and triumph in Buenos Aires. This edition did not have the seven right hand fingerings as modern editions.

It is also an edition autographed on the bottom of the last page by the maestro. This is an extremely rare edition, in that, of the 10 archives used to present the photo history of the golden era of Buenos Aires, there was only one copy remaining in the hands of the professionals on the scene at the time.

Archive: J. Augusto Marcellino

Ruet, J., Método de Guitarra . . . . » 4.—

Sagreras, J. S., Las Primeras Lecciones, obra elemental, perfectamente
digitada para la iniciación del estudio de la Guitarra (indispen-
sable a todo principiante . . . . » 2.50

— Colección de 10 Sonatinas en forma de estudio, cada una . . . . . » 0.60

— Escalas y Arpegios . . . . » 1.20

— Scherzo, Estudio de ligados . . . . » 0.60

— Técnica Superior de acuerdo con la moderna escuela del maestro
Tárrega (obra de gran mérito para perfeccionamiento) . . . . . . » 4.—

Segovia, A., Estudios de técnica elemental, escalas diatónicas, primer
cuaderno. . . . . » 2.50

Sinópoli, A., Ejercicios de Escalas . . . . » 2.50

— Ejercicios técnicos en todos los tonos mayores y menores . . . . . . » 2.50

Sors., F., Método Completo . . . . » 6.—

— 26 Estudios completos revisados por M. Coste . . . . » 3.—

— Idem, 1er. cuaderno . . . . » 1.50

— » 2.º » . . . . » 1.50

— » 3.º » . . . . » 1.50

— » 4.º » . . . . » 1.50

— Op. 6-12 Estudios, 1er. libro . . . . » 3.—

— Op. 29, 12 Estudios 2.º libro del op. 6 . . . . » 3.—

— » 31 24 Lecciones progresivas 1er. libro . . . . » 2.—

— » 24 31 » » 2.º » . . . . » 2.—

— » 35 24 Ejercicios muy fáciles, 1er. » . . . . » 1.80

— » 35 24 » » » 2.º » . . . . » 3.—

METODOS POR CIFRA

Para aprender la Guitarra sin necesidad de maestro

Catalá, A. F., "El Guitarrista", método fácil y rápido, posiciones ilus-
tradas . . . . » 1.50

— "La Guitarra Nacional", Libro práctico de Tonos Mayores y Me-
nores con sus posiciones ilustradas . . . . » 1.—

Cimadevilla, F., Método Completo . . . . » 2.50

Correa, F. M., Método Fácil . . . . » 0.50

Damas, T., Nuevo método al alcance de todas las inteligencias . . . . . . » 3.—

García, M., Nuevo método Americano . . . . » 1.—

Marín, R., Gran método Flamenco completo con una bonita colección
de piezas y aires andaluces. . . . . » 20.—

Villoldo, A. G., Nuevo método Americano con una colección de piezas
criollas . . . . » 1.40

MUSICA

Aguado, D., Andantes, colección de 10 . . . . » 3.20

— Colección completa de: 10 Andantes, 6 Minuetos, 17 Valses de
2 partes, 14 Valses de 3 partes, y 14 Valses de 4 partes. . . . . . » 6.50

ROMERO Y FERNANDEZ

Here is a listing of the Segovia Scales: *"Estudios de técnica elemental, escalas diatonicas, primer cuaderno"*, 2.50 Pesos. It is from page 4 of the *"Metodos y Estudios"* section of the c. 1928 *"Romero & Fernández Catalogo No. 5, Métodos y Musica para Guitarra"* catalog of 34 pages.

Sagreras, J. S., Venecia, barcarola-capricho. 2ª. guitarra .... $ 1.—
— Viajero solitario (Grieg. E.) .... » 0.60
— Violetas, vals muy fácil .... » 0.80
— Zamba y Vidalita oriental .... » 0.50
— Zorzal, E.; estilo muy fácil .... » 0.80
Sainz de la Maza, R., Boceto andaluz .... » 2.50
— Gavota (Bach, J. S.) .... » 1.20
— Preludio .... » 1.20
Sánchez Aranda, E., Tonada sanluiseña .... » 0.60
Segovia, A., Air de la suit X (Haendel) .... » 1.50
— Andante contabile y Marcha militar (Schumann, R.) .... » 1.50
— Andante largo, en La (Sors, F.) .... » 1.—
— Andantino (Sors, F.) .... » 1.—
— Asturias, preludio español (Albéniz, I.) .... » 2.—
— Canción del Norte y Labrador alegre (Schumann, R.) .... » 1.50
— Canción silvestre (Schumann, R.) .... » 1.20
— Canto del campesino (Grieg, E.) .... » 1.20
— Impromptu .... » 1.20
— Mayo, buen Mayo (Schumann, R.) .... » 2.—
— Melodía popular y Pequeño estudio (Schumann, R.(......... » 1.50
— Minueto de la sonata op. 31 N.º 3 (Beethoven, L. V.) ...... » 1.20
— » (Haydn) .... » 1.50
— 3 Pequeños valses (Schubert, F.) .... » 2.—
— 3 Preludios .... » 1.20
— Romanza (Franco, J. M.) .... » 1.50
— » op. 30 N.º 3 (Mendelssohn, F.) .... » 1.50
— Rondino sobre un tema de Beethoven (Kreisler, F.) .... » 1.50
— Zarabanda de la 2ª. sonata para violín solo (Bach, J. S.) .. » 1.20
— Siciliana de la 1ª. sonata para violín solo (Bach, J. S.) .. » 2.—
— 2ª. sonata op. 25 (Sors, F.) .... » 3.—
— Sonatina (escrita para guitarra por Moreno Torroba, F.) .... » 3.—
— Tonadilla .... » 1.20
— Triste N.º 4 (Aguirre, J.) .... » 1.—
— Variaciones sobre un tema de Mozart (Sors, F.) .... » 2.—
— Vidalita (Aguirre, J.) .... » 1.—
Shand, E., Danza de las Ninfas .... » 0.80
— Phyllis, gavota .... » 0.80
Sinópoli, A., Asturias, preludio español (Albéniz, I.) .... » 2.—
— Angélica, gavota ....
— Arreador, El; estilo fácil .... » 0.60
— ¡Ay—ay—ay!, canción cuyana (Pérez Freire, O.) .... » 0.60
— Bourrée (De Viseo, R.) .... » 1.—
— Buenos Aires, tango (Jovés, M.) .... » 1.—
— Canción de los Alpes .... » 0.80
— » indígena .... » 1.—
— Cecilia, zamba .... » 0.70
— Chacarera doble .... » 1.—
— Chimango, tango .... » 1.—

Florida 255. — Cangallo 1574. — B. Mitre 947

Here is a listing of twenty six pieces by Andrés Segovia. It is from page 25 of the *"Musica"* section of the c. 1928 *"Romero & Fernández Catalogo No. 5, Métodos y Musica para Guitarra"* catalog of 34 pages.

SEGOVIA

The Great Spanish Guitarist

From Painting by Miguel del Pino

Last Two Recitals This Season

ENTIRELY NEW PROGRAM	FAREWELL REQUEST PROGRAM
# GALLO THEATRE	# TOWN HALL
254 West 54th Street	113 West 43rd Street
Sunday Afternoon at 3 o'Clock	Saturday Afternoon at 3 o'Clock
## JAN. 29th, 1928	## FEB. 4th, 1928
Seats now at Gallo Theatre Box Office Phone, COL. 1140	Seats Now at Town Hall Box Office Phone, BRY. 9447

Management: METROPOLITAN MUSICAL BUREAU, 33 West 42nd St., N. Y. City

〖OVER〗

This handbill lists the last two concerts of Andrés Segovia's first American concert tour. The Gallo Theatre concert is not mentioned in the Alberto Lopez Poveda book *"Andrés Segovia Vida and Obra"*.

762

ANDRÈS SEGOVIA

Solid Acclaim from New York Critics

"HE gave one of the most extraordinary and engrossing recitals of music that has ever taken place in a N. Y. concert hall. We make no bones about saying that Segovia is one of the most consummate MASTERS of any instrument now before the public. He made the guitar a thing to be spoken of in the same breath with the cello of Casals, the violin of Heifetz."—*Lawrence Gilman, Herald-Tribune.*

"GENIUS on the Guitar. The Guitar in the hands of Mr. Segovia seems to have no limitation whatsoever. He must be heard to be believed."—*Samuel Chotzinoff, World.*

"PLAYS like Poet and Master that he is. Belongs to the very small group of musicians who by transcendent power of execution, by imagination and intuition create an art of their own. Wholly exceptional artist, a man of mark among musicians."—*Olin Downes, Times.*

"ACHIEVES true wonders. Conquered audience completely."—*Leonard Liebling, American.*

GALLO THEATRE	TOWN HALL
Entirely New Program	**Request Program**

GALLO THEATRE — Entirely New Program

1. a) Sonata ....*Ferdinand Sor*
   Allegretto
   Andante
   Menuet
   Rondo
   b) Fandango (dedicated to A. Segovia
   Joaquin Turina
   c) Etude ....*Napoleon Coste*

2. a) Sarabande ....*Handel*
   b) Gavotte
   Menuet }..............*J. S. Bach*
   Bourree
   c) Mazurka ....*Tschaikowsky*

3. a) Sonata (dedicated to A. Segovia)
   Manuel Ponce
   Allegro
   Cancion
   Finale
   b) Cadiz ....*Isaac Albeniz*

TOWN HALL — Request Program

1. a) Etude ....*Ferdinand Sor*
   ✝ b) Théme varié ....*Ferdinand Sor*
   ✝ c) Serenata ....*Joaquin Malats*
   d) Danza in G major..*Enrique Granados*

2. a) Gavotte
   Courante }..............*J. S. Bach*
   Loure
   b) Menuet ....*Haydn*

3. a) Sonatine (dedicated to A. Segovia)
   Federico M. Torroba
   Allegretto
   Andante
   Allegro
   ✝ b) Sevilla
   ✝ Torre Bermeja ....*Isaac Albeniz*
   ✝ Legenda

Management: Metropolitan Musical Bureau, 33 W. 42nd Street, N. Y. City

The quote by Olin Downes is from his concert review published in the New York Times on **January 9, 1928,** the day after Andrés Segovia's debut at the Town Hall. The crosses made by the listener at the **February 4, 1928** concert show the most impressionable pieces they heard.

* * *

Andres Segovia, Spanish guitarist, will open his season with a New York recital at Town Hall on the afternoon of Dec. 29. This will be followed by a second recital on Sunday afternoon Jan. 6, also at Town Hall.

* * *

Andres Segovia, Spanish guitarist, who is to be heard today in Town Hall, in his first appearance in America this season.

These repositioned digital images are from the Musical America magazine of December 29, 1928. They are from a page entitled: "Names and what their Owners are doing."

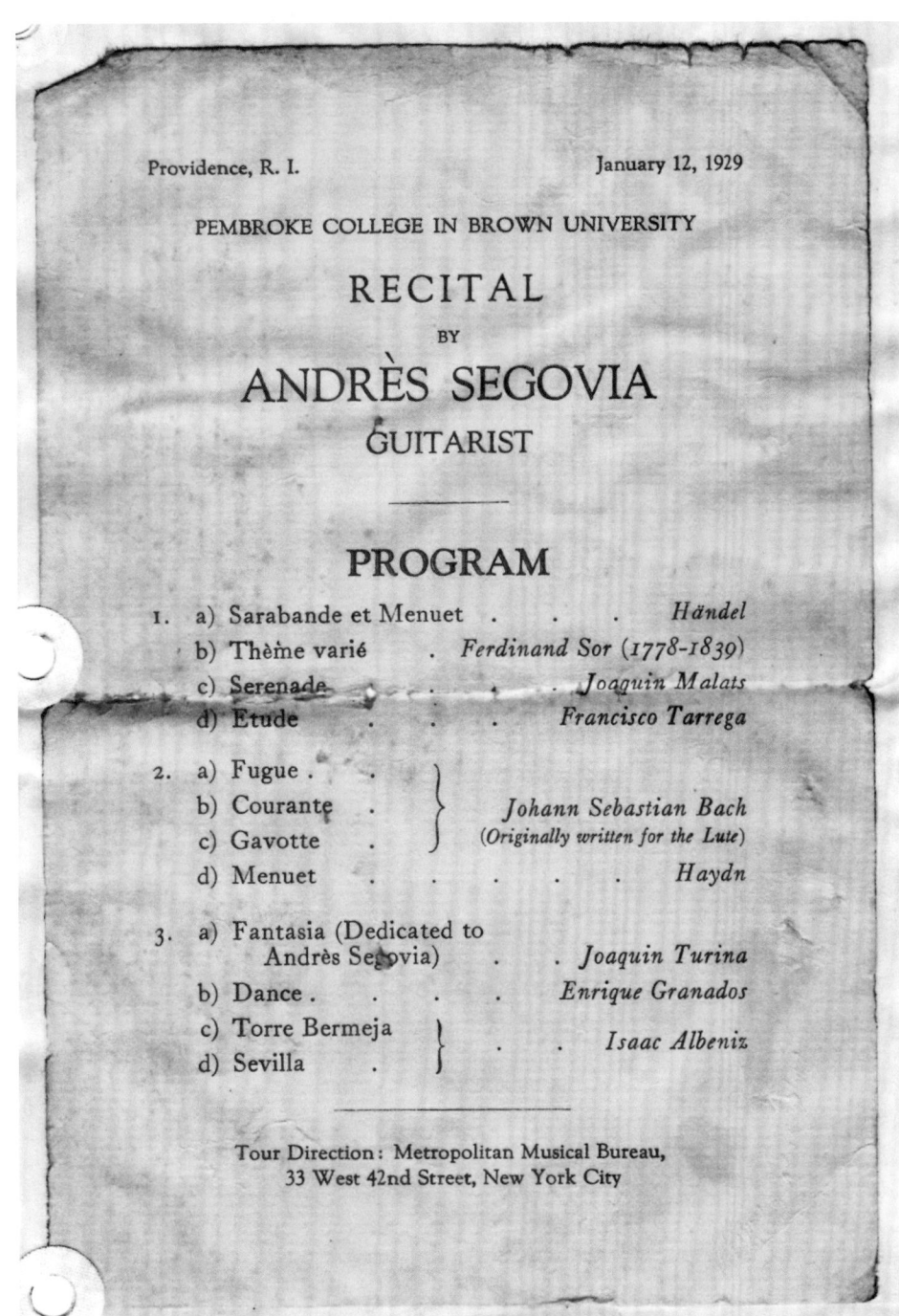

This Saturday January 12, 1929 Concert was held at the Pembroke College in Brown University. These theatre programs belonged to Anna Palmer Coit North (1908-2014), who was the very first female feature writer for Time magazine.

Fourth Concert of the Wellesley Concert Fund Series

ALUMNAE HALL   **WELLESLEY COLLEGE**

Thursday Evening, January 17, 1929

RECITAL

- - - *by* - - -

ANDRES SEGOVIA

Guitarist

Programme

1.	a)	Sarabande	*Handel*
	b)	Thème varié	*Ferdinand Sor (1778-1839)*
	c)	Serenade	*Joaquin Malats*
	d)	Etude	*Francisco Tarrega*
2.	a)	Prelude	
	b)	Courante	*Johann Sebastian Bach*
	c)	Gavotte	(Originally written for the Lute)
	d)	Menuet	*Haydn*
3.	a)	Fandanguillo (Dedicated to Andrès Segovia)	*Joaquin Turina*
	b)	Dance	*Enrique Granados*
	c)	Sevilla	*Isaac Albeniz*
	d)	Legenda	*Isaac Albeniz*

Tour Direction: Metropolitan Musical Bureau, 33 W. 42nd St., New York City
Local Manager, Dr. H. C. Macdougall

The fifth concert in the Concert Fund Series will be given by the Flonzaley String Quartette (their farewell appearance) on Thursday evening, February 14.

This Andrés Segovia second season concert was held at Wellesley College in Massachusetts on Thursday January 17, 1929. This was the alma mater of the Secretaries of State: Madeleine Albright and Hilary Rodham Clinton.

ANDRES SEGOVIA

WHO DESERVED BETTER OF HONG KONG

AN IMPRESSION

The marvel of it is that any true artist ever finds it in him to come to Hong Kong at all. I should say it is doubtful if they ever come twice. In the first place, the promoter of these things is a man who evidently dislikes spending money on advertising. Scarcely an announcement foreshadows the arrival of Mr. Strok's celebrities. If he thinks the mere whisper of their reputation will bring the public of Hong Kong to the City Hall, he has not yet learnt the public of Hong Kong. After all, we don't come to Hong Kong for civilisation; we come to make money out of China as quickly as we conveniently can. Anyone who wishes to make money out of us must adopt strictly commercial methods.

This, of course, is not for the artists themselves. If it was, they would have no need of managers.

But Mr. Strok does not believe in advertisement. Having obtained a little nearly free publicity through the medium of the Hong Kong Musical Society, which circularises its 200 odd members on the advent of any Strok celebrity, our Far East showman expects the public to do the rest. In the case of a singer, this is all right. For some reason or other people will flock in shoals to hear a singer. But the pianist, be he never so famous, is looked on somewhat coldly, and as for the guitar . . .

The second deterrent facing the artist visiting Hong Kong is the conditions under which he has to perform. One of the odd half dozen stragglers who had had the self control to detach themselves from their dinner tables in time to get to the hall before the contest was due to begin, had seen our poor artist, sitting in a room behind the stage, running his fingers miserably over his new strings and shuddering everytime a tram went roaring past.

Considerable Emotion

"He insists on having all the windows shut," said my friend, mopping his forehead with his handkerchief. Segovia spoke in French and not too clearly at that, being under the influence of considerable emotion. He had gleaned little from him.

"Ce bruit 'epouvantable," murmured the poor man, as a chorus of hooting motors rounded the corner outside.

"Absolute silence is necessary . . . ."

I gathered that the vibration of the noise upset the delicate tuning of the strings, quite apart from the noise itself.

My colleague, Jan J. de Kloe, did research and found several newspaper reports about the Andrés Segovia concert in Hong Kong on Saturday September 7, 1929. It was the only concert the maestro played, despite the mention in the Alberto Lopez Poveda book: *"Andrés Segovia Vida y Obra"* of two concerts. These 4 pages are the pages 11-14 of Mr. Kloe's research, this being the coverage by "The China Mail".

The stage was empty, but for a single black chair and a tiny white bamboo footstool.

"I think they might have given him a black footstool," said Jones, little knowing there had been anxiety about getting a footstool at all.

Some lights went out in the auditorium and the hush of the fans being shut off was accentuated by the chatter of the particularly late arrivals (not by any means the last) who happened to choose that moment to find their places. Andres Segovia walked across from the wing to his solitary black chair and with a little bow to acknowledge the perfunctory clapping, bent his thick black mane and his dark rimmed spectacles over his instrument and gently felt the strings for their final tuning up. It took a little time, and in the meanwhile there was a slightly horrified pause as a tram rumbled by. I think he must have been a little reassured. They make less noise from the stage than from that little back room.

With a final flourish of his hand over the strings he embarked on that delighted old "Etude in C" and for a little while the artist was lost to all. This first thing showed us at once the wonderful variety of tones that await his command, the light humorous, seductive twangs, the conversational middle notes, and those deep flute-like tones that bring out the song of the contrapuntal passages.

The Unknown Man

The applause at the end of this was very different to the clapping that greeted the unknown man. Segovia got up, bowed, sat down again, ran his hand lightly over the strings, adjusting the tuning, and then rested his elbow on his instrument and gazed towards the corner of the theatre. The shrill voice of female coolies arguing just outside filled the air with more sound than the guitar gives on its more delicate tones. No one bothered. It is nobody's business to see about unnecessary noise either without or within the theatre, nobody's business to see that we have a theatre fit to give a concert of any finer quality than that of a military band, nobody's business to look after things generally, to provide decent seats for the audience, or oscillating fans that actually oscillate, a piano worthy of a pianist, or even a footstool worthy of a

768

guitarist. All these things occurred to us during that little pause while Segovia sat with his elbow on his instrument and a slight aspect of despair in his thickset intelligent poise, moved as if to begin playing, and then sat again for a little, while the coolies yelled outside. But over all was the easy assurance of the practised artist, and presently with a little gesture of resignation he went on with his programme. After all, the bringers of civilisation have had to cope with misunderstood difficulties ever since civilisation began. In breaking new ground, we do not ask for the comforts of a Metropolis. Singers and musicians found their way in the early days to Western States of America and brought the wonder of their craft to rough-clad hearers and rude log halls. Only—are we, in Hong Kong, so primitive?

However, we had to suffer for our unpreparedness, the programme was altered and instead of some of the delicate things promised us in newspapers, the programme consisted exclusively of mere sob stuff, better capable of penetrating our unwelcoming atmosphere.

Stately Pieces

But Bach remained. A-thining no doubt of the well-known 48, had said that he had heard Bach and enjoyed him on organ, piano and orchestra, and did not particularly relish any experiments on the guitar. He was wrong. These gay and stately of pieces—Fugue, Courante, Sarabande and Gavotte—written originally for the lute, might have been specially designed for the guitar and have been revived, as are many other forgotten lute pieces, for the master hand of Segovia. Probably best of all of these old things was that Menuet of Haydn, delicate, entrancing, with its counter melodies enhanced by subtle changes of tone. And then that seductive Serenata of Malats, with its haunting notes of song, the very notes to find their insinuating way up in clad walls in moonlight. Malats—one of the most promising of the young French musicians of last century: Madame, standing in the warm night outside the theatre told us of our concours that she had attended — Saint Saens, Massanet, all the great men had been there—and she had implored her master to let her go, implored him for weeks, and at last he had let her go, and she had sat for hours, sideways, in a small cramped seat in a corner in the presence of the most famous musicians of France. At that Concours Malats played, and gained the first prize—"And I was there—j'ai assiste a ce concours!", said Madame with rapture. Malats died early of consumption but left the world richer by a few things, of which this Serenata is one.

769

C'est Terrible

Madame also has heard of Segovia, heard he was coming, had called, met him, helped . . . . . He was prostrate with the heat during the voyage. Helas! What would he do? All his strings were broken with the damp, he felt miserable. Also he had forgotten his footstool, "Son petit banc," on the boat. He knew not where to go. Madame assured him she would get him another "petit banc." She came to the theatre and found him in the extreme of worry on account of the noise. "Et le petit banc?" he exclaimed, "Vous l'avez?"

"Oui, oui," reassured Madame, "c'est ici." It was the little bamboo thing, white, incongruous, but just right, Hong Kong's one contribution to the success of the evening.

The latter part of the programme was pure Spanish. And as everyone knows, the guitar is the National instrument of Spain. Forgetting all discomforts and disturbances we gave ourselves up to the enjoyment of these sunny's sinuous melodies.

I say we, but not in any universal sense. Our audience was not only poor in numbers but in appreciation. At the end they gave him one somewhat grudging encore and then hastened to collect themselves. Segovia himself came back thrice without his instrument before giving the encore and I think he was relieved to have the ordeal over. I fancy we shall not see him again in Hong Kong, not at any rate until we have provided accommodation worth calling a concert hall. But for myself I am grateful to the parsimonious Mr. Strok for giving me one of the most delightful evenings of my musical experience.

—G. H.

No. 27,280 HONG KONG. TUESDAY, SEPTEMBER 10, 1929. PRICE $3.00 Per Month.

Page 6

CORRESPONDENCE

ANDRES SEGOVIA

[To the Editor of the "China Mail."]

Sir,—The ordinary errors of the typesetter are fairly obvious and call for no comment, but I must ask you kindly to correct that part of my article on Segovia which reads, "the programme consisted exclusively of mere sob stuff," a statement which is diametrically opposed to fact. The words I used were "sterner stuff."

Yours, etc.,
G. H.

Hong Kong, September 10.

770

プログラム （第二回）

1. A) ソナティナ …………… ショパニ
   B) 主題による變奏曲 ………… ソ ー ル
   C) 組曲 キャスチラナ
      （セゴヴィアの為に作曲）………… トルロバ
      (イ) ブレリュド
      (ロ) ア ラ ダ
      (ハ) ナクレスタ
   D) エボカチオン ………………… ヌ レ ガ

2. A) ブリュウディオ
   B) ア レ マ ンデ
   C) サ ラ バ ンド
   D) ダ ク ラ ンテ ……………… J.S.バッハ
   E) ガ ボ ッ テ
   F) ブ ラ ショウス ……………… ティコフスキー

休　憩

3. A) セゴヴィナ（セゴヴィアの為に作曲）…… チュリナ
   B) ト調マニック ア ……………… グラナドス
   C) カ ディ ス
   D) セ レ ナ ー タ ……………… アルベニス
   E) セ ヴィ ラ

演奏中は扉により静かにお願ひお願ひ申上げます

GUITAR RECITAL
BY
THE GREAT SPANISH GUITARIST
ANDRES SEGOVIA
NOV. 2ND 7P.M.
1929

AT THE ASAHI KAIKAN
MANAGEMENT:
A. STROK

朝　日　會　館

セゴヴィアギター演奏會

Andrés Segovia's 2nd Osaka concert at the Asahi Kaikan on November 2, 1929
Translation of titles by Randy Osborne

"Second Program

1. Part
A. Sonatina Turina
B. Shudai no yoru Kyou so kyokko Sor Theme varié (Mozart-Sor)
C. Suite Castellana Moreno Torroba
(Dedicated to Segovia by the composer)
In A; Prelude
In G: Arada
In C: Burlesca (Fandanguillo is normally the third piece of this Suite. R. O.)
D. Evocacion Tárrega (Recuerdos de la Alhambra)

2. Part
J.S. Bach
A. Prelude
B. Allemande
C. Sarabande
D. Courante
E. Gavotte.
F. Grazioso Tchaikovsky

Intermission

3. Part
A. Sevillana (Dedicated to Segovia by the composer) Turina
B. Danza (No. 5) Granados
Albeniz
C. Cadiz
D. Serenata (Granada)
E. Sevilla

———————

During the concert while listening please be quiet, we beg of you."

The image of the concert program on the previous page is courtesy of Robert Coldwell.

The text below is from the *Armonia* magazine issue No. 18 published in Sendai Aramachi, Miyayagiken, Japan by Chuzaemon Sawaguchi (1902-1948). The Japanese translation by Randy Osborne is on the bottom of the next page.

「通信」欄より

大阪でR.M.G.主催「セゴヴィア氏歓迎茶話会」が開かれ６０余名参加。セゴヴィア氏より『教則本はアグアドのものを使うこと。次にジュリアーニの右手の練習をし、それからソルの全部について勉強して下さい。絃はガット絃を用いること。音楽に対して常に感激を忘れないこと。』とのアドバイスがあり、他に、タルレガの息子は今ドイツで数学の先生をしていること、ギターはミュンヘンのヘルマン・ハウザーが一番よいこと、が話され、大阪での第一夜の演奏楽器は１９２８年製ハウザーだったことが判明した。【第１８号】

After conquering the Old World and the upper and lower parts of the New World, Andrés Segovia set out to tour Asia. While Andrés Segovia was playing in Japan, Miguel Llobet as well as Regino Sainz de la Maza were performing in Buenos Aires.

According to the translation of excepts from the book *"Andrés Segovia Vida y Obra"* by Alberto Lopez Poveda: In 1929 "He played in New York in his second tour of the United States, including at the "Athenaeum" in New Orleans, and also in Toronto, Canada. In this tour he performed four different programs. After spending the month of April in Geneva, he went to Paris where he offered the only concert there on May 15th, in this concert he debuted the *"Sonata Romantica"* by Ponce, and also met Joaquín Rodrigo for the first time. After touring a few other European cities he returned to Geneva.

In the month of August he boarded the Japanese vessel *"Hakore Maru"*. His manager is Mr. Stroch (sic- A. Strok). After a long trip he arrived in Hong Kong where he gave two recitals (Investigation of articles in four Hong Kong newspapers by Jan de Kloe shows only one concert on Saturday September 7, 1929 took place.) He traveled to, Macao, then Shanghai, and arrived afterward in Manila, where he gave one of three scheduled concerts, the theater was suffocating, and upon opening the windows the noise of the street traffic made performing unbearable, he suspended the second and third concerts. (Poveda says similar incident due to extreme heat also happened in Havana, Cuba in 1923.) By coincidence the great tenor Miguel Fleta was there and they offered an emotional performance of homage to the city. Andrés Segovia returned to Shanghai, then to Tientsin-now Tianjin where he gave three recitals. Though he visited Peking-now Beijing, he didn't give any recitals there. He eventually made his way back to Shanghai and left for Japan. At the end of October he arrived and gave the following recitals:

October 26th, 27th and 29th (This was the day of the stock market crash bringing on the depression.) in Tokyo at the Imperial Theater (Teigeki),

October 30th in Osaka at the Asahi Kaikan (Hall),

October 31th in Kyoto at the Okazaki Hall,

November 1st in Osaka at the Asahi Hall (sic-the 2nd program in Osaka program on the previous page says November 2, 1929-due to popular demand maybe another concert was offered-with Andrés having already played three concerts in fours days in Tokyo. Possibly information given to Mr. Poveda was erroneous.)

November 4th in Kobe at the Christian Church Hall,

November 9th and 11th in Tokyo at the Imperial Theater (Teigeki).

Source: Translated from *Andrés Segovia Vida y Obra* by Alberto Lopez Poveda published by the Universidad de Jaen / Ayuntamiento de Linares 2010.

The adjective used in October-November of 1929 to describe Andrés Segovia's first concerts in Japan, "shougeki" (shock) and "kougeki" (attack-on the senses). This description is from the book written by Kikuo Takeuchi: "Deatta gitar- to Nihon jin" (The Guitar meets the Japanese people) This is a history of the Classical Guitar in Japan from 1854-2000. Publisher: Yamaha Music Media Corporation 2011

From the Column "Correspondence"

"Attended by more than 60 people the "Welcome tea party for Segovia" organized by the Revue Mandolin Guitar (RMG) was held in Osaka. Mr. Segovia said: 'Aguado is what we use as didactic study. Then practice the right hand studies of Giuliani, please learn all of the works of Sor. Use gut strings. Always do not forget the inspiring music.' He had advice 'and, besides, the son of Tárrega who is now a teacher of mathematics in Germany, says as for guitars, Hermann Hauser of Munich is said to be the best,' Segovia playing a Hauser instrument that was made in 1928 on the first night in Osaka." (*Armonia* magazine issue No. 18)

In the short lived 3 issue magazine *"A Voz do Violao"* (February to April 1931), published in Rio de Janeiro, edited by F. Acquarone, managed by S. Leal, administrated by B. Polazzi, was the issue No. 2 of March 1931, which in its *"Violao no Extrangeiro"* section (The Guitar Abroad), was the report about Andrés Segovia going to North America and Japan.
Portuguese translation by Randy Osborne:

"Andrés Segovia

In the middle of last year this eminent concert guitarist began an artistic *"tournée"* of North America and Japan. His recitals were so numerous and as we learned, this is the second time Segovia has made the same itinerary.

He possesses enviable technique, along with appreciable musical culture, he has deserved, the hottest applause throughout and the best sympathies of the diverse public, the examination of which has been submitted and won by the marvelous "globe trotter".

Segovia has his own repertoire, vast and selected. Within the greatly distinguished transcribed classics by J. S. Bach, Mozart and César Franck, along with the magnificent pages of modern music, Spanish, where are placed Pedrell, Ponce, Moreno Torroba, Turina and his own by Segovia in an insuperable form."

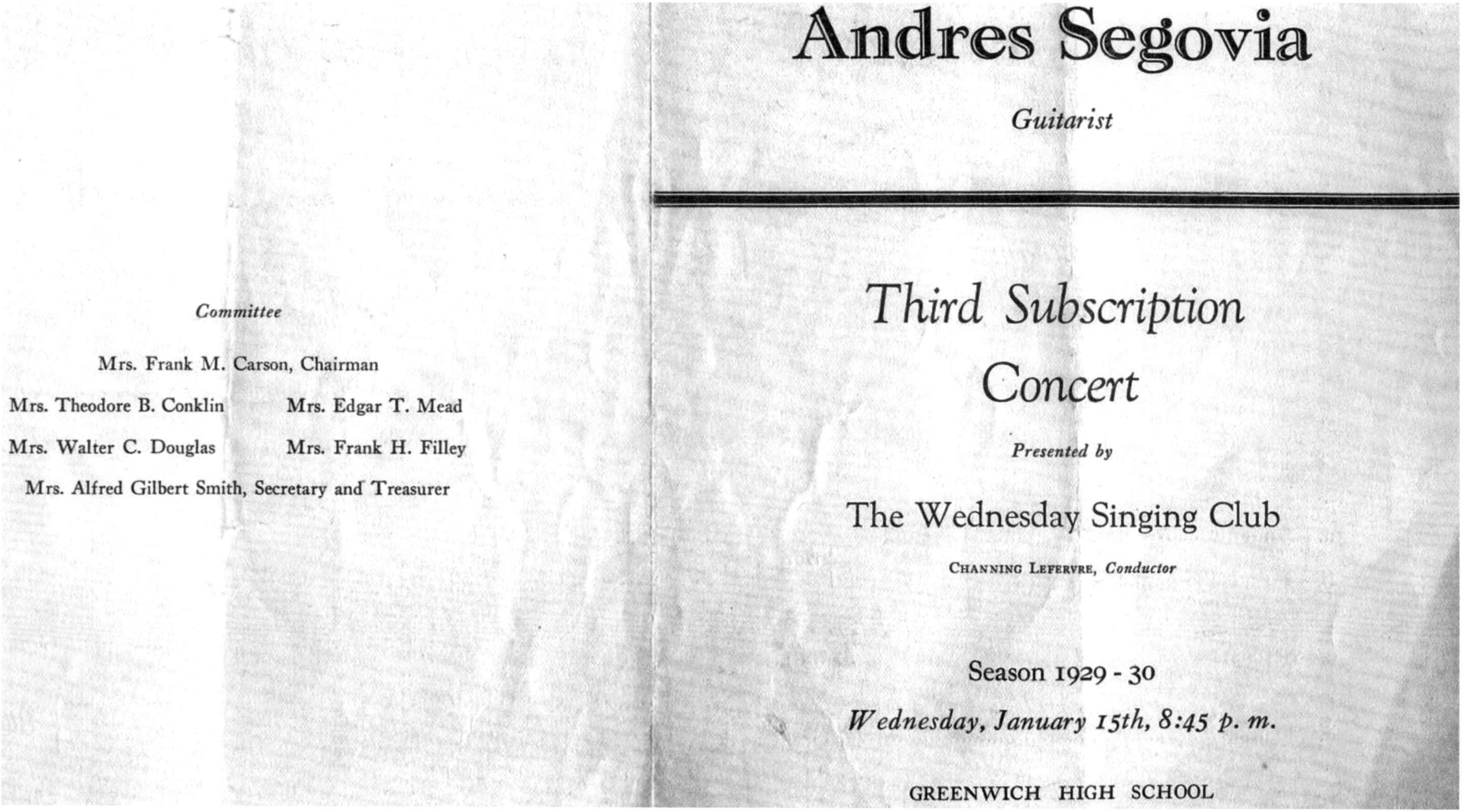

Andres Segovia

Guitarist

Third Subscription

Concert

Presented by

The Wednesday Singing Club

CHANNING LEFEVRE, *Conductor*

Season 1929 - 30

Wednesday, January 15th, 8:45 p. m.

GREENWICH HIGH SCHOOL

Committee

Mrs. Frank M. Carson, Chairman

Mrs. Theodore B. Conklin   Mrs. Edgar T. Mead

Mrs. Walter C. Douglas   Mrs. Frank H. Filley

Mrs. Alfred Gilbert Smith, Secretary and Treasurer

This third season January 15, 1930 concert took place in Greenwich, Connecticut.

ANDRES SEGOVIA

Guitarist

Program

I

a.	Andante et Menuet	⎱ Sor
b.	Folias d'Espagne	⎰
c.	Serenata	Malats
d.	Danza	Tarrega

Program

II

a.	Gavotte	Bach
b.	Menuet	Haydn
c.	Moment Musical	Schubert
d.	Canzonetta	Mendelssohn

III

a.	Sonatina	Torroba
b.	Danza	Granados
c.	Granada	⎱ Albeniz
d.	Sevilla	⎰

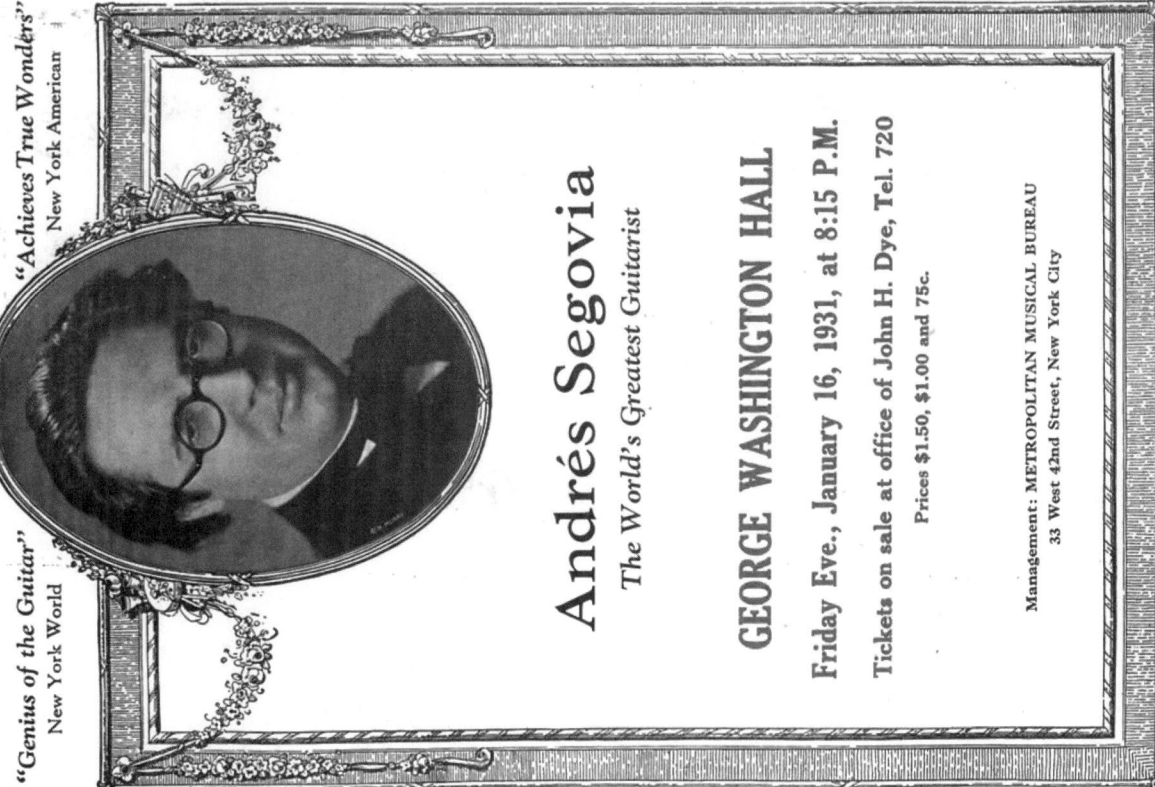

The Spell of the Guitar

ANDRÉS SEGOVIA was born in 1896 in a small city of Andalusia, near Granada, Spain. From his childhood he was greatly interested in music and the guitar was his favorite instrument. Segovia gave his first public concert at the age of fifteen in Granada under the auspices of the artistic circle of that City. This concert was a revelation to the public. Segovia from that time on continued to give public concerts throughout Spain with remarkable success. Later on, he toured South America. He has brought about a renaissance of the art of the guitar. Many prominent European composers have written music specially for Segovia, which fact makes it possible for him to present to the public many varied programs. Segovia has also made personally researches of the old manuscripts of music written by classic composers such as Bach and others for the lute, an instrument similar to the guitar, and has arranged this music for the guitar.

Andrés Segovia's remarkable successes in Europe are already a matter of history. Coming to America unheralded and practically unknown, Senor Segovia made his debut on January 7, 1928 and created a sensation. Music critics, connoiseurs of music and music lovers all agreed unanimously that he was a master virtuoso and a supreme musician. They marveled at his technical prowess, his impeccable taste and the surpassing beauty of the effects he was able to produce on the guitar.

Last season, Senor Segovia played over forty concert engagements in this country and during the current season, he is again making an extensive coast to coast concert tour here.

"In Mr. Segovia's marvelous hands his guitar could be impressively solemn as in the stately Sarabande; it could work a Spanish spell, as in the fascinating Serenata of Malats, or bring out old world grace in the dance, as in Haydn's charming Menuet. But whatever Mr. Segovia played, whether the music had native worth, distinction, or was merely "a piece for the guitar," he adorned it by his command of all artistic resources. The large and expectant audience was quick to appreciate the talent of the visitor, who might justly be called the genius of the guitar." — Boston *Herald*.

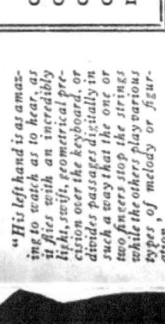

"His left hand is amazing to watch as to hear, as it flies with an incredibly light, swift, geometrical precision over the keyboard, or divides passages dexterally in such a way that the one or two fingers stop the strings while the others play various types of melody or figuration."

"The guitar in the hands of Mr. Segovia seems to have no limitations whatsoever. It is not given us to know just how the anatomy of the guitarist's hands differs from ours, nor how he has acquired a mastery of his instrument so perfect that the most intricate polyphony seems as natural to the guitar as to the piano. The fact remains that Mr. Segovia's performance yesterday was aesthetically and emotionally satisfying to the highest degree.

If comparisons are at all permissable I should compare Mr. Segovia to Pablo Casals. I can think of no other artist who possesses the guitarist's delicate musical perceptions, his refinement, his aristocratic reserve and his sense of rhythm. Mr. Segovia must be heard to be believed."—New York *World*.

This is the cover to a promotion for the Friday February 11, 1931 concert at Yale University.
The program on the two previous pages took place in Andover, Massachusetts on January 16, 1931.

ANDRES SEGOVIA, that serious young Spaniard from the romantic hills of Granada, who has raised the humble guitar to the status of a concert instrument, returns to this country for another season of triumphs.

A guitarist! To those who have never succumbed to the spell of Segovia, the thought may evoke a supercilious smile. In the opinion of some people a guitar is at best a romantic accompaniment to a serenade.

He gave one of the most extraordinary and engrossing recitals of music that has ever taken place in a New York concert hall. He made the guitar a thing to be spoken of in the same breath with the 'cello of Casals, the violin of Heifetz.

claiming over his astounding virtuosity; you end by exclaiming over his beautiful and sincere and exquisite musicianship. The kaleidoscopic variety of effects that he secures baffles comprehension. The elfin wizardry of this playing is in a musical world by itself.

This is the inside cover page of a promotion for the Friday February 11, 1931 concert at Yale University.

DRES SEGOVIA

belongs to the very small group of musicians who by transcendent powers of execution, by imagination and intuition, create an art of their own. He is a wholly exceptional artist, a man of mark among musicians.

OLIN DOWNES in N. Y. Times

But under the magic touch of Segovia, this poor Cinderella of musical instruments is changed into a princess and rides in a coach by his side.

Segovia's first visit to this country was in the early part of 1928.

In five weeks he had piled up astonishing record of six sold-out New York recitals, two Boston recitals, and twenty-five appearances outside of New York. In his second season he filled forty dates in eleven weeks. His third visit here was preceded by a tour of the Far East, thus making him a figure of international acclaim.

His New York debut may safely be said to have made musical history, in that it was the first guitar recital ever to have been given in this city. The novelty of the recital brought a throng of curious, for to the majority the recital could be little more than a freak event.

What the audience saw was a young man bearing a striking resemblance to Franz Schubert, but of true Andalusian type—olive complexion, raven-black hair and the expansive forehead of the scholar.

By sheer genius he demonstrated undreamed-of possibilities. Bending absorbed over his instrument, he drew from it a fairy-like music. He took a Bach Suite and, within the compass of six strings achieved an intricate polyphony, incredible as this may sound. Under his deft fingers one heard a Handel Sarabande, a Haydn Minuet. Sheer wizardry, it seemed.

It is this treatment of the classics that evokes the wonder of musicians and gives Segovia title to "the genius of the guitar." Small wonder that composers like De Falla, Turina, Torroba, and others are writing music especially for him.

But when all is said, there still remains the fact that "Segovia must be heard to be believed." When one has listened to the musical magic of his guitar, only then can one appreciate the marvel of his playing.

The technical proficiency of Mr. Segovia is almost incredible to those who know the character of the instrument. The most remarkable exhibition of technic was the performance of Bach's Fugue, with a contrapuntal clearness that a violinist or a clavecin-

In Mr. Segovia's marvelous hands his guitar could be impressively solemn, as in the stately Sarabande; it could work a Spanish spell, as in the fascinating Serenata by Malata; or it could bring out old-world grace in the dance, as in Haydn's charming Minuet.

The well deserved eulogies were unstoppable.

SEGOVIA

From Painting by *Miguel del Pino*

Astounding Virtuosity; Exquisite Musicianship
LAWRENCE GILMAN

Segovia Achieves True Wonders on Guitar
LEONARD LIEBLING

A Man of Mark Among Musicians
OLIN DOWNES

Aesthetically and Emotionally Satisfying
SAMUEL CHOTZINOFF

Technical Proficiency Almost Incredible
PHILIP HALE

Amazes By Magic of His Art!
WARREN STORY SMITH

"GENIUS OF THE GUITAR"

Andrés Segovia must have enjoyed practicing the guitar with the quality of performance he had achieved at this point in time.

The images on this and the next page are from 2 issues of the B.M.G. magazine No. 315 of July 1931 and No. 317 of September 1931 XXVIII. They discuss the article from the American publication "The Crescendo" of June 1931.

SEGOVIA AND NAIL PLAYING.

On reading the June issue of the "Crescendo," I noticed the following statement by the Editor of our American fretted instrument contemporary:—

"In perusing a copy of the April issue of 'B.M.G.,' published by our London friends Messrs. Clifford Essex Company, we came upon a little article which states that Mr. Alexis Chess plays the Spanish guitar by vibrating the strings with the nails. Mr. Chess

finger tips, or plectrum playing. I had never heard that Segovia and other great guitarists made use of their finger nails for vibrating the strings until I joined the Philharmonic Guitar Society a few months ago, and became acquainted with Dr. Perott and Mr. Alexis Chess.

It was with a certain amount of quiet satisfaction, therefore, that I wrote this paragraph in the April issue :—

"Recent issues of 'B.M.G.' contained articles which advocated the use of the finger nails for vibrating the strings of the banjo. I noticed that Mr. Alexis Chess was picking the strings of his guitar with his finger nails during his 'turn' at the Rally. Later on when I spoke about this to him, he told me that Segovia, Llobet, Louise Walker and other eminent guitarists prefer always to vibrate the strings with the nails, which is rather an interesting thing to know."

advised the Editor of the British paper that Segovia, Llobet and Louise Walker all played the guitar in that manner also, and we are beginning to doubt our powers of observation, or else we are too hopelessly mid-Victorian to notice any change in Segovia's technique.

I have heard the great Spaniard five times, and have interviewed him twice, and have sat at two concerts close enough to him to notice his method of attack, and not once did I detect him picking the strings with the nails of his right hand. A few Mexican players have used this method at times, but I am quite positive that none of our virtuosi to-day would indulge in it. I shall ask Mr. Papas, our guitar authority, to enlighten us further in this respect."

I, although not professing to be a great guitarist, have always vibrated the strings of the guitar with my finger nails, and (on the guitar) I still prefer this method to either picking the strings with the flesh part of the

I sent a marked copy of the "Crescendo" to Mr. Alexis Chess who, confirming his previous statements to me on this subject, has replied as follows :—

"I read the 'Crescendo' Editor's remarks with considerable interest, and am glad to repeat my previous statement that Segovia, Louise Walker and Miguel Llobet always vibrate the strings of the guitar with the tips of their finger nails. I could mention the names of many more famous guitarists including Mozzani, Mazu and Albert, all of whom use the nails exclusively. I have discussed this subject of nail-playing with several of these famous artistes, including Segovia and Louise Walker, and have enquired as to the most suitable length of nail, the advisability of shaping them to a point and so on.

Emilio Pujol (who does not use the nail method) told me that he knows very few great guitarists who vibrate the strings by using the

flesh part of the finger tip, and he mentioned Alfonso, of Barcelona, and Daniel Fortea, of the Argentine.

The tone of a guitar when played with the finger nails tastefully and in accordance with modern technique, is marvellously pure and, even when a close watch is kept, it is difficult to detect the fact that the nails are being used."

*   *   *

NAIL PLAYING ON THE SPANISH GUITAR.

By Alexis Chess.

SINCE my recent article on the subject of nail playing for guitarists appeared in "*B.M.G.*," I have received many letters from players asking various questions about this method of vibrating the strings. They want to know how long the nails should be in order to obtain the best tone; how the nails should be trimmed; should the thumb nail be used; does nail playing cause gut strings to fray more quickly, and many other things. I now reply to all these correspondents through the medium of "*B.M.G.*"

Nail playing on the Spanish guitar is not a modern innovation as many players seem to think. It has been in use for at least two centuries. The native amateur guitarists of Spain mostly vibrate the strings of their instruments with the nails of their right hands exactly as did their ancestors of countless generations past. Their favourite items are commonly known as "Flamenco Songs," which are the folk songs of Spain, the accompaniment consisting of peculiar rapid movements of the right hand called "rasquado." Single strings are accented in a characteristic way, and here it is that the nails are used to produce the desired effect.

Although the great master of the guitar, F. Sor (1780-1839), did not use the nail method of vibrating the strings, this method was used by a great Spanish guitarist and composer named D. Aguado who was a contemporary of Sor.

In his book of instruction for the guitar (Simrock edition) Sor pays tribute to the exquisite art of Aguado's nail playing on the guitar. Another famous contemporary of Sor's was the Spanish virtuoso Chibra, who also played with the nails.

It is probable that authorities will continue to differ with regard to the respective merits of playing the guitar only with the flesh part of the finger-tips or with the nails. There are, however, plenty of opportunities for hearing the instrument played both ways so personal taste and inclination must be the deciding factor. Emilio Pujol told me that his teacher, F. Tarrega, gave up nail playing because he felt that the quality of tone he produced by using that method did not satisfy him as being representative of the spirit of Beethoven's compositions which Tarrega played so exquisitely on the guitar

In order to be able to vibrate the strings of an instrument with the nails, they should be allowed to grow for about a fortnight. It will be found that the strength and quality of the nails will greatly improve after they have been in constant daily use for several months. Two great nail players upon the guitar—A. Segovia and M. Llobet—use special scissors for cutting and shaping the nails; Mozzani uses only a nail file. The natural shape of the nail in its rounded form should be retained, and of course the playing edge of the nail should be kept as smooth as possible. I am referring to the finger-nails only. The thumb nail is never used. Opinions seem to differ as to what is the best length of nail. I was told that Mozzani has the longest nails of all. M. Llobet's nails scarcely extend beyond the finger tips, and L. Walker keeps her nails also very short. On the other hand, Mario Maccaferry prefers his nails to be long and also uses a steel pick which is fitted on the thumb.

When vibrating the strings, I allow the nails of my right hand to give only the final impulse to the strings. The tips of my fingers have the first contact with the strings then the latter pass on to nails. This I consider very important. I find that rapid passages are more easily executed when the nails are used. Moreover, the tremolo is more effective and I find that gut strings last longer because there is less contact with the strings than when only the tips of the fingers are used. Those correspondents of mine who complain about the fraying of their gut strings after a period of nail playing are either playing with rough-edged nails or making other mistakes of which there may be several.

The art of producing good tone from a guitar is considered to be more difficult and complicated than is the art of controlling the left hand. The method of holding the instrument, the position of the player's shoulders and left leg, are important factors in tone production, just as is the correct method of using the fingers. The strength of tone does not depend upon the strength of player's arm, but upon the "elasticity" of the fingers when "striking" the strings. I say "striking" because the player should have a sensation rather of a striking effect than of pulling the strings when vibrating them. All this is of course difficult to explain in written language. The art of playing any musical instrument really well so far as the actual technique is concerned, is most speedily acquired by those wise and fortunate students who are able to have personal lessons from a capable teacher and thus be able to *see* and *hear* the instrument demonstrated in a practical way.

Se SEGOVIA, ANDRES—Guitarrista

Andrés Segovia, reconocido como el exponente máximo de la guitarra, que antes había sido considerado como tan solo un medio secundario en la interpretación de música seria, es otra de las grandes adquisiciones recientes de la Compañía Víctor. La guitarra en manos de este artista no es el instrumento monótono apropiado solamente para acompañamiento de una serenata sentimental: el alcance y el color del instrumento en manos de Segovia a veces supera a los del clavicordio. En la interpretación de las grandes obras clásicas, Segovia conserva inmaculada la intención del autor y el significado de la música. La musicalidad de Segovia no admite duda. Sus arreglos de las obras clásicas compuestas para otros instrumentos, son admirables. Oirle tocar la guitarra es oír un instrumento de una belleza y dulzura que no pueden ser descritas con palabras; un instrumento noble que cautiva desde sus primeras notas, un instrumento que casi canta en sus delicados acentos.

SEGOVIA

Discos de Andrés Segovia		Nº	Med.	Prec.
Courante	Bach	1298	25	4.75
Fandanguillo	Turina	6767	30	6.00
Gavotte	Bach	6766	30	6.00
Fugue	Bach	7176	30	6.60
Preludio y Allemande	Bach	7176	30	6.00
Sonatina en La Mayor	Torroba	1298	25	4.75
Theme Varie	Sor	6766	30	6.00
Tremolo—Estudio	Tárrega	6767	30	6.00

This discography is from the *"Catalogo de Discos Victor 1932"* published in Buenos Aires, with a complete list up to January 1, 1932. Translation:

"Victor Red Seal Discs

Andrés Segovia, Guitarist

Andrés Segovia is recognized as the best exponent of the guitar, that before had only been considered as such a medium of second place for the interpretation of serious music, he is another of the great acquisitions by the Victor Company recently. The guitar in the hands of this artist isn't the monotone instrument that is only appropriated for the accompaniment of a sentimental serenade: the achievement and the color of the instrument in the hands of Segovia at times surpasses that of the clavichord. In the interpretations of the great classic works, Segovia preserves the intention of the composer and the significance of the music immaculately. The musicality of Segovia doesn't allow doubt. His arrangements of the classic works composed for other instruments, is admirable. To hear him play the guitar is to hear an instrument of a beauty and sweetness that can't be described in words; a noble instrument that captivates from its first few notes, an instrument that almost sings in its delicate accents."

The 10″ records sold for 4.75 Pesos, and the 12″ discs for 6.00 Pesos. Other artist's recordings, be it Argentine popular *criollo* singers, orchestras, including American imported icons sold for 2.50 Pesos (10″) or 3.75 Pesos (12″), so the maestro of the Classical Guitar was well paid for his great endeavors.

LA VIDA ARTISTICA EN MEXICO

Impresiones y Crítica

Andrés Segovia, el Virtuoso de la Guitarra.

Oyendo Tocar a Segovia ∽

Por
María Luisa Serrano

(Especial para MEXICO AL DIA)

CON místico fervor guardo en el fondo de la urna de mis devotos recuerdos, aquellos en que el arte, por la magia de sus intérpretes, dejó imborrables, para siempre, imágenes e impresiones.

Abro la urna y se esparcen aromas que de nuevo me saturan..., quemo incienso en el altar de mis recuerdos y van surgiendo las visiones límpidas, precisas!

¿Artistas? Pueden ser muchos. ¿Emociones que despertaron? Quizá a pocos corresponden... Cuántas figuras se van borrando en la lejanía del recuerdo, cuántas se perfilan con mayor relieve y energía!

Ahora, de nuevo, es Andrés Segovia, a quien no borraron años de ausencia y sí lo agigantaron actuaciones similares... Segovia es "único"!

Yo no podría hacer un juicio digno de su arte; mi impresión de entonces, de hoy y de siempre, es de aquellas que por pura, honda y exquisita, no hay palabras que la traduzcan.

Oírlo tocar su guitarra es sentir la caricia más suave, la más dulce vibración, el más delicado recogimiento espiritual, divina ensoñación de la que el alma no quisiera despertar...

Hadas forjaron sus manos. Genio besó su frente. Arte lo eligió por hijo!

Unciosamente mi alma en éxtasis recogió sus notas que, al evocarlas, me dan la sensación de volver a sonar cual si fuesen nacidas no de arpa, sino de guitarra eólica...

Todo en este Virtuoso es impecable: técnica e inspiración.

Es una delicia contemplar sus manos sobre el instrumento, que, dócil a su impulso, gime, ríe, suspira o llora en triunfo o en agonía.

Notas, arpegios, acordes armónicos, lo que sea, la más simple o vulgar melodía a través de su temperamento varonil, sobrio, elegante, enormemente sincero y sinceramente exquisito, soñador y refinado, se ennoblece y vuelve al corazón del pueblo donde nació envuelta en alburas de armiño, en sol hecho de polvo de oro, en trino de ruiseñores, en aroma de flor divina, en bravura de torrente o en murmullo de fuente cristalina; oyendo tocar a Segovia se siente uno ante el paradisíaco esplendor de la Naturaleza; siente uno cerca, muy cerca, a Dios!

Creo con firme convicción que quien no sepa transportarme con su expresión de arte, o no es artista o no supe comprenderlo; pero es innegable que quien tiene poder para impresionar a un iniciado o a un profano en cualquier momento o en cualquier estado anímico hasta el más absoluto recogimiento, para hacer evocar lo más grande, lo más bello o lo más doloroso de nuestra vida, quien hace sufrir y gozar, quien nos arranca un grito sin palabras—homenaje de

entusiasmo—, o una lágrima que asoma a los ojos y vuelve al corazón ahogándonos—santa, delicada ofrenda muda, ese es Artista, ese dejará ya para siempre su imagen y la vibración de su alma en la urna de nuestros recuerdos!

¡Mágico poder de evocación! Oigo a Segovia y surge a su lado, acariciando sus cabellos con el tintineo de sus castañuelas, la grácil y estatuaria Antonia Mercé; sigue la guitarra sonando... y entre las ondas que forman sus notas, asoman los ojos brujos de Pastora Imperio... Brotan melodías que cantan las excelencias de la tierra hispana y junto a Segovia, nimbada de gloria con su arpa de oro se enseñorea la inmortal, la dulce, la nunca olvidada ESMERALDA CERVANTES!... Flota en el ambiente del alma de Sevilla, Cádiz, Granada... quisiera hablar y no puedo, entonces se levanta la figura—también única—de Federico García Sanchiz ¡quién pudiera galana y verbosamente expresarse como él, que, con la donosura de su léxico, pinta, graba en bronce, canta, poetiza...!

¿Suena la guitarra?... ¡No!... es mi corazón que llora... Segovia lo aprisiona entre sus dedos y le arranca gritos de dolor... se perdió la última nota entre aplausos delirantes, tengo preñados de lágrimas los ojos, enclavijadas las manos que se aprietan fuertemente contra el pecho..., mi corazón late emocionado bajo ellas..., no fué el mío el que estrujó Segovia... era el suyo... pero el mío y el de todos, respondía al unísono de sus dolores y místicamente, quizá oraba... Religión es fuente de Arte. Arte engendra religión!...

¡Un regalo más nos brinda Segovia!; nuestras canciones!; entre sus armonías se yergue, coronada con hilos de luz de luna la cara simpática, los expresivos ojos, la amplia sonrisa bondadosa de nuestro querido Manuel M. Ponce!

¡Sentir! ¡Soñar! Eso es la vida, y Andrés Segovia nos la brinda en sus más puras expresiones; por eso siempre que le escucho, no puedo menos de exclamar: ¡Benditas tus manos que me traen la caricia suprema de vivir un instante! ¡Bendita tu alma que las inspira y bendita tu mente que las ilumina!

María Luisa SERRANO

This article is from the *Mexico al Dia* magazine published on April 1, 1933 in Mexico City. The translation of the article by Maria Luisa Serrano begins on the next page.

This article by Maria Luisa Serrano for the *Mexico al Dia* magazine was published on April 1, 1933 in Mexico City. The translation is:

Photo dedication: For *Mexico al Dia,* Andrés Segovia Mexico 1933.

Photo caption: Andrés Segovia, the Virtuoso of the Guitar.

"The artistic life in Mexico.

Listening to Segovia Play.

Impressions and critique.

(Special for the *Mexico al Dia* magazine)

With mystic fervor I keep in the bottom of the urn of my devoted memories, those in which the art, by the magic of his interpretations, leaves uneraseable, forever, images and impressions.

I open the urn and they spread aromas that saturate me again..., burns incense in an altar of my memories and the crystal clear and precise visions come surging!

Artists? There can be many. Emotions that they can awaken? Perhaps a few correspond... How many have been erased in the distance of the memory, how many sketch it with a better relief and energy?

Now, again, is Andrés Segovia, to whom the years of absence haven't erased and if it agitates similar present ones... Segovia is "unique"!

I can't do a dignified judgement of his art; my impression then is, of today and always, is of those by pure, deep and exquisite, there are no words that translate it.

To hear him play his guitar is to feel the softest caress, the sweetest vibration, and the most delicate spiritual recognition, divine playing of which the soul doesn't want to awaken from...

Fairytales are forged in his hands. Genius kisses his forehead. Art has chosen this son.

My soul is salivating in ecstasy, picks up his notes which, to evoke them, they give me the sensation to return to play which if they were born not of a harp, but of an aeolian guitar...

Everything in this Virtuoso is impeccable, technique and inspiration.

It is a delicacy to contemplate his hands over the instrument, which, obedient to his impulse, moans, laughs, sighs or cries in triumph or in agony.

Notes, arpeggios, harmonic chords, whatever, the most simple or common melody throughout his masculine temperament, sober, elegant, enormously sincere, sincerely exquisite, a dreamer, and refined, it ennobles and returns the heart of the place where you were born wrapped in whiteness of ermine, in the sun made from gold dust, in the trill of the hummingbirds, in an aroma of a divine flower, in the ferocity of a torrent, or in the murmuring of a crystalline fountain; to hear Segovia play one feels before the splendor of the paradise of Nature; one feels close, very close to God!

I believe with firm conviction that whoever doesn't know that it transports me with his expression of art, or he isn't an artist or hasn't found it to comprehend; but is undeniable that whoever has power to impress to an initiated or a non believer in whatever moment or animico state up to the most absolute recognition, for making the greatest evocation, the most beautiful or the most painful of our lives, who makes suffer and enjoy, who starts our wordless yell — homage of enthusiasm —, or a tear that begins at the eyes and returns to the heart drowning us — a sanctuary, a silent delicate offering, this is an Artist, this leaves forever his image and the vibration of his soul in the urn of our memories.

Magic power of evocation! I hear Segovia and surge to his side, caressing his hairs with the tinkling of his eyebrows, the graceful and statutory Antonia Mercé; the guitar continues to play... and among the waves that form his notes, begin the bewitching eyes of Pastora Imperio...They produce melodies that sing the excellencies of the Hispanic land and along with Segovia, full of glory with his golden harp, it possesses the immortal, the sweet, the unforgettable, Esmeralda Cervantes!...Floats in a ambiance of the soul of Seville, Cadiz, Granada... it wants to speak and it can't, then the figure arises — also unique — of Federico García Sanchiz who could gallantly and verbosely be expressed as him that, with the elegance of his vocabulary, paint, engraves in bronze, sing, write like a poet...!

Does the guitar ring?... No!...it's my heart that cries...Segovia has imprisoned it between his fingers and he starts the screams of pain... the last note is lost among the delirious applause, I have eyes pregnant with tears, joined hands that are tightly compressed against the chest...my heart flutters emotionally below them...it wasn't mine that squeezed Segovia's...it was his ...but mine and everyone's, might respond to the unison of its pain and mystically perhaps will speak...Religion is the source of art. Art begets religion!

Segovia toasts us with one more gift; our songs; among his harmonies it raises, the kind face crowned with threads of the moonlight, the expressive eyes, the ample kind smile of our Manuel Ponce!

To feel! To dream! That is the life, and Andrés Segovia toasts us with his purest expressions; because of that I always listen to him, I can't less than exclaim Bless your hands that carry me to the supreme caress to live an instant! Bless your soul that inspires those hands, and bless your mind that illuminates them.

Maria Luisa Serrano"

Andrés Segovia, el famoso guitarrista, cuya llegada a esta
capital se anuncia para el presente mes

This photo is from the daily *"La Nacion"* of Sunday August 5, 1934 from an article entitled "Andrés Segovia" by the Argentine folksinger and guitarist Ana Schneider de Cabrera written from Lima, Peru in July of 1934. The photo caption translates to:

"Andrés Segovia, the famous guitarist, for whose arrival the present month to this capital has been announced."

The dedication in the autographed photo is translated to:

"For *"La Nacion"* from an old friend, signed Andrés Segovia Lima July 1934"

Here is the translation of the article:

"In this city, the most Spanish of all the cities of America, where the courteous spirit of the epoch of the viceroyalty has left its deep footprints; where the grace and the beauty of the women and the gentlemanliness and finery of the men are tradition; where its still persists and it is celebrated it's called the fiesta of the color, of the light and of the bravery, the Spanishism of the bullfight; in this Lima, what is music for the spirit, the Spanish guitar, the classic of the polished vihuelists, that which Tárrega elevated so high, almost doesn't exist. The guitar here is the indispensable of the popular jaranas, and Bach and Mozart haven't sung on the beautiful instrument in their solemn graveness, nor the graceful flutter of wings in the minuets of the 18th century.

But Andrés Segovia has arrived, and the unequaled notes of his guitar have flown, they have expanded, and all the soul of this city so spiritual vibrates with the music made. We remember the phrase of Stravinsky, whom, admired Segovia while listening to him in a recital offered at the Opera in Paris, said: "The guitar doesn't sound loud, but it is heard from faraway." The phrase has more sense of, which isn't apparent at first look.

Yes the past brilliant epoch of the guitar, Coste, Sor and Tárrega, were to be erased a little bit, the good guitarists, Llobet, already retired from active artistic life, and now Segovia, not only have made the resurgence of the good that mustn't be forgotten, but that he has initiated what we can call the golden century of the guitar.

In Spain, Granados and Albeniz marked the resurgence of the good music with the depth of a nationalist root; to them follow de Falla, the colorist, Turina, Moreno Torroba and Salazar; the Mexican Ponce; Roussel, Samazeuilh, Collet, Ferroud, Ibert, among the French; Cyril Scott, the distinguished English composer, all of them have contributed to enrich the totality of the productions for the guitar. Besides, Casella, Respighi, Tedesco and some other follows producing suggestive pages and of great artistic height, written especially for this instrument.

Known are the artistic honor and constancy of the Germans. Now then, in Germany the enthusiasm for the guitar is evident, so much so that Segovia prognosticated that among the good guitarists of the future there would be, undoubtedly, some Germans. In England and the Nordic countries, Sweden, Norway and Denmark, the guitar concerts and the associations that have made of it a cult that can be counted in increasing numbers.

In Germany Segovia made the valuable find of a good quantity of the music of the brilliant Bach, written for the classic lute, that duly arranged sounds marvelous on the guitar. Now Segovia has incorporated in his distinguished programs--in quantity and quality — a good number of authors, the group being of a variety and artistic height that charms. The severe and brilliant technique, with the security that is the norm in Segovia, caused a lively impression here and they impatiently awaited the opportunity to hear him again. His style so purified the varied tones and the sonorous effects that enliven the guitar, make it a little orchestra.

It pleases me greatly to congratulate the upcoming arrival of Segovia in Buenos Aires. The great capital of the South among the number of populaces where the guitar has many and good proselytes and where a brilliant nucleus of guitarists have elevated the artistic sense of the instrument, making undeniable and valuable work of popular culture.

I hope we will be able to soon count on good musical literature of authors that reflect aspects of our folklore, so prodigious in noble suggestions as personalism in its distinguishing, beautiful and characteristic senses."

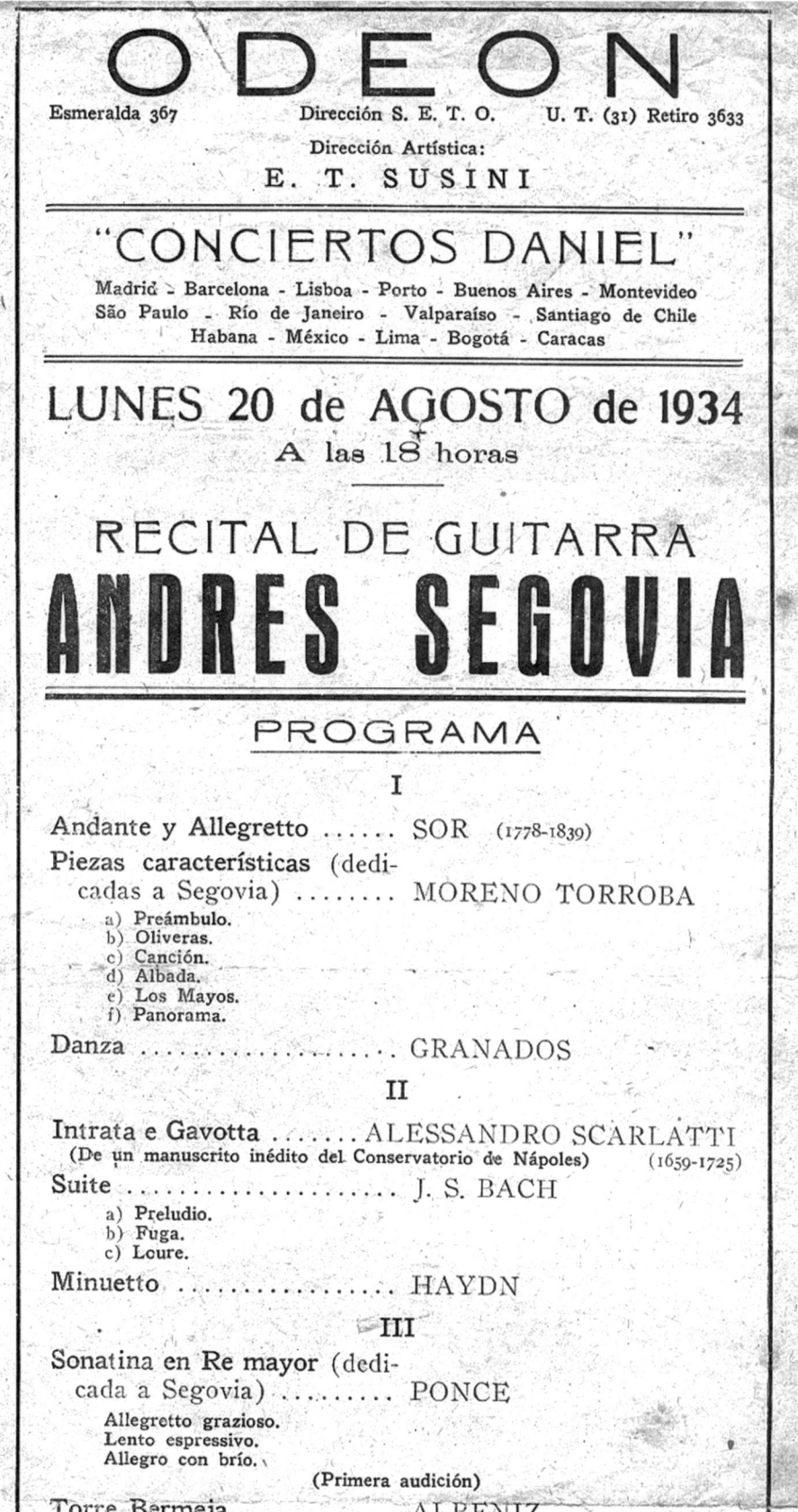

This August 20, 1934 concert of Andrés Segovia, produced by Conciertos "Daniel", in the Teatro Odeon debuts the "*Sonatina* in D Major" dedicated to the maestro by Manuel Ponce.

ODEON

Esmeralda 367   Dirección S. E. T. O.   U. T. (31) Retiro 3633

Dirección Artística:
E. T. SUSINI

"CONCIERTOS DANIEL"

Madrid - Barcelona - Lisboa - Porto - Buenos Aires - Montevideo
São Paulo - Río de Janeiro - Valparaíso - Santiago de Chile
Habana - México - Lima - Bogotá - Caracas

MIERCOLES 29 de Agosto 1934
A las 18 horas

RECITAL DE GUITARRA
ANDRES SEGOVIA

PROGRAMA

I

Andante en re mayor	SOR (1778-1839)
Sonatina	GIULIANI
Fandanguillo	MORENO TORROBA
Arada	,, ,,
Madroños	,, ,,
(Dedicadas a Segovia)	

II

Allegramento .... DAVID KELLNER
     (Primera Audición)   (1659-1748)

Preludio, Fuga y Loure en re
mayor .... BACH
    (Primera audición, primitivamente escrita para laúd)

Minuetto .... SCHUBERT

III

Preludio, Diferencias y Fuga sobre la Folía de España .... PONCE
    (Dedicada a Segovia)
          (Primera Audición)

Guitarreo .... C. PEDRELL
    (Dedicada a Segovia)

Sevilla .... ALBENIZ

This debut of the *Folias de España* by Manuel Ponce dedicated to Andrés Segovia was on Wednesday August 29, 1934 at the Teatro Odeon, in Buenos Aires.

This Friday September 7, 1934 concert takes place in Montevideo at the "Teatro 18 de Julio" theater. It is slated as his last great concert before leaving for other parts of the world. His last major concert in Buenos Aires, for this season, is just 12 days away.

Translation of the dedication: "For Miss Elsa, a friend of the guitar, Andrés Segovia."

Programa del Ultimo Concierto

1.ª Parte

VARIACIONES Sobre un tema italiano...... Sor

SONATINA (Dedicada a Segovia) .... Moreno Torroba
   a - Allegretto.
   b - Andante.
   c - Allegro.

DANZA EN SOL...................... Granados

2.ª Parte

ZARABANDA .... Haendel
BOURRÉE....................... Bach
MINUETO....................... Schubert
CANZONETTA .... Mendelssohn

3.ª Parte

FANDANGUILLO (Dedicado a Segovia)..... Turina

GRANADA .... ⎤
SEVILLA .... ⎥ Albeniz
LEYENDA .... ⎦

In this Friday September 7, 1934 concert Andrés Segovia plays two works that are dedicated to him, the *Sonatina* by Federico Moreno-Torroba and the *Fandanguillo* by Joaquín Turina.

478ª. REUNIÓN

ANDRES SEGOVIA

RECITAL DE GUITARRA

Rosario, Miercoles 12 de Setiembre de 1934
a las 21 y 30 horas

SALA DE LA BIBLIOTECA ARGENTINA

Andrés Segovia played in Rosario, Santa Fe five times between 1928 and 1939. This concert was on Wednesday September 12, 1934. Andrés Segovia performed for "El Circulo" in Rosario, Santa Fe on August 7, 1928 for the first time within that period.

PROGRAMA

I

Sor	- Andante y Allegretto
Moreno Torroba	- Piezas características
	a) Preambulo
	b) Oliveras
	c) Canción
	d) Albada
	e) Los Majos
	f) Panorama
Granados	- Danza

II

Scarlatti	- Intrata e gavotta
Bach	- Suite
	a) Preludio
	b) Fuga
	c) Loure
Haydn	- Minuetto

III

Ponce	- Sonatina en re mayor
	a) Allegretto grazioso
	b) Lento espressivo
	c) Allegro con brio
Albeniz	- Torre Bermeja

Andrés Segovia plays for the second time in Rosario, Santa Fe on this Wednesday September 12, 1934. The maestro plays guitar works by Sor, Moreno-Torroba, Granados, Scarlatti, Bach, Haydn, Ponce and Albeniz.

In earlier tours of Rosario, Segovia played in 1920-21. This can be said by autographs I have viewed. R.O.

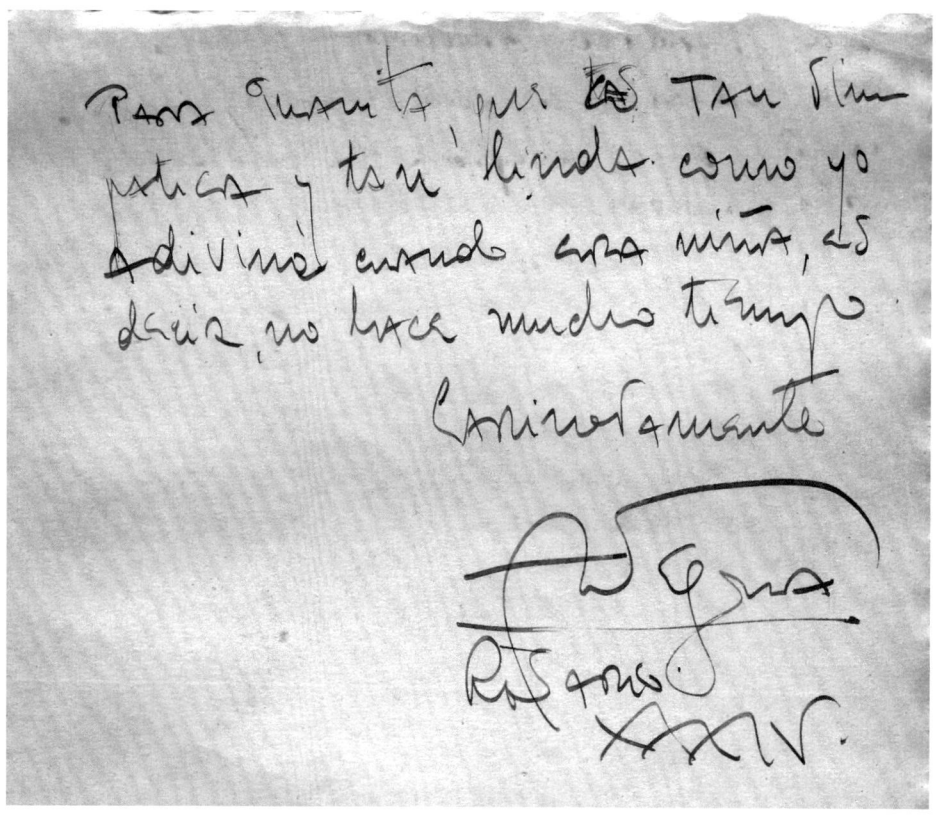

This autographed note to a fan is translated as:

  "For Juanita, that is so charming and so pretty as I predicted when she was young, that is to say, not too long ago.

Affectionately,
Andrés Segovia
Rosario 1934"

Andrés Segovia autograph in Montevideo in 1934.

This photo of Andrés Segovia is from the magazine *"Atlantida"* of September 13, 1934.

Andrés Segovia's last concert in Buenos Aires at the Teatro Odeon in his 1934 tour. He has three debuts of pieces, of which Joan Manen and Manuel Ponce dedicate two of these to him in this Wednesday, September 19th concert.

Translation of the review from the newspaper "*La Nacion*" on September 20, 1934.

"*En el Odeon dio ayer su ultimo concierto el guitarrista A. Segovia.*"

"Guitarist A. Segovia gave his last concert in the Odeon."

"Yesterday in the teatro Odeon the good-bye concert of the guitarist Andrés Segovia, one of the most excellent proponents of this instrument in the present, took place. His labor in the recitals that recently happened shows him to us once again as the interpreter of admirable mechanism and exquisite musicality reediting the success that we know in other seasons as artistic manifestations that have always distinguished to his..."

(incomplete)

MUSICA

En el Odeón dió ayer su último concierto el guitarrista A. Segovia

En el teatro Odeón se realizó ayer el concierto de despedida del guitarrista Andrés Segovia, uno de los más eximios cultores de ese instrumento en la actualidad. Su labor en los recitales efectuados recientemente en dicha sala nos lo mostró una vez más como el intérprete de admirable mecanismo y exquisita musicalidad que conocimos en otras temporadas reeditando el éxito que como manifestaciones artísticas han destacado siempre a sus au-

This concert announcement for Andrés Segovia at Wigmore Hall on December 6, 1935 is from the December 1935 B. M. G. magazine.

December, 1935]

Segovia is giving a recital at the Wigmore Hall, London, on Friday evening, December 6th. Tickets for this recital, which commences at 8.30 o'clock, can be obtained from the usual agencies.

C X 22 — FADA RADIO

Administración: 18 de Julio 1100. - Teléf. 8-59-46
Estudios y Dirección: 18 de Julio 1092. - Teléf. 8-41-20

DOMINGO 22

9.50 Comienza trasmisión.
10. **Rotativo Aéreo por Enrique Noguera.**
10.30 Al Jonson, canciones.
10.45 **Radio Teatro Infantil, por José Macías (h.).**
12. Harry Roy, grab.
12.15 **Carmelo Mazzulo, ctor.**
12.30 Dajos Bela, grab.
12.45 **Carmelo Mazzulo, ctor.**
13. **J. C. Meizoso, recit.**
13.15 Boleros, grab.
13.30 **J. C. Meizoso, recit.**
13.45 "Madame Butterfly", 3 actos, de Puccini.
15.45 Fragm. de películas.
16.30 Gardel, L. Lamarque, I. Corsini y A. Gómez.
17.30 Bailables, por orq. típicas y jazz.
20.15 **V. Amoretti y J. Macías.**
20.30 Cantos reg. españoles.
21.30 Orq. sinfón., grab.
22. Cantos rusos, grab.
22.30 Bailables y jazz, grab.

LUNES 23

10. **Rotativo Aéreo por Enrique Noguera.**
10.30 Sop. ten., barít., contr.
11.30 Orq. típicas, grab.
11.45 **Olbert, cantor.**
12. Vals, grab.
12.15 **Olbert, cantor.**
12.30 E. Duchin, D. Elligton, Ray Noble, grab.
13.30 **Hora Artiguista.**
14.30 Cine-Actualidad.
15.30 Heraldo Klaxon.
16.30 **María A. Bauzé, piano.**
17. Revista del Aire.
18. Rythm Symcopated.
18.30 Canciones.
19. **En el País de las Maravillas.**
20. C. Gardel, grab.
20.15 **Lila Marrone, cancion.**
20.30 Tangos, por típ., grab.
20.45 **Lila Marrone.**
21. Fco. Canaro, grab.
21.30 "Rocambole", episodios (continuación). Cía. de Artistas Unidos. Teatralización de H. Sena. Exclusivo.
23. José Mojica, grab.

MARTES 24

10. **Rotativo Aéreo por E. Noguera.**
10.30 Canc. brasileñas, grab.
11. **Recit. y charlas.**
11.30 "El Conde de Luxemburgo", de F. Lehar.
12.30 Trasm. de la lotería.
14.30 Conj. "Melodía Azul".
15.30 Heraldo Klaxon.
16.30 Prof. Brandino, piano.

16.45 Oscar Rico, violinista.
17. Secretos Cinescos.
18. Varietee. F. Aranaz.
18.30 Hora Artiguista.
19. Euskal Oruna.
20. M. Chevalier, grab.
20.15 **Religión del Aire.**
20.30 A. Vila. Magaldi-Noda.
21. Música de jazz, grab.
21. Jazz.
21.30 "I Pagliacci", óp. de Leoncavallo.
23. Bailables, grab.

MIERCOLES 25

10. **Rotativo Aéreo, por E. Noguera.**
10.30 Sel. de operetas, grab.
11.30 Conj. de mandol., grab.
11.45 **Disertación sobre Enfermedades del ganado.**
12. **Olbert, cantor.**
12.15 Trio Sanducero.
12.30 **Olbert, cantor.**
12.45 Cuart. Machin y Trio Matamoros.
13.30 Orq. sinfónicas, grab.
14.30 Cine-Actualidad.
15.30 Heraldo Klaxon.
16.30 Ortiz Tirado, grab.
17. Revista del Aire.
18. Rythm Symcopated.
18.30 **Hora Artiguista.**
19. **País de las Maravillas.**
20. **Lila Marrone, cancion.**
20.15 Nat Silkret, grab.
20.30 **Lila Marrone, canc.**
20.45 Conj. típico Panchito.
21.15 R. Tauber, grab.
21.30 "Rocambole" episodios. Continuación. Por la Cía. Artistas Unidos. - Teatralización H. Sena.
23. Orq. Hollywood Bowl.

JUEVES 26

10. **Rotativo Aéreo, por E. Noguera.**
10.30 Folklore criollo, grab.
11.30 E. Caruso, grab.
12. Ninon Vallin, grab.
12.15 M. Chamlee, grab.
12.30 Alma Reyles, grab.
12.45 M. Fleta, grab.
13. Tito Schipa, grab.
13.30 **Hora Artiguista.**
14.30 S. violín, piano, cello.
15.30 Heraldo Klaxon.
16.30 **María A. Bauzá, s. p.**
17. Secretos Cinescos. Dix.
17.30 Oscar M. Rico, violín.
18. Conj. "Melodía Azul".
19. Segovia y Barrios.
19.45 **J. Macías (h.), recit.**
20. Rumbas, grab.
20.15 **J. Macías (hijo), recit.**
20.30 **Carmelo Mazzulo, cant.**
20.45 Div. musicales, grab.
21.30 Euskal Orúa.

22.30 "Campo", de Fabini.
23. Por los Caminos del Mundo, por Ariel.

VIERNES 27

10. **Rotativo Aéreo, por E. Noguera.**
10.30 Peric., gatos, rancheras, zambas, etc., grab.
11. Canc. mejic., ton. chil.
11.45 **Olbert, cantor.**
12.15 Trío Sanducero.
12.30 Imp. Argentina, grab.
12.45 Trío Sanducero.
13. Mús. aut, alem., franc.
13.30 **Hora Artiguista.**
14.30 Cine-Actualidad.
15.30 Heraldo Klaxon.
16.30 Solos de órgano, grab.
17. Revista del Aire.
18. Varietés por Aranaz.
19. **País de las Maravillas.**
20. Don Besto, grab.
20.15 **L. Marrone.**
20.30 Harry Roy.
20.45 **Lila Marrone, cancion.**
21. **J. C. Meizoso, recit.**
21.15 Overturas, grab.
21.30 "Rocambole" Episodios Continuación, por la Cía. Artistas Unidos. Teatralización de H. Sena. Exclusivo.
23. Schubert, Lizst, Falla y Albéniz.

SABADO 28

10. **Rotativo Aéreo, por E. Noguera.**
10.30 Inform. Magisterial.
10.45 Sel. de la Discoteca.
11.45 Bandas y rondallas.
12.15 "La Montería", La Pícara Molinera", "Los Flamencos", "Los Claveles", "La canción del olvido", selec. zarz.
13. Euskal Ordúa.
14. **Conferencia.**
14.15 Variedades típicas.
15. "Cavallería Rusticana" de Mascagni.
16.30 Hora gallega.
17.30 Conj. "Melodía Azul".
18.30 **Profesora Brandino.**
19. **Turf-Deportes. Dr. Trigémino.**
20. Conjunto típico brasileño "Panchito".
20.15 Tino Folgar, grab.
20.30 Conjunto típico brasileño "Panchito".
20.45 Gómez. Falcón. Gardel.
21.30 Ten. y barítonos, grab.
22. Lily Pons. Chialiapin.
22.30 Bailables y jazz.

Operas de la semana: Domingo 22, a las 13.45: "Madame Butterfly", 3 actos de Puccini.
Martes 24, a las 21.30: "I Pagliacci", 2 actos de Leoncavallo.
Sábado 28, a las 15: "Cavallería Rusticana", 1 acto de Mascagni.
Zarzuelas y operetas: Martes 24, a las 11.30: "El Conde de Luxemburgo", Franz Lehar.
Sábado, a las 12.15: Gran selección de zarzuelas.
Actuación del cantor nacional Carmelo Mazzulo: Domingos, de 12.15 a 12.30, 12.45 a 13.
Jueves, de 20.30 a 20.45.
Actuación de la "Hora Artiguista": Lunes, de 18.30 a 19; martes, de 13.30 a 14.30;
miércoles, de 18.30 a 19; jueves, de 13.30 a 14.30; viernes, de 13.30 a 14.30.

Here we see on CX 22 Fada radio in Montevideo on Thursday September 26, 1935 Andrés Segovia and Agustín Barrios recordings being played from 7 PM until 7:45 PM. This is from the magazine entitled: *Programa oficial de las estaciones uruguayas de radio* (Official program of the Uruguayan Radio Stations) The Bold text listings are live events.

New York Recital This Season

ANDRES
SEGOVIA
World's Greatest Guitarist

Town Hall—Jan. 22, 1936
Wednesday Evening at 8:30

PROGRAM

I. (a) Sarabande, Menuet, and Gavotte . . . HANDEL
   (b) Sonatine meridionale . . . . . . PONCE
       Dedicated to Andres Segovia—First time in New York
           Allegretto grazioso
           Lento espressivo
           Allegro con brio
   (c) Dance . . . . GRANADOS

II. (a) Fugue and Gavotte . . . . . . J. S. BACH
    (b) Siciliana . . . . C. PH. EM. BACH
    (c) Gigue . . . . S. L. WEISS

III. (a) Capriccio
         (Homage to Paganini) . M. CASTELNUOVO-TEDESCO
         Composed for Mr. Segovia—First time in New York
     (b) Sevillana . . . . TURINA
             Dedicated to Andres Segovia
     (c) Torre bermeja . . . . ALBENIZ

Tickets Now On Sale at Town Hall Box Office

113 West 43rd Street   BRyant 9-9447

Auspices: Sixth Town Hall Endowment Series

Andrés Segovia's program for the Wednesday January 22, 1936 Town Hall, New York concert. These theatre programs belonged to Anna Palmer Coit North (1908-2014), who was the very first female feature writer for Time magazine.

ANDRES
SEGOVIA

The World's Greatest Guitarist

He Looks Like Franz Schubert
This Romantic Spaniard
Critics Have Compared Him
To Kreisler and Casals
He Plays the Classic Music of
Mozart, Handel, Bach ... the Music
of Granados, De Falla, Albeniz ...
Contemporary Composers Such as
Turina, Torroba, Tarrega Compose
Special Music for Him.

These repositioned images on this and the following two pages are from a booking advertisement placed in an oversize edition magazine called Musical America dating from February 10, 1936.

SEGOVIA OPENS RECITAL SEASON

Concert of Guitarist Found Masterly

New World of Beauty and Poetry Is Seen in His Program at Town Hall

By OLIN DOWNES

In Town Hall last night Andres Segovia, the Spanish guitarist, returned to a grateful public for his first American appearance of the season. On the stage, when the audience gathered, was only the diminutive rest which is his sole apparatus. When he entered with his guitar he was his customary self—the Schubertian collar and necktie, the quiet mien and, because of his greatness as a musician, completely master of the situation. He struck two soft chords for attention and began.

Mr. Segovia would be unusual, in these days of ballyhoo, if only for the fact that he uses no exterior means to impress his audience; rather he gathers his audience to him. There is an almost instantaneous transposition of values—a new world of beauty and poetical expression within an incredibly modest scale of sonority, and this from an instrument abused, misunderstood, underestimated. Mr. Segovia makes this instrument not only one of pulsatile effects, but of song. He uses the glide from tone to tone rarely, and the vibrato with the same discretion and infallible taste. It is the art which conceals art, appearing as an intimate and informal improvisation, being in fact a profoundly conceived and precisely planned creation. Within a measure this artist can obtain as many shades of color and sonority as players of grosser perceptions achieve in a page of music.

Mr. Segovia, playing all this in the most artistic manner, can readily point to Bach as the arch-transcriber of all the great composers, who was by no means a purist where transcriptions for various instruments were concerned. After Bach two minutes of Haydn were performed with the most consummate art — in certain places with a very slight and inimitable "rubato," perfectly in order, in fact demanded by the inmost spirit of the music, and indicative of the swing of the popular dances, origins of a great deal of Haydn's music.

Compositions of Turina and Albeniz completed the printed program. An audience of music lovers and of many professional musicians, not only players of the guitar, but of various instruments, listened, applauded and cheered while Mr. Segovia played encores. Whatever instrument they played, they could afford to listen and to learn from such an artist.

N. Y. TIMES, Jan. 23, 1936

THIS IS SEGOVIA'S SEVENTH SEASON IN NORTH AMERICA

From Painting by *Miguel del Pino*

These images on this and the following page that are from a booking advertisement placed in an oversize edition magazine called Musical America dating from February 10, 1936.

This photo is from the magazine Musical America dating from February 10, 1936.

This is the cover to a 4 page flyer for a Monday February 24, 1936 concert at the Philharmonic Auditorium in Los Angeles, and it had been used at least since the Friday February 11, 1931 Yale concert.

This advertisement by Columbia Music, that was owned by Sophocles Papas, for the 35 pieces of sheet music and 7 recordings by Andrés Segovia is from the "Mastertone" magazine, published in Kalamazoo, Michigan of February 1936, No. 11 Year 7.

Mastertone
A FRETTED INSTRUMENT MONTHLY FOR PLAYER, TEACHER AND DEALER

7th Year, Number 11   The Mastertone Publishing Company, Kalamazoo, Michigan $1.00 per year by subscription

FEBRUARY, 1936

AT THIS TIME OF THE YEAR IT IS FITTING FOR US TO GET OUT OUR HISTORY BOOKS AND RE-READ THE LIFE STORIES OF THE TWO GREATEST AMERICANS OF ALL TIMES — ABRAHAM LINCOLN AND GEORGE WASHINGTON.

THE STORY OF THE MAN WHO WAS THE FATHER OF OUR COUNTRY AND THAT OF HE WHO WAS THE SAVIOR OF THE NATION ARE INSPIRATIONAL READING TO EVERYONE.

IN THIS ISSUE

THE SPIRIT OF '36	WHAT IS YOUR ANSWER?	ROMANCE OF THE GUITAR
(Page 3)	(Page 5)	(Page 7)

— PRICE · TEN · CENTS —

Andrés Segovia, is listed in this issue of *"Radio Revista — cancionera"* Issue No. 239 *Año* VI Sunday August 23 — Saturday August 29, 1936, published in Montevideo on August 21, 1936. His records were played on Sunday August 23 from 2:15PM until 2:30 on Radio C X 14 *El Espectador*. The listings in bold text are live performances and the listings in plain text are recordings played for the audience.

C X 14 El Espectador

11. Libertad Lamarque.
11.15 Ignacio Corsini.
11.30 Policromias. Revist. Femen. Dir.: Turquesa.
12.15 Orqs. italianas.
13.30 Organistas.
13. 13 campanadas.
14. Canciones peruanas.
14.15 Andrés Segovia.
14.30 Rondallas.
15. Trasm. cont. de bailables e inf. completa de todos los dep.
19.45 La Perchelerita.

20. 8 campanadas.
20.15 La Perchelerita.
21.15 Canc. brasileñas.
21.45 Vicente Simón.
22. Orq. Tip. y de Jazz.
22.15 Bailables.
22.30 Bolet. de últ. hora.

806

Les Concerts Classiques

ANDRÈS SEGOVIA

Para la siempre amiga y siem-
pre admirada obra Normal.

RÉCITAL DE GUITARE

DONNÉ PAR

ANDRÈS SEGOVIA

This Andrés Segovia c. November 1936 concert took place at the Fox Theater in Casablanca, Morocco. In Alberto Lopez Poveda's book Andrès Segovia Vida y Obra published by the Universidad de Jaen / Ayuntamiento de Linares 2010, on page 260 he says that Andrés first made a tour of North Africa in January of 1934.

Andrès SEGOVIA

Moins de dix ans après le début de sa carrière, *Andrés Segovia* atteint à la célébrité mondiale. Littérateurs et musiciens des deux continents lui consacrent toute une littérature — commentaires techniques, comparaisons fleuries, métaphores subtiles — étrange florilège, où des pages délicates de Gérard d'Houville voisinent avec les éloges solidement motivés de la musicologie allemande.

Le miracle n'est pas dans cet universel consentement, dans cette admiration des élites, en complet accord avec le sentiment du grand public, mais bien dans le fait que, cette unanimité, *Segovia* l'ait obtenue sans concession, au particularisme des avertis, au snobisme salonnier, non plus qu'aux fades tournures de ce qu'on appelle communément (et si injustement) l'art populaire.

Le brillant de l'instrument, la variété de ses coloris, ferraillement du rasgueado, pizzicati nasillards, ironiques ou d'une cinglante netteté, traits volubiles, harmoniques d'or et de cristal, tenues qui se prolongent comme les sons filés d'un violon, toutes ces richesses encloses « au bois creux des guitares », *Segovia* les exploite avec une habileté transcendante.

Mais, dans cette voie, d'autres l'avaient précédé. Il semble bien que ce Huerta qui créa une telle sensation au milieu du siècle dernier ait été, déjà, une sorte de magicien de la sonorité: pourtant, l'oubli le plus complet ne devait pas tarder à retomber sur son nom.

Celui de *Segovia* n'est pas menacé d'une telle désaffection. Détenteur des solides traditions de Sor, de Tarrega, de l'habileté diabolique de Huerta, il apparaît comme le musicien le plus capable de redonner à la guitare sa pleine dignité, d'en faire, comme au temps de Luis Milan et de Robert de Visée, le moyen d'expression d'une musique parfaitement noble.

Bien souvent on l'a comparé à Casals : c'est, en effet, chez les deux interprètes, même clarté dans l'établissement d'un plan, même don, si rare, de continuité rythmique, capable de maintenir à travers les fluctuations du tempo l'unité vitale d'une œuvre, même sobriété, même concentration.

Une musique ressuscite pour la guitare rénovée : les vieux luthistes, exorcisés, secouent leur poudreux linceul. Une autre naît : de Falla, Torroba, Turina, Roussel, Ponce; auprès d'eux, une cohorte de jeunes compositeurs constituent un répertoire dans lequel la sobriété, la justesse des proportions, l'équilibre commandés par le génie de l'instrument et l'ascendant de l'interprète présentent un aspect caractéristique de l'évolution musicale contemporaine et, plus généralement, de l'esprit latin.

The French translation by Randy Osborne is on the next page.

Andrés Segovia

"Less than six years after the debut of his career Andrés Segovia attained worldwide celebrity status. Writers and musicians of the two continents consecrated him in all their articles — the commentaries on technique, flowery comparisons, subtle metaphors — a strange anthology, where by the delicate pages of neighborly Gerard d'Houville along with the strongly motivated praise of German musicology.

It isn't a miracle by universal consent, that the admiration by the elite, in complete agreement with the sentiment of the public at large, but in the fact that, this unanimity, Segovia has obtained without concession, particularism of the sophisticated, the snobbery of the salon, not as bland naming commonly called (if it's unjust) popular art.

The brilliance of the instrument, the variety of colors, the rattle of the rasgueados, the nasal pizzicatos, the ironic or biting sharpness, weaving features, golden and crystal harmonics, prolonged sustain as if they are from the bow of the violin, all the riches enclosed (of the wooden box of the guitar) Segovia exploits them with a transcendent ability.

But, in this way, others have preceded him. Like him Huerta who created the same sensation in the middle of the last century, once again, a kind of a magician of sonority, however, his name is completely forgotten to oblivion.

That of Segovia isn't threatened by the same disaffection. He holds the strong tradition of Sor, of Tárrega, of the diabolical ability of Huerta, he appears as a musician very capable to restore the guitar to its full dignity, to make, as in the time of Luis Milan and Robert de Visée, a perfectly noble means of expressing music.

So often, he is compared to Casals: this in effect, in both interpreters, the same clarity even in a plan, same talent, so rare, of continuing the rhythm, capable of maintaining across the fluctuation of tempos a vital unity of the work, the same sobriety, the same concentration.

A music resuscitated by the renovated guitar: of the lutenists, is exorcised, it shakes their dusty shroud. Another is born: de Falla, Torroba, Turina, Roussel, Ponce; with them, a cohort of young composers are of a repertoire wherein the sobriety, the appropriate proportions, the balance commands for the genius of the instrument and the ascension of the present interpreter a characteristic aspect of contemporary musical evolution and, mainly of the Latin spirit."

The "Tremolo Study" by Tárrega is *"Recuerdos de la Alhambra"*.

PROGRAMME
du Récital de Guitare

DONNE PAR

ANDRÈS SEGOVIA

I

ANDANTE ET ALLEGRO	SOR (1780-1839)
THEME VARIE	SOR (1780-1839)
TARANTELLA (Dédiée à Segovia)	CASTELNUEVO-TEDESCO
MADRONOS (Dédiée à Segovia)	TORROBA
ESTUDIO	TARREGA

II

PRELUDE ET BOURREE	J. S. BACH
GIGUE	WEISS
ANDANTE	MOZART
CANZONETTA	MENDELSOHN

III

FANTASIA (Dédiée à Segovia)	J. TURINA
DANZA	E. GRANADOS
GRANADA	
TORRE BERMEJA	I. ALBENIZ
SEVILLA	

INTERMEDES DE DIX MINUTES

Intermission of ten minutes.

LES CONCERTS CLASSIQUES

20 Rue de l'Horloge - CASABLANCA

Saison 1936-37

DECEMBRE

Lotte Schoene
Cantatrice
Au piano M. Maurice O'Hana

JANVIER

Marcel Dupré
Organiste
Grand Prix de Rome
Titulaire de l'Eglise St-Sulpice

FEVRIER

Misha Elman
Violoniste

HORS SERIE

Niedzielsky
Pianiste
Récital Chopin

MARS

Arthur Rubinstein
Pianiste

AVRIL

Teresina
Danses espagnoles

Représentant pour l'Afrique du Nord des Secrétariats de Jean YSAYE, par entente avec le Bureau des Concerts Marcel de VALMALETE, 45, Rue de la Boétie - PARIS

LES CONCERTS CLASSIQUES

ont lieu à

CASABLANCA .... au VOX

RABAT .... au ROYAL

MEKNES .... au REGENT

ORAN .... au THEATRE MUNICIPAL

ALGER .... à L'Opéra - Théâtre Municipal

CONSTANTINE .... à la Salle de l'Université Populaire

BONE .... au THEATRE MUNICIPAL

TUNIS .... au THEATRE MUNICIPAL

●

CASABLANCA	ALGER
20, Rue de l'Horloge	6, Rue Voinot
Tél. 02-76	Tél. 53-73

814

Andrès SÉGOVIA

This is the cover of the program for the concert held at the Salle du Conservatoire in Geneva, Switzerland on Wednesday, December 16, 1936.

SALLE DU CONSERVATOIRE - GENÈVE

Mercredi 16 décembre 1936

●

Unique Récital

Andrès SEGOVIA

MAURICE VERLEYE, IMPRESARIO, GENÈVE

This unique recital was held at the Salle du Conservatoire in Geneva, Switzerland on Wednesday, December 16, 1936.

Programme

I

(Œuvres écrites originellement pour guitare)

ALLEGRO	Sor
INTERLUDE	Sor
ALLEGRETTO	Sor
CAPRICCIO (omaggio à Paganini)	*Castelnuovo-Tedesco*
TARANTELLA (dédiée à Andrès Ségovia)	*Castelnuovo-Tedesco*

ANDRÈS SÉGOVIA

II

(Œuvres primitivement écrites pour luth)

a) PRÉLUDE	*Bach*
SARABANDE	*Bach*
LOURE	*Bach*
b) COURANTE	*Bach*
BOURRÉE	*Bach*

(Transcription des pièces dont l'esprit et la technique s'adaptent à la guitare)

MINUETTO	*Schubert*
CANZONETTA	*Mendelssohn*

III

TONADILLA	*Granados*
GRANADA	*Albeniz*
TORRE BERMEJA	*Albeniz*
SEVILLA	*Albeniz*

The translation of the French text is:

In the first set Andrés Segovia is playing "works originally written for the guitar". Besides the Sor pieces there are the "homage to Paganini" and the piece "dedicated to Segovia" by the composer Mario Castelnuovo-Tedesco.

In the second set Andrés starts with pieces "originally written for the Lute". These are followed by "transcriptions of which the spirit and technique are adapted to the guitar". (From Piano by Schubert and from String Quartet by Mendelssohn.)

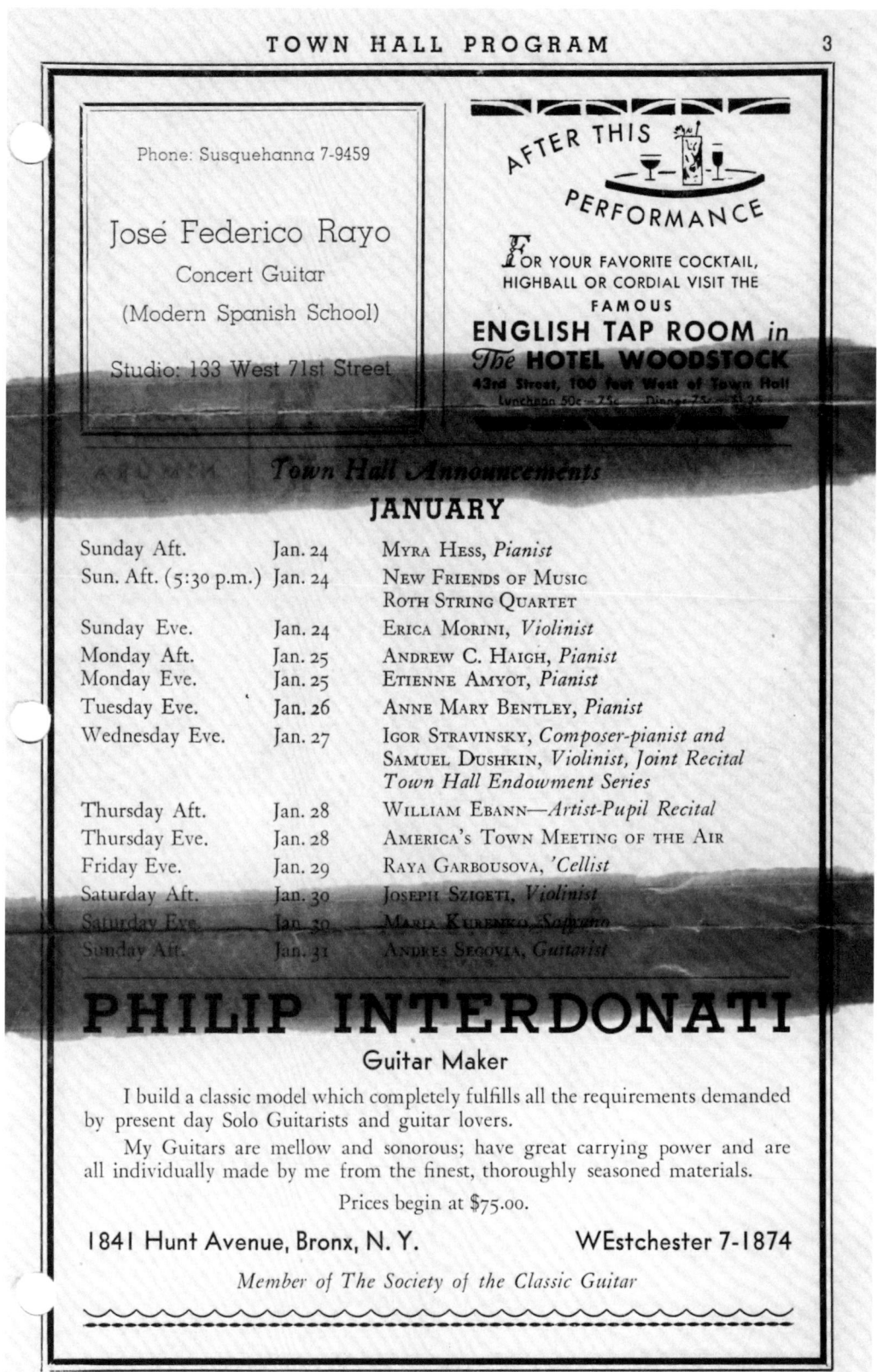

Town Hall Announcements
JANUARY

Sunday Aft.	Jan. 24	MYRA HESS, *Pianist*
Sun. Aft. (5:30 p.m.)	Jan. 24	NEW FRIENDS OF MUSIC ROTH STRING QUARTET
Sunday Eve.	Jan. 24	ERICA MORINI, *Violinist*
Monday Aft.	Jan. 25	ANDREW C. HAIGH, *Pianist*
Monday Eve.	Jan. 25	ETIENNE AMYOT, *Pianist*
Tuesday Eve.	Jan. 26	ANNE MARY BENTLEY, *Pianist*
Wednesday Eve.	Jan. 27	IGOR STRAVINSKY, *Composer-pianist and* SAMUEL DUSHKIN, *Violinist, Joint Recital* *Town Hall Endowment Series*
Thursday Aft.	Jan. 28	WILLIAM EBANN—*Artist-Pupil Recital*
Thursday Eve.	Jan. 28	AMERICA'S TOWN MEETING OF THE AIR
Friday Eve.	Jan. 29	RAYA GARBOUSOVA, *'Cellist*
Saturday Aft.	Jan. 30	JOSEPH SZIGETI, *Violinist*
Saturday Eve.	Jan. 30	MARIA KURENKO, *Soprano*
Sunday Aft.	Jan. 31	ANDRES SEGOVIA, *Guitarist*

Last on the list of Town Hall weekly announcements, Andrés Segovia's Sunday afternoon January 31, 1937 concert is mentioned. These theatre programs belonged to Anna Palmer Coit North (1908-2014), who was the very first female feature writer for Time magazine. Of note is the Italian American Guitar Maker, Philip Interdonati, who made extraordinary ornate guitars. The Society of the Classic Guitar had been formed in 1936.

Segovia Gives Town Hall Recital

Andres Segovia, guitarist. Town Hall, Jan. 31, afternoon:

Prelude and Gavotte..............Scarlatti
Allegremento, Sarabande and Gigue...Weiss
Prelude, Fugue and Loure...........Bach
Allegretto and Variations...........Sor
Sarabande, Menuet and Gavotte.....Handel
Andante ....Mozart
Menuet ....Schubert
Canzonetta ....Mendelssohn
Tarantella ....Castelnuovo-Tedesco
    (First time in New York)
Improvisation ....C. Pedrell
    (First time in New York)
'La Maja de Goya'..........F. Granados
'Granada,' 'Torre bermeja'........Albeniz

One of the foremost interpretative artists of a country that is at present paying small heed to the finer aspects of civilization, Andres Segovia, Spanish guitarist extraordinary, gave a program of eclectic nature in this his first New York recital of the season.

Year after year Mr. Segovia returns, his art in no wise diminished or his powers impaired, but strengthened by the mounting seasons, to acquaint or reacquaint his auditors with small miracles of technique and interpretation. Even if he is somewhat limited by the comparatively small amount of artistic literature written for the six-stringed instrument of which he is the exponent, his programs are often of a surprising scope. That presented at this recital was no exception, for the program began with the Prelude and Gavotte of Alessandro Scarlatti from an unpublished manuscript in the archives of the Conservatory of Naples, and proceeded through music by Bach to the four works by Handel, Mozart, Schubert and Mendelssohn, which were classed in a program note as transcriptions of works whose spirit and technique are adaptable to the guitar.

If any further proof was needed of Mr. Segovia's abilities it would be found in the different treatment accorded Sor's Allegretto and Variations, a work of Latin enthusiasms, appealing in melodic content, and Handel's Suite. When Mr. Segovia played the Sor music, it was with the fingers of a Spaniard, and in the Handel, which followed immediately, with almost purely Nordic viewpoint.

Of his ability to ring the changes in color upon his instrument, notwithstanding its somewhat circumscribed qualities, his remarkable manual dexterity, or range of dynamics, it is almost superfluous to speak. It is sufficient to say that he played with that quality of genius peculiar to him, and

Andres Segovia

that his playing was appreciated. Two works dedicated to Mr. Segovia were given a first performance in New York, the Castelnuovo-Tedesco Tarantella, and the Pedrell Improvisation.   P.

These two images are from a February 10, 1937 Musical America magazine. Of note are the two New York debut pieces: *Tarentella* by Mario Castelnuovo-Tedesco and the piece by Carlos Pedrell: Improvisation.

Harry Zelzer Concert Management
presents
ANDRES SEGOVIA

ORCHESTRA HALL
SUNDAY AFTERNOON, FEBRUARY 14th
AT 3:30 O'CLOCK

Tour Direction: Metropolitan Musical Bureau, Inc.
Division of Columbia Concerts Corporation of Columbia Broadcasting System
113 W. 57th St., New York City

Recital by

ANDRES SEGOVIA

GUITARIST

PROGRAM

(Works Written for Lute and Guitar)

1. Prelude and Gavotte.. A. Scarlatti
     (From an unpublished manuscript in the archives of the Conservatory of Naples)   (1659-1725)

   Allegramento and Gigue.. S. L. Weiss
                                                                                                 (1680-1750)

   Andante and Allegretto... F. Sor
                                                                                                 (1778-1839)

   Fantasia (dedicated to Andres Segovia)... J. Turina

(Transcriptions of Woks Whose Spirit and Technic are Adaptable to the Guitar)

2. Prelude
   Courante
   Sarabande   } Originally composed for the lute................................... J. S. Bach
   Bourree

   Menuet.. J. Haydn

Intermission   Program Continued on Next Page

Program Continued

(Works Written for Andres Segovia or Inspired by the Rhythms or Themes of Popular Andalusian Guitar Music)

3. Tarantella (dedicated to Andres Segovia)............................... Castelnuovo-Tedesco

   Improvisation (dedicated to Andres Segovia)................................... C. Pedrell

   Tropico e Rumba (dedicated to Andres Segovia)................................... Ponce

   Granada .... I. Albeniz

   Legend .... I. Albeniz

Publicity: William R. Harshe

This Andrés Segovia Chicago concert was held on Sunday February 14, 1937.

Last Chicago Recital This Season

... by ...

ANDRES SEGOVIA

TUESDAY EVENING, FEBRUARY 16th, at 8:30 O'CLOCK

TEMPLE ISAIAH-ISRAEL

Hyde Park Blv'd. and Greenwood Ave.

PROGRAM

Canzone e Saltarella	Chilesotti
Suite in D	R. de Visee
Piezas caracteristicas	Torroba
Prelude	J. S. Bach
Menuet	Schubert
Canzonetta	Mendelssohn
Sonatina meridionale	Ponce
Danza	Granados
Serenata	Albeniz

Tickets on Sale at Temple Box Office
Telephone: Kenwood 0155

This Andrés Segovia Chicago concert was held at the Temple Isaiah-Israel on Tuesday, February 16, 1937. This listing was found in the back of the program of Sunday February 14, 1937.

THE TOWN HALL

=123 WEST 43rd STREET, NEW YORK, N. Y.

Andres Segovia

Alfred Scott • Publisher • 156 Fifth Avenue, New York

206-2-27E-37

This Saturday, February 27, 1937 Andrés Segovia concert took place at The Town Hall in New York. The maestro is playing his 1912 Ramírez. He plays a New York debut of Miguel Llobet's Catalan transcriptions, J.S. Bach's *Chaconne,* and pieces dedicated to Andrés Segovia. The images on the next page are repositioned from the program.

THE TOWN HALL

SEASON 1936-1937

Saturday Evening, February 27th, at 8:30 o'clock

ANDRES
SEGOVIA

Guitarist

PROGRAM

I.

Works Written for Andres Segovia or Adaptable to the Guitar

Folias de España, Diferencias, y Fuga.................M. Ponce
Dedicated to Andres Segovia

Six Little Popular Songs of Catalonia................M. Llobet
First New York Performance

(a) El Mestre (*The Teacher*)
L'Hereu Riera (*The Heir*)

(b) El Testament de n'Amelia (*Amelia's Testament*)
El Noy de la mare (*Mother's Boy*)

(c) La Filla del marxant (*The Merchant's Daughter*)
La Filadora (*At the Spinning-Wheel*)

Capriccio diabolico (Homage to Paganini).......Castelnuovo-Tedesco
Dedicated to Andres Segovia

PROGRAM CONTINUED ON SECOND PAGE FOLLOWING

II.

*Transcription of a Work Adaptable to the Guitar
in Its Spirit and Technic*

Chaconne...J. S. Bach

Intermission

III.

*Works Written for Andres Segovia or Inspired by the
Rhythms or Themes of Popular Andalusian
Guitar Music*

Sevillana ⎫
Fandanguillo ⎰ ....J. Turina

Dedicated to Andres Segovia

Two Dances (G major and E major)................E. Granados

Legend...I. Albeniz

Guitar Ramirez, Madrid

Management: METROPOLITAN MUSICAL BUREAU, INC.
Division of Columbia Concerts Corporation
of Columbia Broadcasting System
Steinway Building   113 West 57th Street   New York City

REPERTORY THEATRE

Sunday Afternoon, Feb. 28 at 3:30

AARON RICHMOND presents

ANDRES SEGOVIA

GUITARIST

PROGRAM

I.

Works written for Lute and Guitar

PRELUDE and GAVOTTE　-　-　-　Alessandro Scarlatti (1659-1725)
(From an unpublished manuscript in the archives of the
Conservatory of Naples)

ALLEGRAMENTO— Gigue　-　-　-　-　- S. L. Weiss (1680-1750)

PRELUDE—Fugue in D—Loure　-　-　-　-　-　- J. S. Bach

VARIATIONS　-　-　-　-　-　-　- F. Sor (1778-1839)

II.

*(Transcriptions of Works Whose Spirit and Technic
are Adaptable to the Guitar*

ANDANTE　-　-　-　-　-　-　-　-　-　W. A. Mozart

MINUET　-　-　-　-　-　-　-　-　-　F. Schubert

CANZONETTA　-　-　-　-　-　-　-　F. Mendelssohn

—⁙ INTERMISSION ⁙—

*(Works Written for Andres Segovia or Inspired by the Rhythms
or Themes of Popular Andalusian Guitar Music)*

TARANTELLA　-　-　-　-　-　-　-　Castelnuovo-Tedesco
Dedicated to Andres Segovia

IMPROVISATION　-　-　-　-　-　-　-　. C. Pedrell
Dedicated to Andres Segovia

GRANADA
TORRE BERMEJA ⎫　-　-　-　-　-　-　- I. Albeniz

GUITAR RAMIREZ

Concert Direction: Aaron Richmond, Pierce Building, Boston

Tour Direction: Metropolitan Musical Bureau, Inc., 113 W. 57th St., N. Y.

The next day's concert, with a totally different program by Andrés Segovia on Sunday afternoon February 28, 1937. These theatre programs belonged to Anna Palmer Coit North (1908-2014), who was the very first female feature writer for Time magazine

CONCIERTOS DANIEL

Año XXIX de su fundación. - Presidente: Ernesto de Quesada.

Madrid - Barcelona - Lisboa - Buenos Aires - Montevideo - Río de Janeiro Santiago de Chile - Lima - Bogotá Caracas - Habana - Puerto Rico - Santo Domingo - Guatemala - San Salvador - San José, C. R. Año VI en Bogotá.

Dirección: Domingo y José Mesutti

Temporada oficial de grandes conciertos 1937

Miércoles 5 de Mayo

A las 18 y 30

Reaparición del notable guitarrista

Andrés

Segovia

—PROGRAMA—

PRIMERA PARTE —

INTRATA Y GAVOTA .... Alex Scarlatti
(De un manuscrito inédito del Conservatorio de Nápoles)
(1659 - 1925).

PIEZAS CARACTERISTICAS (Dedicado a Segovia) ... Torroba
Preámbulo
Oliveras
Melodía
Albada
Los mayos
Panorama

ESTUDIO .... Tárrega

SEGUNDA PARTE —

PRELUDIO, FUGA EN RE Y LOURE (Para Laúd) ... Bach

MINUETTO .... Haydn

CANZONETTA .... Mendelssohn

TERCERA PARTE —

CAPRICCIO DIABOLICO .... Castelnuovo
  Homenaje a Paganini, Dedicado a Segovia) 1.a audición   Tedesco

DANZA .... Granados

TORRE BERMEJA .... Albéniz

LEYENDA .... ˮ

GUITARRA RAMIREZ

PRECIO DE LAS LOCALIDADES

Palcos avant - scene sin entrada ..	$ 15.00	Tertulia balcón	$ 3.00
Palcos bajos o balcón sin entrada ˮ	10.00	Tertulias altas 1.a y 2.a filas	ˮ2.00
Palcos altos, sin entrada .... ˮ	8.00	Tertulias altas otras filas	ˮ 1.50
Palcos de Cazuela sin entrada ... ˮ	5.00	Delanteras de Cazuela	ˮ 1.00
Entrada Palco .... ˮ	1.50	Delanteras de Paraíso	ˮ 1.00
Sillón de Platea .... ˮ	3.00	Entrada de Cazuela	ˮ 0.60
		Entrada de Paraíso	ˮ 0.60

Sillón de Platea .... $ 3.00

This is the balance of the program for the Wednesday, May 5th, 1937 concert at the Teatro Solis in Montevideo, where it states he is using his Ramírez guitar (made in 1912 by Santos Hernández.) One can see that the artist chose a slightly different program that he played in Buenos Aires at the Teatro Odeon just two days later. As a concert guitarist he had dozens of pieces in his repertoire. In this concert he is debuting the piece dedicated to him by Mario Castelnuovo-Tedesco: *Capriccio Diabolico*- Homage to Paganini.

The translation of the autograph on the previous page is:

"For Ms. Chela, with all my affection for your musical sensibility.

Andrés Segovia."

ODEON

CONCIERTOS "DANIEL"
AÑO XXVI DE SU FUNDACION
MADRID, BARCELONA, LISBOA, BUENOS AIRES, MONTEVIDEO,
RIO JANEIRO, SANTIAGO DE CHILE, LIMA, BOGOTA, CARACAS,
HABANA, PTO. RICO, STO. DOMINGO, GUATEMALA, SAN SAL-
VADOR, SAN JOSE, COSTA RICA

Debut Viernes 7 de Mayo 1937   a las 18:30

Andrés Segovia's concert debut at the Teatro Odeon Friday, May 7, 1937. In Andrés Segovia's autobiography he states that the sketch for this cover was drawn by Miguel del Pino y Sarda for a Madrid recital in 1920.

PROGRAMA

In this Friday, May 7, 1937 program, Andrés Segovia plays the *Chaconne* by Johann Sebastian Bach, which was highly criticized by non guitarists, as the piece had been written for the violin. He also performs the premier of the homage to Paganini, *"Capriccio Diabolico"*, written expressly for him, by Mario Castelnuovo-Tedesco. He also makes use of his 1912 Manuel Ramírez, which he received as a gift in 1912. The guitar was made by Manuel's shop foreman: Santos Hernández, and it was an 11 string that was made on commission for the blind virtuoso, Antonio Jiménez Manjón. Manjón complained about it and offered Manuel less for the guitar, he wanted to pay for on a time payment plan, so, it went unsold and was reconfigured as a 6 string model.

From the same program, this small ad for Pirastro strings, stating as being the "best in the world", and indicating they would be available for "only a few days" at the Celestino Fernández music store. Pirastro strings had made promotional postcards for Andrés Segovia. He was their best salesman, as he had used their strings for many years.

SEGOVIA

A Segovia guitar concert is something everyone at some time must experience. The first year he appeared in New York City, he gave 20 — TWENTY—recitals by public demand His return is a long awaited event.

New York Times, February 1st, 1937
"Looking like the original sitter for a portrait by Goya, Andres Segovia has long been acclaimed the world's greatest virtuoso on the six-stringed instrument. No rivals have risen to dispute his right to the title."

PROGRAM

I.
THREE SELECTIONS .... PURCELL
SARABANDE .... HANDEL
PREAMBLE; BOUREE .... ALEXANDER SCARLATTI
SONATA .... DOMINICO SCARLATTI
PRELUDE; GAVOTTE .... J. S. BACH

II.
SONATA .... CASTELNUOVO-TEDESCO
TWO STUDIES .... VILLA LOBOS

III.
MALLORCA ....⎫
TORRE BERMEJA (Red Tower) ....⎬ ALBENIZ
LEYENDA ....⎬
SEVILLANA ....⎭

FIRST NEW YORK RECITAL FOLLOWING FIVE YEAR ABSENCE

TOWN HALL
Wednesday Evening, Nov 3rd, at 8:30
Opening Event—14th Season of the Town Hall Endowment Series
For Subscriptions or Segovia tickets: Box office, 113 West 43rd St. BR. 9-9447.

Exclusive Management: HUROK ATTRACTIONS, INC., 711 Fifth Avenue, New York 22, N. Y.
Booking Direction: NATIONAL CONCERT & ARTISTS CORP.

This is the opening concert program listing for a Wednesday November 3, 1937, concert at the Town Hall in New York.

Archive: Anna Palmer Coit North (1908-2014)

830

"DYNAMIC! EXQUISITE! Rarest of the Rare!"

SEGOVIA

A Segovia guitar concert is something everyone at some time must experience. The first year he appeared in New York City, he gave 20— TWENTY—recitals by public demand His return is a long awaited event.

New York Times, February 1st, 1937
"Looking like the original sitter for a portrait by Goya, Andres Segovia has long been acclaimed the world's greatest virtuoso on the six-stringed instrument. No rivals have risen to dispute his right to the title."

"The undisputed Master!"   —*Herald-Tribune*

"An audience that filled every seat and available standing room gave ovation after ovation and cheers at the close!"   —*N. Y. Times*

"He makes a guitar recital a first-rate musical event!"   —*PM*

EIGHTH STREET THEATRE
Wednesday Evening, January 19, 8:30 o'clock

Tickets $1.10, 1.65, 2.20, 2.75 (tax included)
On sale at Civic Opera House, Room 330, Tel. Dea. 2990
Direction Harry Zelzer Concert Mg't.

Exclusive Management: HUROK ATTRACTIONS, Inc. 711 Fifth Avenue, New York 22, N. Y.
Booking Direction: National Concert and Artists Corp.

This is the cover to a 2 page flyer for a Wednesday January 19, 1938 concert at the Eighth Street Theatre in New York.

This mentions his 5 years absence for this venue of his Wednesday January 19, 1938 concert at the Eighth Street Theatre in New York.

Promotional 4 page flyer for Andrés Segovia's January 23, 1938 concert in Jordan Hall in Boston. These theatre programs belonged to Anna Palmer Coit North (1908-2014), who was the very first female feature writer for Time magazine.

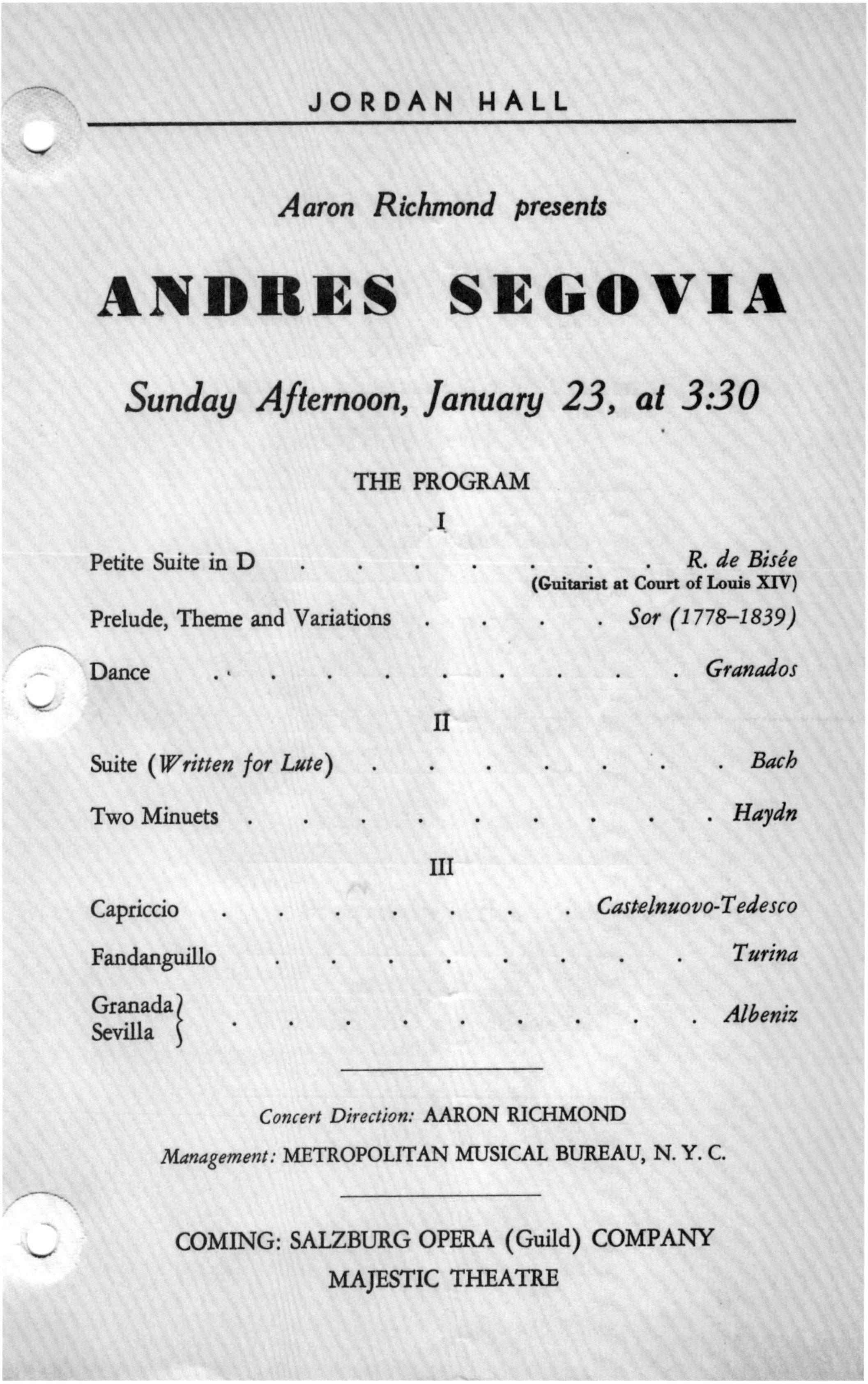

Aaron Richmond presents

ANDRES SEGOVIA

Sunday Afternoon, January 23, at 3:30

THE PROGRAM

I

Petite Suite in D . . . . *R. de Bisée*
(Guitarist at Court of Louis XIV)

Prelude, Theme and Variations . . . . *Sor (1778–1839)*

Dance . . . . *Granados*

II

Suite (*Written for Lute*) . . . . *Bach*

Two Minuets . . . . *Haydn*

III

Capriccio . . . . *Castelnuovo-Tedesco*

Fandanguillo . . . . *Turina*

Granada ⎱
Sevilla ⎰ . . . . *Albeniz*

Concert Direction: AARON RICHMOND

Management: METROPOLITAN MUSICAL BUREAU, N. Y. C.

COMING: SALZBURG OPERA (Guild) COMPANY
MAJESTIC THEATRE

Andrés Ssegovia's Sunday afternoon January 23, 1938 concert program in Jordan Hall, Boston, the opening piece should be by R. de Visée. These theatre programs belonged to Anna Palmer Coit North (1908-2014), who was the very first female feature writer for Time magazine.

Handbill for the Sunday March 6, 1938 concert at the Town Hall in New York, Andrés was now using the 1937 Hermann Hauser I "the guitar of our epoch".

ANDRES SEGOVIA

Program

I

Prelude, Theme, and Variations . . . . F. Sor
(1778-1839)

Sonata . . . . CASTELNUOVO-TEDESCO
Homage to Boccherini
- Allegro con spirito
- Andante quasi canzone
- Tempo di minuetto
- Vivo ed energico

(Dedicated to Andres Segovia)

Fandanguillo . . . . TURINA
(Dedicated to Andres Segovia)

II

Allemande
  Courante
    Sarabande   *Written originally* } . . J. S. BACH
      Bourrée   *for the lute*
        Menuet
         Gavotte

INTERMISSION

III

Homage to Debussy . . . . DE FALLA

Madronos . . . . TORROBA
(Dedicated to Andres Segovia)

Mazurka . . . . PONCE
(Dedicated to Andres Segovia)

Danza . . . . GRANADOS

Torre bermeja . . . . ALBENIZ

Guitar Hauser

Tickets at Box Office:—$1.10 to $2.20

Management: METROPOLITAN MUSICAL BUREAU, INC.
DIVISION: COLUMBIA CONCERTS CORPORATION OF COLUMBIA BROADCASTING SYSTEM
113 West 57th Street • • • New York City

On the next page is the cover of the Sunday March 13, 1938 concert at the Civic Theatre in Chicago.

Chicago Concert Series

HARRY ZELZER CONCERT MANAGEMENT

Presents

ANDRES SEGOVIA

.CIVIC THEATRE ∾ CHICAGO

Sunday Afternoon ∾ March 13 ∾ at 3:30 P·M.

PROGRAM

I.

PRELUDE AND VARIATIONS ....F. Sor
(1778-1839)

SONATA ....Castelnuovo-Tedesco

Homage to Boccherini

Allegro con spirito
Andante quasi canzone
Tempo di menuetto
Vivo ed energico

Dedicated to Andres Segovia

DANCE ....Granados

(Continued on next page)

PROGRAM—Continued

II.

PRELUDE
ALLEMANDE
COURANTE
SARABANDE   Written originally for the lute ....J. S. Bach
BOURRÉE
MENUET
GAVOTTE

INTERMISSION

III.

MAZURKA ....Ponce

Dedicated to Andres Segovia

MADRONOS ....Torroba

Dedicated to Andres Segovia

(Continued on next page)

GRANADA
TORRE BERMEJA } ....Albeniz
SEVILLA

GUITAR HAUSER

Tour Direction: Metropolitan Musical Bureau, Inc.

Division of Columbia Concerts Corporation of Columbia Broadcasting System

Steinway Hall, 113 West 57th Street, New York City

Publicity—A. A. Fierro

CIVIC OPERA HOUSE AND CIVIC THEATRE

Telephone: DEArborn 9737   T. C. MacVICAR, Manager   Telephones in the Main Lobby

THE CIVIC OPERA HOUSE and the CIVIC THEATRE are available for concerts, lectures, public meetings, etc. For terms apply to Manager.

CHECK-ROOMS are provided in main lobby and balcony for the accommodation of patrons. Checking fee ten cents. The theatre will exercise ordinary diligence in safeguarding wraps, but assumes no responsibility in cases of loss.

Chicago Classic Guitar Society, 1229 Jarvis Avenue, Chicago, Illinois

The object of this society is the fostering of mutual understanding among persons who perform on, or are interested in, the classic guitar and its literature.

The society, through its members, furthers interest in the literature of such ancient masters as Guiliani, Sor, and Carulli, and of such modern masters as Tarrega, Segovia, Pujol, and Llobet.

The Chicago Classic Guitar Society aims to stimulate public and private interest in this type of music and its traditional performance.

Maestro Segovia was enchanting his audiences with his 1937 Hermann Hauser guitar, "The Guitar of our Epoch."

C X 20 — MONTE CARLO

Estación y Estudio: Humberto I Nº 4033. - U. T. E. 40-16-83
Administración: Palacio Salvo. 7º piso. - U. T. E. 8-29-87.

DOMINGO 10 DE ABRIL DE 1938
12. Orqs. sinfónicas. 12.30 M. Fleta.
13. O. Fresedo y E. Donato.
13.30 Claire Aronovici: concierto piano.
14. Diversiones musical. 14.30 P. Vargas
15. Sel. de "Rigoletto", de Verdi.
15.30 Sel. clásica. 16. Piano y órgano.
16.30 Tenores, barítonos. 17. V. Phrioda.
17.30 "Eleonore", obertura.
18. Orqs. sinfónicas. Ballet.
18.30 Pedro Vargas. 19. Bailables.
20.45 Julián García Rondeau, con. guitarra
21. Variedades selectas.
21.15 J. García Rondeau, conc. de guitarra.
21.30 Compañía Española de Alta Comedia Concepción Olona. Interpretación de la comedia en 3 actos y en verso de Luis Fernández Ardavin, "Rosa de Madrid".

LUNES 11
11. Canciones mejicanas.
11.15 "Para todas". Notas sociales y arte a cargo de Mirtha.
12. A. Vila. 12.30 Diversiones.
13. Sel. de operetas de E. Kalman.
13.30 Canzonettas y M. Chamlee.
13.45 Diario del éter "Tinta China", bajo la dirección de Abelardo Rondán.
16. Orquestas sinfónicas.
16.15 Juan D'Arienzo.
16.45 Ortiz Tirado. 17. Carlos Gardel.
17.30 Jazz sinfón. 18. Segovia, Montoya.
18.30 Otilia Alarma, recital de piano.
18.45 Selección clásica.
19.15 Orq. O. Fresedo y Dajos Bela.
20. Selección por Tito Schipa.
20.15 Héctor Genta, cantor nacional y sus guitarristas Hnos. Genta y Trías.
20.30 Variedades de la discoteca.
20.45 Héctor Genta, cantor nacional.
21. Variedades de la discoteca.
21.30 Trío Melódico: música selecta.
22. G. Martinelli.
22.15 Concertina inglesa: Prof. N. Yarovoff; piano Mastrángelo.
22.30 Trío melódico. 23. Bailables.

MARTES 12
11. Orq. San Francisco. 11.30 Valses.
12. Orquestas E. Donato y Víctor.
12.30 Divers. musicales. 13. C. Gardel.
13.30 Diario "Defensa de la Industria y del Comercio": Carlos M. Giuria.
13.45 Diario del éter "Tinta China".
16. Selección clásica (violín).
16.30 Fantasía húngara, de Liszt.
17. Sel. de ballet.
17.30 Marta Eggerth y N. Vallin.
17.45 Carmen Bonnet, estilista.
18. Foxtrot. 18.30 Canc. venezolanas.
19. Bailables. 20. Valses vieneses.
20.30 Diversiones musicales.
20.45 Trío Maurente-Schenini-Douglas.
21. Variedades de la discoteca.
21.15 Trío Maurente-Schenini-Douglas.
21.30 Charlas industriales: C. Soriano.
21.45 Noche lírica. Gran sel. de óperas.

MIERCOLES 13
11. Canciones paraguayas. 11.30 Típicas
12. Galli Curci y G. Danise.
12.30 Orq. Philadelphia. 13. Carlos Gardel
13.45 Diario del éter "Tinta China".
16. Selección clásica.
16.30 Aud. de piano por Rubinstein.
17. Max Rosen y M. Quiroga.
17.30 Sel. de "Bohème", de Puccini.

18.15 "Del rodar de las horas". Dir.: S. Dallegri, con Carmen Villanueva y R. Mastrangelo. 19. Bailables.
20. Tenor A. Crotis.
20.30 Sel. de "Noche de Verbena".
21. Operetas de S. Herbert.
21.30 Trío Melódico. Música selecta.
22.15 Prof. Yarovoff. Piano Mastrangelo.
22.30 Trío Melódico. 23. Sel. clásica.

JUEVES 14
11. Films. 11.30 L. Lamarque y A. Vila.
12. Valses y foxtrots. 12.30 C. Gardel.
13. Diario "Defensa de la Industria y del Comercio". Dir.: Giuria.
13.45 Diario del éter "Tinta China".
16. Selección clásica: orquestas.
16.30 Solos de piano: Brailowsky.
17. Lilian Harvey, M. Chevalier.
17.30 Beethoven y Bach.
18. Fresedo y Firpo. 18.30 Foxtrots.
19. Héctor González, cantor nacional, acompañado por R. Dioniggi.
19.30 Diversiones musicales.
20. Danzas húngaras.
20.30 Orquestas típicas y jazz.
20.45 J. García Rondeau: conc. de guitarra
21. Valses y fantasías.
21.15 J. García Rondeau.
21.30 Panoramas del mundo: Caballero Soriano.
21.45 Trío Melódico. Música selecta.
22. F. Chialapin.
22.30 Trío Melódico. 2º. Operetas inglesas.

VIERNES 15
11. Tríos típicos.
11.15 "Para todas". Notas sociales y arte a cargo de Mirtha.
12. Violoncello por P. Casals.
12.30 Canaro, E. Donato. 13. C. Gardel.
13.45 Diario del éter "Tinta China".
16. Música de cámara.
16.15 Orquestas sinfónicas.
17. Selección clásica.
17.30 Audición de bailables.
17.45 Carmen Bonnet, estilista.
18. Oberturas. 18.30 Música popular.
19. Jazz. 19.30 Música por rondallas.
20. O. Fresedo y P. Laurenz.
20.30 Diversiones musicales.
21. Selección de canciones populares.
21.15 Trío Maurente, Schenini, Douglas.
21.30 Variedades selectas.
21.45 Trío Maurente. Schenini, Douglas.
22. Programa de música española.
23. Selección clásica.

SABADO 16
11. Diversiones musicales.
11.30 L. Bori. 12.30 Foxtrots y rumbas.
12. Selección de operetas.
13. Audición Carlos Gardel.
13.30 Diario "Defensa de la Industria y del Comercio". Dir.: C. M. Giuria.
13.45 Diario del éter "Tinta China".
16. Selección clásica.
16.30 Violín por A. Spalding.
17. Audición de bailables.
18. "Del Rodar de las Horas".
18.45 Suplemento Artístico de "Notas Sociales y Arte", a cargo de Mirtha.
19.30 Bailables.
21.30 "El hombre que contesta todas las preguntas", por Caballero Soriano.
21.45 Trío Melódico: música selecta.
22. M. Talley. 22.30 Trío Melódico.
23. Programa de bailables.

Pedidos: 40-16-83

Here we see on CX 20 Monte Carlo radio in Montevideo on Monday April 11, 1938 Andrés Segovia and Ramon Montoya recordings being played at 6 PM. This is from the magazine entitled: Programa oficial de las estaciones uruguayas de radio (Official program of the Uruguayan Radio Stations) The Bold text listings are live events. Notice the request line phone number at the bottom of the page.

Empresa C.E.P.A.
CORRIENTES
y   PARANA

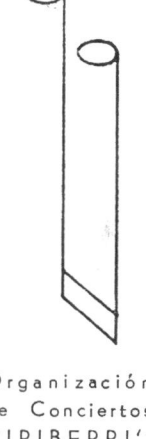

Organización
de Conciertos
"IRIBERRI"
Florida 431

ANDRES SEGOVIA

EMINENTE ARTISTA

PRIMER CONCIERTO

LUNES 8 DE MAYO DE 1939 a las 18.30 hs.

PLATEA 6 Pesos

Andrés Segovia's first concert at the Politeama Theater in Buenos Aires on Monday, May 8, 1939.

Programa

I

1. {
   Preámbulo
   Oliveras
   Madroños
   Albada
   Los Mayos
   Panorama
   } (dedicadas a A. Segovia) F. M. TORROBA

2. Tarantella CASTELNUOVO-TEDESCO
   (dedicada a A. Segovia)

3. Choros (¹) H. VILLA-LOBOS

(Obras para clavicordio cuyo espíritu
y técnica se adaptan a la guitarra)

II

1. {
   Aria "La Frescobalda" con variaciones. G. FRESCOBALDI
   Pasacaglia   (1583-1644)
   Corrente
   }

2. Minueto J. Ph. RAMEAU
   (1683-1764)

3. Sarabande y Gavotta A. SCARLATTI
   (de un manuscrito inédito del Conser- (1660-1725)
   vatorio de Nápoles)

(Obras escritas originalmente para
guitarra inspiradas en ritmos y melodías populares)

III

1. Hommage a Debussy M. de FALLA
   (escrito para guitarra)

2. Fandanguillo J. TURINA
   (dedicado a A. Segovia)

3. Guitarreo C. PEDRELL
   (dedicado a A. Segovia)

4. Torre Bermeja I. ALBENIZ

5. Leyenda id.

GUITARRA HAUSER

_____

(1) De un grupo de obras escritas para guitarra, doce de
las cuales están dedicadas a Segovia.

ORGANIZACION DE CONCIERTOS
"IRIBERRI"
FLORIDA 431   BUENOS AIRES

Monday, May 8, 1939 concert by Andrés Segovia, which has many pieces written for the guitar or those dedicated to him by Federico Moreno-Torroba, Mario Castelnuovo-Tedesco, Manuel de Falla, Joaquín Turina, and Carlos Pedrell. There is also the mention of his Hermann Hauser I guitar made in 1937, which Andrés described as "The Guitar of our Epoch". My colleague, Richard Bruné, says that Segovia mentioned the usage of Hauser I guitars at least from 1929.

Celestino Fernández 's back page advertisement in the Andrés Segovia Monday May 8, 1939 concert program, with the most noteworthy aspect being the Hermann Hauser I bass strings. Richard Bruné says Hermann Hauser III was unaware his grandfather had made these strings.

POLITEAMA ARGENTINO

Empresa C.E.P.A.
CORRIENTES
y PARANA

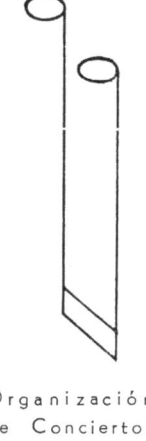

Organización
de Conciertos
"IRIBERRI"
Florida 431

ANDRES SEGOVIA

EMINENTE ARTISTA

SEGUNDO CONCIERTO

LUNES 15 DE MAYO DE 1939 a las 18.30 hs.

PLATEA 6 Pesos

Andrés Segovia's second concert at the Politeama Argentino on Monday May 15, 1939.

Programa

I

1. **Grupo de danzas escritas para guitarra.** R. DE VISEO

2. **Cuatro melodías populares catalanas** M. LLOBET

3. **Trópico** M. PONCE
   (Dedicado a Segovia)

II

1. **Preludio**
   Fuga
   Minuetto (Compuestas original-
   Burrée mente para laúd). J. S. BACH
   Sarabanda
   Gavotta y Musetta

III

1. **Capriccio Diabolico** M. CASTELNUOVO-TEDESCO
   (Homenaje a Paganini)

2. **Danza en Sol** GRANADOS

3. **Sevilla** ALBENIZ

GUITARRA HAUSER

ORGANIZACION DE CONCIERTOS
"IRIBERRI"
FLORIDA 431   BUENOS AIRES

This Monday May 15, 1939 concert has the inclusion of a Manuel Ponce piece *"Tropico"*, dedicated to Andrés Segovia.

Andrés Segovia concert in Montevideo at the Teatro Solis on Friday May 19, 1939. This program comes from the archive of U.S. Ambassador to Uruguay, William Dawson.

Segunda parte

PRELUDIO	....	J. S. Bach
FUGA	....	"
MINUETO	....	"
BOURREE	....	"
SARABANDE	....	"
GAVOTTE Y MUSETTE	....	"

(Compuestos originalmente para laud.

Tercera parte

TARANTELLA (Dedicada a A. Segovia)	....	M. Castelnuovo - Tedesco
FANDANGUILLO (Dedicado a A. Segovia)	....	J. Turina
DANZA EN SOL	....	Granados
TORRE BERMEJA	....	Albéniz

Andrés Segovia's 2nd set was a Lute suite by J. S. Bach. The 3rd set starts with 2 pieces dedicated to the maestro by Mario Castelnuovo-Tedesco and Joaquín Turina.

The other items on this page are also from the archive of U.S. Ambassador to Uruguay, William Dawson.

The translation of the unknown Montevideo newspaper item is:

Yesterday afternoon Mr. Andrés Segovia and his wife Mrs. Paquita Madriguera offered in their elegant residence on calle Massini in Pocitos, a reception in honor of a nucleus of their friends, which provoked a note of elucidation.

The friendly owners of the home and the daughters of Puig Madriguera gathered the invited to all classes of attention, what transpired was a reception in the most pleasant environment.

En lo de Segovia Madriguera —

El señor Andrés Segovia y su esposa señora Paquita Madriguera ofrecieron ayer de tarde en su elegante residencia de la calle Massini en Pocitos, una recepción en honor de un núcleo de sus amistades, lo que provocó una nota de relieves muy lucidos.

Los amables dueños de casa y sus hijas las señoritas de Puig Madriguera colmaron a sus invitados de toda clase de atenciones, lo que hizo que la recepción transcurriera en un ambiente de lo más agradable.

The calling cards of the maestro and his wife, a virtuoso pianist in her own right since the World War One period of time.

ANDRÉS SEGOVIA

PAQUITA MADRIGUERA DE SEGOVIA

Teatro SOLIS

TEMPORADA DE GRANDES CONCIERTOS 1939

LA ORGANIZACION
DE CONCIERTOS
IRIBERRI PRESENTA A

ANDRES
SEGOVIA

In Montevideo, the Friday May 26, 1939 concert, quite a varied repertoire for two concert a week apart. The image on the next page is 85% actual size.

Archive: Alfredo Escande

SEGUNDO CONCIERTO.

Viernes 26 de Mayo de 1939.
A las 18 y 45.

Programa

Primera parte

I - PREAMBULO .... F. Moreno Torroba
  Oliveras
  Madroños
  Aldaba
  Los Mayos
  Panorama
      (Dedicadas a A. Segovia)
II - SEVILLANA (Dedicada a A. Segovia) .... J. Turina
III - TROPICO (Dedicado a A. Segovia) .... M. Ponce

Segunda parte

I - CHACONA .... J. Pachelbel
                                   (1653 - 1706)
II - ZARABANDE .... A. Scarlatti
   GAVOTTE ....   "
                                   (1659 - 1725)
III - MINUETO EN LA .... J. Haydn
IV - CANZONETTA .... Mendelsohn

Tercera parte

I - CHOROS (Escrito para guitarra) ...... Villa - Lobos
II - IMPROVISACION (Dedicado a A. Segovia) ... C. Pedrell
III - GRANADA .... Albéniz
IV - LEYENDA ....   "

GUITARRA HAUSER

849

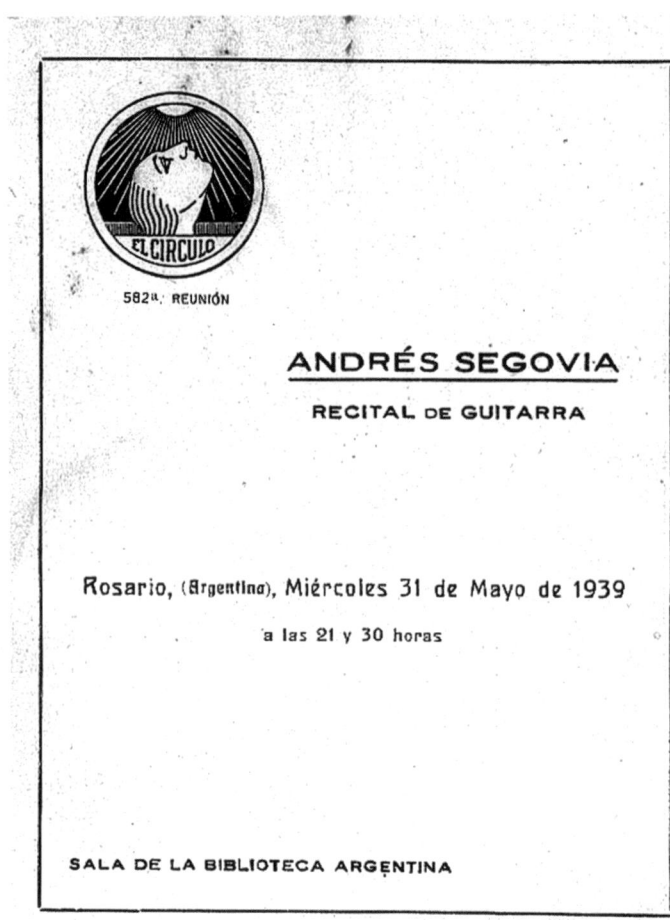

582ª REUNIÓN

ANDRÉS SEGOVIA

RECITAL DE GUITARRA

Rosario, (Argentina), Miércoles 31 de Mayo de 1939

a las 21 y 30 horas

SALA DE LA BIBLIOTECA ARGENTINA

The fifth Andrés Segovia concert in Rosario, Sante Fe Province on Wednesday May 31, 1939. The city of Rosario, Santa Fe Province was home to several guitar virtuosos, Bautista S. Almiron, his daughter Lalyta Delfina Almiron and the last Domingo Prat student creation and early 1940's RCA Victor recording artist, Nellie Ezcaray.

In a largely J. S. Bach concert on May 31, 1939 Andrés Segovia begins by playing a Lute suite. In the middle set the famous *Chaconne* of J. S. Bach. In his last recital set, he plays works by Fernando Sor and works dedicated to himself, such as Joaquín Turina's *"Fandanguillo"* and Mario Castelnuovo-Tedesco's *"Tarantella"*.

This is the world premier of the "*Concierto para guitarra y orquesta*" by Mario Castelnuovo-Tedesco, in Montevideo on Saturday, October 28, 1939.

This was the first Concierto for Guitar and Orchestra.

ESTUDIO AUDITORIO

Calle Andes esq. Mercedes. — Montevideo. — Teléfono de Boletería: 8 72 28

ESPECTACULOS ORGANIZADOS POR EL

S. O. D. R. E.

Temporada Oficial 1939

Sábado 28 de Octubre, a la hora 19

CONCIERTO SINFONICO

BAJO LA DIRECCION DEL MAESTRO

LAMBERTO BALDI

SOLISTA:

ANDRÉS SEGOVIA

GUITARRISTA

PROGRAMA

PRIMERA PARTE

VIVALDI — Concierto para cuatro violines y orquesta, Op. 3 N.º 10

Allegro   (1.a Audición)
Largo
Allegro

Solistas: Juan Fabbri, Armando Coirolo, Enrique Sebastiani y Eduardo Fazzio.

SEGUNDA PARTE

CASTELNUOVO TEDESCO - Concierto para guitarra y orquesta

(1.a Audición en el mundo)

Allegretto justo y un poco pomposo
Andantino a la romanza
Ritmico y caballeresco

Solista: ANDRÉS SEGOVIA

TERCERA PARTE

RIMSKY KORSAKOFF — Suite "Le Coq D'or"

PRECIOS DE LAS LOCALIDADES

Palcos sin entradas	$ 4.00
Platea	» 2.00
Tertulia 1.a fila	» 2.00
Tertulia, otras filas	» 1.50
Entrada a Palco	» 1.50
Galería Baja 1.a fila, numerada, mixta.	» 1.00
Galería Baja otras filas, numerada, mixta	» 0.80
Galería Baja sin numerar mixta	» 0.40
Galería Alta 1 a fila, numerada, mixta	» 1.00
Galería Alta otras filas, numerada, mixta	» 0.80
Galería Alta sin numerar, mixta	» 0.40

Casa Romano __ Sierra 1919

This San Juan, Puerto Rico Andrés Segovia concert held in the Auditorium of the University of Puerto Rico is from January 30, 1940. The cover sketch by Helmut Ruhermann had been a staple of concert program covers for 20 years.

ANDRES SEGOVIA

El célebre guitarrista español Andrés Segovia nació en Linares, provincia de Jaén, el 18 de Febrero de 1894, demostrando desde su infancia excepcionales disposiciones para el instrumento que había de cultivar con hondo fervor consagrándole todos sus esfuerzos y afanes. Trasladado a Granada dió en el Círculo Artístico de esa ciudad su primer concierto a los 14 años, llamando poderosamente la atención sus raras facultades. En Barcelona sentó los primeros jalones de su reputación que más tarde había de cristalizar en sólida fama universal. Su temperamento inquieto y emprendedor hizo que recorriese muy pronto casi todas las provincias españolas, dando innumerables conciertos y consolidando luego su prestigio en Madrid. Trasladóse enseguida a América siendo aclamado por los públicos de casi todo el continente. En abril de 1924 dió un concierto en la Sala del Conservatorio de París cuyo público le acogió con entusiasmo y seguidamente recorrió Alemania, Austria, Bélgica, Holanda, Inglaterra, Suiza, Hungría, Checoeslovaquia, Suecia, Noruega, Dinamarca, Rusia, Italia y Estados Unidos.

Aunque realizó Segovia sus comienzos en la guitarra bajo la dirección de un modesto cultor de este instrumento, el desenvolvimiento de su técnica puede considerarse como uno de los pocos casos autodidácticos. En su arte se destaca la manera especial y vehemente cómo hace cantar la guitarra y una interpretación pasional y muy personal, inconfundible.

Los autores más diversos figuran en su repertorio. Al nombre de Sor, de quien Segovia casi nunca prescinde en la confección de sus programas, se juntan los de Tárrega, Coste, etc., y además los de Bach, Albéniz, Granados y otros de los que ejecuta transcripciones, realizadas por él en su mayor parte.

En los últimos tiempos de consolidación de su fama, músicos modernos de prestigio, tales como Turina, Moreno Torroba, Nin, Manén, Roussel, Jacques Ibert, Cyril Scott, Ponce, Brocqua, Bréville, Migot, Tansman, Respighi, Castelnuovo-Tedesco, Hindemith, Carlos Perell, han compuesto o están componiendo para Segovia obras para guitarra. El renacimiento que en estos últimos años se observa en este instrumento, es debido en gran parte a Segovia, quien en sus peregrinaciones por todo el mundo, puede decirse, ha logrado formar ambiente, con su arte y actividad considerable, elevando la guitarra al nivel de estima y consideración que merece como instrumento de concierto.

The translation of the biography of the maestro is:

"The celebrated Spanish guitarist Andrés Segovia was born in Linares, in the province of Jaen, on the 18th of February of 1894 (sic February 21,1893), demonstrating since his infancy an exceptional disposition for the instrument that he has cultivated with a deep fervor consecreting all of his efforts and worldly labors. Having moved to Granada he gave his first concert in the *Circulo Artistico* in that city at the age of 14, powerfully drawing attention to his rare abilities. In Barcelona, he felt the first tugs of his reputation that later were to crystallize in solid universal fame. His restless and enterprising temperament made such that he was to be touring very soon almost all the Spanish provinces, giving innumerable concerts and consolidating his prestige in Madrid afterward. He then traveled to the American continent being acclaimed by the public of almost all the continents. In April of 1924 he gave a concert in Paris in the Sala de Conservatoire whose public received him with enthusiasm and then he toured Germany, Austria, Belgium, Holland, England, Switzerland, Hungary, Czechoslovakia, Sweden, Norway, Denmark, Russia, Italy and the United States.

854

Although Segovia made his outset on the guitar under the direction of a modest player of this instrument, the unfolding of his technique can be considered as one of the few selves taught cases. In his art he distinguishes the special and vehement manner as making the guitar sing and a passionate and very personal interpretation, unmistakable.

The most diverse authors have a place in his repertoire. To the name Sor, of whom Segovia almost never leaves out in the confection of his programs, he joins those of Tárrega, Coste, etc. and besides those of Bach, Albeniz, Granados and others of them, which he plays transcriptions for the most part made by him.

In the latest times of the consolidation of his fame, modern musicians of prestige, such as Turina, Moreno Torroba, Nin, Manén, Roussel, Jacques Ibert, Cyril Scott, Ponce, Broqua, Bréville, Migot, Tansman, Respighi, Castelnuovo-Tedesco, Hindemith, Carlos Pedrell, have composed or are composing works for the guitar for Segovia. The renaissance of which in those last few years are observed on this instrument, are due in a great part to Segovia, whom in his foreign travels all around the world, it can be said, has succeeded to form an environment, with his art and considerable activity, elevating the guitar to a level of esteem and consideration it deserves as a concert instrument."

These repostioned images from the 20-page concert program were mixed among advertisements and lists of dozens of socios, foreign and domestic. The *Preludio y Danza* by Moreno-Torroba, the *Fandanguillo* by Turina, and the *Guitarreo* by Pedrell were pieces composed and dedicated to Segovia.

Mi entrevista con Andrés Segovia

Por RAFAEL MONTAÑEZ

Andrés Segovia, el gran guitarrista que nos honra con su visita al país.

The photo caption says: "Andrés Segovia, the great guitarist who honors us with a visit to the country."

The journalist Rafael Montañez writes his impressions about the maestro for the San Juan Puerto Rico newspaper *"El Mundo"* on Tuesday, January 30, 1940. Though the title of the article translates to "My interview with Andrés Segovia", there is only a quote at the end.

Translation of the interview by Rafael Montañez with Andrés Segovia for the *El Mundo,* San Juan, Puerto Rico newspaper on Tuesday, January 30, 1940.

"My interview with Andrés Segovia"

"Of Andrés Segovia I have already said — because the unanimous critics of all the towns which had the privilege to hear his miraculous performances let me know, because having studied with meditative analysis the harmony and known structure of many of the transcriptions that for the 6 course lyre he might make of the works by Johann Sebastian Bach, by Domenico Scarlatti, by Frederic Händel; because I know the homage that they honor his genius they had rendered Manuel de Falla, Joaquín Turina, Castelnuovo-Tedesco, Manuel Ponce, Jacques Ibert, Cyril Scott and other celebrated musicians, contemporary composers, writing works for his guitar that is talent of emotion and knowledge; because absorbed in thought before the perfection, the profundity and the beauty of his interpretations I have heard, indefatigably, with sheet music in hand, all of the phonographic transcriptions the maestro has recorded — of Andrés Segovia I've already said he was an "eminent musician" exalter of the guitar to a new level of artistic hierarchy; a learned diver of musical treasures of all times for incorporating them to the unnamed grandeur of his profound and beautiful art; genial artist and incomparable interpreter, by the cause of which the concepts "Guitar" and "Johann Sebastian Bach" have formed the most bold and narrow synonym.

Today we have in front of us the man to which only a facet of his artistic personality might confer the hallowed cape. Andrés Segovia the interpreter, the austere and solemn, interpreter of the profound grandure and essential beauty of Juan Sebastian Bach has achieved the heights that parallel by identical routes, Wanda Landowska has been climbing nobly on her very old *clavecin.* Andrés Segovia, the erudite musician, the knowledgeable investigator, the alchemist of the sonorous transfigurations, has stirred in the centennial books in folio form, has picked up the eternal gold of the old chests, he has blown the breath of his genius and has enriched with jewels of inestimable value the treasure that is already the musical literature of today's guitar. An equal prestige sounded by the eminent violinist Fritz Kreisler, who tricked the critics attributing to Couperin and Pugnani works that he himself wrote. Andrés Segovia, the poetic expounder, the magician of the diamond like sonorities, knows the purity of the timbres that the tactile caress of his meaty fingers start up the six strings of the harmonious trunk like no one, makes sob, sigh, groan or sing. Purity, transparency, velvet like polyphony, as he extracts them also from the egregious instrument like another of his compatriots, the cellist, Pablo Casals.

But I, might already know Andrés Segovia in all those aspects, as perhaps all my readers know for whom by chance it's a redundant result by all that is written being well known, I have approached Andrés Segovia in another admiring attitude. Of an equal manner as a student of philology of the Spanish language can't evoke the figure of the knowledgeable investigator *don* Ramon Menéndez Pidal without rushing to his mind, by association obliged of ideas, the prints of the Romancer, of the Archprelate, of Alfonso X el Sabio, for me to approach Andrés Segovia more than in a *"Fugue"* by Bach, a *"Sonata"* by Scarlatti, or a *"Minuet"* by Haydn, I have thought in the ingenuous beauty of a *"Pavan"* of Luys de Milan, in a *"Galliard"* by Gaspar Sanz or in a *"Suite"* by Robert de Visée. And I have followed a route that they drew up to Dionisio Aguado and Fernando Sor's instrument and I have evoked the impulsive tug that Francisco Tárrega would print. How far is the guitar of Andrés Segovia from the limitations of the vihuelists and the lutenists of antiquity! How far he is from de Fuenllana, de Valderrabano, from Luis de Narvaez, from Alonso de Mudarra, from Carulli, from Giuliani, from Napoléon Coste!

But not by that is it any less beautiful, the work that serves as a pedestal to the structure that today has as a mountain peak a *"Chaconne"* by Bach, the *"Variaciones a través de los siglos"* by Castelnuovo-Tedesco, the creations by Tansman, by Turina, by Ponce and by Villa-Lobos.

858

The work of Andrés Segovia has been to expand the vicinity of the guitar by luck that doesn't make its peak in Spain; but universalizes it. Honored in the profundities of the past, baptized in the pristine sources of the classicism: Bach, Haendel, Haydn, Mozart, Beethoven, Schubert, Schumann, Mendelssohn, and César Franck. To be projecting in this hour, makes the sacrament with the mystical de Falla, by Turina, by Ponce, by Manén, by Salazar, by Glazunov.

The Spanish hour of Isaac Albéniz, of Enrique Granados, of their own Tárrega, that has had very fervent cultivators in the present such as Miguel Llobet, Emilio Pujol, Fortea, Robledo, Sainz de la Maza, would have Andrés Segovia as its top interpreter. That Spanish music that penetrates such deep richeness, such vast beauties; that music that Rimski-Korsakof and Glazunov love, that inspires Ravel, Debussy, and Lalo, has as a heralding town crier and as a glorifier to the guitarist from Jaen. A basic part of his concert programs constitutes a series of works of genuine Iberian character and by Spanish authors; pieces of the luminous works of Isaac Albéniz, compositions by Sor, Moreno Torroba, Joaquín Malats; and all of it of the purest regional flavor and curd of this only module that speaks of its racial ancestry; saturated of those emotional and plaintive ayes that are... "the fatal ends of the Morro race", that Machado said.

We are in the waiting hours before attending one of his concerts. The spirit is temperate for the magnificent and transcendental occasion. We have already done the labor of reviewing the possible polyphonic richness that his miraculous guitar grants us. The ear is covetous for the sonorous captivation of the polychromed well-aimed shades of color of his interpretations that have the bewitching of a seductive singer. The spirit is alert, the intuition is syntonized, for receiving all the range of emotion that the tremolous strings of his lyre send into the ether; for the quiet and tenuous friction that the vague sigh gets mixed in; for the dizzy torrent that it unties in the crushing swell. The will is easily influenced to the subordination of the genius, susceptible to the fluid order, to the aeolian spell of his thrilling messages.

Today I have shaken the friendly hand of the man whose grandeur I have reverently admired for many years. A few initial words and it is evident that to help me even get a glimpse of his emotional sensibility. We spoke of music, and soon we pronounced the name of Johann Sebastian Bach. He knows him fully. I know him vaguely. As soon as the conversation had taken off on this theme. "Music is the most difficult flower of our civilization", he said paraphrasing I don't know what thinker, Shakespeare, Cervantes, Unamuno, Stefan Zweig, that parade among the personalities of our conversation. All the phrases of the artist calibrate the grandeur, the knowledge, the serenity, the simpleness, the generosity and the deep human sense of Andrés Segovia, whose cordial and friendly hand I had the privilege to shake today."

Sociedad Musical Daniel

AÑO XXXI

Presidente: Ernesto de Quesada

Buenos Aires - Río de Janeiro - Sao Paulo - Montevideo - Santiago de Chile - Valparaíso - La Paz - Lima - Quito - Bogotá - Panamá - Caracas - Port of Spain - Kingston - Curaçao - Puerto Rico - Ciudad Trujillo, R. D. - Habana - San José, C. R. - San Salvador - Guatemala - Lisboa - Porto - Barcelona - Madrid — Manila (Filipinas) - China - Japón - Monterrey - México, D. F.

Unico Recital de Guitarra
Andrés Segovia

Viernes 1º de marzo de 1940

a las

8 y 30 p. m.

en el

Teatro Nacional

Andrés Segovia concert in San José, Costa Rica on Friday March 1, 1940 at the Teatro Nacional.

La sonoridad de la guitarra es infinitamente más blanda y tenue que la del piano; menos penetrante que la del violín; más emotiva y suave que la del arpa.

Para percibir plenamente estas vivas cualidades espirituales del más bello de los instrumentos, se requiere un absoluto

SILENCIO

En un ambiente quieto y callado, se destaca su delicado sonido, puro y limpio, escuchándose las obras más claramente y el juego de matices, en que se revela la calidad del artista, no queda obscurecido por los mil ruidos flotantes de un auditorio inatento y distraído. Se ruega en beneficio de las personas hoy congregadas para oír a ANDRES SEGOVIA un riguroso

SILENCIO

En el espacio de obra a obra puede el auditorio descansar de la tensión que la naturaleza de la guitarra le demanda y seguir después el itinerario espiritual del concierto. Pero mientras toca el Artista el mismo auditorio se percatará de que cualquier pequeño movimiento interrumpe la coordinación musical de la obra y se anega la bella sonoridad de la guitarra en una atmósfera falta de transparencia.

Por todo lo dicho y deseando dar al concierto verdadera eficacia emotiva, se ruega un perfecto y unánime

SILENCIO

SOCIEDAD MUSICAL DANIEL

Andrés Segovia's quest for silence on behalf of the beautiful Guitar is revealed here.

Translation of the previous page:

The sonority of the guitar is infinitely blander and faint than that of the piano; it penetrates less than the violin; and is more emotive and smooth than a harp.

To fully perceive these live spiritual qualities of the most beautiful of the instruments, it requires absolute

SILENCE

In a quiet and hush environment, one can distinguish its delicate sound, pure and clean, to be listening to the works more clearly and the set of tones, in which it reveals the quality of the artist, it doesn't remain obscured by the thousand floating noises of an inattentive and distracted auditorium. One is begged for a rigorous SILENCE for the benefit of the persons congregated here today to hear ANDRÉS SEGOVIA.

In the space between each work the audience can relax from the tension which the nature of the guitar demands and afterward follow the spiritual itinerary of the concert. But while the Artist is performing the same audience will be able to perceive whatever small movement shall interrupt the musical coordination of the work and drown out the beautiful sonority of the guitar in an atmosphere that lacks transparency.

By all that has been said and desiring to give the concert true emotive efficiency, we beg for a perfect and unanimous SILENCE.

Sociedad Musical Daniel

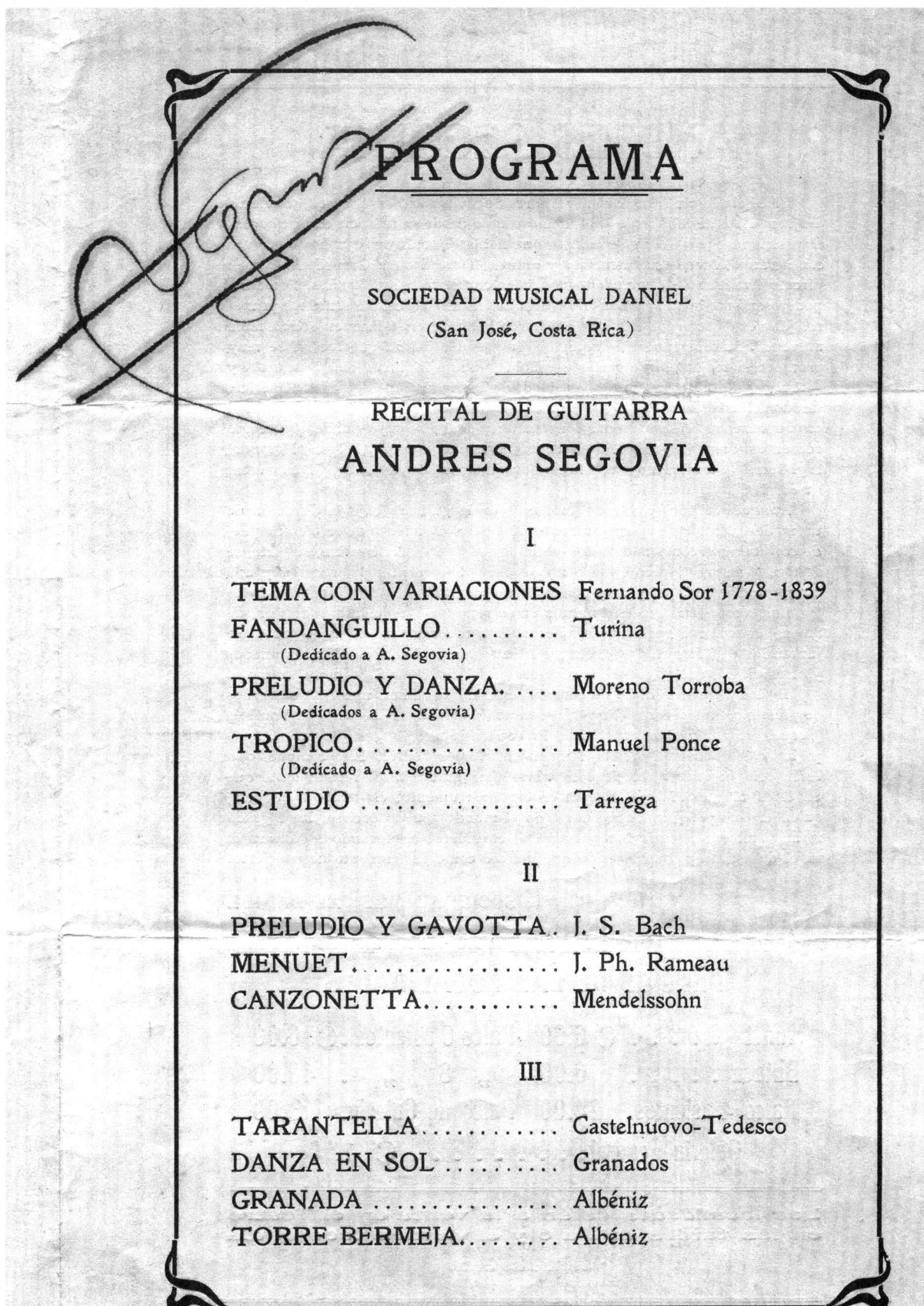

PROGRAMA

SOCIEDAD MUSICAL DANIEL
(San José, Costa Rica)

RECITAL DE GUITARRA
ANDRES SEGOVIA

I

TEMA CON VARIACIONES	Fernando Sor 1778-1839
FANDANGUILLO..........	Turina
(Dedicado a A. Segovia)	
PRELUDIO Y DANZA.	Moreno Torroba
(Dedicados a A. Segovia)	
TROPICO.	Manuel Ponce
(Dedicado a A. Segovia)	
ESTUDIO	Tarrega

II

PRELUDIO Y GAVOTTA.	J. S. Bach
MENUET.................	J. Ph. Rameau
CANZONETTA...........	Mendelssohn

III

TARANTELLA............	Castelnuovo-Tedesco
DANZA EN SOL	Granados
GRANADA	Albéniz
TORRE BERMEJA........	Albéniz

The pieces by Turina, Moreno Torroba and Ponce are dedicated to maestro Andrés Segovia.

ANDRES SEGOVIA

El célebre guitarrista español Andrés Segovia nació en Linares, provincia de Jaen, el 18 de febrero de 1894, demostrando desde su infancia excepcionales disposiciones para el instrumento que había de cultivar con hondo fervor consagrándole todos sus esfuerzos y afanes. Trasladado a Granada dió en el Círculo Artístico de esa ciudad su primer concierto a los 14 años, llamando poderosamente la atención sus raras facultades. En Barcelona sentó los primeros jalones de su reputación que más tarde había de cristalizar en sólida fama universal. Su temperamento inquieto y emprendedor hizo que recorriese muy pronto casi todas las provincias españolas, dando innumerables conciertos y consolidando luego su prestigio en Madrid. Trasladóse en seguida a América, siendo aclamado por los públicos de casi todo el Continente. En abril de 1924 dió un concierto en la Sala del Conservatorio de París cuyo público le acogió con entusiasmo, y seguidamente recorrió Alemania, Austria, Bélgica, Holanda, Inglaterra, Suiza, Hungría, Checoeslovaquia, Suecia, Noruega, Dinamarca, Rusia, Italia y Estados Unidos.

Aunque realizó Segovia sus comienzos en la guitarra bajo la dirección de un modesto cultor de ese instrumento, el desenvolvimiento de su técnica puede considerarse como uno de los pocos casos autodidácticos. En su arte se destaca la manera especial y vehemente como hace cantar la guitarra y una interpretación pasional y muy personal, inconfundible.

Los autores más diversos figuran en su repertorio. Al nombre de Sor, de quien Segovia casi nunca prescinde en la confección de sus programas, se juntan los de Tárrega, Coste, etc., y además los de Bach, Albéniz, Granados y otros, de los que ejecuta transcripciones, realizadas por él en su mayor parte.

En los últimos tiempos de consolidación de su fama, músicos modernos de prestigio, tales como Turina, Moreno, Torroba, Nin, Manén, Roussel, Jacques, Ibert, Cyril, Scott, Ponce, Brocqua, Bréville, Migot, Tansman, Respighi, Castelnuovo - Tedesco, Hindemith, Carlos Pedrel, han compuesto o están componiendo, para Segovia, obras para guitarra. El renacimiento que en estos últimos años se observa en este instrumento, es debido a Segovia, quien en sus peregrinaciones por todo el mundo, puede decirse, ha logrado formar ambiente, con su arte y actividad considerable, elevando la guitarra al nivel de estima y consideración que merece como instrumento de concierto.

SOCIEDAD MUSICAL DANIEL

PRECIOS DE LAS LOCALIDADES

Luneta	₡ 6.00	Palco 6 asientos	₡ 36.00
Butaca	6.00	„ 8 „	48.00
Palco 4 asientos	24.00	Palco de Galería	3.00
Galería General			₡ 1.50

Las localidades están a la venta en el Teatro en las tardes de 1 a 6 y el viernes todo el día

Vestido de calle

Andrés Segovia's biography at this time by Sociedad Musical Daniel. The translation is on the following page. At the very bottom of this page is the dress code: Streetclothes.

864

Andrés Segovia

The celebrated Spanish guitarist Andrés Segovia was born in the province of Jaen on February 18, 1894, (sic February 21, 1893) demonstrating since his infancy, exceptional disposition for the instrument which he has been cultivating with fervor consecrating all of his efforts and desires. Moving to Granada he gave in the *Circulo Artistico* of that city his first concert at the 14 years of age, powerfully calling the attention to his rare facilities. In Barcelona he established the first marks of his reputation which later would crystallize the solid universal fame. With his anxious temperament and enterprising manner, he soon covered almost all of the Spanish provinces, giving innumerable concerts and then consolidating his prestige in Madrid. He then moved to South America and became acclaimed in almost of the continent. In April of 1924, he gave a concert in the Sala del Conservatoire de Paris, whose public welcomed him with enthusiasm and right away he traveled to Germany, Austria, Belgium, Holland, England, Switzerland, Hungary, Czechoslovakia, Sweden, Norway, Denmark, Russia, Italy and the United States.

Although Segovia made his beginning on the guitar under the direction of a modest player of the guitar, the development of his technique can be said to be one of the few self-taught cases. In distinguishing the special and vehement manner such as making the guitar sing and a passionate and very personal interpretation, unmistakable.

The most diverse authors make up his repertoire. To the name of Sor, of whom Segovia almost never does without in the preparation of his program, those of Tárrega, Coste, etc., and besides those of Bach, Albeniz, Granados and others, of those that he performs transcriptions, made for the most part by himself.

In the latest times of the consolidation of his fame, modern musicians of prestige, such as, Turina, Moreno Torroba, Nin, Manén, Roussel, Jacques Ibert, Cyril Scott, Ponce, Bréville, Migot, Tansman, Respighi, Castelnuovo-Tedesco and Carlos Pedrell, have composed or are composing works for the guitar for Segovia. The renaissance which in these latest years is observed on this instrument, is due to Segovia, who in his pilgrimages all over the world, it can be said, has achieved to form an environment, with his art and considerable activity, elevating the guitar to a level of esteem and consideration which it deserves as a concert instrument.

Sociedad Musical Daniel

GUITARRA

ANDRES SEGOVIA

AA	198	Nocturno	Torroba
		Serenata	Malats
AB	273	Fandanguillo	Turina
		Trémulo Estudio	Tárrega

Listing of Andrés Segovia 78 RPM discs from the June 1941 Odeon Catalogo General de Discos La Voz de su Amo, Odeon y Regal. The *tremolo Estudio* is actually Francisco Tárrega's *Recuerdos de la Alhambra* and was recorded in London on May 20, 1927.

ANDRES SEGOVIA
E M I N E N T E   A R T I S T A

EN EL

TEATRO ODEON

El gran guitarrista español antes de partir para su gira Sud Americana ha resuelto ofrecer una corta serie de audiciones en el ODEON iniciándolas

EL DOMINGO 27 DE JULIO A LAS 18.30 Hs.

ORGANIZACION DE CONCIERTOS ''IRIBERRI'', FLORIDA 431, BUENOS AIRES

Andrés Segovia's first concert at the Teatro Odeon on Sunday July 27, 1941.

Translation:
"Andrés Segovia the eminent artist in the Teatro Odeon. The great Spanish guitarist, before leaving for a South American tour, has decided to offer a short series of performances in the Odeon, initiating them on Sunday July 27 at 6:30PM.

ORGANIZACION
DE CONCIERTOS
"IRIBERRI"

ANDRES SEGOVIA
eminente ARTISTA

SEGUNDO RECITAL

SABADO 2 DE AGOSTO DE 1941
A LAS 18.30 HORAS

ODEON

EMPRESA: JOSE P. CARAMBAT
ESMERALDA 367 - U. T. 31-3633

Andrés Segovia's second concert at the Teatro Odeon on Saturday August 2, 1941.

PROGRAMA

·I

Romancesca. (*) (Para vihuela).	ALONSO DE MUDARRA (1541)
Cuatro pequeñas danzas. (Para guitarra).	R. DE VISEO (1650-1725)
Aria la Frescobalda.	G. FRESCOBALDI (1583-1644)
Zarabanda.	HAENDEL (1685-1749)
Menuet.	J. PH. RAMEAU (1683-1746)

II

Prelude.		
Allemande.		
Sarabande.	(Originalmente compuesta para laud).	J. S. BACH
Bourrée		
Menuet.		
Gavotte.		

III

Capriccio (Omaggio a Paganini). (Dedicado a A. Segovia).	CASTELNUOVO TEDESCO
Mazurca. (Dedicada a A. Segovia).	M. PONCE
Danza.	E. GRANADOS
Torre Bermeja.	I. ALBENIZ

GUITARRA HAUSER

(*) Notación moderna, por A. Segovia.

In this recital Andrés Segovia plays an opening set of Renaissance and Baroque works, to be followed by a Lute suite by J. S. Bach, and finishing with works that are dedicated to him by Mario Castelnuovo-Tedesco (*Capriccio "Diabolico"*-Homage to Paganini) and Manuel Ponce, as well as immortal works of three Spanish composers: the late Enrique Granados and Isaac Albeniz, as well as Manuel de Falla. Here he mentions his usage of the Hermann Hauser I guitar, which could be found in number for sale at Celestino Fernández 's music store.

868

In the *"Noticiario Ricordi"* of September 1941, *Año* 5, No. 9, in the Conciertos section this mention of a concert that Andrés Segovia had made the previous month was listed. The translation reads: "The 15th of August, Andrés Segovia offered in the Teatro Odeon a new performance of works for the guitar, that were appreciated by the numerous public attending, which awarded his interpretations of pages of Mozart, Haydn, Mendelssohn, Moreno Torroba, Turina and of the Concierto en Re by Castelnuovo-Tedesco, for guitar and piano, backed by Paquita Madriguera de Segovia, with great applause."

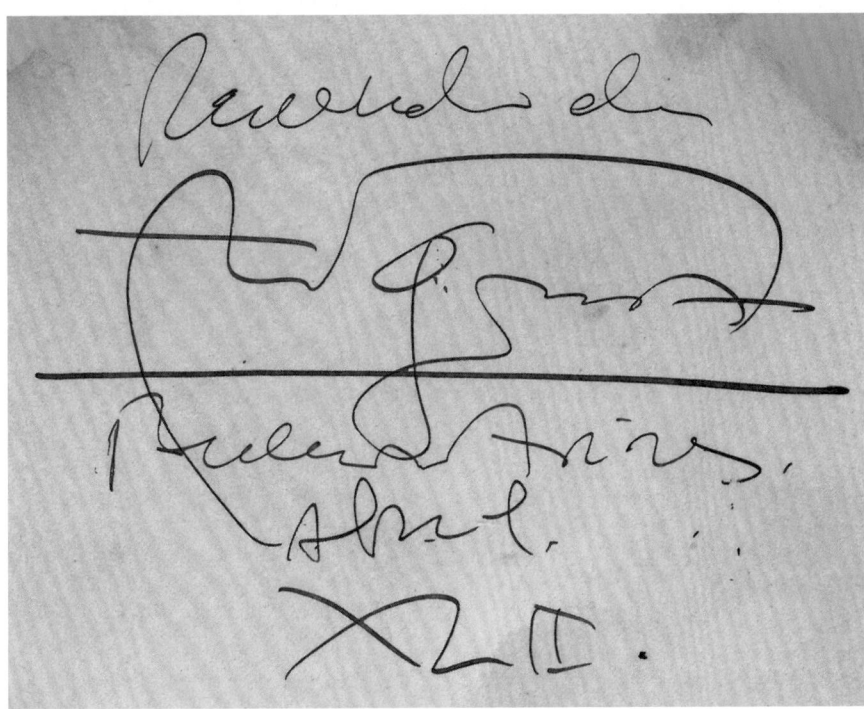

An undedicated Andrés Segovia autograph from April 1942 signed in Buenos Aires to a fan.

ESTUDIO AUDITORIO

Calle ANDES esq. Mercedes — MONTEVIDEO — Teléfono de Boletería: 8 72 28

ESPECTACULOS ORGANIZADOS POR EL

S. O. D. R. E.

Temporada Oficial

1941

Sábado 4 de Octubre, a la hora 18 y 33

CONCIERTO SINFONICO

BAJO LA DIRECCION DEL MAESTRO

MANUEL PONCE

SOLISTA:

ANDRES SEGOVIA

(GUITARRA)

———— PROGRAMA ————

— I —

PONCE MANUEL — **PEQUEÑA SUITE EN ESTILO ANTIGUO**

Preludio

Canon

Pavana

Fughetta

— II —

PONCE MANUEL — **CONCERTO DEL SUR para Guitarra y Orquesta**

Allegro moderato ed espressivo

Andante

Allegro moderato e festivo

(Primera audición en el mundo)

SOLISTA: **ANDRES SEGOVIA**

Dirige el Maestro BALDI

— III —

PONCE MANUEL — **POEMA ELEGIACO**

»   »   — **CHAPULTEPEC** - (Tres bocetos sinfónicos)

Primavera en el bosque

Nocturno romántico

Canto y Danza

Imp. A. B. C.

Manuel Ponce and Andrés Segovia debut concert in Montevideo at the S.O.D.R.E. on Saturday October 4, 1941. Archive: U.S. Ambassador to Uruguay, William Dawson.

Manuel Ponce

La presencia en Montevideo del maestro Manuel M. Ponce, tiene una gran trascendencia para nuestra cultura artística, por tratarse de uno de los creadores, en el dominio de la música, más sólidos y renombrados del Continente Americano.

Nació en Fresnillo, Estado de Zacatecas (México) el 8 de Diciembre de 1886. Hizo sus primeros estudios musicales en la Capital de México. Durante cuatro años (1904 a 1908) estudió el piano en el Conservatorio Stern de Berlín, con el profesor Martin Krause. También vivió algún tiempo en Bolonia, Italia, donde estudió composición con el maestro Enrico Bossi.

A su regreso de Europa se dedica al profesorado y desempeña en el Conservatorio Nacional de Música de México las cátedras de piano, composición e Historia de la Música. En 1915 visita la Habana y Nueva York, dando a conocer en ambas ciudades, con gran aplauso de la crítica y el público, su producción de entonces. Regresa a México en Julio de 1918 y acepta la dirección de la Orquesta Sinfónica Nacional que el Ministerio de Educación le ofrece. Se traslada a París en 1925 donde permanece nueve años; traba allí conocimientos, fecundos para su arte, con los grandes maestros franceses y extranjeros de aquel momento, y con críticos, estetas y literatos. Entre sus amistades más fervorosas ha de señalarse la de Pau' Dukas en cuya convivencia artística el espíritu de Manuel Ponce se acendra y enriquece. Su producción es, desde entonces, copiosísima.

Otro de sus fieles amigos, Andrés Segovia, da origen a que consagre también gran parte de su talento a la guitarra. En efecto, para este bello instrumento, escribe numerosas composiciones de formas y estilos diversos, las cuales, por su noble calidad, honran no sólo a la literatura especial de la guitarra, sino, por encima de cualquier instrumento, a la propia Música.

Su participación en el Festival Ibero-Americano de Barcelona atrae particularmente hacia él la admiración de los maestros españoles y en general el aprecio personal de cuantos colegas a él se acercan y le tratan.

Aproximadamente en la misma época funda en París la Gaceta Musical, en lengua española y cuenta en seguida para colaborar en su redacción con los nombres prestigiosos de Madariaga, Paul Dukas, Heri Prunieres, Mark Pincherle, Henri de Curzon, Marguerite D'Harcourt, Aloys Mooser, Joaquín Turina, etc., etc.

Durante su permanencia en París, fué objeto de frecuentes homenajes. El maestro Dukas organizó, con este carácter, una audición de obras del maestro Ponce y la Sociedad Internacional de Música presidida por Dukas y Ravel, acogió e hizo interpretar uno de sus Cuartetos.

En fin, actualmente desempeña la cátedra de folklore en la Universidad de México y es además Inspector de Jardines de Niños.

Damos a continuación una breve reseña de sus principales obras:

PIANO: 11 Miniaturas, 2 Rapsodias mexicanas, 14 Trozos románticos, 23 Mazurkas, 5 Hojas de Album, Preludio y Fuga sobre un tema de Bach, 10 Canciones mexicanas, 4 Estudios de Concierto, Evocaciones, 4 Preludios encadenados, 4 Piezas, Rapsodia Cubana, Scherzo mexicano, 2 Estudios, 2 Sonatas, Idilio mexicano, para dos pianos, etc.

CANTO Y PIANO: 50 Canciones populares mexicanas, Aleluya, Dos Cantos de Tagore, Granada, Le Mort, 6 Poemas arcaicos, 3 Poemas de Brull, 3 Poemas de González Martínez, 2 Poemas de Urbina, 5 Poemas de Icaza, 4 Poémes Chinois, (F. Toussaint), 50 coros para jardines de niños.

MUSICA DE CAMARA: Sonata para violín y piano, Sonata para chelo y piano, Sonata para violín y viola, Trío para piano, violín y chelo, Cuarteto (Miniaturas), Cuarteto de cuerdas.

ORQUESTA: Chapultepec (3 bocetos sinfónicos), Suite en estilo antiguo, Poema elegíaco, Ferial (Divertimiento sinfónico), Estampas nocturnas, Concierto para piano y orquesta, Concierto para guitarra y orquesta.

ORGANO: Preludio fugado, 3 piezas sobre un coral, 4 Corales (sobre un tema de Bach).

GUITARRA SOLA: Sonata en La Mayor, Sonata Clásica, Sonata en Re Menor, Sonata romántica, Sonatina Meridional, 22 Variaciones y Fuga sobre "Folías", Preludio en Si Menor, Estudio en Re Menor, Tres canciones mexicanas, 12 Preludios, Mazurka, Vals, Trópico y Rumba, Preludio y Final en Re Menor.

Manuel Ponce and Andrés Segovia had a friendship since the 1920's when they met. The translation of the biography of the composer is on the next page.

Manuel Ponce

The presence in Montevideo of Manuel Ponce has a great transcendence for our artistic culture, by being one of the creators, in the dominion of music, most solid and renowned of the American Continent.

He was born in Fresnillo, Zacatecas on December 8, 1886. His first musical studies were made in the capital of Mexico. For duration of four years (1904-1908) he studied piano in the Conservatory Stern of Berlin, with Professor Martin Krause. He also lived for some time in Bologna, Italy, where he studied composition with the maestro Enrico Bossi.

When he returned from Europe, he dedicated himself to the occupation of professor at the Conservatorio Nacional de Musica de Mexico, in the departments of piano and composition and the History of Music. In 1915 he visited Havana and New York, getting to know both cities, with great applause of the critics and the public, of his production at that time.

Manuel returned to Mexico in July 1918, accepting the direction of the National Symphonic Orchestra which the Minister of Education offered. He moved to Paris in 1925 where he stayed for nine years; making himself known there, making his art fertile, with the great French maestros and foreigners of that moment, and with aesthetic and literary critics. Among his friendships the most fervent to be pointed out is with Paul Dukas in whose artistic coexistence the spirit of Manuel Ponce ascended and was enriched. His production is, since then the most plentiful.

Another of his faithful friends, Andrés Segovia, gave rise to the consecration as well of a great part of his talent to the guitar. In effect, for this beautiful instrument, he wrote numerous compositions of diverse styles and forms, which, by his noble quality, honored not only the special literature of the guitar, but, on top of whatever instrument, its own Music.

His participation in the Festival Ibero-Americano de Barcelona brought particularly the admiration of the Spanish maestros toward him and in general the personal appreciation of whatever colleagues that he approached and dealt with.

Approximately in the same epoch he founded the Gaceta Musical in Paris, in the Spanish language and counted on the collaboration of his editing the prestigious names of Madriguera, Paul Dukas, Henri Prunieres, Marc Pincherle, Henri de Curzon, Marguerite D'Harcourt, Aloys Mooser, Joaquín Turina, etc. etc.

During his stay in Paris, he was the object of frequent homage. The maestro Dukas organized, with this character, a performance of works of the maestro Ponce and the International Society of Music presided by Dukas and Ravel, who chose and made interpret one of his Quartets.

In the end, presently his occupation is in the department of folklore in the Universidad de Mexico and is also the Inspector de Jardines de Niños.

We give a brief resume of his principle works: (The works for: Piano, Voice and Piano, Chamber Music, Orchestra, Organ and Solo Guitar are listed on the previous page.)

Andrés Segovia

El célebre guitarrista español Andrés Segovia nació en Linares, provincia de Jaén, el 18 de Febrero de 1894, demostrando desde su infancia, excepcionales disposiciones para el instrumento que había de cultivar con hondo fervor consagrándole todos sus esfuerzos y afanes. Trasladado a Granada dió en el Círculo Artístico de esa ciudad su primer concierto a los 14 años, llamando poderosamente la atención sus raras facultades. En Barcelona sentó los primeros jalones de su reputación que más tarde había de cristalizar en sólida fama universal. Su temperamento inquieto y emprendedor hizo que recorriese muy pronto casi todas las provincias españolas, dando innumerables conciertos y consolidando luego su prestigio en Madrid. Trasladóse enseguida a América siendo aclamado por los públicos de casi todo el continente. En Abril de 1924, dió un concierto en la Sala del Conservatorio de París, cuyo público le acogió con entusiasmo y seguidamente recorrió Alemania, Austria, Bélgica, Holanda, Inglaterra, Suiza, Hungría, Checoeslovaquia, Suecia, Noruega, Dinamarca, Rusia, Italia, y Estados Unidos.

En los últimos tiempos de consolidación de su fama, músicos modernos de prestigio, tales como Turina, Moreno Torroba, Nín, Manén, Roussel, Jacques, Ibert, Cyril, Scott, Ponce, Bréville, Migot, Tansman, Respighi, Castelnuovo-Tedesco, Carlos Perell, han compuesto o están componiendo para Segovia obras para guitarra. El renacimiento que en estos últimos años se observa en este instrumento, es debido a Segovia, quien en sus peregrinaciones por todo el mundo, puede decirse, ha logrado formar ambiente, con su arte y actividad considerable, elevando la guitarra al nivel de estima y consideración que merece como instrumento de concierto.

Suite en estilo antiguo

Esta obra fué estrenada por Arsemet en 1936. El "Preludio" se desarrolla sobre un diseño de dobles corcheas que los instrumentos de arco exponen desde los primeros compases. Las constantes **imitaciones** y su diatonismo dan a este trozo un carácter arcaico, de acuerdo con el espíritu de la obra. En el **Canon** riguroso, a 3, el autor emplea ya en forma dialogada, ya en conjunto los instrumentos de cuerda y de aliento. La "Pavana" está construida, como un primer tiempo de Sonata, con la repetición en la tonalidad principal, del fragmento con que termina la primera parte. En la "Fughetta" encontramos una nueva manera de presentar el tema o sujeto: el quinteto de arcos acompaña con ritmo marcial la exposición del tema y de la respuesta y toda la orquesta prosigue el desarrollo tradicional de esta clase de composiciones, aunque en forma breve.

Concierto del Sur
(dedicado a Andrés Segovia)

El título de esta obra alude al ambiente folklórico de la región andaluza tierra de Andrés Segovia y Patria de la guitarra. Sin apoyo en ningún tema concreto, se desarrolla su fina inspiración musical de acuerdo con las sugerencias de los siguientes epígrafes:

I Allegro

Tu eres alma que dice su armonía
solitaria a las almas pasajeras.
("Guitarra" Antonio Machado)

II Andante

Vuelve a Granada los ojos
y el alma a su Felisarda...
("Romance de Abenumeya")

III Final

Rumores de fiesta lejana

Manuel Ponce's Suite en *estilo antiguo* and *Concierto del Sur* dedicated to Andrés Segovia were performed as a part of this concert in Montevideo.

Andrés Segovia

The celebrated Spanish guitarist Andrés Segovia was born in the province of Jaen on February 18, 1894, (sic February 21, 1893) demonstrating since his infancy, exceptional disposition for the instrument which he has been cultivating with fervor consecrating all of his efforts and desires. Moving to Granada he gave in the Circulo Artistico of that city his first concert at the 14 years of age, powerfully calling the attention to his rare facilities. In Barcelona he established the first marks of his reputation which later would crystallize the solid universal fame. With his anxious temperament and enterprising manner he soon covered almost all of the Spanish provinces, giving innumerable concerts and then consolidating his prestige in Madrid. He then moved to South America and became acclaimed in almost of the continent. In April of 1924, he gave a concert in the Sala del Conservatoire de Paris, whose public welcomed him with enthusiasm and right away he traveled to Germany, Austria, Belgium, Holland, England, Switzerland, Hungary, Czechoslovakia, Sweden, Norway, Denmark, Russia, Italy and the United States.

In the latest times of the consolidation of his fame, modern musicians of prestige, such as, Turina, Moreno Torroba, Nin, Manén, Roussel, Jacques Ibert, Cyril Scott, Ponce, Bréville, Migot, Tansman, Respighi, Castelnuovo-Tedesco and Carlos Pedrell, have composed or are composing works for the guitar for Segovia. The renaissance which in these latest years is observed on this instrument, is due to Segovia, who in his pilgrimages all over the world, it can be said, has achieved to form an environment, with his art and considerable activity, elevating the guitar to a level of esteem and consideration which it deserves as a concert instrument.

Suite en estilo antiguo

This work was debuted by Ansermet in 1936. The *"Preludio"* was developed over a design of sixteenth notes, which the bowed instruments exhibit from the first measures. The constant imitations and their diatonicism give to this passage an archaic character, of agreement with the spirit of the work. In the rigorous *Canon,* to 3, the author already employs in a dialogued form, already in a group of string instruments and woodwinds. The *"Pavana"* is constructed, as a first tempo of Sonata, with the repetition in the principal tonality, of the fragment with the end of the first part. In the *"Fughetta"* we find a new manner of presenting the theme or subject: the quintet of strings accompanies with march rhythm the exposition of the theme and of the reply and all the orchestra continues the traditional development of this class of compositions, although in a brief form.

Concierto del Sur

(Dedicated to Andrés Segovia)

The title of this work alludes to the folkloric environment of the Andalucia region-the land of Andrés Segovia and Fatherland of the guitar. Without support of any concrete tempo, it develops its fine musical inspiration of agreement with the requests of the following inscriptions.

I Allegro   You are the soul which says its solitary harmony to the passing souls.
("Guitarra" Antonio Machado)

II Andante   Return to Granada the eyes and the soul to its Felisarda...
("Romance de Abenumeya")

III Final   Murmur of a distant party

Poema Elegíaco

Dedicado a la memoria del gran poeta mejicano Luis G. Urbina, amigo fraternal del autor, el Poema Elegíaco data de 1934. El compositor intentó evocar, en una síntesis musical, la vida de su amigo, sus ensueños y sus dolores, sus esperanzas e ilusiones. Trátase de páginas escritas con la sinceridad del que sufre la desaparición de un ser querido, de una elegía consagrada al melancólico y suave poeta de "Puestas de Sol" y del "Cancionero de la Noche Serena".

Chapultepec - 3 Bocetos Sinfónicos

Compuestos por el año 1921, estos bocetos sufrieron importantes modificaciones en 1934, quedando esta nueva versión integrada por "Primavera en el bosque", "Nocturno Romántico" y Canto. El primer trozo es descriptivo, es una impresión ante la belleza majestuosa del antiquísimo bosque de los emperadores aztecas. Como se sabe, Chapultepec era el lugar de veraneo del emperador Moctezuma. En medio del parque existe una elevación del terreno donde se hallaba antaño el palacio de los emperadores de México y que fuera reemplazado más tarde por el Palacio que ocupara el Emperador Maximiliano. Fué allí mismo donde defendieron con su sangre la integridad mexicana ante la invasión estadounidense los niños-héroes, o sea, los cadetes de la Escuela Militar.

En el segundo boceto, el autor evoca un plenilunio bajo los ahuehuetes, árboles gigantes y milenarios que aún se conservan. El Canto que inicia el tercer boceto es una melodía de probable origen prehispánico, titulada, **Canto de la Malinche**, el cual alude tal vez a Doña Marina, la india que sirvió de intérprete a Cortés. A esa melodía primitiva, acompañada por instrumentos de percusión que forman de esta manera el ambiente sonoro de los viejos tiempos, sigue una Danza en la que es utilizada una escala indígena que participa de tres tonalidades: mi menor, re menor y la menor.

Acerca de esta obra, que dió a conocer en Filadelfia y Nueva York Leopoldo Stokowski, el crítico del "New York Herald Tribune", Francis D. Perkins, publicó en ese diario (21 de noviembre de 1934), el siguiente juicio: "Música franca, con vitalidad y sustancia. El "Chapultepec" del maestro Ponce que tomó su nombre del famoso jardín cercano a la ciudad de México, demostró ser obra de un verdadero compositor que emplea ventajosamente los recursos de la orquestación moderna y manifiesta ideas musicales que indican en alto grado individualidad y distinción".

SABADO 11 DE OCTUBRE

A LA HORA: 18 y 33

SEGUNDO CONCIERTO SINFÓNICO

BAJO LA DIRECCION DEL MAESTRO

MANUEL PONCE

SOLISTA:

Paquita Madriguera de S

(PIANO)

PRECIOS DE LAS LOCALIDADES

PALCOS BAJOS o Balcón, sin entradas	$ 6.00
PLATEA	" 3.00
TERTULIA, 1.a fila	" 3.00
" otras filas	" 2.50
Entrada a Palco	" 3.00
Galería Baja, 1.a fila (mixta)	" 2.00
" " otras filas	" 1.50
Entrada General (mixta)	" 0.60
Galería Alta, 1.a fila	" 1.50
" " otras filas	" 1.20
Entrada General	" 0.60

Poema Elegiaco

Dedicated to the memory of the great Mexican poet Luis G. Urbina, fraternal friend of the author, the *Poema Elegiaco* dates from 1934. The composer intended to evoke, in a musical synthesis, the life of his friend, his dreams and his hurts, his hopes and illusions. To deal by written pages with the sincerity of the suffering of the disappearance of a loved one, of a consecrated elegy to the melancholic and smooth poet of *"Puestas de Sol"* (Sunsets) and of the *"Cancionero de la Noche Serena"* (Songbook of the Serene Night).

Chapultepec — 3 Bocetos Sinfonicos

Composed in the year 1921, these sketches suffered important modifications in 1934, remaining as this new version integrated by *"Primavera en el bosque"* (Spring in the forest), "Nocturno Romantico" (Romantic Night), "Canto y Danza" (Song and dance). The first passage is descriptive, it is an impression before the majestic beauty of the oldest forest of the Aztec emperors. As it is known, Chapultepec was a summer place of Moctezuma. In the middle of the park exists an elevation of the terrain where the old palace of the emperors of Mexico is found and was replaced later by the Palace that emperor Maximillian occupied. It was there where the child-heroes with their blood or in other words, the cadets of the Military School defended the Mexican integrity before the United States invasion.

In the second sketch, the author evokes a full moon under the trees, the gigantic and very old trees that are still preserved. The *Canto,* which begins the third passage is a melody of probable prehispanic origin, entitled, *Canto de la Malinche,* which alludes maybe to *Doña* Marina, the Indian that serves to interpret Cortez. To this primitive melody, accompanied by percussion instruments that form by this manner the sonorous environment of the old times, continues the Danza in which the indigenous scale is utilized to participate in three tonalities: E minor, D minor and A minor.

About this work, which Leopold Stokowski gave in Philadelphia and New York, the critic of the "New York Herald Tribune", Francis D. Perkins, published in this daily (November 24, 1934) the following judgement: " Frank music, with vitality and sustenance. The *"Chapultepec"* by the maestro Ponce which takes its name from the garden near Mexico City, demonstrates to be a work of a true composer that advantageously employs the resources of the modern orchestration and manifests the musical ideas which indicate a high grade of individualism and distinction."

Below these paragraphs is the advertisement for a second symphonic concert to be given on Saturday October 11, 1941 under the direction of maestro Manuel Ponce with the participation of Paquita Madriguera de Segovia on Piano. The work is unnamed.

TEATRO
COLON

TEMPORADA
1942

The construction of the Teatro Colon was completed in 1909 and was a real splendor.

1942 TEATRO COLON 1942

SABADO 18 DE ABRIL, a las 18. (2ª función del abono a 6 conciertos
sinfónico-corales de Otoño)

PROGRAMA

I

Preludio y fuga en Mi Bemol, para órgano .... **BACH**
    (Orquestación de Arnold Schönberg).

Pastoral del Oratorio de Navidad .... **BACH**

II

Concierto, para guitarra y pequeña orquesta. .... **CASTELNUOVO TEDESCO**
    a) Allegretto giusto e un poco pomposo.
    b) Andantino alla romanza.
    c) Rítmico e cavalleresco.

Solista: ANDRES SEGOVIA

Iberia .... **DEBUSSY**
    I. — Por calles y caminos.
    II. — Los perfumes de la noche.
    III. — Mañana de un día de fiesta.

III

Sinfonía "Matías el pintor" .... **HINDEMITH**
    I. — Concierto de ángeles.
    II. — Entierro.
    III. — Las tentaciones de San Antonio.

Director: JUAN JOSE CASTRO

The Andrés Segovia Teatro Colon concert on Saturday April 18, 1942, and a photo as well of Juan José Castro, composer and conductor, who had just returned from New York where he was under contract with NBC Radio.

The beautiful interior of the Teatro Colon in 1957. The patrons are singing the National Anthem. This is from the magazine *"El Hogar"* of July 19, 1957 issue No. 2485, year LIV.

ASOCIACIÓN WAGNERIANA
DE BUENOS AIRES
Santa Fe 1145 - U. T. 41 - Plaza 6296

RECITAL DE GUITARRA

POR

ANDRES
SEGOVIA

LUNES 4 de MAYO

a las 21.30

EN EL

TEATRO NACIONAL DE COMEDIA
(Cervantes)

CEDIDO POR LA COMISION NACIONAL DE CULTURA

1942

Córdoba y Libertad   Buenos Aires

Andrés Segovia continues to offer different programs weeks apart, this one at the Teatro Nacional de la Comedia for the Asociacion "Wagneriana" on Monday May 4, 1942.

PROGRAMA

I

PREAMBULO ....⎤
SARABANDA ....⎬ Alejandro Scarlatti
GAVOTA ....⎦

(De un manuscrito del Conservatorio de
Nápoles. Adaptación de Andrés Segovia.)

SONATA .... D. Scarlatti

ROMANZA (escrita para guitarra) .... N. Paganini

DOS MINUETOS .... Haydn
    a) en Re
    b) en La

II

* SONATA (Homenaje a Boccherini) .... Castelnuovo Tedesco
    Allegro con Spirito
    Andantino, quasi canzone
    Tempo di minuetto
    Vivo ed energico

* TARANTELA .... Castelnuovo Tedesco

III

* PRELUDIO Y ALLEGRO .... Manuel Ponce
* MAZURKA ... . Alex Tansman
DANZA en Sol .... Granados
LEYENDA .... I. Albéniz

* Dedicado a Andrés Segovia.

Para asistir a esta audición es necesario presentar el CARNET DE ABRIL

Mario Castelnuovo-Tedesco wrote many great pieces for the guitar due to Andrés Segovia's inspiration, here we notice the *Sonata*-Homage to Boccherini as well as the *Tarantella*; which incidentally was a part of the masterclasses in Compostela in the 1960's that were filmed.

EL ACONTECIMIENTO RADIAL DEL AÑO

ANDRES SEGOVIA

CASA AMERICA
"El Hogar de la Música"

auspició los tres únicos conciertos radiales del genial artista, ofrecidos en homenaje a la exquisita sensibilidad musical del público argentino.

Casa América
AV. DE MAYO 959 - Bs. As.
U. T. 38 - MAYO 2066

REVISTA DE LA GUITARRA

This photo of Andrés Segovia for the promotion by Casa America for "The Radio Happening of the Year" is from the *"Revista de la Guitarra"* issue No. 11 of January 1, 1943 to October 31, 1944
Translation: "The Radio Happening of the Year": Andrés Segovia. Casa America "the home of music" will sponsor three unique radio concerts by this brilliant artist, offered in homage to the exquisite musical sensibility of the Argentine public."

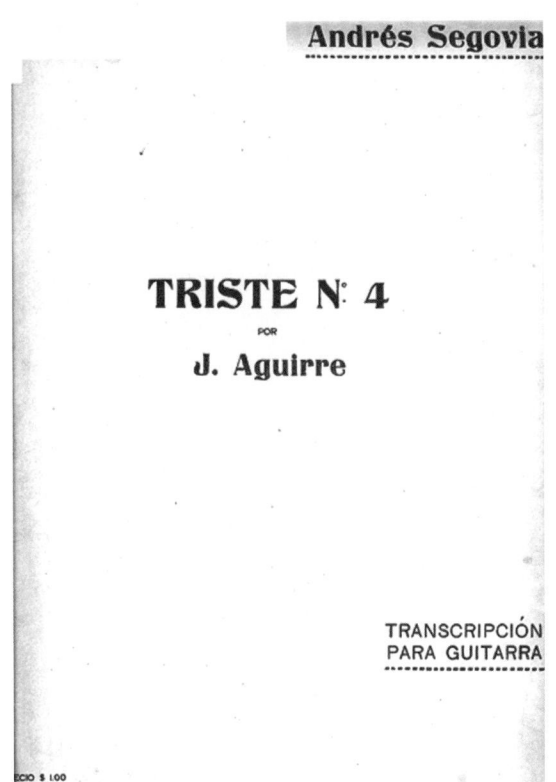

(Left) Daniel Fortea publication in Madrid in 1924 of Andrés Segovia's *"Tres Preludios"*. (Right) Andrés Segovia's transcription of the *"Triste No. 4"* by Julián Aguirre published by Romero & Fernández .

(Left) Diego, Gracia and Co. publication, of 1939 transcriptions by Andrés Segovia.
(Right) Piece dedicated to Andrés Segovia and published by Editorial Fidelio.

ANDRES SEGOVIA, el más eminente de los intérpretes de la guitarra en la actualidad, mundialmente aplaudido. Sus conciertos por Radio "El Mundo" son escuchados por centenares de miles de personas en toda América.

This photo of Andrés Segovia is from the magazine "*Mundo Argentino*" of November 1, 1944, issue No. 1763. The translation of the caption reads: "Andrés Segovia, the most eminent of the present interpreters of the guitar applauded worldwide. His concerts on Radio "*El Mundo*" are heard by hundreds of thousands of persons in all South America.

Archive: Ricardo Muñoz

This is a tour booking advertisement from a 1944 American magazine. At this point Andrés Segovia had been giving guitar concerts for over 30 years.

MUSIC

By VIRGIL THOMSON

ANDRÉS SEGOVIA, guitarist, and small orchestra conducted by Ignace Strasfogel, concert last night in Carnegie Hall. The program:
Concerto in D major......Castelnuovo-Tedesco
Dedicated to Mr. Segovia; first performance in the U. S. A.
Guitar solos:
Air variée.............................Handel
Prelude, Sarabande, Bourree and Lourc..Bach
Variations on a Theme of Mozart........Sor
Torre Berneja.........................Albeniz
Leyenda...............................Albeniz
Concerto del Sur......................Ponce
Dedicated to Mr. Segovia; first performance in the U. S. A.

Andres Segovia

Guitarist who played last night at Carnegie Hall

Guitar With Orchestra

THERE is no guitar but the Spanish guitar, and Andrés Segovia is its prophet. For aficionados of the instrument (of whom your reporter is one) last night's concert of solos and concertos that Mr. Segovia played, in Carnegie Hall offered untold delights. Persons less sensitive to the charms of the guitar usually profess to find it monotonous either in repertory or in musical figuration. But I doubt if there lives a music lover with soul so dead that he could not find reward in attendance at a Segovia concert at least once. This artist's work has, indeed, a nobility of style that is worth going far to hear and that one does not quickly forget.

* * *

Ponce's Concerto del Sur, on the other hand, was a delight. Written in the Andalusian manner, it is rich in expressive variety and musical interest. The orchestral accompaniment, moreover, amplifies the already large range of guitar timbres in the most becoming way imaginable. Here was no overpowering dynamic effect, but a galaxy of wind-instrument and string colorations that made one wonder why the guitar has not more often been used in ensemble works of

some length. It is doubtful whether there are enough guitarists of impeccable musicianship to make an expansion of its usage as a concerto instrument likely just now. But this admirer of Mr. Segovia's art would like to hear it displayed more often in large-scale composition with orchestra. Mr. Ponce's concerto had breadth without the loss of any of the guitar's characteristic intensity of expression. His Concerto del Sur is a completely agreeable work and a unique contribution to repertory.

One of these display works was the Concerto in D major of Castelnuovo-Tedesco, and the other, by Manuel Ponce, Spanish composer, was entitled "Concerto del Sur." In these, Mr. Segovia was assisted by an orchestra made up of twenty musicians from the Philharmonic-Symphony Orchestra, conducted by Ignace Strasfogel.

Although Mr. Segovia had played with orchestra in Latin-America, he had not done so previously here, and curiosity was aroused by the novel procedure. Before the two concertos were written, no works of the kind for guitar and orchestra existed in musical literature. In them, had the composers solved the problem of balancing the fragile tone of the guitar against a score of other instruments? Would the soloist be able to dominate the assembly, and could he even make the guitar part distinctly audible in the spaces of so vast an auditorium?

Well, it happened that the works proved so capably contrived that a fine balance and blending of tone was maintained throughout their respective three movements. And without any undue effort, Mr. Segovia managed to make the sounds from his guitar clearly audible to a surprising degree.

Of the two concertos, the Ponce opus was easily the more important in content and facture. Its thematic material had more substance, and was more interestingly and knowingly treated. Built on Andalusian folk tunes, it had a likable spontaneity, and rhythmic as well as melodic charm. The orchestral scoring never gave the sense of skimpiness felt in the other concerto, and yet was always quite as discreet. Moreover, it afforded far better opportunities for effective solo work on the guitar, and was altogether of a more up-to-date and consequential composition.

Mr. Segovia, in his incomparable fashion, made the most of his chances for virtuosity in these novelties, and the orchestra, under Mr. Strasfogel's capable direction, afforded fine-grained and sensitive support. Between the two concertos, Mr. Segovia played a group of offerings by Bach, Handel, Sor and Albeniz, all of which were further examples of his highly-polished technique and remarkable control of tone, color, dynamics and rhythm, again demonstrating the fact that both as executant and interpreter, he remains peerless in his chosen field. The audience was large and appreciative.. N. S.

These three reviews are from a February 1946 Musical America magazine, the one on the right is from the New York Times. Its headline was masked over in the one page graphic overlay. It read: "Segovia Presents a Novel Program — Guitarist Plays in Carnegie Hall First .... Concertos Written for Him. For the first time in his local career Andrés Segovia the Spanish guitarist makes an appearance .... this city, containing two concertos, written specially for him."

"Segovia's Magic Guitar Captures Carnegie Hall!"

—Louis Biancolli
N. Y. World Telegram
Jan. 14, 1946

B.M.G.

The Monthly Magazine devoted to the interests of the Banjo, Mandolin, Guitar and Kindred Instruments

Vol. XLIII. No. 490.]   FEBRUARY, 1946   [Price Ninepence

SEGOVIA

Banjo Solo (Fgr. or Plec. style): "I'll Be Your Sweetheart"
Hawaiian Guitar Solo (with Gtr. acc.): "Kalakaua March"
Plectrum Guitar Solo: "Reminiscing on the Guitar"
Spanish Guitar Solo: "Andante Pastorale" (Verini)
Banjo Solo: "Some Folks Like to Sigh."

● FORTY-THIRD YEAR ●

B.M.G.

The Monthly Magazine devoted to the interests of the Banjo, Mandolin, Guitar and Kindred Instruments

Published on the 1st of each month at

8, NEW COMPTON STREET, LONDON, W.C.2, ENGLAND

Telephone—Temple Bar 2810
Telegrams—"Triomphe, Westcent, London"

Edited by

A. P. SHARPE

The Editor does not necessarily agree with the opinions expressed by his contributors.

Subscription rate :

12 months .. 8/6 (U.S.A. $2.00)

All news items submitted for the next issue must arrive at this office not later than the 10th.

ADVERTISING RATES ON REQUEST

Vol. XLIII. No. 490.]   **FEBRUARY, 1946**   **[Price Ninepence**

Andres Segovia

By The EDITOR

TODAY, the growing interest in the classical guitar owes much to the playing of Andres Segovia. His world tours, his many broadcasts, his gramophone records, all have done much to stimulate interest in an instrument which has a library of music second only to the piano and a history which can be traced back to 1700 B.C.

Andres Segovia was born in Linares (Jaén), Spain, in 1893, but at an early age his parents moved to the province of Granada, the part of Spain which is rich in artistic tradition.

The boy's innate musical sensitivity steered him to the guitar at an early age. Segovia himself has told how he discovered the guitar.

"In my native Granada I heard many musical instruments, but all of them frightened me. Looking back I think I must have unconsciously blamed the sins of the performer on the instrument he played; but the fact is that I listened to a violin, was conscious of its scratching tone and said, 'Ah! That is bad! Not for me!' Then I heard a piano, and became terrified at its blurred thunder; and again I declined with thanks. Through all of these attempts to find something to love; I loved music with all my heart. And there was the guitar that I heard about me all the time. No matter how indifferently it was played, it sounded musical. So I decided that I must have been waiting for the guitar all the while—from the time before I was born."

Segovia studied music at the Granada Musical Institute, but there was no professor of the guitar so he became his own teacher.

NO INSTRUCTION

The world's most famous guitarist received no instruction beyond what he provided for himself. Not only did he create his own instrumental technique, but he became an avid student of the art and history of the guitar; delving into antiquity in his search for complete knowledge.

At the age of 14 Segovia had attained sufficient musical status to play in public as a serious artist and his first public appearance was acclaimed by Granada's artistic circles.

A few months later he played in Madrid and from there travelled to Barcelona where he gave 15 consecutive recitals.

Then followed a tour throughout Spain and, after the cessation of the

1914-18 war, he visited Argentina, Uruguay, Brazil, Mexico and Cuba, where his playing received the unstinted praise of musical critics.

In 1924 he made his Paris debut at a concert attended by famous musicians, painters, writers and poets. His performance was a brilliant success and public and musical critics alike acclaimed his performance. This unanimous praise, from even the severest of French musical critics, led to increased demands for further appearances and during the next two years Segovia appeared on concert platforms in every country in Europe —including several recitals in this country.

In 1926 he appeared on the concert platforms of Russia and Dr. Perott has already told in these pages how he altered the outlook of many outstanding guitarists in Russia; even to the extent of them discarding their national guitar (with its seven strings) to adopt the six-string Spanish guitar.

Two years later, Andres Segovia took New York by storm and at the present time is making a welcome reappearance in the United States. Appearances in Japan, the Philippines, China, Java, Sumatra and the Celebes next heard the ambassador of the Spanish guitar. He was truly worldfamous.

PERSONAL LOVE

Andres Segovia himself expresses an almost personal love for his chosen instrument. He has said : " My greatest satisfaction has come not from the plaudits of the peoples of many nations, but from the knowledge that I have given the guitar its rightful place in the musical gallery."

Hundreds of compositions for the guitar have been written through the efforts of Andres Segovia. His own transcriptions of ancient vihuella music and the music of Bach, the original compositions by Falla, Turina, Torroba, Ponce, Castelnuovo-Tedesco and many others have all provided welcome additions to the vast library of music for the Spanish guitar.

His many recordings have for a long time been a source of pleasure and inspiration to students of the Spanish guitar and it is welcome news that the maestro has recently recorded six new sides for the American Decca label.

The New Segovia Records

By A. McK. Houston

THE new American Decca Album of Segovia recordings (No. A.384) consists of three 12 in. discs and here, first of all, are the details of the titles with the record numbers :

219154 "Granada (*Serenata*)" — Albeniz.
　　　 "Tonadilla (*La Maja De Goya*)"—Granados.
219155 "Danza Espanola No. 10 in G Major"—Granados.
　　　 "Torre Bermeja"—Albeniz.
219156 "Danza Espanola No. 5"—Granados.
　　　 "Sevilla (*Sevillanas*)" — Albeniz.

The first side consists of four movements; the opening and closing being in 3/4 time. There is a beautiful sense of rhythm throughout the whole piece —the offsetting of bass and treble being carried out most effectively. The tone of Segovia's guitar is gloriously resonant and there is no lack of expression.

The second side is a bright and lively piece with a pleasing melody. Here again, plenty of expression is evident, and the playing throughout can only be described as superb.

Altogether a record which makes one realise the complete mastery which Andres Segovia has over the guitar.

The third side is fast and spirited, as one would expect from the title, although the fourth side appeals to me, personally, less than the three preceding titles.

Granados' "Danza Espanola No. 5" makes the biggest appeal to me from the whole album. It is typically a Spanish piece—played most beautifully—and a composition of which I would never tire.

The sixth side is an attractive composition, the outstanding feature being its peculiarly haunting theme.

INDIVIDUAL PLAYING

No one acquainted with the Spanish guitar could fail to recognise the playing of Andres Segovia. It is decidedly individual. The nearest approach to his tone I have heard is in

ANDRES SEGOVIA
A photograph taken in the Decca studio during the making of the records reviewed on this page.

the recordings of Ida Presti. Perhaps I had better say that this is a comparison of *recordings* only.

I have never heard either of these artists play in person (that is a pleasure to which I look forward and one which I earnestly hope will be possible of realisation in the not too distant future), and so I am unable to judge how their playing compares with other artists whom I have heard in person but not on records.

I say this because I believe that there is a vast difference between being in the presence of an artist actually playing the guitar and listening to a recording. The microphone amplifies and tone controls can be used to give a "flattering" result in

a record, and I always feel—particularly regarding guitar recordings—that they give a different effect to that obtainable "in the flesh."

My one criticism of Andres Segovia's playing (judged from records, be it noted) is that, perfect though it is, it tends to become monotonous. Perhaps this lies more in his choice of compositions, which have a certain "sameness" about them. I, personally, consider that more contrasts in the type of solos played would add immeasurably to one's enjoyment of a recital of Segovia records.

CONTRAST IN STYLE

As it is, to enjoy Segovia to best advantage I feel that I want to intersperse recordings of other guitarists to get this contrast in style and tone.

In these latest six recordings, there is noticeably much artistry, taste and expression. Segovia is undoubtedly —as would be expected—now an even greater exponent of the Spanish guitar than he was when he made the recordings which have been released in this country (excellent as they are).

I have heard Andres Segovia criticised as sacrificing artistic rendering for perfection in technique—but this charge could certainly not be levelled at him in respect of these latest Decca recordings.

And may I end with a plea to the English Decca Company ? It is many years since students of the Spanish guitar in this country have been able to purchase a new recording. Would it not be a generous gesture to reissue this new album over here ? I am sure all lovers of the guitar (and not all of these are in the ranks of players) would welcome the opportunity to purchase them.

SEGOVIA SOCIETY

BULLETIN

2000 N STREET, N. W.   OCTOBER, 1946   WASHINGTON, D. C.

MESSAGE FROM ANDRES SEGOVIA

I ACKNOWLEDGE a deep sense of gratitude to those of you who have organized this Society for two reasons: First, because it is bound to spread understanding and love of the instrument to which I have devoted my life; secondly, because of the honor accorded me in naming the Society after me. I can serve as a useful example to you only in that I have never faltered since my extreme youth, in my all-consuming passion for this instrument. Through my life-long work, motivated by a devotion to the guitar, I have been able to awaken a similar feeling in the hearts of music lovers everywhere. I am happy to say that neither vanity, excessive ambition nor personal gain have marred the catholicity of that love.

Among the Charter members of the Segovia Society there is one name that stands out—that of Sophocles Papas, prime mover in the organization. We all deeply appreciate his continuing and selfless efforts to instill an interest and lay the ground work for a true appreciation of the guitar.

I sincerely hope that the noble objectives of this society will be realized. To do this we must remember that only through the individual effort of each one of the members will we reach final success. Whether this individual contribution be appreciation or advancement of technique, it is nevertheless a valuable one.

The guitar possesses an inherent beauty which becomes more apparent to us as we grow more and more familiar with the instrument. While it may seem limited in the hands of the uninitiated, its range becomes miraculously amplified when we discover its far-reaching possibilities. We see it change from an instrument used as a simple accompaniment to popular songs, to one capable of interpreting the rich polyphony of Bach and the varied color tones of modern music. We must all, according to our individual capacities, do our part toward rescuing the guitar from the state of indifference in which it rests, as well as remedying the present day inadequate knowledge of this instrument.

Such are the aims animating the Segovia Society; and let us hope that this society, based upon the brotherhood of all present and future members, will grow and prosper with the years. For my part, I shall lend my unqualified support to the association in its efforts for greater understanding and artistic encouragement of the guitar. From this day forward, I want each member to regard me as his friend, his advisor or his teacher, and I want him to know that once I discover a true enthusiast for the guitar, I will gladly help to solve any and all problems that may arise.

ANDRES SEGOVIA.

This is the first bulletin of the Segovia Society, from October 1946.

THE SEGOVIA SOCIETY, Inc.

Washington Headquarters
2000 N Street, N. W.
OFFICERS
President
Oliver La Farge
Vice-Presidents
Dr. J. deS. Coutinho
Dr. Benjamin Frank
M. C. Walsh
Mildred O. Waugh
Treasurer
Ona Lee Jeffries
Secretary
Sophocles Papas

EDITORIAL

WHEN the true oracle speaks, it is well for minor witnesses to remain quiet. I who am no more than an eager listener to the guitar cannot expect to add anything of value to Segovia's splendid greetings, published in this issue of the Bulletin.

The fraternity of the guitar, like that of all true arts, is world-wide. In wartime, of necessity, the Segovia Society lay dormant. With the coming of peace, it is most fitting that lovers of this great instrument should unite to spread the knowledge and appreciation of the delights it offers to mankind.

To this end, the Society has been reorganized. Old friends and new have rallied to it. We intend it to become the means of union, mutual encouragement, and stimulating interchange between the members of a natural brotherhood. It will increase public understanding of the full possibilities of the guitar which at present are not fully realized even by many amateurs of music.

New By-laws will be published shortly to decentralize the growing organization and unite the central office in Washington democratically with membership throughout the United States. We expect to be able to establish branches in the near future, to serve as local centers of interchange and communication. Meantime, the Society extends a warm invitation and a hearty welcome to all true lovers of the guitar who join its ranks.

Oliver La Farge
President, The Segovia Society.

OVERTONES

ANNOUNCEMENT will be made in the January issue of the Segovia Society Bulletin of anticipated dates and places of Mr. Segovia's 1947 concert tour. A New York engagement is being arranged for early in the year; there will be a concert in Washington, and a number in important Western and Mid-Western cities, and in Canada.

———

Dr. Ernest Harris of the Music Education faculty, Teachers College, Columbia University, is the author of a pamphlet, just published, entitled "The Guitar—The Modern Approach to Music Education and Recreation." Says the foreword: "The war brought home the fact that one of the most important instruments for musical appreciation and enjoyment is the guitar. Never before has one instrument risen so fast and to such heights of popularity to be acclaimed by the men and women of the armed forces as their favorite musical instrument."

Says Dr. Harris: "From all indications this instrument is headed toward a more widespread popularity than ever before, not as an instrument to be carelessly 'strummed' but performed well and on a high musical level."

———

Great composers still vie to write music for Andres Segovia. A partial list of the new works for the guitar dedicated him includes: "*Serenade*"* by Mario Castelnuovo-Tedesco, and "*Rondo*" by the same composer; "*Suite*" by Guillermo Uribe Holquin; "*Concertino*"* by Alexander Tansman; "*Concerto*"* by Moreno Torroba; also a *Suite* by Ignace Strasfogel, well-known conductor who led the orchestra which accompanied Mr. Segovia in Carnegie Hall last January.

Of interest also is a "*Quintette for Strings and Guitar*," by Manuel Ponce, dedicated to Sophocles Papas.

———

* Numbers marked by asterisks are for guitar and orchestra.

890

PUTTING A COMPOSER TO WORK

ANDRES SEGOVIA, perhaps more than any other person, has been responsible for the modern development of guitar music. A letter from Castlenuovo-Tedesco, written from his Hollywood home, tells how the great guitarist gets music out of a composer! He says:

"If I have written so much for the guitar during the last ten years, the fault is entirely of Andres Segovia! I had never thought of writing for the guitar until I met him at an International Festival in Venice, in 1932.

"At that time he first asked me to write something for his instrument; I answered him that I would be delighted to have my music played by one of the interpreters I most admired, but . . . that I didn't have the slightest idea how to write for the guitar! Anyway, he insisted that I should try; and from Geneva (where he lived at that time) he sent me two sets of Variations (those of Sor on a Mozart theme), and those of Ponce on 'La Follia') as models; therefore I also tried my first work as a set of Variations, which I called 'Variations Through the Centuries' (ranging from a Chaconne . . . to a Fox-Trot!)

"He was so pleased with the work that the next year he asked me something more: 'Your countryman, Boccherini, was very much interested in the Guitar; why don't you write for me a "Homage to Boccherini?"' And so the Sonata (in four movements) was born.

"The following year he told me—'Do you know? Also Paganini was very much interested in the Guitar: why don't you write a "Homage to Paginini?"' And so came to life the 'Capriccio Diabolico'.

"Finally he asked me to write for him a Concerto for Guitar and Orchestra! This time I hesitated . . . I hesitated for several years (although I wanted so much to fulfill his wish) because I was really afraid of the task: not so much of writing for Guitar (which I had largely experienced before) nor of writing a Concerto (which was one of my favorite forms) but of combining the delicate and precious sound of the Guitar with the other instrumental colors: something which had never been experienced before (at least on a larger scale)! It was a problem of 'quality' and of 'quantity' at the same time; it was the problem of giving the 'appearance' of an orchestra, without giving the 'weight' of it . . . Therefore I always postponed the realization of this plan.

"But on Christmas of 1938 Segovia himself came to see me in Florence; he knew that I was about to leave my native country, that I was very much depressed and worried about the future, that I had not been writing music for months; he came to spend these holidays with me, to give me encouragement and faith in the future . . . I was so deeply touched by his friendly gesture, that I suddenly decided to write the Concerto, to prove him my gratitude!

"The first movement was written while he was still in Florence, and we tried it together. Later (during the following January) I composed the second and third movements, which I sent him to South America, while (soon later) I left for North America myself. This is the last work I have written in Italy, and (although Segovia has played it everywhere in South and Central America since the first performance in Montevideo, Uruguay, in 1939) I haven't heard it played with orchestra myself! Strangely enough, although it was composed in one of the saddest periods of my life, it is one of the purest and most serene works I have ever written . . .I don't know yet how it sounds; but I know it was written for one of the artists I most admire: for Andres Segovia."

TO THOSE WHO ARE NOT YET MEMBERS
OF THE SEGOVIA SOCIETY

LIKE Andres Segovia, the Segovia Society seeks to widen the circle of those who appreciate the guitar as a serious instrument and a vehicle of the finest music.

We think that the revival in recent years of popular interest in eighteenth century music foreshadows a renaissance of the guitar. We believe that all who know the classical guitar at its best will agree that for music of refinement, delicacy, and precision, for the most effective rendering of much of the music of masters so divers as Bach, Debussy, and Albeniz, the guitar is the instrument of choice. While serious guitar music may never be everyone's "dish of tea" we are convinced that a great many people do not appreciate it simply because they do not know it.

The Segovia Society is seeking to correct that condition. Beginning with this issue, the Society will publish for its members a quarterly bulletin, giving news of concerts, recordings and other matters of interest to those who play and those who listen to the guitar. A column will answer questions concerning technical problems of the guitarist. The Society also hopes to be of assistance in arranging concerts, making possible the recording and publication of serious guitar music on a wider scale, encouraging the study of the guitar and interesting contemporary composers in writing for the instrument.

Members are encouraged to form local Chapters of the Society. If you have further questions about the Segovia Society I shall be glad to answer them. The membership application, printed below, is for your convenience. If you share our interest in the guitar, we need your help.

SOPHOCLES PAPAS,
Secretary.

———

Dear Colonel La Farge:

Enclosed is check for annual dues as a member of the Segovia Society. All good luck to you and your associates. Next year when my present commitments have slowed down somewhat, I hope to hunt out some pieces of writing I have done on the guitar and send them on to you.

Yours,
(signed) Carl Sandburg

APPLICATION FOR MEMBERSHIP

I, _____

Address _____

Occupation _____

Business Address _____
        hereby apply for membership in THE SEGOVIA SOCIETY, INC., as a
        ☐ PATRON _____ $100.00
        ☐ CONTRIBUTING MEMBER _____ $25.00
        ☐ ACTIVE MEMBER _____ $5.00

_____
                                                    Signature

Please make check payable to
THE SEGOVIA SOCIETY, INC.
and mail to 2000 N Street, N. W.
    Washington 6, D. C.

This extraordinary duet concert took place on October 11, 1946 at the S.O.D.R.E. Auditorium in Montevideo. The image on the next page is 98% actual size.

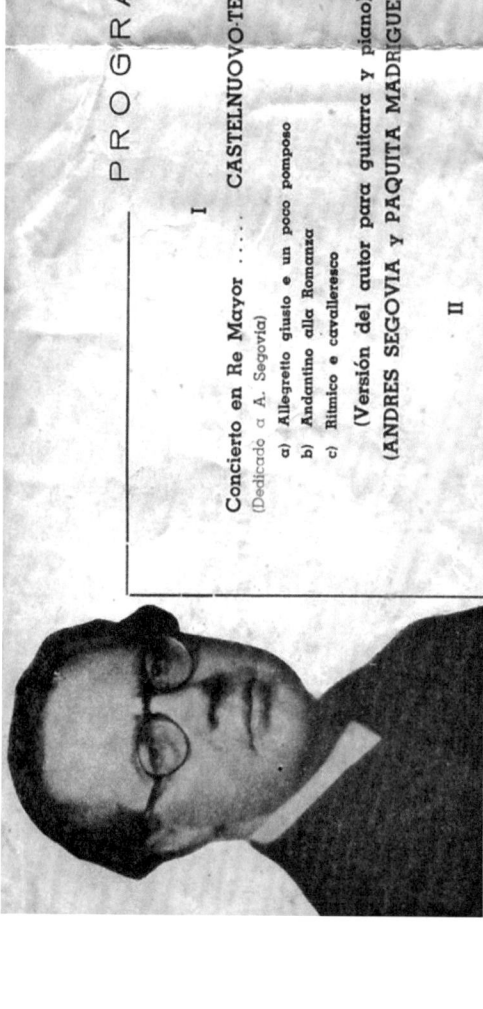

PROGRAMA

I

Concierto en Re Mayor ...... CASTELNUOVO-TEDESCO
(Dedicado a A. Segovia)

a) Allegretto giusto e un poco pomposo
b) Andantino alla Romanza
c) Ritmico e cavalleresco

(Versión del autor para guitarra y piano)

(ANDRES SEGOVIA y PAQUITA MADRIGUERA)

II

Aria con variazioni .... HANDEL
Allegretto .... RAMEAU
Sonata .... DOM. SCARLATTI
Prelude et bourrée (para laúd) J. S. BACH

Mazurka (dedicada a A. Segovia) ALEX. TANSMANN
Fantasía (dedicada a A. Segovia) TURINA
Mallorca } ALBENIZ
Torre Bermeja }

(ANDRES SEGOVIA)

III

Concierto del Sur .... M. PONCE
(Dedicado a A. Segovia)

a) Allegretto moderato ed espressivo
b) Andante
c) Allegro non troppo

(Versión del autor para guitarra y piano)

(ANDRES SEGOVIA y PAQUITA MADRIGUERA)

Concierto del Sur

M. PONCE

Ponce, en homenaje a la tierra de Segovia y a la tierra de la guitarra, buscó inspiración en el ambiente popular de Andalucía, denominando por eso su obra "CONCIERTO DEL SUR".

El título de esta obra alude al ambiente, folklórico de la región andaluza, tierra de ANDRES SEGOVIA y Patria de la guitarra. Sin apoyo en ningún tema concreto, se desarrolla su fina inspiración musical de acuerdo con los siguientes epígrafes:

Adopta esta obra, la forma clásica del Concierto en tres tiempos, en cada uno de los cuales realiza con acierto y pericia admirables, los timbres, a un tiempo suaves y vigorosos de la guitarra y el encanto peculiar de su técnica polifónica.

Con extrema delicadeza y brillantez alternan diálogos nobles, poéticos y humorísticos entre la guitarra y el piano.

I ALLEGRO MODERATO ED ESPRESSIVO.

Tú eres alma que dice su [armonía]
solitaria a las almas pasajeras
("Guitarra" Antonio Machado)

II ANDANTE

Vuelve a Granada los ojos
y el alma a su Felisarda...
("Romance de Abenumeya")

III FINAL (Allegro non troppo)

Rumores de fiesta lejana

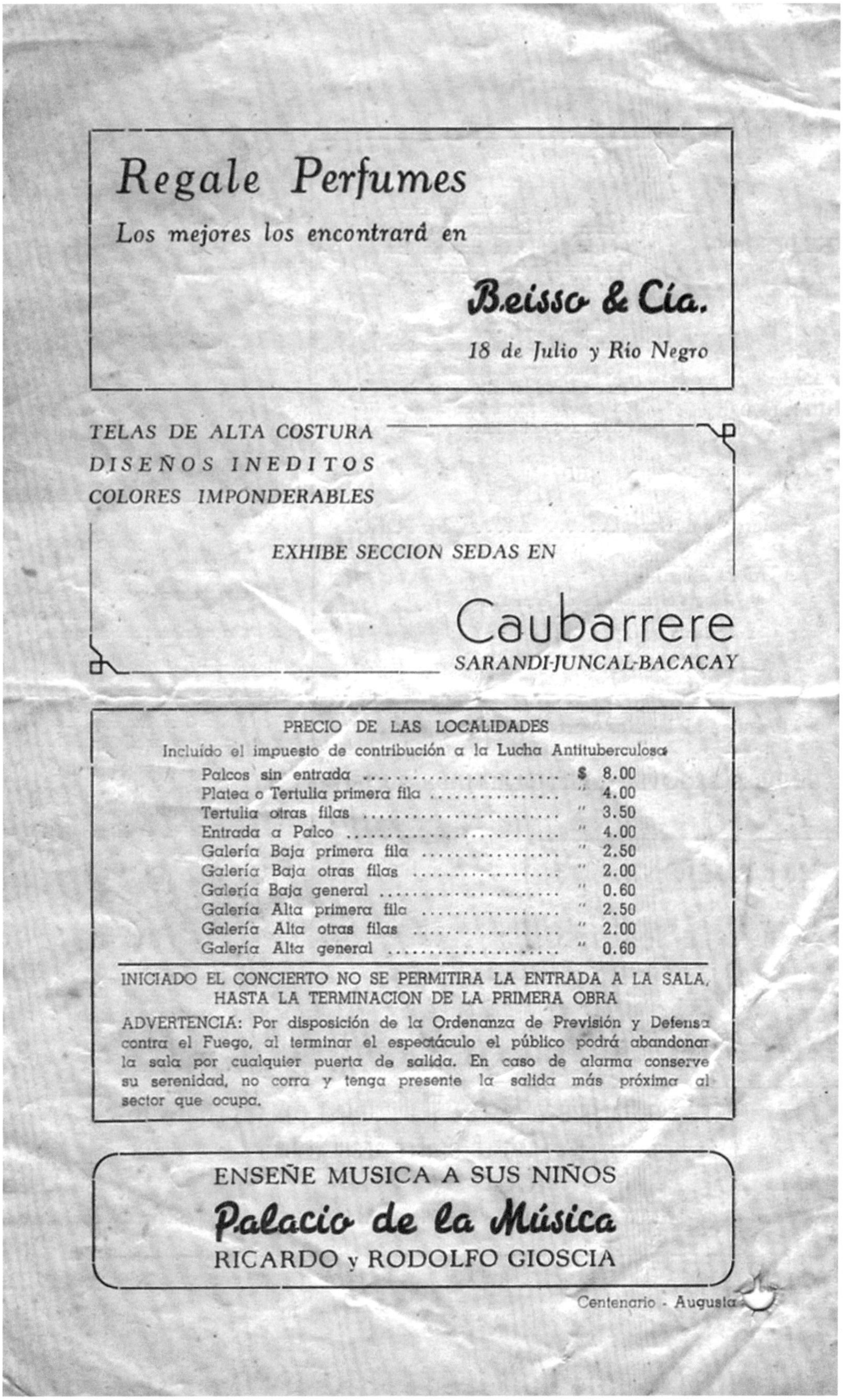

Regale Perfumes
Los mejores los encontrará en
Beisso & Cía.
18 de Julio y Río Negro

TELAS DE ALTA COSTURA
DISEÑOS INEDITOS
COLORES IMPONDERABLES
EXHIBE SECCION SEDAS EN
Caubarrere
SARANDI-JUNCAL-BACACAY

PRECIO DE LAS LOCALIDADES
Incluído el impuesto de contribución a la Lucha Antituberculosa

Palcos sin entrada	$ 8.00
Platea o Tertulia primera fila	" 4.00
Tertulia otras filas	" 3.50
Entrada a Palco	" 4.00
Galería Baja primera fila	" 2.50
Galería Baja otras filas	" 2.00
Galería Baja general	" 0.60
Galería Alta primera fila	" 2.50
Galería Alta otras filas	" 2.00
Galería Alta general	" 0.60

INICIADO EL CONCIERTO NO SE PERMITIRA LA ENTRADA A LA SALA, HASTA LA TERMINACION DE LA PRIMERA OBRA

ADVERTENCIA: Por disposición de la Ordenanza de Previsión y Defensa contra el Fuego, al terminar el espectáculo el público podrá abandonar la sala por cualquier puerta de salida. En caso de alarma conserve su serenidad, no corra y tenga presente la salida más próxima al sector que ocupa.

ENSEÑE MUSICA A SUS NIÑOS
Palacio de la Música
RICARDO y RODOLFO GIOSCIA
Centenario - Augusta

This music store — Palacio de la Musica — (Music Palace) was the shop where one could buy a Santos Hernández or Hermann Hauser I in Montevideo. Source: Richard Bruné.

Argentine Victrola discs of Andrés Segovia that were recorded in London on May 20, 1927. The *"Tremolo-Estudio"* is the first recording of Francisco Tárrega's *"Recuerdos de la Alhambra"*. Joaquín Turina dedicated the *"Fandanguillo"* to Andrés Segovia.

The Gramophone Co.'s "His Master's Voice" British label recordings of Andrés Segovia. There is the Prelude in D Major from the 1st Cello Suite by J. S. Bach and the Alard Study in A Major by Francisco Tárrega.

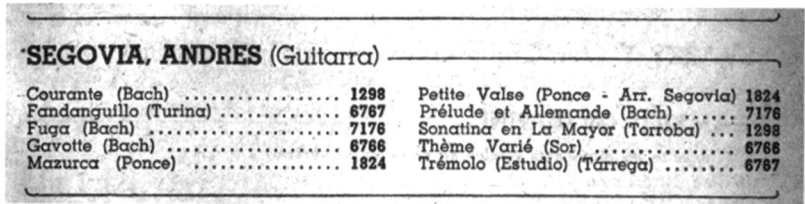

This listing is from the *1949 RCA Argentina Catalogo No. 49* as of August 31, 1949. His first recordings were still in print.

Argentine Victor recordings by Andrés Segovia of Mozart-Sor Op. 9 Variations from the Magic Flute and a *Gavotte* by J. S. Bach. According to the EDVR this *Gavotte* was the first song that was recorded on February 2, 1927. (It was done 4 days after he played the Wigmore Hall concert on January 29, 1927.) This information is from: The Encyclopedic Discography of Victor Recordings (EDVR) web site. A team of researchers based at the University of California, Santa Barbara Libraries edits the database.

Prelude and Allemande by J. S. Bach recorded by Andrés Segovia and pressed for the Argentine RCA Victor label, as well the famous *Fugue* in A minor originally from the Violin Sonata No. 1 in G minor.

American Red Seal Victor recordings by Andrés Segovia of the *Sonatina* in A Major by Federico Moreno-Torroba and the *Courante* from the 3rd Cello Suite by J. S. Bach.

DEL MISMO AUTOR

I	Rondino sobre un tema de Beethoven	Kreisler	$	1.50
II	Minueto de la sonata op. 31 No. 3	Beethoven	"	1.20
III	Minueto	Haydn	"	1.50
IV.	a) Melodia popular b) Pequeño estudio	Schuman	"	1.50
V	a) Andante cantabile (en fa mayor) b) Marcha militar	Schuman	"	1.50
VI	a) Canción del norte b) Labrador alegre	Schuman	"	1.50
VII	Romanza sin palabra op. 30 No. 3	Mendelsohnn	"	1.50
VIII	Leyenda (Preludio Español)	Albéniz	"	2.—
IX	Torre Bermeja	"	"	2.—
X	Romanza en la menor (original para guitarra)	José M.ª Franco	"	1.50
XI	Andantino en re menor, revisado y numerado por A. Segovia	F. Sors	"	1.—
XII	Gran Sonata revisada y numerada por A. Segovia	"	"	3.—
XIII	Variaciones sobre un tema de Mozart		"	2.—
XIV	Triste No 4	J. Aguirre	"	1,—
XV	Vidalita	"	"	1.—

This listing of the 15 transcriptions done by Andrés Segovia is from the back outside cover of *Leyenda* by Isaac Albeniz published by Romero & Fernández in the 1920's. The newest transcriptions are those of the Argentine composer Julián Aguirre.

(*"del mismo autor"* means of the same author.)

Edgar L. Goldsmith   Warren E. Thompson

present

CARMEN TORRES
Soprano

and

ANDRES SEGOVIA
Guitarist

•

The third event in the 1947-48
History and Enjoyment of Music Series
Section II

•

Sunday, January 11, 1948, at 3:30 P.M.

ORCHESTRA HALL

Andrés Segovia concert with Carmen Torres at the Orchestra Hall in Chicago on Sunday January 11, 1948.

I.

Lungi dal caro bene .... G. Sarti

> *Far from my love, I languish, I do not live. Dreams sweet with death*
> *steal o'er me. If she be not before me, fails me the light of day.*

Donzelle Fuggite .... Cavalli

> *O, hasten, ye maidens, from beauty to flee!*
> *If a piercing glance strikes your heart like an arrow,*
> *Beware of the dart, it is laden with sorrow.*
> *Love snares but to chasten, deceiving is he!*

Gia la notte .... Haydn

> *Known as "the father of the symphony", and creator of an immense*
> *amount of instrumental music, Haydn was equally successful in writing*
> *for the voice, as attested by his oratorios and a number of charming*
> *songs.*

Aria: Pensar en El, from "La Marina" .... Arrieta y Correra

Carmen Torres

II.

Sarabanda .... Handel

Prelude et Gavotte .... Bach

Menuet .... Haydn

Variations on a Mozart Theme .... Sor

Andres Segovia

INTERMISSION

III.

Nortena .... Crespo

Prelude .... Villa-Lobos

Etude .... Tarrega

Sevilla .... Albeniz

Andres Segovia

IV.

Cycle of Seven Songs .... Manuel de Falla

El Pano Moruno	Jota
Seguidilla Murciana	Nana
Asturiana	Cancios
	Polo

Carmen Torres

Andrés Segovia did not accompany Carmen Torres, that role was fulfilled by Alexander Astor at the piano.
The Maestro opens his second set with *"Norteña"* by Jorge Gomez Crespo.

V

Pano Murciano . . . . Joaquin Nin

An Andalusian girl asks the jeweler how much it will cost to have her lover's kiss set in her ring that she may preserve it forever.

Coplas de curro dulce . . . . Fernando Obradors

Oh, the tiny little bride, the tiny little groom; the tiny little parlor and the tiny little room. That is why the resting place must be very, very small, as well as the mosquito netting.

La Guitarra Sin Prima . . . . Fernando Obradors

El Vito . . . . Fernando Obradors

This is a popular Spanish song from Madrid written about the year 1800 and is one of many that Obradors has arranged for modern use. It is notable for its unusual rhythms and color.

Carmen Torres

Alexander Aster at the Piano

CARMEN TORRES was born in Geneva, Switzerland, during the period of her father's service as Spanish consul there. She lived in Switzerland for several years, then moved to Paris, where she spent most of her childhood and received her musical training. The historic Liceo Opera House in Barcelona was the scene of Carmen Torres' operatic debut. There she created a sensation as Gilda in "Rigoletto" at the age of seventeen. Returning to her adopted home in Paris, Miss Torres, in her dual role of excitingly beautiful singing actress and virtuoso vocal artist, soon became the toast of the French capital.

ANDRES SEGOVIA, foremost Spanish guitarist of our day, was born at Linares, February 18, 1894. Native of Granada, he commenced the study of the guitar at an early age, and continued his specialization in the instrument at the Granada Musical Institute, making his debut as a recitalist and guitar virtuoso in Granada at the age of fourteen. For six years he toured Europe and South America, and in 1928 made his first New York appearance. After some years he retired to Montevideo, Uraguay, with his wife and small daughter, devoting much of his time to the transcription of classical music by Bach and other composers for his instrument. Five years ago he was brought out of retirement for a tour of North America by S. Hurok. Each of his succeeding visits has served to increase both his popularity and his standing as the preeminent master of his chosen medium, in which he utilizes all the contrapuntal resources of the "king of instruments", as it is affectionately called by the Spanish people.

Andrés Segovia's birthdate is wrong, which is February 21, 1893. The subject of retirement in the biography is a mystery.

TOWN HALL
Sunday Eve., March 7 at 8:40 p.m.
PRICES: $3.00, $2.40, $1.80, $1.20 (Tax Incl.)
Tickets Now At Box Office

This Sunday March 7, 1948 concert by Andrés Segovia is at the Town Hall in New York, where he gave his debut on January 8, 1928, in his first American concert tour.

The praise of Andrés Segovia on this handbill, would change as the years went by, reflecting reviews of the more recents triumphs by the maestro, written in the New York dailies.

This article and interview by Hope Stoddard with Andrés Segovia are from the May 1949 "International Musician" magazine Issue No. 11, XLVII, published in Newark, New Jersey.

Classical Guitarist

WHEN YOU hear—and see—what Andrés Segovia can do with his ten fingers on the guitar, you wonder why men have profaned the strings with bows and key-operated hammers. But there is, after all, only one Segovia, who can produce on his single instrument harmonies and tone-shadings which, with your eyes closed, you would credit to a string quartet, playing softly in the distance. The tone of his guitar is not unlike that of a harpsichord, but it is fuller and mellower, with more sustention and body; and there is none of the harpsichord's plangent "ping" which finally becomes as trying as the drone of the bagpipe.

Segovia's program, in his one New York concert of the season at Town Hall Sunday night, March 6th, exhibited the great range and variety of his art. He played pieces written for the guitar, such as the Suite in D by Vigeo, Louis XIV's court guitarist; a series of adaptations from Scarlatti, Bach, and Haydn; and finally, new works written for him: "Allegro" by M. Ponce; "Study" by Villa-Lobos, and Samazeuilh's "Serenata." He varied his technique for these different period styles with the utmost subtlety, so that each work was a distinct and unique musical experience for the listener.

The music came from his instrument with each phrase molded in the round and fully embodied. He played the classical masters in a thoughtful, almost elegiac mood, so that the polyphonies seemed to come to the listeners as if through a golden haze. Always one sensed the complete mastery of the work as a whole, and one could only puzzle over the miracles of technique which produced such complexities of musical pattern with a single instrument. (It would be a boon to the 2,000,000 fretted-string players in this country if they could watch his fingering close-up on television.) Always the technique was subdued to the purposes of interpretation, and Segovia seemed to be recreating the very moments of creation that the composers had lived through.

He was equally at home with his contemporaries, and conveyed with a fine touch the blend of French and Spanish tradition in the Brazilian Villa-Lobos. In the gay and lively numbers, Segovia infused a high, gallant Quixotic quality, commanding always that grave philosophic treatment of the comic which we associate with Cervantes.

The audience responded to the high seriousness of the guitarist's art by listening with complete quiet—until each number was over, when they were loud with their bravos. They demanded nine encores at the end.

Throughout the program one felt the restful and tranquillizing effect of Segovia's art: no strain, no insistence, but that timelessness and perfect rightness that mark the truly classical style.

An interview with Andrés Segovia appears on page twenty-one.

I ARRIVED at Andrés Segovia's apartment on Central Park, West, New York, somewhat before my scheduled time, and was shown into a room which in its curious blend of austerity and exuberance is typically Spanish. A painting—a Desiano—dark and mellow in tone, caught my eye first, then prints of old Spain and a polytych of the Madonna and Saints. The desk, a Seventeenth Century Bargueno, its innumerable small drawers flanked by tiny gold-leafed columns—later Segovia showed me their various secret compartments—had the appearance of a storied palace in miniature. A leathern pipe-stand with seven pipes and a jar of old ivory rested on it. Rare woods, subdued and rich colors—bronze, rust, aquamarine, touches of crimson—soothed rather than teased the eye.

In the book-case were, among other books, Grove's Dictionaries, histories of Spain, a "Handbook of Legendary Art," Virgil Thomson's "The Musical Scene," Ernie Pyle's "Brave Men." On top of the bookcase stood the photograph of a little girl, Segovia's daughter, as I later discovered. (His son, a painter, lives in Switzerland.) The candelabra on the mantelpiece were heavy with dripped wax. Then there was the low music stand, an Etude by Villa-Lobos spread open on it. Facing it at a convenient distance was a small-backed chair covered in tapestried leaf design.

I seated myself at a table of hard oak, deep-grained and flanked by two bare benches, its only burden a plant with sleek, sparse leaves. Outside the window pigeons strutted on the balcony, their muffled call closing around the stillness like hands encircling a crystal ball.

Then Segovia stood in the doorway, hatless, in a rough overcoat, a red muffler about his throat. He looks less professorial than student-like, an effect brought about by his dark-rimmed glasses, his slightly down-bent head, and the easy yet controlled motion of his body. He crossed the room and took my hand. For all he is so quiet-moving, he has a swift and comprehending glance. Now he turned on the lights, spoke a few words to the maid, motioned me to a comfortable chair, poured cooling drinks —every movement of his hands poised and timed —took a chair, smiled at me slightly, and waited.

I remembered something I had read in his autobiography: "I decided I would be the apostle of the guitar, or, to put it more exactly, her husband before God, swearing to provide her with all that she might need so that in the future the world might respect her and receive her with the honor she deserved . . . And more than all that . . . I would be entirely faithful . . ." This promise Segovia made when he was a very young man. Marriage vows have seldom been more scrupulously observed.

So of course I asked him about his guitar. What had made him choose it as his instrument in the first place?

"I was living in Granada," he told me, "a city in which the musical life was at a very low ebb. Yet my whole soul cried out for music. But it was not so easy for me to begin formalized musical training. The piano teacher I approached was so very bad that the instrument became to me—in the words of a humorous poet—'a rectangular monster which is made to scream when its teeth are drilled.' I approached next a violinist and he, too, was very bad. I had no better luck with the cellist. Of course I had no way of knowing it was the teachers who were at fault, not the instruments. I was scared by the rough sonority. I ran away.

"But when I heard the guitar—even as it was played on the street—the suavity of it, the nuance, the sonority so captivated me, I gave myself up to that soft and nice-voiced instrument."

He smiled the smile of one recalling a stirring encounter. Then he continued. "I realized such an instrument should have a literature. I began to investigate. After long searching I found a few works by Arcas, Sor, and Tarrega. I gave my first concert when I was fourteen. From that day to now I have never stopped."

I asked then of the difficulties he had to face. "With the scanty notions of solfeggio which I possessed at the time," he said, "I could hardly read the music I had found. And as I had to fight against the opposition of my family, there was no question of a teacher. Secretly, therefore, I acquired a solfeggio method and a book of music theory, and when everyone was asleep I taught myself to be a good sight-reader. From that time forward I was my own teacher and pupil, in a comradeship so firm and persevering that the most trying incidents of my life served only to strengthen the union.

"I carefully studied piano exercises, noted how each made the fingers work and what degree of independence, strength and agility it developed in them. Then I would try to apply my observations to the technique of the guitar. It brought me an indescribable joy to discover that the exercises I had worked out were increasing the vigor, elasticity and rapidity of my fingers."

I asked him next about the inclusion in his programs of modern works. "I was impelled by the sound of the guitar," he told me, "to add to the repertoire. I had to break the vicious circle in which the instrument was closed. There were no composers because there were no artists, and there were no artists because there were no composers. Now I have in my repertoire seven concertos written for guitar, two by Castelnuovo-Tedesco, one by Alexander Tansman, one by Joaquin Rodrigo, one by Villa-Lobos, one by

(Continued on page thirty-two)

Segovia is a guitarist—a guitarist without whom the history of the guitar today would lack meaning. If every reference to Segovia were removed from the history of the guitar, he would be present without a name—in the vacuum produced by his absence. The prestige which Segovia has brought to his instrument has attracted many eminent composers, and a flood of talent which might otherwise have been lost has been guided into channels that have enriched the repertory not only of the guitar, but of music as a whole.—Carlos Vega, in "The Guitar Review."

Segovia on the Guitar

(Continued from page twenty-one)

Torroba, and one by Manuel Maria Ponce, all of them dedicated to me. Since the guitar is peculiarly adapted for modern music you can understand how these concertos widen the scope of my instrument.

"For years Ponce hesitated to write his 'Concerto del sur' because he feared that the tenuous sound of the guitar would be swallowed up by the orchestra. But when Castelnuovo-Tedesco, another dear friend of mine, completed his guitar Concerto in D, Ponce, who himself conducted its premiere in Mexico, found his imagination awaken and fell to work. He set down the concerto on the thinnest air-mail paper and sent it to me section by section as he finished it. Whenever the postman brought that bulky envelope to my door, my wife and I suspended our daily study so that we could put our whole hearts into reading and rereading the pages," Segovia smiled, sitting quietly, remembering.

"And it did sound good," he went on. "At the rehearsal of the work by the National Symphony Orchestra, Hans Kindler, who was conducting, exclaimed, at one point where the instruments gave flesh and blood to the spirit of the phrase just whispered by the guitar, 'How beautiful this is.' "

Then Segovia told me that Ponce had composed more than eighty works for guitar before his last illness; that, along with Turina, Falla, Manen, Castelnuovo, Tansman, Villa-Lobos, Torroba, he had given the guitar a status it had never before possessed as an instrument of the highest artistry. Thus, as Segovia explained, "the guitar was saved from the music written exclusively by guitarists."

I recalled in this connection a letter of Castelnuovo's in which he described Segovia's gentle means of persuasion: "On Christmas of 1938 Segovia himself came to see me in Florence. He knew that I was about to leave my native country, that I was very much depressed and worried about the future, that I had not been writing music for months. He came to spend these holidays with me, to give me encouragement and faith in the future . . . I was so deeply touched by his friendly gesture that I suddenly decided to write the Concerto to prove to him my gratitude!"

Now I spoke to Segovia about the intimacy between him and his instrument as he played it, holding it in his lap, looking at it always. "No obstacle between the instrument and the heart," he told me gently. "Only the slight layer of skin on the finger-tips."

I asked then about the attitudes of concert audiences here and in Europe—how did they differ?

"The way to love music is the same all over the world," he answered.

And now I stood up to leave. I dropped my pencil and he stooped to pick it up. I had long since dropped my brave speech, but it was not missed in the silence, rich with the echoes of his talk. Here, one felt, stood that rare person, a man fit for his mission. A man who had created music of a sort we might otherwise never have heard. A man who had created not only beauty but the means of projecting that beauty into ages to come.

—Hope Stoddard.

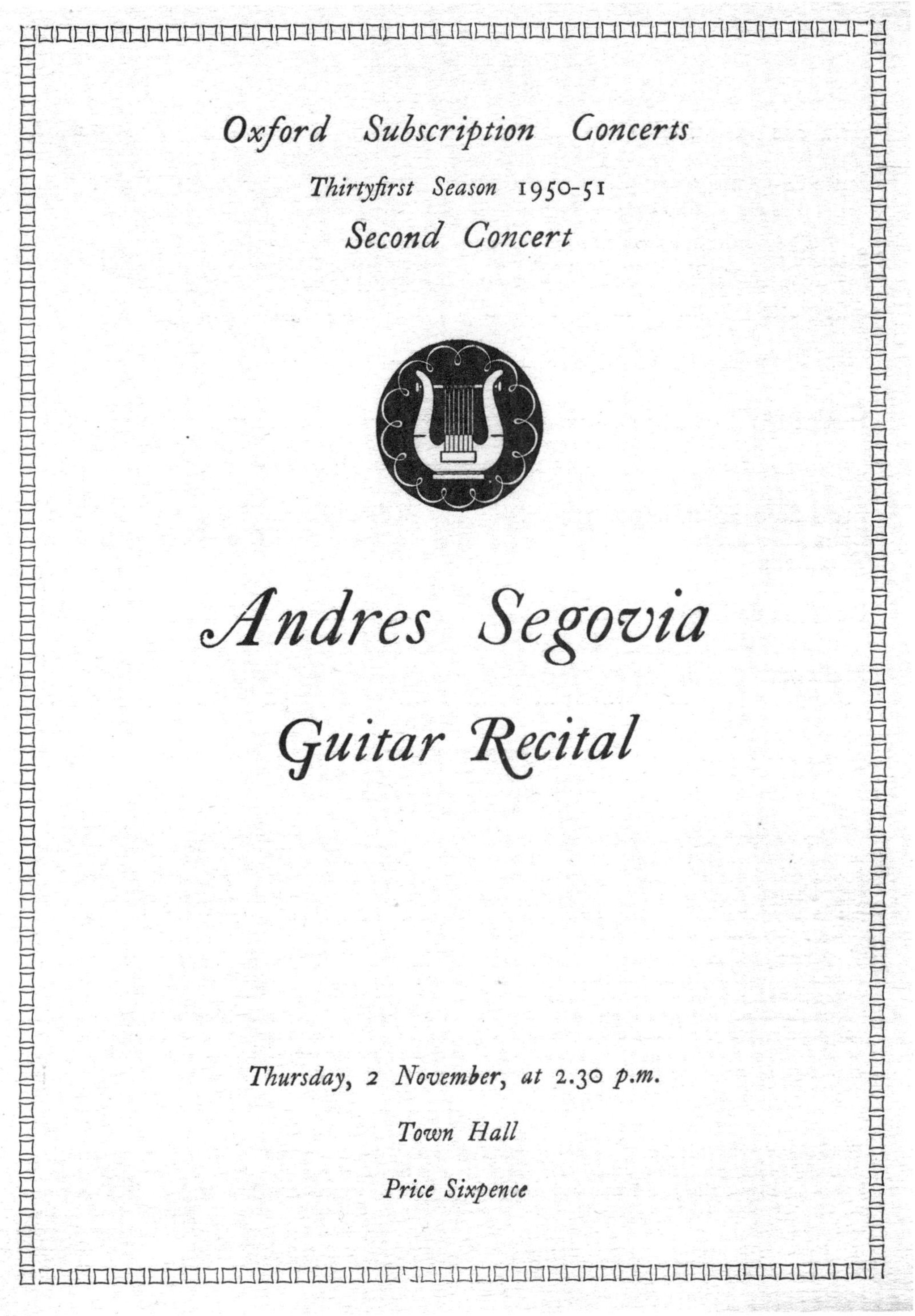
Oxford Subscription Concerts

Thirtyfirst Season 1950-51

Second Concert

Andres Segovia

Guitar Recital

Thursday, 2 November, at 2.30 p.m.

Town Hall

Price Sixpence

This Andrés Segovia concert in Oxford, England on Thursday November 2, 1950 was held at the Town Hall theater.

Programme

Aria con variazioni ... ... *Frescobaldi*

Suite in D major ... ... *de Visée*
Prelude — Allemande — Bourrée — Sarabande — Gigue — Menuet — Courante

Sonatina ... ... *M. Giuliani*

Allegretto ... ... *Sor*

Chaconne ... ... *J. S. Bach*

Preludio quasi un'improvvisazione ⎫ dedicated
Ballata Scozzese   ⎬ to Segovia   *Castelnuovo-Tedesco*
Tarantella   ⎭

La Maya de Goya ... ... *Granados*

Mallorca ⎫
Sevilla ⎭ ... ... *Albeniz*

THE GUITAR

The Guitar, an instrument of ancient Arabian origin, was brought into Spain by the Moors in the XIth or XIIth Century. It then had four strings, but a fifth, added in the XVIth Century, differentiated the Spanish Guitar which, in the hands of the brilliant player, Espinel (1551—1624), became so popular that it soon ranked as the national instrument of Spain, and has in turn exerted a strong influence over Spanish music. The modern instrument has six strings, tuned to E A D G B E.

During the early XIXth Century the guitar became a fashion in Europe; its romantic associations attracted the amateur in that romantic age while players like Sor and Giuliani showed that it could be put to more serious uses. Their musical descendant of our own day, Senor Segovia, has shown the guitar to be a medium for the expression of complex and polyphonic music, brilliant display and poetic emotion. The commonly-held notion of a guitar as something suitable only for thrumming a simple serenade accompaniment has finally been exploded by the brilliant and tireless work of the greatest guitarist of all.

THE COMPOSERS

Frescobaldi (1583—1643). Famous in his day as the finest organist in Europe and ancestor, through Froberger, of the great German school of organ-playing culminating in J. S. Bach, Frescobaldi was also a distinguished composer in whose organ music the gradual development of the polyphonic forms laid the foundation of fugue. He also wrote instrumental fantasies and madrigals.

Robert de Visée (c. 1650—c. 1725). He was a lutenist and guitarist and held the appointments of Guitar-player and Oboeist to the Dauphin and Chamber Musician to King Louis XIV of France from about 1686 to 1721. He wrote music for the guitar, songs, trios for lute, theorbo and guitar, etc.

Mauro Giuliani (c. 1780—?). Famed throughout Italy for his guitar-playing he also showed in his compositions a more serious use of his instrument than was current. He wrote three Concertos for guitar and orchestra, a Quintet for guitar and strings, works for guitar, violin and 'cello, two guitars and a number of solos.

Fernando Sor (1778—1839). Born at Barcelona, where he produced an opera at the age of nineteen, he became a guitar virtuoso and composer. On Napoleon's invasion, he fled to London and later Paris. His playing became all the rage in fashionable circles and he even appeared at the Royal Philharmonic Society's Concerts. He had many aristocratic pupils and his fame spread throughout Europe. He died in Paris.

Castelnuovo-Tedesco (b. 1895). Born at Florence, though resident, since 1939, in the United States, Castelnuovo-Tedesco studied with Pizzetti. His works include Overtures to seven of Shakespeare's plays and settings of all the Shakespearian songs, in English; operas; chamber music; numerous short works, and concertos for piano, violin and guitar.

Granados (1867—1916). A celebrated pianist, Granados had a gift for melody. He wrote several operas but was most successful with his songs (tonadillas) and short pianoforte pieces in Spanish idiom. His best pieces are the two sets inspired by works of the painter Goya.

Albeniz (1860—1909). Albeniz began his career as a pianist at the age of four. He studied with various masters, including Liszt, and for some years travelled as a virtuoso. Having settled for a time in Spain he quitted it for London and Paris, where he studied with Dukas. He wrote several operas and songs and a large number of piano pieces, of which the best are the set of 12 called "Iberia". He is regarded as the originator of the Spanish "National" School.
                                                                                          C.T.

CONCERNING THE CHACONNE OF J. S. BACH
Translation of an Article by MARC PINCHERLE,
Secretary of the French Society of Musicology, Paris

You ask me, my dear Andres, to present your transcription of the Chaconne. To tell the truth, I hardly see how anyone could suspect a musician such as yourself of lacking in respect towards Bach. On the other hand, it may be that certain writings on the Chaconne have surrounded it with taboos and prompted the overzealous to forbid, in the name of Bach, the very things the old Cantor would have been the first to encourage.

While deeply admiring the Chaconne, I have never heard it without a certain dissatisfaction. This, despite the splendour of the music, its nobility and restrained pathos, the variety that never disturbs its perfect balance, the ingenuity displayed in the treatment of the violin. It is only on the rarest occasions that the performance fulfils all our expectations, so great is the disproportion between the meagre resources of strings and the intensity of the message they are asked to convey—between the melodic character of the violin, that pure soprano, and the orchestral fullness that is required of it.

Personalities like Joachim and Ysaye may have known how to reconcile these opposites. A handful of privileged ones have, since their day, succeeded, too. On each occasion one had the impression of having witnessed a triumph of genius—something quite beyond the reach of all the honest and impeccable interpreters of current repertoires.

This feeling of mine must have been shared by those fervent "Bachists"—Mendelssohn, Ferdinand David, Schumann. When during the winter of 1840, David played for the first time the then recently unearthed Chaconne (it had been published in 1802 by Simrock and later by Decombe, but had attracted no attention) Mendelssohn went to the piano and improvised an accompaniment which he later wrote down and had published in London in 1847.

Other means have been tried to make its performance less forbidding. F. Hermann made an arrangement for two violins without accompaniment. Brahms arranged a version for piano, for the left hand alone (No. 5 of the Studies published by Breitkopf). There is also Busoni's over-sumptuous transcription. Finally, that master of the bow, Jeno de Hubay, in an excess of zeal, transcribed the Chaconne for large orchestra, in which the different choirs divide among themselves the polyphonic strands originally assigned to a single violin.

Andrés Segovia spent about a year working on the *"Chaconne"* by J.S. Bach and had performed it since Saturday February 23, 1935 at the The Town Hall in New York. Marc Pincherle (1888-1974) had written this article in France at that time after its European debut on June 4th in Paris at the Salle Gaveau.

Andrés Segovia wrote: *"La Chacona es una de las obras cumbres del arte de musica y Bach como el Himalaya"*.

"The Chaconne is one of the masterpieces of the art of music and Bach as the Himalayas".

Marc Pincherle is mentioned as the President and not the Secretary of the musical society.

Source: Translated from *Andrés Segovia Vida y Obra* by Alberto Lopez Poveda published by the Universidad de Jaen / Ayuntamiento de Linares 2010.

To those who might take exception to such liberties, one has only to recall the musical customs of Bach's own day, and the freedom with which he himself changed the instrumental settings of his works, giving to the harpsichord an adagio in legato style written for the violin, or a prelude for violin alone to the organ with orchestral accompaniment.

Among the instruments to which he gave special attention was the lute, a close cousin of the guitar. Several scholars—among others, N. D. Bruger and H. Neemann, have made an inventory of these works of which we possess several versions—for the violin alone and lute, for lute and 'cello—without being able, for the most part, to ascertain which version was the original and which the transcription. The Chaconne would not be out of place among these ambiguous works, and it is by no means certain that some future discovery may not justify its inclusion among them.

Indeed, who knows but that it may be found to have some kinship with the guitar? One cannot help remarking on the perfect suitability of the key of D; the harmonic scheme in more than one place (and especially in nearly the whole of the last page) is identical with a certain progression found in popular Andalusian music, for which the guitar is the traditional vehicle.

In short, there is nothing against the notion that Iberian origin of the Chaconne might have suggested to Bach's mind that he compose it for a Spanish instrument of whose existence his ever-lively curiosity in all things musical must have made him aware; the more so, since masters like Champion, de Visée, Corbet, had brought the guitar into fashion all over Europe.

I need hardly add that such a hypothesis is too bold to be stated with anything like conviction. The strongest argument in its favour is that the Chaconne, whether written for the guitar or not, is scored as though the composer had this very instrument in mind. Not only is there no change to be made in the dispositions of chords, but everything lends itself to the guitar with perfect ease. The chords, which on the violin must be arpeggiated, can here be played with all the notes sounding simultaneously; the "imitations" keep their independence of line and colour; the arpeggios yield an even harmonic texture, over which the melodic lines stand out in full relief. The violin keeps its superiority in certain legato passages, and others in the register which lose some of their vivid incisiveness when played on the guitar. Almost everything else is better suited to the guitar, which has among other advantages that of sounding an octave below the written note, thus giving deep bass tones which are capable of bearing the weight of the majestic edifice.

But all this need not be dwelt upon. It is a question for the ear and sensibility; your hearers themselves will form their own opinion. I wish only to assure them that the pleasure they are going to derive from hearing you is by no means an illicit one.

It is perhaps a crime toward the Chaconne to present it in lame and scratchy fashion, as though it bristled with difficulties; but to present it in a harmonious, ample, and balanced manner—to give us, in short, the equivalent of the most ideal mental hearing—can make you deserving only of our greatest thanks.

Next Concert :

23 NOVEMBER, 2.30 p.m.   TOWN HALL

The New Italian Quartet

PAOLO BORCIANI, *Violin*   PIERO FARULLI, *Viola*
ELISA PEGREFFI, *Violin*   FRANCO ROSSI, *Violoncello*

Quartet in G, Op. 77, No. 1 ... ... *Haydn*
Quartet in B flat, Op. 168 ... ... *Schubert*
Quartet in E minor ... ... *Verdi*

Tickets 7/6, 5/6, 4/-, on sale from Monday, November 13
Box Office : C. TAPHOUSE & SON, 3 MAGDALEN STREET, OXFORD. PHONE 2674.

Hall the Printer Ltd., 5 Brewer Street, Oxford.

ALLIED ARTS CORPORATION

HARRY ZELZER, *Managing Director*

Presents

ANDRES

SEGOVIA

SUNDAY AFTERNOON, FEBRUARY 10th, 1952

at 3:30 P.M.

ORCHESTRA HALL   CHICAGO

PROGRAM

I.

Romanesca . . . . Alonso de Mudarra
(16th Century)

Pavana and Gallarda . . . . Gaspar Sanz
(17th Century)

Villano . . . . Francisco Guerau
(17th Century)

(PROGRAM CONTINUED ON NEXT PAGE)

PROGRAM—Continued

Andantino Variato (Written for Guitar) . . . . N. Paganini
(1782-1840)

Sonatina . . . . M. Giuliani
(-1771)

Short Intermission

(PROGRAM CONTINUED ON NEXT PAGE)

PROGRAM—Continued

II.

Allegretto grazioso ⎫
Gavota   ⎪
Menuet   ⎬ . . . . G. F. Handel
Folia   ⎭   (1685-1759)

Prelude and Loure . . . . J. S. Bach
(1685-1750)

Menuet . . . . F. Schubert
(1797-1828)

INTERMISSION

(PROGRAM CONTINUED ON NEXT PAGE)

PROGRAM—Continued

III.

Sonata III. (Dedicated to Segovia) . . . . M. Ponce
    Allegro   (1886-)
      Chanson
        Finale

Highland Song (Dedicated to Segovia) . . . . . . M. Castelnuevo-Tedesco
(1895-)

Asturias   ⎫ . . . . I. Albeniz
Torre Bermeja ⎭   (1861-1909)

Exclusive Management: HUROK ATTRACTIONS INC., 711 Fifth Ave., N. Y.

Here we see pieces by Ponce and Castelnuevo-Tedesco dedicated to Andrés Segovia.

912

POLITEAMA ARGENTINO

CORRIENTES 1478 · *Empresario* G. CONTENTO · T.E. 38-5214

MARTES 17 DÉ JUNIO DE 1952, a las 22.30

RECITAL DE

ANDRES SEGOVIA

•

PROGRAMA

PRIMERA PARTE
GRUPO DE OBRAS ESCRITAS PARA GUITARRA

ROMANZA .... Alonso Demadarra (1541)

SUITE EN RE .... R. Dice (1650-1725)
    Prelude
    Allemande
    Bourre
    Zarabande
    Guige
    Menet
    Courante

DOS ESTUDIOS Y TEMAS CON VARIACIONES
            Fernando Sors (1778 - 1839)

SEGUNDA PARTE
**GRUPO DE TRANSCRIPCIONES DE OBRAS CUYA TECNICA
Y ESPIRITU SE ADAPTA A LA GUITARRA**

ZARABANDA Y GRACIOSA .... Haendel

TEMPO DE BOURRE .... Bach

ALLEGRETTO .... J. Ch. Rameau

MINUETO .... Schumann Schubert

TERCERA PARTE
**COMPOSICIONES DEDICADAS A ANDRES SEGOVIA
INSPIRADAS EN EL FOLKLORE ESPAÑOL**

SONATINA MERIDIONAL .... M. Ponce
    Campo, copla, siesta

PRELUDIO Y DANZA .... Torroba

DANZA EN SOL .... Granados

SEVILLA .... Albéniz

Disposición Municipal:

Uso de los sombreros (Art. 1860, 70 y 71 del D. M.): Queda prohibido en las plateas, tertulias altas y demás secciones en común del Teatro, la permanencia de personas de ambos sexos, con sombrero puesto, una vez empezado el acto.

---

(87)   Capacidad: 1.199 localidades)

This Andrés Segovia concert was held at the Politeama Argentino Theater on Tuesday June 17, 1952. There were over 1,000 listeners that attended this concert.

PALACIO DE LA MUSICA

RECITAL

Domingo, 14 de Diciembre 1952
a las 6'30 de la tarde

ANDRÉS
SEGOVIA

PROGRAMA

I
(Obras originales para vihuela o guitarra)

Romanesca.	Alfonso de MUDARRA (1541)
Suite en Re	R. de VISEO (1650-1725)
Allemande - Bourrée - Sarabande - Gigue - Menueto - Courante	
Andantino variato (*)	N. PAGANINI
Andante y Allegretto.	F. SORS (1778-1839)

II
(Transcripciones de obras cuya técnica y espíritu
son adaptables a la guitarra)

Aria con variazioni	G. FRESCOBALDI
Allegretto	J. Ph. RAMEAU
Gavotta	A. SCARLATTI
Sonata	D. SCARLATTI
Bourrée	J. S. BACH

III
(Composiciones escritas para Andrés Segovia o inspiradas
en ritmos y giros melódicos andaluces)

Cavatina (**)	A. TANSMAN
Prelude - Sarabande - Scherzino - Barcarolle	
Tarantella	CASTELNUOVO - TEDESCO
Leyenda catalana y sardana . . .	Gaspar CASSADÓ
Torre Bermeja	I. ALBENIZ

(*) *Revisado por Manuel PONCE.*
(**) *Primer premio en el Concurso Internacional celebrado en la Academia Chigiaux, en 1951.*

This Andrés Segovia concert in Barcelona on Sunday December 14, 1952 was held at the Palacio de la Musica theater. In first set the Paganini piece was revised by Manuel Ponce. In the last set the piece *"Cavatina"* by Tansman was the First Prize winner in the International Competition of Composition at the Academia Chigiana in Siena, Italy in 1951. According to Alberto Lopez Poveda, Andrés played in Santander on the 16th, in Bilbao the 17th, in Vitoria the 18th, in San Sebastian the 19th, then in Barcelona again on the 21st. He had returned to Madrid, Spain for the first time in 15 years on June 21, 1952.

Translation of the liner notes to these concerts from the pen of the severe critic Robert Aloys Mooser:

"Andrés Segovia

Because of the universal fame of this reigning Spanish artist we will dispense with enumerating the habitual biographical dates, and in its place, we are pleased to reproduce the study of his artistic personality, due to the pen of the great Swiss musicologist and critic Robert Aloys Mooser. He says:

'Andrés Segovia isn't only an incomparable virtuoso, whose fingers appear to be pleased in the development of the most arduous and complex problems, but a consummate musician, who possessing the most delicate taste (always growing, in all the qualities of expressive order), is converted into one of the preeminent and complete interpreters of the present epoch.

His prodigious technique, flexible, equal, ignoring the weak, adapts to the realization of polyphonic works without effort, in which he distinguishes the sonoral planes so simply and easily, that permits the instrument to sketch every melodic phrase, illuminating every accent and every inflection.

Segovia finds the most varied and subtle effects. From the six strings of the guitar he draws the variety of colors, such beauty of celestial clouds and such delicate sound, that it confounds us. But in him, the technique always surpasses the ideas of the composers, penetrating fully with them, and manifesting that the virtuoso must be a medium and not a fundamental idea.

This great maestro subtly interprets that testifies to every instant a Latin concept of the measure, of the order and of the clarity of expression, needed in repertoire. You can't be content with the transcriptions and triviality that was all the literature of the guitar for a long time. And among the work that the guitarists of the brilliant epoch, such as Sor, Carulli, Giuliani, Coste and Tárrega left, Andrés Segovia found a great quantity of pieces that deserve to be saved from being forgotten. Much later he investigated among the guitarists and lutenists of the centuries before to enable us to delight with a good number of ancient compositions, among those that exist real masterworks, some of J. S. Bach, who, as a fervent admirer of the lute, wrote or transcribed for the instrument some fifteen pages.

The modern composers weren't late to realize that they heard from him what the guitar in the hands of this great artist is an instrument capable to express the most beautiful color and the most intense emotion, and today are the musicians of our epoch that have contributed the most enrichment to the programs of Segovia, writing the multitude of exquisite pieces expressly for him that witness the definite renaissance of an art that for a long time many believed had disappeared completely. de Falla, Turina, Moreno Torroba, Salazar, Cassado, among other Spaniards; Ponce, Mexican; Villa-Lobos, Brazilian; Roussel, Ibert, French; Cyril Scott, English; Castelnuovo-Tedesco, Italian; Tansman and many others of a difficult enumeration, are his present collaborators.

The service that the great interpreter has done for the instrument isn't little, consecrating him in the whole world by the medium of the flash of his exceptional talent and of his sober mastery and sustaining a renovated interest in the guitar everywhere.'"

Domingo, 21 de Diciembre de 1952
a las 6'30 de la tarde

DESPEDIDA
de
ANDRÉS SEGOVIA

PROGRAMA

I
(Obras escritas para laud o guitarra)

Canción y Villanella	V. GALILEO (1533-1591)
Dos Gallardas	J. DOWLAND (1562)
Suite en *la menor*	S. L. WEISS (1686-1750)
Preludium - Allemande - Ballet - Sarabande - Gigue	
Sonatina	GIULIANI
Fantasía (dedicada a A. Segovia) . .	J. TURINA

II
(Transcripción de A. Segovia)

Chacona	J. S. BACH

III
*(Obras dedicadas a A. Segovia (*) o adaptadas
a la guitarra por M. Llobet (**)*

Suite en *re* (*)	CASTELNUOVO-TEDESCO
Ricercare - Batalla escozesse - Capriccio	
Dos estudios (*)	H. VILLALOBOS
Madroños (*)	F. MORENO TORROBA
Danza en *sol* (**).	GRANADOS

Rómulo y José Pascual Mora - Carmen, 114

This farewell Andrés Segovia concert in Barcelona on the following Sunday December 21, 1952 was held at the Palacio de la Musica theater. The pieces after the Bach *"Chaconne"* in set three were dedicated to the Maestro or were, in the case of the last piece, it was arranged by Miguel Llobet.

916

Andrés Segovia made his way to the Teatro Nacional de São Carlos in Lisbon to perform a concert on January 8, 1953.

917

PROGRAMA

Obras originais para viola ou guitarra

Romanesca	A. DE MUDARRA (1541)
Suite en ré	R. DE VISEU (1630-1725)

  a) — Allemande
  b) — Bourrée
  c) — Sarabanda
  d) — Giga
  e) — Minueto
  f) — Corrente

(*) *Andantino variado (escrito para guitarra)*	N. PAGANINI
Andante e Allegretto	F. SOR (1778-1839)

Transcrições de obras cuja técnica e espírito são adaptáveis à guitarra

Aria con variações	GIROLAMO FRESCOBALDI
Allegretto	J. PH. RAMEAU
Gavota	A. SCARLATTI
Sonata	D. SCARLATTI
Bourrée	J. S. BACH

Obras escritas para A. Segovia e inspiradas em ritmos e cantares andaluzes

(**) *Cavatina (dedicada a A. Segovia)*	A. TANSMAN

  a) — Prelúdio
  b) — Sarabanda
  c) — Scherzino
  d) — Barcarola

Tarantela (dedicada a A. Segovia)	CASTELNUOVO-TEDESCO
Lenda catalã e Sardana (dedicada a A. Segovia)	GASPAR CASSADÓ
Torre bermeja	ALBENIZ

(*) Transcrição de M. Ponce.
(**) 1.º Prémio do Concurso Internacional da Academia Chigiana, em 1951.

Os próximos concertos realizam-se na segunda quinzena de Janeiro com o célebre TRIO PASQUIER

The pieces of the first set are Original works for guitar, the second set pieces are Transcriptions of works whose technique and spirit are adapted to the guitar and the third set pieces are Works written for Andrés Segovia inspired by rhythms and songs of Andalucia. The suite of pieces by Tansman were awarded the 1st Prize at the International Competition at the Academia Chigiana in 1951. Portuguese translation by Randy Osborne.

This Andrés Segovia concert was held at the Politeama Argentino Theater on Wednesday, May 20, 1953. He performed with an orchestra, besides the solos he presented.

PALACIO DE LA MUSICA

UNICO RECITAL

DE

ANDRES SEGOVIA

Retrato de Andrés Segovia, por G. Morcillo

Jueves 17 de diciembre de 1953, a las siete de la tarde, a beneficio de la Sociedad de Socorros Mutuos, Montepío de los Profesores de Orquesta y de las Escuelas de los Suburbios de San José, de Vicálvaro.

This Andrés Segovia concert in Barcelona on Thursday December 17, 1953 was held at the Palacio de la Musica theater.

PROGRAMA

I

CANZONE E GALLARDA. . . . . . . V. GALILEI.

PASSACAGLIA . . . . L. COUPERIN.

ALLEGRETTO . . . .⎫

MENUET . . . .⎬ J. PH. RAMEAU.

PRELUDE, SARABANDE, LOURE. . . . J. S. BACH.

II

CHACONA. . . . . J. S. BACH.

III

CAVATINA (dedicada a Segovia) . . . . . . AL. TANSMAN.

    Preludio.
    Sarabande.
    Scherzino.
    Barcarolle.
    Dause pomposa.

TONADILLA . . . . E. GRANADOS.

MALLORCA . . . .⎫

TORRE-BERMEJA. . . . .⎬ I. ALBÉNIZ.

This Andrés Segovia concert included the Bach "Chaconne". In the last set the piece "Cavatina" by Tansman was still a very popular item, having been written just 2 years before.

According to Alberto Lopez Poveda, Andrés played to 1,710 attendees, including 80 in the standing room only section, with another 80 patrons seated on the stage at the Town Hall in New York on Sunday March 1, 1953, at his second concert, the first was on February 17th.

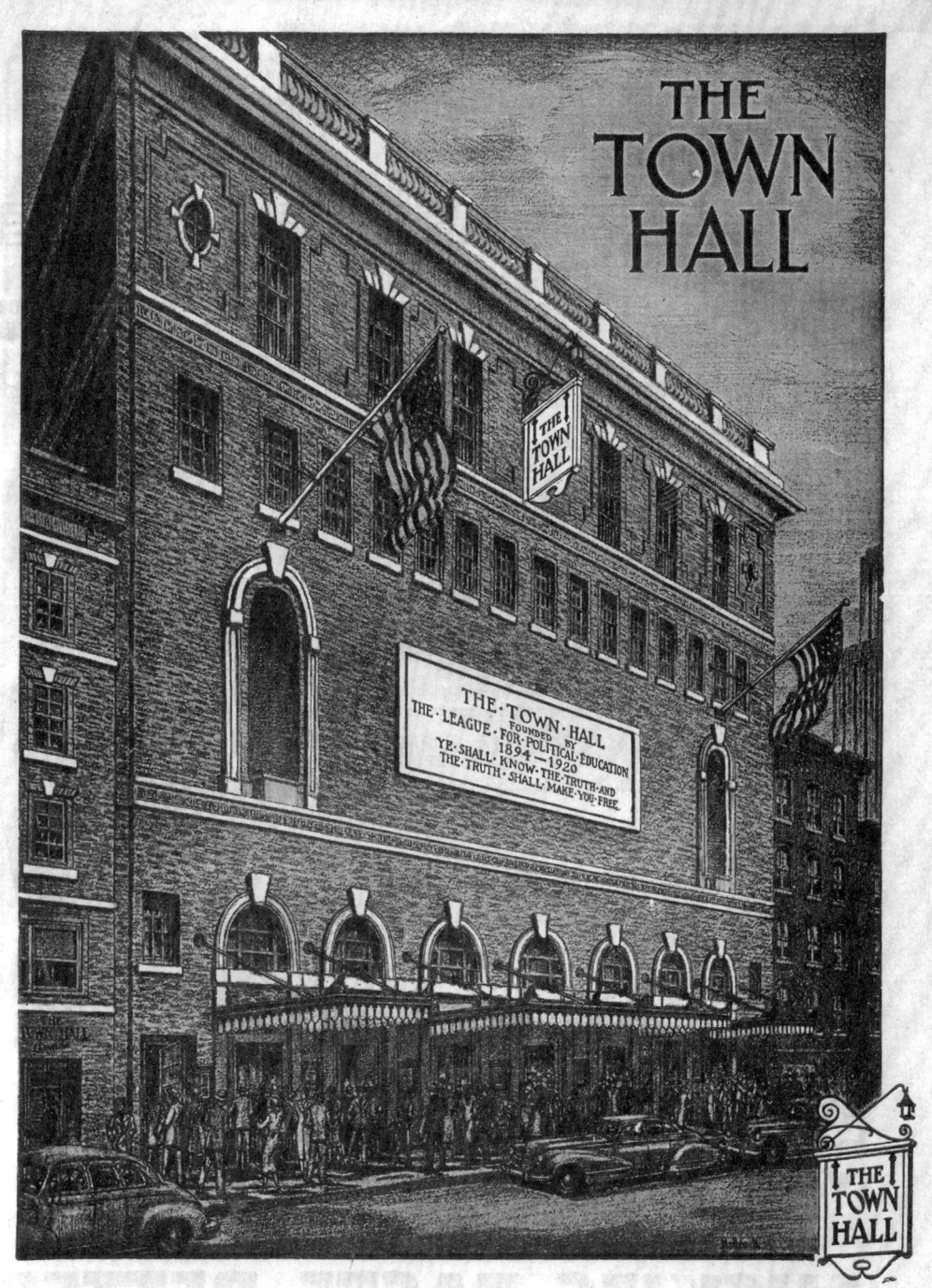

This Andrés Segovia concert was held at the Town Hall in New York on Saturday February 20, 1954.

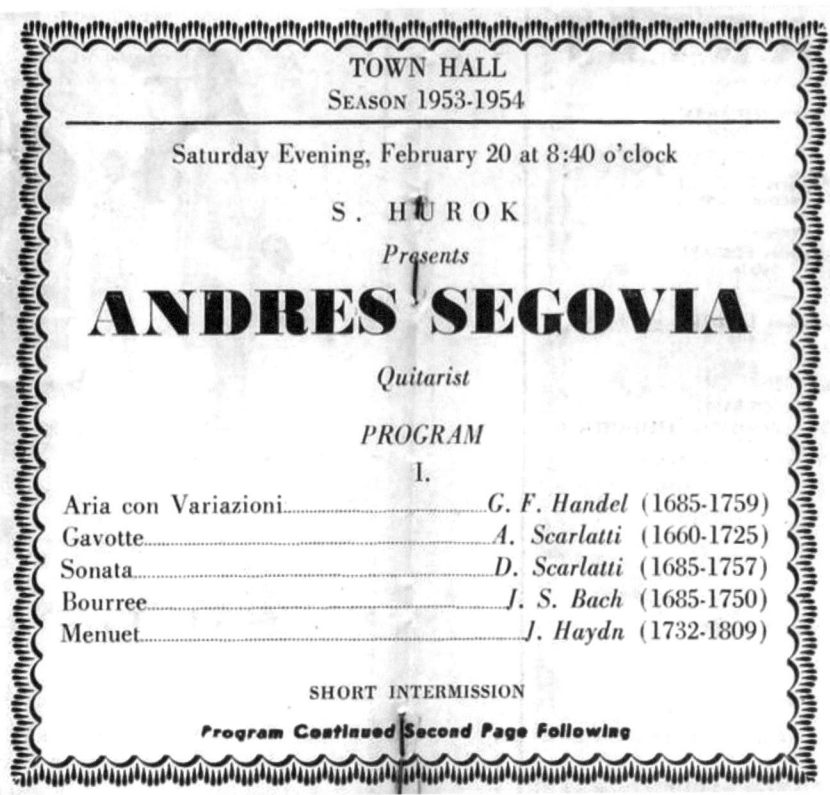

TOWN HALL
SEASON 1953-1954

Saturday Evening, February 20 at 8:40 o'clock

S. HUROK
Presents

ANDRES SEGOVIA

Quitarist

PROGRAM

I.

Aria con Variazioni	G. F. Handel (1685-1759)
Gavotte	A. Scarlatti (1660-1725)
Sonata	D. Scarlatti (1685-1757)
Bourree	J. S. Bach (1685-1750)
Menuet	J. Haydn (1732-1809)

SHORT INTERMISSION

Program Continued Second Page Following

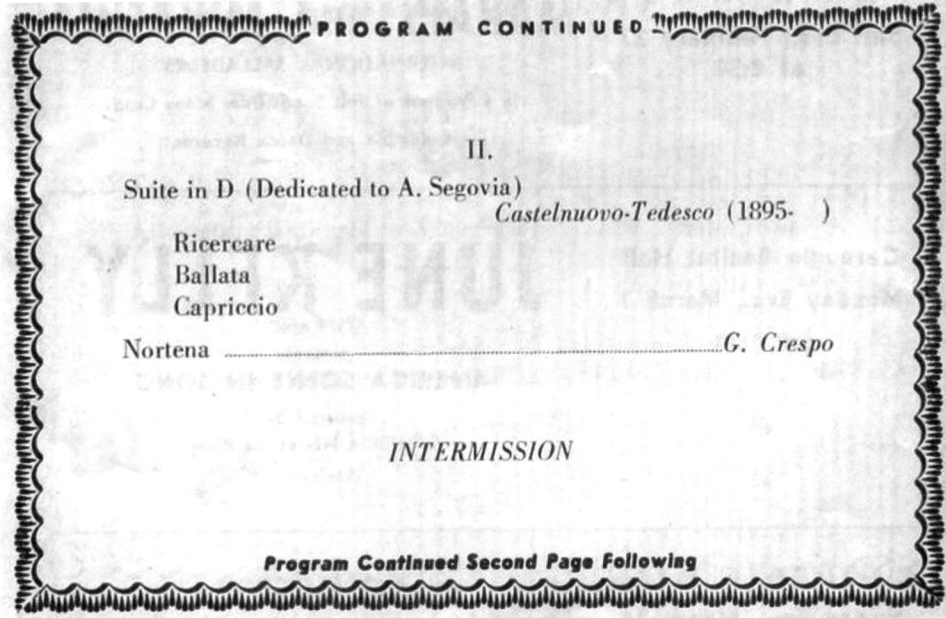

PROGRAM CONTINUED

II.

Suite in D (Dedicated to A. Segovia)
Castelnuovo-Tedesco (1895-)

Ricercare
Ballata
Capriccio

Nortena .... G. Crespo

INTERMISSION

Program Continued Second Page Following

The first and second sets from the 16 page program of the Andrés Segovia concert that was held at the Town Hall in New York on Saturday February 20, 1954.

A most notable aspect of this concert is the inclusion of *"Norteña"* by Andrés Segovia's best friend Jorge Gomez Crespo. Whenever Andrés would arrive in Buenos Aires, he would call Jorge on the phone, before he had even gotten to his hotel.

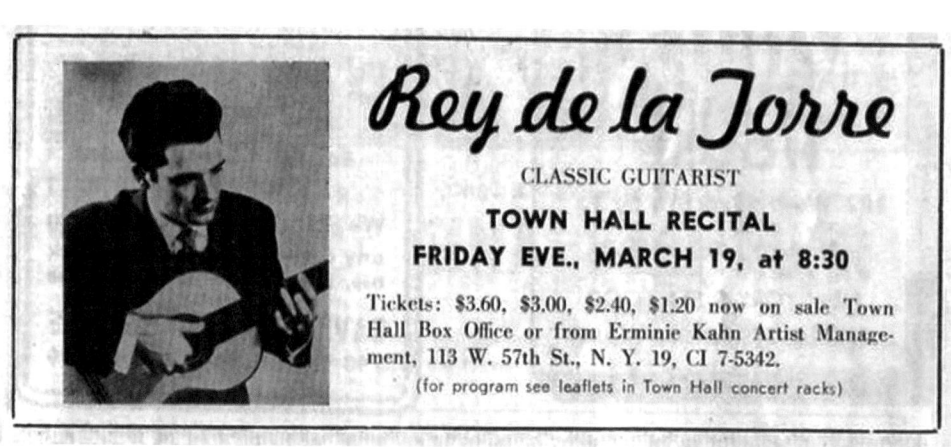
After an eight-year stay beginning in 1934 Julio Martínez Oyanguren left the United States to return to Uruguay in 1941. In America he had been Andrés Segovia's number one rival. Julio also had been called "the greatest guitarist of the world", when living in the United States. This had generally been a phrase earned by Andrés Segovia, since his arrival in the United States in 1928.

José Rey de la Torre, born in Cuba in 1917, became the number one rival. As we see here, he also played the very same venues due to the quality of his tone and three years of perfection instruction with Miguel Llobet in Barcelona from 1932-1934. This concert advertisement is from page 14 of the 16-page program of the Andrés Segovia concert that was held at the Town Hall in New York on Saturday, February 20, 1954.

JOSÉ REY

CUBAN GUITARIST

SATURDAY AFTERNOON at 2:30
MAR. 19
1938

STEINWAY HALL

PROGRAM

1.

Suite in D minor .... VISEE (1535)
      Prélude   Allemande   Sarabande   Gigue
Prelude (1) .... BACH
Bourrée (2) .... BACH
Fugue (2) .... BACH

2.

Etude .... SOR
Minuet .... SOR
Variations on a theme by Mozart .... SOR

3.

Melodía popular catalana .... LLOBET
Canción Mexicana (1) .... PONCE
Mazurca (3) .... BUFFALETTI
Sueño .... TARREGA

4.

Homenaje a Debussy .... FALLA
Ecos del Paisaje .... BROQUA
      (from the Evocaciones Criollas)
Spanish Dance (3) .... GRANADOS
Fandanguillo .... TURINA
Sevillanas (3) .... ALBENIZ

(1) Transcribed by Segovia
(2) Transcribed by Tárrega
(3) Transcribed by Llobet

    Tickets: $1.65 and $1.10   Tax included   On sale at Box Office

According to my teacher, Byron Pang, José Rey de la Torre had the best musicianship of all classical guitarists, whatever the composer suggested on the sheet music was performed by him. José Rey de la Torre was at Steinway Hall in New York on March 19, 1938. These theatre programs belonged to Anna Palmer Coit North (1908-2014), who was the very first female feature writer for Time magazine.

925

REY DE LA TORRE

CUBAN GUITARIST

CARNEGIE CHAMBER MUSIC HALL

154 WEST 57th STREET

FRIDAY EVENING

JUNE 18th, 1943

at 8:30 P. M.

José Rey de la Torre was at Carnegie Chamber Hall in New York on June 18, 1943. These theatre programs belonged to Anna Palmer Coit North (1908-2014), who was the very first female feature writer for Time magazine.

Program

I.

Minuett in D
" " A } . . . . FERNANDO SOR

Prelude
Allemande } . . . . J. S. BACH
Bourree

Variations on a theme by Mozart . . . FERNANDO SOR

II.

Preludes 1, 2 and 3
Marietta } . . . . . FRANCISCO TARREGA

Mazurca . . . . FEDERICO BUFALETTI

Tremolo Study . . . . . . FRANCISCO TARREGA

Intermission

Suite Castellana . . . . MORENO TORROBA
    a) Fandanguillo   b) Arada   c) Danza

Three Mexican Songs . . . . . . MANUEL M. PONCE

Preludio . . . . MORENO TORROBA

Sevillanas . . . . ISAAC ALBENIZ

All these concerts were performed using the last Francisco Simplicio guitar, Miguel Llobet, brought José to meet Miguel in the Simplicio workshop 3 weeks after Francisco had passed away.

927

TED ZITTEL, Inc., *presents*

Rey de la TORRE
CUBAN GUITARIST

in a classical guitar recital

TOWN HALL
TUESDAY EVENING, MAY 23rd, 1944
at 8:30 p.m.

•

Prices
$1, $1.50, $2, and $2.50
including all taxes

•

Tickets available at Town Hall Box Office, or Room 1210, 15 East 40th Street, New York 17, N. Y.

•

See program on reverse side.

José Rey de la Torre was at Town Hall in New York on May 23, 1944. These theatre programs belonged to Anna Palmer Coit North (1908-2014), who was the very first female feature writer for Time magazine.

Program

1

GALLARDAS AND FOLIAS . . . . *Gaspar Sanz*
TWO PAVANAS . . . . *Luis de Milan*
SUITE IN D MINOR . . . . *Robert de Visee*
    Prelude
    Allemande
    Sarabande
    Gigue

2

COURANTE . . . . *J. S. Bach*
BOURREE
FUGUE

STUDY IN B MINOR . . . . *Fernando Sor*
STUDY IN D MINOR
STUDY IN B FLAT MAJOR
STUDY IN A MAJOR·

VARIATIONS ON A THEME BY MOZART . . . . *Fernando Sor*

Intermission

3

THREE CATALONIAN MELODIES . . . . *Miguel Llobet*
    La filla del marxant
    El testament de n'Amelia
    El Mestre

DOLOR (Basque prelude) . . . . *Padre San Sebastian*
THREE MEXICAN SONGS . . . . *Manuel Ponce*

4

PRELUDIO . . . . *Frederico M. Torroba*
SONATINA . . . . *Frederico M. Torroba*
    Allegretto
    Andante
    Allegro
TORRE BERMEJA . . . . *Isaac Albeniz*

Not all of Miguel Llobet's Catalonian folksongs were commercially available until after Miguel had passed away.

929

GUITAR RECITAL

By

Vicente Gomez

(American Debut)

•

TOWN HALL
Sunday Evening, April 24th,
at 8 P. M.

Besides José Rey de la Torre, another artist who played at the Town Hall was Vicente Gomez. He was a Flamenco virtuoso, who also played pieces from Segovia's repertoire. He appeared in the motion picture Blood and Sand and began recording for Decca Rocords immediately. This Sunday April 24, 1938, Concert was his American Debut. These theatre programs belonged to Anna Palmer North, who was the very first female Time magazine writer.

Born twenty-six years ago in Madrid, Spain, before he was ten years of age Vicente Gomez entertained visitors in his father's tavern on Via Agusta Figuero with the magic of his guitar playing. When he was thirteen he made his public debut in a recital at the Teatro Espanol.

After scores of concerts given throughout Spain, he made his first foreign tour in Italy in 1929, followed by equally successful tours of Northern Africa and France in 1932-33. He left Spain in April, 1936, on the European-American tour through Russia, Poland, Austria, Cuba and Mexico which has now brought him to New York.

Acclaimed wherever he has played as one of the world's greatest guitarists, Vicente Gomez is the only guitarist who has ever mastered the widely-differing techniques of classical and Flamenco playing. He is also a noted composer, being the only modern writer of Spanish Gypsy music.

Mr. Gomez may be heard every Sunday at 2:15 P. M. over Station WEAF and the Red Network of the National Broadcasting Company.

Vicente Gomez was a youthful 26 years old, (July 8, 1911 – Madrid, Spain – December 23, 2001 Los Angeles) he had a career that lasted for many decades publishing sheet music and also teaching in Los Angeles. American guitarist, Jack Buckingham, who taught at UC Berkeley in the 1950's and at Laney College in Oakland, California, studied with Vicente in the early 1980's. I have a few hand written manuscripts by Vicente from the Jack Buckingham archive. Between 1938-1969 Vicente Gomez recorded 156 songs. Source: The Encyclopedic Discography of Victor Recordings (EDVR) web site.

Vicente Gomez

Guitarist

PROGRAM

I

Preludio
    Allegro y
        Andante expresivo .... *F. Sors.*
                                                             (1778-1830)

Granadinas (Popular numero "flamenco") .... *V. Gomez*

Fandanguillo .... *Turina*

Vals Brillante (dedicado a Vicente Gomez) .... *Esquembre*

La Farruca (Baile Andaluz) .... *V. Gomez*

II

Dos Pequenas Mazurkas .... *Tarrega*

Recuerdos de la Alhambra .... *Tarrega*

Bourree y Gavota .... *J. S. Bach*

Recuerdos de la Caleta (Malaguenas) .... *V. Gomez*

Playera (Danza 5a.) .... *Granados*

Andalucia (Soleares flamencas) .... *V. Gomez*

III

Homenaje a Debussy .... *M. de Falla*

Granada Arabe (zambra gitana) .... *V. Gomez*

Castellanas (Tiempo de fandango) .... *M. Torroba*

Leyenda .... *Albeniz*

Gran Jota .... *Tarrega*

Fin.

There pieces from all three sets that are also a part of the Segovia repertoire.

Management of Shank and Tuvim
R. K. O. BUILDING - RADIO CITY - NEW YORK

932

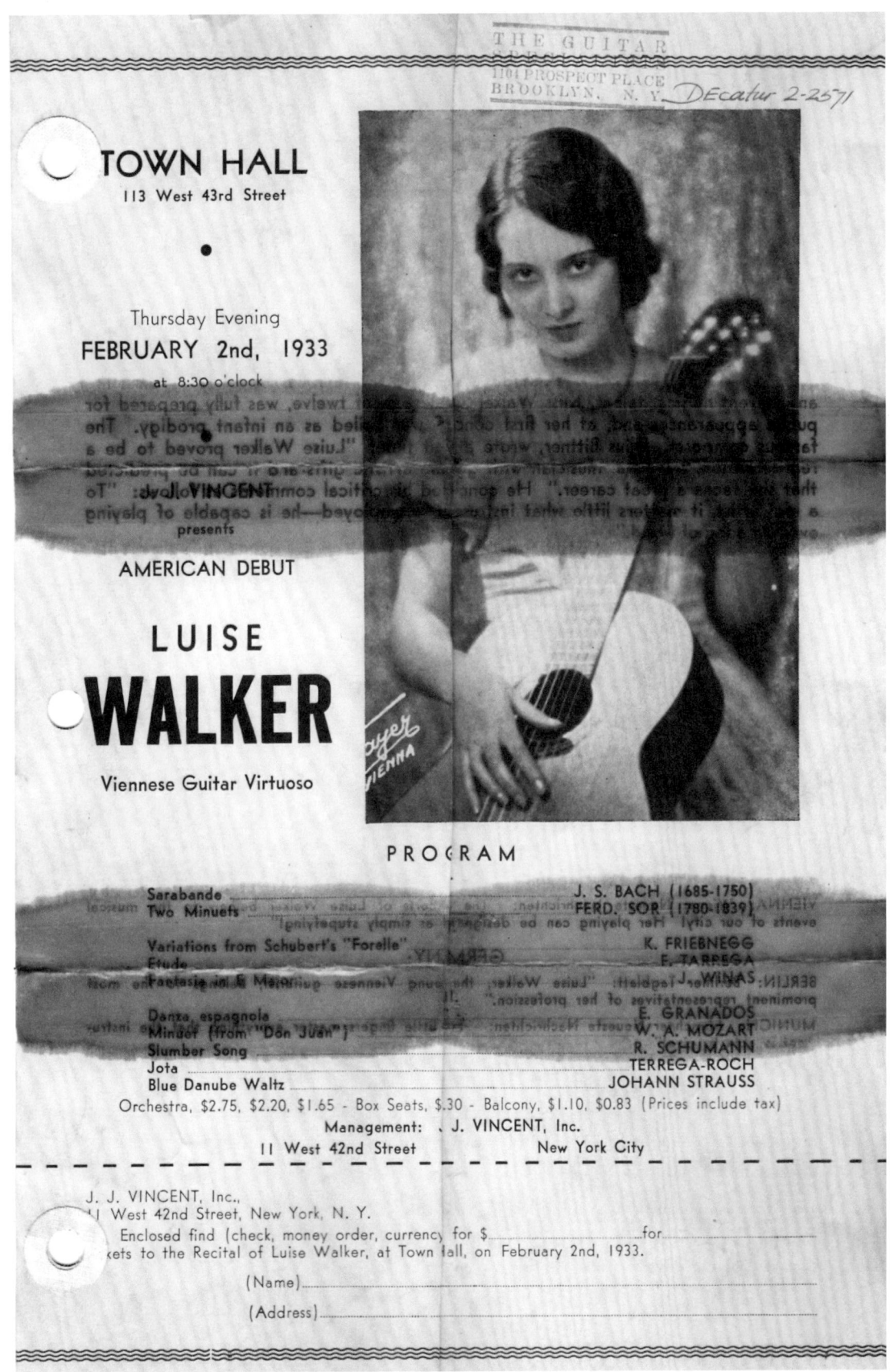

Luise Walker (September 9, 1910 – January 30, 1998) played her American Debut on February 2, 1933, she began recording for Odeon in 1932 and Telefunken in 1934. These theatre programs belonged to Anna Palmer North, who was the very first female Time magazine writer.

BIOGRAPHICAL NOTES

LUISE WALKER, the young Viennese guitar virtuoso, illustrates anew the amazing and potent influence of heredity; for, on both sides of her family, there are to be found a number of prominent and distinguished musical artists. Her mother, who is Viennese, was a noted coloratura soprano and a leading member of the Kroll Opera Company in Berlin; an aunt, sister of her father, was a well-known operatic and concert contralto and her granduncle, Anton Schnittenhelm, was an established favorite with the Vienna State Opera for a lengthy period.

Though her father is an American, a native of Chicago, Miss Walker is Viennese by birth and adoption. It was Mr. Walker who was responsible for her adopting the guitar (an instrument which he admired) as a medium for musical expression. Possessing an inherent musical talent, Miss Walker, at the age of twelve, was fully prepared for public appearances and, at her first concert, was hailed as an infant prodigy. The famous composer, Julius Bittner, wrote at that time: "Luise Walker proved to be a real sensation, a natural musician with genuine artistic gifts and it can be predicted that she faces a great career." He concluded his critical comment as follows: "To a guitarist, it matters little what instrument is employed—he is capable of playing even on a log of wood."

At fourteen, Miss Walker had completed her studies at the Vienna Staats Academy under Professor Jacob Ortner and was immediately engaged for a tour of the Austrian provinces, followed later by extensive tours on the Continent and in England, where, at her last concert, she played before the Royal Family. To date, she has made over six hundred appearances throughout Europe.

Miss Walker holds the unique status of being the only woman guitar virtuoso.

● ● ●

PRESS COMMENTS

AUSRIA:

VIENNA: Neues Wiener Tagblatt: "Miss Walker demonstrated at her last concert what can be drawn out of such an instrument as the guitar.—Her concert, which took place before a packed house, turned out to be a musical sensation!"

VIENNA: Wiener Neueste Nachrichten: "The concerts of Luise Walker belong to the musical events of our city! Her playing can be designated as simply stupefying!"

GERMANY:

BERLIN: Berliner Tagblatt: "Luise Walker, the young Viennese guitarist belongs to the most prominent representatives of her profession."

MUNICH: Munchner Neueste Nachrichten: "Her little fingers master everything that the instrument is able to give!"

ENGLAND:

LONDON: Morning Post: "This player is to be congratulated on her tremendous success, well deserved, namely, that of making a whole evening of guitar music, consistently interesting and enchanting to her auditors."

FRANCE:

MARSEILLE: Le Plectre: "Concerning the young guitarist, Luise Walker, it can only be said, that her playing is simply admirable; no other instrument, neither the piano, the violin, the violoncello, the mandoline, etc., seem to exist besides the guitar if it is played with such a perfection!"

CZECHOSLOVAKIA:

PRAG: Prager Tagblatt: "Miss Walker can be ranged unreservedly among the most celebrated artists of the present time in spite of her youth. Her playing is dazzling and fascinating."

Luise Walker began her studies with Jakob Ortner (in the program-sic), later studying, with Miguel Llobet, Andrés Segovia and Emilio Pujol. The United States was at least the seventh country in which she had delighted audiences by the time of this concert. Even when she was elderly, she had a capacity to enrapture audiences, evidenced by a Japanese produced VHS performance.

Andrés Segovia in New York City at the Academy of Music on Saturday March 14, 1954. This is the front of a flyer advertising the upcoming concert.

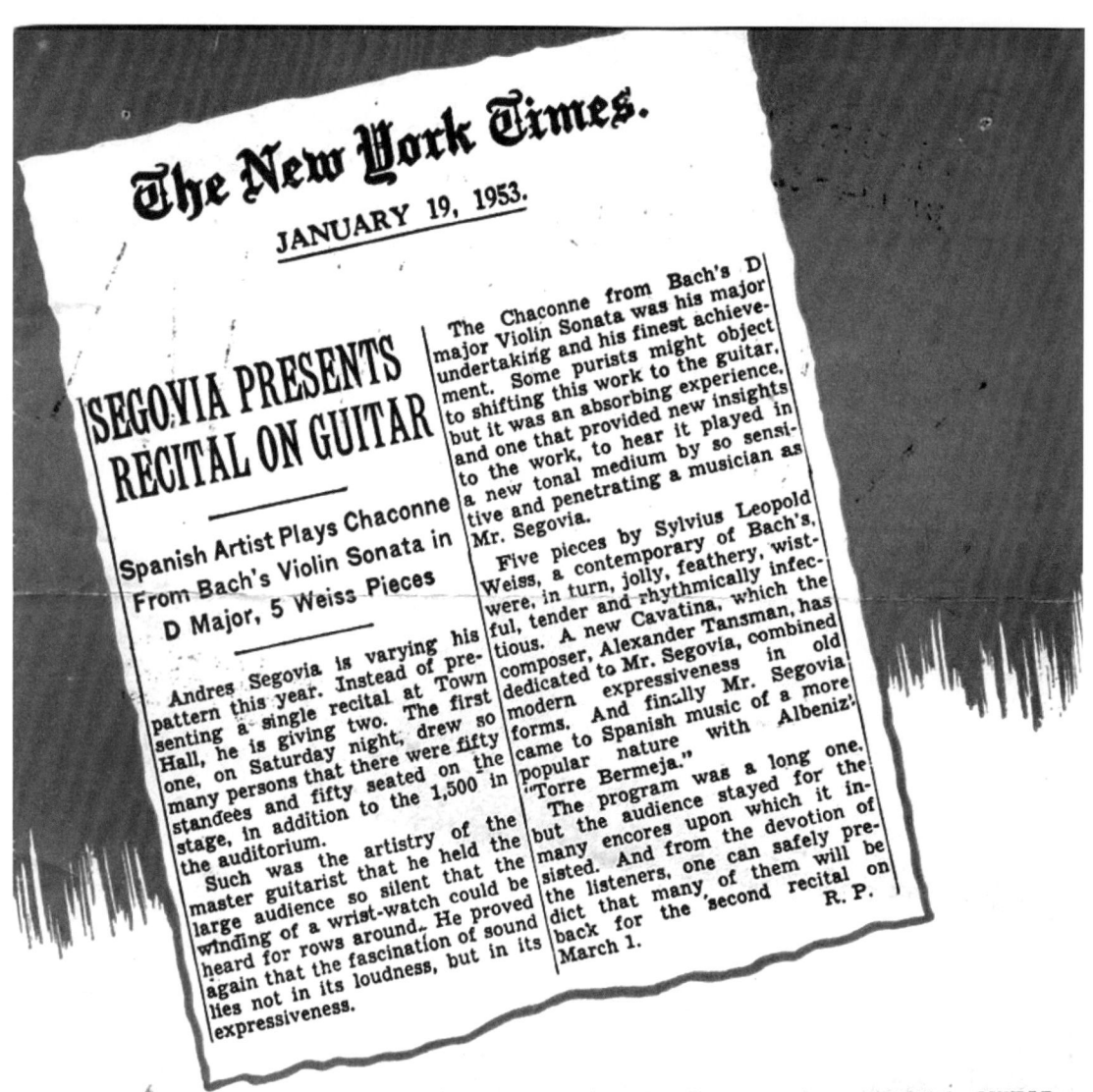

Well deserved praise by critics of this era. This is the back of the flyer advertising the upcoming March 14, 1954 concert.

936

S. HUROK

presents

ANDRES SEGOVIA
GUITARIST

———

Sponsored by THE NEW SCHOOL OF MUSIC

———

ACADEMY OF MUSIC

Sunday Evening, March 14, 1954

8:30

———

EMMA FELDMAN, Local Management

ANDREW J. SERAPHIN, Press Representative

———

Exclusive Management: HUROK ATTRACTIONS, Inc.
711 Fifth Avenue, New York 22, N.Y.

This is the concert program for Andrés Segovia in New York City at the Academy of Music on Saturday, March 14, 1954.

Program

I.

Passacaglia .... **L. COUPERIN (1626-1661)**

Suite (Originally written for the lute)............... **S. L. WEISS (1686-1750)**
    Prelude
    Sarabande
    Ballade
    Capriccio
    Gigue

Chaconne .... **J. S. BACH (1685-1750)**

SHORT INTERMISSION

II.

Cavatina (Dedicated to A. Segovia) .... **A. TANSMAN (1897-   )**
    Prelude
    Sarabande
    Scherzino
    Barcarolle
    Dansa pomposa

Tarantella .... **M. CASTELNUOVO-TEDESCO (1895-   )**

INTERMISSION

III.

Campo (Dedicated to A. Segovia) .... **M. PONCE (1886-   )**

Nortena (Dedicated to A. Segovia) .... **G. CRESPO**

Allegretto Castellano .... **M. TORROBA**

Dance in G .... **E. GRANADOS (1867-1916)**

DECCA RECORDS

The most notable aspect of this concert is the inclusion of *"Norteña"* by Jorge Gomez Crespo.

ANDRES SEGOVIA

"There is no guitar but the Spanish guitar, and Andres Segovia is its prophet. I doubt there lives a music lover with soul so dead that he could not find reward in attendance at a Segovia concert."

So wrote music critic Virgil Thomson in the *New York Herald Tribune* after a recent Segovia performance. Since his American debut more than two decades ago, this distinguished virtuoso has astonished both audiences and critics.

Segovia was born November 21, 1893 in Linares, a village in southern Spain.

Segovia was determined to succeed as a serious artist with an instrument that had never been accorded a place on the concert stage. Unable to find a capable instructor, Segovia became his own guide. "To this day," he says with a twinkle in his eyes, "teacher and pupil have never had a serious quarrel."

He made his first public appearance in Granada at the age of 14. His debut, sponsored by a local cultural organization, was described as a "revelation." Within a short time his name was known throughout Spain. At the age of 22 Segovia appeared at the Paris Conservatory. His success resulted in an extensive concert tour.

In 1919 Segovia's appearance in South

His father, an attorney, hoped Andres would follow the same career. To broaden the youngster's cultural background, he provided the boy with piano lessons. Andres, however, rebelled, having discovered a guitar in the home of a friend. Attempts to have the boy learn a 'respectable' instrument like the violin or cello also failed. Andres, enchanted by the guitar, decided 'for better or worse' to make it his career.

Objections from his family and teachers at the Granada Institute of Music, where he studied, proved of no avail.

America proved to be a sensation. He did not return to Europe until 1923. At that time, many persons attended Segovia's concerts because they expected a novelty, but they came back to admire and to cheer. The critic of the *London Times* confessed, "In the fullness of our ignorance we went, expecting we did not know what, but hoping since Senor Segovia's reputation had preceded him and the name of Johann Sebastian Bach appeared on his program, that we would satisfy our curiosity about an instrument that had romantic associations, without being outraged musically. We remained to hear the last possible note, for it was the most delightful surprise of the season!"

This is the artist biography for Andrés Segovia in New York City at the Academy of Music on Saturday, March 14, 1954. Andrés Segovia and five Francisco Tárrega students performed in South America before radio existed. The advent of radio came to Buenos Aires in the summer of 1920. The wrong month is listed as a birth date, it should be February 21, 1893.

On the next page is the balance of the artist's biography.

Leading composers began to write for the guitarist, among them Alfredo Casella and Mario Castelnuovo-Tedesco, who composed concertos dedicated to Segovia. In January 1928, the virtuoso, still unknown in the United States, arrived in New York for his debut at Town Hall. Olin Downes in the *New York Times* reported: "He belongs to the very small group of musicians who by transcendent powers of execution and imagination create an art of their own, and sometimes seem to transform the very nature of their medium."

Segovia's was the first guitar recital in New York. Within five weeks he had achieved a record of six complete sold out New York concerts. In the next 11 weeks he played forty American engagements!

In 1943, Segovia first began his transcontinental tours of the U.S. and Canada under the direction of S. Hurok. Since then he has appeared as recitalist and as soloist with symphony orchestras.

In addition to Castelnuovo-Tedesco and Casella, the guitarist has had works dedicated to him by Alexander Tansman, de Falla, Villa-Lobos, Manuel Ponce, Albert Roussel, Jacques Ibert, Cyril Scott, and Torroba. Last October with Sir John Barbirolli and the Halle Orchestra in London, the guitarist gave the world-premiere of a concerto for guitar and string quartet by Villa-Lobos.

The busy activity of the maestro is evident from the details in the last page of the artist's biography.

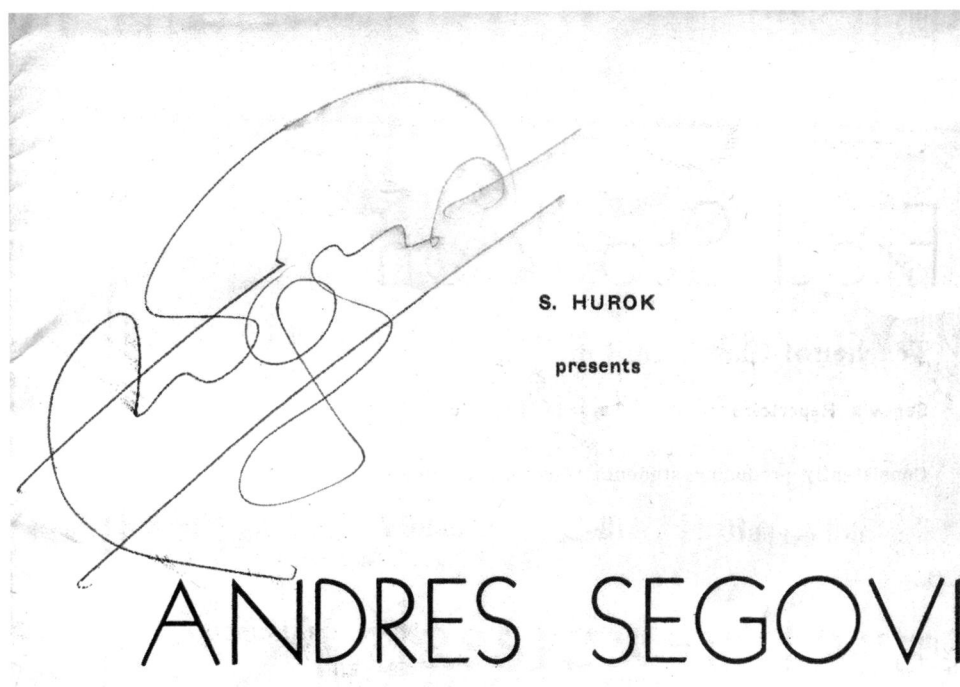

S. HUROK

presents

ANDRES SEGOVIA

Guitarist

Veterans Auditorium   **San Francisco**

TUESDAY, MARCH 23, 1954

8:30 p. m.

* * *

· A SPENCER BAREFOOT ATTRACTION

* * *

This is the concert program for Andrés Segovia in San Francisco at the Veterans Auditorium on Tuesday, March 23, 1954.

Archive: Jack Buckingham

ANDRES SEGOVIA

Program

I

PASSACAGLIA..L. Couperin

PRELUDE, SARABANDE AND LOURE..J. S. Bach

ALLEGRETTO
MENUET..J. P. Rameau

CANZONETTA...F. Mendelssohn

Short Intermission

II

SUITE IN D..M. Castelnuovo-Tedesco

    Ricercare

    Ballata

    Capriccio

RONDO (Hommage to Sor) (Dedicated to Mr. Segovia)................................M. Ponce

FANDANGUILLO (Dedicated to Mr. Segovia)..Turina

Intermission

III

INCA SONG AND IMPROVISATION (Dedicated to Mr. Segovia)..................C. Pedrell

DANCE IN G...E. Granados

MALLORCA...I. Albeniz

SEVILLA..I. Albeniz

* * *

Exclusive Management: HUROK ATTRACTIONS INC. 711 Fifth Avenue, New York

Andrés Segovia in Vancouver, British Columbia, Canada on Friday, April 2, 1954. In this 20 page program it mentions that Andrés had given concerts at times in Canada since 1943.

Presents

Andres Segovia

GUITARIST

Program

I.

ARIA CON VARIAZZIONI.................................G. F. *Handel*
(1685-1759)

Program

SUITE IN D...S. L. *Weiss*
(1686-1750)

    Prelude

    Sarabande

    Gigue

ALLEGRETTO
THEME AND VARIATIONS } ....F. *Sor*
(1779-1839)

SHORT INTERMISSION

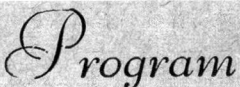

Program

II.

LOURE... *J. S. Bach*
                                                          (1685-1750)

MENUET... *J. P. Rameau*
                                                          (1683-1764)

CANZONETTA .... *F. Mendelssohn*
                                                          (1809-1847)

LITTLE WALTZ... *E. Grieg*
                                                          (1843-1908)

INTERMISSION

Program

III.

STUDY (Dedicated to A. Segovia)............ *H. Villa-Lobos*
                                                          (1888-   )

PRELUDE (Dedicated to A. Segovia)............ *M. Torroba*

DANCE in G.. *E. Granados*
                                                          (1876-1916)

LEYENDE .... *I. Albeniz*
                                                          (1860-1909)

DECCA RECORDINGS

Exclusive Management: HUROK ATTRACTIONS INC.

711 Fifth Avenue, New York

There are two pieces dedicated to the maestro, one by Villa-Lobos and the other by Moreno Torroba.

ANDRÉS

SEGOVIA

GUITAR

Study	
Allegro in D	F. Sor (1780-1839)
Theme with Variations	
Fandanguillo	J. Turina (1882-)

Six Little Pieces	V. Galileo (1520-1591)
Sonata	D. Scarlatti (1685-1757)
Menuet	J. P. Rameau (1683-1764)
Gavotte	J. S. Bach (1685-1750)

INTERMISSION

Sarabande Lointaine	J. Rodrigo (1902-)
Serenata Burlesca	M. Torroba (1891-)
Danza	E. Granados (1867-1916)
Torre Bermeja	I. Albeniz (1861-1909)

Tuesday, November 2, 1954 — 8:00 p. m.

FINNEY CHAPEL

This is the concert program for Andrés Segovia in Oberlin, Ohio at the Oberlin Conservatory of Music held in the Finney Chapel on Tuesday, November 2, 1954.

946

This Andrés Segovia concert program is from the S.O.D.R.E. in Montevideo on Thursday July 4, 1957.

JUEVES 4 DE JULIO • A LA HORA 19

5º RECITAL DEL CICLO DE ABONO

PROGRAMA

PRIMERA PARTE

Luis DE NARVAEZ — Canción del Emperador y Diferencias sobre un aire popular.

John DOWLAND — Tres piezas cortas para laúd.

Alexandro SCARLATTI — Preámbulo y Gavota.

Fernando SOR — Introducción y Allegro en Re.

Héctor VILLA-LOBOS — Preludio, Estudio, Preludio.
(Dedicado a A. Segovia.)

SEGUNDA PARTE

Johann S. BACH
- Siciliana.
- Fuga.
- Corrente.
- Sarabanda.
- Bourré.
- Gavota.

Jean Ph. RAMEAU — Minuetto.

TERCERA PARTE

Alexandre TANSMAN — Cavatina.
(Dedicada a A. Segovia.)

Sonatina.
Lento.
Scherzino.
Barcarole.
Danse Pompose.

Joaquín RODRIGO — Fandango.

Isaac ALBENIZ — Sevilla.

Andrés Segovia plays music spanning from the Renaissance to the 20th century, including pieces dedicated to the maestro, written by Villa-Lobos and Tansman.

PATRICK HAYES

in association with

THE FRIDAY MORNING MUSIC CLUB

and

S. HUROK

Presents

ANDRES SEGOVIA

Guitarist

LISNER AUDITORIUM

Wednesday, April 9, 1958

at 8:30 P.M.

"The month before Andrés Segovia had made the World Debut of the *"Fantasia para un Gentilhombre"* by Joaquín Rodrigo on March 5, 1958 at the Opera House in San Francisco, with Enrique Jorda conducting the Symphony Orchestra. Three thousand persons attended. This was one of 36 concerts played that year in the United States. In this tour he used two guitars, one by Hermann Hauser II and a 1956 Ignacio Fleta."

Source: Translated from *Andrés Segovia Vida y Obra* by Alberto Lopez Poveda published by the Universidad de Jaen / Ayuntamiento de Linares 2010.

This concert on Wednesday April 9, 1958 was at the Lisner Auditorium in Washington, D.C.

PATRICK HAYES

in association with

THE FRIDAY MORNING MUSIC CLUB

and

S. HUROK

Presents

ANDRES SEGOVIA

Guitarist

Program

I

Six Little Pieces for Lute .... *V. Galileo* (16th Century)*
Preambulo ⎫
Oliveras |
Melodia   ⎬ .... *F. M. Torroba* (1891-   )
Albada |
Los Majos |
Panorama ⎭
Study in A Major .... *F. Tarrega* (1854-1909)

II

Prelude, Fuga and Gavotte .... *J. S. Bach* (1685-1750)

Andante and Menuet .... *F. J. Haydn* (1732-1809)

Theme with Variations .... *F. Sor* (1778-1839)

Intermission

III

Berceuse d'Oriente ⎫
Alla pollaca   ⎬ .... *Alex Tansman*
              (Dedicated to A. Segovia)

Fandango .... *J. Rodrigo*
              (Dedicated to A. Segovia)

La Maja de Goya ⎫
Danse in G   ⎬ .... *E. Granados*

DECCA RECORDS

*Father of the Astronomer.

Exclusive Management: HUROK ATTRACTIONS INC., 730 Fifth Ave., New York, N. Y.

Andrés Segovia played two compositions dedicated to him, those by Tansman and Rodrigo in the third set. Around two thousand persons attended this event. The artist drew rave reviews everywhere he played.

SEGOVIA IN JAPAN

THE 1959 visit of Segovia to Japan will long be remembered. From programmes and press reports we gather that the impact of Segovia on the musical life of the country was terrific, resulting in greatly increased interest in the guitar and its music. The tour was extremely well organised. We have seldom seen such a carefully prepared and beautifully printed souvenir programme as that for Segovia's Tokyo concerts—more than 20 pages of portraits, programme notes and biographical articles—some of them in English—written by Syun Ogura.

Different halls were used for the three concerts. The second concert included the Castelnuovo-Tedesco Concerto, Op. 99, with the Japan Philharmonic Chamber Orchestra conducted by Akeo Watanabe. Items played during the recitals included Six Lute Pieces (V. Galilei), Two Pieces (Dowland); Suite (R. de Visée); Theme Varie and other items by Sor; Sinfonia and Gavotte (Bach); works by A. and D. Scarlatti; Menuet (Rameau); Romanza and Canzonetta (Mendelssohn); Study in A major (Tárrega); Melodie and Little Waltz (Grieg); Piezas Caracteristicas and Sonatina (Moreno-Torroba); Prelude and Study (Villa-Lobos); Danza (Granados), Sevilla and Torre Bermeja (Albeniz), etc.

The television recitals naturally reached a vast audience. The picture of Segovia's hands in action was taken by Mr. Ogura who also took the photo of Segovia on page 7.

As for the press, one did not have to be able to understand Japanese to realise by the many portraits of Segovia how enthusiastic was his reception. Some of the magazines had particularly fine portraits, one devoted a page to six interesting shots of his hands in action.

One of the newspapers showed a picture of the Crown Prince of Japan arriving at the hall for a Segovia recital. During the interval Segovia and the Crown Prince had a friendly conversation. The Prince has studied the guitar for more than a year under Syun Ogura.

The
Hands
of
Segovia
(on television)

This is from the "Guitar News" magazine issue No. 51 of January-February 1960. The pioneer of the guitar in Japan and recording artist, Shun Ogura, had met Andrés Segovia 30 years before during his first tour of Japan in October of 1929.

LUNES 16 de MAYO de 1960, a las 22 horas

INAUGURACION DEL AÑO ARTISTICO

RECITAL DE GUITARRA
— POR —

ANDRES SEGOVIA

PROGRAMA

I

SEIS PIEZAS CORTAS PARA LAUD	V. GALILEO * (1533-1591)
ANDANTE, MINUETTO y ALLEGRO en DO	F. SOR (1778-1839)
PRELUDIO y ESTUDIO	H. VILLALOBOS
TARANTELA	CASTELNUEVO-TEDESCO
MODROÑOS	MORENO TORROBA

PRELUDIO	
SARABANDA	BACH
GAVOTA	
ANDANTE y MINUETTO en RE	HAYDN
ROMANZA y CANZONETTA	MENDELSSOHN

II

FANDANGO	J. RODRIGO
ALLEGRO RITMICO	M. PONCE
DANZA	GRANADOS
SEVILLA	ALBENIZ
ESTUDIO Nº 2	*ALARD*
LEYENDA	*HAUG*

* Padre del célebre astrónomo.

Próximos Conciertos: Lunes 30 a las 22 hs. y Martes 31 a las 18.15 hs.

AUDICION de MUSICA de CAMARA por el
Cuarteto de la Asociación Wagneriana
Obras de DITTERSDORF - BRAHMS - MOZART

This Andrés Segovia concert was held at the Gran Teatro Broadway for the Asociacion Wagneriana in Buenos Aires on Monday May 16, 1960.

Translating from Alberto Lopez Poveda's book *"Andrés Segovia: Vida y Obra"*, the daily *"La Prensa"* said about the concert on May 18th said: "The outstanding quality that permits Andrés Segovia to include works of epochs and very different styles in the same program, with the authentic uptake of them, that every one of them appears performed by the specialists, it was one of the most outstanding aspects in this new recital offered in the Wagneriana."

In the same daily the week before on the 11th they said "...To question him if he knew the reason for Casals to not perform in nations reigned by tyranny, the maestro responded that he had discussed the theme with his friend Casals and that he was completely in disagreement with that opinion. 'It is very cruel — he said — to deprive a populace of great artistic expressions for this reason', and he added: 'I believe the mission of the art is more of pacifying and ennoble the minds that are mixed in the political passions. The artist must, therefore, be the messenger of these ennobling spirits, without which otherwise abdicate the love of democracy and liberty within the order and hierarchy.'"

This is from the *"Cantando"– La Revista de Musica Popular* magazine published in Buenos Aires, on May 24, 1960, issue No. 164, *Año* IV.

"The Argentine Tango produces an allergy in the famous guitarist, Andrés Segovia"

Photo caption: "He doesn't like the Tango. He doesn't know who Atahualpa Yupanqui is and has doubts about our folklore."

The text translation is on the next page:

NO... ¡POR FAVOR!

No le gusta el tango. No conoce a Atahualpa Yupanqui y duda de nuestro folklore.

EL TANGO ARGENTINO LE PRODUCE ALERGIA AL FAMOSO GUITARRISTA ANDRES SEGOVIA

INDISCUTIBLEMENTE... el célebre concertista de guitarra don Andrés Segovia, que ofreció su primer recital público en la ciudad de Granada antes de cumplir los 15 años, y que en la actualidad ocupa el primer plano en la guitarrística del mundo entero... ¡nos desconcertó!...

Los argentinos ya le conocemos, pues estuvo en nuestro país en varias oportunidades y hace apenas cuatro años que gustamos de su arte maravilloso, incomparable y pensamos que nuestros aplausos y nuestra auténtica admiración, habían conquistado la simpatía del gran maestro hispano. Lamentablemente, eso no ocurrió. O quizá ocurrió antes y nadie reparó en ello, porque el famoso guitarrista jamás mencionó ese aspecto del pequeño gran problema que acaba de plantearse con sus despectivas declaraciones de "palpitante actualidad" la noche de su arribo a Buenos Aires y de acuerdo a lo publicado el martes 10 de mayo por el prestigioso vespertino "La Ra-

zón". La breve charla del cronista con el maestro Andrés Segovia no tiene desperdicio. Denota claramente que el insigne artista sufre la implacable acción del tiempo, pues no debemos olvidar que desde hace tres cuartos de siglo, gracias a sus excepcionales condiciones, se reivindicó el prestigio de la guitarra en el concierto universal. Existen otros atenuantes que aunque nos desconciertan, restan gravedad a sus palabras: Andrés Segovia estaba evidentemente cansado, de mal humor, impaciente y excitado por el atraso de su llegada. Quizá por ese motivo, el gran maestro subestimó nuestra música con respuestas tajantes y pronunciadas con un tono sumamente despectivo:

Le preguntaron si le agradaba nuestro folklore y qué opinión tenía de Atahualpa Yupanqui. Dijo que el primero era muy interesante, y que no conocía al segundo. Respondió a:

—¿El tango le gusta?
—¡No!... ¡Por favor!...

953

Text translation:

"Unquestionably . . . . the celebrated concert guitarist, Don Andrés Segovia, who offered his first public recital in the city of Granada before he turned 15 years old, and who in the present occupies the first place as a guitarist in the whole world . . . he bewilders us! . . .

Us Argentines we already know, since he has been in our country on several opportunities and it is almost four (sic-forty) years that we have enjoyed his marvelous art, incomparable and we think that our applause and our authentic admiration, we have been conquered by the charm of the great Spanish maestro. Lamentably, that didn't happen. Or perhaps it happened before and no one criticized it, because the famous guitarist never mentioned that aspect of the little great problem that just posed with his pejorative declarations of *"palpitante actualidad"* (highly topical) the night of his arrival to Buenos Aires and of his agreement to have it published Tuesday the 10th of May by the prestigious morning *"La Razon"*. The brief chat by the journalist with maestro Andrés Segovia, doesn't have rubbish. It clearly notes that the notable artist suffered the implacable jet lag, since we mustn't forget that since three-quarters of a century, thanks to his exceptional abilities, he reclaimed the prestige of the guitar as a universal concert instrument. Other extenuating circumstances that bewilder us although, they take away the gravity of his words; Andrés Segovia was evidently tired, in a bad mood, impatient, and excited by the delay of his arrival.

Perhaps because of that motive, the great maestro underestimated our music with sharp and pronounced answers with an extremely pejorative tone.

They asked him if he was pleased with our folklore and what opinion he had of Atahualpa Yupanqui. He said that the first was very interesting and that he didn't know the second. He responded to:

— 'The tango, do you like it?'

— 'No! . . . 'Oh, please!' . . .

PATIO DE LOS LEONES

RECITAL DE GUITARRA

POR

ANDRES SEGOVIA

PRIMERA PARTE

SUITE . . . . R. DE VISÉE (1636-1721)
    Passacaille. Bourrée. Sarabande. Menuet. Gigue. Courante.

RONDO . . . . F. SOR (1778-1839)

SONATA (Ommagio a Boccherini) . . . . M. CASTELNUOVO-TEDESCO
    Allegro con spirito.
    Andantino alla Romanza.
    Tempo di minueto.
    Vivo ed energico.

SEGUNDA PARTE

PRELUDIO . . . .
SARABANDA . . . . } (Del cello por Jack Duarte) . . . . J. S. BACH
GIGA . . . .

FUGA Y GAVOTA . . . . »

LARGO Y MINUETO . . . . J. HAYDN

ROMANZA Y CANZONETTA . . . . F. MENDELSSOHN

TERCERA PARTE

PARA SEGOVIA . . . . A. TANSMAN
    Canzonetta.
    Alla Polaca.
    Berceuse d'Orient.
    Mazurka.
    Barcarolle.
    Danse.

MALLORCA (LEYENDA) . . . . I. ALBÉNIZ
    (Guitarra: Hauser-Junior.)

Andrés Segovia uses a Hermann Hauser II guitar in this concert program from the Patio de los Leones in Granada on Wednesday June 28, 1961. His participation was a part of the 10th Festival Internacional de Musica y Danza de Granada.

955

ANDRES SEGOVIA

SABADO 16 DE JUNIO DE 1962, A LAS 17.30

Primer recital del abono a 2 vespertinos

Presentación del guitarrista

A N D R E S   S E G O V I A

I

L. de MILAN .... Fantasía y Pavana

S. L. WEISS .... Toccata

F. SOR .... Rondó

Estudio en mi menor

A. TANSMAN .... Berceuse d'Orient et Danse

H. VILLA-LOBOS .... Dos preludios

II

G. FRESCOBALDI .... Passacaglia y Courante

J. S. BACH .... Siciliana

Fuga

Bourrée

Sarabande

Gavotte

III

M. CASTELNUOVO-TEDESCO .... Platero y Yo (1ª audición)

Platero

Melancolía

Angelus

Retorno

Golondrinas

Arrulladora

I. ALBENIZ .... Torre Bermeja

DISPOSICIONES GENERALES DE ACCESO A LA SALA

En los conciertos no se permitirá el acceso a la sala durante la ejecución de las obras.
Igual temperamento regirá para los espectáculos líricos y coreográficos, donde se
consentirá unicamente durante la mutación de escenas.

This Andrés Segovia concert was held at the Teatro Odeon in Buenos Aires on Saturday June 16, 1962. This evening he made the debut of *"Platero y Yo"* by Mario Castelnuovo-Tedesco.

At the bottom of the program it says: "In the concerts no one is permitted access to the hall during the performance of the works. The rule applies to lyrical and choreographic spectaculars, where it will only be consented during the lapse between the sets."

TEMPORADA OFICIAL

SABADO 23 DE JUNIO DE 1962, A LAS 17.30

Segundo y último recital del Abono a 2 Vespertinos

Actuación del guitarrista

ANDRÉS SEGOVIA

I

L. de NARVÁEZ .... Canción del Emperador y Variaciones
sobre un tema popular.

R. de VISÉE .... Suite en Re
Passacaille
Bourrée
Menuet I et II
Courante

F. SOR .... Allegro en Re

II

J. S. BACH .... Preludio, Sarabanda y Gavota en
forma de Rondó.

F. J. HAYDN .... Largo assai y allegretto

F. MENDELSSOHN .... Dos romanzas
Canzoneta

III

H. VILLA-LOBOS .... Cuatro estudios

F. MORENO TORROBA .... Romance y Madroños

I. ALBENIZ .... Sevilla

DISPOSICIONES GENERALES DE ACCESO A LA SALA
En los conciertos no se permitirá el acceso a la sala durante la ejecución de las obras.
Igual temperamento regirá para los espectáculos líricos y coreográficos, donde se
consentirá únicamente durante la mutación de escenas.

This Andrés Segovia concert was held at the Teatro Odeon in Buenos Aires a week later on Saturday
June 23, 1962.

ANDRES SEGOVIA

Master Class
for Performers and Auditors

July 20 - August 14, 1964

Music Extension · University of California

Andrés Segovia had given Master Classes in Europe since the early 1950's. In the summer of 1964, he gave a Master Class in Berkeley, California from July 20th-August 14th of 1964.

Andres Segovia

Master Class in Guitar, July 20–August 14, 1964, Berkeley, California

Andres Segovia studied at the Granada Institute of Music as a child and soon decided to make the guitar his major instrument. By his mastery of the guitar, Mr. Segovia established it as an accepted instrument on the concert stage. He has vastly increased the guitar repertoire through his numerous transcriptions and works he has commissioned. Manuel de Falla, Manuel Ponce, Jacques Ibert, and Heitor Villa-Lobos are among the noted composers who have written music especially for him.

The Master Class will meet in Hertz Hall, University of California, Berkeley, Monday through Friday, from 10 a.m. to 1 p.m., July 20 through August 14. Performers will be limited to students who have not reached their 30th birthday as of July 1, 1964.

Mr. Segovia will audition performing applicants by appointment during the week of July 13 in Morrison Hall on the Berkeley campus of the University of California. For those who are unable to attend the auditions, he will listen to tapes during the month of June. Tapes must be received by Music Extension, 11 Morrison Hall, University of California, Berkeley, California, not later than May 22.

Auditors may make reservations for the Master Class by returning the enrollment form. (There are no prerequisites for auditors.)

Fees: Performers, four weeks $100; two weeks $60.
Auditors, four weeks $65; two weeks $40.

Single unreserved admissions ($5) for auditors may be purchased at the door preceding each class.

Andrés Segovia gave advice to students about the works of sixteen composers, from ancient to modern. The photo on the next page is from page four of the Master Class booklet.

WORKS TO BE PERFORMED FOR THE AUDITION ARE:

Mario Castelnuovo-Tedesco, *Tarantella*

Manuel M. Ponce, *Sonata No. 3 in D Minor*

Fernando Sor, *Studies,* from the 10th to the 20th (five to be selected by the pupil) and *Variations on a Theme by Mozart*

STUDENTS SELECTED FOR THE MASTER CLASS WILL PERFORM WORKS FROM THE FOLLOWING LIST:

J. S. Bach, original compositions for lute, transcribed for the guitar by Segovia, and *Chaconne,* Segovia transcription

Mario Castelnuovo-Tedesco, *Sonata "Omaggio a Boccherini," Capriccio Diabolico,* and *Concerto in D*

Luys de Narvaez, *Song of the Emperor* and *Variation on the Theme of "Guardame las Vacas"* (1538)

Robert de Visee, selected works

John Dowland, selected works

Joan Manen, *Fantasia Sonata*

Luis Milan, *Fantasia in F* and *Pavanas* (1535)

Federico Mompou, *Suite Compostelana*

Manuel M. Ponce, *Sonata No. 3, Sonata Romantica, Thème Varié et Finale,* and *Six Preludes*

Fernando Sor, *Studies,* from the 10th to the 20th, *Andantes* and *Andantinos, Variations,* etc.

Alexandre Tansman, *Cavatina, Romanza, Polacca, Mazurka, Berceuse d'Orient*

Federico Moreno Torroba, *Sonatina, Characteristic Pieces, Suite Castellana*

Joaquin Turina, *Sevillanas* and *Fandanguillo*

Heitor Villa-Lobos, *Three Preludes* and *Studies No. 1 in E Minor, No. 2 in E Minor, No. 7 in E Major,* and *No 8 in C Sharp Minor*

Leopoldo Silvius Weiss, selected works.

"Oh, for another four or five years," he replied. "As long as I am healthy and fit enough."

He was on his way to Geneva, where he has a second home, his first being in Madrid. He planned to deposit all the fruits of his English shopping expeditions at his Swiss home, before journeying to Germany, for a concert date in Hamburg.

I pointed out the old man's hands. As you would expect of someone who has wrought a musical revolution with them, Segovia's hands are incredible.

He held up the left one, its third finger brandishing a huge gold, ruby-studded wedding ring, and flexed the muscles — first those between the knuckles, then those in the fleshy part between the thumb and forefinger. The fingers themselves are short (the nails impeccably groomed) and fat with muscle—the result of half-a-lifetime of guitar playing.

EMOTIONAL STRAIN

Did he not feel the strain of his international concert career at 72? Segovia replied: "I am so accustomed to giving concerts. Besides, I practice every day for four hours—two in the morning and two in the afternoon—so the 90 minutes of a concert are not too demanding physically but, of course, there is a great deal of emotional strain."

December sees the 56th anniversary of Segovia's first concert, when he was just 16. For many years he has been giving between 110 and 115 concerts each year, from Britain, to America, to Australia . . . to the whole world. Between December '63 and December '64, he caught 112 planes, he told with amusement!

If it is necessary to prune his annual concert schedule—as it will be, though Segovia tends to skirt the subject—he will confine his concert-giving to Europe; not because of the travelling but because "I like it very much—it is my *own* continent."

Astonishingly, Segovia has only owned four guitars throughout his career. He had a Spanish guitar from 1912-1935; a German model until 1956

and from then on, two Spanish-made guitars; a Fleta (which he keeps at home) and a Ramirez, which he takes on tour.

The requirements? "The timbre must be very beautiful but it must be solid enough never to be affected by the climate.

"The guitar is a very untrustworthy instrument," he explained. "Often the temperature will seriously affect the sound."

His views on electric guitars are well known: "When I see one, I turn the other way," he said firmly.

"The enthusiasm for the Classical Guitar is world-wide," came the reply when I asked him whether he found the English keen guitarists. "It is incredible."

In Japan there were 600,000 amateur enthusiasts. "And in America, 45,000 Classical Guitarists are registered with the Musicians' Union," he added with quiet pride. "As soon as the Philharmonic public has made the acquaintance of the Classical Guitar, it loves it. It is exactly the same with the composer. He hears a work of his played on the guitar and continues to write for it."

BEST PUPIL

Segovia praised John Williams, now 24, as his best pupil. Another promising follower was Spaniard Alirio Diaz, 35.

With the new generation taking up the torch where he left off, I asked him what were his hopes for the future of the instrument.

"I hope the young people will continue its noble tradition," he said simply.

I chose that appropriate moment—as the loudspeakers were calling passengers to board the Geneva plane—to say goodbye. As I shook hands, first with Mrs. Segovia, then with her husband, he rose politely. A living legend, but open and friendly—a truly GREAT man.

As I walked away, I spotted a pop group battling through the swing doors marked "Arivals" under a weight of guitar cases, amplifiers, etc. Suddenly a girl screamed, then another—and in seconds a deafening hue and cry broke out!

My mind went back to Segovia's words and that picture of him sitting, calmly, majestically amongst the chaos and bustle of the world's busiest international airport.

Andres Segovia

By Peter Anderson

SEGOVIA. In one word, all the nobility, the dignity, the majesty of the Spanish Guitar.

Those who have seen this now slightly stooping, grey-haired Spaniard walk on to the stage of a concert hall and charm an audience of thousands into absolute awed silence with the artistry of his short, muscular fingers, know his power.

But only those privileged to meet and talk with him know his politeness, his warmth, his humility, his GREATNESS.

His beautiful wife Emilia at his side, Segovia was sitting calmly amidst the bustle of the final departure lounge at London Airport when I met him.

The night before, he had given the last of the concerts of his British tour—at the Fairfield Halls, Croydon—and he was full of praise for the acoustics there.

I asked the great man, 72 years old this year, dressed in modest grey suit with a familiar black "string" tie, how much longer he would go on giving concerts.

This is from the December 1965 B. M. G. magazine.

CARNEGIE HALL / Diamond Jubilee 75th Season

Fifth Event in the Hurok International Festival Sunday Series

Sunday Afternoon, January 29, 1967 at 3:00 o'clock

S. HUROK

presents

Andres Segovia

Guitarist

PROGRAM

I

(Compositions written for the Guitar)

Suite in D	R. de Visee (1686-1721)
Andante alla Siciliana / Allegretto / Menuet / Rondo	F. Sor (1778-1839)
Melancholia / Primavera	M. Castelnuovo-Tedesco (1895-)

II

Transcriptions of Compositions, the Spirit and Harmony of which have been adapted for the Guitar)

Sarabande and Allegretto	G. F. Handel (1685-1759)
Gavotte	J. S. Bach (1685-1750)
Andante and Allegretto	F. J. Haydn (1732-1809)

INTERMISSION

III

(Compositions dedicated to Mr. Segovia)

Andante (Dreams of the Wedding) Ahuahuete / Ritmos y cantos Aztecas	M. Ponce (1886-1948)
Berceuse de Orient and Mazurka	A. Tansman (1897-)
Preambulo and Sardana	G. Cassado
Torre Bermeja	I. Albeniz (1860-1909)

Decca Gold Label Records

Exclusive Management: HUROK CONCERTS, INC., 730 Fifth Avenue, New York

The next event in the Sunday Series: ARTUR RUBINSTEIN, February 12, 1967

Mr. Segovia will play a second recital at Town Hall on March 11, 1967

Tickets on sale this week

This concert by Andrés Segovia was held at Carnegie Hall on Sunday January 29, 1967, the next page shows the Decca ad from the program, with a list of 21 LPs recorded by that time.

964

This is the cover to the program for a concert by Andrés Segovia at the Royal Festival Hall in London on Tuesday May 30, 1967.

ROYAL FESTIVAL HALL

(General Manager: John Denison, C.B.E.)

SEGOVIA

I

Fantasia and Pavana	LUIS MILAN (1500c—1561c)
Suite in D	R. DE VISEE (1685—1721)
Andante	F. SOR (1778—1839)
Allegretto	
Minuetto	
Rondo	

II

Five Short pieces	PURCELL (1658—1695)
Bourrée	J. S. BACH (1685—1750)
Menuet	SCHUBERT (1797—1828)
Romanza and Andantino Variato	N. PAGANINI (1782—1840)
(written for the guitar)	

INTERVAL

III

Sonatina Meridiona	M. PONCE (1882—1948)
Melancolia—	M. CASTELNUOVO-TEDESCO
Primavera—Arrulladora	(b. 1895)
Torre Bermeja	I. ALBENIZ (1860—1909)

Tuesday, 30th May, 1967 at 8 p.m.

Management: IBBS & TILLETT LTD.

Programme price 1/6

This is the program for a concert by Andrés Segovia at the Royal Festival Hall in London on Tuesday, May 30, 1967.

Below is the courtesy notice from the top of the page of the composer biography notes. The theater seated 2,500 patrons.

During a recent test in the Hall, a note played Mezzoforte *on the horn measured approximately 65 decibels [dB(A)] of sound. A single "uncovered" cough gave the same reading. A handkerchief placed over the mouth when coughing assists in obtaining a pianissimo.*

TEATRO REAL

Lunes, 11 de diciembre de 1967   A las 7,15 de la tarde

UNICO RECITAL DE GUITARRA
POR
ANDRES SEGOVIA

PROGRAMA

Primera parte

Seis piezas breves de un códice anónimo del siglo XV, para laúd, notación moderna, por	O. CHILESSOTTI
Fantasía y Pavana...	L. MILAN (1535)
Suite	R. DE VISEE (1650-1725)
Cinco composiciones cortas...	H. PURCELL (1658-1695)
Fuga y Gavota (originalmente escritas para laúd)	J. S. BACH

Segunda parte

Suite in modo polónico	Al. TANSMAN
Dos estudios	H. VILLALOBOS
Primavera (de la suite «Platero y yo»)... ...	M. CASTELNUOVO
Sonatina meridional	M. PONCE
Preludio y Allegretto...	M. TORROBA
Fantasía sevillana	J. TURINA
Torre Bermeja...	I. ALBENIZ

Localidades para los abonados de los viernes y sábados de la Orquesta Nacional: Lunes 27 y martes 28.

Venta libre a partir del miércoles 29. Taquillas del Teatro Real, plaza de Oriente.

This is a flyer for a concert by Andrés Segovia that was held at the Teatro Real in Madrid on Monday December 11, 1967. This evening he was given the *"Medalla de Oro al Mérito de Trabajo"*— a Gold Medal for Merit of Work.

The third set actually begins with *"Sonata meridional"* by Manuel Ponce, according to a concert program on page 577 from Alberto Lopez Poveda's book *"Andrés Segovia: Vida y Obra"*.

Andrés Segovia played concerts since biplanes could be seen first flying in the air, all the way until he flew on jet airplanes to the wide reaches of the world. My colleague, Jim Westbrook, says he remembers there was a concert in England where Andrés Segovia played on the same stage as Jimi Hendrix.

Andrés Segovia Interview

This is from the *"Digame"* magazine, published in Madrid on January 23, 1968.

Translation: Randy Osborne

The journalist is: Miguel Fernández , the photos by Julio César

Photo captions:

He spent his Christmas vacation days in Costa del Sol.

Andrés Segovia, in Madrid

"Now for me remains the longest tour of South America".

"I can't accept more than one hundred thirty concerts a year."

Andrés Segovia has just arrived in Madrid. Having come from the Costa del Sol where his home "La Herradura" is. There he spent his Christmas vacation, the Maestro says, resting to simply not travel. But now, within a week he leaves, several exhausting months await him, of continuous concerts, flying from one country to another.

"Now for me remains the longest tour. I'll be in South America until April."

M. F. How much concert ground do you cover every year?

"Only one hundred thirty. I can't accept more contracts."

M. F. Do you practice daily?

"I always practice three hours in the morning, another three hours in the afternoon, then whatever I can do in the evening."

M. F. How many guitars have you used in your life?

"Only three. First I had one by Manuel Rodríguez (sic) (Ramírez-real surname). When I went to Germany for the first time, the "Luthier" for the Conservatory of Munich (Hermann Hauser I) asked me for permission to study it. Since then, every year he has sent me one. They were all very good, but I wasn't convinced until he made one in 1937. Now I utilize one fabricated by the grandson of (José) Ramírez."

M. F. Three guitars, only three guitars, have made the world of emotion vibrate. They started every note of painful humanity, festive or passionate. They have converted the tremor of its strings in a moving dialogue maintained in an international idiom. South America, Australia, Tasmania, New Zealand, Europe... The universe is small to welcome our guitarist.

"The countries with the greater musical sensibility are those which follow me with greater interest. Just as they follow the rest of the famous musicians."

M.F. Your guitar gets the sounds of all the musical instruments. Your guitar — we can say — has in its strings a fantastic orchestra.

"I have for about seventy years been playing the guitar. Seventy years of uninterrupted activity."

969

The Guitar is Rising

Andrés Segovia has an apartment on the avenue of Concha Espina, near the Santiago Bernabéu stadium. We speak in the living room. The library takes up a complete wall. On the shelves there are perfectly bound books and small objects that recall the most diverse countries: an exotic naked doll, a ceramic Virgin, a small ivory wizard playing the guitar, a Buddha figure, a large vase of artificial flowers, a silver plaque stating he is the favorite son of Linares.

"Now the guitar is rising, undoubtedly. I'm living the closest to it. The halls that I give my concerts in are insufficient. Since my first concerts, in which the guitar was without a public following, things have varied considerably."

M. F. When Segovia began, they were barely calling guitarists musicians. And the few that they found had a little artistic quality. The North American Virgil Thompson has written: "There is no guitar but the Spanish guitar, and Andrés Segovia is its prophet." The universal Andalucian has dedicated his whole life to redeem the guitar, a rescue for the music of the concert stage.

"One of my greatest prides I have gotten is that composers have written for the guitar."

M. F. Composers such as de Falla, Villa-Lobos, Turina, Casella, Castelnuovo-Tedesco and others have written scores exclusively with him in mind.

I Teach Guitar in Rome

M. F. I observe instinctively the hands of Andrés Segovia. Hands that are sensible, meaty, very wide, and fingers that aren't long. The hands are like two agile gazelles. They are some hands that close in on the strings of the guitar and provoke a fire in the stairway of our dreams.

"Yes, I also teach guitar. I have been giving lessons fourteen years in the Chigiana Foundation, of Count Chigi, in Rome."

M. F. Our guitarist smokes slowly and surely on a small-carved pipe. The tobacco goes out continuously. The maestro with patience lights a new match and nears the tobacco.

"The classical guitar has its own public. A public of smaller numbers, select and philharmonic."

M. F. Among your disciples, are there any that excel on the guitar?

"Yes, some have gotten to be, such as the Englishman, John Williams, a sonorous success."

M. F. Scarce and few strands of hair like white threads of silk. The eyes are seen -noble and sad- behind his black rimmed glasses. The nose is lightly wincing, the lips are thick, and sensual. Andrés Segovia physically has the air of a middle class gentleman with all of his aspirations completed. But it isn't difficult to discover in him a spirit still young, with wide and noble ambitions."

The last concert of Andrés Segovia's 78 year career was in Miami, Florida on Saturday April 4, 1987. The cover photo was from the late 1970's to early 1980's and had been used on a December 1981 "Frets" magazine cover. The maestro has an Ignacio Fleta Cedar soundboard guitar in his hands, despite using a José Ramírez for the concert. He passed away less than 2 months later, on June 2, 1987.

ANDRES SEGOVIA

Biography

Andres Segovia was born in Linares, Jaen, in the region of Spain known as Andalusia on February 21, 1893. From his early childhood Segovia was deeply responsive to the sound of the guitar, an instrument which was part of everyday life in southern Spain. At the age of ten Segovia moved from Linares in order to attend school in Granada. Here he acquired his first guitar. Despite the absence of any competent teachers, Segovia soon gained a prodigious mastery and discovered the existence of fine guitar compositions surpassing the limitations of Andalusia's folkloric guitar styles.

By 1909 Segovia was ready to offer his first public recital at the Centro Artistico in Granada. Concerts in Cordoba and Seville followed and later Segovia moved to Madrid where, in 1912, he gave his debut at the Ateneo and was presented with his first concert guitar of quality by Manuel Ramirez.

Segovia's first international tour was to South America in the early 1920's while his European reputation was established by a resoundingly successful debut in Paris in 1924, attended by many distinguished musicians. From this period of his life onwards Segovia not only enriched the range of the guitar repertoire by transcribing and performing works by great composers of the past, but also persuaded his contemporaries to write new pieces for the instrument.

Composers such as Federico Moreno Torroba and Joaquin Turina of Spain, Manuel Ponce of Mexico, Mario Castelnuovo-Tedesco of Italy, Heitor Villa-Lobos of Brazil and Alexandre Tansman of Poland all wrote significant compositions for him during this crucial period of Segovia's early concert career.

Armed with this new repertoire, Segovia's international esteem rapidly increased. In 1926 he performed in Russia and Britain, in 1927 in Scandinavia, in 1928 came his first tour of the U.S.A., and in 1929 Segovia made his first visit to Japan. Since that time the sound of Segovia's guitar has been heard in almost every country in the world.

Andres Segovia continues to take the guitar to the world's concert halls. This year, he celebrates his ninety-fourth birthday in February and he will make his customary annual tour of the U.S.A. By his dedication and insight the guitar has become established as a respected solo instrument with a wide repertoire and an international following.

Segovia, one of the twentieth century's greatest instrumentalists, has received many high honors from the international community. More than a dozen honorary doctorates from the major universities have been conferred upon him and his numerous medals of distinction include the Grand Cross of Isabel La Catolica, Spain's highest civilian honor. In 1981, Andres Segovia was created Marquis of Salobrena by His Majesty King Juan Carlos I of Spain. In February, he will receive a Lifetime Achievement Award from NARAS when the Grammy Awards are presented.

INTERNATIONAL ARTISTS SERIES
presents

In the Miami Beach Theatre of the Performing Arts
April 4th, 8 PM, 1987

Andres Segovia

GUITAR

Aria con Variazioni*	FRESCOBALDI (1583-1643)
Andante and Minuet	SOR (1778-1839)
Prelude-Little Study-Minuet- Slow Mazurka-Gavotte-Capricho	TARREGA (1852-1909)
Fandanguillo	TURINA (1882-1949)

INTERMISSION

Fuge*	J.S. BACH (1685-1750)
Allegretto*	HAYDN (1732-1809)
Mazurka*	TCHAIKOVSKY (1840-1893)
Cancion and Allegretto	PONCE (1882-1948)

- -

* Transcribed by Segovia

Guitar Ramirez

RCA, Decca/MCA Records

Exclusive Management:
ICM Artists, Ltd.
40 West 57th Street
New York, NY 10019
Lee Lamont, President
A Member of the JOSEPHSON Talent Agency Group

In November of 2011 I acquired 33 letters typed or handwritten in English by maestro Andrés Segovia to the Senior Editor, Ray A. Roberts, at MacMillan Publishing Co., Inc. in New York, regarding his autobiography published in 1976. These were written between May 20, 1973 and June 27, 1977. I only have one letter from Ray A. Roberts from June 13, 1976, so it wasn't possible to read the dialogue.

Initially the maestro had planned on 4 books. The first book was to go from his date of birth until 1920, when he was contracted to play in Buenos Aires, Montevideo, etc. That volume was to end when he took the boat to Buenos Aires. The second volume was to cover from that epoch until his first concert in New York, passing through all his recitals in Europe and Russia. The third book was to cover from that period to the beginning of the Spanish Civil War. The last volume was to cover from that time until the present.

An undated typed page says: MY LIFE — IN FOUR *SONATA TIEMPOS* — *Allegro Appassionato* — *Sherzo* — *Andante Meditativo* — *Finale:* Passionately Toward Death by Andrés SEGOVIA

On June 26, 1976 the maestro wrote that he accepted the general title, valid for all the work, but thought as a subtitle "The Guitar and I" specified the character of what his Memoirs would contain. The name of the second book in the beginning was "The World, The Guitar and I", he asked that "The World" be removed-the first chapter of this was written by May 10, 1976, but due to the ideas of Ray A. Roberts, of publishing all four books one at a time, and then publishing them together in one volume, the name of the first book was changed to as it became known: "Segovia: An Autobiography for the Years 1893-1920." The maestro said he hoped to finish the second volume by August of 1977. It was never published, Mrs. Tana de Gamez (1920-2003) was the sole translator of those chapters.

Advised by friends, he requested to maintain the ownership of the books written in languages other than English. These letters were written from all over the world, from his home in Spain: "Los Olivos" La Herradura, in Granada Province, from hotels where he stayed while on tour, etc. Andrés didn't want his book to be translated by a South American, as he understandably felt, that person would mostly ignore the real Spanish style.

He was always appreciative for the reception of books, such as the "Segovia Technique" in Japanese in 1975. The first translator was a gentleman called Mr. O'Brien who worked as a translator for the United Nations. Andrés wrote to the Spanish Ambassador at the United Nations thanking him for the recommendation of Mr. W. F. O'Brien, who was given credit as the translator. The second translator brought in was Mrs. Tana de Gamez, she was given credit as having edited the book. The maestro said she skillfully softened the sharp edges of certain English sentences, then the reading was smoother. Vladimir Bobri did the design and illustrations.

From Madrid the maestro wrote on June 10, 1976 that he was to make a film for the "Movie Picture Theatre" in July and it would be shown throughout the world in October therefore he hoped the first volume would be out that month. As the first book progressed, in the letter from Ray A. Roberts from June 13, 1976, he states it would be absolutely impossible to publish the book before November of 1976, to have it in stock in late September, with sufficient time to ship it across the United States for healthy Christmas sales. Due to brisk sales the second printing began in 1977.

The typed or handwritten letters by maestro Andrés Segovia to the Senior Editor, Ray A. Roberts, at MacMillan Publishing Co. were to be towards the end of the book, after the Ronoel Simões family member's biographies. In 2012, through Angelo Gilardino, as an intermediary, I approached Segovia's widow, and was told for 2,000 Euros she would allow these letters to be in this book, with the upcoming printing in 2019, I tried to make that payment, and was told, she didn't recall the written conversation and would not accept the funds nor allow the letters to to be included.

Andrés Segovia performed at least 5,204 concerts in his career.

Source: Translated from *Andrés Segovia Vida and Obra by Alberto Lopez Poveda* published by the Universidad de Jaen / Ayuntamiento de Linares 2010.